Guide to
UK Universities 2010

Guide to UK Universities 2010

30th Edition

The One-stop Guide to UK Universities

KLAUS BOEHM
&
JENNY LEES-SPALDING

Formerly The Student Book

Guide to UK Universities 2010

© Macmillan Press Ltd
1979, 1980, 1981, 1982, 1983

© Klaus Boehm and Jenny Lees-Spalding,
Nick Wellings 1984, 1985, 1986, 1987

© Klaus Boehm and Jenny Lees-Spalding & Klaus Boehm Publications Ltd 1988–2007, 2009

The moral right of the authors has been asserted

This 30th edition published in 2009 by Trotman Publishing,
an imprint of Crimson Publishing,
Westminster House, Kew Road, Richond, Surrey TW9 2ND
www.crimsonpublishing.co.uk

Previous editions published by Macmillan Press Ltd (1979–83);
Trotman and Co Ltd (1984–2006)

British Library Cataloguing in Publication Data
A catalogue record for this book is available from the British Library

ISBN: 978–1–84455–185–9

Typeset by IDSUK (DataConnection) Ltd.
Printed and bound in Italy by LEGO SpA

CONTENTS

About the Editors

Klaus Boehm has developed a wide range of reference books with a number of publishers. Titles include the *Dictionary of the History of Science*, *British Archives*, *The Royal and Ancient Golfer's Handbook*, *The Macmillan Nautical Almanac* and the prize-winning *The European Community*. **Jenny Lees-Spalding** was academic registrar at what is now London Metropolitan University, working with students on first degree courses. She has since been involved with undergraduate programmes based at City University and the Open University.

Their joint titles share a common philosophy. Readers are intelligent people who make their own choices; reference books make a good starting point for preliminary investigations and developing a strategy but are **no substitute** for primary sources.

Foreword

Your best buy

If you have decided to apply to university, money must be a major consideration. Not only do you need to make sure you can pay for your university education but also that you get value for money as well – and in the present financial climate this is more important than ever.

University costs a lot – you need money to live on for three or more years and money to pay tuition fees. It may or may not be you that pays, and for UK students there is a load of help around, in the form of loans, grants and bursaries. But whoever pays, it is **your** investment decision.

So is it good value for you? You need to be clear about what you are looking for, and then make sure you choose a subject, a course and a university that meets your criteria. This book helps you do that.

How can you judge if a course offers you good value for money? You can tell next to nothing from the prices that UK students are charged – they are pretty much all the same and set at the government-imposed maximum. A good start is to check out the value placed on the course by the global market. There is no government control over the fees paid by international students, so universities charge what students will pay. Here you get a real feel for the perceived value placed on a course by the global market. Courses taught in laboratories cost more than comparable courses taught in classrooms, and clinical courses cost the most, but within that broad framework there are astonishing variations. Some courses cost international students little more than the maximum subsidised fee that UK students pay, starting at around £5,500 pa. The most sought-after courses have very high global market prices – nearly £9,000 pa for an LSE social science course, or £19,500 pa for an Imperial science course, or over £30,000 pa for clinical medicine at Edinburgh University. These are the most straightforward indicators of the value of the course (see the table on page 58).

If you are an international student, you will be judging these prices against those charged by comparable universities across the globe – and the top universities in the UK are up there with the best of the world-class universities. If you are a home student, check how the open market values your course – and, if you are lucky enough to qualify for one of the elite courses, be glad someone else is picking up the bulk of the course fee for you, at least for the time being. Either way, value for money is one more thing to take into account when looking for the university course that best suits **you**.

Acknowledgements

The *Guide to UK Universities* (formerly *The Student Book*) is, and always has been, a consumer book. More precisely, it is a book for those applying for first degrees, who will become the final consumers of UK higher education. It unashamedly sides with sixth formers and undergraduates, not teachers, not university admissions staff, not UCAS – although it maintains a very good working relationship with all of them.

We are very grateful for the help we have received from the administrators of over 250 universities and colleges and to the central institutions of UK higher education – particularly UCAS itself, SCONUL, HESA and HEFCE. We have relied heavily on their published data.

This book would not be possible without the tremendous help we get from all our student correspondents. And our special thanks go to Anna Boehm, Jenny Dodd, Mike Kenward and Nick Lea, who helped in various ways with redesigning our student contributions and persuading students to complete questionnaires.

To all our readers: the very best of luck with your applications and, equally important, a brilliant start to your degree courses in September 2010.

Klaus Boehm and Jenny Lees-Spalding
January 2009

SHORTLISTING

Choosing your Subject and Course

Points to consider

You're spoilt for choice. There are over 50,000 full-time undergraduate courses on offer in the UK, teaching a tremendous mix of subjects in all sorts of different ways. Not all subjects are taught at every university, and the curricula in one subject (eg history or biology) can be very different at different institutions. You can find out which universities teach a particular subject in 'Where your subject is taught', page 670.

This book (which deals with first degrees and equivalent qualifications) is to help you narrow down your choices to a shortlist that attracts **you**. Before you start, here are some criteria you should consider.

- Whether the subject is likely to suit you ('Suitability', see below)
- How employable you will be when you graduate ('Employability', page 3)
- Whether you are on the right route to qualify for your chosen profession, if you have thought that far ahead ('Qualifying for a profession', page 3)
- How easy or difficult it is to get on to the course ('Getting in', page 3) and whether a particular department is a top research department ('Top departments', page 3)
- 'Course content' (page 4).

Suitability

Are you likely to do well in the subject? Find out from students who are already doing the subject or course whether they are enjoying it – and why (you may be different). Even subjects you have studied at school will change when you get to degree level, so talk to your teachers and do some reading to see if you are still likely to enjoy it. If you are thinking of a vocational course, try out the subject by doing some work experience.

You can try one of the tests intended to suggest subjects that match your interests and abilities. You may be able to take one through your school or you can complete the Stamford Test on the UCAS website.

Increasingly, universities make a real effort to help you sample subjects at first degree level before you apply – for example, sixth-form summer schools and pre-taster courses (information available from UCAS).

Employability

Many degree courses are vocational, which is fine if that is the job for you. Some other degrees may give partial exemption from professional qualifications or lead towards a range of jobs in a more general way.

You should expect to be able to develop the skills that employers want – problem-solving, teamwork, IT literacy, communication and presentation. Courses that include some work experience often produce the most employable graduates. Find out about the employment record of the specific courses that interest you, as employers have their own league tables of what a course is worth to them.

The link between jobs and the specific subject studied at first degree is complex. To be a doctor, you will obviously need to study medicine (although you can still train if you took a first degree in a different subject). But many top law and accountancy firms, for example, positively prefer you to have studied something quite different, as long as it is a 'hard' academic subject (eg economics), and to undertake legal/accountancy training after you graduate.

You usually qualify for the professions faster if you take a specialist degree, but if you are not 100% certain about your future plans, the longer route has many advantages. For example, if you change your mind about being a teacher, you may be more marketable in the wider world with a physics degree than a teaching degree.

What does matter is that you get a good degree, and you're most likely to do so if you study a subject that you enjoy throughout the course. So, if you want to read history or Akkadian, go for it – and get the best possible degree to impress employers.

Qualifying for a profession

If you are thinking of qualifying for a particular profession you need to check with the professional body (or bodies) what is required. Most professions are graduate entry only, although a degree is in itself seldom sufficient qualification – and some degrees will help towards the final qualification, while others will not.

Professional bodies' websites and information packs are usually excellent and tell you what is required, which degree courses they recognise, what you need to do to qualify and how long it takes. Contact details of professional bodies are listed on pages 749–53.

Getting in

It's very easy to get onto some courses and very difficult to get onto others. Courses that are much in demand can ask for much higher grades than less popular courses. Some over-subscribed courses (eg medicine and law) now use aptitude tests in addition to the standard entrance qualification and interviews.

So it's a case of horses for courses: don't waste applications on courses that consistently ask for grades hopelessly higher than you are likely to get. Conversely, high-fliers are likely to be bored on courses where most other students have only minimum grades (and the teaching is pitched at that level). University prospectuses usually give typical offers for each of their courses and will tell you if you need any prior experience.

Top departments

When you have chosen your subject, you then need to look for the right course for you. Some university departments are much more high-powered than others. You may want to study in a top research department or you may prefer somewhere less research-focused. So, however you feel about them, it is worth looking at which are the top research departments in the different subjects – look on pages 754–64.

Course content

There is no national standard for what universities include in their courses, so two courses with the same title will be different at any two universities. For instance, a psychology course might be heavily science-based, involve an understanding of animal behaviour and include practical work on rats, or it might be drawn from the social sciences and studied in a social and cultural context. Similarly, a music technology course may be the offspring of a music or an engineering department – and this will lead to different approaches and a different balance between music and technology. Large numbers of students each year find themselves on courses that differ wildly from their expectations; don't be one of them.

Courses vary not only in their content and approach, but also in their teaching and assessment methods (eg examination, continuous assessment, project work). Final-year options in particular usually reflect the research interests of staff; check out the university prospectuses.

Extras

You may want to select courses that allow you to spend time abroad or in work experience, to learn a language or enhance your IT skills. All are available – either as an integral part of the course, as options or as extras provided by the university. Check prospectuses before you apply.

If you want to study in Europe, there are student-friendly and financially advantageous arrangements under the EU Erasmus programme. Make sure you choose approved courses (see www.britishcouncil.org/erasmus).

Course structure

Each university has its own language to describe its degree courses but there are commonly used terms to label the very real differences in structure (eg single subject or multidisciplinary) and approach (theoretical, vocational). If you are not totally sure precisely what you want to study for the next three or four years, and feel that you may want to change direction, choose a course that is flexible and will allow you to change emphasis as your interests develop. Courses are in general becoming more flexible, but it does make their labels harder to define. Here are a few.

Single subject degrees. One subject is studied for the length of the course, although a wide variety of topics may be covered and the first year may be broad.

Joint Honours degrees. Two subjects are taken equally (but less of each, so you don't do twice as much work).

Combined (multidisciplinary or interdisciplinary) courses. Components from any number of subjects can be put together.

Modular (or unit) schemes. The information taught is parcelled up into discrete units (modules or course units). Students structure their own degrees from a range of units or modules, within the constraints laid down for the particular course. This can allow you to study unconventional combinations of subjects, or to add some IT or a language, while still finishing with a degree that makes sense to employers. It is not total anarchy: there will be specified units you will need to take if you want, for example, professional qualifications or a named degree (eg BSc in Physics). This is an increasingly common structure, but almost all non-modular courses offer some choice.

ANGLO-EUROPEAN COLLEGE OF CHIROPRACTIC (AECC)

The AECC offers a four year, full-time course leading to a Masters degree in Chiropractic (MChiro). The programme of study at the AECC enables its graduates to develop the skills necessary ahead of a demanding and rewarding career in chiropractic.

Chiropractic is an expanding health care profession, primarily concerned with the diagnosis, treatment, prevention and rehabilitation of conditions and complaints of the musculoskeletal system.

The chiropractic profession is known throughout the world as a specialist body of practitioners, giving help and relief to countless thousands of people who would otherwise suffer prolonged pain and illness.

Chiropractors take an holistic approach to the health needs of their patients, considering physical, psychological and social factors. They provide care and support to their patients by reducing pain and restoring motion by musculoskeletal disorders.

There are over 2,200 practising chiropractors in the UK presently, with the profession continuing to grow year-on-year.

The AECC is continuing to grow too. In January 2009 , a new 1,500m² chiropractic teaching clinic was opened at the college's Bournemouth-based campus – a state-of-the-art facility to benefit the local community and AECC students alike. The clinic is where final year students will spend a considerable part of their last 12 months at the AECC, experiencing the reality of treating patients first-hand, while under the supervision of experienced chiropractic tutors.

The AECC has been established for over 40 years and has a world-wide reputation in chiropractic education. The college is set in a grade II listed building, previously used as a convent, just a ten minute walk to a seven-mile stretch of golden coastline.

Chiropractic is a fully regulated profession throughout the UK and in many countries around the world. The MChiro degree is accredited by the European Council for Chiropractic Education and is therefore recognised in many countries across Europe. AECC graduates have a near 100% success record of going into employment, with starting salaries in chiropractic generally above average graduate earnings.

For further information on the AECC visit www.aecc.ac.uk

Vocational courses. The degree is directly linked to work applications and will often include some work experience.

Sandwich courses. Part of the course is spent in a work placement – in professional or industrial training or work (possibly overseas), which is usually paid. There are 'thick' sandwiches (a year out) and 'thin' sandwiches (usually two periods of six months). These courses usually last a year longer than the non-sandwich equivalent.

Foundation degrees. A two-year course with a strong bias towards work-based learning. It should give credit to the first two years of an Honours degree, although you may need to take an extra term or attend a summer school before joining the third year.

Intercalated courses. Where students on a first degree course (usually medicine, dentistry or veterinary medicine) interrupt their studies to complete a one-year course of study in another subject, usually to Honours standard, and then return to their original course.

Length of course

An Honours degree course usually takes three years (four in Scotland), but there are many exceptions. Many first degree courses last four years – for example if you spend a year abroad or in a work placement, if you get an additional qualification (eg QTS or undergraduate Master's) or if the course includes a foundation year. If you are studying architecture, medicine or veterinary medicine your course will normally last five or more years. Foundation degrees last two years and so do a few accelerated degree courses (typically 45 weeks a year).

The final degree

Bachelor's (or Master's) degrees

Most first degrees lead to the award of a Bachelor's degree – so when you graduate, you can put BA, BSc, BEd or LLB after your name (and there are some modern mouthfuls: BSocSci, BPhysChem; the list grows longer each year). Some first degrees lead to a Master's, notably in the older Scottish universities (where many first degrees lead to an MA) and some science degrees (which take four years and qualify you for, eg, MEng, MMath). For the most part, Master's are higher degrees involving further study; but then some Bachelor's degrees (eg BPhil) are higher degrees. All rather confusing. Medics usually take five years and get an MB BS or MB ChB (Bachelor in medicine and surgery, in different languages).

Honours or ordinary degrees

Most degrees are Honours degrees. These are differentiated by classes, depending on how well you have done. You can get a first-class degree (or just a first), upper second-class (sometimes known as a 2:1), lower second (or 2:2) or a third. Do not believe that a first-class degree from one university necessarily equals a first from another; whatever they say, it does not.

An ordinary degree (sometimes called a pass degree) may be awarded if a student fails to achieve Honours standard or if the course does not provide for Honours (eg some Open University courses and courses at some Scottish universities). You can usually top up an ordinary degree to an Honours degree with a further year's study.

Whose degree?

In the vast majority of cases your degree will be awarded by the university (or university college) you attend. Many colleges do not award their own degrees, in which case your degree will be from the university that validates your course. So if you study at, say, Rose Bruford College, you will get a degree from Manchester University.

The Courtauld Institute of Art is the major centre in Britain for the study of art history and conservation. Based in Somerset House in central London, The Courtauld, with its famous Gallery and collections, is close to London's major cultural institutions and provides unsurpassed research resources and learning opportunities. As a college of the federal University of London, students have access to many of the research resources of the University and its other constituent colleges, including the University Library at Senate House and those of other specialised institutions.

THE COURTAULD
Institute of Art

www.courtauld.ac.uk
020 7848 2635/2645
ugadmissions@courtauld.ac.uk
pgadmissions@courtauld.ac.uk

A place to study and learn:
- small group teaching our hallmark
- a dynamic and friendly organization
- teaching rated excellent in student satisfaction surveys
- over four hundred students: a third undergraduates, the rest taught postgraduates or PhD students

A major research community:
- top ranked for AHRC Block Grant partnership scheme
- ranked first for power in art history and conservation research in the 2008 Research Assessment Exercise
- guaranteed funding for 44 PhDs and 60 MAs from the UK and the EU over the next five years

Please look at the website and current prospectus for more details and come to one of our Open Days.

Degree certificates

All this will be recorded on your degree certificate, for example Bachelor of Arts with First Class Honours from the University of Woking. It might also add the subject(s) you studied and/or, increasingly, you will get a transcript, which logs your achievements in the different elements of your degree (the marks for each paper/module/unit). Transcripts are useful evidence of what you have done, either to back up your claims to specialist studies or to explain away your final class of degree.

Specialist courses

Agriculture, horticulture and related land use courses

These are taught both as first degrees and also as non-degree vocational qualifications. They are available at universities and some specialist land use colleges. At degree level, at some universities agriculture is treated as a science (eg Reading University); and at some of the specialist colleges (eg Writtle) as a practical, vocational subject.

Art and design degrees

These vary widely in philosophy, structure and content (critical, contextual, historical), and there is a huge range of subjects, from animation to zoological illustration. Some courses are very rigid or prescriptive (eg painting only); others are completely inter-disciplinary, allowing you to move between areas at will. Some courses are explicitly traditional, others are experimental or use new media. Read the prospectuses carefully – and be sure to visit the university. Courses are offered at multi-faculty universities and some specialist art colleges/universities.

Drama training

Studying drama prepares students for work in the professional theatre and the film and television industries. Courses are offered at a range of universities and specialist colleges. While some are degree courses, others do not involve a large measure of academic work and take less than three years to complete.

You can usually apply for a grant and/or loan in the standard way, but tuition fees at drama colleges may be much higher than at a university (£4k–£10k pa). To be in with a chance of funding, choose a course approved by the National Council for Drama Training – see its website at www.ncdt.co.uk for a full list and more detail about funding options.

Film and TV education

Courses are usually a mix of academic study and practical training, so check what that mix is for a particular course. The courses available are listed on the British Film Institute website (www.bfi.org.uk). Many universities and colleges profiled in this book teach film and TV studies as full first degree courses, or as part of more general media courses. Two colleges specialising in film and TV studies are also profiled (the London Film School and the National Film & TV School) but they only recruit postgraduate or post-experience students.

Medical courses

There is great pressure on places at medical school, despite the opening of several new medical schools. To get in, you will need three good A-levels (or equivalent) and may have to pass a clinical aptitude test as well. Your A-levels will need to be in academic subjects, usually including chemistry plus one other science: some medical schools want applicants to have all three sciences; others prefer one contrasting subject.

All UK medical courses leading to registration as a doctor are approved by the General Medical Council, but teaching differs from school to school. Some teach by independent, problem-based learning, some mainly by formal lectures, etc. At some, clinical teaching is concentrated in primary care rather than hospitals. Some expose students to patients from the start; others keep you away from real patients until the third year. Accelerated four-year courses allow graduates in related subjects to qualify for the medical profession.

Performing arts courses

These are vocational training courses for would-be professional actors, singers and dancers. They are offered by a variety of universities and colleges. They should not be confused with performance arts courses, which provide an education in the understanding of the arts and are also offered by a variety of universities and colleges.

Teacher education and training

To teach in a state school you must have both a degree and Qualified Teacher Status (QTS). Some first degrees include initial teacher training, so you graduate with QTS. Otherwise you qualify after you graduate, normally by taking a one-year PGCE. You should be reasonably confident that teaching is for you before deciding to limit your options by going for a teaching degree as your first degree.

Find out more from the Training & Development Agency for Schools (TDA) website (www.tda.gov.uk) or ring the teaching information line: 0845 600 0991 (0992 for Welsh speakers).

Other routes to a degree

External degrees and distance learning

External degrees are offered to students who study away from university, usually in their own time. They are related to distance learning, which also involves studying at home.

External degrees are still in demand, particularly from overseas. The majority of external students are studying for the wide range of external degrees offered by London University. No formal tuition is provided by the university (though it may be provided locally) and there is a range of learning materials, short courses, informal tutorial assessments and reading lists from which students may pick and choose. Undergraduate programmes last a minimum of three years, but external students usually take longer, and registration is valid for eight years. External students set their own pace and can sit their London University exams in most countries in the world.

Distance learning was pioneered by the Open University, founded 40 years ago, which developed sophisticated course materials to allow mature students to study at home. Many other universities now have distance-learning options, of variable quality, on degree courses. These are essentially part-time courses for which you do not have to attend the university.

Local routes

Some first degree courses can be taken locally, either completely or in part. Sometimes you can study for a year or two at your local FE college (and may qualify for a foundation degree) and then take your final year or two at the university that awards the degree. There are very many permutations and possibilities. Ask your local FE college.

American colleges

Many US universities and colleges have a campus in the UK that admits British students. Their academic standards vary greatly, so students may find it difficult to get British employers and professional bodies to accept their degree as necessarily equal to a UK degree. Some of these American colleges are excellent and of international standing.

Bogus degrees

These may be offered by post or, increasingly, by spam email. Sometimes they are for sale, sometimes a thesis is required, sometimes they are awarded for work experience. There is seldom any course of instruction. No university featured in this book offers or accepts such degrees but there seems to be a real demand for them.

It is a criminal offence to award or seek to offer a UK degree without express government authority.

If in doubt, you can check the list of all recognised degrees and degree-awarding institutions at www.dcsf.gov.uk/recogniseduKdegrees. There is no constraint on offering UK certificates or diplomas, or degrees from overseas, as long as it is clear that they are not UK-approved courses.

Selecting Universities

Your shortlist

Making a shortlist shouldn't be daunting, and this book is here to help you – you need to find a place that suits you physically and which matches your talents academically.

Don't just look at league tables: you are looking for a place that suits **you**, your interests, aptitudes and budget. It's worth accepting guidance from parents, teachers, etc, but do not let them decide for you.

This section of the book should provoke your thinking about different criteria – location, cost of living, student mix, etc.

Location and environment

It is crucially important that you find a congenial place in which you will be happy to spend the next few years of your life.

Do you want to be in a large, busy university with 20,000 students or in a small, cosy place where you will know everyone? Do you want to remain living at home or be at a university within, say, 30 miles of home – or do you want to put several hundred miles between you and your parents? Do you need to study somewhere where you can easily find a part-time job? Or get out to the hills? Or keep your surfing going?

If you have strong views about where you want to study, use the maps on pages 86–9 for guidance.

London

With over 60 universities and colleges and a colossal student population, London is a magnet for students, but there can be difficulties: not all universities and colleges have adequate accommodation, and the private sector can be pricey. Entertainment outside the students' union (SU) can be expensive too. Students are scattered across a very wide area, so you may have to travel some distance for work and play.

London does have huge advantages. For a start, it has some of the country's most distinguished university institutions and specialist colleges – many of international standing. It is second to none on the British cultural scene and is 'cool capital' of the world. If you study in London, your student loan will be marginally bigger to allow you more cash to live on, and you may get student travel concessions. There are infinite opportunities for entertainment – and lots of it is free if you look for it.

If you don't fancy a big city, well, that's another matter.

Different kinds of university

Universities are a pretty mixed bunch.

- Some have been around for 700 years; some are a lot younger than you are.
- Some have 1,500 students; some over 30,000 (London University has 43,000).
- Some are run as a single university; some are federations of separate institutions many miles apart; and others are made up of a collection of independent colleges in the same city.
- Some will be the right place to study philosophy or chemistry; others are the top places for car design or retail management.
- In some, all undergraduates are full-time; in others almost all students are part-time (for instance, Birkbeck is almost entirely for part-time students and the Open University is solely for distance learning).
- Some are world-class, research-intensive universities; some concentrate on teaching rather than research.
- Some universities can pick and choose their students ('selecting universities'); some are more active ('recruiting universities').

Every university has its own unique character. Not only does each have its own range of subjects, teaching and student mix, but it will also have its own rationale and ethos. You can check out the profiles, including indicators to the student body, in the 'University and college profiles' (page 91 onwards). There are some broad categories into which universities fall: see 'Six categories of university' (pages 765–67).

A 'top' university?

A top, research-led university suits some people but not others. If you can identify the top academic universities, you can then be sure to shortlist them or to avoid them like the plague. There are two indicators you might start with: research quality (see next section, page 12) and the standard of new students' entry qualifications. The intake will be different on different courses within the university but this does give a feel for the overall student body. Universities where the average student has 350 points or more are as follows.

Aston University
Brighton and Sussex Medical School
Bristol University
Cambridge University
Cardiff University
Courtauld Institute
Dundee University
Durham University
Exeter University
Glasgow Caledonian University

Glasgow University
Hull York Medical School
Imperial College
Leeds University
Leicester University
Liverpool University
LSE
Manchester University
Newcastle University
Oxford University

Peninsula Medical & Dental College
Queen's University Belfast
Royal Veterinary College
St Andrews University
Southampton University
Strathclyde University
Surrey University
University College London
Warwick University
York University

Teaching and research quality

The amount and quality of research being undertaken in a university is a good measure of its academic standing. If you are highly academic, you will get into and thrive in a top research-led university. If you are not, you will probably waste valuable UCAS choices applying there.

Universities ranked top in the recent Research Assessment Exercise were as follows.

The very top world-class universities

Cambridge University
Courtauld Institute
Imperial College
London Business School
LSE
Manchester University

Oxford University
Royal Academy of Music
Royal College of Art
School of Pharmacy
University College London
Warwick University

Top research-intensive universities

Aberdeen University
Bath University
Birkbeck
Birmingham University
Bristol University
Cardiff University
Central School of Speech & Drama
Dundee University
Durham University
East Anglia University
Edinburgh University
Essex University
Exeter University
Glasgow University
Goldsmiths
Kent
King's College London
Lancaster University
Leeds University

Liverpool University
Loughborough University
Newcastle University
Nottingham University
Open University
Queen Mary
Queen's University Belfast
Reading University
Royal College of Music
Royal Veterinary College
Royal Holloway
St Andrews University
Sheffield University
SOAS
Southampton University
Surrey University
Sussex University
York University

(Source: an analysis of the 2008 Research Assessment Exercise published by *Times Higher Education*, no. 1876, December 2008.)

Teaching quality varies greatly between departments and between institutions; the QAA website has information on the teaching assessments (www.qaa.ac.uk). Poor teaching quality, however, unlike research quality, can be improved relatively fast. It's also worth bearing in mind that an approach that suits others may not suit you – you may get a good idea of the approach from the prospectus.

Oxbridge (Oxford and Cambridge Universities)

The distinctive feature of the universities of Oxford and Cambridge is their collegiate system. You are admitted and belong to a college, which is an independent institution with its own staff, students and finance. Since there are only 200–600 undergraduates in each college, you can get to know most

students and it is relatively easy to participate in drama, sport, etc, but you also have all the advantages and opportunities that go with belonging to a large university – and one of only a handful of world-class universities in the UK.

You usually need to be pretty bright – capable of at least three A-levels at grade A. If you are up to the mark, do not be put off applying, either by their general media image (class bias, etc) or by the prejudice of school teachers. Oxford and Cambridge are not just playgrounds for rich, independent school kids – state-school entrants are in the majority at both; and they both have loads of advantages.

Both are top universities, actively looking for bright students, particularly students from comprehensive schools. There is lots of money around; hardship funds are generous and virtually no students drop out because of financial problems. In fact the drop-out rates at both universities are almost non-existent. Accommodation is available for most, often all, of your course; it is usually reasonably priced and you pay for it only in term time – and terms are relatively short. These are all real pluses.

Some of the teaching is in the college but much is university-based, as are the examinations. Women have been accepted in the universities for nearly 100 years, originally in women-only colleges. Except for a handful of women-only colleges in Cambridge, all colleges are now fully mixed at undergraduate level, though you may find the male:female ratio of the staff interesting.

Choosing a college is a bit like choosing a university (are you good enough in the chosen subject? are the right sort of activities available? etc). At present you are admitted by the college (though this may change in the future), so making your choice can involve some luck – everyone else wanting to do your subject may be applying to the same college. Do not be seduced by the buildings and the lawns. You may find the smaller, newer colleges less daunting than the bigger, grander ones (and for women it can be easier to get into the women-only colleges). You can find the college profiles under 'University profiles'.

Employability

Despite claims to the contrary, employers seldom regard universities or their graduates as equal; they use their own employment criteria. Many are fairly conservative and still prefer graduates from a handful of elite universities; some only interview graduates from places that are dominant in their fields (eg LSE for economics).

Most graduates leaving university have found a job within six months – some 94% of those whose fate is known are in employment or further study. There are some patterns: art students can be slower to find work, so art colleges and universities with a lot of art students have lower percentages; universities with vocational degrees involving work experience have higher percentages. The universities with the highest percentage (97%+) of graduates in employment or further study within six months (2006/2007) are as follows.

Courtauld Institute
Harper Adams University College
King's College London
Leeds College of Music
Liverpool Hope University
Napier University
Robert Gordon University

Royal Academy of Music
Royal College of Music
Royal Veterinary College
Saint George's
School of Pharmacy
Surrey University
Trinity College Carmarthen

To dig deeper into the employment record of an individual university, look at its website; if there is no information there, ask admissions staff direct. The fact that graduates have found work over the past six months does not tell the whole story, of course. No one knows if they are in worthwhile jobs or whether they are enjoying their employment – or indeed whether the graduate recruitment market will be as keen to absorb bright young graduates in three or four years time as it has been in the past.

Cost of living

There are huge differences between the cost of living in different places – and between individual colleges and universities in the same location. For example, living in Bradford is much cheaper than living in London; living at home is probably cheaper than anywhere else (but if you are living at home you get a lower student loan).

The individual university profiles give some information about local rents, opportunities for part-time work and the financial safety nets provided. Most universities now give you some idea of the minimum you will need to live on (excluding tuition fees) on their websites and in their prospectuses, although a few are too coy to do so. These reveal a huge spread – from £5k pa to over £12k pa.

Tuition fees

Almost all UK and EU students are expected to contribute towards the cost of their tuition. In 2009, the tuition fee for most first degree courses is £3,225, but there are various exceptions. Some universities charge less for some or all courses. Some universities charge this fee but give bursaries to all students; fees at all Scottish universities are lower and free to Scottish students; and fees at private colleges and universities can be a great deal higher.

CITY UNIVERSITY LONDON

City University London has one of the highest proportions of international and graduate students of any university in the UK. It successfully combines academic and professional studies with the majority of students gain a professional, as well as an academic award. The University has seven Schools and teaches across a range of subjects in journalism, music, informatics, social sciences, engineering and mathematical sciences, business, law, health and community sciences. With over 23,000 students from 156 countries and teaching staff drawn from nearly 50 international locations, the University has a truly international outlook.

City is ranked fifth amongst the UK's top universities offering graduates the best prospects following their studies according to The Times Good University Guide 2008. This is further evidenced by its alumni. Many former City students go on to reach the top of their chosen field and include countless captains of industry and other household names, such as Brendan Barber, General Secretary of the TUC; Stelios Haji-Ioannou, easyGroup Chairman; Ruby Hammer, Co-Owner of Ruby and Millie Cosmetics and Faisal Islam, Channel 4 News Economics Correspondent.

The University continues to build and maintain its strong links with the City of London and wider industries and prides itself on being 'The University for business and the professions' – it strives to enable students to achieve their goals by preparing them for their careers and providing them with opportunities otherwise unavailable. The University's Chancellor is The Lord Mayor of the City of London.

City students have a new Students' Union venue on the main Northampton Square site and the University Student Centre brings together a comprehensive range of support activities; in one face to face location ensuring students have a dedicated point of contact throughout their university career.

With a long tradition of bringing thought leaders and influencers into the University, there are regular debates, talks and events. Recent event highlights include, Thomas Gensemer – the brains behind President Obama's online election campaign; campaigning criminal barrister, Michael Mansfield QC and Chancellor of the Exchequer, Alistair Darling who divulged his latest plans for maintaining economic stability in the midst of the bank bailout.

www.city.ac.uk

International students pay the full-cost fee for the course – or whatever the university feels the international market will bear. Home students may find it salutary to look at these fees – you may think of your course as a bargain at £3,225 pa if you find that other students are willing to pay £15k pa for it.

International fees are lower for courses taught largely in the classroom (from £7k to over £12k pa) than for those taught in a studio or lab (from around £8k to over £18k pa). Fees for clinical courses are the most expensive, from £18,500 to £30k pa.

A complete list of universities and the fees they charge is given on pages 58–66.

Financial help from universities

Universities have lots of money to help particular categories of students – but the amount that you might get varies enormously from university to university. Almost all universities (certainly all that charge the fee of £3,225 pa) will help students from low-income families. There are also earmarked funds of differing sizes for particular groups of students, for example students on particular courses, those with high entrance requirements and those with nursery costs or those from local partner schools and colleges. Almost all have money for students who suddenly hit unexpected hardship during their course. Check out what's on offer in the university profiles and go for it – bursaries are non-returnable (ie they are not loans), so they are really worth getting.

What a university defines as a low-income family, and what help is on offer, will vary. For example, if your family income is £26k pa, you may qualify for a bursary of £500 pa at one university, of £2k pa at another, a combined scholarship and bursary of £3,500 pa at a third, or nothing at all at another university.

As a simplistic indication, if your family income were approximately £18k, you would be entitled to a bursary of more than £1,400 pa from the following universities listed in the box below, without any extra entitlements. The actual bursary (approximate figure) is in brackets.

BURSARIES

You will get a bursary of at least £1,400 pa or more at the following places if you are a UK student and your family income is approximately £18k pa. (Figures in brackets are pa.)

Bristol Old Vic Theatre School (£1,700)
Cambridge University (£3,150)
Exeter University (£1,500)
Guildhall School of Music & Drama (£1,453)
Hertfordshire University (£1,453)
Heythrop College (£1,453)
Imperial College (£3k)
Leeds University (£1,500)
London Contemporary Dance School (£1,700)
LSE (£1,593)

Northern School of Contemporary Dance (£1,700)
Oxford Brookes University (£1,560)
Oxford University (£3,225)
Peninsula Medical & Dental College (£1,500)
RADA (£1,700)
Royal Agricultural College (£1,500)
Royal Veterinary College (£1,650)
Warwick University (£1,800)
York St John University (£1,570)
York University (£1,436)

Exciting extras universities offer

Beyond their degree courses, universities offer a huge variety of opportunities to develop your own personal skills and interests. There may be free access to language centres and IT courses at all levels of experience and ability; opportunities in sport, for novices and high-fliers; excellent music; lively drama; debating; and more. Or, of course, there may be none of these. There may be stunning libraries and impressive IT provision, and the SU may be large and humming, with an award-winning student mag and major bands at its venue – or not. You can get a flavour of what each university offers in our university profiles.

The lists below shows the universities that spend more than £200 pa per student on information provision, and those that spend less than £50 pa.

£200 per student pa

Buckingham University
Cambridge University
Courtauld Institute
Cranfield University
Glasgow University
Imperial College
Liverpool University
London Business School
LSE
Oxford University
St Andrews University
St George's
School of Pharmacy
Scottish Agricultural College
Spurgeon's College
University College London

Less than £50 per student pa

Arts London
Edinburgh College of Art
Glyndŵr University
Leeds College of Music
Newport
Northern School of Contemporary Dance
Norwich University College of the Arts
Rose Bruford College
Thames Valley University
Trinity College of Music
Writtle College

Student mix

There are huge variations between the student populations in different universities. It's not just the male:female ratio and the proportion of students from state/independent schools but also the drop-out rates (which range from zero to 22% in the first year), the proportion of international students and mature students, full- and part-time students – not to mention the courses they are taking, the standard of qualifications they come with and the level of courses they are studying.

You'll find out more about the student mix in our university and college profiles.

College – does the label matter?

The word 'college' can mean many things – a school (Eton College), a crammer (Garret Tutorial College, Hackney) or a professional institution (Royal College of Surgeons).

Those that teach first degrees might be specialist colleges (Royal Northern College of Music), colleges of a university (University College London, or Pembroke College, Cambridge), independent colleges awarding their own degrees (Falmouth University College) or the degrees of another university (Bradford College).

Further education colleges may also offer some first degree courses in addition to A-level and vocational courses; these are always validated by (and the degree awarded by) a university, not the college itself. Increasingly, it is possible to take the first one or two years of a course at an FE college and complete the course at the validating university.

Anglia Ruskin University research is world-leading

Commitment to research and scholarship enshrines vision to be one of the most successful modern universities

The government's 2008 Research Assessment Exercise (RAE) results for Higher Education institutions have been announced, showing research at Anglia Ruskin University is increasing in strength and scope. More than half of the work in all nine of Anglia Ruskin's submissions was recognized as of 'international quality', with eight submissions having a proportion of their work rated as 'world-leading'.

Out of the 'new' universities, the *Times Higher Education* Tables 2008 rated Anglia Ruskin top for Psychology, second for English Language & Literature and third for History.

The RAE is a periodic analysis of research strengths across the sector and confirms the UK's dominant position in international research. It shows the UK research base in more detail than ever before, and results have been used to allocate more than £1.5 billion each year from 2009-2010.

Vice Chancellor Professor Michael Thorne said: 'I am delighted that the excellence of the work in the areas where we have prioritised research has been recognised in this way. Those colleagues involved will be justly proud that we do so much work of an international standard - not to mention an encouraging proportion of world-leading research. For me, this confirms the content of our newly agreed Research and Scholarship strategy. It amplifies the unambiguous commitment to research and scholarship now enshrined in our Vision and describes a set of actions and investments, totalling some £4.5 million.'

Anglia Ruskin University achieved similar rankings in the *Guardian* and *Research Fortnightly.*

Anglia Ruskin also demonstrates teaching excellence, with nine of it's subjects - Allied health professions (radiography); applied social work; English; music; nursing and midwifery; philosophy; psychology; teacher training; theology and religious studies, being rated 'Excellent' by the *Sunday Times University Guide* 2008.

For further information:
Click **www.anglia.ac.uk/telegraph**
Email **answers@anglia.ac.uk**
Call **0845 271 3333**

Anglia Ruskin
University

Cambridge & Chelmsford

Get More Detail

Prospectuses and websites

All universities and colleges publish prospectuses – both the traditional (usually glossy) paper versions and electronic versions on their websites. These are your primary sources. (Web addresses are given in each university profile.) Each college within the federal universities (eg London, Cambridge) has its own prospectus. So, too, do many individual university departments and faculties; these give lists of teaching staff and their research interests (which can be illuminating) and outline how they teach their subject.

The university website or prospectus is essential if you want to find out more about the place – its departments, the structure and assessment of the courses, typical offers made, the attitude to studying abroad, possible combinations of subjects, accommodation, facilities – in fact almost everything you need to know. It will also tell you if you are likely to be accepted – whether you have the right subjects at the right level and with the right grades or points for the course you want to do. It may express a view about mature students, gap years, repeat A-levels, etc. Some universities and colleges have student profiles on the UCAS website, which describe the sort of students they are looking for. Don't rely on secondary sources. If you have any doubt at all, check direct with admissions tutors.

Don't lose sight of the fact that prospectuses are first and foremost designed to sell the university to you. Use them to try to identify the university's ethos; see what the strengths are (eg sport or religion); these may or may not match yours. They are an essential read before any interview.

Visits and open days

Don't even think of spending three years at a place you haven't visited. You may find you hate it on sight, and it's too late to discover that when you start freshers' week.

All universities and colleges, and most departments, hold open days for prospective students. These give you the opportunity to see the campus and town as well as any facilities that are particularly relevant to your choice of course (computer centre, studios, etc); and, of course, you can meet staff and students. If you can't fit in an open days, at least go and snoop around to make sure you feel you will fit in. Ideally, visit before you apply; certainly before you accept.

Dates of open days are usually published on the university's website and in prospectuses; they are also given on the UCAS website (www.ucas.com). Sometimes open days are only available to those who have been offered a place. When open days are offered – go.

Higher education fairs

These are like markets, with university staff as stallholders hawking their wares. They last for a day or two and are useful for picking up prospectuses and talking to a range of university staff, all under one roof. They are run nationally and regionally, so you should be able to find one near you (it is not worth travelling too far to go to one). Fifty or so are run by UCAS under the label of UCAS Conventions; check the UCAA website for your nearest event. While they are useful, higher education fairs are no substitute for visiting the university itself.

Students' unions

Most SUs have their own websites. These can be useful to see how the union is run, what it does for students and what is going on. Many have special sections for prospective students. The SU may also have an alternative prospectus. Many SUs are pleased to talk directly to sixth formers who take the trouble to contact them (contact details are given in the university profiles).

Entrance Requirements and Offers

Entrance requirements

Each university has its own entrance requirements, and they come in two guises: **minimum entrance requirements**, without which you will not be accepted by the university (though there are exceptions for mature students); and individual **course requirements**, which may be much more specific. The minimum entrance requirements for a university might be five GCSEs at grade C, and two A-level passes (or equivalent); but course requirements for its physics degree might be three A-levels including grade B in physics (or equivalent). Course requirements will vary between different courses at the same university and between the same course at different universities.

Formal entrance requirements should not be confused with the actual requirements a university makes when it offers you a place. In most cases **offers** are much higher than entrance requirements and will reflect both the academic expectations of the course lecturers and the number of other people applying for places on the course.

As for the qualifications that universities accept – all will accept A-levels (rarely AS-levels on their own). The International Baccalaureate (IB) is widely accepted, and with some enthusiasm. Scottish Highers are generally regarded as satisfying the entrance requirements of universities in Scotland, but elsewhere in the UK you will usually need Advanced Highers or A-levels as well. Most universities treat the Welsh Baccalaureate as equivalent to A-levels (and some Welsh universities enthuse about it). The new Advanced Diplomas are scarcely mentioned in university entrance requirements, though this will obviously change: where they are specifically accepted, it is usually only for related degree courses, and you may require an A-level as well. If you have other qualifications, including overseas qualifications, check that they are acceptable on the university website or direct with university admissions staff. You will normally need a recognised English language qualification (eg GCSE grade C or the IELTS test).

And a warning about subjects – do not assume that all A-level (or equivalent) subjects are equally acceptable for the purposes of university entrance. They are not. Some subjects are almost always accepted for university entrance and some are not – particularly where entry is very competitive. School subjects including accounting, art and design, business studies, communications studies, dance, design and technology, drama or theatre studies, home economics, information and communication technology, law, media studies, sports studies or a vocational qualification are likely to be acceptable for degrees in a related subject. However, if you are applying to a mainstream academic course at a competitive university, you will need to combine any of these subjects with two mainstream academic subjects. General studies often does not count as one of the three A-levels required by academic universities.

Each university has its own approach. You can usually find information on the university website, either summarised in their general statements about entry requirements or given on individual course profiles. If you are in any doubt about whether you meet precisely whatever is needed, do not hesitate to check direct with the university admissions staff.

Offers

The offer that a university makes may require you to achieve a lot more than the minimum entrance (or course) requirement – for example up to three A-levels at grade A, or even more for a course with high demand. Some competitive courses may make lower offers of, say, AAB, although they will only bother to look at an application if you were predicted AAA.

Some offers are given in terms of specific grades for specific qualifications (eg you may be required to get three A-levels, with grade B in physics), some in tariff points (eg 300 points). Or some may be a mixture – for example 320 points, of which 240 should be from A-levels; or 310 points to include a grade C in A-level history. Check the 'UCAS tariff points table' below if you are not sure of the relationship between the two.

Typical offers are now published, course by course, in almost all university prospectuses. You need to be clear about what is required before you apply, so that you don't waste your UCAS choices.

University offers relate to demand and can change (rather like prices): if a particular course becomes very popular, the grades required will go up next year; if no one wants to do the course, the offers may go down. So there can be bargains around in summer Clearing, when some universities scrabble to top up their student numbers.

Tariff points table

The tariff system is an attempt by UCAS to equate different grades in various qualifications into a single points system. Not everyone agrees with it and many universities do not use it. The principal qualifications translate as follows.

UCAS tariff points table*

Grade	AS-level GCE/VCE 3 units†	A-level GCE/VCE 6 units	VCE A-level double award 12 units	Scottish Advanced Highers	Scottish Highers
A*	–	140 points	280 points	–	–
A	60 points	120	240	120 (130) points	72 (80) points
B	50	100	200	100 (110)	60 (65)
C	40	80	160	80 (90)	48 (50)
D	30	60	120	72	42 (36)
E	20	40	80	–	–

* Some points change in 2010; new score in brackets
† No double counting – AS-levels continued to A-level do not count

The International Baccalaureate converts into tariff points very generously. The lowest pass (24 IB points) equates to 280 tariff points. Each additional IB point adds approximately 23 tariff points, so the highest pass (45 IB points) comes to an unbelievable 768 tariff points.

New qualifications are constantly being added to the tariff points system: the new sixth-form diplomas, Welsh Baccalaureate, BTEC National Diplomas, key skills, music grades 6–8, British Horse Society, financial services exams, etc. You can find out which have been included, and calculate your own points, on the tariff tables on the UCAS website (www.ucas.com).

Some universities will allow any of these exams to count towards any points offer; most will not.

Admissions tests

As more applicants achieve top A-level grades, academic universities are increasingly using admissions tests to select students for their more competitive courses. If you are interested in one of these courses, you will, whatever your other achievements, have to take the admissions test before they consider your application.

Admissions tests currently being used by groups of universities or individual universities include the following.

- BMAT (BioMedical Admissions Test), used for entry to certain medical, veterinary and related courses at Cambridge, Imperial, Oxford, Royal Veterinary College and University College London (www.bmat.org.uk).
- ELAT (Oxford University's English Literature Admissions Test) (www.admissionstests.cambridgeassessment.org.uk/adt/elat).
- GAMSAT (Graduate Medical Schools' Admissions Test), for entry to many graduate medical schools – six at the last count (www.gamsatuk.org).
- HAT (Oxford University's History Aptitude Test) (www.history.ox.ac.uk).
- HPAT (Health Professions Admissions Test), for certain health courses at Ulster University (http://hpat-ulster.acer.edu.au).
- LNAT (the National Admissions Test for Law), used by a number of universities – 12 at the last count (www.lnat.ac.uk).
- MML (Cambridge University's Modern and Medieval Languages Test) (www.cam.ac.uk).
- STEP (Cambridge University's Sixth Term Examination Papers), used for mathematics (www.maths.cam.ac.uk).
- TSA (Thinking Skills Assessment Test), used by three universities: Cambridge, for courses in computer science, economics, engineering, land economy, natural sciences (physical and biological) and social and political science; Oxford, for courses in politics, philosophy and economics and also economics and management; and University College London, for European social and political studies. You can check out all of them on the same website: www.admissionstests.cambridgeassessment.org.uk.
- UKCAT (UK Clinical Aptitude Test), used by a consortium of UK medical and dental schools – about 28 at the last count (www.ukcat.ac.uk).

If you want to know what any of these aptitude tests involve, you should be able to find past papers, information on how to enter, test dates, etc on the relevant website.

Art foundation courses

You may be accepted onto a degree course in art and design with either A-levels or (preferably) an art foundation course, or both. Like A-levels, the art foundation course – or Diploma in Foundation Studies (Art and Design), as it is formally known – attracts UCAS tariff points: a pass counts for 165 tariff points, a merit 225 and a distinction 285.

Why bother at all? Because art foundation courses allow you to sample a range of disciplines and media, and to develop your portfolio, before deciding which direction you want to follow at degree level. Many sixth formers believe that an art foundation course is not really necessary, particularly as some colleges compete to offer more able A-level students a direct place, but those who have taken an art foundation course tend to start their degree courses with a clearer idea of what they want to do, are better motivated and are less likely to drop out.

Most students take their art foundation course at one of 200 local art colleges. A few universities have four-year degree courses with an integral foundation year, which may look attractive, but from a free-standing art foundation course you can move on to the university or college that best suits your chosen area of specialisation.

Those without formal entrance requirements

There are ways of getting in, even if you do not meet the published entrance requirements. For example, the formal requirements may be waived or modified for mature students (usually defined as students aged 21 or over). You do, however, have to persuade admissions tutors you can cope with the course. Some universities and colleges will decide this by interview; some may require you to take an exam (eg an A-level in a year).

There are many access and foundation courses that help you return to study, or to pick up, for example, science basics before a science degree, or a pre-med course before a medical degree. Some are better than others; and some are linked with particular degree courses.

You will find universities and colleges vary widely in their attitudes, so be sure to check direct with the admissions staff before applying.

And If . . .

. . . you are thinking of taking a gap year

Taking a gap year between school and university can be a very good thing, but you need to make sure that your chosen universities (and course tutors) agree. The university prospectus may welcome students who are taking a year out, while one of its departments doesn't (or perhaps insists that the time is spent gaining relevant experience). Some universities welcome students after a gap year but will not make offers in advance (deferred offers).

If you decide to take a year out, you can apply for your course either during your gap year or in 2009 for deferred entry in 2011. But watch out for those universities (and departments) that are happy about gap years in principle but are not interested in offering places to deferred entry applicants.

Before you apply, ask the admissions tutors to spell out the university and departmental position, and whether others on your course will also have taken a gap year.

. . . you will be over 21 when you start

Nearly half the students in higher education are aged over 21 at the start of their course and universities often make special provision for their particular needs, and may waive some entrance requirements (see 'Those without formal entrance requirements', page 27). At Birkbeck, in London, over 90% (and at the Open University over 75%) of the students are mature students. Both Oxford and Cambridge have colleges specifically for mature students.

Elsewhere, there are very high numbers of mature students at some universities and relatively few at others; the average is 27%. Check the proportions for individual universities in the university profiles. Mature students should feel particularly comfortable at the following institutions, where they constitute more than 60% of the student population.

The list below shows places where more than 60% of students are over 21 on entry:

Anglia Ruskin University
Birkbeck
Colchester Institute
Edge Hill University
Goldsmiths
London School of Theology
Open University
Plymouth University

Spurgeon's College
Thames Valley University
UHI Millennium Institute

At Cambridge University: Hughes Hall, Lucy Cavendish and St Edmund's colleges; at Oxford University: Harris Manchester College.

. . . you have a disability

In addition to all the usual considerations, students with disabilities also need to know if institutions have the facilities and support services they need. Most should have – there are probably over 8,000 students with disabilities at UK universities. A few universities have state-of-the-art facilities, such as libraries for partially sighted people.

Make direct contact with universities and colleges before completing your shortlist. Most universities have a special adviser or co-ordinator with whom you can discuss your needs for studying and daily living; and you will probably be able to arrange a fact-finding visit. Many now provide or help organise specialist support services, such as readers, note-takers and transcription; and many have specialist accommodation available. Provision does vary, so always make individual enquiries. Make contact early; they may be able to improve their facilities in some way before you get there. If you cannot proceed with an application because the facilities are not suitable, you can ask UCAS to substitute an alternative choice.

You can get useful information and advice from Skill (National Bureau for Students with Disabilities). The website is www.skill.org.uk and it links to the individual websites for Skill Scotland, Skill Wales and Skill Northern Ireland.

. . . you have children

Studying when you have children brings its own problems and you need to address them before you apply, particularly if taking your course involves moving from your home.

If you have a young child, find out about nursery facilities. Ring each of your possible choices and speak to the head of the nursery: ask about waiting lists, minimum age and how you book a place (and don't forget to budget for nursery costs). Many university profiles describe nursery arrangements, and some college education departments have a teaching nursery.

If you have an older child or children, find out about local schools and how to get into them. Sort out accommodation possibilities early: halls of residence do not usually accept children, but some universities and colleges have family accommodation.

. . . you want to go straight into the second (or subsequent) year of a course

If you change course (or return to higher education after a break) you may be able to transfer credit for the work you have completed to your new course, and so complete it in less time; you may also be able to get credit for what you have learned in a related job. The jargon for this is APL or APEL – assessment of prior (experiential) learning.

You may be able to carry credit from one university to another, or from one course to another within the same university. You will need the help (and maybe the approval) of the course tutor from your first course, so make sure you keep him/her informed.

Some credit transfers are easier than others. It is usually automatic from an HND or foundation degree to a linked degree course and almost impossible from, say, social science to physics. The overlap between two courses is not simple to assess, and some admissions tutors can be reluctant to try. Their approaches can be very different, so check direct with the university admissions staff.

GETTING IN AND SURVIVING THERE

How to Apply

UCAS – the system

For the vast majority of first degree courses, you apply through UCAS (the Universities and Colleges Admissions Service). It handles nearly half a million applications for over 50,000 courses every year and runs a central applications system for almost all UK universities and colleges.

You make a single application for up to five courses. UCAS forwards your application to the admissions staff at each individual university you have specified, and then makes sure that each university makes a decision about your application. It plays no part in the selection process itself. Each university and college decides for itself whether to offer you a place and on what terms; and you decide whether or not to accept each or any offer. Communication between you and the universities at this stage is through UCAS. The system works according to a strict timetable.

UCAS has an applicants' enquiry line for help and advice: 0871 468 0468 (if you have hearing difficulties, call the RNID Typetalk service on 18001 0871 468 0468 or +44 151 494 1260 from outside the UK).

But the key to its operation is its website (www.ucas.com), which has loads of information on the application procedure, courses with unfilled places, etc. It allows you to apply online (*Apply*), track the progress of your own application (*Track*) and search for course details (*Course Search*).

How UCAS works for you

First choose your courses

First you need to decide which courses you want to apply for, and at which universities (see 'Shortlisting' (pages 1–27)). You choose up to five courses. These may include different courses at the same university, a mixture of degrees at different universities, and more than one subject – the choice is yours (each university will obviously know which of its own courses you have applied to, but it won't see what you have applied to at any other university). *Course Search* on the UCAS website has up-to-date information on courses and their entrance requirements.

Then apply

You make a single UCAS application. You can apply from anywhere in the world with internet access, using the secure web-based application system called *Apply*. You can apply either as an independent applicant or through a UCAS-registered centre (eg a school, college or careers office). If you apply through your school or college, they are responsible for getting your application and reference to UCAS.

When you apply online, you will find pull-down menus and help text to ensure you enter valid university and course information in the choices section of your application.

Apply as early as you can

There are different deadlines to keep your eye on. You can apply any time from mid-September, but the earlier the better – UCAS and admissions tutors are very busy around deadlines. Applications for 2010 entry should be with UCAS by 15 January 2010, unless you are applying for medicine, dentistry or veterinary medicine/science or to any course at the universities of Oxford or Cambridge, when the deadline is 15 October 2009. Some art and design courses have a deadline date of 15 January, some 24 March 2010; you should check this on *Course Search* on the UCAS website.

If you miss the 15 January deadline, all may not be lost. UCAS will still accept your application, but the universities and colleges are not obliged to consider it, so you may miss out on courses in high demand (this does not apply to international applicants from outside the EU). Applications received after 30 June will not be sent on to universities in the normal way but will go straight into the summer Clearing – although you can of course contact your chosen universities and colleges direct in the meantime. UCAS will accept new applications through Clearing until 21 September, but by then most courses will have closed admissions.

Referee

This will usually be your head of sixth form or sixth form tutor. Whoever you choose, make sure you give them enough time to write your reference. Referees will have more than one reference to write, and yours needs to be processed in time to reach UCAS by the appropriate date.

Application fee

If you are applying individually or you are an international applicant, you will normally have to pay by credit or debit card. If you are applying through your school or college, they will let you know how to pay: either by credit or debit card online or direct to the school or college, who will then pay UCAS. The fee is £19 (£9 if you are applying only for one course).

After you have applied

UCAS will then do the following.

- Confirm receipt of your application (electronically).
- Send you a 'Welcome' letter, which confirms details of your application and lists the courses and institutions they have recorded for you. Check these details carefully. This letter also gives you your own, individual Personal ID and *Track* username. Keep them safe; you will need them for all future correspondence and to check the progress of your application on the UCAS website using *Track*.
- Pass your application on to the universities and colleges you have chosen.

The universities decide

The admissions tutors for all your chosen courses consider your application. They decide whether to offer you a place and, if so, whether the offer is conditional (on, say, the results of summer exams) or unconditional. Sometimes this may involve an interview. Once an institution has made a decision, UCAS sends you an email telling you to check *Track* for details. As long as you have applied by the January deadline, you should expect to hear from all your choices by early May 2010.

You decide

When you have had responses from all your choices (and if they include at least one offer), you need to decide whether to accept. If none of your offers depends on exam results, you can make your final decision and accept just one offer. If some or all of your offers are conditional on exam results, you can accept a maximum of two – a first choice and an optional insurance offer (it's usually more sensible to choose a lower offer).

You cannot make a decision before you have heard from all your choices; if you know you have the offer(s) you want, you can cancel your other choices and then accept the offer(s) you want – all using *Track*. You must reply by the deadline given – which is your **own personal deadline**, depending on when your offers were made.

Extra

If you have used all your choices and have either received no offers or turned down the ones you have, you can make further choices (one at a time) through Extra. This operates from the end of February to the end of June. Extra allows you to change direction completely (eg if you've gone off medicine, you can change to sports science). Check vacancies on the courses you are interested in, either with each university or on the UCAS website (*Course Search*).

If you are taking exams in the summer

UCAS will receive your summer exam results direct from the exam boards for most UK qualifications (eg AS and A-levels, IB, BTEC National Diploma, SQA) so you don't need to tell them or any university holding a place for you.

- You definitely have a place if you have (precisely) met the conditions of your offer; you will be able to confirm this on *Track*. UCAS will also send you a confirmation letter, which will tell you if you need to take any further action to confirm your place. If the letter asks you to confirm with the university that you accept the place, you must do this within 14 days or risk losing it. Institutions usually make decisions very quickly after the results come out, so you should take action if you have not heard from UCAS after ten days: check *Track* to see that your place has been confirmed or contact the university direct.

- You might have a place if your results are lower than those specified in the offer (in general, eg three grade Cs instead of a B and two Cs; or, in particular, eg, your grade in history), but that is entirely at the discretion of the university. Ring and persuade them; lots of other people may be in the same boat but you want them to notice you. If they will still take you, they will confirm your place and UCAS will inform you by letter.

- If your results are better than you needed for your accepted offer, you might want to switch to a different course. For a short time, you can look for a course you prefer that still has places available, while still holding your original offer.

Clearing

No place yet? Then you are entered into Clearing, which operates from mid July to September (but mostly after A-level results are published in mid August). If you do not have a place, because your application was late or your results did not match your offer, you will automatically be given a Clearing number (shown on *Track*). Don't wait that long to hassle admissions tutors for a place – there is nothing to prevent you from getting in touch with any university or college direct, and the earlier the better. If you do contact the university, do it yourself; don't expect the university to accept you on the basis of a call from your parents.

Art and design

Applications for art and design courses may have a deadline date of 15 January or 24 March; check this on *Course Search* on the UCAS website.

Music – practice-based courses

For most of the practical music courses at seven of the specialist conservatoires, you apply through CUKAS – the Conservatoires UK Admissions Service.

The conservatoires using CUKAS are: Birmingham Conservatoire, Leeds College of Music, Royal College of Music, Royal Northern College of Music, Royal Scottish Academy of Music & Drama, Royal Welsh College of Music & Drama and Trinity College of Music.

And of course you can apply direct to the two London conservatoires not using CUKAS: Royal Academy of Music and Guildhall School of Music & Drama.

CUKAS

CUKAS works rather like UCAS – it sends your application to the conservatoires you have chosen and notifies you about auditions, offers, etc.

You can make up to six choices through CUKAS (all your choices are seen by the conservatoires you apply to). You can also make another five degree course choices through UCAS, but you cannot hold a confirmed place through both UCAS and CUKAS (UCAS will write and ask which place you will be taking up).

The key to the CUKAS operation is its website (www.cukas.ac.uk). You register online and can then use it for your course research (*Course Search*) and application (*Apply*). The key dates for applications are on the website, but they are all several months earlier than for other courses – for example, applications can be made from early July and the closing date for on-time applications is 1 October. You can monitor the progress of your application through *Track*. There is online assistance if you need it or you can phone the CUKAS customer services line on 0871 468 0470.

Direct applications

Some institutions offering first degree courses do not use UCAS. These include universities offering a wide range of part-time first-degree courses (Birkbeck, the Open University) and some specialist colleges (Guildhall School of Music & Drama, the Architectural Association).

For direct applications, it is important to check early to avoid missing vital deadlines (closing dates, dates for audition, interviews, submission of portfolios, etc). You can apply direct to as many of these colleges and courses as you want, in addition to your UCAS/CUKAS courses.

Application timetables

UCAS applications

Key dates for a 2010 start

Mid September 2009: you can send your completed application to UCAS.

15 October: last date for your application to reach UCAS if you are applying for medicine, dentistry or veterinary medicine/science. Also deadline for Oxford or Cambridge University applications to reach UCAS.

15 January 2010: closing date for on-time UK/EU applications.

Early May: you should have heard from all your choices by now.

Your personal reply date: when you have heard from all your choices, you may have two or more offers. If so, you will have to decide which is your first and which is your insurance offer, within a few days. Beware – this **personal deadline** for replying is important; other people's deadlines will be different.

End February–end June: Extra, when you can make more or different applications. 30 June: closing date for international applications (non-EU) and for late UK/EU applications. Apply after that date and you will go into Clearing.

August: your exam results.

- If you have met the conditions of any offer, you're in. You will usually receive confirmation via UCAS within 10 working days; if asked to do so, you must reply to your university within 14 days.
- If you have not met the conditions of your offer, UCAS will automatically place you in Clearing.

Late August–20 September 2010: Clearing. Ring round the universities and colleges; get help from your school or your local careers office. Look for vacancies on the UCAS website and in the national press.

Practice-based music applications

Key dates for a 2010 start

Early July 2009: you can send your completed application to CUKAS.

1 October: closing date for on-time applications.

Mid October: auditions start.

End January 2010: final date for you to reply to any offers you received by early January.

1 February: you should contact conservatoires to check for vacancies if you want to apply now.

End March/July: final dates for you to reply to any offers you received by early March/July.

August: your exam results. If you have met the conditions of any offer, you're in.

25 August: final date for you to reply to offers received by early August.

31 August 2010: final date for late applications to reach CUKAS.

Applying

Completing your application

The university's sales document is its prospectus; yours is your completed application, so be sure to sell yourself as hard as they do. Remember, you may be interviewed by someone holding your application, so don't overdo it! Also, this is your own application – not the school's, not your parents' – so make your own case. Selectors are looking for good grades and motivation, promise for the future and wide interests and activities. In short, they want to know whether you are likely to benefit from their degree course.

The vast majority of applications – certainly all those to UCAS and CUKAS – are electronic. The system is pretty foolproof: it prevents you entering invalid information on choices, entry requirements, course codes, etc. You may need to complete a paper form for direct applications to some colleges (but this is usually a form downloaded from a website), in which case you will need to make absolutely sure you get the details correct.

However you apply, the information you are asked for is usually as follows.

Personal details: Fairly straightforward. You may be disconcerted to be asked by UCAS to reveal your ethnic origin, occupational background and whether your parents are graduates, but this information is not used for selection purposes; it is sent to the university/college for statistical purposes for students who are accepted.

Choice of course: Up to five choices through UCAS; six through CUKAS. Make sure they include a fall-back choice, so you are still in with a chance if your exam results do not match your expectations. Universities may not see where else you are applying to, but admissions tutors will obviously see which courses you apply to at their university, so think twice before applying for totally different courses at the same university – would admissions tutors feel you were equally committed to either course?

Examinations for which results are known: Put down everything, even failures and low grades. You should also include any AS-levels taken in Year 12 for which you are getting a certificate. You must tell the whole story. Even a poor result might not look as bad as you think: coming back from a failure or disappointing result indicates persistence, motivation and determination.

Examinations to be taken: Again, put in everything.

Employment: If you are applying from school and have worked part time, you can include this information here, particularly if your employment is related to the course you are applying for. You can use your personal statement to expand on your employment record and to mention any casual jobs you have done.

Personal statement: This is the most difficult section, but it is your key selling opportunity, so use the space positively (nb UCAS has a word limit). Be sure you write it yourself. If your parents write it for you, it will show; if you pay a company to write it for you, it could look even worse. Draft it first and make as many changes as you need. When you are happy with it, paste it in to your application. This is your one chance to sell yourself, so give relevant and precise information. Include everything that gives you some depth – don't put 'reading' as an interest; you're expected to read, so be specific. Then you can answer actual questions if you are interviewed. The admissions staff will read dozens – maybe hundreds – of personal statements, so be sure you stand out from the crowd. If you have a career in mind, say so (this shows motivation); but don't lose sleep if you don't know. It can take a lot of time to get this section written. You may find it helpful to work in pairs or groups to decide what to cover.

References

All applications must be supported by an educational reference. A lot of importance is attached to it, so get the best you can. Your sixth form tutor or course tutor is expected to write your reference if you are still at school or college, and to predict your likely results if you are taking summer exams. Don't go out of your way to flatter them, but show interest, motivation, persistence and, above all, that you're teachable. Make sure they know of any activities and interests outside the classroom that are relevant. Some teachers/tutors discuss the reference with students before they write it.

Make sure you give your referee enough time (their diaries are usually more clogged than yours). Messing up your references is one of the easier ways of messing up your application.

References are often thought of as confidential, but under the Data Protection Act, you can get a copy of your reference, and any other personal information UCAS holds on you.

Interviews

If you are called for an interview, find out if it is part of the selection procedure (rather than a visiting or open day). Prepare for the interview by predicting questions like 'Why are you applying here?' 'Why have you chosen this particular course?'. On highly selective courses, you may get questions that are intended to be hard to anticipate and that test your ability to think laterally ('Is this question logical?'). Ask your teacher/tutor to give you a mock interview. Look at one of the many guides available. Here are some thoughts to start you off.

- Show you have the personal qualities needed to undertake a degree, such as enjoying learning, reading, writing essays, doing lab work, wanting to argue and talk about new ideas and being eager to find out things for yourself.
- An interview is a structured conversation, so avoid answering in monosyllables.
- Be positive – avoid answering 'No', when you could answer 'Not precisely, but I have . . .'.
- If you have more than one interviewer, reply to the one who asks the questions and then bring the other(s) in.
- Don't mumble, don't chew gum, don't pick your nose and turn off your phone.
- Relax as much as possible and wear something smart but comfortable.
- Try to repress any distracting mannerisms.
- Prepare questions for the interviewer at the end.
- Above all, don't be cowed: you're interviewing them too.

If you have a disability, make sure you let the college know of any special requirements (such as communicators or parking facilities) before you attend.

How you are chosen

This is not always clear – some people think it is more or less a lottery. The situation is obviously different on a highly competitive course at a popular university than it is on a hard-to-fill course somewhere less popular. On some courses, you will be accepted if you apply with the minimum entrance qualifications; but for some top courses, where all applicants have straight A grades, universities are using extra admissions (or aptitude) tests to help admissions tutors decide.

Each university has a target number of places that it must meet precisely – if possible with teachable students. They adopt one of two ways of going about it (or both): they make a large number of conditional offers so that the exam results do the choosing; or they put more reliance on interviews and references.

Apart from all the other information about you, admissions staff are working on your predicted grades (which may or may not match your final results), so they are playing a futures market, which relies on their experience of assessing student potential.

After the summer results are known, universities that have missed their target numbers may accept applications they would have rejected earlier in the year. Do not lose heart if you do not yet have a place; keep badgering admissions staff – even after the beginning of term.

Offers

You may be offered a place in one of two ways: unconditionally or conditionally.

- Unconditional offers are what they say they are – you're in!
- Conditional offers are dependent upon the results in exams you have still to take. They are expressed as grades in specific exams, or as total points to be achieved, and they may include extra GCSEs or AS-levels. If you are asked for specific grades, they will mean it (a poor grade in one subject cannot be compensated for by a better grade in another, unless your offer is expressed in points). But there is no telling what they will actually accept in August when the results are published and they can see what grades everyone has.

Some offers are expressed so badly they are almost incomprehensible. If you don't understand an offer, contact the university to find out precisely what it means – you can't afford not to know.

Once the universities have made decisions on all your choices, the ball is back in your court and you reply to your offers online using *Track*. After this, you cannot keep more than two offers through UCAS (and if your offers are all unconditional you can keep only one). This means you may have to turn some down. If you still have exams to take, make your best guess as to what grades you will get and compare these with your offers. One strategy is to accept your first-choice course, whatever the offer, together with the course that has made the lowest offer as a fall-back. Another is to accept the two lowest offers to give you the maximum chance of a choice later. Don't accept any university you have not visited and would not be happy to attend.

Just missed your offer? Action points

If you do not get the grades or points to match your offer, all is not lost. You are not alone – over 30,000 people find their place on first-degree courses in Clearing.

To start, check whether your chosen course will take you in spite of your results. If you have only missed your offer by a grade or two, use *Track* and telephone the course tutor (not UCAS). If everyone else has met their offers, the course will be full and the tutor will be inflexible. If hardly anybody did, the admissions tutor may be glad to take you. So don't just assume they don't want you; speak to the course tutors – you may be lucky.

If not, you're into Clearing. UCAS will automatically allocate you a Clearing number, which will go onto *Track*. It should be there by the first week in September, so check as soon as you can – most of the action takes place immediately after A-level results day and speed is of the essence.

To find out which courses are still available, look at the official list on the UCAS website under *Clearing Course Search*. This information is also published in the national press (from the third Thursday in August). If you want to study locally, check out the local press and local radio and TV. If you want to talk to somebody, your school/college should have staff available, and the DCSF runs a helpline (0808 100 8000). Universities with places available often have specially staffed units and open days during Clearing.

Now is the time for you to contact universities and colleges direct. Keep focused. Do your research well. Keep shopping around, but move fast – don't be away on holiday or stuck in a job; lots of other people will be on the phone too and you want to get in first. And do it yourself; don't leave it to your parents to do it for you – that hardly shows you're keen.

If a university offers you a place that you want to accept, give them your Clearing number so that they know you do not already have a place. UCAS will send an official letter when the process is over.

Many people make the wrong decision in Clearing. These are the students most likely to drop out in their first year or be dissatisfied with their university experience. Don't compromise on your basic criteria: for example, if you know you can't stand big cities, don't accept a place in central London just because it's on offer. Use this book to make sure you only accept the right sort of place for you.

Good luck!

Completely unstuck?

It's tough, but not the end of the world. You can think about the following immediate options.

- Resit your A-levels (or take different A-levels).
- Aim lower – for example, if you have passed one A-level, try an HND or foundation degree course. If you choose somewhere with a linked degree course, you might be able to transfer later.
- Try for an Open University degree.
- Forget all about university for the time being and get on with your life.

The last option is not as silly as it may sound – there are plenty of second chances for mature students with indifferent A-levels (or none) at university. You will almost certainly be able to come back to education later – thousands do. About 25% of current undergraduates started their degree course when they were over 21.

Once you have a place

When you have a place, you will have to adjust to it all becoming a reality at last, and you will have a lot to do.

- Start by accepting your place (check your confirmation letter for instructions on any action you need to take).
- Make sure you have accommodation.
- If you haven't already got one, open a bank or building society account.
- Make sure your student support is organised (loans, bursaries, scholarships – see 'Cash for courses', below).

- Check that your parents really are going to pay their share (and when).
- Get lots of passport photos (essential for university ID in the first week of term).
- Read the mass of administrative information the university will send you.
- Find your exam certificates (results slips will only be acceptable for the most recent exams).
- Get an NHS exemption certificate if you think you will qualify for free prescriptions, dental charges, etc.
- Get yourself vaccinated against meningitis (free from your GP or university health service).
- Buy supplies of stationery, suitable clothes, etc.
- Check whether you need to take bedding, cooking equipment, etc for your accommodation.
- Do not let the gigantic reading list you will be sent put you into a cold panic.
- Sort out travel arrangements and make sure you get there when you need to.
- Arrange cash for the start of term.

Cash for Courses

You will need money to pay your tuition fees and money to live on.

Tuition fees

These vary throughout the UK. How much you are charged depends primarily on whether you are defined as a home student (from the UK or EU) or an international student (from anywhere outside the EU). It might also depend on your course and where you study.

International students are charged the full (unsubsidised) cost of their course – a very wide range of tuition fees starting at around £7k pa and rising to around £30k pa for some clinical courses. You can check each university's tuition fees in the 'University Profiles' section, and compare them against the complete list of university tuition fees on pages 58–61.

Home students' tuition fees are highly subsidised (and capped by the government). They range from nil (eg for Scottish students studying in Scotland and some NHS courses) to £3,225 pa (for students on most degree courses in the rest of the UK). However, in some cases there is no government subsidy, so home students may be charged the full cost of tuition – for example at some private colleges/universities, or if you already have a degree. Then the university or college may charge you anything up to the full international fee (although you will still be charged the lower home fee if your new course is in medicine, veterinary science, architecture, social work or initial teacher training).

Tuition fees usually increase annually in line with inflation.

Money to live on

How much you need to live on depends on where you study (eg Bradford is cheaper than London) and your personal life choices (a studio flat will cost more than a shared room). Most universities estimate you need a minimum of around £6k to live on per academic year. Many universities recommend considerably more than that – £12k pa or even more in London.

Total course costs

If you add up the cost of tuition and your own living costs over the three (or more) years of your course, you may get a nasty shock. For a UK student, the total is unlikely to be less than £28k and could be over £45k – twice that much for an international student. So you need to know where that money is coming from.

Where to get the money?

UK students are eligible for a patchwork of student support (loans, grants, bursaries, etc), as well as help that may be expected from your family. In particular, there is generous (and non-returnable) money for students from low-income families.

The names of the various elements of student support, and the arrangements for applying, differ in England, Scotland, Wales and Northern Ireland. So **check out the country you live in** (and ignore the other three).

There is some help available from the UK government for EU students. Those from outside the EU get no UK government help, but their own government may provide assistance. See 'Non-UK students' (page 54).

If you live in England

Paying for your tuition fees

You do not have to pay your tuition fees up front. As long as you are eligible for student support, you can apply for a tuition fee loan to cover your actual fees, up to a maximum of £3,225 pa (in 2009). This loan is not means-tested; the money is paid direct to your university (so you can't spend it on anything else); and you repay the loan later (when you are earning at least £15k pa).

You have to apply for the loan: if you don't, you may be charged the full cost of the course, not just £3,225 pa.

Money to live on

You are expected to live on money from a variety of sources, depending on your personal circumstances. (If you are already a graduate, you should check carefully; you may not be eligible for any of this help.)

- **Student loan and your family.** Almost all UK undergraduates are entitled to take out a student loan to provide money to live on, which you pay back after graduation. Most (72%) of this is not means-tested. If your family income is above a certain threshold, your family (parents, spouse/civil partner) will be expected to make a contribution.
- **Maintenance grant.** If your family income is less than £50k, you will also qualify for a non-returnable maintenance grant (or a special support grant, if, eg you are eligible for income support or housing benefit).
- **Special help.** There is additional special help (see pages 51–52) for certain categories of student, including those with a disability, those with children or other dependants.
- **Bursaries.** Universities usually provide some (non-returnable) bursary help for the lowest-income students (they are obliged to do this if they charge the fee of £3,225 pa).

For more information, check out the Student Finance England website, www.studentfinanceengland.co.uk.

How much to live on

How much you have to live on will depend both on your family income and on where you live while you are at university.

The maximum student loan is £4,950 pa. Only 28% of this is means-tested so, even if your family is comfortably off, you will still get £3,564 pa and your family will be expected to contribute £1,386 pa. The maximum student loan is reduced to £3,838 pa if you are living with your parents and increased to £6,928 pa if you are studying in London.

A non-repayable maintenance grant of £2,906 pa is available to anyone whose family income is £25k or less. The value of the grant gradually decreases as family income goes up – down to nil if your family's income is more than £50k pa. The amount of student loan you can take will be reduced (by half the value of your grant), so you have less to pay back later.

University bursaries should be available if your family income is below £25k, unless you are studying in Scotland. Bursaries are not repayable. Each university has its own bursary schemes, helping different groups of students with varying amounts of cash – from £319 pa to perhaps £5k pa for bright students from low-income families who are taking specified subjects. These schemes are outlined in the university profiles. To see how much you might get if your family income is around £18k–£20k pa, see the list on page 62.

The table shows the approximate amount of help available to a student, depending on their family's income.

Help with living costs (if you live in England)

If your family income is:	£20k	£40k	£50k	£80k+
Your student loan (more in London, less if you live with your parents)	£3,497	£4,595	£4,924	£3,564
Maintenance grant	£2,906	£711	£52	Nil
Bursaries from university	£319+	Unlikely	None	None
Total help	**£6,722+**	**£5,306**	**£4,976**	**£3,564**
Assuming your parents pay	Nil	Nil	Nil	£1,386
What you have to live on will be:	**£6,722+**	**£5,306**	**£4,976**	**£4,950**

All figures are pa.

Some small print. There are allowances against your family's gross income before you arrive at the figure used in the calculation (whether you have siblings still in education, etc). If your parents (or spouse/civil partner) don't want to complete the financial assessment, you will only be able to claim the non-means-tested loan, ie £3,564 pa. This maintenance money is all in addition to the tuition fee loan.

Applying for student support

Applying: Apply for student support as soon as possible (though it's rarely possible before March). Do not wait until you have received an offer of a place, or you risk not having your money by the start of the academic year. You need to apply for each year of your course, but you make a single application. Go to the Student Finance England website, (www.studentfinanceengland.co.uk) and you can then track your application with the password you will be given.

Eligibility: The first decision is whether you are eligible for student support or not, and this is made on the basis of your application (you may not be eligible if you are already a graduate). This first stage is important because it caps the tuition fee that you can be charged (ie you won't be charged the full cost of your course). It also entitles you to take out the non-means-tested loans – the tuition fee loan (£3,225 pa maximum) and 72% of the basic student loan for maintenance (£3,564 pa); you indicate on your application if you only want to take the non-means-tested loans. Otherwise, you and your family must also complete the financial sections.

Financial assessment: Once you have completed the financial sections of the application, a financial assessment is made. You will then be told how much help you are entitled to for that year – that is, how much you can take out as a tuition fee loan and how much maintenance money is available (the student loan for maintenance, whether you are eligible for a maintenance grant, and if so how much, whether you qualify for a disabled student's allowance, etc).

You will be sent a payment schedule. You will normally get a third of the total at the start of each term. Make sure you take your payment schedule or financial assessment with you when you register at the start of your course.

Getting the money: Once your university has confirmed you are registered, your maintenance money will be paid into your bank/building society account. The tuition fee loan is paid direct to your university.

Your eligibility for university bursaries is often also based on your financial assessment (make sure you tick the box that will allow the university access to the information); in this case you should get the bursary money automatically. At other universities you need to apply for help. So make sure you know the procedure at your university if you think you will qualify.

You can get more information and apply for student support on the Student Finance England website, (www.studentfinanceengland.co.uk) or ring the helpline, 08456 077577.

If you live in Scotland

Paying for your tuition fees

If you live in Scotland and are studying at a Scottish university, you will not be charged any tuition fees. They will be paid for you, as long as you eligible for student support and have not done a degree course before.

If you are studying elsewhere in the UK (England, Northern Ireland or Wales), you will be charged tuition fees (up to £3,225 pa) but you do not have to pay these up front. As long as you are eligible for student support, you can apply for a student loan to cover your actual tuition fees, up to a maximum of £3,225 (in 2009). This loan is not means-tested; the money is paid direct to your university (so you can't spend it on anything else), and you repay the loan later (when you are earning at least £15k pa).

But you have to apply: you will not get your fees paid (in Scotland) or the student loan for fees (elsewhere in the UK) unless you do; and if you don't, you may be charged the full cost of the course, which will be many thousands of pounds.

Money to live on

You are expected to live on money from a variety of sources, depending on your personal circumstances. (If you are already a graduate, you should check carefully; you may not be eligible for any of this help.)

- **Student loan and your family.** Almost all UK undergraduates are entitled to take out a student loan to provide money to live on, which you pay back after graduation. A small proportion (20%) of this is not means-tested. If your family income is above a certain threshold, your family (parents, spouse/civil partner) will be expected to make a contribution.
- **SAAS bursary.** If you come from a low-income family, you may also qualify for a bursary. These bursaries are means-tested, but you will not have to repay them. There are different schemes, depending on whether you are under 25 and studying in or outside Scotland.
- **Special help.** Additional special help (see pages 51–52 is available for certain categories of student, including lone parents, those with a disability and those leaving care.
- **University bursaries.** If you qualify for an SAAS bursary and are studying outside Scotland (and so paying higher fees), you should also be eligible for bursary help from your university.

For more information, check out the SAAS website (www.saas.gov.uk).

How much to live on

How much all this amounts to will depend on your family income and on where you live while you are at university. The information for 2009 was not yet available at the time of writing, but the following was what was on offer for 2008.

The maximum student loan was £4,510 pa, 80% of which was means-tested, so if your family income was over about £54k, you would only get a loan of £890 pa and your family would be expected to provide you with the remainder. The maximum student loan was reduced to £3,570 pa if you were living with your parents, and increased to £5,565 pa if you were studying in London.

SAAS bursaries were payable to students whose family income was below £33k. These bursaries are paid instead of part of your loan (though your loan is increased), and they do not have to be repaid. The Young Students' Bursary (YSB) applies if you are under 25 and studying in Scotland, the Students' Outside Scotland Bursary (SOSB) if you study elsewhere. In 2008 you would get up to £2,575 pa under the YSB (£2,095 under the SOSB) if your family income was £18,800 or less, down to nil if it was over £33,300.

University bursaries certainly should be available if your family income is below £25k and you are studying outside Scotland. Bursaries are not repayable. Each university has its own bursary schemes, helping different groups of students with varying amounts of cash – £319 pa up to perhaps £5k for bright students from low-income families who are taking specified subjects. These are outlined in the university profiles. To see how much you might get if your family income is around £18k–£20k pa, see the list on page 66.

The table below shows the approximate amount of help available to a student, depending on their family's income.

Help with living costs (if you live in Scotland)*

If your family income is:	£20k	£30k	£40k	£60k+
Your student loan (more in London, less if you live with your parents)	£2,144	£3,170	£2,650	£890
YSB (Young Students' Bursary)	£2,366	£591	Nil	Nil
Bursaries from university	Possibly	Maybe	Unlikely	Rarely
Total help	**£4,510+pa**	**£3,761pa**	**£2,650pa**	**£890pa**
Assuming your parents pay	Nil	£749	£1,861	£3,620
What you have to live on will be:	£4,510	£4,510	£4,510	£4,510

All figures are pa.

* 2008 figures.

Applying for student support

Applying: Apply for student support as soon as possible (though it is rarely possible before March). Do not wait until you have received an offer of a place. Certainly try and apply before the summer rush. For courses starting in September, the absolute deadline is the end of the academic year. You make a single application to the Student Awards Agency for Scotland – fill in an application form or apply online through its website, (www.saas.gov.uk). You have to apply for each year of the course.

Eligibility: The first decision is whether or not you are eligible for student support, and this is made on the basis of your application (you may not be eligible if you are already a graduate). This first stage is important because it ensures the SAAS will pay your fees if you are studying in Scotland, or caps the tuition fee that you can be charged elsewhere (so that you won't be charged the full cost of your course). It also entitles you to take out the non-means-tested loans – the student loan for fees and 20% of the basic student loan for maintenance; you indicate on your application if you only want to take the non-means-tested loans. Otherwise, you and your family must also complete the financial sections.

Financial assessment: If you have completed the financial sections of the application, a financial assessment is made. You will then be told how much help you are entitled to for that year – that is, how much you can take out as a student loan for fees and how much for maintenance money (the student loan for maintenance, whether you are eligible for an SAAS bursary, and if so how much, whether you qualify for a disabled student's allowance, etc). This will then be confirmed to you in an award notice; make sure you take this with you when you register at the start of your course.

You will be sent a payment schedule, telling you when and how your maintenance money will be paid to you.

Getting the money: Once your university has confirmed you are registered, your maintenance money will be paid into your bank/building society account; your fees (in Scotland) or student loan for fees (elsewhere) are paid direct to your university.

Your eligibility for university bursaries is often based on your financial assessment (you need to make sure you tick the box that will allow the university access to the information); at other universities you need to apply for help. So make sure you know the procedure at your university if you think you will qualify.

You can find out more information and apply for student support on the Student Awards Agency for Scotland website (www.saas.gov.uk).

If you live in Wales

Paying for your tuition fees

You do not have to pay your tuition fees up front, as long as you are eligible for student support.

If you live in Wales, and are studying at a Welsh university, you will be entitled to a fee grant of £1,940 pa towards your tuition fees. Then you can apply for a student loan to cover the remainder of the fee.

If you are studying elsewhere in the UK, you can apply for a student loan to cover the actual fees you are charged, up to a maximum of £3,225 pa (in 2009).

Student loans for fees are not means-tested; the money is paid direct to your university (so you can't spend it on anything else); and you repay the loan later (when you are earning at least £15k pa).

You have to apply: you will not get the fee grant or the student loan for fees unless you do (and if you don't, you may be charged the full cost of the course, not just £3,225 pa).

Money to live on

You are expected to live on money from a variety of sources, depending on your personal circumstances. (If you are already a graduate, you should check carefully; you may not be eligible for any of this help.)

- **Student loan and your family.** Almost all UK undergraduates are entitled to take out a student loan to provide money to live on, which you pay back after graduation. Most (75%) of this is not means-tested. If your family income is above a certain threshold, your family (parents, spouse/civil partner) will be expected to make a contribution.
- **Assembly Learning Grant.** If your family income is less than £39k, you will also qualify for a non-returnable Assembly Learning Grant.
- **Special help.** There is additional special help (see pages 51–52) for certain categories of student, including those with a disability, those with children or other dependants.
- **Bursaries.** Universities usually provide some (non-returnable) bursary help for the lowest-income students (they are obliged to do this if they charge the fee of £3,225 pa). In Wales, some of this is from the Welsh National Bursary Scheme.

For more information, check out the Student Finance Wales website (www.studentfinancewales.co.uk).

How much to live on

How much this all amounts to will depend on your family income and where you live while you are at university.

The maximum student loan is £4,745 pa. This maximum is reduced to £3,673 pa if you are living with your parents, and increased to £6,648 pa if you are studying in London.

An Assembly Learning Grant of £2,835 pa is payable to students whose family income is up to £18,400; you do not need to repay this. The value of the grant gradually decreases as family income goes up – down to nil when family income is more than £39,300 pa. The first £1,255 of your Assembly Learning Grant will be deducted from the amount of student loan you can take, so you have less to pay back later.

Bursaries should be available through your university if your family income is below £18,400, unless you are studying in Scotland. Bursaries are not repayable. In Wales, most are paid from the Welsh Bursaries Scheme. Elsewhere, each university has its own bursary schemes, helping different groups of students with varying amounts of cash – £319 pa up to perhaps £5k pa for bright students from low-income families who are taking specified subjects. These are outlined in the university profiles. To see how much you might get if your family income is around £18k–£20k pa, see the list on page 61.

The table shows the approximate amount of help available to a student, depending on their family's income.

Help with living costs (if you live in Wales)

If your family income is:	£20k	£30k	£40k	£60k+
Your student loan (more in London, less if you live with your parents)	£3,457	£3,689	£4,673	£3,559
Assembly Learning Grant	£2,628	£1,056	Nil	Nil
Bursaries from university	£319+	Maybe	Unlikely	None
Total help	£6,404+	£4,745	£4,673	£3,559
Assuming your parents pay	Nil	Nil	£72	£1,186
What you have to live on will be:	£6,404+	£4,745	£4,745	£4,745

All figures are pa.

Some small print. There are allowances against your family's gross income before you arrive at the figure used in the calculation (whether you have siblings still in education, etc). All these figures go up in line with inflation each year. This maintenance money is all in addition to the student loan for fees.

Applying for student support

Applying: Apply for student support as soon as possible. Do not wait until you have received an offer of a place or you risk not having your money by the start of the academic year. You need to apply for each year of your course.

You make a single application, either online or paper. To apply online, go to the Student Finance Wales website (www.studentfinancewales.co.uk), and you can then track your application with the password you will be given. For a paper application, either download a form from the website or apply to your Local Authority (LA).

Eligibility: The first decision is whether you are eligible for student support or not, and this is made on the basis of your application (you may not be eligible if you are already a graduate). This first stage is important because it caps the tuition fee that you can be charged (ie you won't be charged the full cost of your course); if you are studying in Wales, it entitles you to the fee grant. It also entitles you to the non-means-tested loans – the student loan for fees (£3,225 pa maximum) and 75% of the student loan for maintenance (£3,559 pa). You indicate on your application if you only want to take the non-means-tested loans. Otherwise, you and your family must also complete the financial sections.

Financial assessment: If you have completed the financial sections of the application, a financial assessment is made. You will then be told how much help you are entitled to for that year – that is, how much you can take out as a student loan for fees and how much for maintenance money (the student loan for maintenance, whether you are eligible for an Assembly Learning Grant, and if so how much, whether you qualify for a special support grant, etc).

You will be sent a payment schedule (usually you will get a third of the total at the start of each term). Make sure you take your payment schedule or financial assessment with you when you register at the start of your course.

Getting the money: Once your university has confirmed you are registered, your maintenance money will be paid into your bank/building society account; the student loan for fees is paid direct to your university.

Your eligibility for university bursaries is often based on your financial assessment (you need to make sure you tick the box that will allow the university access to the information); at other universities you need to apply for help. So make sure you know the procedure at your university if you think you will qualify.

You can find out more information and apply for student support on the Student Finance Wales website (www.studentfinancewales.co.uk).

If you live in Northern Ireland

Paying for your tuition fees

You do not have to pay your tuition fees up front. As long as you are eligible for student support, you can apply for a student loan for fees to cover your actual fees, up to a maximum of £3,225 pa (in 2009). This loan is not means-tested; the money is paid direct to your university (so you can't spend it on anything else); and you repay the loan later (when you are earning at least £15k pa).

You have to apply: you will not get the student loan for fees unless you do (and if you don't, you may be charged the full cost of the course, not just £3,225 pa).

Money to live on

You are expected to live on money from a variety of sources, depending on your personal circumstances. (If you are already a graduate, you should check carefully; you may not be eligible for any of this help.)

- **Student loan and your family.** Almost all UK undergraduates are entitled to take out a student loan to provide money to live on, which you pay back after graduation. Most (75%) of this is not means-tested. If your family income is above a certain threshold, your family (parents, spouse/civil partner) will be expected to make a contribution.

- **Maintenance grant.** If your family income is less than £40k, you will also qualify for a non-returnable maintenance grant (or a special support grant, if, eg, you are eligible for income support or housing benefit).
- **Special help.** There is additional special help (see pages 51–52) for certain categories of student, including those with a disability and those with children or other dependants.
- **Bursaries.** Universities usually provide some (non-returnable) bursary help for the lowest-income students (they are obliged to if they charge the fee of £3,225 pa).

For more information, check out the Student Finance NI website (www.studentfinanceni.co.uk).

How much to live on

How much this all amounts to will depend on your family income and where you live while you are at university.

The maximum student loan is £4,745 pa. Only 25% of this is means-tested so, even if your family is comfortably off, you will still get £3,559 pa and your family will be expected to contribute £1,186 pa. The maximum student loan is reduced to £3,673 pa if you are living with your parents and increased to £6,643 pa if you are studying in London.

A maintenance grant of £3,406 pa is available if your family income is £18,800 or less; you do not need to repay this. The value of the grant gradually decreases as family income goes up – down to nil when family income is more than £40k pa. The first £1,792 of your maintenance grant will be deducted from the amount of student loan you can take, so you have less to pay back later.

University bursaries certainly should be available if your family income is below about £20k, unless you are studying in Scotland. Bursaries are not repayable. Each university has its own bursary schemes, helping different groups of students with varying amounts of cash – from £319 pa to perhaps £5k pa for bright students from low-income families who are taking specified subjects. These are outlined in the university profiles. To see how much you might get if your family income is around £18k–£20k pa, see the list on page 62.

The table shows the approximate amount of help available to a student, depending on their family's income.

Help with living costs (if you live in Northern Ireland)

If your family income is:	£20k	£30k	£40k	£60k+
Your student loan (more in London, less if you live with your parents)	£3,014	£3,617	£4,670	£3,559
Maintenance grant	£3,147	£1,128	£75	Nil
Bursaries from university	£319+	Possible	Unlikely	None
Total help	£6,480+	£4,745	£4,745	£3,559
Assuming your parents pay	Nil	Nil	Nil	£1,186
What you have to live on will be:	£6,480+	£4,745	£4,745	£4,745

All figures are pa.

Some small print. There are allowances against your family's gross income before you arrive at the figure used in the calculation (whether you have siblings still in education, etc). If your parents (or spouse/civil partner) don't want to complete the financial assessment, you will only be able to claim the non-means-tested loan, ie £3,559 pa. All these figures go up in line with inflation each year. This is all in addition to the student loan for fees.

Applying for student support

Applying: Apply for student support as soon as possible. Do not wait until you have received an offer of a place or you risk not having your money by the start of the academic year. You need to apply for each year of your course.

You make a single application, either online or paper. To apply online, go to the Student Finance NI website (www.studentfinanceni.co.uk), and you can then track your application with the password you will be given. For a paper application, either download a form from the website or apply to your Education and Library Board (ELB).

Eligibility: The first decision is whether you are eligible for student support or not, which is made on the basis of your application (you may not be eligible if you are already a graduate). This first stage is important because it caps the tuition fee that you can be charged (ie you won't be charged the full cost of your course). It also entitles you to take out the non-means-tested loans – the student loan for fees (£3,225 pa maximum) and 75% of the basic student loan for maintenance (£3,559); you indicate on your application if you only want to take the non-means-tested loans. Otherwise, you and your family must also complete the financial sections.

Financial assessment: If you have completed the financial sections of the application, a financial assessment is made. You will then be told how much help you are entitled to for that year – that is, how much you can take out as a student loan for fees and how much for maintenance money (the student loan for maintenance, whether you are eligible for a maintenance grant, and if so how much, whether you qualify for a disabled student's allowance, etc).

You will be sent a payment schedule (usually you will get a third of the total at the start of each term). Make sure you take your payment schedule or financial assessment with you when you register at the start of your course.

Getting the money: Once your university has confirmed you are registered, your maintenance money will be paid into your bank/building society account; the student loan for fees is paid direct to your university.

Your eligibility for university bursaries is often based on your financial assessment (you need to make sure you tick the box that will allow the university access to the information); at other universities you need to apply for help. So make sure you know the procedure at your university if you think you will qualify.

You can find out more information and apply for student support on the Student Finance NI website (www.studentfinanceni.co.uk).

Repaying student loans

UK students who have taken out their full loan entitlement – to cover fees and living expenses – will be borrowing over £8k a year, so it is worth being realistic about the repayment arrangements.

You pay back the amount you have borrowed, adjusted for inflation – so the amount you pay back is equivalent in spending terms to the amount you borrowed. At today's rate of inflation, if you have borrowed £10k, the debt will increase by about £40 a month.

You start paying back your student loans through the tax system, after you have finished your studies and are earning over £15k pa. You pay at the rate of 9% of those earnings over the £15k threshold. Here are some examples.

- If you are earning £14,999 pa, you pay nothing.
- If you earn £20k a year, you will pay 9% of £5k (the difference between £15k and £20k). This means you will pay £450 pa (£37.50 a month).
- If you earn £50k a year, you will pay 9% of £35k (the difference between £15k and £50k). This means you will pay £3,150 pa (£262.50 a month).
- If your earnings never reach £15k, you never repay your loan nor any part of it.
- The outstanding balance of your loan is cancelled after 25 years (35 years if you live in Scotland) or if you die.

More information can be found on the student support websites for England, Scotland, Wales and Northern Ireland, or visit the Student Loans Company website (www.slc.co.uk).

Special help

Students from low-income families

Government and university money is available for UK students from low-income families, but what you get depends on your actual family income, where you live and where you are studying.

Each of the four UK countries helps students from low-income families in its own way (eg maintenance grants in England and Northern Ireland, Assembly Learning Grants in Wales and various SAAS bursaries in Scotland). The amount you get is not standard in the four countries, and neither is the maximum family income at which help is available (though you should qualify for the maximum if your household income is less than £18k). Check your country's student support website to see what money you are eligible for.

The universities (particularly those charging fees of £3,225 pa) all help UK students from low-income families, in addition to the money you get from your own government. If your family income is under £20,000 you should certainly get at least £319 pa, so make sure you do. Sometimes you need to apply for it; increasingly often, you will get it automatically on the basis of your student support assessment (as long as you have ticked the box that allows the information to be shared with your university).

Different universities have bursary schemes (sometimes called scholarships, even when they are not competitive): these are outlined in the university profiles. At some universities you will only get the minimum of £319 pa if your family income is £25k or less; at others there will be help for students whose family income is £50k or less. You may get more if you are from a designated school, have high entrance qualifications, are on a specified course, etc – which can all total up to as much as £5k pa. You can get an idea of the range by looking at the list on page 62. Bursaries are not repayable.

Students with children or other dependants

UK students with children or other dependants qualify for additional grants and allowances; this is assessed with your main student support application. The names and amounts of this help vary (so the figures given here are approximate). They are all means-tested.

If you have children, you may qualify for a parent's learning allowance of up to about £1,508 pa, and a childcare grant of up to 85% of your actual costs to a maximum of about £150–£160 per week for one child.

If you have an adult dependant, you may be eligible for up to around £2,645 pa.

Students with dependants are some of the few who may be entitled to some benefits (such as housing benefit); find out before you start from your local Jobcentre Plus office or, if appropriate, One Parent Families (www.oneparentfamilies.org.uk).

Many universities also have money to help students with children or other dependants – check the individual university profiles.

Students with disabilities

UK students who have a disability that will increase the cost of their course should qualify for one or more of the disabled students' allowances (DSAs). These are not means-tested and you will be assessed for the DSA along with the rest of your student support application.

Depending on what help is required, you may be eligible for DSAs to help towards general course expenditure (up to about £1,700 pa), for a personal helper (up to £20,500 pa) or a one-off payment for specialist equipment (up to £5,200). There may also be money available from your university or college – check the individual university profiles.

Most graduates who want to do a further degree course are not eligible for student support; disabled students are exempt from this bar. You can get useful information and advice from Skill (National Bureau for Students with Disabilities, www.skill.org.uk).

Academic years longer than 30 weeks

The student loan is increased for UK students whose course lasts longer than 30 weeks in the year. The basic amount is some £83 per week – less if you are living with your parents, more if you are in London or abroad.

Health professions courses

There is extra help for UK students who have been accepted on NHS-funded pre-registration courses in one of a number of health professions (including nursing, chiropody, dietetics) and for medical and dental students in their fifth and subsequent years (including graduate entrants for most of their course). These students are entitled to a non-returnable NHS bursary, a reduced rate student loan that is not means-tested and their tuition fees will be paid for them. For further information, see www.nhsstudentgrants.co.uk.

Other cash sources

Sponsorship

Sponsorships are offered by some employers in industry, government and professional partnerships and by professional bodies. They are much sought after because they can solve two student problems at a stroke – financing yourself through university and getting a job when you graduate. You are normally responsible for gaining your own admission onto an appropriate degree course.

Competition is fierce for sponsorships, so you need to apply early. Several sponsorships are advertised on the UCAS website and in the press. Some firms offer sponsorship for the final year only; you apply in your second year.

Career development loans

You may be able to get a career development loan (CDL), offered by a partnership of the Learning and Skills Council and some high street banks. They are designed to cover vocational education or training for two years. You cannot hold a CDL along with a student loan.

The maximum CDL is £8k – up to 80% of your course fees (possibly 100% if you have been unemployed) and 100% of your living expenses.

You can get information leaflet on the Lifelong Learning website (www.lifelonglearning.co.uk/cdl).

Jobs

You can work during the vacations to supplement your income – some 90% of students do; and many students also have part-time jobs during term time. The university profiles give some of the local possibilities.

See also 'Jobs' on page 73 and 'Work (paid or voluntary)' on page 65.

University scholarships, bursaries and other help

Some universities' scholarships or bursaries are open to all students; others are targeted at specific categories of student. The most common approaches are as follows:

- Most bursary help is for students from low-income families and/or those from partner schools and colleges.
- Scholarships are usually for high academic performance (or sport or music). They usually require either high entry qualifications or high marks in the first-year assessment. For sports scholarships, you often need to be competing at national level – or even be in with a chance of a gold medal at the 2012 Olympics. Some scholarships may be awarded to students from low-income families, international students, etc.
- Hardship funds and access to learning funds usually help disabled students, those with dependant children or adults, those with high costs or existing students who are experiencing unexpected financial difficulties. They may also cover the costs of computers, field trips, etc.

Universities have their own priorities and many earmark funds for particular groups of students (mature students, students from the Commonwealth, etc) or for special expenditure (eg travel, childcare); so the same person might qualify for help in one university and not in another. The key thing is to talk to someone in the university (student advice, SU, your tutor – anyone) as soon as you are in trouble and before you are in real difficulties. UK students do not usually qualify for any help unless they have taken out their full student loan entitlement.

Universities also administer government funds to help students on low incomes who need extra financial support to stay on their course. These funds are only available after you have started the course and, again, come in different guises in each different country, for example access to learning funds in England, financial contingency funds in Wales.

Check the individual university profiles and universities' own websites; also look at the table on page 62.

Educational trusts and charities

There are lots of impoverished students chasing the little money handed out by educational charities, so don't pin your hopes on getting a lot.

Most charities are very specific about who or what they can help (eg students from Hackney, cats homes in Derbyshire). You need to focus on those whose remit includes you. You can get advice from Educational Grants Advisory Service (EGAS) on www.egas-online.org.

Benefits

Few students qualify for state benefits – some disabled students, student parents and part-time students are exceptions. If you think you qualify, try telephoning your local Jobcentre Plus office. The

Department for Work and Pensions (DWP) will give you information. Contact your local authority if you think you are eligible for any benefits.

Borrowing more

Borrowing is a fact of student life these days. Consider the costs carefully. A business-like approach is to take the cheapest loan first.

- Free overdraft. Most banks offer interest-free overdrafts to students if you ask for one – though who knows who banks are lending to these days.
- Student loan (interest at inflation rate only).
- Agreed overdraft (variable interest rate, bank base rate plus).
- Credit cards (ferocious interest rates).

You could also try a career development loan if you, or your course, is eligible.

Non-UK students

EU students

If you are an EU national who has been resident in the UK for the past three years, you will be treated as a home student. You will be charged the home rate of fees (see 'Tuition fees', page 40) and you can apply for student support in the same way as other UK students – check the information on the country where you live.

If you have been resident elsewhere in the EU for the past three years, you will be treated as a home student for fees purposes only. You can apply for a student loan to cover your fees, but you are not entitled to any government help with living costs.

UCAS should automatically send you the form to apply for the student loan for fees. Otherwise, email euteam@slc.co.uk or find the application form at www.studentfinancedirect.co.uk (link through 'My home is not in England').

International students (from outside the EU)

International students are not normally entitled to any UK student support and you will be charged the full cost of your tuition.

Help and advice: Many countries have their own system of funding their students, administered by their embassy or high commission. Some universities also have some scholarships and bursary help for certain international students, for example those from specific countries.

If you are still living overseas, contact the British Council locally (see its very useful website, www.britishcouncil.org). If there is no office locally, ask the British High Commission or Embassy.

If you are already in the UK, contact the British Council or the UK Council for International Student Affairs (www.ukcisa.org.uk).

Most universities have international student offices with dedicated staff to help, who will be sympathetic to your problems, so get in touch with them. The international office will also have a separate section of the university website – make sure you find that, or you may find very misleading information about tuition fees, for example.

Tuition fees: If you are from outside the EU, you are expected to pay the full cost of your course. You can look up the tuition fees in the university profiles. Currently the fee range is £7k–£12k pa for courses based in the classroom; some £8k–£18k pa for courses based in a lab or studio; and from £18,500 to nearly £30k pa for clinical years (medicine or veterinary medicine).

The definitions are complicated, but you will be classified as an international student for fees purposes unless you:

- have been resident ('settled status') in the UK for three years
- are a UK national who has been resident in the EU for the last three years
- are a European Economic Area (EEA) migrant worker or
- are a recognised refugee.

These definitions are open to a range of interpretations and you may want to check your status with each university that offers you a place. If in doubt, consult the British Council or UKCISA.

British students living abroad

If you are British and live outside the EEA, the chances of getting government financial assistance are pretty slim unless you or your family have been temporarily working abroad (eg in the armed services). Worse still, you could be in danger of being classified as an international student, which means your fees will be a great deal higher (£7k+ pa, up to £29k pa on clinical courses). It is worth being crystal clear about your own residential status early on.

The fact that you are British is not enough. You must also have been resident ('settled') in the British Isles (possibly the EEA) for three years preceding the course – and time spent at a UK boarding school is almost never sufficient. The rules are complicated and can be interpreted differently by the various universities and authorities.

To check out your own status, get advice from the UK Council for International Student Affairs (www.ukcisa.org.uk).

Managing your money

Course budget

Money is likely to be tight and it is important that you know how you are going to spend it, rather than just let it trickle through your fingers. It really is worth working out an income and expenditure budget for each year of the course, including any period spent overseas.

You should expect the costs to go up as you progress through your course: in the second year most students move out of university accommodation (so costs may go up); and in the final year you will need to devote more time to your studies (more fast food, less time for a part-time job).

When you work out your expenditure, be realistic about how many weeks/months it covers: will your rent be for 30, 40 or 52 weeks? Will you go home (so no electricity bills) each vacation?

Look at the range of prices given in the university profiles – there is also good information on many university websites; and talk to friends and siblings already at university.

Here is a blank form to get you started. You can then add up your three or four annual budgets, get a glimpse of your financial position at the end of the course and see whether you need to add to your income to get there – get vacational work, apply for an overdraft, etc.

Your course budget form

Income (annual is probably easiest)		Expenditure (monthly is probably easiest)	
Savings/cash in bank	£	Tuition fees	£
Student loan for maintenance	£	Exam fees	£
Student loan for fees	£	Rent	£
Parental contribution (actual)	£	Gas/electricity	£
Grant (if any)	£	Telephone	£
Vacation earnings (net of tax/NI)	£	TV licence	£
Term-time earnings (net)	£	Insurance	£
Any special benefits (eg DSA)	£	Council tax (if any)	£
Any other income (eg bursary)	£	Food	£
		Car/motorbike/ bicycle	£
		Rail card/bus pass	£
		Fares	£
		Field courses	£
		Lab or other course costs	£
		Vacation travel home	£
		Books	£
		Stationery	£
		Equipment	£
		Clothes	£
		Laundry	£
		Leisure (booze, fags, societies, contraceptives, etc)	£
		Other (eg childcare)	£
		Interest (eg on overdraft)	£
TOTAL ANNUAL INCOME	£	**TOTAL MONTHLY EXPENDITURE**	£
Multiply the expenditure figure by the number of months you will be supporting yourself:			
		TOTAL ANNUAL EXPENDITURE	£
		less TOTAL ANNUAL INCOME	£
		BALANCE	£

Monitoring the amount you spend

To stop your expenditure getting out of control, you usually need to undertake a more detailed exercise.

Estimate your weekly outgoings and check (at least once a month) how closely your actual expenditure corresponds to your estimates. You can estimate your costs over three different time frames – a week, a term or a calendar year – depending on what you do in the vacations.

Banking

You will definitely need a student-friendly bank or building society that offers students preferential terms, such as free banking and overdrafts. You do not get student packages automatically – you have to ask for them (or even open a new student account, even if you already have an account).

Get yourself a bank account before you start your course. This means your money will be paid directly into it – and you won't have to worry about it once you get to university.

Take a four- or five-year view of your banking arrangements – from when you first apply for your student support to the time you graduate, with or without a job to go to. Between those dates, you will probably face a succession of cash crises and will need a bank overdraft to see you through (eg to pay a deposit at the end of term in July to secure your accommodation for September).

Always keep the bank informed, especially if you know that you will face a financial crisis; most banks will try to help you through it, as long as they know what is going on.

Basic bank equipment is a cash/debit card, a monthly bank statement and (probably) a cheque book. You might find a credit card useful, but beware of the ferocious interest rates. The rest are additional services – authorised overdraft, commission-free travellers' cheques or discounted student insurance. With telephone and internet banking, it no longer matters about having a bank that is represented on your campus – you will hardly ever need to visit it and, for the most part, all you will need is a cash point.

Cash to start with

However well organised you are, don't assume that the system will be too. Make sure you have enough cash in the bank to survive for a few weeks, in case your student loan is not waiting for you at the beginning of term; you need to eat as well as settle in.

Annual tuition fees – value for money?

The table below shows the annual tuition fees charged by each university. Some rules of thumb for price comparisons: courses largely taught in the classroom cost less than those taught in an art studio or a science lab, or business courses (so the minimum cost will be higher at a specialist - art or business college than at a multi-faculty university); clinical courses are the most expensive.

University	International fee (fee for clinical courses in brackets)	Home student fee
Aberdeen University	£9,000–£11,250 (£22,040)	£1,820–£2,895
Abertay Dundee University	£8,150	£1,820
Aberystwyth University	£8,475–£10,750	£3,225
ALRA	£11,500	£11,500
Anglia Ruskin University	£9,300–£12,050	£3,225
Architectural Association	£14,475	£14,475
Arts London	£10,700	£3,225
Aston University	£10,200–£12,300	£3,225
Bangor University	£8,500–£9500	£3,225
Barts & The London	£12,700–£14,600 (£23,350)	£3,225
Bath Spa University	£9,000–£9,580	£3,225
Bath University	£10,000–£12,750	£3,225
Bedfordshire University	£8,000–£8,200	£3,225
Birkbeck	£3,810	£1560
Birmingham City University	£8,800–£13,500	£3,225
Birmingham Conservatoire	£12,500	£3,225
Birmingham University	£9,880–£12,800 (£23,350)	£3,225
Bolton University	£7,800	£3,225
Bournemouth University	£8,000–£13,000	£3,225
Bradford College	£7,100–£7,950	£2,000
Bradford University	£8,325–£10,755	£3,225
Brighton & Sussex Medical School	£23,678 (£23,678)	£3,225
Brighton University	£9,240–£10,740	£3,225
Bristol Old Vic Theatre School	£13,340	£3,225
Bristol University	£11,450–£14,750 (£26,600)	£3,225
Bristol UWE	£8,250–£8,700	£3,225
British School of Osteopathy	£8,600	£3,225
Brunel University	£8,300–£10,200	£3,225
Buckingham University	£9,000–£9,400	£5,360–£5,760
Bucks New University	£7,800–£8,450	£3,225
Camberwell College of Arts	£10,700	£3,225
Cambridge University	£9,747–£12,768 (£23,631) + college fees of £3,300–£4,400	£3,225
Canterbury Christ Church University	£7,650–£8,375	£3,225
Cardiff University	£9,600–£12,300 (£22,500)	£3,225
Central Saint Martin's College of Art & Design	£10,700	£3,225
Central School of Speech and Drama	£13,068–£13,454	£3,225
Chelsea College of Art & Design	£10,700	£3,225
Chester University	£7,182–£8,388	£3,225
Chichester University	£7,400–£8,200	£3,225
City University	£7,750–£12,000	£3,225
Colchester Institute	£7,200	£3,225
Courtauld Institute	£11,804	£3,225
Coventry University	£7,900	£3,225
Creative Arts University	£6,780–£8,910	£3,225
Cumbria University	£7,900	£3,225

University	International fee (fee for clinical courses in brackets)	Home student fee
De Montfort University	£8,500–£9,000	£3,225
Derby University	£7800–£8415	£3,225
Dundee University	£8,500–£10,500 (£20,800)	£1,820–£2,895
Durham University	£10,560–£13,770	£3,225
East Anglia University	£10,610–£13,900 (£25,480)	£3,225
East London University	£9,000–£12,500	£3,225
Edge Hill University	£7,900	£3,225
Edinburgh College of Art	£9,630	£1,820
Edinburgh University	£11,050–£14,500 (£30,400)	£1,820–£2895
Essex University	£9250–£11,990	£3,225
European Business School London	£12,300	£12,300
Exeter University	£10,000–£12250	£3,225
Falmouth University College	£9,097–£9,581	£3,225
Farnborough College	£5,500	£1,255
Glamorgan University	£9,250	£3,225
Glasgow Caledonian University	£8,500–£10,000	£1,820
Glasgow School of Art	£9,600–£10,560	£1,820
Glasgow University	£9,400–£12,350 (£21,600)	£1,820–£2,895
Gloucestershire University	£8,200	£3,225
Glyndŵr University	£5,850	£3,225
Goldsmiths	£9,870–£13,690	£3,225
Greenwich University	£8650–£12,300	£2835–£3,225
Guildhall School of Music & Drama	£15,200	£3,225
Harper Adams University College	£8,200	£3,225
Heriot-Watt University	£9,000–£11,350	£1,820
Hertfordshire University	£8,000	£3,225
Heythrop College	£5,490	£3,225
Huddersfield University	£8,250–£9250	£3,225
Hull University	£9,500–£11,500 (£22,000)	£3,225
Hull York Medical School	£22,000 (£22,000)	£3,225
Imperial College	£15,500–£19,450 (£35,500)	£3,225
Keele University	£8,500–£11,300 (£20,700)	£3,225
Kent	£9,870–£11,990	£3,225
King's College London	£12,020–£15,080 (£27,980)	£3,225
Kingston University	£9,000–£10,050	£3,225
Laban	£12,950	£3,225
Lampeter University	£8,988	£3,225
Lancaster University	£9,200–£11,100	£3,225
Leeds College of Music	£9,800	£3,225
Leeds Met University	£8,000–£8,700	£2,000
Leeds Trinity	£7,425–£7,985	£3,225
Leeds University	£9,700–£12,600 (£23,500)	£3,225
Leicester University	£9,450–£12,650 (£22,900)	£3,225
Lincoln University	£8,524–£9,038	£3,225
Liverpool Hope University	£6,600	£3,225
Liverpool John Moores University	£8,320–£8,950	£3,225
Liverpool University	£9,400–£12,000 (£18,600)	£3,225
London College of Communication	£10,700	£3,225

University	International fee (fee for clinical courses in brackets)	Home student fee
London College of Fashion	£10,700	£3,225
London Contemporary Dance School	£13,340	£3,225
London Film School	£10,000–£21,111	£10,000–£21,111
London Met University	£8,200	£3,225
London School of Theology	£4,995–£5,979	£4,995–£5,979
London South Bank University	£8,360–£8,600	£3,225
London University Institute in Paris	£9,000	£3,225
Loughborough University	£9,850–£12,800	£3,225
LSE	£12,840	£3,225
Manchester Met University	£7,785–£12,900	£3,225
Manchester University	£10,500–£12,900 (£23,500)	£3,225
Marjon	£8,200	£3,225
Middlesex University	£9,200	£3,225
Myerscough College	£8,000	£3,225
Napier University	£8,600–£9,990	£1,820
National Film & Television School	£10,000–£17,500	£3,500–£7,500
Newcastle University	£10,415–£13,620 (£25,220)	£3,225
Newport	£7,750–£8,750	£3,225
Northampton University	£7,450–£8,250	£3,225
Northern School of Contemporary Dance	£13,340	£3,225
Northumbria University	£8,300–£8,700	£3,225
Norwich University College of the Arts	£8,750	£3,225
Nottingham Trent University	£8,450–£9,600	£3,225
Nottingham University	£10,610–£13,910 (£25,900)	£3,225
Open University	£1,050–£1,410	
Oxford Brookes University	£9,780–£10,000	£3,225
Oxford University	£11,750–£13,450 (£24,500) + college fees of £4,800–£5,200	£3,225
Peninsula Medical & Dental College	£12,500 (£20,000)	£3,225
Plymouth University	£8,650–£9,150	£3,225
Portsmouth University	£8,350–£9,650	£3,225
Queen Margaret University	£8,800–£9,700	£1,820
Queen Mary	£9,000–£10,900 (£23,350)	£3,225
Queen's University Belfast	£8,970–£10,990 (£22,920)	£3,225
RADA	£13,340	£3,225
Ravensbourne College of Design and Communication	£9,000	£3,225
Reading University	£9,630–£11,610	£3,225
Regent's Business School London	£11,250	£11,250
Robert Gordon University	£8,750–£10,600	£1,820
Roehampton University	£8,875	£3,225
Rose Bruford College	£11,025	£3,225
Royal Academy of Music	£15,500	£3,225
Royal Agricultural College	£7,300	£3,225

University	International fee (fee for clinical courses in brackets)	Home student fee
Royal College of Music	£15,280	£3,225
Royal Holloway	£11,555–£13,120	£3,225
Royal Northern College of Music	£13,150–£14,300	£3,225
Royal Scottish Academy of Music & Drama (RSAMD)	£11,499	£1,820
Royal Veterinary College	£8,030–£8,300 (£18,400)	£3,225
Royal Welsh College of Music & Drama	£11,045	£3,225
St Andrews University	£11,350–£17,300 (£17,300)	£1,820–£2,895
St George's	£12,020–£15,200 (£26,655)	£3,225
Saint Mary's University College	£7,200	£3,225
Salford University	£8,400–£10,500	£3,225
School of Pharmacy	£12,300	£3,225
Scottish Agricultural College	£7,400	£1,820
Sheffield Hallam University	£8,000–£10,000	£3,225
Sheffield University	£9,920–£13,050 (£23,580)	£3,225
SOAS	£11,460	£3,225
Southampton Solent University	£8,200	£3,225
Southampton University	£9,380–£12,000 (£21800)	£3,225
Spurgeon's College	£5,665–£6,450	£5,665–£6,450
Staffordshire University	£8,850	£3,225
Stirling University	£9,100–£11,200	£1,820
Strathclyde University	£8,930–£11,465	£1,820
Sunderland University	£8,150	£3,225
Surrey University	£9,000–£11,400	£3,225
Sussex University	£9,975–£12,750 (£22,550)	£3,225
Swansea Met University	£6,950	£3,225
Swansea University	£8,200–£11,900	£3,225
Teesside University	£8,000–£8,500	£3,225
Thames Valley University	£7,600–£8,900	£3,225
Trinity College Carmarthen	£6,500	£3,225
Trinity College of Music	£12,950	£3,225
UCLan	£8,950–£9,450	£3,225
UHI Millennium Institute	£6,410–£7,565	£1,820
Ulster University	£8,540	£3,225
University College Birmingham	£7,300	£3,225
University College London	£11,810–£15,460 (£23,060)	£3,225
UWIC	£7,800–£11,000	£3,225
Warwick University	£10,250–£13,350 (£21,720)	£3,225
West of Scotland University	£7,500–£8,300	£1,820
Westminster University	£9,830	£3,225
Wimbledon College of Art	£10,400	£3,225
Winchester School of Art	£9,380	£3,225
Winchester University	£7,740	£3,225
Wolverhampton University	£8,350	£3,225
Worcester University	£8,000	£3,225
Writtle College	£7,500	£2,835
York St John University	£7,800	£3,225
York University	£9,510–£12,555	£3,225

Bursaries table

Universities have lots of money to help particular categories of student – but the amount that you might get varies enormously. For example, if your family income is below £25k pa, you might qualify for a bursary of £500 pa at one university, or a combined scholarship and bursary of £5k pa at another, or nothing at all at a third.

Most universities give help to students from low-income families, but they may also have earmarked funds, for example for students on particular courses, those with high entrance qualifications, those with nursery costs or those from local partner schools and colleges. The following lists show the approximate level of bursary paid by different universities, solely on the basis of a student's low family income – around £18k–£20k pa (though you may also qualify for scholarships, help with nursery costs, etc).

Bursaries of £1,500 pa and more

Bristol Old Vic Theatre School	Oxford Brookes University
Cambridge University	Oxford University
Exeter University	Peninsula Medical & Dental College
Imperial College	RADA
Leeds University	Royal Agricultural College
London Contemporary Dance School	Royal Veterinary College
LSE	Warwick University
Northern School of Contemporary Dance	York St John University

Bursaries of £1,001–£1,499 pa

Bath Spa University	London University Institute in Paris (ULIP)
Bath University	Loughborough University
Brighton & Sussex Medical School	Manchester University
Brighton University	Newcastle University
Bristol University	Nottingham Trent University
Cardiff University	Nottingham University
Chichester University	Plymouth University
Cumbria University	Queen Mary
Durham University	Queen's University Belfast
Guildhall School of Music & Drama	Reading University
Hertfordshire University	Royal Northern College of Music
Heythrop College	St George's
Hull York Medical School	Southampton Solent University
King's College London	Teesside University
Lancaster University	Thames Valley University
Leeds College of Music	Ulster University
Leicester University	University College Birmingham
Liverpool John Moores University	University College London
Liverpool University	York University

Bursaries of £1k pa

Aberystwyth University	Kent
Bangor University	Leeds Trinity
Bristol UWE	London Met University
Brunel University	Manchester Met University
Chester University	Northampton University
Goldsmiths	Rose Bruford College
Hull University	Royal College of Music

Southampton University
Staffordshire University
Surrey University

Sussex University
Trinity College of Music
Winchester School of Art

Bursaries of £500–£999 pa

Anglia Ruskin University
Aston University
Bedfordshire University
Birmingham City University
Birmingham Conservatoire
Birmingham University
Bradford University
British School of Osteopathy
Bucks New University
Canterbury Christ Church University
Central School of Speech and Drama
City University
Derby University
East Anglia University
Edge Hill University
Falmouth University College
Greenwich University
Harper Adams University College
Huddersfield University

Keele University
Kingston University
Laban
Lincoln University
Liverpool Hope University
London South Bank University
Norwich University College of the Arts
Portsmouth University
Roehampton University
Royal Holloway
St Mary's University College
School of Pharmacy
Sheffield Hallam University
SOAS
Sunderland University
UWIC
Winchester University
Wolverhampton University
Worcester University

Bursaries of less than £500 pa

Arts London
Bolton University
Bournemouth University
Camberwell College of Arts
Central Saint Martin's College of
    Art & Design
Chelsea College of Art & Design
Colchester Institute
Courtauld Institute
Coventry University
Creative Arts University
De Montfort University
East London University
Essex University
Gloucestershire University
Glydŵr University

London College of Communication
London College of Fashion
Middlesex University
Myerscough College
Northumbria University
Ravensbourne College of Design and
    Communication
Royal Academy of Music
Salford University
Sheffield University
Swansea Met University
UCLan
Westminster University
Wimbledon College of Art
Writtle College

University Life

Gap years and long summers

Gap years

Taking a year out (before or after university) can be a very good thing – especially if you are sick of annual exams and your interests go beyond simply getting a degree and a job. A year out can help you get all sorts of experience that schools and universities cannot provide. So, what to do with it? Doing nothing is definitely not recommended (and boring). So be ambitious. You can mix and match travel, voluntary work and paid work, and spend time both at home and overseas.

Gappers often take paid work in the UK for a few months, then voluntary work overseas for another two or three months and round off the year with international travel until the end of the summer.

Overseas travel obviously 'broadens the mind' but it also forces you to live on a budget – a vital experience for your years as a cash-starved student. Working overseas (paid or unpaid) can be more interesting and useful than just travelling in a country (see 'Work (paid or voluntary)', page 65). Paid work, particularly if it is lucrative, can help pay for your travel and contribute to the cost of doing voluntary work or of your university course.

Even in difficult economic circumstances, there are plenty of ways of filling the year actively. Wonderful opportunities are on offer – teaching English in Bolivia, saving turtles in Sri Lanka, working in a hospital in Thailand, leading adventure training courses in Canada . . .

Do you really need to plan your gap year a very long time ahead? The pundits say you should plan two years in advance, which means starting when you are in Year 12. Clearly this makes no sense for most sixth formers, and many successful gap years are arranged in far less time; but if you wait until you have left school and got your results, you may well find you have missed out on some opportunities.

Where to start searching for these opportunities? There are many professional gap year organisations, which offer structured programmes in many parts of the world. These will have local support arrangements in place – worth it if it's your first time away, even if it just allows your parents to sleep at night. A good start is to check out organisations in the Year Out Group, a self-regulatory group of 35 non-profit organisations. Its website (www.yearoutgroup.org) has lots of good advice, information about how to assess what's on offer and links to member organisations.

What is on offer, how well it's organised and how much it costs obviously varies. Gap year providers charge £1k–£4k or even more; but in the current economic climate it will be worth shopping around. Make sure you compare like with like, so check whether the fee covers, for example, accommodation, flight, food, training, visa, insurance, meeting you at the airport, coping if you are sick, etc.

Placement organisations do not offer Club 18–30 holidays for the brainy. If you want to go to the developing world, get ready for basic conditions and don't expect everything to be handed to you on a plate.

Long summers

Make the most of them – you are not likely to get holidays this long once you graduate. Most of the opportunities available to gappers are open to you too and you can pick up a bit of useful work experience to impress employers at the end of your course. You can mix and match work and travel, home and abroad; and, because most universities finish before schools, you may be able to catch some of the early summer air travel bargains before fares rise for the school holidays.

Work (paid or voluntary)

Most work is useful for bolstering your CV; and paid work helps to finance your university costs as well. The right balance for you will depend on your personal finances, the type of work you hope to do and where – in some places work permits and/or job opportunities are hard to get. You can start by looking at as some specialist books such as *Summer Jobs Worldwide* or *Green Volunteers* (www.crimsonpublishing.co.uk).

In the UK, the leading volunteer agency is Community Service Volunteers (www.csv.org.uk). Young people work as full-time volunteers, living away from home with free accommodation, spending money, food allowance and travelling expenses. No offer of service is refused.

If you want to work abroad, there are many organisations that will arrange placements, either for a few months in the summer or for a whole year (before or after university). They offer very different types of work, from EFL teaching to coral conservation. On some you are paid, on most you pay to go; some are in remote areas of the developing world, some on the ski slopes of Canada. There may be age limits (upper or lower). You can also get information about work in international aid and development, at home or overseas, from World Service Enquiry (www.wse.org.uk).

International travel

Student travel offices: Start with your university student travel office (eg STA Travel) if there is one. It will have lots of good advice on student travel deals, insurance, etc. STA has a very good website (www.statravel.co.uk), which can help you plan your trip, fix appointments with travel consultants and sell you cheap air tickets and student/youth deals.

Air: You will find countless cheap flights advertised on the web and in the press, and Google throws up loads of interesting/complex round-the-world ticket deals. You may be able to get student reductions with a valid ISIC card – check your student travel office for what's available.

Rail: You can travel cheaply by train in 30 European countries by buying an inter-rail pass. You can buy a pass for all countries (for a minimum of £125, if you are under 25, for five days' travel in a specified ten-day period); it costs less if you restrict your travel to one country (eg £25 for three days' travel in Bulgaria, in a specified month). Check out details or buy a pass on the Rail Europe website (www.raileurope.co.uk).

Coach: There is good, cheap coach travel to destinations in Europe, and you may get a discount if you are under 26. See the Eurolines website (www.eurolines.co.uk).

International travel notes: There's a wealth of information around, but here are some key points to keep your eye on.

- **Foreign Office travel advice.** To check on the situation in the countries you plan to visit, look at the Foreign Office website (www.fco.gov.uk). It has country-by-country travel advice, which is excellent and up-to-date, and lots of general advice on drugs, terrorism, etc in countries where these are serious dangers to young travellers.

- **Money.** In some countries, ATMs are widespread and work well; in others it would be better to take travellers' cheques, maybe in dollars, maybe sterling. Check in guidebooks specific to the countries you are visiting.

- **Student card.** You will need an ISIC card to get any student discounts abroad (www.isiccard.com). If you are on a gap year, you can get an ISIC card as soon as you have a confirmed offer of a university place.
- **Hostels.** You will find cheap accommodation in youth hostels throughout most of the world. Membership of Hostelling International gives you access to 4,000 youth hostels in 80 countries; find out more from its website (www.hihostels.com).

Gap year and travel organisations

Foreign and Commonwealth Office (for up-to-date travel advice by country)	www.fco.gov.uk
STA Travel	www.statravel.co.uk
Lonely Planet	www.lonelyplanet.com
Rough Guides	www.roughguides.com
Year Out Group	www.yearoutgroup.org
ISIC card	www.isiccard.com
Youth Hostel Association	www.yha.org.uk (in Scotland www.syha.org.uk; in Northern Ireland www.hini.org.uk)
Hostelling International	www.hihostels.com
Eurolines	www.eurolines.co.uk
Rail Europe	www.raileurope.co.uk
British Institute in Florence	www.britishinstitute.it
BUNAC (British Universities North America Club)	www.bunac.org.uk
Camp America	www.campamerica.co.uk
Community Service Volunteers (CSV)	www.csv.org.uk
Kibbutz Representatives	www.kibbutz.org.il
World Service Enquiry	www.wse.org.uk

A–Z of surviving your first year

Accommodation

Take this seriously, for two reasons. First, where you live makes a huge impact on the quality of your student experience. The friends you make in the first year are frequently the ones you keep, and where you live plays a large part in meeting them. Second, it is expensive: it is difficult to over-estimate the impact of your accommodation costs (rent and bills) on your total student budget.

Most universities house you for the first year. What you get depends on your university. Some have very little accommodation, while a very few (including Oxford and Cambridge) house most students for their whole course. There may be university halls (on or off campus), university-owned or managed accommodation (such as local houses), privately run halls or private-sector housing, or a mixture of all of these.

University accommodation: Opt to live in university housing if you can. Standards and rents vary but it is easier to make friends, you have more clout with the landlord and it may be closer to the SU and teaching areas.

What's on offer? Usually you have a choice of rooms in different halls at different rents. Traditional halls are based on corridors; modern halls are usually clustered in flats, and some rooms may have ensuite bathrooms (although the rent will be higher). Most university accommodation is self-catered but catered halls are sometimes an option. Check the university profiles for a summary of what is on offer, and the university's own website for detailed descriptions. If at all possible, go and see the accommodation you are applying for. Find out before you arrive what is supplied and what you need to bring with you (eg bedding).

How much does it cost? From around £55 a week for something basic in a cheap area, to £120 or more a week for an ensuite room with broadband connection in swish new halls. The university profiles tell you roughly how much it costs at each university and, crucially, how many weeks your contract runs for. This matters. Some are on a term-time contract (perhaps requiring you to move out over the Christmas and Easter vacations) – which is fine if you have a home to go to in the holidays and not so good if you don't. Other contracts are for the 36–40 weeks of the academic year – this is best if you want a base for most of the year and plan to travel in the summer. Some are for the full 52-week year – a must for those with a family or with no other home, but a great waste of money for others.

How do you get university accommodation? It usually involves filling in yet another form, usually online. You may be asked about your interests, whether you smoke, etc, so the accommodation office can attempt to group compatible students together. Make sure you get your application in well before the closing date because some accommodation is allocated on a first-come-first-served basis.

Private halls: In cities with lots of students, there are commercial student halls managed by private companies, for example UNITE (www.unite-students.com). They are usually central and purpose-built, and you may share with students from a number of other universities in the city.

Private accommodation: If you need to rent privately, the university accommodation service will almost certainly help and, if you are lucky, it may also have vetted the accommodation on its lists. Colleges without first-year accommodation sometimes organise 'housing days', where new students come and meet each other and local estate agents to sort out house-shares. There is much information about local prices on our university profiles; also look at some of the national websites covering major student cities (www.studentpad.co.uk or www.accommodationforstudents.com). For accommodation in London, try the joint London universities' site (www.studenthousing.lon.ac.uk)

Cheap rented accommodation is harder to find in leafy suburbs or holiday areas (where term starts before the holidaymakers go home). Self-catering accommodation is usually cheaper, as long as you know how to feed yourself cheaply. Remember to add in the travel costs when assessing rents (there's no point living somewhere dirt cheap if it costs a fortune getting to lectures).

There is a lot to think about when looking at accommodation (and you **must** look). Here are a few pointers.

- **Security.** Is it in an area where you will be able to get burglary insurance?; is it on a bus/tube route?; will you feel safe walking home from your nearest stop?
- **Electricity/gas/water safety.** Do sockets, pipes, wiring and appliances look safe and regularly serviced? Particularly look at gas water heaters and fires; landlords now have to have gas appliances serviced annually and they must provide you with proof of this. (If you are concerned about a gas appliance, the Health and Safety Executive runs a carbon monoxide advice line (0800 300363) or via the website (www.hse.gov.uk/gas).)
- **Fire safety.** Check smoke alarms, exits, windows and doors.
- **Damp.** Any sign of it? Check ventilation.
- **Vermin and pests.** Check for signs, smells, etc.
- **TV licence.** Has it been paid? If not, it is legally down to you to pay for one.

Get accommodation organised before the start of term if you possibly can; you will be at a long-term disadvantage if the course starts while you are still sleeping on friends' floors.

Living at home: If it's close enough, it will almost certainly be cheaper to live at home; but you may miss out on some of the social facilities and be less involved in student life. You should move out if you do not have proper study facilities – at least a room of your own.

Buying: Some mortgage companies have special packages for students who can afford to buy a flat or house and sub-let rooms. You may need a parent to act as guarantor. Alternatively, some parents find that buying a house or flat is the most cost-effective way of making their parental contribution.

Other options: If all else fails, renting a caravan can be an option in some rural areas.

Arrival

Everyone experiences culture shock when they start university. Whatever school or college you come from, it is all new and unnerving – but don't worry, almost everyone gets used to it quickly.

Here's some general advice:

- Arrive in good time to settle into your accommodation and meet housemates, etc before you have to register.
- Get a diary and maps – a campus map is a must, but you will need a city map too. Use them to make sure you know where you are supposed to be and when (don't rely on other freshers having much more of a clue than you).
- Get yourself to induction meetings (IT facilities, library, SU, etc), to enrolment, course briefings, meeting your tutors for the first time, at the right time and right place (see also 'Registration and enrolment', page 77). Induction meetings can bore you to death, but you will see the faces in power and you might sit next to someone interesting.
- Find out where your lectures, seminars, tutorials and laboratory sessions are held and when, and where you hand in your essays, etc.
- Start making your own academic timetable for the term or semester, noting dates that assessments have to be handed in (to avoid being penalised if they are late). Don't rely on other people on your course – they may have a different tutor, be taking different optional classes, etc.
- Submerge yourself in the first week's entertainment – usually a Freshers' Fair, endless parties and bar promotion nights. This is also when all the clubs and societies will try to recruit you – but don't be hassled and don't waste money joining loads of them. Some people find freshers' week a real trial that seems to last for ever, but you can always use the time to explore the locality or do some background reading as well as party.

Books

You will be given an exhaustive reading list. Do not go to the bookshop and buy everything – you won't be able to afford it, and you should be able to find the books you need in the library.

Second-hand textbooks are often for sale for a fraction of the price – look on SU and departmental notice boards. If you're lucky they might be available from Amazon too. Or you can try borrowing, or splitting the cost with others, or be inventive in your use of the library. It is (just about) possible never to buy a book, but most students buy the essentials (eg if your tutor has written the definitive work on your subject).

Changing course

Lots of students find that their chosen course, or subject, is not for them and want to change – but don't take it for granted that you can. If you are sure you know what you want to change to, act as soon as you can. The longer you leave it, the more difficult it can be. Your newly chosen course may be completely full (or filling up fast), or you may have already missed too much teaching (so have to start from scratch the following year).

Most universities are sympathetic, but they are aware of the dodges (get on an under-subscribed course and then switch). Start by talking to your tutors; then you will need approval from both the course you are leaving and the one you are joining. The SU may be able to help.

Transferring from one university to another can be more difficult and there is no agreed procedure. Different course tutors will have different attitudes to giving credit for earlier study. Check out your loan position before you decide, particularly if your overall period of study will be longer when you transfer.

Complaints

All universities have a formal complaints procedure. If this does not lead to a satisfactory outcome, you can take up your complaint with the relevant national complaints organisation. Start by talking to the SU, though.

In England and Wales, the relevant national organisation is the OIA – the Office of the Independent Adjudicator for Higher Education (www.oiahe.org.uk). This provides an independent system for students to make complaints about universities – but only if they relate to a study or research programme, a service provided by the university, or a final decision by a university disciplinary or appeal board. It cannot deal with matters of academic judgement, court actions or employment, etc. In Scotland, a similar system is operated by the SPSO – the Scottish Public Services Ombudsman (www.spso.org.uk). It deals with complaints against any organisation providing public services in Scotland, including higher education.

Disabled students

Many disabled students study successfully for a degree and enjoy their time at university. They may meet difficulties and barriers, due to the physical environment (particularly in old buildings) or maybe financial difficulties, but good organisation can help overcome some of them.

Most universities have a designated adviser to help and support students with disabilities. Otherwise, try the welfare officer, student services officer or your personal tutor – and the library and SU may offer support too. If you are a UK student, you should get extra disabled students' allowances (DSAs) and some universities have targeted bursaries too. Support agencies may be able to help you, for example RNIB or the Dyslexia Institute.

If you are not yet in touch with your local branch of Skill (National Bureau for Students with Disabilities), this is the time to do so. It is a charity promoting opportunities for young people with any kind of impairment in post-16 education, training and employment. Check out its website (www.skill.org.uk) which also has links to Skill Scotland, Skill Wales and Skill Northern Ireland.

Distress

Many people, particularly students, may find themselves in distress and want to talk to someone immediately. This may be due to stress, bereavement, financial problems or just feeling miserable. If you find yourself in this situation, there are two basic options:

- **Local nightline.** Many SUs run their own nightlines for students who need someone to talk to. Your student handbook should give the telephone number.
- **The Samaritans.** A national organisation that will have someone you can talk to if you ring their national number: 08457 909090 (calls charged at 2p a minute from residential numbers); or you can email via the website (www.samaritans.org.uk).

Dropping out and intermitting

There are hundreds of reasons why students drop out. It may be shortage of cash or family pressure to do something else. They may fall ill or in love. Perhaps they don't like their course, their subject, the university or its location. Maybe they find that university was a mistake in the first place or discover that they hate it even before the end of freshers' week. Mature students, those without formal entry qualifications, students who got there through Clearing, and men, are statistically the most likely to drop out.

From a financial standpoint, if you are going to drop out, do it early. If you leave it until later, you will end up with larger debts, and no academic qualification to show for them. Your fifth term (of a nine-term course) is probably the final cut-off time; after that, you will probably be better off financially to stay on and get your degree.

Alternatively you can 'intermit' – take a year out from your course (to earn enough money or recover your motivation). Normally this is best done after you have completed your second year.

If you are seriously thinking of dropping out or intermitting, make sure you talk to tutors and student advisers first.

Drugs

If you get into trouble with the police for taking or supplying drugs, you can get advice from Release (www.release.org.uk). They have a helpline (0845 450 0215), or you can email ask@release.org.uk.

If you are worried about a drug problem and want to stop, contact Narcotics Anonymous (www.ukna.org). They run a helpline (0845 373 3366 or NAHelpine@ukna.org), which is open 10am–10pm, seven days a week. If alcohol is the problem, you could approach Alcoholics Anonymous (www.alcoholics-anonymous.org.uk); it also runs a helpline (0845 769 7555).

Emotional problems

Homesickness may be inevitable – some 60% of students are supposed to suffer from it at some stage, though far fewer (nearer 10%) find they cannot cope. Making friends is important and, remember, everyone else is in the same boat. Try to avoid rushing into ephemeral friendships – but equally do not avoid human contact for fear of getting hurt. Lasting friendships will form, but not in the first five minutes.

If you find it hard to cope, use university welfare services, nightline (many SUs run one) or ring the Samaritans (08457 90 90 90). They'll be more helpful (and cheaper) than a bottle of vodka.

Gays, lesbians and bisexuals

If you are homosexual or bisexual (and it is estimated that 5–10% of the population are), a university provides a better than average environment to come to terms with your own sexuality.

Most universities have lively LGBSs (lesbian, gay and bisexual societies), which are often active socially and maybe politically. If you face any discrimination, contact the Campaign for Homosexual Equality (www.campaignforhomosexualequality.org.uk).

Hardship funds

Universities often have substantial funds to help students in financial difficulties, whether these are long-term or short-term.

If you are a UK student from a low-income family (certainly if your family income is below £25k pa), you should automatically be entitled to a bursary from your university of at least £319 pa, but it may be much more. Sometimes you need to apply for it, or it may be assessed automatically along with your loan and grant entitlement. Individual universities may have other categories of student they will help, such as local students coming through designated schools or colleges. Details can usually be found on the university's website.

In addition, a lot of money is available for which you have to apply – you need to make a case to get it. This may be given as large or small handouts to students who can prove hardship, or as small loans to tide you over if your money is delayed. Each university has its own procedure. The best are quick (to avoid financial catastrophe while they think about it) and rigorous (to weed out those who are just after a quick buck). You will normally need to have applied for all your student loans before you are considered for any financial help from your university.

If you are running out of money, make sure you talk to someone in the university or SU student services office; they are not telepathic and you won't get help unless you ask.

Health – advice and information

You can get health advice and information 24/7 through NHS Direct. This is a truly brilliant service, particularly for students a long way from home. You can ring any time and speak to a nurse for advice and confidential health information – to find out what to do if you are feeling ill, about your specific health conditions, about your local healthcare services (finding and contacting doctors, dentists, late-night opening pharmacies, minor injury clinics, etc) and about self-help organisations. You can also research your symptoms online.

To speak to a nurse because you are feeling unwell or have common health questions, ring NHS Direct on 0845 4647. In Scotland, ring NHS24 on 08454 242424; this is a similar service, which also integrates with the ambulance service, GP out-of-hours service and hospital A&E departments.

Online you can research your symptoms and local services through the NHS Direct website, which has a wealth of self-help information, a health encyclopaedia and an information and advice enquiry service, check out www.nhsdirect.nhs.uk. The corresponding websites in Wales and Scotland are www.nhsdirect.wales.nhs.uk and www.nhs24.com. The BBC website has loads of excellent information on health and wellbeing (www.bbc.co.uk/health).

Health – NHS charges

Students have no special NHS status. Once you are 19 years old, you cease to be exempt from NHS charges and are expected to pay for prescriptions, dental treatment, sight tests, glasses, etc.

You are only exempt from these charges if you can demonstrate that your income is really low (and your capital almost non-existent) or for other specified reasons, for example if you are pregnant or have a chronic health problem. Many students will qualify, but you do need to get the appropriate form to avoid paying health charges. Get one from your student health centre, GP, dentist, optician or pharmacist. Further information on health charges is published in the NHS booklet *Help with Health Costs: HC11 Student's Guide*, available online on the Department of Health website (www.dh.gov.uk).

Health – student health services

All universities have student health centres. At larger universities this will include, for instance, a counselling service, a family planning centre, a psychiatrist, help for eating disorders and sexually transmitted diseases and somewhere you can get inoculations for your summer travel.

You should register with a doctor as soon as you arrive. Do not wait until you get ill. You register either with the university health centre or with a GP practice near your student accommodation. Your medical records will come to your new doctor but you can still see your home doctor in the vacations (as a temporary patient).

All the health professionals dealing with university students will be experienced at dealing with the problems of young people and you should find them hard to shock. You can expect them to be experts in dealing with, for instance, eating disorders, sexual problems, pregnancy – or to help if you find you are spending your day staring at your bedroom wall instead of getting on with student life. They are also clear about issues of confidentiality, so what you tell them will not get back to your course tutor or your parents.

ICT

Most universities have sophisticated ICT systems. The ICT service usually works closely with the library – often the two services are merged and operate together out of a learning resource centre. You will almost certainly have an induction to both services; don't miss it. Most universities run beginners' courses for those left behind by the electronic revolution.

What's on offer varies from university to university. Specifically, libraries may have information in the form of CD-ROMs, databases, electronic journals, online services, etc; tutors may have their own personal websites for communicating with students, or a website for a particular course, etc. At some universities, you can access the university network from each student room; at some smaller colleges, you still have to queue up for a handful of PCs in the library. You will almost certainly be expected to use a computer to type up coursework (if you aren't up to that, make the most of any beginners' courses on offer). You can find out more about what's on offer at each university in the profiles.

If you can afford it, get yourself a computer of your own. The best solution is probably a notebook/laptop that you can take around with you. A desktop is cheaper and should work fine; you shouldn't need to move it more than twice a year. Even a three- or four-year-old machine will allow you to type up your essays – if you have a memory stick you can print them on the university computer. You may be able to hire a computer from the university or get technical and financial help when buying one. Some universities have deals that allow you to buy specific computers cheaply.

Insurance

The standard advice is not to take expensive items to university: if you do, the next best thing is to make sure you insure your property, wherever you live.

At some universities, insurance of your personal effects is included in your rent – but is not the case everywhere, so check. If you are not in university accommodation you will certainly need to arrange insurance yourself.

Companies that specialise in student insurance include Saxon Insurance (www.saxoninsurance.com) and Endsleigh (www.endsleigh.co.uk), which also has branches on many campuses. Apart from your personal possessions, you need to think about insuring musical instruments, computers, bikes, etc. The most important thing is to get your insurance sorted out immediately.

And the less money you have, the more important it is to be insured so that you can replace anything that is stolen.

International students' survival

Any student can find the first few weeks at university disorientating, but international students often face additional problems. If you have not spent much time in the UK before starting your course, you will have to learn to live with the English language and British culture as well as a new educational experience. There is now a good deal of help available.

Most UK universities take international students seriously. There is always an international office, with dedicated international student advisers; and the SU usually has an international student orientation programme. The international office will offer counselling, help and support, as well as special social events. While you may not want to surround yourself with your compatriots all the time, it can be helpful to know that others share your specific worries and problems. Most university websites have full information tailored to international students' needs, so you are unlikely to be wholly ignored by or isolated from the locals, whether staff or students.

You can also get useful advice and information – and a contact at most universities – from the UK Council for International Student Affairs (www.ukcisa.org.uk).

The British Council runs an information and advice service for international students. Its website has useful information about studying and living in the UK – finding accommodation, seasonal foods, etc (www.britishcouncil.org).

If you have a problem with a UK visa, contact your university's international office. The British government visa service website has specific guidance for students and deals fully with many common visa-related questions (www.ukvisas.gov.uk).

Jobs

It is highly unlikely that you will go through university without working (for cash) at some point – over 90% of students do. Most work in the vacations, but an increasing number also have part-time jobs in term time. ·

Students' motivations vary. Most work out of financial necessity, but many find it also helps with time management, gives contact with the real world and is an advantage when looking for a job on graduation. Some find mindless work (stacking shelves, working in a petrol station forecourt, etc) can relieve the pressure of intensive courses.

If, however, you find yourself struggling to keep up with your coursework or to get to 9am lectures, a term-time job is probably not a sensible option; and examiners will not make allowances for fatigue affecting your examination performance.

Very few universities forbid term-time work, but there is often a limit (advisory or absolute), usually of 10–15 hours per week. In general, research indicates that this level of work has a minimal impact on study; longer hours have a negative effect, which may be reflected in your final class of degree. It is particularly hard to fit in a job on intensive courses such as drama or science. You should, in any case, give yourself some free weeks around exam time.

Most universities, or their SUs, have their own employment offices (or jobshops) to help students find work. Indeed, there are often jobs on campus – in libraries, bars, administration, catering, etc. Check out job opportunities quickly – there is often a waiting list for SU bar jobs by the end of the first day of term. Use the local newspaper, look for advertisements in shop windows, network and don't be afraid to approach potential employers on spec.

Wages vary across the country and according to what type of work you undertake. Work in bars, restaurants, shops, offices and call centres is widely available and hours are flexible, but you will probably only get the minimum wage (though working in a restaurant should at least ensure you are fed). You can earn more if you can type, are IT-literate or have some specialist expertise (lifeguard or sporting qualification, care work or programming skills). If you can do translation work or coach GCSE candidates, you could earn up to £30 an hour. You may need to pay national insurance and income tax (check the current limits). Make sure you are not being paid less than the minimum wage for your age group; you can check this at the HM Revenue and Customs website (www.hmrc.gov.uk).

In vacations, virtually all students try to find a job – to pay off the overdraft, fund some travel or gain relevant work experience – though vacation wages are much more variable. Some students go home, if there are jobs there (and living costs can be lower), but many remain in their university towns, if there is more work there and they are paying for accommodation anyway. Others go further afield, for example to work in US summer camps. Do not underestimate the value of real training and work experience; many a new graduate has wished they had done more of it (see 'Gap years and long summers', page 64).

Library and information services

University libraries will loom large in your academic life. You will probably discover early on that the other students are all after the same books and articles as you are, just when you want them. So suss out the library early and get on top of its catalogue and reservation systems. The catalogue will probably be held electronically and you may be able to access it at home through the internet. Check which days the library is open (some hardly open at weekends, others are open 24/7). Work out ways of getting your hands on recommended texts and make sure you know how to photocopy them (there may be restrictions on how long you can borrow them). There will be an induction to show you how it all works. Don't skip it.

University libraries operate at a completely different level from those you are likely to be used to. Compare your school library with, say, that at UCL, which has two main libraries and 15 specialist libraries; a total of 2 million volumes and 12,000 periodicals; generous access to e-books, e-journals, databases and the main London University Library round the corner; and it spends £259 pa for each student. Of course, not all universities have, or need, that amount of library and information provision. Those specialising in art, dance or drama, for example, will concentrate on studios rather than library and IT resources. While the mean number of books per student is around 63, some universities have more than twice this figure, some less than half.

The amount that universities spend on all information provision varies hugely, ranging from £28 to £558 pa for each full-time equivalent (FTE) student. The mean spend is about £121 pa. This may be used for books but is increasingly spent on sophisticated online facilities such as e-journals, national databases, CD-ROMs, etc. Indeed, ICT plays such a significant role in accessing information that many universities have merged their library and ICT service to form integrated learning resource centres. Some of these are deliberately set up as study centres, with lots of seating, computer terminals and photocopiers. Most are central, warm and welcoming, providing a haven for students living off-campus.

Living at home

More university students now choose to live at home – some because they prefer it, more often because it is likely to be cheaper. It is worth checking how much rent your parent(s) will charge you and how much travel will cost. You may find that, financially, there is not much in it – especially when you take into account the lower student loan you will get if you live at home.

Practically it has its difficulties – most obviously because it can be harder to participate fully in student life; less obviously because it may make participation in academic studies more isolating and late night use of university libraries impossible (though you will usually be able to access your university's electronic resources from home).

If you are going to live at home, make sure you have established the ground rules from the start: you are a student on a degree course, not a superannuated sixth former. Different considerations obviously apply to mature students with family constraints.

If you attend a university that has large numbers of students living at home, or where many students commute rather than live on campus, it should be relatively easy to fit into student life.

Living away from home

Many students will be living away from home for the first time. You need to work out how to study and socialise effectively, while keeping on top of the nitty gritty of everyday living. Otherwise your university career could be dominated by personal logistics – travelling, eating, sleeping and keeping clean (not to mention dealing with dentists, plumbers and bank managers). While it may be cool to be scruffily dressed, you will keep more friends if you know how to wash your clothes. So, if you are one of the many who are not yet 100% confident of every aspect of living away from home, here are some things you could think about.

Cash: Make sure you have some money to take with you at the start of term and a bank or building society account (with some money in it) so you can access more. Be sure you really know how to use a cash point, can deposit a cheque/cash and understand a bank statement.

Budgeting: You will find this easier if you have done it before – for example, if you have managed a personal clothes allowance or travelled on a fixed budget. The 'Course budget' form on page 56 might help.

Transport: Get yourself maps of the campus and the town, so you can find your way around. Find out about student deals and off-peak travel on local buses, trains, etc. Don't be frightened about taking taxis: they are not always expensive, particularly if several students share one. Only hail licensed taxis (not minicabs) in the street; it is worth keeping the number of one of the national taxi companies on your mobile. When you ring for a minicab, ask them to tell you the (approximate) fare and confirm this with the driver. Before you get into a minicab, ask the driver which company he is from, to check it was the one you called.

Staying in touch: Make sure you have your email address list with you. Shop around for a mobile phone deal that will allow you to phone home without running up huge bills. Most university halls will have a telephone (though they can be expensive to ring out on, and communal phones are not always answered). If you are sharing a flat, you may need a landline for the internet, but you can bar it from outgoing calls. Does anyone write letters any more?

Dentists and doctors: Sign on to an NHS practice – do this before you get ill. The college/university will have its own health centre or will advise on good practices (see also 'Health – student health services', page 71). For immediate health problems contact NHS Direct, which is open 24/7 (see 'Health – advice and information', page 71).

Shopping and cooking: Shopping to a budget is a skill you will have to develop. Find your nearest market and cheap supermarket. Make a list before you go to the shop, buy own brands, look for the loss leaders and special offers. Food prices are often reduced just before closing time (bread can be as cheap as 10p on Sundays). Get hold of a student cookbook, which will have cheap recipes and money-saving ideas.

Laundry: Get to grips with the laundry arrangements early. Use your own soap powder (it is expensive in laundrettes) and try using half the recommended amount. You will find a drying rack is cheaper than using a tumble drier. An iron is rarely provided in your accommodation; if your wardrobe needs one, get a travelling iron.

Locals

If there are good relations between students and locals, you will feel welcome in the streets, shops and pubs, and comfortable about travelling late at night. If relations are antagonistic, life is much harder.

University towns often have a mix of student-friendly localities and areas where students are not so welcome; the SU will almost certainly give you guidance as part of its induction. Some students can be made to feel so uncomfortable that they stick within their campus, rather than mixing with the locals – particularly where youth unemployment is high. You may feel that you are a cash-starved student; local unemployed people may see you as privileged, state-subsidised and middle class. If you have problems with locals, contact the SU.

Money management

Money is a constant problem for students, so money management matters. Start with a sound budget (use our 'Course budget' form, page 56) so you know you can manage and keep your costs down.

You will probably have to borrow – first, obviously, taking out your student loan, then borrowing from banks and parents (or other sympathetic family members); you may have to use credit cards, but only if you're desperate. Most students will get a job to make ends meet – maybe in term time, almost certainly in the vacations. The key is not to let your money get out of control.

Most universities try to help. The more forward-thinking run seminars on how to manage your money. Almost all try to help if your finances get out of hand – they will offer advice and, if you are lucky, money from hardship funds. The best advice is to tell your university about impending financial catastrophe before it occurs.

Parents

Agree the ground-rules – if possible while you are still at home. Start with cash – the amount they are prepared to give you by way of parental contribution, and when and how it is to be paid. Then define contact frequency – how often they expect you to be in contact and how often (if at all) they expect you to visit home. Make an agreement about transport, if you need them to help you move at the beginning and end of term.

You should be able to preserve your independence, but without distancing yourself too much, or it will make your parents anxious and Christmas impossible. You are an adult with a separate life to lead. Pride and/or concern will usually mean they will want to visit you at university. Before they come, warn them what to expect. Don't let them just turn up – it will be at the most inconvenient moment. Fix an exact time and date when your more disreputable friends are out of the way.

Plagiarism and cheating

Do not be tempted to cheat – either by getting off-the-peg essays online, original essays written on commission or just getting another student to write them for you. Cheating may seem a simple solution to ensure academic success, but the truth will out, penalties are severe and you will probably be sent down without a degree if you are caught.

Plagiarism means lifting other people's work without attribution, which is easily done when working from web sources. While it may seem like an easier option than writing original essays, don't fall for it – university software makes it increasingly easy to detect plagiarism and it, too, can cost you your degree.

However, it can be hard to define precisely what constitutes plagiarism in the context of your course: the difference between quoting sources for the ideas in your written work and simply lifting text verbatim can be unclear. Most universities take pains to see that you understand the difference between plagiarising (lifting) and using arguments from sources which you quote (attribution). Your university or course handbook, given out at the start of your course, should spotlight how the university defines it.

Some universities make you certify every individual piece of work you hand in as being your own work – that it is not plagiarised and not written by anyone else.

Poverty – how to cope with it

Once you have collected all your money – loans, grants, bursaries, scholarships and/or parents' handouts – it will probably be more than you have ever had in your bank account before. You will need all of it (and probably more) to keep you afloat until the start of next term, so find ways of making it stretch.

Start with your own university. There will be lots of cheap deals for students in and around your university if you look for them. Then there are some general ways of keeping your costs down:

- Cheap accommodation that is not too far away from the university. Add your travel expenses to the rent; you may find that pricier accommodation within walking distance of lectures is a better bet than living further away.
- Buying a second-hand bike is usually cheaper than a year's bus fares.
- You can spend a fortune replacing your belongings if they are stolen and you are not insured.
- Food, drink and entertainment are usually cheapest at the SU and its shops. Meat can be expensive, so try vegetarian food.
- Plenty of locals will compete for your business, so keep your eyes open for local deals, for example Chinese and Indian restaurants, student discounts at theatres and cinemas, student nights at pubs and clubs.
- Banks offer interest-free overdrafts to students, up to a specified limit. This is (obviously) the cheapest way to borrow commercially. If your overdraft is beyond the interest-free limit, bank borrowing is still cheaper for you as a student than for others, but keep within the agreed limit. Credit cards are an outrageously expensive way to borrow.
- Your student loans do not attract interest but go up in line with inflation. This is almost certainly the cheapest way for you to borrow in the longer term.
- Avoid lending money to your cash-starved student friends – it can be embarrassing if you need it back and it is hard to collect.

But don't be put off. Although you will not have much spare cash, neither will anybody else. Try not to skimp on food. Most students enjoy themselves in spite of their lack of money. After all, the best things in life are free . . . so they say.

Racism

Students from ethnic minorities may find less racial prejudice at university than elsewhere – although they may be surprised by some other student minorities and a small number of staff.

Most universities now have well-organised student groups and societies representing international students and different national and religious minorities (eg black, Jewish or Irish students). Many of these groups are extremely active in the social and political life of the university and are a good place to meet other students of a similar background.

SUs are often involved in campaigns against racism. Contact SU officers or your tutor if you have a problem on account of your race – on or off the campus. See also 'Victimisation', page 82.

Registration and enrolment

Put up with registration and enrolment – it only happens once a year (and the first year is the worst). It is vital to get your university student card, which is your passport to libraries and the SU and may be an actual key to the university buildings. Expect queues (take a book, a crossword or try busking).

Make sure you take everything you will be asked for, which might include information about your fee status and original exam certificates. You will usually have to take all your certificates, including GCSE certificates, so get duplicates in advance if you have lost them (results slips are usually only accepted for the most recent exams). Take a pen and don't lose your papers.

Take lots of passport photographs for ID, membership cards, etc.

Safety and security

Universities are very conscious about safety and security issues. Some run late-night buses (some for women students only) and issue personal alarms and security leaflets; they may have security systems, such as smart cards, and 24-hour porters or security patrols. If these are not available at your university, well, start badgering. Start with the SU.

Keep out of any area that the SU says is a no-go area for students.

Check that you can get to and from your lectures/parties, etc safely – that your accommodation is close to public transport, footpaths are well lit, you know which local routes are safe and which are not.

Be sensible and follow local police guidance – which is usually not to walk around on your own late at night, to stick to main roads where possible, to avoid using your mobile in the street, not to use cash machines at night and to make sure your room/flatmates know where you are going and generally to leave a trail.

There are some useful personal safety tips on the Suzy Lamplugh Trust website (www.suzylamplugh.org).

Sects

Students are easy targets for religious sects, and a few sects are banned from campuses. If you are bothered by them, complain to the SU and tutors.

Self-catering checklist

Here are some points you may find useful if you are catering for yourself.

- Find out what cooking facilities you will have – oven, rings, grill, microwave, gas or electricity?
- How many others share them?
- Are there restrictions as to when they can be used?
- Make sure you know how to operate them properly.
- What about cooking utensils: pots, pans, cutlery, crockery, etc?
- Make a list of things you know you will need and check whether they are provided. A basic list could start with:
  o kettle
  o saucepan(s)
  o frying pan
  o chopping board/surface
  o sharp knife
  o bread knife
  o wooden spoon/spatula
  o ovenproof dish/bowl
  o dishtowels
  o tin opener
  o jug
  o mugs
  o glasses
  o plates and bowls
  o cutlery.

Then add whatever else you personally cannot do without – bottle opener, fish slice, lemon squeezer, garlic press, potato peeler, cheese grater, sieve, corkscrew.

- What food storage space is available? How big is the fridge and who uses it? It can make a big difference if there is somewhere secure for you to store supplies rather than shopping each day.

- Many students prefer to share buying and cooking food – it saves time and it's good for bonding in a flat/house. It pays to be organised about it, especially where money is involved: set up a kitty, or a book where everyone writes down what they spend on communal food. Agree early what is communal and what is not: milk, coffee, cleaning materials, etc. Keep some sort of emergency supplies so you will not starve if your cook gets a last-minute invitation on the way home.

- If you have not done much cooking before, there are lots of student cookbooks – you'll find them in supermarkets and bookshops in university towns, or check out student cookbooks on Amazon (www.amazon.co.uk).

Sex

Many students spend much of their time thinking about sex, but relatively little time actually doing it. For students living in close proximity to each other, often for the first time free from parental disapproval, the opportunity to experiment with sex can be irresistible. Stick to safe sex; condoms are usually available in the SU, and they're sometimes free.

Sexual harassment

If you are being sexually harassed (by a member of staff or a fellow student), make sure you tell someone. Most SUs have an officer responsible for women's issues.

If you are raped, you (women and men) can ring the Rape and Sexual Abuse Support Centre on its helpline: 01483 546400 (open 7.30pm–9.30pm except Saturdays and bank holidays) or visit their website (www.rasasc-guildford.org). This is part of a national network of such centres – for one nearer you, check the list of members on www.thesurvivorstrust.org.

There is also a male-only rape centre, Survivors UK. It runs a helpline on 0845 122 1201 (open 7pm–10pm, Monday, Tuesday and Thursday); or email through the website (www.survivorsuk.org).

When either of these is closed, ring the Samaritans on its central number: 08457 909090.

Staff–student sex

It happens. Both male and female students, heterosexual or homosexual, can be at risk. It can be very ego-boosting (but not much more) to be 'courted' by an older, and apparently wiser, person. At worst it is simply sexual harassment (see previous section).

An affair with a tutor can lead to awkwardness, and more important from your point of view, it can increase pressure on you; and it can be very tacky if your tutor is your examiner. Permanent relationships have (very occasionally) been known, but tread warily. Some universities have codes of conduct to regulate staff–student sexual conduct. Others now require staff to report their sexual relationships with students (rather like the House of Commons Register of Members' Interests, but more entertaining). If a member of staff is making unwelcome advances to you, talk to the SU or your student counsellor (unless he/she is the offending party).

Student discounts

You can get lots of student discounts with your student ID – locally, you can get reduced prices at shops, theatres, bookshops, cinemas, etc and discounted newspapers, insurance, driving lessons and mobile phones nationally and on the internet. Your SU website may list the discounts they have negotiated, or check with your SU office. To prove your student status, your university student card or NUS democracy card usually does the trick.

To get discounts overseas you need an International Student Identity Card (ISIC) – which also gives you free email and discounted international phone calls as well as some UK discounts. You can apply online (www.isiccard.com) or get it from your local STA travel office. You will need proof that you are a full-time student, proof of age and a passport-size photo. It currently costs £9 pa.

The NUS has some additional cards to get student discounts. You can also pay £10 a year for an NUS Extra card, which gives you a wide range of extra discounts – online and in shops – and a free ISIC card. If you are an OU student or a sixth former, you can get an NUS Associate card, which gives some discounts. There is more information on the NUS website (www.nusonline.co.uk).

Students' unions

Almost all universities and colleges have their own SU, sometimes called a Students' Guild or Students' Association (SA). It is normally, but not always, affiliated to the NUS (National Union of Students). Whatever the slant of the union (left, right or apolitical), it is run by students for students – more or less.

At a small college, the SU will be based around a common room. At a large university, it will have its own building with a union shop, bar and maybe other eating and drinking spots. The SU is responsible for entertainments (club nights, quizzes, entertainment) and for funding clubs and societies. The larger SUs may run multiple bars and eateries, as well as nightclubs, a nightline for personal problems, newspapers and radio stations. There's usually an SU welfare service, which can help with accommodation, jobs (in the SU and locally), hardship funds, changing course, and general advice and know-how. Most SUs have their own website (see our university profiles) so you can see what is going on.

How much you get involved in union activities is up to you. They encompass a huge range – sport, politics, debating, drama, media, etc – and the standard can be very high. Joining in helps to widen your circle of acquaintances, beyond those on your course and in your halls, and taking part in running activities can be useful experience for life after graduation.

Study skills

Many universities run short courses at the beginning of the first term to help you develop study skills, particularly essay-writing and IT skills. Don't be embarrassed or too snooty to attend: some of the best students need these courses.

Studying and time management

You will be responsible for your own academic development at university, far more than you were at school. Approaches differ, depending on the course and university, but you should expect little spoon-feeding and will probably experience unfamiliar ways of learning – seminars, lectures, maybe problem-based learning. You may be asked to make PowerPoint presentations of your work to groups of other students (and tutors) and to write extended essays or dissertations (of maybe 10,000 words), based on your own research.

It is assumed that you enjoy your subject, are committed to it and want to find out more about it. You may be given a booklist but are not advised which of the books you really need to read; you will need to use your judgement. You will be expected to use a much wider range of sources than the lecturers' handouts, such as international academic journals. Your timetable may be different from your friends', and you will probably be expected to work it out for yourself. It may include lectures and tutorials, seminars and practicals – some will be compulsory, some not (but think hard before you decide not to attend). Your timetable will probably leave you with what looks like masses of free time, but this is for your own reading, analysis and writing.

Not having a busy schedule can lead to much time-wasting. Get a grip on it from the start. A well-known technique for time management is to analyse your diary in detail for a whole week, recording what you do hour by hour. The results can be illuminating. Remember, it is your own time you are wasting, nobody else's.

Watch out for deadlines – you need to deliver work when it is due. Excuses, however real, may not be accepted and you can be marked down for missing a deadline, even by a minute; on some courses, late work may not be accepted at all (so late submission means you fail that paper). Always make sure you have back-up copies of your work and that you give yourself enough time to print out all the copies you need to hand in.

Sometimes a number of pieces of work have to be handed in by the same deadline, which means you really have to be organised. Make a careful schedule, with enough slack to accommodate a bout of flu or a computer breakdown; and make sure you have at least something to hand in for each segment, rather than one piece of work that is perfect and several that are blank.

Don't be put off by students who appear to be more sophisticated; they are not necessarily brighter than you. Use your own common sense and go your own way.

Travel – local

At some universities, you live, socialise and are taught on a single site so there is not much need for local travel. At others, local travel between your accommodation and university can be costly and difficult – especially if you have to join commuters in the rush hour. Where different sites are spread all over town, there is often free connecting transport; and some SUs run night-time minibuses to get students home safely.

Cash-starved students find they can walk further than they thought possible – and that a pushbike, scooter or pair of roller blades can be useful. Public transport always costs, and it's worth shopping around for your cheapest local travel options. In general, buses are cheaper than trains, and both are usually cheaper than the tube in London.

There are sometimes (but not always) student discounts on local public transport. This usually depends on the individual company, but sometimes on the university – for example, in London, the 18+ Student Oyster Scheme is only available to students at participating universities (see the Transport for London website (www.tfl.gov.uk)). Check out what is available locally from your SU.

Travel – national

You can get major discounts, on top of any cheap fares, if you get a rail and/or coach card – your ordinary student card is not enough.

Coachcards: National Express Young Person's Coachcards (or 16to26 Coachcards) are for young people aged 16–26 and for full-time students. They cost £10 for a year and save up to 30% off National Express journeys in the UK and some Eurolines fares too. The simplest way to buy one is on the National Express website (www.nationalexpress.com).

Railcards: A 16–25 Railcard, which is for those aged 16–25 and for full-time students, costs £24 for a year and gives you a third off most rail fares (though there may be certain restrictions; for example, you may not be allowed to use it in the rush hour). There are also special offers with railcards, which are worth looking out for. You can apply online (www.railcard.co.uk) and the card will be posted to you first class – and they give you free YHA membership worth £9.95! If you are applying for the first time, you need your passport number or UK driving licence number plus a passport-size photograph.

If you are over 25 years old or you prefer to apply in person, you can buy a railcard at a station ticket office, a rail-appointed travel agency or student travel office. You can print a blank application off the website first to save time, and take it with you, together with a passport-size photograph. Also, if you are under 26 years old, you will need proof of age (birth certificate, passport, driving licence or ISIC card); if you are over 26 years old, you will need proof that you are a full-time student at a recognised institution (either an ISIC card or the mature students section of the application form completed and certified).

You can also buy a card by phone; start with National Rail Enquiries: 08457 484950.

Victimisation

If you think you are being victimised for reasons of politics, race, religion or sex, you should contact your own SU, or you can try one of the following national organisations:

- Campaign for Homosexual Equality (CHE) www.c-h-e.org.uk
- Conservative Future www.conservativefuture.com
- Equality and Human Rights Commission www.equalityhumanrights.com
- Federation of Student Islamic Societies in the UK and Eire (FOSIS) www.fosis.org.uk
- Labour Students www.labourstudents.org.uk
- Liberal Youth (Liberal Democrat Youth and Students) www.liberalyouth.org
- Liberty (National Council for Civil Liberties) www.liberty-human-rights.org.uk
- National Union of Students (NUS) www.nusonline.co.uk
- Union of Jewish Students (UJS) www.ujs.org.uk

Voting

If you are a UK student, make sure you can vote in any British election – general elections, local elections, referendums and European parliamentary elections. Your name must be on the electoral register, which is updated annually in October.

If you have a different address in term time from your permanent home address, you can lawfully be on the electoral register at both addresses. You will then be eligible to vote in local elections in the two different areas. You can only vote once in a national election – it is an offence to vote twice in any one election. It is now easy to get a postal vote in England, Scotland and Wales, and you don't need to give a reason (there are different arrangements in Northern Ireland).

You can register, or check your details on the register, at your local electoral registration office. This is generally at your local council office in England and Wales, the Valuation Joint Board in Scotland and EONI in Northern Ireland. You can find downloadable voter registration forms and applications for postal voting at www.aboutmyvote.co.uk.

It is important to be able to vote, even if you don't actually bother when the time comes. You can get more information on voting at www.electoralcommission.org.

Welfare

Universities and SUs are generally very supportive and provide specialist help for a range of welfare problems. Check out what is on offer from the university and your SU.

In general, students are not entitled to government welfare benefits unless there are other reasons – for instance, if you are a single parent. If you think you might qualify, get in touch with the Citizens

Advice Bureau. You can find your local CAB office on www.citizensadvice.org.uk or get online advice from their national service (www.adviceguide.org.uk).

What if you don't survive?

Work out what went wrong:

- If higher education is not for you, look for a job – maybe one with an element of occupational training, so that you will have a marketable skill and a qualification to certify you have it. Or take a practical, job-related course locally.
- If you think higher education is for you, but you chose the wrong course, the wrong college, or the wrong place, apply for a different course next year.
- If the reasons are personal or financial, try taking a break. You may be able to return later, transfer credit to another institution or continue part time somewhere else.

When you have settled in

When you have settled in, and before you forget the *Guide to UK Universities* completely, how about telling us what you think? We would particularly like to know about anything you wish you had known before you applied or when you got to university or college – and any money-saving tips.

Please write to:

Guide to UK Universities

c/o Trotman Publishing

Westminster House

Kew Road

Richmond

Surrey TW9 2ND

UNIVERSITY PROFILES

Map 1 Scotland, Northern Ireland and Wales

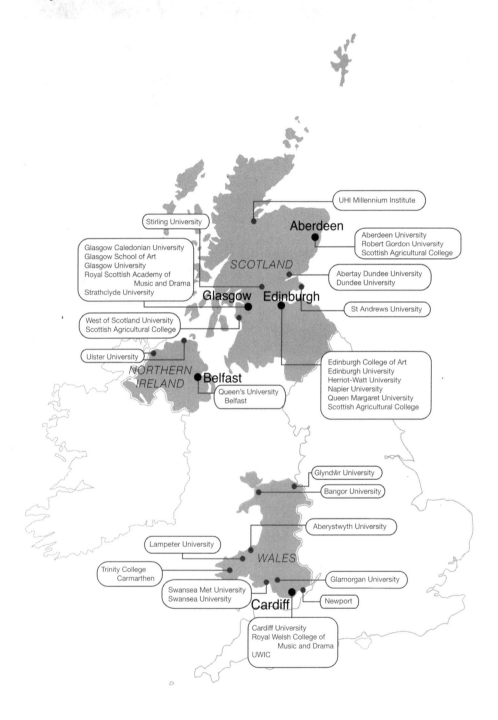

UHI Millennium Institute

Stirling University

Aberdeen

Aberdeen University
Robert Gordon University
Scottish Agricultural College

Glasgow Caledonian University
Glasgow School of Art
Glasgow University
Royal Scottish Academy of
          Music and Drama
Strathclyde University

SCOTLAND

Abertay Dundee University
Dundee University

Glasgow   Edinburgh

West of Scotland University
Scottish Agricultural College

St Andrews University

Ulster University

NORTHERN
IRELAND   Belfast

Queen's University
Belfast

Edinburgh College of Art
Edinburgh University
Herriot-Watt University
Napier University
Queen Margaret University
Scottish Agricultural College

Glyndŵr University

Bangor University

Aberystwyth University

Lampeter University

WALES

Trinity College
Carmarthen

Glamorgan University

Swansea Met University
Swansea University

Cardiff

Newport

Cardiff University
Royal Welsh College of
          Music and Drama
UWIC

Map 2 England

ENGLAND

Huddersfield University

Cumbria University
Lancaster University

Bradford College
Bradford University

Myerscough College
UCLan

Newcastle University
Northumbria University

Durham University

Sunderland University

Teesside University

Hull York Medical School
York St John University
York University

Leeds College of Music
Leeds Met University
Leeds Trinity
Leeds University
Northern School of
Contemporary Dance

York

Leeds

Hull University
Hull York Medical School

Manchester Met University
Manchester University
Royal Northern College of Music
Salford University

Bolton University

Edge Hill University

Manchester

Sheffield Hallam University
Sheffield University

Liverpool Hope University
Liverpool John Moores University
Liverpool University

Chester University

Liverpool

Lincoln University

Nottingham Trent University
Nottingham University

Derby University

Loughborough University

Coventry University
Warwick University

Keele University
Staffordshire University

Birmingham

East Anglia University
Norwich University
College of the Arts

Wolverhampton University

Harper-Adams University College

De Montfort University
Leicester University

Worcester University

Northampton University

Anglia Ruskin University
Cambridge University

Bedfordshire University

Cambridge

Cranfield University

Aston University
Birmingham City University
Birmingham Conservatoire
Birmingham University
University College Birmingham

Buckingham University
Bucks New University
National Film & TV School

Oxford

Colchester Institute
Essex University

Hertfordshire University

Gloucestershire University

Bristol

London
Page 88–89

Reading University

Anglia Ruskin University
Writtle College

Oxford Brookes
University
Oxford University

Bristol Old Vic Theatre School
Bristol University
Bristol UWE

Canterbury Christ
Church University
Kent University

Bath Spa University
Bath University

Creative Arts University

Royal Agricultural
College

Brighton

Plymouth

Winchester School of Art
Winchester University

Surrey University

Brighton and Sussex
Medical School
Brighton University
Sussex University

Exeter University

Southampton Solent
University
Southampton University

Chichester University

Bournemouth University

Farnborough College

Exeter University
Falmouth University
College

Marjon
Peninsula Medical
and Dental School
Plymouth University

Portsmouth University

Map 3 Greater London

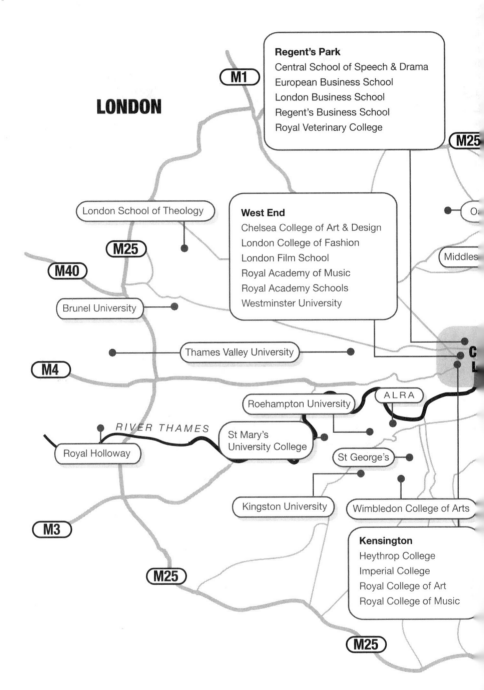

LONDON

M1

Regent's Park
Central School of Speech & Drama
European Business School
London Business School
Regent's Business School
Royal Veterinary College

M25

London School of Theology

M25

West End
Chelsea College of Art & Design
London College of Fashion
London Film School
Royal Academy of Music
Royal Academy Schools
Westminster University

O

Middles

M40

Brunel University

Thames Valley University

M4

C
L

ALRA

Roehampton University

RIVER THAMES

St Mary's
University College

Royal Holloway

St George's

Kingston University

Wimbledon College of Arts

M3

Kensington
Heythrop College
Imperial College
Royal College of Art
Royal College of Music

M25

M25

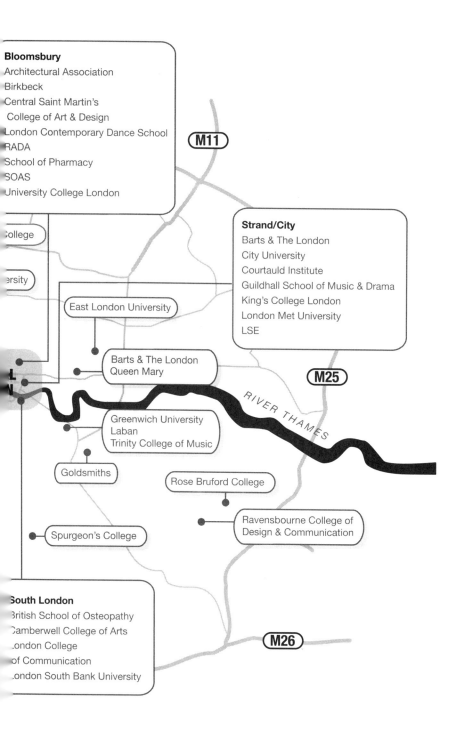

Bloomsbury
Architectural Association
Birkbeck
Central Saint Martin's
 College of Art & Design
London Contemporary Dance School
RADA
School of Pharmacy
SOAS
University College London

College

ersity

East London University

Strand/City
Barts & The London
City University
Courtauld Institute
Guildhall School of Music & Drama
King's College London
London Met University
LSE

M11

M25

Barts & The London
Queen Mary

RIVER THAMES

Greenwich University
Laban
Trinity College of Music

Goldsmiths

Rose Bruford College

Ravensbourne College of
Design & Communication

Spurgeon's College

South London
British School of Osteopathy
Camberwell College of Arts
London College
 of Communication
London South Bank University

M26

What the Profiles Cover

Formal name and contact details. Also where to make enquiries and where to apply.

Location & number of sites. Where to find them and how many campuses or sites there are, for example whether the university is in one location or spread over two cities, for example Cheltenham and Gloucester. Partner colleges where you can study for a part or all of the university's courses.

In brief

This is a brief outline of the university: the type of university or college it is, the broad study areas taught, the profile of the student population and staff numbers. There is also information on freshers, including numbers, drop-out rates, points on entry and how likely you are to get accommodation in your 1st year.

The broad study areas are sometimes very broad (often described in very few words, eg arts, sciences) and may be the names of the university's faculties; or they may be a selection of subjects or a single discipline (eg osteopathy, music), It is **not** a catalogue of courses. To find out if a specific subject is taught (eg popular music), look it up in the search index, 'Where your subject is taught (pages 670–748) and see if the university or college is listed.

The information on students, which is drawn from data published by HESA (Higher Education Statistical Agency), will show you whether they are full time or part time and the proportion who are postgraduate, international, mature on entry, etc, so you can judge for yourself whether this is the right sort of student body for you.

Icons

These come at the beginning of each university profile and provide information on the student population at each university. Each figure of a person represents 10,000 students. There are three other icons following this; firstly, the percentage of undergraduates and postgraduates that make up the total student population. Secondly, the socio-economic backgrounds of students, which includes the percentage of mature students, students from lower socio-economic groups, full-time students and UK students and finally the male to female ratio at every university.

Profile

This includes information on the **institution** (date of foundation, how to get there, etc); **courses** (degrees offered, awarding body, etc); **Study opportunities & careers** (libraries and IT, spending on information provision (according to Sconul, the Society of College, National and University Libraries), opportunities for study abroad, etc); **Student services & facilities** (eg amenities, accommodation); and **money** (eg how much you need to live on, bursaries offered, tuition fees charged).

Student view

An impression of student life at the university or college, written by a student.

These profiles are to help you start shortlisting. Then start looking at individual universities' websites and prospectuses.

University and College Profiles

Aberdeen University

Location:
Aberdeen, north of
Scotland (map 1)
**Main teaching centre
plus medicine, both
within city**

University of Aberdeen, King's College,
Aberdeen AB24 3FX
☎ Tel 01224 272000
✉ Email sras@abdn.ac.uk
💻 Website www.abdn.ac.uk/sras

Student enquiries: Student Recruitment and Admissions
Service (tel 01224 272090/1,
fax 01224 272576)
Application: UCAS

In brief

otal Students: 14,025

72% undergraduate
28% postgraduate

Undergraduates: 10,155
87% full-time
17% mature on entry
87% UK students
25% lower socio-economic groups
55% female
45% male

- **A top UK research-intensive university.**
- **Teaching staff:** 1400 full-time.
- **Broad study areas:** Arts, sciences, education, engineering, medicine, dentistry, law, divinity, social sciences, music.

Freshers
- **Admissions information:** AS-levels accepted on some courses; most require A-levels or Highers and Advanced Highers.
- **First degree entrants:** 2105 UK, full-time.
- **Points on entry:** 270 (average).
- **Drop-out rate:** 10% in 1st year.
- **Accommodation:** All new students housed who wish it.

Profile

Institution
Founded: 1495 (King's College). **Site:** 2 sites: King's College in Old Aberdeen; medical sciences at Foresterhill. **How to get there:** Fast coach services from Edinburgh, Glasgow and all major cities; rail services north and south. For university, bus from Union St (nos 1, 2, 14, going east); by road, follow signs for A90 and Old Aberdeen. **Special features:** Institute of Scottish and Irish Studies, medical sciences, plus initiatives in ethnology and cultural studies.

Courses

Academic features: Access courses and summer school. Courses in animal care, health and welfare, anthropology, Celtic civilisation, off-shore engineering, petroleum geology, cultural history, safety engineering, sports and exercise science, social research and all biosciences including tropical environmental science. **Awarding body:** University of Aberdeen. **Main undergraduate awards:** MA, BSc, BD, BTh, LLB, MB ChB, BSc Med Sci, MEng, BEng, BScEng, BEd, BMus. **Length of courses:** 3 years (ordinary/designated), 4 years (Hons and Divinity), 5 years (MB ChB, MChem, MEng).

Study opportunities & careers

Library and information services: 4 library buildings, over 1.05 million volumes, inter-library loan service, short loan collections for course books in heaviest demand. Annual expenditure £178 per student (FTE), plus departmental purchases. IT and library services converged. 1000+ networked PCs have access to internet and so to library catalogue (ratio workstations to students 1:8), open 24 hours/day. IT support from 4 help desks in main library and in computing centre. Information skills week for new students, plus departmental inductions; informal classes on use of library. **Other learning resources:** Interactive video; satellite TV for language teaching. Specialist collections: Jacobite material, transport and photographic collections, pre-1800 British and European works, first editions of early science and medical volumes. Almost 250,000 maps, many historical. **Study abroad:** 6% of students spend part of their course abroad, including those on courses in law with European law (or French, German, Spanish law) who study abroad for local diploma. Erasmus links with 155 European institutions, plus 5 formal scholarship exchanges (Lausanne, Rennes, Zurich, Geneva and Kiel) and exchanges with 20 American and 4 Canadian universities. Careers: Information and advice service; regular vacancy bulletins.

Student services & facilities

Student advice and services: Medical practice; chaplaincy; counsellors; nursery; international student adviser; welfare, disability and financial advisers; information and advice centre. **Amenities:** Student centre; late buses, vacation employment office, university music groups; SA, student newspaper, SA babysitting agency. **Sporting facilities:** Swimming pool; two extensive sports fields including running tracks; cardiovascular performance gym; squash and tennis courts; rowing on River Dee; Cairngorms and Grampians (mountain hut) within easy reach for climbing, walking and skiing; 150 sports clubs and societies. **Accommodation:** All new students who wish it are guaranteed university accommodation, if they apply by 31 August (38% of students overall). 3000 places available: 800 catered places (some ensuite) at £116–£137 pw, term time only; 2200 self-catering (some ensuite) at £72–£103 pw, rentals 38–48 weeks; utility charge in addition to rent. University can offer accommodation to most students, though many prefer to live in privately owned accommodation for 1+ years: approx £70–£90 pw for self-catering. 25% of first-degree students live at home.

Money

Living expenses budget: Minimum budget of £5280 (excluding tuition fees) recommended by university, for 9-month academic year. **Term-time work:** University allows term time work for full-time students (30% believed to work); limit of 15 hours pw. Some work on campus in catering, bars, library and (in vacs) as porters, gardeners, groundsmen; also SU-based Joblink agency helps in finding work off campus. **Financial help:** Entrance scholarships and access awards of up to £1k pa: access awards for those who need financial support to enter higher education; scholarships for academic merit or, eg music, sport, agriculture. **Tuition fees:** Scottish and EU students pay no fees during their course; other UK students pay £1820 pa for first degrees (£2895 for clinical courses). International students: £9k (classroom), £11,250 (lab), £22,040 (clinical).

Student view

Angela Fraser, Student President (4th year, MA Economics)

Living

What's it like as a place to live? Aberdeen is the perfect size for a city. Big enough that it has everything – pubs, clubs, music scene, theatre and football club – but small enough to get around easily and not get lost. **How's the student accommodation?** University accommodation is amongst the cheapest in Scotland. It is spacious and very close to the campus with some accommodation in the heart of the campus. **What's the student population like?** A large number of students come from Aberdeen and Scotland but the university also has students from 120 different countries and a hugely active International Students' Society. **How do students and locals get on?** Aberdeen, which is the oil capital of Europe, is very diverse and students and locals get along fantastically well, with no areas a no-go for students. The student charities campaign donates £80k (approx) every year to local charities.

Studying

What's it like as a place to study? Probably the most flexible degree programme in the UK. You can arrive with the intention of studying chemistry, then get a degree four years later in Economics: I did! **What are the teaching staff like?** The university has a real commitment to students and all students will meet international and 5-star lecturers during their time at the University of Aberdeen.

Socialising

What are student societies like? With more than 95 different societies there are societies for everyone. Harry Potter to Dance, French to Economics. Most students are a member of a society or sports club or both. **What's a typical night out?** Going to one of the great nights at the Union, then a club. **And how much does it cost?** £20ish, depends if you're thrifty. **How can you get home safely?** Loads of taxis, night bus at the weekend, not far to walk.

Money

Is it an expensive place to live? Rental prices are similar to Edinburgh and Glasgow but cost of living is cheap. **Average price of a pint?** £2.10 in city centre, £1.90 on campus. **And the price of a takeaway?** Cheap curry and rice with naan and snack, £5! **What's the part-time work situation?** Lots of well-paid work in city readily available, SA has joblink service.

Summary

What's the best feature about the place? The history, established in 1495, Aberdeen University is in its sixth century! When the whole of England had two universities, so did Aberdeen! **And the worst?** In the winter its get dark very early in Aberdeen, as early as 3.30pm in deep winter. **And to sum it all up?** The University of Aberdeen is the most beautiful, ancient-meets-modern university in the UK.

Past students: Sandy Gall (ITN newscaster), Iain Cuthbertson (actor), Douglas Henderson MP, James Naughtie (BBC broadcaster), David McLean MP, Alistair Darling MP, Sir Denys Henderson (ICI), Earl of Strathmore, Ian Crichton Smith, Catherine Gavin (authors), Nikki Campbell (radio broadcaster), Kenneth McKellar (opera singer), Evelyn Glennie (percussionist). **More info?** Ring SA on 01224 272965, ask for Freshers' Mag or look at www.ausa.org.uk.

Abertay Dundee University

Location:
Dundee, on east coast of Scotland (map 1)
Main teaching centre in city, plus partner colleges

✉ University of Abertay Dundee, Kydd Building, Bell Street, Dundee DD1 1HG
☎ Tel 01382 308080
📠 Fax 01382 308081
✉ Email sro@abertay.ac.uk
💻 Website www.abertay.ac.uk

Student enquiries: Student Recruitment Office
Applications: UCAS

In brief

Total Students: 4180

84% undergraduate
16% postgraduate

Undergraduates: 3500
91% full-time · 83% UK students
35% mature on entry · 37% lower socio-economic groups

50% female · 50% male

- **A modern university.**
- **Teaching staff:** 240 full-time, 230 part-time.
- **Broad study areas:** Law, business, computing, tourism, sports studies, forensic sciences, food and nutrition, psychology, health and nursing, media.

Freshers

- **Admissions information:** All applicants considered on individual basis; no policy on UCAS tariff.
- **First degree entrants:** 960 UK, full-time.
- **Points on entry:** 175+ (average).
- **Drop-out rate:** 8% in 1st year.
- **Accommodation:** Almost all 1st years housed who apply by the deadline.

Profile

Institution
Founded: 1888 as Dundee Technical Institute; university status from 1994. **Site:** City centre; all buildings within 5 mins' walk. **How to get there:** Close to bus and rail stations (good road and rail connections; daily flights from London). **Special features:** Good staff links with commerce and industry.

Courses
Academic features: All courses have strong vocational bias; many have supervised work placements. Small class sizes. **Awarding body:** University of Abertay Dundee. **Main undergraduate awards:** BA, BSc. **Length of courses:** 4 years (Hons), 3 years (ordinary degrees).

Study opportunities & careers
Library and information services: Purpose-built library: 140,000 volumes, 500+ journals and periodicals, 700 study places. Information provision, £99 pa spent for each student (FTE). IT and

library services converged. 1100+ PCs with access to library and internet (ratio 1:4 workstations to students), open 13 hours/day. IT support from helpdesk 9 hours/day. Module for all new students on using, eg databases, spreadsheets, internet and wordprocessor; some evening and weekend classes also available on IT skills. **Other learning resources:** Audio-visual laboratories, self-access language centre; bibliographic and full text databases. Specialist collections: Faculty of Procurators' legal collection. **Study abroad:** Several courses include opportunity to study abroad in Europe or America. **Careers:** Information, advice and placement service.

Student services & facilities

Student advice and services: 4 part-time counsellors; advisers for students with disabilities and for international students; information on childcare; health and money advice. Chaplaincy centre for all faiths (full-time chaplain plus associate chaplains; Christian Union; room for Muslim prayers). **Amenities:** New student centre. **Sporting facilities:** Gym on campus; access to all city sporting facilities including swimming pools and AstroTurf pitches. **Accommodation:** 20% of all students in university accommodation – almost all 1st years who apply by deadline (1 September). Single rooms (some ensuite) in self-catering flats for 1st years, approx £70 pw (up to £100.66 pw ensuite), contracts 36 or 38 weeks Sept–May. Privately owned accommodation, rent £50 pw upwards.

Money

Living expenses budget: Minimum budget of £5250 pa (excluding tuition fees) recommended by university. **Term-time work:** University does not discourage students from part-time work, as long as it does not affect their studies. Student employment centre (SCOPE) helps students find part-time work. **Financial help:** £337k government funds. Scholarships for overseas students and elite athletes; fee waiver for part-time students on state benefits. Apply for help to Student Finance Adviser. **Tuition fees:** Scottish and EU students pay no fees during their course; other UK students pay £1820 pa for first degrees. International students pay £8150 pa.

Student view) **Gav Herron,** Student President (1st year, Computer Arts)

Living
What's it like as a place to live? Dundee as a whole is a great place to live. It may not be as big or as flashy as larger cities but with two universities it really is a student-friendly place to live. A real hidden gem. **How's the student accommodation?** Accommodation is really quite good here, particularly at Abertay. I've had my room with them for 3 years and still stay there as Student President. Students have a varied choice of accommodation too, both uni and privately owned, that seems to cater for all tastes and budgets. Our SA always gives plenty of advice on finding the right place. **What's the student population like?** Abertay has a hugely diverse student population with representatives present from all over the globe; plenty of locals and those across the country to people from as far as India, China and beyond. **How do students and locals get on?** Like all cities there are areas that wouldn't be recommended for students, but these are few and far between. There doesn't really seem to be much interaction; we both on the whole co-exist quite happily.

Studying
What's it like as a place to study? Abertay is a great place to study, famed for its computer-based courses, often at the forefront of advances. A very contemporary institution that's constantly adapting to the ever-changing face of the student body. **What are the teaching staff like?** When I speak to my counterparts at other institutions some

of them tell me what a struggle it is to get the university's support or attention, but I have found that here, the staff try their best to think of students at every stage; my job is almost done for me!

As with every uni, there are some staff that you can't help but fall asleep to, but in the main, the lecturers are engaging and have novel ways of getting their point across.

Socialising

What are student societies like? At Abertay we have 16 societies and 3 more on the way. We have just over 600 students registered as members of these societies and with around 4000 students, this is quite a good number.

We have a wide variety of societies; from the law society and the Christian Union to the Circus Society and Rock Society, we have something for most tastes but there's always room for more – our vice-president's door is always open for students to suggest societies and hopefully start a few up. **What's a typical night out?** There is a wide variety of things to do. Dundee has rock clubs, dance clubs, cinemas and an ice rink, Abertay has all of these bar the ice rink. **And how much does it cost?** Depending on where you go, it can be anything from £20 (Abertay) to upwards of £40 (nightclubs) . . . but that's entrance, drinks and a taxi home too. **How can you get home safely?** I'm sure it's the same everywhere else, but the taxi drivers know where the most fares are going to be and so there are several points in town where there is normally a line of taxis.

Money

Is it an expensive place to live? That's a hard one to answer, really; it's different from student to student I guess. All depends on how much money they have, what bills are like, price of rent. As with everything there's a mix. **Average price of a pint?** On average £2. **And the price of a takeaway?** £5–£7. **What's the part-time work situation?** The university runs the JobShop, which is used as a point of contact for local businesses wishing to employ workers. With 2 institutions in Dundee, employers see students as a hard-working, flexible, friendly source of workers. The downside is, with such a large pool of potential workers, there is no incentive to offer much more than minimum wage.

Summary

What's the best feature about the place? Not too big, not too small. **And the worst?** GIANT SEAGULLS!

Past students: Maurice Malpas (footballer), Andy Nicol (rugby player), David Jones (Inventor of 'Lemmings'), Stuart Wilson (golfer). **More info?** Ring UADSA on 01382 308307 or check out the website (www.abertaystudents.com).

Aberystwyth University

Location:
Aberystwyth, on west coast of Wales (map 1)
3 sites in and around town

🖳 Aberystwyth University, Penglais Campus,
Aberystwyth SY23 3DD
☎ Tel 01970 622021
🖷 Fax 01970 627410
✉ Email ug-admissions@aber.ac.uk
🖥 Website www.aber.ac.uk

Student enquiries: Recruitment and Admissions
Applications: UCAS

In brief

Total Students: 12,245

12% FE students
67% undergraduate
20% postgraduate

Undergraduates: 8255
75% full-time ● ● 92% UK students
11% mature ● ● 29% lower
on entry ● socio-economic groups

53% female · 47% male

- **Traditional and research-intensive.** Constituent member of University of Wales.

- **Teaching staff:** 320 full-time.

- **Broad study areas:** Biological sciences; computer sciences; education; English; European languages; geography and earth sciences; history; information studies; international politics; law and criminology; management and business; maths and physical sciences; rural sciences; sport and exercise sciences; theatre, film and TV studies; Welsh-medium studies.

Freshers

- **Admissions information:** AS-levels accepted, usually in combination with 2+ A-levels (4 AS and 1 A-level may be acceptable in some cases). Key Skills level 3 (IT, communication, application of number) if offered, count towards UCAS tariff.

- **First degree entrants:** 1770 UK, full-time.

- **Points on entry:** 245 (average).

- **Drop-out rate:** 6% in 1st year.

- **Accommodation:** All 1st years housed.

Profile

Institution

Founded: 1872, received charter in 1889. Founding college of University of Wales, with Bangor and Cardiff, in 1893. **Structural features:** Part of University of Wales, though awarding its own degrees. **Site:** Old College on sea front; Penglais 400-acre campus overlooking Cardigan Bay; Llanbadarn campus and accommodation within walking distance of Penglais. (Nearly all students live within walking distance of main teaching buildings.) **How to get there:** Regular rail service from London Euston via Birmingham (5 hours) and coach service (Trans Cambria). For university, bus service from station (Waun Circular). **Special features:** Extensive package of entrance scholarships and bursaries.

Courses

Academic features: Wide range of programmes, including HND, foundation degrees and year-in-employment options. Flexible degree schemes allow students to keep options open until end of first or 2nd year. **Awarding body:** Aberystwyth University. **Main undergraduate awards:** FdSc, BA, BSc, BScEcon, LLB, MPhys, MMath, BEng, MEng. **Length of courses:** 3 years; 4 years (BEng, MMath, MPhys, language and sandwich courses); 5 years (MEng); 2 years (FdSc).

Study opportunities & careers

Library and information services: 4 libraries, with total of 750,000 volumes, 3500 periodicals, 1100 reader places; also departmental collections. Information provision, £147 pa spent for each student (FTE). Access to National Library of Wales (copyright). IT and library services converged. Approx 700 PCs available in public rooms and halls of residence, 2600 residential rooms with network access points, 700 in academic departments. IT facilities open 24 hours/day; IT support from helpdesks. Talks, tours and courses on library and information services for new students; introductory and follow-up IT courses on various software. **Other learning resources:** Film, audio and video facilities; video conferencing; language laboratories. Specialist collections: 600 books printed pre-1701; private press books; first editions collection (Matthew Arnold, Swinburne and Shelley); 1747 edition of Shakespeare annotated by Samuel Johnson. **Study abroad:** Formal exchange links with universities across central and eastern Europe – many open to non-linguists. **Careers:** 17 full-time staff. Information, education and guidance for both students and graduates. Work experience and placements, graduate work and optional year-in-employment schemes.

Student services & facilities

Student advice and services: Student health centre, university chapel (available for baptisms and marriages), SU student advice and counselling service, learning support unit, childcare manager, nursery, after-school club, half term and holiday schemes. **Amenities:** SU houses nightclub venue, bar, travel shop, food outlets, bank, shop, etc. Over 100 societies. **Sporting facilities:** 50+ acres of playing fields, swimming pool, all-weather floodlit pitch, dance studio, climbing wall, 2 sports halls, squash courts, computerised technogym, health suite, weights room, boathouse at marina, equestrian centre. 45 student-guild sports clubs. **Accommodation:** All 1st years guaranteed university accommodation (50% of all students housed). 4000+ places, including 2940 self-catering places, £69–£90 pw (£65 pw shared), term time or longer; 1070 catered places (£3.20 per day food allowance), £96 pw single, £83.50 pw shared, term time only. Students usually live in privately owned accommodation for 2nd year: rent approx £60–£90 pw self-catering (plus bills). Very few students live at home.

Money

Living expenses budget: Minimum budget of £5k pa (excluding tuition fees) recommended by university. **Term-time work:** Part-time work restricted to 15 hours pw during term. Some work on campus in bars and library (plus office work out of term time); Job Link scheme helps students find work (term time and vacation). **Financial help:** Means-tested bursaries (£200–£1k pa) for students where families income is up to £40k; residential bursaries giving £500 discount on 1st-year accommodation fee; bursaries for care leavers of £1k or £1800 pa. Around 50 annual entrance scholarships (up to £1200 pa), 100 merit awards (of £1k; must sit exams in UK), audition-based music bursaries (£400), sports bursaries (£500 pa); excellence bursaries (£2k for the duration of the course), based on entrance qualifications, in science, European languages and Welsh. £437k government funds, £16k own funds (average award £600). Special help for mature students, those with disabilities or childcare costs or whose financial circumstances worsen suddenly; also available for international students. Apply for help to Student Financial Support Office. **Tuition fees:** Home students pay £3225 pa for first degrees (though Welsh residents may be eligible for fee grant). International students pay £8475 pa (classroom), £10,750 (lab/studio).

Student view   Samantha Lumb, President (2nd year, PhD Law)

Living

What's it like as a place to live? Aberystwyth is an absolutely wonderful place to live. Students love the surroundings of the beach, the friendly atmosphere and the cheap cost of living. **How's the student accommodation?** Accommodation in Aberystwyth is a mixed bag. Most university accommodation competes with the best of other institutions, some ensuite and some central housing posts. Private accommodation depends on how much you are willing to spend! In general, accommodation is reasonably priced and all 1st-year students are guaranteed university accommodation, which makes starting uni a bit easier! **What's the student population like?** Aberystwyth is known for its friendly party environment. We have a diverse range of students from over 90 different nationalities, which helps keep Aberystwyth the lively place that it is. There is a strong community network in Aberystwyth but the locals do love students really! **How do students and locals get on?** Locals need the students to sustain the economy, but essentially Aberystwyth is a student town so everybody gets on just fine. There are no areas where students cannot go. It is a very student-centred town.

Studying

What's it like as a place to study? Aberystwyth is an amazing place to study. With access to the National Library of Wales, finding materials for research is second to none. We have good IT facilities and the environment makes Aber a great place to study as you can watch the sun set over the sea from the library. I think Aber has a good vibe for those who like to study. **What are the teaching staff like?** Aberystwyth has a large international community and a number of well-established departments. We have also just launched the new IBERS Department, which is proving to be a big recruiter of excellent academics. Most students seem to like teaching staff although I am sure some would disagree!

Socialising

What are student societies like? Sports and societies are the biggest part of student life in Aber. We have over 56 active sports clubs and 52 societies. They drive the entertainment and everyone is keen to be involved – these include traditional sports like football and rugby to climbing, caving and show jumping. Societies play an equal role, from political societies to conservation societies to the volunteering side of student life. **What's a typical night out?** Everybody generally heads to their sports club sponsors then ends up in the union for an amazing night of banter. The union is by far the best place to be on a Wednesday, Friday or Saturday. **And how much does it cost?** Really depends but £20 will see you through the night including taxis! Its dirt cheap. **How can you get home safely?** There is a main taxi rank in town and one outside the union. They cost about £1 a person.

Money

Is it an expensive place to live? It's not expensive to live in Aber because most things are organised for free by sports clubs and societies so life is pretty cheap and the lifestyle great, especially with the beach being so close – beach parties are the way forward. **Average price of a pint?** £1.60. **And the price of a takeaway?** 3 for £10 in the Chinese, or 2 for £10 in the Indian; both include rice and nibbles. It's a bargain! **What's the part-time work situation?** The union offers a lot of part-time employment and the university itself employs a number of students as guides and in similar jobs. Being a student town, Aberystwyth is very much catered to supporting the student network.

Summary

What's the best feature about the place? Being so close to the sea and having the opportunity to study somewhere where most people are so friendly. That's what keeps the crime rate so low! **And the worst?** Travelling to or from Aber without a car is a bit of a problem but the truth is, once you get to Aber, you don't really want to leave. **And to sum it all up?** Its a place full of beauty and banter, with a great union making sure there is fun to be had all year round. It's so much fun, ex-students try to find permanent work in Aber just so that they don't have to leave!

Past students: Lord Cledwyn of Penrhos, Arthur Emyr (rugby player), Most Rev. George Noakes (Archbishop of Wales), Berwin Price (Olympic athlete), Angela Tooby (Olympic athlete), Prince Charles. **More info?** Ring 01970 621700, email union@aber.ac.uk or see the website (www.aberguild.co.uk).

ALRA

Location:
south-west London
(map 3)
Single site on
Wandsworth Common

✉ Academy of Live & Recorded Arts, Royal Victoria
Patriotic Building, John Archer Way, London SW18 3SX
☎ Tel 020 8870 6475
🖨 Fax 020 8875 0789
✉ Email info@alra.co.uk
💻 Website www.alra.co.uk

Student enquiries: Registrar
Application: UCAS

In brief

Total Students: 110

  10% postgraduate
90% undergraduate

 95% full-time ● ● 90% UK students

 60% female / 40% male

- **Specialist vocational drama school.**
- **Teaching staff:** 4 full-time, 20 part-time.
- **Broad study areas:** Acting, stage management, TV and radio, technical theatre.

Freshers

- **Admissions information:** 2 A-levels at grade D, BTEC National Diploma or GNVQ Advanced in performing arts required.
- **Accommodation:** No academy accommodation.

Profile

Institution

Founded: 1979. **Site:** In listed (Grade II) Victorian building on Wandsworth Common. **How to get there:** Rail (Clapham Junction or Wandsworth Common); tube (Tooting Bec); buses from central London. **Special features:** Guest directors and speakers from the industry, including BBC casting department. Acting for Camera teaching throughout the course.

Courses

Academic features: Courses range from foundation degree in stage management to Master's course in professional acting. NCDT-accredited acting courses: modern approach and a concern for the individual student; courses cover television, radio, film and theatre and include screen acting, radio, voice, movement, improvisation, dance, singing, stage combat. Stage management and technical theatre course includes stage management, production management, event management, prop making, lighting, sound, technical drawing/design, model-making and special effects. **Awarding body:** Greenwich University, Trinity College London. **Main awards:** BA, FdA, National Diploma/Certificate, MA. **Length of courses:** 3 years (BA); 2 years (FdA); 1 year (MA).

Study opportunities & careers

Library and information services: Library with 6000 resources, including DVDs, books, recordings, etc. 8 computers in library with access to internet; IT and learning support from staff member.

Induction days for new students include introduction to library and information services. **Other learning resources:** Fully equipped theatre; TV and radio studios; digital television and radio editing facilities; rehearsal studios; stage management workshop; wardrobe. **Careers:** Information and advice given; graduation showcase for agents, directors, producers and casting agents (80% acquire agents on graduation). Postgraduate support service.

Student services & facilities

Student advice and services: Information pack given to new students covering local housing, public libraries, doctors and health centres, banks, etc. Welfare support system. Registrar and course director supervise welfare and progress. Student counselling service. **Amenities:** Student kitchen, common room, drinks machines, showers. Next to Wandsworth Common. Royal Victoria Patriotic Building also has wine bar/restaurant on site. **Sports:** Good local sports facilities. **Accommodation:** No academy accommodation. Students given active help in finding self-catering accommodation locally; prices £100–£120 pw.

Money

Living expenses budget: Minimum budget of £8k pa (excluding tuition fees) recommended by Academy. **Term-time work:** Plenty available locally. **Financial help:** Scholarships up to full fees available through Drama and Dance Awards Scheme (DADAs); smaller amounts from private sponsors, charitable trusts and bursaries. Possible to apply for career development loan for stage management course (up to £8k pa). **Tuition fees:** All students pay £11,500 pa for first degrees (£12,550 pa for MA); on FdA, home students pay £1535 pa; international students pay £8k pa.

Student view

Sticking out of the south London gloom like a gothic sore thumb, the Royal Victoria Patriotic Building, ALRA's home, sits comfortably on the cusp of Wandsworth Common. The common is a wonderful neighbour for a drama school, lending itself as a teaching space in the summer or a refuge from the day-to-day grind where you can run, cycle or just collect your thoughts whilst ambling through its pleasant green space. Mercifully divorced from the hustle and bustle of Central London, it is very easy to immerse yourself in the work, with very few distractions, and yet with Clapham Junction station only a short walk away, you are no more than a ten-minute train journey from the heart of the city. Accommodation in Wandsworth and Clapham tend to be expensive, so most opt for the less pricey Tooting or Streatham (also adds to the community vibe). ALRA offers a disciplined, strenuous and in-depth learning experience for all involved. Its facilities are ideal for both the acting and stage management courses, with on-site sound, television and radio studios; large halls and performance spaces and library, as well as its own theatre. The hundred or so students are given the freedom to explore their craft in an intimate and professional environment. They are led by dedicated and experienced staff who know the workings of the profession and bring their knowledge and contacts, so students feel they are being thoroughly and realistically prepared for the professional industry. What all the courses share, and benefit from, is the close-knit feel of the place. Since there aren't too many students, everyone gets to know one another pretty quickly.

Student footnotes

Housing: School helps with accommodation days. Rents in Tooting and Streatham £300 upwards a month. **Eats:** Well-priced on-site café; more expensive 2–3 courses in bar/restaurant on site.

Drink: Average £2.80 a pint (£3.50 in central London). **Nightlife:** Tends to be one size fits all south of the river: Clapham for Cocktails; Brixton for Bohemia. For variety, you'll have to venture to the centre (but as choice increases, so do prices). Plenty of night buses to get you home. **Locals:** Fine! **Financial help:** No student loans at present. DADAs fund most places; some maintenance grants. Seek out sponsorship or charities if strapped for cash. **Jobs:** Part-time work in term time is difficult (volume of work) but no shortage of local bars and restaurants crying out for evening and weekend staff. **Best features:** Close-knit peer community in picturesque surroundings not far from city life. **And worst:** Drink prices.

Anglia Ruskin University

Location:
East Anglia (map 2)
Campuses in Cambridge and Chelmsford, plus partner colleges

Anglia Ruskin University,
Rivermead Campus, Bishop Hall Lane,
Chelmsford, Essex CM1 1SQ
Cambridge Campus, East Road, Cambridge CB1 1PT
⊠ Email answers@anglia.ac.uk
💻 Website www.anglia.ac.uk

Student enquiries: Contact Centre, 0845 271 3333
Applications: UCAS (GTTR for PGCE courses)

In brief

Total Students: 23,970

 22% postgraduate
78% undergraduate

Undergraduates: 18,620
 64% full-time · 85% UK students
66% mature on entry · 37% lower socio-economic groups

 68% female · 32% male

- **A modern university.**
- **Teaching staff:** 1181 full-time and part-time.
- **Broad study areas:** Art and design, built environment, business, education, humanities, languages, drama and performing arts, law, science, social sciences, computing, technology, nursing, planning, engineering.

Freshers
- **Admissions information:** AS-levels normally accepted in combination with 2+ A-levels or equivalent. UCAS tariff used for almost all offers (plus any specific course requirements).
- **First degree entrants:** 2300 UK, full-time.
- **Points on entry:** 180 (average).
- **Drop-out rate:** 12% in 1st year.
- **Accommodation:** Most 1st years housed (unless local).

Profile

Institution
Founded: 1989 as Anglia Polytechnic, from Essex Institute and Cambridgeshire College of Arts and Technology; university status in 1992 (as Anglia Polytechnic University). **Site:** 2 main sites: Chelmsford

(including new Ashcroft International Business School); Cambridge city centre. **How to get there:** Good train connections with London from both sites. M25 and M11.

Courses

Academic features: All courses available on modular, credit accumulation basis. Large number of franchised courses in other East Anglian colleges. **Awarding body:** Anglia Ruskin University. **Main undergraduate awards:** BA, BEd, BSc, LLB, BOptom, BEng. **Length of courses:** 3 and 4 years.

Study opportunities & careers

Library and information services: Library at each site: 350,000 volumes, 1800 printed periodicals and extensive digital collections; 1060+ study places. 24-hour opening on main sites, staffed services 12+ hours. Information provision, £71 pa spent for each student (FTE). Separate IT service: 1200 mixed IT/study places, group study and casual spaces; most general open access provision within libraries, supported by IT help desks; growing number of students have own PCs with access to internet and university library. IT skills courses available in, eg wordprocessing, spreadsheets. Specialist collections: law, education and management, music, nursing and midwifery, French Resistance archive. **Other learning resources:** CAD/CAM centre; language centres; learning resource centres; computer centres. **Study abroad:** Many students spend a period abroad. Exchange links for eg business studies and technology students in France, Germany, Netherlands and Spain. **Careers:** Information, advice and placement.

Student services & facilities

Student advice and services: Counselling, medical and health services; disability advice and support; learning support, finance. **Amenities:** SU buildings with bars, bookshops. Nursery (Cambridge). Mumford Theatre (Cambridge). **Sporting facilities:** Sports hall, fitness room (Chelmsford); gym and pitches (Cambridge). **Accommodation:** At Cambridge, most 1st years housed unless they live within 35 miles; in Chelmsford, single 1st-year students guaranteed a hall place (if offer accepted before deadline), 24% of all students in university accommodation. 1600+ self-catering places, most with broadband internet access: 960 in Cambridge (£63–£123 pw), 510 in Chelmsford (£77.50–£83.50 pw), all for 40+ weeks/year. Students live in privately owned accommodation for minimum of 1 year: rent for self-catering (excluding bills) £65–£105 pw in Cambridge, £42–£70 pw in Chelmsford.

Money

Living expenses budget: Minimum budget of £7k per academic year (excluding tuition fees) recommended by university. **Term-time work:** University allows term-time work for full-time first-degree students on most courses. Student employment office helps find work on and off campus. **Financial help:** £305 pa for all UK students whose family income is approx £25k. £1k award for academic progression in Year 1, £500 in each of Years 2 and 3 for all home/EU students (full-time, publicly funded). Also sports scholarships (£500–£1k pa) and 12 scholarships of £750 to allow students to study abroad. £160k government funds, £200k own funds (average award £250). Priority given to mature students, students with dependants, students from low-income families, students from Foyers and care leavers, students with disabilities. Apply for help to Student Support Services. **Tuition fees:** Home students pay £3225 pa on most first degree courses. International students pay £9300 pa (classroom), £10,925 (lab/studio), £12,050 (optometry).

Student view (Cambridge campus)
Nick Evangelista, Students' Union President

Living
What's it like as a place to live? Cambridge is a fantastic place to live; there is always something to do, especially within the union. **How's the student accommodation?**

Relatively new on-campus halls. Students who live in the nearby Mill Road area will not forget the experience. You can buy nearly everything you want here. **What's the student population like?** The student demographic is wide and varied. Increasing numbers of international students also create a fascinating yet friendly atmosphere. **How do students and locals get on?** Very well. Locals recently commented to the Union on how well behaved students were after leaving our venue.

Studying

What's it like as a place to study? Courses are wide and varied with facilities being upgraded all the time. 24/7 library in Cambridge through union consultations with the university. **What are the teaching staff like?** Teaching staff very much student-centered and focused on creating a better learning environment all the time.

Socialising

What are student societies like? There is a wide range of clubs, ranging from traditional football and rugby to ski and snowboard and Afro-Caribbean. People encouraged to become involved and set up new societies. **What's a typical night out?** Flirt at the SU on a Friday is very popular. **And how much does it cost?** Union = £25. Into town = £40, more at weekends. **How can you get home safely?** Walking in groups from the union or town as it is not far. Taxi fares can be expensive but worth it if you're alone.

Money

Is it an expensive place to live? Can be expensive. Most students work part-time to help pay rent and other costs. **Average price of a pint?** SU = £1.90. Town = £2.80. **And the price of a takeaway?** Chinese = £12, Pizza = £10, Indian = £12. **What's the part-time work situation?** SU offers bar, gym, shop and office work. There are more than enough shops around to get a Saturday job.

Summary

What's the best feature about the place? The city of Cambridge is the hub of student life and a fantastic place to live and study. **And the worst?** The prices of private renting accommodation and some of the letting agents.

Past students Kim Howells MP, Peter Turnbull (crime writer), Sacha Count (own lingerie firm), John Swinfield (TV presenter), Adam Ant (musician), Fluck and Law (Spitting Image). **More info?** Contact SU on 01223 460008, email info@angliastudent.com or look at website (www.angliastudent.com).

Student view (Chelmsford campus)
James Green, Student Experience Officer

Living

What's it like as a place to live? Chelmsford is a friendly place to live with easy access to London. **How's the student accommodation?** The university accommodation is a clean and bright area. Cost is reasonably expensive but halls are located on campus. **What's the student population like?** Friendly and from a diverse background consisting of full-time, international and nursing students. **How do students and locals get on?** Very well, with great student nights in town used by local people and students alike.

Studying

What's it like as a place to study? Very much practice-based with nursing, teaching and science and technology being prominent, but with a large business and law school. **What are the teaching staff like?** Friendly and always there to help, sometimes hard to contact.

Socialising

What are student societies like? More of a minority involved. Around 20 on campus ranging from an International Society to an American football team. **What's a typical night out?** Start at SU bar and go to club in town. **And how much does it cost?** £30 for a good night including taxis. **How can you get home safely?** Student bar on campus. 5-min walk to centre of town.

Money

Is it an expensive place to live? Most students work to subsidise costs. **Average price of a pint?** £2.10 town/£1.70 SU bar. **And the price of a takeaway?** £3.50. **What's the part-time work situation?** Loads of jobs with strong uni and SU support.

Summary

What's the best feature about the place? It's a big town that has the safety of a small town. **And the worst?** Parking and travel is near impossible. **And to sum it all up?** Friendly place with new and expanding features within the uni.

Past students Jerry Hayes (former MP), Mike Smith (DJ and musician), Tom Sharpe (author). **More info?** Visit SU website (www.angliastudent.com) or email info@angliastudent.com.

Architectural Association

Location:
central London
(map 3)
Principal site in
Bloomsbury, smaller
site close by plus
satellite site in Dorset

Architectural Association School of Architecture, 34–36 Bedford Square, London WC1B 3ES.
☎ Tel 020 7887 4000
🖷 Fax 020 7414 0779
✉ Email undergraduateadmissions@aaschool.ac.uk
💻 Website www.aaschool.ac.uk

Student enquiries: Admissions Co-ordinator,
Registrar's Office
Application: Direct

In brief

Total Students: 500

 100% full-time ● ● 10% UK students

 45% female 55% male

- **Specialist architecture school.**
- **Teaching staff:** 104 contracted staff plus consultants.
- **Broad study areas:** Architecture.

Freshers

- **Accommodation:** No school accommodation.

Profile

Institution

Founded: 1847. **Site:** Single site in Bloomsbury; smaller site close by plus satellite site in Dorset. **How to get there:** Tottenham Court Road underground station. **Special features:** International character.

Offers a wide range of design options and teaching styles. Students recognised as individuals and expected to demonstrate a high level of self-motivation to benefit from programme (including seminars and tutorials with professional consultants and members of allied disciplines).

Courses

Academic features: 1-year foundation course offered to develop creative skills through intensive programme of studio work. 5-year RIBA/ARB recognised course in architecture has emphasis on developing personal creativity with strong self-directed tutorials. **Awarding body:** AA, RIBA/ARB. **Main awards:** AA Diploma, AA Intermediate Examination (RIBA/ARB Part 1), AA Final Examination (RIBA/ARB Part 2). **Length of courses:** 5 years; 1 year (foundation).

Study opportunities & careers

Library and information services: 30,000+ books, 100,000 images, 100 study places. IT and library services separate. 60 networked PCs/Macs with access to internet and so to library catalogue (ratio workstations to students 1:5), open 12 hours/day. IT support provided by 4 members of staff. Library and computer induction sessions in introduction week. Specialist collections: 1930s photographs by FR Yerbury. **Study abroad:** Study trips worldwide. **Careers:** Information and advice from practical training adviser.

Student services & facilities

Student advice and services: Pastoral care and individual counselling available. **Amenities:** International exhibition gallery, specialist bookshop, dining room, bar, audio-visual department, model workshops, digital prototyping lab, digital photo studio, electronic media studio, drawing materials shop. 350-acre woodland site in Dorset, with workshops and accommodation. **Accommodation:** No accommodation provided by the school. Accommodation office open for 3 weeks before each academic year. Most students live in shared self-catering accommodation, £75–£125 pw.

Money

Living expenses budget: Minimum budget of £12k pa (excluding tuition fees) recommended by school. **Financial help:** Limited number of scholarships and bursaries awarded annually. **Tuition fees:** Home and international students pay £14,475 pa (£12,870 for foundation course).

Student view

It's a private school with affiliated professional association, the oldest and arguably number one architectural school in the world, located a stone's throw away from the British Museum. Features a 5-year programme for RIBA Parts I and II and AA Diploma, plus a range of postgraduate courses and a foundation course. Choice of units ranging from conceptual to rigorously architectonic – all experimental, none aims to advocate any house-style. Throughout the year a series of juries take place, where a panel of internal and external professors, registered architects and professionals from other disciplines offer guidance and criticism based on a short presentation. Pass from year to year is based on your final oral presentation of unit work, also known as the Final Tables, and successful fulfilment of submissions from complementary course groups (general studies, technical studies and media studies). No traditional structure is imposed, but high standards are expected and academic excellence a must. Students are given a great deal of independence, which requires more resilience to maintain one's own standards without being spoon-fed; sometimes a mild shock to those arriving from A-level but the perfect opportunity to develop one's interests. An intense, but often friendly, competitive atmosphere prevails, diluted in the evenings as students and tutors collect themselves at the elegant school bar, aptly named the AA Bar. The school year consists of very intense work alongside exhibitions, lectures, workshops and other events specially co-ordinated to complement study (some quite provocative and diverse); several superb evening lecture series given by speakers from all over the world in many disciplines. A variety of student exhibitions throughout the year; end-of-year projects review in July – the highlight of the London architectural calendar, taking over all three Georgian buildings and gardens; a transformation to see. School not cheap, with full-costs fees, but recently more bursaries and scholarships for local students. International mix of students, cosmopolitan environment, a variety of influences and dialogues. AA Student Forum is an independent organisation, run by students, that provides creative and financial support to any AA student or group of students who wish to make something happen – an exhibition, publication or social event – alongside the AA radio. Well-stocked bookshop includes in-house publications and a slide library. Workshop for working with metal, wood, some plastics, etc, now fitted with a CNC machine for computerised modelling; also mobile darkroom sessions conducted guerrilla style. If you really love the cutting edge of architecture, and you can't wait to express your commitment and fascination without being stifled, then apply, but be prepared to take the initiative.

Student footnotes

Housing: As varied as London itself – students prefer old factory buildings and loft spaces in Hackney and City. Good accommodation service at beginning of term; co-ordinators can advise on house/flat shares. Look in Loot and watch school noticeboards. **Eats:** Charlotte Street has exciting options (pizza at ICO to Thai green curry at Thai Metro); Pollo Restaurant on Old Compton Street, Bar Italia on Frith Street. AA lunchtime restaurant/bar (meal for £3.50+). **Drink:** Own bar, no time for anything else! **Nightlife:** Christmas party, fireworks night and other impromptu events throughout the year; watch the school transform with themed parties. West End theatres and galleries (reduced rates). **Locals:** Very friendly. No local problem areas. **Sports:** None at AA; but ULU and YMCA facilities very close. Local Camden facilities open to students. **Travel:** Travel scholarships from AA, and other architectural institutes. STA Travel. **Financial help:** Some scholarships and bursaries available. **Jobs:** Working part-time within school or in practices possible during term time. **Informal name:** AA, commonly mistaken for Alcoholics Anonymous. **Best features:** The 'best architectural school'. **And worst:** Very expensive. **Past students:** Richard Rogers (Lloyd's Building, Pompidou Centre, etc), Mark Fisher (designer of Pink Floyd concerts), Ron Arad (furniture designer), Zaha Hadid (Rosenthal Centre for Contemporary Art, Phaeno Science Centre), Eileen Gray (architect, designer), Janet Street Porter (notorious), Nigel Coates (architect, designer), Nick Grimshaw (DJ and TV presenter), Michael Hopkins (Manchester Art Gallery, Westminster Underground Station). **More info?** Enquiries to AA Student Forum Co-ordinators (email aasf@aaschool.ac.uk).

Arts London

Location:
mostly in central
London (map 3)
**6 constituent art
colleges across
London**

🖳 University of the Arts London, 65 Davies Street, London W1K 5DA
☎ Tel 020 7514 6000
🖷 Fax 020 7514 6131
✉ Email info@arts.ac.uk
🖳 Website www.arts.ac.uk

*Student enquiries: 020 7514 2067 or through website
Applications: to the individual colleges through UCAS*

In brief

Total Students: 20,835

61% undergraduate

11% postgraduate
28% FE students

Undergraduates: 10,535
95% full-time
29% mature on entry

64% UK students
29% from state schools

71% female   29% male

- **Europe's largest university for the creative arts**, a federation of six prestigious London art colleges.
- **Teaching staff:** 3000+ (including 2000+ associate lecturers).
- **Broad study areas:** Art and design, fashion, media, communications, performing arts.

Freshers

- **First degree entrants:** 2855 UK, full-time.
- **Drop-out rate:** 4% in 1st year.
- **Accommodation:** Most 1st years housed in university halls.

Profile

Institution

Founded: 1986 as London Institute; university status in 2004. Colleges' histories date back to the nineteenth century. **Structural features:** Europe's largest university for the arts, bringing together six of the most celebrated colleges of art, design and communication, all of which have their own strong traditions and distinctive character. Each has its own prospectus and admits its own students. All students benefit from access to university resources. You can look up college profiles separately:

Camberwell College of Arts
Central Saint Martins College of Art and Design
Chelsea College of Art & Design
London College of Fashion
London College of Communication
Wimbledon College of Art

Site: 17 sites in London, from Oxford Street to Archway, Hackney, Wimbledon and Southwark.
Special features: Newly refurbished Arts Gallery in Mayfair exhibits work of students and graduates from all six colleges.

Courses

Academic features: University offers a distinctive education in art, fashion, design, communication and performance; learning is practice-based, creative and strongly linked with the creative arts through live briefs, placements, exhibitions and performances. Strong links with the creative industries, employing 2000+ practicing professionals as associate lecturers, all leading practitioners in their fields. Courses range from access and first diploma to PhD. Students often progress from a foundation course at one college to a degree course at another.

Study opportunities & careers

Library and information services: Centrally located Learning Zone, for students across the university, combines traditional and modern learning facilities, including key texts, wi-fi, laptops, projectors, whiteboards and lightboxes, in a flexible and informal space. 8 libraries, with 400,000+ titles, 3500 journals and periodicals (art to web design), 10,000 videos and DVDs; electronic resources including databases, e-periodicals and e-books. Information provision, £49 pa spent for each student (FTE). Ratio 1:7 workstations to students; 9024 internet access points, including 158 wi-fi points. IT help in open access areas and specialist help from schools. Library and IT induction to all new students; some IT skills courses. **Special collections:** 50+ collections, eg 800+ paper dressmaking patterns at London College of Fashion, archive of Stanley Kubrick at London College of Communication. **Other learning resources:** Cochrane Theatre (a working public theatre); newsrooms, TV and broadcast studios. **Study abroad:** Increasing numbers of students complete part of their course abroad. **Careers:** Specialist careers service (Creative Careers) provides 1:1 guidance to students, regular workshops, invitations to networking events, podcasts of creative professionals revealing the trade secrets of how to secure that dream creative job.

Student services & facilities

Student advice and services: Central student services, with satellite offices in each college, provide advice and guidance about accommodation, careers and finance plus support, counselling and day nursery facilities. Also chaplaincy and advice for students with disabilities. **Amenities:** College shops sell art and design materials. Central social and learning space for all university students in the Student Hub, including Arts Gallery, Learning Zone, café bar and open-access computing. Discounted access to many sporting, social and cultural facilities (including 200+ galleries and museums). SU runs sports clubs and societies (martial arts to ballroom dancing) and a number of college bars, and organises events and parties, including pathfinding week; also helps students with academic and accomodation issues, complaints and general advice. **Accommodation:** 2244 places in 12 residences across London; rent £76 –£167 pw, contracts 42 or 51 weeks (depending on residence). Privately rented accommodation available at £70–£120 pw plus bills.

Money

Living expenses budget: Minimum budget of £6k–£10k pa (excluding tuition fees) recommended by university. **Term-time work:** No official university policy on term-time work. Students are encouraged to be aware of study needs and, if work is necessary, to seek work related to their course of study; careers service helps. **Financial help:** Bursaries of £310 pa for students whose family income is up to £25k (ie receiving a full grant). In addition, 500 bursaries each year of £1k for students whose family income is up to £50k (priority to those from families with no tradition of higher education or from areas of low participation). **Tuition fees:** Home students pay up to £3225 pa for first degrees. International students pay £10,700 pa.

Student view

It's one of the most exciting creative institutions in the world. Made up of 6 colleges spread across London, Arts is a great place to study a wide range of disciplines. Regardless of which college they study at, every student has access to all the university's facilities, including the new Student Hub development at Davies Street. Collectively, the college libraries are the best art and design resource in Europe, with thousands of books, journals, periodicals, videos and DVDs. Brand new SU office at Davies Street. SU has a constantly growing number of sports clubs (including men and women's football, rugby, basketball, netball, hockey teams) and various faith and cultural societies; also other services, including a social mentoring scheme for international students. Pathfinding week (university's version of freshers week) is university-wide, as are the Christmas party and summer fayre. Alumni include huge names in every area of art and design, many of whom remain close to the university through lectures, events and even, in some cases, tutoring. Although London can be a very daunting place, it has such a massive cultural diversity, it is anything but boring.

Student footnotes

Housing: University halls of residence. Private accommodation: look in Loot, noticeboards, housing office at Davies Street; expect to pay £100 pw in shared house in zone 2. **Eats:** College cafeterias (meal for £2.50+); various sandwich shops around each college site. **Drink:** College bars and various pubs and bars near colleges. **Nightlife:** University SU runs parties and regular bar events; bar football, Sky sports. And there's London. Student nights at venues across London every night; most clubs offer student discount. **Locals:** Mixed (depends where you live); SU and housing office can advise on a safe place to live. **Sports:** No university sports facilities but student rates at sports centres near most colleges. **Travel:** No travel scholarships. Travel in London cheaper with student card, but a bike will save you £60 a month if you don't mind getting wet. **Financial help:** Access fund; hardship loans. **Jobs:** Plenty of part-time work in London. Tutors can sometimes help (good contacts). SU bar, design work, restaurants, NFT and other cinemas; retail hours easier than bar work. **Informal name:** Arts. **Best features:** It's big, yet friendly and very well-respected place to study. **And worst:** Lack of interaction between courses and cost of living. **Past students:** Trevor McDonald (broadcaster), Stella McCartney, Hussein Chalayan (fashion designers), Amish Kapoor (sculptor), Shonagh Marshall (fashion buyer); Jimmy Choo, Manolo Blahnik (shoe designers); Peter Blake (artist), Pierce Brosnan (actor).

More info? Contact SU President on 020 7514 6270, email president@su.arts.ac.uk or check out the website (www.suarts.org).

Aston University

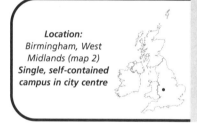

Location:
Birmingham, West
Midlands (map 2)
**Single, self-contained
campus in city centre**

Aston University Birmingham, Aston Triangle,
Birmingham B4 7ET
☎ Tel 0121 204 3000
✉ Email ugenquiries@aston.ac.uk
🖥 Website www.aston.ac.uk

*Student enquiries: Registry
Applications: UCAS*

In brief

Total Students: 9800

28% postgraduate
72% undergraduate

Undergraduates: 7085
96% full-time   85% UK students
11% mature   36% lower
on entry   socio-economic
groups

49% female   51% male

- **A top UK research-intensive university.**
- **Teaching staff:** 460 full-time.
- **Broad study areas:** Business and management, modern languages and European studies, engineering and applied sciences, life and health sciences, social sciences.

Freshers

- **Admissions information:** 3 A-levels or equivalent expected (2 AS-levels may be accepted in place of a 3rd A-level, additional AS/A-levels welcomed). Wide range of other qualifications accepted. UCAS tariff used for many programmes.
- **First degree entrants:** 1750 UK, full-time.
- **Points on entry:** 350–360 (average).
- **Drop-out rate:** 4% in 1st year.
- **Accommodation:** All 1st years housed who apply by deadline.

Profile

Institution
Founded: 1895. University charter 1966. **Site:** Single, modern, green 40-acre campus in centre of Birmingham. **How to get there:** Birmingham is at the centre of England's rail, coach and road networks: mainline stations (New Street, Snow Hill and Birmingham International); coaches connect directly from 500 destinations; many motorway links; Birmingham International Airport close by. University is 5 mins' walk from city centre; extensive local transport.

Courses
Academic features: Close links with industry and business. All courses have strong vocational element; unusually high numbers of students on sandwich or year-abroad programmes (70% of students on sandwich courses). Combined Honours programme allows wide combinations of subjects, including languages in many courses. Engineering faculty offers BEng and MEng. Large business school and vision science department. **Awarding body:** Aston University. **Main undergraduate awards:** BSc, BEng, MEng, MPharm. **Length of courses:** BSc 3 years (full-time), 4 years (sandwich); BEng/MEng 3–5 years (full-time and sandwich).

Study opportunities & careers
Library and information services: Library with 250,000 monographs, 1000 current periodicals, over 3850 electronic journals, 315 CD-ROM and self-service online databases, computerised catalogues, circulation and information services, online access to databases throughout the world; audio-visual laboratory, 800 reader places (over 100 with IT facilities). Library open 80 hours/week (24 hours/day April–June). Information provision, £124 pa spent for each student (FTE). 1100 workstations (ratio workstations to students 1:6), all with access to library catalogue, intranet and internet; Blackboard Virtual Learning Environment; internet access from all student accommodation, plus most cafés, lecture theatres and common rooms. IT facilities open 24/7; helplines for IT support and staff on hand in open-access IT rooms. Tours and presentations on library and information services for new students; core courses/modules on IT skills. IT infrastructure means all courses now available in virtual learning environment. **Other learning resources:** Multimedia language suites; CAD laboratories; extensive computing facilities; design studios and model shop; mathematics support centre, learning and development centre. Social and study spaces on each floor of main building and the Loft (Students' Union/Guild), with wi-fi access. **Study abroad:** 15% of students spend 6–12 months abroad. Strong European/international focus in many degrees, eg international business and modern languages, sociology and French, etc. **Careers:** Information and advice service. 83% of graduates employed within 6 months, in graduate-level jobs (one of highest in UK).

Student services & facilities
Student advice and services: NHS health centre (with 24-hour cover), dental surgery, optician, chaplaincy, student advice, careers advice, counselling service, accommodation office and nursery on campus. Student advice centre provides financial help and support for students with disabilities (special accommodation on campus). Study skills programmes. **Amenities:** Students' Guild has bars, disco/concert hall, games room, general store, eating places, sandwich bar, print shop, secondhand book and stationery shop, laundrette, bank, hairdresser, also runs 40 non-sporting societies and interest groups. Supermarket, computer shop and bookshop on campus; city facilities close by – 5 mins walk to nearest major supermarket. **Sporting facilities:** 2 well-equipped sports halls, 25m swimming pool, squash courts, fitness suite (75 stations), sprung gym space for aerobics and martial arts, multigym, bouldering wall and floodlit all-weather pitch on campus. Sports ground, 20 mins away, has 10 pitches (including floodlit all-weather pitch), tennis and squash courts, cricket pitch and pavilion (with bar and café). Athletic Union offers 37 sports clubs. **Accommodation:** On-campus accommodation for all 1st years who want it, many final year students and international students for their whole course (provided they apply by deadlines). 2150+ places, all on campus and with internet access: 1500 self-catering

places at £65 pw, 650 ensuite at £101 pw; contracts 39 weeks, Sept–June. Catered meal plan (half board) at approx £300 per term. Additional residences owned by Guild of Students. Most 2nd year students live in privately owned accommodation (student apartments in city centre, 5 mins walk from campus, or in suburbs of Erdington or Selly Oak): rent £45–£70 pw self-catering.

Money 💰

Living expenses budget: Minimum budget of £5500 pa (excluding tuition fees) recommended by university. **Term-time work:** Student jobshop advertises vacancies of up to 15 hours a week (60% believed to work). Work on campus in bars, restaurants, travel agency and summer catering. University helps finding holiday work off campus (many opportunities for part-time work in city centre, 10 mins walk) and short-term course-related placements. Many students on sandwich courses (sandwich year salary £14k pa). **Financial help:** Means-tested bursaries of up to £800 pa for UK students with family incomes of less than £18k, then on a sliding scale for incomes of £18k–£38k. Also placement bursaries of £1k–£1500 for all students on year abroad or placement year. £300k government access to learning funds, around 250 students helped (average award £500- £600); plus own funds including some for international students (mostly short-term help). Special help: single parents with childcare needs, students who are self-financing, mature or who are subject to financial difficulties for reasons beyond their control. Some international bursaries available (up to £3k pa); also some travel bursaries. European Social Fund bursaries, up to £200k (awards of £750–£1k). Apply to Student Services for help. **Tuition fees:** Home students pay £3225 pa for first degrees (£1610 in placement year). International students pay £10,200 pa (classroom), £12,300 (lab-based); £1800 in placement year. Fees can be paid termly.

Student view

Ria Joyce, SU Market Research Officer (2nd year, International Business, Spanish and French)

Living

What's it like as a place to live? Aston is based in the centre of Birmingham, home to over 50,000 students and one of Europe's liveliest and most welcoming cities. Aston is a very friendly campus with a sense of community. There's always something going on for the students and with a city centre 5 mins walking journey, everybody's needs are catered for. Aston is a very homely campus that houses a close-knit community. **How's the student accommodation?** Aston has plenty of options for living. We have standard and ensuite rooms, which are the perfect combination for students who have preferences with living. The campus accommodation is a key component to why Aston is such a tight-knit community in the heart of Birmingham city centre. The rooms are at a very affordable price; you pay more for the ensuite accommodation, but the value for money is brilliant. **What's the student population like?** The students are the life and soul of Aston. Aston is a multicultural university (as all universities should be), all the students are friendly and get along with one another. At Aston there are students from all different walks of life – from all around the UK, Europe and the rest of the world. No matter where you are from, your interests and culture, you will find lots of people like you at Aston. **How do students and locals get on?** The location of the Aston University campus is perfect. It is so close to the city centre, yet it is secluded from everyone that's not a student. Everyone that is walking on campus is either a student or works in the university. Locals are rarely seen on campus, apart from students of course! Students would not need to go into the smaller towns of Birmingham to shop, as everything can be found in the city centre.

Studying

What's it like as a place to study? There are a wide array of subjects to study at Aston. There are 5 schools within the university that cover all the courses in Aston. For example, the Business School for all business-related courses and the Life and Health Sciences

School that covers Optometry, Pharmacy and Audiology. Aston technology is always increasing. Aston being very active in research allows the students to be pro-active with all new technology and resources. **What are the teaching staff like?** All students and staff get along with one another. Staff are always welcoming in open office hours, and many lecturers remain in their office during the day to help. Tutorials are always an effective method to build relationships with lecturers. In addition, Aston houses a peer mentoring scheme for additional help. Lecturers are mentors for 1st years in many courses.

Socialising

What are student societies like? At Aston there are 4000 people involved in sport clubs and societies, which is brilliant for a university that has under 8000 students. There are 40 sport clubs and 50 societies, ranging from the original football clubs to the zombie society! There are social societies as well as cultural societies, so there is always something for everyone. To sign up to these societies or sport clubs we hold a freshers' fair at the beginning of the year where they are all present, but if you miss out you can always join later in the year. **What's a typical night out?** There are student nights out every night of the week, for all different genres of music. **And how much does it cost?** It costs an average of £4 entry, but drinks are always cheap! Sometimes £1. **How can you get home safely?** Taxis are always available all over Birmingham, and fairly cheap too! The city centre social areas are 5–10 mins walk from the campus.

Money

Is it an expensive place to live? Students are always known to be skint. Birmingham being so heavily populated with students, all the local companies always offer students discounts. Student loans can be stretched to the end of each term, as long as you manage your money. Usually students work part-time to fund their social activities. **Average price of a pint?** £1.80. **And the price of a takeaway?** £2.50. **What's the part-time work situation?** Being so close to the city centre, part-time jobs in the massive shopping centre, the Bullring, are always available. The Guild helps students find jobs in and around Birmingham; the Student Jobshop is managed by the Guild and is constantly busy finding students jobs.

Summary

What's the best feature about the place? A brilliant, vibrant, multicultural university, right in the middle of England's second city! With one of the best city centres a stone's throw away! **And the worst?** Honestly? There's too much to do! The weather isn't always brilliant but where in the UK is it?

And if you had to sum it all up in a sentence (or two)? Astonfantastic!

More info? Visit www.astonguild.org.uk or get the alternative prospectus from the Guild President (tel 0121 204 4826).

Bangor University

Location:
Bangor, north Wales
(map 1)
Main site in city
centre; partner
colleges

✉ Bangor University, Bangor, Gwynedd LL57 2DG
☎ Tel 01248 351151
🖨 Fax 01248 370451
🖥 Website www.bangor.ac.uk

Student enquiries: Academic Registrar
Applications: UCAS

In brief

Total Students: 12,710

68% undergraduate

17% postgraduate

15% FE students

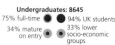

Undergraduates: 8645
75% full-time · 94% UK students
34% mature on entry · 33% lower socio-economic groups

64% female · 36% male

- **A top research-intensive institution.**
- **Teaching staff:** 663 full-time and part-time.
- **Broad study areas:** Arts, media, languages, business and management, social sciences, law, science, engineering, education, agriculture and forestry, biological and ocean sciences, environmental sciences, health, psychology, sports science, Welsh-medium studies.

Freshers

- **Admissions information:** Normally 3 A-levels or equivalent (minimum of 2 A-levels or equivalent); most qualifications accepted, including new 14–19 diplomas. Some courses have subject-specific requirements.
- **First degree entrants:** 2020 UK, full-time.
- **Points on entry:** 268+ (average).
- **Drop-out rate:** 8% in 1st year.
- **Accommodation:** All 1st year undergraduates guaranteed place in halls.

Profile

Institution
Founded: 1884. **Structural features:** Academic schools organised into 6 colleges. **Site:** City centre. **How to get there:** 1/2 hours travelling distance from M56, which links with M6. A55 is coastal expressway and A5 the scenic route through North Wales. Regular fast trains from London, Birmingham and Manchester.

Courses
Academic features: Number of courses taught in Welsh. **Awarding body:** University of Wales. **Main undergraduate awards:** BA, BD, BM, BMus, BN, BSc, BEng, LLB, MChem, MEng, MEnvSci, MMSci, MMBiol, MOcean. **Length of courses:** 3 years; 4 years (languages, undergraduate Master's).

Study opportunities & careers
Library and information services: 6 libraries; 798,000 printed items, 5920 electronic journals, 3050 print journals; short-loan scheme for texts in heavy demand (catalogue on http://library.bangor.ac.uk); study areas; IT facilities; specialist librarians for research, law and health studies. Library tours for new students. Additional services available for dyslexic and disabled users. Information provision, £140 pa spent for each student (FTE). IT and library service separate. 180 points with access to library, 160 to internet. Some IT facilities open 24/7; IT support from helpdesks, manned in office hours. **Other learning resources:** Ocean-going research vessel, centre for hill and upland management, botanic garden, natural history museum, multimedia language centre; listening and viewing facilities for DVDs and CDs, computer-assisted learning unit, audiovisual services, media centre (TV and radio), computerised graphics suite. **Study abroad:** Some 90 students annually go on exchanges; over 120 partners in 20+ countries in Europe and North America. **Careers:** Information, advice and programme of work placements.

Student services & facilities
Student advice and services: Health service through local GPs; student services centre incorporates counselling and mental health services; disability services including a specialist dyslexia unit; money

support unit; private-sector housing service; international student welfare; and general welfare help. Also chaplaincy team. Students' union has separate advice centre and nightline service. **Amenities:** Professional theatre, concert halls, museum, art gallery. **Sporting facilities:** University sports centre (2 sports halls, cardiovascular and weights rooms, gymnasium, climbing wall, squash courts and AstroTurf), athletics track, playing fields; unparalleled opportunities for outdoor activities in Snowdonia. **Accommodation:** All 1st-year students guaranteed a place in halls (provided they apply by 31 August). 2300 places (some ensuite), all self-catered and with internet connection: self-catering from £63–£98 pw, 40–51-week contracts. Privately rented accommodation approximately £55 pw (plus bills).

Money

Living expenses budget: Minimum budget of £6k pa (excluding tuition fees) recommended by university. **Term-time work:** Careers centre has Jobzone, which advertises part-time work on and off campus; also paid work experience opportunities. **Financial help:** Variety of scholarships and bursaries available: £500 or £1k pa for those with family income of £39k or less; £500 pa for those on specific courses, eg chemistry, law; £300 start-up bursaries for mature students or those who were in care; various scholarships worth £500–£1500 pa, eg academic (specified courses), sport, excellence (top achieving entrants in psychology and music). See website for details. Total of £450k government funds, 600 awards made. Special consideration given to mature students, students with disabilities, single parents, students with dependants, care leavers and final-year students. Apply for assistance to money support unit (student services centre). **Tuition fees:** Home students pay £3225 pa for first degrees (though Welsh residents may be eligible for a fee grant). International students pay £8500 pa (classroom-based courses), £9500 (lab-based).

Student view   Carolan Goggin, Deputy President 2007–08 (Music)

Living
What's it like as a place to live? Cosy, very much a student town. Over a third of the population are students and you'll meet someone you know everywhere you go. **How's the student accommodation?** A huge redevelopment of uni halls opened in September '08 – very plush, hardly any older halls left. Neuadd Willis is a large private hall in the town: a combination of that and the new uni halls has forced the rest of the private sector to up their game. **What's the student population like?** *Very* friendly, laid back, lots of outdoorsy types. About 1 in 10 students are international and 1 in 5 are Welsh. **How do students and locals get on?** As in any student-dominated town, there is some friction, mostly stirred up by the local papers, but the SU's volunteering department works closely with the local community and the SU is a strong proponent of the Welsh language, which also strengthens ties with the community.

Studying
What's it like as a place to study? Flexible courses, module-based teaching so plenty of options. Especially strong departments are Music, Psychology and Ocean Sciences. **What are the teaching staff like?** Good personal tutor system. Some focus on research, others more on student contact.

Socialising
What are student societies like? Wide range of extra-curricular activities with 35 societies and 45 sports clubs, two newspapers and a radio station. From ghost hunting to politics to drama, from rugby to climbing to underwater hockey, there really is something for everyone. **What's a typical night out?** Visit a couple of pubs (probably including the Yellow Pub), end up in one of the SU nightclubs. **And how much does it cost?** £20. **How can you get home safely?** Very low crime rate. Most people walk with a couple of

friends or maybe get a taxi. During freshers' week the SU takes freshers back to their halls in minibuses.

Money

Is it an expensive place to live? Fourth cheapest place to study in the UK. Everyone's still broke though – we're students! **Average price of a pint?** £2. **And the price of a takeaway?** £3. **What's the part-time work situation?** Jobs available in supermarkets and bars, usually minimum wage. Uni has a job centre to help you find work.

Summary

What's the best feature about the place? Friendly atmosphere, everyone takes care of each other. **And the worst?** Doesn't have the bustle or options of a big city. **And to sum it all up?** Friendly, petite, down-to-earth city WLTM laid-back students, GSOH, likes long walks and living by the sea.

Past students: Dr Robert Edwards (pioneer of test-tube babies), Roger Whittaker (singer, songwriter), Dr David Rees (Director of National Institute for Medical Research), Ann Clwyd MP, Robert Einion Holland (Chief General Manager, Pearl Assurance), Lord Dafydd Elis Thomas (Chairman, Welsh Language Board), John Sessions (poet and impressionist), Frances Barber (actress), Danny Boyle (director). **More info?** Enquiries to SU President on 01248 388001, email president@undeb.bangor.ac.uk. Handbooks and guides available from SU or on its website (www.undeb.bangor.ac.uk).

Barts & The London

Location:
central London
(map 3)
Sites in City and east
London

✉ Barts & The London, Queen Mary's School of Medicine & Dentistry, Turner Street, London E1 2AD
☎ Tel 020 7882 2239
🖷 Fax 020 7882 7206
✉ Email medicaladmissions@qmul.ac.uk
🖳 Website www.smd.qmul.ac.uk

Student enquiries: Admissions Assistant
Applications: UCAS

In brief

Total Students: 2,350

35% postgraduate
65% undergraduate

Undergraduates: 1550
95% full-time
10% mature on entry
95% UK students

MEDICINE
50% male
50% female

DENTISTRY
65% male
35% female

- **A top UK research-intensive medical school.** Part of Queen Mary University of London.
- **Teaching staff:** 300 full-time and part-time.
- **Broad study areas:** Medicine, dentistry.

Freshers

- **Admissions information:** High grades required in 3 A-level subjects, including chemistry or biology and 1 other science (both chemistry and biology to at least AS-level). Offers expressed in terms of grades, not UCAS tariff.
- **First degree entrants:** 300 UK, full-time.

- **Points on entry:** 330 (average).
- **Accommodation:** All 1st years housed unless local.

Profile

Institution

Founded: St Bartholomew's in 1123, London Hospital Medical College in 1785, Dental Teaching Hospital in 1911. Became school of Queen Mary in 1995. **Structural features:** Part of Queen Mary University of London. **Site:** City and East London: Whitechapel, West Smithfield, Charterhouse Square and Mile End. **How to get there:** Whitechapel, St Paul's, Barbican or Mile End underground stations; many buses to each site.

Courses

Academic features: Integrated teaching at Mile End and Whitechapel campuses; clinical teaching at hospital sites. Problem-based learning (PBL) is a central element of the medical curriculum. 10 pa join clinical course after pre-clinical at, eg Oxbridge. Intercalated BSc or BMedSci course open to students who have completed 4th year of MBBS (competitive, not automatic). **Awarding body:** University of London. **Main undergraduate awards:** MBBS, BDS, BMedSci, BSc. **Length of courses:** 5 years; 6 years (intercalated BSc/BMedSci).

Study opportunities & careers

Library and information services: Three main collections: Whitechapel, West Smithfield and Mile End, all with audio-visual learning aids, computer resources and study places. Separate IT services; 600 workstations; helpdesk 8 hours/day. New students have library introduction; IT courses (eg on Windows, most software packages, basic programming languages). **Study abroad:** Erasmus and Socrates programme.

Student services & facilities

Student advice and services: Pastoral pool scheme for all students, senior tutor allocated to students. Health centre, in-house dental treatment, nursery, Nightline, counsellors, chaplains. **Amenities:** Association of Medical and Dental Students plus Queen Mary SU. Bookshops, travel centre, bank, snackbars, billiards room, common rooms, nightclub, bars. **Sporting facilities:** Numerous sports clubs, multigym, squash courts, gymnasium, swimming pool, athletics grounds, rowing club with boats at Chiswick. **Accommodation:** All 1st years in campus accommodation, if home address outside the M25. See also *Queen Mary*.

Money

Financial help: See Queen Mary. **Tuition fees:** Home students pay £3225 pa for first degrees. International students pay for medicine: £14,600 pa (pre-clinical), £23,350 (clinical); for dentistry: £12,700 pa (Year 1) to £21,900 (Years 2–5).

Student view
Chendoran Thavamokankanthi, President, Barts & The London Students' Association (Year 4 MBBS)

Living
What's it like as a place to live? When students see the two words East and London, they seem to relate it back to 'Old Kent Road' and 'Whitechapel' on the Monopoly board – the two cheapest assets in the game. However, Barts & The London School of Medicine & Dentistry is probably one of the best places to not only study but also to live. It

is based in 3 sites: Whitechapel, Mile End and Charterhouse Square. Each of these sites are very accommodating and are undergoing many new developments with the Olympics in the horizon. **How's the student accommodation?** The halls of residence are generally quite good. The best website to visit is www.ccrs.qmul.ac.uk/residences – it has all the information you will need. Medical and dental students are normally based in ether Pooley House (Mile End), Folyer House (Whitechapel) or Dawson Halls (Charterhouse Square). Halls of residence are reasonably priced, ranging from £70 pw to £115 pw. There are many options for private accommodation around this area where students live; however, they tend to be more pricey than the halls of residence. **What's the student population like?** Students at Barts & The London are extremely friendly, and there is a good mix between year groups so sharing of experiences is always a bonus. Students come from all over the country to this medical and dental school. We also have a good international intake of students. **How do students and locals get on?** Students tend to keep themselves to themselves here. There are not any 'No-go areas' per se; however, students are always advised to avoid travelling alone.

Studying

What's it like as a place to study? You can apply to do a 4- or 5-year medical course or a 5-year dental course. Teaching methods throughout the years adopt the format of lectures, problem-based learning (PBL), self-directed learning (SDL), GP lead teaching, clinical skills with bedside teaching and special study components (SSC). We have an amazing Clinical Skills Centre at St Bartholomew's Hospital: visit www.cetl.org.uk and you will know exactly what I'm talking about! For those students who are also interested in taking an additional year for in-depth study/research, the school offers a variety of intercalated degrees. **What are the teaching staff like?** The teaching staff are really good at Barts & The London School of Medicine & Dentistry. The staff have a wide range of academic qualifications and adopt a proactive way of teaching. They are always willing to answer any questions and are always on hand to help. There are many school and student body events where many staff and students attend.

Socialising

What are student societies like? At Barts & The London, the SA has many clubs and societies affiliated with it. All the major sports have a good mix of teams competing at high standards. We have over 50 clubs and societies in total. These range from rugby, football, netball, hockey, water polo, rowing, basketball to the Kenyan Orphan Project, Medsin, BL Lifesavers to RAG – Raising and Giving. I need to give RAG a special mention because here at Barts & The London we remain the best at it. Last year we raised over £96k for charity! **What's a typical night out?** We have our own student bar based at Whitechapel and we should have new facilities at our other campus at Charterhouse Square soon. There are many union events held at our bar by our entertainment officers. The SU is located at Whitechapel, so conveniently close to the halls of residence! Once a year all medical schools in London come together to host the annual inter-medical school event, '999', at Ministry Of Sound. From the university, it only takes about 20 mins to get into central London – so there are many choices for students. **And how much does it cost?** A union night normally costs around £15 (including entry). A night out in central London would come to about £35–£40, which includes entry and transport back. **How can you get home safely?** The union is walking distance back to the halls of residence. However the Number 25 Bus runs 24 hours and can take you back to your halls from central London. There are many taxi firms that would also be able to take you back. A taxi telephone service is located at the main entrance of the SU for students.

Money

Is it an expensive place to live? London tends to be expensive. However, once you have lived here for a few weeks you will begin to learn how and where you can save money and you will also begin to budget a lot better. Your student loan should last you, provided you don't go crazy during freshers' fortnight. **Average price of a pint?** £1.80 (SU). **And the price of a takeaway?** £5. **What's the part-time work situation?** Studying medicine or dentistry is a full-time degree, students are not advised to work. It would be difficult to fulfil the academic requirements throughout the course with a job. Many students do have part-time jobs at the weekends; however, it is difficult to hold down a job during the week. There are many flexible jobs at the SU that can be worked around your academic agenda.

Summary

What's the best feature about the place? The student body and staff are extremely friendly and helpful. There is a very tight-knit community here with so many opportunities. The school and the SA have a strong link and work closely together throughout the year, making sure that students gain the best experience from studying at Barts & The London. The school and university maintain a supportive environment and the students currently present are able to express their satisfaction with their choice in selection. **And the worst?** Can't think of anything! **And to sum it all up?** Great medical and dental school offering immense opportunity for discovery of not only the medical and dental fields, but of the capital city London. Not only will you be in the heart of the East End, but you will be taught by some of the best professors and clinicians around and meet the greatest people and just generally have the time of your life.

Past students: Frederick Treves (physician to John Merrick, the 'Elephant Man'), Professor Winston (BBC's *The Human Body*), Dr Thomas Barnado (of the children's charity), William Harvey (discovered circulation of blood), John Abernethy (founder of St. Bartholomew's Medical College), Richard Gordon (*Doctor in the House*, etc), Graham Chapman (Monty Python), Thomas Vicary (surgeon to Henry VIII), W G Grace (cricketer). **More info?** Tours available from the SA and on open days. Ring BLSA on 020 7377 7640, email president@bartslondon.com or see the BLSA website (www.bartslondon.com).

Bath Spa University

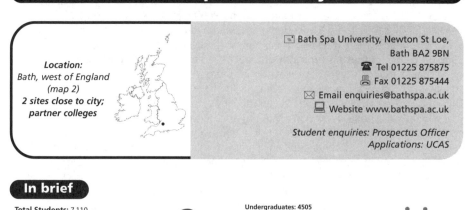

Location:
Bath, west of England
(map 2)
**2 sites close to city;
partner colleges**

Bath Spa University, Newton St Loe,
Bath BA2 9BN
☎ Tel 01225 875875
🖷 Fax 01225 875444
✉ Email enquiries@bathspa.ac.uk
💻 Website www.bathspa.ac.uk

*Student enquiries: Prospectus Officer
Applications: UCAS*

In brief

Total Students: 7,110

37% postgraduate
63% undergraduate

Undergraduates: 4505
91% full-time ● ● 96% UK students
28% mature ● ● 31% lower
on entry   socio-economic
                 groups

31% female   69% male

- **A modern university.**
- **Teaching staff:** 175 full-time, 70 part-time.

- **Broad study areas:** Art and design, English and creative studies, education, historical and cultural studies, social sciences, science and environment, music and performing arts.

Freshers

- **Admissions information:** AS-levels accepted, in combination with 2+ A-levels or equivalent. UCAS tariff used on most courses.
- **First degree entrants:** 1310 UK, full-time.
- **Points on entry:** 220–280 (average).
- **Drop-out rate:** 6% in 1st year.
- **Accommodation:** Most 1st years housed.

Profile

Institution

Founded: 1983 from Bath College of Higher Education and Bath Academy of Art. University status in 2005. **Site:** Newton Park (4 miles from city centre) and Sion Hill (1½ miles from centre). **How to get there:** Rail, road (M4/A4), local buses.

Courses

Academic features: Most courses part of a flexible modular scheme. **Awarding body:** Bath Spa University. **Main undergraduate awards:** BA, BSc, FdA, FdSc, DipHE. **Length of courses:** 3 years; 4 years (BA/BSc with PGCE); 2 years (FD/DipHE).

Study opportunities & careers

Library and information services: Library at each site; 178,000 volumes, 8,000 journals, including e-journals; 370 study places; slide library. Information provision, £53 pa spent for each student (FTE). IT and library services converged. 272 computers including open access. IT facilities open average 14 hours/day; student computer support desk open 10 hours/weekday. Introductory talk and self-guided tour of library and information services; IT skills courses within curriculum and on voluntary basis. **Study abroad:** Erasmus/Socrates programme; links with 28 European institutions. **Careers:** Information, advice and placement service.

Student services & facilities

Student advice and services: Guidance and support through careers office (including Job Shop), counselling, disability and welfare offices. Advice on managing study and other commitments and financial issues. **Accommodation:** Approx 85% of 1st years in university accommodation. 890 self-catering places: rent £59–£92 pw (£103.50 pw ensuite), £58–£76 pw sharing; 38- or 42-week contracts. Students live in privately owned accommodation for 2+ years: rent £280–£320 per month self-catering.

Money

Living expenses budget: Budget of £6800 pa (excluding tuition fees) recommended by university for the academic year. **Term-time work:** 15 hours pw recommended maximum. Job Shop helps students find work on and off campus. **Financial help:** Bursaries up to £1200 pa for UK students whose family income is up to £16,900 tapered down to £100 pa where family income is £38,900 (60% of all students qualify). Also science scholarships of £1k pa for UK students. Government funds of £359k; some 760 students helped (awards £75–£3k) due to exceptional circumstances. Apply to Welfare Office for help. **Tuition fees:** Home students pay £3225 pa for first degrees. International students pay £9k–£9580 pa.

Student view
James Anderson, President 2007–08 (Business and Management)

Living
How's the student accommodation? Waterside Court – off campus, good value for money, clean and ensuite. On campus accommodation: adequate, some ensuite, generally ok. Private accommodation varies. **What's the student population like?** Small, friendly population. Quite local to south west. Few international students. Good sense of community. **How do students and locals get on?** Generally very well. Most students live in one area – Oldfield Park – but students are welcome almost everywhere.

Studying
What's it like as a place to study? Very flexible in terms of courses and choice. University sports facilities are quite poor but library and ICT services are improving annually. **What are the teaching staff like?** As a teaching-led institution the lecturers are very interested in students and want them to fulfil their potential.

Socialising
What are student societies like? Very wide range of societies and clubs with many students involved. Good volunteering opportunities. Student societies have a very powerful voice. **What's a typical night out?** Wednesday night at the SU is Flirt! night! **And how much does it cost?** £2.50 entry then cheap drinks. **How can you get home safely?** 418 bus nearby or taxis.

Money
Is it an expensive place to live? Rent is expensive and food and drink are a little more expensive compared to other cities. **Average price of a pint?** £2.70 in town, £1.70 at the SU. **And the price of a takeaway?** £7–£15. **What's the part-time work situation?** Good job shop in university. Students are encouraged to find part-time work. Easy to get a job in town.

Summary
What's the best feature about the place? Small student population with a good sense of community, peaceful countryside campus.
And the worst? Not a great deal of sport facilities on site. **And to sum it all up?** A small university that offers good tuition to students on a personal level.
Past students Anita Roddick (Body Shop), Howard Hodgkin (painter), Martin Potts (painter); Nicholas Pope, Veronica Ryan, Peter Randall-Page (sculptors); Jason Gardener (athlete). **More info?** Enquiries to SU on 01225 875578, or check out the website (www.bathspasu.co.uk).

Bath University

Location:
Bath, west of England (map 2)
Single campus; associated colleges

The University of Bath, Claverton Down, Bath BA2 7AY
☎ Tel 01225 383019
Fax 01225 386366
Website www.bath.ac.uk

Student enquiries: Admissions Office
Applications: UCAS

In brief

Total Students: 14,255

37% postgraduate
63% undergraduate

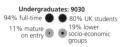

Undergraduates: 9030
94% full-time
11% mature on entry
80% UK students
19% lower socio-economic groups

45% female   55% male

- **A top UK research-intensive university.**
- **Teaching staff:** 450 full-time, 60 part-time.
- **Broad study areas:** Engineering, science, languages, architecture, management, social sciences, pharmacy.

Freshers

- **Admissions information:** AS-levels accepted in combination with 2+ A-levels or equivalent. UCAS tariff not usually used.
- **First degree entrants:** 1720 UK, full-time.
- **Points on entry:** 315 (average).
- **Drop-out rate:** 3% in 1st year.
- **Accommodation:** All 1st years housed.

Profile

Institution

Founded: 1894, as Merchant Venturers' Technical College; full university status 1966. **Site:** Campus 1 mile from Bath city centre. **How to get there:** By train to Bath Spa station (London Paddington 90 mins, Bristol 15 mins) or coach; bus from railway and bus stations (18/418). Close to the M4, then A4 and A36 to Claverton Down; easily accessible from Bristol and Heathrow airports.

Courses

Academic features: Most students are on sandwich degrees; possible to include a language in most courses. **Awarding body:** University of Bath. **Main undergraduate awards:** BA, BSc, BEng, MEng, MArch, MPharm. **Length of courses:** 3 years; 4 years (sandwich, MPharm, MEng); 5 years (MEng sandwich).

Study opportunities & careers

Library and information services: 450,000 volumes, 2200 periodicals, 1000 study places, 18,000 course books on short loan. Information provision, £161 pa spent for each student (FTE). IT and library services separate, both open 24 hours/day. Ratio 1:6 workstations to students; 400 PCs in Learning Centre, open 24 hours/day, others in departments – all PCs with access to library and internet. IT support by email, telephone or walk-in helpdesk. IT skills courses outside teaching hours. **Study abroad:** 10% spend time abroad. Erasmus links with large number of European universities and colleges in many subjects.

Student services & facilities

Student advice and services: Counsellor, doctors, psychiatrist, chaplain, dentist, learning support manager. Some accommodation for disabled students; nursery (£27–£33 per day). **Amenities:** Bookshop, banks, general shop (SU), chaplaincy, supermarket, travel agency, post office, newsagent, hairdresser, cafés, bar, food court, plus SU-run café. **Sporting facilities:** Indoor and outdoor tennis courts, sports hall, 2 swimming pools (1 Olympic), running track, AstroTurf floodlit pitches. **Accommodation:** All 1st years in university accommodation (33% of all students). 2200 places, mostly on campus, many ensuite, all self-catering and connected to university network: rent £75–£115 pw, for term time or longer. Students live in privately owned accommodation other years, rent £65–£90 pw for self-catering plus utility bills.

Money 💰

Living expenses budget: Budget of £7250 pa (excluding tuition fees) for an academic year recommended by university. **Term-time work:** University understands necessity for term-time work for some full-time students (20% believed to work). Student job shop helps find part-time and holiday work, including in bars, offices, library, registry, conferences office on campus; help for work off campus and sandwich placements. **Financial help:** Bursaries of £1200 pa for UK students whose family income is up to £25k pa (less in placement years), tapered down to £300 for those with a family income of £35k–£50k. Also a number of entrance scholarships of £1k+ pa (sports, choral and several subject scholarships). Also government access to learning funds. **Tuition fees:** Home students pay £3225 pa for first degrees (less in placement years). International students pay £10k pa (classroom), £12,750 pa (lab-based).

Student view

It's perched on top of Claverton Down, boasting spectacular views of the city and surrounding countryside. But the university is far from being just a pretty face. Since receiving its royal charter (1966), it has gone from strength to strength, proving itself to be one of the finest universities and securing its place among graduate employers. But there is much more on offer than just a degree. The SU has around 100 different societies, ranging from Gravity Vomit (Juggling Society) to the award-winning student newspaper, Impact. There are also 50 sports clubs – rock climbing, hot air ballooning, fencing and football to name but a few. And with the sports training village, all students have the opportunity to train alongside Olympic athletes in a truly state-of-the-art facility. Pace of life is refreshingly unhurried, but when you feel the need to liven things up a bit (as students do pretty much every night), there is plenty on offer to suit all but the most outlandish tastes. The SU club on campus, Elements, has a variety of different nights on every week, and regular live bands. With two student bars as well, it is hard to find a reason ever to leave campus!

Student footnotes

Housing: All 1st years on campus (including places for disabled students); some university accommodation for final years, on or off campus. City accommodation often expensive and sometimes hard to find; help from (excellent) uni accommodation office. **Eats:** Range of food on campus (meal for £2-ish); good selection of restaurants in town including vegetarian and wholefoods, kebabs, curries and fish and chips, pizzas and burgers; Thai, Lebanese, Japanese and (excellent) Indian, the Rajpoot; Manuel's, Café Martini (meal £10–£15 a head). **Drink:** £1.90+ a pint in SU bar. Plenty of pubs, lots of real ale pubs and student pubs (eg Pultney Arms). Local brews: Bath Gem, Ushers, 6X; Scrumpy Paradise. **Nightlife:** Events held almost every night in SU venue; discos, live ents and student-run nights; Sunday cinema. Moles, good student club. Extensive freshers' week, discount card for shops, cinemas, restaurants. **Locals:** Harmless enough, no real problems (can sometimes be more studenty than the students). **Sports:** Olympic-size swimming pool and excellent facilities for squash, badminton and tennis on campus; AstroTurf and 8-lane athletics track (free to students); many teams and clubs from snooker to skiing. Sports centre in town more expensive. Sports scholarships available. **Travel:** Buses frequent and reasonable (run to 3am). Good rail and coach links: London 75 mins by train, Bristol 15 mins. SU travel shop on campus for discounts. **Financial**

help: University access fund; money advice centre. **Jobs:** Some tourism, part-time shop work; standard availability. About 30% of students work part-time in term-time. Large tourist industry means summer and Christmas work available. Job Centre advertises in SU; student employment centre on campus. **Best features:** Friendly campus; beautiful town. **And worst:** Cold wind and rain. **Good news:** New radio mast so can broadcast campus-wide. **Past students**: John Kiddey (TV reporter), Martin Hedges (world champion canoeist), Chris Martin (singer and composer), David Trick, Gareth Adams and John Sleightholme (England rugby players), Dr Fox (Capital Radio DJ), Don Foster MP. **More info?** Contact SU on 01225 826612, fax 01225 444061, website www.BathStudent.com.

Bedfordshire University

Location:
Bedfordshire,
north-west of London
(map 2)
2 sites in Luton, 1 in
Bedford; partner
colleges, hospital sites

The University of Bedfordshire, Park Square,
Luton, Bedfordshire LU1 3JU

☎ Tel 01234 400 400
🖷 Fax 01582 486260
✉ Email info@beds.ac.uk
💻 Website www.beds.ac.uk

Student enquiries: Admissions Office (admission@beds.ac.uk)
Applications: UCAS

In brief

Total Students: 14,550

15% postgraduate
85% undergraduate

Undergraduates: 12,320
67% full-time ● ● 79% UK students
50% mature ● ● 43% lower
on entry socio-economic
groups

68% female   32% male

- **A modern university.**
- **Teaching staff:** 415 full-time, 145 part-time.
- **Broad study areas:** Advertising, marketing and public relations; art and design; biomedical sciences; business, management, finance and accounting; computing and information systems; education and teaching; English; healthcare, nursing and midwifery; human resource management; language and communication; law; leisure, tourism and sport management; media and performing arts; psychology; social sciences and social work; sport and physical education.

Freshers

- **Admissions information:** AS-levels welcomed and Key Skills qualifications recognised; applicants still expected to complete 2–3 A-levels or equivalent. UCAS tariff fully used.
- **First degree entrants:** 1955 UK, full-time
- **Points on entry:** 160–200 points (180 average).
- **Drop-out rate:** 13% in 1st year.
- **Accommodation:** All 1st years who apply by deadline are housed

Profile

Institution

Founded: 1957 as Luton College, with roots back to 1904. University status in 1993. **Site:** Main campuses in Luton town centre and Bedford; also Putteridge Bury (business) and Butterfield Park (healthcare), both 4 miles from Luton town centre; also hospital sites in Aylesbury (23 miles from Luton) and High Wycombe (31 miles away). **How to get there:** Luton is 30 mins north of London by train; university is 5 mins from M1, bus and railway stations; 10 mins from Luton Airport. Bedford on coach and mainline train network (40 mins to King's Cross); on A6 and close to A1 and M1; good local buses and cyclists well catered for.

Courses

Academic features: Specialises in career-related education. **Awarding body:** University of Bedfordshire. **Main undergraduate awards:** BSc, BA, BEd, LLB, FdA, FdSc, DipHE, ExtD. **Length of courses:** 3 years; 4 years (BEd, sandwich, extended degrees); 2 years (foundation degrees, DipHE).

Study opportunities & careers

Library and information services: Resources on 6 sites: 315,000 volumes and reference materials, 20,000 journals (including e-journals), audio-visual resources (eg slides, microforms, DVD/videos); 1585 study places. Information provision, £68 pa spent for each student (FTE). Library and IT services converged in learning resources centres. 700 PCs in libraries (open to 2am most nights), others in departments. Guidance via helpdesks, printed guides and internet; information skills embedded in curriculum; IT skills workshops; IT training facilities at 2 sites, educational technology, wireless access at all sites. **Other learning resources:** Psychology, sports therapy, biological and cognitive labs; centre for excellence in teaching and learning; centre for media arts. **Study abroad:** Opportunity to spend an academic year abroad; 65 partner institutions across Europe, Canada, Japan, and USA – open to non-language specialists. **Careers:** Advice and guidance services available for 3 years after graduation. Personal and career development programmes integrated across the curriculum. Support for, eg cv writing, online applications, interview skills. Subject-focused employer conferences.

Student services & facilities

Student advice and services: Subject-based academic advisers, personal tutors, chaplaincy, student health centre (doctors, nurses and clinics), counselling service; student services advice on welfare, housing, childcare support service, and advice for disabled students and international students; advice to students and applicants on tuition fees, funding and financial support. **Amenities:** Luton has a shopping centre, theatre, cinema, restaurants, bars, pubs and clubs. Bedford has a beautiful river, many bars, pubs and clubs; also live music and comedy acts at the Corn Exchange. **Sporting facilities:** At Luton, fitness suite, sports massage clinic, Vauxhall Recreation Club (including tennis and squash courts, football and hockey arena, sauna, sports bar, snooker and pool tables). At Bedford, state-of-the-art gymnasiums and new physical education and sports science centre, Priory Marina golf and squash complex and Bedford Athletics Stadium. **Accommodation:** All 1st years are housed, if they apply by the deadline. 1500+ places in halls at Luton and Bedford campuses, mostly for 1st years, £68.50–£81 pw (including utilities and personal contents insurance). Most students live in privately owned accommodation for 2+ years; rent £60–£80 pw self-catering.

Money

Living expenses budget: Minimum budget of £5500 pa (excluding tuition fees) recommended by university. **Term-time work:** University job shop helps students, recent graduates and local residents find local, part-time, casual and vacation work; aim is to help students gain work experience and enhance transferable skills. Some work available on campus (SU bars, offices, library, recruitment fairs, admissions, etc). **Financial help:** Bursaries of £820 pa for home students whose family income is up to £18,400; of £615 pa where family income is £18,400–£27,800; of £460 pa where it is £27,800–£39,300; and £310 pa where it is more than £39,300. Scholarships and awards between £310–£1025 pa (eg sports, academic, local students, those from specified colleges). Government access funds available for all UK students on eligible courses: special help for those with disabilities. Apply for help to Student Finance Unit. **Tuition fees:** Home students pay £3225 pa for first degrees (except nursing and midwifery); £1285 pa for foundation degrees, £1615 for sandwich year. International students pay £8k pa (classroom), £8200 (lab/studio).

Student view

It has 3 campuses: main campus, Park Square, is in centre of Luton about 2 mins (by taxi) from coach and railway stations, 10 mins from Luton International Airport and only 1/2 hour from London by train; Bedford Campus is 3 miles from Bedford train station; and Putteridge Bury campus (mostly postgraduate) is 4 miles from Luton and is a magnificent neo-Elizabethan mansion in attractive grounds. Luton has usual shops and a good indoor market. Many 1st years in self-catering halls of residence; private sector is cheaper but you must shop around to get the best deals. Diverse student population in both Luton and Bedford. Socially, SU is centre of all activities. It's the cheapest place to drink so is always packed out. Underground nightclub (Sub-Club) at Luton, and a bar where you can watch television and videos on a large screen plus a fantastic new food menu. Regular discos and live bands plus all the usual happenings in a thriving SU. Bedford has bar and night club – Bar Soviet and Oxygen. Clubs and societies include religious, political and hobbies; excellent opportunities for students to develop portfolio material with a newly launched newspaper, The Blend – articles or design – or work on the website (www.ubsu.co.uk). Luton has new multiplex cinema and arts complex; Luminar Leisure (with 600 nightclubs around the UK) is based there, and many clubs put on weekly student nights. All usual fast food joints and pizza places; excellent Chinese and Indian restaurants; odd Italian and French restaurants, usually hidden up some obscure side street. Luton and Bedford are fun places to study. It's no problem to change courses in first term (usually in first six weeks). Typical students are conscientious and hard-working but when necessary can go through a metamorphic change and become the ultimate party animal.

Student footnotes

Housing: University halls; private housing through local letting agency. **Eats:** Refectories on campus. Vicarage Street, good food incl vegetarian. Plenty of chip shops, kebab, Chinese and Indian (veggie curry). New canteen at Bedford. **Drink:** SU bar cheapest (£1.50 a pint). Pubs generally cater for students, eg Bar Soviet. **Nightlife:** SU has band nights with local and national talent, a variety of shows. SU nightclub (Sub-Club) cheapest and safest; student nights at local nightclubs in both towns. **Locals:** Averagely friendly. Students tend to avoid Bury Park for safety reasons; town centre is well lit but nobody should walk home alone at night. **Sports:** University uses Vauxhall facilities (1/2 mile away): gym, playing fields for tennis, rugby, football, etc. Many private gyms and leisure complexes; swimming pool 20-min walk from university at Luton, 5 mins at Bedford. **Travel:** Local transport good and student discount. **Financial help:** Very good. Hardship fund and hardship loans available. **Jobs:** Jobshop has local and national vacancies, in and out of term. Work in SU at Luton allows shifts to work round classes. **Best features:** Learning resources suite. **Past students:** Paul Young (pop singer), Sir David Plaistow (Chairman of Vickers). **More info?** Contact SU (tel 01582 743265).

Birkbeck

Location:
central London
(map 3)
**Single site in
Bloomsbury**

☞ Birkbeck University of London, Malet Street,
London WC1E 7HX
☎ Tel 0845 601 0174 or +44 (0)20 7631 6692/6435
from outside the UK
🖷 Fax 020 7079 0649
✉ Email info@bbk.ac.uk
🖳 Website www.bbk.ac.uk

*Student enquiries: Information Unit
Applications: Direct*

In brief

Total Students: 19,350

16% postgraduate
22% undergraduate

62% undergraduate
certificate

Undergraduates: 16,255

99% part-time
99% mature
on entry

97% UK students

63% female   37% male

- **A top UK research-intensive institution.** A college of University of London, specialising in evening higher education.
- **Teaching staff:** 405 full-time and part-time.
- **Broad study areas:** Arts, computer science, economics, languages, law, management, mathematics, natural sciences, psychology, social sciences.

Freshers
- **First degree entrants:** 1033 UK, part-time.

Profile

Institution
Founded: 1823. **Structural features:** A college of University of London. **Site:** In the heart of University of London's central precinct in Bloomsbury, central London. **How to get there:** Easily reached by underground (Russell Square, Goodge Street, Warren Street, Euston Square and Euston stations), mainline stations (Euston, St Pancras, King's Cross) and well-served by central London bus routes. **Special features:** London's only specialist provider of evening higher education, allowing students to earn while they learn and graduate without debt.

Courses
Academic features: Multi-faculty institution teaching 170+ postgraduate, 75+ undergraduate degrees and 80+ undergraduate certificates courses. **Awarding body:** University of London. **Main undergraduate awards:** FdA, FdSc, BA, BSc, BSc(Econ), LLB. **Length of courses:** 4 years (part-time).

Study opportunities & careers
Library and information services: Integrated library in main building: 353,182 books, 4179 periodicals; 335 study places. Open 7 days/week, plus remote access facilities, designed to meet the needs of part-time students. Information provision, £73 pa spent for each student (FTE). Students may also use Senate House Library next door, research students also the British Library. Networked IT

service across campus and from the outside world; IT support with technical bulletins, regular newsletter and advisory service. **Other learning resources:** Centre for Film and Visual Media (including a state-of-the-art 70-seat cinema); languages and film centre; self-tuition elements to several language programmes, with language laboratory and computer-assisted packages; expanding collection of recordings in major European languages, sound-recording studio and tape facilities. **Study abroad:** No formal arrangements for periods abroad but French, Spanish and earth sciences departments have European links.

Student services & facilities

Student advice and services: Links to local health centre. College provides advice on accommodation and careers, disability support, study skills courses. Evening nursery. **Amenities:** Snack bar (open day and evenings); restaurant (weekdays). SU counselling service and advice centre. ULU (University of London Union, next door) has all major sports and social facilities. Waterstone's university bookshop close by.

Money

Financial help: College has variety of awards, bursaries, etc, some restricted to students in particular subjects, some for students on low incomes who are not eligible for government help. **Tuition fees:** Home students pay £1560 pa (totals £6240 for 4-year course). International students pay £3810 pa. Students can pay in 8 instalments at no extra cost.

Student view

Unique college catering primarily for those in full-time employment who wish to gain a London University degree through evening study (most classes are held between 6 and 9pm). Wide age range but most students are in their 30s and 40s; those without formal qualifications often accepted. Undergraduate degrees take 4 instead of 3 years and students may transfer to full-time study after 2 years. Almost half of students are on postgraduate and research degrees, which can be taken by part- or full-time study. College services cater for both full-time and part-time students: SU office, library and snack bar are open in the evenings and during the day; also restaurant, serving hot meals all weekdays. SU magazine welcomes student contributions. Other facilities include a nursery, lively bar, a freshers' fair, and over 20 SU-funded clubs and societies, covering a wide range of interests. SU also offers free counselling service, advice centre and Skills for Study programme. Birkbeck students highly motivated, and some manage to put time into union activities, clubs and societies on top of work, study and family life. ULU (University of London Union) is next door with all major sports and social facilities, as are Senate House Library and Waterstone's university bookshop. Located in the heart of academic London, it is well served by public transport, and nearby shops, entertainment and places of interest abound.

Student footnotes

Housing: Most students have their own accommodation. Can get help from accommodation office, noticeboards. **Eats:** College snack bars; meal £2+ on campus. ULU and Pizza Paradiso also good. **Drink:** SU bar good value; ULU also good. Carling is favoured brew. **Nightlife:** Occasional events in bar. **Locals:** Very friendly. **Sports:** All facilities at ULU. Football teams. **Travel:** ULU Travel is next door. **Financial help:** Some college assistance possible. **Jobs:** Some casual work (SU can help). **Best features:** Variety of students; wide range of age/background. **And worst:** Everyone has too many commitments to get to know each other – work, study, family . . . **Past students:** Baroness McFarlane (Manchester University), Dame Elizabeth Estève-Coll (Vice Chancellor, East Anglia

University), Frank Sidebottom (cabaret singer), Sidney Webb (founder of LSE and other things), Helen Sharman (first British astronaut), Laurie Taylor (sociologist and journalist). **More info?** Contact President of SU (President@bcsu.bbk.ac.uk).

Birmingham City University

Location:
Birmingham, West Midlands (map 2)
*Sites across city;
partner colleges*

Birmingham City University, Franchise Street, Perry Barr, Birmingham B42 2SU
☎ Tel 0121 331 5595
🖷 Fax 0121 331 7994
✉ Email info@bcuchoices.com
🖳 Website www.bcu.ac.uk

*Student enquiries: Choices (tel 0121 331 5595)
Applications: UCAS (direct for some courses)*

In brief

Total Students: 24,460

80% undergraduate

2% FE Students
18% postgraduate

Undergraduates: 19,470
67% full-time ● ● 95% UK students
40% mature ● ● 46% lower
on entry socio-economic
groups

60% female

40% male

- **A modern university.**
- **Teaching staff:** 2935 full-time and part-time.
- **Broad study areas:** Accountancy and finance; art, design and visual communication; business and management; computing, IT and software engineering; criminal justice and law; education and teacher training; engineering; English; health and social care; jewellery; marketing and PR; media, multimedia and new media; music; nursing and midwifery; property, construction and planning; social sciences. You can look up the *Birmingham Conservatoire* separately.

Freshers

- **Admissions information:** AS-levels accepted in combination with 2+ A-levels or equivalent on most degree courses. UCAS tariff used.
- **First degree entrants:** 3175 UK, full-time.
- **Points on entry:** 255 (average).
- **Drop-out rate:** 12% in 1st year.
- **Accommodation:** Most 1st years houses; all from outside Birmingham

Profile

Institution

Founded: 1971 as Birmingham Poly, from colleges of art, commerce, education, music and PE. University status in 1992 as UCE Birmingham; changed name 2007. **Site:** Split across 8 sites: City

North is main site at Perry Barr, 3 miles north of city centre (SU, business, education, law, humanities, development and society); Millennium Point, in city centre (technology innovation centre, acting); Edgbaston, south of city centre (midwifery and nursing); Conservatoire in the city centre. Also Birmingham Institute of Art and Design on 4 sites: at Gosta Green, close to city centre (art and design, digital media), Bourneville, in the Bourneville Village Trust (visual arts), Margaret Street, a Venetian Gothic building in city centre (art); and Vittoria Street in city's jewellery quarter (jewellery department). **How to get there:** Birmingham is at the centre of England's rail, coach and road networks: mainline stations (New Street and Birmingham Snow Hill); coaches connect directly from 500 destinations; many motorway links; Birmingham International Airport close by. An extensive bus and train network ensures easy access to all sites from Birmingham city centre.

Courses

Awarding body: Birmingham City University. **Main undergraduate awards:** BA, BSc, BEng, BMus, LLB. **Length of courses:** 3 years; others 4 years.

Study opportunities & careers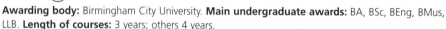

Library and information services: Main library (recently refurbished) contains 950,000 books, 9000 journals (print and electronic), course books on reference; also seven specialist libraries and digital library. Extensive information on other media, eg CD-ROM, slides, video and DVD. Specialist collections: rare books collection; collection of children's books; large collection of sheet music. Information provision, £61 pa spent for each student (FTE). IT service converged with library (access 13+ hours/day). Network/internet points for workstations and loan laptops; wireless access points in recreation areas and halls of residence; open-access facilities within faculties. IT support from technician in library opening hours; faculty librarians give induction for new students; electronic information workshops throughout the year. **Other learning resources:** University's virtual learning environment (Moodle) allows 24-hour access to, eg lecture notes, background information, video lectures, journals, discussion forums. **Study abroad:** Formal exchange links with partner institutions in Europe and North America. **Careers:** Information and advice, employer contact, recruiters' events, vacancies and job shop. Mentoring and work experience schemes for ethnic minority students.

Student services & facilities

Student advice and services: SU student advice service; student services: chaplaincy (3 full-time RC and Anglican, 2 part-time Orthodox and Progressive Jewish). Counsellors, doctors, nurses, disability service, mental health advice, personal assistance scheme, student finance advisers, jobshop, international advice service. **Amenities:** General shop, cashpoints, insurance broker, 2 nurseries, hairdresser, cafés, restaurants. **Accommodation:** Most 1st-year students in university halls. Approx 1500 places in halls, rent £73.50–£96 pw self-catering. Many students live in privately owned accommodation from 2nd year: rent £65+ pw self-catering.

Money

Living expenses budget: Minimum budget of £6k–£7k pa (excluding tuition fees) recommended by university. **Term-time work:** University guideline of 15 hours/week for full-time students. Some part-time work on campus and course-related work. **Financial help:** Bursaries of £525 pa for students whose family income is up to £25k; tapered down to £285 pa where family income is £50k. Also government funds for students in need; and other funds may be available, depending on individual circumstances. **Tuition fees:** Home students pay £3225 pa for first degrees (£1225 for foundation degree). International students pay £8800–£13,500 pa.

Student view

George Campbell, Tiger TV Assistant Manager, SU TV Station (Year 2, BSc Television Technology and Production)

Living

What's it like as a place to live? It is an ok place to live. There are a couple of student bars nearby and two superstores down the road. I live close to the university and the union, which is helpful. **How's the student accommodation?** Uni accommodation was good last year. I lived in Hamstead, which was catered. It was good for the money and, because it was catered, it was very social and I met a lot of people. **What's the student population like?** Student population is very wide-ranging. Loads of international and mature students as well as undergraduates. **How do students and locals get on?** There are a couple of dodgy places locally, like some pubs and areas, but it isn't too bad and students know about them. It is a highly student–populated area and the locals seem to be used to it and are generally fine.

Studying

What's it like as a place to study? The facilities are good and the courses are wide. Some of the courses are newer, like some specialist art and design courses. You always get one day off in the week! **What are the teaching staff like?** My tutor has worked in the industry that I am studying so he knows what he is talking about. He is a regional chair of an industry union and has many contacts that he bases information on.

Socialising

What are student societies like? The union is always working on this and they do get a good turnout. There have been loads of new societies made this year; the climbing society is successful in recruiting new people and setting up meetings. **What's a typical night out?** 'Toons' in the SU bar on a Friday night.

And how much does it cost? It is £2 to get in so it is very cheap compared to going somewhere in town. **How can you get home safely?** I, like most other students in the area, live across the road so it isn't too bad. Although I still make sure that I am walking home with someone else.

Money

Is it an expensive place to live? Rent isn't too bad but at the beginning of the first term I had to buy a bus pass to get into uni in town so that is an extra expense on top. Most people I know are skint but we generally sort out our money spending by the second term. **Average price of a pint?** £1.50. **And the price of a takeaway?** £6. **What's the part-time work situation?** The university have a Job Shop where you can go and seek help on getting a job. We have two superstores and one shopping centre close by as well as a city centre so jobs aren't too hard to find. However, most of the time employers are looking for Christmas staff. Jobs tend to pay above the minimum wage as far as I know.

Summary

What's the best feature about the place? The fact that it is a student area. My friends are just a short walk away and you feel a lot safer that everyone close by is in the same boat. **And the worst?** It's bad that the main campus is far away from town. If you want to get into town you have to use a bus or a taxi. It would be better if we were closer to the city centre so we could have more nights out/trips without using public transport. **And to sum it all up?** An opportunity to meet new people, experience new things not to be missed. It's your last chance to be irresponsible and young before you have to start working!

Past students: Alfred Bestall (creator of Rupert Bear), Kathy Cook (Olympic athlete), Betty Jackson (fashion designer), Zoë Ball (radio presenter), Kirsten O'Brian (children's TV), Nigel Mansell (ex-F1 driver), Frank Skinner (comedian). **More info?** Contact SU President (tel 0121 331 6811) or visit website on www.birminghamcitysu.com.

Birmingham Conservatoire

Location:
Birmingham, West Midlands (map 2)
Single site in city centre

Birmingham Conservatoire, Birmingham City University, Paradise Place, Birmingham B3 3HG
☎ Tel 0121 331 5901/2
🖷 Fax 0121 331 5906
✉ Email conservatoire@bcu.ac.uk
🖥 Website www.conservatoire.bcu.ac.uk

Student enquiries: The Registrar
Applications: CUKAS

In brief

Total Students: 585

75% undergraduate
10% FE Students
15% postgraduate

Undergraduates: 450
90% full-time ● ● 90% EU students
10% mature on entry ●

50% female 50% male

- **Specialist music college**, part of Birmingham City University.
- **Teaching staff:** 20 full-time, 190 part-time.
- **Broad study areas:** Music: performance, composition, jazz, music technology, community music, musicology, world music.

Freshers

- **Admissions information:** AS-levels accepted in combination with 2 A-levels.
- **First degree entrants:** 135 UK, full-time.
- **Points on entry:** 80 (minimum).
- **Accommodation:** All 1st years housed unless local.

Profile

Institution

Founded: 1886 as part of Birmingham and Midland Institute. **Structural features:** Part of Birmingham City University (formerly UCE Birmingham) since 1970. **Site:** City centre. **How to get there:** Birmingham is at the centre of England's rail, coach and road networks: mainline stations (New Street and Birmingham Snow Hill); coaches connect directly from 500 destinations; many motorway links; Birmingham International Airport close by. Conservatoire 10 mins' walk from New Street and Snow Hill railway stations, 15 mins from coach station. **Special features:** Individual teaching, workshops and masterclasses with internationally renowned musicians. Purpose-built complex includes 150-seat recital hall customised for performance with live electronics, 520-seat Adrian Boult Hall and specialist music library. Many CBSO principals teach at Conservatoire.

Courses 🎵

Academic features: BMus, first study performance or composition with range of options (eg world music, early music, chamber music, jazz, improvisation, conducting, music technology and recording, teaching skills and school studies). Also specialised BMus course in jazz. Final year of BMus (music or jazz) can be taken over two years with integrated PGCE. Good record of professional placements; professional schemes with, eg CBSO, BRB, BCMG, Philharmonia Orchestra. **Awarding body:**

Birmingham City University. **Main awards:** BMus, MMus, PGDip, AdvPGDip, PGCert, Grad Dip, MPhil, PhD. Also HND, BSc, MA offered as joint courses. **Length of courses:** 4–5 years (BMus); 1 year (GradDip, PGCert); 1–2 years (other postgraduate).

Study opportunities & careers

Library and information services: Newly rebuilt library: over 8000 books, 1300 orchestral and band sets, 1100 sets of vocal scores, 100,000 individual scores and parts, 12,000 sound recordings, including over 6000 CDs. Audio room with suite of listening and recording equipment, plus 2 cubicles for listening and viewing. 23 fixed computers, 15 MacBooks, 3 catalogue terminals, plus printing facilities (plus 9 PCs and 16 specialist music computers in separate labs). **Study abroad:** Exchange links with several European and American universities and colleges. **Careers:** Professional development embedded in course structures.

Student services & facilities

Student advice and services: Wide range of support services available through the University. **Accommodation:** See *Birmingham City University*.

Money

Living expenses budget: Minimum budget of £6k–£7k pa (excluding tuition fees) recommended by university. **Term-time work:** Students allowed to work part-time, some on campus as, eg cleaners, porters, concert stewards. **Financial help:** Own hardship funds. Entrance scholarships awarded on audition results. See also *Birmingham City University*. **Tuition fees:** Home students pay £3225 pa for first degrees. International students pay £12,500 pa (undergraduate or postgraduate).

Student view

Ideally situated, in modern purpose-built city centre development. Easy access to relatively cheap transport (no parking at college) and main arts centres, including town hall, symphony hall and repertory theatre. Recent developments (library, canteen, keyboard lab and further practice rooms) together with concert hall, listening room and computers make the college well equipped. Ample opportunities for dedicated musicians with emphasis on professional discipline within a lively and friendly atmosphere. Courses combine a high level of practical and academic standard with concentration on the first study; modern teaching methods used in all areas. Established orchestras, choirs, bands and chamber music and students encouraged to develop own activities with staff guidance. Ethnomusicology and community music being developed – both courses and work experience. Staff/student relationships excellent. Growing emphasis on student welfare with active on-site student body and help and advice from SU office. Hardship funds available in some cases. Places in halls of residence for most 1st years (Cambrian Hall most accessible, four mins' walk); other accommodation also available. Birmingham social life ranges from cheap student pubs to international clubs, reasonable restaurants, sports facilities and good shops. Some work available, including gigs and stewarding, although often competitive. Very few students fail to complete the course and most leave Birmingham having enjoyed their time there.

Student footnotes

Housing: Uni housing list can be expensive. Halls good, some very close. **Eats:** Lots of reasonable restaurants and sandwich bars. College canteen reasonably priced. **Drink:** Summer Row and Broad Street on the doorstep, Shakespeare (MandB), Prince of Wales (Ansell's), the Grapevine, the Wellington, Atkinson's (local ale). 4 union bars across the city. **Nightlife:** Rock and classical concerts with regular big names. City centre excellent for a good night out; everyone catered for. **Sports:** Can join any uni sports clubs. Student reductions at most sports centres and shops. **Travel:** Good public transport, discounts with taxi companies, cheap buses. **Financial help:** Limited funds available. **Jobs:** Some Christmas shows offer work plus chance to gain experience; pub work in term time; stewarding at the symphony hall. Can use musical talents to earn money, eg gigs or teaching, but very competitive.

Past students: Ernest Elemont (violinist), Peter Aston (singer/songwriter), Brian Ferneyhough (singer), Jean Rigby (opera singer). **More info?** Ring SU President on 0121 331 6811.

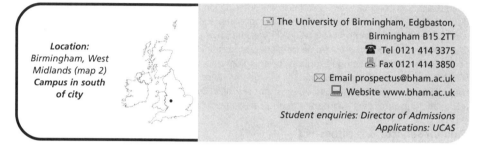

Birmingham University

Location:
Birmingham, West Midlands (map 2)
Campus in south of city

📠 The University of Birmingham, Edgbaston, Birmingham B15 2TT
☎ Tel 0121 414 3375
🖨 Fax 0121 414 3850
✉ Email prospectus@bham.ac.uk
💻 Website www.bham.ac.uk

Student enquiries: Director of Admissions
Applications: UCAS

In brief

Total Students: 30,415

39% postgraduate
61% undergraduate

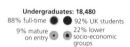

Undergraduates: 18,480
88% full-time — 92% UK students
9% mature on entry — 22% lower socio-economic groups

55% female — 45% male

- **A top UK research-intensive university.**
- **Teaching staff:** 1302 full-time, 175 part-time.
- **Broad study areas:** Arts, languages, literature and history; education; business and commerce; social sciences, government and politics; law; engineering; medicine, dentistry and health sciences; science.

Freshers
- **Admissions information:** AS-levels accepted in combination usually with 3 A-levels or equivalent. UCAS tariff partially incorporated.
- **First degree entrants:** 4360 UK, full-time.
- **Points on entry:** 300 (average).
- **Drop-out rate:** 5% in 1st year.
- **Accommodation:** All 1st years guaranteed accommodation (subject to certain conditions).

Profile

Institution 🏛

Founded: 1828, as Birmingham School of Medicine and Surgery, and 1875 Mason College; granted charter in 1900. **Site:** At Edgbaston, 2½ miles from city centre. **How to get there:** Birmingham is at the centre of England's rail, coach and road networks: mainline stations (New Street and

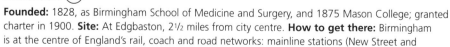

Birmingham International); coaches connect directly from 500 destinations; many motorway links; Birmingham International Airport close by. University is just off A38; buses between university and city centre; trains between University Station (on campus) and New Street Station in city centre. **Special features:** Barber Institute of Fine Arts and Music.

Courses

Awarding body: University of Birmingham. **Main undergraduate awards:** BA, BDS, BEng, MEng, BMedSc, BMus, BNurs, MSci, BSc, LLB, MBChB. **Length of courses:** 3 years; 4 years (language courses, MEng, MSci, MNatSc, BCom, BNurs); 5 years (MBChB and BDS).

Study opportunities & careers

Library and information services: 10 libraries and resource centres. 2.6 million volumes (books and periodicals), 3 million manuscripts and archives. Information provision, £149 pa spent for each student (FTE). Library, IT and learning support services converged. Ratio workstations to students 1:8. IT support from large academic information service; computer officers in university schools. Comprehensive induction programme for all new students, introducing library, computing resources and facilities. **Other learning resources:** Learning development unit. Botanic Garden at Winterbourne House. **Study abroad:** 2% of students spend time abroad. Formal exchange links with over 157 European universities and 40+ rest of the world. **Careers:** Information centre, individual advice and guidance; employer presentations, careers fairs, on-campus interviews; skills development.

Student services & facilities

Student advice and services: Student support and counselling service (www.sscs.bham.ac.uk) offers support with practical welfare, learning or emotional/psychological difficulties and disability/dyslexia; international office gives specialist welfare and immigration advice; financial support office. Guild of Students welfare service. **Amenities:** Union building with hall, bars, places to eat, etc; bookshop, banks, supermarket, travel agent, opticians and hairdressers on site. **Sporting facilities:** Excellent facilities include AstroTurf pitches, floodlit athletics track, 3 sports halls, gym and extensive free weights room, 7 squash courts, gymnastics hall, swimming pool, numerous grass pitches, a dedicated unit for sports medicine, human performance and fitness services; own outdoor activities centre on the shores of Coniston Water in the Lake District. Consistently in top 3 in BUCS competition (More info on www.sport.bham.ac.uk) **Accommodation:** All 1st years guaranteed accommodation, subject to certain conditions (40% of all students). 5500 places available: self-catering places at £78–£96 pw (up to £115 pw ensuite), catered £115–£142 pw, almost all 42-week contracts (so £3271–£4834 pa self-catering, £4817–£5975 pa catered). 90% of accommodation has unlimited access to the internet and university network. (Accommodation office on www.housing.bham.ac.uk.) Many students live in privately owned accommodation for 2 years: rent £60+ pw plus bills for self-catering. Small number of students live at home.

Money

Living expenses budget: Budget of £7950–£9820 for an academic year (excluding tuition fees) recommended by university. **Term-time work:** Students recommended to keep term-time work below 12 hours pw Guild-run Job Zone helps find part-time work. **Financial help:** Bursaries of £840 pa for UK undergraduates whose family income is up to £35,500; additional scholarships of £1290 pa for bursary holders with high grades on entrance (10% of students expected to qualify). Also subject scholarships in physics, engineering, computer science, and for music and sport. £850k government hardship funds, average award £1k. Own funds of £30k (average bursaries £1k pa, discretionary payments £300). Special categories: hardship payments to single parents, those with dependants and mature students with families; other funds available for academically able students without sufficient funding; some scholarships for international students. Apply for help to Student Funding Office. **Tuition fees:** Home students pay £3225 pa for first degrees. International students pay £9880 pa (classroom), £12,800 (lab/studio), £23,350 (clinical).

Student view

Birmingham is an ideal city for students, easily accessible, diverse and thriving. Attractive, leafy campus in Edgbaston, some 2 miles from city centre. Excellent academic reputation and usually easy to change course in first term (but depends on tutor). Graduate employment levels exceptional. Excellent Guild of Students, with wide range of services. Opportunities for involvement enormous, with 160+ student groups and standing committees: you can run a show on the student radio station (Burn FM), volunteer in the community with ComAc or burn up dance floors across the country with Twelve-Ten, the clubbing society. The guild has an excellent advice and representation centre (ARC), giving access to welfare facilities, academic representation and information about all important aspects of student life, and the Job Zone, visited by thousands of students every term. Large and successful athletic unions, based at Munrow sports centre on campus; sports teams can use all facilities (swimming pool to Olympic-standard hockey pitches). Wide range of entertainment at guild, with regular open mic and quiz nights, 3 bars and nightclub; Joe's is the main student bar, Beorma bar for a quieter drink; nightclub venue, The Underground, has famous Fab'n'Fresh on Saturday nights; 5 club nights a week, local bands, up-and-coming comedians, student-run plays and musicals. 1st years mostly housed in university's mix of catered and self-catering accommodation. Rented accommodation in pleasant surroundings in Selly Oak, Selly Park and Harborne. Birmingham is a cultural haven and excellent retail centre. Redeveloped BullRing resulted in Europe's brightest shopping capital and other shopping complex developments in the city planned; exciting mix of high street stores and unique boutiques. Symphony Hall, National Indoor Arena, NEC and revamped Birmingham Academy all within striking distance, so you can catch top chart acts, classical extravaganzas and up-and-coming artists on the city's thriving music scene. Excellent small art gallery on campus, Barber Institute of Fine Art; also city centre has art gallery with fine Pre-Raphaelite collection, a sealife centre for monsters of the deep and a science museum with a full-size steam train.

Student footnotes

Housing: Catered and self-catering accommodation on campus; guaranteed place for all 1st years, if Birmingham their first choice. Supply exceeds demand in local rented accommodation; uni housing services and ARC (in the guild) will help find good deals and reputable landlords (landlord accreditation scheme recently introduced). **Eats:** Bristol Road dotted with the curry houses that make Birmingham so popular! 2 catering outlets in guild, including Subway, Spar (jacket potatoes and pastries). **Drink:** Guild bars have best deals; 4 pubs in Bristol Road, close to campus. **Nightlife:** All sorts provided by guild, eg Wednesday's 'I Love Risa' on Broad Street, Friday night Foam Party, Saturday's Fab'n'Fresh. City-centre clubs offer midweek student nights (cheap drinks promos but long queues!). **Locals:** Need to be treated with respect but no real 'town v gown' problems. **Sports:** University routinely in BUCS's top three. Excellent facilities, including swimming pool. Birmingham has 2 football teams: Birmingham City and Aston Villa; county cricket ground within walking distance, NIA and Alexandra Stadium for basketball and athletics. **Travel:** Easy access via international airport 10 miles from city centre; New Street Station; train station on campus; plenty of cycle paths around city. **Financial help:** Guild and university provide some; well publicised. Advice at the ARC. **Jobs:** 500+ jobs in guild (bar work to marketing); guild's Job Zone for part-time and vacation work in the city and beyond. **Best features:** Location and reputation. **And worst:** Bureaucracy. **Past students:** Desmond Morris (writer and broadcaster); Phillipa Forrester and Chris Tarrant (broadcasters); Alex Jarratt (Jarratt Report); Sir Austin Pierce (British Aerospace); Sir Peter Walters (BP); Victoria Wood (comedian); Ben Shephard (TV presenter). **More info?** Contact the Guild President at president@guild.bham.ac.uk, or check out the website (www.guildofstudents.com).

Bolton University

Location:
*north-west England
(map 2)*
**Single campus in
Bolton town centre;
partner colleges**

University of Bolton, Deane Road,
Bolton BL3 5AB
Tel 01204 903903
Fax 01204 903809
Email enquiries@bolton.ac.uk
Website www.bolton.ac.uk

*Student enquiries: Student Services
Applications: UCAS*

In brief

Total Students: 10,000

80% undergraduate

1% FE Students
19% postgraduate

Undergraduates: 8000
76% full-time
54% mature on entry
74% UK students
46% lower socio-economic groups

50% female
50% male

- **A modern university.**
- **Teaching staff:** 320 full-time and part-time.
- **Broad study areas:** Arts, media and education; built environment and engineering; business; games, computing and creative technologies; health and social sciences; logistics and information systems.

Freshers

- **Admissions information:** AS-levels accepted in combination with full A-levels (or equivalent). Also welcomes applicants with Access or vocational qualifications, eg AVCE, National Diplomas or new level 3 Advanced Diploma.
- **First degree entrants:** 1500 UK, full-time.
- **Points on entry:** 160–280 (average).
- **Drop-out rate:** 22% in 1st year.
- **Accommodation:** Most 1st years housed.

Profile

Institution
Founded: 1824 as Bolton Mechanics Institute; following mergers it became Bolton Institute in 1982. University status in 2005. **Site:** Single campus in Bolton town centre, Deane Campus. **How to get there:** Town easily reached by road and rail (10 miles north of Manchester). Campus is a 10-min walk from bus and train stations.

Courses
Awarding body: University of Bolton. **Main undergraduate awards:** BA, BEng, BSc. **Length of courses:** 2–4 years (full-time/sandwich); 3–6 years (part-time).

Study opportunities & careers
Library and information services: 175,000 books and other materials, including video cassettes, DVDs and audiocassettes, 11,500+ print and electronic journals, 7000 electronic books; online access

to electronic resources. Information provision, £92 pa spent for each student (FTE). 672 workstations with access to library and internet; 50 loan laptops for students; ratio 1:10 workstations to students; 24 hours/day open access IT facility; free wireless networks across the whole campus. Library and IT support from computer information officers. 1-hour introduction to library and information services for all new students. **Study abroad:** Exchanges abroad for students on some degree courses. **Careers:** Professional careers advisers offering guidance, counselling and information.

Student services & facilities

Student advice and services: Specialist staff in counselling, welfare and special needs; also international office and multi-faith service. **Amenities:** New SU and student social learning zone in centre of campus. **Sporting facilities:** Sports centre on campus (gym, climbing wall, multi-use sports hall); access to Bolton Arena (20 mins away). **Accommodation:** All 1st-year students who apply usually offered place in halls of residence. 700 single self-catering study bedrooms, on two sites: rent £62 pw, 38-week contract (Sept–July). Private sector rent from £40 pw (plus bills).

Money

Living expenses budget: Budget of £6500–£7500 pa (excluding tuition fees) recommended by university. **Term-time work:** University jobshop helps students find part-time temporary work on and off campus. **Financial help:** Bursaries of £350 pa for all UK students whose family income is up to £25k; sliding scale down to nil where family income is £50k. Scholarships of £750 pa for students who have taken a preparatory course at a partner college; of £500 pa for those entering with 300+ tariff points; of £1k pa for care leavers; and a one-off award of £15k to the most academically gifted 1st-year student. **Tuition fees:** Home students pay £3225 pa for first degrees (no fee in sandwich year). International students pay £7800 pa.

Student view

Now on a single campus, Deane Campus, with over 7000 students; just outside the town centre and about 15 mins' walk between the two. Bolton is a large town (about 330,000 people) just north of Manchester and easily accessible by both train and the M61 (main route from Manchester to Preston). Halls of residence at Orlando Village and the Hollins both modern and comfortable: plenty of car parking space in security-patrolled grounds. Orlando Village better suited for 1st years and a bit livelier; the Hollins is better suited to PGCE students and anyone wanting a quieter year. Plenty of private accommodation dotted about the town. SU plays a big part in campus life and many students belong to one of its many sports clubs or societies. Union runs bar and catering services: bar has cheap beer and a terrific atmosphere. Its catering services have really good tasty food at low prices. Town caters well for total student experience, with many great events throughout the year – old classics like 3-legged pub-crawl (beat 13 pubs in 28 mins!), annual sportspersons dinner, comedy nights and new ideas all the time. Relatively easy to change course in first term; just ask the course leader.

Student footnotes

Housing: Good, comfortable halls. Plenty of private housing in town; look at university lists, SU noticeboard and in the *Bolton News*. **Eats:** Massive array of restaurants, takeaways and cafés. **Drink:** SU cheapest; many other classy bars. Bolton hosts major beer festival each October. **Nightlife:** Several big clubs, some nice classy bars and delights of Manchester only 15 mins by train. **Locals:** Not bad (many other northern towns worse). **Sports:** Cracking range of clubs and societies (leads to very good social life). On campus sports hall, squash courts. Local sports centres, gyms, swimming pools. **Financial help:** Only in exceptional circumstances. Make an appointment with the advice unit by calling reception. **Jobs:** Work if you want it: SU bar, or bars in town. **Best feature:** The friendly and close atmosphere. **And worst:** Typical northern weather!

More info? Contact SU President (tel 01204 900850, email supres@bolton.ac.uk) or Vice President Finance and Recreation (tel 01204 900850, email suvpfr@bolton.ac.uk); some info on the website (www.bisu.co.uk).

Bournemouth University

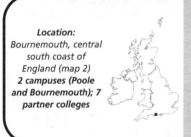

Location:
Bournemouth, central south coast of England (map 2) 2 campuses (Poole and Bournemouth); 7 partner colleges

🖃 Bournemouth University, Fern Barrow, Poole, Dorset BH12 5BB
☎ Tel 01202 524111
🖷 Fax 01202 962736
✉ Email askBUenquiries@bournemouth.ac.uk
💻 Website www.bournemouth.ac.uk

Student enquiries: future student enquiries tel 08456 501501 or, from outside UK, +44 (0)1202 961916
Applications: UCAS

In brief

Total Students: 16,205

11% postgraduate
89% undergraduate

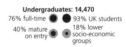
Undergraduates: 14,470
76% full-time
40% mature on entry
93% UK students
18% lower socio-economic groups

57% female
43% male

- **A modern university.**
- **Teaching staff:** 580 full-time and part-time.
- **Broad study areas.** Accounting and finance; archaeology and heritage; business and management; computing and business information technology; computer animation; conservation sciences; design; food and nutrition; forensic science; health and social care; law; marketing; media and communications; psychology and computing; tourism, sport and hospitality.

Freshers

- **Admissions information:** AS-levels accepted in combination with 2+ A-levels or equivalent. UCAS tariff used.
- **First degree entrants:** 3170 UK, full-time.
- **Points on entry:** 287 (average).
- **Drop-out rate:** 7% in 1st year.
- **Accommodation:** All 1st years housed who apply by the deadline.

Profile

Institution

Founded: 1992 as a university; previously Dorset Institute (1976) from merger of various colleges of technology and education. **Sites:** Talbot Campus, 2 miles from centre of Bournemouth, and

Lansdowne Campus in near town centre. Partner colleges: Bournemouth and Poole, Bridgwater, Kingston Maurward, Weymouth colleges, Wiltshire College Salisbury and University Centre Yeovil. **How to get there:** By air, rail, National Express or road to Bournemouth. Unilinx bus service plus good local bus network links campuses and accommodation; limited parking but extensive cycle routes in town.

Courses

Academic features: Placement year in a third of degree programmes. **Awarding body:** Bournemouth University. **Main undergraduate awards:** BA, BSc, LLB, FdA, FdSc. **Length of courses:** 2 years (foundation degrees); 3–4 years (full-time); 4 years (sandwich); 4–5 years (extended programme).

Study opportunities & careers

Library and information services: Large library and learning centre plus libraries on both campuses; total of 292,000 books 1405 journals, 48,000 e-books and 41,000 e-journals and report series; 1172 study places. Information provision, £89 pa spent for each student (FTE). Separate IT service: 1620 points with internet access, some open 24 hours (ratio 1:10 workstations to students). IT support from helpdesks in term time; some IT skills included in courses, some self-managed learning packages available. **Other learning resources:** Virtual learning environment, internet radio station, musical centre with music rooms, product design computer studios and workshops; national centre for computer animation, HD TV Studio. **Study abroad:** Wide range of opportunities to engage with international activities. Exchange links with universities in Europe and Canada (funding available through Erasmus and university travel bursary scheme). **Careers:** Information, advice and placement. 90+% of graduates in employment or further study within 6 months, 75% in graduate-level employment.

Student services & facilities

Student advice and services: Doctors, nurse, counsellors, multi-faith chaplaincy, accommodation staff, family planning advisers, SU welfare officer. **Amenities:** Large SU entertainment facilities, including nightclub (in refurbished fire station), 3 bars, bistro internet café. Nursery. **Sporting facilities:** All-weather and turf pitches, county-standard cricket ground, 4-court sports hall, 2 activity studios, large climbing and bouldering centre, fitness suite, golf simulator and elite sports training suite. Individual athlete sport scholarship and performance scheme. **Accommodation:** All 1st years housed who apply before 1 September (later applicants in private-sector houses). 2485 self-catering university-allocated places: 989 in university halls; 575 in university-managed houses; 920 in partner-provided halls (Unite plc/Signpost Homes) allocated by university; rent £75–£91 pw (including bills and internet connection in most rooms). Most students live in local privately owned accommodation for 2 years (university letting service helps); self-catering rent typically £65–£85 pw plus bills.

Money

Living expenses budget: Minimum budget of £7300–£8200 pa (excluding tuition fees) recommended by university **Term-time work:** Some work on campus in bars, library, help with open day tours; off-campus in retail, hotels, etc (local temping agencies keen to place students). **Financial help:.** Bursaries of £319 pa for all UK students whose family income is £25k or less; also bursaries for students from partner colleges. Annual scholarships, mostly £1k, for music, sport and citizenship, and others based on high entry qualifications and in specified departments. Government funds of £396k: special help for students with additional needs/disability, students with childcare needs, mature students and those with high travel and housing costs. **Tuition fees:** Home students pay £3225 pa for almost all first degrees (lower in placement years; fee at Bridgwater College expected to be approx £2110 pa). International students pay £8k–£13k pa (lower in placement year); international fees do not rise during the course.

Student view
Angela Smith, Vice President, Communications
(BA Public Relations)

Living
What's it like as a place to live? Bournemouth is a lovely place to live with a great beach and night life as well as shops and activities for both day and night time. Bournemouth is a great town and many students stay after finishing their studies. **How's the student accommodation?** Uni accommodation has been improved recently and more and more halls are being built to get more freshers into halls, but the uni-let houses are just as good to live in. There are some great private lets around but students need to be careful of some letting agents that rip students off, but the university is trying to stop this happening. It isn't very difficult to find somewhere to live and prices aren't too bad for the area, but Bournemouth is a bit more expensive than a lot of other UK towns and cities. **What's the student population like?** The student community is good and includes a lot of people with different and diverse backgrounds as well as international students. Bournemouth attracts a lot of people from all over the world but the community is generally friendly and there are no obvious splits. **How do students and locals get on?** The local community aren't too happy with the amount of students now in Bournemouth but there are no major issues or anything that affects students.

Studying
What's it like as a place to study? Bournemouth is undergoing development and there are a lot of new facilities being built, such as HD studios for the media school. The courses are generally vocational and quite practical, which is good after graduation, having some actual experience to help sell yourself when trying to get a job. **What are the teaching staff like?** The staff are quite helpful and many inform students of their free time from teaching so students can go and talk to them if they need to.

Socialising
What are student societies like? There are lots of ways to socialise at Bournemouth, with the Union offering lots of opportunities to do something to meet new people. There are over 50 clubs and societies, TV, radio and magazine media to contribute to, as well as fundraising, personal development and volunteering. The uni also offer a wide range of sports. **What's a typical night out?** There are a range of bars and clubs in Bournemouth, including a club run by the SU offering competitive prices. There is generally something for everyone. **And how much does it cost?** During the week is cheaper than weekends, but there is generally something for everyone's budget. **How can you get home safely?** There are always taxis around and night buses so it is easy to get home safely.

Money
Is it an expensive place to live? Bournemouth is quite expensive with being a seaside tourist town, but it is not over-priced and every budget is catered for. Depending on what your lifestyle is like the loan is fine, but quite a few people who have no support from parents with rent etc will often get a part-time job. **Average price of a pint?** £2.70. **And the price of a takeaway?** £7 depending on how much you want. **What's the part-time work situation?** There are plenty of part-time jobs and the Union provides a job shop that advertises suitable positions so students can balance work and uni.

Summary
What's the best feature about the place? The beach – it is a great place to go. **And the worst?** It's a very busy place with lots of people, meaning there is a lot of traffic around so it can cause delays and make it difficult getting to places sometimes. It's best to

use public transport. **And to sum it all up?** Bournemouth is great, I loved doing my degree here and had a great time. This is an amazing place to study and live and offers the chance to have a fantastic university experience.

More info? Enquiries to the SU (tel 01202 965765, email studentsunion@bournemouth.ac.uk) or visit the website (www.subu.org.uk).

Bradford College

Location:
Bradford, north of
England (map 2)
**Single site in city
centre**

✉ Bradford College, Great Horton Road,
Bradford BD7 1AY
☎ Tel 01274 433333 (voice and minicom)
🖷 Fax 01274 433241
✉ Email admissions@bradfordcollege.ac.uk
💻 Website www.bradfordcollege.ac.uk

*Student enquiries: Admissions Officer
Applications: UCAS (Admissions Office for part-time courses)*

In brief

Total Students: 3305

20% postgraduate
80% undergraduate

Undergraduates: 2645
70% full-time ● ● 90% UK students
30% mature ●
on entry

60% female 40% male

- **Associate college of Leeds Met University.**
- **Teaching staff:** 570 full-time, 500 part-time.
- **Broad study areas:** Art and design; beauty therapy; business, information technology and finance; education; health and social care; law; ophthalmic dispensing,

Freshers
- **First degree entrants:** 750 UK, full-time.
- **Points on entry:** 120–180.
- **Accommodation:** Majority of 1st years housed.

Profile

Institution
Founded: 1982 from merger of Bradford and Ilkley colleges. **Site:** One main site in Bradford. **How to get there:** By bus or train to Bradford Metro Travel Interchange or train to Forster Square Station; college is 10 mins' walk from both. By road, exit junction 26 from M62, follow signs to M606 and A641 and city centre and then to college/university.

Courses
Academic features: Open and distance learning facilities available. **Awarding body:** Leeds Metropolitan University. **Main undergraduate awards:** BA, BEd, BSc, LLB. **Length of courses:** 3 years; others 4 years.

Study opportunities & careers

Library and information services: 195,000 volumes; 1200 current periodicals, 590 study places. Separate IT service: centres in main teaching buildings, varying opening times. IT skills courses. Specialist collections: art and design collection of over 65,000 slides. **Other learning resources:** Open workshops in English and mathematics. **Careers:** Advisory service.

Student services & facilities

Student advice and services: Student service centre, including counsellors and nursing staff. Learning support (disabilities) tutor and day nurseries. **Amenities:** SU building. **Sporting facilities:** Gym; many sports facilities in city. **Accommodation:** 200 ensuite rooms/apartments at Arkwright Hall, rent £73–£81 pw, self-catering; 42 week contract..

Money

Living expenses budget: Minimum budget of £6535 pa (excluding tuition fees) recommended by the college. **Financial help:** Total available approx £350k. Help is given through access to learning fund; own funds for repayable loans, special travel scholarships, small prizes and awards. Special help: emergency situations/changes of circumstances and towards completion of qualification. Apply for help to Learner Services. **Tuition fees:** Home students pay £2k pa for first degrees. International students pay £7100–£7950 pa.

Student view

Non-elitist community college, with high proportion of mature and especially local students. Active and campaigning SU; students represented on all college committees with direct and uncompromising stance. Union now located in principal college building, making it easily accessible for students. Book early for accommodation – new block is expensive but very tasty. Exciting, diverse and very affordable social scene. Local community has friendly and easy-going attitude to strangers but, like in any big city, be aware of personal safety.

Student footnotes

Housing: Many cheap properties available (but beware of standards). Many students spend 2 years in college accommodation. **Eats:** Meals good value on campus (including big breakfast). Can get a large meal for £4 locally at, eg Walkabout, Revolution, Lunch Box, Love Apple. **Drink:** Union building has cheap drinks and promos; no question, best in town. Several large student-orientated pubs in easy reach of campus; the Sound Gallery is cheap. Tetley's is the local brew. **Nightlife:** SU has regular club night and events (eg Comedy Club, DFD at the Union); a few bands. Bradford Film Theatre and Pictureville for ultimate independent releases, new and old. Queen's Hall, Chicago's and the Sound Gallery good student clubs. **Sports:** Full range of sports facilities, mostly shared with university. **Locals:** Area is student-friendly (though city centre sometimes not good at weekends). **Travel:** Cheap buses, trains and taxis. **Financial help:** Limited funds for the very desperate via college student services. **Jobs:** Plenty about, if you look, on and off campus. **Best features:** Union and college student services. **And worst:** Lack of sports facilities. **Past students:** David Hockney (painter); New Model Army (rock band); Bernard Ingham (journalist); Terry Rooney MP; Michael Jack MP; Terrorvision (rock band); Robbie Paul (rugby player, Bradford Bulls). **More info?** Contact SU President (tel 01274 414314/5).

Bradford University

Location:
Bradford, north of England (map 2)
Main city-centre campus plus 2 further sites

 University of Bradford, Bradford, West Yorkshire BD7 1DP
☎ Tel 0800 073 1225
🖷 Fax 01274 236260
✉ Email course-enquiries@bradford.ac.uk
💻 Website www.bradford.ac.uk

Student enquiries: Enquiries Office
Applications: UCAS

In brief

Total Students: 11,485

23% postgraduate
77% undergraduate

Undergraduates: 8860
90% full-time ● ● 81% UK students
29% mature ● ● 48% lower socio-economic groups
on entry

52% female 48% male

- **Research-intensive university.**
- **Teaching staff:** 489 full-time, 617 part-time.
- **Broad study areas:** Animation and games; archaeological sciences; cybernetics and robotics; computing and informatics; design and technology; economics; electronics and telecommunications; engineering; geography and environmental sciences; health studies; humanities (incl history and English); ICT; law; life sciences (incl biomedical, chemical and forensic, clinical sciences, optometry, pharmacy); management and business (incl finance, HR, marketing); media studies; philosophy; psychology; social sciences; peace studies.

Freshers

- **Admissions information:** UCAS tariff used together with specific requirements relating to subjects and grades; Key Skills may contribute for most courses. Range of qualifications (UK and international) accepted; applications from mature students particularly welcome.
- **First degree entrants:** 2030 UK, full-time.
- **Points on entry:** 266 (average).
- **Drop-out rate:** 11% in 1st year.
- **Accommodation:** All 1st years (who apply by deadline) guaranteed a place in halls.

Profile

Institution

Founded: Royal Charter in 1966; originally Bradford Technical College founded in 1860s.
Site: Main campus close to city centre; school of health studies 10 mins walk from main campus; school of management in parkland 2 miles away. **How to get there:** Good rail and coach links to Bradford Interchange; well connected to motorway network via M62 and M606; also Leeds/Bradford Airport. For university, No. 576 bus from Bradford Interchange and Nos 610/1/2/3/4 from city centre.
Special features: University promotes ethos of teaching in an atmosphere of research. University-wide

Ecoversity programme, aims to embed the principles and practices of sustainable development (sustainable education, healthy environment, social wellbeing, thriving economy).

Courses

Academic features: Non-standard and mature applicants encouraged; combined studies, informatics, engineering and science courses foundation year for those with non-standard qualifications. Many courses have a practical orientation; 18% of students are on sandwich degree courses. Distinctive courses include chemistry with pharmaceutical and forensic science, archaeological sciences, robotics with artificial intelligence, virtual design and innovation, peace studies. **Awarding body:** University of Bradford. **Main undergraduate awards:** BA, BEng, BSc, MEng, MPharm, MChem, FdA, FdSc, FdEng. **Length of courses:** 3 years; 4 years (some sandwich courses, those with foundation year); 5 years (sandwich). Foundation degrees, 1–5 years.

Study opportunities & careers

Library and information services: 3 sites: 600,000 volumes, 1100+ print and 5000+ electronic subscriptions; 1090 study places. Information provision, £122 pa spent for each student (FTE). IT and library services converged. 1500 workstations with access to library and internet (plus free broadband points in most student bedrooms) and wi-fi hotspots across campus; ratio workstations to students 1:8 (plus many students have own machines). IT and library facilities open 24 hours/day; support from advisory service, PC and network clinics. All new students offered introductions to library and information resources; more advanced help with information retrieval (when required); IT core skills integrated into all appropriate academic programmes. **Study abroad:** 1% of first-degree students spend a period abroad. Formal exchange links with 50 universities and colleges around the world plus many departmental links. **Careers:** Guidance, advice and substantial careers information library (including overseas section); website; careers information events; employer recruitment visits and fairs; regular vacancy bulletins; vacation work.

Student services & facilities

Student advice and services: The Hub, a one-stop support centre, incorporates accommodation office, international student adviser, fees and bursaries officer, mature students adviser. Also learner development unit (for academic and maths support, counselling service, health service). 69-place day nursery. SU welfare office, disability office. Online social network at http://developme.ning.com. **Amenities:** Communal building with 4 bar/café areas, dance floor, disco bar; shop, bank, bookshop on campus; studio theatre, music centre, art gallery, campus radio. **Sporting facilities:** Indoor sports centre, with sports halls, dance/aerobics studio, solarium, sauna, 2 squash courts, 100-station fitness suite, 25m swimming pool. 35-acre sports ground (3 miles away). Artificial turf areas, squash courts at halls of residence. **Accommodation:** All 1st years guaranteed accommodation (if Bradford is their firm choice and they do not live within travelling distance) plus all students coming through Clearing (if they apply before 5 September) and all international students. Approx 1700 self-catering places in university-owned or approved halls, on or near campus (some ensuite, those on campus with data points and internet access): £65–£72 pw (£75–£86 pw ensuite), contracts 42 weeks. Most 2nd and 3rd years in privately owned accommodation, rent locally £45–84 pw self-catering plus bills.

Money

Living expenses budget: Minimum budget of £6k–£7k for the academic year (excluding tuition fees) recommended by university. **Term-time work:** Job Shop helps students find part-time and summer work, on and off campus. **Financial help:** Bursaries for those whose family income is up to £40k, of £500 in 1st year, rising to £900 in 3rd and any subsequent years; and of £400 (1st year) rising to £600 (3rd year) where family income is £40k–£60k. Further £300, as one-off payment in 1st year, for those coming through partner schools and colleges. Various subject-based scholarships. Government funds £457k (average award £800). Special help: students incurring childcare costs; mature students; self-financing students; care leavers. Own funds available as loans for international students with unexpected financial difficulties. Apply for help to The Hub (tel 01274 236504). **Tuition fees:** Home students pay £3225 pa for first degrees (£625 in a sandwich year, £1200 for foundation year except in clinical sciences). International students pay £8325 pa (classroom), £10,755 (lab-based) for most courses.

Student view

Small, friendly campus university, 10 mins' walk from city centre. School of Health Studies is walking distance from main campus; management 2 miles away (on main bus routes). A technological university, academic strengths are, eg, pharmacy, optometry and archaeology, as well as rare humanities courses such as peace studies and interdisciplinary human studies. Popular for electronic communication courses such as telecommunications, and electronic imaging and media communication. Workloads vary hugely depending on course and time of year. Many courses include a placement (industrial or educational); university's ethos is applied rather than theoretical knowledge. Easy to change course in first term and dropout rate is low. Very good sports facilities and loads of different sports to try; sports centre on campus has a swimming pool, sports hall, gym, weights room, etc; AstroTurf pitches within walking distance and playing fields easily accessible by bus. University halls of residence are good standard. Plenty of private accommodation in Bradford, mostly in large Victorian terraced houses within a mile of campus; standards vary but Unipol (student housing standards agency) aims to iron out poor housing. Active SU, with campaigns running all the time. SU runs 4 bars and 3 nightclubs, 2 shops and an advice centre. 40 sports clubs, ranging from traditional rugby and football to more adventurous frisbee and sub-aqua; 35 societies, eg clinical sciences, twirling, karaoke and CND. Hardship funds and budgeting advice from SU and university (but Bradford inexpensive, so money stretches well!). Students from over 90 nationalities and no two people there for the same reason; cosmopolitan atmosphere and always new people to meet. Teaching methods a good balance of traditional stuffy academia to off-the-wall experimentation; university committed to whole-student experience. Small but varied nightlife in city; usually something for everyone. Union events predominately cheese-based, but also regular hip hop, rock, reggae and drum and bass nights. Flirt on Fridays is night to remember; Rio's is one of the best rock/alternative clubs in the north. Not many live national bands but lots of student bands do gigs and we're close enough to Leeds, Manchester and Sheffield so it's never far to a decent gig. Mainstream and independent cinemas in town; SU cinema on campus. National Museum of Film, Photography and Television nearby, and only 10 mins on the train to the Yorkshire Dales!

Student footnotes

Housing: Halls reasonable. Plenty of inexpensive housing in city; check shop windows and Unipol. **Eats:** You can't starve in Bradford. The best curry houses in Britain; get a meal for £3+. Union bars and loads of international restaurants. **Drink:** Usual suspects, eg Revolution, Walkabout and Wetherspoons; lots of local student bars and real ale pubs in town. JB's is local brew. **Nightlife:** SU nights: Flirt, cheese, hip hop, DandB; rock, Rio's close by. **Locals:** Quite friendly. Some dodgy areas (as in any large city). **Sports:** Very good, cheap sports centre on campus. AstroTurf pitches on campus; playing fields 3 miles away on direct bus route. **Travel:** Well placed to reach, eg London, Leeds, Manchester, Sheffield. Student travel agent provides great cheap deals. **Financial help:** Excellent; union and university funds. **Jobs:** Lots of casual work, in SU and locally (bars, shops, etc). University-run JobShop helps find work. Most tutors now expect students to have jobs. **Best feature:** Friendly, cosmopolitan community atmosphere. **And worst:** The atmosphere tends to suck people in – you might never leave! **Past students:** Dr Barry Seal MEP; Roland Boyes, Ian Bruce, David Hinchcliffe,

Alice Mahon, Ann Taylor, all MPs; Tony O'Reilly (chairman of Heinz International); John Hegley (poet); Ifem Onura (Gillingham FC); John McGregor (author). **More info?** Enquiries to SU Communications Officer (tel 01274 233300, email ubu-comms@bradford.ac.uk) or check out the website (www.ubuonline.co.uk).

Brighton & Sussex Medical School

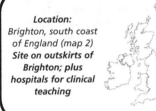

Location:
Brighton, south coast of England (map 2)
Site on outskirts of Brighton; plus hospitals for clinical teaching

⌨ Brighton & Sussex Medical School, Mithras House, Lewes Road, Brighton BN2 4AT
☎ Tel 01273 644644
🖷 Fax 01273 642825
✉ Email medadmissions@bsms.ac.uk
💻 Website www.bsms.ac.uk

Student enquiries: BSMS Admissions
Applications: UCAS

In brief

Total Students: 1200

55% postgraduate
45% undergraduate

Undergraduates: 560
100% full-time
25% mature on entry
95% UK students
65% lower socio-economic groups

60% female   40% male

- **Specialist medical school**, a partnership between Brighton and Sussex universities.
- **Teaching staff:** 20 full-time; 210 part-time/module lecturers/teaching clinicians.
- **Broad study area:** Medicine.

Freshers

- **Admissions information:** 3 A-levels required (or 2 plus 2 AS-levels); both biology and chemistry to AS-level, one with an A at A-level.
- **First degree entrants:** 135 UK, full-time.
- **Points on entry:** 340+ (average).
- **Accommodation:** All 1st years housed who apply by the deadline.

Profile

Institution

Founded: 2002. **Structural features:** A partnership between the universities of Brighton and Sussex. Clinical teaching at the Royal Sussex County Hospital (medical education centre) and within the University Hospitals NHS Trust. **Site:** Falmer, 4 miles from Brighton town centre (years 1–2); Brighton (Royal Sussex County Hospital, years 3–4); various teaching hospitals in the south east (Year 5). **How to get there:** Falmer site close to station; buses and trains from Brighton. Royal Sussex County Hospital well served by buses.

Courses

Academic features: Integration of academic and clinical aspects throughout course. Small group teaching (both academic and clinical). Students gain experience undertaking research projects.

Awarding body: Joint award by University of Brighton and University of Sussex. **Main undergraduate awards:** BM BS. **Length of courses:** 5 years.

Study opportunities & careers

Library and information services: Libraries at Falmer site and at medical education centres (Brighton), with study places, work rooms and IT suites; extended access hours. Library inductions, self-help guides. IT support staff and advice online, at library help desks and by phone. Large number of PC clusters on site (some with 24-hour access); dedicated medical suites, on campus and in clinical sites, all linked to campus network giving access to information sources, eg library catalogues, medical school e-learning resources and internet. **Study abroad:** Year 4 elective normally taken overseas.

Student services & facilities

Student advice and services: All students have personal and academic tutors. Medical and counselling services on campus including psychologists and psychotherapists. Welfare and pastoral support including chaplaincies and crèche/nursery. SU provides help on, eg loans, accommodation, benefits. **Amenities:** Grocery shops, catering outlets, laundrette, bookshop, banks, cash dispensers, post office. **Sporting facilities:** Sports halls, fitness rooms, dance studios, squash and tennis courts, soccer and rugby pitches, floodlit artificial turf pitches, sauna and solarium plus many facilities of city. **Accommodation:** All 1st years who apply by the deadline are in self-catering university accommodation (see *Brighton University* and *Sussex University*). Private rented accommodation for 4 years, but hospital accommodation for on-call duties.

Money

Living expenses budget: Budget of £7k pa (excluding tuition fees) recommended by medical school. **Financial help:** Bursaries of £510–£1020 pa for UK students whose family income is £38,300 or less. Also scholarships of £1k pa for some students from low-income families with no tradition of going to university. Merit- and sport-based scholarships and international scholarships available. **Tuition fees:** Home students pay £3225 pa. International students pay £23,678 pa.

Brighton University

Location:
Brighton, south coast of England (map 2)
Major sites in Brighton and Eastbourne; partner colleges

University of Brighton, Mithras House, Lewes Road, Brighton, East Sussex BN2 4AT
☎ Tel 01273 600900
🖷 Fax 01273 642825
✉ Email admissions@brighton.ac.uk
💻 Website www.brighton.ac.uk

Student enquiries: Admissions Office
Applications: UCAS

In brief

Total Students: 11,485

23% postgraduate
77% undergraduate

Undergraduates: 8860
90% full-time
29% mature on entry
81% UK students
48% lower socio-economic groups

52% female 48% male

- **A modern university.**
- **Teaching staff:** 930 full-time and part-time.

- **Broad study areas:** Art and architecture; education and sport; engineering; health; management and information sciences; medicine. See also the entry for *Brighton & Sussex Medical School*.

Freshers

- **Admissions information:** AS-levels accepted in combination with 2+ A-levels or equivalent. UCAS tariff used.
- **First degree entrants:** 3085 UK, full-time.
- **Points on entry:** 260 (average).
- **Drop-out rate:** 8% in 1st year.
- **Accommodation:** Majority of 1st years housed (guaranteed for international students who meet application dates and criteria).

Profile

Institution

Founded: University status 1992. Formerly Brighton Polytechnic, from merger of colleges of technology and teacher training, and school of art. **Site:** 3 major sites in Brighton, one at Eastbourne. Also manages University Centre Hastings. **How to get there:** Under 1 hour by train from London, 35 mins from Gatwick Airport; M/A23 from London/Gatwick to Brighton, A22 to Eastbourne. A27 connects two towns. Bus and train services provide regular inter-site travel. **Structural features:** Brighton & Sussex Medical School, joint with Sussex University.

Courses

Academic features: 4-year degree programme including preparatory year (UK4) for students from Gulf States. **Awarding body:** University of Brighton. **Main undergraduate awards:** BA, BA QTS, BSc, BEng, MEng, MPharm, FdA, FdSc. **Length of courses:** 3 years; others 4 years (BEd, MEng and sandwich, some part-time courses); 2 years (FdA/Sc).

Study opportunities & careers

Library and information services: 5 libraries, 612,500+ volumes. 1500+ study places. Library and IT services converged. Information provision, £73 pa spent for each student (FTE). Library and computer induction sessions; information advisors on each site. **Other learning resources:** Media units for film and video, including darkroom and graphic design studio. **Careers:** Careers counsellor and information rooms on all sites.

Student services & facilities

Student advice and services: Welfare and accommodation officers, doctor, personal counsellor, chaplain, disability support services at each site; 2 nurseries. Community liaison officer. **Amenities:** Bars; bookshops at Moulsecoomb and Falmer sites. **Sporting facilities:** At Falmer site, playing fields, 2 gymnasia, access to well-equipped Brighton Health and Racquets Club; Eastbourne is a regional centre for elite athletes with swimming pool, sports hall, activity halls, fitness suite, synthetic pitch; at Moulsecoomb, sports centre, fitness suite, 2 badminton courts. **Accommodation:** 1900 places in halls of residence in Brighton and Eastbourne (many ensuite), and with 24-hour staff cover; rent £66–£100 pw self-catering (plus bills), £105–£128 pw catered (plus bills), most on 39–40-week contracts. Also 300 places in university-managed flats. Most students in privately owned accommodation for 2+ years: self-catering rent £85–£95 pw in Brighton, £75 pw in Eastbourne. Accommodation office runs house-hunting days (students can meet potential flatmates and househunt together); Brightonstudentpad is online search service.

Money 💰

Living expenses budget: Minimum budget of £7k pa (excluding tuition fees) recommended by university. **Term-time work:** University recommends maximum of 15 hours/week term-time work for full-time students (35% believed to work). Some jobs available on campus, eg student ambassadors; university student employment office (careers centre) helps find work in and out of term. **Financial help:** Bursaries of £1080 pa for home students with a family income of up to £25k pa; reducing on a sliding scale to £540 pa for those with a family income of up to £43,300. Between 40%–50% of students likely to receive a bursary. Also 210 merit-based scholarships (of £1k), based on end-of-year assessments; 5 scholarships of £1k each for disabled athletes; range of sports scholarships and international scholarships awarded on merit. **Tuition fees:** Home students pay up to £3225 pa for first degrees (£710 for sandwich years). International students pay £9240 pa (classroom), £10,740 (lab/studio); international fees are fixed for the duration of the course.

Student view

Joel Andrews, Vice-President, Communications and Finance, Brighton Students' Union, and Editor of Student Newspaper

Living

What's it like as a place to live? It's a fun, vibrant city with something to offer everyone. **How's the student accommodation?** Due to there being 2 unis in the area, there are many student houses available that are generally of a good quality. **What's the student population like?** 10% of Brighton residents are students, which, coupled with Brighton's unique, friendly feel, make this an awesome place to study. **How do students and locals get on?** Students are spread throughout the community, and as such town-gown relationships are good.

Studying

What's it like as a place to study? There are a huge variety of courses available; I found my tutors fantastic and always around to help. **What are the teaching staff like?** Staff take the view that students are the future researchers and innovators and provide great support accordingly.

Socialising

What are student societies like? Huge range of societies with a large budget to bid for, lots of support for starting a new society. **What's a typical night out?** No such thing in Brighton! **And how much does it cost?** £20–£40 a night, loads of student deals. **How can you get home safely?** CityCabs offering 10% student discount and set fares to halls.

Money

Is it an expensive place to live? With so many bars and clubs there is always work to keep you in money! **Average price of a pint?** £2.80. **And the price of a takeaway?** £8. **What's the part-time work situation?** University runs part-time and full-time job workshops to help you find employment whilst at uni.

Summary

What's the best feature about the place? The friendly, diverse and 100% unique feel whilst studying here.

And the worst? Having to leave uni at the end of it! **And to sum it all up?** Most people who come here to study don't leave – that speaks for itself!

More info: Check out the union website on www.ubsu.net.

Bristol Old Vic Theatre School

Location:
Bristol, west of
England (map 2)
Main site in
Clifton plus other
venues

📧 Bristol Old Vic Theatre School, 2 Downside Road,
Clifton, Bristol BS8 2XF
☎ Tel 0117 973 3535
📠 Fax 0117 923 9371
✉ Email enquiries@oldvic.ac.uk
💻 Website www.oldvic.ac.uk

Student enquiries: Admissions
Applications: Direct

In brief

Total Students: 160    100% full-time ● ● 95% UK/EU students   40% female   60% male

- **Specialist drama school.** A member of the Conservatoire for Dance & Drama.
- **Teaching staff:** 24 full-time, 40+ visiting lecturers.
- **Broad study areas:** Acting, stage management, theatre arts and technique, broadcast skills, theatre design and costume, scenic art, production management, theatre management, television and radio drama, directing.

Freshers

- **Admissions information:** All applicants auditioned or interviewed; academic qualifications are only part of entry criteria. Acting auditions also in London. Mature applicants welcomed.
- **Accommodation:** No School accommodation.

Profile

Institution

Founded: 1946. **Structural features:** Member of the Conservatoire for Dance & Drama; associate school of Bristol UWE. Close ties and working arrangements with Bristol Old Vic Company, BBC Radio, ITV and both local universities. **Site:** Main Clifton site, former BBC Christchurch Studios, and other performance venues around the city. **How to get there:** City is well served by rail (mainline west to Bristol Parkway) and coach; close to M4 (for London, Heathrow and south Wales) and M5 (Birmingham and the north and west country). School adjacent to Dart bus stop.

Courses

Academic features: Vocational training for theatre and related media by working professionals; visiting specialists in all fields of the profession. Acting and stage management courses accredited by NCDT. **Awarding body:** Bristol UWE (University of the West of England). **Main undergraduate awards:** BA, Diplomas (professional and postgraduate). **Length of courses:** 3 years; others 2 and 1 years.

Study opportunities & careers

Library and information services: Link to Bristol UWE library, a stock of play sets, individual texts and music. Also local libraries and certain students use Bristol University theatre collection. All courses work with School's IT service, open 10 hours/day. 1:10 workstations to students, all with internet access; IT support from 2 technicians. **Other learning resources:** Facilities for stage management, lighting, sound, television and radio, prop making, carpentry, stage design, costume, scenic art, production management. **Careers:** Information and advice given. No guarantee of placement.

Student services & facilities

Student advice and services: Access to local health centre. **Sporting facilities:** Local facilities only. **Accommodation:** No school accommodation. Private accommodation in nearby areas, approx £75–£100 pw; accommodation officer helps find digs 3 weeks before commencement.

Money

Living expenses budget: Minimum budget of £6k pa (excluding tuition fees) recommended by school. **Term-time work:** Many students find evening work locally, but pressure of coursework may prohibit this in the final year. **Financial help:** Conservatoire bursaries of £1700 pa (£2100 in final year) for UK students whose family income is up to £25k; tapered down to £100 pa (£500 in final year) where family income is £37,900–£39,300. No school personal loans; advice about grant-making trusts available. **Tuition fees:** Home students pay £3225 pa for first degrees. International students pay £13,340 pa.

Student view

Tiny but highly regarded school, close to one of the most exciting city centres. It runs both technical and performance courses in a caring but rigorous and professional manner. High ratio of tutors to students and low intake ensure a high-quality and dedicated, friendly learning atmosphere. Long, long hours and total dedication needed (not much time left for life outside). Students get out of it what they put in and more! Students get access to the best technical expertise and equipment in Christchurch Studios (ex-BBC, also home to the Insects), which are owned by the school. Unique middle year on 3-year acting course takes students on tour round West Country schools, theatres and churches, offering invaluable lessons in voice, performance, stamina and diplomacy skills. By the time they graduate, students will have been in nearly 200 performances in 18 months and many television, film and radio programmes. The courses give actors and technical students a wide range of experience, which makes us well-rounded, highly employable professionals. Away from the traffic and rent of London, BOVTS attracts top agents, casting directors and producers to auditions and shows every year, and prides itself on producing an enormous variety of versatile and dedicated graduates.

Student footnotes

Housing: No school housing but accommodation officer helps. **Eats:** Cheap snacks and sandwiches on premises. **Drink:** Beaufort Arms, Renatos, King's Arms, Coronation Tap, Channings. Bristol packed with bars, restaurants, etc. **Nightlife:** Theatre Royal and New Vic, Watershed, Arnolfini. 5 cinemas including multiplex, ice skating, go-karting, bowling, quasar, etc; countless late bars nearby as well as clubs in town. **Sports:** Both Bristol universities have large sporting facilities; city packed with health clubs and gyms. **Financial help:** Some government support; number of school funds and trusts. **Jobs:** Front-of-house work at the Bristol Old Vic, bar/restaurant work, hotel security, supermarket staff. Very difficult with long working day – weekends best. Almost impossible in final year. **Informal name:** BOVTS. **Past students:** Brian Blessed, Samantha Bond, Simon Cadell, Annette Crosbie, Daniel Day-Lewis, Jeremy Irons, Jane Lapotaire, Tim Pigott-Smith, Miranda Richardson, Patricia Routledge, Gene Wilder, Aled Jones, Helen Baxendale, Sean Pertwee, Pete Postlethwaite, Richard Coyle, Oded Fehr, Olivia Williams. **More info?** Email students@oldvic.ac.uk.

Bristol University

Location:
Bristol, south-west of England (map 2)
Main teaching site in Clifton; veterinary science 15 miles away

University of Bristol, Senate House, Tyndall Avenue, Bristol BS8 1TH
☎ Tel 0117 928 9000
📠 Fax 0117 925 1424
✉ Email ug-admissions@bristol.ac.uk
🖥 Website www.bristol.ac.uk

*Student enquiries: Undergraduate Admissions Office
Applications: UCAS*

In brief

Total Students: 21,135

19% postgraduate
81% undergraduate

Undergraduates: 17,085
75% full-time ● ● 90% UK students
35% mature on entry ● ● 29% lower socio-economic groups

63% female   37% male

- **A top UK research-intensive university.**
- **Teaching staff:** Approx 2400 full-time.
- **Broad study areas:** Arts; engineering; medical and veterinary sciences; medicine and dentistry; science; social sciences and law.

Freshers

- **Admissions information:** AS-levels welcomed in combination with 3 A-levels or equivalent; alternative qualifications are often acceptable, particularly access courses. Offers normally in terms of grades, rather than UCAS tariff.
- **First degree entrants:** Approx 3215 UK, full-time.
- **Points on entry:** 445 (average).
- **Drop-out rate:** 4% in 1st year.
- **Accommodation:** Almost all 1st years housed.

Profile

Institution
Founded: 1876, charter granted 1909. **Site:** University precinct ¼ mile from city centre. Clinical veterinary science in Langford, 15 miles south west. **How to get there:** City well served by rail (main line west to Bristol Temple Meads) and coach; close to M4 (for London, Heathrow and south Wales) and M5 (Birmingham and the north and west country). Good bus services around Bristol; many students use bikes.

Courses
Academic features: Many science and engineering courses include year in industry or year abroad. BSc deaf studies was first in UK (Centre for Deaf Studies now 30 years old). **Awarding body:** University of Bristol. **Main undergraduate awards:** BA, BDS, BEng, MEng, BSc, MSci, BVSc, LLB, MBChB. **Length of courses:** 3 years; 4 years (MEng, MSci and degrees involving languages, study abroad or industrial experience, MBChB graduate entry); 5 years (MBChB, BDS, BVSc, MEng); 6 years (MBChB, BDS, BVSc with pre-medical/dental/veterinary year).

Study opportunities & careers

Library and information services: 13 branch libraries. About 1.4 million volumes of printed books and periodicals, around 10,000 electronic journals; 2000+ study places. Short loan collections for heavily used items. Late-night opening in arts and social sciences library. Professional subject liaison and support for academic users; induction and training for new students; courses and materials to develop personal and computing skills. Information provision, £180 pa spent for each student (FTE). Library and IT services merged. Many computer rooms in university precinct (some open 24 hours/day) and in halls of residence; wireless access to university network in many areas. IT helpdesks in computer centre and arts library, ResNet help for residential networking facilities; information handling skills courses (including web searching, databases, etc). Specialist collections include original notebooks and sketchbooks of Isambard Kingdom Brunel, collection of election manifestos since 1892. Further information: www.bristol.ac.uk/is. **Study/work abroad:** Nearly 500 students a year spend time abroad as part of their degree; depending on their course, maybe 3–12 months at one of over 140 universities in Europe, North and South America, Australia and Asia or in a work placement in Europe.

Student services & facilities

Student advice and services: These include student health centre, multi-faith chaplaincy, nurseries, counselling service, international advice and support, careers service, access unit for deaf and disabled students. **Amenities:** Three theatres, university bookshop. Active SU with bars, restaurants, recreational facilities. **Sporting facilities:** 33-metre indoor swimming pool, fitness training facilities, squash courts, sports centre, playing fields including indoor tennis centre, 2 synthetic pitches (1 water-based) and grass pitches for all outdoor sports. **Accommodation:** 1st years guaranteed accommodation, so long as they live outside the Bristol area, have firmly accepted their offer and apply for accommodation by the deadlines (about 96%). 3630 places (3470 for 1st years; 140 places in shared rooms), half catered, half self-catering. Rents: catered places £109–£136 pw (£92 pw if sharing) for 38-week let; self-catered places £73–£116 (£52 if sharing), 38- or 46-week lets. Most students live in privately owned accommodation after the 1st year, rent £70–£100 pw plus bills.

Money

Living expenses budget: Most students have a budget of £6500–£8500 pa for living expenses (excluding tuition fees). **Term-time work:** University suggests term-time work limited to 14 hours a week for full-time students. Some work on campus in bars, offices and libraries. University jobshop helps students find work off campus. **Financial help:** Bursaries of £1200 pa for most UK students with a family income of up to £50k; further £1075 pa for those resident in BA or BS postal codes. Scholarships for musical, dramatic and sporting talent. Also government funds for home students in greatest financial difficulty; hardship loans and short-term loans available for students in unexpected financial difficulty. **Tuition fees:** Home students pay £3225 pa for first degrees (but £17,200 pa if taking veterinary science as a second undergraduate degree). International students pay £11,450 pa (classroom-based), £14,750 pa (lab/studio-based), £26,600 pa (clinical).

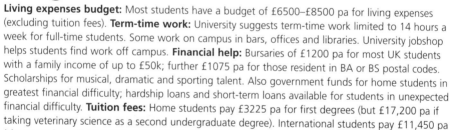

Student view

Bristol really has something for everyone. The city itself is big enough to offer a diverse range of restaurants, cafés and clubs whilst being small enough to feel a sense of community. The university is in the heart of the city and is widely considered to be academically excellent. Students play an important part in the local community and there is a real sense that they are accepted. They tend to stay close to the main university site, living in Clifton (by far the most expensive but popular with some students), Redland or Cotham (hundreds of large houses to let). Expensive city to live in but still possible to find reasonably priced housing and the university's accommodation office is invaluable. Very student-friendly city with loads to offer socially; literally hundreds of pubs and clubs (including the famous Whiteladies Road that 1st years experience on pub crawls!). Established comedy scene is popular; several art galleries and cultural centres including the Watershed and Arnolfini. Music scene not as famous as it was, but loads of venues for new bands to play, and big bands play at SU Bristol Academy and Colston Hall. Hundreds of places to eat, with cuisine from around the world. Large, busy SU offers commercial services (eg 3 bars, theatre, swimming pool and shop) and second largest gig venue in Bristol. It has 7 full-time sabbatical officers, who represent students, offer advice (eg tips to avoid exam stress). Loads to get involved in; hundreds of clubs and societies, from ballroom dancing to real ale. Diverse student base although disproportionate number of students from independent schools and home counties/London (but stereotypes worse than the reality). Hardship funds available for those who do have problems. Careers service and graduate employment record both good. Bristol students work hard and there is a culture of success. Courses vary in structure: some assessed continually with essays; others rely largely on end-of-year examinations. The university is famed for its medical and veterinary schools. A great city to study and work in.

Student footnotes

Housing: Halls in Stoke Bishop. House/flat shares in Clifton, Cotham, Redland or Hotwells (contracts usually for 52 weeks/year); look in *Bristol Evening Post* or through the Accommodation Office. **Eats:** Union restaurant and burger bar, Café Zuma. Good local takeaways. York Café in Clifton serves one of the best fry-ups and is a popular hangover hangout. **Drink:** Epi (Union) bar or hall bars; beer £1.70+ a pint. Smiles bitter is the popular local brew, sold widely but especially at the Highbury Vaults. Cider in Coronation Tap. Kings Street/Clifton popular but expensive. **Nightlife:** Lots of national bands, comedians etc in SU; local/student bands in pubs (eg Bristol Bridge, Kings Arms). **Locals:** Quite friendly. Hard to get insurance if living in St Pauls. **Sports:** University sports centre on campus; pool attached to Union; 46 sports clubs. Sports grounds 1 mile from halls, 4 miles from SU. **Travel:** University scholarship schemes. Lift shares available. **Financial help:** Access funds, payments of £20–£200. **Jobs:** Careers service jobshop helps find work. **Best features:** City and social life; good teaching. **And worst:** A little pricey. **Past students** Sue Lawley (BBC), Susan Engels (actress, RSC), Frances Horovitz (poet), Hugh Cornwell (lead singer with the Stranglers), Paul Boateng MP (cabinet minister), David Hunt MP, Alistair Stewart (newsreader), Lembit Opik MP, Emily Watson (actress); Matt Lucas, David Walliams (comedians); Michael Winterbottom (film director), Chris Morris (satirist), Simon Pegg (actor). **More info?** Check out the union website (www.ubu.org.uk).

Bristol UWE

Location:
Bristol, west of England (map 2)
4 campuses in and around city; partner colleges

University of the West of England, Frenchay Campus, Coldharbour Lane, Bristol BS16 1QY
☎ Tel 0117 328 3333
🖷 Fax 0117 328 2810
✉ Email Admissions@uwe.ac.uk
🖳 Website www.uwe.ac.uk

Student enquiries: Admissions and International Applications: UCAS

In brief

Total Students: 31,075

21% postgraduate
79% undergraduate

Undergraduates: 24,405
79% full-time
26% mature on entry
91% UK students
29% lower socio-economic groups

57% female   43% male

- **A modern university.**
- **Teaching staff:** 1013 full-time equivalent.
- **Broad study areas:** Art and design; built environment; business; computing; education; engineering; health; humanities; languages; law; science; social science.

Freshers

- **Admissions information:** AS-levels accepted in combination with 2+ A-levels equivalent. UCAS tariff used.
- **First degree entrants:** 4970 UK, full-time.
- **Points on entry:** 260 (average).
- **Drop-out rate:** 9% in 1st year.
- **Accommodation:** All 1st years housed who require it.

Profile

Institution

Founded: 1969 as Bristol Polytechnic, from technical, commerce, art, education and health colleges; university status in 1992. **Site:** 4 campuses and 3 regional centres (school of health and social care). **How to get there:** City well served by rail (main line to Bristol Parkway and Temple Mead stations) and coach; close to M4 (for London, Heathrow and south Wales) and M5 (Birmingham, the north and the west country). Buses from Bristol city centre to all campuses; inter-campus/city centre buses free for most students in UWE-managed accommodation.

Courses

Awarding body: University of the West of England (Bristol UWE). **Main undergraduate awards:** BA, BA(ITE), BSc, BEng, LLB. **Length of courses:** 3 years; 4 years (sandwich).

Study opportunities & careers

Library and information services: 5 service points, total of 723,000 books, 16,000+ periodicals (75+% electronic); 2010 study places, electronic information retrieval facilities in all libraries; faculty librarians run introduction and in-depth information retrieval skills sessions for new students. Information provision, £87 pa spent for each student (FTE). Separate IT service. 1700 networked PCs with access to library catalogue, internet, mail and specialist software; 24-hour facilities; wireless access in all libraries and many communal areas; access from 4000+ accommodation rooms. IT assistance available at support centre during working hours and by phone including at evenings and weekends. **Study abroad:** Language students spend a period abroad; opportunities on some degrees for study or work placements in Europe through Erasmus (some teaching in English) plus exchanges in USA. Students can study a language as part of their degree or as an additional module or through self-tuition facilities. **Careers:** Information, advice and careers events.

Student services & facilities

Student advice and services: Student welfare, counselling, health and wellbeing services, nursery (student discount); faith and spirituality centre; advice centre. **Amenities:** Bookshop, bank, SU shop on 4 campuses; centre for performing arts, snooker room, sport and activities centre, media centre, jobshop, print shop, 5 bars, 100+ clubs and societies. **Sporting facilities:** Multi-purpose sports centre, including sports hall (badminton, basketball, netball and volleyball courts, indoor hockey and cricket), glass-backed squash courts, aerobics studio, 70-station fitness suite and weights; climbing wall; also international-standard water-based astropitch. **Accommodation:** All 1st years who require it (and apply by 1 July) are guaranteed university-approved accommodation. 4079 self-catering places available, £87–£122 pw, Sept–July. Students live in privately owned accommodation for 2+ years: rent £60–£130 pw self-catering. Demand high in January–March each year.

Money

Living expenses budget: Minimum budget of £8k pa (excluding tuition fees) recommended by university (for students who go home in vacations). **Term-time work:** Students advised not to work more than 14 hours pw (average) during term time. SU Jobshop offers (free) part-time job-seeking service. **Financial help:** Bursaries of £1k pa for UK students whose family income is up to £25k. Also bursaries of £1k pa for students from Access courses. Some £750k government funds; plus short-term loans, £30k international students' hardship fund; awards range from £100–£3500 pa. Special help for student parents. Apply for help to Student Advice and Welfare Services. **Tuition fees:** Home students pay £3225 pa for first degrees. International students pay £8250 pa (classroom), £8700 pa (lab-based).

Student view — Katy Phillips, Vice-President, Student Representative Council (Marketing course)

Living

What's it like as a place to live? Bristol is a busy and vibrant city, there's always something going on. **How's the student accommodation?** The new student village has allowed us to create a UWE community on campus as well as offer a range of city centre accommodation and student housing. **What's the student population like?** Varied: from local undergraduates to postgraduates and international students. **How do students and locals get on?** Students do loads of community volunteering with both the SU and the university.

Studying

What's it like as a place to study? There are a wide variety of courses and options for Joint Honours study at UWE so students can find a course to suit them.

Socialising

What are student societies like? There are a huge range from religious groups to sporting and interest societies. Also if a student wants to set something up, they are given funding and training on doing so. **What's a typical night out?** Again, there is much on offer: bars, clubs, comedy nights, etc. **And how much does it cost?** Fun can be had on a budget in Bristol. Great for students! **How can you get home safely?** With student and public buses as well as taxis, transport is in abundance.

Money

Is it an expensive place to live? It depends where you go; the prices on the whole reflect city living. **Average price of a pint?** Less than £2. **And the price of a takeaway?** Depends on what you fancy! **What's the part-time work situation?** The union offers a jobshop with over 6500 jobs every year, which are flexible around student studies.

Summary

What's the best feature about the place? The diversity of our campuses. **And to sum it all up?** A really exciting and fun-filled place.

Past students: Jack Russell (England wicket keeper), Mark Knopfler (Dire Straits guitarist), Kyran Bracken (England rugby player), Dawn Primarolo MP. **More info?** Union website (www.uwesu.net).

British School of Osteopathy

Location:
*central London
(map 3)*
**Single site
south of London
Bridge**

The British School of Osteopathy, 275 Borough High Street, London SE1 1JE
☎ Tel 020 7089 5316
🖷 Fax 020 7089 5300
✉ Email admissions@bso.ac.uk
💻 Website www.bso.ac.uk

*Student enquiries: Student Recruitment and
Admissions Officer
Applications: UCAS for full-time
(direct for 'mixed mode' pathway)*

In brief

Total Students: 520

15% postgraduate
85% undergraduate

Undergraduates: 450
80% full-time   90% UK students
50% mature
on entry

60% female   40% male

- **Specialist osteopathic college.**
- **Teaching staff:** 16 full-time, 120 part-time.
- **Broad study area** Osteopathy.

Freshers
- **First degree entrants:** 90 UK, full-time.
- **Accommodation:** No college accommodation.

Profile

Institution
Founded: 1917. **Site:** One teaching site and a clinic in Borough. **How to get there:** Close to London Bridge (over- and underground) and Borough (underground) stations; various bus routes.

Courses
Academic features: Course is student-centred with a focus on problem-solving in a clinical context: includes clinical supervision, practical sessions, tutorials, seminars and self-managed learning. Nearly all clinical tutors run their own practices. Course can be taken by mixed mode (3 years mixed distance- and on-site learning then 2 years full-time). **Awarding body:** University of Bedfordshire. **Main undergraduate award:** MOst. **Length of courses:** 4 years (full-time); 5 years (mixed mode).

Study opportunities & careers
Library and information services: 10,000 volumes, 30 periodicals, 100 study places; also videos and DVDs. Specialist collections: rare books on osteopathy. Separate IT service, open 60 hours/week in term time. Ratio workstations to students 1:10, access to internet from all computers; IT support available. 2-hour introduction to library and information services for new students; computer training given if needed.

Student services & facilities

Student advice and services: Dyslexia tutor, counselling service, student learning adviser, welfare officer. **Amenities:** SU active in organising social functions with similar institutions. **Sporting facilities:** Student sports clubs make arrangements for playing facilities with other institutions, eg local medical schools, London South Bank and Bedfordshire universities. **Accommodation:** No college accommodation. Reasonably priced accommodation locally or in halls of local universities; most students share rented accommodation. Rents locally £76–£100 pw.

Money

Living expenses budget: Minimum budget of £6k pa (excluding tuition fees) recommended by school. **Financial help:** Bursaries of £510 pa for UK students where the family income is £25k; bursary holders may be eligible for a further £205 pa if they are either local or from an access course. Some welfare funds available for students experiencing severe hardship. **Tuition fees:** Home students pay £3225 pa for first degree. International students pay £8600 pa (for mixed mode study, home students pay £3600 pa, international students £6150 pa).

Student view

The largest alternative-medicine training centre in Europe, on Borough High Street just south of London Bridge. It's in a large 1960s-style building; inside it is spacious and light, providing a good atmosphere for both students and patients. An extensive library containing a large collection of osteopathic as well as conventional medical literature. It's virtually next door to Borough tube station, 10 mins' walk to London Bridge station (tube and rail) and around 30 mins' walk to the West End (less by tube); there is storage for bicycles. Small union, not politically active, but channels its resources into welfare, sports, entertainments and staff relations. The course involves a good deal of physical contact between students whilst learning and practising osteopathic technique; this doesn't mean it is a 4-year orgy but does mean that the prospect of stripping down to underwear becomes almost an everyday occurrence and physical intimacy becomes demystified. A demanding course: a part-time counsellor provides confidential support for students (even the most resilient can feel vulnerable sometimes). Workload is phenomenal; the course is much the same as medical school (one year less to do it in!) but training is holistic, ie health and illness are looked at in terms of the patient rather than the disease. Much less emphasis on biochemistry and pharmacology than at med school, since osteopathy is a drug-free system of medicine. Anatomy vitally important: students learn the entire body at a level of detail doctors only approach during postgraduate surgical training. Much of the course is on osteopathic technique. Clinical training starts with observation in 1st year and gradually increases, under supervision, until fourth-year students see patients right through from taking their case histories to providing final treatment. Work assessed by a combination of written exams, viva voces, essays and Objective Structured Practical Examinations (OSPEs). There is inevitably some attrition, mostly 1st year. Some 40% of students are 18–22-year-olds, mostly straight from sixth form; another 40% are between 25–35, many of them graduates; the remainder are in their late 30s, even into their 40s, doing what they have always wanted to do before it is too late!

Student footnotes

Housing: No school halls, but some available for BSO students in local unis. **Eats:** Small canteen with sandwiches and limited hot food. Very good value. **Drink:** SU has cheapest drinks locally. Stella is main beer. **Nightlife:** Lots of SU social events; good connections with nearby bars. **Locals:** Very friendly in bars and sandwich shops. **Sports:** Weight-training room. Off-campus access to any sport you can think of if enough people interested. **Financial help:** Osteopathic Education Foundation help some students from 2nd year. **Jobs:** The heavyweight courses mean students do clinical work during the so-called holidays. Good time management and masses of energy enable some students to earn some money. **Informal name:** BSO. **Best features:** Good atmosphere – close knit. **More info?** Enquiries to any SU member via the school.

Brunel University

Location:
west of London,
within M25
(map 3)
**Single campus
in Uxbridge**

✉ Brunel University, Uxbridge, Middlesex UB8 3PH
☎ Tel 01895 274000
🖷 Fax 01895 203096
💻 Website www.brunel.ac.uk

*Student enquiries: Admissions Office (applications) or
Marketing (course information, open days)
Applications: UCAS*

In brief

Total Students: 13,885

26% postgraduate
74% undergraduate

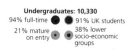
Undergraduates: 10,330
94% full-time   91% UK students
21% mature   38% lower
on entry   socio-economic
                 groups

50% female   50% male

- **Research-intensive university.**
- **Teaching staff:** 593 full-time, 471 part-time.
- **Broad study areas:** Biosciences, business and management, design, drama, economics and finance, education, electronic and computer engineering, English, film and TV studies, health studies, history, information systems and computing, law, mathematical sciences, mechanical engineering, media studies, music, politics, psychology, social anthropology, social care, sociology, sports sciences,

Freshers
- **Admissions information:** AS-levels accepted in combination with 2+ A-levels or equivalent. UCAS tariff scores for most courses plus specific subject grades.
- **First degree entrants:** 2950 UK, full-time.
- **Points on entry:** 310 average.
- **Drop-out rate:** 9% in 1st year.
- **Accommodation:** Most 1st years housed.

Profile

Institution
Founded: 1966; merged with West London Institute 1995. **Site:** Single campus at Uxbridge. **How to get there:** West Drayton mainline station or Uxbridge tube station (Metropolitan and Piccadilly lines). Close to M4, M25 and M40. **Special features:** Music and sport bursaries. Associate student scheme for mature part-time returners. 27 research centres including contemporary music, bioengineering, cancer

genetics, environmental research, international law and multimedia systems, public health, infant behaviour.

Courses

Academic features: Many degree courses, with or without sandwich element, emphasise relevance and practical application. Modular structure allows some students to add, eg languages, management, computer science, or to take Joint Honours in a range of disciplines. Foundation courses in IT and engineering for applicants without science A-levels. Optional 1-year extensions to BEng courses for MEng/Diploma in engineering management. **Awarding body:** Brunel University. **Main undergraduate awards:** BSc, BA, BEng, LLB. **Length of courses:** 3 year; 4 years (sandwich); up to 6 years (part-time, some courses).

Study opportunities & careers

Library and information services: Library stocks 458,000+ books, 17,000 journal titles (of which 16,500 are electronic); 1200 study spaces and 280 PCs; open 73+ hours/week in term time. Information provision, £139 pa spent for each student (FTE). New students have subject-specific induction on library, IT, online learning and effective learning services. Separate IT service: 1300 open-access workstations, 5000 access ports in halls and remote access; wireless provision; all linked to library and internet. Access to workstations 24 hours/day; IT facilities with staff support (and further support by email) open 10 hours/weekday. Some schools offer IT skills courses. **Other learning resources:** Learning and teaching development unit, audio-visual centre, EFL/language centre, web-based learning remote IT access, arts centre. **Study abroad:** Students can take language modules as assessed part of degree; many opt for extra-curricular courses. Some student exchanges with Europe and USA. **Careers:** Information and advice services.

Student services & facilities

Student advice and services: Medical centre, chaplaincy, counsellors, assistive technology centre, placement and careers centre, jobshop, welfare unit. **Amenities:** Dedicated student centre, bank, 2 supermarkets, pharmacy, student newspaper, radio station, refectory, coffee and snack bars, university art gallery, art and music classes, student music bursaries. **Sporting facilities:** 2 multi-purpose sports halls; indoor athletics centre; all-weather facilities, eg 6-lane 400m athletics track, full field events facilities, with sports pavilion; pitches for football (5), rugby (2), floodlit all-weather hockey pitch; 2 full-sized floodlit, synthetic playing fields; 4 squash courts; artificial climbing wall; fitness suite; 'free-weight' strength training room; sports injury and health promotion services from fully trained and qualified staff; sportsbar. **Accommodation:** Most 1st-year students in university accommodation. 4571 self-catering halls places (most ensuite), rent £81.50 pw (£98–£100 pw ensuite); places in ex-RAF flats £94 pw (incl bills); studio flats for couples, £150 pw. Most students in privately owned accommodation for 2+ years; rent locally £85–£90 pw. for self-catering.

Money

Living expenses budget: Minimum budget of £7k pa (excluding tuition fees) recommended by university. **Term-time work:** University allows term-time work for full-time students. University jobshop helps find part-time and vacation work, locally and on campus. **Financial help:** Bursaries of £1k pa for UK students whose family income is up to £25k, and of £500 pa where family income is £25k–£50k. Up to 25 scholarships, up to £3k pa, for students from targeted schools or colleges. **Tuition fees:** Home students pay £3225 pa for first degrees (£815 for year out on 'thick' sandwich course, £2020 pa on 'thin'; foundation course £1615). International students pay £8300 pa (classroom), £10,200 (lab/studio).

Student view — Rosanne Mallett (4th year Psychology)

Living

What's it like as a place to live? When living on campus, all the halls are close together and all are good quality. As a town, Uxbridge is fine, shopping and eating are good. Bit chavvy at the weekend though! If on campus you pretty much never have to leave – there's shops, a bank, 2 good bars, a gym . . . and of course library and 24-hour computers. **How's the student accommodation?** Uni accommodation is good, quite expensive but apparently not bad compared with other London unis (if we are to be considered in London!). Most are ensuite, but the standard ones are still fine too. In the last three years lots and lots of new halls have been built, all in the style of flats with ensuites and good disabled facilities. There are also couples flats in the new halls that have just been built, which are more like a riverside complex of flats than halls. Off-campus housing is a mix. There are some grotty, awful places, but if you look hard enough and early enough there are good houses there to be had. Some local estate agents do try and rip you off, charging £370 a month whatever the quality of the house, as they know that in the end people will be forced to take their houses and pay whatever they have to. **What's the student population like?** Brunel is very 'ethnically diverse'; it's a mix of people, some who have travelled from all over the country to go to uni and have the uni experience, and another half who live in Harrow and have come here with their friends from college and see it as more of a college than a uni. There are also many international students, and there seem to be more disabled students this year with the new halls being completed too. It can be a friendly place, but at times it can get tense. Sometimes walking through campus at night time can be scary, with groups of people hanging around as if it's a street corner of a housing estate. This is, however, a minority, and the few incidents of muggings, etc in the area have been off campus, and I haven't heard of any in the past year or so. The student population is very diverse, but not really mixed. I work in the SU bar; in the daytime it is full of Asian students who probably live locally and use it as a place to spend their gaps in between lectures and play pool, etc, and in the evenings the bar is full with sports teams and the people who have moved away from home to come here and want to get drunk and have a good time, etc! **How do students and locals get on?** I don't think there is a problem between locals and students, although I can't say I've ever really met someone around here who isn't a student. It wouldn't surprise me if there was trouble in town if uni boys clashed with some local guys, if they went into the wrong pubs, etc. But it's not something that you would be aware of as a student.

Studying

What's it like as a place to study? I chose to come to Brunel mainly because they offer placement courses. In engineering, design, business, social sciences and probably more, there is the option to do a thin or thick sandwich course. This means you get to spend more time at uni and get good work experience whilst you're here and still getting your loan. Many of the engineering, design and law placements are paid placements; however, many of the social science placements are unpaid. But it's better to work unpaid when getting your student loan than once you've graduated and can't get a job because you haven't had any experience. The facilities on campus are as you would expect. It gets hard to find a computer in the library, but I think this would be the case however many computers they put in the library. The organisation of some courses and some schools leaves something to be desired and this can hinder students' progress. For example, my boyfriend is the only one on his course, a combination of engineering and computer design, and he has lots of lecture clashes, with most lecturers being very unsympathetic; when one seminar could be cancelled they chose to cancel the one last thing on a Friday rather than cancel the one that he couldn't go to. **What are the teaching staff like?** Academically I think there are staff who are well regarded in their disciplines, but no one is actually well known as far as I am aware.

Socialising

What are student societies like? There are loads of societies, a massive range. There are the obvious sports teams, then there are others like Hindu society, Iranian society, every ethnicity and religion you could think of! And then hobbies such as circus skills, rock society; RAG (raise and give) is a good one to be part of; also snow club, scuba, sky diving. A lot of people are members of societies; however, I would imagine that these are mainly students who are on campus, rather than those who travel in from home. I think this is why Brunel may come off badly in some surveys, etc, as the many groups at Brunel have different experiences at Brunel. **What's a typical night out?** For me: the Academy, the SU club on campus, or Liquid in Uxbridge on a Wednesday night. Others go to Kingston (to Oceana), venture to Watford on a Monday or maybe even be daring and go into central London, risking getting stranded at the Hayes bypass by the night bus! The Academy and Liquid are your typical cheap student drunky, dancy nights. **And how much does it cost?** Academy and Liquid are a few pounds to get in on the door, £2 or so for a drink. **How can you get home safely?** If you live on the campus, getting back from the Academy is nice and easy; from Liquid it's either a 20-min walk or a £5 taxi, lots of which hang around outside the club.

Money

Is it an expensive place to live? I've never had a problem, but then I work and I'm sensible with my money! If people want to go into London regularly and get drunk all the time, then yes! **Average price of a pint?** £2 in Locos, up to £3.50 in the nice places in town. **And the price of a takeaway?** Depends what you have! **What's the part-time work situation?** University has a good 'job shop'; bar jobs, etc are snapped up early in term, I'm sure most who really want a job will manage to find one!

Summary

What's the best feature about the place? The new halls. **And the worst?** There's no grass. **And to sum it all up?** Brunel is an urban university. It's concrete, has a diverse student population . . . too many rude boys, but a campus university near London nonetheless. Good campus atmosphere and facilities.

Past students: Audley Harrison (boxer); Jo Brand (comedian); James Cracknell, Tim Foster (rowers); Kathy Cook, Iwan Thomas (athletes); Tony Adams (footballer). **More info?** Contact Vice-President (marketing and communications) (tel 01895 462200, email vp.communications@brunel.ac.uk) or check out the website at www.brunelstudents.com.

Buckingham University

Location:
north-west of
London (map 2)
**3 sites in
and near
Buckingham town**

⌨ The University of Buckingham, Hunter Street,
Buckingham MK18 1EG
☎ Tel 01280 814080
🖷 Fax 01280 824081
✉ Email admissions@buckingham.ac.uk
🖥 Website www.buckingham.ac.uk

*Student enquiries: Admissions Office
Applications: UCAS*

In brief

Total Students: 1010

29% postgraduate
71% undergraduate

Undergraduates: 720
94% full-time ● ● 32% UK students
45% mature ●
on entry

48% female 52% male

- **UK's only independent university.**
- **Teaching staff:** 75 full-time, 52 part-time.
- **Broad study areas:** Business, law, applied computing, humanities, social sciences, international studies.

Freshers

- **Admissions information:** UCAS tariff used.
- **First degree entrants:** 85 UK, full-time.
- **Points on entry:** 280 (average).
- **Drop-out rate:** 5% in 1st year
- **Accommodation:** All 1st years housed.

Profile

Institution

Founded: 1976 as an independent university. **Site:** 3 sites near Buckingham town centre. **How to get there:** By train to Milton Keynes, then taxi; by air to Heathrow (then 1½ hours drive); by car close to M1 (junction 13/15 and follow signs to Buckingham) and M40 (junction 10 and follow signs for Northampton then Buckingham). Buses from Aylesbury, Milton Keynes, Oxford and Bicester (all with railway stations). **Special features:** Britain's only independent university; receives no direct government financial support. High staff:student ratio (approx 1:10).

Courses

Academic features: 2-year degree courses, and a range of cross-disciplinary supporting courses. Academic year is 4 terms long and runs January–December. Entry to courses is available in January, July and September. Applications welcomed from mature students. **Awarding body:** University of Buckingham. **Main undergraduate awards:** BA, BSc, LLB. **Length of courses:** 2 years (8 terms); others 2¼, 2½ or 3 years.

Study opportunities & careers

Library and information services: 2 libraries: 91,620 volumes in total, 325 periodicals (plus many more electronic subscriptions), computerised catalogue; 205 study places, short loan collection. Information provision, £279 pa spent for each student (FTE). Separate IT service, access up to 24/7. 140 computers with access to internet (ratio 1:5 workstations to students). IT support from helpdesk, open 8 hours/day. One-to-one and small group instruction. **Other learning resources:** Dedicated computer-aided language learning, multimedia and computer labs. Audio-lingual language labs; satellite TV viewing room for live broadcasts in 6 European languages; video facilities; library of audio and video materials in over 12 languages. **Careers:** Information and advice service, full-time careers adviser.

Student services & facilities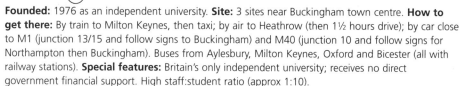

Student advice and services: University medical officer, advisory system, counsellor. Full-time support available for students with disabilities, particularly dyslexia. **Amenities:** Student social centre; concert hall. Oxford 23 miles, Milton Keynes 12 miles away. **Sporting facilities:** Varied sports and recreational facilities. **Accommodation:** All new students guaranteed university accommodation. 450 self-catering places available, £950–£1400 per term. Some students live in privately owned accommodation for 2nd year, from £500 per month (1-bed self-catering flat).

Money 💰

Living expenses budget: Minimum budget of £7500–£8k pa (excluding tuition fees) recommended by university. **Financial help:** Limited funds available for severe hardship during the course. Financial help primarily aimed at helping students with living expenses. Apply for help to Admissions Office. Scholarships available to well-qualified students. **Tuition fees:** Home students pay £8040–£8640 pa for first degrees (ie £16,680 for the whole course, whether 2, 2^1/$_2$ or 3 years). International students pay £13,500–£14,100 pa (ie £27,600 for whole course).

Student view — Duane Orridge, Students' Union President (2nd year BSc Economics)

Living
What's it like as a place to live? Buckingham is a quiet town situated in the countryside. It's the perfect place for those serious about their study. There's everything you would need, but Milton Keynes and London are not too far away. It is a real diamond in the rough. **How's the student accommodation?** Accommodation at the university is of a good standard. Students have a choice of many different locations. Beloff is usually the most popular due to its ensuite bathrooms, whilst Sunley is the quiet block reserved for mature students and those who are keen on studying. **What's the student population like?** Buckingham University has a very diverse student population. The atmosphere is extremely friendly and with such diverse cultures you get a taste of the bigger picture of the world. We have students from Australia, China, Russia, France and Germany to name a few. **How do students and locals get on?** The locals and students have an active relationship. We have a group called the Friends of the University who help organise events, such as 'meet and greet the students', to help students integrate into the town. Students from other countries get a taste of old English dinners provided by the Friends.

Studying
What's it like as a place to study? The University of Buckingham has a very personal approach to teaching. You are taught as an individual instead of another face in the crowd. Class sizes are very small, with about 12 people per lecture and 4–5 per tutorial. Buckingham is a very quiet town and the ideal place to study. **What are the teaching staff like?** The teaching staff at Buckingham are very helpful, and their sole goal is to help its students. Staff are always willing to have a one-on-one chat to help with studies or anything else for that manner. With the university's small size, staff are able to give greater attention to their students.

Socialising
What are student societies like? At Buckingham we have a number of societies: the European Society, Nigerian Society, Law Society, Football Society and many others. These societies plan events that enlighten others about their culture, objectives and goals: from events such as parties, culture days where one can indulge in different foods from around the world, to fundraising for charities. The societies are a big part of the university and students are actively encouraged to participate. **What's a typical night out?** There is the university bar, Old Tanlaw Mill, where parties are usually held. There are local English pubs in the Buckingham town where students are always welcome. You can travel 15 mins to Milton Keynes or 50 mins to London, where you can visit nightclubs, ice skating, bowling and, most important, shopping. **And how much does it cost?** A night in Buckingham

would be around £20; with the close proximity of the town to the university there are no real travel costs. To Milton Keynes you would expect to spend around £40 including taxi fare, although there are bus routes running regularly. To London would be around £50–£70 due to the taxi fare and train ride. **How can you get home safely?** Calling a local Buckingham taxi firm is usually the best bet. You can obtain the telephone number from the SU Office or the noticeboards around campus. As in most cities there is usually a line of taxis waiting for customers.

Money
Is it an expensive place to live? It all depends on whether you live on or off campus. On campus is obviously less expensive as bills are included but it depends on the student's lifestyle. **Average price of a pint?** On average £3 on a happy hour, £1 a pint at uni bar. **And the price of a takeaway?** £6–£8. **What's the part-time work situation?** With Buckingham being such a small town, employment is scarce. But Bicester Village and Milton Keynes are not far away and have plenty of part-time vacancies. Our careers office sends out regular mails with part-time work opportunities.

Summary
What's the best feature about the place? Small, private and personal with two-year degrees. **And the worst?** Crazy loud ducks along the river! **And to sum it all up?** The University of Buckingham is a diamond in the rough. We're the only private university in the UK and we've been top of the National Student Survey for the past 3 years. You can gain a first-class education from a prestigious institute where you not only complete your degree in just two years but you also take away a truly multicultural experience. Our world-class lecturers are always happy to help, be it work-related or not, and our small class sizes deliver an excellent student to staff ratio, ensuring greater attention to your progress.

Bucks New University

Location:
north-west of London
(map 2)
Campuses in High Wycombe and Uxbridge; associated colleges

Buckinghamshire New University, Queen Alexandra Road, High Wycombe, Bucks HP11 2JZ

☎ Tel 0800 0565660

📠 Fax 01494 524392

✉ Email advice@bucks.ac.uk

💻 Website www.bucks.ac.uk

Student enquiries: Directorate of Marketing, Communications and Recruitment
Applications: UCAS

In brief

Total Students: 9045

92% undergraduate

1% FE Students
7% postgraduate

Undergraduates: 8295
64% full-time ● ● 88% UK students
37% mature ● ● 37% lower
on entry ● ● socio-economic groups

51% female   49% male

- **A modern university.**
- **Teaching staff:** 350+ full-time.
- **Broad study areas:** Creativity and culture; enterprise and innovation; society and health.

Freshers
- **Admissions information:** AS-levels accepted in combination with 2+ A-levels or equivalent. All qualifications in UCAS tariff acceptable, on their own or in combination.
- **First degree entrants:** 1285 UK, full-time.
- **Points on entry:** 200–280.
- **Drop-out rate:** 10% in 1st year.
- **Accommodation:** Majority of 1st years housed.

Profile

Institution
Founded: 1893, from High Wycombe School of Science and Art; university status in 2008. **Site:** 3 campuses, 2 in High Wycombe (1 near town centre; 1 at Wellesbourne on outskirts) and 1 in Chalfont St Giles (12 miles away). **How to get there:** All sites well served by roads and railways; about 40 mins from London. Chalfont also on London Underground. Free university bus links all campuses.

Courses
Academic features: 300+ employment-orientated courses, with excellent industry contacts. **Awarding body:** Buckinghamshire New University. **Main undergraduate awards:** BA, BSc, FDSc, FDA. **Length of courses:** 3 years (full-time); 2 years (FDA, FDSc).

Study opportunities & careers
Library and information services: Main library in new Gateway building at High Wycombe; nursing library at Uxbridge. Total of 113,000 volumes, multimedia services, 2000 periodicals; electronic resources available, including remotely; 500+ study places, some with internet access. Information provision, £79 pa spent for each student (FTE). Separate IT service: 180+ computer points with access to library and internet. Information and IT skills seminars. **Study abroad:** Many courses offer international exchanges with partner institutions (including to Europe through Socrates/Erasmus scheme). **Careers:** Information, workshops, vocational guidance and careers management.

Student services & facilities
Student advice and services: Doctor, dentist, FPA, solicitor, chaplain, disabilities adviser, financial adviser. **Amenities:** SU bars, High Wycombe site. **Sporting facilities:** Brand new multi-purpose sports hall, sports performance labs, gyms, playing fields, local sports centres. **Accommodation:** Most 1st-year students housed. 650 places in self catering halls on 2 sites, in walking distance of campus and all with internet access; rent £76–£88 pw (inclusive of bills), 37-week contract. Also places in university-managed accommodation, on 44-week lets. Most students live in privately owned accommodation locally, approx £50–£75 pw self-catering.

Money
Living expenses budget: Minimum budget of approx £6k pa (excluding tuition fees) recommended by university. **Term-time work:** Students allowed term-time work (45% believed to work). Some work available on campus in SU bars, offices and casual summer work, eg decorating, office work, catering. SU runs a jobshop to help find off-campus work. **Financial help:** Non-means-tested bursaries of £500 pa for all UK/EU students, plus free entertainment, sports and course-related support, etc. Further help for students in hardship from Access to Learning Fund (UK students) and

university fund (international students). **Tuition fees:** Home students pay £3225 pa for first degrees. International students pay £7800 pa (classroom-based), £8450 pa (lab-based).

Student view — Kim Briggs, Ladies' Hockey Chairman (BA, Graphic Design and Advertising)

Living
What's it like as a place to live? High Wycombe has everything you need to live here; shops, bars, parks . . . everything! **How's the student accommodation?** Halls of residence are good value and lots of fun but when you go private you need to shop around as it can be expensive. **What's the student population like?** Everyone seems to know everyone else and there are people from all over the country and a few international students too. **How do students and locals get on?** Students and locals are completely different but we get on, and of course there are no-go areas – every town has them!

Studying
What's it like as a place to study? Bucks tends to specialise in some courses but it's not good at everything. **What are the teaching staff like?** Lecturers are helpful and professional; a lot have worked in the industry they lecture in, which is a bonus.

Socialising
What are student societies like? With the Big Deal, sports and recreational activities are free, which means more and more students are getting involved. **What's a typical night out?** Local pub, then SU bar, then kebab. **And how much does it cost?** Around £20. **How can you get home safely?** Union runs a free night bus and there are plenty of cabs.

Money
Is it an expensive place to live? Loan does last but a part-time job eases the pain! **Average price of a pint?** £2. **And the price of a takeaway?** £3. **What's the part-time work situation?** I got my part-time job through the recruitment fair, which the uni told me about.

Summary
What's the best feature about the place? Bucks has a close-knit student community. **And the worst?** The town needs some better clubs. **And to sum it all up?** Bucks has given me loads of friends, lots of fun and plenty of memories. I'll miss it when I leave. **More info?** Contact SU president on 01494 446330, email President@bucks.ac.uk or check out the website (www.bucksstudent.com).

Camberwell College of Arts

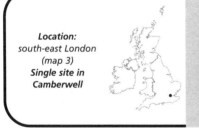

Location: south-east London (map 3) **Single site in Camberwell**

Camberwell College of Arts, Peckham Road, London SE5 8UF
☎ Tel 020 7514 6302
Fax 020 7514 6310
✉ Email enquiries@camberwell.arts.ac.uk
Website www.camberwell.arts.ac.uk

Student enquiries: College Information Officer
Applications: UCAS

In brief

Total Students: 1400
15% postgraduate
60% undergraduate

 25% FE Students

Undergraduates: 800
100% full-time ● ● 85% UK students

 60% female 40% male

- **Specialist arts college.** Part of University of the Arts London.
- **Teaching staff:** 70 permanent staff (full- and part-time), 200 visiting tutors.
- **Broad study areas:** Art and design, including ceramics, conservation, drawing, graphic design, illustration, painting, photography, sculpture, 3-D design.

Freshers
- **Accommodation:** Some 1st years housed.

Profile

Institution
Founded: 1898. **Structural features:** Constituent college of Arts London (University of the Arts London, previously London Institute). **Site:** 2 main buildings and an annexe in Camberwell, south London. **How to get there:** Train to Peckham Rye or Denmark Hill, both a 15 min walk. Buses from Waterloo, Peckham Rye, Elephant and Castle, New Cross, Oval, Vauxhall and Victoria stations.

Courses
Academic features: Courses include major subject, cross-disciplinary elective (eg philosophy, book arts, curation), as well as personal and professional development. **Awarding body:** University of the Arts London. **Main undergraduate award:** BA.

Study opportunities & careers
Library and information services: 40,000 volumes, 170 periodicals, 60 study places. Open access to computing facilities 10 hours/day, 7 days/week with staff support: 65 points with access to internet. Induction to learning resources services, subsequent sessions if required; IT training as part of personal and professional development programme. Also access to facilities of the university's central Learning Zone. **Other learning resources:** DVD/video viewing, photographic facilities. **Careers:** Information and advice service.

Student services & facilities
Student advice and services: Easy access to university's central student services (including day nursery at London College of Communication); see *Arts London*. College has own student services office, providing advice on eg grants, careers, disability and dyslexia co-ordinator. **Amenities:** College shop, bar, students' union facilities. **Accommodation:** Some students in university's halls of residence, see *Arts London*. University accommodation service helps find privately rented accommodation: rent approx £75–£115 pw, excluding bills and meals.

Money
Living expenses budget: Minimum budget of £6k–£10k pa (excluding tuition fees) recommended by university. **Term-time work:** College allows term-time work for full-time students. Some work available in college in SU bar, library work and during exhibition period; also careers service circulates lists of jobs outside college. **Financial help:** See *Arts London*. **Tuition fees:** Home students pay £3225 pa (£1570 in placement year) for first degrees. International students pay £10,700 pa.

Student view

Three buildings: the main one on Peckham Road is a 1960s monstrosity tacked, rather uncomfortably, onto a beautiful Victorian, purpose-built art school. There is also a prefab sculpture annexe and an old grammar school. South London Gallery is next door. Train stations at Peckham and Denmark Hill, but most students use buses. The great thing about Camberwell is that students can live and work in the same area, as it's so cheap! The whole area has a very arty, chilled-out vibe, and lots of students end up staying in the area when they graduate. Goldsmiths is nearby, which adds to the laid-back student atmosphere. The area is laden with a mixture of crusty pubs and slick bars. Loads of cheap shopping in Peckham (particularly vegetable markets). Peckham also has the cheapest cinema in London. Fewer international students than elsewhere at Arts, but they are also far less pretentious and more student-orientated. It's small, friendly and cosy; there is an endless stream of social events put on by students. Small classes allow for much interaction between tutors and students, and there is a good balance between structured and less-structured teaching.

Student footnotes

Housing: 3 halls of residence nearby: Brooke Hall (near Camberwell Green), Bernard Myers Hall (virtually next door) and Ewen Henderson Court (New Cross). Rent in Peckham and Camberwell is cheap, £70–£90 pw. **Eats:** College refectory; loads of cafés and restaurants locally. Tadim (amazing Turkish place, serving mezes, dolma and baklava, etc and not too expensive); BrB (two for one pizzas on Tuesdays); Fez's (greasy-spoon opposite college, simple and cheap). Camberwell and Peckham have loads more places, including curry shops, Chinese, fish and chips, etc. **Drinks:** Camberwell bar at Peckham Road: small and cosy, with reasonably priced drinks. The Castle (more posh, very nice), Hermit's Cave (old-man by day, student by night; jammed after degree show night); Joiner's Arms (like Hermit's Cave with a pool table and younger crowd). **Nightlife:** The Red Star (very boho, bit like a free party and hosts DJs and sound systems); Funky Munky (open till late, function room upstairs, DJs mostly). **Locals:** Mix! Mad people, sane people, rude people, polite people. **Sports:** Couple of small sports centres but little else locally; better sports facilities elsewhere in London. **Financial help:** Some from the university. **Jobs:** Loads of bars to work in – in Central London, locally or at college bar; library. University setting up jobshop. **Best feature:** You can live, study, work and play in one area without travelling (a lifestyle not easily attainable in London). Half the building, built in 1898, is really pretty. **Worst feature:** Half the college is in an ugly 1970s block; there is no tube; and whilst working in the studio you don't get masses of space. **Past students:** Howard Hodgkin, Gillian Ayres (painters), Mike Leigh (screenwriter and playwright), Mark McGowan (performance artist), Gillian Carnegie (Turner prize nominee 2006), the Pipettes (musicians). **More info?** University SU on 020 7514 6270 or www.suarts.org.

Cambridge University

Location:
Cambridge, East Anglia (map 2)
29 constituent colleges and university teaching centres across city

University of Cambridge, Cambridge, CB2 1TN
☎ Tel 01223 337733
Fax 01223 366383
✉ Email admissions@bradfordcollege.ac.uk
💻 Website www.cam.ac.uk
Student enquiries: Cambridge Admissions Office, Fitzwilliam House, 32 Trumpington Street, Cambridge CB2 1QY (tel 01223 333308, email admissions@cam.ac.uk); or the Admissions Tutor of any Cambridge college (website www.cam.ac.uk/admissions/undergraduate) Applications: UCAS

In brief

Total Students: 11,665

40% postgraduate

60% undergraduate

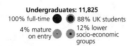

Undergraduates: 11,825
100% full-time
4% mature on entry
88% UK students
12% lower socio-economic groups

48% female   52% male

- **World-class research-intensive university.**
- **Teaching staff:** 2000 full-time and part-time.
- **Broad study areas:** Arts, education, social sciences, law, science (including engineering), technology, medicine, veterinary medicine.

Freshers

- **Admissions information:** AS-levels accepted only in combination with 3+ A-levels; AEAs welcomed. UCAS tariff not used.
- **First degree entrants:** 3420 UK, full-time.
- **Points on entry:** 360 (average).
- **Drop-out rate:** 1% in 1st year.
- **Accommodation:** All 1st years housed.

Profile

Institution

Founded: 13th century. **Site:** Scattered throughout city centre. Most colleges and university facilities (faculties, departments, libraries, labs) and sports grounds within walking or cycling distance. **How to get there:** Two mainline links from London (King's Cross and Liverpool St), rail and coach links around the country; close to A14/M11. Within city, walk or bike; also Uni 4 bus passes many university and college sites. **Special features:** Distinctive collegiate system. All staff and students of the university live within a few miles of city centre. University is committed to admitting the most able students. **The colleges:** Each college is a self-governing community that elects its own fellows, admits its own undergraduates and provides academic, sporting and social facilities as well as accommodation. Each has its own prospectus, in addition to the university prospectus. Most colleges admit undergraduates to study all the subjects at Cambridge. For most undergraduates the college is the focal point of their Cambridge life.

Courses

Academic features: Teaching in university lectures, labs, etc, as well as in college. Courses are usually very broad for first one or two years followed by more specialist final year(s) – a flexible system, which allows you to study additional subjects. **Awarding body:** University of Cambridge. **Main undergraduate awards:** BA, MB/BChir, MB/VetMB, MEng, MSci. **Length of courses:** 3 years; others 4 years (eg languages, MEng, MSci); 5+ years (MB/BChir).

Study opportunities & careers

Library and information services: All students have access to at least three libraries: university library (copyright library receiving all books published in the UK); department/faculty specialist library; and college library. Computerised catalogue links all three. Information provision, £385 pa spent for each student (FTE). Separate IT service. Students have IT access through college, department and university sites. University computer network links all colleges and departments; open 24 hours/day; most college rooms linked into it. Many IT courses (taught and self-guided) on use of internet, software applications, programming. **Other learning resources:** Language centre (open to all students, computer-assisted learning). 8 specialist museums, eg Fitzwilliam; Botanic Gardens. **Careers:** University careers service.

Student services & facilities

Student advice and services: Pre-entry advice from central university admissions office and colleges. University counselling service, disability resource centre, childcare information and financial support administrator. Most other support services (eg welfare, religion) are college-based. **Amenities:** University provision for wide range of societies in addition to college facilities. **Sporting facilities:** First-class university sports grounds, boat club, etc, in addition to facilities in colleges.
Accommodation: All 1st years in college accommodation (colleges guarantee to house all single undergraduates without a family for three years). Provision and price varies between the colleges: approx £70–£90 pw without meals (ensuite £80–£100 pw) for 30-week year. Hardly any students live at home.

Money

Living expenses budget: Estimated at £6k–£7500 pa (excluding tuition fees). **Term-time work:** University does not normally allow term-time work for full-time students (terms are only 8 weeks long and very intense). **Financial help:** Bursaries of £3150 pa (£5250 pa if mature) for UK students whose family income is up to £25k; reduced bursaries (tapered down to £50 pa) where family income is £25k–£60k. Some 33% of students qualify. £310k government access to learning funds available, 290 students helped (awards £100–£3500). Numerous university and college scholarships, awards and hardship funds available, particularly for self-financing students. Apply to the college for help in the first instance. **University tuition fees:** Home students pay £3225 pa for first degrees. International students pay £9747 pa (classroom), £12,768 (lab), £23,631 (clinical). **College fees:** Home and EU students who are publicly funded (eg are eligible for a student loan) are exempt from paying college fees; international students pay £3300–£4400 pa, depending on the college.

Applying to Cambridge

You need to submit your application to UCAS by **15 October**, specifying Cambridge as one of your choices. You should include the appropriate campus code for the college you have chosen, or '9' for an open application. Once your application has been received, you will be sent an email asking you to complete a Supplementary Application Questionnaire (SAQ), so the university can ensure it has consistent information about all applicants. (If you are applying from outside the EU, irrespective of your nationality, you should check the university website as there is a special form to be completed and there may be an earlier deadline.)

You may not apply to Oxford as well as Cambridge in the same year, unless you are an applicant for an organ award or an affiliated student.

The colleges

There are 29 undergraduate colleges. You can look up their profiles below.

Men and women:

Christ's
Churchill
Clare
Corpus Christi
Downing
Emmanuel
Fitzwilliam
Girton
Gonville & Caius
Homerton
Hughes Hall (mature only)

Jesus
King's
Magdalene
Pembroke
Peterhouse
Queens'
Robinson
St Catharine's
St Edmund's (mature only)
St John's
Selwyn

Sidney Sussex
Trinity
Trinity Hall
Wolfson (mature only)

Women only:
Lucy Cavendish (mature only)
Murray Edwards (previously New Hall)
Newnham

Student view
Andy McGowan, CUSU Access and Funding Team (2nd year Law)

Living
What's it like as a place to live? Theoretically a city, Cambridge feels like a large campus, which sprawls over the town. It's easy to get round, with most accommodation, lecture halls, social activities and shops within walking distance. By far the most common mode of transport is bike, with nearly every student owning one. **How's the student accommodation?** Accommodation varies between colleges but practically all undergraduates receive accommodation for the entirety of their degree. Some colleges have new ensuite accommodation, the majority of rooms each have a sink in the room and you tend to share a kitchen and bathroom with three other people (on average). A bonus is that each college has a maintenance team, who will fix any dripping taps, blown fuses or other day-to-day issues. **What's the student population like?** Cambridge really does have a fairly diverse and international population. There are people from state schools, people from private school, people from cities, people from the middle of nowhere. In terms of extra-curricular activities and interests, Cambridge is equally diverse, with over 600 university-wide sports clubs and societies. **How do students and locals get on?** There's an historic town vs gown divide – locals are irritated by the students and students are irritated by the tourists – but it doesn't go so far as any antagonism. In reality, though, relations are absolutely fine.

Studying
What's it like as a place to study? The courses are pretty much all academic subjects, with a lot of work involved – but there is plenty of time for fun as well! The facilities within colleges and on a university-wide scale are impressive. Every college has its own library, which tends to be stocked to suit most students' needs. The faculties have extensive libraries, with a good range of journals and online resources, and there's the university library, which hosts every book published in the UK. **What are the teaching staff like?** You really are being taught by leading experts in your subjects. More often than not you will be lectured or supervised (taught in smaller groups of 1–3) by academics who have written the leading textbooks on their subject! Despite being so intelligent, they are all willing to help you and are genuinely interested in what you have to say.

Socialising
What are student societies like? There are hundreds and hundreds of societies – ranging from the normal ones (football club, drama societies, etc) to some of the more obscure (Winnie the Pooh Society, Assassins Guild, etc.) There is no central SU, but instead each college has its own bar. In terms of sports and music, you can get involved on a college level, which caters for a range of standards from complete beginner to competitive, or on a university level, where you get professional coaching and very high standards. **What's a typical night out?** It really depends on the person – maybe start off at the college bar with friends, play a few games of pool in the common room or watch TV, have a few drinks then off out to one of the nightclubs. However, other people may prefer to go and see a gig or watch a production or eat with friends and watch DVDs. **And how much does it cost?** College bar £1.70 a pint, pool 50p a game, entry to nightclub £3–£4, drinks once inside £3 each. **How can you get home safely?** Most colleges are within walking distance so groups of students walk back together. For those living outside of the centre, there are buses and also numerous taxi services with a taxi rank in the centre by the clubs.

Money
Is it an expensive place to live? Cambridge isn't as expensive to live as some people think. The college subsidises your room rent so rent can be anything from £50 a week to £100 pw

and you only pay for it when you're there and not during the vacations. Food in college is cheap as well (meal, dessert and drink for about £3.30). There are also very generous bursaries so money should never be a big issue for people. **Average price of a pint?** £1.70. **And the price of a takeaway?** A cheeseburger is about £2.70 from the food van. The curry houses do student deals that are quite cheap, and there are several pizza chains. **What's the part-time work situation?** As a rule of thumb, you're not allowed to have a part-time job during term time, because the terms are shorter than everywhere else. However, there are occasional exceptions (working in college bar, etc) where college may allow you to work for a maximum of 6 hours pw. There are exceptional bursaries, so if you find you do need the extra money, the college will help you out.

Summary

What's the best feature about the place? It would have to be the people – you meet some great friends and you are taught by world-class academics. The accommodation does tend to be nice as well (especially when you consider how old some of the buildings are!) **And the worst?** There is a lot of work to do – but as long as you balance your time properly, you will be fine. **And to sum it all up?** I'm really glad I came to Cambridge. You get a top-class education and plenty of opportunities to get involved in activities, especially things you haven't done before. You meet loads of great people.

Past students: Samuel Pepys, Desiderius Erasmus, William Wilberforce, Isaac Newton, John Milton, Christopher Marlowe, William Pitt the Younger, Charles Darwin, Lord Byron, Samuel Taylor Coleridge, Rupert Brooke, J M Keynes, Dame Frances Dove (campaigner for women's rights), Bertrand Russell (philosopher), Constance Herschell (chemist), Ethel Sargat (research botanist), Miriam Margolies, John Cleese, Emma Thompson, Hugh Laurie, Ian McKellen (actors), Joan Bakewell, Stephen Fry (writers and broadcasters), David Baddiel, Griff Rhys Jones, Sandi Toksvig (comedians), Margaret Drabble, A A Milne, E M Forster, Graham Greene, Sylvia Plath, Germaine Greer (writers), Rajiv Gandhi, Shirley Williams (politicians), Lord Mountbatten, Clive James, Brian Redhead, Carol Vorderman, Jeremy Paxman (broadcaster), David Attenborough (naturalist and broadcaster), Diane Abbott MP, Baroness Warnock. **More info?** Get Alternative Prospectus from Cambridge University SU (tel 01223 761691, email access@cusu.cam.ac.uk, website www.applytocambridge.com).

Cambridge – Christ's

Christ's College, Cambridge CB2 3BU
Tel 01223 334953
Fax 01223 334967
Email admissions@christs.cam.ac.uk
Website www.christs.cam.ac.uk

Profile

Staff & students

Undergraduates: 260 men, 170 women. **Postgraduates:** 70 men, 50 women. **Teaching staff:** 65.

College & admissions

Founded: 1505; women undergraduates first admitted 1978. **Admission:** Pre-A-level, by matriculation or conditional offers; some places offered on A-level results, school reports and interview. Applications not accepted for architecture or veterinary medicine.

Study opportunities

Study abroad: 60 students learn a language or spend time abroad. **Library and information service:** Modern college working library; old library with antiquarian collection; separate law library. IT facilities open 24 hours/day, ratio 1:6 workstations to students. 10 points with access to library, 50 to internet (plus points in all college rooms). IT courses on request.

Living

Eating arrangements: Choice of formal or informal meals. Facilities charge of £101 per term, plus meals taken at cost. **Gate/guest hours:** None. **Other college facilities:** Theatre, concert hall, auditorium, playing fields, boathouse, squash courts and modern public rooms. Medieval dining hall. Chapel. **Accommodation:** All students in college: rent £70-£90 pw (£80–£100 pw for ensuite); average is £85 pw, term-time only. No first-degree students live at home.

Money

Term-time work: College does not allow term-time work. **Scholarships:** Approx 100 scholarships (£100), mainly awarded on results of university examinations. **Travel grants:** Approx 100 available each year (£60–£1k). **Financial help:** £75k college own funds, 40% of students helped according to need. £80k available for international students prior to course, approx 15 helped.

Student view

Anna Horvai, JCR President 2007–08 (3rd year, Education Studies with English)

Living

What's it like as a place to live? Christ's College is a beautiful place to live and study. The college is composed of 3 courts with old college rooms, with New Court at the back of the college being the more modern accommodation block (refurbished this past year). The expansive Fellows' Garden is perfect in the summer, either for exam revision or relaxation in the sunshine. **How's the student accommodation?** Most of the student accommodation is located in college. Almost all of these rooms are extremely nice and a lot are surprisingly spacious. Although the rooms in the newly renovated New Court are smaller than most of the others in college, they are all ensuite. **What's the student population like?** Christ's students are very welcoming. Due to the college's small community, students in all years mix together and get to know one another. Students tend to come from all over the country, and there is a distinct international community as well. **How do students and locals get on?** Students and locals don't tend to mix very much because they go out on different nights. Cambridge students tend to go out on Tuesdays, Wednesdays and Sundays, whilst the locals will go out on Fridays and Saturdays. There isn't very much interaction between the two groups.

Studying

What's it like as a place to study? Cambridge terms are very intense because a lot of work, lectures and supervisions are included in the course of eight weeks. The amount of lectures/supervisions per course varies, although scientists tend to have more rigid schedules than arts students because they often have lab work and practicals to do. The library facilities in Cambridge are great – Christ's has its own library, which has most books you would need, whilst the university library has absolutely everything and your individual faculty library will have more specialised books. There are also a variety of bookstores in the town centre that have useful resources. **What are the teaching staff like?** The amazing thing about studying at Cambridge is getting the chance to be supervised by academics who are experts in their field. The majority of the time these individuals are truly interested in students' work and opinions, and will commit time and effort to ensuring that supervisions are productive and that students get extensive feedback on their work.

Socialising

What are student societies like? There are many student societies within Christ's – all of them are open to any student who would like to join, regardless of experience. These societies range from sporting societies (football, rugby, basketball, badminton, netball – all with men's and women's teams, whilst there are some mixed teams as well) to academic and special interest groups (Darwin society, English society, Christ's Amateur Dramatics society, Christ's Shakespeare Company, Christ's Film society, etc). Students do tend to get involved in these societies because they don't require huge time commitments or previous experience. Most societies also plan social events. **What's a typical night out?** Wednesday and Sunday are the biggest nights – students will sometimes go on Formal Hall swaps (dinners together) with other college societies before going out to one of the 4 major clubs in Cambridge. The main club on Wednesday has massive queues until about midnight, so it's best to get there early (around 9.30pm; it gets busy around 10.30pm). The music here is usually cheese. There are a few other club options in Cambridge that offer a greater variety in terms of music. **And how much does it cost?** About £3–£4 for the entrance fee – drinks inside start from £1.50. **How can you get home safely?** Christ's is about a 2-min walk from the 4 major clubs in Cambridge, so it's not a dangerous walk at all (since these clubs are in the city centre, in well-lit areas). However, you can always take a taxi home if you live farther away – many taxis stand opposite Christ's.

Money

Is it an expensive place to live? Yes, Cambridge is a very expensive place to live, but you can make it significantly cheaper if you eat all of your meals in college and limit your spending. **Average price of a pint?** About £2.50. **And the price of a takeaway?** Depends on what you get – probably around £3–£4. **What's the part-time work situation?** You aren't technically allowed to have a job during term time.

Summary

What's the best feature about the place? The beautiful city (especially the fact that it's student-orientated) and the people. Not to mention the incredible, albeit demanding, academics. **And the worst?** Probably the intensity of the terms (although this isn't as bad as it sounds, but can get stressful). Also, it gets very cold and windy in the winter. **And to sum it all up?** Cambridge is an incredible experience – it is unlike anything I have ever been a part of, and I feel so lucky to be here. Christ's has been a wonderful home for the past 2+ years, and I know I will be extremely sad and nostalgic when it all comes to an end.

Past students: John Milton, Charles Darwin, Lord Mountbatten, C P Snow (novelist), David Mellor (politician), Richard Whiteley (*Countdown*), Ali G (Sacha Baron-Cohen), Lord Irvine of Lairg, the Lord Chancellor, Kieran West (Olympic gold medallist for rowing). **More info?** Write to JCR President at the college, telephone 01223 334900 and ask for JCR President or email jcr@christs.cam.ac.uk.

Cambridge – Churchill

Churchill College, Cambridge CB3 0DS
Tel 01223 336202
Fax 01223 336180
Email admissions@chu.cam.ac.uk
Website www.chu.cam.ac.uk

Profile

Staff & students
Undergraduates: 330 men, 150 women. **Postgraduates:** 200 men, 100 women. **Teaching staff**: *Men:* 42 fellows, 10 research fellows. *Women:* 8 fellows, 9 research fellows.

College & admissions
Founded: 1960; women undergraduates first admitted 1972. **Admission:** Conditional offers: usually AAA at A-level (or equivalent) for both arts and science courses. For science courses, conditional offers may include grades in STEP and/or AEA papers. Undergraduates not admitted for land economy or theology.

Study opportunities
Academic features: ICT courses; modern language courses for non-linguists. Churchill Archive Centre: 20th-century British history. **Library and information service:** Undergraduate library open 24 hours a day. Books in greatest demand lent for limited period only. IT services open 24 hours/day (ratio workstations to students 1:11). 30 PC workstations and 5 Apple Macs for student use, 2 OPAC for accessing the university library, 2 for accessing the college library, 1 laptop with LAN access; ethernet and telephone connections in all student rooms. IT support from 3 full-time, 2 part-time staff. **Study abroad:** 4% of students learn a language as part of their course and spend 6 months or more abroad.

Living
Eating arrangements: All meals self-service plus formal dinner. Vegetarian available. **Gate/guest hours:** None. **Other college facilities:** Buttery; bar; theatre; multigym; extensive playing fields; tennis and squash courts within college grounds; boathouse (rowing); music recital and practice rooms; visual arts studio. Late-night taxi service to provide safe travel back to college at college expense. **Accommodation:** All students in college accommodation for 3 years (modern bedsitting rooms, 36% ensuite). £541–£991 for 10-week term (most around £705) plus meals at subsidised prices. No first-degree students live at home.

Money
Travel grants: Small long-vacation travel fund. **Term-time work:** Term-time work strongly discouraged. Some vacation work available in college and help offered in finding gap year and vacation work out of college. **Financial help:** £35k own funds used to help 40 students encountering financial hardship.

Student view) Harry Bullivant, JCR (Undergraduate) President (3rd year, Manufacturing Engineering)

Living
What's it like as a place to live? Churchill is unique among Cambridge colleges for its sense of community. It's a dynamic, forward-looking college. **How's the student accommodation?** Accommodation is of a consistently good standard. Rooms are priced at an appropriate range for the types of room. The college as a whole is a great environment and was one of the best pieces of architecture to come out of the 1960s. **What's the student population like?** Churchill has a very diverse population and the highest proportion of students from state school backgrounds. It also has a vibrant international and graduate community. It is a very sociable, friendly environment, partly because most students spend all three years in college. **How do students and locals get on?** Generally fine – there are few issues.

Studying

What's it like as a place to study? Cambridge is an amazing place to study. The courses are all very well taught and generally rank among the highest in the world. **What are the teaching staff like?** Generally experts in their fields or PhD students. Very interested in the success of students and the college. Many are undertaking fascinating research in their departments.

Socialising

What are student societies like? There are a huge range of societies, both in college and the university. Colleges all have their own sports teams and there are inter-collegiate matches in most common sports. Students can also compete on a university level and there is a wide range of participation. Outside sport, there are societies covering almost every area imaginable, from ballet, to music, to launching balloons to the edge of space. **What's a typical night out?** Either to some bars, then a club or a 'formal swap'. Formal swaps are a tradition where a group of guys from one college, or sports team, will go out with a group of girls (or vice versa) from another. This is usually to a formal dinner at college or a curry house/restaurant, followed by bars and a club. They are a great way to get to know people well, in a short space of time – they're also great fun, and fuelled by sufficient quantities of (usually) wine. The JCR (Undergraduates) also host a free weekly party (an 'ent') for students from Churchill and nearby colleges every Friday. **And how much does it cost?** Drinks in bars tend to be around £2.50–£3. College bars are much cheaper. Club entry is usually £4. Formal dinners tend to range between £5–£10 and a bottle of wine is about £4. **How can you get home safely?** Walk, or get a taxi (if you're feeling lazy).

Money

Is it an expensive place to live? Generally slightly more expensive than other universities; however, there are a lot of bursaries available for students on low incomes, so finances should never be an issue. **Average price of a pint?** £3.50 in a bar. £2ish in a college. **And the price of a takeaway?** £7? Pizzas are £6.50 delivered. Most students often eat in college. Formal dinner costs £8.50. **What's the part-time work situation?** Students are generally not allowed, and wouldn't have time, to take part-time jobs during term time. Churchill allows students to work a few hours pw for the College (eg in Bar, maintenance, etc). Outside term, there are no restrictions, and there is often work available with the college.

Summary

What's the best feature about the place? Sense of community, diversity, sociability. **And the worst?** Slightly out of town (15 mins walk from centre). 1960s building, mid-range in wealth compared to other colleges. Occasionally difficult relationships with the college body (ie staff and fellows). **And to sum it all up?** Churchill is a diverse, communal and sociable college, which considers itself forward looking whilst retaining the good traditions of Cambridge colleges.

Cambridge – Clare

- Clare College, Cambridge CB2 1TL
- ☎ Tel 01223 333246
- Fax 01223 333219
- ✉ Email admissions@clare.cam.ac.uk
- 🖥 Website www.clare.cam.ac.uk

Profile

Staff & students
Undergraduates: 240 men, 230 women. **Postgraduates:** 110 men, 90 women. **Teaching staff**: 65.

College & admissions
Founded: 1326; women undergraduates first admitted 1972. **Admission:** Conditional offers, usually AAA at A-level (or equivalent). Most candidates apply during fourth term in sixth form; normally A-levels plus STEP for maths.

Study opportunities
Library and information service: 25,000 volumes. Some computing and word-processing facilities and links to university computer network in all college rooms. **Study abroad:** Some international links for linguists.

Living
Eating arrangements: Self-service buttery; formal dinner in hall. **Other college facilities:** Playing fields. **Accommodation:** Students in college accommodation for three years, rent £705–£980 per term (most £820–£950) plus £107 fixed kitchen charge per term. No first-degree students live at home.

Money
Scholarships: Organ scholarship (£300 pa) and choral scholarships (£100 pa). **Term-time work:** Vacation work available in college library and helping with conferences; also with care of applicants during interview fortnight.

Student view
Danielle Kaminski, Clare College Access Officer (2nd year, Natural Sciences)

Living
What's it like as a place to live? Bustling city. Diverse community. Full of stimulating conversation. **How's the student accommodation?** Fantastic. High quality and reasonably priced. **What's the student population like?** Both friendly and diverse. Students come from all over the world but all have a common passion to learn. **How do students and locals get on?** There is some tension between the two, and going out in the city is inadvisable on a Friday/Saturday night but there are plenty of student nights within colleges to make up.

Studying
What's it like as a place to study? Hard work but courses are second to none. Interesting, stimulating and generally flexible. **What are the teaching staff like?** Many international academic stars. Generally interested in students.

Socialising
What are student societies like? Almost any society one can think of and if what you want doesn't exist, there is funding to set up new societies. **What's a typical night out?** College ents, or local club/bar. Also theatre productions, concerts, jazz nights, etc. **And how much does it cost?** Very much depends. Can easily have a good night out on £10. **How can you get home safely?** Within walking distance, easily. Walk in pairs to be on the safe side.

Money
Is it an expensive place to live? Reasonably expensive city although no more so than other southern cities, and Cambridge has one of the best bursary systems in the country. **What's the part-time work situation?** Not advisable to work in term although there are some vacancies in the college bar and library.

Summary

What's the best feature about the place? Always something to do. **And the worst?** If you're used to big city clubs, you won't find many here. **And to sum it all up?** Standard in societies second to none, top international academics, intellectually challenging and fantastic people.

Past students: David Attenborough (naturalist and broadcaster), Paul Mellon (philanthropist), Harvey and one of his Wallbangers (musicians), James Watson (Nobel Laureate – DNA), Chris Kelly (broadcaster), Hugh Latimer (martyr), Siegfried Sassoon (poet), Peter Lilley MP, Matthew Parris (journalist), Norman Ramsey (Nobel Laureate), John Rutter (composer). **More info?** Contact JCR President at ucspres@clare.cam.ac.uk.

Cambridge – Corpus Christi

Corpus Christi College, Cambridge CB2 1RH
Tel 01223 338056
Fax 01223 338057
Email admissions@corpus.cam.ac.uk
Website www.corpus.cam.ac.uk

Profile

Staff & students

Undergraduates: 160 men, 120 women. **Postgraduates:** 100 men, 90 women. **Teaching staff:** *Men:* 40 fellows, 2 research fellows, 23 lecturers, 19 life fellows, 20 honorary fellows. *Women:* 7 fellows, 7 lecturers, 3 research fellows, 2 life fellows.

College & admissions

Founded: 1352; women undergraduates first admitted 1983. **Admission:** Primarily based on public examination results, school report and interview. Undergraduates not admitted for architecture, education or land economy.

Study opportunities

Library and information service: Taylor Library (working undergraduate library); Parker Library (medieval and Anglo-Saxon manuscripts and early books). IT and library services converged. 15–20 computers, access 24 hours for keyholders; 2 points with access to library catalogue, 18 to the internet plus all student rooms; IT support from computer officer.

Living

Eating arrangements: All meals provided in hall and/or bar. **Gate/guest hours:** Entry after 11pm by key. **Other college facilities:** Extensive sports grounds; 7-acre garden with open-air swimming pool; river boathouse; craft and music rooms; strong music and drama activities. **Accommodation:** All students in college accommodation (sets and single rooms), mostly around £750 per term plus meals; allow £3500 pa to live in college. No first-degree students live at home.

Money

Scholarships: Awarded to those already in residence on the basis of academic performance. Organ and choral scholarships also available. **Travel grants:** Considerable sums annually. **Term-time work:**

No work in term-time. Some bar work in college and domestic work in vacs. **Financial help:** Generous provision of access funds and hardship support for those in need.

Student view

In the middle of Cambridge, with only 250+ undergraduates, it is one of the smallest and most central colleges, with a reputation for friendliness. The buildings comprise Old Court, the oldest court in Cambridge, and the gothic New Court. Accommodation varies from old and spacious rooms to a few that are pretty small. All have internet and phone connections. Furthest hostel is 5 mins' walk away. Good quality food from hall, with vegetarian options and popular guest nights. Snacks from bar throughout the day. Bar is popular and offers occasional events and special entertainments. Rugby and football pitches, squash and tennis courts and rowing machines at sports ground, 15 mins away. Boathouse shared with 3 other colleges; many continue rowing after novice term. A strong college for drama with the college society, the Fletcher Players, running the college-owned Playroom in conjunction with the Arts Theatre. One of the best student-run chapel choirs and all are encouraged to play in informal concerts and recitals. Lecture theatre for talks by visiting speakers and presentations by the college film society. College library is small but most departmental libraries are close by. Undergraduates are discouraged from keeping cars. Cambridge has high workloads generally and Corpus is no exception, though the college is continually seeking to improve support for students. Most people can expect to have some but not all supervisions within college. College deals sympathetically with money problems: bursaries are available, along with travel awards and prizes for performance in tripos.

Student footnotes

Housing: Guaranteed for whole course but rent increasing; 4 college hostels. **Eats:** College food relatively expensive locally but good quality. Vegetarian choices. Many other local places, varied prices. **Drink:** Good college bar; other college bars and several pubs nearby. **Nightlife:** Lots of student drama and music, college film socs, variety of student orchestras, college bops. ADC Theatre. Big names to Corn Exchange nearby. **Locals:** No real town/gown problems. **Sports:** Good college facilities; everyone encouraged to join in regardless of abilities. **Travel:** College travel grants awarded annually. **Jobs:** Not permitted in term time. **Best features:** Friendly atmosphere and small size makes it easy to get involved in sport, drama, music, etc. **And worst:** Some find it claustrophobic. **Past students:** Christopher Marlowe (poet and playwright), Christopher Isherwood (author), Sir Frederick Lawton (Lord Justice of Appeal), Lord Sieff (Marks and Spencer), Sir Eric Faulkner (Lloyds Bank), Mark Elder (conductor), Joe Farman (discoverer of hole in ozone layer), Christopher Booker (journalist/writer), E P Thompson (historian/nuclear disarmer). **More info?** Write to JCR President at the college.

Cambridge – Downing

✉ Downing College, Cambridge CB2 1DQ
☎ Tel 01223 334826
✉ Email admissions@dow.cam.ac.uk
🖥 Website www.dow.cam.ac.uk

Profile

Staff & students
Undergraduates: 215 men, 190 women. **Postgraduates:** 160 men, 90 women. **Teaching staff:** *Men:* 34 fellows. *Women:* 14 fellows, 2 research fellows.

College & admissions
Founded: 1800; women undergraduates first admitted 1978. **Admission:** All offers based on school or college reference, interviews and exam results. Conditional offers usually AAA at A-level (or equivalent). Undergraduates not admitted to study education.

Study opportunities
Library and information service: Well-stocked college library. Separate IT service, open 24 hours/day. Access to college network and internet from all student rooms. IT support from 3 computer officers.

Living
Eating arrangements: Undergraduates may take all meals in hall. Facilities provided for self-catering. **Gate/guest hours:** Gates shut 11pm to 6am. Guests not booked in overnight must leave by 12.45am. **Other college facilities:** Coffee and reading room, auditorium, bar and café; computer room; 2 tennis courts and 2 squash courts in college precincts; sports ground 10-min cycle ride away; boathouse. **Accommodation:** All undergraduates in college accommodation for at least 3 years: rent £74–£106 pw, term-time only. No first-degree students live at home.

Money
Scholarships: Scholarships on performance in university exams. Annual organ scholarship and instrumental awards. Substantial awards available for Downing graduates intending to train for the legal and medical professions or for careers in management or business. **Travel grants:** Available for students undertaking overseas study or attending conferences. **Term-time work:** College does not allow term-time work except in college (eg in library, as computer assistants). **Financial help:** College support and hardship grants available.

Student view
Dan Chapman, JCR President, Downing College
(3rd year, MSci Natural Sciences; Geological Sciences)

Living
What's it like as a place to live? Cambridge in general and Downing College in particular are great places to live and work. The college buildings are beautiful, the location is fantastic for most lectures, the city is reasonably safe and there are lots of things to do around the city. **How's the student accommodation?** In general the college accommodation is of a very good standard and is much cheaper than you could find on the private market – one of the plus sides of Cambridge Uni is that most colleges (and Downing is no exception) can house almost all of its undergraduates, not just those in their 1st year. **What's the student population like?** Trying to define the student population is like trying to push water uphill. There is so much diversity and cross-college friendships that the whole university becomes one massive community, with almost every possible background represented. **How do students and locals get on?** Cambridge does have some problems with local teenagers occasionally taking issue with members of the university but this is thankfully rare. Cambridge is a safe city, and even in the so-called 'trouble hotspots' it can't be described as a no-go area. As long as people are sensible and never walk alone after dark in poorly lit areas then there should be no problems.

Studying

What's it like as a place to study? Cambridge has an unfair reputation for being stuffy and full of tradition, that courses are archaic and teaching methods hark back to the early 1900s. In reality, teaching at Cambridge is world-class and cutting edge. The unique supervision system gives Cambridge students such a head start over other universities that we even get longer holidays! Studying at Cambridge can be challenging, but as long as you put the effort in, the rewards are fantastic. **What are the teaching staff like?** Students at Cambridge are taught by the same people who publish the research papers that make Cambridge renowned the world over as a hotbed of academic excellence. All teaching staff are world-class experts in their field and they take a real interest in how their students are progressing. As you learn more you will find that the supervisors will be discussing things with you that concern current and cutting-edge research that they are carrying out, and you will gain a fantastic insight into the future of your field.

Socialising

What are student societies like? Cambridge students may work hard, but we know how to party just as hard as well. Having a busy social life is essential to remain happy at uni, and Downing College has an abundance of societies who try to take your mind of studying for a while. Downing is a keen sports college, and even those who have no interest in participating will often find themselves watching the rowing on the river with bated breath. Clubs for everything from drama to tea drinking are catered for in college, and then there are the hundreds of uni-wide societies for more niche things. **What's a typical night out?** Cheap drinks in the student bar before hitting the town and a nightclub called Cindies (real name Ballare). **And how much does it cost?** The Downing student bar has pints at around £1.80, shots at around £1.20 and bottles at around £1.50, and that doesn't include the regular special offers. Cindies is usually about £5 to get in, and then drinks are quite cheap (but more than the student bar . . . obviously!). **How can you get home safely?** Downing is ridiculously close to Cindies and so it is very easy to just walk home, but if you want a taxi, and have no money, there is an emergency taxi scheme operated by the porters who will pay for your taxi for you when you arrive at college, on the proviso that you repay them at a later date.

Money

Is it an expensive place to live? Time to bust another popular myth about Cambridge – you don't need to be rich to survive. Cambridge is actually quite a cheap place to live, and accommodation is usually cheaper than at other universities. Your student loan, combined with an unrivalled bursary system, means no student need ever leave Cambridge due to financial concerns. **Average price of a pint?** £1.80 in the student bar, anything from £2.10 to £3 in pubs and clubs. **And the price of a takeaway?** £5.95 for a pizza, £4.60 for a Chinese, £4.40 for an Indian and all within a 30-second walk of the College's main gates. **What's the part-time work situation?** The university discourages people from getting part-time jobs as the studying at Cambridge is considered to be a full-time commitment. However, for those who are worried, terms are much shorter than at other universities and so you can earn more money during the vacations. There is the opportunity to earn some spare cash by doing shifts on the college bar, or by working in the library.

Summary

What's the best feature about the place? The beauty of the college, combined with the world-class teaching and the fantastic supervision system – also the kudos having a degree from Cambridge will give you when you are job hunting. **And the worst?** Lots and lots of work at a level that is much harder than A-level means some people find it difficult to adjust at first, but perseverance is the key, as well as maintaining a healthy balance between work and socialising. You may also find you are having to explain to friends that not everyone at Cambridge is a rich snob, and most of us are perfectly normal! **And to sum it all up?** Always apply, even if you think you won't get an offer at Cambridge; it is only one space on your UCAS form, and you might just end up at one of the best universities in the world!

Past students: Sir Graham Smith (Astronomer Royal); John Cleese (comedian); F R Leavis (literary critic); Lord Goodman (lawyer, political adviser), Prof Lord John Butterfield (medical scientist, Vice-Chancellor of the university); Michael Winner (film director); Mark Cox (tennis player); Michael Atherton (cricketer); Sir Peter Hall, Trevor Nunn (theatre directors); Thandie Newton (actress). **More info?** Visit www.downingjcr.co.uk and www.downingents.com.

Cambridge – Emmanuel

Emmanuel College, Cambridge CB2 3AP
Tel 01223 334290
Fax 01223 762073
Email admissions@emma.cam.ac.uk
Website www.emma.cam.ac.uk

Profile

Staff & students
Undergraduates: 254 men, 237 women. **Postgraduates:** 120 men, 123 women. **Teaching staff:** *Men:* 48 fellows, 9 research fellows. *Women:* 11 fellows, 4 research fellows.

College & admissions
Founded: 1584; women undergraduates first admitted 1979. **Admission:** Conditional offers usually AAA at A-level (or equivalent); STEP papers also required for mathematics. Post-A-level applications welcomed. Undergraduates not admitted for land economy.

Study opportunities
Library and information service: Large college library; Sancroft Library (old books) and Watson Collection (illustrated books).

Living
Eating arrangements: No compulsory eating arrangements. **Gate/guest hours:** Main college gate locked at 2am; duty porter will open gate if required. **Other college facilities:** Grand piano, harpsichord and organ; 2 squash courts, table tennis room, tennis courts and open-air swimming pool in college precincts; playing fields and boathouse; Queen's Building with theatre and concert facilities. **Accommodation:** All students are in college accommodation (1st and 3rd years in college, old or modern rooms; 2nd and 4th years in college or college hostels); average rent £680 per term. Ethernet connections available in all rooms. For an average room and 3 meals daily, approx £4576 pa No first-degree students live at home.

Money
Term-time work: College does not allow term-time work apart from 2 college bar managers. **Financial help:** Funds available to undergraduate and graduate students.

Student view
Grace Jackson, President, Emmanuel College Students' Union (3rd year, English)

Living
What's it like as a place to live? Very lively, occasionally stressful – but with beautiful views! A nice community spirit, open to everyone. **How's the student accommodation?** We get it for all 3 years. The quality varies – a few beautiful ensuite rooms, quite a lot of sets (bedroom and study), lots of average-sized rooms with a sink. Very reasonably priced, rent vary according to size and quality. **What's the student population like?** Diverse – lots of internationals, plenty of Londoners and lots from around the UK. A favourable ratio of state and independent students. **How do students and locals get on?** Not much interaction. We are 'warned' at the beginning of the year about bike theft, no-go areas (not nearby though) and homeless people – rather patronising; there is *very rarely* any trouble.

Studying
What's it like as a place to study? Currently our library is being redeveloped – which is and will be a lovely place to study. People revise on the paddock in the summer! **What are the teaching staff like?** Great! Lots of celeb-academics! Most are 100% committed in their students. They work you hard.

Socialising
What are student societies like? There are loads! Every sport is represented. We also have the Real Ice Cream Society, a thriving drama society, an art society, an active SU . . . etc. **What's a typical night out?** Drinks in the bars, cheesy club night. **And how much does it cost?** £10–£15. **How can you get home safely?** By walking. Cambridge is tiny and Emma is very near the bars and clubs.

Money
Is it an expensive place to live? Cambridge is expensive but college is reasonable. The college has the cheapest bar in town! People make their loans last. **Average price of a pint?** College bar: £1.60. **And the price of a takeaway?** £5–£6. **What's the part-time work situation?** You aren't allowed. But you can work in the college bar or the college library (for minimum wage). Employment opportunities during vacations – summer schools, etc.

Summary
What's the best feature about the place? The bar, with our great club nights, cheap drinks and student-friendly atmosphere. **And the worst?** It can feel like a pressure cooker during exam term – you need to get away sometimes! **And to sum it all up?** There's something for everyone at Emmanuel, but you'll be expected to work (and play) hard.

Past students: Griff Rhys Jones, Graeme Garden (comedians); John Harvard (who founded Harvard University); Cecil Parkinson MP.

Cambridge – Fitzwilliam

Fitzwilliam College, Cambridge CB3 0DG
Tel 01223 332030
Email admissions@fitz.cam.ac.uk
Website www.fitz.cam.ac.uk

Profile

Staff & students

Undergraduates: 285 men, 185 women. **Postgraduates:** 140 men, 60 women. **Teaching staff:** *Men:* 40 fellows, 4 bye-fellows, 1 research fellow. *Women:* 9 fellows, 3 bye-fellows, 2 research fellows.

College & admissions

Founded: 1869; women undergraduates first admitted 1978. **Admission:** Conditional and unconditional offers on basis of interview and school report and usually AAA at A-level (or equivalent).

Study opportunities

Library and information service: College library and separate law library. 2 dedicated computer rooms open 24 hours; 27 workstations in 4 locations (ratio workstations to students 1:26). Network connections in all college rooms. IT support from 3 full-time staff and team of volunteers. **Study abroad:** Modern linguists study at a European university.

Living

Eating arrangements: Breakfast and lunch in hall; choice of self-service and formal dinner. There is an amenities charge but most meals paid for as required. **Other college facilities:** Café/bar, laundrette, music rooms, photographic darkroom, auditorium, chapel, fully-equipped kitchen, dining room (for student dinner parties), society room, weights room, squash and badminton courts, playing fields near college, boathouse on river. **Music:** Very active music society; students can be involved in all kinds of music-making (chapel choir and chamber opera to jazz and rock bands). Hosts termly residences, including concerts and master classes, by Fitzwilliam String Quartet (founded in college in 1968); professional concert series. **Accommodation:** All students guaranteed accommodation, on site or in college-owned houses nearby. 368 rooms on site (174 ensuite); rent £735–£1039 per term. Some overnight accommodation for guests (certain conditions apply).

Money

Scholarships: Scholarships awarded on basis of performance in university examinations. **Travel grants:** Contributions to travel costs made from various college sources. **Financial help:** Funds available through the college funds, including E D Davies Fund.

Student view

It's not only Fitzwilliam's red-brick exterior that distinguishes it from the traditional Cambridge college – the diverse student intake helps too. Students from state schools make up 70% of the undergraduate population. The atmosphere is down-to-earth and friendly and there is a strong sense of community, perhaps due to the college's location slightly out of town. It is, however, still only a 5-min cycle ride into the centre, and the rest of the colleges are close enough to be able to enjoy what the university as a whole has to offer. On the social front, its termly event, Soundcheck, is reckoned the biggest and best in Cambridge (attracting high-profile performers, eg Annie Mac and High Contrast, plus a popular Christmas ball. Clubs and societies range from martial arts to aerobics; lots of music, with an active choir, swing band, barbershop and numerous other less formal groups. Sport is extremely well provided for and, with opportunities for all; 3 squash courts in college and the sports ground is 5 mins away. Strong representation in all major sports but the emphasis is on activity as relaxation, with many social teams and minority sports on offer (eg volleyball, netball, basketball); female sport is particularly active.

College accommodation guaranteed for all 3 years (half of 2nd years live off-site in college-owned houses). Most on corridors of eight rooms; most rooms in college with their own showers or are fully ensuite. Kitchen facilities are basic, though adequate, and improve in 2nd- and 3rd-year rooms. Active JCR involved in a wide range of issues; fairly apathetic politically but proactive in college matters. Few restrictions on visitors or overnight guests; contraceptive, drinks and games machines can all be found. An award-winning 1990s chapel available for use by the students. Excellent bar.

Student footnotes

Housing: Rooms for all (if desired); those wanting to live out, look on noticeboards. **Eats:** Cafeteria good; subsidised by fixed charge. Varying standard but always a vegetarian option and salad bar. Locally, Gardenia's, La Margherita (prices fair to steep). **Drink:** College bar (£1.70+ a pint) cheaper than pubs; also other college bars. Broadside is good local brew. **Nightlife:** 2 excellent large events per term, bands 3 times a term. Films, concerts; superhalls; Christmas revue. **Locals:** All right. **Sports:** All free – athletics, basketball, badminton, chess, croquet, darts, football, hockey, rugby, martial arts, mountaineering, netball, squash, softball, tennis, volleyball, waterpolo, table football. **Travel:** Number of college and university awards. **Financial help:** On individual basis. **Jobs:** No term-time employment by university regulations (bent for fundraising); some holiday jobs in college or part-time in area. **Informal name:** Fitz. **Best features:** Friendly and compact. **And worst:** Cycling up the hill. **Past students:** Lord St John of Fawsley, Norman Lamont, Rt Hon Andy Burnham MP, Jim Knight MP, Vince Cable MP, Dr A Szent-Gyorgi (Nobel prizewinner), Derek Pringle (cricketer and sports journalist), Phil Edmonds (cricketer), Christopher Martin Jenkins (cricket commentator), Nick Clarke (Radio 4), Dr David English (President of Methodist Conference), Dr David Starkey (historian, media personality). **More info?** Enquiries to JMA President (tel 01223 332000; email Pres@fitz.cam.ac.uk).

Cambridge – Girton

Girton College, Cambridge CB3 0JG
Tel 01223 338972
Email admissions@girton.cam.ac.uk
Website www.girton.cam.ac.uk

Profile

Staff & students

Undergraduates: 255 men, 232 women. **Postgraduates:** 109 men, 98 women. **Teaching staff:** *Men:* 23 fellows, 6 research fellows, 25 lecturers, *Women:* 19 fellows, 5 research fellows, 20 lecturers.

College & admissions

Founded: 1869; men undergraduates first admitted 1979. **Admission:** Conditional offers usually AAA at A-level (or equivalent). Post-A-level and candidates for deferred entry welcomed.

Study opportunities

Library and information service: 90,000 volumes in college library. IT and library services converged. Ratio workstations to students 1:10, open 24 hours/day; 40 points with access to library and internet (students with own machines have access via college network). Support from 3 computer officers 8 hours/day. **Study abroad:** Formal exchange link with Utrecht University (for modern language students).

Living

Eating arrangements: No compulsory meals. Lunch arrangements with Clare, Downing and Pembroke colleges. Formal dinner in hall once a week. **Guest/gate hours:** College members must be back in college by 6am (if without overnight exeats); guests after 10.30pm only if accompanied by college member. **Other college facilities:** Playing fields, croquet lawns, swimming pool, cricket, soccer and rugby pitches, boathouse, tennis courts, squash court. **Accommodation:** All students in college accommodation: £1165 per term (incl heating) and kitchen fixed charge. No first-degree students live at home.

Money

Scholarships: Scholarships and exhibitions awarded on results of tripos examinations; organ scholarships, choral and instrumental awards. **Travel grants:** Some available. **Term-time work:** College discourages term-time work. **Financial help:** Emily Davies bursaries and Buss Fund for undergraduates; bursaries for international students.

Student view

Set in pleasant, extensive grounds about 2½ miles from city centre (most find a bike essential). It has a friendly and relaxed atmosphere. College accommodation for all: Wolfson Court (housing 140) is modern and includes a law library, reading room and computer room complex; several college houses, most undergraduate housing next to college. Fixed rent for all rooms regardless of size. Food quite cheap and very good – several choices, including salads and vegetarian meals (vegan on request). Self-catering facilities on each corridor and coin-operated washing machines. Large, extensive library with convenient opening hours. Workloads realistic and, despite traditional atmosphere of degrees, interesting and unpressurised. Academic standards average and it's fairly easy to change subjects. Good relations between senior and junior college members. Intake is mixed: male/female ratio nearly equal; strong international contingent; varied educational and home backgrounds; down-to-earth and unpretentious. College societies range from subject-related to music, drama (GADS) and film club. Good sports facilities on site for hockey, lacrosse, tennis, basketball, netball, rugby, soccer, squash, cricket, croquet; also heated indoor swimming pool (water polo), multigym and a successful rowing club. Lively, busy bar in atmospheric college cellars (with pool table, darts board, table football, jukebox, etc) – also it's cheap and has unique bar staff. Party rooms, TV room; JCR hires out discotheque and organises the garden party and spring ball, as well as band nights and discos. All rooms, facilities, library, bar etc contained within one building. Front gate locked at 2am but porter always on duty. Security keys can get you into college too, and can be used in the canteen. JCR bikes available for students; frequent buses (every 10 mins).

Student footnotes

Housing: All live in; extra houses close by. **Eats:** Best eating places in town on Castle Hill: several Indian restaurants and Dojo's serves good (inexpensive) Chinese food. College meals about £3, vegetarian available. **Drink:** Guinness, Carlsberg Export, Stella, Tetley's – good selection of bottled beers in college bar from £1.90 a pint. Other college bars (have to know people in a college to drink in its bar) and Girton village pub; also the Anchor, Mitre, Pickerel and the Castle. **Nightlife:** Local bands in college bars – some more famous play in Corn Exchange (fairly expensive); film, bop, band or other ents (eg bingo, generation game) each week in college. Also ADC Theatre, Arts Theatre. Good ents in

Clare Cellars, Emma bar, Queens; also Fez Club, Life and Soultree. **Locals:** Friendly to students who are friendly. **Sports:** Good facilities; new AstroTurf cricket nets. **Travel:** Bikes essential. Bus frequent. Taxi to/from town £7. Travel grants available for summer vacation. **Financial help:** Hardship funds. Can pay bill in instalments. **Jobs:** Some work in college kitchens and development office – otherwise not officially allowed during term time; temping possible in holidays. **Best features:** Friendly atmosphere; inexpensive. **And worst:** Small town so social life is whatever you make of it. **Past students:** Arianna Stassinopoulos-Huffington (writer and broadcaster), Angela Tilby (writer and TV producer), HM Queen Margarethe of Denmark, Prof Rosalyn Higgins (Professor of International Law, University College, London), Doris Wheatley (Chairman and Managing Director, Cambridge Communications Ltd), Prof Dorothy Wedderburn, Joan Robinson (economics), Baroness Warnock, Prof Gillian Beer, Sandi Toksvig (comedian). **More info?** Contact JCR President on 01223 338898.

Cambridge – Gonville & Caius

- Gonville & Caius College Cambridge CB2 1TA
- ☎ Tel 01223 332447
- 🖷 Fax 01223 332456
- ✉ Email admissions@cai.cam.ac.uk
- 💻 Website www.cai.cam.ac.uk

Profile

Staff & students
Undergraduates: 310 men, 230 women. **Postgraduates:** 140 men, 85 women. **Teaching staff:** *Men:* 82 fellows. *Women:* 11 fellows.

College & admissions
Founded: 1348; women undergraduates first admitted in 1970s. **Admission:** Conditional offers usually AAA at A-level (or equivalent). Those wishing to study maths often also asked for STEP.

Study opportunities
Library and information service: College library contains collection of modern books (4500 new acquisitions pa); also a large medieval collection in college and various collections bequeathed by Fellows. IT and library services converged. Ratio of 1:13 workstations to students, access 24 hours/day; 60 points with access to library and internet (plus 250 in students' rooms). IT support from 3 computer officers.

Living
Eating arrangements: Self-service breakfast and lunch; dinner either formal or informal. **Gate/guest hours:** No restrictions. **Other college facilities:** Music practice rooms; college boathouse and boatman; cricket pitch; sports ground and pavilion; squash court; health centre; auditorium; 2 computer centres and 3 out-stations. **Accommodation:** All students in college accommodation: rent £844–£1013 per term, average rent £93 pw. No first-degree students live at home.

Money
Scholarships: Unlimited scholarships and exhibitions for exceptional performance in university examinations. **Travel grants:** Numerous minor travel grants plus Paton-Taylor travelling scholarship

for projects of an academic nature; awards from Leonard Gluckstein Memorial Fund for travel associated with historical or archaeological studies; grants from Handson Bequest for medical projects. **Term-time work:** No college policy on term-time work. Occasional vacation work available in college library. **Financial help:** College bursaries to £900; no limit to number awarded (approx 50). Additional hardship funds available if required (up to £3k awarded occasionally). International students eligible for overseas bursaries (for maintenance or fees).

Student view

Main college buildings (Old Courts) are attractive and ornate – pretty flower beds and trees!; in the centre of town, next to the Senate House. Most 1st years live in Harvey Court (1960s monstrosity, admired by architects!), 10 mins' walk away on the Backs and next to the arts faculties and university library. 2nd years live out in college houses, allocated by ballot (ballot order reversed to choose 3rd-year rooms in the Old Courts). All staircases are mixed. Old Court Porter's Lodge closes at 1am (but access possible afterwards). Washing machines/irons etc are readily available, and 2–5 people share a kitchen with fridge and cooking rings. Officially only minor cooking is allowed, as it's compulsory to buy 45 meal tickets a term for hall; this means that generally the whole college meets up at least once a day, so everyone knows everyone else. Some find it insular but many Caians are involved at university level in various activities, including various sports, RAG, CUSU, etc. Relations between the students and administration are friendly and each student has a personal tutor. SU (GCSU) is active and affiliated to the university SU and to NUS; it concentrates on welfare issues rather than party politics; advice is available from specific officers (eg welfare or women's officer) on any problems with college life or work. Generally a relaxed atmosphere; college bar and courts tend to be very sociable. History and medicine particularly strong; law, economics and natural science also well respected. It is easy to change subject for Part II. Workloads vary hugely between individuals and between courses; arts subjects require self-reliance (generally 1–2 supervisions a week and few lectures); natural sciences and medicine are much more structured. Standard of teaching is excellent, though courses tend to be fairly theoretical and demanding. College library (highly regarded in Cambridge) open 17 hours a day. College excels at rowing; football, rugby and hockey are also popular and other sports are played at a laid-back level. Some 50+ clubs and societies in college and easy to start up a new one (eg karting, Amnesty International); debating, drama, music and RAG are all thriving. Some 50% of students are women, 5%–10% of students are international (more in graduate, MCR) and special efforts are made to ensure their integration into college life. Little ostentatious wealth amongst students; few leave without an overdraft.

Student footnotes
Housing: All students in college accommodation, 85% of which is excellent. Rents average, but contracts for only 30 weeks. Married quarters; some rooms with disabled access. **Eats:** College caters for all diets although dinner can be expensive, but reasonable quality. Good vegetarian restaurants and health food shops in town; masses of choice (decent meal £8, cheaper alternatives). **Drink:** Bitter £2 pint in college bar. Nice old pubs in town (though some becoming trendy wine bars). Local Wetherspoons, Rat and Parrot for cheap drinks, etc. Local club (Life), very popular. **Nightlife:** Frequent (cheap) college bops) and other events. Thriving drama society; regular concerts and plays. Art Picture House in town is excellent; also a mainstream cinema. Life, Cindies, Fez, Po Na Na's and Coco all good, cheap student clubs. **Sports:** Excellent sports ground with clubhouse (best sports bar in Cambridge) and squash and tennis courts. Standard generally good but opportunities for all abilities. **Travel:** Get a bike and you're sorted! Approximately £8 return to London (coach) and regular

trains around the country. **Financial help:** Ever-increasing grants and bursaries. All students get a £40 book grant. Relatively easy to get a travel grant. Good university bursary scheme. **Jobs:** Students allowed to stay in accommodation outside term time (especially for academic reasons) but most find work closer to home. **Informal name:** Caius (pronounced Keys). **Best feature:** Size and facilities means atmosphere is friendly. **And worst:** College regulations! **Past students** Titus Oates (revolutionary), David Frost (broadcaster), Stephen Hawking (scientist), John Venn (of Venn diagrams), Harold Abrahams (Olympic sprinter), Sir Nevill Mott (Nobel laureate, physics), Kenneth Clarke MP, Mark Bailey (England rugby player), Alastair Campbell (Blair communications guru), Jimmy Carr (TV comedian). **More info?** Contact GCSU Access Officer (access.officer@cai.cam.ac.uk).

Cambridge – Homerton

🖃 Homerton College, Hills Road, Cambridge CB2 8PH
☎ Tel 01223 507252
✉ Email admissions@homerton.cam.ac.uk
🖳 Website www.homerton.cam.ac.uk

Profile

Staff & students
Undergraduates: 290 men, 315 women. **Postgraduates:** 200 men, 440 women. **Teaching staff:** 41.

College & admissions
Founded: 1695 in London. Teacher training since 1850; moved to Cambridge in 1894. Became a college of the university in 2001. **Admission:** Conditional offers usually AAA at A-level (or equivalent). Offers full range of university subjects except architecture, medicine and veterinary medicine.

Study opportunities
Library and information services: 45,000 volumes, 40 periodicals; about 90 study places; 24-hour access. Separate IT service, access 24 hours/day. 50 computers for student use, with access to internet and university network; internet connections in all student bedrooms. IT support from 6 full-time staff; induction to library and information services on each course.

Living
Other college facilities: Tennis courts, playing fields (soccer and hockey), indoor facilities for squash. Drama studio and auditorium. College sick bay on site, with nursing sister.
Accommodation: All undergraduates offered college accommodation for their whole course. 570 places available (500 ensuite), 190 for 1st years; half-board places at approx £112 pw, term-time only.

Money
Financial help: Generous university help for students from low-income families.

Student view

It's the 'up and coming' college in Cambridge – fresh-faced, having become a full member of the university less than 10 years ago. However, it has been based in the city for 100+ years, with some fine-looking Victorian buildings. There's a huge amount of energy swirling around as it bids to establish itself amongst the Cambridge colleges. New societies are constantly being set up and it has a new, and very large, bar – which is useful! Fantastic mix of students; excellent college SU (only college to have a sabbatical president and welfare service available by phone 24/7). A little way out from the centre, which has its benefits, eg own football and hockey pitch. And you are allowed on the grass, a novelty for a Cambridge college! Library and computer room open 24 hours/day. Large amount of modern ensuite accommodation – which is very nice!

Student footnotes

Housing: College accommodation excellent; most students live in for at least 2 years (quality of local houses variable). **Eats:** New café serves cold food; snacks and cheap food in hall (meal £3+). Formal hall's always good banter. Takeaways close by; fine restaurants in Cambridge. Local leisure park full of usual chains (eg Nando's) with good lunch-time menus! **Drink:** Homerton Bar cheap(ish) compared to pubs (£2 a pint). Great pubs in the vicinity. **Nightlife:** Friendly college bar with cheap pool, jukebox, quiz machine; nearby pubs and clubs; cinema/bowling complex over the road. Good college drama and music groups, steel pan band, large Christian Union, strong les-bi-gay group. Good SU organised events (2 big ones a term and a few mini ones) **Sports:** Most sports possible at college level, strong netball and football. **Travel:** Pilkington travel award, Erasmus scheme, other bursaries and info. **Financial help:** Easily available; range of college and university funds. **Jobs:** Not recommended (though not forbidden, as is commonly perceived) due to work commitments, but many work in local pubs as well as college bar. **Best features:** Friendly, relaxed and fun! **And worst:** Cost. **Past students:** Julie Covington (singer), Dawn French (comedian), Cherie Lunghi (actress), Nick Hancock (comedian), Nick Hornby (author), Kieran West (Olympic gold medallist). **More info?** Enquiries to SU President at hus-president@homerton.cam.ac.uk or on 01223 507235.

Cambridge – Hughes Hall

Hughes Hall, Cambridge CB1 2EW
Tel 01223 334897
Fax 01223 311179
Email ugadmissions@hughes.cam.ac.uk
Website www.hughes.cam.ac.uk

Profile

Staff & students
Undergraduates: 56 men, 26 women. **Postgraduates:** 210 men, 170 women. **Teaching staff:** *Men:* 32 fellows. *Women:* 9 fellows.

College & admissions
Founded: 1885. **Admission:** Primarily a graduate college for research students in the humanities and sciences and for students taking postgraduate professional courses in, eg education, medicine. Also

admits undergraduates over 21 and affiliated students but not to medicine (except 4-year graduate course), veterinary medicine or architecture.

Study opportunities

Library and information service: New library resources centre, with ample space for library materials, computers and study facilities. All college rooms have access to the library and internet.

Living

Eating arrangements: Cafeteria system for all meals, except 2 formal dinners a week. **Gate/guest hours:** Gate closed 8pm to 6am; evening porter. **Other college facilities:** Sitting rooms, bar, television room, gardens. 2 boats; informal links with other colleges for field games and squash. **Accommodation:** All undergraduates can be accommodated. 270+ study bedrooms and several college houses nearby: rent £92–£108 pw, inclusive of utilities.

Money

Scholarships: A small number of bursaries and other student support funds available.

Student view
Adrian Leonard, President, Hughes Hall MCR; President, Hughes History Society (2nd year, BA History)

Living
What's it like as a place to live? Friendly, cosmopolitan and grown-up, in the most interesting district of Cambridge. Always some activity going on, and the best food of any Cambridge College dining hall. **How's the student accommodation?** Mostly rather new (less than 20 years old), with plenty of ensuite rooms. Competition is high for rooms, although undergraduates are guaranteed accommodation for all 3 years. **What's the student population like?** International, with scores of countries represented. We are all over 21, so vomiting in the MCR is almost unheard of. Hughesians are also extremely social, and study the spectrum of disciplines. Roughly three-quarters are graduates. **How do students and locals get on?** Cambridge, after 800 years, is just about getting used to us. This city is really geared up for students.

Studying
What's it like as a place to study? You study the Cambridge University curriculum. Hughes benefits from a new Library and Learning Resources Centre (open March 2009), which will significantly extend study facilities. A stimulating multidisciplinary environment. **What are the teaching staff like?** At Cambridge all students benefit from all academics within the collegiate and faculty system, including, eg, Stephen Hawking, who supervises a Hughesian this year. Hughes Senior Members include two members of the Royal Society.

Socialising
What are student societies like? With over 20 societies, from poker to politics, Hughes has everything going. The college also boasts a very strong boat club, plus all the expected sports clubs, most of which have a few internationals in their number. **What's a typical night out?** Hughes MCR Bar, to Fez Club, to late hours at the Fountain pub, then a Faghito's takeaway. **And how much does it cost?** That depends on how much you drink! Cambridge prices are middling. **How can you get home safely?** Walk or cycle; Cambridge is safe.

Money
Is it an expensive place to live? Cambridge is much cheaper than London. Most people have enough for a tin of Red Stripe. **Average price of a pint?** £2.60. **And the price of**

a takeaway? £4.50. **What's the part-time work situation?** Undergraduates at Cambridge are not permitted to hold part-time jobs.

Summary

What's the best feature about the place? Mature environment. **And the worst?** Hughes isn't the richest college. **And to sum it all up?** Hughes Hall delivers the complete Cambridge educational experience without the young, screaming undergraduates, in a stimulating and multinational environment.

Cambridge – Jesus

🖃 Jesus College, Cambridge CB5 8BL
☎ Tel 01223 339455
🖨 Fax 01223 339313
✉ Email undergraduate-admissions@jesus.cam.ac.uk
🖥 Website www.jesus.cam.ac.uk

Profile

Staff & students

Undergraduates: 295 men, 250 women. **Postgraduates:** 135 men, 95 women. **Teaching staff:** *Men:* 45 fellows, 1 research fellow, 2 lectors. *Women:* 15 fellows, 2 research fellows, 1 lector.

College & admissions

Founded: 1496; women undergraduates first admitted 1979. **Admission:** Candidates admitted on basis of A-levels, school reports and interviews; conditional offers usually AAA at A-level (or equivalent); STEP for maths only.

Study opportunities

Library and information service: Quincentenary library, 30,000+ volumes. 30+ machines for student use in college computer centre, open 24 hours/day. All machines, and all student rooms, have internet access. 5 full-time computing officers plus part-time assistants.

Living

Eating arrangements: Self-service with alternative formal hall dinner. Each undergraduate pays kitchen fixed charge (£105+) plus cost of meals taken. **Gate/guest hours:** Free access until 2am. Overnight guests have to be signed in. **Other college facilities:** Bar, common room, shop, party room, stereo-reproduction room, multigym, snooker room, laundrette, sports fields within the college grounds, boathouse nearby. **Accommodation:** All students in college accommodation: rent £637–£1216 per term (depending on room and whether en suite). No first-degree students live at home.

Money

Scholarships: Foundation scholarships and exhibitions on performance in university examinations. **Travel grants:** Available in Lent term. **Term-time work:** College does not allow term-time work. **Financial help:** Named funds plus college loans.

Student view

Friendly, medium-sized college just off the tourist track (an advantage in summer). Only 3 mins' walk to city centre with full range of shopping facilities. College is one of the few in Cambridge that has all its sports grounds and facilities on site, giving an atmosphere of openness as well as producing a strong sporting tradition; participation is possible at all levels, including very active women's teams. Rowers are head of the river and football team are cup champions. Significant number of international students but few mature. Students are well integrated, from all social backgrounds, and very active in university activities. Flourishing college music society and drama. College rooms tend to be warm and well-furnished. All students housed – 1st years in college, most 2nd and 3rd years in college houses (literally opposite). Students can have paintings in their room for a year from the college art collection. Food is quite good and formal hall (3-course, waitress-served meal to which gowns must be worn) is cheap, high quality and served 5 nights a week. Lively and popular student bar, full-sized snooker table, reading room and TV room. New library and computing centre. Jesus positively encourages applications from the state sector, and across the board in terms of subjects; no strict quotas in operation. Usually somewhere in the middle of the Cambridge academic league tables. Most fellows approachable and willing to listen to students and their problems.

Student footnotes
Housing: All students housed; rent average for Cambridge. **Eats:** Meals in college good value. Pizza Express in same street, cheap burger bars nearby. **Drink:** Last orders late (11.30pm) in student bar; good brands. Good cocktails at the Maypole. **Nightlife:** Balare, Fez Club, Twenty Two are good student clubs. **Locals:** Generally friendly. **Sports:** Sport free on college site. **Travel:** Travel scholarships available. **Financial help:** Very generous system of college grants and loans. **Best features:** Friendliness. **And worst:** Difficulty in getting permission for parties or entertainments. **Past students:** Alastair Cooke (journalist), John Biffen MP, Jacob Bronowski (scientist, writer and broadcaster), Raymond Williams (writer, cultural commentator), Sir Sam Brittan (ecomonic commentator), S T Coleridge (poet), Archbishop Cranmer, Laurence Sterne (author), Thomas Malthus (economist), Prince Edward, Nick Hornby (author). **More info?** Enquiries to JCSU President (tel 01223 339339 (leave message); email jcsu-president@jesus.cam.ac.uk).

Cambridge – King's

King's College, Cambridge CB2 1ST
Tel 01223 331417
Email undergraduate.admissions@kings.cam.ac.uk
Website www.kings.cam.ac.uk

Profile

Staff & students
Undergraduates: 215 men, 190 women. **Postgraduates:** 145 men, 111 women. **Teaching staff:** *Men:* 36 fellows. *Women:* 12 fellows.

College & admissions

Founded: 1441; women undergraduates first admitted 1972. **Admission:** Conditional offers usually AAA at A-level (or equivalent). Undergraduates not admitted for education or veterinary science.

Study opportunities

Library and information service: 110,000 volumes; extensive music section. Record library.

Living

Eating arrangements: Self-service cafeteria. Standing charge covers kitchen overheads; individual meals are paid for. **Gate/guest hours:** None. **Other college facilities:** 2 bars, laundrette, darkroom, arts centre, computer room, film projection room, picture loan collection, croquet garden, punts, sports grounds. **Accommodation:** All students in college accommodation: £680–£1075 per term, rent incl heating. No first-degree students live at home.

Money

Scholarships: Choral scholarships and organ studentships awarded at entrance; academic scholarships also awarded on university examinations. **Travel grants:** Many undergraduates awarded travel grants (up to £400), usually for 2nd-year summer vacation. **Term-time work:** College does not allow term-time work. **Financial help:** General funds available for those with financial needs; around 250 students helped per year.

Student view

King's effectively has the best of both worlds – from outside it presents the best-known and most impressive exterior in Cambridge; within, it is informal and relaxed. In nearly every field (social, academic, artistic – even sport, at a pinch), it can hold its own (at least) with the rest of the university. It is the King's breakdown of the Cambridge cliché that makes it stand out – here, students, staff and fellows do actually achieve some sense of community. High ratios for women, state school, mature and graduate intake, resulting in a mature and well-balanced student body: it actively welcomes and encourages applicants from all backgrounds. Minority subjects are a speciality. The student activism of the 60s and 70s that led to the tag of Red King's has left its legacy – the college offers a unique degree of student representation and involvement. The college is home to most shades of opinion and is seen as a tolerant place to be. Student hardship is taken seriously; a very sympathetic finance tutor runs workshops during freshers' week (though not just for freshers) with help and advice. College is relatively affluent and can bail people out. It also welcomes the disabled – a set of rooms specially converted for wheelchair access. It's a nice place but be prepared to work hard!

Student footnotes

Housing: College accommodation ranges from not bad to pricey-but-good (bedroom plus sitting room for many final years). **Eats:** Adequate choice in canteen. Town tends to be either McDonald's or expensive, with lots of restaurants and two kebab vans. **Drink:** College bar the only financial relief for the real drinker. **Nightlife:** Good for films and student plays both on and off campus. **Sports:** College facilities improving. **Travel:** Town is compact so little need for transport. Travel abroad can be funded by college. **Financial help:** Lots and lots of lovely lolly. **Jobs:** Lots of badly-paid tourist industry work in summer, also colleges themselves are quite good. Many students get work in their home area out of term time. **Good news:** Hardship funds being improved. **Past students:** Sir Robert Walpole (politician); Rupert Brooke (poet); J M Keynes (economist); the King's Singers; Michael Mates MP; Alan Turing (mathmatician); E M Forster, Salman Rushdie, Zadie Smith (authors).

Cambridge – Lucy Cavendish

- Lucy Cavendish College, Lady Margaret Road, Cambridge CB3 0BU
- ☎ Tel 01223 330280
- ✉ Email lcc-admissions@lists.cam.ac.uk
- 💻 Website www.lucy-cav.cam.ac.uk

Profile

Staff & students
Undergraduates: 128 women. **Postgraduates:** 123 women. **Teaching staff:** *Women:* 30 fellows, 5 research fellows.

College & admissions
Founded: 1965 as a women's college. **Admission:** Mature (21 and over) women only. For undergraduate admissions, normally 2 or 3 A-levels, an access course, OU level 1 or above, or equivalent recognised qualifications as evidence of recent academic achievement. College written entrance tests and interviews. College also admits graduates. Supervisions in college and at other colleges by men and women.

Study opportunities
Library and information service: Purpose-built college library (20,000 books, currently expanding). Ratio 1:10 workstations to students, access 24 hours/day; 20 points with access to library and internet (all student rooms connected). IT support from computer officer.

Living
Eating arrangements: Lunches every day; evening meal 3 times a week. Cooking facilities for residents. **Other college facilities:** Computer facilities, fine gardens, gym. **Accommodation:** All students offered college accommodation (some ensuite): rent £71–£91 pw (most are £808 a term), plus food.

Money
Scholarships: Small supplementary awards (details available from college). **Travel grants:** Limited number of small grants. **Term-time work:** No term-time work permitted except in college bar, library, invigilation, etc. **Financial help:** Own funds available plus some supplementary funding from charitable foundations. All candidates given details of awards for which eligible.

Student view

Affectionately known as 'Lucy', it's unique in Cambridge catering solely for mature (over 21), female students. About 250 students, a good mix of undergraduates and postgraduates. This creates an exciting and diverse mixture of age, background, culture and experience. A few mins' walk or cycle ride to the city centre, close to the Backs and River Cam. It comprises a mixture of several Victorian houses, a number of modern buildings situated in beautiful gardens in a 3-acre site and 4 houses for married students or those with families. New library houses excellent computer facilities and a multimedia suite. College members have 24/7 access to library and other buildings, providing a flexible service for the individual needs of different students. Most students live in during term time – in shared flats, study bedrooms or single rooms (all with internet connections). Food is excellent – always a choice of hot/cold dishes and vegetarian option (lunch available daily; weekly formal dinner on Thursdays, supper 2 other evenings). Lectures and teaching rarely more than a few mins away by bike – definitely the preferred method of transport within the town! Work is intense and demanding, but also exciting and stimulating. Standard of teaching generally good, and Lucy staff are approachable, friendly and supportive. Demands of academic life can be difficult to balance for students with family and other commitments, but mature students are generally well motivated and most achieve good results. College staff always willing to help and give advice as well as practical help, including financial (from hardship funds, bursaries, etc); also excellent, confidential, free university counselling service. Lucy SA (affiliated to the university SU and NUS) is mainly a social rather than political body; its aim being to enhance the life of the students; organise parties and other social gatherings and formal hall 'swaps' with other colleges. It also supports various sporting activities, eg a successful rowing team, regular yoga class and aerobics group; opportunities to take part in football and other sports in other colleges. Lucites enjoy weekly video nights, regular jazz nights in the college bar, pub quiz nights, cheese and wine events and a garden party. City is a lively place to be: cosmopolitan population and mixture of students, residents and tourists. Plenty of places to go – pubs, restaurants, cinema, theatre, clubs and concert venues, as well as the market, the museums and the old, traditional colleges. Cambridge is an excellent place to study, and Lucy is a very special place to be. It is small enough to be friendly and welcoming, but large enough to offer a unique, often life-changing experience.

Student footnotes

Housing: Nice study bedrooms, most ensuite (rent includes heating); some married or family accommodation. Those living out, look in *Cambridge Evening News* or ask university accommodation office. **Eats:** Good college food; vegetarian option. Margherita, Anatolia, Dojo's locally (meal for £10-ish) plus various Indian, Thai, Italian, Turkish places. **Drink:** £1.80 a pint in college bar; Cambridge Union also cheap. Greene King is local brew. **Nightlife:** Active social committee in college; other colleges full of entertainment. Bands at the Corn Exchange; student nights at local clubs, eg Po Na Na, Fez, Chicago's. **Locals:** Very friendly. **Sports:** Lucy joins other colleges for most sport. College has small, well-equipped gym. **Financial help:** College bursaries help. **Jobs:** About 20% find work in summer holidays. **Informal name:** Lucy. **Best features:** Environment; friendly and very supportive. **And worst:** None.

Cambridge – Magdelene

Magdalene College, Cambridge CB3 0AG
Tel 01223 332135
Fax 01223 462589
Email admissions@magd.cam.ac.uk
Website www.magd.cam.ac.uk

Profile

Staff & students

Undergraduates: 111 men, 128 women. **Postgraduates:** 148 men, 85 women. **Teaching staff:** *Men:* 27 fellows, 8 research fellows, 22 lecturers. *Women:* 7 fellows, 2 research fellows, 2 bye-fellows, 7 lecturers.

College & admissions

Founded: 1428; women undergraduates first admitted 1988. **Admission:** Conditional offers usually AAA at A-level (or equivalent), plus STEP for maths and computer science; IB and Scottish Highers also accepted. All eligible candidates interviewed.

Study opportunities

Library and information service: Over 26,000 volumes; also Wigglesworth Law Library, Pepys library (including the diaries) and Old Library. Ratio workstations to students 1:25; all college rooms on network, giving access to library and internet. IT support from 3 computer officers.

Living

Eating arrangements: Meals at cost (dinner £3.95), both formal and self-service facilities. **Other college facilities:** Bar, film society; 2 grand pianos, harpsichord and organs; laundrettes; boathouse, squash court, fives court, gym, table tennis room, 25 acres of playing fields nearby (shared); 26 computer terminals. **Accommodation:** All students in college accommodation: 420 rooms in halls of residence at £65–£98 pw incl heating and lighting; kitchen charge £147 per term. No first-degree students live at home.

Money

Scholarships: Choral and music awards every year, organ scholarship most years. Generous scholarships and bursaries available in all subjects, plus some bursaries for international students. **Travel grants:** Available (including research) in all subjects. **Term-time work:** College does not allow term-time work. Vac work available (housekeeping, clerk of works). **Financial help:** Various special funds exist including access bursaries, hardship funds, travel grants.

Student view

Jon Romer-Lee, Magdalene College JCR President 2007–08 (3rd year, MEng)

Living

What's it like as a place to live? It's great – near enough to the town centre to walk everywhere but far enough for there not to be too many tourists. And we're surrounded by places to eat! **How's the student accommodation?** Really lucky as every undergrad (even 4th years) are accommodated on the college site. Whether you want old or new, big, small, cheap or less cheap, the way the college has been gradually built up over 600 years means we have them all! **What's the student population like?** Awesome. We're quite small (340 undergraduates) and from all over the place. Despite everyone's different backgrounds, there's a really good, friendly, almost family atmosphere where everyone knows everyone. **How do students and locals get on?** As we're not in the town centre, it's not really an issue. Pubs etc are happy to see locals and students – it's just not a great idea to go clubbing on Saturdays or Fridays but that's the same at most unis.

Studying

What's it like as a place to study? We have a decent library that's about to have a huge extension, and the college generally can cater for most subjects – only very rarely is your

Director of Studies not at Magdalene. **What are the teaching staff like?** A few famous names in their fields, but most are totally unaffected by this and love the college's close student–fellow relationships.

Socialising

What are student societies like? Excellent – most sports, musical ambitions, drama etc can be catered for in college, regardless of talent, which just adds to the atmosphere. If we don't have it, or if you are really talented, the uni can provide! **What's a typical night out?** Drinks with friends, then maybe a curry, then clubbing to cheese! **And how much does it cost?** £20 will get you floored. **How can you get home safely?** Grab a friend by the arm, and take a 5-min stroll back to bed – via the 'van of death' for some chicken nuggets or a kebab!

Money

Is it an expensive place to live? Not really – rent's not too high and you can easily live as frugally or as lavishly as you like. **Average price of a pint?** £2.20 in college bar. **And the price of a takeaway?** £5.95. **What's the part-time work situation?** Undergrads are not allowed to work during term – there just isn't enough time. However, with terms only 8 weeks long, there's loads of time to work on vacation.

Summary

What's the best feature about the place? The size – it's small enough always to feel like a community, but big enough for you not to see *too* much of people. **And the worst?** The terms are too short! **And to sum it all up?** A great place to live, work and play; the most welcoming and inclusive college in Cambridge.

Past students: Lord Ezra (Chairman National Coal Board, Liberal Democrat peer), Lord Justice Cumming-Bruce, Sir Michael Redgrave (actor), Lord Ramsay, Nick Estcourt (mountaineer), Gavin Hastings (rugby player), Bamber Gascoigne (presenter and broadcaster), Samuel Pepys (diaryist), Charles Kingsley (author), Lord Pilkington, Jonathan Ridgeon (athlete), William Burt (writer), Lord Derby, Prince Szudek (of Poland), Rob Wainwright (rugby player), John Simpson (journalist and broadcaster), George Mallory (explorer). **More info?** Contact JCR President at the college (jcr-president@magd.cam.ac.uk).

Cambridge – Murray Edwards

Murray Edwards College, Huntingdon Road, Cambridge CB3 0DF
Tel 01223 762229
Fax 01223 762216
Email admissions@murrayedwards.cam.ac.uk
Website www.murrayedwards.cam.ac.uk

Profile

Staff & students

Undergraduates: 390 women. **Postgraduates:** 100 women. **Teaching staff:** *Men:* 23 fellows, 7 external directors of studies. *Women:* 27 fellows, 1 external director of studies.

College & admissions

Founded: 1954 as New Hall; changed its name to Murray Edwards College in 2008. **Special features:** Mixed fellowship, but student places open only to women. Major contemporary art collection.

201

Admission: Mostly following interview. Conditional offers usually AAA at A-level (or equivalent); STEP usually required for maths. Post-A-level and mature applications assessed on record and interview.

Study opportunities

Library and information service: Large undergraduate library and computer suite, both with access 24 hours/day. Wi-fi and network access to library and internet from all college rooms. IT support from 3 staff and several student computer officers. **Study abroad:** All language students and some law students spend a year abroad as part of course. College promotes exchanges with some universities abroad.

Living

Eating arrangements: Cafeteria system (including salad bar and Saturday brunch); formal meals; vegetarian and other diets catered for. Student kitchens. **Other college facilities:** Music rooms, grand piano, drama society, art room, darkroom, multigym, shared sports grounds and boathouse, gardens, squash/tennis courts, bar, freeview widescreen TV, common room, public rooms and lecture rooms with projection cable TV. **Accommodation:** College accommodation available for almost all students: rent £750–£1k per term of 30 weeks. No students live at home.

Money

Travel grants: Many small and a few large grants for non-work-related travel. **Term-time work:** Paid work in term-time strongly discouraged. College can sometimes help find work in vacations. Internship scheme. **Financial help:** Generous student support funds for those in need.

Student view

A modern, female college, unique in architecture and outlook. Students can be found in every sphere of university life, owing greatly to the supportive environment at the college. Not the richest college, but it will throw everything it can at you to help you realise your potential (eg various travel grants, substantial rewards for high achievers). After all, what makes it stand out from the crowd is its atmosphere and students. Not lacking when it comes to its facilities: 24-hour access to Rosemary Murray library, new computer suite, fully-equipped multigym, tennis and squash courts, various music rooms, art room and photographic dark room. And of course, the newly revamped bar, with vending machines, pool, darts and huuuuuge TV! Accommodation ranges from impressive new rooms (40% ensuite) to unique split-level rooms – all with phone and internet connection; rooms and rates to suit everybody. Great food served in the Dome, college's impressive central venue. Access to fully equipped kitchens for when you need to unleash your own culinary skills – some with dining tables for 20 and comfy seats! Academically, its students do well compared to other university women, particularly in, eg English, SPS, natural sciences and medicine. Extra-curricularly, college is well represented both on a university and college level. A good range of college clubs and societies – Amnesty International, boat club, the Harlots (drinking society), fair-trade group and numerous academic, sport and religious societies. College enjoys good relationships with the other Hill colleges with whom there is a joint orchestra (Orchestra on the Hill), rugby club and drama society.

Student footnotes

Housing: All students housed, in and around college. **Eats:** Excellent range of affordable meals in the Dome (£2–£2.50); no breakfast but a mean brunch on Saturdays. Several shops and restaurants in walking distance. **Drink:** Recently refurbished college bar, wide selection of drinks at decent prices.

Nightlife: Excellent regular events, varying in themes, topped off by renowned summer garden party! **Locals:** Generally OK; occasional town and gown tension. No areas unsafe for students. **Sports:** Full-equipped multigym, squash and tennis courts. Most sports represented by successful college teams. **Travel:** Travel grants and vacation grants available. **Financial help:** Various grants available to anyone who may require them. **Jobs:** Not allowed during term. 5–10% get work locally out of term, 50% elsewhere. **Best features:** Relaxed atmosphere: college is made by its people, not the buildings we're in or their history! **And worst:** Falling asleep on the heated floors. People's misconceptions about female colleges. **Past students:** Tilda Swinton (actress), Joanna MacGregor (concert pianist), Sonia Ruseler (TV news presenter), Sue Perkins (comedian), Claudia Winkleman (presenter), Lisa Burke (Sky Weather), Jane Rogers (author), Jocelyn Bell-Burnell (discoverer of pulsars), Haruko Fukuda (World Gold Council), Barbara Stocking (Director of Oxfam), Frances Edmonds (author and broadcaster), Julia King (Institute of Physics), Deborah Swallow (Director, Courtauld Institute). **More info?** Write to JCR President.

Cambridge – Newnham

- Newnham College, Cambridge CB3 9DF
- ☎ Tel 01223 335783
- 🖶 Fax 01223 357898
- ✉ Email adm@newn.cam.ac.uk
- 💻 Website www.newn.cam.ac.uk

Profile

Staff & students

Undergraduates: 380 women. **Postgraduates:** 155 women. **Teaching staff:** (men and women): 43 college lecturers and directors of studies, 5 research fellows, 27 special supervisors, 4 associate lecturers.

College & admissions

Founded: 1871, as a women's college. **Admission:** Women only. Conditional offers based on exam performance (usually AAA at A-level or equivalent) and interviews. STEP required for maths only. Undergraduates not admitted to study education.

Study opportunities

Library and information service: 85,000 volumes, 6000 antiquarian books. New library building with excellent IT facilities, networked to database search facilities. Separate IT service, access 24 hours/day; network connections to all student rooms; wi-fi in some college areas. IT support from 3 full-time computer officers. **Study abroad:** Formal exchange links with some universities.

Living

Eating arrangements: Brand new buttery for cafeteria service, and hall for formal dinners (cash or charged to college bill). **Other college facilities:** Large computer centre; bar, student common rooms; washing machines; performing arts centre with grand piano and full stage lighting; practice rooms with pianos; art room; dark room; multigym, playing fields and tennis courts on site in large college grounds. **Accommodation:** Available in college for all undergraduates for 3 years: £993 for 10-week term includes heating, kitchen facilities and catering contribution.

Money

Scholarships: Prizes awarded for outstanding performance in university exams. **Travel and book grants:** Generous funds available. Also equipment grants. **Term-time work:** Term-time work discouraged (as terms are short and very intense, and a number of grants are available for those in financial difficulties); jobs of over 6 hours a week only with tutor's agreement. Some part-time work available in college bar, library, waitressing and with admissions events. **Financial help:** Approx 50 college bursaries (£250–£1k pa) for those in special need, and a general hardship/emergency fund, in addition to university's bursary fund.

Student view

Freya Morrissey, Newnham College JCR President (3rd year, English)

Living

What's it like as a place to live? Beautiful, homely and inspirational. Newnham has some of the most beautiful gardens in Cambridge, and the Victorian ivy-covered red-brick buildings are lovely. The college is situated a perfect distance from the hubbub of the city centre: close enough that it's a short walk, but far enough away to avoid all but the most intrepid tourists. **How's the student accommodation?** The rooms are, on the whole and compared with most university accommodation, pleasantly sizeable. Each part of the building has a very different feel, and in 2nd and 3rd year, students choose their own rooms. On-site accommodation is provided throughout the course. Not many ensuite facilities (though there are some), but wonderful garden views often make up for it! Most rooms have large windows, letting in loads of light, as well as quirky features like beautiful old furniture and fireplaces. **What's the student population like?** Female! Newnham is an all-women's college, and proud of it (men are welcome to visit at all times of the day and night, of course – it's not a convent). The student population comes from all over the world, and represent many different religions and cultures. Diversity is something we celebrate, as are friendship, thoughtfulness and ambition. Newnham has a real buzz about it, and a dynamism radiating from its huge range of students. **How do students and locals get on?** Most university societies are open for anyone living or working in Cambridge to join, and of course there is a city outside of the university. Plenty of community projects and campaigns to get involved with – recommended as a way to escape the 'Cambridge bubble'!

Studying

What's it like as a place to study? Newnham has one of the very best college libraries in Cambridge. When the college was founded, and for many years afterwards, women were not permitted to use the central university library, so Newnham had to provide its own impressive facilities. Today, the library is at the centre of the college, and comprises two parts: the old Victorian section and a 2004 extension that blends beautifully with the old surroundings whilst housing all the attendant mod cons (internet access at every desk; photocopying and computer room, etc). The courses are centrally determined (ie by the university not the college), but taught with a mix of college and university supervisions, classes and lectures. Newnham provides the support, encouragement and freedom necessary and desirable for a thorough and exciting education. **What are the teaching staff like?** Dedicated and brilliant. Students have very close contact with the teaching staff, which means continual support, encouragement, goading and stimulation.

Socialising

What are student societies like? Too numerous to do justice to! Sports, music, academic, community-oriented, food-related, religious, political, silly, serious . . . definitely something for everyone. The university has hundreds of societies, and each college also has its own (you can mix and match which you belong to, depending on what you want). There is a society for any activity you could possibly wish for – though if you find a gap in the provision there is plenty of funding for you to set something up yourself, too. Life here is a case of 'work hard, play hard', and there is more than enough opportunity to do both. **What's a typical night out?** Everyone does different things. Some drink, some don't, and there is more than enough to do! Really does depend on what you're interested in doing – whether it's going clubbing, or playing chess, or playing chess in a club, you can go out (or stay in) and do it. **And how much does it cost?** However much you want it to. **How can you get home safely?** It's always a good idea to walk home with friends once it's late or dark, and there are several taxi firms should you find yourself stranded. If you're caught without cash and think a taxi is a good idea, the porters at Newnham will pay for it and the amount will simply be added to your college bill.

Money

Is it an expensive place to live? Unless you are quite unusual, you will leave any university in debt – such is the state of current HE funding. At Cambridge and Newnham, however, there is an extensive and very generous system of bursaries and grants readily available for anyone who finds themselves in a financial pickle. Newnham offers substantial book grants to all students, as well as generously funding many vacation projects. It is a myth that Cambridge is a more expensive place to live: we're some of the financially best-supported students in the country! Newnham has a dedicated financial tutor, who is always available to offer advice and direction in these matters. **Average price of a pint?** Newnham's is currently one of the cheapest bars in Cambridge. **And the price of a takeaway?** £5+. **What's the part-time work situation?** Students are discouraged from working in term time, because of the sheer intensity of the academic work and other activities. There are opportunities for occasional work, however – Newnham's College Bar is currently run and staffed by students, which will earn you £30 for one night's shift. The admissions office offers payment for helping out with open days and other access events; and the development office runs a well-paid telephone campaign every year. All of these things are great fun to be involved with, too! In addition, the vacations are very lengthy, and provide ample opportunity to get long-term well-paid work.

Summary

What's the best feature about the place? That's like asking an English student what their favourite book is – almost impossible to answer! Newnham's atmosphere, generated by a combination of its proud history, its students, and its ambitions, is pretty awesome. **And the worst?** Probably the fact that people make inaccurate and annoying assumptions about what it's like to be at an all-women's college. **And to sum it all up?** Life-changingly, eye-openingly, mind-expandingly brilliant. Come and visit us, and see for yourself.

Past students: Julia Neuberger (author and broadcaster), Frances Gumley (author), Sarah Rowland Jones (immunology specialist), Dorothy Hodgkin (scientist); Margaret Drabble, A S Byatt, Germaine Greer (authors), Sylvia Plath (poet), Joan Bakewell (broadcaster and author), Susie Menkes (fashion writer), Shirley Williams (politician), Ann Mallalieu (lawyer and Labour peer), Emma Thompson (actress), Diane Abbott MP, Clare Balding (presenter), Patricia Hewitt MP. **More info?** Email jcr.president@newn.cam.ac.uk.

Cambridge – Pembroke

✉ Pembroke College, Cambridge CB2 1RF
☎ Tel 01223 338154
🖷 Fax 01223 766409
✉ Email admissions@pem.cam.ac.uk
🖥 Website www.pem.cam.ac.uk

Profile

Staff & students
Undergraduates: 235 men, 215 women. **Postgraduates:** 130 men, 75 women. **Teaching staff**: *Men:* 45 fellows, 7 research fellows. *Women:* 10 fellows, 2 research fellows.

College & admissions
Founded: 1347. Women undergraduates first admitted 1984. **Admission:** Either on the basis of results gained or by conditional offer (usually AAA at A-level or equivalent). Undergraduates not admitted for education or geography.

Study opportunities
Library and information services: Reading and borrowing facilities in all degree subjects. Separate IT service, access 24 hours/day; ratio 1:8 workstations to students; all student rooms linked to university data network and internet. IT support from 3 staff members.

Living
Eating arrangements: Self-service breakfast, lunch and evening meal; formal dinner. **Meals:** £3–£3.50 breakfast; lunch or dinner £5–£7. Café Pembroke for daytime snacks; Sunday brunch. **Gate/guest hours:** Gates closed 7.30pm until 6am, but access for keyholders. Overnight guests permitted by prior arrangement; other guests leave by midnight. **Other college facilities:** Sports (cricket, hockey, rowing, rugby, soccer, squash, netball, tennis, table tennis, multigym), music (rehearsal rooms, pianos, organ, instrumental awards scheme), drama room, photographic darkroom, art room, junior parlour, bar, party cellar, extensive gardens. **Accommodation:** All students in college or nearby college hostels, some 2-roomed sets but mainly single study bedrooms (most with central heating, wash basins and telephone points): rent £1950–£2805 a year. The college operates an automatic means-tested rent rebate scheme. No first-degree students live at home.

Money
Scholarships: College and foundation scholarships, exhibitions and prizes awarded for merit in university examinations. **Travel grants:** Grants towards cost of vacation travel for suitable projects. **Term-time work:** College does not allow term-time work. **Financial help:** Significant bursaries on means-tested basis.

Student view

A happy, friendly community, easy-going in every way. Pleasant architecture and beautiful, well-maintained gardens; very central and well located for most subjects. College provides accommodation for all (1st years in college, remainder in college-owned hostels nearby). Standards vary but good on the whole; rent vary from very low to average for good rooms. Friendly porters and staff. Limited provision for married students. Good food available on cafeteria basis; formal hall served every night. Cooking facilities are limited in college but better in hostels. JP (Junior Parlour – college SU) active socially rather than politically. Relations with college authorities and teaching staff very friendly; joint JP/college committee, numerous student/fellow contacts, both academic and social. Progressive admissions tutors who welcome applications from all backgrounds and ethnic groups. Undergraduates are friendly, outgoing and going places. Bike is useful, depending on subject/sporting interests. Recently extended college library; refurbished bar; soundproof music rooms; good gym; video and TV rooms; party rooms; well-resourced computer rooms; college-catered private functions; large sports ground. Sport is strong, particularly rowing, rugby, netball, football and hockey. Also strong emphasis on drama and music opportunities. Strong subjects: natural science, English, history, economics, engineering – a nice mix. Changing subject is fairly easy.

Student footnotes

Housing: College rent relatively cheap. **Eats:** Local market great for fresh food, and 10 mins' walk to Sainsbury's. A range of restaurants nearby. Meal in college £3–£5; buttery food generally good. Reciprocal arrangements with other colleges. **Drink:** Excellent, newly refurbished, cheap college bar (£1.90 a pint). Well situated for other college bars and local pubs – Mill, Anchor, Eagle. **Nightlife:** College bops, karaoke, stand-up, Pembroke May Ball or June Event. Much cheap and often good student theatre and close to Arts Theatre. Regular cheap films and events at nearby colleges. Weekly university-wide student nights at local nightclubs. **Locals:** Very friendly in general. **Sports:** Wide range of facilities – own boathouse; football, rugby and cricket grounds; squash and tennis courts; multigym in college; free access to university gym. **Travel:** Number of travel awards – easy to get. **Financial help:** University bursary scheme; other hardship funds and many college bursaries. Access funds well organised. Financial pressures as anywhere but many safety nets, fair rent and rebates, etc. **Jobs:** Various in vacation. **Best feature:** Friendly relaxed atmosphere. **Worst:** Some feel suffocated (but a Cambridge problem, not just Pembroke). **Past students:** Ted Hughes (poet); Tom Sharpe (author); Clive James (comedian); Edmund Spenser, Thomas Gray (poets); Tim Brooke-Taylor, Peter Cook (comedians); Eric Idle (comedian and actor); Bill Oddie (conservationist and presenter); Ray Dolby (Dolby Laboratories); William Pitt (Prime Minister); Christopher Hogwood (conductor and harpsichordist); David Munroe (author); Lord (Jim) Prior (former Northern Ireland Secretary); Lord Chief Justice Taylor; Chris Smith MP. **More info?** Email JP Committee at jp@pem.cam.ac.uk.

Cambridge – Peterhouse

Peterhouse, Cambridge CB2 1RD
Tel 01223 338223
Email admissions@pet.cam.ac.uk
Website www.pet.cam.ac.uk

Profile

Staff & students

Undergraduates: 102 men, 75 women. **Postgraduates:** 96 men, 65 women. **Teaching staff**: *Men:* 32 fellows, 3 research fellows, 5 bye-fellows. *Women:* 12 fellows, 2 research fellows, 3 bye-fellows.

College & admissions

Founded: 1284; women undergraduates first admitted 1985. **Admission:** Conditional offers usually AAA at A-level (or equivalent). No undergraduates admitted for geography, education, land economy, social and political sciences or veterinary medicine.

Study opportunities

Library and information service: Approx 80,000 volumes. **Study abroad:** Students use university exchange with the universities of Paris, Poitiers and Utrecht and with MIT.

Living

Eating arrangements: All meals provided in hall, cost depends on choice. **Gate/guest hours:** Gates close at 2am, when guests (other than overnight guests) required to leave; gate keys issued for out-of-hours use. **Other college facilities:** Bar, croquet lawns, squash court, multigym, computer room, punts, washing machines, playing fields, boathouse. Library, theatre and concert hall.
Accommodation: All students in college-owned accommodation: £851 per term average (range £545–£1075). No first-degree students live at home.

Money

Scholarships: Examination, prizes, scholarships and exhibitions (£50–£150) for performance in tripos; annual organ scholarship (£250); music awards (£50 plus tuition); further named college examination prizes in many subjects. **Travel grants:** Approx 95 travel grants awarded pa (average value £400).
Term-time work: Students may not work during term time, except in college library (1% believed to work). **Financial help:** Fund administered by tutors. Help given to any student suffering financial hardship.

Student view

Friendly, lively and unpretentious, it is the oldest and almost the smallest college. The student body is diverse, and the bar is always full of merriment (and cheap alcohol) towards closing. In a small and intimate college, everyone knows everyone else. Sportingly it is comfortably in the middle of the Cambridge range. The library is good for most subjects and excellent for some. Full computing facilities are free. There are male and female teams for most sports, including rugby, football, cricket, rowing, hockey, badminton, squash, water polo, skiing, table tennis and tennis. Because of its relatively small size, it's possible to play all sports as a beginner, yet at the same time Peterhouse has a good share of blues. The shared sports ground comprises 3 football pitches, a rugby pitch (or a cricket pitch in summer) and all-weather tennis courts. Accommodation is provided for all students, most on main college site and all in a safe area; most has been renovated recently and are now a high standard; telephone and internet sockets in all rooms. New kitchen provides good food with plenty of choice. The JCR provides DVDs, videos, newspapers and are a pool table. There are several societies – musical, sporting, theatrical, academic and film – that provide entertainment additional to the bar and the regular events. Bursaries are available in case of hardship; extensive travel grants for all. Peterhouse is continually developing as students' needs and preferences change. Essentially though, it's fantastic fun.

Student footnotes

Housing: All live in. **Eats:** Cheap (or reassuringly expensive) restaurants are 2 mins away.
Drink: College bar is loud and cheap. Local pubs include the Mill, with alfresco dining, on Coe Fen; and the Spread Eagle, with a big-screen TV. **Nightlife:** Cambridge is not the best for nightlife but there's enough to keep most happy. Clubs range from cheesy to mainstream. Multiplex cinema down

the road; plenty of theatres. **Sports:** Kelsey Kerridge Sports Hall is cheap and cheerful. **Financial help:** Very good. College bursaries and university funds. **Locals:** Mostly OK, although they're sometimes a bit bemused by the vast amount of Cambridge jargon.

Cambridge – Queens'

Queens' College, Cambridge CB3 9ET
Tel 01223 335540
Fax 01223 335522
Email admissions@queens.cam.ac.uk
Website www.queens.cam.ac.uk

Profile

Staff & students
Undergraduates: 310 men, 230 women. **Postgraduates:** 170 men, 150 women. **Teaching staff**: *Men:* 45 fellows (3 research fellows, 42 lecturers). *Women:* 9 fellows (3 research fellows, 6 lecturers).

College & admissions
Founded: 1448; women undergraduates first admitted 1980. **Admission:** Entry in all subjects is via conditional offers, usually AAA at A-level (or equivalent); STEP may be used only for mathematics.

Study opportunities
Library and information service: Undergraduate library with copies of all course books; full borrowing facilities both in and out of term. Law library. Separate IT service. Ratio 1:2 workstations to students; computer suite with micro-computers linked to university network; 240 points with access to library and internet. IT support from 1 full-time computer officer.

Living
Eating arrangements: Self-service for all meals; formal dinner also available. **Gate/guest hours:** Very relaxed. **Other college facilities:** Bar, 220-seat theatre, squash courts, table tennis, badminton, croquet, punts, organ, piano, darkroom, laundrette, rooms for TV, college nursery; boathouse and playing fields with tennis courts nearby. **Accommodation:** All students in college accommodation: £798–£976 per term. No first-degree students live at home.

Money
Scholarships: Awarded on performance in university examinations. **Travel grants:** Awards from college expedition fund and other funds. **Term-time work:** College does not allow term-time work outside college. Some work available in college bars and computer room. **Financial help:** Some funds to help those who suffer financial difficulty. Bursaries available for eligible students.

Student view
Ben Wright, Queens' College JCR President
(3rd year, Veterinary Medicine)

Living
What's it like as a place to live? Friendly. By far the most sociable college. There is a strong sense of community at Queens' and this is fostered by lots of inter-year and inter-

subject socialising. **How's the student accommodation?** All undergrads get 3 years' accommodation on site. Rooms vary between old and new, big and small, nice and nasty. The price generally reflects the quality. Graduate accommodation tends to be off site in private housing or nearby Owlstone Croft. **What's the student population like?** Very very friendly. People from all over the world (though majority are British), but everyone tends to settle in quickly and form a close friend network. **How do students and locals get on?** Few locals in college (mainly tourists). No Queens' specific interaction with locals, just the usual uni-wide issues, which tend to include very few problems.

Studying
What's it like as a place to study? Offers almost all courses at the uni. College sticks to the traditional teaching hierarchy at Cambridge (supervisors, tutors and director of studies, etc). Traditionally an academically strong college. **What are the teaching staff like?** Many tutors/directors of studies are experts in their fields. Some supervisors are PhD students, but the quality is still very, very high!

Socialising
What are student societies like? Good range of societies in Queens', especially sports. All sports/societies welcome beginners as well as pros, and many compete at a uni level. Music is very strong at Queens'. Socs range from a few people to 50. If there isn't a soc you are interested in then you can set one up (ie salsa club was set up just last year). **What's a typical night out?** No typical night out – variety of things to do – depends on person. **And how much does it cost?** Again, very dependent. On average, about £20 for a night out. **How can you get home safely?** Cambridge is essentially safe. Can get taxis, walk with friends, cycle, bus (if not too late – a bus stop is right outside Queens').

Money
Is it an expensive place to live? No. Everyone complains about prices and overspends anyway, but compared to national prices, very good. **Average price of a pint?** £1.75. **And the price of a takeaway?** £8. **What's the part-time work situation?** Uni strongly discourages part-time jobs. Plus the terms are so short and busy that it isn't worth it. There are some available though, as so few students get them.

Summary
What's the best feature about the place? The people. The bar. The location. The mix of old and new buildings. The ents. **And the worst?** Some shoddy rooms. Sports pitches about a mile away. Listening to punting tours telling fake tales about the Mathematical Bridge! **And to sum it all up?** The social hub of the university – something for everyone!

Past students: Stephen Fry (comedian); Archbishop of Sydney; Erasmus; Graham Swift, T H White (authors); Michael Foales (first Briton in space).

More info? Enquiries to JCR President (tel 07761 680912, email jcr-president@quns.cam.ac.uk).

Cambridge – Robinson

Robinson College, Cambridge CB3 9AN
☎ Tel 01223 339143
🖷 Fax 01223 339743
✉ Email apply@robinson.cam.ac.uk
🖥 Website www.robinson.cam.ac.uk/admissions

Profile

Staff & students

Undergraduates: 249 men, 153 women. **Postgraduates:** 86 men, 48 women. **Teaching staff**: *Men:* 53 fellows. *Women:* 23 fellows.

College & admissions

Founded: 1977 as first college for men and women (undergraduates admitted from 1979). **Admission:** Offers made on basis of interview and exam performance (usually AAA at A-level, or equivalent). STEP required for mathematics.

Study opportunities

Library and information service: Extensive college library (24-hour access) and law library. Separate IT service, access 24 hours/day; all student rooms connected to college network and internet. IT support from 3 full-time computer officers. **Study abroad:** Formal exchange programme with certain universities in France and USA.

Living

Eating arrangements: Cafeteria-style Garden Restaurant; formal hall (optional, twice weekly, costing £7.65). **Gate/guest hours:** No gate hours; guest rooms available. **Other college facilities:** Computer room, café, bar, music rooms, party room, TV room, theatre, auditorium; Frobenius organ, harpsichord, pianos, joint sports ground with Queens', boathouse shared with St John's, squash and tennis courts, extensive gardens. **Accommodation:** All students can be in college accommodation: residence charge £965–£1460 per term. No first-degree students live at home.

Money

Scholarships: Academic awards after 1st year, based on examination results. Organ and choral scholarships. **Term-time work:** No term-time work without college permission. Vacation work available in college (eg housekeeping, catering). **Financial help:** Financial assistance fund and bursaries available and book and travel grants.

Student view

Youngest college and one of the most relaxed and friendly atmospheres – yet still maintains the highest standards traditionally associated with Cambridge. Attracts a good mix of students from a diverse range of backgrounds. Variety of societies including numerous successful sporting teams and a thriving theatrical and musical community. Designed as a conference centre out of term, so catering and accommodation are well above the student norm (most rooms are ensuite). Some criticise the modern architecture but the picturesque gardens, ideal for lazing about during the summer term, more than make up for this. The benefits of being tourist-free should not be underestimated. Being new, there is a wide range of modern facilities, including a large JCR, a TV room, one of the biggest and best college bars, a large theatre (which doubles as a Dolby digital cinema!) and a beautiful chapel. Well-organised ents team puts on a broad range of regular events in both the main bar and the college party room. Robinson successfully treads the line between traditional Cambridge and the real world, and should seriously be considered by anyone thinking of studying at the university.

Student footnotes

Housing: All undergraduates housed – most in or adjoining the college, some 2nd years in college houses off the main site. **Eats:** Cafeteria open every weekday, lunch only at weekend (but well-equipped kitchens on each staircase). Quality of food high, range of options and good provision for vegetarians and special diets. **Drink:** College bar, open at lunchtimes as well as evenings; prices higher than other student bars (lower subsidies). Pubs in town not far for change of scene. **Nightlife:** Regular ents, films twice a week (recent releases); popular, reasonably priced May ball. **Locals:** Relations generally good; Cambridge is a safe area for students with common sense. **Sports:** Boathouse shared with John's; tennis courts and pitches (hockey, football, rugby) reasonably close; squash and badminton courts over the road. Croquet lawn. **Travel:** Grants for study-related travel. College prizes for non-study-related travel. **Financial help:** College generous with what it has. Bursaries for those in trouble. Book grants available to every student. **Jobs:** No termly work allowed; college employs many students outside term, good wage and free accommodation. **Best features:** Good community atmosphere; refreshing outlook and modern facilities. **And worst:** Limited nightlife in Cambridge itself. **More info?** Contact RCSA President c/o the college.

Cambridge – St Catharine's

St Catharine's College, Cambridge CB2 1RL
Tel 01223 338319
Email undergraduate.admissions@caths.cam.ac.uk
Website www.caths.cam.ac.uk

Profile

Staff & students
Undergraduates: 240 men, 230 women. **Postgraduates:** 100 men, 90 women. **Teaching staff**: *Men:* 55 fellows, 7 research fellows. *Women:* 14 fellows, 1 research fellow.

College & admissions
Founded: 1473; women undergraduates first admitted 1979. **Admission:** Conditional offers (usually AAA at A-level, or equivalent); STEP examinations for mathematics only. Undergraduates not admitted for architecture or history of art.

Study opportunities
Library and information service: 2 college libraries, 3 computer rooms with access 24 hours/day; 4 computers in library, further 27 with internet access; all college rooms have network connections. Ratio workstations to students 1:20. IT support from 2 full-time and 1 part-time computer officers. **Study abroad:** Formal exchange links with Heidelberg (open to all undergraduates) and California Institute of Technology (summer programme for science students).

Living
Eating arrangements: All meals available in college dining hall. No compulsory meals. **Gate/guest hours:** Keys issued on payment of deposit; guest rooms for limited periods. **Other college facilities:** Large 3-manual organ; music practice room with grand piano; sports field with pavilion, AstroTurf hockey pitch, squash, badminton and tennis courts; boathouse; graduate and undergraduate common room; college bar (fair-trade): **Accommodation:** All undergraduates accommodated for at

least three years of their course: residence charges £503–£820 per term, including heating and lighting (no vacation rent unless students stay out of term).

Money

Travel grants: Various grants available. **Term-time work:** College forbids paid employment during term. **Financial help:** Various funds available.

Student view

Described by students from many other colleges as the most fun, least pretentious and friendliest college in the university. It is medium sized (around 135 undergraduates a year) with a good mix of male/females, as well as state/independent school. It also consistently finishes near the top of the academic tables. Centrally placed in the city and near to most faculties. Well over 500 years old (9th oldest in the university) and thus synthesising tradition and culture with a fresh and pleasant attitude and atmosphere. Sounds too good to be true but you would struggle to find any Catz student who regrets the choice. Sports facilities are very good, especially the sports pitches (including AstroTurf) and sports hall. Students can play almost any sport at any level – from rowing to rugby and cricket to squash; the college enjoys a good sporting reputation and considerable success. Many other activities and societies to get involved with – from the superb choir to the Shirley Society (oldest literary group in Cambridge). Nightlife in Cambridge is varied: popular clubs tend to appeal to the fans of 'cheese' rather than your more hard-core clubbers but there is generally something to suit everyone (eg college ents). College bar is very popular (amongst those from other colleges as well as Catz students) and prices cheaper than local pubs and many other colleges; normally a very lively atmosphere, especially at bops (3 times a term). JCR is not politically active but deals with college issues and caters efficiently and effectively for the students' needs. Catz was first Cambridge college to gain Fairtrade certification.

Student footnotes

Housing: All live in college rooms or flats. **Eats:** College: good choice including vegetarian options; cheap and average quality; formal hall excellent value (£7.50 for 3 courses, cheese and coffee). Town: good sandwich shops, fast food outlets; restaurants fairly expensive but Pizza Express, Zizi's, Strada, the Depot reasonable. **Drink:** Several good pubs nearby (Anchor, Granta, Bath House) but quite expensive. College bar cheaper (£1.95 a pint). **Nightlife:** College bops regularly; Cambridge good for films and plays; Ballare, 22, Soultree and the Fez all good clubs; ADC for comedy (including world-famous Footlights); great college music scene. Something for everyone. **Locals:** Averagely friendly. Lots of tourists! **Sports:** Superb college facilities 10 mins walk (include rugby, football, tennis, cricket, squash, badminton and AstroTurf hockey pitch – only a swimming pool and full gym are missing). Very strong in university sports. **Travel:** Many students get summer travel bursaries – £200 approx. **Financial help:** Students have to be very definitely in need but plenty of help available. **Jobs:** Very few students get paid work during term – officially not allowed. College has work during (summer) conference season; many seasonal jobs in Cambridge tourist industry. **Best features:** The people; the atmosphere; bar; sports; accommodation. **Past students:** Howard Brenton (controversial playwright), Sir Ian McKellen (actor), Steve Punt (Mary Whitehouse Experience), Jeremy Paxman (TV presenter), Allan Green (MSP), Sir Peter Hall (director), Kevin Greening (former Radio 1 DJ). **More info?** Contact JCR President c/o the college.

Cambridge – St Edmund's

St Edmund's College, Cambridge CB3 0BN
Tel 01223 336086
Fax 01223 336111
Email admissions@st-edmunds.cam.ac.uk
Website www.st-edmunds.cam.ac.uk

Profile

Staff & students

Undergraduates: 75 men, 55 women. **Postgraduates:** 160 men, 80 women. **Teaching staff**: *Men:* 50 fellows including 7 professors, 2 readers, 1 lecturer, 8 senior research fellows, 4 university executive fellows. *Women:* 13 fellows including 4 research fellows, 1 university executive fellow.

College & admissions

Founded: 1896; college of university since 1975. **Admission:** Primarily a graduate college but also admits a number of mature students (21 and over) and affiliated undergraduates for any subject.

Study opportunities

Library and information service: Library and IT services separate. Modern computing facilities open 24 hours; 15 computers in 2 rooms, all with internet access. IT support from 1 part-time computer officer. Brief voluntary inductions to library services; uni-led courses for IT skills.

Living

Other college facilities: Bar, football pitch, tennis courts, croquet lawn, boat club; also number of facilities shared with other colleges. **Accommodation:** 60% of all students in college and college houses: rent £720–£1060 per term plus £175 fixed kitchen charge per term. All rooms have internet connections. Also accommodation for couples and families. Students may live in privately owned rooms.

Money

Term-time work: Permitted at the discretion of student's tutors. Small amount of work available in college library.

Cambridge – St John's

St John's College, Cambridge CB2 1TP
Tel 01223 338703
Email admissions@joh.cam.ac.uk
Website www.joh.cam.ac.uk

Profile

Staff & students

Undergraduates: 330 men, 225 women. **Postgraduates:** 200 men, 135 women. **Teaching staff:** *Men:* 100 fellows, 11 research fellows. *Women:* 20 fellows, 7 research fellows, 1 lectrice.

College & admissions

Founded: 1511; women undergraduates first admitted 1981. **Admission:** Candidates apply for conditional offers (usually AAA at A-level or equivalent) or on the basis of exams already taken. STEP required for mathematics.

Study opportunities

Library and information service: New college library (plus early 17th-century Old Library) with over 120,000 volumes, ranging from medieval manuscripts to modern university textbooks; full set of Law Reports; skeletons for medical students. 3 computer rooms (2 in library) open 24 hours/day. 4 IT support staff. Training sessions in first week; university runs free IT courses.

Living

Eating arrangements: Self-service buttery dining room; formal dinner in Great Hall available 6 evenings a week (£4.08). **Gate/guest hours:** College members may come and go as they wish; certain regulations regarding overnight guests. **Other college facilities:** Bar, 2 choirs and musical society, theatre in School of Pythagoras; badminton court, fitness centre, multigym, disco cellar; music practice rooms, art studio, drawing office and large auditorium; cinema; 26-acre playing fields and pavilion near college; modern squash courts, table tennis and billiards rooms, college punts. **Accommodation:** All students in college: rent and service charge £1k–£1167 per term. No first-degree students live at home.

Money

Scholarships: Scholarships awarded to members of the college on the basis of performance in university examinations. Scholars receive generous book grants and other privileges. **Travel and other grants:** Travel grants available to all undergraduates for course-related travel. All receive book grants and financial help with extra-curricular expenses. **Term-time work:** Not permitted.

Student view

It's a large, friendly, beautiful college right in the heart of Cambridge – on the river (idyllic in summer) and very central (so nothing far away). 3rd biggest college in terms of undergrad size means it's big enough to meet lots of new people, always finding someone who shares your interests. A rich college, with excellent facilities and resources (including financial assistance). Plenty of societies and clubs to cater for most interests, and funding available to set up new ones if you can't find yours. Central playing fields just across the road, squash courts and a gym on site and a well-equipped boathouse on the river all make for some of the best sporting facilities in Cambridge. Fantastic ents include alternative music events in the Boiler Room venue, open mic nights; Jazz@John's is hugely popular; and May ball (voted '7th best party in the world' by *Time* magazine). Accommodation in college for all 3 years (all 1st years in single rooms). College food is good; cooking facilities for the keen are basic but adequate. Cosy, welcoming bar is a good place to get to know people, whether or not you drink. Pastoral support is good (chaplain; peer support system; and college nurse). Johns people are the friendliest around; it is unpretentious and exciting, with great diversity – a great place to spend the best years of your life.

Student footnotes

Housing: Available in college for all 3 years; large rooms, all with internet and phone access, fantastic architecture. Rents relatively pricey. **Eats:** Buttery meal about £2; excellent formal hall, £4+ for 3-course meal in stunning 'Harry Potter' hall. Vegetarian options at both, halal food served twice a week in the buttery, other dietary requirements catered for. **Drink:** College bar, plenty of nice pubs nearby. **Nightlife:** Ents in college and other colleges (Queens', Clare), several nightclubs in town (but more a fun night out than serious clubbing). Plenty of drama, bands at the Corn Exchange, etc. **Sports:** Fantastic sporting facilities on site, well-equipped boathouse on river. **Travel:** Many travel grants available. **Financial help:** Plentiful, bursaries match the means-tested part of loan. Hardship funds, book grants for all, etc. **Jobs:** University discourages term-time jobs. **Best features:** Historic, beautiful buildings and friendly atmosphere. **And worst:** Sometimes difficult to communicate feelings to college staff, but this is improving. **Past students:** William Wilberforce (social reformer), Paul Dirac (physicist), William Wordsworth (poet), Derek Jacobi (actor), Rob Andrew (rugby player), Douglas Adams (author), Piers Paul Read (author and playwright), Jonathan Miller (satirist, director), Manmohan Singh (Prime Minister of India).

Cambridge – Selwyn

Selwyn College, Cambridge CB3 9DQ
Tel 01223 335896
Email admissions@sel.cam.ac.uk
Website www.sel.cam.ac.uk

Profile

Staff & students
Undergraduates: 210 men, 180 women. **Postgraduates:** 135 men, 65 women. **Teaching staff**: *Men:* 50 fellows, 5 research fellows, 33 lecturers. *Women:* 7 fellows, 3 research fellows, 4 lecturers.

College & admissions
Founded: 1882; women undergraduates first admitted 1976. **Admission:** By conditional offer (usually AAA at A-level, or equivalent) after interview; some places offered on A-levels, school reports and interviews. Most applicants resident in the UK are invited for interview.

Study opportunities
Library and information service: College library (45,000 books), with law and history reading rooms. Separate IT service, access 24 hours/day. 2 computer rooms, ratio 1:42 workstations to students.
450 points with access to library and internet (points in every student room for use with own PCs). IT support from 3–5 staff.

Living
Eating arrangements: Breakfast, lunch and dinner taken in hall; informal self-service and formal dinner. **Gate/guest hours:** College gates closed 2–6am; late keys obtainable. Undergraduates permitted to put up a guest in their own rooms. **Other college facilities:** Bar, shop, 3 rooms for private functions, drama facilities; music practice rooms; photographic darkroom; shared sports ground with King's College. Choral evensong 3 times weekly. **Accommodation:** All students in college: most charged £850 a term (range £520–£1098), including utilities. No first-degree students live at home.

Money
Scholarships: Organ scholarships awarded 2 years out of 3; annual choral and instrumental exhibitions; book prizes, scholarships and exhibitions awarded to those achieving outstanding

performances in university examinations. **Travel grants:** Some available. **Term-time work:** College strongly discourages term-time work (negligible number do). University careers service helps finding vacation jobs. **Financial help:** Variety of awards and funds including Chadwick Fund, Keasbey awards.

Student view — Olivia Wilkinson, Selwyn JCR President (3rd year, Theology)

Living

What's it like as a place to live? We live in colleges – sometimes it can feel like boarding school but that's not always a bad thing! **How's the student accommodation?** Quite expensive but there are a range of options so if you're feeling broke you can get a grottier room for less. The best rooms are ensuite and really new but leave a hole in your bank account. **What's the student population like?** There's quite a few international students, an equal mix of state and private school pupils (contrary to popular belief) and a cosy atmosphere. **How do students and locals get on?** Townies vs gownies lives on. There's not much mixing at all but the locals are welcoming and pleasant so there are very few no-go areas, if any at all.

Studying

What's it like as a place to study? The courses are quite traditional but there are lots of people around who will help you get the most out of your course and therefore it's quite flexible too. **What are the teaching staff like?** We certainly have the academic stars and the eccentrics but if you're not suited to someone it's quite easy to change.

Socialising

What are student societies like? Every possible society exists – there's a societies fair at the beginning of first term to introduce people, and most people are a member of at least one. **What's a typical night out?** Cindies! Cheesy music and drunk toffs. **And how much does it cost?** Entrance £3–£4; drinks cheapest about £1.50. **How can you get home safely?** Taxis, but everyone lives so close that walking home with just one other person is perfectly safe.

Money

Is it an expensive place to live? People have money here so lots of students aren't skint – it's quite expensive if daddy isn't funding you. **Average price of a pint?** £2++. **And the price of a takeaway?** Kebab £2.50. **What's the part-time work situation?** We are not allowed to work during term time.

Summary

What's the best feature about the place? You know you're at the best possible place and it spurs you on to do your best. **And the worst?** The pressure to constantly do your best. **And to sum it all up?** Hard work but the most enjoyable and stimulating hard work you're ever likely to do.

Past students: Malcolm Muggeridge (journalist and broadcaster); Lord Rayner (managing director of Marks and Spencer); Simon Hughes MP, John Selwyn Gummer (politician); Huw Davies (broadcaster); Clive Anderson, Hugh Laurie (comedians).

More info? Contact the JCR President (email JCRpresident@sel.cam.ac.uk).

Cambridge – Sidney Sussex

Sidney Sussex College, Cambridge CB2 3HU
Tel 01223 338872
Email admissions@sid.cam.ac.uk
Website www.sid.cam.ac.uk

Profile

Staff & students
Undergraduates: 180 men, 190 women. **Postgraduates:** 105 men, 60 women. **Teaching staff**: *Men:* 30 fellows, 5 research fellows. *Women:* 15 fellows, 2 research fellows, 2 lektorin/lectora.

College & admissions
Founded: 1596; women undergraduates first admitted 1976. **Admission:** Places are given on the basis of performance in public examinations, aptitude tests, academic references and interviews. Undergraduates not admitted to study education.

Study opportunities
Library and information service: Modern library, open 24 hours; computing suite; all rooms internet connected. **Study abroad:** Exchange links with MIT and European universities in some subjects.

Living
Eating arrangements: All meals may be taken in hall (£2.95 for 2-course meal; formal hall £5.72); also self-catering facilities. **Gate/guest hours:** 24 hours via student room keys. **Other college facilities:** Music practice room with piano, grand piano and harpsichord; organ. Sports field shared with St John's, boathouse with Corpus Christi, Girton and Wolfson; squash and tennis courts; gym. Three common rooms, bar. **Accommodation:** All undergraduates in college-owned accommodation: rent £65–£95 pw (average £80) plus kitchen charge of £380 pa. Typical student pays £2800–£3500 pa full board (rent and food).

Money
Scholarships: A number of scholarships, exhibitions and prizes awarded on performance in university examinations and various graduate studentships. **Financial help:** UK undergraduates may be eligible for a variety of bursaries, grants and hardship funds. Additional funding available for the purchase of books and for academic travel.

Student view

It's small and friendly – and famous for being 'the one opposite Sainsbury's (Sidney students are the envy of those from other colleges, who have to cart their shopping home). It's a pretty college, with some beautiful architecture and pleasant gardens. Decent facilities include 24-hour library and computer suite (recently upgraded), TV room, student-run bar, recently updated gym, squash court and off-site sports grounds and boathouse. A good mix of students; 50:50 male:female split, around 65% from state schools and 10% international. Everyone is very friendly, which contributes to the family-like feel in college. Relations between students, fellows and other college staff are good, with student representation on many college committees, and an approachable pastoral system. Tripos results improving recently; fellows always keen to hear student opinions. Active SU which puts on bops, runs the bar, and organises welfare provisions and recycling facilities. Many different clubs and societies – from the active history society (Confrat) to the not-so-active HobNob and other biscuit appreciation society (NobSoc). Sporting teams are generally about participation rather than ability and if there isn't a society that grabs your fancy, the union has provisions for you to start your own!

Student footnotes

Housing: Guaranteed for all undergraduates; prices significantly below university average. Most on site, some hostels a couple of mins away and a couple of houses across city; variable standard though all pretty good (about 90 ensuite). 2nd- and 3rd-year rooms assigned by ballot (order of which is reversed in 3rd year). **Eats:** 3 meals a day in hall (except Sunday when dinner only served), standard pretty good and prices fair. Formal hall (3 times a week) not compulsory. College central, so good food never far away. **Drink:** College bar is very cheap. Lots of pubs nearby, including the Regal (Britain's biggest). **Nightlife:** University theatre (ADC) nearby, weekly productions. Arts Cinema nearby – excellent variety. Bops organised by different colleges and advertised throughout. Close to main Cambridge nightclubs. **Sports:** Town sports centre relatively expensive. Wide variety of sports available – no great skill required at college level (emphasis on fun). College gym. **Travel:** Small amount (about £100) for vacation travel available quite easily for 2nd years. £300 for 'deserving cases'. **Financial help:** Various hardship funds, several travel grants, book grants, financial awards for academic achievement. **Jobs:** Very few get paid term-time work (lack of time), although some work in student-run bar. **Best features:** Awesome friends; Sainsbury's. **And worst:** State of the TV room, post-bop. **Past students:** John Patten (former MP), David Thomson (journalist), C T R Wilson (physicist), Lord David Owen, Oliver Cromwell, Asa Briggs (author), Carol Vorderman (Countdown). **More info?** Enquiries to President SSCSU (tel 01223 338860, email sscsu.president@sid.cam.ac.uk, website www.jcr.sid.ucam.org).

Cambridge – Trinity

Trinity College, Cambridge CB2 1TQ
☎ Tel 01223 338422
✉ Email admissions@trin.cam.ac.uk
🖥 Website www.trin.cam.ac.uk

Profile

Staff & students

Undergraduates: 428 men, 242 women. **Postgraduates:** 218 men, 129 women. **Teaching staff:** *Men:* 34 fellows, 27 research fellows, 48 professorial fellows. *Women:* 16 fellows, 7 research fellows, 4 professorial fellows.

College & admissions

Founded: 1546; women undergraduates first admitted 1978. **Admission:** Pre-A-level candidates considered for conditional offers, which will include STEP for mathematics applicants. Post-A-level candidates considered on their record. Most candidates will be interviewed.

Study opportunities

Library and information service: Magnificent Wren Library with over 50,000 volumes plus a reading room; also law reading room. IT and library services converged. Ratio 1:25 workstations to students (access 24 hours/day). 1200 points with access to library and internet (all college rooms). IT support from member of computer staff.

Living

Eating arrangements: Breakfast, lunch and dinner available in hall on cafeteria system, plus formal dinner. Fixed annual price of £378 plus cash payment for individual meals. **Gate/guest hours:** Great Gate locked at 2am but college members may enter or leave at any time. **Other college facilities:** 3 large common rooms; 2 student computer rooms; bar; games and party rooms; buttery; 6 laundrettes; CD lending library; music practice rooms; 2 sports grounds; gym, squash, tennis and badminton courts; boathouse with excellent modern facilities. **Accommodation:** All students in college: most charged in range £707–£1044 per term, including heating.

Money

Scholarships: Scholarships awarded on university examinations; organ scholarship (£300 pa) offered in alternate years, 6 choral exhibitions (£100 pa) annually; numerous college prizes. **Travel grants:** Grants for projects and research; small grants for vacation travel. **Term-time work:** College discourages term-time work. **Financial help:** Any student experiencing financial difficulty considered.

Student view

Trinity probably epitomises what most people imagine when they think of Cambridge: it is large, wealthy, grandiose and architecturally stunning but its population is not stereotypically 'Cambridge'. It's the largest college in the university and has an exceptionally varied student body – one of its best features; there's almost certainly someone who shares your passion, however obscure! There are people from all over the world, a variety of schools and backgrounds; high proportion of international students (about 10%) and a large graduate population. It's conveniently placed in the centre of Cambridge – most faculties less than 10 mins' walk and Sainsbury's is handy. The SU (TCSU) runs ents (dances/band nights, etc) and provides welfare services. College also has a wide range of student-run clubs and societies for sports, hobbies and interests; several teams for most sports at any level; Dryden Society for drama; student art lending; cultural societies; fairtrade and even a houmus society. Several music rooms and myriad of choirs and bands, so plenty of opportunities to make beautiful (?!) noises. As the wealthiest Cambridge college, there is financial help to students in many forms – bursaries, hardship funds, prizes. College provides housing for all undergraduates throughout their degree and it varies considerably. 1st year rooms are all around the main college site, mostly modern and all with internet. Choice of room in subsequent years, traditional rooms with high ceilings, oak beams and decidedly variable amenities, or apartment-style, modern rooms with all mod cons in Burrells Field across the river. Impressive facilities for study: 2 computer rooms (Macs and PCs), well-stocked library (any vital books missing will be ordered at your request) and Wren library (contains Newton's original manuscripts and first notes on Winnie the Pooh). Stylish (if small) bar, a games room with pool and table football, 2 comfortable common rooms with a 32" TV (with Sky Digital) and separate common room for graduates. Small party room for club nights, with variety of music. Can sometimes be a bit boggling to be in such a large, grand college but the benefits far outweigh any disadvantages – loneliness just isn't an option! Don't make any decisions about Trinity without seeing it – it probably isn't quite what you expect.

Student footnotes

Housing: College rooms for all (subsidised, so cheap). **Eats:** Palatable, filling fare served up in hall – breakfast, lunch and dinner, plus kitchen fixed charge per term. Vegetarian option always available; halal meat on Mondays. Good selection of local restaurants and sandwich bars, variety of prices. **Drink:** Student bar with cheap drinks (£1.80+ for a pint, £1.30+ a shot). **Nightlife:** Ents in colleges plus 4 main clubs in town catering for a variety of tastes but mainly dominated by student staple – cheese. Lots of pubs and bars, with different atmospheres – something for everyone. **Locals:** Very friendly (trouble is so rare it's reported in the university newspapers). **Sports:** Excellent, at both college and university levels. **Travel:** Lots of travel grants and bursaries for both study and fun. **Financial help:** Plenty of money for anyone with a justifiable claim. **Jobs:** Term-time jobs not allowed (but some people manage it). **Best features:** Excellent academic facilities, enormous variety of people, financial benefits. **Worst features:** Hard work squashed into short terms; people feeling that they should live up to the Trinity stereotypes. **Past students:** A E Housman (poet), Francis Bacon (artist), Field Marshal Montgomery, Sir Isaac Newton (scientist), Lord Butler (civil servant), J Nehru (prime minister of India), A A Milne (author), R Vaughan Williams (composer), G M Trevelyan (historian), Betrand Russell (philosopher); Byron, Tennyson (poets), Lord Rutherford (scientist), Macaulay (historian), Wittgenstein (philosopher). **More info?** Contact tcsu-president@trin.cam.ac.uk.

Cambridge – Trinity Hall

Trinity Hall, Cambridge CB2 1TJ
Tel 01223 332535
Fax 01223 332537
Email admissions@trinhall.cam.ac.uk
Website www.trinhall.cam.ac.uk

Profile

Staff & students

Undergraduates: 195 men, 190 women. **Postgraduates:** 130 men, 100 women. **Teaching staff:** *Men:* 38 fellows, 2 research fellows. *Women:* 10 fellows, 3 research fellows.

College & admissions

Founded: 1350; women undergraduates first admitted 1977.

Study opportunities

Library and information service: New library; also historic library (chained books). Internet access from all PCs in library and points in all student rooms in college. Computer officer and undergraduate support team give IT support.

Living

Eating arrangements: All meals available in hall and charged to end of term bill. Super hall (special dinner) on some Thursdays. All rooms have access to cooking facilities. **Gate/guest hours:** Gate closed at 2am; all undergraduates on central site may have gate key. **Other college facilities:** Bar; music room with piano; washing machines and driers; boathouse; squash and tennis courts; playing fields. **Accommodation:** All students guaranteed college accommodation for 3 years (4th years offered graduate accommodation): rent average £80 pw including heat but not including meals. No first-degree students live at home.

Money

Scholarships: Scholarships awarded on the results of university examinations taken while in residence; numerous college prizes. **Travel grants:** Elmore travel exhibition annually on result of modern and medieval languages tripos; grants from Benn and Gregson funds for vacation travel of educational or adventurous nature. **Term-time work:** College does not allow term-time work for first-degree students (term-time work in college only in exceptional circumstances). University careers service helps find work out of term time. **Financial help:** Number of funds available, as well as university funds (see college website); all cases are considered individually on merit. Travel funds also available according to need.

Student view

Andy McGowan, Trinity Hall JCR Access Officer (2nd year, Law)

Living

What's it like as a place to live? It is a really friendly college and as it's quite small you can walk through college and know at least the names of practically everyone that you will walk past. The porters really have a reputation for being friendly and helpful (whether you've locked yourself out of your room, have injured yourself playing football or are just stressed in exam term and want a chat over a cup of tea at 3 in the morning). **How's the student accommodation?** Trinity Hall accommodates all of its undergraduates for the entirety of their degrees. There is some new ensuite accommodation that is quite posh (heated towel rails, leather sofa in the common room, big kitchen) but all other rooms have a sink and a mirror in them and you share a bathroom and kitchen (normally between 4 people or so). The accommodation is quite nice and there is some within the centre of Cambridge, and some just a bit outside. **What's the student population like?** Trinity Hall has quite a diverse population with a sizeable international community. On its JCR Committee, there are welfare reps and also an international rep who looks after the needs of international students.

Studying

What's it like as a place to study? Trinity Hall has a rather new library, which is pretty well stocked – they also operate a scheme where you can request a book and if your course director sees it as helpful to your course, then the library will get it in (usually within 2–3 days!). Trinity Hall is quite good at balancing academic and extra-curricular activities so that you have the time to do both. **What are the teaching staff like?** The teaching staff at Trinity Hall really do their best to help you both academically and non-academically. They have some leading experts in numerous subjects, as well as PhD students who are really, really enthusiastic, so it's quite a mix. As it's quite a small college, you may find yourself having 1 or 2 supervisions in a different college.

Socialising

What are student societies like? Trinity Hall has a large range of societies ranging from football, rugby and choir to a film society and a pool club. The college has a reputation for letting anyone be involved who wants to be involved – even if they have never done it before and aren't very good. It does have a reputation for 'punching above its weight', especially in rowing. **What's a typical night out?** Most Wednesdays, you will find students going out to the local club for the students' night, starting at the college bar, having a few drinks with friends and relaxing, and then going to one of the clubs (after queuing for a while!) before stopping off for some food on the way back at the end of the night for a burger or kebab. **And how much does it cost?** Probably around £20 in total (including entry to nightclub and the food). **How can you get home safely?** Most of the accommodation is within the centre of town and only a couple of mins' walk from most of the clubs/bars. There is some accommodation a bit further away but everyone walks up in a group (about a third of the college live up at that second site).

Money

Is it an expensive place to live? Accommodation within college is reasonably cheap. The college has some new ensuite accommodation which costs around £100 pw – but on average, the typical price of a room varies between £50 and £80 pw. **Average price of a pint?** £1.70. **What's the part-time work situation?** Generally you're not allowed a part-time job, but they do employ some students to work behind the college bar (for 1 or 2 nights a week); they also pay students to help out with open days and similar events at the start of vacations.

Summary

What's the best feature about the place? It really does have a reputation for being a very friendly college – people in the 1st year socialise with people in the 3rd year. Even the porters do their best to make sure they learn your name (and even invite you for tea and biscuits!) **And the worst?** The food is quite expensive compared to other colleges, but still cheap in comparison to in town. **And to sum it all up?** Trinity Hall is a very friendly place to study, and everyone is encouraged to get involved in all aspects of college life as much or as little as they want – whether it's standing for a position on the committee, playing a sport for fun or even going to watch a drama production just to support the people in it.

Past students: Rt Rev Robert Runcie (former Archbishop of Canterbury), Lord Geoffrey Howe, Sir Norman Fowler MP, J B Priestley (writer), Tony Slattery (comedian), Rachel Weiss (actress), Lord Phillips of Sudbury (lawyer and politician), Nicholas Hytner (Director of the National Theatre), Terry Waite (author, former hostage).

More info? Enquiries to JCR President (email jcr@trinhall.cam.ac.uk).

Cambridge – Wolfson

Wolfson College, Cambridge CB3 9BB
☎ Tel 01223 335918
✉ Email ug-admissions@wolfson.cam.ac.uk
🖥 Website www.wolfson.cam.ac.uk

Profile

Staff & students

Undergraduates: 70 men, 70 women. **Postgraduates:** 290 men, 215 women.

College & admissions

Founded: 1965. **Admission:** Primarily graduate college but mature undergraduates over 21 admitted (some are affiliated students, who already have a first degree, reading for BA in 2 years).

Study opportunities

Library and information service: 13,000 books, 44 periodicals, many study places. Separate IT service; points with access to library and internet in each study bedroom. IT support from 1 computer officer.

Living

Eating arrangements: Meals in hall (average meal for £3). Formal hall £10. Vending machines, cafeteria in club room. **Other college facilities:** Tennis court, multigym, boathouse and boats. **Accommodation:** 90% in college accommodation. Rents £74–£96 pw (more for flats).

Money

Travel grants: College travel fund. **Term-time work:** No college policy on part-time work for undergraduates. Some term-time work available in college as bartender and porter. **Financial help:** College hardship fund.

Student view

One of the newest Cambridge colleges, Wolfson is relaxed, unpretentious and friendly. Students are all postgraduates or mature undergraduates, with over 70 countries represented. It's next to the M11, a little way from the town centre (15 mins by foot), compensated by campus set in safe and quiet area. Good library (especially for law) and computer facilities, open all hours. Excellent gym, recently extended. Within easy distance of university library and many language and humanities faculties. Food improving all the time. Members can live in college accommodation for all 3 years if they want; some married and family flats available. SA (WCSA) represents all students. Very active; it's pragmatic rather than political and oversees the running of a wide range of clubs and societies.

Student footnotes

Housing: All college rooms have phones and internet connections. **Eats:** College food good (meals £3-ish); 3 meals weekdays (weekends lunch only). Vegetarians catered for. Twice weekly formal halls popular. **Drink:** Cheap college bar, open daily 9pm–midnight; range of drinks being extended. **Nightlife:** All college events free. Weekly disco, live bands, ceilidhs, etc. **Locals:** Area safe for students. **Sports:** Excellent gym and tennis court on site. Most sports supported. **Travel:** Travel funds available. College good for contacts as highly international. **Financial help:** Some from college; much more from university. **Jobs:** In college bar, porter's lodge, kitchens or around town. **Best features:** Cosmopolitan atmosphere. **And worst:** Apathy. **More info?** Check out the website (www.srcf.ucam.org/~wcsa).

Canterbury Christ Church University

Location:
south-east England
(map 2)
Main campus at
Canterbury plus
Broadstairs, Medway
and Folkstone;
partner colleges

Canterbury Christ Church University,
Canterbury, Kent CT1 1QU
☎ Tel 01227 767700
🖨 Fax 01227 470442
✉ Email Admissions@canterbury.ac.uk
💻 Website www.canterbury.ac.uk

Student enquiries: Admissions and Recruitment Department
Applications: UCAS

In brief

Total Students: 14,495

 24% postgraduate
76% undergraduate

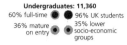 **Undergraduates: 11,360**
60% full-time ● ● 96% UK students
36% mature ● ● 35% lower
on entry ● ● socio-economic
groups

 72% female 28% male

- **A modern university.**
- **Teaching staff:** 270 full-time, 36 part-time.
- **Broad study areas:** Initial teacher training, nursing, midwifery and professions allied to medicine, arts and humanities, science and business.

Freshers

- **Admissions information:** AS-levels accepted in combination with 2+ A-levels or equivalent. UCAS tariff used.
- **First degree entrants:** 1855 UK, full-time.
- **Points on entry:** 180 (average).
- **Drop-out rate:** 10% in 1st year.
- **Accommodation:** 1st years from outside the immediate area guaranteed accommodation.

Profile

Institution

Founded: 1962 as a Church of England foundation; merged with various schools of nursing and radiography. University status in 2005. **Site:** Main campus in Canterbury, 10-min walk from city centre; other sites in city centre, eg Sidney Cooper Gallery; other campuses at Broadstairs, Tunbridge Wells, Medway and Folkstone (joint with Greenwich University). **How to get there:** By car, A2/M2; frequent coach service from London Victoria to Canterbury; by rail from London (Victoria, Charing Cross or Waterloo East) to Canterbury East/West, both 20-mins walk from campus. **Special features:** Own radio station.

Courses

Largest fields of study: Teacher education, health-related studies. **Awarding body:** Canterbury Christ Church University. **Main undergraduate awards:** BA, BSc. **Length of courses:** 3 years.

Study opportunities & careers

Library and information services: Library with 231,000 volumes, 800 periodicals, 400 study places. Information provision, £59 pa spent for each student (FTE). Separate IT service: 370 points with access to library, 440 to internet (410 PCs, 30 Macs); access 4–10 hours/day. IT support from computer services help desk; computer skills training and library tours and talks for all new students; various IT skills courses each term. **Careers:** Information and advice.

Student services & facilities

Student advice and services: Chaplain, counsellor, student adviser, disability adviser, study support unit, personal tutors; nursery facilities nearby. **Amenities:** Student building. **Sporting facilities:** Sports centre; tennis courts, gymnasium and fitness centre. **Accommodation:** 70% of 1st years in university-owned accommodation (guaranteed for overseas students). Places in catered and self-catering halls: rent for self-catering £65–£91 pw (£85–£96 pw ensuite), for catered places £112.50 (£117.50 pw ensuite); all 39-week contracts. Also head-leased places (not for 1st years) at £67–£76 pw, Sept–July. Halls in Broadstairs at £86 pw.

Money

Living expenses budget: Minimum budget of £540 per month (excluding tuition fees) recommended by university. **Term-time work:** Many first-degree students believed to work; term-time work available on campus in library, bars, etc. JobShop (in careers service) helps find work up to 15 hours/week, mostly in Canterbury and Thanet. **Financial help:** Bursaries of £840 pa for UK students whose family income is up to £25k, of £520 pa if family income is £25k–£49,300. Also sports scholarships. Government access to learning funds of £75k, 340 students helped. **Tuition fees:** Home students pay £3225 pa for first degree courses. International students pay £7650–£8375 pa.

Student view

Main sites in the shadow of Canterbury Cathedral and 5 mins from the town centre. A new university, Christ Church has grown over the last few years, and continues to do so while maintaining its friendly and personal atmosphere. A growing international programme integrates students from all over the world. Originally a teacher training college, it now runs a wide range of degree courses. Student numbers are high and accommodation expensive. Driving in Canterbury is a nightmare and parking is almost impossible (but improving slowly). The SU is the place to be, with varied entertainments bringing it to life at night. During the day the building acts as one large coffee shop selling hot and cold food and drink, tickets to events and alcohol. The SU has an award-winning radio station (and is working with Kent University on an FM radio station for the Canterbury area) and has its own TV station; it has sports teams that compete in both BUCS and SESSA, not to mention societies such as trampolining and lacrosse.

Student footnotes

Housing: Accommodation scarce and expensive. Look early in papers, noticeboards and Accommodation Office. SU runs an accommodation database. **Eats:** Canteen on campus; wide range of food in town (loads of student discounts). Meals from £3 on campus, Wetherspoons burger and chips £4. **Drink:** SU bar is cheapest place (pint from £1.80). Many pubs: Wetherspoons, the Scream; most student-friendly. **Nightlife:** SU events most nights on campus and local venues; 5 formal balls a year, culminating in all-night extravaganza, the Summer Ball. Local nightclubs include Chicago Rock Café, Baa Bars, the Bizz and Studio 41. Also the Venue is student-only (belongs to Kent University). **Locals:** Fairly friendly; *loads* of tourists. **Sports:** Reasonable facilities, including gym; brilliant teams. **Travel:** Easy, quick links to London and Europe. **Jobs:** Mainly in pubs, restaurants and shops, also in SU bar. University JobShop (also online). **Best features:** Entertainment. **And worst:** Lack of parking. **Informal name:** Christ Church. **More info?** Enquiries to SU President on 01227 782416, email su.president@canterbury.ac.uk, website www.ccsu.co.uk.

Cardiff University

Location:
Cardiff, south-east
Wales (map 1)
All sites near
city centre, plus
hospital site

📧 Cardiff University, 46 Park Place, Cardiff CF10 3BB
☎ Tel 029 2087 4455
📠 Fax 029 2087 4457
✉ Email enquiry@cardiff.ac.uk
🖥 Website www.cardiff.ac.uk

Student enquiries: Undergraduate Recruitment Office
Applications: UCAS

In brief

Total Students: 30,930

70% undergraduate
25% postgraduate
5% FE Students

Undergraduates: 21,800
75% full-time
14% mature on entry
93% UK students
22% lower socio-economic groups

61% female
39% male

- **World-class research-intensive university.**
- **Teaching staff:** 1433 full-time, 419 part-time.
- **Broad study areas:** Business; law; health and life sciences; medicine, dentistry and nursing; professions allied to medicine (including occupational therapy, physiotherapy and radiography); physical sciences; engineering; architecture; town planning; humanities and social studies.

Freshers

- **Admissions information:** Normally at least 3 A-levels, excluding general studies, required; detailed policy depends on subject area.
- **First degree entrants:** 4325 UK, full-time.
- **Points on entry:** 389 (average).
- **Drop-out rate:** 5% in 1st year.
- **Accommodation:** All 1st years guaranteed student accommodation (unless through Clearing).

Profile

Institution

Founded: 1883. **Structural features:** Merged with University of Wales College of Medicine in 2004. **Site:** Close to Cardiff city centre. Healthcare students also at hospital site, Heath Park Campus, 1 mile away. **How to get there:** Cardiff Central Station on the national rail network; coaches to bus station (next to train station); M4 from London and M5 (west country and midlands). For university, frequent trains from Central Station to Cathays station (on campus), local buses from bus station (53, 79, 81 for main campus; 8 or 9 for hospital site).

Courses

Academic features: 4-year integrated sandwich degree programmes, 5-year two-tier degree programmes in architecture and town planning. 5-year medical and dental courses, plus foundation year for those without science backgrounds; clinical teaching throughout Wales. **Awarding body:** Cardiff University; University of Wales (for medicine and dentistry). **Main undergraduate awards:** BA, BD, BDS, BMus, BN, BSc, BEng, BScEcon, LLB, MArch, MB BCh, MPhys, MChem, MEng, MPharm. **Length of courses:** 3 years; others 4 and 5 years.

Study opportunities & careers

Library and information services: Integrated library, IT and media services: 17 libraries, 25 computer rooms, 7 media resources units. Over 1.3 million books, 14,000 printed and electronic journals, access to numerous web-based databases, 3220 study places. Specialist collections: include Salisbury Library of Celtic and Welsh material; Cochrane Archive of evidence-based healthcare; South Wales Europe Direct Centre. Also special collections in law, architecture. Information provision, £164 pa spent for each student (FTE). IT network to all parts of campus, 5500 connections in student residences, 24-hour access. IT support (on-site or via telephone/email); IT and information literacy skills courses, some in liaison with academic departments. **Study abroad:** 2% of students spend a period abroad. Active Erasmus programme, with 250+ European links. Student exchange agreements worldwide. **Careers:** Information, advice and individual guidance available; workshops, careers talks, employers presentations, skills sessions. Careers library, online vacancy bulletin, careers fairs. Careers management skills modules in many departments and work experience opportunities.

Student services & facilities

Student advice and services: Student support centres offer general advice, financial support, counselling, services for disabled and dyslexic students. Health centre. Chaplains (Anglican, Catholic, Methodist) work alongside other local faiths/denominations. Some residential facilities for students with families or with disabilities; day-care centre. **Amenities:** Large purpose-built SU houses, eg 9 bars, nightclub, concert venue, cafés, TV lounge, IT and games rooms, shops, letting agency, jobshop, IT shop and repair service, athletic union, societies lounge, media centre (radio and television stations and student newspaper). **Sporting facilities:** Indoor and outdoor facilities at Talybont: floodlit AstroTurf pitch, tennis courts, fitness suite, sports halls and a martial arts dojo. At Park Place: squash courts, fitness suite and classes, wellbeing clinic. Sports fields at Llanrumney: 33 acres of pitches, changing rooms, pavilion. Heath Hospital site: swimming pool, sauna, jacuzzi, squash and badminton court, sports hall, multigym. **Accommodation:** All 1st years guaranteed a single place in university residences (unless through clearing): 5054 self-catering places at £56–£82 pw; 82 catered places (female only) at £79 pw; 193 part-catered places at £70–£80 pw; all on 38-week contracts (ie including Christmas and Easter vacations). Most students in private-sector housing after 1st year, £55–£60 pw plus bills.

Money

Living expenses budget: Minimum budget of £5640 (excluding tuition fees) recommended by university for each academic year (Sept–June), £7520 for full calendar year. **Term-time work:** Part-time work in university and SU (in bars, restaurants, offices, libraries, labs, sports centre, etc) through Unistaff Jobshop; also jobs locally in bars, shops and offices. **Financial help:** Bursaries of £1050 pa for students whose family income is up to £25k, of £500 pa where family income is £25k–£39,300. Total of 100 scholarships awarded annually, worth a total of £3k, for high-achieving students in particular disciplines (eg physics, maths, music, Italian). £1m government funds; also hardship loans. Some charitable trust funds, eg for students encountering unexpected hardship (including final-year students from Commonwealth and SE Asia), self-financing students, female students whose health is affected during course. Apply for help at Student Support Centre. **Tuition fees:** Home students pay £3225 pa for first degrees (though Welsh residents may be eligible for annual fee grant; NHS pays fees on some courses). International students pay £9600 pa (classroom), £12,300 pa (lab/pre-clinical), £22,500 pa (clinical).

Student view

Cardiff is a young, vibrant city; it recently celebrated its centenary as a city. A blend of beautiful old architecture (Civic Centre, Cardiff Castle) and new, cutting-edge developments (eg Cardiff Bay waterfront). Cosmopolitan, with a large student population (38,000 of them, some 10% of the city's population). Main student areas are Cathays, Roath and Plasnewydd. It's the fastest growing capital in Europe, so all the amenities you would expect with the bonus of being small enough to access it on foot and via the excellent transport links. Limited parking at halls (you need to buy a permit) but easy to live without a car. City centre is 5 mins from Cathays Park campus and has a vast array of cafés, restaurants, bars and clubs (excellent nightlife), especially St Mary Street, the Hayes, the Bay and the student heartland of Cathays; all from student-friendly to expensive. Good shops – indoor centres, eg St David's Centre, Capitol and Queen Street Arcade. Many traditional arcades with an array of boutiques; thriving indoor market; plus many shops on St Mary and Queen streets. Terrific world-class venues, (eg Millennium Stadium, Millennium Centre and Cardiff International Arena (CIA). Also beautiful parks near the university so, overall, excellent lifestyle. University has very large SU, based both at Park Place and the Med Club at Heath

Park. At Park Place, a massive array of services – 59 sports clubs, 140 societies, dedicated media suite (which houses award-winning gair rhydd, Quench and Xpress radio), advice and representation centre, student development unit, volunteering unit and representation for all students. It boasts 4 main venues: the Taf bar (modern, 600 capacity), Solus nightclub (3 rooms, 1900 capacity) and CF10 (café by day, venue by night). Also jobshop, Endsleigh insurance, STA Travel and specialist shops selling booze, computers, books, mobile phones, etc; and it is the centre of most social activities. Med Club at Heath Park has legendary Med Club bar, which hosts many social events and has a shop. University has a reputation for being well-rounded in terms of courses – 31 academic schools from architecture to Welsh; medicine, business, philosophy, psychology and optometry are among its strengths. Quite demanding to get into (need 350+ points). Good libraries and internet points in most student rooms. A relatively cheap and exciting place to live.

Student footnotes

Housing: Places in halls guaranteed for 1st years; good standard and reasonably priced. Most is at Talybont (within easy walking distance of university); some 10 other halls, including large University Hall (farthest from uni but great atmosphere) and Aberdare Hall (all-female). Private rentals relatively inexpensive; most live in the north of the city. Cathays and Roath are student-ville; avoid Grangetown and Riverside; Bay area popular for those with bigger budgets. Get help from the Residence office and SU (it has a housing guide). **Eats:** Zushi (sushi restaurant), The End (£3-ish), Cantaloupe, Henry's and Tiger Tiger all good. **Drink:** SU consistently cheap. Many bars throughout city centre. **Nightlife:** Plenty happening in SU: club nights throughout the week, eg alternative music (Fun Factory), sports nights (Rubber Duck), Fat Friday, and Come Play on Saturdays. Loads of good clubs in city. **Locals:** No student animosity in Cardiff and no problem areas in town; cheap area to get insured; good local taxi services. **Sports:** Gyms and sports centres range from free SU/university facilities to excellent but more expensive Cannons fitness centre. Swimming pools, velodrome and an ice rink. **Travel:** Discounted travel from STA Travel. **Financial help:** Range of funds, including for women with health problems; some for students on specific courses or backgrounds; short-term loans and grants for finalists. **Jobs:** Many students work but best apply early (as soon as possible after arriving). Jobshop helps and some employers give flexible hours for students. Some jobs in SU bars and shops. **Best features:** Cardiff is relatively small but has all you expect from a big city – always something on, day or night, whatever interests you. **And worst:** The Welsh weather. **Past students:** Neil Kinnock MP, Glenys Kinnock MEP, Tim Sebastian (presenter), John Peters (former RAF pilot and Gulf War veteran), Doreen Vermeulen-Cranch (anaesthetics), Vincent Kane (presenter), Mark Lamarr (presenter and DJ), Huw Edwards (BBC). **More info?** Cardiff University SU (Park Place, Cardiff CF10 3QN, tel 029 2078 1419, email studentsunion@Cardiff.ac.uk, www.cardiffstudents.com).

Central Saint Martins College of Art & Design

Location:
central London
(map 3)
Main sites in Holborn
plus specialist centres;
single site King's
Cross from 2011

🖳 Central Saint Martins College of Art & Design,
Southampton Row, London WC1B 4AP
☎ Tel 020 7514 7022/7023
🖷 Fax 020 7514 7254
✉ Email info@csm.arts.ac.uk
🖳 Website www.csm.arts.ac.uk

Student enquiries: Information Office
Applications: UCAS

In brief

Total Students: 4000

65% undergraduate
20% postgraduate
15% FE Students

Undergraduates: 2700

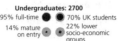

95% full-time
14% mature on entry

70% UK students
22% lower socio-economic groups

65% female   35% male

- **Specialist art and design college.** Part of University of the Arts London.
- **Teaching staff:** 80 full-time, 70 visiting lecturers.
- **Broad study areas:** Fashion and textiles; fine art; communication design; graphic design; media arts; theatre design and performance; 3-D design (including jewellery, ceramics, industrial, furniture design); acting; directing.

Freshers
- **Admissions information:** UCAS tariff not yet used.
- **Accommodation:** Some housed in university halls.

Profile

Institution
Founded: 1989 from Central School of Art & Design (1896) and St Martin's School of Art (1852). **Structural features:** Constituent college of Arts London (University of the Arts London, previously London Institute). Drama Centre and Byam Shaw School of Art both part of college. **Site:** Sites in Charing Cross Road, Holborn, Back Hill and Archway. Moving to single site at King's Cross in 2011.

Courses
Academic features: Majority of applicants are foundation students; academic qualifications are secondary to portfolio and practical work assessment. Courses range from fashion and textile design to sculpture and product design; also fine art at Byam Shaw, acting and directing at Drama Centre. **Awarding body:** University of the Arts London. **Main undergraduate award:** BA. **Length of courses:** 3 years, 4 years (sandwich); 5 years (part-time).

Study opportunities & careers
Library and information services: Libraries on main sites. 80,000 volumes, 250 periodicals, 126 study places, slide libraries, 100,000 transparencies. Separate IT service, access 10+ hours/day. All computers access library and internet (ratio 1:9 workstations to students). IT support from technicians; IT skills training on some courses. Also access to facilities of the university's central Learning Zone. **Other learning resources:** TV and ciné equipment; reprographic centre, computer room, language centre. At new site at Kings Cross: new library, innovation centres, gallery and performance spaces; flexible, purpose-built workshops; social learning spaces to allow students to interact and learn from each other; also publicly accessible spaces to allow connection with wider community. **Study abroad:** Opportunities to spend 6 months or more abroad on some courses. **Careers:** University careers service.

Student services & facilities
Student advice and services: Easy access to university's central student services; see *Arts London*. Student service office in college for general enquiries. **Amenities:** Shop selling course materials; cafés; canteen. Entertainment organised by SU. **Accommodation:** Some students in university's halls of residence; see *Arts London*. University accommodation service helps find privately rented accommodation: rent approx £75–£115 pw, excluding bills and meals.

Money
Living expenses budget: Minimum budget of £6k–£10k pa (excluding tuition fees) recommended by university. **Term-time work:** College allows term-time work for full-time first-degree students. Occasional term-time work on campus during exhibitions and private views; also college has

placement contacts for work outside college. **Financial help:** See *Arts London*. **Tuition fees:** Home students pay £3225 pa for first degrees. International students pay £10,700 pa.

Student view
Kit Friend, Campaigns and Communications Officer (recently graduated from BA Arts, Design and Environment)

Living
What's it like as a place to live? London's a fantastic mix of exciting opportunities and resources for any creative person. **How's the student accommodation?** University halls are few and far between; private accommodation is the most expensive in the UK and ranges from 5 star to squalor. **What's the student population like?** Diverse, international, exciting and fiercely independent. A thrilling mix of the world's top talent. **How do students and locals get on?** With around a million students in the capital, the city is a great place to be.

Studying
What's it like as a place to study? Creative courses that promise lots and deliver most of the time. Facilities and buildings are seriously outdated but the future's brighter. **What are the teaching staff like?** Plenty of potential but frequently isolated and unavailable.

Socialising
What are student societies like? A good range existing but steadily growing. Our sports teams are doing fantastically. **What's a typical night out?** No such thing as typical in the metropolis. **And how much does it cost?** From £5 to £1000s. **How can you get home safely?** If you're rich, a cab; for the rest of us mortals, post-midnight it's the sporadic night bus service.

Money
Is it an expensive place to live? Incredibly expensive. **Average price of a pint?** £3+. **And the price of a takeaway?** £5–£10. **What's the part-time work situation?** Loads of jobs for all sorts of careers and wages! Everyone works part-time; it's a fact of life in London.

Summary
What's the best feature about the place? The other students, their creativity and culture. **And the worst?** Outdated facilities, lack of social space in the university, staff not around enough. **And to sum it all up?** We've got a great reputation and for some that's enough, but there's a way to go before we provide a proper 'university experience'.
Past students: Stella McCartney, Alexander McQueen (fashion designers), Gilbert and George (artists).
More info? Contact SU President on 020 7514 6270 or check out (www.suarts.org).

Central School of Speech & Drama

Location:
north London
(map 1)
Single site in Swiss Cottage

The Central School of Speech & Drama, Embassy Theatre, 62–64 Eton Avenue, London NW3 3HY
☎ Tel 020 7722 8183
Fax 020 7722 4132
✉ Email enquiries@cssd.ac.uk
Website www.cssd.ac.uk

Student enquiries: Registry
Applications: UCAS (GTTR for postgraduate teachers)

In brief

Total Students: 870

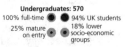

34% postgraduate
66% undergraduate

Undergraduates: 570

100% full-time
25% mature on entry

94% UK students
18% lower socio-economic groups

66% female   34% male

- **Specialist drama and arts college.** Part of London University.
- **Broad study areas:** Drama, performing arts and theatre making; arts management; stage management and technical theatre production; design for the stage; drama and media education; applied theatre; voice and movement studies; musical theatre; physical and visual theatre.

Freshers

- **Admissions information:** Minimum of 2 A-level passes or equivalent; usually interview or audition. UCAS tariff not used.
- **First degree entrants:** 180 UK, full-time.
- **Points on entry:** 230 (average).
- **Drop-out rate:** 3% in 1st year.
- **Accommodation:** Some 1st years housed through London University.

Profile

Institution

Founded: 1906. **Structural features:** A college of London University since 2005. **Site:** Swiss Cottage. **How to get there:** Swiss Cottage tube stations; rail to Finchley Road and Frognal; many buses. **Special features:** Many well-known guest directors and tutors from the theatre, teaching and related professions.

Courses

Academic features: Unique provision of academic study and professional/practical training in related fields of performance arts and theatre-making, drama for specific communities, education, stage management and technical theatre production and design. **Awarding body:** University of London. **Main undergraduate award:** BA. **Length of courses:** 3 years.

Study opportunities & careers

Library and information services: 38,000 items, across a range of media, 50 journal subscriptions, 200 e-journals, 180 e-books, electronic bibliographic databases, etc. Also access to Senate House library. Information provision, £50 pa spent for each student (FTE). Separate IT department. Open-access computers in library, 30 in computer room, all with internet access; also 18 in media lab. On-site support from IT and library staff, induction for new students; weekly IT clinics. **Other learning resources:** Media services providing digital sound and video editing, camcorders and data projectors. Proscenium theatre (seating 230); 14 modern studios and range of design studios, editing suites and workshop facilities, lecture theatres, full drama technical workshops.

Student services & facilities

Student advice and services: Student counselling and advisory service for finance, careers and disabilities. **Accommodation:** Some places in London University halls; rent £100–£180 pw. College runs accommodation advice service June–Oct, to help students find private accommodation; rent locally £110–£170 pw self-catering, £90–£130 further afield.

Money

Living expenses budget: Minimum budget of £8500–£16,500 pa (excluding tuition fees) recommended by the School. **Term-time work:** Some jobs occasionally in School (eg student bar, library). **Financial help:** Bursaries of £500 pa for students whose family income is up to £25k. Various other awards and bursaries (see website for further information). **Tuition fees:** Home students pay £3225 pa for first degrees. International students pay £13,068 pa (but £13,454 for BA acting).

Student view | Hannah Bourgault (2nd year, BA Drama, Applied Theatre and Education)

Living

What's it like as a place to live? Willesden Green's quite nice. Good transport links. **How's the student accommodation?** No university accommodation – all self-found residence. **What's the student population like?** Friendly, quite cliquey after first term, generally open-minded. **How do students and locals get on?** No particular interaction.

Studying

What's it like as a place to study? Interesting, small compared to other unis but that makes it more of a community. **What are the teaching staff like?** Interested in what the students have to say; know their stuff.

Socialising

What are student societies like? Only one society but poorly attended – degrees demand a lot of time so students don't ask for them. **What's a typical night out?** SU bar then to Camden/walkabout. **And how much does it cost?** £20ish. **How can you get home safely?** Night buses/taxis.

Money

Is it an expensive place to live? YES (it is London!). **Average price of a pint?** £3.10. **And the price of a takeaway?** £6 minimum. **What's the part-time work situation?** Can get a job at SU bar but it's small so few opportunities. Jobs are self-motivated and not linked to uni. Jobs noticeboard has industry jobs (that have been sent to SU President).

Summary

What's the best/worst feature about the place? Both the best and worst: small uni so everyone knows everyone else – part of a community but also results in a lot of gossip. **And to sum it all up?** It's a drama school – does what it says on the tin.

Past students: Peggy Ashcroft, Jerome Flynn, Wendy Craig, Graham Norton, Lynn Redgrave, Laurence Olivier, Judi Dench, Amanda Donohoe, Carrie Fisher, Dawn French, Vanessa Redgrave, Cameron Mackintosh, Tony Robinson, Jennifer Saunders, Zoe Wanamaker, Deborah Warner, James Nesbitt, Christopher Ecclestone. **More info?** Ring SU President on 020 7559 3944.

Chelsea College of Art & Design

Location:
central London
(map 3)
Single site on Millbank

Chelsea College of Art & Design, 16 John Islip Street, Millbank, London SW1P 4JU
☎ Tel 020 7514 7751
🖨 Fax 020 7514 7778
✉ Email enquiries@chelsea.arts.ac.uk
💻 Website www.chelsea.arts.ac.uk

Student enquiries: General Enquiries
Applications: UCAS

In brief

Total Students: 1600

10% postgraduate
55% undergraduate

35% FE Students

Undergraduates: 900
90% full-time
10% mature on entry

70% UK students
18% lower socio-economic groups

60% female   40% male

- **Specialist art and design college.** Part of University of the Arts London.
- **Teaching staff:** 35 full-time, 120 part-time.
- **Broad study areas:** Art and design: communication; digital arts; digital media; drawing; film and video; fine art; furniture; graphic design; interactive multimedia; interior design; knitwear; model making; new media; painting; photography; printmaking; printed textiles; screenprinting; sculpture; stitch/embroidery; textile design; visual design and display.

Freshers
- **Accommodation:** 20% of 1st years housed.

Profile

Institution
Founded: 1891, later incorporating art departments of Regent Street Polytechnic and Hammersmith College of Arts and Crafts. **Structural features:** Constituent college of Arts London (University of the Arts London, previously London Institute). **Site:** Single site on Millbank, opposite Tate Britain. **How to get there:** Pimlico tube station and buses along Millbank.

Courses
Largest fields of study: Painting, sculpture, fine art media, textile design, interior and spatial design, design communication. **Awarding body:** University of the Arts London. **Main undergraduate award:** BA. **Length of courses:** 3 years; 4–5 years (part-time or mixed mode).

Study opportunities & careers
Library and information services: Single new library: 70,000 volumes, 300 periodicals, also exhibition catalogues, slide collection (120,000 images). Special collections: Afro-American art,

Afro-Caribbean British art and Asian British art. Also access to facilities of the university's central Learning Zone. **Careers:** Information and advice. **Employment:** Strong tradition of freelance work in fine art, industrial employment in design.

Student services & facilities

Student advice and services: Easy access to university's central student services; see *Arts London*. **Amenities:** Shops for students' materials on 3 sites. **Accommodation:** Some students in university's halls of residence; see *Arts London*. University accommodation service helps find privately rented accommodation: rent approx £75–£115 pw, excluding bills and meals.

Money

Living expenses budget: Minimum budget of £6k–£10k pa (excluding tuition fees) recommended by university. **Term-time work:** College allows term-time work for full-time students (20% believed to work). Job vacancies bulletin issued by university. **Financial help:** See *Arts London*. **Tuition fees:** Home students pay £3225 pa for first degrees. International students pay £10,700 pa.

Student view

Now on Millbank, on the site of the Royal Army Hospital and right next door to Tate Britain (all students get free entry to exhibitions). The move is definitely viewed positively and has been great for providing a strong identity (previously college buildings were scattered over west London). Now all students are in one self-contained space, there is very intense social cohesion. It's one of the smallest colleges at Arts London, with some 1600 students and a reputation for being one of the most friendly and social colleges. There is masses of interaction between students on all courses, from foundation to postgraduate. Even lecturers and admin staff are often found drinking in the SU bar with the students. The strong social aspect of the college also prompts students to be pro-active about getting their portfolio on display; there are student shows running a few times a week in college studios and gallery spaces – great opportunities for networking and making new friends. All the print-rooms and darkrooms have been eradicated with the move, although the advantage is obviously the cutting-edge digital facilities.

Student footnotes

Housing: Hardly anything affordable close to college; halls limited. Students rent all over London, particularly in north and east London. Rents typically £100 pw. **Eats:** College refectory fairly cheap; few restaurants and little café culture in vicinity but Victoria and St James only 5–10 mins walk. **Drink:** SU bar cheapest; also local pubs (some embrace students, some blatantly hostile; Spread Eagle always a safe bet). **Nightlife:** Arts SU puts on large parties at Heaven, Ministry of Sound, Fabric and SU bars. Also students put on nights in local bars. **Locals:** Extremely safe area; not remotely 'dodgy'. **Sports:** Main Arts SU runs lots of different sporting and club activities. **Travel:** Brilliant location; Victoria Line makes it easily accessible from anywhere in London by tube; buses cheaper. **Financial help:** Access fund. **Jobs:** Loads of part-time work in college, in galleries around London. Very easy to get jobs; student services helps. **Best features:** Fantastic interaction between students. **And worst:**

Slack teaching; lack of structure. **Past students:** Alexei Sayle (comedian); Steve McQueen (artist); Alan Rickman (actor); Sir Dirk Bogarde (actor); Graham Gough (gardener); Dame Elizabeth Frink, Henry Moore (sculptors); Simon Edmonson, Patrick Caulfield (painters); Sarah Jane Hoare (stylist with Harpers and Queen); John Berger (author); Anish Kapoor (sculptor, Turner prize winner), Peter Doig (painter); Helen Chadwick, Gavin Turk, Richard Deacon, Kerry Stewart (artists). **More info?** SU President (tel 020 7514 6270) or visit www.suarts.org.

Chester University

Location:
north-west England
(map 2)
Main site in Chester;
campus at
Warrington; partner
colleges

🖳 University of Chester, Parkgate Road, Chester CH1 4BJ
☎ Tel 01244 511000
🖷 Fax 01244 511302
✉ Email enquiries@chester.ac.uk
🖥 Website www.chester.ac.uk

Student enquiries: Marketing Recruitment and Admissions
(tel 01244 512471)
Applications: UCAS

In brief

Total Students: 15,095

23% postgraduate
77% undergraduate

Undergraduates: 11,655

63% full-time
18% mature on entry
97% UK students
37% lower socio-economic groups

69% female   31% male

- **A modern university.**
- **Teaching staff:** 373 full-time, 117 part-time.
- **Broad study areas:** Applied and health science; arts and media; business and management; education and children's services; health and social care; humanities; law; social sciences; sport and exercise sciences.

Freshers

- **Admissions information:** All post-16 qualifications accepted, including Key Skills; students expected to have at least 240 points from A-level or equivalent. UCAS tariff fully adopted.
- **First degree entrants:** 2295 UK, full-time.
- **Points on entry:** 270 (average).
- **Drop-out rate:** 11% in 1st year.
- **Accommodation:** Many 1st years housed.

Profile

Institution 🐾
Founded: 1839 by Church of England; university status in 2005. **Site:** Main 32-acre campus 10-mins walk from Chester city centre; departments all walking distance from main campus. Also campus at

Warrington (Padgate); health and social care education centres at Birkenhead, Chester, Crewe and Warrington. **How to get there:** Chester Campus: bus and coach service from Vicars Lane bus depot, 10 mins from campus; Chester railway station 15 mins; 10 mins from M56, 30 mins from M6. Warrington Campus: bus service from Warrington town centre; 5 mins from M6 and M62. Free university shuttle service between two campuses.

Courses

Academic features: Modular structure for all first degrees allows subject combinations, named pathways and single subject degrees; includes work-based learning modules with range of employers. **Awarding body:** University of Chester. **Main undergraduate awards:** BA, BSc, BEd, BTh, LLB. **Length of courses:** 3 or 4 years.

Study opportunities & careers

Library and information services: Libraries at both campuses. Total of 325,000 volumes, 3250 periodicals, 5000 e-journals, 40+ databases, 850+ study places, electronic resources and internet access. 8 hospital nursing and midwifery libraries. Information provision, £70 pa spent for each student (FTE). Introductory literature, web information, tours, etc of libraries; workshops on information retrieval and internet searching. Integrated IT service, access 68+ hours pw, 1300 workstations for student use; Dual boot iMacs in open-access IT suites in libraries; ratio workstations to students 1:11. IT support from 25 staff, both central and departmental; IT training suite. **Other learning resources:** Human performance laboratory; satellite remote-sensing suite; seminar/group study rooms for student use, digital video edit suite, TV and sound studios; commercial music production suite; darkroom; integrated live arts building (art, design and technology), drama studio; fully equipped theatre; interactive newsroom (journalism). **Study abroad:** Opportunities for students to study in countries worldwide (some open to non-language specialists). **Careers:** Individual guidance available.

Student services & facilities

Student advice and services: Chaplaincy; student counsellor, student support and guidance services; student development programme (including mentoring); personal tutorial system; learning support unit. **Sporting facilities:** Fitness suite, swimming pool, sports hall, squash courts, all-weather floodlit pitch. **Accommodation:** 65% of 1st years in university accommodation. 930 1st-year places at Chester (277 ensuite; all with internet access): £53–£83.50 pw self-catering, £63–£97.50 pw semi-catered (40-week contracts), £97.50–£126 pw full-board (mainly term time only). Meal schemes for those in self-catering accommodation of £195 a term (lunch only) or £355 (lunch and dinner). At Warrington, £60–£73 pw self-catering, £97.50 semi-catered; most term time only. Most students live in privately owned accommodation for 2+ years: rent £55–£95 pw self-catering. 20% of first-degree students live at home.

Money

Living expenses budget: Minimum budget of £6k pa (excluding tuition fees) recommended by university. **Term-time work:** University allows term-time work for full-time students; (45% believed to work). Some work on campus (in learning resources, bar, schools liaison, fitness centre). **Financial help:** Bursaries of up to £1k pa for UK students whose family income is up to £25k. Access funds of £510k to provide discretionary help. **Tuition fees:** Home students pay £3225 pa for first degrees. International students pay £7182 pa (classroom-based), £8388 pa (lab/studio-based).

Student view

It's a small, compact campus with a few departments situated elsewhere. The city is one of the nicest in the country – lots of history, tourists, shops, restaurants and pubs. Both city and university very friendly; everyone knows pretty much everyone. Atmosphere great. It's easy to reach by car and train; buses and taxis very cheap (although almost everything is in walking distance). A women's safe transport service operates in the city. Library and computer facilities are good (all students have free email and internet access). Sporting facilities very good and sports clubs successful. All courses popular, most filled to capacity: largest are English, psychology, drama, PE/sports science and teacher education. Most students undertake a work-based learning placement. Drop-out rate low and workloads realistic. Variety of assessment methods, from essays and exams to presentations and seminars. University has several halls of residence and runs a head lease scheme but is still unable to house all 1st years; but plenty of reasonably priced housing locally and accommodation office has good links with landlords. Fair number live at home (part-time and mature students mostly). Hundreds of part-time jobs in city and on campus, so never difficult to earn extra money. Majority of students are from the north of England (particularly the north west) but also from all over the country and the world; a large proportion are female. Staff for the most part are very student-friendly. Personal academic tutor system and size of uni means that most students know the staff well and relationships are good. Largely apolitical union is affiliated to NUS. Based in De Bunsen Centre, it is the focal point for student representation, information, advice, entertainment and services: a strong welfare service, a job board (helps find temporary employment) and it runs all sporting and non-sporting clubs and societies, from hockey and football to outdoor pursuits and scuba diving. SU bar is hub of student social life; combination of low prices, pool, video games and big-screen TV ensures that the venue is busy most nights. SU also organises popular, inexpensive student nights with local nightclubs. Rag week highlights students' commitment to charity fundraising.

Student footnotes

Housing: Off-campus, look on SU noticeboards; accommodation office. **Eats:** Meal for £2–£3 on campus. Locally, Chez Jules, Dos Americos, Mamma Mia, many more – all reasonably priced. **Drink:** Uni bar (£1.50+ a pint). Drink promotions and many cheap deals in town. **Nightlife:** Good ents in SU bar. Clubs include RB's, Brannigans, Destiny and Elite. Discounts at theatres, cinemas, etc. **Locals:** Friendly. No major problem areas. **Sports:** Sports hall, squash courts, gymnasia, swimming pool, sauna and solarium, tennis courts, AstroTurf and grass pitches. Some funding for sporting representation available. **Travel:** Train station near campus. **Financial help:** Access and hardship funds; some loans. **Jobs:** Loads of jobs on and off campus including 50+ in SU, eg shops, restaurants, bars; minimum wage upwards. **Best features:** Small and compact; very friendly atmosphere. **And worst:** Rains a lot. **Past students:** John Carlton (rugby international), Carol Lewis (HM Borstal), Walter Winterbottom (Sports Council), Richard Palmer (British Olympic Committee), The Venerable Francis William Harvey (Archdeacon of London), Lynn Davies (British long jump record-holder), George Courtney (football referee), Rob Wotton (Sky Sports). **More info?** Contact President on 01244 513398 (fax 01244 392866), email csupres@chester.ac.uk or visit the website (www.chestersu.com).

Chichester University

Location:
south coast of
England (map 2)
*Two sites, Chichester
and Bognor; partner
colleges*

University of Chichester, Bishop Otter Campus,
College Lane, Chichester, West Sussex PO19 6PE
☎ Tel 01243 816000
🖷 Fax 01243 816080
✉ Email admissions@chiuni.ac.uk
💻 Website www.chiuni.ac.uk

*Student enquiries: Admissions Office (tel 01243 816002)
Applications: UCAS (for full-time study)*

In brief

Total Students: 4930

25% postgraduate
75% undergraduate

Undergraduates: 3715
82% full-time
31% mature on entry
95% UK students
36% lower socio-economic groups

66% female   33% male

- **A modern university.**
- **Teaching staff:** 200 full-time, 80 part-time.
- **Broad study areas:** Business; dance; education; English; history; IT; music; performing arts; social studies; sports studies and sciences; theology; tourism.

Freshers

- **Admissions information:** Minimum of 2 A-level passes (one in a relevant subject), and 3 further subjects at, eg GCSE level. AS-levels accepted on some courses. UCAS tariff adopted but specific requirements on some courses.
- **First degree entrants:** 915 UK, full-time.
- **Points on entry:** 210+ (average).
- **Drop-out rate:** 5% in 1st year.
- **Accommodation:** Most 1st year students housed.

Profile

Institution
Founded: 1977 as West Sussex Institute from Bishop Otter College Chichester (1839) and Bognor Regis College (1947); university status in 2005. **Site:** 2 sites seven miles apart at Chichester and Bognor Regis. **How to get there:** Trains from London (Victoria or Waterloo) to both Chichester and Bognor; coach station in central Chichester; by road, A27 from Worthing or Portsmouth to Chichester, A29 and A259 to Bognor. Both sites within easy walking distance of respective town centres; free inter-campus transport.

Courses
Academic features: Maths enhancement course for secondary teaching. **Awarding body:** University of Chichester. **Main undergraduate awards:** BA, BA(QTS), BSc. **Length of courses:** 3–4 years.

Study opportunities & careers

Library and information services: Library on each site. 260,000 volumes in total, 1270 periodicals, 480 study places; short-loan collections. Information provision, £74 pa spent for each student (FTE). IT and library services converged in modern learning resources centre. 2 PC networks, 177 workstations with internet access (ratio 1:24 workstations to students), access 13 hours/day. IT support from helpdesk, specialist staff at each campus. All students have training in information sources and skills. **Other learning resources:** Media centre; reprographics; video edit suites; media production space; photographic centre; physiology laboratories; 2 dance studios (with computerised sound and light systems); music rehearsal rooms and recording studio; art centre and gallery. Specialist collections: Bishop Otter collection of 20th-century British art, Gerard Young local history collection, art slides, 19th-century British parliamentary papers, Historical Association pamphlets, music scores, dance videos, specialist theological collection. **Study abroad:** Erasmus European exchanges for students in dance, maths and sports studies. **Careers:** Information and advice, both individually and as part of course.

Student services & facilities

Student advice and services: Accommodation officers, health centre, doctors, counsellors, chaplain, welfare officer for international students and for finance, disability and learning support service, student money advice. **Amenities:** SU with bar at both campuses, many societies and clubs. Chapel, Otter Gallery, art collection, laundrette. **Sporting facilities:** Sports research and activity centre: gym, pitches (including floodlit all-weather pitch), running track, 4 badminton courts, indoor and outdoor climbing walls, cricket pitch and nets, tennis and netball courts. Local leisure centres, swimming pools, tennis club, sea sailing, windsurfing, bowling and canoeing. **Accommodation:** 647 places: 435 at Chichester (catered and self-catering), 212 catered at Bognor Regis. Rents £74–£85 pw self-catering (£104 ensuite); £111 pw catered (£94 for shared room; £126 ensuite); contracts 40 weeks. Rent includes heat and 12 meals a week in catered accommodation. Students live in privately owned accommodation for 2+ years: £62–£70 pw self-catering, £60–£75 BandB, £92–£98 pw half board.

Money

Living expenses budget: Minimum budget of £5k–£6k pa (excluding tuition fees) recommended by university. **Term-time work:** Careers Office jobshop: official pay-scale for part-time work on campus (eg SU bar, contract catering, IT and library) and off campus (plenty of summer work locally in tourism, etc). **Financial help:** Bursaries of £1077 pa for UK students whose family income is up to £25k; tapered bursaries down to £256 pa where family income is £49,900; over 50% of students expected to qualify. £208k government funds. **Tuition fees:** Home students pay £3225 pa for first degrees. International students pay £7400 pa (classroom-based), £8200 (lab/studio-based). Fees payable in instalments.

Student view) **Alvin Ramsamy,** President of the Students' Union (graduated from Media Studies with Performing Arts)

Living
What's it like as a place to live? Chichester's a nice place to live. Originally coming from London, I wasn't used to the nice relaxed atmosphere but you quickly get used to it. Thanks to the student population you can always find something to do. Or if you are a culture vulture there's plenty for you in this cathedral city. You may also choose to live in Bognor Regis where the other campus is located. There is more to do in Bognor, being a British holiday hotspot, and the atmosphere is different to Chi. The houses are also bigger and cheaper to live in. **How's the student accommodation?** Whilst at uni I lived in shared facilities in my 1st year and in the new blocks when I was a warden. Shared facilities are amazing: the rooms are bigger and you get fed (breakfast, if you wake up,

and dinner). Your 1st year is always the best and being in halls plays a big part of that. When I became a warden the uni had just built brand new halls so I left my allegiance to shared facilities and went for not posh blocks but the new posh-er blocks! (posh means having your own toilet and shower!). They were really nice, self-catering and the showers were amazing power showers. The rooms are a bit smaller due to the toilet and shower. I was happy with either – it was the people that made the halls, not the facilities! You can get nice houses and you can get rubbish ones. Myself and a lot of students would advise you to stay away from a certain letting agency (email me and I'll tell you who!). Like I said, Bognor is cheaper and bigger to rent. But if you can, go with private landlords in Chi. The union and the accommodation department of the uni work closely and we have a housing fair and will strive to find you a house. **What's the student population like?** Smallish student population (around 5500) and a few internationals. The people who engage with the campus and social side of things know each other. It's quite an intimate atmosphere, which helps not only socially but also educationally as your tutors will know you better and be able to offer tailored advice. **How do students and locals get on?** They do get on. The union has also been getting involved with the community to help break down traditional stereotypes of students. We have joined in the campaign to save a local hospital, many of our students work in local business or volunteer in many different ways. We also have seats on the council so we can talk directly about students issues.

Studying
What's it like as a place to study? Facilities are good: big library, good sports facilities. If you came to university to study then you won't have much to complain about here. **What are the teaching staff like?** The ones I had were amazing, dedicated to their field and didn't mind some banter.

Socialising
What are student societies like? There's a fair range, not many but ones like Christian Union, Poker, BAM (Business and Management), Beatfiend (clubbing), Musical theatre, etc. Very easy to set up one if you wish. **What's a typical night out?** Monday: Zee Bar (Chi) for Skint (cheap drinks), Club DJ or In MII in Bognor for Karaoke or Comedy Night. Tuesday: MII (Bog) for Broke (same as Skint) or head to student night at the club Thursdays (some Tuesdays are comedy night or big jazz band in Zee). Wednesday: Big Wednesday at Chi or Poker or Open Mike in Bog. Thursday: Pre-club party in both bars with Karaoke in Chi! Friday: live music in Chi, Quiz in Bog. Various things at weekends. **And how much does it cost?** Depends on how much you drink! Some people spend about £10 on a Monday. On Thursday everyone goes to Club Vision (Sheiks) in Bog; £30 should be enough but if you go a lot and are used to spending money, then £50. **How can you get home safely?** Everything's drunken walking distance in Chi, but there are taxis that wait outside the library and there's a taxi rank outside the club in Bognor. You'll always get home safely!

Money
Is it an expensive place to live? West Sussex is a little bit cheaper than London but not much! **Average price of a pint?** £2.50–£3. SU is £2. **And the price of a takeaway?** £5. **What's the part-time work situation?** In my 1st year finding a job was quite easy; I got one by Christmas when I started running out of money!

Summary
What's the best feature about the place? It's just easy living here. **And the worst?** Is dead and boring when there's no students around! **And to sum it all up?** I had a good time all the time at uni. Chichester is different to other unis due to the courses it offers and you get a wide range of personalities here!

More info? Ring SU on 01243 816392 or check out the website (www.chisu.org).

City University

Location:
*central London
(map 3)
Single site near
Islington plus medical
sites*

✉ City University London, Northampton Square,
London EC1V 0HB
☎ Tel 020 7040 5060
🖷 Fax 020 7040 8559
💻 Website www.city.ac.uk

*Student enquiries: Undergraduate Admissions Office
Applications: UCAS*

In brief

Total Students: 21,400

32% postgraduate
68% undergraduate

Undergraduates: 14,530
54% full-time ● ● 84% UK students
38% mature ● ● 40% lower
on entry socio-economic
groups

56% female   44% male

- **Mid-sized research-intensive university.**
- **Teaching staff:** 641 full-time and part-time.
- **Broad study areas:** Business, management, finance, actuarial science, engineering, informatics, mathematics, nursing, allied health professions, social sciences, journalism, law, music.

Freshers

- **Admissions information:** AS-levels accepted in combination with full A-levels or equivalent, preferably in a contrasting subject (some departments may accept 2 AS-levels in place of a 3rd A-level but often with higher grades). UCAS tariff used for some offers, grades for others (or combination).
- **First degree entrants:** 1490 UK full-time
- **Points on entry:** 310 (average).
- **Drop-out rate:** 11% in 1st year.
- **Accommodation:** All 1st years guaranteed accommodation (if from outside London and fulfil certain conditions).

Profile

Institution

Founded: 1894 as Northampton Institute; university status in 1966. **Site:** Islington, close to City of London. Also business near Moorgate, law in Gray's Inn, optometry off City Road and health sites in West Smithfield and Whitechapel. **Access:** Angel, Farringdon or Barbican underground stations for main site; several bus routes. All other sites well-served by tube and bus.

Courses

Academic features: Many courses include optional 1-year professional placement and lead to exemptions from professional exams. All courses offer introduction to IT, development of communication skills and opportunities for learning languages; major individual project in final year. **Awarding body:** City University London. **Main undergraduate awards:** BA, BSc, BEng, LLB, BMus, MEng. **Length of courses:** 3–4 years; others 4–5 years (eg MEng).

Study opportunities & careers

Library and information services: Library with 350,000 volumes, 25,000+ periodical titles online; 900 study places. 4 further libraries: Cass Business School, City Law School and for community and health sciences. Information provision, £120 pa spent for each student (FTE). Separate IT service, access 24 hours 6/7 days/week (IT support all hours). 900 points with internet access plus others in halls of residence (ratio 1:14 workstations to students). IT skills courses on all supported software. **Careers:** Information, advice and placement service, and student employment service.

Student services & facilities

Student advice and services: Student centre gives access to all support services; SU information and representation centre; health centre; counselling services; centre for careers and skills development. **Amenities:** Bookshop on site; SU recreational facilities, including café, bar, shop and social venue. **Sporting facilities:** Saddlers sports centre (including fitness centre and sauna); squash courts; playing fields in north London; variety of SU clubs and societies. **Accommodation:** Guaranteed for all 1st years who live outside Greater London, are aged 18 and who apply before the deadline. 1344 self-catering places available (600+ for 1st years); rent £97–£180 pw, mostly 39-week contracts, Sept–June. Most students live in privately owned accommodation for 2 years, rent £95–£150 pw for self-catering (plus bills).

Money

Living expenses budget: Budget of £7500–£10,900 for the academic year (excluding tuition fees) recommended by university. **Term-time work:** Centre for career and skills development helps students find part-time jobs. **Financial help:** Bursaries of £770 pa for UK students with family income of up to £25k; partial bursary for students with family income of £25k–£30k. Additional school-based scholarships in specific subjects. Also help available from government access to learning funds. Apply to student centre for help. **Tuition fees:** Home students pay £3225 pa for first degrees. International students pay £7750–£12k.

Student view

In one of the most vibrant and upcoming areas of London, between Islington, Clerkenwell and Hoxton (known as CitySide). This is the centre of the new creative industries, art and entertainments and new designer restaurants, bars and clubs are opening apace (Fabric, Fluid, Dust, Cantaloupe, Schneke) – an exciting and trendy area. The main site, Northampton Square, is in the triangle formed by the Angel, Old Street and Barbican (or Farringdon) tube stations, with other academic sites, halls of residence and the sports centre close by. A city-style university, most activity and services (including the SU) are in Northampton Square. University accommodation is within walking distance for first- and some third-year students (priority goes to those from outside London). Welfare advice and support is mainly provided by the SU although there are trained counsellors in the university's health centre. The SU consists of a lovely bar, student shop and book exchange. A full ents programme caters for the diverse student population both on the premises and at some of London's most prestigious venues. The SU is committed to student development and provides a valuable service helping students gain some of the skills needed in the world of work, and a bureau for finding students volunteer work in the local community. City attracts a wide mix of people due to its Central London location. Top subjects include business and finance, law, social and health sciences, journalism, computing and engineering.

Student footnotes

Housing: 3 main sites, all close. Off-campus, look in *Loot*, estate agents, uni accommodation office. **Eats:** University refectory, meal for £3.50+. Good range on Upper Street. The Quiet Revolution in Old Street (£5). **Drink:** SU bar on site is cheap; close to Islington's busy Upper Street with many restaurants/bars. **Nightlife:** Professionally run ents on site and in local clubs. Good prices with further discounts for card holders. London on your doorstep! **Locals:** Sometimes difficult locally but becoming increasingly wealthy as City boys and designers move into new loft-style developments. **Sports:** Sports centre with weight gym, aerobics, step boxercise classes. Over 50 SU clubs and societies. **Travel:** All university sites within walking distance. Tubes and buses run good local service, but at central London price. **Financial help:** Some available; also SU has 'funder finder' to help find sponsorship and trust donations. **Jobs:** Many available in SU, catering, bars, shop, admin, etc all with full training. **Best features:** Location; good mix of students; union. **And worst:** Increasing cost of local private-sector rent. **Past students:** Charles Farnecombe (conductor), Michael Fish (meteorologist), Dermot Murnaghan (news presenter), Kate Adie (reporter), Jo Whiley (presenter and DJ), Stelios (Easyjet).

Colchester Institute

Location:
East Anglia (map 2)
Single site near
Colchester town
centre

🖳 Colchester Institute, Sheepen Road, Colchester, Essex CO3 3LL
☎ Tel 01206 712000
📠 Fax 01206 763041
✉ Email info@colchester.ac.uk
💻 Website www.colchester.ac.uk

Student enquiries: Course Enquiry Line (tel 01206 712777)
Applications: UCAS

In brief

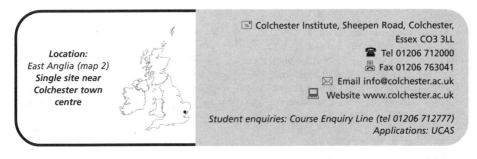

Total Students: 10,500

85% FE Students
15% undergraduate

Undergraduates: 1570
40% full-time
90% mature on entry

99% UK students

55% female   45% male

- **College offering Essex University degrees.**
- **Teaching staff:** 218 full-time, 347 part-time.
- **Broad study areas:** Art, design and media; music and performing arts; business and management; health and care; education; engineering; computing and administration; construction.

Freshers

- **Admissions information:** All applications treated on merit.
- **First degree entrants:** 400 UK, full-time.
- **Points on entry:** 40–160.
- **Drop-out rate:** 1% in 1st year.
- **Accommodation:** Some 1st years housed.

Profile

Institution

Founded: 1976 from technical and art colleges. **Site:** Main campus at Colchester. **How to get there:** Campus near town centre and railway station. **Special features:** Strong links with industry; regional work placements.

Courses

Awarding body: University of Essex. **Main undergraduate awards:** FdA, FdSc, BA, BSc. **Length of courses:** 3 years.

Study opportunities & careers

Library and information services: Single library. 100,000+ items including books, music, audio-visual materials; 360+ periodicals, online journals and databases; inter-library loan service. 40+ networked computers, with internet access in library. Subject specialist advisers. **Other learning facilities:** Technical learning resources (TLR) has specialist facilities, eg cameras, video-editing suites, television studio, digital image and audio workshops; copying, binding and laminating.

Student services & facilities

Student advice and services: Student counsellor, guidance on accommodation and finance. **Amenities:** Refectories, 2 restaurants (in catering centre). **Sporting facilities:** Gymnasia and fitness gym. **Accommodation:** Limited accommodation in Essex University halls, mostly for international students (rent approx £90 pw). Local rent approx £55–£80 pw for self-catering, £95–£105 full-board.

Money

Living expenses budget: Minimum budget of £6400 for an academic year recommended (excluding tuition fees). **Term-time work:** Institute allows term-time work for full-time students. **Financial help:** Bursaries of £319 pa for UK students with a family income of up to £25k, of up to £1,574 for students with family income of £25k–£60k on a sliding scale. Access to learning fund for any student in financial difficulty. Apply to the student finance adviser for help. **Tuition fees:** Home students pay £3225 pa for first degrees. International students pay £7200 pa.

Student view — Holly Sara Freeman, SU President (graduated in 2008)

Living

What's it like as a place to live? I don't live in the same town. **How's the student accommodation?** As this is a college there are no living-in facilities; however, the student services do try to help with getting housing for certain students. **What's the student population like?** There is such a large population of students from all walks of life, even across seas. All the students are very friendly and all want to be involved the college. **How do students and locals get on?** They are students, loud and out for fun, and the locals know this is a mutual relationship.

Studying

What's it like as a place to study? Plenty of places students can go to study and most of the time they take advantage of that. **What are the teaching staff like?** Staff and students get on very well in general and the students are able to approach staff with anything.

Socialising

What are student societies like? Students tend to stick to the course groups but will go out together around the local town. **What's a typical night out?** Don't have time to go out.

Money

Is it an expensive place to live? It depends on where you go. Most places in town will do discounts for student but there are a couple of clubs that will charge a lot. **Average price of a pint?** £1 on student night, £3.50 other days. **And the price of a takeaway?** £5ish. **What's the part-time work situation?** Always jobs available; we help advertise jobs and try and get students more involved with Connexion.

Summary

What's the best feature about the place? It is a historic town that has a lot of tourism. **And the worst?** Not big enough. **And to sum it all up?** Could be better, could be worse.

Past students: Graham Coxon (Blur's guitarist), Martin Litton (jazz pianist), Farnaby Brass Quartet, Ebony Wind Quartet, Simon Cornelias (footballer).

More info? Contact Colchester SU on 01206 518705 or email student.union@colchester.ac.uk.

Conservatoire for Dance & Drama

Location:
London, Bristol and Leeds
8 affiliated schools

📧 Conservatoire for Dance & Drama, 1–7 Woburn Walk, London WC1H OJJ
☎ Tel 020 7387 5101
🖨 Fax 020 7387 5103
✉ Email info@cdd.ac.uk
💻 Website www.cdd.ac.uk

Student enquiries and Applications: To individual affiliate schools

In brief

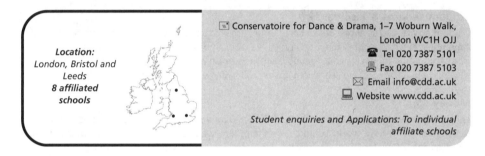

Total Students: 1190
91% undergraduate
6% postgraduate
3% FE Students
Undergraduates: 1085
99% full-time
39% mature on entry
72% UK students
62% female
38% male

- **A federation of prestigious dance and drama colleges.**

- **Broad study areas:** Acting, classical ballet, contemporary dance, stage management, theatre directing, lighting, costume and scenic design.

Freshers

- **First degree entrants:** 165 UK, full-time.

- **Drop-out rate:** 8% in 1st year.

Profile

Institution

Founded: 2001. **Structural features:** A conservatoire comprising some of the top schools providing vocational training in dance, drama and circus arts. Applications, teaching, student services and tuition fees are dealt with by the 8 affiliate schools. You can look up 4 of the schools profiled individually in this book:

Bristol Old Vic Theatre School (BOVTS)
London Contemporary Dance School (LCDS)
Northern School of Contemporary Dance (NSCD)
Royal Academy of Dramatic Art (RADA)

For information on the other schools, visit the Conservatoire website (www.cdd.ac.uk) or their
individual websites below.

Central School of Ballet (CSB)   www.centralschoolofballet.co.uk
London Academy of Music and Drama (LAMDA)   www.lamda.org.uk
Rambert School of Ballet and Contemporary Dance   www.rambertschool.org.uk
The Circus Space (TCS)   www.thecircusspace.co.uk

Study opportunities, student services, etc.

For information on library, student services, accommodation, etc, see individual affiliated schools.

Money

Financial help: Conservatoire bursaries of £1700 pa (£2100 in final year) for UK students whose family
income is up to £25k; tapered down to £100/£500 for those with family income of £37,900–£39,300.
Tuition fees: Home students pay £3225 pa for first degrees. International students pay £13,340.

Courtauld Institute

Location:
central London
(map 3)
**Single site on the
Strand**

Courtauld Institute of Art, University of London,
Somerset House, Strand, London WC2R 0RN
Tel 020 7848 2777
Fax 020 7848 2410
Email ugadmissions@courtauld.ac.uk
Website www.courtauld.ac.uk

*Student enquiries: Undergraduate Admissions
(tel 020 7848 2645/2635)
Applications: UCAS*

In brief

Total Students: 455
66% postgraduate
34% undergraduate

Undergraduates: 900
100% full-time ● ● 84% UK students
10% mature ● ● 23% lower socio-economic groups
on entry

84% female   16% male

- **A top UK research-intensive institution.** A specialist college of University of London.
- **Teaching staff:** 31 full-time.
- **Broad study area:** History of art (western civilisation, from antiquity to the present day).

Freshers

- **Admissions information:** All offers based on A-levels (or equivalent).
- **First degree entrants:** 50 UK, full-time.
- **Points on entry:** 340 (average)
- **Drop-out rate:** 2% in 1st year.
- **Accommodation:** Most 1st years housed.

247

Profile

Institution

Founded: 1932. **Structural features:** College of the University of London. **Site:** The Strand, in central London. **How to get there:** Close to many underground/rail stations (Charing Cross, Embankment, Temple, Covent Garden, Waterloo); many buses down the Strand.

Courses

Academic features: Postgraduate courses in the history of art, history of architecture, curating the art museum, history of dress, and conservation of wall and easel paintings. **Awarding body:** University of London. **Main undergraduate award:** BA. **Length of course:** 3 years.

Study opportunities & careers

Library and information services: Over 180,000 volumes, 300 current periodicals, approx 150 study places; a slide library with over 250,000 b/w and coloured slides. Information provision, £220 pa spent for each student (FTE). Separate IT service, open 12 hours/day. 30+ points with access to library and internet (ratio workstations to students 1:30). IT support from 3 staff members. Introductory computing sessions on demand for small groups in first term. Specialist collections: Witt and Conway Image Libraries (photographs and reproductions of paintings, drawings, graphics, sculpture and architecture). Courtauld Institute Gallery (French Impressionist and Post-Impressionist paintings, Flemish and Italian Old Master paintings and drawings, Turner watercolours). **Careers:** University information and advice service.

Student services & facilities

Student advice and services: London University facilities and in-house welfare and counselling officers. **Amenities:** SU is affiliated to ULU and students can use its gymnasium, swimming pool, squash courts, etc. **Accommodation:** Most 1st years housed in accommodation owned by The Courtauld or University of London. 26 places in Courtauld accommodation in The Strand, rent £110–£155 pw. Other places allocated to Courtauld in university halls of residence (mostly in Bloomsbury), rent £100–£180 pw for catered places. Most students live in privately owned accommodation for 2 years; rent £70–£120 pw.

Money

Living expenses budget: Minimum budget of £7k pa (excluding tuition fees) recommended by Courtauld. **Term-time work:** Term-time work allowed for full-time students (50% believed to work); limit of 10 hours pw. Some work available on campus in library, and assistance with open days. **Financial help:** Bursaries of £319 pa for UK students from low-income families. 4 additional bursaries of £4k pa for eligible students (as grant, fee waiver, book vouchers and/or travel grant). £8k government hardship fund for home students (average award £300). Travel and postgraduate scholarships also available. **Tuition fees:** Home students pay £3225 pa for first degrees. International students pay £11,804 pa.

Student view

It's in Somerset House, one of the most splendid buildings in London, together with the Courtauld's world-famous art collection. The Strand is on one side, the Thames on the other. It has superb library facilities (Book Library and the Witt and Conway libraries for pictorial reference) teaching rooms and its own fully-modernised lecture theatre. Comfortable common room space for students and a smart refectory selling quality food. It's small, with a friendly atmosphere; the 'finishing school' reputation is long gone. Very high academic standards; all tutors expect complete dedication. Social life revolves around frequent parties and a summer ball. Added to this is the more informal social life whereby, when the college closes, anyone left in the building is encouraged to go to the pub. Some accommodation on the Strand, otherwise students are referred to London University intercollegiate halls. As members of the university, students can make use of all ULU sporting facilities at Malet Street. London's galleries and libraries within walking distance and, of course, the West End and all the entertainments London has to offer.

Student footnotes

Housing: Institute housing close by plus intercollegiate halls. **Eats:** Cheap refectory. **Drink:** The Lyceum pub substitutes for a union bar. **Nightlife:** Parties. **Sport:** ULU facilities. **Travel:** Institute travel scholarships. **Financial help:** Emergency hardship loans. **Jobs:** Several jobs in libraries and galleries for those that need them. **Informal name:** CIA. **Past students:** Giles Waterfield, Anita Brookner (authors); Neil McGregor (director, British Museum); Alan Bowness (former director, Tate Gallery); Anthony Blunt (art historian); Vincent Price (actor); Jeremy Deller (artist).

Coventry University

Location:
West Midlands
(map 2)
Single campus in Coventry; partner colleges

🖳 Coventry University, Priory Street,
Coventry CV1 5FB
☎ Tel 024 7688 7688
🖨 Fax 024 7688 8638
💻 Website www.coventry.ac.uk

Student enquiries: Recruitment and Admissions Office
Applications: UCAS

In brief

Total Students: 19,415

15% postgraduate
85% undergraduate

Undergraduates: 16,430
67% full-time
28% mature on entry
90% UK students
39% lower socio-economic groups

49% female   51% male

- **A modern university.**
- **Teaching staff:** 480 full-time, 620 part-time.
- **Broad study areas:** Art and design; business; civil, aerospace and automotive engineering and computing; health and life sciences; international studies and law; mathematical and information sciences; science and environment; performing arts; forensics; geography; transport; product design; wine studies.

Freshers

- **Admissions information:** Minimum of 2 A-levels (or equivalent) required; 1-year course, eg AS-levels, accepted.
- **First degree entrants:** 2930 UK, full-time.
- **Points on entry:** 200+ (average).
- **Drop-out rate:** 11% in 1st year.
- **Accommodation:** Most 1st years housed.

Profile

Institution

Founded: 1970 as Coventry Poly, from Coventry College of Design (founded 1843) and other colleges of engineering technology and art; university status in 1992. **Site:** Coventry city centre; 33-acre modern campus. **How to get there:** 5 miles M6/M1 intersection; 20 mins Birmingham by train, 90 mins London Euston; adjacent to bus and coach station.

Courses

Academic features: Courses are modular; credit transfer possible. **Awarding body:** Coventry University. **Main undergraduate awards:** BA, BSc, BEng, LLB. **Length of courses:** 3 years; 4 years (sandwich).

Study opportunities & careers

Library and information services: State-of-the-art library: 350,000 volumes in total; 9200 journals (incl some 8000 electronic); 1200 study places (450 connected to university network) and wireless internet access. Information provision, £85 pa spent for each student (FTE). 800+ open-access PCs around university, some 24 hours/day (workstation ratio to students 1:7). IT support from advisory service and helpdesk in library; full induction to library and computing services for all new students. **Study abroad:** Several courses (eg law, environmental sciences) have European routes with year abroad. 100+ formal exchange links across Europe, which are given full credit (some open to non-language specialists). **Careers:** Information and advice service.

Student services & facilities

Student advice and services: These include careers and employability service, funding advice, accommodation, medical services, nursery, welfare and disabilities, spirituality and faith, counselling and sport and recreation. **Amenities:** Restaurants, sporting and social areas. **Sporting facilities:** 34-acre playing field and new indoor sports centre. City sports centre and Olympic-standard swimming pool is adjacent to the campus. **Accommodation:** 62% of 1st years who apply are in university accommodation. 2400+ places available (most with internet points): catered places at £94 pw, Sept–June contracts; self-catering places £78–£128 pw (£60 if sharing). Coventry has an abundance of student accommodation.

Money

Living expenses budget: Minimum budget of £6500 pa (excluding tuition fees) recommended by university. **Financial help:** Bursaries of £320 pa for UK students whose family income is up to £50k. Also scholarships of £2k pa for students with high entry qualifications or excellence in enterprise, creative or performing arts; and of £2k–£4k pa for sports scholars. £517,706 government access to learning funds, payments range from £100–£3500; own funds of £20k used for, eg emergency loans up to £100. Apply to Student Funding Office for help. **Tuition fees:** Home students pay £3225 pa for first degrees (but £2220 pa for foundation degrees, £615 for sandwich year). International students pay £7900 pa (fee fixed for the duration of the course).

Student view
Rich Hayward, Vice President, Communications (Marketing and Economics)

Living

What's it like as a place to live? The city is very compact so it's so easy to get around, the people are mostly friendly and the university is located right in the city centre so everything is so convenient. **How's the student accommodation?** The accommodation is generally good; there is both private and university accommodation. The private accommodation tends to be better quality but has less of a social life. The most social 2 halls, Priory and Singer, are both university-owned. **What's the student population like?**

Coventry has a very diverse campus and has a large commuter population because it is so close to other major cities such as Birmingham and Leicester. Everyone is really friendly and it is really easy to make friends. **How do students and locals get on?** They tend not to mix; there are not any no-go areas but there do seem to be set places and nights for students and the locals to go out.

Studying

What's it like as a place to study? The courses are generally very good and tend to be aimed at getting a job at the end of the course. The university has a new library, which is a fantastic resource for learning. **What are the teaching staff like?** The teaching staff are good and easy to track down; they all make their office times known and are always willing to help out with anything you do not understand.

Socialising

What are student societies like? There are over 80 sports and societies, covering a diverse range of subjects. We currently offer societies in everything from football, cheer-leading and karting to mountaineering, Sikh and geography. All our sports teams compete against other universities in the BUCS leagues and tournaments ensuring a high level of competition. **What's a typical night out?** All the city's nightclubs and pubs do a student night offering cheap drinks. **And how much does it cost?** The typical cost on a student night is between £2 and £4 entry and most drinks start from as low as 50p! **How can you get home safely?** Taxis are everywhere in Coventry; there are so many, so it's easy to just jump in a cab at the end of the night.

Money

Is it an expensive place to live? Coventry is one of the cheapest places to live in the country; if you choose the right bars to go to and the right places to shop you can make your loan last a long time. **Average price of a pint?** £2. **And the price of a takeaway?** £2.99 for a pizza. **What's the part-time work situation?** It is easy to find a part-time job in Coventry, there are loads of opportunities with both the university and the SU.

Summary

What's the best feature about the place? The city centre location, meaning everything is so convenient. **And the worst?** It's the furthest city away from the sea in the country. **And to sum it all up?** A good modern university that is always innovating, with a fantastic social life and an active SU.

Past students: Steve Ogrizovic (Coventry City goalkeeper), David Yelland (*Sun* Editor), Alan Smith (Arsenal and England striker), John Kettley (TV weatherman), Peter Hadfield (founder of Two Tone), Jerry Dammers (The Specials).

More info? Contact CUSU (tel 024 7657 1200) or visit website www.cusu.org.

Cranfield University

Location:
Bedfordshire
(map 2) and Wiltshire
Main campus in
Cranfield plus site at
Shrivenham

⌨ Cranfield University, Cranfield, Bedford MK43 0AL
☎ Tel 01234 758008
🖷 Fax 01234 752462
✉ Email enquiries@cranfield.ac.uk
🖥 Website www.cranfield.ac.uk

Student enquiries: Enquiries Office
Applications: Direct (or online)

251

In brief

Total Students: 4350

100% postgraduate

60% full-time  53% UK students

24% female 76% male

- **A research-intensive postgraduate university.**
- **Academic/research staff:** 650.
- **Broad study areas:** Aerospace; automotive and motorsport; computing; defence; engineering; the environment; management; manufacturing, health and water engineering and management.
- **Accommodation:** Most students housed.

Profile

Institution

Founded: 1946 as College of Aeronautics, subsequently merging with National College of Agricultural Engineering and working in partnership with Royal Military College of Science at Shrivenham. Royal Charter in 1969. **Site:** Main campus at Cranfield, including an airfield; also site at Shrivenham (Defence College of Management and Technology). **How to get there:** To Cranfield, by road from M1 (10 mins); by coach and rail to Bedford or Milton Keynes. To Shrivenham, train, coach or by road (M4) to Swindon.

Courses

Awarding body: Cranfield University. **Main awards:** MBA, MSc, PhD, EngD, MDes, MRes.

Study opportunities & careers

Library and information services: Library and information service with books, 8500 electronic journal titles, 200 databases, subject gateways to the internet. Information provision, £502 pa spent for each student (FTE). Separate IT service, access 24 hours/day. Ratio 1:2 workstations to students, all with access to internet and library (library catalogue on internet); specialist IT support in normal working hours. Orientation on library and information services for new students, further course-related sessions on searching skills and databases; on-going courses on, eg specific databases (eg Inspec), information sources on internet (eg patent information) and general course on how to manage references for theses. **Other learning resources:** Wind tunnels, airfield, extensive networked computer facilities and various specialist facilities. **Study abroad:** Many 'double degree' programmes with institutions in France, Belgium, Germany, Greece, Spain and China. **Careers:** Information, advice and counselling service.

Student services & facilities

Student advice and services: Welfare office and medical centre; crèches. **Amenities:** Many and varied student societies and SA. **Sporting facilities:** Gym, sports hall, cardio and resistance gyms, tennis/squash courts and playing fields. **Accommodation:** Range of university accommodation. Catered hall (£355 pm); self-catering halls (£338–£483 pm); places in shared houses (£338–£411 pm). Also flats/houses for couples and families.

Money

Living expenses budget: Minimum budget of £8500–£9k pa (excluding tuition fees) recommended by university for a single student. **Financial help:** Some scholarships and bursaries; help in seeking funds from outside sources, eg sponsorship. **Tuition fees:** Home students pay £3300–£28k pa, international students £16k–£28k.

Student view

It's about a mile out of Cranfield village, just off the M1 motorway and 10 miles from both Bedford and Milton Keynes; buses from both railway and bus stations in both towns (taxis widely available). Free university shuttle service between the campus, MK, railway station, coachway and shopping centre (must be booked in advance). Rural location makes local travel difficult on foot, risky on bike, but ok if you have a car. On-site facilities include a 24-hour computer centre, award-winning library, gym, sports hall and pitches. Campus has a newsagent and grocers, bookshop, barber, garage and airport. Student accommodation ranges from shared self-catered houses, single full-board rooms, family houses and flats for couples. An entirely postgraduate campus, the average age of students is 27 and majority are male; large proportion of EU and international students, encompassing a broad spectrum of cultures and religions. Family-friendly university: has pre-school, activity centre, play park and family housing. Most of the academic work is supported directly by industry and there are opportunities for students to make the most of those links. Cranfield SA (CSA) is the heart of student activities and provides a shop, lounge, bar, dancefloor, meeting rooms, photo-machine and photocopier. Wide variety of clubs and societies, facilitated by the CSA, cater for most tastes. Local area has a variety of sports and leisure centres, swimming pools, nightclubs, restaurants and cinemas. Miles of public footpaths and bridleways around, through open countryside.

Student footnotes

Housing: Good standard of competitively priced housing on campus. Off-campus lists available from housing office. **Eats:** CSA and halls provide food (£3–£5). The Swan in North Crawley (£5 upwards), the Carpenters' Arms in Moulsoe cooks fresh food before your eyes (£12+). **Drink:** CSA bar has low prices, fabulous deals and a friendly atmosphere. Couple of other establishments on campus. **Nightlife:** Regular events in CSA (themed nights, pool comps, bands, films, discos). MK and Bedford nearby. **Locals:** Very friendly. **Sports:** Numerous sports clubs, sports hall and fitness suite; swimming pool in MK, Flitwick or Bedford. **Travel:** Double degree offered with various universities overseas. Some travel available as part of industry-funded courses/projects. **Hardship:** Some funds available. **Jobs:** Bar and shop work through CSA, other casual work on campus (bar, hotel, library reshelving). **Best features:** Small size, multitude of cultures and quality of education. **And worst:** Rural location and small proportion of females! **More info?** Contact CSA President on csapresident@cranfield.ac.uk or visit the website (www.cranfield.ac.uk/csa).

Creative Arts University

Location:
Kent and Surrey, southern and south-east England (map 2)
Sites at Canterbury, Epsom, Farnham, Maidstone and Rochester

🖥 University for the Creative Arts, Falkner Road, Farnham, Surrey GU9 7DS
☎ Tel 01252 892883
🖨 Fax 01252 892616
✉ Email enquiries@ucreative.ac.uk
💻 Website www.ucreative.ac.uk

Student enquiries: Enquiries (tel 01252 892883)
Applications: UCAS (direct for part-time courses)

In brief

Total Students: 7460

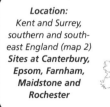

67% undergraduate

3% postgraduate
29% FE Students

Undergraduates: 5035
95% full-time ● ● 88% UK students
17% mature ● ● 35% lower
on entry ● ● socio-economic groups

65% female

35% male

- **Specialist creative arts university.**
- **Teaching staff:** 130 full-time, 350 part-time.
- **Broad study areas:** Art, architecture, design, fashion, media and communication.

Freshers

- **Admissions information:** Many courses require 160+ points from 2 A-levels or equivalent, of which 80 points are in an art/design-related subject. Kent recruits predominantly from foundation art courses.
- **First degree entrants:** 1440 UK, full-time.
- **Points on entry:** 160–175 (average).
- **Drop-out rate:** 10% in 1st year.
- **Accommodation:** Many 1st years housed (allocated by distance).

Profile

Institution

Founded: 2005, from amalgamation of Kent Institute of Art and Design and Surrey Institute of Art and Design; university status in 2008. **Site:** 2 main centres: Kent with campuses in Canterbury, Maidstone and Rochester, each shared with other educational establishments and close to the town/city centre; Surrey with campuses in Farnham and Epsom town centres. **How to get there:** All sites easily accessible from London and Europe by coach, bus, rail and road. **Special features:** Academic staff are practising artists, designers, film makers, media and crafts people. Many students win major awards, participate in festivals/trade fairs and receive external commissions.

Courses

Academic features: International links. Range of design specialisms. Record of student awards and commissions; professional facilities (eg computers, video studios). **Awarding body:** University for the Creative Arts. **Main undergraduate award:** BA. **Length of courses:** 3 years; 4 years (including foundation year); 5 years (part time) .

Study opportunities & careers

Library and information services: Library and learning centre (LLC) on each campus. Total of 150,000+ volumes, 600 journals, 350,000+ slides, 10,000 videos; open 9 hours/day in term time (7 hours outside term time). Information provision, £60 pa spent for each student (FTE). 240+ PCs and Macs for students in LLCs across all campuses, plus others in departments; some laptops can be loaned. Software includes Adobe Creative Suite (Illustrator, In Design and Photoshop). Support from IT staff in LLCs. **Other learning resources:** TV studios, newsrooms, photographic studios, editing suites, specialist workshops, machinery, tools, sewing machines, cutting tables and easels. **Study abroad:** Students can study abroad as part of degree course; links with colleges in 16 European countries, India, Australia, USA and New Zealand. **Careers:** Specialist library, one-to-one guidance, online help, presentations and events. Career planning an essential part of each course.

Student services & facilities

Student advice and services: Visiting doctor, nurse. Counsellors, accommodation officer, chaplains, international student support officer, special needs co-ordinator, student welfare advisers. **Amenities:** Shop on each site. **Sporting facilities:** Games hall at Surrey and local sports centres in town. Kent students have subsidised access to local leisure centres. **Accommodation:** Many 1st-year students housed (priority to those from greatest distance). 1055 self-catering places, rent £49–£105 pw depending on campus (some have modern halls, student villages and/or local houses and flats); all contracts 41 weeks. 188 places at Canterbury, rent £85–£90 pw; 147 at Epsom, rent £87–£105 pw; 372 at Farnham, rent £49–£89 pw; 134 at Maidstone, rent £87 pw; 214 at Rochester, rent £87 pw. Privately owned accommodation approx £65–£85 pw for self-catering.

Money

Living expenses budget: Minimum budget of £6500 for an academic year (excluding tuition fees) recommended by university. **Term-time work:** University allows term-time work for first-degree students. Some work available on campus. **Financial help:** Bursaries of £319 pa for all UK students whose family income is up to £25k. Also 160 scholarships of £1k pa awarded to academically promising students from low-income families. Additional financial help may be available on a campus basis. **Tuition fees:** Home students pay £3225 pa for first degrees (Year 0 pay £1725, foundation degrees £2100 pa). International students pay £6780–£8910 pa.

Student view

It's a new university, made up of five campuses across Kent and Surrey. With a wide range of facilities and strong student support there are opportunities for students to develop themselves in a variety of different fields within and beyond their chosen courses. Each campus is in a diverse and culturally individual area and is just out of town – excellent for students and close enough to enjoy city life. Each has its own social space for entertainment and individual openings for development. SU encompasses all five campuses; vice president at each campus organises clubs and societies.

Student view
(Kent campuses)

Canterbury is a great place to study; not large but has high student to resident ratio. Beautiful, historic city; great cathedral; lively pubs and bars and lots to do. A small but friendly campus. University provides a creative environment in which students' energy and passion for their subject is given free range. Regular live bands and DJs in SU bar, also theme nights – most musical tastes accommodated. Hundreds of pubs in Canterbury. Halls have ensuite facilities, communal kitchens and dining rooms; some on campus, some 20 mins walk. Student services can help find private accommodation in 2nd year, mostly in rented houses. Many students have part-time jobs. Students and staff get along well; all courses elect representatives who meet in a well-organised student/staff forum to sort out any problems. At *Maidstone*, it is in a purpose-built 70s building with some new additions, in a pleasant park within walking distance of the town centre. Halls midway between town and college. Illustration, graphics, photography, video, animation and further education are here; high standard facilities, eg studios and IT kit. Well-stocked library, specific to art and design. Small and friendly campus so everyone knows everyone. Large refectory and fully licensed bar. Students have highly subsidised use of huge local sports centre and there are organised sports teams at the college. Lively social life – Maidstone is known as the clubbing capital of the south-east. Large number of international students, so there is a diverse group of people. Courses also offer foreign exchanges, which have had good feedback. At *Rochester*, a 70s-style building with lots of character sits at the top of the hill overlooking the city and surrounding area. 5 mins walk from halls and city centre. It houses many creative courses, including design, fashion, photography and foundation studies.

Student footnotes

Housing: Rents can be high, so look around. **Eats:** *Canterbury:* excellent value food, wide range, in college refectory; in town, good restaurants to suit all tastes and budgets. *Maidstone:* Canteen ok but pricey; in town, Maidstone Grill (good when you've had a few), various pizzas, Mexican and Mongolian restaurants, good Chinese and Indian buffets and takeouts, Nandos, etc. *Rochester:* good-value food in refectory suits most tastes, plus snacks in vending machines and from SU bar. **Drink:** College bar at all sites. Trendy wine bars, Weatherspoon's (two of them), the Ashes sports bar in Maidstone. Plentiful bars and pubs in Rochester (20 in immediate area). **Nightlife:** Excellent mix of parties, theme nights and live gigs, etc at all union bars. In town, cinema, bars, bowling, comedy club, theatre. Limited gay scene. Business park near Rochester site, with cinema, bingo, variety of restaurants, bars and Kent's largest nightclub. **Sports:** No sports facilities on Canterbury campus but 2 local universities help out. At Maidstone, Mote Park complex, swimming, etc. College football and basketball teams. **Travel:** Some exchanges to Europe, Russia, Canada, etc. **Jobs:** Some work helping at college gigs; restaurant, bar, shop, cleaning work and summer fruit picking. **Financial help:** Limited loan fund. Government funds allocated in extreme and specific hardship. Welfare and accommodation officers very helpful. **Past students:** Tracey Emin (Brit-art artist), Karen Millen (fashion designer), Arnold Schwartzman (Oscar-winning film maker), Colin Banks (graphic designer/typographer), Humphrey Ocean (portrait artist), Zandra Rhodes (fashion designer), Tony Hart (TV artist), George Rodger (photo-journalist), Babette Cole (writer and illustrator). **More info?** Enquiries to SU (tel 01227 817337, website www.uccasu.com).

Student view
(Surrey campuses)

Both campuses, in Farnham and Epsom, relatively central to the town centres. Farnham is a small market town and has a good choice of pubs, restaurants and wine bars – as does the leafy town of Epsom (home of the famous racecourse). London is easily accessible by train; Epsom 30 mins, Farnham 50 mins. Both towns have sports centres and offer good discounts to students. Well-stocked specialist libraries at both sites, and resource centres with good computer access. It's a specialist art, design and media college with a good reputation. Many students have won acclaimed prizes and awards both internationally and nationally. Design faculty has a good reputation and offers one of the few degree courses for the study of glass, plus others in design management and packaging. The arts and media faculty offers degree courses in most modern technologies. The majority of degrees are 100% coursework, so although the workload is constant there isn't the pressure of end-of-year exams. Relatively easy to change course in first term, so long as there is space. Both campuses have bars and offer a wide range of clubs and societies.

Student footnotes

Housing: New accommodation in Epsom. Farnham has a student village and very helpful accommodation office. Halls/shared rooms, self-catering, for some 1st years (including all international students). Student houses, bedsits, etc found through SU noticeboards, accommodation lists, word of mouth. **Eats:** University refectory; meal deals all year round. Lots of restaurants around town (Indian, Chinese, Italian); lots of pubs to eat in. **Drink:** SU bar (the Glasshouse) is cheap, has late licence and large selection of beers, spirits, lagers and cocktails. **Nightlife:** Students' union – very well established and unique; SU nightclub with discos, bands, cabarets, films etc. **Locals:** Friendly enough. **Jobs:** Work available in local restaurants, supermarkets and cleaning. **Financial help:** Very good. **Best features:** Students' union ents – it's the only nightclub to go to in Farnham. **And worst:** Not enough places to go out. **Past students:** Annabelle Jankel (cucumber animation – *Max Headroom*), Dave Banks (editorial photographer – *Face*, etc), Mark Bauer (Grand Prix, Annely), Mark Baker (Oscar nomination 1994), Dan Greaves (Oscar winner 1992), Hugh Miles (director, BAFTA winner), Mike Edwards (camera CBS, Emmy award winner), Stephen Dodd (TV director), Kate Broom (director BBC2), Nick Sinclair (portrait photographer). **More info?** Contact SU on 01252 710263 or visit the website (www.uccasu.com).

Cumbria University

Location:
north-west England
(map 2)
Sites at Carlisle,
Ambleside, Lancaster,
Penrith; teaching site
in London

⌨ University of Cumbria, Fusehill Street,
Carlisle CA1 2HH
☎ Tel 01228 616234
💻 Website www.cumbria.ac.uk

Student enquiries: Undergraduate
Admissions (tel 0845 606 1144)
Applications: UCAS (direct for part-time)

In brief

Total Students: 13,875

75% undergraduate
21% postgraduate
4% FE Students

Undergraduates: 10,365
54% full-time
36% mature on entry
98% UK students
35% lower socio-economic groups

75% female   25% male

- **A modern university.**
- **Teaching staff:** 350+ full-time, 80+ part-time.
- **Broad study areas:** Art and design; performance arts; business; nursing and health-related subjects; humanities; IT and science; teaching; sport, tourism and leisure.

Freshers

- **Admissions information:** AS-levels may be considered, but only in combination with 2+ A-levels or equivalent. UCAS tariff used, to which AS-levels and Key Skills can contribute.
- **First degree entrants:** 1555 UK, full-time.
- **Points on entry:** 200 (average).
- **Drop-out rate:** 10% in 1st year.
- **Accommodation:** Almost all 1st years housed who apply.

Profile

Institution

Founded: 2007, a regional merger of 3 HE institutions: St Martin's College (an HE college in Lancaster, Carlisle and Ambleside), Cumbria Institute of the Arts (Carlisle) and the Central Lancashire University campuses at Penrith and Carlisle. **Site:** Sites at Ambleside (in the Lake District); Carlisle (2 campuses); Lancaster (single open campus 5 mins from city centre); Penrith (rural campus a mile from town); plus London teaching site in Bow. **How to get there:** Ambleside: rail to Windermere and taxi ride, or by road via M6 then A591. Carlisle: rail (London–Glasgow) or by road via M6 then A69. Lancaster: rail (London–Glasgow line) or by road via M6; frequent local bus service. Penrith: rail (London–Glasgow) then taxi, or by road (M6). **Special features:** University has strong links with 4 local FE colleges.

Courses

Academic features: Range of modular studies and professional courses in, eg nursing, teaching, occupational therapy and radiography, law, youth and community work. **Awarding body:** University of Cumbria. **Main undergraduate awards:** BA, BSc, BA/BSc(QTS), BEng, LLB. **Length of courses:** 3 years; 4 years.

Study opportunities & careers

Library and information services: Libraries on 10 sites: total of approx 300,000 items, including books, journals, multi-media items. Plentiful study places; networked PCs. Information provision, £100 pa spent for each student (FTE). Specialist collection: teaching practice collections. **Other learning resources:** Multi-media facilities and media equipment, computer laboratories, art and ceramic studios, dance and drama studio, music recital and rehearsal rooms. Paramedical building for OT, radiography and imaging science. **Study abroad:** 5% spend a period abroad. European university links. **Careers:** Information and advice service on main campuses.

Student services & facilities

Student advice and services: Student development and advisory service has one-stop shops on main campuses, including student finance, international student advice, disability and specific learning difficulties, residence life, academic skills, counselling, mental health and wellbeing and careers guidance. SU adviser, chaplain, SU solicitor; chapel, medical centre, counselling. **Amenities:** Campus bookshop, SU bar and social club; shop. **Sporting facilities:** Sports centre with 4 badminton courts, gymnastics area, conditioning room, sports injury clinic. Floodlit all-weather pitch, tennis and squash courts, gymnasia, multigym with equipment for aerobic exercise at Lancaster. Similar facilities at Penrith. Varied facilities at other sites. **Accommodation:** Most 1st-year students housed. Some accommodation self-catering, some catered, depending on campus; rent £70–£100 pw. Students live in privately owned accommodation for 2+ years: rent £45–£60.

Money

Living expenses budget: Minimum budget of £6k pa (excluding tuition fees) recommended by university. **Term-time work:** University allows term-time work for full-time students. Some work available on Lancaster campus in bar, catering or sports centre (careers service advertises jobs off campus). **Financial help:** Bursaries of £1290 pa for UK students whose family income is up to £25k, tapered (down to £215 pa) where family income is £25k–£60k. Also 35 scholarships of £1k pa for achievement or potential in sport, community, environment, business enterprise and entrepreneurship, or creative arts by students from low-income families or low-participation groups. Small bursaries may be awarded, if eligible, from university hardship funds. **Tuition fees:** Home students pay up to £3225 pa for first degrees. International students pay £7900 pa.

Student view
(Ambleside Campus)

Located in the heart of the Lake District, with stunning views, this campus is certainly a great place to study. Ambleside is a busy little tourist town, with many jobs available (but living costs and public transport fairly expensive). Majority of 1st years live in halls, 2 mins walk from college. SU bar (the Overdraught) is largest venue in town and has many events throughout the week. Brand new library with state-of-the-art equipment. Sports facilities are limited at best but plans underway to improve them. Despite this, there is still a strong BUCS participation, as well as many other clubs, eg mountaineering, kayaking and dodgeball.

Student footnotes

Housing: Halls for 1st years (self-catering, fully- or semi-catered). Sufficient private-sector houses off campus. **Eats:** College refectory and snack bar. Loads of local cafés and bars but few student discounts. **Drink:** SU bar, the Overdraught; pubs in town average £2.20 a pint, £1.80 a shot. **Financial help:** Good grant/loan schemes in place through student services. **Best features:** You get to know everybody and it's very friendly. **And worst:** Everybody knows you (can be hard for some people). And it rains – a lot. **More info?** Contact Vice President Ambleside (tel 015394 30376, email info@su.cumbria.ac.uk, website www.thestudentsunion.org.uk).

Student view
(Carlisle Campus)

It's next to the city centre, on the site of the old infirmary, which has been extensively refurbished. Recent developments include a sports complex, halls of residence and student bar. Learning gateway centre and SU building planned. Carlisle is an historic border city surrounded by beautiful countryside with excellent shopping, restaurants and entertainment. Student body is growing and the SU is very active, running many clubs, societies and organising entertainment events. Halls are stylish, modern and comfortable; housing off-campus arranged through the accommodation office as a head lease scheme (so students only have to deal with the university and can be guaranteed housing that meets all safety and living standards). Sports are very diverse and the sporting facilities offer virtually endless opportunities at extremely reasonable rates with big discounts for student users.

Student footnotes

Housing: Reasonable rates for halls; head lease scheme for housing off-campus. **Eats:** University dining room. Wide range of restaurants in town. **Nightlife:** SU bar on campus, with friendly staff. Excellent variety of student-friendly pubs and clubs in Carlisle. **Sports:** Newly established sports and societies use the local sports centre for reduced price. **Jobs:** Part-time work available in shops and pubs in town. **Financial help:** Really good, and you can apply throughout the year. **More info?** Enquiries to Vice President Carlisle (tel 01228 616253, email info@su.cumbria.ac.uk, website www.thestudentsunion.org.uk).

Student view
(Lancaster Campus)

A very friendly campus, only ½ mile from Lancaster, which has the usual high street stores, great little boutiques and specialist shops; also pubs and restaurants for all tastes and great places for theatre, music and films. It's close to coastal and countryside activities, including the Lake District, and 60 miles from Manchester and Liverpool. Seven halls on-site (all with irons, kettles, etc); self-catering residences are in town, 15 mins' walk from college. Campus has medical centre, laundry, TV lounges, coffee bars, bookshop and SU shop (stationery, food, etc); 2 bars sell alcoholic and soft drinks at cheap prices. Active SU campaigns on student issues, runs student advice centre, organises entertainments, eg themed nights; also runs successful sports clubs and societies. Great sport facilities. A place of opportunities where people can be themselves and participate in or initiate activities.

Student footnotes

Housing: Above-average standard on campus. **Eats:** Refectory, including vegetarian provision, coffee bars have snacks. Chinese, French, Mexican, Indian, Italian, all in town. **Drink:** SU bar very cheap. Vast range of pubs in town. **Nightlife:** SU ents include themed nights, quiz night, visiting bands, balls. **Sports:** Sports complex, multigym, AstroTurf. Access to Lancaster University facilities; private clubs have student rates. **Travel:** Trust funds and travel scholarships through the chaplaincy. **Jobs:** Easy to get part-time work, eg SU bar and shop. **Past students:** David Coates (broadcaster). **More info?** Contact SU President or Vice President (tel 01524 526567, email info@su.cumbria.ac.uk, website www.thestudentsunion.org.uk).

Dartington

Location:
*south-west England
(map 2)
**Single site near
Totnes; moving to
Falmouth in 2010***

Dartington Hall Estate, Totnes,
Devon TQ9 6EJ
☎ Tel 01803 862224
🖷 Fax 01803 861666
✉ Email admissions@dartington.ac.uk
🖥 Website www.falmouth.ac.uk

*Student enquiries: Registry
Applications: UCAS*

In brief

- **Specialist arts college**, now part of University College Falmouth.
- **Broad study areas:** Music, performance writing, theatre, visual performance, choreography.

Freshers
- **Accommodation:** All 1st years housed who apply.

Profile

Institution
Founded: 1961. **Structural features:** Now part of Falmouth University College. **Site:** In beautiful grounds on River Dart until 2010, when Dartington will close and all remaining courses move to Falmouth. **How to get there:** Road and rail access from Plymouth and Exeter (within half hour), Totnes 2 miles.

Courses 📖
Awarding body: University College Falmouth. **Main undergraduate award:** BA. **Length of courses:** 3 years.

Study opportunities & careers 🎓
Library and information services: 84,000 items (books, scores, sound recordings, slides, films, CD-ROM). IT and library services converged; access 12 hours/day. 3 points with access to library

catalogue, 36 to internet; ratio 1:10 workstations to students. IT support from specialist IT and library staff. **Other learning resources:** Specialist performance technology centre, studios, workshops and practice rooms. For further information, see *Falmouth University College*.

Student services & facilities

Student advice and services: Health centre, part-time nurse; counselling service; welfare officer. **Amenities:** Refectory, bar, laundrette; extensive grounds. Dartmoor, Torbay, Exeter and Plymouth within easy reach. **Accommodation:** All 1st years who request it housed on site. Partial self-catering and self-catering places at £68–£73.50 pw including utilities, Sept–June contracts; some rooms have internet access, charge £60 per term. For further information, see *Falmouth University College*.

Money

Term-time work: Limited part-time work on Dartington Estate and in Totnes. **Financial help:** See *Falmouth University College*. **Tuition fees:** Home students pay £3225 pa for first degrees. International students pay £9097–£9581 pa.

De Montfort University

Location:
Leicester, Midlands
(map 2)
2 sites in city centre; many partner colleges

De Montfort University, The Gateway, Leicester LE1 9BH
☎ Tel 0116 255 1551
🖷 Fax 0116 250 6204
💻 Website www.dmu.ac.uk

Student enquiries: Enquiry centre (tel 08459 45 46 47)
Applications: UCAS

In brief

Total Students: 19,380
88% undergraduate

1% FE Students
11% postgraduate

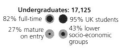

Undergraduates: 17,125
82% full-time ● ● 95% UK students
27% mature ● ● 43% lower
on entry ● ● socio-economic
groups

58% female 42% male

- **A modern university.**
- **Teaching staff:** 660 full-time, 140 part-time.
- **Broad study areas:** Art and design, business and law, computer science and engineering, health and life sciences, humanities.

Freshers
- **Admissions information:** UCAS tariff being used.
- **First degree entrants:** 3825 UK, full-time.
- **Points on entry:** 235 (average).
- **Drop-out rate:** 10% in 1st year.
- **Accommodation:** Almost all 1st years housed who request it.

Institution

Founded: 1969 as Leicester Poly; university status in 1992. **Site:** Main campus near city centre plus further site to east of city. **How to get there:** Leicester easily accessible from across the UK by rail and coach; campus approx 20-min walk from bus and train stations; close to M1 (junctions 21 and 22).

Courses

Academic features: Modular courses available in all disciplines. Wide range of 1st year courses available at franchise centres around the country. Policy of encouraging mature students. **Awarding body:** De Montfort University. **Main undergraduate awards:** BA, BSc, BEng, MPharm, LLB. **Length of courses:** 3 years; others 4 years (sandwich), 5 years (extended).

Study opportunities & careers

Library and information services: Network of information centres (libraries, bookshops, communication facilities and resources), access often through electronic links. Library on both campuses (incl specialised law library) plus computers, internet, CD-ROMs, videos, study areas, audio material and video conferencing. Information provision, £77 pa spent for each student (FTE). Specialist collections: National Art Slide Library. **Study abroad:** Formal exchange links with European universities and colleges, available to wide range of students. **Careers:** Information, advice and placement service at each site. Strong links with textile, fashion and engineering industries.

Student services & facilities

Student advice and services: Counselling, student health service, chaplaincy, legal information service at Leicester. **Amenities:** Bookshop, exhibition hall, SU, health centre. **Sporting facilities:** Good sporting facilities. **Accommodation:** Most 1st years housed; guaranteed for all 1st years under 23 from outside the LE postal district, for all students under 18, international students, and anyone with disabilities. 2300 self-catering places, £70–£90 pw, most contracts Sept–June. Most students live in privately owned accommodation for 2+ years, rent £60–£70 pw plus bills.

Money

Living expenses budget: Minimum budget of £6500–£8500 for academic year (excluding tuition fees) recommended by university. **Term-time work:** University allows term-time work, to a limit of 12 hours a week (45% believed to work). University employs some 60 students as ambassadors. DMU Works recruitment service helps find jobs off campus. **Financial help:** Bursaries of £400 pa for UK students whose family income is up to £60k; of £400 pa for local students; and of £1k pa for students who were in care. Also scholarships (of £1k–£1500 pa) for those with high entry qualifications, some restricted to those on creative industry courses. £1.6 million access to learning funds; 1500 students helped. Special help to those with high costs, eg childcare costs, health/disability costs or high travel/accommodation costs. Apply to Student Services for help. **Tuition fees:** Home students £3225 pa for first degrees. International students pay £8500–£9k pa.

Student view

Now based solely in Leicester, it prides itself in the quality of teaching and research, in professional, vocational and creative education. Interesting courses include: radio broadcasting to contour fashion design (recently awarded Karen Millen an honorary degree). Strong links to industry and local community so good opportunities for placements; brilliant library and excellent computer provision. Good mix of students – international, mature, local, rich and poor students – chimes with the cultural diversity of the city. Leicester is a really cool city: not so big that you feel out of your depth, but big enough to be an excellent place to spend your student years. Main shopping mall being extended and much regeneration going on. Many bars and clubs, theatres, sports facilities and clubs (Leicester City FC, Leicester Tigers RFC, Leicestershire CCC). University is accessible, particularly by train, and you are as safe as anywhere else in the country. Plenty of opportunities for work; university runs its own Workbank and also has loads of hardship fund money for those in need. Housing guaranteed for pretty much all 1st years who want it. New private accommodation competes with the traditional landlord. Narborough Road is the city's student-ville. Plenty of bars and restaurants around campus, so there is no excuse not to find bargains around! SU is the heart of most students' social experience. Many sports and societies to join, as well as award-winning media (radio and TV stations, website and newspaper).

Student footnotes

Housing: New halls and student flats. Off-campus, hundreds of terraced houses (look on union noticeboards, housing agents). **Eats:** Basic meal from £1.50+ on campus. SU food good, varied and cheap, as are takeouts on Narborough Road. Couple of local pubs do vegetarian and vegan food. **Drinks:** SU good and cheap. **Nightlife:** Live acts on campus (including performances from East 17, Tim Westwood, Zane Lowe and appearances from *Neighbours* stars); also a range of music to suit all audiences. Plenty of other clubs in the city. **Sports:** University sports centre – keep fit, step-aerobics, etc and fitness suite. Swimming pool at Aylestone leisure centre. **Travel:** Good local bus service has student rates. Travel shops in city centre. **Jobs:** Local shops, call centres, pubs and restaurants. Work in SU bar (but can be waiting list of 1–6 months). **Buzz-words:** DMU (De Montfort University), the Narb (abbreviation of Narborough Road – the student area). **Best features:** SU – venue and evening entertainment. **And worst:** Leicester's road system and cycling paths! **Past students**: Charles Dance (actor), Gary Lineker (footballer), Sarah Wooliscroft (Arsenal ladies football), Stephen Bates (England kayak), Sam Cook (England women's rugby). **More info?** Call the SU or visit www.demontfortstudents.com.

Derby University

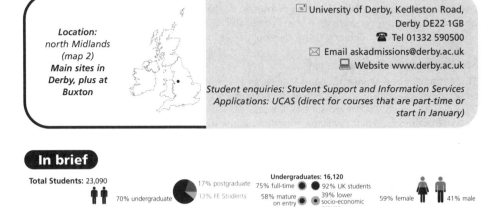

Location:
north Midlands
(map 2)
**Main sites in
Derby, plus at
Buxton**

University of Derby, Kedleston Road,
Derby DE22 1GB
☎ Tel 01332 590500
✉ Email askadmissions@derby.ac.uk
💻 Website www.derby.ac.uk

*Student enquiries: Student Support and Information Services
Applications: UCAS (direct for courses that are part-time or
start in January)*

In brief

Total Students: 23,090

70% undergraduate
17% postgraduate
13% FE Students

Undergraduates: 16,120
75% full-time
58% mature on entry

92% UK students
39% lower socio-economic groups

59% female 41% male

- **A modern university.**
- **Teaching staff:** 414 full-time, 648 part-time.
- **Broad study areas:** Art and design; beauty, spa and complementary therapies; business and management; computing; criminology; education; engineering; hospitality, catering

263

and events management; humanities; law; maths; media; professions allied to nursing; science and technology; social science; sport; travel and tourism.

Freshers

- **Admissions information:** AS-levels accepted usually in combination with 2+ A-levels or equivalent. UCAS tariff used for offers.
- **First degree entrants:** 2560 UK full-time.
- **Points on entry:** 160–300.
- **Drop-out rate:** 14% in 1st year.
- **Accommodation:** Guaranteed for all 1st years who apply by end of August.

Institution

Founded: 1851 as a teacher training college, becoming Derbyshire College of HE in 1983; university status in 1992. **Site:** Derby Campus consists of Kedleston Road, Markeaton Street and Britannia Mill sites; separate Devonshire Campus in Buxton. **How to get there:** Good road and rail links to Derby and Buxton. Subsidised Unibuses between Derby city centre and halls of residence, and between Derby and Buxton; free shuttle bus links Derby sites.

Courses

Academic features: Joint Honours scheme involves 60 subjects. Range of entry qualifications accepted. **Awarding body:** University of Derby. **Main undergraduate awards:** BA, BEd, BSc. **Length of courses:** 3 years; 4 years (sandwich).

Study opportunities & careers

Library and information services: Learning centres at both campuses; 329,000 volumes, 2100 periodicals, 10,000 electronic periodicals; 1700 study places. Information provision, £74 pa spent for each student (FTE). Internet access from all workstations; access to university network and internet 24/7 from rooms in halls. **Other learning resources:** Multimedia and graphics centre. **Study abroad:** Opportunities for students to spend period abroad. Formal exchange links with some EU universities and colleges. **Careers:** Career development centre.

Student services & facilities

Student advice and services: Support from student services, assistant deans, wardens and university nurse, doctor, chaplaincy, student counsellors. **Amenities:** SU shop, student employment agency, bank, hairdressers, bar, bookshop at Derby Campus; SU shop, travel agency, bistro and restaurant at Buxton. **Sporting facilities:** Gymnasia, sports pitches (for rugby, football, hockey), running track, health club, sports clubs at both campuses. **Accommodation:** Place in halls guaranteed for all 1st years who apply by end of August. 2600 self-catering places, £60–£87 pw; 42- or 50-week contracts. Most students live in privately owned accommodation for 2 years; rent £65–£70 pw.

Money

Living expenses budget: Minimum budget of £6500 for academic year (excluding tuition fees) recommended by university. **Term-time work:** Student employment agency helps find work on and off campus. **Financial help:** Bursaries of £830 pa for UK students whose family income is up to £25,600; of £520 pa where family income is £25,600–£35,900; and £210 pa where family income is £35,900–£51,300. Also bursaries of £300 or £400 for those from local area or from specified partner schools or colleges. Access and hardship funds. **Tuition fees:** Home students pay £3225 pa for first degrees (£2055 for foundation degrees; £625 for placement years). International students pay £7800 pa (classroom-based), £8415 (lab-based); fees fixed for whole course.

Student view

Split across several sites in Derby – one even reaching as far as Buxton. Main campus is Kedleston Road, with great views of the countryside from all sides. Satellite sites are all close and linked by a regular uni bus service. Accommodation ranges from new halls of residence (some ensuite) to various university-approved houses, all in walking distance of university. Student body is very diverse, with many international and mature students. Diversity reflected in the facilities: new multi-faith centre and numerous sports pitches. SU has its own gym, bars, shops, coffee shop and advice centre; it also runs a monthly magazine and newsletter, radio station, website, various campaigns and even more sports teams, societies and volunteering opportunities – plenty of chances to get involved. SU exists to support, advise, represent and entertain so that students have a unique, enjoyable and safe student experience. It also offers a thriving nightlife for all tastes – something on every night. City centre has many restaurants, bars, clubs and cinemas; many offer student discounts. Students are friendly, with a strong community spirit, and it is very easy to integrate and have a fantastic time.

Student footnotes

Housing: Reasonable prices. Use uni housing department. **Food:** Many restaurants: Fat Cats, Zizzi, Pizza Express, La Tasca, Vines, as well as various takeaways and Indian restaurants. **Drink:** SU bars, SUB and Lonsdale are cheap, friendly and safe. Many city bars and clubs have student nights. **Nightlife:** SU-affiliated nights (eg Spank, Bed); many nightclubs, eg Bluenote (indie), Blu Bamboo (cheese), Firstfloor (rock). Cinemas; Victoria Inn for live music. SU runs 3 annual balls (Freshers, Graduation and May balls); many famous acts come to them, eg Fun Lovin' Criminals, Girls Aloud, Beat Freaks. **Locals:** Friendly. Medium-sized city, so still cosy and less scary! **Sports:** Gym, swimming pool, football, rugby, netball and hockey pitches. **Travel:** A good uni bus service, regular local buses and plenty of taxis. Relatively easy and cheap to get to larger cities too. **Jobs:** Easy to get part-time work (bars, shops) and work experience; use uni student employment agency. **Best features:** The atmosphere; the SU, the Atrium. **And worst:** Satellite sites can mean communication is sometimes lost and some fragmented facilities. **Past students:** Barry Evans (rugby player, Leicester/England), Berni Yates (fashion designer), Greg Tucker (accountant), Ryan Cook (graphic designer), Alisdair Mackie (high roller). **More info?** Contact the SU on 01332 591507 or visit the website (www.udsu.co.uk).

Dundee University

Location:
Dundee, east coast of Scotland (map 1)
Main campus in city centre; hospital site in suburbs

✉ University of Dundee,
Dundee DD1 4HN
☎ Tel 01382 384160
🖷 Fax 01382 388150
🖥 Website www.dundee.ac.uk

Student enquiries: Admissions and Student Recruitment
Applications: UCAS (except for nursing and midwifery)

In brief

Total Students: 18,225

33% postgraduate
67% undergraduate

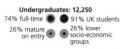

Undergraduates: 12,250

74% full-time · 91% UK students
26% mature on entry · 26% lower socio-economic groups

65% female 35% male

- **A top UK research-intensive university.**
- **Teaching staff:** 715 full-time, 227 part-time, 866 honorary (mainly medicine and dentistry).
- **Broad study areas:** Medicine, dentistry and nursing; law and accountancy; arts and social sciences; art and design; engineering and physical sciences; life sciences; architecture; town and regional planning; education and social work.

Freshers

- **Admissions information:** UCAS tariff used, maybe with additional subject requirements; S-grades, core skills and Key Skills not included.
- **First degree entrants:** 2500 UK, full-time.
- **Points on entry:** 388 (average).
- **Drop-out rate:** 10% in 1st year.
- **Accommodation:** All 1st years housed who require it (and apply by deadline).

Profile

Institution

Founded: 1882; university status in 1967. **Site:** Near city centre; teaching hospital in suburbs. **How to get there:** Motorway links and direct rail and bus services from other parts of UK; rail and bus stations in walking distance.

Courses

Academic features: Students able to switch between arts and social sciences and science and engineering subjects respectively before entering the 2nd year. **Awarding body:** University of Dundee. **Main undergraduate awards:** BA, BAcc, BArch, BDes, BDS, BEd, BEng, BFin, BMSc, BSc, LLB, MA, MB ChB. **Length of courses:** 3 or 4 years; others 5 years (architecture, dentistry, medicine, enhanced physics and engineering courses).

Study opportunities & careers

Library and information services: Main library with approx 700,000 volumes; medical, law, nursing, art, design, education and social work and departmental libraries; archives department; inter-library loan scheme. Information provision, £131 pa spent for each student (FTE). Separate IT service, open 11–24 hours/day; ratio 1:8 workstations to students. 1000 computers with access to library and internet, plus multiple access points in, eg halls of residence; wireless networking zones across campus. Tours of library for new students and compulsory IT induction course. **Other learning resources:** Online resources (my dundee, advance@dundee); language centre. **Study abroad:** 1% of students spend 6 months or more abroad. Formal exchange links with a number of universities and colleges in western Europe and North America, open to a range of students. **Careers:** Information and advice service.

Student services & facilities

Student advice and services: Student advisory and counselling services; health service offers routine medical examinations by local GP. **Amenities:** SU building with swimming pool, shop, bars, restaurant, bookshop, coin laundry; chaplaincy centre; civic repertory theatre adjoining campus. **Sporting facilities:** Large indoor sports complex (recently extended); university sports grounds and tennis courts; more than 20 golf courses including St Andrews and Carnoustie within half an hour's drive; skiing, climbing and hill walking in surrounding countryside. **Accommodation:** 65% of 1st years in university accommodation (all those that require it and apply by end of July). 1750 self-catering places, £67–£99 pw for 38 weeks (ie total of £2550–£3990). Dundee has buoyant private-sector housing at reasonable costs; rent from £50 pw. 20% of first-degree students live at home.

Money (💰)

Living expenses budget: Minimum budget of £500–£600 per month (excluding tuition fees) recommended by university. **Term-time work:** University does not encourage term-time work but realises it is inevitable (20% believed to work); advisory limit of 15 hours pw. Some work available on campus in SU and residences. **Financial help:** Total available £800k government funds, 990 students helped; some one-off donations, disbursed by university hardship panel. Special help for students with children, self-financing students and others in severe financial hardship; other funds available for those of Scots birth or extraction studying medicine, dentistry, science or engineering. Also some scholarships (varying value) for academic ability of potential, computing, medicine and dentistry, music. **Tuition fees:** Scottish and EU students pay no fees during their course; other UK students pay £1820 pa for first degrees (£2895 for clinical courses, £6500 for full-cost LLB). International students pay £8500 pa (classroom-based courses), £9900–£10,500 (lab/studio), £13,100 (pre-clinical), £20,800 (clinical).

Student view

Campus is about 5 mins from city centre and easily accessible by both train and road – students rarely require local transport as most things are within walking distance. Excellent medical department (recent award for keyhole surgery) and biochemistry department is world leader in cancer research; Dundee scientists also gave the world 'hole in the wall' cash dispensers and liquid crystal displays. Courses span a broad spectrum, many including industrial placements in Europe, Canada, USA and Australia. Semester system makes it even easier to change course in 1st year (even changing faculty). 5 university libraries; main library open until midnight and during the vacation. The SU boasts 2 nightclubs (combined capacity of 1350), 5 bars and games room with pool tables and video games; good catering facilities and state-of-the-art debating chamber. SU shop, Under Union, sells all essentials. Union has over 100 societies, many sports-based; also excellent student newspaper and good debates union. It also provides support services and system of representation. Excellent sports centre on campus, with multigym and swimming pool.

Student footnotes

Housing: Generally reasonable; 2 luxury halls of residence available. **Eats:** Union eatery (Yum Yum), meal £4+. **Drink:** Union definitely cheapest; regular drinks promos. **Nightlife:** Varied SU ents programme and many society events; Dundee has rep theatre, numerous cinemas, ice arena. **Sports:** Sports centre on campus. Public leisure centre 10 mins from campus. **Travel:** Cheap fares available through travel agent near SU. **Jobs:** SU bars, library, security, PR or local work in pubs, etc. DUSA jobshop helps find work. **Financial help:** Available through faculties, SA and university. **Best features:** SU: combines quality entertainment with cheap drink. **Good news:** Hardship fund increased; major refurbishment of union. **Past students:** George Robertson (politician); Selina Scott (presenter); Fred McCauley (author, presenter). **More info?** Contact SA (tel 01382 221841, email vpc@dusa.co.uk) or check out the website on www.dusa.co.uk.

Durham University

Location:
North-east England
(map 2)
**Teaching departments
and colleges, Durham
city centre; separate
campus Stockton**

Durham University, University Office,
Durham, DH1 3HP
Tel 0191 334 2000
Fax 0191 334 6250
Email admissions@durham.ac.uk
Website www.durhamac.uk

*Student enquiries: Undergraduate Admissions Office
Applications: UCAS*

In brief

Total Students: 15,505
84% at Durham
16% at Stockton

26% postgraduate
74% undergraduate

Undergraduates: 11,410
98% full-time
5% mature on entry
93% UK students
15% lower socio-economic groups

51% female
49% male

- **World-class research-intensive university.**
- **Teaching staff:** 600 full-time.
- **Broad study areas:** Arts; humanities; sciences; social sciences; health.

Freshers

- **Admissions information:** AS-levels accepted in combination with A-levels or equivalent; some departments may accept 2 AS-levels in place of a 3rd A-level but often with higher grades; general studies not generally accepted. University welcomes applications from students with non-traditional qualifications and backgrounds. UCAS tariff not used.
- **First degree entrants:** 3240 UK, full-time.
- **Points on entry:** 458 at Durham, 348 at Stockton (average).
- **Drop-out rate:** 3% in 1st year.
- **Accommodation:** All 1st years live in college.

Profile

Institution

Founded: 1832. **Site:** 2 sites: at Durham, in city centre (and short walk south of river); and Queen's Campus at Stockton (10 mins from Stockton town centre, 26 miles from Durham). **How to get there:** Durham: mainline trains and coach services to Durham from London and all main UK regions; frequent local buses within the region; by road Durham is just off the A1. Stockton: by rail to Darlington, connecting services to Thornaby, 5 mins from campus; frequent local buses; by road, A66 and A19, under 10 miles from A1. **Special features:** University consists of 16 colleges and societies; most are in Durham, 2 in Queen's Campus, Stockton. Teaching is organised centrally, not by college.

Courses

Academic features: 200+ undergraduate degrees across 3 faculties (arts and humanities, science, social sciences and health). Most courses based at Durham; some at Queen's Campus, Stockton. Medicine (at Stockton) offered in partnership with Newcastle University. **Awarding body:** Durham

University. **Main undergraduate awards:** BA, BSc, MB BS, LLB, MSci, MEng, MMath. **Length of courses:** 3 years; others 4–5 years.

Study opportunities & careers

Library and information services: Main library has 1.5 million + printed volumes plus digital resources; also departments and colleges have libraries and IT facilities. Information provision, £168 pa spent for each student (FTE). IT facilities in libraries plus open-access points (including in college bedrooms) with access 24/7. Library induction pack and guided tours; IT support on dedicated helpline 10+ hours/weekdays; certified IT skills courses available. **Other learning resources:** Various special collections and archives; museums (oriental art and archaeological); botanic garden. **Study abroad:** Links with 100+ universities across Europe, through Socrates-Erasmus. Also exchanges in, eg Russia, Singapore, USA. **Careers:** Dedicated careers advisory service.

Student services & facilities

Student advice and services: Student health centre in Durham, access to local medical practices at Stockton; sick-bay facilities in each college; support for students with disabilities. **Amenities:** Wide range of facilities in colleges; bar, minibus, etc centrally in modern DSU building, Dunelm House. **Sporting facilities:** Sports hall; 64 acres of playing fields. Also college sports facilities, including boat clubs. **Accommodation:** All 1st years live in university accommodation in colleges. Range of options and length of contract at Durham, eg £150 pw fully catered, 29 week contract (ie total of £4347 pa); from £95.50 pw self-catering for 38 weeks (£3630 pa). At Stockton, £92 pw self-catering (total £3489 pa). Private accommodation in Durham approx £70–£75 pw, in Stockton £43 pw.

Money

Living expenses budget: Minimum budget of £7k pa (excluding tuition fees) recommended by university, £7500 if not in university accommodation. **Financial help:** Grants of £1300 pa for students whose family income is up to £25k. Also 25 scholarships of £3k pa awarded each year for music, sport and performing arts. Access funds and university's own hardship fund can help students with a sound financial plan that has been compromised by unforeseen circumstances. Funding available for personal development, scholarships and prizes awarded for academic achievement. **Tuition fees:** Home students pay £3225 pa for first degrees. International students pay £10,560 (classroom), £13,770 pa (lab-based).

Student view

Durham is a brilliant place to live and study. Picturesque city with a fascinating history and breathtaking natural and human architecture. The 14 colleges based there have as their backdrop the stunning castle and cathedral. It has a vibrant and varied social scene (bars, cafés, nightclubs, theatres, restaurants and a cinema) but small enough to be able to walk just about anywhere. Bill Bryson (the university Chancellor) described it as 'a perfect little city – if you have never been to Durham, go there at once. Take my car. It's wonderful.' The bailey is encapsulated by the river and has on it the castle, cathedral and several colleges (University, Hatfield, Chad's, John's and Castle). Hild and Bede college is on the river bank, overlooking the city. The hill, to the south of the bailey, has most of the university buildings and 8 of the colleges (Josephine Butler, Ustinov, Collingwood, Grey, St Aidan's, Van Mildert, Trevelyan and St Mary's). Most of the colleges on the hill were built in the 1960s and '70s and have great facilities and accommodation; the bailey has the charm of old buildings and cobbled streets. Queen's Campus is in Stockton-on-Tees and the student body and campus are an integral part of the regeneration of the area. Stephenson and John Snow colleges are at Queen's, as are some subject areas, including medicine; all departments are on the main campus (including the Wolfson Research Institute). About one sixth of students are based at Queens. The colleges on both campuses provide a good sense of community for students and are the main focus of their lives. Each has its own individual character and college rivalry is intense! The junior and middle common rooms of the colleges regularly put on plays, host balls and formal dinners and provide a social hub for their students. College facilities include libraries, computer rooms, study areas, common rooms and bars. Teaching is done mainly in departments: sciences are in the designated science park next to the library; others are scattered throughout the city. Many departments retain a tutorial system combined with cutting edge research. Students come from all over the world; over 120 countries are represented. The SU is in the centre of Durham (in Dunelm House), a building that makes extremely good use of concrete: split over four levels, it has a bar, café and a shop selling all sorts. Union holds regular events (eg Jazz Café, Revolver Indie nights on Saturdays, and Durham blasts off to Planet of Sound on Fridays). DSU also publishes an independent student newspaper (*Palatinate*) and airs Purple Radio, both run by students. SU is a collaboration of colleges, supporting 100+ societies across both campuses. These include student community action and award-winning Charity Kommittee (DUCK), which supports hundreds of local and national charities (students raise money by taking part in expeditions, hitch hikes, rag raids and more). Student theatre group, and light opera group (DULOG), regularly run productions; many student drama, revue, musical and performance companies. Both campuses have great transport links and stations in walking distance. Newcastle and Middlesbrough are nearby if you want to get out of the student bubble. It's a university with character, a lively and active student population as well as strong academic record and connections around the world.

Student footnotes

Housing: Accommodation all good standard, but varies, eg Collingwood, ensuite rooms fully catered; University College, living in a castle! For those living out, excellent SU accommodation office. **Eats:** For something a bit special try Hide, Hollathans or Oldfields. **Drink:** Most colleges have student-run bars, prices reasonable. **Nightlife:** Regular SU events including weekly sell-out Planet of Sound. Klute has cult status: plenty of cheese. Other clubs both big and small. **Sports:** College sports teams, most facilities on Durham site. All levels so there will be a team to suit you. **Jobs:** Careers service runs a employment service. **Best features:** Opportunities to get involved in whatever interests you. **And worst:** Cobbles, hills and cobbled hills! **Past students:** Judith Hann (presenter, *Tomorrow's World*), Harold Evans (newspaper editor), Will Carling (England rugby captain), Nasser Hussain (England test cricketer), Hunter Davies (writer), Jonathan Edwards (world triple jump record holder), Mo Mowlam (politician, former Northern Ireland Secretary), George Alagiah (journalist). **More info?** Contact SU on 0191 334 1775, email enquiries@dsu.org.uk or visit the website (www.dsu.org.uk).

East Anglia University

Location:
Norwich, East Anglia
(map 2)
Single campus
on outskirts
of city

University of East Anglia, Norwich, Norfolk NR4 7TJ
☎ Tel 01603 456161
🖷 Fax 01603 458553
✉ Email admissions@uea.ac.uk
💻 Website www.uea.ac.uk

Student enquiries: Admissions Office (tel 01603 59 1519/1515)
Applications: UCAS

In brief

Total Students: 19,585

22% postgraduate
78% undergraduate

Undergraduates: 15,190
66% full-time
32% mature on entry
91% UK students
24% lower socio-economic groups

62% female   38% male

- **A top UK research-intensive university.**
- **Teaching staff:** 590 full-time, 97 part-time.
- **Broad study areas:** Biological and chemical sciences; environmental sciences; development studies; mathematics; computing and information systems; medicine; pharmacy; professions allied to health; nursing and midwifery; management and business; history; education; economics; political, social and international studies; law; English and creative writing; philosophy; drama; American studies; art history and music; film and TV studies; modern languages; social work; psychology.

Freshers

- **Admissions information:** 2 A-levels or equivalent required as minimum. In practice, AS-levels accepted in combination with 3+ A-levels or equivalent. UCAS tariff not widely used.
- **First degree entrants:** 2440 UK, full-time.
- **Points on entry:** 311 (average).
- **Drop-out rate:** 7% in 1st year.
- **Accommodation:** Almost all 1st years housed.

Profile

Institution

Founded: 1963. **Site:** 2 miles from centre of Norwich. **How to get there:** Coach service from all major cities to Norwich, and to university from London airports; rail service from London (2 hours) every ½ hour. For university, regular bus services from city (nos 25, 35, 21/22). By road from London on M11/A11, then A47 and B1108. **Special features:** Renowned for creative writing (Ian McEwan and Kazuo Ishiguro studied there) and environmental sciences (climatic research unit and Tyndall Centre for climate change research are on campus). University is part of the Norwich Research Park, one of the largest UK groupings of research expertise for bioscience. Innovative programmes in development studies, international relations, art history and allied health professions. New network of HE provision in East Anglia, jointly with Essex University.

Courses

Academic features: Around 180 degree courses across 23 schools of study. Modular course structures allow combination of specialist study alongside related disciplines, with continuous assessment. **Awarding body:** University of East Anglia. **Main undergraduate awards:** BA, LLB, BSc, MChem, MComp, MNatSci, MMath, MPharm, MBBS. **Length of courses:** 3 years; 4 years (courses involving study abroad/in industry); 5 years (medicine).

Study opportunities & careers

Library and information services: Over 818,500 volumes, including books, DVDs, periodicals, music scores and material on microfilm; 1200+ study places. Extra copies of books in heavy demand; online catalogue available on and off campus. Information provision, £144 pa spent for each student (FTE). Library open 7 days/week in term time. 24-hour access to IT areas and wireless network service for laptop users including from student halls; off-campus free internet access, personal email address and web pages are supplied. Ratio 1:12 workstations to students. IT and library helpdesks plus self service issue and return facilities. **Other learning resources:** James Platt Centre for language learning; audio-visual centre (including TV studio). **Study abroad:** Some 2% of students spend a period abroad. UEA participates in many European research projects and has exchange agreements in 30+ countries. **Careers:** On-campus centre provides information, guidance and advice to all students and graduates (including interview skills and cv workshops). 90% of graduates are in work or further study within six months of graduating.

Student services & facilities

Student advice and services: Purpose-built campus medical centre with pharmacy and dentist; student counselling service; learning enhancement team; resident tutor system and chaplaincy. Nursery on campus; married students' accommodation; disability co-ordinator. **Amenities:** Union House has gig venue, advice centre, bars, coffee shop and travel agent. Newsagents, supermarket, post office, banks, laundrettes, bookshop, cafeteria, and restaurants on site. Sainsbury Centre for Visual Arts, music centre and drama studio also on campus. **Sporting facilities:** Sportspark (major expansion being built) with Olympic-size pool, climbing wall, fitness centre, squash and tennis courts, martial arts studio, dance/aerobics studio, badminton and 5-a-side facilities; 40 acres of playing fields, AstroTurf pitches and 8-lane athletics track. 45+ sports clubs. **Accommodation:** 1st years guaranteed university accommodation (if they apply before a specific date and live more than 12 miles away). 3500+ self-catering places available: £58–£93 pw, Sept–June or longer. Students live in privately owned accommodation for 1–2 years: average rent £50–£60 pw (excluding bills).

Money

Living expenses budget: Minimum budget of £6500 pa (excluding tuition fees) recommended by university. **Term-time work:** University allows term-time work for first-degree students. EmployAbility (run jointly between uni and SU) helps students find part-time/casual work in term time and vacation positions. Work available on campus for SU or as student ambassadors and guides. **Financial help:** Bursaries of up to £600 pa for UK students whose family income is up to approx £25k (ie is on maximum grant). Scholarships of £500–£4k available based on academic merit. £90k hardship fund, nursery fund of £47k and short-term cash loan fund for financial emergencies also available through Dean of Students Office. **Tuition fees:** Home students pay £3225 pa for first degrees. International students pay £10,610 pa (classroom), £13,900 (lab/studio), £14,660–£25,480 (medicine).

Student view

The focal point for students is the Square, next to the union and flanked by other important buildings and features; it only takes a few rays of sunlight for people to congregate on the steps. It's a campus university set in 300+ acres of mostly green land, with a large picturesque lake overlooked by some of the halls of residence. Many campus buildings, although a little grey, are architecturally listed. 30 mins' walk to the centre of Norwich, or 10 mins by (frequent) bus – but you always feel part of city life. Easy to get to the Norfolk Broads and less than 2 hours to London (trains half-hourly). University facilities always improving: newly extended library is well-stocked, although you may need to be quick for popular course texts. Lecturers increasingly use the internet as a teaching resource: vast numbers of computers around campus – plenty of terminals for everyone and online access – and wireless internet connections in nearly all major buildings. Lottery-funded Sportspark made on-campus sport even better with price concessions for UEA students. As for entertainment – there's something to do on campus every night of the week, besides going to the bar. The Norwich Waterfront (owned by the SU) together with the union LCR (1800 capacity) is the premier venue in East Anglia for live music . . . just check out the listings section in any music magazine. All genres are regularly catered for, with sell-out chart and retro club nights. Large and successful SU aims to improve students' lives by providing great entertainment, cheap beer in 3 bars and a professional support service; it also helps with housing, jobs, academic appeals, personal problems and more, and funds over 100 different clubs and societies, sporting and non-sporting. Student population is diverse and well integrated; known for its variety of international students and number of mature students. Students are attracted by high academic standards and research achievements, while still maintaining the stereotypical student ambience. Course structures make it easy to pick a degree that suits your own preferences and to add subjects to your timetable. Well known for environmental sciences, American studies, film and TV, history of art and English literature (particularly creative writing, which has produced many renowned novelists). It's a great place to study because, while academic standards are high, students realise there is more to life than study.

Student footnotes

Housing: Guaranteed on campus for 1st years and international students; mostly single rooms (some ensuite). Private sector, much of it in Golden Triangle (west of the city centre). **Eats:** £3–£4 for a meal on campus; sandwiches and snacks in shops and bars. In town, some vegetarian, hundreds of cheap Indian takeaways (meal for about a fiver), Chinese, Mexican, Italian; some more up-market restaurants and usual fast food. Endless pizza/kebab delivery outlets in city centre. **Drink:** Loads of pubs in Golden Triangle, reasonable prices (£2.80 a pint) and student nights at most places. Union bar's cheapest (£1.80 a pint). **Nightlife:** Riverside development with restaurants, trendy bars and clubs – Lava/Ignite, Mercy, Optic and Po Na Na's. Union's LCR and Waterfront between them host all types of events for all genres. 2 multiplex cinemas and an independent; films also shown on campus. **Locals:** Extremely tolerant and welcoming. Feel safe walking the streets and very low crime. **Sports:** Big on rugby, hockey and football but huge range of other sports (including ultimate frisbee and korfball) all with teams funded by the SU. Athletics and hockey centre next to campus; state-of-the-art gym, swimming pool, climbing wall, studios, etc. **Travel:** 2 hours to London, 4 to Newcastle by car or train. SU travel shop gives best deals. **Jobs:** Available on and off campus, help from SU employment agency, EmployAbility. Bar work at SU best paid. **Financial help:** Access funds, VC loans and other hardship funds and scholarships. Help available from SU advice centre and Dean of Students Office (also gives interest-free loans). **Informal name:** UEA. **Best features:** Events, gigs, balls, film showing, nice accommodation, very safe. **And worst:** Travel to other parts of country (usually have to go through London on train). The concrete buildings in wintertime (in summer you don't notice it!). **Past students:** Johnathan Powell (BBC); Selina Scott (TV presenter); Jenny Abramski (Radio 4); Ian McEwan, Kazuo Ishiguro, Ruth Rendell (authors); Noelle Walsh (editor, *Good Housekeeping*); Vanessa Evans (editor, *Country Homes and Interiors*); Tim Bentinck, David Vann (actors); Andy Ripley (rugby player); Dennis Callopy (MD, E6 Music Group); Clive Sinclair (entrepreneur); Paul Whitehouse (comedian). **More info?** Student handbook (also student newspaper and union newsletter) from SU on 01603 592504 or email su.comms@uea.ac.uk. Check out the website (www.ueastudent.com).

East London University

Location:
east London
(map 3)
2 campuses in
East London;
several partner
colleges

University of East London, University Way,
London E16 2RD
☎ Tel 020 8223 3333
✉ Email Admiss@uel.ac.uk
💻 Website www.uel.ac.uk

Student enquiries: Department of Student Administration
Applications: UCAS

In brief

Total Students: 19,305

26% postgraduate
74% undergraduate

Undergraduates: 14,230
66% full-time ● ● 89% UK students
55% mature ● ● 46% lower
on entry socio-economic
groups

60% female   40% male

- **A modern university.**
- **Teaching staff:** 440 full-time, 195 part-time.
- **Broad study areas:** Architecture and visual arts, business, law, psychology, computing, technology, education, social sciences, media and cultural studies, health and bioscience.

Freshers

- **Admissions information:** AS-levels accepted in combination with 2+ A-levels or equivalent. UCAS tariff used on some courses.
- **First degree entrants:** 3090 UK, full-time.
- **Points on entry:** 160 (average).
- **Drop-out rate:** 13% in 1st year.
- **Accommodation:** Some 1st years housed.

Profile

Institution
Founded: 1970 as North East London Poly; university status in 1992. **Site:** 2 campuses, at Stratford and Docklands (waterside location at Royal Albert Dock). **How to get there:** Close to mainline stations, underground and bus routes; Docklands campus has its own station (Cyprus).

Courses
Academic features: Broad-based programmes allow students to study 2 or 3 subjects, eg psychology and criminology. **Awarding body:** University of East London. **Main undergraduate awards:** BA, BSc, BEng, LLB. **Length of courses:** 3 years; 4 years (sandwich); 4 or 5 years (part-time).

Study opportunities & careers
Library and information services: 3 libraries with subject bias; over 300,000 books in total, 1000 study places. Information provision, £68 pa spent for each student (FTE). IT and library services converged. 182 points with internet access; IT helpdesk. Docklands halls of residence connected to

UEL network. **Study abroad:** Formal exchange links with a number of universities/colleges in Europe and worldwide. **Careers:** Information, advice and placement service. Enterprise zone helps ex-students interested in setting up their own businesses.

Student services & facilities

Student advice and services: Professional welfare officers, with access to external agencies, eg charities and aid centres; also doctor, FPA, chaplain. **Amenities:** SU officers and premises on each campus. **Sporting facilities:** Very close to new Olympic park.

Accommodation: 1180 self-catering places (all ensuite and with internet access); rent £92–£105 pw (£122–£128 pw for a flat), all 39-week contracts (Sept–June). Priority for university accommodation given to international students and those living furthest away. Also some private halls and flatshares locally, approx £80 pw self-catering (plus bills). Large number of first-degree students live at home.

Money

Living expenses budget: Minimum budget of £7k for an academic year (excluding tuition fees) recommended by university. **Term-time work:** University allows term-time work for full-time students. Work available on campus in SU bars and shops; employment unit helps find work locally off campus. **Financial help:** Bursaries of £319 pa for UK students whose family income is up to £25k. Progress bursaries for all home/EU students progressing to second semester, of £500 credits (£300 in second and subsequent years) to be spent on university services, eg books, computers, rent, travel. Some scholarships of £1k pa (for sport, citizenship, creative activities or academic achievement). Also access to learning fund for those facing exceptional financial difficulties; summer support fund for those not able to work in the summer (eg single parents, disabled students); emergency loans. More information from student money advice team (020 8223 6200). **Tuition fees:** Home students pay £3225 pa for first degrees. International students pay £9k–£12,500 pa.

Student view — Joseph Bitrus, Students' Union President (3rd year, International Development)

Living

What's it like as a place to live? Vibrant, diverse and cosmopolitan. **How's the student accommodation?** Buildings close to the waterfront. It has amazing, breathtaking halls of residence and scenary. Sometimes expensive but wide choice. **What's the student population like?** Friendly, diverse; a lot of international students, EU and home. **How do students and locals get on?** No problems as far as I know, although we have few locals near us. You can also find many more locals 15 mins away.

Studying

What's it like as a place to study? Wide range of courses. Teaching facilities at business school are quite good. Our multi-cultural identity makes us stand out among other universities. We take pride in this as the main heart of UEL so we promote that extremely well and allow people of diverse backgrounds to engage in cross-cultural discussions. **What are the teaching staff like?** Experienced and supportive.

Socialising

What are student societies like? We boast of many successful registered societies and have more than 70 societies and more than 1000 members. This year, there is great demand for expansion, personal development and workable supported societies. **What's a typical night out?** Underground bar, thematic nights, fashion night, rock n roll, R'n'B with variety of drinks and seating arrangements. **And how much does it cost?** From

£0 to £5 depending on the event. **How can you get home safely?** We have good transport network connecting our campuses and the city of London. In case the night catches up with you, there are 24-hour night buses right into the campus; the train connection ends at 1am; and a jet flight if you want to fly privately to your destination.

Money

Is it an expensive place to live? I am not entitled for a loan as an international student, but I'm sure the student loan is usually not enough to cover all expenses as this is a tiny amount as compared to the needs of students. **Average price of a pint?** About £2.20 in the SU bar. The credit crunch is behind the rise of the prices in the bar. We have a cheap and affordable student price for an average pint. **And the price of a takeaway?** £3.50–£5 depending on the combination of food and choice of area. **What's the part-time work situation?** There are part-time jobs but it depends on the situation in London generally. The SU and the University has a culture of employing our own students. The employability unit is fantastic in preparing students for a competitive job.

Summary

What's the best feature about the place? Modern campus with modern facilities, our library is open 24 hours a day, 7 days a week. **And the worst?** City airport is nearby. **And to sum it all up?** A great place to be – be proud of it.

Past students: Garry Bushell (TV editor, the *Sun*), Mark Frith (journalist, *Smash Hits*), Dame Vera Lynn (singer), Trevor Brooking (Football Association). **More info?** Check out the website (www.uelsu.net).

Edge Hill University

Location:
north-west England
(map 2)
Main campus at
Ormskirk, 3 other
centres; partner
colleges

🖳 Edge Hill University, St Helen's Road, Ormskirk, Lancashire L39 4QP
☎ Tel 01695 575171
🖷 Fax 01695 579997
✉ Email enquiries@edgehill.ac.uk
🖥 Website www.edgehill.ac.uk

Student enquiries: Enquiries Unit (freephone 0800 195 5063)
Applications: UCAS

In brief

Total Students: 22,080

36% postgraduate
64% undergraduate

Undergraduates: 14,050
49% full-time ● ● 98% UK students
71% mature ● ● 40% lower
on entry ● socio-economic
groups

78% female | 22% male

- **A modern university.**

- **Teaching staff:** 366 full-time, 68 part-time, 384 associate tutors.

- **Broad study areas:** Business and management; computing; education; English; geography; health, nursing and midwifery; law; media; performing arts; social and psychological sciences; sport.

Freshers

- **Admissions information:** AS-levels accepted in combination with 2+ A-levels or equivalent. UCAS tariff used, in addition to course-specific criteria.

- **First degree entrants:** 2425 UK, full-time.
- **Points on entry:** 260 (average).
- **Drop-out rate:** 13% in 1st year.
- **Accommodation:** Many 1st years housed.

Profile

Institution
Founded: 1885; university status in 2006. **Site:** Main campus in Ormskirk (semi-rural); others at Chorley (education), Aintree and Stockport (both health). **How to get there:** To Ormskirk by coach or rail (from Liverpool Central); both train and bus stations 10 mins' walk (or university bus service). By road on M6 and M58 or A59. Liverpool, Manchester and Southport 20 mins away. **Structural features:** Partner colleges include Knowsley Community College, Hugh Baird College, Liverpool College, MANCAT and Blackburne House.

Courses
Academic features: Modular BA/BSc scheme. **Awarding body:** Edge Hill University. **Main undergraduate awards:** BA, BSc, BA/BSc(QTS). **Length of courses:** 3 years.

Study opportunities & careers
Library and information services: 247,000 books, 10,000 full-text e-books, 9880 journals (980 print, 8900 electronic); 500 study places. 14,000 audio-visual and reference materials; short loan collections. Information provision, £77 pa spent for each student (FTE). IT and library services converged. Ratio PCs to students 1:8, all with access to internet and electronic resources. Resource centre and IT facilities open 12 hours/weekdays (7 hours at weekends). Helpdesks at all sites give library and IT support in person, by phone or email; induction to library and information services (including use of the network, basic IT information); embedded information skills training throughout the year and bookable one-to-one sessions on eg Word, Excel, use of electronic resources. Dedicated centre provides support for IT, study skills and dyslexia. **Other learning resources:** TV studio, language laboratories, multimedia, satellite and CD-ROM facilities. **Study abroad:** Opportunities for those taking French to study abroad. **Careers:** Careers centre and website; volunteering and mentoring programmes linked to degrees.

Student services & facilities
Student advice and services: Finance and welfare rights advisers, counsellors, accommodation officers, health centre, childcare, support for students with disabilities. Majority of buildings adapted for wheelchair access. **Amenities:** SU building with café, restaurant, fast food outlet, bar and shop; bookshop on campus. **Sporting facilities:** Indoor and outdoor sports complex for use by students and local community. **Accommodation:** Many 1st years in university accommodation (two-thirds of those who apply are successful); priority given to those living furthest from campus. 678 places available: 313 half-board, at £82 pw for 38–40 weeks (including term-time catering package); 365 self-catering (some ensuite), at £51–£66 pw. Students live in privately rented accommodation for 1–2 years: average £60–£70 pw for self-catering, plus bills.

Money
Living expenses budget: Minimum budget of £5300–£6k pa (excluding tuition fees) recommended by the university. **Term-time work:** Job club run by careers centre. **Financial help:** Bursaries of £500 pa for UK students whose family income is up to £25k. Also help for siblings (£1k pa fee remission), students who have been in care (£750 pa). 4 bursaries annually for those who have been disadvantaged by, eg illness, bullying, dyslexia. Unicard for all UK students worth £200 for

photocopying, book purchase, etc. Also scholarships of approx £250–£1k pa for excellence in, eg academic, sport, performing arts, volunteering. Additional government funds £1+ million: £700k access to learning fund (660 students helped); £607k secondary shortage subject scheme (180 students helped). **Tuition fees:** Home students pay £3225 pa for first degrees. International students pay £7900 pa.

Student view — **Nic Bouchard,** Students' Union President (recently graduated from BA Media: Television and Film)

Living
What's it like as a place to live? Edge Hill and Ormskirk are fantastic places to live, great fun and lively atmosphere that's safe and secure. **How's the student accommodation?** Student accommodation both on and off campus is well maintained and clean and tidy. Halls are well looked after and each has a student assistant living in them, who helps all students with settling in and throughout their year in halls. **What's the student population like?** Students are friendly and easy-going. A number of the students are from Liverpool but there is a diversity of backgrounds and there is a strong number of students from America. **How do students and locals get on?** The students and the locals are not always the best of friends although there are some good times had between the locals and the students.

Studying
What's it like as a place to study? Edge Hill is a great place to study with multiple computers and facilities. The library has a number of books, most of which can be accessed online. Computer room so students can have access to the internet and computers all day and all night. **What are the teaching staff like?** The teaching staff are helpful and interested in the students, and the students' wellbeing and success.

Socialising
What are student societies like? There are a number of sports teams. The SU doesn't have many societies; however, they are looking to have more, getting the new students involved to get these set up. **What's a typical night out?** A typical night out is a few drinks in the numerous pubs and bars that Ormskirk has and then off up to the University Club bar where all the students come together. **And how much does it cost?** The night would usually cost around £20. **How can you get home safely?** There are mini-buses that run at the end of the night back into town to drop off students so they can get home safe.

Money
Is it an expensive place to live? Edge Hill is not an excessively expensive place to live. **Average price of a pint?** £2.35. **And the price of a takeaway?** £3.50. **What's the part-time work situation?** There are some average paid jobs in the surrounding area and the university has a Job Club where they will help you find placements and part-time work. The uni also employs students for open days and other one-off events.

Summary
What's the best feature about the place? The best feature about Edge Hill and Ormskirk is that it's a nice pretty place to live and study. Everywhere is in easy walking distance and there are trains and buses to the surrounding areas of Southport and Liverpool. **And the worst?** Ormskirk town is very quiet on a Sunday and bank holidays, and not much is open. Also the campus and university is very quiet at the weekend. **And to sum it all up?** A beautiful place to work, study and play.

Past students: Ann McCormack (commercial planner, Metal Box Co.), Jonathan Pryce (actor), Russell Slad (football manager), Paul Deacon (Bradford Bulls and England rugby league). **More info?** Contact the SU on 01695 575457 or visit the website (www.edgehillsu.com).

Edinburgh College of Art

Location:
Edinburgh, central Scotland (map 1)
Single site in city centre

✉ Edinburgh College of Art, Lauriston Place, Edinburgh EH3 9DF
☎ Tel 0131 221 6000
🖷 Fax 0131 221 6001
✉ Email enquiries@eca.ac.uk
💻 Website www.eca.ac.uk

Student enquiries: Academic Registry
Applications: UCAS

In brief

Total Students: 1710

19% postgraduate
81% undergraduate

Undergraduates: 1380
97% full-time ● ● 82% UK students
23% mature ● ● 21% lower socio-economic groups
on entry
62% female 38% male

- **Independent specialist college of art, design, architecture and landscape architecture.** An accredited institution of the University of Edinburgh.
- **Teaching staff:** 55 full-time, 67 part-time plus visiting lecturers.
- **Broad study areas:** Architecture; landscape architecture; fashion, performance costume and textiles; glass, interior design, jewellery and silversmithing; product design; animation, film and TV; graphic design, illustration and photography; intermedia art; painting; sculpture.

Freshers
- **Admissions information:** Portfolio is most important feature.
- **First degree entrants:** 430 UK, full-time.
- **Points on entry:** 240 (average for architecture, art and design), 260 landscape architecture.
- **Drop-out rate:** 5% in 1st year.
- **Accommodation:** Many 1st years housed.

Profile

Institution
Founded: 1907. **Structural features:** Accredited institution of Edinburgh University. **Site:** Purpose-built art school, overlooking castle rock in city centre. **How to get there:** Easily accessible by train or coach from all over the UK: Waverley railway station and central bus station (St Andrew's Square) nearby. Airport 8 miles (cheap flights from London and other centres).

Courses 📖
Awarding body: University of Edinburgh. **Main undergraduate awards:** BA, BArch, MA. **Length of courses:** 4 years; others 5 years.

Study opportunities & careers ◉
Library and information services: 80,000 volumes, 150,000 slides, 390 periodicals, 100 study places. Information provision, £46 pa spent for each student (FTE). Separate IT service. Ratio 1:6 workstations to students, access around 15 hours/day (but varies through academic year). 270 student

279

computers, all with access to internet and library. Wireless campus for student laptops. Technical IT support and helpline. Introductory talk and seminar for new students on library and information services; IT skills course integrated into 1st year studies. **Study abroad:** Extensive exchange opportunities across Europe and elsewhere (though no students learn a language). **Careers:** Employability and career guidance service.

Student services & facilities

Student advice and services: Academic and study skills support; language support; disability advice; international student support; student counselling. **Amenities:** College shop, reprographics, student common room with bar, canteen, snack bar, music room and photographic dark room.
Accommodation: No college halls but accommodation arranged with other institutions; priority given to those under 19 and those who live furthest from Edinburgh. Limited number of places in self-catering flats, rent £96–£114 pw for 41 weeks. The college holds a list of places to rent through the website; rent £260–£320 per month.

Money

Living expenses budget: Minimum budget of £6560–£7200 per academic year (£160–£175 pw) recommended by college, excluding tuition fees. **Financial help:** 20 international awards of £2k.
Tuition fees: Scottish and EU students pay no fees during their course; other UK students pay £1820 pa for first degrees. International students pay £9630 pa (£2220 in a sandwich year).

Student view

Right in the middle of town, with a brilliant view of the castle, it is near just about everything – art galleries, theatres, cinemas, shops, libraries, pubs, restaurants and Wonderland toyshop. The main building is a fascinating piece of Victorian architecture, dominated inside by the sculpture court – the main exhibition space. Associated with Edinburgh University, it still retains its own governing body, is independently funded and has retained its own identity. The college consists of 2 faculties – environmental and art and design, both very highly thought of. SU (aka SRC – who knows what it's really called?) is very active within the college; its office is busy but friendly and there's always someone on hand for welfare, accommodation or legal advice. SU has internet PCs; photocopying and telephone facilities; darkroom available for black and white processing and printing (in and out of college hours), and a much-used music room. SU-run snack bar, Albertina's, offers the cheapest chip buttie in town and the Wee Red Bar, at weekends, is a legendary club venue. College shop is first port of call for art materials; lots of good swap shops around. There are numerous societies active within the college, including the Christian Union, Archie (architects), Slag (landscape architects), Scoop (sculpture co-operative), film, entertainments and painting, and *Wee Red Herring*, the student newspaper.

Student footnotes

Housing: Cowgate flats, central and cheap (usually for international students and those leaving home for the first time). Can also apply for Edinburgh Uni-leased flats. Excellent college accommodation service; also look in *The List*, the *Scotsman*, *Edinburgh Evening News*. **Drink:** Edinburgh has huge range of pubs (Hog's Head, K Jackson's are popular), lots licensed until late. Beer £1.70+ in SU bar. Popular brews are Caledonian 80, Deuchars IPA, Coillespiel Stout. **Eats:** Albertina's (SU café) has to be cheapest, meal £2–£2.50. Lots of lunchtime student specials in local pubs; plenty of good cheapish restaurants in town, eg Forest Café, Ndebele (African), Urban Angel (organic, fairtrade), Cosgrave. **Nightlife:** SU runs clubs in Wee Red Bar. Many different clubs cater for all different tastes. Numerous cinemas and theatres nearby as well as cabaret and live band venues. Pigpen, guitar band spawned in art college. **Locals:** Very friendly in general (Leith can be a bit rough at night). **Sports:** Edinburgh University sports facilities available; numerous Edinburgh sports facilities, especially swimming pools. Leisure access cards give good discounts for council pools and gyms. **Travel:** Travel scholarships given on merit. Various travel award schemes plus some organised outings and trips abroad. **Financial help:** Little available except for short-term emergencies. **Jobs:** If you're determined, it's possible to find term-time work (50% do): cleaning, catering on campus, lots of pub work (minimum wage). Holiday work available (majority find it necessary) especially during summer festivals; some find work at home. **Informal name:** ECA. **Best features:** Small; easy to meet everyone. **And worst:** Small; not many resources; sometimes lack of interest in events. **Past students:** John Bellamy, John Houston, Gwen Hardy and Elizabeth Blackadder (painters); Suzie Wighton (primary healthcare worker, Palestinian camps), Ron Brown and Roy Williamson (the Corries), Albert Mallard (comic). **More info?** Contact SU President on 0131 229 1442, email src@eca.ac.uk or find everything you might ever need to know on eportal.eca.ac.uk.

Edinburgh University

Location:
Edinburgh, central Scotland (map 1)
Main site in city centre plus sciences 2 miles away

📧 The University of Edinburgh, Old College, South Bridge, Edinburgh EH8 9YL
☎ Tel 0131 650 1000
📠 Fax 0131 651 1236
✉ Email rals.enquiries@ed.ac.uk
💻 Website www.ed.ac.uk

Student enquiries: Student Recruitment and Admissions (tel 0131 650 4360)
Applications: UCAS

In brief

Total Students: 25,750

29% postgraduate
71% undergraduate

Undergraduates: 900
96% full-time
11% mature on entry
88% UK students
16% lower socio-economic groups

57% female 43% male

- **A top UK research-intensive university.**
- **Academic staff:** 2983 full-time, 714 part-time.
- **Broad study areas:** Humanities and social sciences, science and engineering, medicine and veterinary medicine.

Freshers

- **Admissions information:** Minimum required for most courses is 4 Highers, or 3 A levels – all with grade B.
- **First degree entrants:** 3635 UK, full-time.
- **Points on entry:** 300+ (average).
- **Drop-out rate:** 5% in 1st year.
- **Accommodation:** All 1st years guaranteed offer of accommodation (unless local and so long as they apply by deadline).

Profile

Institution
Founded: 1583. **Site:** Main sites: city centre (majority of buildings); King's Buildings, 2 miles south (science and engineering); New College in city centre (divinity); Holyrood in city centre (education); Little France, 4 miles south (medicine). **How to get there:** Easily accessible by train or coach from all over the UK: Waverley railway station and central bus station (St Andrew's Square) nearby. Airport 8 miles (cheap flights from London and other centres).

Courses
Academic features: Over 300 degree programmes, including more than 200 joint degrees. **Awarding body:** University of Edinburgh. **Main undergraduate awards:** BA, BD, BEd, BEng, BMus, BN, BSc, BVandMS, LLB, MA, MBChB, MEng, MChem, MChemPhys, MPhys. **Length of courses:** 4 years (Hons), 3 years (general); 5 years (medicine, veterinary medicine, fine art, MEng, MPhys, MChem, MChemPhys).

Study opportunities & careers
Library and information services: Main library (largest university library in Scotland), also various site libraries. 3.5 million volumes, journals and pamphlets, long- and short-loan services. Library online. Information provision, £178 pa spent for each student (FTE). Ratio workstations to students 1:6, access up to 24 hours/day; technical IT staff support when facilities are open. 39,900 points university-wide with internet access (wireless networking in most university spaces). Online and print instruction on services available. IT skills courses for beginners and on software packages. Specialist collections: special collections and archives in all subjects (main library); Reid Music Library; Erskine Medical Library; Europa Institute Library; New College (divinity); Russell collection of early keyboard instruments; also historic collection of wind instruments; Talbot Rice Art Gallery with permanent and visiting exhibitions of contemporary art; Cockburn Museum of Geology; Natural History Museum. **Study abroad:** Formal exchange links with over 150 European universities/colleges and wide links with North America, Japan, Singapore, China, New Zealand and Australia, many open to non-language specialists. Member of Coimbra Group and Universitas 21. **Careers:** Provides career education, information and guidance; employer information and vacancies; further study information and skills/career insight courses.

Student services & facilities
Student advice and services: Nursery, student counselling service, drop-in advice centres. Disability office arranges support, including financial help from the disabled student support fund. **Amenities:** SA bars, shops, catering, club venues; 170 societies, 50+ sports clubs, chaplaincy centre. **Sporting facilities:** Sports centre, playing fields, outdoor pursuits centre on Loch Tay. **Accommodation:** All 1st years from outside the Edinburgh area are guaranteed an offer of university accommodation, if they apply by deadline (30% of all students housed). 5700 places available (4300 for 1st years); full-board places at £110.50–£173 pw, 33-week contracts; self-catering places at £56–£97.50 pw, 38-week contracts. University flats or private flats after 1st year £70–£80 pw. Under 20% of first-degree students live at home.

Money
Living expenses budget: Minimum budget of £6700 pa (excluding tuition fees) recommended by university. **Term-time work:** University allows term-time work for full-time students (35% believed to work); limit of 15 hours pw max. Some work available on campus. Help from student and graduate employment (SAGE) in careers service. **Financial help:** Total available £839,832 government hardship funds; £205,690 childcare fund; some help for international students. Amounts awarded £500–£3k. See www.scholarships.ed.ac.uk for details. **Tuition fees:** Scottish and EU students pay no fees during their course; other UK students pay £1820 pa for first degrees (£2895 for clinical course).

International students pay £11,050 pa (classroom), £14,500 (lab/studio), £19,950 (veterinary science) £17,950–£30,400 (medicine).

Student view

It's a fantastic city, unlike any other, with its main street exposed on one side to reveal the famous castle overlooking Princes Street Gardens. University itself almost entirely located in the city centre, apart from the main science campus (King's Buildings), which is well connected by a free bus. Great university sports facilities and good computer facilities at 2 locations, with 24-hour access. SA (EUSA) includes both the students' representative council (which undertakes most of the representational work), and the union (which runs 4 well-equipped buildings, shops, all university catering outlets and extensive entertainments programme). Good welfare and counselling provided by EUSA advice place (on main campuses), student counselling service and the student-run nightline (telephone listening and information service). Extremely wide range of courses and it is generally easy to change if you find that things don't work out just as planned. As you might expect from the Festival city, there are all forms of entertainment. Exceptionally well endowed with theatres, museums and galleries and a large number of pubs – with Scotland's most liberal licensing hours, this proves a winner with most students. City is packed at weekends and evenings with students and generally friendly locals. Common places for students are the union houses, especially the popular Friday nights in Teviot and Potterrow. Over 200 societies offer something for everyone. Excellent freshers' week. The gay scene in Edinburgh is well catered for in various parts of the town.

Student footnotes

Housing: 1st years usually in halls of residence. Large number of furnished flats/houses owned or approved by student accommodation services (look also on union noticeboards, newspapers); some for married students. University accommodation generally good but can be expensive in Pollock. **Eats:** Meals from union good value for money. Many good restaurants in city. **Drink:** Union bars cheap (£1.65 a pint for most of the day), hundreds of pubs in town. **Nightlife:** All unions have clubs at night: Teviot Fridays; Pleasance comedy; big cheese at Potterrow. Music for every taste and many big names regularly in the city. **Locals:** Fine. Best to avoid Cowgate or Meadows at 4am. Sports: Sports union has huge range of facilities and clubs. Sports facilities at newly refurbished King's Buildings House and commonwealth pool. **Travel:** Many exchange schemes. Many discounts through Edinburgh travel centre. **Hardship fund:** Small university short-term loans and crisis funds for students in desperate long-term financial need. **Jobs:** Large number of on-campus jobs, huge number off-campus – if you want a job you can generally find one: 30% get paid work during term-time (many get bar jobs). Majority get employment for at least part of the summer (eg tourist industry and festival). Student employment service helps find part-time jobs, maximum 15 hours pw in term-time. **Buzzwords:** EUSA (Yoo-sah) is Edinburgh University SA; Pollock (main halls of residence); KB (King's Buildings, ie science campus). **Best features:** Great social life, festival. **And worst:** Cold, frosty weather. **Past students:** David Hume (philosopher); Charles Darwin (scientist); James Africanus Horton (first African graduate from a British university); Sally Magnusson (TV journalist); Peter Roget (of *Thesaurus*); Sir Walter Scott, Robert Louis Stevenson, Sir Arthur Conan Doyle (authors); Sir David Steel MP, Malcolm Rifkind MP, Gordon Brown MP; David Livingstone (explorer). **More info?** Ring EUSA office on 0131 650 2656 or check out the website (www.eusa.ed.ac.uk).

Essex University

✉ University of Essex, Wivenhoe Park, Colchester
CO4 3SQ
☎ Tel 01206 873666
🖷 Fax 01206 873423
✉ Email admit@essex.ac.uk
🖥 Website www.essex.ac.uk

Student enquiries: Undergraduate Admissions Office
Applications: UCAS

Location:
East Anglia (map 2)
Main campus at
Colchester, 1 at
Southend; partner
colleges

In brief

Total Students: 8400

25% postgraduate
75% undergraduate

Undergraduates: 6340
86% full-time
24% mature on entry
80% UK students
33% lower socio-economic groups

54% female   46% male

- **World-class research-intensive university.**
- **Teaching staff:** 470 full-time.
- **Broad study areas:** Humanities and comparative studies; social sciences; science and engineering; law and management.

Freshers

- **Admissions information:** AS-levels accepted in combination with 2, usually 3, A-levels or equivalent. Points assessed on a maximum of 3 A-levels and 1 AS-level or equivalent.
- **First degree entrants:** 1740 UK, full-time.
- **Points on entry:** 310 (average).
- **Drop-out rate:** 8% in 1st year.
- **Accommodation:** All 1st years housed who have applied by deadline.

Profile

Institution

Founded: 1964; Royal Charter received 1965. **Site:** Main campus Wivenhoe Park, 2 miles east of Colchester; new campus at Southend (schools of entrepreneurship and business, health and human sciences, East 15 acting school). **How to get there:** By rail (frequent trains from London take under an hour; also from Harwich and East Anglia); by coach (from most parts of Britain including Stansted airport); by road on A12. For Colchester campus, local buses from train and bus stations (61,78 and 78A; 74, 75, 77 from bus station). **Structural features:** Partner colleges: Writtle and Colchester Institute (you can look these up separately) and South East Essex College (Southend); also new University Campus Suffolk, a network of HE provision across Norfolk and Suffolk, run jointly with East Anglia University.

Courses

Academic features: Degrees in, eg finance and management, art history, drama and acting, American studies, Latin American studies, entrepreneurship and business, health and human science, philosophy, sports and exercise science, computing and electronic systems. **Awarding body:**

University of Essex. **Main undergraduate awards:** BA, BSc, LLB, BEng. **Length of courses:** 3 years; others 4 years (eg modern languages, marine and freshwater biology).

Study opportunities & careers

Library and information services: Collection of 1 million+ books, pamphlets, e-publications; 1000 study places; 3-hour loan system for certain course books. Specialist collections: Latin American and Russian collections; Sigmund Freud collection; Harsnett Collection of religious works from Henry VIII. Information provision, £137 pa spent for each student (FTE). Separate IT service, access up to 24 hours/day. Ratio 1:7 workstations to students. 110 points with access to the library, 400+ networked computers with internet access (100 open 24 hours/day); internet points in all student accommodation. IT support from computing helpdesk (12 hours/weekday plus some weekend cover) and some departments. Library induction course for new students, information leaflets, assistant librarians available to help; IT induction training if needed, based on self-assessment by new students; some IT courses arranged by departments. **Study abroad:** 3% of students spend a period abroad. Formal exchange links with 80 universities and colleges across Europe, open to students in a variety of subjects. **Careers:** Information, advice and placement service.

Student services & facilities

Student advice and services: Advice service, student support office; doctors; FPA; multi-faith chaplaincy centre; counsellors; welfare rights advice. Some residential facilities for married and disabled students; day nursery. **Amenities:** Bookshops; general shop; photocopy centre; insurance shop; banks and post office; 217-seat theatre; exhibitions gallery; bar; SU building with shop, 3 bars, games room, nightclub, print room, newspaper; film society plus 100 other societies for sports, academic and cultural interests; RED (radio station); multimedia studio. **Sporting facilities:** Sports hall, weights room, aerobics studio, fitness room, indoor climbing wall, fitness testing lab, gymnasium, squash courts; floodlit all-weather playing area and tennis courts (40 acres for sporting activities); wide range of sports including water sports association with club house and dinghies. **Accommodation:** All 1st years who apply by the deadline are in university accommodation (60% of all students). 3100 self-catering places available at Colchester, rent £61.50–£95 pw, academic-year-long contracts; self-catering rooms at Southend, rent £90–£99 pw, 39 or 50 week contracts. Students live in privately owned accommodation for 1–2 years: £55–£80 pw self-catering. 20% of first-degree students live at home.

Money

Living expenses budget: Minimum budget of £6k–£7500 (excluding tuition fees) recommended by university. **Term-time work:** University allows term-time work for first-degree students. Some work available on campus in SU bars and entertainment and university offices; holiday work available in domestic, catering, language teaching. SU advertises other local vacancies and jobshop helps students find part-time work. **Financial help:** Bursaries for UK students whose family income is under £32,500, so that students receive a total of £3225 pa from the combination of government grant and university bursary (so bursary of £319 pa where family income is up to £25k, rising to £1560 where family income is £32,500). Then bursaries of £1574 where family income up to £33k, down to nil where family income is up to £60k. Scholarships (mostly of £1k–£3k pa) for, eg students from specified countries, for sport, acting, maths, computing. Also £350k government funds plus various university bursaries and loan schemes. Special support for international students in exceptional financial circumstances; also students from Worthing and from Jamaica, mature students, those with refugee status or non-traditional backgrounds. Apply to Student Support Service for help. **Tuition fees:** Home students pay £3225 pa for first degrees (except foundation year). International students pay £9250 pa (classroom), £11,990 (lab/studio).

Student view

Based in stunning Wivenhoe Park campus, about 2 miles from Colchester. Compact but diverse campus community has a friendly atmosphere and a cosmopolitan feel. Range of residential options from 4–16 people per flat with varying levels of kitchen and bathroom facilities (some ensuite). 1st years guaranteed university accommodation with phone, internet connection, access to 24-hour campus laundrette. Regular local bus services, good transport links (only 50 mins by train to Central London). SU provides nationally accredited advice centre and supports cultural, religious, sporting and society activities – run by students for students. Diverse entertainments programme: regular music, comedy and quiz nights as well as fantastic end-of-year summer ball. Opportunities to get involved almost endless with clubs, societies and many other ways to volunteer. Also student-run newspaper, radio and new TV station (R:TV, now streamed on the SU website). Excellent new SU facilities, including 2 bars, 2 venues and newly refurbished nightclub, second-hand bookshop and large campus supermarket.

Student footnotes

Housing: Reasonably priced off-campus accommodation (standards monitored by university). **Eats:** On campus, hot and cold food outlets; fast food, healthy options, coffee and salad bar (average meal £2.50+). Caters for vegetarian, vegan and halal. Not far for, eg Pizza Express, Noodle Bar. Drinks: SU bar, pint average £1.80. Locally, trendy bars (Edwards, V Bar, Yates's) with good atmosphere. **Nightlife:** SU provides diverse range of daily entertainments. Excellent nightclub, Sub Zero. Recent events include Babyshambles, the Subways, Ronny Size, Rachel Stevens, Trevor Nelson, Young Knives, Tim Westwood. Good university theatre. **Sports:** Refurbished sports centre with gym and fitness room; AstroTurf training ground. **Hardship:** University and SU funds available. **Jobs:** Work available in union and university outlets (summer and term time); jobs off-campus (locally and further afield) from jobshop. **Past students:** Nick Broomfield (documentary film-maker); Daniel Libeskind (architect); Virginia Bottomley MP; President Oscar Arias of Costa Rica (Nobel Peace Prize 1987); Ben Okri (writer); Alison Steadman (Olivier Best Actress award); Mike Leigh (film director); David Triesman (General Secretary Labour Party). **More info?** SU website (www.essexstudent.com).

European Business School London

Location:
Regent's Park, central London (map 3)
Single campus in Regent's Park

European Business School London, Regent's College, Inner Circle, Regent's Park, London NW1 4NS
☎ Tel 020 7487 7505
📠 Fax 020 7487 7425
✉ Email EBSL@Regents.ac.uk
💻 Website www.ebslondon.ac.uk

Student enquiries: External Relations Department
Applications: UCAS or direct

In brief

Total Students: 800

25% postgraduate
75% undergraduate

Undergraduates: 600
100% full-time ● ● 10% UK students

60% male

- **Specialist business school**, part of an international network.
- **Teaching staff:** 80 full-time, 60 part-time.
- **Broad study areas:** International business studies, events management, modern languages.

Freshers

- **Points on entry:** 200+ (average).
- **Drop-out rate:** 10% in 1st year.
- **Accommodation** 50% of 1st years housed.

Profile

Institution
Founded: 1979. **Structural features:** Part of an international network with 70 partner universities worldwide. **Site:** Single 26-acre campus in the heart of Regent's Park. **How to get there:** 5 mins' walk from Baker Street underground and buses.

Courses
Academic features: Integrated courses in language with international business or international events management, including study abroad and work experience. **Special features:** February and September start dates. 36 weeks in-company training in at least 3 countries and 5 companies. 1-year foundation year for those who do not meet the BA entry requirements. **Awarding body:** Open University. **Main undergraduate award:** BA. **Length of courses:** 3½ years.

Study opportunities & careers
Library and information services: 36,000 volumes; 500 periodicals including daily newspapers from UK and overseas; 30 online catalogues with CD-ROM access; 300 academic videos; 120 study places. Specialist collections: Business and Institute of Linguists libraries. Information provision, £69 pa spent for each student (FTE). Separate IT service; access 24 hours/day, staffed helpdesk all opening hours. Ratio 1:6 workstations to students, 340 points with access to library and internet. Induction to library and information services for new students; instruction in major IT applications 4+ hours/week in 1st year. **Other learning resources:** CALL and language laboratories. **Study abroad:** All students spend a year studying abroad at a partner institution. **Careers:** Information, advice and placement service; links to 6500+ companies worldwide. **Employment:** Managerial positions throughout the world; all those seeking work are employed within 6 months of graduation.

Student services & facilities
Student advice and services: Personal tutors. **Amenities:** Music practice room, art gallery, sports bar, internet café, bookstore, cinema, student lounge. **Sporting facilities:** Tennis and basketball courts, weights room, multigym, dance studio. Students can join University of London Union and use its sports facilities. **Accommodation:** 50% of students in school accommodation. 250 places available: full-board at £188–£270 pw (shared room), £270–£290 pw (single), term-time only. 5% of first-degree students live at home.

Money
Living expenses budget: Minimum budget of £9500 pa (excluding tuition fees) recommended by school. **Financial help:** 3 scholarships available. **Tuition fees:** All first-degree students pay £12,300 pa.

Student view

It's in the beautiful Regent's College campus, surrounded by 500 acres of Regent's Park yet only 15 mins from the West End and City of London. 2 tube stations are 5 mins' walk; easy access from all mainline stations and airports. Excellent state-of-the-art IT centre with 250 networked PCs and Macs and extensive opening hours; internet and email for all students; Janet and CD-ROM available. Tennis, basketball, multigym and sauna on campus. Truly international in flavour, with 80+ nationalities represented in the student body. Few mature students. The small size makes EBS personal and friendly. Courses are intensive, all involve at least 1 foreign language and a minimum of 48 weeks' work experience in at least 3 countries; strong emphasis on developing personal, leadership and networking skills alongside teamwork. Result is 100% employment rate and graduates further their careers in international business around the globe. SU is mainly social, organising eg trips to theatre; also counselling service and active football and basketball teams.

Student footnotes

Housing: Expensive: single, double and triple rooms, all full-board. Accommodation office helps find off-campus housing. **Eats:** School refectory – good food, great variety, nice surroundings, reasonable prices (meal £2–£5). Also restaurant and a coffee/lunch bar on campus. **Drink:** School bar – nice, panelled and reasonable prices (£1.80 a pint). **Nightlife:** Student centre organises theatre trips, etc. One of the most exciting cities is on your doorstep. **Sports:** On-campus tennis courts (2 grass, 1 hard), fitness centre, basketball court. Football pitches in Regent's Park. **Jobs:** About 5% work part-time in term (most get sufficient funding from parents or corporate sponsorship); limited number of casual jobs on campus. Approx. 25% work placements are paid. **Informal name:** EBS. **Best features:** Location; international student body. **And worst:** Too many mobile phones. **More info?** Ring SU on 020 7487 7454.

Exeter University

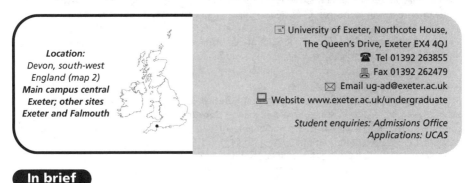

Location:
Devon, south-west
England (map 2)
**Main campus central
Exeter; other sites
Exeter and Falmouth**

University of Exeter, Northcote House,
The Queen's Drive, Exeter EX4 4QJ
☎ Tel 01392 263855
🖨 Fax 01392 262479
✉ Email ug-ad@exeter.ac.uk
💻 Website www.exeter.ac.uk/undergraduate

*Student enquiries: Admissions Office
Applications: UCAS*

In brief

Total Students: 15,720
95% at Exeter
5% at Cornwall

31% postgraduate
69% undergraduate

Undergraduates: 10,815
85% full-time
11% mature on entry
91% UK students
17% lower socio-economic groups
55% female
45% male

- **A top UK research-intensive university.**
- **Teaching staff:** 1060 full-time and part-time.

- **Broad study areas:** Modern and classical languages and culture physical and natural sciences (pure and applied); engineering (in engineering); computing; social studies; business and economic medicine and dentistry. You can look up the *Peninsula Medical*

EXETER UNIVER
software pack
journals, da
to supply
from
serv

Freshers

- **Admissions information:** Two AS-levels are acceptable in ᴄᴄ subjects; see prospectus for specific subject requirements. Offers expressᴜᴜ tariff points or grades.
- **First degree entrants:** 3260 UK, full-time (2880 at Exeter, 460 at Cornwall)
- **Points on entry:** 393 (average).
- **Drop-out rate:** 4% in 1st year.
- **Accommodation:** All 1st year undergraduates guaranteed accommodation (if they apply by the deadline).

Profile

Institution

Founded: 1885 as a school of art, becoming a university college in 1922, a university in 1955.
Structural features: Peninsula College of Medicine & Dentistry, joint with Plymouth University. Cornwall Campus (includes Camborne School of Mines), part of Combined Universities in Cornwall initiative. **Site:** 3 campuses. 2 in Exeter: Streatham Campus, a 300-acre garden site 1 mile from city centre; St Luke's Campus 1 1/2 miles away and 1/2 mile from city centre. Also Cornwall Campus, shared with others, near Falmouth. **How to get there:** *Exeter campuses:* by train (2 1/2 hours London to St David's Station); by coach (links from most other areas of country); by road (M4/M5 links Exeter with London, midlands, south Wales and the north); by air to Exeter, Plymouth or Bristol airports. Main campus is 15 mins' walk from St David's station or minibus service (weekdays 8–9.30am and 4–6pm). *Cornwall Campus:* by train (4 hours London to Truro, 15 mins from Truro to Penryn Station); by coach (links from most other areas of the country); by road (A30 from Exeter then A39 from Truro to Falmouth and Penryn); by air to Newquay airport.

Courses

Academic features: Flexible combined Honours programme allows students in some subjects to design their own 3-year degree programme around 2 fields of study. Subjects available at Cornwall Campus include history, politics, law, geography, geology, biosciences, Cornish studies, English, mining engineering, renewable energy. **Awarding body:** University of Exeter. **Main undergraduate awards:** BA, BSc, BEng, LLB, LLB (Eur), BM BS, MEng, MMath, MPhys. **Length of courses:** 3 years; 4 years (eg courses with education, European study or languages and undergraduate Master's).

Study opportunities & careers

Library and information services: *Exeter campuses:* 1.2 million volumes and journals; online access to over 12,500 journals, plus newspapers and reference works; extensive audio-visual section; separate subject libraries, especially law and education. Specialist collections: rare editions, examples of early printing, Sir John Betjeman, Agatha Christie. Bill Douglas Centre (history of cinema and popular culture); also runs Devon and Exeter Institution Library (West Country material). Information provision, £142 pa spent for each student (FTE). IT service, access up to 24 hours/day. All open-access PCs connected to library and internet; virtually all student rooms have network points for own PCs; special IT equipment for disabled users. IT support in person, by phone or email on weekdays. Introductory talk to new students on library and information services; IT courses on use of major systems and

...ages. *Cornwall campus:* 110,000 volumes and journals; online access to over 8000 ...abases, newspapers and reference works. Dedicated law collection; inter-site loan service ...items from Exeter campus libraries. Specialist collections: videos and maps, archive collections ...amborne School of Mines and Institute of Cornish Studies. **Careers:** Careers and employment ...e has searchable jobs database (graduate jobs, training opportunities and careers events).

Student services & facilities

Student advice and services: Health centres serving each campus; counselling service; chaplaincies (Exeter and Cornwall); family centre (Exeter, run jointly with Students' Guild), day nursery (Cornwall); welfare advice from Students' Guild (Exeter), SU (Cornwall). Advice and support for students with disabilities and on study skills, and English language support for international students. **Amenities:** *Exeter:* Shops, bank, etc on campus; Guild buildings with licensed bars, laundrettes, etc; Northcott Theatre (with own professional company and for amateur productions). *Cornwall:* 2 shops on campus; bar and regular events, theme nights and live music held in the Stannary; 400-seat restaurant. **Sporting facilities:** *Exeter:* 60-acre and 23-acre sites provide playing fields for rugby, football and cricket plus an all-weather cricket square (and major a new cricket centre); sports hall with, eg, squash courts, exercise, health and fitness studios; open-air swimming pool; all-weather pitches; tennis centre (4 indoor, 4 outdoor floodlit courts); athletics track; indoor swimming pool and gymnasia at St Luke's. Sports scholarships. *Cornwall:* Sports centre with exercise studio, air-conditioned gym and fitness suite, and 3 tennis courts; multi-use games area; range of sports clubs. **Accommodation:** All 1st year undergraduates in university accommodation (guaranteed for those who apply by deadline). *Exeter:* 4000 places, some ensuite: 1800 full-board places at £112–£156 pw (£98–£134 shared), term time only (31 weeks); and 2,000 self-catering places at £64.50–£104 pw (£78 pw shared), most Oct–June (40 weeks); 240 places in university-owned houses close to campus; also 16 family flats and 65 studios for postgraduates. Most students live in privately owned accommodation for 2 years, £55–£100 pw self-catering. *Cornwall:* 500 ensuite places in student village on campus, rent £98.50 pw, self-catering.

Money

Living expenses budget: Minimum budget of £6700 (excluding tuition fees) recommended. **Term-time work:** Some regular work available on campus in halls of residence, plus casual work in bars, refectories, stewarding, office work, cleaning and waitressing. Careers and employment service has searchable jobs database; also runs jobshop jointly with the Guild for term-time and vacation work. **Financial help:** Bursaries of £1500 pa for students whose family income is up to £25k, of £1k pa where it is £25k–£30k, of £500 pa where it is £30k–£35k and of £250 pa where family income is £35k–£45k. Also awards of up to £1500 pa for local students with family incomes of up to £45k. Some subject-specific scholarships; merit scholarships £2k–£5k for students with ability in science, leadership, entrepreneurship, music, sport or community involvement. £388k government (access to learning) funds; 720 awards made, average £440. Help targeted towards disabled students, mature students and those with dependants, in cases of financial hardship and those with serious domestic difficulties; mostly as grants but some emergency loans. Apply to student funding team for help. **Tuition fees:** Home students pay £3225 pa for first degrees. International students pay £10,000 pa (classroom), £12,250 pa (lab/studio).

> ## Student view
> ## (Exeter campus)
>
> **Francesca Litchfield,** Welfare and Equal Opportunities Officer (recent graduate, Law)

Living

What's it like as a place to live? Whenever anyone asks what Exeter is like, the first response is usually 'green'. And it's true. The campus is a truly unique and beautiful environment to live and study in, which encapsulates services and facilities for students over a reasonably small and navigable campus, whilst also integrating with the city. You could say that we have the best of both worlds as students – the green, beautiful valley and historic buildings of campus, together with the modern convenience of a growing city. **How's the student accommodation?** There is a variety of accommodation on and off campus run by the university, a lot of which is relatively newly built. A lot of the accommodation is really nice – for the more expensive halls you definitely get what you pay for (ensuite, double bed, etc), but there are also cheaper options which are just as good. There is a mix of old halls with lots of tradition, and new halls – but wherever you are the atmosphere is usually what makes your year in 1st year! There is also plenty of good private accommodation in Exeter, so you will always be able to find a house for your second and third or 4th-years. The university provides a housing list of private-let accommodation, which is a bible for anyone looking for a house! The price range is pretty good too, with the cheapest houses ranging from about £60–£65 a week. **What's the student population like?** Everyone I know at Exeter has found their own niche. There is so much going on that it would be difficult not to find a group of like-minded people! Campus is very friendly, and the population is growing more diverse with each year. In comparison to other campuses, Exeter isn't particularly international, and campus can seem a little homogenous sometimes, but the atmosphere is always really friendly. **How do students and locals get on?** The Students' Guild does a lot of work with the community to try and engage them with the positive aspects of what students bring to the wider Exeter community. Particularly through volunteering through Community Action and RAG (Raising and Giving). However, like any other university, students and residents do sometimes come into conflict over issues such as noise. I wouldn't say there were any no-go areas per se, except perhaps a few of the pubs which are known to be very local!

Studying

What's it like as a place to study? There is a mixture of traditional and non-traditional courses at Exeter, and most degree programmes offer the flexibility to include different degree areas into your course. Facilities vary from department to department, but the library has recently had some investment put into it, and there is a decent amount of flexible work space around campus. **What are the teaching staff like?** A lot of schools benefit from having renowned academics teaching courses. The university is research-led, so there are sometimes cases where the staff can seem more interested in their own research priorities than student concerns. However, in most cases the staff are generally helpful and interested in encouraging and supporting students to fulfil their potential.

Socialising

What are student societies like? There are hundreds of societies run by students as part of the Students' Guild. From archaeology society to wine society; from beats and bass to jazz orchestra; from stop Aids society to international society. There is a wide range of societies to cater for all your interests, and if there is something that you would like to see that isn't currently being done then you can set up your own society. There is also a strong volunteering community at Exeter – Community Action runs a variety of student-led projects in the community, and Raising and Giving (RAG) runs a range of events and activities raising money for different charities. Media is also very strong, with *Exepose* (the campus newspaper), X-TV, Xpression FM and X-media online, all with a keen student membership. **What's a typical night out?** There's a range of activities that students get involved in during their time at Exeter. Many students frequent the Ram and the Lemmy, the student bar and club on campus. During the week students will also venture into town to clubs and bars, especially as part of society socials – most notably in Arena and Timepiece. If you're up for something a bit different then there is a good music scene with lots of gigs on campus (recently we've had the Zutons, Feeder, Seth Lakeman, Razorlight, the Fratellis) and there are large-scale events such as the Summer Ball (a full night of revelry going on till 5am!) going on throughout the year. **And how much does it cost?** On campus you might spend £10–15 in a night – depends how many rounds you buy! In town might be slightly more expensive, but prices on campus range from £2 a pint to £2.10 for spirits and mixers. **How can you get home safely?** Exeter isn't a particularly large city so you'll never be far from home, but you should still think about your safety. Students should, and usually do, stick together in groups to walk home after a night out, and there are good taxi services around the city.

Money

Is it an expensive place to live? Your loan should last the term so long as you are sensible about what you spend your money on – ie if you stay away from Princesshay, the almighty shopping centre! **Average price of a pint?** £2 on campus in the union bar. Slightly more expensive in town. **And the price of a takeaway?** About £8 for a pizza (half-price with a RAG card!), £2 for cheesy chips. **What's the part-time work situation?** A lot of students work part time while they study, both in town and on campus (either for the Students' Guild or the university). Pay will obviously vary depending on the type of job, but the relatively new shopping centre in town has created a lot more student-friendly jobs. The Students' Guild and university jointly run 'The Works' (the jobshop), which will help you find a part-time job to suit you.

Summary

What's the best feature about the place? Probably the compact nature of the campus, and the city. Everything is accessible and really close – you can escape from the city in 20 mins and find yourself on a beach or up in the moors, and yet you're still living in a city that has everything you could need to hand. **And the worst?** The hills and the rain! **And to sum it all up?** It may be hilly, and it does rain a lot, but that all adds to the charm of Exeter. It's a place that you will always find yourself coming back to long after you've graduated – not least because the experience Exeter provides both academically, and in terms of extra-curricular activities, such as societies and volunteering, gives students an all-round grounding whilst living in a beautiful campus in the heart of Devon.

Past students: Richard Hill, Mike Slemen (England rugby players), Paul Jackson (BBC comedy producer), Tony Speller MP, Bowen Wells MP, Paul Downton, Richard Ellison (England cricketers), Thom Yorke (Radiohead), Emma B (Radio 1 DJ), Peter Phillips (Princess Anne's son), J K Rowling (author), Will Young (singer). **More info?** Contact Guild President (tel 01392 263540, email president@guild.ex.ac.uk, website www.exeterguild.org).

Student view (Cornwall campus)

Studying at the Cornwall campus of Exeter University is a unique and exciting experience – you get a degree from a top university, but in wonderful settings. Atlantic is close by so plenty of chances for water sports such as surfing, kite surfing, sailing, kayaking and swimming; the campus's rural environment offers opportunities for horse riding, running and cycling – and it's useful for academic work with great scope for field trips. Campus itself, Tremough, has commanding views of the Fal Estuary and the surrounding countryside, and frequent buses to Falmouth. It is in an 18th-century manor house with beautiful Italian gardens to add flavour to the brand new campus buildings and teaching facilities. All 1st years guaranteed a place in one of the 800 student rooms on site. Campus is shared with art college (Falmouth University College), so there is a diversity of courses and people. The 2 institutions share campus facilities (library, IT services, accommodation, bar, canteen, reprographics, gym, etc) and the union, FXU (Falmouth and Exeter Students' Union). Campus bar, the Stannary, has a 1300-person capacity and has seen some big acts (eg Jack Johnson, 100 Reasons, Pendulum, Mr Scruff and Thirteen Senses) but also student and local bands, open mic nights, quizzes, poker and much more. Falmouth town has a vibrant student community and most students move there in their second and 3rd years. The town has 4 clubs, lots of bars and pubs, with live music, DJs and quizzes, and is where most people go out in the evening. Falmouth and Cornwall have rich cultural heritages, so there are many interesting things going on; maritime museum, Tate at St Ives and the Eden Project are great places to explore. The town, campus services and the university employ a lot of students in a range of ways, from campus tours to bar work.

Student footnotes

Housing: All students guaranteed university accommodation for 1st year. Good deal of private housing available in Penryn and Falmouth. **Drink:** Stannary Bar. **Nightlife:** Some big acts in bars/club on campus and expect more. Lots of live music, good bars and clubs in Falmouth. Larger bands and theatre companies visit the Hall for Cornwall in Truro. **Sporting facilities:** Outdoor activities (surfing, rock climbing, scuba-diving and gliding). Main team sports include rugby (men's and women's), football and hockey (men's and women's); all in county leagues. On campus health and fitness studio; classes, eg martial arts, table tennis, spinning and yoga. **More info?** Contact FXU President UECC (tel 01326 370774, email presidentuecc@fxu.org.uk) or check out the website (www.fxu.org.uk).

Falmouth University College

Location:
Cornwall, south-west England (map 2)
2 campuses in Cornwall

University College Falmouth incorporating Dartington College of Arts, Woodlane, Falmouth, Cornwall TR11 4RH
☎ Tel 01326 211077
🖷 Fax 01326 213880
✉ Email admissions@falmouth.ac.uk
💻 Website www.falmouth.ac.uk

Student enquiries: Admissions Office
Applications: UCAS

In brief

Total Students: 2800

10% postgraduate
6% FE Students
84% undergraduate

Undergraduates: 2350
97% full-time ● ● 96% UK students
19% mature ● ● 32% lower socio-economic groups
on entry

59% female 41% male

- **University college, specialising in art, design, media and performance.**
- **Teaching staff:** 159 full-time, 246 part-time.
- **Broad study areas:** Art, design, media and performance.

Freshers

- **Admissions information:** foundation diploma, national diploma, AVCEs and A-levels accepted; each applicant considered on individual merit.
- **First degree entrants:** 675 UK, full-time.
- **Points on entry:** 220 (average).
- **Drop-out rate:** 8% in 1st year.
- **Accommodation:** Majority of 1st years housed.

Profile

Institution

Founded: 1902 as private venture; incorporated in 1989; university college since 2005. Merged with Dartington College of Arts in 2008. **Structural features:** At the centre of the Combined Universities of Cornwall at Tremough with other HE institutions in the region. **Site:** Woodlane Campus near Falmouth town centre, 5 mins from the sea; Tremough Campus a few miles away in Penryn; Dartington Campus near Totnes in Devon (performance courses based here until 2010). **How to get there:** Regular train services to Truro from all major cities, then branch line to Falmouth (20 mins) and Penryn (15 mins); daily National Express coaches to Falmouth; by road A30 from Exeter, A3076 to Truro, and A39 to Falmouth. Inter-campus bus; improving facilities for cyclists and pedestrians; committed to green transport.

Courses

Academic features: Unit-based courses across 3 schools: art and performance (fine art, illustration, choreography, theatre and music); design (fashion design, contemporary crafts, garden design, graphic design); media (digital animation, photography, broadcasting, film, journalism, English with creative writing). **Awarding body:** University College Falmouth. **Main undergraduate award:** BA. **Length of courses:** 3 years.

Study opportunities & careers

Library and information services: Collection of 180,000+ items including books, journals, databases, newspapers, DVDs, slides and maps. Information provision, £52 pa spent for each student (FTE). Computer suites with latest applications plus wi-fi across all campuses and student residences. Induction to library and information services at enrolment; IT skills part of curriculum on most courses. **Study abroad:** 5% of students spend a study period abroad in 2nd year. Formal exchange links with institutions in Europe, Canada and Japan; developing links in USA and Australia; industrial placements in Europe. **Careers:** Advice service available to all students.

Student services & facilities

Student advice and services: Specialist counselling and careers services; disability service; dyslexia support; advice on hardship fund applications. SU also gives financial and general advice. **Amenities:** SU arranges social and sports activities; excellent sailing; shops and crèche. **Accommodation:** Over 1000 places (mostly at Tremough), rent £89–£98 pw, 40–51 week contracts. List of approved lodgings; average rent £70–£100 pw (most students pay £85–£90).

Money

Living expenses budget: Minimum budget of £5500 pa recommended (excluding tuition fees). **Term-time work:** College allows term-time work (30+% believed to work); some jobs available on campus. **Financial help:** Bursaries of £850 pa for UK students whose family income is up to £25k, of £500 pa where income is £25k–£30k, and £325 pa where income is £30k–£40k; additional help for those with dependants (£250) and for care leavers (£1k pa). **Tuition fees:** Home students pay £3225 pa for first degrees. International students pay £9097–£9581 pa.

Student view

It nestles near the bottom of the Cornish peninsula, surrounded by golden beaches, stunning countryside, and where the culture is rich with history. Student population spreads across 2 campuses: at Woodlane and the fantastic Combined Universities of Cornwall (CUC) development at Tremough. At first glance Falmouth seems a quiet town but it can be as exciting as anywhere; plenty of pubs, bars, cafés and restaurants in which to socialise and venues to suit all tastes and budgets. SU is known as FXU – Falmouth (University College Falmouth) and Exeter (University of Exeter, Cornwall) SU. It is the driving force behind student support and entertainment – everything from poker nights to black tie events. Great facilities for entertainment at Tremough in the Stannary bar, so bigger gigs can be held (have included Mr Scruff, Zero 7, Squarepusher and Jack Johnson). FXU is committed to offering a complete service to students, to ensure they enjoy their time at Falmouth; present on both campuses and lots of opportunities to be involved in lots of different ways. It has trained advisers offering confidential and impartial help, co-ordinators for community action and sports/recreation. Students like Falmouth for its relaxed, laid-back lifestyle and the beautiful environment of Cornwall.

Student footnotes

Housing: 2 student residences: Henry Scott Tuke House (central Falmouth); Glasney Parc (Tremough). Locally, many self-catering bedsits, shared houses and self-contained properties (flats, houses, small annexes, etc), £60–£75+ pw plus bills. Look for landlords in voluntary council accreditation scheme. **Locals:** Very friendly. **Sports:** Everything from sailing, surfing, horse riding, rugby, football, hockey, basketball and many more. **Jobs:** Mainly available during the tourist season (bar, hotel and shop work). **Informal name:** UCF. **Best features:** People and scenery. **And worst:** Occasional wet weather! **Past students:** Fergus Walsh (BBC Radio 4), Juliet Morris (BBC TV), Martyn Perks (graphic designer), Ed Hall (TV presenter), Daniel Boetcher (news presenter), Tacita Dean (Turner nominee), Serena de la Hay (Willow man on the M5), Tim Shaw (sculptures, Eden), Katie Haswell (news presenter), Angus Walker (TV news reporter); of Dartington: Josie Lawrence (presenter). **More info?** Enquiries to FXU (tel 01326 370447 (Tremough), 01326 213742 (Woodlane), email presidentucf@fxu.org.uk) or check out the website (www.fxu.org.uk).

Farnborough College

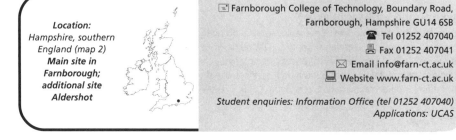

Location:
Hampshire, southern England (map 2)
Main site in Farnborough; additional site Aldershot

Farnborough College of Technology, Boundary Road, Farnborough, Hampshire GU14 6SB
☎ Tel 01252 407040
🖨 Fax 01252 407041
✉ Email info@farn-ct.ac.uk
💻 Website www.farn-ct.ac.uk

Student enquiries: Information Office (tel 01252 407040)
Applications: UCAS

In brief

Total Students: 7945
0.5% postgraduate
12% undergraduate
88% FE Students
Undergraduates: 720
75% full-time
40% mature on entry
90% UK students
40% female   60% male

- **Specialist college of technology.**
- **Teaching staff:** 500 full-time and part-time.
- **Broad study areas:** Aerospace and motorsport engineering, business, computing, media, leisure and sport studies.

Freshers

- **Admissions information:** UCAS tariff adopted and Key Skills taken into account in students' profile.

- **First degree entrants:** 325 UK, full-time.
- **Points on entry:** 80+ (average).
- **Drop-out rate:** 10% in 1st year.
- **Accommodation:** No college accommodation.

Profile

Institution
Founded: 1957, originally as training wing of former Royal Aircraft Establishment. **Site:** Farnborough. **How to get there:** Easy reach of London; Farnborough campus on A325, close to M3 (junctions 4 and 4A); short walk to railway station. Good local bus service. **Special features:** Maintains close links with industry, commerce and local community, giving good work placements for students in their chosen field.

Courses
Academic features: Wide range of courses (A-levels, vocational and professional courses, foundation degrees, first degrees, Master's degrees). **Awarding body:** University of Surrey. **Main undergraduate awards:** BA, BSc. **Length of courses:** 2, 3 or 4 years.

Study opportunities & careers
Library and information services: LRC (learning resource centre) with 45,000 items, both print and electronic, including books, journals, audiovisual and electronic information. 144 study places. Open-access PCs on college network and with internet access. Information provision, £50 pa spent for each student (FTE). Library and computing services converged. LRC staff give general and IT support. **Other learning resources:** Language and science laboratories, engineering workshops, fitness suites, TV and radio stations. **Careers:** Information, advice and placement service.

Student services & facilities
Student advice and services: Counselling service, occupational health unit, student finance adviser, accommodation officer, learning support unit. Weekday nursery school throughout the year. **Amenities:** SU arranges live bands, discos, theatre, films, charity and fund-raising events. **Sporting facilities:** Local recreation centre has indoor sports facilities (10 mins' walk). **Accommodation:** Help with finding local accommodation; rent approx £60–£70 pw self-catering.

Money
Living expenses budget: Minimum budget of £5500 pa recommended (excluding tuition fees). **Term-time work:** College allows term-time work for full-time students (approx 80% believed to work). Some work available on campus, eg cleaning, admin during summer; also college careers adviser helps students get work off campus. **Financial help:** Learner support fund. **Tuition fees:** Home students pay approx £1255 pa for first degrees. International students pay £5500+ pa.

Student view

Based on the main Farnborough Road, the campus is 100 yards from Farnborough Airfield – great for the air show but can cause major traffic problems. College has parking facilities; 5 mins' walk from town centre. Well-stocked library and recently improved computer facilities for all students. Sports centre and playing fields rented. Large refectory offers snacks, hot drinks and food. Loads of courses for mature students through to under-18s. Quite a few foreign students. Very friendly college with helpful staff and lecturers. Easy to change course in 1st year. Part-time work available with local business. SU building, with 2 bars, is open all day but closed at night; since there are few pubs and no clubs in Farnborough, most students go out in nearby Guildford, Farnham or Reading. London is another option (but expensive). Students run a college radio station and TV production company. A nice place to study (especially media or engineering) although lacks the feel of a big university.

Student footnotes

Housing: College student services help. **Eats:** £2 for a meal in college. Domino's Pizza, Ham and Blackbird £7–£10. **Drink:** Most beers £1.60+. **Nightlife:** SU organises events nights; trips to clubs and pubs. **Locals:** Commuters and families. **Sports:** Gym and basketball court; good teams. **Jobs:** Ask union or local agencies. **Financial help:** Good record of hardship loans. **Best features:** SU building; other students, Westminster theatre. **And worst:** Lack of young life in town centre. **Past students:** Verity Larby (walker), Peter Hull (Olympics), Beverley Kinch (long jump and 100 metres), Steve Benton (national cyclist), Vicki Elcoate (Deputy Director of Council for National Parks), Jet (*Gladiators*). **More info?** Contact SU President (tel 01252 407142, email su@farn-ct.ac.uk).

Glamorgan University

Location:
south Wales (map 1
2 campuses near
Pontypridd, new
campus central
Cardiff; number of
partner colleges

🖻 University of Glamorgan, Pontypridd,
Mid Glamorgan CF37 1DL
☎ Tel 0800 716925
🖷 Fax 01443 480558
✉ Email enquiries@glam.ac.uk
🖥 Website www.glam.ac.uk

Student enquiries: Student Enquiry Centre
Applications: UCAS

In brief

Total Students: 25,465

13% postgraduate
15% FE Students
72% undergraduate

Undergraduates: 18,280

56% full-time ● ● 87% UK students
42% mature ● ● 42% lower
on entry socio-economic
groups

52% female 48% male

- **A modern university.**
- **Teaching staff:** 995 full-time and part-time.
- **Broad study areas:** Art and design, built environment, business, computing and mathematics, engineering, English and creative writing, geography and environment, health sciences, humanities and social sciences, law, policing and crime, life sciences, media and drama studies, physical sciences, sport.

Freshers

- **Admissions information:** AS-levels accepted in combination with 2+ A-levels or equivalent. UCAS tariff used, in addition to any subject requirements.
- **First degree entrants:** 3295 UK, full-time.
- **Points on entry:** 210 (340 on some courses)
- **Drop-out rate:** 18% in 1st year.
- **Accommodation:** Most 1st years housed.

Profile

Institution

Founded: 1913; university status in 1992. **Site:** 2 safe, modern campuses at Pontypridd (Treforest and Glyntaff); new campus in Cardiff city centre (creative industries). **How to get there:** Cardiff campus: mainline rail to Cardiff (from London, Manchester, Swansea). Pontypridd campuses: mainline rail to Cardiff then frequent trains on Valley Line to Treforest station (next to campus); National Express coaches to Cardiff Bus Station and bus to Treforest; 20-min drive from Cardiff and M4, follow A470 Merthyr Tydfil and take exit at signpost A473/Llantrisant; close to Cardiff International Airport.

Courses

Academic features: All courses are modular, so students can design own study programme. **Awarding body:** University of Glamorgan. **Main undergraduate awards:** BA, BSc, BEng, LLB, MEng, FdA, FdSc. **Length of courses:** 2 years (FdA/Sc); 3 years; 4 years (with sandwich year).

Study opportunities & careers

Library and information services: Approx. 250,000 volumes, 7000 serial publications (including electronic), 800 study places. Specialist collections: Welsh writing in English. Information provision, £90 pa spent for each student (FTE). 24-hour access to e-journals, e-books and databases; laptops and media equipment can be borrowed. Separate IT service; computer labs open 24/7; 1600 computer workstations for students; wireless networking also available. IT staff support available for 12+ hours/weekday (8/weekend days). Induction sessions on library and information services for new students, plus support booklets. **Other learning resources:** Education drop-in centre eg for extra tuition in maths, statistics, exam techniques, researching and writing assignments. Media services and state-of-the-art audio studios. All students entitled to free language tuition at the Unilang Centre. **Study abroad:** Many students can study abroad: active collaboration with many institutions in USA and most countries in Europe. **Careers:** Free professional guidance to all students and graduates; practical help with job hunting (96+% of graduates in employment or/and further study after 6 months). Careers service has excellent links with national and local employers, organises (paid) work experience programme, links to regional and national recruitment fairs (more information on www.glam.ac.uk/careers)

Student services & facilities

Student advice and services: Health centre, student money service with advisers and loan officers, counselling and advisory service, childcare crèche, advice shops, chaplaincy, international student support service, disability and dyslexia service, resident tutor team. **Amenities:** SU with bars and nightclub, cafés, restaurants, shop, travel centre, laundrette, welfare advice, etc. **Sporting facilities:** 9 football and rugby pitches (including 3 floodlit), floodlit all-weather pitch and cricket pitch, large indoor sports hall, 4 squash courts, 6 badminton courts, 60-station conditioning room, free weights room, sauna, 9m climbing wall, 20m traversing wall, bouldering room, accessible to wheelchair users. **Accommodation:** Most new students offered a place in halls (first-come-first-served). 1108 self-catering places (75+% ensuite), rent £64 pw (£78 ensuite) including utilities, internet and insurance; 39 week contracts. Students live in privately owned accommodation for 2+ years, average £50 pw (+ utility bills of £8 pw).

Money

Living expenses budget: Minimum budget of £6295 per academic year (excluding tuition fees) recommended by university. **Term-time work:** SU employment service helps students find work on campus (eg in SU) and off campus. **Financial help:** Scholarships of £1k pa for students with 300+ points on entry; residential allowance of £500 pa for students from more than 45 miles away; scholarship of £1500 pa for international students; sports scholarships of £500+ pa. Further help eg for some nursing students, care leavers. Total available £1.85 million government funds to alleviate hardship. **Tuition fees:** Home students pay £3225 pa for first degrees (though Welsh residents and EU students may be eligible for a fee grant, reducing fee to £1225). International students pay £9250 pa (£2220 in a placement year).

Student view

Based 10 miles from Cardiff in Treforest, near Pontypridd, it's easy to reach either by road (close to the M4) or rail (from Cardiff every 20 mins or so). Main campus is superbly equipped, offering all the facilities you need, including SU, recreation centre, library, 24-hour computer rooms and halls of residence. SU has a nightclub, 2 pubs, laundrette and whole range of student support (including trained welfare officer, a women's and equal opportunities officer, and education officer for all academic, health, housing and other welfare needs). SU team also represents students to the university, local council and NUS; it runs campaigns to promote student awareness and get the student voice heard (eg grants-not-fees and cancer awareness). SU provides opportunities for all to get involved with sports and activities, from football to snowboarding, LGB to ghost and paranormal societies; whatever you're into, it's covered, and if not, you can start a club yourself with SU support. Well-equipped recreation centre with gym, sauna and sunbeds; many national and high-profile teams use the playing fields and AstroTurf pitches. Large number of international students and opportunities for student exchanges. Wide range of courses; premier chiropractic school and good business school, as well as great courses in media, drama, design, engineering, astronomy. Nursing and law schools nearby at Glyntaff campus. Library good but demand is high at peak times. Workloads vary from 10- to 30-hour weeks and most courses are assessed with mix of coursework, exams or presentations; on many courses you can play to your strengths and interests. Campus halls are either new, well-equipped and ensuite or are more traditional corridor structure. Most students live within 10 mins of campus. Union is one of the main venues for student life, providing a varied and exciting programme of events and entertainments. Also an array of local pubs with much to offer and, with Cardiff on the doorstep, you are never short of ways to entertain yourself.

Student footnotes

Housing: Full range on campus; university housing association. Relatively cheap. **Eats:** Meal about £2+ on campus. At the union, Smiths and Butties offer a range of hot and cold food. Not much choice locally but some good pub grub; plenty of good restaurants in Cardiff. **Drink:** Union bars cheapest in area (£1.65 a pint). Plenty of good local pubs, eg the Rickards. **Nightlife:** Shafts (union nightclub) open nightly with ents, eg live bands, discos, cabaret, quiz, films. Cardiff has several top nightclubs, cinemas, theatres and venues. **Locals:** Not too bad and getting better. **Sports:** On-campus sports centre offers a range of facilities (good climbing wall, squash courts). Local swimming pools. **Travel:** Train service from Treforest to Cardiff every 20–30 mins (then access to other mainline stations easily reached). Buses from campus to Pontypridd and surrounding area. Free SU shuttle bus takes off-campus students home after evening ents. Good union travel shop. **Hardship fund:** University access funds – no problems if your case can be documented. Small emergency loans from union. **Jobs:** Union employs many students, eg stage crew, receptionists, bar staff, DJs; also has info on jobs in uni and locality. **Informal name:** Glam Uni. **Best features:** SU nightlife; friendly, community atmosphere. **And worst:** Uni is on a steep hill and it rains. **More info?** Check out the website (www.glamsu.com) or contact SU President (tel 01443 483500, email supres@glam.ac.uk).

Glasgow Caledonian University

Location:
Glasgow, central Scotland (map 1)
City centre site

Glasgow Caledonian University, Cowcaddens Road,
Glasgow G4 0BA
Tel 0800 027 9171
Fax 0141 331 3005
Email helpline@gcal.ac.uk
Website www.gcal.ac.uk

Student enquiries: to helpline by telephone, email or via the website
Applications: UCAS (CATCH for some nursing and midwifery)

In brief

Total Students: 17,450

22% postgraduate
78% undergraduate

Undergraduates: 13,690

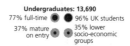
77% full-time ● ● 96% UK students
37% mature ● ● 35% lower
on entry   socio-economic groups

61% female   39% male

- **A modern Scottish university.**
- **Teaching staff:** 750 full-time and part-time.
- **Broad study areas:** Built and natural environment; business; engineering, science, design and computing; health and social care; law and social sciences; life sciences; nursing, midwifery and community health.

Freshers

- **Admissions information:** Programme entry requirements vary; see prospectus.
- **First degree entrants:** 3210 UK, full-time.
- **Points on entry:** 367 (average).
- **Drop-out rate:** 13% in 1st year.
- **Accommodation:** Small number of 1st years housed.

Profile

Institution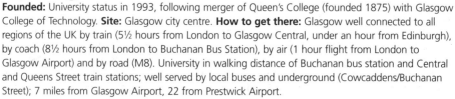

Founded: University status in 1993, following merger of Queen's College (founded 1875) with Glasgow College of Technology. **Site:** Glasgow city centre. **How to get there:** Glasgow well connected to all regions of the UK by train (5½ hours from London to Glasgow Central, under an hour from Edinburgh), by coach (8½ hours from London to Buchanan Bus Station), by air (1 hour flight from London to Glasgow Airport) and by road (M8). University in walking distance of Buchanan bus station and Central and Queens Street train stations; well served by local buses and underground (Cowcaddens/Buchanan Street); 7 miles from Glasgow Airport, 22 from Prestwick Airport.

Courses

Awarding body: Glasgow Caledonian University. **Main undergraduate awards:** BA, BSc, BEng, BN, BM, LLB. **Length of courses:** 3–5 years.

Study opportunities & careers

Library and information services: 370,000+ volumes, 12,600 journals (12,000 electronic); 1800+ study places in learning centre, open 72 hours/week. Information provision, £110 pa spent for each student (FTE). Separate IT service: ratio 1:8 workstations to students (1800 computers for student use). Induction to library and IT for new students. **Other learning resources:** Effective learning service (ELS) provides support and information on study skills (open to all); aims particularly to meet learning needs of disabled students, including those with dyslexia. **Study abroad:** Exchange schemes established on many programmes. **Careers:** Information, guidance and recruitment service.

Student services & facilities

Student advice and services: Student counsellors, disability advisers, funding advisers, international student advisers and chaplaincy. **Sporting facilities:** Sports and recreation centre with 2 games halls, 2 multigym areas. Range of classes and sports teams. **Accommodation:** 15+% of 1st years in university accommodation (priority given to 1st years from some distance, particularly international students or those with special needs). 660 self-catering places (340 ensuite), all with internet access in secure, modern accommodation next to campus: £72–£82 pw, contracts Sept–June. Many students live in privately owned accommodation, from £70 pw self-catering plus bills. Many first-degree students live at home.

Money

Living expenses budget: Minimum budget of £8500–£9500 pa (excluding tuition fees) recommended by university. **Term-time work:** SA jobspot helps find work locally. **Financial help:** Total of £783k (£410k hardship, £133k childcare, £240k mature students), 1600 students helped. Apply to student funding office for help (tel 0141 331 3873 or email funding@gca.ac.uk). **Tuition fees:** Scottish and EU students pay no fees during their course; other UK students pay £1820 pa for first degrees. International students pay £8500–£10k pa.

Student view

It's a modern city-centre campus – 5 mins' walk of shops, pubs, clubs, restaurants, cinemas and theatres and with excellent transport links. Halls of residence, Caledonian Court, has all modern facilities. Wide range of courses in its 8 schools – many with industrial work placements and opportunities to study abroad. Newly built Saltire Centre is learning centre and social space for students: spacious environment, a café and wireless internet access. Caledonian students are renowned for their active social life. The SU, Bedsit, has 2 bars and a games room offering food and drinks at student-friendly prices; also a wide range of regular entertainments, eg Wednesday nights Caleyoke, quiz nights and other one-off events. Main bar screens all major sporting events and doubles as a club venue (big-name acts like Cream and Babyshambles). SA supports a wide range of sports and societies, from rugby club to the music society. Welfare department, based in Bedsit, provides confidential information, advice and support. University welcomes vast numbers of students from all backgrounds, making it a fun and friendly place to study and socialise.

Student footnotes

Housing: Uni accommodation good. Otherwise West End, Southside and Dennistoun areas popular, flats from £210 pm upwards. Help from accommodation department; look on noticeboards, *Evening Times*, *The Herald*. **Eats:** Wide range of food at cheap prices at Bedsit. Lots of cheap fast food and restaurants around city. **Drink:** Bedsit good cheap drinks and range of promotions (£1.50 a pint). Tennents is popular local brew. **Nightlife:** Bands and quiz nights in Bedsit. Loads to do in city centre. **Locals:** Very friendly (mostly students as well). **Sports:** Modern gym, sports hall; range of affordable exercise classes. 28 clubs and 10 societies, from skiing to sub aqua. **Travel:** Campus next to underground, bus station and 2 central train stations. **Financial help:** Short-term loans and access fund, and fund for direct emergencies. **Jobs:** SU Jobspot advertises jobs and offers advice. **Informal name:** Caley. **Best features:** SA and Saltire Centre. **And worst:** No outdoor sports facilities. **Past students:** Jim Delahunt (TV presenter), Pat Nevin (Chelsea FC and Scotland), Gordon Smith (Rangers), Colin Calder (BBC radio producer), Claire English (TV presenter), Andy Kerr (health minister), Craig Wright (Scottish cricket captain), Cathy Jamieson (Justice Minister). **More info?** Visit website (www.caledonianstudent.com).

Glasgow School Of Art

Location:
Glasgow, central
Scotland (map 1)
Single city centre site

The Glasgow School of Art, 167 Renfrew Street, Glasgow G3 6RQ
☎ Tel 0141 353 4512
🖷 Fax 0141 353 4408
✉ Email info@gsa.ac.uk
💻 Website www.gsa.ac.uk

Student enquiries: Academic Registry
Applications: UCAS Route B for art and design courses,
Route A for architecture and product design engineering

In brief

Total Students: 1840

16% postgraduate
84% undergraduate

Undergraduates: 1555
95% full-time   82% UK students
16% mature   18% lower
on entry   socio-economic
groups

60% female   40% male

- **A top specialist art college.**
- **Teaching staff:** 77 full-time, 80 part-time.
- **Broad study areas:** Fine art, design (including interior design, silversmithing and jewellery, textiles, visual communication), architecture, product design.

Freshers

- **Admissions information:** AS-levels accepted but not as alternative to A-levels. UCAS tariff not used.
- **First degree entrants:** 270 UK, full-time.
- **Points on entry:** 265 (average).
- **Drop-out rate:** 2% in 1st year.
- **Accommodation:** Some 1st years housed.

Profile

Institution 🏛

Founded: 1845. **Structural features:** One of the few independent art schools remaining in the UK. Close relationship with Glasgow University, which validates all its degree courses; students have access to university library and other facilities. **Site:** Glasgow city centre. **How to get there:** Glasgow well connected to all regions of the UK by train (5½ hours from London to Glasgow Central, under an hour from Edinburgh), by coach (8½ hours from London to Buchanan Bus Station), by air (1 hour flight from London to Glasgow or Prestwick; Glasgow Airport 7 miles from centre, Prestwick 22 miles) and by road (M8). School in walking distance of main train/bus stations and well served by local buses, underground (Cowcaddens) and train (Charing Cross).

Courses

Awarding body: University of Glasgow. **Main undergraduate awards:** BA, BArch, BDes, BEng, MEng. **Length of courses:** 4 years.

Study opportunities & careers

Library and information services: 80,000 volumes, 250 periodicals, 150 study places, 60,000 slides, 200 video cassettes. Information provision, £52 pa spent for each student (FTE). Central library and IT services converged (but also specialist departmental computing resources; sophisticated computer clusters throughout school). Ratio 1:10 workstations to students, access 11 hours on most weekdays. 130 points with access to library and internet. 10 full-time staff give IT support; library induction and 1-hour introduction to computer centre; IT skills, eg word-processing, various image manipulation courses. **Study abroad:** Links with 80+ US liberal arts schools. Exchange opportunities with 80 partner institutions worldwide.

Student services & facilities

Student advice and services: Full-time welfare officer and student services administrators. **Amenities:** Active SU, activities committee organises programme of exhibitions, annual fashion show and social functions (eg dances, gigs and clubs). **Accommodation:** 10% of all students in school accommodation; priority to 1st years from outside the area and international students. 196 self-catering places in 4–8 bedroom flats in school halls of residence: £897 per term for standard room, £962 for ensuite room; 39-week contracts. Most students live in privately owned accommodation, £280–£310 pm self-catering, plus bills; school database on available accommodation.

Money

Living expenses budget: Minimum budget of £7500 pa recommended (excluding tuition fees) recommended by school. **Term-time work:** School allows part-time work for first-degree students. Limited work available on campus. **Financial help:** Total available £35,500 government funds, minimum £100 awarded. **Special help:** mature students, those with children, final-year students. **Tuition fees:** Scottish and EU students pay no fees during course; other UK students pay £1820 pa for first degrees. International students pay £9600 pa (£10,560 for BEng/MEng).

Student view

It's between the city centre and the West End of Glasgow. The majority of students live in the west, a 15–30-min walk to college; there are some halls of residence (handy but best suited to 1st years from beyond Scotland's central belt). GSA is spread among several buildings, the most famous of which is the Charles Rennie Mackintosh building, bringing tourists in throughout the year. Wide range of courses, falling broadly into architecture, design and fine art. It also maintains a pivotal role in the creative life of a vibrant and renovated city. The SA, with its own well-loved Vic Café Bar, provides a focal point for socialising and other activities as well as offering welfare and academic advice through the Student Representative Council (SRC). The Vic is a haven to slake your thirst on anything from espresso to beer, from 9am till late; and SA runs highly-regarded club nights from

Thursday to Saturday. Host of cafés and pubs in nearby Sauchiehall Street (1 of the 2 main city-centre streets); check out Nice and Sleazy, Griffin and the Centre for Contemporary Arts – CCA.

Student footnotes

Housing: Some halls, but expensive; rooms small, in flats of 4–8. Private accommodation locally or in West End; info from GSA, shop windows, etc. **Eats:** Usual city centre offerings as well as bar food in the Vic and a refectory on campus (meal for £2.50); £3+ at Nice and Sleazy's. **Drink:** SU Vic Café bar (£2 a pint). Local bars, eg Variety Bar, Brunswick Cellars, Nico's, Uisgebeatha (pronounced Ischkibar) and the 13th Note. Tennent's SD is good local brew. **Nightlife:** Glasgow can satisfy most hedonists: art house cinema (GFT) one minute away; live music in the Vic as well as Record Playerz, Divine and Freakmoves, which are popular club nights. Glasgow gay scene leaves much to be desired but Delmonica's, Polo Lounge, Moda and Bennets are all in east of centre and union has monthly gay night. **Locals:** Quite friendly. **Sports:** No sports facilities on campus except a ping-pong table but various public facilities 15-min walk away, and full access to Glasgow Uni's sports facilities. **Travel:** Many student discount schemes. **Financial help:** Access funds for home students. **Jobs:** Difficult to find, mainly waiting, bar work, odd jobs (minimum wage); word of mouth. **Best features:** The Vic Bar. **And worst:** No sports facilities. **Past students:** Steven Campbell, Peter Howson, Adrian Wiszniewski, Ken Currie (artists); Jenny Saville (Saatchi collection); Douglas Gordon (Turner prize winner 1996); Christine Borland (Turner nominee 1997); Alisdair Gray and John Byrne (artists/writers); Peter Capaldi, Robbie Coltrane (actors); Pam Hogg (fashion designer); Toby Patterson (Beck's Futures Prizewinner 2002). **More info?** Ring SA on 0141 353 4530.

Glasgow University

Location:
Glasgow, central
Scotland (map 1)
**Main campus, West
End of Glasgow; plus
site at Dumfries**

University of Glasgow, Glasgow G12 8LG
Tel 0141 330 6062
Fax 0141 330 4045
Website www.glasgow.ac.uk

Student enquiries: Recruitment, Admissions and
Participation Service
Applications: UCAS

In brief

Total Students: 21,000

27% postgraduate
73% undergraduate

Undergraduates: 15,395
78% full-time
13% mature
on entry

75% UK students
22% lower
socio-economic
groups

52% female 48% male

- **A top UK research-intensive university.**
- **Teaching staff:** 2446 full-time and part-time.
- **Broad study areas:** Arts and social sciences; divinity; education; engineering; law and financial studies; medicine; science; veterinary medicine.

Freshers

- **Admissions information:** 5 AS-levels required except in courses/faculties where A-levels required. UCAS tariff not used.
- **First degree entrants:** 3700 UK, full-time.
- **Points on entry:** 396 (average)

- **Drop-out rate:** 7% in 1st year.
- **Accommodation:** All 1st years housed who require it.

Profile

Institution
Founded: 1451. **Site:** Compact campus in West End of city; also Garscube Campus (veterinary medicine), a green-field site 4 miles away; and Dumfries Campus in South-West Scotland (interdisciplinary programmes) shared with West of Scotland University. **How to get there:** Glasgow well connected to all regions of the UK by train (5½ hours from London to Glasgow Central, under 1 hour from Edinburgh), by coach (8½ hours from London to Buchanan Bus Station) and by air (1 hour flight from London to Glasgow or Glasgow Prestwick; Glasgow Airport 7 miles from centre, Prestwick 22 miles); by road (M8). University well served by local buses (No. 44), underground (Hillhead and Kelvinbridge stations) and trains (Partick); cycle racks on campus.

Courses
Awarding body: University of Glasgow. **Main undergraduate awards:** BAcc, BArch, BD, BDS, BEd, BMus, BN, BSc, BEng, MEng, LLB, MA, MB ChB, MSci, BVMS, BTechEd, BTheol, BTechnol, BTechS. **Length of courses:** 4 years (Hons); others 3 years and 5 years.

Study opportunities & careers
Library and information services: Main academic library with 2 million volumes; separate reading areas with all 1st year texts; individual departmental libraries. Information provision, £221 pa spent for each student (FTE). IT service separate; 400 points with access to internet, 3000+ to the library. IT facilities and library open 18+ hours/day with user support staff. Familiarisation sessions with library and information services as part of general induction; certificate in IT compulsory for all new students. **Other learning resources:** Computer centre, language laboratories. Specialist collections: extensive and valuable collection of books and manuscripts. Also Hunterian Museum (anatomical and surgical drawings, instruments, etc); Hunterian Art Gallery (old masters, Whistlers, Chardins, Charles Rennie Mackintosh House), ethnographic and Roman collections. **Study abroad:** 5% of students spend a period abroad. Wide range of exchanges with universities and colleges across the EU, North America, Canada and Australia for students in many subject areas. **Careers:** Advice (including summer jobs) and placement service.

Student services & facilities
Student advice and services: The Hub (newly opened), housing admission, recruitment, careers service, registry, health centre and bookshop. Counselling service (including effective learning advisers, special needs adviser); academic advisers for all students. Student disability service with advisers for any student (or potential student) with a disability or specific learning difficulty. **Amenities:** SRC shops, travel bureau, bank, insurance bureau, printing and photocopying facilities; 2 SUs with lounges, bars, TV rooms; mature SA. **Sporting facilities:** Physical education building offering wide range of indoor sports, 25m swimming pool, 3 activity halls, cardiovascular and muscle-conditioning suites and sauna. Athletic grounds with bar and pavilion about 2 miles from campus. Access to international sports facilities in Kelvin Hall sports arena. **Accommodation:** All 1st years who require it are in university accommodation. 3800 places available (3000 for 1st years), most with telephone and data points: catered room £107 pw (£111 pw ensuite), self-catering £82–£99 pw (£66–£76 pw shared); 39 week, academic-year contract. Private accommodation locally £60–£70 pw, self-catering. 40% of first-degree students live at home.

Money 💰

Living expenses budget: Minimum budget of £7200 pa (excluding tuition fees) recommended by university. **Term-time work:** No university policy on part-time work in term time (30% of students believed to work). Some work available on campus in registry, helping with student recruitment, admissions, matriculation; also SRC operates a jobshop. **Financial help:** Total available £750k government funds, 1800 students helped. Special help for those in private or university owned/sublet accommodation, those with child-minding costs (including travel), extra costs arising from a disability or special needs, or mature students. £53k own funds, 100 students helped, including 50 pa scholarships for home students facing financial hardship. **Tuition fees:** Scottish and EU students pay no fees during their course; other UK students pay £1820 pa for first degrees (£2895 for clinical courses). International students pay £9400 pa (classroom), £12,350 (lab-based), £17,500–£21,600 (clinical subjects).

Student view — Gavin Lee, SRC President (studying Law)

Living

What's it like as a place to live? Glasgow is an extremely vibrant city, which manages to cater to many different interests while retaining a friendly and relaxed feel. Food and drink is relatively cheap, and you can get a lot of good deals around the city in unusual or international cuisine restaurants. **How's the student accommodation?** There are 6 or 7 different halls of residence based around the West End of Glasgow. All but 2 are self-catering, and based around a more intimate flat-based environment rather than hallways of rooms. Each flat has a bathroom and kitchen along with the private bedrooms. It's relatively well priced since electricity and internet connections are covered in the rent. Standards of finishings, etc can vary, but overall the accommodation is of a good standard. **What's the student population like?** About 40% of students at Glasgow live at home or come from Glasgow, but within the other 60% there is a diverse range of people with a large proportion of international students. **How do students and locals get on?** The vast majority of students will spend their time in the West End of Glasgow, where the University is and where many of the most popular and coolest pubs, bars and restaurants can be found. Students and 'locals' live side by side and there isn't a lot of tension: especially since, as previously mentioned, 40% of students at Glasgow are from the city.

Studying

What's it like as a place to study? The course system at Glasgow is flexible, and allows for students to explore different subjects that may be of interest to them before choosing a final degree subject. Students in 1st and 2nd year can choose up to 3 subjects to study, specialising in one of these subjects during 3rd and 4th year. This allows students to really experience the learning environment before making that important decision of their degree choice. The library has recently been renovated, and with 12 floors of books you're likely to find exactly what you're looking for, plus there's a large number of computers to work at all over campus. There's also a great redeveloped gym so you can keep fit while you're working hard! **What are the teaching staff like?** Glasgow scored very well in the National Student Survey. Staff are friendly and there are supportive tutors and Advisors of Studies allocated to each student to ensure any help needed is given.

Socialising

What are student societies like? Glasgow is very unusual in its set-up of student organisations: there are 3 on campus. The Students' Representative Council deals solely with the wellbeing of students, and campaigns for improvements at the university while providing a range of services such as cheap photocopying, a secondhand bookshop, and a free minibus service to halls of residence. There are 2 SUs, which each have their own atmosphere, events and board of management. As a result of this, students can really choose what sort of experiences they want to have, and have a much greater choice of entertainment. There are over 80 clubs and societies affiliated to the SRC, so students are sure to find a group of people with similar interests. If not, they can create their own society! **What's a typical night out?** There is no 'typical' night out in Glasgow. Because of the range of bars and clubs there's a lot of choice. Glasgow has a vibrant and much-praised music scene, so often students go to gigs around the city. The SUs provide clubnights and quizzes. Clubs in the city cater for every type of music taste, from pop and cheesy 80s music to metal to cutting edge techno and DandB. There is also a plethora of small pubs and bars throughout the city for students who want a quieter night. **And how much does it cost?** Many clubs grant you free entry, but most will charge £4–£5 for students. Gigs depend on the band, but usually you can visit most smaller venues for £8 or under. **How can you get home safely?** Glasgow taxis are relatively cheap: you can usually get from the city centre to most places in Glasgow for under a fiver. The SRC operates a free minibus service during the week for students to get from campus to their halls of residence. A lot of students walk home after a night out, and while this is usually safe, we would always recommend taking a taxi home. Night buses run all night throughout the city, run by local companies.

Money

Is it an expensive place to live? Glasgow is a cheap place to live in, but the West End, where most students live, is more expensive than the rest of Glasgow. There are lots of student deals available, so it's possible to get by on your loan with a few well-chosen bargains. **Average price of a pint?** This ranges from about £2.30 in local pubs to about £3.20 in the pricier bars in town. The SUs have pints for under £2. **And the price of a takeaway?** Around £4 for a pizza or kebab, but the local specialty of chips and cheese will cost around £2. **What's the part-time work situation?** The SRC has a Jobshop that allows employers to advertise roles primarily for students. The university is understanding of the fact that many students have to work during their time at university, and as such can be quite flexible. There are a number of jobs available, ranging from call-centre work to bar jobs, but the competition for employment increases significantly during the summer months, and often students find it difficult to get a job during that time.

Summary

What's the best feature about the place? The city as a whole is vibrant, cosmopolitan and exciting. Glasgow University is full of opportunities and there's so much on offer to students to take advantage of. **And the worst?** The weather in Glasgow during winter is absolutely miserable: rain and cold for about 5 months. **And to sum it all up?** One of the most exciting cities in the UK that's full of culture, music and brilliant banter. Definitely worth considering if you want to learn an awful lot, not just from your degree.

Past students: Teddy Taylor MP, John Smith (former Labour Party leader), William Boyd (author), Pat Kane (Hue and Cry), Donald Dewar MP, Charles Kennedy MP, Lord Irvine (ex-Lord Chancellor).

More info? Websites for GUU (www.guu.co.uk), QMU (www.qmu.org.uk) and SRC (www.glasgowstudent.net).

Gloucestershire University

Location:
*West of England
(map 2)*
**Three sites
Cheltenham, one
Gloucester; partner
colleges**

University of Gloucestershire, The Park, Cheltenham,
Gloucestershire GL50 2QF
☎ Tel 08707 201100
✉ Email admissions@glos.ac.uk
💻 Website www.glos.ac.uk

*Student enquiries: Admissions and Recruitment Office
(tel 01242 714500, fax 01242 714827)
Applications: UCAS*

In brief

Total Students: 8745

 19% postgraduate
77% undergraduate

 4% FE Students

Undergraduates: 6730
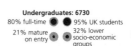 80% full-time ● ● 95% UK students
21% mature ● ● 32% lower
on entry ● ● socio-economic
groups

 57% female   43% male

- **A modern university.**
- **Teaching staff:** 490 full-time and part-time.
- **Broad study areas:** Accounting, business and finance; arts, design and media; computing and multimedia; environment and biology; humanities; leisure, tourism, hospitality and heritage; social care and social sciences; sport and exercise; teacher education.

Freshers

- **Admissions information:** UCAS tariff adopted.
- **First degree entrants:** 1680 UK, full-time.
- **Points on entry:** 200 (average).
- **Drop-out rate:** 7% in 1st year.
- **Accommodation:** Approx. half of 1st years housed.

Profile

Institution
Founded: 1990 as Cheltenham and Gloucester College from 2 education colleges (founded 1847 by the Church of England); university status in 2001. **Site:** 3 campuses in Cheltenham; new campus in Gloucester (9 miles away), 5 mins drive from centre; also teacher training in East London. **How to get there:** Train, coach, M5 motorway, Birmingham and Bristol airports. **Special features:** Voluntary C of E foundation; admissions policy not affected but Christian ethics underpin university ethos. Strong emphasis on sustainability.

Courses
Academic features: Modular structure for most undergraduate courses. Links with industry and commerce. **Awarding body:** University of Gloucestershire. **Main undergraduate awards:** BA, BEd, BSc. **Length of courses:** 3 years; 4 years (with work placement).

Study opportunities & careers
Library and information services: 350,000 volumes, 1900 periodical titles. Information provision, £90 pa spent for each student (FTE). IT service converged with library; learning centre on each

campus. 300 points with internet access (ratio 1:12 workstations to students). IT facilities open 11–12 hours/weekday (4–7 weekends); basic IT support during opening hours, specialist support 8 hours/day. Induction video and introduction to learning centres for all new students; on-going programme of IT courses on, eg Word, Excel, email. **Other learning resources:** TV and film, journalism, dance and drama studios; language laboratories. Specialist collections: college archives from 1847; Dymock poets archive; Bristol and Gloucestershire Archaeological Society Library; history of sport collection; slide collection of fine art and fashion. **Study abroad:** Formal exchange links with a number of European universities/colleges, all open to non-language specialists. **Careers:** Information and advisory service; drop-in sessions; computer guidance system.

Student services & facilities

Student advice and services: Counsellors; medical officer and nursing staff; chaplains. **Sporting facilities:** Sports centre including dance hall, gymnasium, physiology and biomechanics laboratories; 17-acre playing fields. **Accommodation:** Approx. half of 1st years in university halls (most rooms with broadband). 1000 self-catering places available, £69–£102 pw; 38-week contracts (Sept–July). Some students live in privately owned accommodation for their whole course: rent £55–£65 pw self-catering, £75–£85 pw for half board.

Money

Living expenses budget: Minimum budget of £6k–£6500 for an academic year (excluding tuition fees) recommended by university. **Term-time work:** University allows term-time work (60+% believed to work). Some work available on campus in SU bar, catering, registry, libraries; SU employment agency helps find work off-campus. **Financial help:** Bursaries of £310 pa for students whose family income is approx £25k (ie who qualify for full maintenance grant); bursary of £1k in 1st year for students from local partner colleges (continued into 2nd and 3rd year if family income is under £25k). Scholarships of £500 in 1st year for those with 360 points on entry; also music and sports scholarships. £296k government funds (awards £100–£3500, average £300); also some university bursaries. Apply to student finance support team for help (tel 01242 714236). **Tuition fees:** Home students pay £3225 pa for first degrees (£900 for sandwich year). International students pay £8200 pa.

 Student view) **James Durant,** Student Union President (Graduate, Broadcast Journalism)

Living
What's it like as a place to live? The town appears regal from the outside, but there is such a vibrant student community and great nightlife. **How's the student accommodation?** Halls of varying quality (most very high standard though). We have new halls being built for September 2010 (at the latest). **What's the student population like?** Very friendly from all over the country. Strong intake of international students. **How do students and locals get on?** Generally ok, a few minor problems at one campus, but overall very well.

Studying
What's it like as a place to study? Always introducing new courses and constantly expanding. **What are the teaching staff like?** Vast majority are interested in their students and want to get the best out of them.

Socialising
What are student societies like? Extremely varied, from the Mountain Bike Society to the Geographical Society. **What's a typical night out?** SU bar for majority of the night, club in town later on. **And how much does it cost?** £0–£30. **How can you get home safely?** Taxi, walk home in large groups, subsidised night buses.

Money

Is it an expensive place to live? Halls can be expensive, house rent is much cheaper. Have to be careful with the loan, like everywhere. **Average price of a pint?** £2. **And the price of a takeaway?** £3. **What's the part-time work situation?** SU Jobshop helps well over 1000 students each year, plus loads of jobs available.

Summary

What's the best feature about the place? The students! **And the worst?** Things not getting done quick enough by the university. **And to sum it all up?** Without doubt, the best 3 (or 4) years of your life. You'll get whatever you put in out of it!

Past students: David Bryant (journalist), Howard Newby (author), Graham Brookhouse (swimmer), Don Hale (investigative journalist), Chris Broad (cricketer), Beverley Knight (soul singer), Chris Beardshaw (garden designer). **More info?** Contact the SU (tel 01242 532848) or visit www.yourstudentsunion.com.

Glyndŵr University

| Location: north Wales (map 1) Four sites in north Wales: 2 in Wrexham; Denbighshire; Flintshire | ⬛ Glyndŵr University, Plas Coch, Mold Road, Wrexham LL11 2AW ☎ Tel 01978 293439 📠 Fax 01978 290008 💻 Website www.glyndwr.ac.uk *Student enquiries: email sid@glyndwr.ac.uk Applications: UCAS or direct* |

In brief

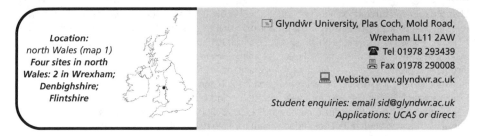

Total Students: 6300

9% postgraduate
91% undergraduate

Undergraduates: 5735
49% full-time ● ● 79% UK students
57% mature ● ● 46% lower socio-economic
on entry groups

49% female 51% male

- **A new university, accredited institution of University of Wales.**
- **Teaching staff:** 190 full-time, 140 part-time.
- **Broad study areas:** Art and design; built environment; business; communications technology; computing; education; engineering; health and social care; humanities; science and environment; social work and criminal justice; sport and exercise sciences; youth and community.

Freshers

- **Admissions information:** AS-levels accepted in combination with 2+ A-levels or equivalent. UCAS tariff used on most courses.
- **First degree entrants:** 720 UK, full-time.
- **Points on entry:** 200+ (average).
- **Drop-out rate:** 16% in 1st year.
- **Accommodation:** Some 1st years housed.

Profile

Institution

Founded: 1975 from merger of teacher training and 2 technical colleges; associate college of Wales University in 1993, full member in 2002; university status in 2008, and changed its name (from North East Wales Institute). **Site:** Main site on edge of Wrexham; art and design, 10 mins walk. Further sites in St Asaph, Denbighshire and Northop, Flintshire. **How to get there:** Local and national bus services to Wrexham bus station (King Street, 10 mins' walk from campus); rail service to Wrexham from Chester or Shrewsbury, daily direct trains from Birmingham, Cardiff and Holyhead; by road from M56, M53, M54 to A483 Chester–Oswestry, then A541 towards city centre. Airports at Manchester (45 miles) and Liverpool (37 miles).

Courses

Awarding body: University of Wales. **Main undergraduate awards:** BA, BA(QTS), BEng, BNursing, BSc, FdA, FdSc, FdEng. **Length of courses:** 3 years, 2 years (FdA, FdEng, FdSc).

Study opportunities & careers

Library and information services: Approx. 10,000 volumes, 500 periodicals, 410 study places. Information provision, £45 pa spent for each student (FTE). IT and library services converged. Ratio workstations to students 2:3, all with access to library and internet; IT facilities open 12 hours/day with support from tutors. **Other learning resources:** Laboratories, computer suites, reprographic services, radio studio, recording studio, theatre studios, art gallery, art workshops, graphic design laboratories, engineering facilities. **Study abroad:** Some opportunities to spend time abroad. **Careers:** Information and advice service. Student placement scheme and employment bureau.

Student services & facilities

Student advice and services: Welfare officer, counsellors, nurses, doctor surgery on campus, nursery, chaplain. **Amenities:** Bookshop and café; Students' Guild bar, restaurant, coffee shops and shop; 900-seater concert venue; art gallery. **Sporting facilities:** 6-court sports centre with all-weather pitch. International-standard playing field and water-based hockey pitch. Swimming pools and sports centres in Wrexham. Area excellent for water sports and outdoor pursuits. **Accommodation:** Student village on campus, hostel and hall in town centre. Approx. 400 self-catering places available (most ensuite); rent £60 pw, £72 pw ensuite. Most students live in privately owned accommodation for 2+ years, £50–£57 pw self-catering.

Money

Living expenses budget: Minimum budget of £120 pw (excluding tuition fees) recommended by university. **Financial help:** Bursaries of £1400 pa for UK students not from Wales, whose family income is up to £18,400, of £1k pa where it is £18,400–£22k, and of £600 pa where family income is over £22k; bursaries for Welsh students are £500, £450 and £400 pa, depending on family income. Also help for gifted athletes, careleavers, international students and those with, eg childcare or travel costs; £248k funds available (average award £575). **Tuition fees:** Home students pay £3225 pa for first degrees (though Welsh residents may be eligible for annual fee grant). International students pay £5850 pa.

Student view — **Matthew Hart,** President, Student Guild

Living

What's it like as a place to live? Wrexham has the best North Wales has to offer. Close to everything including mountains, but not too far from major city centres like Manchester and Liverpool. But much much more affordable! **How's the student accommodation?** Student accommodation on campus is mainly single rooms with their own bathroom and sharing a kitchen, although some accommodation has shared bathroom facilities. Other accommodation in town varies from private halls to shared houses to individual landlord-offered properties. All university accommodation is very reasonably priced with good support for student tenants. **What's the student population like?** The student population is very diverse with large numbers of resident international and European students studying alongside more local students of various age groups. This wide range of students from other places gives excellent opportunities to experience many different cultures and has a positive impact on the social life. **How do students and locals get on?** Wrexham is quite a small town, so meeting local people is easy. On the whole, the town is very accepting of its students. Studying and socialising in Wrexham lets you meet new friends not just on campus but in the wider community, depending on how active you are socially.

Studying
What's it like as a place to study? Wide range of courses – there's something for everyone! Small class sizes and lots of personal attention. **What are the teaching staff like?** Very personable and friendly, most have real world work experience that they bring into the classroom. Not just 'out there' academics!

Socialising
What are student societies like? There are a number of active societies and clubs ranging from photography to mountaineering; and there are easy-to-access structures and support from the Student Guild to encourage and help students engage with a wide range of social opportunities run for students by students. **What's a typical night out?** 'Typical?' **And how much does it cost?** Whatever you spend – some people like to spend a lot, some like to spend a little. **How can you get home safely?** The centre of town has one of the best CCTV and policed areas in Wales, and is very safe. Alternatively taxis are never more than £4 within the town even after 12am.

Money
Is it an expensive place to live? Wrexham is certainly not the most expensive place to live, very reasonable in fact. **Average price of a pint?** Student Bar £1.40/£1.57. Town Bars £2–£3. **And the price of a takeaway?** £4 upwards depending on which of the many food outlets you choose. **What's the part-time work situation?** The university has excellent careers and job shop facilities that is really useful to students seeking part- and full-time work. Jobs available both on and off campus.

Summary
What's the best feature about the place? The best things are the diversity of the student body, and the fact that the student opinions and voice are taken seriously by the university, along with the easy access to other parts of the country. **And the worst?** Some facilities are not as good as they could be but they are improving all the time. **And to sum it all up?** It's an ambitious place where anybody who has the desire will get the support they need to succeed, both in their studies and beyond.

More info? Contact SU on 01978 293296 website or visit the (www.newisu.com).

Goldsmiths

Location:
*south-east London
(map 3)*
Single campus in New Cross

⬛ Goldsmiths University of London, New Cross,
London SE14 6NW
🖥 Website www.goldsmiths.ac.uk

*Student enquiries: Admissions Office (tel 020 7919 7766,
e-mail admissions@gold.ac.uk)
Applications: UCAS*

In brief

Total Students: 7980

35% postgraduate
65% undergraduate

Undergraduates: 5030

85% full-time ● ● 70% UK students
79% mature ● ● 30% lower
on entry socio-economic
groups

65% female   35% male

- **A top UK research-intensive institution.** Part of London University.
- **Teaching staff:** 388 full-time, 386 visiting tutors.
- **Broad study areas:** Anthropology; art; community and youth work; computing; cultural studies; design; drama and theatre arts; education; English; history; history of art; media and communications; music; politics; psychology social work; sociology.

Freshers

- **Admissions information:** AS-levels accepted, usually in addition to at least 1 full A-level or equivalent; courses may have subject-specific requirements. UCAS tariff not used for offers.
- **First degree entrants:** 1265 UK, full-time.
- **Points on entry:** 240 (average).
- **Drop-out rate:** 9% in 1st year.
- **Accommodation:** Most 1st years housed.

Profile

Institution
Founded: 1891. Became a full school of London University in 1988. **Site:** Campus in south-east London. **How to get there:** Buses; New Cross Gate and New Cross rail stations; Deptford Bridge DLR station.

Courses 📖
Academic features: Interdisciplinary approach to subjects. Extensive evening study programme (open to all students). Many degree courses available part-time; many in combined subjects. **Awarding body:** University of London. **Main undergraduate awards:** BA, BA(Ed), BMus, BSc. **Length of courses:** 3 years; others 4 years (eg those involving work experience, foundation year and extension degrees). Many degree programmes available part-time.

Study opportunities & careers 🎓
Library and information services: Information services building combines library, computer services, digital media suite and languages resource centre. Over 225,000 volumes, 2600 periodicals,

audio-visual collections with facilities; 450 study places. Information provision, £65 pa spent for each student (FTE). Ratio 1:11 workstations to students. 622 computers, of which 275 networked in library. IT facilities open 15+ hours/day; staffed IT helpdesk. Tours and demonstrations of equipment in library and information service for new students; IT skills courses. **Other learning resources:** Language laboratories, computer-enhanced learning facilities, satellite reception, audio and video CDs and DVDs. **Study abroad:** Formal exchange links with EU universities and colleges. **Careers:** College and university careers services.

Student services & facilities

Student advice and services: Doctors, counsellors, solicitor (via SU), chaplains, nursery (23 places). **Amenities:** College shop, refectory and bar; audio-visual facilities, theatre; SU building with facilities centre, coffee bar, etc. **Sporting facilities:** New gym/fitness centres; sports grounds and playing fields near Sidcup (30 mins); tennis courts, practice field on site; swimming pool nearby. **Accommodation:** Majority of 1st years housed; priority given to 1st years from outside London (international students for their whole course). Approx. 1000 self-catering places in halls (majority ensuite), either on campus or in walking distance; rent £85–£114 pw (including bills). Private-sector rent £80–£110 pw (plus bills).

Money

Living expenses budget: Minimum budget of £7k–£9k pa (excluding tuition fees) recommended by the college. **Term-time work:** Careers service helps students find part-time work; weekly job opportunities bulletin (JOB) and noticeboard of local vacancies. **Financial help:** Bursaries of £1k pa for UK students whose family income is up to £19k; bursaries to a maximum value of £500 pa where family income is £19k–£40k. Also residential bursary reducing halls bills by 10%–20% for those with a low family income. Variety of scholarships: for students with highest entrance scores (2 of £5k, plus 1 per department of £500 pa); for students educated in Lewisham with strong academic ability (2 a year of £10k); for those educated in London and who are facing financial hardship (32 scholarships worth £500 pa); and for string players on BMus (of £500 pa). Also £387k government funds, over 700 payments made; small amount of own funds for hardship loans, available subject to student's circumstances. **Special help:** students who hit unforeseen crises; some part-time students. Apply to Student Funding and Information Office for help. **Tuition fees:** Home students pay £3225 pa for first degrees (£1613 part time). International students pay £9870–£10,360 pa (classroom), £12,630–£13,690 (lab/studio).

Student view

Famous for its drama, music, visual arts, communications and sociology. It's located in the heart of south-east London, near Greenwich, Blackheath and Lewisham and with easy access to the centre of town by train and bus. Student population very diverse and interesting; large numbers of female, mature, ethnic and international students. Majority of 1st years guaranteed a place in halls but the facilities available depend on the hall. SU is very active; has an inclusive and welcoming environment and an equal-opportunities policy. Many active clubs and societies including the LGBT (lesbian, gay, bisexual and transgender), athletics and Afro-Caribbean to name just a few. SU also funds a variety of student-led media including a radio station, Wired (broadcast on FM and over the internet at www.wired.gold.ac.uk) and an autonomous student newspaper, *Smiths* (publishes 5 times a year with a variety of news, music and arts features). SU entertainments try to cater for most of the students: comedy, quiz, live music and club nights ranging from urban and indie nights to student-led events, which could be anything wanted. And if that isn't enough, there are plenty more things to do and places to go in the city centre. A good place to study for city lovers wanting a university that is fun, stimulating, eventful and a refreshing change.

Student footnotes

Housing: College halls (generally good). Otherwise, cheap area for London (look on noticeboards and on London University accommodation website). Many live at home. **Eats:** Quality of food on campus is good and at reasonable price (meal for £3.50+). Number of reasonable cafés locally – greasy spoons to health food cafés – eg Raj Bhojan, Mary's Café and Goldsmith's Café. **Drink:** Good value drinks in union bar, open late 3 times a week. Local pubs reasonable (eg Goldsmiths Tavern, the Hobgoblin) and some open late. **Nightlife:** Union has good ents programme (including bands from local area plus recently Art Brute, Graham Coxon, Kano, Electric Soft Parade). On campus, Club Sandwich is good. If that isn't enough there are endless clubs in London. **Locals:** Fairly friendly if you are sensible. **Sports:** Wide range of sporting provision (eg football, badminton) nearby for all abilities. Also non-competitive activities, eg yoga and aerobics. Brand new gym on site; also ULU facilities (bit of a trek). **Travel:** Tube, train and bus. Local underground out of action until 2010 (being extended for the Olympics). **Financial help:** Variety of funds available such as access to learning funds. SU hardship fund (£50) can tide over students until further financial help can be found. **Jobs:** SU offers part-time jobs and has a jobshop. Loads of pubs employ students and plenty of local agencies. **Best features:** So close to central London; diversity of students. **And worst:** Could do with a lick of paint. **Past students:** Linton Kwesi Johnson (poet and musician); Mary Quant (fashion designer); Tessa Jowell, Merlyn Rees (politicians); Colin Welland (actor); Jack Brymer (clarinettist); Graham Sutherland (painter); Malcolm McLaren (former Sex Pistols manager); John Cale (Velvet Underground); Blur; Placebo; Damien Hirst, Tom Keating, Gillian Wearing (artists); Derek Hatton (politician); Julian Clary (comedian); Antony Gormley (sculptor); Julia Carling (presenter); John Illsley (Dire Straits); Vic Charles (world karate champion). **More info?** Enquiries to SU President on 020 8692 1406, email gcsu@gold.ac.uk or visit www.goldsmithsstudents.com.

Greenwich University

Location:
south-east London and Kent (map 3)
Campuses at Greenwich and Eltham (London), Chatham (Kent); partner colleges

🖳 University of Greenwich, Greenwich Campus, Old Royal Naval College, Park Row, Greenwich, London SE10 9LS
☎ Tel 0800 005 006
🖷 Fax 020 8331 8145
✉ Email courseinfo@gre.ac.uk
💻 Website www.greenwich.ac.uk

Student enquiries: Enquiry Unit (tel 0800 005 006; from outside UK +44 20 8331 8590)
Applications: UCAS

In brief

Total Students: 24,915

28% postgraduate
72% undergraduate

Undergraduates: 17,990
71% full-time ● ● 86% UK students
48% mature ● ● 46% lower socio-economic groups
on entry

53% female　　47% male

- **A modern university.**
- **Teaching staff:** 552 academic, 126 research staff.

- **Broad study areas:** Architecture; business; built environment; chemical and pharmaceutical sciences; computing; earth and environmental sciences; education and teaching; engineering; health, nursing and midwifery; humanities; languages; law; life sciences; mathematics; social sciences.

Freshers

- **Admissions information:** AS-levels accepted in combination with 2+ A-levels or equivalent. UCAS tariff used.
- **First degree entrants:** 3125 UK, full-time.
- **Points on entry:** 200 (average).
- **Drop-out rate:** 7% in 1st year.
- **Accommodation:** All 1st years housed.

Profile

Institution

Founded: University status in 1992. Formerly Thames Poly (founded 1970), an amalgamation of Woolwich Poly (1890) and a number of colleges of building, art, education and healthcare. **Site:** 3 main campuses: Greenwich Campus (Old Royal Naval College and adjacent buildings, Greenwich), Avery Hill Campus (Eltham) and University of Greenwich at Medway (Chatham). **How to get there:** To Greenwich by DLR (close to Cutty Sark station), by tube (Jubilee line to North Greenwich then 188 bus) or by train (to Greenwich from London Bridge, Cannon Street or Charing Cross). To Avery Hill by road (A2 off the M25, then A210) or by train (from Waterloo East, Charing Cross and London Bridge to Falconwood or New Eltham, 20 mins' walk). For Medway, M26, M20 or A/M2 to Chatham, or train from London, Ramsgate or Dover. **Special features:** Mature students may be admitted without normal entry requirements. Considerable transferability between courses allowed.

Courses

Awarding body: University of Greenwich. **Main undergraduate awards:** BA, BSc, BEng, LLB, MPharm. **Length of courses:** 3 years (full-time); 4 years (sandwich); 4–6 years (part-time).

Study opportunities & careers

Library and information services: 3 libraries developed into learning centre; 600,000 volumes, 3000 periodicals, 1000 study places; short loan for course texts; photocopying; online information services; access 60+ hours/week. Library and IT services converged. Induction to library and IT tutorials; IT support staff. Information provision, £62 pa spent for each student (FTE). **Other learning facilities:** Computer centre and PC facilities on all sites. **Study abroad:** 6% of students spend a period abroad. Exchange programmes with many universities in Europe and USA. **Careers:** Jobshop and careers centre for information, advice and support.

Student services & facilities

Student advice and services: Mentoring, counsellors, advisers (including disability adviser), nurses, medical officers and consultant psychiatrist, Anglican and RC chaplains. **Amenities:** SU; stationery and bookshop; dance and drama hall; crèche at Avery Hill. **Sporting facilities:** Multigyms, playing fields, tennis, netball, squash courts, fitness rooms, sailing, sub-aqua, many varied sporting clubs. **Accommodation:** All 1st years in university accommodation who apply by the deadline (20% of all students). 2500 self-catering places available + 204 at Medway. Rents, £84–£103 pw at Avery Hill, £91–£100 pw at Medway, £78–£110 pw (studio flats £113–£151 pw) at Greenwich; all on 40-week contract. Also some university-managed accommodation. Privately owned accommodation rent: £75–£105 pw for self-catering.

Money

Living expenses budget: Minimum budget of £6400–£7500 pa (excluding tuition fees) recommended by university. **Financial help:** Bursaries of £500 pa for UK students who qualify for a maintenance grant (ie family income of £50k). Also bursaries for those who join the university choir (3 bursaries of £1k), for sons and daughters of naval ratings (£3k pa), for those from partner colleges (£500 pa), for those on MPharm on a full maintenance grant (£310 pa) and for those with appropriate rugby experience. Scholarships of £500 pa for UK students with 300 tariff points on entry. Hardship fund for UK students with unexpected difficulties. Separate arrangements for the MPharm and partner colleges. Also financial support fund of £1.25 million to help those who encounter unexpected hardship. **Tuition fees:** Home students pay £2835 pa for first degrees except MPharm (£3225 pa), some foundation degrees (£1700 pa), placement years (£625) and courses at partner colleges (£2270 pa). International students pay £8650 pa, except £12,300 for MPharm.

Student view

It's up-and-coming and with huge ambition. It's based at 3 campuses: at Greenwich, Avery Hill in Eltham and Medway in Chatham (as well as partner colleges in the south-east). Each campus houses complete university schools, so the subject you study determines where you'll spend your time. The majority of schools and students are at Greenwich Campus – part of a World Heritage Site on the River Thames, designed some 300 years ago by Sir Christopher Wren. The area is full of history and tourist sites: the Cutty Sark and Gypsy Moth IV are both in dry dock nearby; the Royal Observatory (home of Greenwich Mean Time), Royal Naval College and Painted Hall; and then of course there are Greenwich markets, which are a real part of local life. Avery Hill, at Eltham, is a vibrant campus of nearly 6000 students, with modern facilities and the up-to-date equipment needed for education and training, health and social care and architecture and construction. Eltham is full of surprises such as Eltham Palace. Medway campus offers the high-tech research and science facilities needed for engineering and science, as well as the Natural Resources Institute, which is based there. Chatham Dockyard and other sights are nearby. There are halls of residence at (or near) all 3 campuses. The Avery Hill village is open to students on all campuses (a free bus service so lectures are easy to get to!). It's a courtyard development of shared flats, some rooms are ensuite and all have a small fridge, telephone and internet access; it's set in parkland and has a great community feel; there is a general shop, laundrette, gym and bars and food court at the Dome. Four halls near to Greenwich campus, offering a variety of accommodation, some ensuite, many with internet connections. 2 halls on site at Medway campus (all rooms ensuite). A huge part of the Greenwich experience is the social life. SU creates a variety of social and cultural events to meet the needs of a diverse student population – from live music, different acts and club nights to comedy, quiz and film nights. SU bars at all campuses are a great place to relax and escape the pressures of academic life. Annual events (eg freshers', valentine's ball, May ball, sports and societies awards dinner) are special dates in the calendar and attract lots of interest. Wide range of sporting activities, from BUCS premiership football to newly created American football. Also massive choice of societies (Amnesty International to LGBT); there's generally something for everyone – but if not, the SU can help you set it up. If you want something different, central London is only a train ride away. Whichever campus you are on, with over 20,000 students from 80+ countries, the university's policy on equal opportunities and diversity encourages a vibrant multicultural atmosphere.

Student footnotes

Housing: University accommodation for all new students. Then local rented housing (look on noticeboards, estate agents). **Eats:** SU food outlets on all sites – value-for-money food. Meal

£3+ on campus. Usual variety of local eateries at all sites; good restaurants in Greenwich, Chatham and Gillingham. **Drink:** SU bars at all campuses. Earl of Chatham (Woolwich), brand new bar in Greenwich – Bar Latitude – very popular. London Pride, Ramrod Special, good local beers. **Nightlife:** Loads of ents at the SU. Incredible number of bars and clubs in central London. Multiplex and nightclub bars on outskirts of Chatham and Gillingham. Zen's club in Dartford popular. **Locals:** Friendly in Dartford and Chatham, less so in Woolwich. **Sports:** Multi-purpose (and cheap) gym at Avery Hill site. Charlton Athletic Football Club has massive sports facility on site (used for training purposes) and new sporting facilities (eg sports hall, dance studios) at Avery Hill. **Jobs:** Lots about, at minimum wage, through the SU (bars, stewarding, ents work), university (registry, recruitment and marketing, lab work), off-campus (all sorts!), and work experience programmes operated through the Jobshop. **Best features:** Diverse campuses and societies. **Past students:** Hale and Pace (TV comedians), Brian Jacks (Olympic judo medallist), Ann Packer (Olympic athletics medallist), Rachel Heyhoe-Flint (cricketer), Professor Ian McAllister (Professor of Politics, University of New South Wales). **More info?** Ring SU on 020 8331 7629 or visit website www.suug.co.uk.

Guildhall School of Music & Drama

Location:
central London
(map 3)
Single site in the
Barbican

Guildhall School of Music & Drama, Silk Street, Barbican, London EC2Y 8DT
☎ Tel 020 7628 2571
🖷 Fax 020 7256 9438
💻 Website www.gsmd.ac.uk

Student enquiries: Registry
Applications: Direct

In brief

Total Students: 865

 42% postgraduate
58% undergraduate

Undergraduates: 500
100% full-time  72% UK students
21% mature on entry

49% female 51% male

- **World-class music, drama and technical theatre school.**
- **Teaching staff:** 30 full-time, 500 part-time.
- **Broad study areas:** Acting; music; stage management and technical theatre.

Freshers
- **Admissions information:** Entry by audition. 2 A-levels or equivalent required.
- **First degree entrants:** 95 UK, full-time.
- **Accommodation:** Most 1st years housed

Profile

Institution
Founded: 1880; degree status granted in 1945. **Site:** Barbican, central London. **How to get there:** Moorgate underground station; many buses. **Special features:** All teachers active in their professions outside the school. Visiting ensembles include Kungsbacka Trio, Takacs Quartet; Belcea Quartet, and masterclasses by high-profile visiting artists. Collaborative partnerships with Barbican Centre, LSO, and BBC Symphony Orchestra.

Courses

Awarding body: Guildhall School of Music & Drama, City University. **Main undergraduate awards:** BA, BMus. **Length of courses:** 4 years (BMus); 3 years (BA).

Study opportunities & careers

Library and information services: Over 75,000 volumes, 60 periodicals, 44 study places; separate drama library and study area. IT service separate; 5 points with access to library, 12 to internet. Introductory tutorial on library use, and series of leaflets; library staff give individual IT help. Specialist collections: Alkan Society Collection, Appleby Collection (guitar music), Harris Collection (opera vocal scores), Merrett Collection (double bass), Worshipful Company of Musicians Westrup Collection. **Other learning resources:** Professional 16-track recording studio; listening facilities. Audio-visual room with 17 study carrels, special resources room with computer facilities and multimedia/electronic music workstations. **Careers:** Advice from senior staff.

Student services & facilities

Student advice and services: Student services officer, student health advisors, counsellors, chaplain. **Amenities:** Music hall, theatre (orchestra pit of 80), lecture recital room, John Hosier Practice Annexe (46 practice studios), theatre-training gymnasium, Barbican Centre. **Accommodation:** Most 1st years housed. Hall of residence (Sundial Court) with 177 rooms in flats; rent £112 pw. Student services officer gives information and advice about external accommodation, rent from £85 pw.

Money

Living expenses budget: Minimum budget of £9600–£15k pa (excluding tuition fees) recommended by school. **Financial help:** Bursaries for UK students whose family income is less than £50k, equivalent to 50% of the maintenance grant for which they qualify, ie £1453 pa for those whose family income is up to £25k, down to nil where family income is £50k. Variety of other bursary and scholarship schemes. Hardship fund to help those meeting unexpected financial hardship. **Tuition fees:** Home students pay £3225 pa for first degrees. International students pay £15,200 pa.

Student view

Ensconced in the Barbican – one of the world's cultural hubs – it has a distinctly urban aspect: in one direction the West End, with all it offers; in the other, the East End (the school has active links and outreach work in Tower Hamlets). The main building buzzes with activity and music all day. It houses a theatre, concert hall, studio theatre, extensive stage workshop with CAD facilities, recording and MIDI studios, nearly 100 teaching/practice rooms (most with pianos), recital room and rehearsal studios. A good library with an extensive listening facility; students can also join the Barbican library and City University library. There are no on-site sports amenities, but students have access to cheap fitness facilities at nearby City University and many local gyms and swimming pools offer student rates. The school attracts students from throughout the country and a large number of international students. Courses are challenging and progressive, with an emphasis on practical skills; relatively easy to change course in 1st year. Teaching chiefly by leading professionals in the field (many staff from major orchestras, the National Theatre, RSC, Royal Opera House, ENO, etc) and many outstanding visitors (eg Simon Rattle, Murray Perahia and Gangiro Nakamura III). Schedules are busy, especially on acting and stage management courses, and music students can expect long hours of practice on top of formal schedules. Varied assessment pattern reflects diversity of skills required. Self-reflective skills are developed on all courses. A number of exchange programmes exist with similar institutions in Europe and beyond. Many music students work part-time (bars, stewarding, teaching private pupils or at gigs or other engagements secured through the school); acting and stage management courses do not allow much time. SU organises health and fitness and social activities. Cheap bar with activities including regular jam, karaoke and disco nights and extraordinary events like infamous Bar Olympics. Occasional guest speakers invited; active Christian Union, contemporary music society (collaborates with Royal College of Art and co-ordinates 2 festivals a year) and an international students' buddying scheme. But a lot of social activity is not organised into societies. Students may also join City University societies.

Student footnotes

Housing: 40 flats in halls, 3 mins' walk away, with refectory, rehearsal/performance spaces and (cheap) SU bar. Otherwise houseshares; always pricey but Stratford and (trendy) Hackney offer some cheaper options. Don't expect a palace. **Eats:** Canteen under Sundial Court, top-quality food at competitive prices. **Drink:** Basement bar. **Nightlife:** Whole of London easily accessible. Numerous events in SU; nightclubs Fluid and Fabric are 10 mins' walk, and number of late-night bars. Barbican Arts Centre (next door) and many other London arts venues have student discounts on cinema, theatre and concert tickets. **Sports:** Swimming pool and sports facilities at City University. **Travel:** Close to Moorgate and Liverpool Street tube stations. **Jobs:** SU, welfare department and music assistant collate work offers. **Financial help:** School funds, very good and pretty quick for cases of serious need. Guildhall Trust offers some bursaries. **Informal name:** GSMD; or just 'Guildhall' to arts bods. **Past students:** Orlando Bloom, Eileen Atkins, Fred Astaire, Claire Bloom, Joseph Fiennes Ewan McGregor, Julia MacKenzie, Dudley Moore, Damian Lewis, Fay Ripley, Mollie Sugden (actors); Alastair McGowan (comedian); George Martin (music producer); Geraint Evans, James Galway, Max Jaffa, Tasmin Little, Benjamin Luxon, Jacqueline du Pré, Peter Skellern, Bryn Terfel, Anne Sofie von Otter (musicians). **More info?** Visit the website (www.gsmdsu.co.uk).

Harper Adams University College

Location:
West Midlands
(map 2)
Single campus at
Newport, Shropshire;
1 partner college in
Cheshire

⌨ Harper Adams University College, Newport, Shropshire TF10 8NB
☎ Tel 01952 820280
🖷 Fax 01952 814783
💻 Website www.harper-adams.ac.uk

Student enquiries: Admissions Officer
Applications: UCAS (or direct if early)

In brief

Total Students: 2755

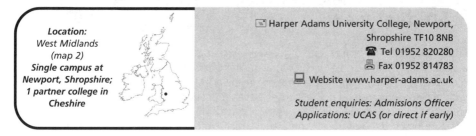

4% postgraduate
2% FE Students
94% undergraduate

Undergraduates: 2590
54% full-time / 96% UK students
18% mature on entry / 58% lower socio-economic groups

46% female / 54% male

- **Specialist land-based university college.**
- **Teaching staff:** 90 full-time and part-time.
- **Broad study areas:** Agriculture; bioveterinary science and veterinary nursing; business, marketing and agri-food; countryside and environment; engineering and design; land and estate management; leisure, tourism and outdoor recreation.

Freshers

- **Admissions information:** AS-levels accepted in combination with A-levels or equivalent. UCAS tariff used.
- **First degree entrants:** 335 UK, full-time.
- **Points on entry:** 220 (average).
- **Drop-out rate:** 9% in 1st year.
- **Accommodation:** All 1st years housed.

Profile

Institution

Founded: 1901. **Site:** Single campus for all teaching, living accommodation and recreation, surrounded by college farm. **How to get there:** By train (Telford station 15 mins by taxi); by road (M54 from the south, M6 and A519 from the north); by air (Birmingham airport 45 mins drive; Manchester, Liverpool John Lennon and East Midlands airports also within 1¼ hour drive).

Courses

Academic features: Modular system for most courses allows a range of options. All degree courses are sandwich courses. **Awarding body:** Harper Adams University College. **Main undergraduate award:** BSc. **Length of courses:** 4 years (sandwich).

Study opportunities & careers

Library and information services: Learning resources centre. 49,500 volumes, 650 periodicals. Links with university libraries on joint courses. Information provision, £130 pa spent for each student (FTE). Ratio of 1:4 workstations to students; 310 workstations with internet access. Most IT facilities open 13+ hours a day (7 hours at weekends); open-access area open 24/7; 700 students access college portal from own computers. First line e-learning and IT support from 9 full-time staff; initial introduction to library and information services; further application training and on-going information skills programmes. **Other learning facilities:** Covered soil working area, specialised laboratories, glasshouse complex, mixed commercial farm, purpose-built engineering design centre, biomass generator. **Study abroad:** 5% of students spend a period abroad. Formal exchange links with colleges in Turkey, Greece and many EU countries. **Careers:** Information, advice and placement service.

Student services & facilities

Student advice and services: Doctors, counsellors and chaplaincy on campus. **Amenities:** Common room with pool table, table football, TV, DVD and sofas; 2 SU bars (1 with dance stage and nightclub lighting for discos and live bands); 2 cafeterias; prayer room; band/music room; student garage/workshop; bookshop; stage and auditorium; hall; SU shop. **Sporting facilities:** Multigym, squash and tennis courts, swimming pool, indoor sports hall, sports fields, 3 floodlit rugby pitches, 3 football pitches, cricket pitch and all-weather floodlit AstroTurf pitch, bowls green, darts board, 4x4 track – all on campus. Own clay-pigeon-shooting ground nearby. **Accommodation:** All new students in college accommodation (40% of students overall). 420 full-board places at £90–£121 pw, 183 self-catering places (100 ensuite) at £78 pw; 32-week contracts, term time only. Rents include utilities, internet, weekly laundry and daily cleaner (plus 3 meals each weekday in catered halls). Students live in privately owned accommodation for 2 years: rent £58–£65 pw for self-catering, £50–£60 for BandB or half-board. Very few live at home.

Money

Living expenses budget: Minimum budget of £5870 pa (excluding tuition fees) recommended by college, for students in college halls. **Term-time work:** College helps find industrial placements only;

holiday jobs posted. Many term-time jobs on campus and locally. **Financial help:** Means-tested scholarships for UK students whose family income is up to £38,300: of £1k pa where family income is up to £17,900; of £750 pa when it is £17,900–£28,500; and £500 where it is £28,500–£38,300. Also merit scholarships of £250–£750 (may not be combined with means-tested scholarship). Also £60k government funds, 60 students helped. **Special help:** mature students, self-financing, those with children. Scholarships (industry and private) and prizes awarded on a competitive basis. **Tuition fees:** Home students pay approx £3225 pa for first degrees (£2732 pa for foundation degrees; but £893 for placement years). International students pay £8200 pa (£4100 in placement year; £7600/£3800 for foundation degrees).

Student view) **Helen Plant,** Students' Union President (Recent graduate, BSc Agri-food Marketing with Business Studies)

Living

What's it like as a place to live? Harper Adams is a really friendly and safe place to live. **How's the student accommodation?** All 1st year students usually live on campus, which is run by the university college, and you can choose to be catered Monday to Friday or to cook for yourself. You can also choose to be ensuite or not, and all on-site accommodation includes your laundry being done for you once a week and full cleaning! Other students live off campus in private accommodation, which tends to range from £45 pw to £65 pw. **What's the student population like?** Very friendly place with a strong community spirit. Quite a strong rural background of students attracted by the location and courses but they come from a wide range of locations. **How do students and locals get on?** Newport is a close community, there are no no-go areas and as long as you park your car considerately (ie not over their drive!) and can remember to put the rubbish out most weeks, students and locals get on fine. The SU even had a float in the town carnival this year.

Studying

What's it like as a place to study? Originally an Agricultural College, Harper Adams has a large number of agriculture (with specialisms) students, and a college farm as a teaching facility. However the range is now much broader, with courses in engineering, business, food, animals, leisure/tourism, land and countryside management and great facilities to match. **What are the teaching staff like?** Lecturers are supportive, easy to contact and generally on first name terms with all their students.

Socialising

What are student societies like? Clubs and societies form a large part of the social life at Harper Adams and there's pretty much something for everyone – and if there isn't one to suit you, we would love for you to set your own club/society up, just see our SU Societies Representative or Sports Secretary. Our clubs and societies include rugby (union and league), hockey, netball, football, shooting, 4 x 4 off-roading, Gaelic football, equestrian, Harper Ireland, Harper Cymru, Harper Scotland, Harper Forum, LGBT, Christian Union and HOPS (Harper Outdoor Pursuits Society). **What's a typical night out?** There's something on every night of the week but the main student night is Wednesday in the legendary Union bar. **And how much does it cost?** Entry is free to all members of the SU, who pay a one-off membership fee at the start of their course. **How can you get home safely?** Walk (normally takes about 40 mins to walk back to town after a few drinks!) or taxis are cheap. Quinny from the Phez (Pheasant Inn) also runs a free mini-bus service on a Wednesday night.

Money

Is it an expensive place to live? Not really, but with Waitrose as one of the 2 supermarkets in town, if you have expensive taste the money soon runs out! **Average· price of a pint?** £2.20 in the SU but around £2.40 in town. **And the price of a**

takeaway? A large margarita pizza is around £4.80. **What's the part-time work situation?** There is some part-time work available in the college bar or as a student ambassador for the college, and there's also work available in Newport. However, a lot of students tend to work during the holidays, especially Easter and summer. The college provides considerable help here with good links with employers and it regularly posts vacancies on the college website.

Summary

What's the best feature about the place? The community atmosphere, also known as Harper Spirit! Everyone gets involved to make things happen, a fantastic example of which are the 4 annual balls organised by student committees. **And the worst?** There's so much going on that it can be difficult to get time just to relax and chill out. **And to sum it all up?** The college motto is 'work hard, play hard', and in my opinion nothing describes Harper Adams better. Harper students know they're here for a reason but that it's also important to enjoy themselves!

Past students: Barbara Woodhouse (dog trainer and TV personality). **More info?** Check out the SU website on www.harper-adams.ac.uk/su.

Heriot-Watt University

Location:
Edinburgh, central Scotland (map 1)
Main campus on outskirts of city; campus in Galashiels

✉ Heriot-Watt University, Riccarton, Edinburgh EH14 4AS

☎ Tel 0131 451 3451

🖷 Fax 0131 450 3630

✉ Email edu.liaison@hw.ac.uk

💻 Website www.hw.ac.uk

Student enquiries: Admissions Office
Applications: UCAS

In brief

Total Students: 10,560

50% postgraduate

50% undergraduate

Undergraduates: 5315

90% full-time

14% mature on entry

77% UK students

28% lower socio-economic groups

41% female   59% male

- **A top UK research-intensive university.**
- **Teaching staff:** 1000 full-time, 100 part-time.
- **Broad study areas:** Management, accountancy and economics, engineering, building and architecture, science, textiles and design, languages, marine science and environmental management.

Freshers

- **Admissions information:** Most offers made in terms of A-levels or equivalent. UCAS tariff partially used.
- **First degree entrants:** 1175 UK, full-time.
- **Points on entry:** 245+ (average).
- **Drop-out rate:** 9% in 1st year.
- **Accommodation:** All 1st years housed who require it.

Profile

Institution

Founded: 1821 as the School of Arts of Edinburgh; granted university charter in 1966. Merged in 1998 with Scottish College of Textiles, Galashiels. **Site:** Edinburgh Campus in west Edinburgh parkland. Also Scottish Borders Campus in Galashiels (textiles; some management and languages); 35 miles away. **How to get there:** Edinburgh easily accessible by train, coach from all over the UK: Waverley railway station and central bus station (St Andrew's Square) nearby; airport 3 miles (cheap flights from London and other centres); for university, bus from central Edinburgh. Scottish Borders Campus: by road A7, approx 1 hour's drive from Edinburgh; by bus (hourly service from Edinburgh); from Berwick-on-Tweed or Carlisle, both 1½ hours by bus or by train. **Special features:** Institute of Petroleum Engineering in Orkney.

Courses

Academic features: All courses on modular system. Combined studies degrees offer scope for choice and flexibility. Unusual specialist degrees, eg brewing and distilling, interpreting and translating, actuarial mathematics. **Awarding body:** Heriot-Watt University. **Main undergraduate awards:** MA, BA, BEng, BSc, MChem, MEng, MPhys. **Length of courses:** 4 years; 3 years (some ordinary degrees); 5 years (MEng, MPhys, MChem).

Study opportunities & careers

Library and information services: 150,000 volumes, 2500 periodicals; online information system. Separate library at Galashiels, 18,000 volumes, 300 periodicals, 80 study places. Information provision, £135 pa spent for each student (FTE). Access to IT facilities 24 hours/day; IT support in open-access computer centre. **Other learning resources:** Television centre, computer-based learning. At Galashiels, handloom weaving workshop, studios, textile and clothing workshops, special collections of fabric samples and shawls. **Study abroad:** 5% of first-degree students (plus language specialists) spend a period abroad. Large number of formal exchange links in EU, some allowing an additional qualification from partner institution. Some industrial placements abroad. **Careers:** Information and advice service; close links with employers.

Student services & facilities

Student advice and services: GP and dental services. Counsellor, tutor/mentors, university chaplains, nursery. **Amenities:** Purpose-built SUs at both campuses, with shop, bank, travel office, hairdresser. **Sporting facilities:** Excellent sports centre with football academy on main campus. Sports hall at Galashiels. **Accommodation:** All new students who require it in university accommodation (40% of all students). 1600 places in Edinburgh (300 of which are catered, 70% ensuite), 200 self-catering places at Borders: catered halls £53–£62 pw, plus £41.50 meal charge; self-catering £57–£68 pw (£82 pw ensuite); contracts 37 weeks. Most students live in privately owned accommodation for 1–2 years, rent average £260–£320 pm 10+% of first-degree students live at home.

Money

Living expenses budget: Minimum budget of £5800 pa (excluding tuition fees) recommended by university. **Term-time work:** No university policy on part-time work. Holiday work only available on campus in catering and residences; careers service helps find work off campus. **Financial help:** Government funds. **Tuition fees:** Scottish and EU students pay no fees during course; other UK students pay £1820 pa for first degrees. International students pay £9k–£11,350 pa.

Student view (Edinburgh campus)

Ruth Bush, SA President (Final year, Maths)

Living

What's it like as a place to live? Heriot-Watt is on a campus just outside Edinburgh. The campus atmosphere is fantastic and you've got everything you need in one place. There's catering, cafés, shops, a bank, and most importantly the SU for nights out. The city is a 25-min bus ride away as well, so really you've got the best of both worlds. **How's the student accommodation?** Our accommodation is university owned, which is a real plus point because they employ older students to be wardens and they organise inter-hall competitions, etc. The rooms are quite small, but the atmosphere is great, people have their doors open and are always chatting to each other. There are communal areas in most of the halls, which are nice to hang out in. **What's the student population like?** 30% of Heriot Watt's students are international, which makes for a really multicultural atmosphere. It's great because you make friends from all over the world and learn so much about other people's cultures. **How do students and locals get on?** We don't have many problems as we are a campus out in the countryside. Most people live in the centre of Edinburgh after their 1st year though and it's a great place to live. We're lucky in Edinburgh that there is plenty of accommodation available for students, and in the majority of places there's a good relationship with the local community.

Studying

What's it like as a place to study? Heriot-Watt's courses are pretty special as courses are much more applied than most universities and you get to see real applications of what you're learning. **What are the teaching staff like?** Teaching at Heriot-Watt is generally really good. The staff are supportive and there's a really good staff–student relationship; students aren't afraid to ask questions and tutorials are much more interactive than just going through a few questions on a white board.

Socialising

What are student societies like? There are a wide range of societies and there's more being affiliated all the time. The university and the SA are really interested in giving students more opportunities to help out in the local community and further afield, and although they're not the centre of most people's social lives I'd say this area is really starting to thrive. **What's a typical night out?** There's a really wide range of things to do so it varies from person to person. The big 1st-year night out is an event called The Big F in the SU. It's themed differently each week and it's full of the best student music anthems around! **And how much does it cost?** A pint or a spirit and mixer in the centre of Edinburgh is normally about £2–£3, but since there are 4 universities situated in Edinburgh, you can find a student night most nights of the week with drinks offers and cheap entry prices. **How can you get home safely?** Buses run to Heriot-Watt campus and other parts of the city 24 hours a day so there's always a way of getting home.

Money

Is it an expensive place to live? Edinburgh isn't too expensive a place to live. People do watch their pennies, but there are loads of student deals for eating, drinking and socialising so you don't have to spend a fortune here to have a good time. Rent prices in the city are quite high, especially for Scotland, so a lot of people live slightly out of the centre to get the cheaper flats. **Average price of a pint?** £2.80. **And the price of a takeaway?** £5. **What's the part-time work situation?** The university understands that part-time jobs are hugely important to students nowadays and offers support wherever it can. The careers service is great for finding part-time jobs and there are even quite a few jobs available on campus. It's normally pretty easy to find a job in the city centre as well. We're lucky in Edinburgh that it gets tourists all year round so there's plenty of random part-time jobs available. Wages are normally pretty good.

Summary

What's the best feature about the place? The atmosphere on campus is fantastic. You've got all your friends, social space and sports facilities in one place so when you need a break from studying it makes life so much easier. **And the worst?** Study spaces are too few and far apart in my opinion. However, the university is aware of the need to update them and we hope to see this happen in the next few years. **And to sum it all up?** Heriot-Watt has the best of both worlds: a strong campus community in a safe, countryside environment, and a buzzing city full of excitement only a short bus ride away. Its unusual applied courses attract people from all over the world.

Past students: Irvine Welsh (author), Gary Younge (writer for the *Guardian* and past HWUSA Officer), Sir Russell Fairgrieve MP, Lord Sanderson, Sir Alan Smith. **More info?** Ring SA on 0131 451 5333, email president@hwusa.org or log on to website (www.hwusa.org).

Student view
(Scottish Borders campus)

Campus is 15 mins' walk from the centre of Galashiels – a small but growing town in the beautiful Scottish Borders, 35 miles south of Edinburgh. It's home to the school of textiles, and a small section of the management department. Formerly known as the Scottish College of Textiles, it's internationally recognised for the high calibre of its design graduates; excellent employment in the textile industry. Most students come from Scotland but lots of international students too (around 100 students from 30 nations). High female:male ratio (around 85% female). With only 600 students on campus, there is a good staff:student ratio and a very relaxed atmosphere. Many courses have industrial placements and assessment by a mix of coursework and exams. Excellent facilities; newly refurbished workshops and High Mill building containing specially designed laboratories and studios. Design department has a vast hand-weaving shed, extensive high-speed weaving and knitting looms so students get first-hand experience of designing fabrics; the printing facilities are some of the best in Europe. Library is in the halls of residence, so excellent access. Hot food available on campus on weekdays. Halls of residence (self-catering) is 2 mins' walk, on hillside overlooking campus and close to new multi-purpose gym (has classes and student membership rates). Also flats in town (some university-owned), good links with the Edinburgh campus: a shuttle bus runs twice daily. SA provides welfare, social and cultural facilities; student societies include fashion show, textile design society and graduation ball. SA runs a full term-time entertainments programme, eg ICE and Bright Light events.

Student footnotes

Housing: Halls and university-owned accommodation (cheap but go quickly). Local rented accommodation through welfare, estate agents and notice boards. **Eating:** Food on campus at reasonable prices (8am-4pm); plenty available in town. **Drink:** Bar in halls with competitively priced drinks. Many pubs in town (Wetherspoons to local old men's pubs). **Nightlife:** Good entertainments programme through SA. 2 nightclubs in town. **Sports:** Multi-purpose gym on campus; aerobics, basketball, rugby, football, hockey and a swimming pool locally. **Financial help:** Good access and hardship funds – well distributed and easily accessible. Short- to medium-term loans from the SRC.

Jobs: Lots of bar and restaurant work in town, and in supermarkets and new retail park; some holiday work in local mills. **Best features:** Quality of facilities and staff; campus community. **Worst:** Girls complain about the lack of guys; building work on campus. **More info?** Contact Vice President Galashiels on 01896 892170, email vpsbc@hwusa.org.

Hertfordshire University

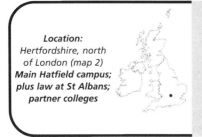

Location:
Hertfordshire, north
of London (map 2)
**Main Hatfield campus;
plus law at St Albans;
partner colleges**

⌨ University of Hertfordshire, Hatfield,
Hertfordshire AL10 9AB
☎ Tel 01707 284800
🖷 Fax 01707 284115
✉ Email admissions@herts.ac.uk
💻 Website www.herts.ac.uk

*Student enquiries: University Student Centre
Applications: UCAS*

In brief

Total Students: 23,725

81% undergraduate
17% postgraduate
2% FE Students

Undergraduates: 19,170
84% full-time
27% mature
on entry
89% UK students
40% lower
socio-economic
groups

55% female   45% male

- **A modern university.**
- **Teaching staff:** 670 full-time.
- **Broad study areas:** Aerospace, automotive and design engineering; art and design; business; computer science; education; electronic, communication and electrical engineering; film and media; humanities; law; life science; music; nursing and midwifery; paramedic sciences, physiotherapy and radiography; physics, astronomy and mathematics; psychology; social, community and health studies.

Freshers
- **Admissions information:** UCAS tariff used; all qualifications count towards tariff but minimum of 2 A-levels or equivalent required.
- **First degree entrants:** 4235 UK, full-time.
- **Points on entry:** 230 (average).
- **Drop-out rate:** 9% in 1st year.
- **Accommodation:** All 1st years housed who apply by deadline.

Profile

Institution
Founded: 1952; Hatfield Poly; then university status in 1992. **Site:** Twin campuses (Hatfield College Lane, and Hatfield de Havilland) 20 miles north of London; campuses 1km apart, linked by paths, cycle routes and continuous shuttle bus. Law school at St Albans. **How to get there:** Hatfield at Junction 3, A1(M); St. Albans campus near A414. All fairly near railway stations with regular fast (20 mins) services from London (King's Cross).

327

Courses

Academic features: Most courses on modular structure; high proportion are sandwich courses. Many Joint Honours and combined programmes available. **Awarding body:** University of Hertfordshire. **Main undergraduate awards:** BA, BEd, BEng, MEng, MPhys, BSc, LLB. **Length of courses:** 3 years; 4 years (sandwich); 4–5 years (extended degrees); 2 years (LLB).

Study opportunities & careers

Library and information services (LIS): 500,000 volumes, over 10,000 journal titles; networked online information services on and off campus, including StudyNet virtual learning environment. Information provision, £121 pa spent for each student (FTE). Integrated computing, library and media services open 24/7. Learning resources centres with 2900 study spaces, 1500 computer workstations (all with internet access) and wireless network for use of personal laptops; ratio workstations to students 1:8. Induction to LIS for all new students; expert advice and support (on-campus helpdesks, telephone helpline, online help guides and drop-in skills sessions). **Other learning resources:** Field centre, observatory, audio-visual aids service, sports science laboratories, multimedia centre. **Study abroad:** Formal exchange links with 70 universities and colleges across Europe, North America, South-east Asia and Australia. **Careers:** Advisory and placement service; recruitment fair.

Student services & facilities

Student advice and services: Specialist help and personal tutorial system. General medical and nursing facilities, professional counsellors, chaplaincy, day nursery, disabled student officer, financial and legal advisory services. Some residential accommodation on each campus for disabled students. **Amenities:** SU buildings; music and drama centres. **Sporting facilities:** Sports village at de Havilland campus has 100-station health and fitness centre, 12 badminton court sports hall, 8-lane swimming pool, exercise studio, 12-metre climbing wall, squash courts, 4-lane indoor cricket hall, 3 AstroTurf pitches, 3 grass football pitches and 1 rugby pitch. Over 30 sporting clubs. **Accommodation:** All 1st years who apply and meet university criteria are in university residences. All places are self-catering, rent £80–£96.50 pw (£61.50–£63 pw shared), contracts Sept–June. Lodgings locally £80 pw full-board, £65 pw self-catering; places in shared house £65–£75 pw plus bills.

Money

Living expenses budget: Minimum budget of £7250–£7600 pa (excluding tuition fees) recommended by university. **Term-time work:** University allows term-time work for full-time students (80% believed to work). Some work available on campus in bars, offices, sports coaches, grounds staff, library, catering, etc (own students employed wherever possible); also UHSU employment office helps find work off campus. **Financial help:** Means-tested bursaries for UK students from families with incomes of up to £40k, valued at 50% of maintenance grant for which they qualify (eg £1453 pa where family income is up to £20k). Also bursaries for students from designated partner colleges. Scholarships for science and engineering, entrepreneurial excellence and for gifted and talented students (value £500–£3k pa). Also government funds of £841k. **Special help:** single parents, low-income families, plus students in severe hardship due to exceptional circumstances (demand for funds always exceeds supply). **Tuition fees:** Home students pay £3225 pa for first degrees. International students pay £8k pa.

Student view
Ricky Valdiny, SU President (Cognitive Science)

Living
What's it like as a place to live? Hatfield at first sight looks like a pretty bleak town, but after living here for 4 years it has developed a subtle charm. The town itself is made up of little more than a shopping mall and a supermarket but its links with other cities is

outstanding. In 20 mins you can be in London and a 15-min ride will take you into the historic city of St Albans. **How's the student accommodation?** Student accommodation varies a great deal in Hatfield. On campus it comes in 2 forms: cheap and cheerful or expensive and stylish. Cheap and cheerful are halls on the College Lane campus and although at first sight they look like reformed prison cells, actually feel very homely once you get used to it. On de Havilland campus you will find luxury accommodation but this is rather pricey. Off campus generally is of less quality and more expensive, with a few exceptions. **What's the student population like?** Student population is incredibly diverse with around 80 different nationalities, with a sizeable international cohort from China, India and Africa. **How do students and locals get on?** Students and locals for the most part do not get on but the university and SU are developing a new £37 million venue, which will be open to the public in an attempt to mend this rift.

Studying

What's it like as a place to study? It is highly dependent on the course you study. Subjects such as business and law are particularly good, engineering has a good tradition at UH and psychology has some world-class lecturers. Subjects such as art and humanities can be less fulfilling. **What are the teaching staff like?** Again, depends on course, but there are some amazing lecturers with world-class reputations and a few that aren't.

Socialising

What are student societies like? Societies have really taken off in the past year or so with the addition of around 10 new ones emerging since 2007. These include everything from the discussion society to Slick and Glamorous (a talent society). **What's a typical night out?** SU bar followed by the Font (SU club). **And how much does it cost?** Varies. Because of our proximity to London, prices are higher than some competitor unions but, with numerous promotions like pound-a-pint, this restores value. **How can you get home safely?** Shuttle buses are available to ferry students home safely.

Money

Is it an expensive place to live? It's affordable for most students but not cheap. **Average price of a pint?** £2.10. **And the price of a takeaway?** £4. **What's the part-time work situation?** The SU has its own employment agency and actively seeks to pair students with part-time jobs. The university is also a large employer of students.

Summary

What's the best feature about the place? Old Hatfield and Hatfield House. **And the worst?** Hatfield town centre. **And to sum it all up?** Don't judge a book by its town centre. **More info?** Contact UHSU on 01707 285000 or visit www.uhsu.herts.ac.uk.

Heythrop College

Location:
central London
(map 3)
**Single site in
Kensington**

Heythrop College, University of London,
Kensington Square, London W8 5HQ
☎ Tel 020 7795 6600
🖶 Fax 020 7795 4200
✉ Email enquiries@heythrop.ac.uk
🖳 Website www.heythrop.ac.uk

*Student enquiries: Assistant Registrar
Applications: UCAS*

In brief

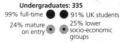

Total Students: 850

61% postgraduate
39% undergraduate

Undergraduates: 335
99% full-time
24% mature on entry
91% UK students
25% lower socio-economic groups

45% female   55% male

- **Specialist college**, part of London University.
- **Teaching staff:** 27 full-time, 10 part-time.
- **Broad study areas:** Theology, philosophy, psychology, biblical studies.

Freshers
- **Admissions information:** UCAS tariff used.
- **First degree entrants:** 125 UK, full-time.
- **Points on entry:** 240–300.
- **Drop-out rate:** 13% in 1st year.
- **Accommodation:** Some 1st years in London University accommodation.

Profile

Institution
Founded: In 17th century Liège as a Jesuit college. Later providing a residential seminary for Jesuits and other students in Oxfordshire until transfer to London in 1970. **Structural features:** Part of London University (since 1970). **Site:** Collegiate scheduled buildings in Kensington Square. **How to get there:** Kensington High Street underground station; many buses.

Courses
Awarding body: University of London. **Main undergraduate awards:** BA, BD. **Length of courses:** 3 years.

Study opportunities & careers
Library and information services: 250,000 items (many 17th-century), 150 study places. Information provision, £131 pa spent for each student (FTE). Separate IT service (although located with library), access 10 hours/day. Ratio 1:20 workstations to students, 10 points with access to library and internet. IT support from 2 full-time staff; 1-hour introduction to library and information services for new students; ad hoc IT skills courses. **Study abroad:** Some Erasmus exchanges with a number of universities in Europe. **Employment:** Christian ministry, teaching, social work, media, police force, etc.

Student services & facilities
Student advice and services: Students use university health service. **Amenities:** Refectory, college choir; proximity to theatres, cinemas, museums, galleries. **Sporting facilities:** Tennis courts; football team. **Accommodation:** No college halls of residence. Some students in London University inter-collegiate halls, rent approx £125 pw (see university website: www.lon.ac.uk/accom). Rents locally from £100 upwards.

Money
Living expenses budget: Minimum budget of £8k pa (excluding tuition fees) recommended by college. **Term-time work:** No college policy on part-time work (50% believed to have jobs); term-time work available in college library. **Financial help:** Bursaries of £1453 for students whose family income is up to £25k, tapering to nil when family income is £50k (ie bursary of 50% of maintenance

grant for which they qualify). Small access and hardship fund. **Tuition fees:** Home students pay £3225 for first degrees. International students pay £5490 pa.

Student view

A small college of London University, specialising in philosophy and theology. Being small, there is a strong communal atmosphere and the eclectic mix of ages, cultures and (usually rather strong) opinions makes for common room interaction unlike any other. SU (HSU) works hard to promote a more active social life within the college, and is an excellent way for all students to make sure their viewpoint gets across. It runs 3 JCRs (one loud, one smoky and one painted pink), with hot drinks (tea, coffee, chocolate) and biscuits (all fairtrade) and use of a microwave, toaster, fridge, pool table, table football, widescreen TV/DVD player and music system – all for a small payment each term. Shop offers popular course texts at reduced prices, together with branded college clothing, etc. Small number of students means that class sizes are small and one to one tutorials with specialised teaching staff. 1st years usually get a place in inter-collegiate halls (a women's hall is on campus), thereafter moving into shared flats and houses, or into various chaplaincies. What isn't available in college is surely on offer at ULU or one of the other London University colleges – all open to Heythrop students – especially via the reciprocal agreement with neighbouring Imperial.

Student footnotes

Housing: Inter-collegiate halls of residence then private housing (look in university accommodation lists, or *Loot*). **Drink:** ULU cheap, with promos; Greyhound, local and well patronised. **Eats:** Meal very reasonable in College; also ULU or anything on High Street Ken. **Nightlife:** ULU; also HSU trips to West End, theatres, cinemas (often with discounts). **Locals:** Posh, but good for a laugh. **Sports:** ULU facilities good; college too small for anything above 5-a-side. **Travel:** Very accessible (next to High St Ken tube) but London notoriously expensive (travel cards are available for discounts). **Financial help:** Discretionary college hardship fund. **Jobs:** Reasonable amount of work if you're not fussy; college library, local stores, etc. **Best feature:** Fun union. **And worst:** Weigh-and-pay salad (expensive). **More info?** Contact HSU (tel 020 7795 4255, email enquiries@hsu.org.uk).

Huddersfield University

Location:
Yorkshire, north of England (map 2)
Main Huddersfield campus plus centres in Barnsley and Oldham

🖳 University of Huddersfield, Queensgate, Huddersfield HD1 3DH
☎ Tel 01484 422288
📠 Fax 01484 516151
✉ Email prospectus@hud.ac.uk
💻 Website www.hud.ac.uk

Student enquiries: Admissions Office
Applications: UCAS

In brief

Total Students: 23,140

15% postgraduate
85% undergraduate

Undergraduates: 19,755

62% full-time
37% mature on entry

92% UK students
42% lower socio-economic groups

56% female   44% male

- **A modern university.**
- **Teaching staff:** 595 full-time, 647 part-time
- **Broad study areas:** Accountancy, business, law and management; marketing and retailing; logistics; hospitality, tourism and leisure; sciences; food sciences; architecture; advertising, graphic design and 3D design; fashion and textile design; fine art; multimedia and virtual reality design; multimedia and internet technology; computing and information technology; engineering and technology; audio and music technology; education and community work; human and health sciences; music and humanities; psychology; nursing; pharmacy.

Freshers

- **Admissions information:** UCAS tariff used in most cases, specific grades in others. Foundation courses available in many areas
- **First degree entrants:** 5400 UK, full-time.
- **Points on entry:** 230+ (average).
- **Drop-out rate:** 10% in 1st year.
- **Accommodation:** All 1st years housed who wish it.

Profile

Institution

Founded: 1825; university status in 1992. **Site:** Main Queensgate campus in town centre. University centres also in Barnsley and Oldham. **How to get there:** By train to Huddersfield (from Leeds or Wakefield), by road via M62, by air to Leeds/Bradford or Manchester airports. Campus within walking distance of bus and railway stations. **Special features:** Hosts annual Huddersfield Festival of Contemporary Music and Literature Festival.

Courses

Academic features: All degree courses within modular scheme. Large number of sandwich courses. **Awarding body:** University of Huddersfield. **Main undergraduate awards:** BA, BSc, BEng, LLB, BMus, BEd, MEng. **Length of courses:** 3 years; 4 years (sandwich); 2 years (BEd).

Study opportunities & careers

Library and information services: 400,000 volumes and printed journals (multiple copies of recommended books), 22,000 e-journals; 1000 study places. Information provision, £89 pa spent for each student (FTE). Separate IT service; extensive computing facilities across university, many available 24 hours/day, with access to internet and virtual learning environment. IT support from helpdesk. Introduction to general library and specific subject staff for all new students, IT induction with follow-up sessions. Resource centres at Oldham and Barnsley. **Other learning resources:** Specialist resources eg for multimedia, music technology, science and language laboratories. **Study abroad:** Small number of students spend a period abroad. Formal exchange links with universities and colleges in Scandinavia and central Europe. **Careers:** Information, advice and placement service.

Student services & facilities

Student advice and services: Student support advisers, including for overseas students; disability support; counselling; faith centre; health centre close to campus. Residential facilities for disabled students. **Amenities:** SU with bar, societies, social events. **Sporting facilities:** University sports hall with fitness centre. Municipal sports centre with Olympic-standard facilities close to campus. **Accommodation:** 2338 self-catering places (many ensuite), mainly for 1st years: £66–£86 pw (£67 sharing), 42- and 43-week contracts Sept–July (rent includes utilities and internet access). University accommodation run by private provider, Digs (see www.campusdigs.com). Plentiful private accommodation locally, approx £55 pw self-catering, plus bills.

Money

Living expenses budget: Minimum budget of £5500 pa (excluding tuition fees) recommended by university. **Term-time work:** University allows term-time work, up to maximum of 15 hours pw (estimated up to 90% 1st-year students work). University jobshop. **Financial help:** Bursaries of £500 pa for UK students whose family income is up to £25k (40% of student intake). University and government funds provide special help for self-financing students, those with dependants and students with disabilities; average award £1140. Apply to Student Finance Office for help. **Tuition fees:** Home students pay £3225 pa for first degrees, except foundation year (£1285) and placement year (no fee charged). International students pay £8250 pa (classroom), £9250 (lab/studio).

Student view

Huddersfield is on the western tip of Yorkshire and has changed in many ways over the past few years, with many exciting developments in the town centre. Now a metropolitan centre but still with the quaint, friendly feeling it's renowned for – and the university is a central part of it. Campus is compact enough for everyone to know everyone and always be a stone's throw from whatever a student wants. Numerous pubs and clubs, all student-friendly, and a new one seemingly opening every week; maybe that's why the town boasts 18,000+ students from over 80 countries. University offers range of courses, from postgraduate to HND; many are sandwich courses with an industrial placement – vital practical training. Much refurbishment and expansion at Queensgate campus, with derelict mills restored into award-winning facilities. 7-storey library and resource centre has everything students need for their studies, including 24-hour computing service for those late-night assignment sessions. Also new centres in Barnsley and Oldham. SU is social centre, in brand new building, housing a large-capacity, multi-purpose venue/bar (where there is a range of events, theme nights, guest DJs, comedy and live bands). Lounge is an alcohol-free eating area. Union also has its student advice centre and shop. Clubs and societies are growing – from rugby to fencing, caving to juggling, there's something for everyone. SU has its own newspaper, *Huddersfield Student*, for its budding student journalists. Weekends in town centre are reminiscent of Greek holiday resorts, with packed streets, open bars with music pumping out – a friendly place without trouble at the weekend.

Student footnotes

Housing: Most at Sorthes Hall student village (15 mins in free bus to/from campus), with bar and sports facilities including gym. Great new halls in town (some have Sky TV, swimming pools). For other accommodation, check out the *Examiner*, uni accommodation service or SU. **Eats:** SU coffee bar (cheap meals); Blue Rooms (vegetarian meal for £10), O'Neills (£5), the New Wharf, Nawaab (£15) and more food emporiums than you could get through in 3 years. **Drink:** Prices reasonable in SU. Numerous student-friendly bars around town: Warehouse, Yates, Evos, Zephyr, Revolution and Sharkeys all have good student deals. **Nightlife:** Good clubs all have student nights, eg Camel (Mon and Thurs), Visage (Tues), Tokyo (Wed). **Locals:** Mainly friendly and welcoming. **Sports:** University sports centre and good community sports centres, pools, etc. **Travel:** Good public transport. **Financial help:** SU can give advice about hardship funds. **Jobs:** Lots of jobs; university jobshop advertises everything suitable in town. **Informal name:** Hudds Uni. **Best features:** State-of-the-art campus. Always someone to talk to, and fun to be had. **And worst:** State-of-the-art campus. Always someone to talk to, and fun to be had! **More info?** Check out the website (www.huddersfieldstudent.com).

Hull University

Location:
north of England, on
east coast (map 2)
**Main Hull campus,
plus campus at
Scarborough**

✉ The University of Hull, Hull HU6 7RX
☎ Tel 01482 466100
🖷 Fax 01482 442290 (Scarborough campus 01723 362392)
✉ Email admissions@hull.ac.uk
💻 Website www.hull.ac.uk

*Student enquiries: Admissions Service. Prospectus hotline
(tel 0870 126 2000)
Applications: UCAS*

In brief

Total Students: 22,275

16% postgraduate
84% undergraduate

Undergraduates: 18,710
56% full-time ● ● 91% UK students
26% mature ● ● 31% lower
on entry ● ● socio-economic
groups

59% female   41% male

- **Traditional well-established university.**
- **Teaching staff:** 1000 full-time and part-time.
- **Broad study areas:** Sciences, engineering, accounting and finance, business, European languages, computing, social sciences, humanities, nursing, law, education, drama and dance, music, psychology, medicine. You can look up the *Hull York Medical School* separately.

Freshers

- **Admissions information:** AS-levels accepted in combination with 2–3 A-levels or equivalent.
- **First degree entrants:** 3005 UK, full-time.
- **Points on entry:** 260+ (average).
- **Drop-out rate:** 6% in 1st year.
- **Accommodation:** Almost all 1st years housed.

Profile

Institution

Founded: 1927, charter granted in 1954. **Site:** Hull Campus, main campus 2 miles north of city centre; Scarborough Campus, small campus 1 mile from Scarborough town centre, about 40 miles from Hull. **How to get there:** Inter-city rail services, M62, Humberside Airport; bus to university from city centre. **Structural features:** Hull York Medical School, joint with York University. Logistics Institute.

Courses

Academic features: Teaching year of 2 semesters, 15 weeks each. Modular degree structure. Foundation year business, science, engineering degrees for students without relevant A-levels. **Awarding body:** University of Hull. **Main undergraduate awards:** BA, BEng, MBBS, MEng, BMus, BSc, LLB, MBMSci, MPhys, MChem, MPhysGeog. **Length of courses:** 3 or 4 years; 5 years (medicine).

Study opportunities & careers

Library and information services: 2 university libraries (Brynmor Jones library at Hull, Keith Donaldson library at Scarborough). 1 million+ volumes; 2700 print, 8000 electronic periodical titles, 84 electronic bibliographies and databases, 2200 study places. Information provision, £106 pa spent for each student (FTE). Specialist collections: Philip Larkin collection, history of Labour and left-wing movements, family and estate papers, 20th-century poetry; distinguished art collection specialising in British art 1890–1940; Thompson collection of Chinese ceramics. Computer centre with 12 public clusters, plus departmental facilities, network connections in all study bedrooms, dial-in access to network. Helpdesk support. ICT training and documentation available. **Other learning resources:** Audio-visual centre and language institute. **Study abroad:** Under 10% of students spend time abroad. Exchange links with 120+ institutions in USA, Europe and elsewhere, all open to non-language students. **Careers:** Information, advice and placement service.

Student services & facilities

Student advice and services: Advice centre, counselling service, nightline, chaplains. Nursery with 50 full-time and some part-time places (cost according to income). Facilities for disabled students. **Amenities:** Bookshop on campus; snack bars, restaurants, SU bars and nightclub, shop, travel bureau, internet café, laundrette, television rooms, 150+ active student societies; Middleton Hall (auditorium of over 500). **Sporting facilities:** Indoor purpose-built sports and fitness centre and playing fields (including floodlit all-weather surface) all on campus. **Accommodation:** All 1st years, except very late admissions, offered university-owned or head-leased accommodation (40% of all students). In Hull: catered halls £106–£123 pw, semi-catered £84–£98 pw, all 31-week contracts; self-catering £58–£84 pw, contracts vary (31, 38, 42 and 50 weeks). In Scarborough: catered halls £109 pw, 31–37-week contracts; self-catering £55.50–£109.50, 42 or 50 week contracts. 20% of 1st-year students live at home or make own arrangements. Local rent approx £160 pm.

Money

Living expenses budget: Minimum budget of £5500 pa (excluding tuition fees) recommended by university. **Term-time work:** University allows term-time work for full-time students. SU job exchange. **Financial help:** Bursaries of £1k pa for students whose family income is up to £25k; of £500 pa where family income is £25k–£40k. Also a range of scholarships (£1500 pa) awarded on academic merit; some competitive bursaries (£500 pa) for local students. Plus £850,780 government hardship funds, 484 students helped (from £100–£3500, average award £1140). All cases of financial hardship are assessed; various special university funds to help, eg students who are disabled, or with childcare or travel costs. Apply for help to student support services. **Tuition fees:** Home students pay £3225 pa for first degrees. International students pay £9500 pa (classroom), £11,500 pa (lab/studio), £22k pa (medicine).

Student view

Helen Gibson, SU President (recent graduate, British Politics and Legislative Studies)

Living

What's it like as a place to live? Fantastic, just the right size for a city, friendly and cheap. **How's the student accommodation?** OK–average. Some houses good, some not so much. 'Student village' 5-min walk from university. **What's the student population like?** Quite diverse, though not as much as some larger cities. Lots of part-timers and international students. **How do students and locals get on?** Fine, no major problems. Lots of residents live near and in the same area as students.

Studying

What's it like as a place to study? Good, all on one campus. Union currently lobbying for 24-hour opening of library. **What are the teaching staff like?** Good teaching university, lots of support staff.

Socialising

What are student societies like? Brilliant, run by union, over 70 different societies. 60 sports clubs, run by union, and lots of volunteering. **What's a typical night out?** SU nightclub, Asylum. **And how much does it cost?** £3.50 to get in, need about £15–£20. **How can you get home safely?** Taxi rank just outside, free buses during welcome week.

Money

Is it an expensive place to live? Loan just about lasts if you're sensible, very cheap. **Average price of a pint?** £1.70. **And the price of a takeaway?** £4. **What's the part-time work situation?** University doesn't object. Lots of jobs. Union runs job exchange.

Summary

What's the best feature about the place? The SU, HUU. One of the top nightclubs and one of the top UK SUs. **And the worst?** Geographical location. **And to sum it all up?** Surprisingly brilliant.

Past students: Roger McGough (poet and broadcaster), Philip Larkin (poet, was librarian), John McCarthy (former hostage, journalist), Jill Morrell (humanitarian and author), John Prescott MP, Anthony Minghella (film director), Sally Lindsay (*Coronation Street* barmaid).

More info? Visit website (www.hullstudent.com).

Hull York Medical School

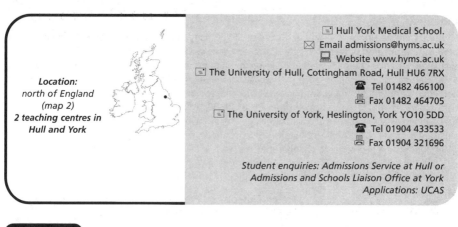

Location:
north of England
(map 2)
2 teaching centres in
Hull and York

Hull York Medical School.
Email admissions@hyms.ac.uk
Website www.hyms.ac.uk
The University of Hull, Cottingham Road, Hull HU6 7RX
Tel 01482 466100
Fax 01482 464705
The University of York, Heslington, York YO10 5DD
Tel 01904 433533
Fax 01904 321696

*Student enquiries: Admissions Service at Hull or
Admissions and Schools Liaison Office at York
Applications: UCAS*

In brief

Total Students: 670

25% mature on entry ● 95% UK students

60% female 40% male

- **Specialist medical school.** A partnership between the universities of Hull and York and the NHS.
- **Teaching staff:** 79 full-time and part-time.
- **Broad study area:** Medicine.

Freshers
- **Admissions information:** Typically 3 A-levels (AAB, including biology and chemistry; excluding general studies and critical thinking) and 1 AS-level (at least grade B); all applicants must sit UKCAT.
- **First degree entrants:** 130 UK students, full-time (11 places for international students).
- **Points on entry:** 390+ (average).
- **Drop-out rate:** 1–2% in 1st year.
- **Accommodation:** All 1st years housed who apply in time.

Profile

Institution

Founded: 2002. **Structural features:** A partnership between universities of Hull and York and the NHS. **Sites:** First two years spent at either Hull University or York University. Teaching in Years 3–5 in centres across NHS area of Hull and East Riding, York and North Yorkshire and Northern Lincolnshire. **Special features:** Hull's existing postgraduate medical school has strong research in cardiovascular medicine, cancer surgery, oncology and medical imaging. York's bioscience, health science and social science departments have particular strengths in molecular medicine, psychology and health and social services research.

Courses

Academic features: Academic and clinical aspects of the course fully integrated. Course outcome-based, with extensive use of problem-based learning in first 2 years. 50% clinical experience outside hospitals. Extensive use of electronic resources. **Awarding body:** Joint award by universities of Hull and York. **Main undergraduate awards:** MB BS. **Length of courses:** 5 years.

Study opportunities & careers

Library and information services: Libraries and IT services at both universities with access 24-hours/day (see descriptions for *Hull University* and *York University*). **Study abroad:** Option of taking elective overseas in Year 5.

Student services & facilities

Student advice and services, amenities and sporting facilities: See descriptions for *Hull University* and *York University*. **Accommodation:** All 1st years who apply in good time can be in university accommodation; most in privately rented accommodation thereafter. For details, see *Hull University* and *York University*. When away from Hull or York, NHS accommodation usually available.

Money

Living expenses budget: Minimum budget of £6k–£7k (excluding tuition fees) recommended by medical school. **Financial help:** Bursary of £1024 pa for UK students whose family income is up to £23k, of £512 where family income is £23k–£38,300. **Tuition fees:** Home students pay £3225 pa. International students pay £22k pa (fee fixed for full 5 years of course).

Imperial College

Location:
*central London
(map 3)
Single Kensington
campus and London
hospitals*

✉ Imperial College London, South Kensington,
London SW7 2AZ
☎ Tel 020 7589 5111
✉ Email admissions@imperial.ac.uk
💻 Website www.imperial.ac.uk

*Student enquiries: Admissions Office
Applications: UCAS*

In brief

Total Students: 13,410

38% postgraduate
62% undergraduate

Undergraduates: 8350
100% full-time   66% UK students
6% mature   18% lower
on entry   socio-economic
               groups

36% female   64% male

- **World-class research-intensive institution.**
- **Teaching staff:** 1200 full-time and part-time plus some 180 visiting.
- **Broad study areas:** Engineering and computing; physical and life sciences; medicine; management.

Freshers

- **Admissions information:** College minimum entrance requirements fully accept AS-levels although most courses have A-level requirements. Virtually all offers made on basis of specified subject grades.
- **First degree entrants:** 1370 UK, full-time.
- **Points on entry:** 340+ (average).
- **Drop-out rate:** 3% in 1st year.
- **Accommodation:** All 1st years housed.

Profile

Institution

Founded: 1907. Previously part of London University; became university in its own right in 2007. **Site:** 16-acre site in South Kensington. Medical school sites in Hammersmith, Paddington, Chelsea, Fulham. **How to get there:** South Kensington and Gloucester Road underground stations and buses for main site; all medical school sites close to tube and buses. **Special features:** Established 'to give the highest specialised instruction and to provide the fullest equipment for the most advanced training and research in various branches of science especially in its application to industry'. Applications from women are strongly encouraged. Director of Music leads a variety of musical activities.

Courses

Academic features: MSci in chemistry with conservation science; 6-year MB BS. Humanities programme offering weekly lectures in associated studies and foreign language courses. **Awarding body:** Imperial College London. **Main undergraduate awards:** MEng, BEng, BSc, MSci, MB BS. **Length of courses:** 3, 4 or 5 years (science, agriculture and engineering); 6 years (medicine).

Study opportunities & careers

Library and information services: Central library and 5 departmental libraries at South Kensington campus; 5 medical and 2 life science campus libraries. Over 1 million volumes, 20,000+ periodical titles (print and electronic); 2000 study places. Information provision, £317 pa spent for each student (FTE). Also provides literacy training. Separate IT support service, high speed and wireless network access to on-site and off-site resources. Workstations in every department offer wide range of application programs with further general workstation access provided in the central library. Helpdesk and additional support via specialist IT staff. **Other learning resources:** 240-acre college field station at Silwood Park (near Ascot). Specialist collections: Haldane collection covers humanities, general reading and music including CDs and scores. **Study abroad:** Wide range of exchange schemes with prestigious technological institutions across Europe allows students to undertake project work for 3–12 months abroad. Strong commitment to year abroad courses (available in most departments); extensive network in EU through Socrates-Erasmus scheme. **Employment:** Traditionally industry; but increasing number of graduates enter accountancy, banking, insurance, etc, as well as general commercial areas.

Student services & facilities

Student advice and services: Vacation training scheme, careers advisory service, student accommodation office, health centre, student counsellor, welfare adviser, nightline, nursery, disabilities officer, college tutor. Information and advice centre, chaplaincy. **Amenities:** SU building with refectory, bar, bookshop, etc; wide range of societies. **Sporting facilities:** Sports centre at South Kensington campus (indoor 25m deck-level swimming pool, sauna, steam room and spa, 5-court sports hall, climbing wall, 70-station fitness gym, aerobics studio, squash courts, juice bar). Other sites have own sporting facilities. Boathouse at Putney, includes gym, workshop, physiotherapy and sports therapy. **Accommodation:** 1st years guaranteed accommodation (subject to certain conditions) in college or university inter-collegiate halls (25% of all students housed). 3000 undergraduate places: all self-catering, £92–£142 pw (£112–£156 ensuite, £55–£110 shared); 39-week contracts. Intercollegiate halls approx £112–£175 pw for catered places. Privately owned accommodation locally approx £105+ pw for self-catering.

Money

Living expenses budget: Minimum budget of £10,500 for each academic year recommended by college (excluding tuition fees), £14k for a calendar year. **Term-time work:** College allows term-time work; limit of 6–8 hours pw. Some work available in college bars, offices, library. **Financial help:** Bursaries of £3k pa for UK students whose family income is up to £25k (plus £300 for those with 3 A-levels grade A); bursary of £2k pa where family income is £25k–£30k, tapering down to £50 where family income is £55k–£60k. Range of scholarships, value £100–£5k pa eg for engineering, medicine, rowing, music. Also £390k government funds (average award £990); £318k own funds (average award £780). Own funds also available for those experiencing unforeseen short-term need. Apply to student finance office for help. **Tuition fees:** Home students pay £3225 pa for first degrees. International students pay £15,500 (maths), £18,200–£19,450 (lab-based courses), £23,800–£35,500 (medicine).

(Student view)

Right next to the tube in South Kensington, it's a mixture of old and new, surrounded by museums and the Albert Hall; also various other medical sites (eg St Mary's Paddington, Charing Cross and Westminster hospitals). Well known for clubs and societies – 248 of them – including most religions and nationalities, theatre productions and own cinema (3rd largest independent screen in London); several sports clubs are UK leaders. College owns 3

339

sports fields, a sports centre, tennis courts, several gyms and swimming pools. All freshers get a place in halls, either Imperial hall or London University inter-collegiate hall. Good variety of accommodation available and halls are safe, friendly places. Really cosmopolitan: third of students originate outside the UK. Work is tough but drop-out rate is low and there is a strong support network. Graduates get more than the average graduate salary and increase their salaries faster and higher. Humanities programme, covering the arts and languages, to broaden education. Some courses include years abroad or in industry. Still people find time for part-time work, many within the union, which is a safe and friendly environment. If the money is really tight, union adviser can help find money from hardship funds, etc. Union (ICU) is biggest student venue in central London. Events throughout the year including comedy nights, music, live bands and bar nights. 6 sabbatical and whole host of student officers to help you. ICU handbook is a guide to all the activities and life in London. Anyone can fit in at IC and there's plenty of union support.

Student footnotes

Housing: Never cheap but then it is London; shared rooms cheaper. Small chance of married quarters. For private accommodation, look in *Loot* and ask Accommodation Office. **Eats:** Union runs Da Vinci's café/bar, burger bar, pizza bar, refectory and DBs baguette bar. **Drink:** Many bars – 3 union, cocktail, college bars; others at medical campus. London Pride is good local brew. **Nightlife:** Weekly nights, bands, quizzes, comedy, cocktail and bar nights. Many free gigs/exhibitions in London (pub gigs good value). Union cinema (large screen). **Locals:** Reasonably friendly. **Sports:** Sport generally cheap; campus sports centre for, eg, swimming, squash, weights (free for gym and swim). Grounds at Heathrow, Teddington and Cobham. **Travel:** *A-Z London* essential! Car parking near to impossible. Good for bikes, tubes and buses. STA branch on campus; expedition fund available. **Financial help:** Access fund arranged by College (rarely used up). **Jobs:** Term-time work easy to get. SU employment service, loads of opportunities. Good prospects for holiday jobs, temping or in the City. **Best features:** Social life; brilliant degree; extra-curricular opportunities. **And worst:** Undeserved 'geeky' image. **Informal name:** IC. **Past students:** H G Wells (author), Sir Lewis Casson (actor and director), Sir Granville Bantock (composer), Joan Ruddock (politician), Sir John Egan (ex-BAA), Sir Alexander Fleming (discovered penicillin), Thomas Huxley (biologist), Dr David Livingstone (explorer), Raj Persaud (psychiatrist), Francis Wilson (meteorologist), Brian May (Queen guitarist), Trevor Philips (Equality and Human Rights Commission). **More info?** Call ICU President (tel 020 7594 8060) or visit website (www.union.imperial.ac.uk).

Keele University

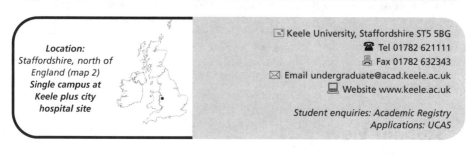

Location:
Staffordshire, north of England (map 2)
Single campus at Keele plus city hospital site

Keele University, Staffordshire ST5 5BG
☎ Tel 01782 621111
🖷 Fax 01782 632343
✉ Email undergraduate@acad.keele.ac.uk
💻 Website www.keele.ac.uk

Student enquiries: Academic Registry
Applications: UCAS

In brief

Total Students: 10,670

34% postgraduate
66% undergraduate

Undergraduates: 7010
86% full-time   93% UK students
23% mature   27% lower
on entry   socio-economic
                 groups

63% female   37% male

- **A top UK research-intensive university.**
- **Teaching staff:** 455 full-time and part-time.
- **Broad study areas:** business; health; Humanities; law; medicine; sciences; social sciences

Freshers

- **Admissions information:** AS-levels accepted in combination with 2+ A-levels or equivalent. UCAS tariff used on most courses (except medicine, physiotherapy, pharmacy).
- **First degree entrants:** 1495 UK, full-time.
- **Points on entry:** 265+ (average).
- **Drop-out rate:** 9% in 1st year.
- **Accommodation:** Almost all 1st years housed.

Profile

Institution

Founded: 1949, from University College of North Staffordshire. **Site:** Campus 2 miles from Newcastle-under-Lyme. **How to get there:** By rail to Stoke (5 miles away) or Crewe (14 miles) and then by bus to campus; by coach (to Hanley bus station in Stoke); by road on M6 (junctions 15/16 about 20 mins from campus).

Courses

Academic features: All courses modular. 500+ dual Honours combinations available. **Awarding body:** Keele University. **Main undergraduate awards:** BA, BSc, MGeoscience, LLB, MPharm, MBChB. **Length of courses:** 3 years; 4 years (foundation programmes, undergraduate Master's); 5–6 years (medicine).

Study opportunities & careers

Library and information services: 475,000 volumes, 1700 print journals, 20,000 electronic journals, plus electronic databases, e-books etc; 700+ study places, separate short-loan library. Information provision, £122 pa spent for each student (FTE). Library open 13 hours/day (10 at weekends). Networked PCs in library, plus wireless network for students' laptops; plus computers for student use around campus; almost all rooms in halls on university network. IT service desk available 55+ hours/week in term time; online IT skills courses. Special collections include: Arnold Bennett papers, Warrillow photographs, Wedgwood archives. **Study abroad:** Over 100 students spend 5–10 months at one of 60 partner universities in 13 different countries worldwide, most open to non-language specialists (in addition to language and sandwich placements). Most students may study a foreign language as part of their course. **Careers:** Information and appointments service.

Student services & facilities

Student advice and services: Doctors, dentist, FPA, counsellor, solicitor (SU), chaplains, financial adviser, counselling service, nursery. **Amenities:** Bookshop on campus; SU premises; supermarket, newsagent and bank; variety of bars and restaurants. **Sporting facilities:** Multi-purpose sports centre with adjoining playing fields, all-weather pitches, tennis courts; squash courts, climbing wall and fitness centre (incorporating state-of-the-art kinesis equipment). **Accommodation:** University accommodation guaranteed (for first and final years) for students with Keele as their firm choice. 3200 self-catering places available at £61–£95 pw (contracts of 33–37 weeks). Private accommodation locally approx £50–£60 pw + bills.

Money (💰)

Living expenses budget: Minimum budget of £5k–£6500 pa (excluding tuition fees) recommended by university. **Term-time work:** University allows term-time work for full-time students. Some work available on campus in bars, catering outlets, etc; also SU jobshop helps find work on or off campus. **Financial help:** Bursaries of £800 pa for UK students whose family income is up to £25k; and of £400 pa for students from partner colleges and schools with family income up to £40k. Scholarships of £1k pa for students with 3 A-levels at grade A (or equivalent), whose family income is up to £40k. Also help for students who have been in care and those studying abroad. Access to learning fund helps students experiencing financial hardship (some 500 students a year). Also short-term loans. Apply to student financial support office for help. **Tuition fees:** Home students pay £3225 pa for first degrees. International students pay £8500–£9k pa (classroom), £10,200–£11,300 (lab-based), £17k–£20,700 (medicine).

Student view | Talah Omran, KUSU President

Living

What's it like as a place to live? Keele has an amazing vibe that is unique and different from anywhere else. It has one of the biggest campuses in Europe and you truly feel an amazing community vibe. Most of the resources you need are found on campus and it has such a great and all-inclusive social buzz that you feel at home from the minute you get here. **How's the student accommodation?** Accommodation here is quite varied. It ranges from your standard student room to brand new ensuites in flats, with over 70% of our student population living on campus. One of the brilliant things we have here at Keele is that third-year students are guaranteed on-campus accommodation as well as the normal 1st years, which is a major plus. Keele also offers family flats to students with children, and a health centre and dentists is also located on campus. **What's the student population like?** We have one of the most diverse populations here at Keele, with students coming from as far away as New Zealand, Burma, China and so on. We are located in the Midlands, at the heart of the country, which means that we get students from absolutely every corner of the UK. There truly is a sense of belonging here at Keele, which is sometimes hard to find in other places. **How do students and locals get on?** Keele Village is found on the outskirts of Keele and we have a few events that take place there organised by some of our societies. They are very successful events that the local village love to partake in. A unique feature of Keele is that we have members of staff living on campus too. This might sound a little odd but it actually works quite well and once again builds up a strong community feel.

Studying

What's it like as a place to study? Keele is a fantastic place to study. We are one of very few universities that offers dual Honour degrees in most of our courses, which allows students to gain qualifications in 2 subjects. This not only provides our students with multi-discipline learning techniques but is a unique selling point with potential future employers. We are 11th in the graduate prospects table and have some of the most amazing departments in the country. **What are the teaching staff like?** They are extremely helpful. Not only are students able to approach them during the day or via email whenever they want but there is also an office hours system where you can drop in and talk about any problems or queries you may have.

Socialising

What are student societies like? At Keele we have 60 – yes, that's 60 – societies! These range from rock societies, dance sport, law societies to our Athletic Union, which has over

1000 members. And if you don't like any of the above you can set up your own really easily! **What's a typical night out?** Here is where the SU shines! Our best nights out are at the SU. We have a wide range of events, such as arranging for amazing acts to come in and play on gig nights. This includes Taoi Cruz and Less than Jake at fantastic prices. We also host many other events that are applicable to a wide range of students, both alcoholic and non-alcoholic. However, your typical night out would start at one of our many halls bars, found at each of the halls of residence, to socialise with a group of friends. It would then follow with a brilliant night out at the Union where you can boogie on down! We have won 'best bar' 2 years in a row and have 4 main bars with a shots bar and a bottle bar. We also have a cocktail bar, which doubles up as a coffee bar during the day. **How can you get home safely?** Keele University SU runs a safety bus service, which is completely free of charge. This is available to all Keele students and will take you home whether you live on campus or not. It is run by our security staff and so is incredibly safe. We have 2 minibuses that provide this service and it's even available to pick students up if they are out in the local area. The SU also has a free direct line to one of the local cab firms.

Past students: David Pownall (author and dramatist); Claire Short, Alan Michael, Ian Taylor, Jack Straw (politicians); Gerry Northam (reporter and presenter); Sue Robbie (presenter); Bernard Lloyd (actor); Michael Mansfield QC; Slash (Guns n' Roses). **More info?** Contact SU President (tel 01782 583701) or visit the website (www.kusu.net.)

Kent

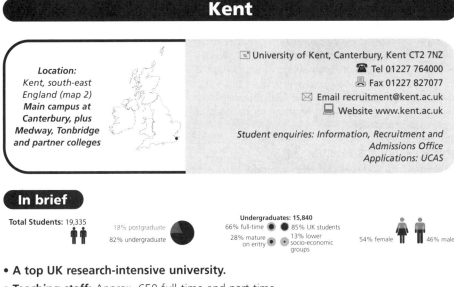

Location:
Kent, south-east England (map 2)
Main campus at Canterbury, plus Medway, Tonbridge and partner colleges

University of Kent, Canterbury, Kent CT2 7NZ
☎ Tel 01227 764000
🖨 Fax 01227 827077
✉ Email recruitment@kent.ac.uk
💻 Website www.kent.ac.uk

Student enquiries: Information, Recruitment and Admissions Office
Applications: UCAS

In brief

Total Students: 19,335
18% postgraduate
82% undergraduate

Undergraduates: 15,840
66% full-time | 85% UK students
28% mature on entry | 13% lower socio-economic groups

54% female | 46% male

- **A top UK research-intensive university.**
- **Teaching staff:** Approx. 650 full-time and part-time.
- **Broad study areas:** Humanities, maths and statistics, natural sciences, law, social sciences, information technology, pharmacy.

Freshers

- **Admissions information:** AS-levels accepted in combination with 2+ A-levels or equivalent. UCAS tariff used on basis of best 21 units.
- **First degree entrants:** 3280 UK, full-time.

- **Points on entry:** 300+ (average).
- **Drop-out rate:** 7% in 1st year.
- **Accommodation:** All 1st years housed that need it.

Profile

Institution

Founded: 1965. **Site:** 300-acre campus, on outskirts of Canterbury; also Medway Campus (Chatham), plus centres in Tonbridge and in Brussels. **How to get there:** Good road and rail links between Canterbury, London and Europe: 55 mins by train from London Victoria or Charing Cross; served by M2, M20 and M25. Heathrow and Gatwick airports, Channel ports (Dover, Ramsgate) and Channel Tunnel all 1+ hour drive. **Structural features:** Campus in Chatham joint with Greenwich University (and a joint school of pharmacy) and Canterbury Christ Church University. Association with Imperial College at Wye in Ashford. Links with 4 French universities and a centre in Brussels.

Courses

Academic features: Wide range of courses: single subject, joint and multi-disciplinary and those with a year abroad or working in industry. **Awarding body:** University of Kent. **Main undergraduate awards:** BA, BEng, BSc, LLB, BBA, MDrama, MPharm. **Length of courses:** 3 years; others 4 years.

Study opportunities & careers

Library and information services: Over 1 million books, periodicals, pamphlets, slides, microfilms and electronic media. Special collections: Early and rare materials, research collections and archives; close links with Cathedral library. Information provision, £114 pa spent for each student (FTE). Separate IT service, access 24 hours/day. 600+ public access computer terminals on site, with access to library and internet (ratio 1:16 workstations to students). IT support from computing reception, helpdesk, online help and documentation. Library skills training programme, online packages; IT skills courses including html and European Computer Driving Licence. **Study abroad:** Formal Erasmus and other exchange links with many EU universities/colleges – open to students in a range of disciplines, eg computer science, drama, economics, law, maths and social psychology. **Careers:** Careers advisory service.

Student services & facilities

Student advice and services: Personal tutorial system; health and counselling service; disability support unit; learning resources centre; SU provides legal and financial advice; day nursery; chaplaincy; travel bureau. **Amenities:** Blackwells bookshop; Gulbenkian Theatre; Cinema 3 (regional film theatre); own radio station; purpose-built nightclub with bars and bistro all on site. **Sporting facilities:** Sports centre provides facilities for over 30 different activities (including coaching to international standard). **Accommodation:** All 1st-year students offered accommodation. 4300 places in Canterbury, some ensuite and all with internet connections: rent £83–£140 pw self-catering, 39-week contracts; £101–£156 pw BandB, 31-week contracts or longer. Privately owned accommodation locally £70–£110 pw plus bills, 52-week contracts.

Money

Living expenses budget: Minimum budget of £7k–£12k pa (excluding tuition fees) recommended by university. **Term-time work:** Student Jobshop. **Financial help:** Bursaries of £1k pa for UK students whose family income is up to £25k; of £750 pa where family income is £25k–£28,500; £500 pa where it is £28,500–£34k; and £250 where family income is £34k–£40k. Also 25 pa scholarships (mostly of £1k pa) for academic excellence, sport and music. £346k government funds, 740 students helped (almost all who applied), average amount £200–£500. Special help to students not publicly funded (assigned prior to start of course). **Tuition fees:** Home students pay £3225 pa for first degrees (less on foundation year). International students pay £9870 pa (classroom), £11,990 (architecture and lab-based courses).

Student view

Canterbury is a great campus, especially in the summer when the winds aren't blowing you off the hill! Beautiful, well-kept grounds, with an amazing view overlooking the city and cathedral. Just out of town (20-min walk down the hill) but buses every 15 mins and plenty of taxis around. Security escort service available to all students 24 hours a day and free night bus either to town or surrounding areas. 6 computer rooms open 24 hours a day, and the library has long opening times (extended around exam periods). Relatively easy to change course during first term, depending on faculty and space available on new course. Job opportunities both on and off campus – jobshop helps students find work. Hardship funds available (lots of forms and all are interviewed). Courses are varied and workload depends on course. Multicultural university (over 120 different nationalities) but large number from London and the south/south-east. Active SU (6 full-time sabbatical officers), a nightclub on campus (the Venue), student advice centre, campus shop, jobshop, bars, etc 110 societies which cater for all tastes, including 38 sports clubs (good sporting facilities). Student nightlife focuses around the Venue and the other 6 campus bars – each has its own personality, all are friendly. Pubs and bars in town are great and a good variety (a different pub for every day of the year!). Nightclubs not so good – limited selection in town. Cinema and theatre in town; Gulbenkian theatre and films also shown on campus. Events continually put on by SU, eg Summer Ball; Winter Ball organised by RAG (Raising and Giving). Housing in Canterbury not cheap and of variable quality; list of vetted landlords and agencies available. Most students live off campus in their 2nd and 3rd years. One of the best things is that it becomes a community – great college spirit and it is impossible to walk from one end of campus to the other without seeing people you know!

Student footnotes

Housing: Little that is cheap in Canterbury; check accommodation lists, letting agencies. **Eats:** Meals reasonable on campus. Wide variety of cheap places, including ethnic (Mexican to Indian); the Lighthouse, Marlowes also good (£6–£15 a head). **Drink:** Shepherd Neame is excellent local brewer. Pubs: Hobgoblin, the Cherry Tree. Union bar cheapest by far (£1.80+ a pint). **Nightlife:** SU club (late licence 6 nights/week), comedy, live music. The Venue, Works, Chicago Rock Café and Penny Theatre are popular. Marlowe Theatre gets all major touring plays. **Locals:** Generally quite friendly; lots of students in the area. **Sports:** Good sports centre on campus. In town, sports centre and swimming pool. **Travel:** Buses cheap, trains adequate. **Financial help:** Union welfare fund – limited budget. Access funds. **Jobs:** Available if you are prepared to search and to work for peanuts; usually bar work in town. **Buzz-words:** K, R, E, D – the 4 colleges: Keynes, Rutherford, Eliot, Darwin (all references to rooms, abbreviate the college names). JCC – Junior College Committee (college part of the SU). **Best features:** Great setting, lots of bars, good atmosphere. **And worst:** Very windy. **Past students:** Kazuo Ishiguro (author), Paul Ross (TV presenter), Gavin Esler (news reporter), Alan Davis (comedian), Tom Wilkinson (sculptor). **More info?** Enquiries to SU President (tel 01227 824200, email union-president@kent.ac.uk) or visit www.kentunion.co.uk.

King's College London

Location:
central London
(map 3)
**4 main campuses in
central London,
1 in south-east
London
(Denmark Hill)**

King's College London, Strand, London WC2R 2LS
☎ Tel 020 7836 5454
💻 Website www.kcl.ac.uk

*Student enquiries: specific School Office for course
Applications: UCAS*

In brief

Total Students: 22,275

 16% postgraduate
84% undergraduate

Undergraduates: 18,710
56% full-time ● ● 91% UK students
26% mature ● ● 31% lower
on entry   socio-economic
            groups

 59% female   41% male

- **A top UK research-intensive institution.** Part of University of London.
- **Teaching staff:** 2827 full-time and part-time.
- **Broad study areas:** Biomedical and health sciences, dentistry, humanities, law, medicine, nursing and midwifery, physical sciences and engineering, social sciences and public policy.

Freshers

- **Admissions information:** AS-levels accepted in combination with 2 (usually 3+) A-levels or equivalent. UCAS tariff not used; offers expressed in terms of grades.
- **First degree entrants:** 2560 UK, full-time.
- **Points on entry:** 310 average.
- **Drop-out rate:** 5% in 1st year.
- **Accommodation:** Almost all 1st years housed.

Profile

Institution

Founded: 1829. **Structural features:** Founding college of University of London (together with University College) and remains part of the university; fourth oldest in England. **Site:** 4 central riverside campuses plus one in Denmark Hill: Strand Campus, between House of Parliament and St Paul's Cathedral (law, humanities, physical sciences and engineering, social science and public policy); Waterloo Campus, next to South Bank Centre (nursing and midwifery, education, biomedical and health sciences); Guy's Campus at London Bridge (medicine, dentistry, biomedical and health sciences); St Thomas' Campus, opposite Houses of Parliament (medicine, dentistry); Denmark Hill Campus in south-east London (medical and dental research and teaching, Institute of Psychiatry). **How to get there:** Good underground and bus services to all campuses. Strand Campus close to many underground/rail stations (Charing Cross, Embankment, Temple, Covent Garden, Waterloo) and bus routes; Waterloo and Guy's campuses are adjacent to Waterloo and London Bridge stations respectively. **Special features:** Excellent connections to academic and cultural resources of London. Teaching informed by world-class research and strong commitment to advances in educational technology.

Courses

Academic features: 9 schools of study, offering 170 undergraduate programmes. **Awarding body:** King's College London (for most programmes). **Main undergraduate awards:** BA, BDS, BEng, MEng, BMus, MPharm, BSc, MSci, LLB, MBBS, BSc with RGN. **Length of courses:** 3 years; others 4–6 years.

Study opportunities & careers

Library and information services: Integrated library, archive and IT service: access to multi-disciplinary, multi-campus information resource base including special collections, over a million books and thousands of journals; on-campus and remote access to electronic information. Lending, reference, copying and scanning facilities. Subject information specialists; help desks with qualified staff. Network of 1600 PC workstations (many open out of hours); wireless capability at each main campus as well as halls of residence. Email and training opportunities to improve use of information tools, self-paced web tutorials and hands-on information literacy training. Information provision, £190 pa spent for each student (FTE). Specialist collections: Enk (classics); Burrows (modern Greek and Byzantine studies); Box (Old Testament); Liddell Hart (military studies); Ford (science); Adam Archive; Marsden (travel, history and philosophy). **Study abroad:** Student exchange programmes with prestigious universities in Europe, North American, Asia and Australia. **Careers:** Information, advice, job-seeking help and vacancy service for part-time, vacation and permanent employment.

Student services & facilities

Student advice and services: Doctors, counsellors, psychotherapists, chaplains, disability advisers, student advisers. **Sporting facilities:** 3 outdoor sports facilities (at New Malden, Honor Oak and Cobham); teams in rugby, football, netball, lacrosse, cricket in BUCS and ULU competitions. Rifle range at Strand; kinetic gym at Waterloo; swimming pool and gym at Guy's Campus. (Guy's and St Thomas' rugby club is oldest in the world.) **Accommodation:** All new students offered 1 year in college or university intercollegiate accommodation. 3254 places available: 1338 in halls, 1321 in self-catering apartments, 595 in intercollegiate halls. College halls: self-catering places at £92–£99 pw (£67 pw shared), catered places £108 pw; apartments £119 pw; all 40-week contracts (but extensions possible). Intercollegiate halls £106–£175 pw (£102–£106 pw shared). Privately rented accommodation locally, rent £60–£95 pw.

Money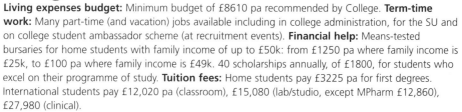

Living expenses budget: Minimum budget of £8610 pa recommended by College. **Term-time work:** Many part-time (and vacation) jobs available including in college administration, for the SU and on college student ambassador scheme (at recruitment events). **Financial help:** Means-tested bursaries for home students with family income of up to £50k: from £1250 pa where family income is £25k, to £100 pa where family income is £49k. 40 scholarships annually, of £1800, for students who excel on their programme of study. **Tuition fees:** Home students pay £3225 pa for first degrees. International students pay £12,020 pa (classroom), £15,080 (lab/studio, except MPharm £12,860), £27,980 (clinical).

Student view
(Main campus)

A multi-site institution right in the heart of London, it's a vibrant go-ahead college of London University. Impressive academic standards are reached in a wide range of subjects with diverse course structures. KCLSU, the SU, boasts a varied and high-quality ents programme centred mainly on the Strand campus and at Guy's (London Bridge). Strand and Waterloo campuses are within walking distance of the major tourist attractions and theatreland. An exciting and stimulating place to enjoy student life.

Student footnotes

Housing: Halls – varied, all over London, some expensive. Excellent college-run head-leasing scheme. **Eats:** KCLSU has an original and varied menu at all bars in the evening, and coffee shops on all 3 sites; also College outlets. Restaurants everywhere. **Drink:** SU runs The Waterfront and Tutu's at the Strand, and Guy's Bar and Inverse at London Bridge. **Nightlife:** Various club nights throughout the week: cheese, indie, R'n'B, hip-hop. Lots of new bands. **Sports:** College sports ground at Berrylands and Honor Oak Park; KCLSU gym at Waterloo. Also good indoor sports facilities at ULU. **Travel:** Extensive exchange programme, scholarships, STA travel shop at the Strand. **Financial help:** Access funds, Principal's fund and overseas students' fund. **Jobs:** KCLSU casual work (bars, catering, shops and venues). **Past students:** Archbishop Desmond Tutu (South African peace campaigner), Sir Shridath Ramphal (former Commonwealth Secretary-General), Chapman Pincher (investigative journalist), Lord Edmund-Davies (High Court judge), Susan Hill (author), Angela Rumbold (former MP), Arthur C Clarke (science fiction writer), Ivison Macadam (founder NUS), Rory Bremner (comedian), Archbishop Carey (former Archbishop of Canterbury). **More info?** Tel 020 7848 1588, email student.life.support@kclsu.org or visit www.kclsu.org.

Student view
(Medical and dental school)

The first 2 years are spent at the Guy's campus at London Bridge, a traditional old medical school across from a spacious park. It comprises a brand new building, New Hunt's House (lecture theatres, laboratories, huge library, 24-hour computer and study rooms) and the original 18th-century buildings (with the dissection rooms and Gordon Museum). Excellent travel connections (buses, underground and London Bridge overground station) so getting around is easy and as safe as in any big city. Clinical teaching at Guy's, St Thomas's, King's (Denmark Hill) and Lewisham hospitals; plus district general hospital attachments at Medway Maritime Hospital (Kent) and Queen Elizabeth Hospital (Woolwich); GP placements around London and attachments across the south-east. Courses are well arranged, standards of teaching high, and students well supported. An intercalated BSc optional and highly encouraged (around two-thirds of medics take one), though this may be changing. The atmosphere is friendly and exciting; nursing, physiotherapy and biomedical students share the campus, allowing for good integration of all professions during and after training. Annual events include Diwali and Christmas shows, a musical, one of the country's largest RAG weeks (£103k raised recently), fashion show and summer ball. Students with good ideas are encouraged to set up their own events, societies and interest groups, if they do not already exist. Social life centres on Guy's SU including a newly refurbished, smart bar/nightclub, with events throughout the week. London's throbbing heart a stone's throw away, and even the bars, cafés and restaurants around the corner are good fun. There are over 100 societies and sports clubs to join (sports grounds are a train ride away in Honor Oak Park and Dulwich). Halls of residence dotted around London but most medics are housed nearby on Great Dover Street, Wolfson House or Stamford Street – all with good connections to London Bridge. Newest halls have ensuite rooms arranged in apartments; older halls in corridors with shared bathrooms. Accommodation in London is relatively expensive compared with many other parts of the country but is on a par with major cities.

Student footnotes

Housing: Guaranteed halls in 1st year. Private accommodation plentiful. Rotherhithe and Walworth, Camberwell and Old Kent Road are popular areas, expect to pay £75–£110 pw + bills. Some students live further out or at home. **Eats:** Lunchtime deals from union bar and Borough High Street cafés. Some reasonable restaurants around. **Drink:** Pints about £1.90 in union with regular drinks promotions. **Nightlife:** Union events for all tastes with London on your doorstep opening up countless cafés, clubs, pubs, bars, eateries, cinemas and theatres. **Locals:** A diverse bunch, from students to city types to authentic Saaf Laandaners! **Sport:** Popular, both for fun and competition. The union gym at Waterloo, hospital gyms at Guy's and St Thomas's with discounted student rates **Travel:** Public transport between halls, campus and clinical placements is all accessible, reasonably priced, especially with student discount cards. **Financial help:** Hardship fund and certain bursaries available but eligibility can vary depending on year of study, etc. **Jobs:** Available at union's bars and shops; shifts to suit your timetable. Lucrative hospital guinea pig research work for the right students. **Best features:** One of the finest medical and dental schools, part of large, diverse university, in one of the world's greatest capitals. **And worst?** Can seem to be rather expensive, but with the right know-how this can be avoided! **Past students (and staff):** Phil Hammond (comedian, TV doctor), Tony Gardner (actor, comedian), Thomas Hodgkin, Thomas Addison and Richard Bright (who had diseases named after them), John Keats (poet, apothecary). **More info?** See GKT MedSoc website (www.kclmedsoc.org).

Kingston University

Location: south-west of London, within M25 (map 3) **Four campuses in and around Kingston; many partner colleges**

✉ Kingston University, River House, 53–57 High Street, Kingston upon Thames, Surrey KT1 1LQ
☎ Tel 020 8417 9000
✉ Email admissions-info@kingston.ac.uk
🖥 Website www.kingston.ac.uk

Student enquiries: Applicant Services
Applications: UCAS

In brief

Total Students: 23,135

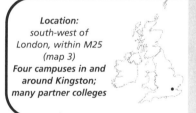

21% postgraduate
79% undergraduate

Undergraduates: 18,200
89% full-time   86% UK students
34% mature on entry   37% lower socio-economic groups

51% female   49% male

- **A modern university.**
- **Teaching staff:** 719 in total.
- **Broad study areas:** Architecture; art and design; business; chemistry and pharmaceutical sciences; computing; economics; education; engineering; environment; geography and geographical information systems; geology and earth sciences; health and social care sciences; humanities; languages; law; life sciences; mathematics and statistics; performance, film, media and music; social sciences; sports sciences; surveying.

Freshers

- **Admissions information:** AS-levels accepted in combination with 2+ A-levels or equivalent. UCAS tariff used; most offers expressed in terms of units to be passed, at what level and points to be attained. All applications considered on individual basis.
- **First degree entrants:** 4440 UK, full-time.
- **Points on entry:** 205 (average).

- **Drop-out rate:** 9% in 1st year.
- **Accommodation:** Many 1st years housed.

Profile

Institution

Founded: 1970 as Kingston Poly, from colleges of technology, art and education; university status in 1992. **Site:** 4 campuses: Penrhyn Road, Knights Park, Kingston Hill and Roehampton Vale – all in 3-mile radius and linked by free university bus service. **How to get there:** Kingston or Surbiton railway stations, buses. **Special features:** Links with St George's for courses in health and social care sciences.

Courses

Academic features: Courses include aerospace engineering, geographical information systems, landscape architecture, furniture design, forensic science. Extended degree scheme in technology and science for mature students or those without traditional qualifications. **Awarding body:** Kingston University. **Main undergraduate awards:** BA, BSc, LLB, BEng, MEng, FdSc. **Length of courses:** 3 years; 4–5 years (sandwich, language and extended degree courses); 2 years (FdSc).

Study opportunities & careers

Library and information services: Libraries on each campus, total of 426,000 books, 2700 printed periodicals, 15,000 electronic journals; 1800 study places; short loan service for course books; slide library at Knights Park (160,000+ slides), music library at Kingston Hill. Information spend, approx £78 pa spent for each student (FTE). 1800 workstations, open 24 hours/weekdays (less at weekends). **Study abroad:** Formal links with a number of European and US universities and colleges. **Careers:** Information, advice and placement service.

Student services & facilities

Student advice and services: Holistic health and counselling centre on main site (GPs, dentists, nurse-counsellors, psychotherapist, hypnotherapist, osteopath, chiropodist, aromatherapists, reflexologists); ecumenical chaplain and contacts in all faiths. **Amenities:** SU facilities on each campus; wide range of clubs and societies; bars, shops, catering outlets. **Sporting facilities:** State-of-the-art fitness centre and aerobics studio, gym, playing fields for all major sports, tennis courts; wide range of sporting activities and sports clubs. **Accommodation:** 45+% of 1st years housed; 3100 students in university accommodation: self-catering places at £87.50–£110 pw, 40-week contracts. Also head tenancy management schemes. Students live in privately owned accommodation for 2+ years: £80–£90 pw for lodgings.

Money

Living expenses budget: Minimum budget of £7k–£10,500 pa (excluding tuition fees) recommended by university. **Term-time work:** University allows term-time work for first-degree students. Some work available on campus; also help finding work off campus; plenty of part-time work in town centre. **Financial help:** Bursaries of £1k for UK students whose family income is less than £1k, of £600 where it is £1k–£25k, of £310 if family income is £25k–£39,300. Also bursaries of £300 pa for students from partner colleges and for students experiencing unexpected hardship. Also access to learning funds, one-off payments up to £3500 for unexpected financial difficulties (see www.kingston.ac.uk/money). Advice also given on benefit claims, applications to charitable trusts, etc. **Tuition fees:** Home students pay £3225 pa for first degrees (£1255 for foundation year; £1570 for year on placement or abroad). International students pay £9k–£10,050 pa (£850 for year on placement or abroad).

Student view

Spread across 4 sites, all within 3 miles of the town centre. Main site on Penrhyn Road is uni administrative centre and SU, plus faculties of science, arts and social science. Faculty of design is at Knights Park, business and healthcare at Kingston Hill and engineering at Roehampton Vale. Often rated among the top 10 new universities; teaching quality is high. The 1st year of many courses can be quite relaxed but pressure increases in the 2nd year. Support is available to any student struggling with the course demands and it is relatively easy to change course in first term (so drop-out rate effectively managed). Opportunity for study abroad or a year out in industry on many courses – valuable cultural and work experience, and gives the cv a competitive edge. Kingston is 15 miles and a fast train and bus ride from London. Its fully pedestrianised town centre is always buzzing and offers superb shopping, lots of pubs and restaurants (for all budgets), 4 nightclubs and cinema complex. Easy to get away from the hustle and bustle to Richmond Park; Twickenham and Wimbledon are a stone's throw away for sports fans. Uni has housing vacancy list and a head-tenancy scheme. Students can find it traumatic finding accommodation (private housing is expensive and estate agents charge high rates or won't deal with students). Many students live at home, which diminishes the overall student experience. Most have part-time jobs in pubs, shops and the union. SU runs 3 bars, 2 shops, 2 Subways and a Gannet eatery; also the sporting and recreational clubs and societies, from the ordinary (football, rugby, politics, etc) to the rather less ordinary (sub-aqua, film and cult television society). Recently refurbished university fitness centre has weights room, aerobics classes, sun bed and lots of contemporary dance classes (salsa, lambada and breakdancing, etc). SU not party political but is involved in campaigning on issues directly relevant to students (end to student hardship, sexual health, freeing Wednesday afternoons). Range of SU-run entertainments – all music tastes are catered for and ethnic diversity of Kingston students is represented in the theme nights on offer (from bhangra and cheesy pop to special events with artists such as Jools Holland).

Student footnotes

Housing: Expensive. **Eats:** Subway and Gannets cater for everyone. Good restaurants (Indian, Italian, Chinese) everywhere. **Drink:** SU bars average 30–35p per pint cheaper than pub prices. The Mill and O'Neill's among favourites. **Nightlife:** Odeon cinema. SU provides major Kingston venues – weekly bands, discos, films. **Sports:** University fitness centre, playing fields, tennis courts. SU has over 70 sports and societies. **Travel:** Good public transport. Hitching bad. **Financial help:** Average. Small loans and access funds via university. **Jobs:** Many part-time jobs in the SU; in Kingston, work in pubs, shops, restaurants. **Past students:** Glenda Bailey (editor of Marie Claire), Lawrence Dallaglio (England rugby). **More info?** Enquiries to SU (tel 020 8547 8868) or visit www.kusu.co.uk.

Laban

Location:
south-east London
(map 3)
**Single site in
Deptford**

Laban, Creekside, London SE8 3DZ
☎ Tel 020 8691 8600
🖷 Fax 020 8691 8400
✉ Email info@laban.org
🖥 Website www.laban.org

*Student enquiries: Course information office
Applications: Direct*

In brief

Total Students: 380

55% undergraduate
5% FE Students
40% postgraduate

Undergraduates: 200
100% full-time   50% UK students
5% mature on entry

80% female   20% male

- **Specialist dance college.**
- **Teaching staff:** 22 full-time, 25 part-time.
- **Broad study areas:** Dance theatre; contemporary dance artist training.

Freshers

- **Admissions information:** 2+ A-levels or equivalent required. UCAS tariff not used.
- **First degree entrants:** 85 UK, full-time.
- **Points on entry:** 120 (average).
- **Drop-out rate:** 5% in 1st year.
- **Accommodation:** No college accommodation.

Profile

Institution

Founded: 1945 (in Manchester; moved to London 1975). **Structural features:** Merged with Trinity College of Music in 2005, to form Trinity Laban – the UK's only conservatoire for music and dance. **Site:** Award-winning, state-of-the-art building in Deptford, south-east London. **How to get there:** DLR Cutty Sark station 5 mins' walk; also Greenwich or Deptford mainline or DLR stations (trains from Charing Cross, London Bridge, Lewisham or Bank stations); many bus routes. **Special features:** Visiting artists as teachers and performers. Annual international Easter and summer schools; study year abroad scheme for US students. EFL taught.

Courses

Academic features: In addition to degree courses, offers diploma and postgraduate (MA, MSc, PhD, MPhil) courses, eg community dance studies, teaching and notating dance, dance science, choreography, scenography (dance). **Awarding body:** City University. **Main undergraduate award:** BA. **Length of courses:** 3 years.

Study opportunities & careers

Library and information services: Large dance collection (130,000 items) comprising books, scores, theses, publications, videos, including the Laban Collection, Peter Williams, Peter Brinson and Shirley Wynne archives; internet resource guide; 75 study places. 26 computers, ratio 1:14 workstations to students. IT facilities open 11 hours/weekday (4 hours Saturdays); induction tours for all students, supplemented by focused sessions. Also access to City University library and IT facilities. **Other learning resources:** 13 dance studios, 300-seat theatre, dance health facilities, pilates studio, production and wardrobe department. **Careers:** Information and advice. **Employment:** Dance performers, choreographers, teachers, directors, community dance workers, arts administration and management.

Student services & facilities

Student advice and services: Physiotherapist, osteopath, remedial masseur, counsellors. Access to buildings for the disabled. **Amenities:** In-house publications: *Dance Theatre Journal*, *Labanlink* and *Discourses in Dance*. **Accommodation:** No college accommodation but some students live in Greenwich University accommodation (close by). Students live in privately owned accommodation for whole course; rent approx £90–£130 pw self-catering. Few first-degree students live at home.

Money

Living expenses budget: Minimum budget of £250 pw (excluding tuition fees) recommended by college. **Term-time work:** Centre allows term-time work for full-time students, to limit of 3 hours per day (50% believed to work). Some work occasionally available on campus. **Financial help:** Bursaries for UK students whose family income is up to £60k, of 25% of the maintenance award for which they qualify: so a bursary of £709 pa where family income is up to £25k, tapering down to £50 bursary where family income is £60k. Some scholarships (variable value). Small interest-free loans available for short term. **Tuition fees:** Home students pay £3225 pa for first degrees; international students pay £12,950 pa.

Student view

Housed in a terrific new building on Creekside (Stirling architecture prize, 2003). It's purpose-built for dance training with great facilities: a pilates studio, in-house physiotherapist and osteopath, a dance-related library with helpful staff, the Bonnie Bird Theatre (which features student performances as well as visiting artists) and Feast Your Eyes Café (mainly fairtrade and organic, which offers nutritious food at student prices). On the border of Deptford and Greenwich, it is close to mainline and DLR stations for easy access to central London in about 20 mins (use common sense when travelling alone!). Since the merger with Trinity College of Music, there are increasing opportunities for collaboration between music and dance. SU for Trinity and Laban organises many joint events and parties throughout the year; mainly socially active within college but increasing interest in political, ethical and environmental issues. Challenging course focuses on contemporary dance. Mainly release-based training but daily classes in ballet and changing modern techniques (eg Cunningham, Graham) throughout the 3 years. Choreography is a big element throughout the course, with many opportunities to show own work and dance in pieces of visiting artists. Academic modules in the 1st and 2nd year, with many essays and presentations; choices in many dance-related subjects in 2nd year (eg visual/costume design, Labanotation, community dance, teaching technique, sound scores, theatre, and dance science); even more freedom to choose area and direction of study in 3rd year. Very heavy timetable – 8.45am until 6pm most days plus weekend and evening rehearsals when necessary. Drop-out rate high. Many international and mature students. High teaching standards. Laban also offers 1-year course, many different MA studies and community classes. Good relations between students and management; very free thinking, open to student views.

Student footnotes

Housing: Deptford area relatively cheap. Newly built Mcmillan student village (across the road) has tidy ensuite rooms. Many people get together to share houses; check out local estate agencies and SU offers advice. **Eats:** Café on site; good variety of reasonably priced eateries nearby. Good local food markets, Deptford for cheap food, Greenwich for organic and delicatessen. **Drink:** Friday night drinks in Laban Bar, all nights drinks in Trinity bar. Many local pubs in Deptford, New Cross and Greenwich. **Nightlife:** Goldsmiths SU very active with regular club, comedy and film nights; also comedy club (Up The Creek), Greenwich Theatre and Picture House cinema nearby. Few cafés feature small jazz bands or jams. Also some gay-friendly bars. Bonnie Bird Theatre, the Venue (club) for bands, the Fridge at Brixton. **Sports:** Student discounts at local leisure centres, with swimming pools. **Travel:** Very good rail connections from Greenwich and Deptford; many bus routes including night buses. **Financial help:** Small college hardship fund (small amounts, and not for long). **Jobs:**

Local work in cafés, supermarkets, shops, pubs, restaurants and the market; also at Bonnie Bird Theatre for performances and in bar; some administrative work at Laban. **Best features:** The chance to train professionally on a very diverse and intensive course, in a very open-minded and contemporary institution! **And worst:** Long hours and heavy workload. **Past students:** The Cholmondeleys (contemporary dancers); David Massingham (National Dance Agency); Matthew Bourne, Lea Anderson, Jacob Marley (choreographers); Mark Murphy (director and movement specialist). **More info?** Telephone Trinity Laban SU on 020 8694 9501 or email su@laban.org.

Lampeter University

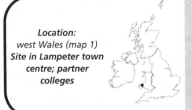

Location:
west Wales (map 1)
Site in Lampeter town
centre; partner
colleges

University of Wales, Lampeter, Ceredigion, SA48 7ED
☎ Tel 01570 422351
🖶 Fax 01570 423423
✉ Email recruit@lamp.ac.uk
💻 Website www.lamp.ac.uk

Student enquiries: Admissions Officer
Applications: UCAS

In brief

Total Students: 8925

21% postgraduate
79% undergraduate

Undergraduates: 7090
16% full-time
42% mature on entry
89% UK students
39% lower socio-economic groups

62% female   38% male

- **A top UK research-intensive institution**, part of University of Wales.
- **Teaching staff:** 80 full-time, 40 part-time (excluding those in partner institutions).
- **Broad study areas:** Liberal arts, humanities, divinity, management, social sciences.

Freshers

- **Admissions information:** AS-levels accepted in combination with 2+ A-levels or equivalent. UCAS tariff used on some courses.
- **First degree entrants:** 295 UK, full-time.
- **Points on entry:** 240 (average).
- **Drop-out rate:** 9% in 1st year.
- **Accommodation:** All 1st years housed.

Profile

Institution

Founded: 1822. **Structural features:** Part of University of Wales (since 1971). **Site:** Lampeter town centre. **How to get there:** By rail from Carmarthen or Aberystwyth, then bus; Transcambrian coach service from Cardiff, Aberystwyth and Bangor; bus from Carmarthen and from Aberystwyth (No. X40); by road from M4 to Carmarthen, then A485, or from north via A487/A44 to Aberystwyth, then A487 via Aberaeron. **Special features:** Very large numbers of part-time and distance-learning students.

Courses

Academic features: Modular structure; course options in, eg Church history, Islamic studies, anthropology, media studies, information technology. Many courses can be started in January. **Awarding body:** University of Wales. **Main undergraduate awards:** BA, BD. **Length of courses:** 3 years; 4 years (philosophy, Welsh).

Study opportunities & careers

Library and information services: Main and Founders' libraries; 200,000 volumes, 530 periodicals, large collection of e-books; 190 study places. Specialist collections: Tracts collection; early Welsh periodicals; bibles, prayerbooks, hymnals, catechisms and ballads; manuscript collection including 15th-century Books of Hours. Information provision, £62 pa spent for each student (FTE). Separate IT service, access 24 hours/day; 200 workstations with access to library and internet; all student rooms connected to network. IT support on demand 8 hours/weekdays; induction sessions to library and computing service for all new students covers, eg email and wordprocessing; other IT training on request. **Study abroad:** 5% of students spend a period abroad. Formal exchange links with universities/colleges in western Europe, USA and Canada. **Careers:** Information, advice and placement service.

Student services & facilities

Student advice and services: Nurse, chaplain, 24-hour welfare service, student support officer, special needs, etc; doctor and clinic close by. Residential facilities for disabled students; purpose-built crèche. **Amenities:** SU shop on campus. **Sporting facilities:** Sports hall; squash courts; multigym; playing fields less than 5 mins from campus; free use of town swimming pool; sailing club at Aberaeron. **Accommodation:** Guaranteed on campus for all 1st-year students. 518 self-catering places (some ensuite) £60–£75 pw, 30 or 36 week contracts; all rooms have network connection included in price. Local private accommodation at £40–£45 pw for self-catering (exclusive of bills).

Money

Living expenses budget: Minimum budget of £5900–£6400 pa (excluding tuition fees) recommended by university. **Term-time work:** University allows term-time work for first-degree students (50% believed to work). Some work available on campus in kitchens, sports hall and SU bars. Locally jobs available in, eg restaurants, pubs, shops, supermarkets. **Financial help:** Total available £30,700 government funds, about 170 students helped. **Tuition fees:** Home students pay £3225 pa for first degrees (though Welsh residents may be eligible for annual tuition fee grant of £1940). International students pay £8988 pa.

Student view

It's in one of the most beautiful locations in the country; the seaside is only 13 miles away where there are regular sightings of seals and dolphins. Originally a theological college, and the oldest degree-awarding institution in Wales, it now has a diverse range of arts degree programmes (undergraduate and postgraduate); most popular subjects are archaeology, theology and religious studies and most recently film and media studies. Local transport system is not brilliant but there are buses to surrounding towns and villages, and to bigger towns such as Aberystwyth, Swansea and Cardiff. Computing facilities on campus are good; internet access in all halls of residence and a variety of workstation rooms (one open 24 hours/day). Students and staff come from all over the world, making it a very multi-cultural campus. Staff are approachable and many have an open-door policy and are welcoming to students. SU is the main provider of social activities, and boasts a wide variety of clubs, societies and associations – and further development and more clubs and societies planned. Union bar is the watering hole for the student population; warm and welcoming atmosphere makes it an ideal venue for bar quizzes, bands, student acoustic nights as well as the occasional slam poet. SU nightclub (the Extension) is open at least twice a week for themed discos, bands and society nights. SU also runs a welfare service, aimed at supporting students (health, finance, housing, etc), running campaigns and awareness days (from breast cancer, Aids awareness to drink-spiking and safe sex). Many sports teams (eg rugby, football, fencing, ultimate frisbee). Welsh countryside offers excellent opportunities for mountain biking, hiking, walking and camping. University provides housing for most students – mostly self-catering, some ensuite. Plenty of student housing in the town as well, generally under 10 mins' walk from the main campus – all fairly safe as Lampeter is a safe town (but, as anywhere, insure valuable items). On-campus employability unit gives students and graduates advice on where to find jobs and work placements. It's a very welcoming and friendly community, which gives you the opportunities to make what you want of your experience at university.

Student footnotes

Housing: 1st years in halls. Accommodation in town relatively cheap; country dwellings and caravans often available out of town. **Drink:** Union bar cheapest in town. 12 pubs in town so plenty of choice. **Eats:** Dewi's, the SU café, is reasonable and open 10am–4pm on weekdays (generous portion of chips and a big slice of pizza for modest amount). **Nightlife:** Regular bands; DJs incl Cash Money and Radio1 Mike Davies, DJ Yoda and the Scratch Perverts; karaoke, discos, pub quizzes, themed nights, regular trips to other universities and towns for gigs and lots, lots more. Film society has 3+ films a week (foreign, classics and blockbusters). **Locals:** Very friendly. **Sports:** Many sports teams. No charge for sports hall on campus; squash courts; town swimming pool (free student sessions). **Travel:** Rely on local buses. **Financial help:** Access (hardship) fund and hardship loan; many bursaries and scholarships available. **Jobs:** Jobs in SU; in town (in cafés, pubs, shops and factories), most pay minimum wage. Try local Job Centre or on-campus employability unit. **Best features:** Welcoming, friendly community, with many opportunities. **And worst:** Can feel a bit small; distance to bigger towns and cities. **Past students:** T E Lawrence (of Arabia fame), Sulak Sivaraska (Thai human rights campaigner), Sue Slipman (National Council for One Parent Families). **More info?** SU (tel 01570 422619, email president@lamp.ac.uk) or check out www.lamp.ac.uk/su.

Lancaster University

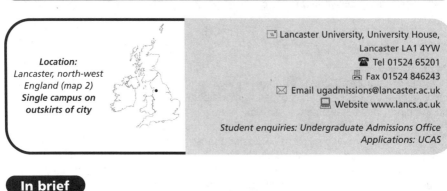

Location:
Lancaster, north-west England (map 2)
Single campus on outskirts of city

📧 Lancaster University, University House, Lancaster LA1 4YW
☎ Tel 01524 65201
📠 Fax 01524 846243
✉ Email ugadmissions@lancaster.ac.uk
💻 Website www.lancs.ac.uk

Student enquiries: Undergraduate Admissions Office
Applications: UCAS

In brief

Total Students: 17,410

20% postgraduate
80% undergraduate

Undergraduates: 13,855
58% full-time
8% mature on entry
91% UK students
22% lower socio-economic groups

53% female   47% male

- **A top UK research-intensive university.**
- **Teaching staff:** 714 full-time and part-time.
- **Broad study areas:** Arts and humanities; creative arts; engineering; management; medicine; sciences; social sciences.

Freshers

- **Admissions information:** Most offers based on best 3 A-levels; AS-levels sometimes accepted in combination with 2+ A-levels or equivalent (providing one is taken in last year of study). Non-A-level qualifications also considered. Most offers specify grades, UCAS tariff only occasionally.
- **First degree entrants:** 2250 UK, full-time.
- **Points on entry:** 308 (average).
- **Drop-out rate:** 5% in 1st year.
- **Accommodation:** All 1st years housed.

Profile

Institution

Founded: 1964. **Site:** Single campus at Bailrigg, south of Lancaster. **How to get there:** Lancaster on main London–Glasgow line; A6 and M6 main roads. **Structural features:** Collegiate system (8 undergraduate colleges, 1 graduate): all students join a college on arrival and remain part of that community throughout their time at the university

Courses

Academic features: Flexible course structure makes it easy to change course and allows specialisation. Undergraduate Master's degrees in engineering, maths, statistics and physics. Flexible BSc combined science. Mature students welcomed. **Awarding body:** Lancaster University. **Main undergraduate awards:** BA, BBA, BMus, BSc, LLB, BEng, MEng, MPhys, MBChB, MSci. **Length of courses:** 3 years; 4 years (language and sandwich courses, undergraduate Master's); 5 years (sandwich MEng and MBChB)

Study opportunities & careers

Library and information services: About 1 million items; access to 16,000+ journals, special collections and a rare book and archive suite; 900 reader places, 150 workstations; short-loan system for books in heavy demand. Information provision, £147 pa spent for each student (FTE). Separate IT service. **Other learning resources:** Language resource centre, TV studio. Specialist collections: Redlich collection (music); Ruskin Library (John Ruskin's collection of watercolours, manuscripts, books and photos); Lord Hesketh's rare book collection currently housed at Lancaster; Quaker collection; library of Burnley Grammar School. **Study abroad:** Most students can spend 2nd year abroad. Many departments have exchange programmes in Europe and USA. **Careers:** Information, placement and advice service.

Student services & facilities

Student advice and services: Central student services, collegiate advisers, doctors, dentists, psychiatrist, chaplains, professional student counsellors. Residential facilities for disabled students and some families; nursery. For details see student support section of website. **Amenities:** Bookshop; varied and numerous eating places; various shops and banks on campus; Peter Scott art gallery; Ruskin library; Jack Hylton music rooms; Nuffield theatre. **Sporting facilities:** Swimming pool, sauna, solarium, rock-climbing wall, 6 football pitches, 1 floodlit synthetic pitch, 8 tennis courts, 3 hockey pitches, golf driving area and jogging routes on campus; outdoor centre in the Yorkshire Dales. **Accommodation:** All 1st years guaranteed housing on campus if they want it and have accepted a firm offer (most 2nd and 3rd years also housed). 6600 self-catering places, rent £65.50–£76 pw (£88–£97 ensuite; £108–£125 for studio apartments). All rooms have telephones and internet points. Some family flats of varying sizes/rents. Head-lease scheme for houses off campus, average rent £55 plus bills.

Money (💰)

Living expenses budget: Minimum budget of £6560 pa (excluding tuition fees) recommended by university. More information and budget planning on website. **Term-time work:** Students should balance need for paid employment with academic demands of the course; 10–14 hours maximum advised. Some work available in college bars, etc. Help finding jobs, placements and vacation work through SU job-shop, university volunteering unit or careers service. **Financial help:** Bursaries for UK students on first degrees of £1315 pa where family income is up to £18,300 pa; or of £500 pa where family income is £18,300–£27,800 pa. Some 420 scholarships of £1k pa for UK students with high grades who make Lancaster their first choice. Access to learning fund (of £150k pa) to help UK students facing a shortfall between income and reasonable expenditure or unexpected emergency costs; around 400 pa students helped. Further information on university website. **Tuition fees:** Home students pay £3225 pa for first degrees. International student pay £9200 pa (classroom-based), £10,600 (management courses), £11,100 (lab-based).

Student view

An attractive modern site in pleasant grounds 2 miles south of Lancaster. Very accessible from most major cities via M6 and London–Scotland rail link. Excellent location for outdoor activity, particularly water sports, walking or general adventures! Close proximity to the Lake District, Blackpool and Morecambe. All students can live on campus, including 2nd and 3rd years. 4–18 people share flats; all rooms have telephones and many have data (internet) points. A collegiate university with 9 colleges, each with its own bar, student-run junior common room and traditions; quite boisterous college spirit and a touch of rivalry between colleges so there is constantly a passionate and lively atmosphere. SU is university-wide; proactive and always campaigning for Lancaster students. Services range from an SU-owned nightclub in town (the Sugarhouse) to a strong advice centre (offers, eg international and academic support, and advice on loans, pregnancy worries, HIV and disabilities awareness, campus watch scheme). SU is also home to athletic union with 30+ sporting clubs. If sport is not your thing, there are also 70+ non-sporting and cultural societies – but if you can't find something you fancy, you are welcome to set your own society up! SU also runs shops, union newspaper (*SCAN*), radio station (Bailrigg FM), RAG and off-campus housing office. University is flexible academically. You study up to 3 subjects in your 1st year; sounds a bit crazy but it allows you to explore different subject areas or something new (all subjects are assessed so there is no easy get out!). Your 2nd year is often the chance to study abroad so, if you fancy a change, ask about your options. Individual departments offer their own support networks and guidance, creating a welcoming and friendly atmosphere. Overall Lancaster is a friendly university; excellent atmosphere with an international flavour.

Student footnotes

Housing: University head lease scheme; flats on campus (including for couples). Off-campus, SU housing office has an accreditation scheme for safe and secure housing. **Eats:** Excellent burger bar, Chinese and Indian takeaway on campus; also university-run food outlets. Usual fast food takeaways plus good international (eg Mexican, Italian, Swiss) restaurants in town; meal £3 upwards. **Drink:** 9 bars on campus (£1.80+ a pint); lots of local pubs; good choice, reasonable prices (cheaper than down south, a lot cheaper!). **Nightlife:** Excellent student nightclub (Sugarhouse), recently refurbished. Local live music scene constantly changing; live acoustic sets to karaoke, something for everyone! Cinema on campus showing latest releases; active theatre group; excellent live ents, comedians, etc. **Locals:** Good relations. **Sports:** Sports centre on campus; swimming pool; active athletic union, which competes in BUCS league. **Travel:** Good car-share schemes; women's safe transport; cycle paths. Buses regular from campus to town and train station, including late-night buses (1-, 2- or 3-term bus passes to reduce costs). Free transport on certain club nights from the Sugarhouse. Some travel scholarships available from colleges. **Financial help:** Access to learning fund from university; college awards. **Jobs:** Good term-time work, some in Sugarhouse and bars; SU jobshop for current vacancies. Holiday work in catering department for tourist and conference trade. **Buzz-words:** LUSU (Lancaster University Students' Union), JCR (Junior Common Room), major subject (your degree subject), minor subject (your supplementary 1st-year courses). **Best features:** The collegiate system; great social and friendly atmosphere. **And worst:** The campus is big and constantly changing; may take a while to find your bearings. **Good news:** Disability access greatly improved; environmental co-ordinator increasing promotion of green and recycling issues. **Past students:** Eric Bolton (Senior Chief Inspector of Schools); Robert Fisk (award-winning newspaper correspondent); Simon Smith (rugby union England international); Gary Waller MP; Michael Handley MEP; Green Gartside (Scritti Politi, rock band); Jason Queally (Olympic gold medallist). **More info?** Check out www.lusu.co.uk.

Leeds College of Music

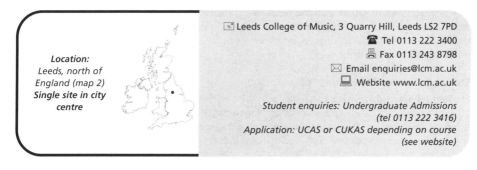

Location:
Leeds, north of England (map 2)
Single site in city centre

✉ Leeds College of Music, 3 Quarry Hill, Leeds LS2 7PD
☎ Tel 0113 222 3400
🖷 Fax 0113 243 8798
✉ Email enquiries@lcm.ac.uk
💻 Website www.lcm.ac.uk

Student enquiries: Undergraduate Admissions
(tel 0113 222 3416)
Application: UCAS or CUKAS depending on course
(see website)

In brief

Total Students: 590

4% postgraduate
96% undergraduate

Undergraduates: 565
100% full-time   96% UK students
14% mature   20% lower
on entry   socio-economic
groups

25% female   75% male

- **Specialist college**, specialising in education and training of musicians, music teachers and associated technologists.
- **Teaching staff:** 52 full-time, 180 part-time.
- **Broad study areas:** Music (including jazz, popular music), music production for film and TV, music technology, music production.

Freshers
- **Admissions information:** UCAS tariff used. Also auditions for most music courses.
- **First degree entrants:** 155 UK, full-time.

- **Points on entry:** 240 (average; 280 for music production).
- **Drop-out rate:** 5% in 1st year.
- **Accommodation:** Most 1st years housed.

Profile

Institution
Founded: 1966. **Site:** Purpose-built building in Leeds city centre. **How to get there:** Leeds very accessible by road (M1 and M62), by national coach services, by rail (2 hours from London Kings Cross) and by air (Leeds/Bradford airport 8 miles from city centre; Manchester airport just over 1 hour). College close to coach and train stations. **Special features:** Artists-in-residence Dennis Rollins (jazz trombonist) and David Greed (Opera North).

Courses
Academic features: Courses in jazz, popular music, classical music, music production; foundation degrees in music production (commercial music and for film and television). **Awarding body:** Open University. **Main undergraduate awards:** BA, FD. **Length of courses:** 3 years; 2 years (FD).

Study opportunities & careers
Library and information services: 36,000 volumes, 55 periodicals; 60 study places. IT and library services converged. Annual expenditure £42 pa spent for each student (FTE). 15 workstations with access to library, 60 to internet. IT facilities open 11 hours/day; IT support from technician 8 hours/day. Introduction to library, its catalogue and specialist software for all new students. Specialist collection: jazz archive. **Other learning resources:** Virtual learning environment; recital room (regular recitals); state-of-the-art 350-seat performance space; 9 fully upgraded recording studios. **Careers:** Information and advice service; placement service for some courses. Main employment areas are teaching, performance, music sales.

Student services & facilities
Student advice and services: 2 student counsellors; advisers for funding, careers and 2 for welfare; SU liaison officer; equality and diversity officer. **Amenities:** College bar; all the amenities of Leeds. **Sporting facilities:** None on campus; use of gym and swimming pool nearby. Rugby league and union teams. **Accommodation:** 190 ensuite rooms in flats next to college; rent from £93 pw (incl utilities, broadband and contents insurance), 42-week contract. Plenty of privately owned accommodation available, rent approx £67+ pw for room in shared, self-catering house. College uses Unipol bureau.

Money
Living expenses budget: Minimum budget of £6k–£7k pa (excluding tuition fees) recommended by college. **Term-time work:** College allows term-time work for full-time students (12 hours/week maximum recommended). **Financial help:** Bursaries of £1055 pa for UK students whose family income is up to £18,400, of £790 pa where it is £18,400–£27,800, and of £540 pa where family income is £27,800–£39,300 pa; also help with audition expenses where needed. Various scholarships (mostly £1500 pa) for those studying particular instruments, Yorkshire young musicians, and for UK students from low-income backgrounds who are studying shortage instruments (eg oboe, strings, tuba). £20k government funds, some 71 students helped (awards £100–£500; average £300). **Tuition fees:** Home students pay £3225 pa for first degrees (fixed fee for whole course). International students pay £9800 pa.

Student view

Danielle Le Cuirot, Student Union Communications Officer (3rd year, BA Popular Music Studies)

Living

What's it like as a place to live? Friendly. Everything you need is within walking distance and it's not hard to find your way around. **How's the student accommodation?** University accommodation is fairly expensive but well located. Private housing is cheap but not necessarily great quality. **What's the student population like?** Very friendly with diverse backgrounds, bringing people in from all around the UK and internationally. **How do students and locals get on?** Locals are friendly but a clear division can be seen between locals and students when it comes to areas each group will spend time in, venues where groups go to socialise, areas students live in and areas locals live in.

Studying

What's it like as a place to study? All courses become more flexible over time and students specialise towards the end of their degree. Facilities are good but there tends to be a shortage during the lead-up to assessments/exams/auditions. **What are the teaching staff like?** Teaching staff are friendly, helpful and take an interest in their students. Guest speakers are frequent and beneficial.

Socialising

What are student societies like? There are several societies for sport, plus a Christian Union and LGBT Scociety. There is a SU in college run by the students with the help of a part-time liaison officer. They organise a good range of gigs and parties through the year including Freshers' Week, Hallowe'en, Christmas and end of year ball. **What's a typical night out?** Leeds has a great nightlife. You can choose from pubbing, clubbing, gigs, restaurants, bars and much more. **And how much does it cost?** Many venues are free or only a few pounds entry, unless you go to a popular club or gig where it will be more. **How can you get home safely?** There are a number of taxi services and several late night bus routes. Most areas of Leeds are well lit and relatively safe but it's always best not to go out alone late at night.

Money

Is it an expensive place to live? It is not an expensive place to live and there is a local market nearby, which helps keep expenses down. **Average price of a pint?** £2.50. **And the price of a takeaway?** £5. **What's the part-time work situation?** College is very helpful for students looking for work or having financial issues. There are jobs available, mainly in theatres, bars and shops.

Summary

What's the best feature about the place? The shopping and the nightlife, and, within college, the community atmosphere. **And the worst?** Being at a music college, you're surrounded by music and other musicians all day, every day, whereas at a university you meet people with completely different interests. **And to sum it all up?** Leeds College of Music is a friendly, vibrant place to study and its location makes it perfect for gaining experience in the live music scene.

Past students: Chris 'Snake' Davis (sax player, M People, Lisa Stansfield), Alan Barnes (jazz saxophonist), Andrew Colman (Young Jazz Musician of the Year 1999), Matthew Bourne (BBC Radio Jazz Innovation award 2002), Damon Gough (aka Badly Drawn Boy). **More info?** Contact SU President (tel 0113 222 3507, email studentunion@lcm.ac.uk) or try the website (www.lcmsu.com).

Leeds Met University

Location:
Leeds, north of
England (map 2)
Two campuses in
Leeds, one in
Harrogate

Leeds Metropolitan University, Civic Quarter,
Leeds LS1 3HE
☎ Tel 0113 812 3113
🖶 Fax 0113 812 3129
✉ Email course-enquiries@leedsmet.ac.uk
💻 Website www.leedsmet.ac.uk

Student enquiries: Course Enquiries Office
Applications: UCAS

In brief

Total Students: 50,000

30% FE Students
10% postgraduate
60% undergraduate

Undergraduates: 29,135
65% full-time   90% UK students
25% mature   33% lower
on entry   socio-economic
                groups

50% female   50% male

- **A modern university.**
- **Teaching staff:** 631 full-time, 687 part-time.
- **Broad study areas:** Sport and education; arts and society; health; information and technology; business; languages; tourism, hospitality and events.

Freshers

- **Admissions information:** Points score usually to be made up of GCE A-level, AS-level and double awards (Key Skills can contribute). Range of alternative qualifications also accepted; prior learning and/or experience considered, particularly from mature students.
- **First degree entrants:** 5310 UK, full-time.
- **Points on entry:** 253.
- **Drop-out rate:** 9% in 1st year.
- **Accommodation:** All 1st years housed (if they have accepted a place).

Profile

Institution

Founded: 1970 as Leeds Poly, from amalgamation of various 19th-century colleges (earliest 1824); university status in 1992. **Site:** 2 campuses in Leeds: 1 in the Civic Quarter and 1 in the leafy woodland of Headingley. Also several key city centre buildings (eg Cloth Hall Court, Old Broadcasting House, Electric Press in Millennium Square) and the Rose Bowl houses the business school from 2009. **How to get there:** Leeds very accessible by road (M1 and M62), by national coach services, by rail (2 hours from London Kings Cross) and by air (Leeds/Bradford airport 8 miles; Manchester airport just over 1 hour). Civic Quarter Campus is walking distance of train and bus/coach stations; frequent bus services link campuses.

Courses

Academic features: Focus on applied learning. **Awarding body:** Leeds Metropolitan University. **Main undergraduate awards:** BA, BSc, BEng, FdA, FdSc, LLB. **Length of courses:** 3 years (full-time); 4 years (sandwich); 2 years (FdA/Sc).

Study opportunities & careers

Library and information services: Integrated library, computing and media facilities on all campuses; 365,000+ volumes, approx 11,900 periodical subscriptions; extensive access to media and electronic resources; 2000+ study places. Ratio 1:5 workstations to students, networked with access to electronic information, email and internet. Library and IT facilities open 24/7 throughout the year. IT staff support from help desks; off-campus support via the web. IT skills taught within students' courses. Induction to library and information services for all new students including making best use of electronic and print information sources. Information provision, £59 pa spent for each student (FTE). **Other learning resources:** Language laboratories, audio-visual resources, special needs support area, off-site library services for distance learners. **Study abroad:** Opportunity to study or undertake work placements abroad on many courses. Formal exchange links and voluntary opportunities with universities and colleges in western Europe, USA and beyond. **Careers:** Personal and impartial service to students and graduates.

Student services & facilities

Student advice and services: Helpzones for student queries at all campuses: disability support team (with dyslexia specialist and technical help); student counselling service; financial adviser; international students adviser; childcare services including play scheme and crèche; 2 health centres, staffed by nurses; multi-faith chaplaincy with Islamic prayer facilities. Also SU advice service. **Amenities:** Shops, cybercafé, coffee lounge, refectories on both campuses, cashpoints, repro services, bars, the Met club venue. **Sporting facilities:** Carnegie sports centre at Headingley Campus (for PE and sports courses, students and public use), with floodlit synthetic pitches, 5-a-side pitch, athletics track, 2 large sports halls, gymnasia, swimming pool, dance studio, fitness and weights rooms, squash courts and indoor climbing wall. Regional tennis and gymnastics centre. Fitness facilities at Civic Quarter Campus and 2 main halls. **Accommodation:** Almost all 1st years housed (guaranteed for those who have firmly accepted a place). 4500 self-catering places: rent £63–£85 (ensuite) plus bills or £85.50–£103 (ensuite) including bills; 41- or 43-week contracts. Newest development, Opal One, all rooms ensuite and on-site fitness suite, swimming pool, sauna, jacuzzi. Some students live in privately owned accommodation for whole course (plentiful and cheap); rent £60+ pw plus bills. Help through Unipol Student Homes (www.unipol.leeds.ac.uk).

Money

Living expenses budget: Minimum budget of £6500 pa (excluding tuition fees) recommended by university. **Term-time work:** University recommends limit of 15 hours' work a week for full-time student. Some jobs available on campus; university Jobshop helps find work on or off campus. **Financial help:** Limited number of bursaries (£1k in Year 1, £500 in following years) for local students whose family income is up to £23k. Also £1.12 million government access funds, 1800 pa students helped; priorities are childcare, commuting costs, mature students, students with disabilities, finalists. Range of sports and academic scholarships. Apply to financial support and advice team and student services for help. **Tuition fees:** Home students pay £2k pa for first degrees. International students pay £8k–£8700 pa.

Student view
Will Watson, SU Associate President of Education and Representation 2007–08 (2nd year, Peace and Politics)

Living
What's it like as a place to live? Leeds – amazing, cultural melting pot, 24-hour city, exotic, friendly, value for money! **How's the student accommodation?** Reasonably priced, lots of it! Ranges from very nice to very not nice. **What's the student population like?** Very diverse in age, gender, ethnicity and nationality. **How do students and locals get on?** Better in recent years due to student volunteering in the community.

Studying

What's it like as a place to study? A very wide range of places to study and courses to take in both HE/FE. **What are the teaching staff like?** Again, from dedicated, exciting and friendly too. . . . not!

Socialising

What are student societies like? Both universities have a wide range of societies, which are growing every year. **What's a typical night out?** Leeds has been voted the best city for going out! **And how much does it cost?** Food, drink and events are well priced. **How can you get home safely?** Taxis are available at reasonable cost.

Money

Is it an expensive place to live? No! Most people find it reasonably ok to live. **Average price of a pint?** £1–£3.50. **And the price of a takeaway?** £5–£7. **What's the part-time work situation?** The university helps you find work and supports you with time commitments.

Summary

What's the best feature about the place? It is both a big city and a small town at the same time! **And the worst?** Local Leeds citizens are missing out on 54 hugs per person pw! **And to sum it all up?** Big, fun, cheap, lush, happy and full of friendly students. **Past students:** Marc Almond (Soft Cell), Sir Henry Moore (sculptor), Ron Pickering (athlete), Ricky Wilson (Kaiser Chiefs), Bill Slater (footballer; last amateur to play in FA Cup Final); Les Bettinson and Austin Healy (England and Leicester rugby union). **More info?** Contact SU President (tel 0113 209 8439) or try the website (www.leedsmetsu.org.uk).

Leeds Trinity

Location:
Leeds, north of
England (map 2)
Single campus close
to Leeds

Leeds Trinity & All Saints, Brownberrie Lane,
Horsforth, Leeds LS18 5HD
☎ Tel 0113 283 7150
🖶 Fax 0113 283 7321
✉ Email enquiries@leedstrinity.ac.uk
💻 Website www.leedstrinity.ac.uk

Student enquiries: Student recruitment team
Applications: UCAS

In brief

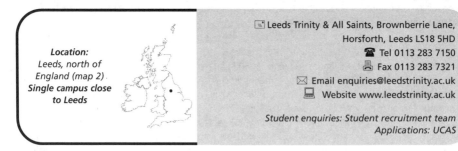

Total Students: 2690

15% postgraduate
85% undergraduate

Undergraduates: 2280
94% full-time · 96% UK students
14% mature on entry · 33% lower socio-economic groups

64% female · 36% male

- **College accredited by Leeds University.**
- **Teaching staff:** 110 full-time.
- **Broad study areas:** Business enterprise and marketing; childhood and youth; humanities; film and TV; journalism; management; media; primary education; psychology and forensic psychology; sport, health, leisure and nutrition.

Freshers

- **Admissions information:** AS-levels accepted in combination with 2+ A-levels or equivalent. UCAS tariff used.
- **First degree entrants:** 690 UK, full-time.
- **Points on entry:** 160–240 (average).
- **Drop-out rate:** 11% in 1st year.
- **Accommodation** Most 1st years housed.

Profile

Institution

Founded: 1966. **Structural features:** A Catholic college accredited by Leeds University. **Site:** Single campus in Horsforth, 6 miles from central Leeds. **How to get there:** Leeds very accessible by road (M1 and M62), by national coach services, by rail (2 hours from London Kings Cross) and by air (Leeds/Bradford airport 2 miles from campus; Manchester airport just over 1 hour). Direct bus services from Leeds and Bradford stop at the campus entrance, local rail station 10 mins' walk with regular service to Leeds city centre and Harrogate.

Courses

Academic features: All courses modular with single and combined Honours available. Strong emphasis on graduate employability, with practical experience and work placements integral to all courses. **Awarding body:** University of Leeds. **Main undergraduate awards:** BA, BSc, BA(QTS). **Length of courses:** 3 years; 4 years (QTS).

Study opportunities & careers

Library and information services: Andrew Kean Learning Centre with 150,000 volumes, 2000 journals (print and electronic); 180 study places; open 66 hours/week in term time. 160 PCs in learning centre (35 available 24/7); ratio 1:9 PCs to students, all with web-based library, email and internet access. All students have induction programme and electronic- and paper-based library and IT guides. Information provision, £84 pa spent for each student (FTE). **Other learning resources:** Computer labs, language lab, sound recording studio, radio studio, video editing suite, TV studio, science labs, primary and secondary education bases. **Study abroad:** Exchange links with universities/colleges in the EU and USA. **Careers:** Information, advice and well-stocked careers library in careers service (open all year). Jobshop advertises part-time job vacancies.

Student services & facilities

Student advice and services: Health centre, counselling service, disability and dyslexia support, careers service, student finance adviser, international office. Nursery on campus (ages 1–5). **Amenities:** SU (sports teams, student societies and social events). Bar and cafeteria on campus. **Sporting facilities:** Sports centre with fitness suite, 2 sports halls with badminton, basketball, volleyball, 5-a-side football and table tennis; also squash courts, floodlit multi-sport outdoor practice area, tennis courts, all-weather pitch, running track, rugby and soccer pitches. **Accommodation:** Most 1st years can live on campus. 626 rooms on campus, normally for 1st years, many with internet access; £65.50–£66.50 pw (£82.50 ensuite) for self-catering; £86–£87 pw (£105 ensuite) for catered, which includes £30 pw food allowance; all contracts 39 weeks. Students live off campus for 2+ years, rent approx £60 pw. Good supply of privately rented accommodation within easy reach. Popular areas: Horsforth, Headingley and Kirkstall.

Money (💰)

Living expenses budget: Minimum budget of around £600 per month (excluding tuition fees) recommended by college. **Term-time work:** Students permitted to work part-time; jobshop can help find jobs. Some work available on campus (bars, events support, conference support). **Financial help:** Means-tested bursaries for UK students, of £1k pa for students whose family income is up to £25k, or £500 pa where family income is £25k–£60k. Also scholarships (£1k) for students demonstrating excellence in their subject area or related extra-curricular activity; progress awards (50% of tuition fee) for students progressing from foundation degree to Honours degree course at Leeds Trinity. Advice from student finance adviser. **Tuition fees:** Home students pay £3225 pa for first degrees. International students pay £7425 pa (classroom based), £7985 (lab/studio based).

Student view
John Joe Mulherin, Student Union President (graduate, Theology Single Honours)

Living
What's it like as a place to live? Leeds Trinity & All Saints is surrounded by stunning scenery – great headspace for learning. **How's the student accommodation?** The accommodation is varied. You can choose self-catered or part-catered; shared facilities or ensuite; there's old and new buildings. **What's the student population like?** The ethnic minority groups are small here. You get a good few locals and the rest are mainly British. **How do students and locals get on?** There are no concerns about student safety really. Horsforth's a proper nice place; you'll have no trouble if you use your common sense.

Studying
What's it like as a place to study? Nearly all the classrooms have SMART Board facilities and the interior of the buildings are clean and modern. **What are the teaching staff like?** Very supportive and keen on student success.

Socialising
What are student societies like? The SU is open and approachable and many new societies start each year – it's all down to what the students want. **What's a typical night out?** Down to HQ bar for pre-drinks then into the city centre. **And how much does it cost?** You can survive on £20 a night. **How can you get home safely?** Buses are put on for a lot of the nights.

Money
Is it an expensive place to live? Average house prices are £62–£70 pw. **Average price of a pint?** £1.50–£2. **And the price of a takeaway?** Pizza £4.50, cheeseburger and chips £3. **What's the part-time work situation?** There's loads of part-time work about and uni has a Job Shop specifically to help students find work.

Summary
What's the best feature about the place? It's surrounded by stunning scenery and yet is 15 mins from Leeds city centre. **And the worst?** The on-campus bar needs a refurb and there's no student common room. **And to sum it all up?** An exceptional place to learn about life and your subject choice.

More info? Contact SU on 0113 283 7241 or check out the website at www.leedstrinity.ac.uk/su.

Leeds University

Location:
Leeds, north of
England (map 2)
**Main city-centre
campus; plus partner
colleges**

▣ University of Leeds, Leeds LS2 9JT
☎ Tel 0113 243 1751
✉ Email ask@leeds.ac.uk
🖥 Website www.leeds.ac.uk

*Student enquiries: Course Enquiries Office
(tel 0113 343 2336)
Applications: UCAS*

In brief

Total Students: 33,000

26% postgraduate
74% undergraduate

Undergraduates: 24,510
93% full-time ● ● 91% UK students
11% mature ● ● 19% lower
on entry ● ● socio-economic
groups

60% female   40% male

- **A top UK research-intensive university.**
- **Teaching staff:** 1750 full-time and part-time.
- **Broad study areas:** Business and economics, science and engineering, medicine and dentistry, humanities, fine art, social science, law, modern languages, music and performing arts.

Freshers

- **Admissions information:** AS-levels accepted in combination with 2+ A-levels or equivalent; individual courses may require specific subjects and grades. International qualifications welcome.
- **First degree entrants:** 6355 UK, full-time.
- **Points on entry:** 392 (average).
- **Drop-out rate:** 6% in 1st year.
- **Accommodation:** 1st years guaranteed university accommodation.

Profile

Institution

Founded: 1904. **Site:** Main site ½ mile from city centre. **How to get there:** Leeds very accessible by road (M1 and M62), by national coach services, by rail (2+ hours from London Kings Cross) and by air (Leeds/Bradford airport 8 miles from city centre; Manchester airport just over 1 hour). University close to bus and railway stations; bus or walking distance to halls of residence.

Courses

Academic features: Many degrees modularised and available part-time. 700 first-degree programmes, including many Joint Honours. **Awarding body:** University of Leeds. **Main undergraduate awards:** BA, BBcS, BChD, BEng, MEng, BSc, MBChB, LLB. **Length of courses:** 3 years; 4 years (those involving period abroad, foundation year, undergraduate Master's); 5 years (medicine, dentistry, MEng with foundation year).

Study opportunities & careers

Library and information services: Over 2.6 million volumes including microfilm, electronic resources and internet access; 4000 study places. Information provision, £189 pa spent for each student (FTE). Computing service, language centre, media services. **Study abroad:** Most degree programmes offer a study abroad period, either optional or compulsory. Formal exchanges with 100+ institutions in Europe (through Socrates), 30+ outside Europe. **Careers:** Advice and placement service.

Student services & facilities

Student advice and services: Health centre, advisers for disabled students, counselling service, day nursery, chaplaincies, union welfare service. **Amenities:** SU building at centre of campus: largest venue for live music in Leeds, award-winning nightclub, facilities for clubs and societies, retail complex, welfare services centre, student newspaper and radio. **Sporting facilities:** 3 sports halls, 4 squash courts, climbing wall, fitness room on campus; extensive sports ground within 3 miles; outdoor huts in Lake District and Pennines. Major investment in sport underway. Olympic-standard swimming pool and golf in city. **Accommodation:** 90% of 1st years in university accommodation (all who choose it). 7830 places available (5850 for 1st years): 1880 catered places from £90–£136 pw, some term-time only contracts; 5948 self-catering places from £63–£124 (some ensuite). Most students live in privately owned accommodation for 1–2 years, £60–£75 pw in shared self-catering house; £95 in bedsit (other types of accommodation limited); little inexpensive accommodation for couples and families.

Money

Living expenses budget: Minimum budget of £7500 pa (excluding tuition fees) recommended. **Term-time work:** LUU joblink employment agency helps students find part-time jobs. **Financial help:** Bursaries of £1500 pa for UK students whose family income is up to £25k; tapered bursaries of £1300–£325 pa where family income is £25k–£36k; approx 20% of students qualify. Scholarships of up to £3k pa for students in specific groups, eg students entering university through access programmes, residents of Barnsley, or where there is no family tradition of going to university (not to be held with a bursary). Scholarships of £1700–£2500 pa for students intending to study specified subjects (eg engineering or environmental science) and of £1k pa for students with high A-level grades. Also £960k government funds; and charitable trusts and university funds, especially for international students facing hardship through no fault of their own, usually in final year. Apply to union welfare services for help. **Tuition fees:** Home students pay £3225 pa for first degrees (£1500 part-time). International students pay £9700 pa (arts), £12,600 (science), £23,500 (clinical).

Student view

It's at the centre of a cosmopolitan metropolis that is one of the fastest growing and most prosperous cities in Europe. University is just to the north of the city centre, a mishmash of differing architectural styles, ranging from neo-classical to 1970s concrete and modern glass and steel. Easy access on foot or by fantastic public transport to all areas, especially studenty areas of Headingley and Hyde Park. Leeds is easy to reach, being slap-bang in the middle of the country where the 2 main motorways (M1 and M62) intersect; it has an international airport and the busiest train station outside London. Leeds students are a friendly bunch! The university has one of the biggest and best ranges of courses in the country (from geography to aviation studies); its sheer size (33,000+ students) makes it able to offer more courses and modules than elsewhere. A great emphasis on students and their pastoral care; drop-out rate among the lowest, due to fantastic help and advice available to all students. The union (LUU), at the heart of the campus, is one of the most active and well-resourced in the country. Its multi-functioning building includes, yes, that legendary establishment, the SU bar – or 2 in Leeds' case. From a pint while fixated on Arsenal v Man U in the Old Bar, to a cocktail over the latest *Heat* magazine in the Terrace, there is something to suit everyone's tastes; and because of the low prices your student loan will last that little bit longer! Union also has a couple of the city's best clubs – Stylus and Pulse (home to fantastic club scene including Fruity, the official student night of the year); also the city's largest live music venue, playing host to some of the most exciting gigs around. LUU also prides itself on the services it offers its members: the student advice centre and great student employment service, Joblink; one of the broadest ranges of recreational societies and sports clubs in the UK (from aikido to yoga); and, to ensure you are safe while you study, a range of safety services and information (from free transport home to personal alarms and self-defence classes). All 1st years are guaranteed a place in university halls if they apply on time; great variety to choose from – swanky city centre flats to traditional catered halls on campus. City has plenty of rented accommodation; most students are in shared houses in Headingley and Hyde Park areas (the famous LS6). Unipol (backed by union and university) establishes housing standards in the private rented sector. Plenty to do in the city – West Yorkshire Playhouse, Opera North, Back-2-Basics and Speedqueen. Main nocturnal student activity based in 3 areas: Headingley, the union and the city centre. City has a fantastic gay scene, is home to some of the best urban music nights and is truly multicultural in nature. Great shopping: national chains along with local retailers; and Kirkgate market is a sight to behold, both for value and range of products.

Student footnotes

Housing: Most 1st years in halls. Plenty of private accommodation, mostly in Headingley and Hyde Park; check out Unipol (www.unipol.leeds.ac.uk). **Eats:** LUU for daytime eating. At night, it's good to get out: major chains; plenty of small cafés and restaurants for all tastes in city centre and Headingley. **Drink:** LUU bars serve cheap drinks. Huge variety of bars in Leeds. **Nightlife:** LUU nightclub, hosts variety of exciting gigs (Keane, Maroon 5, Joss Stone). City has endless clubs and bars, art-house cinemas, bowling alleys, lots of venues, West Yorkshire Playhouse and lots more. **Locals:** Quite friendly relationship, couple of city pubs to avoid. **Sports:** Loads of clubs, well-equipped sports centre on campus; international swimming pool in city centre. **Financial help:** Available from welfare service. **Jobs:** Jobshop on campus. **Best features:** Student-friendly city, large numbers of students (10% of the population). **And the worst:** One-way system with university in the middle of it (it makes buses look very, very attractive). **Past students:** Mark Thomas (comedian), Judi Dench (actress), Nick Witchel (BBC News), Jack Straw MP, Clare Short MP, Marc Almond (Soft Cell), Andy and Liz Kershaw (BBC Radio), most of the League of Gentlemen, Alan Yentob (BBC supremo), Mark Byford (another BBC supremo), Alistair McGowan (BBC TV), John Godber (playwright), Sir Phillip Watts (Shell), Dr Shuhei Toyoda (developed the Toyota Yaris), Sir Duncan Michael (built the Sydney Opera House), Kimberley Jane Walsh (Girls Aloud), Kay Mellor (actress), Corinne Bailey Rae (musician), Wole Soyinka (writer), Mark Knopfler (musician), Piers Sellers (astronaut). **More info?** See www.LUUonline.com.

Leicester University

Location:
Leicester, Midlands
(map 2)
Single campus close
to city centre

University of Leicester, University Road,
Leicester LE1 7RH
☎ Tel 0116 252 2522
🖷 Fax 0116 252 2200
✉ Email enquiry@le.ac.uk
💻 Website www.le.ac.uk

Student enquiries: Enquiry Management Team
(tel 0116 229 7477;
fax 0116 252 2447)
Applications: UCAS (direct if occasional,
part-time or study abroad)

In brief

Total Students: 19,375

49% postgraduate
51% undergraduate

Undergraduates: 565
80% full-time   83% UK students
13% mature   26% lower
on entry   socio-economic
                  groups

53% female   47% male

- **A top UK research-intensive university.**
- **Teaching staff:** 718 full-time, 48 part-time.
- **Broad study areas:** Arts and humanities, science and engineering, social sciences, law, medicine, education.

Freshers

- **Admissions information:** AS-levels accepted in combination with 2 (usually 3) A-levels or equivalent; Key Skills viewed favourably. UCAS tariff used in addition to subject-specific requirements.
- **First degree entrants:** 1945 UK, full-time.
- **Points on entry:** 370+ (average).
- **Drop-out rate:** 6% in 1st year.
- **Accommodation:** All 1st years housed who confirm their offer by the deadline.

Profile

Institution

Founded: 1921, receiving charter in 1957. **Site:** Campus 1 mile from Leicester city centre. **How to get there:** By train (London or Sheffield 75 mins, Birmingham 60 mins), station 15 mins' walk; by road, M1 and M69 motorways 5 miles from campus; by air – direct buses from regional international airports (Birmingham and East Midlands) and from Gatwick and Heathrow, direct train from Stansted. **Special features:** University leads technical design on Beagle 2 (UK's mission to Mars); DNA genetic fingerprinting discovered here; centre for South Asian studies; research centres focusing on football hooliganism, public order and labour market studies.

Courses

Academic features: All courses except medicine are modular (basic teaching unit a 12-week 10-credit module). **Awarding body:** University of Leicester. **Main undergraduate awards:** BA, BSc,

BEng, LLB, MBChB, MChem, MEng, MGeol, MMath, MPhys, MSci, FdA. **Length of courses:** 3 years; 4 years (eg those with foundation year, year abroad or in industry); 5 years (medicine, those with foundation year or year in industry/abroad).

Study opportunities & careers

Library and information services: Main library has 1.14 million items, including books, journal volumes, microforms, etc; multiple copies of prescribed textbooks on short loan; 1100 study places (library recently refurbished and doubled in size, with improved study rooms, IT facilities and lecture and seminar rooms). Information provision, £197 pa spent for each student (FTE). IT centre with a campus-wide network, open 24 hours/day in some departments. 740 points of access to library and internet (ratio workstations to students 1:11). IT support from helpdesk; information skills courses. **Other learning resources:** Computer centre, PC and Apple Mac labs, student learning centre to develop study skills. Specialist collections: English Local History; some 20,000 rare books and manuscripts; papers of Joe Orton. **Study abroad:** 150 placements at European universities. Some courses allow study in USA and elsewhere. Formal exchange links with over 75 EU and 14 US universities and colleges plus links in Australia, South Africa and Singapore in a wide range of subjects. **Careers:** Information and advice service, information and recruitment fair.

Student services & facilities

Student advice and services: AccessAbility centre for students with special needs, doctors, health education, welfare officers, financial advice for student budgeting, pastoral care in university accommodation, FPA counsellors, chaplains, student legal advice centre, Nightline telephone contact service. Nursery (independent) with favourable terms for student parents, playscheme at half terms. **Amenities:** Bookshops, bar, nightclub, disco, general shops and banks on site; Leicester University Theatre (link with Phoenix professional theatre in Leicester); Archduke Trio (resident chamber music group), university radio, TV station and newspaper. 90+ student societies. **Sporting facilities:** Excellent sports facilities including floodlit all-weather pitches, 2 fitness centres and 2 sports halls; 30 sports clubs. **Accommodation:** All 1st years who accept the offer of a place by the deadline are in university-managed accommodation; some halls of residence set in Botanic Gardens. 3935 places available, 3350 for 1st years: 2006 half-board places at £104–£138 pw (£93 pw shared), term time only; 1929 self-catering places at £67–£83 pw, Sept–June or longer. Privately owned accommodation: £40–£50 pw self-catering (current info available from SU).

Money

Living expenses budget: Minimum budget of £600–£620 a month (excluding tuition fees) recommended by university. **Term-time work:** University allows term-time work, up to 15 hours/week, for first-degree students. Some work available on campus in bars, accommodation, clerical; careers office and SU employment centre, WorkBank, help find work on and off campus. **Financial help:** Bursaries of £1310 pa for UK students whose family income is up to £20k; tapered bursary of £1010–£100 pa where family income is £20k–£39,300. Scholarships of £1k in some departments for 1st-year students with top entrance qualifications (ABB at A-level, 36 in IB). Also £450k government funds, grants and loans, 1200 students helped; particular help for students with special needs, those with dependants, mature students, self-financing students and those with field course requirements during summer. Various scholarships for international students, in particular from South East Asia. Apply to welfare office for help. **Tuition fees:** Home students pay £3225 pa for first degrees. International students £9450–£10,600 pa (classroom), £12,650 (lab), £22,900 (clinical).

Student view

Two of them: RH is Rob Hicks, Student Activities Officer (Graduate, American Studies); KD is Kirsten Dyer, Sabbatical – Academic Affairs Officer (Graduate, BA Economics)

Living

What's it like as a place to live? (RH) Big and diverse yet compact enough to easily travel around. **How's the student accommodation?** (KD) Very good. Mostly university-owned with a number of price ranges to suit different budgets. All halls are very sociable with great spirit. **What's the student population like?** (RH) Many diverse backgrounds from within the country, also a large international community. **How do students and locals get on?** (KD) There is a good atmosphere with many local shops offering student discounts.

Studying
What's it like as a place to study? (RH) Good mix of traditional and modern courses, excellent library facilities (new £32 million refurb last year). **What are the teaching staff like?** (KD) Very keen staff, they love incorporating their research into teaching!

Socialising
What are student societies like? (KD) We have many societies ranging from geography to ju-jitsu. They always love welcoming new people and they're a great way of making new friends. **What's a typical night out?** (KD) Mad-fer-it on Fridays at the SU. (RH) Hall bars then onto the SU venue. **And how much does it cost?** (KD) £3 entry with NUS card. (RH) £10–£20. **How can you get home safely?** (RH) Safe transport service run by the SU for £1.

Money
Is it an expensive place to live? No, as long as you budget well you can live very comfortably. A cheap city to live in, in particular private homes for 2nd and 3rd years. **Average price of a pint?** £1.90. **And the price of a takeaway?** £3–£10 **What's the part-time work situation?** Many jobs available, average wages. University doesn't like students working too much as it may interfere with study. Union bar/shop staff, other part-time work plentiful within university and SU as well as in city centre (10 mins from uni). Work bank housed within SU.

Summary
What's the best feature about the place? (RH) Brilliant campus and entertainments. Good community at halls. (KD) Location – very close to city and great entertainment for everybody. **And the worst?** (RH) Have to get a bus from halls to campus. (KD) None! **And to sum it all up?** (KD) A vibrant and exciting place, with something always going on! (RH) Brilliant social opportunities and excellent academic facilities.

Past students: Bob Mortimer (comedian), Professor Laurie Taylor (sociologist and radio presenter), Prof Malcolm Bradbury (author and academic), David Puttnam (film producer), J H Plumb (historian), C P Snow (scientist and novelist), Ron Pickering (athlete), Michael Nicholson (ITN reporter), Sue Cook (presenter), Jeff Hoffman (astronaut), Philip Larkin (poet), Sir John Robertson (High Commissioner to India). **More info?** Campaigns and development officer (tel 0116 223 1125), academic affairs officer (tel 0116 223 1128) or look at www.le.ac.uk/su.

Lincoln University

Location:
Lincoln, east Midlands
(map 2)
Lincoln city centre
(three sites), Hull and
Holbeach; partner
colleges

University of Lincoln, Brayford Pool,
Lincoln LN6 7TS
☎ Tel 01522 882000
🖷 Fax 01522 882088
✉ Email enquiries@lincoln.ac.uk
🖥 Website www.lincoln.ac.uk

Student enquiries: Student Support Centre
Applications: UCAS

In brief

Total Students: 16,705

24% FE Students
8% postgraduate
68% undergraduate

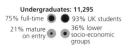
Undergraduates: 11,295
75% full-time 93% UK students
21% mature 36% lower
on entry socio-economic
groups

56% female 44% male

- **A modern university.**
- **Teaching staff:** 360 full-time, 405 part-time.
- **Broad study areas:** American studies; animal sciences; architecture; art and design; biomedical sciences; business; computing; English; food technology and manufacturing; forensic sciences; health and social care; history; journalism; law; management; media; performing arts; psychology; social sciences; sports sciences; theology.

Freshers

- **Admissions information:** Each case considered individually.
- **First degree entrants:** 2940 UK, full-time.
- **Points on entry:** 240–260 average.
- **Drop-out rate:** 7% in 1st year.
- **Accommodation:** Many 1st years in university accommodation.

Profile

Institution

Founded: 2001, building on a history of education in Lincolnshire and Hull dating back to 1850s. **Site:** 3 campuses in Lincoln (Brayford Pool Campus and Cathedral Campus both in city centre, Riseholme Campus 2 miles north); 1 in Hull city centre (Hull City Campus), approx 45 miles north of Lincoln; 1 in Holbeach, South Lincolnshire, approx 45 miles south of Lincoln. **How to get there:** To Lincoln: by train (2¼ hours from London Kings X, 1 hour from Nottingham); bus services from Newark, Retford, Doncaster; by road via A1 and A46/A57; or by air (campus 40 mins from Humberside International Airport and Doncaster Robin Hood Airport). Brayford Pool and Cathedral campuses both short walk from station; shuttle bus runs between 3 Lincoln sites. To Hull, by rail (2¾ hours from London Kings X, 1 hour from Leeds); by road (M62); by air (Humberside Airport); or by ferry (daily crossings from Rotterdam and Zeebrugge). To Holbeach: by train (Spalding, ½ hour from Peterborough); or by road via A52 and A17.

Courses

Academic features: Specialises in relevant courses. Applications encouraged from those from all age groups and communities, including mature students without formal qualifications. **Awarding body:** University of Lincoln. **Main undergraduate awards:** BA, BSc. **Length of courses:** 3 years; 4 years (sandwich).

Study opportunities & careers

Library and information services: Total of 282,000+ volumes, 1100+ print periodicals; extensive e-library, including 2400 e-journals and multiple online databases, newspapers, audio-visual items, dissertations and theses. 980+ study places. Main Lincoln library open 100 hours/week. Information provision, £74 pa spent for each student (FTE). 1184 PCs across campuses, all with free internet and email; ratio of 1:10 computers to students. IT skills courses available on request. **Other learning resources:** Language labs, photographic studios, broadcast-quality TV studios at Lincoln; video editing facilities, high-speed network at Hull. **Study abroad:** Students can study in Europe, USA, Australia. Formal exchange links with 60 EU universities or colleges (range of subjects), and growing number in the USA, China and other countries. **Careers:** Information and advice; placement service at Hull and Lincoln.

Student services & facilities

Student advice and services: Advice, student funding and information team, counselling, chaplaincy, prayer room, disability services (Dart), accommodation office, international office. **Amenities:** SU in student centre Lincoln, with bars, learning environment (the Hub), snack bar, shop. Bar and shop at other sites. SOAP centre (Student Opportunities, Activities and Participation), education and welfare centre, extensive SU societies and sports clubs, community volunteers and job shop. **Sports facilities:** On-campus sports centre at Lincoln; use of local facilities in Hull at good rate. **Accommodation:** 40% of 1st years in university halls. 1037 self-catering places at Brayford Pool Campus, £84 pw (including bills); 180 half-board places at Riseholme Campus, £112 pw. Private purpose-built student accommodation abundant in both cities, £65–£105 pw; university operates code of practice and lists of member landlords.

Money

Living expenses budget: Minimum budget of £7800 for a 9-month academic year (excluding tuition fees) recommended by university. **Term-time work:** Majority of students work part-time. Plenty of part-time available in Lincoln and Hull. **Financial help:** Bursaries of up to £600 pa for UK students whose family income is up to £25k; tapered (down to nil) where family income is £25k–£60k. Also awards for local students taking science and technology courses (£1k pa), for students who had been in care (£1,500 pa), international students (£1k in 1st year) and athletes (£500 or £1k); faculty scholarships for students entering with high points score. Also approx £324k government funds; apply to student revenue office for help. **Tuition fees:** Home students pay £3225 pa for first degrees. International students pay £8524 pa (classroom), £9038 (lab/studio).

Student view

Main campus, Brayford, is ideally sited at the bottom of modern Lincoln, with fantastic views up to the top of Steep Hill and the historic city. The cathedral dominates the skyline and provides a wonderful contrast to the modern university buildings: original building (the Atrium) is very impressive; also learning resources centre, science building and state-of-the-art sports centre. The university has also developed and breathed life into derelict buildings on campus: old great central warehouse has been transformed into the library and the old locomotive engine sheds into the SU. The newly opened Engine Shed is one of the region's largest and most impressive student venues, consists of bars, concert hall and union offices; in its 1st year the venue attracted a number of big-name artists. University has a number of campuses. Riseholme Park, a 240-hectare estate (housing agriculture, animal-related and biological science courses), is very close to the city, making it possible to enjoy both countryside and city life. Cathedral campus (majority of art and design courses) is in impressive historic buildings around the cathedral. The university also has campuses in Hull and Holbeach. SU is very active and aims to work with the university to improve the student experience; very successful athletic union, education and welfare elements, community volunteers encouraging involvement in the union, university and the community. Many sports and societies. Amazing growth in nightlife in last few years: many new pubs and bars battling hard for student market. There's plenty to do and many laughs to be had.

Student footnotes

Housing: University-approved list; fairly cheap, good quality and standards rising with lots of new developments. Halls on campus getting old. **Eats:** Meal for £2.50–£3.50 on campus. Pub food OK;

some 2-for-1 offers. Loads of takeaways and fast-food outlets. **Drink:** SU bar has a great atmosphere. Some good, new bars in the city and Brayford Waterfront. **Nightlife:** SU bars all open late; big names in SU venue include the Zutons, Babyshambles, Dirty Pretty Things, Kings of Leon and the Beautiful South. Nights hosted at Ritzy, Po Na Na's, Sugarcubes and Scream. Cinema on Brayford Waterfront. **Locals:** Generally fine, most friendly (minority hostile to students). **Sports:** Local clubs. Lincoln FC has good student offers. **Financial help:** University student services helpful; applications processed quickly. **Best features:** Modern campus in beautiful surroundings with city centre 5 mins away. **And worst:** Can't get away with anything without being found out! And transport links not that hot. **Past students:** Jon Fox and Tom Rhys (Viking FM breakfast show; Sony Newcomer award winners), Ann Brown and Christine Ford (England women's basketball), Eliot Morley MP. **More info?** Visit www.lincolnsu.com.

Liverpool Hope University

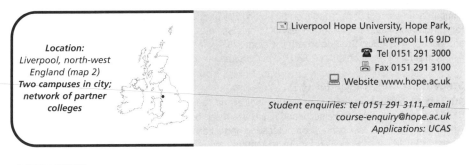

Location:
Liverpool, north-west
England (map 2)
Two campuses in city;
network of partner
colleges

Liverpool Hope University, Hope Park,
Liverpool L16 9JD
☎ Tel 0151 291 3000
🖨 Fax 0151 291 3100
💻 Website www.hope.ac.uk

Student enquiries: tel 0151 291 3111, email
course-enquiry@hope.ac.uk
Applications: UCAS

In brief

Total Students: 7885

21% postgraduate
79% undergraduate

Undergraduates: 6190

73% full-time — 93% UK students
28% mature on entry — 42% lower socio-economic groups

73% female — 27% male

- **A modern university.**
- **Teaching staff:** 646 total.
- **Broad study areas:** Art and design, business, education, environment, health, information technology, law, media, music and performing arts, psychology, sport, theology.

Freshers

- **Admissions information:** Currently offers of 240–280 points to include a minimum of 2 A-levels or equivalent plus any subject-specific entry requirements; Key Skills considered at confirmation of results time. UCAS tariff used on all courses.
- **First degree entrants:** 1565 UK, full-time.
- **Points on entry:** 224 (average).
- **Drop-out rate:** 12% in 1st year.
- **Accommodation:** All 1st years housed.

Profile

Institution

Founded: From 3 Church teacher training colleges (earliest founded 1844); university status in 2005.
Site: Hope Park is main campus in Childwall; the Cornerstone is at Everton. Network of partner

colleges in Blackburn and Bury. **How to get there:** Liverpool well served by rail (to Lime Street Station; from Manchester 40 mins, London 3 hours), by road (via M6 or M62), by coach (to City Centre Coach Station), by air (Liverpool John Lennon Airport) and sea (ferries from Dublin and Isle of Man). Hope Park close to Broad Green station, the Cornerstone close to Lime Street station.

Courses

Academic features: Degree courses in a range of subjects including education, theology and religious studies, performing arts, sports studies. **Awarding body:** Liverpool Hope University. **Main undergraduate awards:** BA, BA(QTS), BSc, BDes. **Length of courses:** 3 or 4 years.

Study opportunities & careers

Library and information services: Sheppard-Worlock library has 250,000+ items, 700+ print journals, 250+ electronic journals and information sources. Also non-book material, range of electronic information including CD-ROMs, indexes, abstracts, datasets and research facilities. 600 computers for student use. Information provision, £81 pa spent for each student (FTE). **Other learning resources:** Satellite and terrestrial broadcasts, music laboratory, sound recording equipment and video edit facilities. **Study abroad:** Exchange links in many subject areas with Europe, USA and Asia. **Careers:** Information, advice, work experience and placements.

Student services & facilities

Student advice and services: On-campus medical and counselling service; ecumenical chapel and multi-faith prayer room; chaplaincy team; financial adviser; co-ordinator for students with disabilities. **Amenities:** SU has unisex barber, computer shop and a bar. Also refectory, common rooms and café. **Sporting facilities:** At Hope Park, sports hall, fitness centre, floodlit AstroTurf pitch. Facilities for range of sports (5-a-side, badminton, tennis, volleyball, netball, basketball, hockey). Access to squash courts, football and rugby pitches. **Accommodation:** All 1st years offered a place in halls. Self-catering rent £66.50 pw, catered £81 pw (£75–£89 pw ensuite); optional catering packages extra. Contracts of various lengths (ie 36 and 40 weeks) available. Students living in privately owned accommodation pay approx £60 pw for self-catering.

Money

Living expenses budget: Minimum budget of £5850–£7k pa (excluding tuition fees) recommended by university. **Term-time work:** University allows term-time work for full-time students (40% believed to work). A variety of work available on campus. **Financial help:** Bursary of £500 pa for all UK and EU students with a family income of up to £39,300. A number of scholarships (up to £2k pa) for excellence, performance or for students from partner schools and colleges. Also access to learning fund for students on low incomes in particular circumstances. Apply to student funds office for information. **Tuition fees:** Home students pay £3225 pa for first degrees. International students pay £6600 pa.

Student view
Sean Clift, Entertainments Officer (Graduate, Business Studies)

Living
What's it like as a place to live? Brilliant. Liverpool is a lively town, especially with the 2008 capital of culture; there is always something to do. **How's the student accommodation?** Really good, free cleaners for common areas and its's really modern and quite reasonable. **What's the student population like?** Genuinely friendly. There are people from all sorts of diverse backgrounds along with local students so you have the opportunity to get to know many different people and cultures. **How do students and locals get on?** Great community atmosphere. The locals understand it's a student area.

CITY UNIVERSITY LONDON

The University for business and the professions

CHALLENGE YOUR MIND, INVEST IN YOUR FUTURE

Actuarial Science
Business & Finance
Computing & Information Technology
Communications
Cultural Policy and Management
Economics
Engineering
Journalism
Law

Maths
Midwifery
Music
Nursing
Optometry
Politics
Psychology
Radiography
Sociology
Speech and Language Therapy

To find out more visit **www.city.ac.uk**

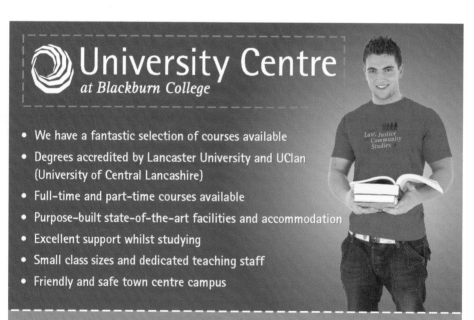

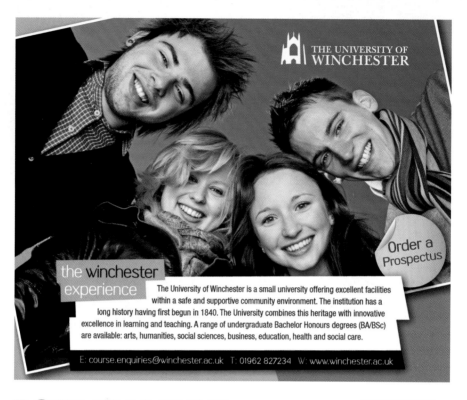

Anglia Ruskin University

Cambridge & Chelmsford

Why choose Anglia Ruskin?

£85 million invested in new facilities for students

We have invested over £85m in new study facilities, additional social and sports facilities for students. Amongst our specialist study facilities we have a:

- Art Gallery
- Complementary medicine suite
- Forensic Science Laboratory, complete with scene-of-crime workshops
- Human energetics and performance laboratory
- Mock courtroom
- Optometry Clinic
- Simulated hospital wards and operating theatres
- Suite of multimedia sound and recording studios.

Prestigious, high quality and practical courses

Our degree courses are designed to be not only vocational and relevant to the needs of industry and the professions, but also engaging and stimulating with a great emphasis on practical skills.

91.4%* of our graduates go into work or further study within six months of graduation, one of the highest employability rates in the Higher Education sector.

* The Higher Education Statistics Agency (HESA) Performance Indicator Employment of Graduates 06/07.

We can help you get real work exposure

We have links with over 120 local employers to help you get the work experience you need to compliment your studies.

Industry experts help us design our courses

These currently include:

Former Human Resources Director for Lloyds TSB.

Former Managing Director of Aston Martin and Jaguar Cars.

Current Head of Logistics for Mercedes Benz.

For a full list of all our courses please visit our website, **www.anglia.ac.uk/telegraph**

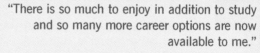

For more information: | **Click** www.anglia.ac.uk/telegraph
Email answers@anglia.ac.uk
Call 0845 271 3333

www.anglia.ac.uk/telegraph

Studying

What's it like as a place to study? Flexible courses and great tutors plus excellent facilities. **What are the teaching staff like?** Interesting and also entertaining. They very much engage the students.

Socialising

What are student societies like? The union is the heart of the university with different events 3 times a week. The guy who does it really works hard for the students! **What's a typical night out?** Starts with cheap drinks in the union then a taxi into town, which is relatively inexpensive due to the student bars, which are there in plenty. **And how much does it cost?** Usually around £20–£25. **How can you get home safely?** Inexpensive taxis.

Money

Is it an expensive place to live? It depends how you manage your money but an OD (overdraft) is helpful! **Average price of a pint?** £1.40. **And the price of a takeaway?** £3.50. **What's the part-time work situation?** University helps you find work, provides lots of jobs for students within university.

Summary

What's the best feature about the place? The union and the community feel. **And the worst?** The hard work! **And to sum it all up?** Liverpool Hope is like a home away from home but without the rules and with a lot of other people in your situation!

Past students: David Alton (politician), Willy Russell (playwright), Paul Tulip (*The Apprentice*, series two). **More info?** SU (tel 0151 291 3651, email vpres@hope.ac.uk) or visit www.hopesu.co.uk.

Liverpool John Moores University

Location:
Liverpool, north-west England (map 2)
Sites across the city; partner colleges

✉ Liverpool John Moores University, Roscoe Court, 4 Rodney Street, Liverpool L1 2TZ
☎ Tel 0151 231 5090
🖷 Fax 0151 231 3462
✉ Email recruitment@ljmu.ac.uk
💻 Website www.ljmu.ac.uk

Student enquiries: Customer Relationship Team
Applications: UCAS

In brief

Total Students: 24,370

17% postgraduate
83% undergraduate

Undergraduates: 20,270
73% full-time
22% mature on entry
92% UK students
41% lower socio-economic groups

55% female   45% male

- **A modern university.**

- **Teaching staff:** 1000 full-time and part-time.

- **Broad study areas:** Art; biological and earth sciences; biomolecular sciences; built environment; business; computing and maths; education and community studies; engineering and technology; health; human sciences; law and applied social studies; media and creative studies; pharmacy and chemistry; science; social studies.

Freshers

- **Admissions information:** A-levels, AS-levels (GCE and VCE) accepted plus alternative qualifications; Key Skills viewed favourably. Many courses have specific subject and grade requirements. UCAS tariff used.
- **First degree entrants:** 4295 UK, full-time.
- **Points on entry:** 180+ (average).
- **Drop-out rate:** 11% in 1st year.
- **Accommodation:** All 1st years housed.

Profile

Institution

Founded: 1823 as Liverpool Mechanics and Apprentices' Library; became Liverpool Polytechnic 1970; university status in 1992. **Site:** Broadly concentrated on 3 sites: City Campus, Mount Pleasant Campus and one in southern suburb (IM Marsh Campus); also number of buildings around city centre. **How to get there:** Liverpool well served by rail (Lime Street Station from Manchester 40 mins, London 3 hours), by road (via M6/M62), by coach (to city centre coach station), by air (Liverpool John Lennon Airport) and sea (ferries from Dublin, Belfast and Isle of Man). Main sites close to Lime Street and Liverpool central stations and many bus routes. **Special features:** Links with local access courses through various partnerships. Positively welcomes (and long experience of supporting) mature students with non-standard qualifications or from access courses.

Courses

Academic features: Modular framework offers a range of subjects, single, joint and combined awards (Honours), major/minor degree choice. All degrees courses make work-related learning and development of graduate skills explicit; students also encouraged to develop higher level World of Work (WoW) skills. **Awarding body:** Liverpool John Moores University. **Main undergraduate awards:** BA, BEd, BA/BSc (QTS), BSc BDes, BEng, LLB, MEng, MChem, MPharm. **Length of courses:** 3 years (full-time); 4 years (sandwich). Extended degree courses 4 years (full-time); 5 years (sandwich).

Study opportunities & careers

Library and information services: Learning resource centres (library, IT, multimedia, audio-visual centres) on all sites; 570,000 printed monographs, 7500 electronic books, 24,000+ periodicals (22,000 e-journals, 1850 print); 1640 study places. Information provision, £98 pa spent for each student (FTE). Access to IT facilities 24 hours/day; helpdesks on all sites and help in open-access IT suites. Induction to all library and information services for new students; IT skills tutorials, 'next steps' guide, student computer helpers assist students with LJMU software. **Study abroad:** 6% of students spend a period abroad. **Careers:** Information, advice and guidance on career development, training and study support. New graduate development centre provides training and assessment and supports students in developing WoW skills.

Student services & facilities

Student advice and services: Nurses, chaplains, counsellors, accommodation office, disability staff, welfare and money advisers, international student adviser, study support and mental health liaison. **Amenities:** SU facilities include bar, nightclub, coffee bar, art shop, newsagent, cash machine, advice centre, clubs and societies on 3 sites. **Accommodation:** All new students guaranteed accommodation (many also have senior students living in, providing support and advice to new students). Approx. 3000 places (most ensuite) in hall-style accommodation in city centre or IM Marsh campus (university or privately owned), rent £72–£86 pw Plenty of houses and flats in private sector, co-ordinated by Liverpool Student Homes (run jointly with other city universities), £59–£69 pw.

Money

Living expenses budget: Minimum budget of £6k–£7k pa (excluding fees) recommended by university. **Term-time work:** Workbank, based in SU, finds temporary work in and out of term time (and graduate employment). Part-time vacancies include bar work, call centre, general admin. More info, telephone 0151 231 4964. **Financial help:** Bursaries of £1050 pa for students with a family income below £25k, and of £420 pa where family income is £25k–£50k. Scholarships: of £10k pa for up to 6 academically gifted students a year (360 UCAS points and a level of excellence and achievement above their peers); of £1k pa for students with 360 UCAS points from 3 units or equivalent; of £1k pa for students demonstrating commitment or excellence in eg volunteering, the arts or citizenship; sport scholarships; and a range of course-specific scholarships. Childcare bursary for students not eligible for an LA childcare grant (up to £148 pw for the first child, or 70% of actual cost). Hillsborough Trust Fund helps disadvantaged students from Merseyside for 2+ years. Also £30k hardship funds; £75k for part-time students, students with children and care leavers; £795k government access to learning funds (some 1304 student helped). **Tuition fees:** Home students pay £3225 pa for first degree courses. International students pay £8320 pa (classroom), £8950 (lab/studio).

Student view

2 main sites in the city centre plus education faculty 3 miles away. Accommodation all pretty good and well located. Lots of work going into new buildings and facilities. Recently implemented 'world of work' skills make each LJMU graduate highly attractive to prospective employers. Active SU, socially and politically balanced: supports around 50 clubs and societies, and BUCS teams competing to a high level; runs award-winning radio station (Shout Radio); also runs 3 shops and 4 bars (cheap and plush). The Haigh has very trendy entertainments bar/venue (the Cooler) and pub (Scholars) and a relaxing coffee bar (Wicked Café) selling fair-trade food and drink. SU puts on regular, quality entertainments 5 nights a week. Sport-for-all philosophy (national champions in several sports recently, including Gaelic football and rugby league). Good staff/student relations. Wide range of subjects; mix of continuous assessment and exams. Industry years and field trips on some courses. Normally very easy to change course in first 4 weeks. Facilities average – 3 good learning resource centres; student services and careers service; a jobshop (workbank); comprehensive welfare advice from university and SU – strictly confidential. Good relationship with community. City was Capital of Culture 2008; has wide range of theatres (from enormous Empire to tiny Unity), art galleries and museums and a good shopping centre from the Albert Dock to the St John's Centre and Church Street. 2 large cinemas, including 1 8-screen (home to MTV Europe Music Awards 2008). Excellent town clubs and good pubs in abundance. High north-west intake (around a third from Liverpool), mainly from state schools; but students from all over country and a growing number international. Ugly racism minimal. Easy to get attached to Liverpool – a vibrant, exciting city, despite what the media say, with a tremendous night life.

Student footnotes

Housing: Uni accommodation in city centre, mostly excellent and much less than private; Liverpool Student Homes co-ordinates off-campus accommodation. **Eats:** All sorts of food in city; meals and snacks in the union; excellent Chinatown; try Quick Chef, Egg Café (veggie), Kimos, Eddie Rockets, Soul Cafe, – lunch £2+, dinner £4.50. **Drink:** From £1.80 a pint in SU (and lots of weekly promotions); Haigh Building, Medication@Cream on Wednesdays, Concert Square; Slaters Street, Garlands on Thursdays. All city-centre bars cheap Mon–Thurs. **Nightlife:** Haigh Building, the Cooler on campus; excellent regular entertainments 3 nights/week, special events include bands, off-the-wall comedy, etc. **Locals:** City has good mix of locals and students, most locals are really friendly, kids can be mouthy. Most student areas are in high insurance brackets. **Sports:** Everton, Kirkby and Toxteth sports centres. Union sports facilities at IM Marsh. **Travel:** Cheap, regular buses to most areas; train network to further parts of Liverpool; can get to London in 4 hours. **Jobs:** In city – bars to clothes shops, cafés to restaurants. SU employs 150 students (bars, admin, café). Successful university jobshop (3700 students registered). **Financial help:** Considerable uni access fund (advice free); quick and available for those in serious need. **Informal name:** JMU. **Best features:** Excellent SU; good mix of students; location. **And worst:** Some parts of uni admin. **Past students:** Debbie Greenwood (presenter), Martin Offiah (rugby league), Julian Cope (Teardrop Explodes), Desmond Pitcher (chairman of North West Water), Caroline Aherne (comedian), Stephen Byers MP, Philip Gayle (Big Breakfast). **More info?** Contact President (tel 0151 231 4901) or visit student website at www.l-s-u.com.

Liverpool University

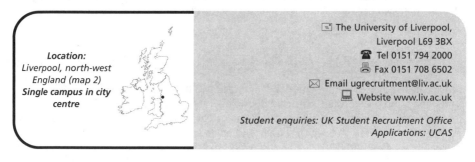

Location:
Liverpool, north-west
England (map 2)
**Single campus in city
centre**

▣ The University of Liverpool,
Liverpool L69 3BX
☎ Tel 0151 794 2000
🖶 Fax 0151 708 6502
✉ Email ugrecruitment@liv.ac.uk
💻 Website www.liv.ac.uk

*Student enquiries: UK Student Recruitment Office
Applications: UCAS*

In brief

Total Students: 20,665

19% postgraduate
81% undergraduate

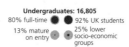

Undergraduates: 16,805
80% full-time   92% UK students
13% mature   25% lower
on entry   socio-economic
groups

54% female   46% male

- **A top UK research-intensive university.**
- **Teaching staff:** 1109 full-time, 254 part-time
- **Broad study areas:** Arts, engineering, law, science, social and environmental studies, medicine and dentistry, veterinary science, health sciences.

Freshers

- **Admissions information:** AS-levels accepted in combination with 2 (usually 3+) A-levels or equivalent, depending on programme to be studied.
- **First degree entrants:** 3650 UK, full-time.
- **Points on entry:** 377 (average).
- **Drop-out rate:** 5% in 1st year.
- **Accommodation:** All 1st years housed.

Profile

Institution

Founded: 1881. **Site:** 85-acre campus in city centre. **How to get there:** Liverpool well-served by rail (to Lime Street Station; from Manchester 40 mins, London 2½ hours), by road (via M6 or M62), by coach (to City Centre Coach Station), by air (Liverpool John Lennon Airport) and sea (ferries from Dublin and Isle of Man).

Courses

Awarding body: University of Liverpool. **Main undergraduate awards:** BA, BArch, BDS, BEng, BN, BSc, BVSc, LLB, MBChB. **Length of courses:** 3 and 4 years; others 5 years (medicine, dentistry, vet science).

Study opportunities & careers

Library and information services: 2 main libraries plus others in departments; 1.8 million books, 9000 e-journals, 2700 print journals; 1000 study places. Specialist collections: Spanish Civil War, science fiction, early children's books, manuscripts, gypsy collection, private press publications, children's welfare organisations, science fiction collection. Induction to library and information services available (varies by dept/course) plus IT skills courses for non-specialist students. Information provision, £244 pa spent for each student (FTE). Separate library and IT services. 2302 PCs available to students plus 2200 in departments; network accessible from all rooms in halls, some 60+ wired data sockets around campus and 70 wireless points; network gives access to library, university network and internet. 24-hour access; helpdesk and online support available. **Other learning resources:** Ness botanic gardens; Leahurst veterinary field station. **Study abroad:** Less than 1% of students spend a period abroad. Exchanges with universities across EFTA and EU, most open to non-language specialists. **Careers:** Information, advice and limited placement service.

Student services & facilities

Student advice and services: 2 full-time, 2 part-time student counsellors, student mental health advisory service (1 full-time adviser), student health service, disability support team, chaplains. **Amenities:** Over 100 cultural, social and sports clubs and societies. Several theatres, concert hall, places of worship, etc. in city. **Sporting facilities:** 2 sports halls on campus: swimming pool, fitness suite including cardiovascular and resistance gyms. Playing fields near halls of residence. **Accommodation:** All 1st years who apply by deadline in university accommodation, plus most late applicants. Some 3360 places available: 2075 full-board places in halls (all for 1st years), average £107 pw, term time only; 1285 self-catering places, average rent £69 pw, 32–42 week contracts. Students live in privately rented accommodation for 2 years or more, at approx £46–85 pw (over-supply of private accommodation in city).

Money

Living expenses budget: Minimum budget of £5500–£7k per academic year (excluding tuition fees) recommended by university. **Term-time work:** No university policy on part-time work for full-time students; free service (PULSE) provides information on vacancies available. **Financial help:** Bursaries of £1400 pa for UK students whose family income is up to £25k. Scholarships of £4k pa for UK students with high entrance points whose family income is up to £20,800; of £1500 pa to students on specified courses who have high entrance points or perform well during their course; others for residents of Merseyside and for international students. Also £763,527 government grants. Special help: students with children, self-financing or mature students. **Tuition fees:** Home students pay £3225 pa for first degree courses (£625 for year abroad/industry; £1255 for Year 0). International students pay £9400 pa (arts), £10,400 (architecture), £12k (science), £18k–£18,600 (clinical).

Student view

Liverpool has much to offer everyone, particularly as the 2008 Capital of Culture – a multitude of bars, restaurants, pubs, clubs, galleries, museums and shops cater for all tastes, and are generally cheaper and friendlier than in the rest of the country. University is 5 mins from heart of the city centre, with regular buses to and from main student areas, halls, town centre and main train station; taxis charge reasonably. 2 main libraries (one open 24 hours); both have good computing facilities. Sports centre recently extended; athletic union, based in the guild of students, is extremely active with around 50 clubs. Courses and teaching are high standard, some of international standing; fairly diverse with traditional courses such as law, veterinary science, dentistry, medicine, English, etc. complemented by rarer ones such as Irish studies and popular music. Most 1st years live in traditional halls in the leafy suburb of Mossley Hill, a few miles out of town; 2nd and 3rd years share one of the surplus of student houses along the main bus routes into town, or increasingly go into one of the private self-catered halls in the city centre; Liverpool Student Homes is excellent at finding appropriate accommodation. Diverse student community with a good combination of students from all over the country, local and international students, and mature students. The guild is run for and by students; offers everything from entertainment to advice, representation to skills training. You name it: from snowboarding to pot-holing, clubbing to juggling, theatre to fundraising, there's a club or society dedicated to it (if there isn't, the guild will help you set one up). Great ents programme, boasting 10 bars, the biggest and best members-only club nights in the city; weekly comedy nights, gigs galore in the Mountford Hall and Stanley Theatre; also runs Liverpool Academies 1, 2 and 3 (largest music venue in city, holds 180 concerts a year). Guild has banks, hairdressers, travel agent, optician and shop (cut-price newspapers, stationery, snacks), pool rooms and a choice of cheap eateries. Budding broadcasters can get involved in the radio station, ICON; newshounds have the *Liverpool Student*, the newspaper produced by the guild and read by 40,000 students. The Guild's own charity, Student Community Action, offers work on rewarding local projects, and LUSTI (Liverpool University Student Trainers Initiative) provides free skills training run by students. Guild advice centre runs a free, confidential drop-in service – everything from welfare matters to your rights as a tenant. Guild and university together offer commitment to academic success, welfare support and personal development, at the heart of one of the warmest, friendliest cities in the country.

Student footnotes

Housing: Good-quality self-catering; limited for married students. Liverpool Student Homes for off-campus accommodation. **Eats:** Meal for £3 on campus; excellent range of food in guild until late (including new bar/restaurant, international cuisine); good food on rest of campus – but rarely at awkward hours. Vegetarian restaurants and food shops in town; great cheap eating places near university do lunchtime student specials. Meal for £3 in the Egg Café, No 7 Café. **Drink:** Guild good for cheap drink. Slaters (Slater Street) and midweek pint in some clubs cheap. **Nightlife:** Great ents, good value for money; great variety – comedy, bands (include Zutons, Lost Prophets, Embrace, Primal Scream and Lilly Allen). Good student clubs, eg Krazy House. **Locals:** Tremendously friendly and welcoming. No particular bad spots (though many students prefer not to live in Kensington). **Sports:** Excellent university sports centre and swimming pool. **Travel:** Travel shop in the Guild can sort out train/coach fares. **Financial help:** Generous bursary scheme. Hardship fund gives grants or loans for any student in financial difficulties to enable them to stay at uni. **Jobs:** In many bars, clubs, shops and the guild; careers service also helps. **Jargon:** Guild (SU); the other place (Liverpool John Moores University). **Informal name:** Liverpool Uni. **Best features:** Students and guild; almost all teaching on one site (except vet field station and some research units). **And worst:** None. **Past students:** Patricia Routledge (actress), Jon Snow (ITN reporter), Steve Coppell (footballer), Dame Rose Heilbron (High Court Judge), Phil Redmond (TV writer – *Brookside*), Ann Leuchars (TV newscaster), Maeve Sherlock (Refugee Council). **More info?** Contact guild on 0151 794 6868, email guild@liv.ac.uk or visit website (www.lgos.org.uk).

London Business School

Location:
central London
(map 3)
**Single site in
Regent's Park**

✉ London Business School, Regent's Park, London NW1 4SA
☎ Tel 020 7000 7000
🖷 Fax 020 7000 7001
✉ Email webenquiries@london.edu
🖥 Website www.london.edu

*Student enquiries: Information Officer
Applications: Direct (application form or online via
the website)*

In brief

Total Students: 1495

100% postgraduate

Undergraduates: 565
58% full-time ● ● 30% UK students

24% female   76% male

- **World-class research-intensive graduate business school**, part of London University.
- **Teaching and research staff:** 92.
- **Broad study areas:** Business administration; corporate finance; management.
- **Accommodation:** Limited on-campus accommodation.

Profile

Institution

Founded: 1965. **Structural features:** Graduate school of London University. **Site:** Elegant Nash terrace overlooking the Regent's Park lake; and nearby in Taunton Place (information/IT facilities and sports complex). **How to get there:** Underground (Baker Street station closest); buses. **Special features:** Research centres include economic forecasting, finance, business strategy, entrepreneurial management and new and emerging markets.

Courses

Academic features: Case teaching, group assignments, visiting speakers, student consultancy projects, shadowing projects, assessed class participation, computer simulation, large variety of corporate partners. Significant number of international professors – over 60% non-UK. Joint global executive MBA with Columbia University (New York). MBA can be taken full-time or part-time; all study a language other than English. **Awarding body:** University of London. **Main awards:** MBA, EMBA, EMBA-Global, Dubai-London Executive MBA, Master's in Finance (MiF), Sloan Fellowship, PhD. **Length of courses:** MBA 15–21 months, full-time; EMBA and EMBA-Global 20 months part-time; Dubai-London Executive MBA 16 months, part-time; MiF 10 months, full-time; Sloan Fellowship 10 months, full-time; PhD 4 years, full-time.

Study opportunities & careers

Library and information services: Corporate library includes comprehensive stock of annual reports and Extel cards – online database facilities available. Information provision, £350 pa spent for each student (FTE). Computer labs (including innovation centre) and high-tech networks running through campus. **Study abroad:** 35% of MBA programme students go on international exchange for a term in one of 33 top business schools worldwide. **Careers:** Career services (CV writing, case presentation, careers fair, company presentation and interviews on campus). Personal professional development portfolio. **Employment:** E-commerce, start-ups, finance, strategy consulting, manufacturing and service industries worldwide.

Student services & facilities

Amenities: Close to West End and City. MBA bar. **Sports:** On campus – gym, aerobics room and swimming pool; off campus – squash at Lord's cricket ground; football, tennis and other sports in Regent's Park. **Accommodation:** Students rent accommodation and share with other students close to campus.

Money

Living expenses budget: Minimum budget of £1k per month – average £1880 – recommended by school (excluding tuition fees). **Financial help:** London University access funds. Loan schemes and substantial scholarship programme. Approx. average award ranges from £1k to £10k. **Tuition fees:** £44,490 for full-time MBA; £45,900 for EMBA; US$132,840 EMBA-Global; US$79,950 Dubai-London Executive MBA; £29,700 MiF; £42,900 for Sloan Fellowship.

Student view

A Nash terrace overlooking Regent's Park lake; an elegant facade hiding very well-equipped lecture theatres, computer rooms – and supposedly the best business library and IT facilities in Europe. No on-campus student housing. A subsidised restaurant and cafeteria. LBS is fun but incredibly demanding – not for the faint-hearted. Students typically put in 80–90-hour weeks during the 1st year; weekends and evenings off are rare! The top European business school (*Financial Times*); both students and faculty totally motivated and committed, with a strong career ethos among students. High percentage of women students and very international. International focus in curriculum, as well as in various projects and field visits. An international exchange programme allows students to spend a term in another top business school (in Europe, Asia, North and South America). Average graduating salary £50k plus, although they will swear that is not why they are here! Average age of entrants is 29. An exclusive, multi-layer admissions procedure with tough entry requirements, including average of 3–4 years' professional experience (apply early – places are quickly filled). Low drop-out rate and few overall failures. Part-timers on MBA programme are usually sponsored and take 2 years to complete course. Great emphasis on high quality of teaching and research; most staff have experience in business schools abroad and consulting links with industry/commerce. Students are very vocal if they are not getting value for time or money; students formally assess lecturers each term. Almost everyone is there to work hard – not for fun. Football, rugby, aerobics and squash are popular and there's a lot of jogging and boating around Regent's Park; gymnasium on site. Careers clubs (such as finance, entrepreneurs, women in business and consultancy) are well attended; students can mix freely with guest speakers, generally senior business figures (eg Michael Dell, Bill Gates). SA non-political, purely administrative and social. 3 or 4 large events per term, well attended, especially the unforgettable summer ball!

Student footnotes

Housing: Look on noticeboards, ask agencies and leaving students. **Drink:** Windsor Castle pub adjacent to campus. Breakspear is good local brew. **Eats:** Meals reasonably priced on campus. Windsor Castle, Light of India and Singapore Gardens good, cheap. **Nightlife:** Many on-campus parties. Own band. **Locals:** Very friendly. **Loans:** Clearing banks offer low-interest loans to UK students, which most take up. **Jobs:** All students earn money for their project work and in the summer. **Best features:** The people. **And worst:** Expense of London. **Past students:** John Egan (ex-BAA), Iain Vallance (BT chairman), Martin Sorrell (CEO of WPP Group), Matthew Carrington MP, Sir Ron Dearing (Dearing Report into Higher Education), Bernard Taylor (CEO Medeva), Sir Richard Greenbury (ex-Marks and Spencer), David Currie (Ofcom), Gary Hamel (business strategist and author).

London College of Communication

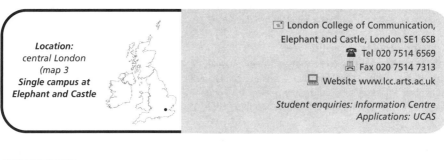

Location:
central London
(map 3
**Single campus at
Elephant and Castle**

London College of Communication,
Elephant and Castle, London SE1 6SB
☎ Tel 020 7514 6569
🖷 Fax 020 7514 7313
🖵 Website www.lcc.arts.ac.uk

*Student enquiries: Information Centre
Applications: UCAS*

In brief

Total Students: 9000

50% undergraduate
15% postgraduate
35% FE Students

Undergraduates: 3500
100% full-time ●

- **Specialist design, media and communication college.** Part of University of the Arts London.
- **Teaching staff:** 270 full-time.
- **Broad study areas:** Media (journalism, photography, broadcasting, film, animation, sound arts, production for live events and TV); design (graphic, interior, surface, display and floral design); printing (print production, print media management, digital media); publishing (book, magazine and online publishing, book arts and crafts); interactive media (interactive games, interactive digital media, graphic moving image); creative enterprise (marketing/ advertising, public relations, retail, travel and tourism).

Freshers
- **First degree entrants:** 1220 UK, full-time.
- **Accommodation:** Some 1st years housed.

Profile

Institution
Founded: 1895. Was London College of Printing until 2004. **Structural features:** Constituent college of University of the Arts, London (previously London Institute). **Site:** Newly built campus at Elephant and Castle. **How to get there:** Close to Elephant and Castle underground station (Bakerloo, Northern lines) and several bus routes.

Courses
Academic features: Range of entry points to wide spectrum of media, design and communication specialisms, including access courses, 1-year diplomas, undergraduate and postgraduate degrees and

research. Provides highly practical, hands-on experience. **Awarding body:** University of the Arts, London. **Main undergraduate awards:** BA, FdA. **Length of courses:** 3 years (Hons); 2 years (FdA).

Study opportunities & careers

Library and information services: College library of specialist material – books, periodicals, slides, audio and visual. Also access to facilities of the university's central Learning Zone and facilities at other colleges of university. Special collection: Stanley Kubrick archives; history of the book. **Other learning resources:** Language laboratories; open-access IT facilities, state-of-the-art equipment in printing, DTP, multimedia, film, video and photography; computer suites. **Careers:** University information and advice service. Free enterprise centre for graduate use.

Student services & facilities

Student advice and services: Easy access to university's central student services; see *Arts London*. Student adviser at LCC. **Amenities:** Canteen, coffee/snack bar, student bar. **Accommodation:** Some students in university's halls of residence; see *Arts London*. University accommodation service helps find privately rented accommodation: rent approx £75–£115 pw, excluding bills and meals.

Money

Living expenses budget: Minimum budget of £6k–£10k pa (excluding tuition fees) recommended by college. **Financial help:** See *Arts London*. **Tuition fees:** Home students pay £3225 pa (less in placement year) for first degrees. International students pay £10,700 pa.

Student view) **Daryl Cichorz,** Students' Union College Officer (BA Graphic and Media Design)

Living

What's it like as a place to live? Great place in a big cosmopolitan city, great for independence but can be hard for meeting up with friends. **How's the student accommodation?** University halls are based throughout central London. Reasonably priced compared to independent housing companies. Bad for meeting students from different halls. Most rooms offer ensuite. Halls are in easy access to university. Some halls share with only 4 students and may not be mixed. Average university halls price £123 pw; independent £200 pw; shared housing £110 pw. **What's the student population like?** Diverse from a variety of backgrounds. International student population with some Londoners also. **How do students and locals get on?** Different backgrounds. Busy vibe throughout the day. A lot less crowded at night so students should travel in groups. Always keep your guard at night and don't flash goods and gadgets. The local area is somewhat grubby and is need of renovation. At edge of central London so council estates are in sight!

Studying

What's it like as a place to study? Good printing facilities and advantage of different workshops in different arts. Big student population and some courses have too many students. Little sense of community among the bigger courses. Course materials and printing will add up and will be expensive. **What are the teaching staff like?** Staff with experience in the industry. Visiting leaders of industry allow students to utilise their questioning in these special lectures. Staff are not especially student-focused, not concerned with wellbeing or the student experience. Course leaders need improved induction/bonding sessions with students and need to have more involvement in student affairs rather than sitting back on the bench after the lesson!

Socialising

What are student societies like? SU arranges events throughout the year. The college has a student-led bar, which hosts a weekly social night every Wednesday until the early hours. Many clubs and societies available for students include a variety of sports, arts, cultural and societies of a subculture variety. Societies often meet up and go out on socials. Countless ways for students to get involved including fundraising and campaigning. There's the Pathfinding Week – the other students' version of a Freshers' Week – and there are big SU parties at Hallowe'en, Christmas and summer as well. You can always suggest something new for the SU! **What's a typical night out?** Going to the SU bar with friends and having some cheap drinks before hitting London. Sometimes somewhere local is cheaper and even better for a night out. The main club a few mins walk from the college is Ministry of Sound. Leicester Square is a centrepoint for having a night out in London, but it's not cheap! Having a few before hitting a club is needed in this expensive city. **And how much does it cost?** SU offer standard drinks for only £1.50 on Wednesday nights. Otherwise drinks at a lot of places can be £4 for a standard drink. SU-led nights will be better for a cost-effective option. **How can you get home safely?** Don't stand out and better when in a group. Public transport is readily available in central London. Use your eyes!

Money

Is it an expensive place to live? Don't expect the loan to last. That little bit more you receive because it's London doesn't mean anything. Everything here is more than anywhere else; food, travel, materials, and the list continues. After all, it is the world's most expensive city! **Average price of a pint?** SU around £2; London £3–£5. **And the price of a takeaway?** Depends what you get and where you go. Locally £4, £20 more central. **What's the part-time work situation?** Jobs are available but demand is high and so is very competitive amongst students from all universities. Christmas time would be the best time to apply. Part-timers can get £6/hour with many companies. If everything else fails, the SU can offer various paid opportunities, which is helpful.

Summary

What's the best feature about the place? A world-recognised college for the arts. Diverse blend of students from a universal environment. **And the worst?** Student interaction is poor and staff interest in students' experience is absent. **And to sum it all up?** A world-class university with endless opportunity, but there's something missing.
Past students: Jane Root (Controller, BBC2); Nick Bell (Nick Bell Design); Helen Boaden (Controller, BBC Radio 4); Dave Bennett (Fulmar Colour Printing); Trevor McDonald (newsreader), Neville Brody (designer, *City Limits*, *The Face*), Dave King (Arts Council designer). **More info?** University SU (tel 020 7514 6270 or visit www.suarts.org).

London College of Fashion

Location:
central London
(map 3)
6 teaching centres
across London

London College of Fashion, 20 John Princes Street, London W1G 0BJ
☎ Tel 020 7514 7400
🖨 Fax 020 7514 7484
✉ Email enquiries@fashion.arts.ac.uk
💻 Website www.fashion.arts.ac.uk

Student enquiries: tel 020 7514 7344
Applications: UCAS or direct to college

In brief

Total Students: 3225

2% postgraduate
30% undergraduate

68% FE Students

Undergraduates: 950
90% full-time ● ● 85% UK students

85% female   15% male

- **Specialist fashion college.** Part of University of the Arts, London.
- **Teaching staff:** 125 full-time, 56 part-time.
- **Broad study areas:** Fashion design and technology; fashion promotion; fashion journalism; fashion management; fashion marketing; styling; menswear, womenswear, accessories and footwear; jewellery; tailoring; cosmetic science; beauty therapy; technical effects; costume; make-up and prosthetics; fashion photography.

Freshers

- **First degree entrants:** 200 UK, full-time.
- **Accommodation:** Some 1st years in university-managed accommodation.

Profile

Institution

Founded: 1906; became part of London Institute in 1986. **Structural features:** Constituent college of University of the Arts, London (previously London Institute). **Site:** 6 sites across London: 2 around Oxford Street in the West End; 2 in the City/Hoxton, 1 in Hackney (Foundation Art and Design course), 1 in Lime Grove, west London. **How to get there:** Oxford Circus and Bond Street underground stations for West End sites. Old Street and Liverpool Street stations for City sites. Bethnal Green for Hackney site. Shepherds Bush for Lime Grove. **Special features:** Largest specialist fashion college in the UK, with courses covering the whole industry.

Courses

Academic features: Degrees in wide range of fashion design, technology, promotion, journalism, management, etc. Top-up years available for foundation degree students. **Awarding body:** University of the Arts, London. **Main undergraduate award:** BA, BSc, FdA, FdSc. **Length of courses:** 3 years (full-time); 4 years (sandwich); 2 years (FdA/Sc).

Study opportunities & careers

Library and information services: 59,000 books, 250 periodicals, 160 study places. Separate IT service, access 11 hours/day. IT support available. Library orientation and internet induction; IT skills taught as part of course. Also access to facilities of the university's central Learning Zone. **Other learning resources:** Specialist fashion collection of unique interest. Textile lab, computer centres, all specialist fashion facilities, CAD/CAM suites. **Study abroad:** 5% of students spend a period abroad. Exchange links with universities in eg Amsterdam, Trier, Berlin, Florence, Madrid and Budapest. **Careers:** Fashion Business Resource Studio (FBRS) provides careers information and advice to all students and for 2 years after graduation; also helps find industrial placements.

Student services & facilities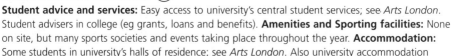

Student advice and services: Easy access to university's central student services; see *Arts London*. Student advisers in college (eg grants, loans and benefits). **Amenities and Sporting facilities:** None on site, but many sports societies and events taking place throughout the year. **Accommodation:** Some students in university's halls of residence; see *Arts London*. Also university accommodation service helps find privately rented accommodation (ie rooms/flats/houses rented from private landlords); rent approx £75–£115 pw, excluding bills and meals.

Money

Living expenses budget: Minimum budget of £6k–£10k pa (excluding tuition fees) recommended by college. **Term-time work:** College allows term-time work for full-time students (65% believed to work). No work in college but industrial liaison unit publicises part-time and vacation jobs. **Financial help:** See *Arts London*. **Tuition fees:** Home students pay £3225 pa (less in placement year) for first degrees. International students pay £10,700 pa.

Student view

It spans the capital with 6 sites, each reverberating with the energy of their particular location. Headquarters, in John Prince's Street (JPS), is in the heart of London's fashion space at Oxford Circus, opposite the flagship Topshop store (both a blessing and a financial curse to the college's urban students). JPS library has a world-class collection of fashion works and magazines. Davies Street (next to Bond Street tube station) recently refurbished, although erratically, creating a thoroughly modern exhibition space, chichi entrance hall and bistro to supply espresso to the sociable student body. Broad range of cutting-edge programmes in certain courses. Computer facilities at the central sites are unfortunately strained and there is a shortage of space overall. Ample opportunity to become involved in student politics and the staff–student liaison system is well organised. Sport facilities cannot match those of non-arts universities and despite the presence of a few dynamic groups, little drive is apparent in the unions. Both central locations provide a constant reminder of both the job opportunities and the demands of the retail market. In terms of high street, prêt à porter, bespoke and haute couture fashion, the heritage of the West End shopping district infuses the college. While creativity is fostered, and designers, journalists and media students are trained to an extremely high level, there is an emphasis on the practicalities of the industry. An interdisciplinary approach is encouraged to ensure a holistic understanding: so the designer gains an understanding of the mechanics of fashion marketing, while the journalist is educated in the mores of the fashion photographer. The other sites are significantly smaller, with a more intimate atmosphere. Cordwainers, in Golden Lane, specialises in accessories and footwear; strong commercial links are complemented by the proximity of museums and galleries, including the Barbican. Technical construction is taught at Curtain Road, in Shoreditch; and art foundation students are in Mare Street, Hackney. All students have access to the facilities at all sites – and to those of the rest of Arts London (library at Central Saint Martins useful). Certain courses are extremely time-intensive (especially the design departments, in common with all fashion design courses) but opportunities for holiday work are promoted to students. Frequent lectures from industry big players give an insight into the realities of fashion as a career (recently Alexandra Shulman, editor UK *Vogue*, Lily Cole and Erin O'Connor) and there are seminars by fashion academics and business gurus, many of whom teach in the college. You constantly feel you are at exactly the right place to absorb what you need for a career in fashion; definitive texts will often be written by an authority who teaches in the college. Students have a bewildering range of professional and national backgrounds, are of all ages and appear to represent every niche. There are both male and female students (although some courses are overwhelmingly female), with a visible gay male student contingent. London, the city for original creation and direction, can be both exhilarating and exhausting, but for the fashion student is flavoured by the quintessential British interpretation of the industry.

Student footnotes

Housing: Halls of residence for 1st years. Private accommodation in zone 1–2 (approx £100 pw for shared flat or house). **Eats:** Café at JPS reasonable (sandwiches £1+). **Nightlife:** Intermittent union evenings (generally superfluous with the selection of bars, clubs and restaurants in London). **Sports:** £20 a month for student membership of council gym (Oasis in Endell Street); great facilities and classes but dingy changing rooms. **Financial help:** Student support office (Davies Street) helps home and international students. **Jobs:** Notices in college about work placements and part-time jobs (general acknowledgement that London living demands a part-time job). **Best features:** Friendly, international students who defy the stereotypical image of factious fashion students. **Worst features:** London in general not conducive to student interaction. And if you like to wear a tracksuit and leave your hair unwashed, you may feel a bit grubby compared to the well-dressed student body (although if you wear a tracksuit every day, perhaps fashion isn't for you . . .). Be prepared to negotiate a certain level of pretension and pseudo-intellectualism. **Past students:** Jimmy Choo, Patrick Cox (footwear designers); Sarah Harris (journalist); Linda Bennett (LK Bennett); Nicola Jeal, Karen Kay, Mandi Norwood (editors); Katarzyna Szczotarska (fashion designer). **More info?** University SU (tel 020 7514 6270) or visit www.suarts.org.

London Contemporary Dance School

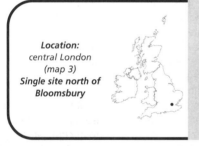

Location:
central London
(map 3)
Single site north of Bloomsbury

✉ London Contemporary Dance School, The Place, 17 Duke's Road, London WC1H 9PY
☎ Tel 020 7121 1111
🖷 Fax 020 7121 1145
✉ Email LCDS@theplace.org.uk
🖥 Website www.theplace.org.uk

Student enquiries: School Office
Applications: Online

In brief

Total Students: 200

73% undergraduate
2% research Students
25% postgraduate

Undergraduates: 145
100% full-time ● ● 56% UK students

74% female   26% male

- **Specialist dance school.** Member of the Conservatoire for Dance & Drama.
- **Teaching staff:** 20 full-time, 15 part-time.
- **Broad study areas:** Contemporary dance, choreography, contextual studies.

Freshers

- **Admissions information:** All must pass a dance audition. Academic qualifications to university entry level expected (including a score of 6.5 on the IELTS where English is not the first language).
- **First degree entrants:** 80 UK, full-time.
- **Accommodation:** No school accommodation.

Profile

Institution

Founded: 1966. **Structural features:** Founding member of Conservatoire for Dance & Drama. **Site:** The Place; a large building with its own theatre, off Euston Road. **How to get there:** King's Cross and Euston tube and train stations, Russell Square/Warren Street tube, buses. **Special features:** Part of The Place, an international centre for dance, also home to the Robin Howard Dance Theatre, Richard Alston Dance Company and Centre for Advanced Training and Professional Development. Leading European centre for training professional dancers in contemporary dance and choreography; also runs recreational classes and courses.

Courses

Academic features: Core of the degree course is professional training, with at least 3 hours of technique classes a day. **Awarding body:** University of Kent. **Main undergraduate award:** BA. **Length of courses:** 3 years (BA); 1 year (Postgraduate Diploma).

Study opportunities & careers

Library and information services: Extensive collection of dance, arts, psychology and related studies in addition to a general collection. CD-ROM collection. Information provision, £52 pa spent for each student (FTE). Separate IT service, access 8 hours/day. Ratio 1:15 workstations to students, 1 point with access to the library and internet. Induction to library and information services to new students; basic word-processing course. **Careers:** Personal contact service for jobs, career talks.

Student services & facilities

Student advice and services: Full-time body-conditioning tutor and part-time osteopath. Resident full-time student support officer and counsellor. **Amenities:** 11 dance studios, music studio, body conditioning suite, the Robin Howard Dance Theatre for student workshop performances; bar, café, full disabled access. **Accommodation:** Student services officer gives advice on accommodation. Rents locally from approx £100 pw.

Money

Living expenses budget: Minimum budget of £8500 pa (excluding tuition fees) recommended by school. **Term-time work:** School allows term-time work for full-time students (90% believed to work). Some work available in bar, as ushers or in office admin. **Financial help:** Conservatoire bursaries of £1700 pa (£2100 in final year) for UK students whose family income is up to £25k; tapered bursaries, down to £100/£500 for those with family income of £39,300. For 2nd and 3rd year students only – competitive scholarship/endowment fund. Limited number of government Dance and Drama Awards (DADAs) for degree students and some others. School's own funds offer limited financial support in cases of extreme hardship (does not offer full scholarships for fees). **Tuition fees:** Home students pay £3225 pa for first degrees. International students pay £13,340 pa.

Student view

Based at The Place in central London, which is also home to the Robin Howard Dance Theatre and resident professional company Richard Alston Dance Company. It has 10+ state-of-the-art dance studios, changing rooms, library, body-conditioning room, theatre, bar and café and more. Euston and King's Cross tube and rail stations only a few mins' walk away and good bus services. No halls of residence but there are many local hostels and usually fairly easy to find flats. Rent gets cheaper out of central London but travel more expensive. Close, friendly atmosphere – international, multicultural and more women than men. School is small and environment is intimate and student-centred. Helpful student support services and each student is allocated a tutorial group. School library open throughout college hours. SU small but active, providing social events and links between students and admin. Degree course consists of practical work with theoretical contexts of dance and is designed to train students as professional dance artists. All courses are full-time and timetables require attendance from 8.30am until at least 4.30pm most weekdays (until 6pm weekends). There are also evening rehearsals and performances at certain times of the year. Plenty of entertainment available in London with a wide range of activities and interests accommodated. Exchange programmes are available with various different dance centres around the world.

Student footnotes

Housing: No college accommodation; advice on local housing available from student services office. **Eats:** Delicious, cheap, healthy, home-made food at café on premises; caters for vegetarians. Many local cafés, health food store and juice bar. **Drink:** Local pub, Mabel's, just across road; drink generally expensive in London. **Sports:** School body-conditioning room. **Hardship funds:** Helpful staff and access to information on sponsorship. **Jobs:** Some available in theatre as ushers, theatre bar and admin. Part-time work quite easy to find but can interfere with training. **Best features:** Being based at a major dance centre. **And worst:** Lots of hard work. **Informal name:** LCDS. **Past students:** Richard Alston (Artistic Director of The Place); Ian Spink (choreographer and director); Darshan Singh Bhuller (Phoenix); Jonzi D (choreographer and rap artist); Etta Murfitt (New Adventures); Henri Oguike (Henri Oguike Dance Company); Robert North, Anthony Van Laast, Kim Brandstrup, Arthur Pita (choreographers); most performing members of Richard Alston Dance Company.

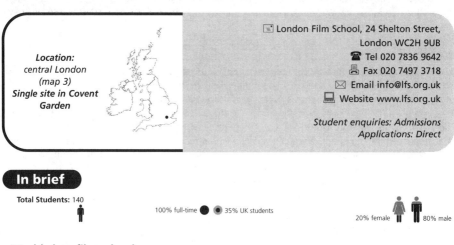

London Film School

Location:
central London
(map 3)
Single site in Covent Garden

📠 London Film School, 24 Shelton Street, London WC2H 9UB
☎ Tel 020 7836 9642
🖷 Fax 020 7497 3718
✉ Email info@lfs.org.uk
💻 Website www.lfs.org.uk

Student enquiries: Admissions
Applications: Direct

In brief

Total Students: 140

100% full-time ● ◉ 35% UK students

20% female ┊┊ 80% male

- **World-class film school.**
- **Teaching staff:** 24 full-time plus various part-time visiting lecturers.
- **Broad study areas:** Film-making.
- **Admissions information:** Students can enrol in September, January and May.
- **Accommodation:** No school accommodation.

Profile

Institution

Founded: 1956 as London School of Film Technique. Then (and still formally) London International Film School. **Site:** Converted warehouse in Covent Garden. **How to get there:** Covent Garden and many other tube stations; close to many bus routes. **Special features:** Acceptance depends upon educational achievement and examples of relevant work, eg photography, previous films, video, film scripts, story boards; experience in film, TV or related areas taken into account.

Courses

Academic features: Writing drama for film scripts. Directing workshops. Practical sessions with actors. Courses begin each term. Time equally divided between practical film-making and formal tuition. **Awarding body:** London Metropolitan University. **Main awards:** MA. **Length of courses:** 2 years (MA film-making); 1 year (MA screenwriting).

Study opportunities & careers

Library and information services: Technical books, periodicals, 17 study places. Access to British Film Institute library. **Other learning resources:** 2 viewing theatres, 2 fully equipped studios, video rehearsal studio, comprehensively equipped camera, sound and editing departments. Equipment includes 35mm Panavision, 16mm and 35mm Arriflex cameras, 2 moviecam SuperAmericas, Nagra sound recorders, Steenbeck editing tables, Avid editing systems, video camera and editing equipment. **Study abroad:** Opportunities exist to make films worldwide in the final term. **Careers:** UK graduates are automatically acceptable as members of BECTU, with access to vacancy registers covering film and TV.

Student services & facilities

Student advice and services: Student services department, personal tutor system and national health services nearby. **Amenities:** LFS Film Society run by students. SU plays large part in school. Free entry often available to National Film Theatre. **Accommodation:** No school accommodation. Privately owned accommodation varies considerably, eg from £127–£133 pw in International Students House (less if sharing).

Money

Living expenses budget: Minimum budget of £9k–£10k pa (excluding tuition fees) recommended by school. **Financial help:** 17 Skillset bursaries for UK/EU students on MA filmmaking, 4 on screenwriting (of approx £5k pa). Some students have Career Development Loans. **Tuition fees:** All students on MA screenwriting pay £10k; MA filmmaking pay £21,111 pa.

Student view

One of 7 film schools accredited by Skillset as a centre of excellence in film education. Great location – in Covent Garden (middle of the West End), occupying a 19th-century fruit warehouse. Near Covent Garden, Leicester Square and Tottenham Court Road tube stations, so access easy. An exciting, international mix of students from Europe, Asia, Africa and the Americas as well as a number of UK students. 2-year filmmaking course, divided into 6 terms; students arrange themselves into groups and make a film each term. Everyone takes courses in various areas of film-making, so gain a broad base of skills. Some students try to specialise by taking on the same role in their group films, while others prefer to try different jobs to broaden their experience – it's up to the individual.

Theory lectures involve watching and discussing films; as the course progresses, students spend more time actually making their group's films or working on other students' films. This is a great strength of the school – many students leave having worked on 15–20 short films in the space of 2 years – and it has a high reputation for technical expertise. Qualification recognised by BECTU (automatic membership for graduates who find work). Graduates have achieved leading positions in the film industry worldwide. There are irregular visits by guest speakers (eg Mike Leigh, Simon Channing-Williams); guests from the film and television industry are invited to the end-of-term screenings. A number of school documentaries have been screened on television, and films are shown at film festivals all over the world including the London Film Festival. Students also participate in various student film competitions such as the Fuji Film Scholarship Awards and the Kodak Student Commercial Awards. Facilities are not plush – spartan but functional.

Student footnotes

Housing: An expensive school in an expensive area. Look on the noticeboard, in *Loot* and in the housing list provided by the school. **Eats:** LFS coffee shop cheapest (but not worst). Covent Garden and Soho full of places (meal for £5+). **Drink:** Two Brewers, Seven Dials, Café Boheme, Freuds; various places around Covent Garden. **Nightlife:** Film society evening screenings; numerous cinemas and theatres around London; Covent Garden is full of fun. **Informal name:** LFS. **Financial help:** Some bursaries available from Skillset and Channel 4. **Jobs:** Limited work within school. **Best features:** Very practical. **And worst:** Expensive. **Past students:** Arnold Wesker (playwright); Mark Forstater (film and documentary producer); Mike Leigh, Horace Ove (directors, screenwriters); George Cosmatos, John Irvin, Franc Roddam, Les Blair, Michael Mann, Mark Kasdan, Don Boyd, Bill Douglas, Simon Lourish, Tak Fujomoto (directors).

London Met University

Location:
central and north London (map 3)
2 teaching centres (City and Holloway Road); partner colleges

📧 London Metropolitan University, 31 Jewry Street, London EC3N 2EY
☎ Tel 020 7423 0000
💻 Website www.londonmet.ac.uk

Student enquiries: tel 020 7133 4200; fax 020 7133 2677
Applications: UCAS

In brief

Total Students: 29,495

2% FE Students
23% postgraduate
74% undergraduate

Undergraduates: 21,955
67% full-time ● ● 80% UK students
53% mature ● ● 44% lower
on entry ● ● socio-economic groups

55% female | 45% male

- **A modern university.**
- **Teaching staff:** 820 full-time, 1100 part-time.
- **Broad study areas:** Accounting, applied social sciences, architecture, biosciences, business, chemistry, communications, computing, design, economics, education, finance, fine art, furniture, health studies, history, languages, law, music technology, politics, psychology, social work, sports science.

Freshers

- **Admissions information:** AS-levels accepted in combination with 2+ A-levels or equivalent. UCAS tariff used.
- **First degree entrants:** 3495 UK, full-time.
- **Points on entry:** 210 (average).
- **Drop-out rate:** 14% in 1st year.
- **Accommodation:** Most 1st years housed who live more than 25 miles away.

Profile

Institution

Founded: 2002 from merger of London Guildhall and North London universities – both formed from 19th-century institutions and awarded university status in 1992. **Site:** 2 campuses: City Campus with 6 teaching sites in Moorgate, Aldgate and Tower Hill; North Campus based on Holloway Road. **How to get there:** Both campuses have good transport connections: City Campus close to 4 major railway stations, DLR, tube stations and buses; North Campus has tube stations (Holloway and Highbury and Islington), bus routes and rail links to major London stations. **Special features:** Positive attitude to mature students and those with disabilities. Strong community involvement, including community education and information centre.

Courses

Academic features: Many courses linked with industrial bodies/companies, eg BBC, Chartered Institute of Insurers, Goldsmiths Company, Reed, FSA. Flexible modular scheme. Courses start in September and February. **Awarding body:** London Metropolitan University. **Main undergraduate awards:** BA, BEng, BSc. **Length of courses:** 3 years; 4 years (sandwich and language)

Study opportunities & careers

Library and information services: 5 libraries plus 2 special collections, 716,000 printed books, 16,195 periodical titles (print and electronic), 52 electronic databases, 314 e-books; 2400 study spaces. Integrated library, media, IT and specialist services (learning development unit, independent learning unit, video-conferencing). Computing suite, with 700+ computer workstations. Range of IT staff support. Information provision, £76 pa spent for each student (FTE). Specialist collections: Women's Library, TUC Library. **Other learning facilities:** New science 'superlab' with 280 workstations, life-size basketball court and other facilities for sports therapy; TV, sound and media studios. Multimedia resources (CD-ROM, workstations, databases, etc.), IT labs, TV studio, language labs (incl an interpreting suite); specialist wood-working and machine tool labs, upholstery and furniture design studios, silversmithing and jewellery workshops, dark rooms and printing studios. **Study abroad:** Option for students to spend a period abroad (under 10% do), including to Mexico, Cuba and US. Formal exchange links with 50 universities and colleges in Europe. Dual qualification (French licence) possible for students in tourism, business and economics at Poitiers University. **Careers:** Information, advice and placement. Law graduates employability network; jobshop. Active alumni association and teaching company schemes.

Student services & facilities

Student advice and services: Student counsellors; chaplain; part-time nurse and doctor; access to solicitor; money advisers; dyslexia support; childcare facilities. **Amenities:** Refectories or snack bars on all teaching sites; SU buildings with bars, TV and games rooms, entertainment venue, on-site banking. **Sporting facilities:** New fitness centre and multi-sport hall complex including basketball court at North Campus; fully equipped fitness centre at City Campus with resistance and cardiovascular machines. Dance and fitness studios for classes in eg aerobics, pilates and yoga. **Accommodation:** Majority of 1st-year students are housed in private halls (rooms allocated on first-come-first-served basis). Total of 4000 places, provided by 10 halls providers; rent £91–£280 pw. Most students live in private accommodation for 2+ years, rent £80–£150 pw (incl or excl of bills). About 50% of students live at home.

Money

Living expenses budget: Minimum budget of £9k–£10k pa (excluding tuition fees) recommended by university. **Term-time work:** University allows term-time work for full-time students; high proportion have part-time jobs. Some work available on campus in SU bars, registries, at one-off events. University jobshop. **Financial help:** Bursaries of £1k pa for UK students whose family income is up to £18k, tapered down to £310 where family income is £40k; also discretionary hardship fund. Subject scholarships for academic achievement. Government funds, awards of £100–£500. Additional help for students with disabilities, with dependants under 16, partners on low income and for single parents. Various special awards. Merit scholarships (£2k pa) for international students. Apply for help to students records and awards unit. **Tuition fees:** Home students pay £3225 pa for first degrees. International students pay £8200 pa (fee fixed for whole course).

Student view
Bruno Selun, Course Representative (Graduate, BA Education Studies with Philosophy)

Living
What's it like as a place to live? London is boiling with so many things to do! **How's the student accommodation?** I lived in university halls for 2 years, and private accommodation for 1. The university accommodation depends on individual halls, so be careful about the place you pick; try to visit it beforehand, visit online forums about it, and so on. If you don't like where you live, the rest will look and feel much worse! **What's the student population like?** Oddly, internationals tended to stick together whilst the British stayed together on their own. The backgrounds are very diverse, and it'll depend who you like and become friends with. **How do students and locals get on?** Usually, pretty well! Don't be a loser; respect the local communities you live with, and be sensible how you affect those around you (loud singing in the courtyard at 2am on Saturday night, anyone?).

Studying
What's it like as a place to study? I loved being at London Metropolitan University, but I know other people prefer central places like Birkbeck or UCL. Wherever you go, make the most out of it! **What are the teaching staff like?** That just depends on each teacher, no universal rule!

Socialising
What are student societies like? A plethora, you'll find something to your taste, whatever you're interested in! **What's a typical night out?** For me, meal at home with friends, cinema and drinks out in a central bar. But some people have it much more expensive in big clubs and eating out! **And how much does it cost?** About £20 for me. **How can you get home safely?** Bus and tubes are pretty safe, but I'm a guy, so it could be different for other people. It also depends on the area you live in, but if everything else fails, get a taxi home!

Money
Is it an expensive place to live? You just need to be careful. You become very aware of what you spend, and you begin to spend smartly instead of impulsively. **Average price of**

a pint? I don't drink pints . . . But a nice glass of wine would be around £3, and an orange juice £1.50 for the less adventurous. **And the price of a takeaway?** Don't do that! Cook at home, you'll pay less, it will last longer, be healthier, and you can invite friends over. Much nicer than the takeaway. **What's the part-time work situation?** It's pretty hard to land a nice job, but some places are nice to work at (for instance Pret a Manger gives pretty decent working conditions and wages). Try to look for jobs you'll like, or at least that you won't hate. University is good at helping you find work!

Summary

What's the best feature about the place? International, lively and never boring! **And the worst?** Ask the wallet. **And to sum it all up?** If you're hesitating about whether or not to come to London, just do it!

Past students: Kate Hoey, Graham Allan (MPs); Jim Moir alias Vic Reeves (comedian); Mark Thatcher (businessman and son of Margaret); Zoë Ball (DJ and presenter); Alison Moyet (singer); Nick Leeson (trader who brought down Barings); Charlie Whelan (former press secretary to Gordon Brown); Sonya (Echobelly), Anna Nolan (*Big Brother* 1).

London School of Theology

Location:
north-west of London, within M25 (map 3)
Single site in Northwood

London School of Theology, Green Lane, Northwood, Middlesex HA6 2UW

☎ Tel 01923 456000
🖷 Fax 01923 456001
✉ Email registrar@lst.ac.uk
💻 Website www.lst.ac.uk

Student enquiries: Registrar
Applications: Direct

In brief

Total Students: 345

35% postgraduate
65% undergraduate

Undergraduates: 225
79% full-time ● ● 73% UK students
80% mature on entry ●

50% female 50% male

- **Specialist theological college.**
- **Teaching staff:** 19 full-time, 7 part-time + visiting lecturers.
- **Broad study areas:** Religious studies, theology.

Freshers

- **Admissions information:** Requires academic qualifications and life skills appropriate to theological studies in a Christian setting. UCAS tariff not used.
- **First degree entrants:** 55 full-time.
- **Drop-out rate:** Nil in 1st year.
- **Accommodation:** Some 1st years housed, who want it.

Profile

Institution

Founded: 1943. Name changed from London Bible College in 2004. **Site:** 9-acre site, north-west of London. **How to get there:** Metropolitan line to Northwood; by road off A404 Rickmansworth Road.

Courses

Academic features: Courses in theology; theology, music and worship; and theology and counselling. Subjects fall into 4 main categories: biblical studies; theological studies; missiological studies and applied theology (including placements). Postgraduate programmes, taught and research-based. **Awarding body:** Middlesex University. **Main undergraduate awards:** BA. **Length of courses:** 1–3 years.

Study opportunities & careers

Library and information services: 50,000 volumes, 200 periodicals, 100 study places. Information provision, £100 pa spent for each student (FTE). Separate IT service, access 24 hours/day. Ratio 1:22 workstations to students. Wireless access and internet in library, plus network points in all student rooms (for students' own machines). IT support from 2 full-time staff; full induction to library and information services for new students. **Study abroad:** Partners in training mission sandwich – run in conjunction with Latin Link in South America. **Employment:** Christian ministry, missionary work, RE teaching, youth and children's work, Christian counselling.

Student services & facilities

Student advice and services: Doctor, counsellor. **Amenities:** Bookshop on premises; games room, tennis courts, football pitch, gym, music rooms, kitchens, TV lounge. **Accommodation:** 100 students (all years) in school accommodation (28% of all students); full-board £4071 pa, term time only.

Money

Living expenses budget: A minimum budget of £8k–£10k pa (excluding tuition fees) recommended by the school. **Term-time work:** The school allows term-time work for full-time students (but encouraged to discuss this with tutors). Work sometimes available on campus in kitchen, waiting on tables during conferences, maintenance. **Financial help:** Total available £157,974 own funds, 84 students helped. **Special help:** international students, self-financing students. **Tuition fees:** All students pay £4995 pa (£5979 on music and worship). Those eligible for a student loan may also take out a loan for fees of £3225 pa towards tuition fees.

Student view

An interdenominational evangelical centre for undergraduate and postgraduate theology. Its academic record is impressive due to both the high standard of teaching and the characteristic dedication of students – the vast majority have a real desire to learn. It's an international community: around 25% of students are international, many studying with English as their second language. Roughly a third of students live on campus – a spacious site in the suburb of Northwood – just 30 mins from central London. Reasonable on-site facilities include a sports pitch, tennis courts, a laundry and a student centre, which has TV rooms, gym, kitchen and games room. The college embraces new technology and boasts an outstanding level of hi-tech equipment for student use; all rooms have points for both advanced phone system and high-speed internet connection. Good music facilities form part of the theology, music and worship course. As well as the more traditional theology degrees, theology and counselling is offered to keep up to date and equip the Church with trained Christian counsellors. Excellent library facilities; well-stocked by the prolific authorship of the LST faculty. Student–faculty relations are excellent; the faculty are friendly and approachable. Confidential pastoral support provided. The college has a warm and friendly atmosphere, fostering mutual respect and encouragement.

Student footnotes

Housing: Expensive housing area but college has a list of cheap digs. **Eats:** College meals not bad; most special dietary needs catered for. Several pubs and restaurants in Northwood offer good, reasonably priced food. **Nightlife:** Not much in immediate vicinity but Watford and Harrow are close at hand, as is London. **Sports:** LST Tigers is successful college football team. Most sports facilities available locally. **Financial help:** Independent, so without government support. Tuition fees are high although bursaries are available and a fee loan helps. **Past students:** Os Guinness (author and social critic), Clive Calver (Evangelical Alliance), Terry Virgo (New Frontiers). **More info?** Enquiries to Student President.

London South Bank University

Location:
central London
(map 3)
Southwark campus
plus hospital sites;
partner colleges

London South Bank University,
103 Borough Road, London SE1 0AA
☎ Tel 020 7815 7815
🖨 Fax 020 7815 6031
✉ Email enquiry@lsbu.ac.uk
🖥 Website www.lsbu.ac.uk

Student enquiries: Course Enquiries Office
Applications: UCAS

In brief

Total Students: 23,215
6% FE Students
25% postgraduate
69% undergraduate

Undergraduates: 15,950
56% full-time ● ● 90% UK students
59% mature ● ● 45% lower
on entry socio-economic
groups

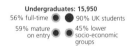

59% female  41% male

- **A modern university.**
- **Teaching staff:** 600 full-time, 600 part-time.
- **Broad study areas:** Business, science, professions allied to medicine, engineering, computing and IT, design and technology, built environment, law, humanities, media, social sciences, health.

Freshers

- **Admissions information:** AS-levels accepted in combination with 1+ A-level or equivalent; many courses have specific requirements in terms of subject and level. UCAS tariff not used.
- **First degree entrants:** 1995 UK, full-time.
- **Points on entry:** 185+ (average).
- **Drop-out rate:** 13% in 1st year.
- **Accommodation:** Most 1st-year students housed.

Profile

Institution

Founded: 1970 as South Bank Polytechnic, from 6 colleges of further education; university status in 1992. **Site:** Southwark Campus, central-south London (near Elephant and Castle); plus 2 devoted to nursing education: Havering Campus (at Harold Wood) and Whipps Cross Campus. **How to get there:** Elephant and Castle, London Bridge and Waterloo stations, plus many bus routes. For nursing sites, trains from Liverpool Street Station to Harold Wood and Wood Street.

Courses

Awarding body: London South Bank University. **Main undergraduate awards:** BA, BEng, BSc, LLB, FdA, FdSc. **Length of courses:** 3 or 4 years.

Study opportunities & careers

Library and information services: 1 main library: 280,000 volumes and other catalogued items; 29,500 bound volumes of periodicals and some 2200 subscriptions to periodicals; 1400 study places. Specialist collections in education, law, computing and the built environment. Information provision, £81 pa spent for each student (FTE). Separate IT system, open 12 hours/day. Approx. 1000 machines with internet access, many with access to library (ratio 10:1 students to workstations). Specialist IT support staff available; all new students inducted to library and information services; IT skills courses. **Other learning resources:** Language lab. Microcomputers in departmental computing labs. Learning resource centre. **Study abroad:** Some students spend a period abroad. Formal exchange links with EU universities and colleges open to non-language students. **Careers:** Information and counselling.

Student services & facilities

Student advice and services: Housing service, professional counsellors, chaplain, visiting medical officers, nursery. **Amenities:** Shops, bars, food outlets. **Sporting facilities:** Sports complex at London Road with sports hall, gymnasium and fitness suites; 21-acre sports ground at Dulwich.
Accommodation: University accommodation for 75% of 1st-year students who want it, in halls 10 mins' walk from main campus. Approx. 1400 self-catering places, £86.50–£88.50 pw (£106 ensuite), inclusive of insurance, bills, etc.; most contracts 39 weeks, but some 40, 42 or 52 weeks. Most students live in privately owned accommodation for whole course, rent approx £85–£95 pw plus bills. 60% of first-degree students live at home.

Money

Living expenses budget: Minimum budget of £8320–£8500 for academic year (excluding tuition fees) recommended by university. **Term-time work:** University allows term-time work for full-time students (some 25% believed to work). University jobshop. Summer work (admissions) available on campus. **Financial help:** Bursaries for all UK and EU students (not means-tested): £500 in Year 1, £750 pa in Years 2 and 3 plus graduation grant of £250. Also scholarships, eg sports (£3k pa), for Asian or West Indian students (£1k pa) and bursaries for disadvantaged young people (£1k pa). Government funds plus limited university hardship funds available. **Tuition fees:** Home students pay £3225 pa for first degrees (£1225 for FdA/Sc). International students pay from £8360 pa (classroom), £8600 (lab/studio).

Student view
Nordin Jahar, SU President and Governor of the London South Bank University (Business Management)

Living
What's it like as a place to live? It's a nice place to live. It's located in central London. Very easy to travel around. **How's the student accommodation?** The accommodation is nice and reasonable. They are affordable for any students. **What's the student population like?** We have a lot of international students. It's a diverse university. There are 23,000 students studying at London South Bank University from different backgrounds and religions. **How do students and locals get on?** The relationships between students and the communities are very good. There isn't any issue or a problem. The university and the SU are working very closely with the communities.

Studying
What's it like as a place to study? The London South Bank University offers a lot of courses. Students do like the courses and the facilities. The university is still working a lot on facilities to provide better services and student experiences. **What are the teaching staff like?** In general the staff are very friendly and helpful. The university is working to improve relations between the students and staff.

Socialising
What are student societies like? We have a good amount of societies and sport clubs that students can relate to. We've got the student bar where everybody comes together. **What's a typical night out?** Tuesday night, student night, Milkshake!!!! **And how much does it cost?** £5. **How can you get home safely?** By night bus or taxi.

Money
Is it an expensive place to live? London is always expensive for students. You need to have a part-time job to live well as a student. **Average price of a pint?** Around £1.50 to £2. **What's the part-time work situation?** Students can find part-time jobs in London that are well paid. The university does help students to find and to prepare them for a part-time job.

Summary
What's the best feature about the place? It's a diverse university with people of all backgrounds and religions. **And the worst?** There are a lot of part-time students that you only see once a week or 2 evenings a week. **And to sum it all up?** If you want to change your life, then South Bank is the place to be!!!
More info? Visit www.lsbsu.org.

London University

Location:
Mostly central London
Many teaching centres – see constituent colleges

▣ University of London, Senate House, Malet Street, London WC1E 7HU
☎ Tel 020 7862 8000
✉ Email enquiries@london.ac.uk
🖥 Website www.london.ac.uk

Student enquiries: To constituent colleges
Applications: To constituent colleges, mostly through UCAS
(see individual college profiles)

In brief

Total Students: 134,200

40% postgraduate
60% undergraduate

Undergraduates: 81,900
75% full-time

- **Federal university,** including world-class and top UK research-intensive institutions.
- **Broad study areas:** All the main subjects are taught in London University by one or more of its constituent colleges.

Freshers

- **Admissions information:** See profiles of constituent colleges.
- **Accommodation:** Most 1st years housed (see constituent colleges).

Profile

Institution

Founded: 1836, bringing together 2 existing London colleges, King's College and University College.
Structural features: A federal university consisting of 19 colleges and the postgraduate School of Advanced Study, in which teaching and research are carried out. Students belong both to the college or institute at which they study and to the university. All the separate teaching institutions select their students themselves and you apply to them, not to the university. You can look up the profiles of the following that offer undergraduate courses:

Barts & The London (part of Queen Mary)
Birkbeck
Central School of Speech and Drama
Courtauld Institute
Goldsmiths
Heythrop College
King's College London
London University Institute in Paris (ULIP)
LSE (London School of Economics and Political Science)
Queen Mary
Royal Academy of Music
Royal Holloway
Royal Veterinary College
St George's
School of Pharmacy
SOAS (School of Oriental & African Studies)
University College London

Site: University site in Bloomsbury, including 35 acres between British Museum and Euston Road, on which University College, Birkbeck and SOAS are located. Almost all London University colleges are within a radius of 3 miles of the Bloomsbury site except for Royal Holloway (Surrey) and the London University Institute in Paris.

Courses

Academic features: Colleges, institutes and London's unique external system collectively offer 4500 course options – the biggest choice of courses in the UK. Most degrees are on modular system. Most courses are offered on a full-time basis but there are many opportunities to study part-time or at home by distance learning. **Awarding body:** University of London. **Length of courses:** 3 or 4 years; 5–6 years (medicine/dentistry). **External students:** The university will register and examine eligible students world-wide who are not registered at colleges of London University: first degrees in arts subjects, computing, divinity, economics, law, mathematics, music; Master's degrees with full distance-learning materials include agriculture, economics, environment. Enquiries to the External Programme (enquiries@london.ac.uk). **Study abroad:** A number of degree courses involve a year abroad.

Study opportunities & careers

Library and information services: Senate House Library has 2 million books and 5500 current periodicals; particularly strong in the humanities and has many distinguished specialist collections. In addition, colleges all have their own libraries. **Summer schools:** London University runs annual taster courses to allow sixth formers to sample a subject and the university environment (prospectus from Senate House). **Students' union:** University union (ULU) is in Malet Street. All undergraduate colleges also have their own unions. **Sporting facilities:** Athletic ground in Motspur Park, Surrey; university boathouse at Chiswick; sailing clubhouse at Welsh Harp Reservoir, Brent.

Student services & facilities

Student advice and services: Central institutions health service for Birkbeck, School of Pharmacy, SOAS; other colleges make their own arrangements. **Accommodation and financial help:** See individual college profiles. **Tuition fees:** Each college sets own fees; see individual colleges.

Student view

Possibly the most diverse university in the UK – with well over 100,000 students, it's certainly the largest. You could be studying at a Senate Institute with 300 students or a large multi-faculty college with nearly 20,000 students but you are at the same university. Because of this, it is possible for everyone to find their place. There's the opportunity to participate fully in university life at the various colleges, but it is just as easy to lead your own separate life outside college – or do both. In London you can do anything you have never done before and now wish to do – but it's up to you to seek it out and get involved. You will have to get used to spending large amounts of your day travelling; even if you live close to the centre, the specialist libraries, research centres, etc. may not be. It's also relatively expensive, although there's a range of rented accommodation available, so you can live quite cheaply. SUs make the expense easier to bear, offering cheaper food and drink, etc.; each college and institute has its own and you can use the University of London Union (ULU) in Malet Street. It is easy to get lonely in London – but it is also easy to make friends with so many different activities going on. All the colleges have student sport clubs and societies and ULU has many federal ones; ULU also has a very good and comprehensive range of sports facilities. Great opportunities for part-time work in London with so many retail and service outlets. Whatever you are looking for from a university, London offers it.

Student footnotes

Housing: Inter-collegiate and college-run halls available for most 1st years and some 3rd years. College and university accommodation offices and head lease schemes. *Loot* (published daily) lists all types and prices of rentals. Students live in all parts of London, from Mayfair to Brixton. **Eats:** Every type of food you could possibly wish to try is served somewhere in London. Meals for about £5 easy to find if you hunt for them. **Drink:** Everywhere expensive except for SU bars (about £1.80 a pint). Some cheaper pubs out of the centre. **Nightlife:** Cheapest ents at SUs. ULU has top bands. Opportunity to see every film, play and exhibition released and most have student rates (even the West End shows offer reduced, last-min student tickets; see *Time Out*). **Sports:** Nearly all colleges have grounds, boathouse, etc.; but only Royal Holloway has everything on site – everyone else has about 30 mins' journey for most facilities. Best and cheapest indoor facilities are at ULU (including swimming pool). **Travel:** London travel expensive but 30% student discount on monthly and seasonal travelcards. For travel awards, etc, see the individual colleges. **Financial help:** Available from each college. **Jobs:** Most SUs offer paid work; enormous number of part-time jobs available (some don't advertise, so often worth going and asking). **Best features:** Opportunities; reputation; size. **And worst:** Expensive to live in London. **Good news:** Many more student discounts now available. **Past students:** Loads – see individual colleges. **More info?** See www.ulu.co.uk.

London University Institute in Paris (ULIP)

Location:
Paris, France
Single site in city
centre

🖹 University of London Institute in Paris, 11 rue de
Constantine, 75340 Paris Cedex 07, France
☎ Tel 00 331 44 117383
🖷 Fax 00 331 44 117382
✉ Email french@ulip.lon.ac.uk
🖥 Website www.ulip.lon.ac.uk

Student enquiries: Student Services Office
Applications: UCAS (degree courses), direct
(year abroad programme)

In brief

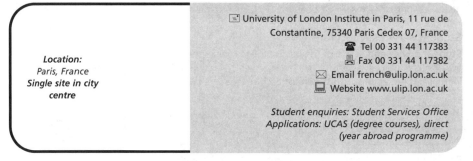

Total Students: 160

10% postgraduate
90% undergraduate

Undergraduates: 145
100% full-time   95% UK students
8% mature
on entry

70% female   30% male

- **Specialist, research-intensive institute of University of London.**
- **Teaching staff:** 6 full-time, 8 part-time.
- **Broad study areas:** French studies, film and cultural studies.

Freshers
- **Admissions information:** Principles of UCAS tariff followed.
- **Points on entry:** 310+ (average).
- **Accommodation:** No Institute accommodation.

Profile

Institution

Founded: 1894, as private organisation. **Structural features:** Incorporated into University of London in 1969. Changed name from British Institute in Paris in 2005. **Site:** Central Paris, on eastern side of Esplanade des Invalides, 10 mins' walking distance just across the river from Champs Elysées. **How to get there:** Invalides metro station; bus routes (Nos 28, 63, 69, 83, 93). From UK, Eurostar to Gare du Nord, metro towards Porte d'Orléans, change at Strasbourg-Saint Denis to Balard line to Invalides; from Charles de Gaulle airport, take train (RER ligne B) heading for Robinson, change at Pont Saint-Michel to RER ligne C towards Versailles and alight at Invalides; from Orly airport, take Air France airport bus direct to Invalides.

Courses

Academic features: BA in French studies (entirely in Paris). MA in Paris studies (history and culture). Also provides courses for students reading French at British universities, on their year abroad.
Awarding body: University of London. **Length of courses:** 3 years (BA); 1 year (MA).

Study opportunities & careers

Library and information services: Learning resources centre has 10,000 volumes. IT and library services converged. Ratio workstations to students 1:6. Access to internet from 25+ computers and wi-fi access. **Other learning resources:** Online resources, cinema room, film resources, multimedia laboratory, AV and computing support services.

Student services & facilities

Student advice and services: Recommendations on health insurance. French social security benefits and Mutuelle (ie supplementary health scheme). **Amenities:** Student cafeteria, SU facilities.
Accommodation: Institute is non-residential, but accommodation secretary has address register. Some places for students at the central Cité Universitaire (apply by late April); good rooms in city, hostel, flatlet and paying-guest accommodation for early birds; rent £300–£800 a month.

Money

Living expenses budget: Minimum budget of £6k pa (excluding tuition fees) recommended by institute. **Term-time work:** Institute allows term-time work for full-time students; limit of approx 10 hours pw (50% believed to work). **Financial help:** Bursaries of £1050 pa to UK students whose family income is up to £25k; £839 pa for those whose family income is £25k–£34,600. Modest student support funding available in the form of bursaries and emergency relief. **Tuition fees:** Home students pay £3225 pa for first degrees. International students pay up to £9k pa.

Student view

James Beard, Union President (3rd year, BA French Studies)

Living

What's it like as a place to live? Paris is an amazing place to live. Very diverse, socially, culturally and ethnically, and cheaper than London. A good place to learn French too.
How's the student accommodation? Technically non-existent. ULIP is too small to have halls but does have connections with student accommodation providers and an accommodation service, which makes things a bit easier. **What's the student population like?** With less than 200 of us (of which 90% are undergraduates) the community is very close-knit, friendly and welcoming – and Union policies, events and activities affect the whole student body! **How do students and locals get on?** Very well. The French young male demographic are exceptionally sleazy but, with most people, speaking a *little* bit of French goes a long way to building mutual respect.

Studying

What's it like as a place to study? ULIP has a decent library and cinema room and the off-site resources (eg Bibliothèque Nationale de France) are world class. Courses range from ridiculous to sublime, most in the middle. The BA is currently being gradually and holistically remodelled. **What are the teaching staff like?** Again, ranges from world-renowned authors and researchers to lecturers who've been booted out of lesser universities. The core language units are traditionally taught by native French 'professeurs' – a unique benefit to ULIP.

Socialising

What are student societies like? FC ULIP always pulls a strong team together, and an even stronger crowd of supporters. From the Bakers' Guild to Theatre Society to *Parlons* magazine, there's something for everyone, and starting new societies is very simple. **What's a typical night out?** Pre-lash at home, Beer Pong at Place Mange, clubbing at Le Mix. **And how much does it cost?** Wine + cocktails + supermarket alcohol usually cheap; clubs often let foreign students in for free. **How can you get home safely?** Last metro around 12.30am (1.30am weekends); night buses every 15 mins (ish) thereafter.

Money

Is it an expensive place to live? Yes, there are no SU bars like in the UK, so we have to rely on Happy Hours and student nights. On the whole, though, food and accommodation *slightly* cheaper than in London. **Average price of a pint?** €5–€6. **And the price of a takeaway?** €6–€7. **What's the part-time work situation?** Anglophone magazine *FUSAC* (free and readily available) helps students break into the Parisian job market. Part-time jobs are often cash in hand.

Summary

What's the best feature about the place? The unique university experience, both in terms of size and location. **And the worst?** ULIP, though vastly improved since 2004, is still not up to par with UK mainland unis in terms of quality assurance and student support services. **And to sum it all up?** A unique and richly rewarding university experience for those willing to brave the language and culture barriers.

Past students: Michael Sadler (dramatist); Sir Christopher Mallaby (HM Ambassador to Paris); Charles de Gaulle.

Loughborough University

Location:
Midlands (map 2)
Single campus in Loughborough

📧 Loughborough University, Loughborough, Leicestershire LE11 3TU
☎ Tel 01509 223522
📠 Fax 01509 223905
✉ Email admissions@lboro.ac.uk
💻 Website www.lboro.ac.uk

Student enquiries: Undergraduate Admissions Office
Applications: UCAS

In brief

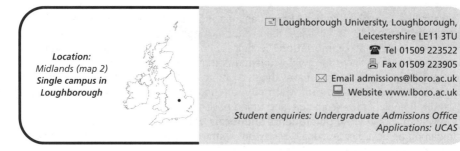

Total Students: 13,195

4% FE Students
13% postgraduate
83% undergraduate

Undergraduates: 10,915
97% full-time — 90% UK students
4% mature on entry — 22% lower socio-economic groups

37% female — 63% male

- **A top UK research-intensive university.**
- **Teaching staff:** 648 full-time, 75 part-time.
- **Broad study areas:** Engineering, science, business, physical education and sport science, social science and humanities, art and design.

Freshers

- **Admissions information:** AS-levels accepted in combination with 2+ A-levels or equivalent. UCAS tariff used in addition to some course-specific requirements.
- **First degree entrants:** 3105 UK, full-time.
- **Points on entry:** 300+ (average).
- **Drop-out rate:** 4% in 1st year.
- **Accommodation:** All 1st years housed if Loughborough is first choice.

Profile

Institution

Founded: 1909; university status in 1966. **Site:** Single campus (433 acres) approx 1 mile from Loughborough town centre. **How to get there:** 1 mile from M1; 1½ miles from railway station; 8 miles from East Midlands airport; bus service between town, railway station and campus. Miles of cycle paths on and off campus. **Special features:** Excellent business and industry links: many staff with industrial experience; number of professors seconded from business.

Courses

Academic features: Range of specialised centres and institutes, including polymer technology and materials engineering, hazard and risk management, water engineering, computer–human interface research, construction management, landscape ecology, sport management, ergonomics, surface science and technology, sustainability, media and cultural analysis. **Awarding body:** Loughborough University. **Main undergraduate awards:** BA, BSc, BEng, MChem, MComp, MEng, MMath, MPhys. **Length of courses:** 3 or 4 years; some 4 or 5 years.

Study opportunities & careers

Library and information services: Pilkington Library with 500,000+ volumes, 6000 serials; 800 study places. Information provision, £128 pa spent for each student (FTE). Access to internet and range of university databases from student rooms. **Study abroad:** Formal exchange links with 90+ universities and colleges in Europe and overseas in many disciplines. **Careers:** Active careers service providing advice and guidance to all students.

Student services & facilities

Student advice and services: Medical services, counsellors, advice centre, chaplains, personal tutors, disabilities and additional needs support unit, mathematics education centre. **Amenities:** Purpose-built SU building with bars, cafés, shops, travel office, banks, bookshop, optician, hairdresser, laundrette; performance area for 2000; day nursery/playgroup; student arts centre with darkroom, studio equipment, record and cassette library; associated music centre; drama studio with workshop; media centres; campus radio station. **Sporting facilities:** Sports halls, gymnasia, squash courts, floodlit all-weather areas and athletics stadium, tennis courts, fitness centre, dance studio, numerous playing pitches, Olympic-standard swimming pool, cricket centre. **Accommodation:** 60+% of all students in university accommodation (all 1st years guaranteed hall place if the university is first choice). 5000 places available, some ensuite: full-board at £109–£134 pw, contracts 31–35 weeks; self-catering at £60–£124 pw, contracts 39–50 weeks. Students live in privately owned accommodation for 1+ years: rent £60–£75 pw for self-catering (up to £105 for single flat). 5% of students live at home.

Money

Living expenses budget: Minimum budget of £6800–£7060 for 38-week academic year (excluding tuition fees) recommended by university. **Financial help:** Bursaries of £1360 pa for UK students whose family income is up to £25k; tapered bursaries where family income is £25k–£34,700 (eg £650 pa where it is £25k); all bursaries doubled for mature students (over 21 on entry). Merit-based entry scholarships of £1k in some science and engineering subjects. Also £250k government funds, £20k own funds, 1100 students helped. Special help: students with special needs, disabled students, those with dependants, mature students or those experiencing unforeseen financial pressures particularly finalists. **Tuition fees:** Home students pay £3225 pa for first degrees (£625 for placement year). International students pay £9850 pa (classroom), £12,800 pa (lab/studio).

Student view

It has an excellent reputation for engineering, sport science, business, social sciences and art. Workloads tend to vary according to course (time on practicals for the science-based). Many courses allow you to spend a year working in industry or abroad. Assessment through coursework, exams and practicals. Very easy to change at the beginning of first term (by seeing the 2 heads of department). Effective academic representation through system of trained course reps. Good facilities for students with special needs. Accommodation excellent – over 5000 places. For those living out, there are many clusters of student-inhabited streets; good atmosphere and generally centred on a pub! Area is flat so good for biking, and a campus bus goes to/from town every 15 mins. SU serves a diverse membership of around 18,000 students (from university, Loughborough FE College and RNIB Vocational College); it supports and represents students as well as providing good facilities. It aims to enhance the Loughborough experience through participation in the many clubs and societies, voluntary projects, charity fundraising or taking a role as a representative – all of which help to develop leadership, organisational and communication skills. Union building provides a base for a fully professional advice centre, employment exchange and a nursery with subsidised places; also catering outlets, shop, smoothie and juice bar, banks, hairdresser, opticians and dentist. Its venue is open for events every night, with 8 bars and recently refurbished Room 1. As well as 40+ clubs and societies, there is also Rag (charity fundraising, £693,938 raised last year), Action (local volunteering community projects), an award-winning media centre, bi-weekly magazine (*Label*) and very successful athletics union (winning men's BUCS competition for 28 consecutive years, the women's for 29 years). Everything is on campus – some students don't leave it for the whole 3 years! Lots of pubs, markets twice a week, cinema, etc. It's only 20 mins to Nottingham and Leicester by train.

Student footnotes

Housing: In halls (some married quarters). Many 2nd-year students choose to live out – noticeboards, uni, word of mouth. **Eats:** Plentiful food in halls of residence. SU fast food outlets and pleasant piazza coffee bar. Meal on campus £3–£4. Town has many restaurants and takeaways (student discounts available); curry and Chinese houses popular. One vegetarian restaurant and a number of wholefood shops. Ashby Road filled with catering outlets. Good meal for £8 in Toby Carvery. **Drink:** Good bars in SU building; regular drinks promotions, a pint of 'purple nasty' is £1.90 and £1 on a Wednesday night and there are plenty of soft drinks available. Loads of student pubs in town: The Griffin and Orange Tree both funky and popular. **Nightlife:** Brilliant in union – live bands every Thursday at SU (eg the Twang, the Feeling, the Automatic, Babyshambles, Scouting for Girls); regular films, discos and top cabaret acts, nightclub with alternative nights. Drama on campus as well as in adjacent cities. In town, 4 student nightclubs (Wild, Rain, Echos, Rapture), 6-screen cinema. **Locals:** Very friendly, no problems. **Sports:** Excellent facilities on campus – open to SU sports clubs members. **Financial help:** Widely available; loans and grants and very good links between uni and SU. Brilliant SU student advice centre. Subsidised nursery places. **Jobs:** Casual jobs available in SU, as well as shop/bar work in town. SU employment exchange has plenty of jobs in range of places. **Best features:** Unique student experience. **And worst:** Too much to do and not enough time to do it! **Good news:** Hall bedrooms have phones and internet access. **Past students:** Alastair Biggart (Channel Tunnel); Peter Bonfield (ICL); Rob Dickens (British photographic industry); Sebastian Coe (athlete and politician); David Moorcroft, Steve Backley, Chris Rawlinson (athletes); Forbes Robinson (singer); Sir Clive Woodward (rugby); Monty Panesar (cricketer); Tanni Grey-Thompson (paralympic athlete and presenter); Paula Radcliffe (runner); Ben Challenger (high jump); Lawrie Sanchez (football); Fran Cotton (rugby). **More info?** Ring SU president on 01509 635000, email president@lborosu.org.uk or visit website at www.lufbra.net.

LSE

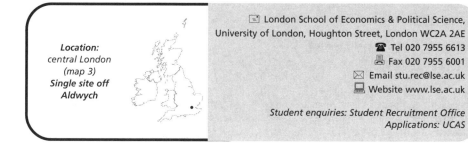

Location:
central London
(map 3)
Single site off
Aldwych

✉ London School of Economics & Political Science, University of London, Houghton Street, London WC2A 2AE

☎ Tel 020 7955 6613
📠 Fax 020 7955 6001
✉ Email stu.rec@lse.ac.uk
🖥 Website www.lse.ac.uk

Student enquiries: Student Recruitment Office
Applications: UCAS

In brief

Total Students: 9600

56% postgraduate
44% undergraduate

Undergraduates: 4200
99% full-time
3% mature on entry
42% UK students
18% lower socio-economic groups

49% female 51% male

- **World-class research-intensive institution.** A college of University of London.
- **Teaching staff:** 420 full-time, 36 part-time.
- **Broad study areas:** All social sciences.

Freshers
- **Admissions information:** AS-levels accepted in combination usually with 3+ A-levels or equivalent. UCAS tariff not used.
- **First degree entrants:** 1200 UK, full-time.
- **Points on entry:** 360 (average).
- **Drop-out rate:** 5% in 1st year.
- **Accommodation:** All 1st-year undergraduates housed.

Profile

Institution
Founded: 1895. **Structural features:** Part of London University since 1900. **Site:** Central London (just off Aldwych). **How to get there:** Holborn and Temple underground stations; numerous buses. **Special features:** Number of public lectures from leading figures from business, politics, academia. Very international student body.

Courses

Academic features: Unique concentration on economic and social sciences, taught in 18 departments.1-year courses for visiting international students. **Awarding body:** London School of Economics. **Main undergraduate awards:** BA, BSc, LLB. **Length of courses:** 3 years.

Study opportunities & careers

Library and information services: The library (also known as the British Library of Political and Economic Science) is a national social science research collection as well as the school's working library; over 1 million books, 10,000 current periodicals. Course collection: 92,000 volumes, with additional copies of more important course books, 20,000 e-journals. Shaw Library, collection of general literature. Information provision, £251 pa spent for each student (FTE). Separate IT service, 1000 points with access to internet (ratio 1:6 workstations to students), 24-hour facility available. IT support from help desk, free tuition and help sheets; all major software packages supported. Introductory tours and courses on library and information services. **Study abroad:** Under 1% spend a period abroad. Limited range of Erasmus exchange links. **Careers:** Information and advice service.

Student services & facilities

Student advice and services: Doctor, dentist, FPA, psychiatrist, nursing sister, chaplains, women's adviser, disabled students' adviser. Nursery with 60 places. **Amenities:** SU with café, bar, shop, legal advice centre, newspaper and magazine; also ULU facilities in Malet Street. **Sporting facilities:** Sports grounds at New Malden; circuit room, squash court and gymnasium on site. **Accommodation:** Guaranteed for all 1st year undergraduates (incl London-based), in LSE or London University residences. 3400+ LSE places available: rent £89–£210 pw self-catering (from shared room to single ensuite). Intercollegiate halls £130–£180 pw incl dinner. Privately owned accommodation, rent £80–£120 pw.

Money

Living expenses budget: Minimum budget of £10k a year (excluding tuition fees) recommended by school. **Term-time work:** Part-time work accepted as financial necessity for some students. Work available in school library, SU and departments. **Financial help:** Bursaries of £2500 pa for UK students whose family income is up to £3k, tapered down to nil where family income is £60k. Also discretionary bursaries (up to £2500 pa) for UK students with exceptional needs. Some scholarships of £5k–£11k pa, mostly subject-specific. Also £140k government funds, £405k own hardship funds for students facing unanticipated financial difficulties (following registration). Special help: students with health problems, disabilities, childcare problems. Apply to financial support office for help. **Tuition fees:** Home students pay £3225 pa for first degrees. International students pay £12,840 pa.

Student view

Aled Dilwyn Fisher, General Secretary of the Students' Union (Graduate, International Relations and History)

Living

What's it like as a place to live? LSE students live all over London, but mainly in places like Islington, Hackney, Tower Hamlets, Camden, South Central (Camberwell, Peckham, Waterloo, Borough, etc.) and centrally around LSE in Westminster or the City. London is a really exciting place to live, with so much to do – you can never really see it all, and there are always new things to try! **How's the student accommodation?** Of all London universities, LSE has the best beds-to-students ratio. Naturally, London accommodation even in halls is very expensive. Some LSE halls are very expensive (if very nice), but there are some at the cheaper end that have a great community atmosphere as well as decent but affordable rooms. There have been numerous problems in LSE halls recently but the union and the school are working on these. Many people have a fantastic time in their halls that they never forget, and make friends for life! Private accommodation can be extremely expensive unless you live further out (and therefore have to commute), and balancing transport costs is essential. Experiences with landlords can be notoriously difficult so it's wise to check out trustworthy services like the University of London Housing Service. **What's the student population like?** LSE has the most international student body of any university in the country. The best represented countries are the UK, the USA, China, South-east Asian countries and European countries but, at times, LSE has had more countries represented than the UN! This means the student body is highly diverse, and you'll meet and make friends with people from all over the world. This is what makes LSE so unique. Furthermore, given that 50% of the student body is postgraduate, this adds to the blend of diversity and different experiences. **How do students and locals get on?** Given that LSE doesn't have 'locals' as such, and our students tend to live in a scattered way across different areas, there are no real community tension problems like there are in other university cities. There are no real 'student-dominated' areas of London.

Studying

What's it like as a place to study? LSE is generally 100% exams based – very few courses have coursework, and for most undergraduates and postgraduates, the dissertation or long essay module is the only non-exam form of assessment. Classes are compulsory; lectures are not. There are usually about 4 essays a year for each of the 4 modules you take in qualitative degrees; quantitative degrees have more regular exercises, like problem sets. The 1st year at LSE counts towards your degree, but not as much as the 2nd and 3rd year (which count equally with each other). LSE is very competitive and this can cause heightened stress. Many courses are flexible and offer outside options in other departments, and even other University of London colleges. Changing course is possible and fairly easy if you have a good reason. **What are the teaching staff like?** The majority of class teaching is down by graduate teaching assistants (GTAs) – postgraduate students – although some professors take classes, particularly at postgraduate level. Some GTAs are excellent, some are not. LSE has received a lot of media attention for its teaching problems. These are being tackled by mass lobbying by the union and investment from the school. LSE is nonetheless full of some of the top academics in the world of economics, law, finance, political science, history, sociology, anthropology, international relations, human rights, climate change research and every other discipline it does. LSE regularly ranks in the top 5 of league tables.

Socialising

What are student societies like? There are around 200 student societies in the LSE SU. There are national, cultural, religious, careers, campaigning, political, special interest, activities and other societies. LSE is notable for how many of its students are involved in societies. Undergraduates and postgraduates mix well within societies. The campus is always alive with society events, campaigns and other visible activities. The Athletics Union (AU) is a very visible presence, particularly on Wednesday nights in the pub! LSE has sports grounds down in Surrey that are accessible by the train network. There are over 30 sports clubs. **What's a typical night out?** There is no such thing as a typical London night out – anything can happen and there's something for everyone! **And how much does it cost?** Potentially, a lot, so be careful. **How can you get home safely?** Use licensed taxis only and night buses (sit downstairs to avoid trouble and be careful).

Money

Is it an expensive place to live? London is very expensive, so it's advisable to budget carefully. There are ways to live cheaply if you're careful! **Average price of a pint?** In central London, probably £2.50–£3. **And the price of a takeaway?** Over £5. **What's the**

part-time work situation? At LSE, there are many part-time jobs available as stewards for public lectures, fundraising callers, library staff and so on. The SU employs students only, and pays the best part-time work rate of any union in the country. Part-time work opportunities are good in London, but make sure employers pay a living wage of at least £7.40/hour.

Summary
What's the best feature about the place? Its international community in the heart of an amazing city. **And the worst?** Pressure – be that peer pressure, academic, financial, etc. **And to sum it all up?** Top-quality university, with unrivalled diversity, rich history and central importance in the political, economic, legal and social world.

Past students: LSE alumni and former staff include 13 Nobel Prize winners, around 28 heads of state (past or present), 28 current UK MPs and 34 members of the House of Lords; John F Kennedy (former US President), George Soros (billionaire financial speculator), Mick Jagger (Rolling Stones), Maurice Saatchi (advertising mogul), Lloyd Grossman (chef and presenter), Carlos the Jackal, F Hayek (economist and political philosopher), Cherie Booth QC, Romano Prodi (Italian and European politician), Monica Lewinsky. **More info?** Get SU handbook from the SU (tel 020 7955 7158, email su.gensec@lse.ac.uk) or visit the website (www.lsesu.com).

Manchester Met University

Location:
Manchester, north-west England
(map 2)
Central campus,
others across city and
in Cheshire; partner
colleges

📄 The Manchester Metropolitan University,
All Saints, Manchester M15 6BH
☎ Tel 0161 247 2000
🖨 Fax 0161 247 7383
✉ Email prospectus@mmu.ac.uk
💻 Website www.mmu.ac.uk

Student enquiries: Academic Registrar
Applications: UCAS

In brief

Total Students: 33,200

17% postgraduate
83% undergraduate

Undergraduates: 27,435
88% full-time ● ● 90% UK students
31% mature ● ● 36% lower
on entry socio-economic groups

58% female 👩 👨 42% male

- **A modern university.**
- **Teaching staff:** 1312 full-time, 777 part-time, plus 111 research staff.
- **Broad study areas:** Art and design; business; clothing and food technology; education; hotel, catering and tourism management; humanities; law, social science; science and engineering; sport science;.

Freshers
- **Admissions information:** Offers made using UCAS tariff, by specifying grades, or by a combination of the 2 methods. AS-levels may be accepted in combination with 2+ A-levels or equivalent.

- **First degree entrants:** 7060 UK, full-time.
- **Points on entry:** 190+ (average).
- **Drop-out rate:** 11% in 1st year.
- **Accommodation:** Most 1st years housed.

Profile

Institution

Founded: 1970 as Manchester Poly, incorporating various colleges of art, technology, commerce and education; university status in 1992. **Site:** Main site, All Saints Campus, close to city centre; also Didsbury site (6 miles away), Hollings (3 miles), Elizabeth Gaskell (2 miles) and 2 campuses at MMU Cheshire (40 miles south). **How to get there:** Manchester well-connected by coach and rail (to Manchester Piccadilly and Victoria stations; 2 hours 40 mins from London), by road (M6/M56, M61, M62, M67) and by air to Manchester International Airport (10 miles south of city centre). Regular bus service to Didsbury, Hollings and Elizabeth Gaskell sites. Good rail service between Crewe and Manchester.

Courses

Awarding body: Manchester Metropolitan University. **Main undergraduate awards:** BA, BEd, BSc, BEng, LLB, FdA, FdEng, FdSc. **Length of courses:** 3 years; 4 years (sandwich); up to 7 years (part-time); 2 years (FdA/Eng/Sc).

Study opportunities & careers

Library and information services: 7 libraries, 850,000 volumes, 14,000 periodicals; 2800 study places. Information provision, £83 pa spent for each student (FTE). Extensive computing facility. Special collections include: book design, children's collection, local collection, artists' books, north-west film archive. **Study abroad:** 200 pa students spend a period abroad. Exchange links with universities in many European countries (Erasmus), the USA, Canada, Hong Kong. **Careers:** 3 information centres, web-based services; individual guidance and advice, including specialist support for students with health and disability issues, for postgraduate law and for volunteering service.

Student services & facilities

Student advice and services: Counsellors; learning support advisers (for disabled and dyslexic students); student support officers in faculties (one-to-one study skills support and workshops); student volunteering service; chaplains; nursery facilities (shared with Manchester University); campus medical facilities; legal advice from solicitors via SU; accommodation for disabled students.
Amenities: Horniman Theatre, art galleries and studios. SU building including bar, restaurant, shop and games room. **Sporting facilities:** Gymnasia, sports halls, fitness rooms, 5-a-side pitches, tennis and squash courts, weight training and swimming pools at Alsager and Manchester (which includes an athletics centre). Playing fields at Hough End and at MMU Cheshire; track and field athletics.
Accommodation: In Manchester, approx 3400 places in owned or leased halls, most for 1st years. 140 catered rooms (catering in term time only), others self-catered. Rents £87 pw catered, £70–£98 pw self-catering (£82–£130 ensuite); term-time or academic year contracts. Students live in privately owned accommodation for 2+ years, rent £45–£150 pw self catering. In Cheshire, 1200 places in owned or leased halls (sufficient for all 1st years and many returning students), some self-catering, some traditional catered halls. Rents: £80 pw for ensuite self-catering rooms, 42-week contracts; £88.50 pw in catered halls, 34-week contracts. Some students in private accommodation (large supply of flats and houses to share in Crewe, sufficient in Alsager); rent from £40 pw plus bills, usually 40-week contract, sometimes 52 weeks.

Money

Living expenses budget: Minimum budget of £7800 pa (excluding tuition fees) recommended by university. **Financial help:** Bursaries of £1k pa for UK students whose family income is up to £20,500; bursaries tapered (down to £100 pa) where family income is £20,500–£39,300 pa. Also £968k government funds (average award £1500). **Tuition fees:** Home students pay £3225 pa for first degrees. International students pay £7785 (classroom-based), £8420 (lab/studio) but more for architecture and physiotherapy (£12,900 and £10,685 pa).

Student view | Jamie Dickinson, Publications Officer/Editor of *PULP* (Graduate, Film and Media)

Living

What's it like as a place to live? Manchester is a fantastic place to live. It's a vibrant and dynamic place with a variety of things to do; it has a big city feel, but because of the large student population it isn't nearly as intimidating as you might think. **How's the student accommodation?** Again, because of the large student population, there is a wide variety to choose from, both private and uni-owned. Most of it is very reasonable and there are always places close to your campus. If you have the bucks to spend there are some very plush private halls and city centre flats; and if you are renting after your 1st year there are plenty of houses and flats in the South Manchester area. Some places in large student areas like Fallowfield can be quite grotty, but nothing's too expensive. **What's the student population like?** Because Manchester is home to Manchester Metropolitan and Manchester University, it has one of the biggest student populations in the country; as such it's hugely diverse with a great mix of students from the local community and surrounding cities to international and students from the other end of the country. It's very, very mixed. **How do students and locals get on?** As with any large city, there are certain areas that are considered 'no-go'; however, most of this is down to rumours and hearsay rather than fact. Generally speaking areas are very student-friendly and have decent amenities and facilities, especially areas like Fallowfield, Burnage, Withington and Didsbury, which have large student populations.

Studying

What's it like as a place to study? This year the SU has a big focus on student services and faculties at MMU and has succeeded in improving these services with Student Information Points and extended library hours. Personally I had a mix of studying options, which suited me, and I'm led to believe this is the case for most students. The university and SU are also looking at the methods of assessment and establishing new means of assessment. **What are the teaching staff like?** MMU is very proud of its teaching staff and its reputation as being an institute of very high standards, to which I would agree. Some well-known and established lecturers and academics have taught me during my time at MMU and I know that others agree, especially within the business school and on our Hollings and Didsbury campuses, where a large majority of students are placed on industry placements with reputable companies and organisations.

Socialising

What are student societies like? MMU SU has over 100 different sports and societies and is increasingly becoming a mainstay on the top of the BUCS leagues as the level of sport at MMU is increasingly rising. There is a huge and diverse selection for everyone; whatever your experience or skill level, everyone's encouraged to get involved, from rugby league to ultimate frisbee and cheerleading. On the societies front, there's Beer and Real Ale Society, LGBT, religious and political groups and a variety of dance societies. And if there isn't something you want to do, you are free to set up your own sport or society. **What's a typical night out?** In Manchester there is no typical night out. You never get bored of the variety. There's student nights on every corner, alternative and mainstream clubs and venues, live music from megastars to local unsigned bands and everything in between. **And how much does it cost?** Depends, really, but usually between £20 and £30. **How can you get home safely?** Night buses run all night, which almost everyone uses, which are reasonably safe – as are taxis, which are never hard to find. As long as you use common sense, both of these options are safe.

Money

Is it an expensive place to live? For a city, Manchester is fairly reasonably and your money goes some way, especially compared to cities like London, Birmingham and Bristol. **Average price of a pint?** Most student nights do pints for £1, other than that it's usually £2.50 to £2.80; in the city centre it goes up to about £3. **And the price of a takeaway?** £3ish. **What's the part-time work situation?** The university is increasingly aware that a lot of students need to work part-time and have other commitments, and so accept this as part of the student life and try to help out. There is no shortage of part-time work in Manchester, from venue work, retail and bars; most people can find something to suit them. I've found, in my own jobs, that it is usually slightly over minimum wage; however, venue work can be higher.

Summary

What's the best feature about the place? Diversity and variety. **And the worst?** Rain and possibly the scallies, the little scrots that inhabit the city centre on the weekend asking for a fag. **And to sum it all up?** Plenty to do and even more people to meet.

Past students: L S Lowry (painter), Ossie Clark (fashion designer), Julie Walters (actress), Bryan Robson (footballer), Mick Hucknall (lead singer of Simply Red), Steve Coogan (comedian). **More info?** Look at website (www.mmsu.com) or contact MMSU President on 0161 273 1162, email s.u.president@mmu.ac.uk or visit www.mmunion.co.uk.

Manchester University

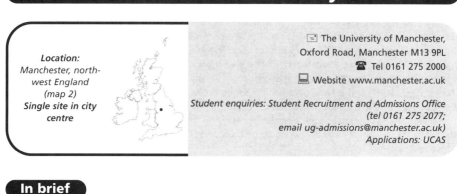

Location:
Manchester, north-west England
(map 2)
Single site in city centre

📧 The University of Manchester, Oxford Road, Manchester M13 9PL
☎ Tel 0161 275 2000
💻 Website www.manchester.ac.uk

Student enquiries: Student Recruitment and Admissions Office (tel 0161 275 2077; email ug-admissions@manchester.ac.uk) Applications: UCAS

In brief

Total Students: 37,715
38% postgraduate
62% undergraduate

Undergraduates: 23,430
96% full-time • 84% UK students
8% mature on entry • 21% lower socio-economic groups

54% female 46% male

- **World-class research-intensive university.**
- **Teaching staff:** Approx. 3800.

415

- **Broad study areas:** Engineering and physical sciences; humanities; life sciences; medical and human sciences.

Freshers

- **Admissions information:** 3 A-levels or equivalent required. In most cases 2 AS-levels accepted in place of 1 A-level. UCAS tariff not used.
- **First degree entrants:** 7000 UK, full-time.
- **Points on entry:** 353 (average).
- **Drop-out rate:** 5% in 1st year.
- **Accommodation:** All 1st years housed.

Profile

Institution

Founded: 2004 as a single university, from merger of Victoria University of Manchester (founded in 1851) and UMIST (founded in 1824), after 100 years of working together, sharing accommodation, welfare, etc. **Site:** Single campus, a mile south of city centre. **How to get there:** Manchester is well-connected by coach and rail (to Manchester Piccadilly and Victoria stations; just over 2 hours from London), by road (M6/M56, M61, M62, M67) and by air to Manchester International Airport (9 miles south of city centre). Many buses from city centre run down Oxford Road. **Special features:** Jodrell Bank Radio Telescope; Nuffield radio astronomy laboratories at Jodrell Bank; Contact Theatre; Science Park; Manchester Museum; Whitworth Art Gallery. Joint Centre for European Studies.

Courses

Awarding body: The University of Manchester. **Main undergraduate awards:** BA, BSc, BEng, BSocSci, BDS, BNurs, LLB, MBChB, MusB, MChem, MEng, MMath, MNeuroSc, MOptom, MPharm, MPhys, MMatSci. **Length of courses:** 3 years; 4 years (eg pharmacy, u/g Master's); 5–6 years (medicine, dentistry).

Study opportunities & careers

Library and information services: John Rylands University Library, over 3.5 million volumes, 8900 periodicals, 1800 study places, course books on reference, CD-ROMs, national databases. Also over 1 million manuscripts and 800,000 microform titles. Specialist collections: Joule Library (science and engineering), Lewis Library (humanities), Charters, early printed and rare books, manuscripts, military documents, archives (eg of *Manchester Guardian*). Information provision, £199 pa spent for each student (FTE). Separate IT service; over 6000 PCs with access to library and internet (ratio 1:3 workstations to students). Induction sessions to library and information services; guides and information sheets (printed and electronic); dedicated training suites and courses in IT skills. **Study abroad:** 14% of students spend a period abroad. **Careers:** Careers service provides information, advice and placement service

Student services & facilities

Student advice and services: Central academic advisory service, counsellors, student health service, SU welfare office, inter-denominational chapel, 2 day nurseries. **Amenities:** SU bars, live music venues, second-hand bookshop, weekly term-time student markets, etc. **Sporting facilities:** Indoor sports centres, wide range of outdoor sport (Firs Athletic Ground, athletics union, boathouse, yacht club, football pitches), partner in Commonwealth Games swimming pool; Manchester Aquatics Centre. **Accommodation:** All 1st-year students guaranteed university accommodation (under certain conditions); international students for their whole course. 9200+ places, rent £63–£108 pw self-catering, £82–£118 pw for catered halls; mainly 40-week contracts. Most students live in privately owned accommodation for 1–2 years, at £55–£70 pw self-catering; private lettings co-ordinated by Manchester Student Homes.

Money 💰

Living expenses budget: Minimum budget of £7480 for an academic year (excluding tuition fees) recommended by university. **Term-time work:** No university policy on term-time work or maximum hours. Part-time and casual work in university (eg in library, university offices) and SU (in cafés, bars); many jobs in shops, cafés, bars in city or in Trafford Centre. Term-time and vacation jobs advertised by Tempwise (run by careers service). **Financial help:** Bursaries of £1250 pa for UK students whose family income is up to around £25k. Scholarships of £3k pa for UK students with 3 A grades at A-level (or equivalent) and whose family income is up to around £25k; of £1250 pa for UK students with 3 A grades (or equivalent) on a range of designated programmes; or of £1750 pa for local students who have taken certain access courses; also various subject and faculty scholarships and awards for talented athletes and musicians. **Tuition fees:** Home students pay £3225 pa for first degrees. International students pay £10,500 pa (classroom), £12,900 (lab/studio-based course), £23,500 (clinical).

Student view
Susannah Birkwood, Student Newspaper Editor
(Graduate, Spanish and Linguistics)

Living
What's it like as a place to live? Extremely multicultural; there's something going on every night of the week. **How's the student accommodation?** There's a huge range of choices; uni accommodation tends to be friendlier than private halls. **What's the student population like?** Extremely diverse: around 1 in 5 is international, more state school pupils than any other Russell Group uni. **How do students and locals get on?** Students completely dominate in areas such as Fallowfield, which is known as the 'the student ghetto'!

Studying
What's it like as a place to study? Courses tend to be traditional, leading to recognised academic qualifications. Not enough books in library. **What are the teaching staff like?** Can be very difficult to get extra help needed.

Socialising
What are student societies like? Large range of societies, very varied selection and lots of involvement, in everything from scuba diving to union newspaper. **What's a typical night out?** Drinks followed by cheesy club in Fallowfield. **And how much does it cost?** £15. **How can you get home safely?** Regular buses, taxi.

Money
Is it an expensive place to live? Yes, but everyone is skint. Reasonable prices compared to other cities. **Average price of a pint?** £1.50. **And the price of a takeaway?** £7. **What's the part-time work situation?** Yes, the university has one of the best careers services in country – very helpful.

Summary
What's the best feature about the place? The mix of nationalities and cultures. **And the worst?** The weather/crime. **And to sum it all up?** A buzzing cosmopolitan city with theatres, cinemas, international cuisine and entertainments galore.

Past students: Mark Carlisle, Sir Rhodes Boyson, Margaret Beckett (MPs); Sir Maurice Oldfield (MI6); Robert Bolt (playwright); Anthony Burgess (novelist); Christabel Pankhurst (suffragette); Peter Maxwell Davies (composer); Sir Frank Worrall (sport); Lord Lever (politician); Alan Gowling (sport); John Tomlinson (music); Anna Ford (broadcaster); C A Lejeune (film critic); Rik Mayall (actor); Francis Thompson (poet); Ben Elton (comedian and author); Sir John Cockroft (Nobel prize for physics); Gary Bailey (football); Sophie Grigson (food writer), Terry Leahy (Tescos). **More info?** Contact SU (tel 0161 275 2930, email umu@man.ac.uk, website www.umsu.manchester.ac.uk).

MARJON

Location:
Plymouth, south-west England (map 2)
Single site outside city

University College Plymouth St Mark & St John, Derriford Road, Plymouth PL6 8BH
☎ Tel 01752 636700
✉ Email admissions@marjon.ac.uk
💻 Website www.marjon.ac.uk

*Student enquiries: Admissions Office
Applications: UCAS*

In brief

Total Students: 3750

43% postgraduate
57% undergraduate

Undergraduates: 2135
97% full-time ● ● 95% UK students
49% mature ● ● 44% lower
on entry ● socio-economic groups

65% female · 35% male

- **University college, awarding its own degrees.**
- **Teaching staff:** 108 full-time, 24 part-time.
- **Broad study areas:** Sports, media, community studies, public relations and management, sociology, humanities, teaching.

Freshers

- **Admissions information:** All applications considered on merit. AS-levels accepted in combination with A-levels or equivalent.
- **First degree entrants:** 645 UK, full-time.
- **Points on entry:** 180+ (average).
- **Drop-out rate:** 10% in 1st year.
- **Accommodation:** College arranges accommodation for almost all 1st years.

Profile

Institution

Founded: 1923, from St John's Battersea (1840) and St Mark's Chelsea (1841); moved to Plymouth in 1973. **Structural features:** Church of England university college. **Site:** 22-hectare campus, 5 miles from Plymouth city centre and overlooking Dartmoor, Plymouth and Plymouth Sound. **How to get there:** Intercity trains to Plymouth from London Paddington, Birmingham and the north; coaches from major cities and airports throughout Britain; M5 and A38 (London 4 hours by road); by air

(Plymouth and Exeter airports connect with number of centres); or ferry (France and Spain). Local bus service to College.

Courses

Academic features: Modular framework for all BA courses, allowing full- and part-time study. Teaching practice opportunities in London and in Europe, as well as Devon and Cornwall. **Awarding body:** University College Plymouth St Mark & St John. **Main undergraduate awards:** BA, BEd, BSc. **Length of courses:** 3 years.

Study opportunities & careers

Library and information services: 150,000+ volumes (including 18,000 children's books), 500 print journals, 5000 electronic journals. 200 study places. Information provision, £71 pa spent for each student (FTE). Separate IT service, open 24 hours/day. 400 PCs in 2 suites, all with internet access, all with access to library catalogue (ratio of workstations to students 1:6); wireless network. IT support (4 technicians, 2 administrative); library and computing induction courses for new students. **Other learning resources:** 3000 videos and DVDs. **Study abroad:** Teaching practice opportunities in Germany, Cyprus, Gibraltar and Channel Islands; study opportunities in USA. **Careers:** Specialist careers adviser and information room. Careers fairs, career management workshops.

Student services & facilities

Student advice and services: Student services department, counselling service, chaplain, disability support, essay workshops and job shop. Christian Fellowship and study groups. **Amenities:** SU bar and snack bar, shop, laundrette, minibus, printing service, specialist bookshop, part-time banking service, chapel, drama theatre, coffee and snack bars; many amenities in Plymouth. **Sporting facilities:** Floodlit all-weather sports pitch; sports centre incl sports halls, gym, weight-training room, squash courts, climbing wall, indoor 25-metre pool. Also Dartmoor and the coast for walking, climbing, water sports. **Accommodation:** Almost all 1st-year students in accommodation arranged by College. 490 college places available (for 1st-year, final-year and international students), in 7 catered halls and 38 self-catering houses: rent average of £63–£67 pw (including internet access, insurance, etc) plus £750 pa for dining-in scheme (compulsory in halls of residence, optional in student village). Privately owned accommodation: £70 pw for self-catering, £120 pw for half-board.

Money

Living expenses budget: Minimum budget of £6k pa (excluding tuition fees) recommended by college. **Term-time work:** College allows part-time work for full-time students. Part-time jobs advertised in student services office, local paper and Job Centre. **Financial help:** Free wireless enabled laptop for all new students. Hardship fund can provide loans and non-returnable grants to students needing financial support. Apply to student services for help. **Tuition fees:** Home students pay £3225 pa for first degrees. International students pay £8200 pa.

Student view

It's situated in a rural, picturesque position 5 miles from the centre of Plymouth, within easy reach of the moors, sea and Cornwall. Public transport to and from campus improving. Reasonable accommodation on campus, including houses in student village and halls of residence; priority given to 1st-and final-year students, other accommodation also available in Plymouth. Small but very active SU, which provides great entertainment. There is a handy 'corner shop' (with alcohol), 3 lively bars, laundrette, games area, transport services and many clubs and societies. Sports centre on campus for related courses, eg PE and sports science (sports halls, fitness suite, squash courts and swimming pool) and available to students at restricted times for a yearly subscription. Extensive sports ground; full-sized AstroTurf pitch, football and rugby pitch, also local pitches are available. High proportion of mature and international students on most courses. Expanding library and IT facilities. Confidential student services and college provides medical, careers, finance, accommodation and counselling staff. Good shopping in city (lots of hypermarkets for bargains), theatres, cinemas, ice skating, pubs, arts centre, arena (many famous people perform) and home of Plymouth Argyle.

Student footnotes

Housing: Good campus accommodation. Approved lodging system off campus (letting agencies, notices everywhere). **Eats:** Adequate campus dining-in scheme; snack food through SU shop; meal £2+ on campus. Wetherspoons, the Mutley Crown, Goodbody's are good (£5–£10); loads of cheaper places. **Drink:** 3 SU Bars (SUB), incl. late bar, Café Del Rosa serves hot drinks and alcohol (licence till 2am Wed and Fri); very cheap, pint from £1.50. More variety in city centre. **Nightlife:** Very good on-campus entertainment. Off campus, clubs, eg Walkabout, Oceana and C103 and pubs with live entertainment. **Locals:** Plymouth as a whole is friendly. **Sports:** Good training and fixture facilities on campus. Involved with BUCS; lots of teams in the premier leagues; many international players; successful basketball, hockey and rugby teams. **Travel:** Minibuses can be hired by the SU. **Jobs:** SU and bar employs 50+ plus jobs in catering and the student shop; plenty of work in city centre or on outskirts. **Financial help:** Access to learning fund. **Best features:** Its small size and relaxed friendly atmosphere, near the sea and moors. **And worst:** It rains too much! **Informal name:** Marjon. **Past students:** Cat Stevens (musician), Peter Duncan (*Blue Peter*), Ron Pickering (athlete), Kate Bush (singer), David Icke (conspiracy theorist). **More info?** Contact President on 01752 636771 (ext 3071) or visit www.marjonsu.co.uk.

Middlesex University

Location:
north of London,
within the M25
(map 3)
4 teaching centres
in north London;
partner colleges

✉ Middlesex University, North London
Business Park, Oakleigh Road South, London N11 1QS
☎ Tel 020 8411 5555
🖷 Fax 020 8411 5649
✉ Email enquiries@mdx.ac.uk
🖥 Website www.mdx.ac.uk

Student enquiries: Enquiries Office
Applications: UCAS

In brief

Total Students: 23,290

24% postgraduate
76% undergraduate

Undergraduates: 17,755
71% full-time ● ● 85% UK students
35% mature ● ● 48% lower
on entry ● ● socio-economic
groups

58% female   42% male

- **A modern university.**
- **Teaching staff:** 575 full-time, 245 part-time.
- **Broad study areas:** Art and design; biological sciences and environment; business; computing and IT; dance, music and theatre arts; English; health and sport sciences; language and translation studies; law; media, culture and communication; nursing and midwifery; philosophy and social sciences; teaching and education.

Freshers

- **Admissions information:** UCAS tariff used wherever possible; Keys Skills contribute. Special procedures for mature students, including those without formal qualifications.
- **First degree entrants:** 3245 UK, full-time.
- **Points on entry:** 240 (average).
- **Drop-out rate:** 13% in 1st year.
- **Accommodation:** Most 1st years who apply housed.

Profile

Institution

Founded: 1973 as Middlesex Poly, incorporating various colleges of technology, education, speech and drama, art, dance and health; university status in 1992. **Site:** 4 distinctive campuses in north London: Hendon is main, flagship campus (business, computing, law, many health and social sciences); Archway campus and hospitals (nursing, midwifery, Centre for Excellence in Teaching and Learning (CETL) for mental health, social work, complementary health); Trent Park, a serene country park, (teacher training, dance and drama); Cat Hill (arts, fashion and design) – Trent Park and Cat Hill are very close. **How to get there:** All campuses easily accessible from central London. Hendon tube and rail stations for Hendon campus; Upper Holloway rail station and Archway tube station for Archway campus; Cockfosters and Oakwood tube stations, New Barnet and Enfield Chase/Oakleigh Park rail stations for Trent Park and Cat Hill; various buses to all campuses. **Special features:** Pioneered student work placements; offers range of placements and overseas exchanges.

Courses

Academic features: Courses include media, nursing, herbal medicine and traditional Chinese medicine, jazz, journalism, computer networks, business, art and design and computer science. Research centres include performing arts, modern European philosophy, higher education, enterprise and economic development, flood hazard, electronic arts, criminology, work-based learning. **Awarding body:** Middlesex University. **Main undergraduate awards:** BA, BEng, BSc. **Length of courses:** 3 years (full-time); 4 years (sandwich); 5–7 years (part-time).

Study opportunities & careers

Library and information services: 3 main learning resource centres, 3 hospital libraries. Total of 600,000 volumes, 8000 periodicals (paper and electronic), 2100 study places, 28,000 audio and video tapes, 2175 CDs, course books for reference; at Trent Park 7000 CDs and tapes, 10,000 music scores; at Cat Hill 225,000 slides and illustrations. Specialist collections: Runnymede Trust library and archive, Black Theatre Forum archive, Bernie Grant collection, Lesbian and Gay Newspaper archive, collections of eg comics, fashion items; further collections in the Museum of Domestic Design and Architecture. Information provision, £54 pa spent for each student (FTE). Library, AV and IT services converged. Ratio 1:6 workstations to students; some 3000 computers with access to internet; IT facilities open up to 14 hours/day; IT support on each campus (approx 50 staff) for enquiries, documentation and workshops. Induction to library and information services for new students, workshops for all levels. **Other learning resources:** 3 TV studios, 4 computer centres, 2 language centres. Study skills workshops (including dyslexia and numeracy support), pre-sessional English language for international students. **Study abroad:** Most disciplines can be studied partly at an institution abroad, sometimes gaining an additional overseas qualification. Many work placements in Europe. **Careers:** Information centres; careers and employer fair; career development module; individual interviews with careers advisers.

Student services & facilities

Student advice and services: Counsellors; advice staff; 2 nurseries; half-term play schemes. English language support (including dyslexia and numeracy support); support for students with disabilities and for international students; information service (money, welfare, finance); nightline. **Amenities:** Bookshops at Hendon, Trent Park and Cat Hill; art supplies shop at Cat Hill. Forum, new café at Hendon, Deadend Gallery café at Cat Hill. Museum of Domestic Design and Architecture (MoDA) at Cat Hill. **Sporting facilities:** Sports halls and fitness centres at 2 major campuses; Burroughs Club at Hendon campus has large fitness centre, health suite, real tennis and outdoor tennis courts; outdoor swimming pool (Trent Park); indoor tennis dome. Outdoor sports pitches, use of 3 AstroTurf pitches (at Southgate Hockey Club – Trent Park campus). **Accommodation:** 75% of 1st years who wish it are in university accommodation (priority to 1st years and international students). 1100+ self-catering places (70+% ensuite), rent £81.50–£97 (ensuite). Privately rented accommodation, £75–£90 pw plus bills. 40% of first-degree students live at home.

Money

Living expenses budget: Minimum budget of £8k pa (excluding tuition fees) recommended by university. **Term-time work:** University allows term-time work for full-time students (60% believed to work). Some jobs on campus (catering, library, administration, etc.); careers service helps find work off campus. **Financial help:** Bursaries of £319 pa for UK students whose family income is up to £25k. Over 100 pa scholarships, eg for those with high points on entry (£1k pa), for academic, community or sporting excellence (£2k pa), for outstanding sporting potential (£10k pa); and one-off scholarships for fashion (£5k) and for contribution to north London community (£2k). Also £1.3 million access to learning fund, 1000 students helped (average £1100 awarded). Special consideration to single parents or students with dependants and students with special needs. Apply to academic registry for help. **Tuition fees:** Home students pay £3225 pa for first degrees. International students pay £9200 pa.

Student view) Nik Roberts, SU President

Living
What's it like as a place to live? The campuses differ: Hendon is in a nice area with good transport and on-campus facilities, and Trent Park also has good links to London but is set in beautiful parkland. **How's the student accommodation?** Uni halls but run by a private contractor. Some are newer than others but most are ensuite. Typical rent for London, but some halls appear to be better value than others. **What's the student population like?** Students from across the world, plenty of local students, mature students, etc. **How do students and locals get on?** A lot of students are locals, so that helps! No student–locals animosity to speak of.

Studying
What's it like as a place to study? Generally facilities are good, as are teaching support and library facilities. Some difficulties with timetabling, etc. after a huge shake-up in the academic framework. **What are the teaching staff like?** Mostly very good and will go the extra mile to see you, even if they are stretched.

Socialising
What are student societies like? Around 50 societies with 1500 members – ranging from religious to cultural to hobbies and sports (competitive teams run separately from societies). We even have a woodland animal appreciation society. **What's a typical night**

out? A few drinks in the uni bar then into London. **And how much does it cost?** Depends where you go to in town, or you could go to one of the nights at uni; entrance average £3.50. **How can you get home safely?** Plenty of trustworthy cabs with freefones. Night buses stop outside campuses. Free shuttle bus from tube station to Trent Park.

Money

Is it an expensive place to live? As it's London, it's not cheap. But with plenty of opportunities for part-time work you should be ok. **Average price of a pint?** On campus £2, off campus £2.60-ish **And the price of a takeaway?** £5–£10. **What's the part-time work situation?** University careers service website plus SU notice boards to help you find a job. Most students have no problem finding something close, with some jobs on campus available. Most wages will recognise the higher cost of living.

Summary

What's the best feature about the place? Diversity of students and dedication of academics. **And the worst?** Expensive living costs and a quite sterile looking campus at Hendon (the VC said no posters anywhere!). **And to sum it all up?** Middlesex is different in a fantastic way, offering the best of the traditional and modern with a huge diversity in students and opportunities.

Past students: Adam Ant (musician); Ally Capellino (Alison Lloyd and Jonathan Platt), Wendy Dagworthy (fashion); Ray Davies (musician); Lynsey de Paul (musician); Richard Torry; Gerard Hoffnung, Anish Kapoor (international artists); Richard Wilson (sculptor); Vivienne Westwood, Yasmin Yusuf (fashion designers); Omar, David McAlmont (singers); Nick Harvey MP; Dermot O'Leary (TV presenter), Ben Onwukwe, Peter Polycarpou, Matthew Marsden (actors); Johnny Vegas, Arabella Weir (TV entertainers); Mike Figgis (film director); Laura Hird (author); Frederick Salle (athlete); Alison Goldfrapp (musician). **More info?** Check out the SU website on www.musu.mdx.ac.uk.

Myerscough College

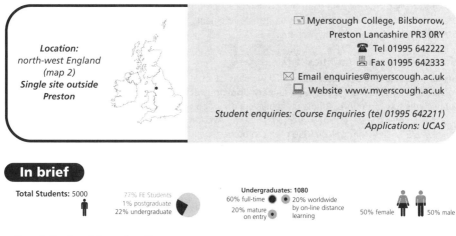

*Location:
north-west England
(map 2)
**Single site outside
Preston***

🖳 Myerscough College, Bilsborrow,
Preston Lancashire PR3 0RY
☎ Tel 01995 642222
🖨 Fax 01995 642333
✉ Email enquiries@myerscough.ac.uk
💻 Website www.myerscough.ac.uk

*Student enquiries: Course Enquiries (tel 01995 642211)
Applications: UCAS*

In brief

Total Students: 5000

77% FE Students
1% postgraduate
22% undergraduate

Undergraduates: 1080
60% full-time
20% mature on entry
20% worldwide by on-line distance learning

50% female   50% male

- **Specialist land-based college.**
- **Teaching staff:** 140 full-time, 280 part-time.
- **Broad study areas:** Agriculture, countryside and wastes management; animal studies; arboriculture; floral and garden design; equine studies; golf, football, cricket, watersports

and sports coaching; horticulture; landscape; mechanisation; motorsports; sportsturf; veterinary nursing.

Freshers

- **Admissions information:** 2 years post-16 education required; college encourages applications from those with alternative qualifications or with relevant careers experience.
- **First degree entrants:** 320 UK, full-time.
- **Points on entry:** 220 (average on BA/BSc; 80 on FdA/FdSc).
- **Accommodation:** Most 1st years housed.

Profile

Institution

Founded: 1894. **Structural features:** Partner college of UCLan (University of Central Lancashire). **Site:** Single countryside campus, 6 miles north of Preston. **How to get there:** M6/A6 Preston to Lancaster road. Train to Preston. **Special features:** Strong links with allied industries ensure industry-led courses.

Courses

Academic features: Modular courses allowing a range of options. Also offers short courses, work-based training and online learning. **Awarding body:** University of Central Lancashire. **Main undergraduate awards:** BA, BSc, FdA, FdSc. **Length of courses:** 2–4 years.

Study opportunities & careers

Library and information services: Library has 45,000 books, 100 current periodicals, 700 videos, 100 CD-ROMs, 100 PCs, video player and seating for approx 100 students. Open 7 days/week in term time. **Other learning resources:** International equine arena, animal academy and veterinary theatre, working farm and over 500 hectares of farmland, 30 hectares of woodland, motorsports workshop and track/rally cars, 2-hectare plant nursery, landscaped grounds, 9-hole golf course and golf academy. **Study abroad:** Students on industrial placements world-wide. Exchanges with USA (Ohio State and Cremson universities).

Student services & facilities

Student advice and services: Residential wardens, student counsellor. **Amenities:** TV/common rooms, SU bar, café/shop, restaurants, laundry. **Sporting facilities:** Extensive recreation facilities: 20-hectares sports grounds, 9-hole golf course, indoor golf academy, sports centre with gym and sports hall, international equine arena (30m x 80m). **Accommodation:** Priority given to 1st years who live 25+ miles from college. 650 places in modern halls: rent for self-catering £75 pw, full-board £110 pw (ensuite); 36-week contracts. Students in privately owned accommodation pay approx £60 pw self-catering, plus bills.

Money

Living expenses budget: Minimum budget of £5500 pa (excluding tuition fees) recommended by college. **Term-time work:** College allows term-time work for first-degree students (25% believed to work) but only provides help finding industrial placements. **Financial help:** Bursaries of £1k in 1st year for all UK students where the family income is up to £60k. Through UCLan; awards of £200–£1k. **Tuition fees:** Home students pay £3225 pa for first degrees. International students pay £8k pa.

Student view
Chloe Gregsoni, Student Rep (2nd year, ND Sport and Exercise Sciences)

Living
What's it like as a place to live? Quality place, good community, good people. Fair discipline when needed. **How's the student accommodation?** Fairly new, in good working order, well built. No private accommodation but can get that in Preston. **What's the student population like?** People from all over the country come. It's great. Most people get along brilliant. Everyone's always up for a laugh and having fun. **How do students and locals get on?** Our college is fairly out of the way but locals come to the college to join in with the open days and no complaints really.

Studying
What's it like as a place to study? The facilities are endless; the college specialises in subjects such as golf and it has a 9-hole course, which is also open to the public. **What are the teaching staff like?** Staff get on very well with students, make sure assignments are on time and done correctly and up to standard.

Socialising
What are student societies like? Gym, pub, sporting activities; at night, quizzes, DJs, bands. There are a good range of things to do at night. **What's a typical night out?** Stumble Nights, Preston. **And how much does it cost?** Stumble (50p on Tues); Preston varies – depends where you go. **How can you get home safely?** College mainly uses Millers taxis and the taxis give discounts for students.

Money
Is it an expensive place to live? All different prices. Reasonable price includes food (optional), cleaning, good facilities. **Average price of a pint?** On site (Stumble) £1.90; Preston £2.50. **And the price of a takeaway?** Preston: doner meat £2 a box, chips £1.50. **What's the part-time work situation?** Jobs on campus, about £5 an hour: cleaning, in the canteen, behind bar on campus.

Summary
What's the best feature about the place? People, friendly atmosphere, range of people, friendly staff – always willing to help. Myerscough is the place to be. **And the worst?** You can only be here 36 weeks a year. **And to sum it all up?** Hmmmm – been at college now for 2 years and planning to stay at least 2 more!!
More info? Contact SU (email supresident@myerscough.ac.uk, tel 01995 642 111).

Napier University

Location:
Edinburgh, central Scotland (map 1)
Sites across city plus health sites; partner colleges

Edinburgh Napier University, Craiglockhart Campus, Edinburgh EH14 1DJ
☎ Tel 08452 606040
🖷 Fax 0131 455 6464
✉ Email info@napier.ac.uk
🖳 Website www.napier.ac.uk

Student enquiries: Information Office
Applications: UCAS (direct for part-time, CATCH for nursing and midwifery)

In brief

Total Students: 14,540

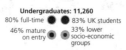
23% postgraduate
77% undergraduate

Undergraduates: 11,260
80% full-time
46% mature on entry
83% UK students
33% lower socio-economic groups

57% female   43% male

- **A modern university.**
- **Teaching staff:** Approx. 800 + 70 research staff.
- **Broad study areas:** E-business and information management, social sciences, alternative medicine, built environment and civil engineering, financial services and accounting, computing and IT, hospitality and tourism, life sciences, health and nursing, design and media arts, communication arts, business management, law, engineering.

Freshers

- **Admissions information:** Minimum 3–4 Highers or 2 A-levels at grade C or above; AS-levels may count in addition.
- **First degree entrants:** 1880 UK, full-time.
- **Points on entry:** 242 (average).
- **Drop-out rate:** 18% in 1st year.
- **Accommodation:** Most 1st years housed (if not local and apply by deadline).

Profile

Institution

Founded: 1964 as Napier College; university status in 1992; changed name to Edinburgh Napier University in 2009. **Site:** 6 campuses across centre and south-west of Edinburgh city, plus nursing sites beyond. 3 main sites: Craighouse (grade A listed Victorian campus); Merchiston (historic site, birthplace of John Napier); and Craiglockhart campus (19th-century site, newly developed; home to business school). 2 further campuses at Canaan Lane in Morningside (health and life sciences), and one in Comely Bank in north of city. Further nursing campuses in Livingstone (West Lothian) and Melrose (Borders). **How to get there:** City easily accessible by train and coach from all over the UK; airport 8 miles (cheap flights from London and other centres). All campuses within 15 mins of city centre, well-served by frequent bus services and linked by cycle paths. **Special features:** Flexible learning, wide access routes, credit accumulation system; advanced entry possible on relevant degrees for those with HNC and HND.

Courses

Academic features: All courses are vocationally oriented, modular and taught in semesters. New degree courses include maintenance surveying, transport management, sports technology, internet computing. **Awarding body:** Napier University. **Main undergraduate awards:** BA, BEng, BDes, BMus, BN, BSc, LLB. **Length of courses:** 3 years (ordinary degrees and nursing); 4 years (Hons).

Study opportunities & careers

Library and information services: 7 libraries; 450,000 volumes, 2500 periodicals, 1100 study places. Information provision, £107 pa spent for each student (FTE). Separate IT service. 1400 computers, some sites open 24 hours/day (including 500-PC computer centre at Merchiston Campus); all students have free email and access to library and internet. IT support from 80 staff across main campuses. All rooms in halls have internet access. **Careers:** Information, advice and placement service. Work placements part of many courses.

Student services & facilities

Student advice and services: University mentoring scheme (new students work with existing students on the same course, to help orientation and problem-solving). Student finance support, student advisers, special needs co-ordinators, medical officers, nurses, counselling and a chaplaincy. **Amenities:** SA (NSA) facilities at each campus. Shops and bars at main campuses, incl restaurant, café and bar. **Sporting facilities:** Sports dome, small gym; discounts at all local authority gym/sports centres. **Accommodation:** 85% of all 1st years housed – guaranteed for applicants living 30 miles outside city centre who apply by deadline. 900 rooms in university accommodation, all for 1st years: rent from £82 pw for 10 months. Many students live in privately owned accommodation for whole course, rent approx £70–£80 pw self-catering.

Money 💰

Living expenses budget: Minimum budget of £590 per month (excluding tuition fees) recommended by university. University has advice booklet covering student funding. **Financial help:** Various scholarships for international students. Hardship fund of £369k (approx 1300 students helped; average £290); mature students' fund of £76,700 (65 students helped; average £1180), childcare fund £69k (52 students helped; average £1335). Apply to student support services for help. **Term-time work:** University recommends a maximum of 15 hours/week in term-time jobs. University careers service and NSA Job Bank both have information on part-time jobs. **Tuition fees:** Scottish and EU students pay no fees during course; other UK students pay £1820 pa for first degrees. International students pay £8600 pa (classroom), £9990 (lab/studio).

Student view) **Carys Evans,** Students' Association President (1st year, MSc Business Management)

Living
What's it like as a place to live? Edinburgh is an historic city with lots to see and do. There is a wide spread of accommodation available. **How's the student accommodation?** Average flatted accommodation – 5–4-bedroom flats, some newly decorated, close to all campuses and centre of town. **What's the student population like?** The population in Edinburgh has a high percentage of students who are local, plus international, making it easy to make new friends. **How do students and locals get on?** Locals are very much used to having students around due to the city being heavily populated by students.

Studying
What's it like as a place to study? Courses are flexible and up to date with the majority having industry links making students more highly employable. **What are the teaching staff like?** Always interested in the students' needs and there to listen, helping to solve any problems the student may have.

Socialising
What are student societies like? Societies are becoming increasingly popular at Napier as more people have an interest in sport. Societies and sports teams include archery, cricket, football, subaqua, drama and whiskey, to name but a few. **What's a typical night out?** Pub/club. Cinema. Wide range of gyms available. **And how much does it cost?** £10–£20 weekday. **How can you get home safely?** Night buses, taxi, short distances are ok to walk.

Money
Is it an expensive place to live? Edinburgh is expensive but every penny is worth it! A student loan will cover accommodation. **Average price of a pint?** £2.50–£3. **And the price of a takeaway?** £6. **What's the part-time work situation?** There are always part-time jobs available, which are reasonably paid. Timetables are planned so that students have time to have part-time work.

Summary
What's the best feature about the place? It is a friendly, informal environment with a modern feel – everything is approachable! **And the worst?** There are not adequate

427

sporting facilities, although the new campus being built at present has excellent facilities for the future. **And to sum it all up?** A modern university with a friendly atmosphere and an active learning environment.

Past students: Ian Buchanan (Edinburgh Councillor), Steve Jacks (Radio Forth DJ), Jane Franchie (BBC Scotland), Greg Kane (Hue and Cry), Gavin Hastings (Scottish rugby), Ali Paton (Siren in *Gladiators*).
More info? Ring NSA on 0131 229 8791 or email nsa@napier.ac.uk. See what's on at www.napierstudents.com.

National Film & TV School

Location:
Buckinghamshire,
north-west of London
(map 2)
**Single site in
Beaconsfield**

✉ National Film & Television School, Beaconsfield Studios, Station Road, Beaconsfield, Bucks HP9 1LG
☎ Tel 01494 731425
🖷 Fax 01494 674042
✉ Email info@nfts.co.uk
🖥 Website www.nfts.co.uk

Student enquiries: The Registry
Applications: Direct

In brief

Total Students: 260   100% postgraduate    90% full-time ● ◐ 60% UK students   50% female   50% male

- **Leading specialist film school.**
- **Broad study areas:** Film production; television programme-making.
- **Admissions information:** 100 students admitted to MA course annually, 30–40 to diploma course; average age 25 years. Normal requirements are first degree or equivalent professional qualification or relevant practical experience in chosen specialisation.
- **Accommodation:** No school accommodation.

Profile

Institution

Founded: 1970. **Site:** Beaconsfield (Buckinghamshire) 25 miles west of London. **How to get there:** Train takes 30+ mins from London Marylebone to Beaconsfield, station 15 mins' walk; by car via M40 (junction 2); close to Heathrow Airport (hourly bus). **Special features:** Professional level, post-experience school. Range of prestigious resident and visiting tutors. School year runs from January to December, based on 3 terms.

Courses

Academic features: MA courses specialising in cinematography, composing for film and television, computer games design and development, digital post production, directing (animation, documentary or fiction), editing, producing, producing and directing television entertainment, production design, screenwriting, SFX/VFX, sound post-production. Diploma courses in production management, sound recording and script development. 10-week documentary summer school. **Awarding body:** Royal College of Art. **Main awards:** MA. **Length of courses:** 2 years (MA); 12–18 months (Diploma).

Study opportunities & careers

Library and information services: 4000+ volumes, 35 periodicals, 20,000+ DVDs and videos. Introduction to library for new students. Separate IT service, open 24 hours/day. **Study abroad:** Strong links with other international film schools. Corporate membership of CILECT (Centre International des Écoles de Cinéma et Télévision); school is founding member of GEECT (European Association of Film and Television Schools); staff and student exchanges with other schools. **Careers:** Advice on career development forms part of each course. Range of schemes to help new graduates establish themselves as professionals.

Student services & facilities

Amenities: Student membership of BAFTA; corporate membership of BFI, and CILECT. **Accommodation:** No school accommodation. Most students are in flatshares or lodgings in Beaconsfield or London.

Money

Living expenses budget: Minimum budget of £6k+ pa (excluding tuition fees) recommended. **Financial help:** Maintenance bursaries up to £6k pa for UK students on basis of financial need; most receive scholarships for some or all of cost of tuition. Own small fund for cases of severe hardship. All students get subsidised rail season ticket London–Beaconsfield. **Tuition fees:** MA courses: home students pay £7500 pa, international students £17,500 pa. Diploma courses: home students pay £3500–£6k for the whole course (depending on course); international students pay £10k for the whole course (but £3500 for script development).

Student view

It has an excellent reputation in the industry as a competitive and well-respected film school, and has many famous alumni. Students specialise before they arrive in one of 10 disciplines: fiction, direction, producing, screenwriting, documentary, animation, production design, cinematography, post-production sound or composing. There are also short courses, and 1-year diplomas. Courses are very much hands-on, with the emphasis on practical projects rather than classroom learning, although the MA involves seminars on screen studies and a dissertation. School is difficult to reach. Most students live in London and commute via Marylebone (a reduced-price rail pass available through the school for this). The school offers no accommodation; it's up to students to find their own place. Specialist equipment at the school is excellent and there are 3 large studios but facilities such as computers and internet are mediocre. Having a job during term-time is next to impossible; fees are heavily subsidised, and many scholarships are available. Life at the school is fun but very intense. Most of the students treat the place as a job and socialise outside the school, but the atmosphere is friendly. Very international and a huge range of backgrounds represented. Maximum of 6 places on each course a year, so very competitive.

Past students: Beeban Kidron, Peter Hewitt, Michael Coton Jones, Elaine Proctor, Michael Redford, Danny Cannon (directors); Molly Dineen, Nick Broomfield, Jane Bokove, Chris Cox (documentary makers); Dianne Tammes, Oliver Stapleton, Gabriel Berenstein, Cinders Forshaw, Andrez Sekula (cinematographers); Nick Parks, David Anderson, Joanne Woodward, Mark Baker (animators); Shawn Slovo, Alrick Riley, Nicholas Martin (writers); Julian Wastall, Trevor Jones, Philip Appleby, Julian Nott (composers). Ena Lind, Alex Mackie, David Freeman. Sound: Ronald Bailey, Danny Handbook, George Richards (editors); Jennifer Howarth, Steve Morrison, Steve Bayly (producers); Laurence Dorman, Carmel Collins (art directors).

Newcastle University

Location:
Newcastle, north-east England (map 2)
Single site in city centre

▣ Newcastle University, 6 Kensington Terrace, Newcastle upon Tyne NE1 7RU
☎ Tel 0191 222 5594
🖷 Fax 0191 222 8685
💻 Website www.ncl.ac.uk

Student enquiries: Enquiries Service, (www.ncl.ac.uk/enquiries)
Applications: UCAS

In brief

Total Students: 18,365

24% postgraduate
76% undergraduate

Undergraduates: 14,040
99% full-time • ● 94% UK students
9% mature on entry ● ● 20% lower socio-economic groups

50% female   50% male

- **A top UK research-intensive university.**
- **Teaching staff:** 2099 full-time and part-time.
- **Broad study areas:** Arts, social sciences, business, law, biological sciences, medicine, dentistry, agriculture, science, engineering.

Freshers

- **Admissions information:** Wide range of academic qualifications accepted; entrance requirements in prospectus and on website. Offers specified in terms of grades rather than in tariff points.
- **First degree entrants:** 3890 UK, full-time.
- **Points on entry:** 394 average
- **Drop-out rate:** 4% in 1st year.
- **Accommodation:** All 1st years guaranteed accommodation (unless local).

Profile

Institution
Founded: 1834 as an institution of higher education; part of Durham University from 1852 until awarded university charter in 1963. **Site:** 45-acre site, in city centre. **How to get there:** By road via A1, junction A167 to Newcastle, follow signs to universities. Ferry services (from Scandinavia and Holland) from nearby North Shields. Newcastle Airport (7 miles outside city) with national and international flights. University adjacent to Haymarket metro station (local rapid-transit system) and close to local bus routes and city coach station. Railway station (20-min walk or short metro ride away) has good links from all major cities. **Structural features:** Medical school partnership with Durham University.

Courses
Academic features: 200+ different degree courses. **Awarding body:** Newcastle University. **Main undergraduate awards:** BA, BSc, BEng, MEng, MPhys, MMath, MChem, LLB, MBBS, BDS. **Length of courses:** 3 and 4 years; 5 years (dentistry, medicine).

Study opportunities & careers

Library and information services: Over 1 million books, 15,000 electronic journals, 2000 study places, computerised online catalogue. Specialist collections: History of medicine; agriculture; mathematics and education; 19th- and 20th-century political and social history; English and Scottish literature and history; local history; Middle Eastern culture; music. Information provision, £194 pa spent for each student (FTE). Separate IT service; ratio 1:8 workstations to students. 2050 computers for student use: 1300 networked in 42 clusters across campus (including in halls), plus 750 in academic schools. 95% of student rooms are wired for internet access. Also wireless access across main campus and a number of docking stations for students' own computers. IT support from helpdesk and training packages; some IT skills courses run as part of degree courses. **Other learning resources:** Great North Museum (incorporating important collections from city and university), Hatton Gallery, Northern Stage theatre. 2 farms, marine biology station, research vessel (RV Bernicia), Dove Marine Laboratory, Moorbank Botanic Gardens. **Study abroad:** 220+ students spend a period abroad each year. Formal links with universities and colleges in 20+ countries including the USA, Canada, East and South East Asia and Europe. **Careers:** Careers service including opportunity awareness (networking, commercial awareness and skills development) and job application (self presentation, action planning, cv support).

Student services & facilities

Student advice and services: Student advice centre, services for counselling, for mature students and for disability support; union society welfare; chaplaincy. **Amenities:** SU one of largest in UK (building owned by the students themselves); wide range of facilities including food and drink outlets, shops, sporting and cultural facilities. Excellent local shops, theatres, cinemas, bars, music venues, etc. **Sporting facilities:** Sports centre, 18-hole golf course, tennis courts, extensive outside sporting facilities incl all-weather pitch. Elite athletes squad provides support for outstanding athletes; sports bursaries available. **Accommodation:** Almost all 1st-year students in university accommodation (guaranteed unless they are local), so long as they meet certain criteria. 4194 places: half-board £93–£108 pw (ensuite); self-catering £65.50–£90.50 pw (minimum £80 for ensuite); contracts Sept–June. Most students live in privately owned accommodation after 1st year: average £64 pw for self-catering.

Money

Living expenses budget: Budget of approx £6k per academic year (excluding tuition fees) recommended. **Term-time work:** Job shop in SU and careers service help students find part-time work (and full-time work in holidays). Plenty of part-time work in the area. **Financial help:** Bursaries of £1280 pa for UK students whose family income is up to £25k; of £640 pa where family income is £25k–£32,300. Bursaries may be enhanced for students with high grades on entry: a further £500 pa for 3 A-levels at grade A, £200 pa for 2 A-level s at grade A (or equivalent). **Tuition fees:** Home students pay £3225 pa for first degrees (except those funded by the Department of Health; reductions for years abroad or on placement). International students pay £10,415 pa (classroom), £13,620 (lab/studio), £25,220 (clinical).

Student view

Attractive and lively city, close to beautiful Northumbrian countryside and east coast. Very accessible by train (3 hours to London); excellent local bus and metro services, going all over Newcastle, with CCTV at all metro stations for extra safety. Recently ranked number one tourist city in England and one of the world's best party cities. Nights out are buzzing with atmosphere, offering everything from wild nights in the Bigg Market to a touch of class by the Quayside. Excellent student discounts throughout the week in most bars. Variety of clubs with great drinks promos throughout the week – student night every night! SU is excellent in terms of entertainment, offering a fantastic line-up of DJs, bands and cheap bars (7 in all!). Weekly club night, Solution, is often a sell-out, as is termly all-nighter, Arcane. Telewest arena attracts all the big names from the music world and many pubs and cafés host up-and-coming bands. 2 multiplex cinemas and 4 theatre venues in city centre, as well as numerous art galleries, showing works of national, local and student artists. University offers a broad spectrum of courses, with high teaching standards. It's quite easy to change courses up to the 3rd week of the 1st semester (with agreement of heads of schools). Students from many different backgrounds including many international students from over 100 different countries. Holds an enviable reputation across a wide range of sporting activities, with very good provision and support. Newcastle is a fantastic place to study, offering a great nightlife, sound courses and friendly locals.

Student footnotes

Housing: 1 year in halls; then most students in private accommodation – cheap, plentiful and close to city centre. Uni accreditation scheme helps avoid dodgy landlords; rent vary depending on area (and size of wallet!). **Eats:** Excellent value in SU with meal deals and other promos (£3-ish). Lots of reasonable places to eat out in town, eg Komal Curry House in Fenham (BYOB), Nachos, Uno's, Est Est Est, Old Orleans (£10–£25 incl wine). **Drink:** Cheap. **Nightlife:** Union has great gigs all year round, eg the Darkness, Kosheen, Elbow, Super Furry Animals, etc. Nightclubs, eg Ikon, Baja's, the Boat, Blu Ba Bu, Cuba Cuba, Foundation, Legends. **Locals:** Very friendly and footie mad (new St James' most prominent feature of the skyline). **Financial help:** Some available. **Jobs:** Available through union jobshop (advertises reputable companies with decent wages). **Best features:** Campus slap bang in city centre. **And worst:** Can be very cold. **Past students:** Rowan Atkinson (comedian), Brian Ferry (musician), Miriam Stoppard (TV doctor), Richard Hamilton (painter), Kate Adie (reporter), the Lighthouse Family (musicians), Russ (Futureheads). **More info?** Check out Union Society website (www.unionsociety.co.uk).

Newport

Location: south-east Wales (map 1) 2 sites in and near Newport; partner colleges	🖳 University of Wales Newport, Caerleon Campus, Lodge Road, Caerleon, Newport NP18 3QT ☎ Fax 01633 432046 ✉ Email uic@newport.ac.uk 🖥 Website www.newport.ac.uk Student enquiries: Information Centre (tel 01633 432432) Applications: UCAS

In brief

Total Students: 9780

3% FE Students
21% postgraduate
76% undergraduate

Undergraduates: 7480
43% full-time ● ● 97% UK students
41% mature ● ● 38% lower
on entry ● ● socio-economic groups

59% female 41% male

- **A university college, member of University of Wales.**
- **Teaching staff:** 175 full-time.
- **Broad study areas:** Business; art, media and design; education; computing; engineering; health and social science.

Freshers

- **Admissions information:** AS-levels accepted in combination with 2+ A-levels or equivalent. UCAS tariff used; course requirements vary from 160–300 points.
- **First degree entrants:** 1170 UK, full-time.
- **Points on entry:** 200 (average).
- **Drop-out rate:** 12% in 1st year.
- **Accommodation:** Guaranteed for all 1st years who apply before deadline.

Profile

Institution

Founded: 1975 as Gwent College of HE, origins from 1841; became a university college of University of Wales in 1996; full constituent member in 2003. **Site:** 2 sites: 1 in residential area on edge of Newport; 1 in Caerleon, a picturesque town 3 miles away. **How to get there:** Regular bus, coach and rail services to Newport; by road from M4; free bus service between campuses.

Courses

Awarding body: University of Wales. **Main undergraduate awards:** BA, BSc, BSc (Econ), BEng, Foundation degrees. **Length of courses:** 3 years (full-time); 2 years (foundation degrees); longer for part-time courses.

Study opportunities & careers

Library and information services: 185,000 volumes, 760 periodicals plus 750 electronic journals; 412 study places; networked CD-ROMs, open-access computer suites available. Specialist collections: David Hurn collection (books and journals on documentary photography); Primrose Hockey collection (local history); collection of 35,000 slides on art and design; 5000 video programmes on film and animation. Information provision, £49 pa spent for each student (FTE). 1000+ computers with access to internet and thence the library (plus remote access for students at home); ratio 1:8 workstations to students. IT facilities open 24 hours/day in term-time; IT helpdesk, software support from library and information services staff and IT technicians. New students have introduction to information resources; various IT workshops, regular drop-in sessions and one-to-one support available. **Study abroad:** Some opportunities for short periods of study in Europe. Formal exchange links with some universities/colleges in western Europe. **Careers:** Information, advice and placement service. Employment liaison officer provides work experience or placements for undergraduates and graduates.

Student services & facilities

Student advice and services: Student health service (medical officer, 2 nurses), welfare service (2 welfare officers, access fund, childcare and disability coordinators), 3 counsellors – all available on each site. **Amenities:** Shop on each campus; bar and recreational area on residential site at Caerleon. **Sporting facilities:** Sports centre at Caerleon for all sports, many to national level; aerobics; dance and martial arts; gymnasium; fitness suite; floodlit tennis and netball courts; rugby pitch. **Accommodation:** All 1st-year students housed who request it (by deadline). 660 self-catering places, with internet access; rent £60–£67 pw (£81 ensuite); 39-week contracts. Private-sector rent: £60 pw self-catering (excl bills).

Money

Living expenses budget: Minimum budget of £8k pa (excluding tuition fees) recommended by university. **Term-time work:** University allows term-time work for full-time students (30% believed to work). Some work available on campus (marketing, library, estates assistants, telephone operators, IT, bar and shop work); work-link officer helps with term time and holiday work. **Financial help:** Bursaries awarded (on first-come-first-served basis) of £1k pa for students whose family income is up to £20k, of £600 pa where it is £20k–£30k, and of £300 pa where family income is £30k–£40k. Also bursaries eg for students needing help for extra-curricular activities, for final-year students needing interview clothes; sports bursaries and scholarships. Government fund of £350k (670 students helped); average award £600. Special help: students with disabilities, those with dependant children; short-term loans available to final-year students.

Tuition fees: Home students pay £3225 pa for first degrees (though Welsh residents may be eligible for annual fee grant). International students pay £7750 pa (classroom-based), £8750 pa (studio).

Student view

Jonny Roberts, Entertainments and Media Officer (2nd year, Film and Video)

Living

What's it like as a place to live? Fun, very different but charming in a strange way! Plenty to do always. **How's the student accommodation?** Shop around very carefully for off-campus accommodation. On-campus accommodation is small but nice and well maintained. **What's the student population like?** Friendly atmosphere. As it's a smaller uni it has a real community feel – everyone knows everyone! **How do students and locals get on?** Students are welcome in the village and in the city. The city isn't the safest on weekends but there is enough going on on-campus to happily stay there.

Studying

What's it like as a place to study? A great variety of courses, most of which have a great national reputation. **What are the teaching staff like?** The majority of lecturers are very approachable and helpful to students' questions and concerns.

Socialising

What are student societies like? Not as many societies as some bigger unis but some great ones like rock climbing, kayaking, circus and entrepreneurs. **What's a typical night out?** Wednesdays are mad; every venue in town has mad offers and a variety of music. **And how much does it cost?** £20–£30. **How can you get home safely?** Taxis – some do discount student rates.

Money

Is it an expensive place to live? Cheaper than most of the UK. Clever spending will make your loan last. **Average price of a pint?** £2 Wednesdays, £3 weekends. **And the price of a takeaway?** £7–£10. **What's the part-time work situation?** Not a great deal of jobs. Make sure you're at the Freshers' Fayre and have a CV ready!

Summary

What's the best feature about the place? The spirit of the city – it's got a great vibrancy around the place. **And the worst?** There is a large chav contingent in the city. **And to sum it all up?** A very special city and a special uni – both are smaller than your standard but that means there is a greater community feel.

Past students: Justin Kerrigan (*Human Traffic*); Kirk Jones (*Waking Ned*); Deiniol Morris and Mike Mort (*Gogs*). **More info?** Check out the website (www.newportunion.com).

Northampton University

Location:
Northampton, north-west of London
(map 2)
**2 sites on outskirts of Northampton;
partner college**

The University of Northampton, Park Campus, Boughton Green Road, Northampton NN2 7AL
☎ Tel 01604 735500
🖷 Fax 01604 720636
✉ Email admissions@northampton.ac.uk
💻 Website www.northampton.ac.uk

Student enquiries: Course enquiry line (tel 0800 358 2232)
Applications: UCAS

In brief

Total Students: 10,645

15% postgraduate
85% undergraduate

Undergraduates: 9065
76% full-time ● ● 93% UK students
46% mature ● ● 35% lower socio-economic groups
on entry

67% female 33% male

- **Teaching staff:** 497 full-time.
- **Broad study areas:** Environmental sciences, leather technology, healthcare education, technology and design, land and environment, art and design, behavioural studies, cultural studies, education, social studies, business and economics.

Freshers

- **Admissions information:** AS-levels accepted in combination with 1+ A-levels or equivalent. UCAS tariff widely used; Key Skills accepted.
- **First degree entrants:** 1775 UK, full-time.
- **Points on entry:** 180+ (average).
- **Drop-out rate:** 12% in 1st year.
- **Accommodation:** Almost all 1st years housed.

Profile

Institution

Founded: 1975 as Nene College, from colleges of education, art and technology; university status in 2005. **Site:** 2 main sites, 2 miles apart: Park Campus on northern edge of Northampton; Avenue Campus 2 miles from town centre; plus hospital sites. **How to get there:** 5 miles from M1; good rail links (1 hour from London Euston or Birmingham New Street); coaches to Greyfriars bus station and then bus (4 and 4A to both campuses). Free bus between campuses. **Special features:** Unique international leather technology centre.

Courses

Academic features: Joint and Single Honours degrees. **Awarding body:** University of Northampton. **Main undergraduate awards:** BA, BA(QTS), BSc, FdA, FdSc. **Length of courses:** 3 and 4 years.

Study opportunities & careers

Library and information services: 2 libraries; 240,000 volumes, some 1100 print periodicals, 3900 e-journals, 850+ study places. Information provision, £68 pa spent for each student (FTE). Resource centres at both campuses; IT and library services separate. 800+ computers with access to internet and library; ratio 1:10 workstations to students. 24-hour access to IT facilities; staff support up to 9pm weekdays. New students have introduction, tour and registration with both library and IT services; IT skills courses on eg internet, spreadsheets, literature searching, etc. **Other learning resources:** Media services, language labs, performance studios, professional practice unit, workshops and gallery space. **Study abroad:** 2% of students spend a period abroad. Formal exchange links for European business students with 20+ European universities and business schools. US intern programme and exchanges on some courses.

Student services & facilities

Student advice and services: Student centre; doctor, chaplain, counsellors, dyslexia support tutor, disabled students' office, mental health office, system of personal tutors and student peer support. **Amenities:** SU buildings and rooms, bookshop, mini-supermarket, computer shop, restaurant on both sites, snack bar, bars, cashpoints. **Sporting facilities:** Sports hall, access to all-weather pitch, tennis courts, playing fields, dance studio. **Accommodation:** 98% of 1st-year students who require it in university accommodation (all who are not local and make the university their first choice). 1630+ self-catering places available (1130 ensuite and most with internet connection): £56–£80 (ensuite) pw for single room, £37.50–£55 (ensuite) pw shared room; 40-week contracts. Students live in privately owned accommodation for 2+ years: rent £50–£55 pw self-catering, plus bills. 25% of first-degree students live at home.

Money

Living expenses budget: Minimum budget of £5k–£6500 pa (excluding tuition fees) recommended by university. **Term-time work:** University allows term-time work for first-degree students (60% believed to work). Some work available on campus (eg bar, security, shop, student ambassadors, libraries); plenty of local temporary work; university jobshop. **Financial help:** Bursaries of £1k pa for UK students whose family income is up to £25k, of £700 where is £25k–£30k, and of £500 where family income is £30k–£40k. Also some scholarships and bursaries eg for local students, academic attainment, travel abroad or for students of leather technology. Also £540k access to learning funds available; special consideration to students with additional financial commitments. Apply to financial guidance services for help. **Tuition fees:** Home students pay £3225 pa for first degrees (£2050 for foundation degrees). International students pay £7450–£8250 pa.

Student view) **Richard Hardwick,** President 2007–08 (Business and Management)

Living
What's it like as a place to live? It's a lively and exciting town, centrally located with great access to the country. Locals are very student-friendly. **How's the student accommodation?** Many types of halls to suit all budgets. New ones have an ensuite and older ones are being refurbished. Private housing must stick to strict quality guidelines. **What's the student population like?** Very diverse, very friendly, 40% local learners. 400+ international students. **How do students and locals get on?** Very well.
Studying
What's it like as a place to study? Very flexible, great place to study. **What are the teaching staff like?** Good interaction, great NSS scores in student feedback.
Socialising
What's a typical night out? Student nights in town – Monday. Union – Wednesday, Thursday, Friday, Saturday. **And how much does it cost?** £20. **How can you get home safely?** Uni buses on Monday nights.

Money

Is it an expensive place to live? Well priced. **Average price of a pint?** £2. **And the price of a takeaway?** £5. **What's the part-time work situation?** Many jobs – uni/union job shops.

Summary

What's the best feature about the place? Campus community; beauty of Park Campus. **And the worst?** Poor sports facilities. **And to sum it all up?** A great green campus community, lots going on for all types of student, great place to study and meet friends for life. **More info?** Call the president on 01604 892550 or check out the SU website at www.northamptonunion.com.

Northern School of Contemporary Dance

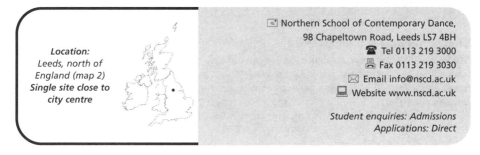

Location:
Leeds, north of England (map 2)
Single site close to city centre

Northern School of Contemporary Dance,
98 Chapeltown Road, Leeds LS7 4BH
☎ Tel 0113 219 3000
🖶 Fax 0113 219 3030
✉ Email info@nscd.ac.uk
💻 Website www.nscd.ac.uk

Student enquiries: Admissions
Applications: Direct

In brief

Total Students: 195

- 15% FE Students
5% postgraduate
80% undergraduate

Undergraduates: 155
100% full-time ● ● 86% UK students

60% female   40% male

- **Specialist dance college.** Member of the Conservatoire for Dance & Drama.
- **Teaching staff:** 10 full-time, 5 part-time.
- **Broad study areas:** Contemporary dance, including: choreography; movement studies; performance opportunities.

Freshers

- **Admissions information:** 4 AS-levels or 2 A-levels or 1 AVEC (1 AGNVQ overseas) or 4 Highers or equivalent.
- **First degree entrants:** 60 UK, full-time.
- **Drop-out rate:** 12% in 1st year.
- **Accommodation:** No school accommodation.

Profile

Institution

Founded: 1985. **Structural features:** Member of Conservatoire for Dance & Drama. **Site:** Leeds (Chapeltown), close to city library/art gallery and universities. **How to get there:** Leeds very accessible by road (M1 and M62), by national coach services, by rail and air.

Courses

Academic features: Courses include contemporary technique and ballet for contemporary dancers, choreography, movement studies, performance. Also supplementary techniques (eg yoga), contextual studies (eg critical and reflective studies, ideas in art). **Awarding body:** University of Kent. **Main award:** BPA. **Length of courses:** 3 years (full-time).

Study opportunities & careers

Library and information services: 5242 books, 1114 DVD/video, 35 study places. Information provision, £31 pa spent for each student (FTE). IT and library services converged. Ratio 1:10 workstations to students; 18 computers with internet access, 1 to library catalogue. IT facilities available 57 hours/week with continuous staff support. All new students have short induction to library and information service plus IT study skills sessions. **Other learning resources:** 3 audio-visual viewing places (+ computer DVD drives), 2 audio places (+ computer CD drives), comprehensive collection of dance company information. Own theatre, the Riley Theatre. **Careers:** Information and advice available.

Student services & facilities

Student advice and services: Tutorial system; specialist learner and welfare support officers; English language support for international students; health, fitness and injury support scheme. **Amenities and Sporting facilities:** City facilities only. **Accommodation:** No school accommodation. Students live in privately owned accommodation close to the school: rent £50–£60 pw self-catering. Help in finding accommodation from the school and through Unipol. 10% of first-degree students live at home.

Money

Living expenses budget: Minimum budget of £6k for academic year (excluding tuition fees) recommended by school. **Term-time work:** School allows term-time work for full-time students (98% believed to work). **Financial help:** Conservatoire bursaries of £1700 pa (£2100 in final year) for UK students whose family income is up to £25k; tapered down to £100 pa (£500 in final year) where family income is £37,900–£39,300. Plus £13k government funds, £8k own funds; average amount awarded £25 pw (any student with less than £40 pw eligible to apply). **Tuition fees:** Home students pay £3225 pa for first degrees. International students pay £13,340 pa (plus validation fee of £370 in 1st year).

Student view

Based in a beautiful, green, domed synagogue, converted to a working theatre in which blood, sweat, tears and laughter are shed daily. College takes pride in accommodating a diverse range of characters, regardless of background. You have to be committed to survive the intensity of the course. There are 2–4 classes a day, depending on year of study, including ballet technique, contemporary technique, body awareness, choreography, music, history of ideas, movement studies, history of dance, combined arts and dance as education. Everyone is in the same boat, so there is a very close-knit feel to the college. Staff form close working relationships with their students. Technical progress is continually assessed while written assignments are variable, set in accordance with individual course structures. At the end of each term, students work through a choreographic process with professional choreographers, culminating in a showcase at the Riley Theatre. Course is vocational, with greater emphasis on the practical as opposed to the academic element. However, it is extremely demanding, both mentally and physically. Previous dance training is not required but at the audition they are looking for people with spirit and the will to dance. Leeds has a massive student population, so there are numerous bars, clubs, restaurants, theatres and cinemas, catering for all tastes. No student accommodation, but college runs house-hunting days before the course starts to help new students find private accommodation.

Student footnotes

Housing: Student digs; affordable housing possible to find. **Eats:** Cheap, informal – Indian, vegetarian. **Drink:** Good mixture of pubs, cheap/good atmosphere. **Nightlife:** Cheap student nightclubs, theatre, bars. **Sports:** No time for extra sports – occasional swim/sauna and gym workout. **Travel:** Student fares; hitching. **Financial help:** Scarce. **More info?** Enquiries to SU (tel 0113 219 3000).

Northumbria University

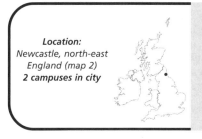

Location:
Newcastle, north-east England (map 2)
2 campuses in city

✉ University of Northumbria at Newcastle, Ellison Building, Ellison Place, Newcastle upon Tyne NE1 8ST
☎ Tel 0191 232 6002
💻 Website www.northumbria.ac.uk

Student enquiries: Student Administration Office (tel 0191 243 7420)
Applications: UCAS

In brief

Total Students: 31,660

1% FE Students
14% postgraduate
85% undergraduate

Undergraduates: 27,080
72% full-time
34% mature on entry
84% UK students
32% lower socio-economic groups

55% female   45% male

- **A modern university.**
- **Teaching staff:** 2521 full-time and part-time.
- **Broad study areas:** Art and design, business, health, community and education, humanities, law, social sciences, engineering and technology, applied sciences, sports studies.

Freshers

- **Admissions information:** UCAS tariff used to make offers on many courses. AS-levels accepted in combination with 2+ A-levels or equivalent.
- **First degree entrants:** 4525 UK, full-time.
- **Points on entry:** 240 (average).
- **Drop-out rate:** 9% in 1st year.
- **Accommodation:** Most 1st years housed who need it.

Profile

Institution

Founded: 1969 as Newcastle Poly, university status in 1992. **Site:** 2 sites: Newcastle City Campus in city centre; Coach Lane Campus 3 miles from city centre. **How to get there:** For Newcastle, coach (Gallowgate) and railway (Central) stations both with good links from all major cities; by road via A1, junction A167 to Newcastle, follow signs to universities; also ferry services (from Scandinavia and Holland); airport 7 miles outside city (services from European and British cities). Bus and metro to all campuses. **Special features:** National coaching centre. Specialist centres include microelectronics education, small businesses, centre for industrial design.

Courses

Academic features: Degree courses include biomedical sciences, law, media production, travel and tourism, design and film; business information technology, fashion marketing, communication engineering. **Awarding body:** University of Northumbria. **Main undergraduate awards:** BA, BA(QTS), BSc, BEng, LLB, MEng. **Length of courses:** 3 years (full-time); 4 years (sandwich); 3–6 years (part-time).

Study opportunities & careers

Library and information services: Library at each site; over 500,000 volumes, 3000 paper periodicals (+ 7000 electronic), 1700 study places, short loan only for recommended volumes. European Documentation Centre. Information provision, £102 pa spent for each student (FTE). IT and library services converged. Wireless access throughout campus including in halls. Access to IT facilities 24/7; e-learning portal for online course info, noticeboards, etc; IT support from full- and part-time staff, helpdesks, support helpline. Voluntary IT induction. **Study abroad:** 5% of students spend a period abroad. Formal exchange links with a number of EU universities and colleges. **Careers:** Information, advice and placement service.

Student services & facilities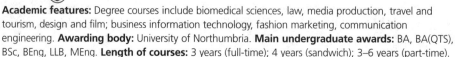

Student advice and services: Health services, welfare officer, student counsellor, accommodation service, chaplains, disabilities advisers, international student advisers. Some places in halls for disabled students, 24 places in local authority flats for married students. **Amenities:** Large SU buildings, including new café-bar; 300-seat theatre, ballroom, second-hand bookshop. **Sporting facilities:** Indoor sports at City Campus (major refurbishment to facilities) and at Coach Lane; outdoor sports 3 miles away. **Accommodation:** 55% of 1st years in university accommodation (most non-local students that need it); 20% of all students housed, including international students. 3000+ places (2150 for 1st years): self-catering places £72–£86.50 pw (£87.50–£112 pw ensuite); catered rooms £89–£99 pw; most contracts 43–44 weeks (Sept–June). Students live in privately owned accommodation for 2+ years: rent £46–£80 pw for self-catering.

Money

Living expenses budget: Minimum budget of £6500 pa (excluding tuition fees) recommended by university. **Term-time work:** University allows term-time work for full-time students; no work on campus. **Financial help:** Bursaries of £319 pa for UK students whose family income is up to £25k. Additional scholarships (of £250, £500 or £1k pa, depending on the study programme) for all students in Year 1 who meet their offer, and in subsequent years depending on end-of-year assessments. Also £1 million+ government funds, 880 full-time students helped (250 part-time). Special help to lone parents, parents on low incomes, mature students, final-year students, those with high travel costs. **Tuition fees:** Home students pay £3225 pa for first degrees (unless covered by the Department of Health or General Social Care Council); reduced fee for year out on sandwich courses. International students pay £8300 (classroom-based), £8700 (lab/studio).

Student view   Dave Wright, Students' Union President

Living

What's it like as a place to live? Newcastle is a vibrant city, with a great range of cultural diversity. It is world renowned for its nightlife, and many would say the city comes alive at night. There is a very large student population owing to its 2 large universities, and the local population is very friendly. Newcastle is small in size, but there's lots going on all the time. **How's the student accommodation?** Northumbria has been investing in accommodation recently. Most 1st-year students will find places in a range of different halls of residence, both privately owned and university-owned. Most of the newer halls are ensuite and have all the modern facilities you would expect. Some of the older halls lack modern features, but make up for this with locality in the city centre and a great sense of community that exists within them. Most prices are reasonable and usually competitive. **What's the student population like?** Northumbria has a large number of students from the north east. Many students stay at home and travel in each day. There is also a large contingent of international students, coming from all over the world, particularly from Asia. Northumbria students are generally a friendly bunch, and the sense of community amongst the student body grows stronger each year. **How do students and locals get on?** There is some unrest with the local population with regard to students. This is probably because of the large number of students living and studying in the Newcastle area. Having said that, most areas of the city and surrounding suburban areas are friendly and very accommodating. Strong links between local community groups and the university exist to try and resolve any issues that arise.

Studying

What's it like as a place to study? Northumbria is undergoing constant improvements. The brand new £125 million City Campus East opened 2 years ago and is state of the art. The rest of the campus is also being developed, with a new £25 million sports complex due to be completed in 2010. Teaching facilities are generally superb, and Northumbria has climbed dramatically up the league table for student satisfaction over the last year. There is a great range of courses offering a mixture of traditional and current courses across the 9 schools. **What are the teaching staff like?** Teaching staff at Northumbria are dedicated to furthering the student experience. Methods of programme delivery are constantly being improved, and feedback from students is taken on board at the highest levels and used to improve teaching across the university. Most students would agree that their lecturers are genuinely interested in them as students, with many going out of the way to further the academic progress of their students.

Socialising

What are student societies like? The SU co-ordinates societies at Northumbria. We have over 70 different active societies ranging from snowsports to *Hollyoaks* appreciation. There is something for everyone, and the union will help anyone set up a society according to their interests with financial support and guidance. There are also many volunteering opportunities through our Student Community Action programme, as well as year-long RAG events. **What's a typical night out?** There's something for everyone any night of the week. Whether it's rock, indie, ska, punk, RandB, dance, electro or just good old-fashioned cheese, somewhere in Newcastle has a night for you. The city centre has both the SU and a mixture of bars and clubs, all with different styles and atmospheres. **And how much does it cost?** During the week, expect to pay anywhere between £3 to £8 to get into a club. On Friday and Saturday, town can be as expensive as £15 to get in, but there are a few places, especially the SU, that cater for the student populations with prices from £1 to get in. **How can you get home safely?** There's an abundance of taxis at any time of day or night, and they're always outside the clubs. Alternatively, there's loads of companies you can call and they can usually get a car to you within 10 mins. And there is a night bus service that operates every hour throughout the night along the most common No. 1 route, and the SU offers a night bus service after the Saturday club night that will take you to your door for only £3. Bargain.

Money

Is it an expensive place to live? Generally speaking, no, it's fairly cheap. However, if you're careless with your cash, then it is possible to spend your entire loan in a few weeks and struggle. There is, however, plenty of part-time work available for students, so money usually isn't a problem. **Average price of a pint?** On average £2. **And the price of a takeaway?** £4–£6. **What's the part-time work situation?** The university runs the JobShop, which is used as a point of contact for local businesses wishing to employ workers. It's co-ordinated by the careers service within the Student Services department. Staff are great at helping students to find work, and will support them through the whole process. Part-time work isn't too hard to find, depending on what you're after and how many hours you want to work. However, with loads of students looking for work, and with the current financial climate, many employers don't offer much more than the minimum wage.

Summary

What's the best feature about the place? Vibrant, friendly, you will never be bored. **And the worst?** It's cold! **And to sum it all up?** Great place to live and study. Friendly and fun atmosphere. There's always something to do, and a general buzz and excitement around the city. Newcastle is one of those places you will love for life, whether you're only here for a month or stay forever! Truly one of the best cities in the world!

Past students: Steve Cram (athlete); Paul Shriek, Karen Boyd, Jeff Banks (fashion designers); Sting (musician); Robson Green (actor); Rodney Bickerstaff (Unison). **More info?** Contact NSU President (su.president@northumbria.ac.uk) or check out the website (www.mynsu.co.uk).

Norwich University College of the Arts

Location:
Norwich, East Anglia
(map 2)
**Single site in city
centre**

Norwich University College of the Arts,
Francis House, 3–7 Redwell Street, Norwich NR2 4SN
☎ Tel 01603 610561
🖷 Fax 01603 615728
✉ Email info@nuca.ac.uk
🖥 Website www.nuca.ac.uk

*Student enquiries: Academic Registrar
Applications: UCAS*

In brief

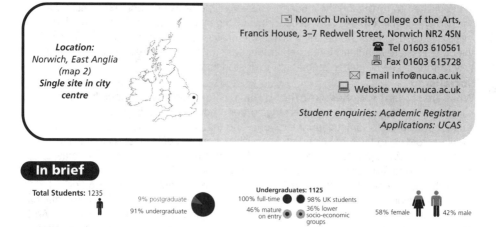

Total Students: 1235

9% postgraduate
91% undergraduate

Undergraduates: 1125
100% full-time
46% mature
on entry
98% UK students
36% lower
socio-economic
groups

58% female   42% male

- **Specialist art and design university college.**

- **Teaching staff:** 23 full-time, 130 part-time.

- **Broad study areas:** Animation; design for publishing; film and video; fine art; games design; graphic design; illustration; photography; textiles; visual studies.

Freshers

- **Admissions information:** Admissions policy not necessarily based on AS/A-levels. 4–5 GCSEs, BTEC, GNVQ or equivalent required. Tariff not used.

- **First degree entrants:** 440 UK, full-time.
- **Points on entry:** 215+ (average).
- **Drop-out rate:** 6% in 1st year.
- **Accommodation:** Some 1st years housed.

Profile

Institution
Founded: 1845; merged in 1989 with Great Yarmouth College of Art and Design; university college status in 2007. **Site:** City centre site. **How to get there:** By train (under 2 hours from London Liverpool Street); by coach (college is 10 mins' walk from coach station); by road via M11 and A11; by air to Norwich International Airport.

Courses
Awarding body: Norwich University College of the Arts. **Main undergraduate award:** BA. **Length of courses:** 3 years.

Study opportunities & careers
Library and information services: 30,000 volumes, 120 journal titles, 2500 videotapes and DVDs, 80,000 slides; 50 study places. Information provision, £30 pa spent for each student (FTE). IT facilities open 8 hours/day; support from workshop manager and technician. Tour and induction to library and information services for new students. **Study abroad:** Formal exchange links with various universities and colleges in Europe, the USA and Japan.

Student services & facilities
Student advice and services: Student counselling service available. **Amenities:** SU bar, shop. **Accommodation:** 30% of 1st years in College accommodation (priority given to those living farthest away or with special needs). 118 self-catering places available (all for 1st years) at £74–£98 pw, term-time contracts or longer. Most students live in privately owned accommodation for whole course: self-catering rent £50–£65 pw + bills.

Money
Living expenses budget: Minimum budget of £5500 pa recommended (excluding tuition fees). **Term-time work:** University College allows term-time work for full-time students. Some work available on campus in library or as student ambassadors. **Financial help:** Bursaries of £800 pa for UK students whose family income is up to £25k (ie qualify for a full grant), of £300 for those whose family income is £25k–£50k. Also government funds: special help to those with dependants, self-financing students or those with medical expenses, course materials costs, etc. **Tuition fees:** Home students pay £3225 pa for first degrees. International students pay £8750 pa full-time.

Student view

Beautifully set overlooking the River Wensum, and close to the centre of this attractive, old city. There are 3 sites within 500 yards of each other. Courses all challenging and diverse (eg new games design course); assessment termly. Great opportunities for 2nd years to spend a term in Europe and sometimes worldwide. Close relationship between staff and students. There is a very good community and social life within the college (though virtually no sporting facilities). SU has its main hall and bar (with cheap drinks) in an attractive converted church. SU very active socially, with abundance of gigs; also big name bands at nearby UEA. College accommodation very limited; students tend to live in good privately rented accommodation within 15 mins' walk of college. Most students come from in and around London but also many international (and mature) students. Free welfare and counselling service available, fully confidential. Everything is within walking distance and cycling is popular. Many discounts in theatres, cinemas, clothes shops and restaurants in city. Rumoured to be a pub for every day of the week and a church for every week! City has lots of parks and green places; London is 2 hours by train, beautiful Norfolk coast about 30 mins' drive.

Student footnotes

Housing: Plenty within walking distance; check local press, college housing lists, noticeboards. College also has 2 sets of halls (1 larger complex, other is 5 separate houses on their own street). **Eats:** Meal for £3+ on campus. Diverse range of restaurants: half-price meals at Indian restaurants, student discounts in some. **Drink:** £2.30 a pint in SU bar/£1.90 double and mixer. 300+ pubs and some sophisticated bars, many with student nights. Adnams is good local brew. **Nightlife:** Eclectic clubs (and some cheesy ones)! Parties, field parties (Fire, Poi, Juggling in the Park), karaoke, bingo, quiz nights. Several good clubs around Norwich, many acoustic, funk, hip hop, reggae, drum and bass, electronica and indie nights; bands include Le Tetsuo, the Porn, Neutrinos. Excellent film choice at Cinema City; good theatre. **Locals:** Very friendly (compared to London), makes for a relaxed atmosphere in the city. **Sports:** Aqua Park, 20 mins' bus ride from city; UEA sports centre, local yoga classes for instant stress relief or a bit of fishing on the river. Boats are always available to hire to explore the wonderful Norfolk Broads. **Financial help:** Limited access funds; also college emergency loans. **Jobs:** Many bar jobs, telesales, waiter/essing – standard pay. **Best features:** Small and intimate; bohemian and beautiful, medieval old buildings (2 cathedrals); the diversity! **And worst:** The diversity. **Informal name:** NSAD. **More info?** Contact the SU on 01603 766846.

Nottingham Trent University

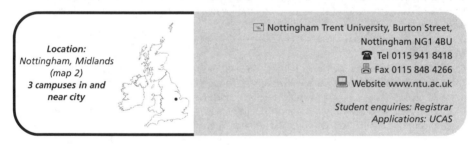

Location:
Nottingham, Midlands
(map 2)
**3 campuses in and
near city**

Nottingham Trent University, Burton Street, Nottingham NG1 4BU
Tel 0115 941 8418
Fax 0115 848 4266
Website www.ntu.ac.uk

*Student enquiries: Registrar
Applications: UCAS*

In brief

Total Students: 23,910

1% FE Students
22% postgraduate
77% undergraduate

Undergraduates: 18,410
84% full-time 95% UK students
28% mature 36% lower
on entry socio-economic
groups

 53% female  47% male

- **A modern university.**
- **Teaching staff:** 1638 full-time and part-time.
- **Broad study areas:** Animal, rural and environmental sciences; arts and humanities; art and design; built environment; business; education; law; science and technology; social sciences.

Freshers

- **Admissions information:** AS-levels accepted in combination with 2+ A-levels or equivalent. Some subject-specific requirements (subjects and grades).
- **First degree entrants:** 6175 UK, full-time.
- **Points on entry:** 270 (average).
- **Drop-out rate:** 7% in 1st year.
- **Accommodation:** Most 1st years housed.

Profile

Institution

Founded: University status in 1992; previously Nottingham Poly, then Trent Poly. **Site:** 2 main sites: City site, close to centre of Nottingham, and Clifton Campus, about 4 miles from city centre; subsidiary site at Brackenhurst, 15 miles away. **How to get there:** Close to M1 and East Midlands Airport; by rail and coach (City site near rail and coach stations); bus services from Clifton site. **Special features:** Credit accumulation and negotiated study programmes, online enrolment.

Courses

Awarding body: Nottingham Trent University. **Main undergraduate awards:** BEd, BA, BSc, BEng, LLB, MChem, MEng, MPhys. **Length of courses:** 3 or 4 years.

Study opportunities & careers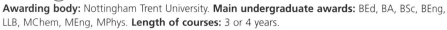

Library and information services: Main library on each site; 478,000 volumes in total, 14,000 journals (many electronic); 900 study places in Boots Library on main campus, 500 at Clifton, 70 at Brackenhurst. Information provision, £84 pa spent for each student (FTE). Separate IT service but integrated support for students across libraries and IT facilities. Ratio 1:15 workstations to students; 1200 computers with access to library (700 in libraries), all with internet access. Most IT facilities open 12 hours/day (some 24/7 on main sites); dedicated support team patrol library and help at point of use. Comprehensive introductory sessions to library and information services, including self-directed i-pod tours; full information skills programme for all students. **Other learning resources:** Modern, open-access language laboratories; science and engineering laboratories. **Study abroad:** Some choose to work or study abroad as part of their degree course. **Careers:** Information, advice and placement.

Student services & facilities

Student advice and services: Integrated student services (including finance, wellbeing and disability services) at drop-in centres on all campuses. Health centres at City and Clifton sites. **Amenities:** Shops, bars, bookshops, banks, travel bureau, CCTV. **Sporting facilities:** Fitness studio, squash courts, small gyms, playing fields, sports hall and all-weather pitch at Clifton; health and fitness studios at City. **Accommodation:** 1st-year students guaranteed university-allocated accommodation if they apply by the deadline (1 July). Self-catering places, rent from £68 pw, £95 pw (ensuite), £118 pw for studio-style room. Private rented accommodation from £55–£80 pw plus bills.

Money

Living expenses budget: Minimum budget of £620–£680 pm (excluding tuition fees) recommended by university. **Financial help:** For UK students whose family income is up to £25k, bursaries of £1075 pa (£1340 if permanent address is in Nottinghamshire); these students may also be considered for one of 50 scholarships (of £2k pa), based on academic performance in 1st year. Bursaries of £665 pa (£780 for Notts residents) where family income is £25k–£30k, of £515 pa (£630 for Notts) where it is

£30k–£35k, and bursary of £360 pa (£475 for Notts residents) where family income is £35k–£40k. Also discretionary hardship fund to help those not able to work in the vacations. Additional £550k government funds plus others; awards £50–£3500. Apply to student support services for help. (tel 0115 848 2621). **Tuition fees:** Home students pay £3225 pa for first degrees. International students pay £8450–£8500 (classroom), £9500–£9600 pa (lab/studio-based).

Student view

Based in the centre of a lively cosmopolitan city, it offers a spectacular range of activities and venues that aid studying and socialising. University is spread over 3 campuses: largest being in the heart of the city; another on the outskirts, in Clifton; and the smallest is Brackenhurst, in the picturesque town of Southwell. Each campus has a SU with shops, bars and restaurants as well as services such as employment store, ticket express, training and development schemes, volunteering opportunities and also confidential student advice centres. SU also offers over 42 sports clubs, 26 societies, *Platform* (the bi-weekly student magazine), Fly FM and Trent TV.

Student footnotes

Housing: All 1st years live in halls (many rooms ensuite). Others have the option to stay in halls but many prefer private accommodation; union offers advice and uni accommodation service has list of accredited properties. **Eats:** Plenty of reasonably priced food on campus. Huge range of restaurants and cafés in city offering wide choice. **Drink:** Nottingham is infamous for its 400+ pubs, bars and clubs!! Prices vary dramatically, depending on venue, so sure to be one in your price range. SU and many other bars have minimum price of £1.50, as part of responsible drinking scheme. **Nightlife:** This is where Nottingham excels! Official SU nights including: Kiss Kiss at Ocean on Tuesdays, Campus (sports and society night) on Wednesday; DV8 at Walkabout (Thursday), Flirt and Climax at SU (Friday and Saturday); also Kinki fancy dress at Ocean once a month. There is always somewhere to go!! **Sports:** 42+ SU sports clubs, gym on campus, sports teams (semi-pro to general kick-arounds), so something for everyone. City has 2 league football teams (Forest and County), National Ice Centre, National Water Sports Centre and world-famous Trent Bridge Cricket Ground! **Travel:** Travelling round city is very easy. SU offers ticket express service for national travel. Easy reach of Nottingham East Midlands Airport. **Jobs:** SU employment store offers range of part-time and holiday jobs. **Best features:** Fantastic atmosphere in university and city that promotes studying as well as enjoyment. **Worst feature:** You'll be spoilt for choice!! **More info?** Call SU office (0115 848 6220) or check out the website at www.trentstudents.org.

Nottingham University

Location:
Nottingham, Midlands
(map 2)
Main campus, plus 2
other sites nearby

The University of Nottingham, University Park, Nottingham NG7 2RD
☎ Tel 0115 951 5559
Fax 0115 846 8062
✉ Email undergraduate-enquiries@nottingham.ac.uk
Website www.nottingham.ac.uk

Student enquiries: The Enquiry Centre (Marketing, King's Meadow Campus, Lenton Lane, Nottingham NG7 2NR)
Applications: UCAS

In brief

Total Students: 30,445

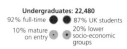

- **A top UK research-intensive university.**
- **Teaching staff:** 1523 full-time, 234 part-time.
- **Broad study areas:** Arts and humanities; biosciences; business; computer science; engineering; food sciences; law; medicine, veterinary medicine and health sciences; modern languages; science; social science.

Freshers

- **Admissions information:** Normally 3 A-levels required (an additional AS-level on some courses); 2 A-levels and 2 AS-levels may be accepted. UCAS tariff not used.
- **First degree entrants:** 5215 UK, full-time.
- **Points on entry:** 300 approx (offers range from AAA–CCC).
- **Drop-out rate:** 3% in 1st year.
- **Accommodation:** All full-time 1st years guaranteed accommodation.

Profile

Institution

Founded: 1881; university status in 1948. **Site:** University Park (330-acre campus to west of city centre). 2 further sites: Sutton Bonington 10 miles south (biosciences, veterinary medicine and science); Jubilee Campus under 1 mile away (business, computer science, education). Also campuses in China and Malaysia. **How to get there:** Close to M1 and East Midlands Airport; by rail and coach to Nottingham. Buses from city centre and Beeston railway station; free hopper bus service between campuses.

Courses

Academic features: Flexible modular degree course structure; teaching in 2 semesters. New school of veterinary medicine and science. **Awarding body:** The University of Nottingham. **Main undergraduate awards:** BA, LLB, BSc, BEng, BMBS, BMedSci, BVM BVS, BVMedSci, BArch, DipArch, MEng, MMath, MNutr, MPhys, MChem, MPharm, MSci, MNursSci. **Length of courses:** 3 and 4 years; 5 years (medicine, veterinary medicine); 6 years (architecture).

Study opportunities & careers

Library and information services: Refurbished libraries (including student cinema, self-service lending, recording space, pioneering 'thunderwall'). 1 million+ printed volumes; 13,000 journals; electronic journals and databases; digital materials; manuscripts and special collections. Short loan collection for books most in demand. Information provision, £159 pa spent for each student (FTE). IT and library services converged. All workstations have access to library and internet; IT access from all student rooms. Libraries open 24 hours/day at exam times. IT support via helplines, email, advisory desks, school IT reps. Induction to library and information services on school basis for new students; IT modules available as part of modular scheme. **Other learning resources:** University language centre, museum and arts centre. **Study abroad:** Many departments have established Erasmus links. Founder member of Universitas 21, which offers a number of study abroad opportunities. Possible also to study at Malaysia and China campuses, depending on course. **Careers:** Centre for career development.

Student services & facilities

Student advice and services: Academic support, disability policy advisory unit, fees and financial support at University Park and Jubilee Campus. Also counselling service; childcare service; health services (including GPs, physiotherapist, psychiatrist, nurse practitioner in mental health, dental practice, pharmacy); international office; student advice and representation office; faith support and advice and disability liaison officer in every school. **Amenities:** SU with shop; minibuses; cinema; travel agency; hairdressers; campus bookshops; cafés and coffee bars; performing arts studio; theatre; DH Lawrence lakeside pavilion; banks; on-campus nightclub. **Sporting facilities:** Indoor sports centre, playing fields, 2000-metre international rowing course nearby, swimming pool, fitness centre. **Accommodation:** All full-time 1st years accommodated (if they confirm before specified date). Approx. 8000 places, a mixture of catered, part-catered and self-catered (12 halls in University Park, 2 at Jubilee Campus, 1 at Sutton Bonington): annual rent from £3139–£5472. Privately rented accommodation locally £55–£80 pw plus bills.

Money

Living expenses budget: Minimum budget of £700 a month (excluding tuition fees) recommended by university. **Term-time work:** University-run student employment service; recommended limit of 20 hours pw. **Financial help:** Bursaries of £1080 pa for UK students whose residual family income is less than £34,500, and of £270–£1080 pa where family income is £34,500–£44,500; additional bursaries of £1080 pa to such students coming via an access or vocational qualification or who have children or elderly dependents; bursaries of £1080 pa for graduates of the Lincoln Health Certificate. Some 50% of students expected to qualify for a bursary. Also hardship funds, access to learning funds, first-in-the-family scholarships, childcare support scheme. Information from Student Services Office. **Tuition fees:** Home students pay £3225 pa for first degrees (reduced fees eg for placement year). International students pay £10,610 pa (arts-based), £13,910 (science-based), £14,660–£25,900 (medicine), £18,980 (veterinary medicine/surgery).

Student view
Rob Barham, Editor of *Impact* Magazine (4th year, International Relations)

Living
What's it like as a place to live? Nottingham's got a really vibrant student scene – on campus, in the areas we live in town, and with the nightlife. **How's the student accommodation?** Accommodation is really varied, but generally quite expensive. The university accommodation is generally good, especially the halls on campus. **What's the student population like?** The student population is quite diverse, and people are generally laid-back and friendly. The proportion of middle-class students is surprisingly high. **How do students and locals get on?** The area most students live is so colonised by us that we rarely see locals. Generally, though, there are few problems.

Studying
What's it like as a place to study? The courses are generally of high quality, although we have little contact with our tutors. Facilities and the libraries are good. **What are the teaching staff like?** They're varied, but most are good and have an interest in students.

Socialising
What are student societies like? There's a large range of societies, from salsa dancing to ultimate frisbee. We also have a very vibrant and successful student magazine. **What's a typical night out?** Fancy dress and vodka Red Bulls at ISIS. **And how much does it cost?** £20. **How can you get home safely?** Easily. Taxis are very cheap.

Money

Is it an expensive place to live? No. Taxis are cheap, as are drinks and takeaways. Accommodation is generally reasonable. **Average price of a pint?** £2. **And the price of a takeaway?** £3.50. **What's the part-time work situation?** Not great. It's fairly hard to get a job right now, although with persistence you will find one.

Summary

What's the best feature about the place? The campus is amazing. It's huge, green and has great architecture. **And the worst?** Limited contact time with tutors. **And if you had to sum it all up in a sentence (or two)?** Bodacious.

Past students: D H Lawrence (author), Brian Moore (rugby), Jim Moir alias Vic Reeves (comedian), Clive Granger (economist). **More info?** Call 0115 846 8800, email studentsunion@nottingham.ac.uk or check out the SU website (www.su.nottingham.ac.uk).

Oak Hill College

Location:
North London, within M25 (map 3)
Single site in Southgate

Oak Hill College, Chase Side, Southgate, London N14 4PS
☎ Tel 020 8449 0467
🖷 Fax 020 8441 5996
✉ Email clareo@oakhill.ac.uk
💻 Website www.oakhill.ac.uk

Student enquiries: Development Officer
Applications: Direct

In brief

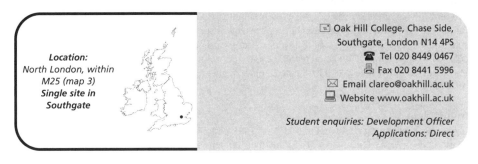

Total Students: 200
5% postgraduate
95% undergraduate

Undergraduates: 190
70% full-time

25% female   75% male

- **Specialist theology college.** An associate college of Middlesex University.
- **Teaching staff:** 13 full-time, 2 part-time.
- **Broad study areas:** Theology, pastoral studies, youth and children's ministry training.

Freshers

- **First degree entrants:** 45 UK, full-time.
- **Drop-out rate:** Under 5% in 1st year.
- **Accommodation:** Most 1st years housed.

Profile

Institution

Founded: 1932. **Site:** Single site in 60 acres of parkland, north London. **How to get there:** Underground to Southgate (Piccadilly line), then walk or bus (about 1 hour from Westminster).
Special features: Exists to train people for Christian ministry.

449

Courses

Academic features: Courses in biblical studies, Christian doctrine, church history, preaching, youth and children's ministry training, ethics, biblical/pastoral counselling, New Testament Greek, biblical Hebrew, theology and world mission; some modules taken with Middlesex University. Mature students may be admitted without the formal qualifications. Successful Dip HE candidates can transfer to degree course. **Awarding body:** Middlesex University. **Main undergraduate award:** BA. **Length of courses:** 3 years; others 1–4 years.

Study opportunities & careers

Library and information services: 49,000 volumes, 180 periodicals, 30 study places; course books placed on temporary reference; tape library, video library. IT service separate. Ratio 1:10 workstations to students; 3 machines have access to library, 8 to the internet; open 24 hours/day. Support from part-time IT technician. Library induction for new students; IT skills courses can be arranged via Middlesex University. **Careers:** Advice service; vocational placement scheme; Church of England training college.

Student services & facilities

Student advice and services: Chaplain, personal tutor. Houses for married couples plus families; crèche. **Sporting facilities:** All-weather tennis courts; football/rugby field on site; municipal squash courts and swimming pool nearby; also cricket pitch. **Accommodation:** Most students in college accommodation. Additional rental for flats/houses. Few students live at home. The annual fee covers a room in college (study bedroom for those that need it, a study for those living off campus).

Money

Living expenses budget: Minimum budget of £12k pa for a single student (incl fees). **Term-time work:** College allows term-time work for full-time students if absolutely necessary. **Fees:** All students pay approx £8700 pa, which covers tuition, term-time meals and a room in college.

Student view

Purely a theological college, primarily training people for Christian ministry. Although Anglican, increasing numbers are from other denominations and independent churches. For some, a qualification in theological and pastoral studies is an end in itself. Set in 60 acres of parkland and woods, housed in a Georgian mansion with a new academic centre nearby; expanding library (access 24/7) and good bookshop. Excellent relationships with staff (first-name basis). Students are represented on all committees and involved in interviewing new staff. Prayer and worship start each day. All students are in fellowship groups. Long-standing links, and possible exchanges, with colleges in Africa and Australia (students fundraise for a college in Uganda). College courses include: biblical studies, doctrine, ethics, sociology, counselling, youth and children's work, communication/preaching, Church history, apologetics, other religions, biblical languages. Teaching styles vary (seminars, lectures, workshops, tutorials, placements in college missions, chaplaincy, etc.); assessments by coursework and/or exam. London easily accessible, 30 mins on tube from station 1 mile away. Families very well catered for: green spaces and playground equipment for children to play, playgroup, babysitting rota. Evening programme for spouses who may also attend lectures free or take the course at half price.

Student footnotes

Housing: Singles usually in study bedrooms in main building; many married couples in college-owned houses and flats on campus. Individual studies available. All on-campus accommodation on college network (and so internet). **Eats:** Food on campus good and cheap (Monday–Friday). Lots of variety locally. **Drink:** No bar. Local pubs ok (especially those in Hertfordshire countryside, few miles north). **Nightlife:** TV/video room, table tennis, snooker, table football, tennis/basketball courts, football (college team), cricket, croquet! Classical music programme, college drama productions, may ball, Christmas parties, bonfire night, parties, etc. **Sports:** Swimming (1 mile), squash (next to college), golf. Saracens RFC is opposite college entrance. **Travel:** Expenses reimbursed for placements. **Financial help:** Various hardship funds. In cases of real need the college community will try to meet the need itself. **Jobs:** Various part-time and vacation work available. **Informal name:** Oak Hill (former students known as Old Oaks). **Best features:** Great courses and grounds, fantastic people, sense of community (visitors often comment on the happy and friendly atmosphere). **And worst:** Can be quite 'academic'. **Past students:** Sir Cliff Richard (singer), John Pantry (musician), various bishops and Anglican big-wigs! Rt Rev George Carey (former Archbishop of Canterbury) was a tutor.

Open University

Distance learning only

🖳 Open University, Walton Hall,
Milton Keynes MK7 6AA
☎ Tel 01908 274066
🖳 Website www.open.ac.uk

*Student enquiries: Customer Contact Centre
(tel 01908 653231 – answering service out of office hours;
evening and weekend advice line tel 0870 333 1444)
Applications: Direct*

In brief

Total Students: 176,560

10% postgraduate
90% undergraduate

Undergraduates: 160,55

100% part-time ● ● 100% UK students
75% mature on entry ●

61% female 39% male

- **World-class distance-learning university.**
- **Teaching staff:** Approx. 1100 full-time, 8800 part-time.
- **Broad study areas:** Arts, childhood and youth studies, environment, education, mathematics and computing, science, social science, technology, languages, health and social welfare, law, business and management.

Freshers

- **Admissions information:** No educational qualifications required (although 30% of new students already hold an HE qualification). Students should be 18 or over and resident in the EU or certain other countries. Early applications take precedence over later ones, so apply early.

Profile

Institution 🚢

Founded: 1969. **Special features:** Students study at home through unique OU method of study (OU-supported open learning), using specially written course texts, set books, online in virtual learning environments and interactive audio-visual materials. Also face-to-face tuition at OU regional tutorial venues and, for some courses, home kits and OU residential schools. OU increasingly attracts students under 25.

Courses

Academic features: Approx. 650 courses, many multi- or inter-disciplinary. Degrees built up by CATS (credit accumulation and transfer scheme): a minimum of 360 points for an Honours degree (120 of these at Level 3) and 300 points for an ordinary degree. Individual courses may be taken on a one-off basis for vocational, updating or as refresher courses. Community education study packs available. Wide range of courses provided for professionals in commerce, industry, education and the caring services (including a certificate, diploma and Master's degree in management). Postgraduate study also possible (taught or research-based and PGCE). **Awarding body:** Open University. **Main undergraduate awards:** BA, BSc, MEng; selection of Honours degrees in named subjects. **Length of courses:** 4–5 years average, 5–6 years average for Honours (individual courses 6–12 months).

Study opportunities & careers

Library and information services: On-campus library for staff and full-time or visiting students. Electronic library resources available to students via the web. **Careers:** Personal and online advice and literature to support students (prospective, current and former) in course choice, career planning and career change.

Student services & facilities

Amenities: Network of more than 300 tutorial venues. All registered students belong to Open University SA (OUSA), which provides support services in education and welfare.

Money

Financial help: Funds for students experiencing financial hardship. Some LEAs may also help and give funds for residential school. **Tuition fees:** For UK residents, £495–£845 for each 60-point course (up to £935 for a language course, £680–£1720 for law). All fees include cost of residential schools if an integrated part of the course. Stand-alone residential school courses are available for a separate fee. Higher fees charged for students resident outside the UK. Average cost £3150–£4225 for a complete Honours degree.

Student view

Primarily a distance-learning organisation – most students are part-time, studying a wide range of courses leading to BA, BSc, MBA, PGCE and various diplomas, Master's and PhDs. There are some full-time research students based on campus but the majority of students never visit Walton Hall in Milton Keynes, where the university is based. Students study at home in between their family and work commitments and on average they are expected to study for 10–15 hours pw although this varies greatly. It takes a lot of self-discipline and motivation to be an OU student; but with nearly 200,000 students across the UK and Europe studying this way, it is clearly an attractive option for many – and an increasing number of young and career-orientated students join every year. Most courses have locally based tutorials and a small number of courses have a residential element, a week (sometimes a weekend) of concentrated study. OUSA plays an extremely active role in the life of the university, from its participation and representation at every level of the OU government structure to its many and varied social activities. It has a network of local branches where students can meet in a social environment and discuss not only their studies but their concerns on student issues. You can get an NUS-OUSA associate card, which gives you discounts and special offers and includes the ISIC card. There is a huge virtual OU community, using OUSA's website and its computer-based conferencing systems, where OU students from all over the country, Europe and beyond can talk to each other, discuss their studies and socialise virtually as well. OU students can obtain various forms of financial support towards their fees and study costs, and as a final safety net, OUSA set up its own separate, registered charity OUSET (Open University Students' Educational Trust). OU students are well motivated: they study to enjoy the experience of learning and to enhance their career and personal development.

Summary
What's the best feature about the place? Choice, flexibility and quality of courses **And the worst?** It is hard work and you have to be focused and committed to succeed. **And to sum it all up?** Studying with the OU is a fantastic experience – it opens doors and changes lives. Also it may be a surprise to know that students have a thriving community through their SA; rather than it being the lonely, isolated experience that many imagine, it can lead to a busy social life, friendships and more!!

More info? Contact OUSA at Walton Hall (tel 01908 652026, email ousa@student.open.ac.uk, website www.ousa.org.uk).

Oxford Brookes University

| Location: Oxford (map 2) Main campus, plus 2 others around Oxford; partner colleges | Oxford Brookes University, Gipsy Lane, Headington, Oxford OX3 0BP Tel 01865 741111 Fax 01865 483983 Website www.brookes.ac.uk Student enquiries: Enquiry Centre (tel 01865 484848, email query@brookes.ac.uk) Applications: UCAS |

In brief

Total Students: 19,070

2% FE Students
27% postgraduate
72% undergraduate

Undergraduates: 13,645
79% full-time ● ● 86% UK students
34% mature ● ● 42% lower
on entry ● ● socio-economic groups

58% female 42% male

- **A modern university.**
- **Teaching staff:** 431 full-time, 204 part-time.
- **Broad study areas:** Arts and humanities (art, history, art history, music, languages, literature, publishing, arts management); built environment (architecture, construction, planning, real estate management); business (including hospitality, leisure and tourism management); health and social care; social sciences (including anthropology, politics, psychology), law, life sciences (biological, human and environmental sciences), technology (computing, maths, engineering); teacher training; religious studies.

Freshers
- **Admissions information:** AS-levels accepted in combination with 1 (usually 2+) A-levels or equivalent. UCAS tariff not used.
- **First degree entrants:** 2620 UK, full-time.

- **Points on entry:** 299 (average).
- **Drop-out rate:** 9% in 1st year.
- **Accommodation:** Almost all 1st years housed who need it.

Profile

Institution

Founded: 1865 as a school of art, becoming Oxford Poly in 1970; university status in 1992. **Site:** 3 main campuses: Headington Campus (1 mile east of city centre), Wheatley Campus (7 miles south-east of city centre; business, maths, technology and engineering), Harcourt Hill Campus (2½ miles west of city centre; education). **How to get there:** Good rail links to Oxford (from London, Birmingham, Heathrow), station 2 miles by bus. By road, close to M40; coach service from London every 15 mins during the day, stops outside Headington Campus; buses to city centre. Brookes bus service between sites and accommodation.

Courses

Academic features: Modular courses allow study on a full-time, part-time or mixed-mode basis. Academic year divided into 2 semesters of 12 weeks teaching and 1 week of exams. Courses in arts administration, environmental sciences, publishing, sports science. Access courses at 7 local centres give entry to university courses. **Awarding body:** Oxford Brookes University. **Main undergraduate awards:** BA, BA (QTS), BSc, BEng, LLB. **Length of courses:** 3 years; others 4 years.

Study opportunities & careers

Library and information services: 3 libraries, 460,000 volumes, 2150 current journals, over 1000 study places. Information provision, £80 pa spent for each student (FTE). IT and library services converged. 971 PC student workstations (including email and internet access), some available 24/7; all student rooms have internet points; ratio of workstations to students approx 1:14. IT helpdesk 12 hours/day during term time; tours, demonstrations and podcasts of library and information services for new students; module on microcomputer applications available to all students. **Other learning resources:** Multimedia graphics workshop; study skills service. **Study abroad:** 20% of students spend a period abroad. Formal exchange links with 100+ universities and colleges throughout Europe, Canada, the USA, Australia, Japan and Hong Kong.

Student services & facilities

Student advice and services: Counsellors, careers, accommodation, housing and chaplaincy staff; nurses; FPA; dentist on campus, visiting GPs; specialist advisers for international students, mature students and students with disabilities; SU welfare advice centre; nursery (60 places). Mentoring schemes. Study skills programme. **Amenities:** SU with bars, entertainments venue, shops, banks. **Sporting facilities:** Sports centre with badminton and squash courts, dance and martial arts studio, weights training room, climbing room; fitness suite; 12 tennis courts, playing fields, artificial turf pitch, 2 golf courses; swimming pool; land-based rowing facility. **Accommodation:** Almost all 1st-year students who need it in university halls (priority to those living furthest away). 3406 places, self-catering and catered: catered rooms at £110–£129 pw (total of £4200–£4900 pa), self-catering £101–£120 pw (total £3850–£5450 pa); most contracts 38 weeks, some 50 weeks. Also some university-managed housing, average rent £75 pw. Students usually live in privately rented accommodation after 1st year: rent approx £60–£105 pw for self-catering, 52-week contracts.

Money

Living expenses budget: Average budget of £8060 for an academic year (excluding tuition fees) estimated by university. **Term-time work:** University allows term-time work (50% believed to work).

Some work available on campus in SU bars, ents and in registry, student recruitment, accommodation, catering; SU Job Shop helps find work on and off campus. **Financial help:** Bursaries of £1560 pa for UK students with family income of £20k; tapered bursaries (down to £150 pa) where family income is £20k–£36k. Also scholarships for excellence, certain local students; and bursaries of up to £2k pa for those who have been in care. Means-tested access to learning fund: £437k government funds, approx 800 students helped; £453k own funds. £60k emergency fund, 100 helped (international and part-time students with unforeseen difficulties; some part-time students or local students on benefit). Apply for help to financial aid office. **Tuition fees:** Home students pay £3225 pa for first degrees (except on healthcare courses, year in placement, foundation year). International students pay £9780 pa (standard), £10k pa (most business courses).

Student view — Antoinette Kyuchukova, OBSU President (4th year, BA Business Innovation and Enterprise)

Living
What's it like as a place to live? Oxford is a vibrant, diverse and very student-centred city. Oxford Brookes offers a modern student experience. **How's the student accommodation?** There are university and private accommodations. Uni-run accommodations are well maintained and of good standard, vary in type and location. There is choice. **What's the student population like?** Very diverse, friendly, plenty of interesting talented people from all sorts of backgrounds. **How do students and locals get on?** Very good community atmosphere, mainly student town, so the locals are young, easygoing and friendly.

Studying
What's it like as a place to study? Brookes is a progressive modern university with a flexible academic programme and opportunities for various curricular and extra-curricular activities. **What are the teaching staff like?** Teaching staff are very friendly, student-focused, professional and committed to delivering a good student learning experience.

Socialising
What are student societies like? The SU is a fantastic place to meet people, develop talents further, learn new skills, socialise and have fun, get advice and support. Societies range from hobby-based to course-based and is worth signing up to them. **What's a typical night out?** At the SU venue on Wed and Fri – over 1200 student club nights. **And how much does it cost?** You can get away with spending as little as £5–£6 pounds at the SU but obviously prices go up in town. **How can you get home safely?** Oxford Brookes is considered a very safe university. The SU runs safety bus schemes that ensure the welfare and safety of students. University and SU work closely with the police to provide a safe environment for Brookes students.

Money
Is it an expensive place to live? It is not very cheap as it near London. The prices are competitive. **Average price of a pint?** £1.20 at the SU, over £1.50 in town. **And the price of a takeaway?** Varies from £1.20 kebab shop to £6.99 Domino's. **What's the part-time work situation?** Plenty of jobs available on campus through the SU. Advertisement of jobs can be found at the SU's Jobshop or on www.thesu.com – jobshop section. Jobs can be found on and off campus.

Summary
What's the best feature about the place? Very lively, diverse and great balance between social and academic life. Beautiful town. **And the worst?** No parking spaces. **And to sum it all up?** Oxford Brookes is a great place to live and study and offers a dynamic environment for personal career and development.

Past students: Adrian Reynard (Reynard Racing), Tim Rodber (England rugby).
More info? Enquiries to SU reception (tel 01865 484715, email obsu@brookes.ac.uk) or visit www.thesu.com.

Oxford University

⊡ University of Oxford, University Offices, Oxford OX1 2JD
☎ Tel 01865 270000
🖷 Fax 01865 270708
💻 Website www.ox.ac.uk

Student enquiries:
(1) (University) Undergraduate Admissions Office, University Offices, Wellington Square, Oxford OX1 2JD (tel 01865 288000, email undergraduate.admissions@admin.ox.ac.uk, website www.admissions.ox.ac.uk (2) (Colleges) The Tutor for Admissions, xxx College, Oxford Applications: UCAS

Location:
Oxford (map 2)
38 constituent colleges and university teaching centres across city

In brief

Total Students: 20,015

40% postgraduate
60% undergraduate

Undergraduates: 11,915
95% full-time ● ● 86% UK students
4% mature ● ● 10% lower socio-economic groups
on entry

48% female 52% male

- **World-class research-intensive university.**
- **Teaching staff:** 1478 full-time, 66 part-time.
- **Broad study areas:** Arts; humanities; life, biological and medical sciences; social sciences; mathematical and physical sciences.

Freshers
- **Admissions information:** Entrance requirements usually at least 3 A-levels at grade A, or the IB with at least 38 points (6 or 7 in higher subjects) or equivalent qualifications.
- **First degree entrants:** 2770 UK, full-time.
- **Points on entry:** 420+ (average).
- **Drop-out rate:** 1% in 1st year.
- **Accommodation:** All 1st years housed.

Profile

Institution
Founded: 12th/13th century. **Site:** Scattered throughout the city centre. Most college and university facilities (departments, libraries, labs) and sports grounds are within walking or biking distance. **How to get there:** Good coach and rail links from London, Birmingham, the north, Heathrow and

Gatwick; close to M40. Walk and bike within city. **Special features:** Distinctive collegiate system. **University and the colleges:** The university is a federation of 38 independent, self-contained and self-governing colleges, 30 of which admit first-degree undergraduates. There are also 6 private halls, founded by different Christian denominations. Each college selects its own students, houses them (most for at least 2 out of 3 years), provides meals, common rooms, libraries, sports and social facilities and is responsible, through the tutorial system, for its students' academic work. The majority of colleges teach most, but not all, of the university courses; so you need to check that the course you want is available at the college you prefer. Your college will be the hub of your life. They have their own prospectuses, in addition to the university prospectus (see list below).

Courses

Academic features: The university provides the curricular framework within which college teaching takes place, as well as providing a wide range of resources for teaching and learning – libraries, labs, museums, computing facilities, etc. It sets the exams and awards degrees. **Awarding body:** University of Oxford. **Main undergraduate awards:** BA, BFA, BM BCh, BTh, MBiochem, MChem, MEng, MEarthSc, MMath, MPhys. **Length of courses:** 3 years; 4 years (eg for languages, undergraduate Master's).

Study opportunities & careers

Library and information services: Bodleian Library is main university library (a copyright library, so may claim a copy of all books published in the UK). Faculties, departments and colleges also have their own libraries. All new students have library induction pack and induction sessions from libraries relevant to their studies. Information provision, £300+ pa spent for each student (FTE). Separate IT service, ratio workstations to students in colleges and libraries at least 1:4. Some college and departmental facilities open 24 hours/day. All colleges offer in-house help. OUCS (university computing service) has extensive website and offers self-paced material, help and advice and courses in basic IT skills, training for European Computer Driving Licence (ECDL) and advanced subjects (eg programming, web publishing, statistics). **Other learning resources:** University museums of art and archaeology, history of science, anthropology and natural history; musical instruments; botanic garden; university language centre. **Study abroad:** Approx. 10% of undergraduates spend a period abroad. Most exchanges are for language specialists but there are opportunities in other subjects, eg 4-year law course with a year at a European university. Links with a large number of European universities and with Princeton University, USA. **Careers:** University careers service. 50% of graduates go straight into employment, 46% to further study.

Student services & facilities

Student advice and services: Mainly in individual colleges. University counselling service and careers service. **Amenities:** Many university societies, eg Oxford Union, OUDS (dramatic society) as well as college activities. 4 theatres in city, several cinemas, variety of venues for music of all kinds, ice rink and 3 swimming pools. Also University Parks, Christ Church Meadow. **Sporting facilities:** Excellent university sports facilities (and high standards for high fliers) including swimming pool; also college facilities (range of standards). **Accommodation:** All colleges provide accommodation for 1st-year undergraduates. Most also house 3rd-year students and many house all undergraduates for their whole course. Students have to live within 6 miles of the centre of the city, so living at home is extremely rare.

Money

Living expenses budget: Minimum budget of £6500 pa for an academic year (excluding tuition fees) recommended by the university, £11,500 for full calendar year. **Term-time work:** Opportunities for limited amount of paid work in college during term time. **Financial help:** Bursaries of £3225 pa (£4100 in Year 1) for students whose family income is up to £25k; and partial awards (minimum

£200) available where family income is £25k–£50k; bursaries may be enhanced by further £1k pa on certain courses. Also government hardship funds plus a variety of other college and university funds to help students eg from particular countries/areas, studying particular subjects or suffering financial hardship; awards generally made on the basis of academic merit or financial need (awards generally range from £100 to £3k). **Tuition fees:** Home students pay £3225 pa for first degrees. International students pay £11,750 pa (classroom-based), £13,450 pa (lab-based), £24,500 (clinical medicine). College fees (£4800–£5200 pa) are paid in addition to university tuition fees, except by home and EU students who are publicly funded (eg those eligible for a student loan).

Applying to Oxford

You no longer need to make a separate application to Oxford as well as to UCAS. You only need to complete a UCAS application, which must be with UCAS by 15 October (slightly earlier if you need to be interviewed at one of the international interview centres).

You may choose a college of preference, or put in an open application to the university. Candidates will be allocated 2nd and 3rd choice colleges and if you are not accepted by any of these colleges, your application may then be available to other colleges for consideration. It is not possible to apply to both Oxford and Cambridge in the same admissions year, unless you are a candidate for an organ award.

The colleges

You can look up each of the following 30 Oxford colleges that admit undergraduates (all colleges now accept both men and women).

Balliol	Lincoln	St Hilda's
Brasenose	Magdalen	St Hugh's
Christ Church	Mansfield	St John's
Corpus Christi	Merton	St Peter's
Exeter	New College	Somerville
Harris Manchester (for students	Oriel	Trinity
over 25)	Pembroke	University College
Hertford	Queen's	Wadham
Jesus	St Anne's	Worcester
Keble	St Catherine's	
Lady Margaret Hall	St Edmund Hall	

There are also 6 permanent private halls that admit undergraduates: Blackfriars (principally members of the Dominican Order); Campion Hall (men only, principally members of the Society of Jesus); Regent's Park (many members of Baptist churches); St Benet's Hall (men only, principally for Benedictines); St Stephen's House; and Wycliffe Hall.

Student view

It's the oldest university in the English-speaking world, laden with tradition and with many beautiful buildings dating from every century since the 1200s. The university is made up of a number of semi-autonomous colleges. Students live, eat, socialise and are taught there and the college identity is strong. Most colleges guarantee students accommodation for at least 2 years –sometimes the whole course – but some live in rented accommodation for 1 year. All colleges are mixed (even St Hilda's from 2008). There is a low proportion of mature students (although Harris Manchester caters specifically for them) but a high percentage of international students, particularly graduates. Most high-street chains are represented in town; a fantastic range of restaurants and cafés; less choice when it comes to clubs but the pubs are great. Oxford is easily accessible by train and 2 bus services from London (every 12 mins by day and most of the night). Reasonable city bus service, especially along Cowley Road, which is a popular student area. Most people use bikes as it's a small place and car parking is extremely restricted. Every college has a JCR (Junior Common Room) for undergraduates and an MCR (Middle Common Room) for graduates – some more political than others. These are separate from, but affiliated to, the university-wide students' union, OUSU – an umbrella organisation that provides representation and services for all students. There are over 300 university societies and voluntary groups. The academic year is short, with 3 terms of 8 weeks. Relatively easy to change course in 1st term (as long as you are qualified). Courses are highly specialised with heavy workloads. Instruction is largely by tutorial, with a tutor to student ratio of 1:3 at the most. Most courses have no continuous assessment – entire degree hinges on one set of exams at the end of the course. University libraries very well stocked and college libraries open 24 hours. Public schools and the south are over-represented but there is an active Target Schools programme (run by OUSU), aimed at encouraging state school applicants: statistics show that public and state school applicants have equal chances of success (about 1 in 3). Employment prospects after graduation much better than average, with many firms recruiting only in Oxbridge. Oxford is becoming an increasingly diverse place.

Student footnotes

Housing: Colleges provide accommodation for 2 or more years, either in college or in flats/houses nearby (rent vary greatly between colleges). Private accommodation very expensive (second only to London); east Oxford saturated with students. University accommodation office produces good info. **Eats:** Huge variety ranging from 5 star to kebab vans, £5 a head to £50. Meals in college about £2.50, food varies in quality but vegetarian food universally available. **Drink:** College bars much less expensive than town equivalents. Loads of good pubs, traditional and themed. **Nightlife:** Many nightclubs, most with student nights; best bands at Zodiac; 1 gay night at the Coven. Colleges hold sweaty events called 'bops'. **Locals:** Few problems; worse on the outskirts where students don't go anyway. **Sport:** Good provision at college level; university sports federation operates. University swimming pool. **Travel:** College travel grants, sometimes generous. **Financial help:** Very good: many sources and lots of cash. Oxford bursary scheme and all colleges have bursaries and are keen to help students (loans, grants, combinations). **Jobs:** Students can find work in college during term but aren't supposed to look elsewhere. Oxford has a huge student population but is an important tourist destination so not too much competition for holiday employment. **Oxford-speak:** Lots: battels (college bill); blue (someone who played for the university against Cambridge in a major sport, eg cricket blue; minor sports warrant a half blue); boatie (rower); Bod (Bodleian Library, the university library); Collections (termly mock exams); come up (to arrive at Oxford) and go down (to leave); Greats or *lit hum* (classics, ancient history and philosophy); hall (college dining room and sometimes refers to evening meal in college – often formal, as in formal hall); JCR (Junior Common Room – undergraduate or junior members of a college), MCR (ditto but Middle – graduates) and SCR (Senior – fellows); Norrington Table (league table of colleges by finals results); PPE (philosophy, politics and economics course); sets (set of rooms, usually 1 or 2 bedrooms with a sitting room); subfusc (cap and gown over formal suit worn for exams). **Best features:** The teaching; the opportunities; busy lifestyle; diverse, interesting people from all walks of life. **Past students:** Oscar Wilde (author and playwright); Margaret Thatcher, Tony Blair (among other former Prime Ministers); Tony Benn, Michael Heseltine, Denis Healey (politicians); Benazir Bhutto (former Prime Minister, Pakistan); Roger Bannister (4-min mile); Rowan Atkinson, Dudley Moore, Willy Rushton (comedians); Melvyn Bragg (writer and broadcaster); Kris Kristofferson (singer and actor); Bill Clinton (ex-US President). **More info?** Get a

free Alternative Prospectus from OUSU, Thomas Hull House, New Inn Hall Street, Oxford OX1 2DH
(tel 01865 288450, fax 01865 288453, email enquiries@ousu.org, website www.ousu.org).

Oxford – Balliol

Balliol College, Oxford OX1 3BJ
☎ Tel 01865 277777
✉ Email admissions@balliol.ox.ac.uk
💻 Website www.balliol.ox.ac.uk

Profile

Staff & students
Undergraduates: 249 men, 153 women. **Postgraduates:** 134 men, 84 women. **Teaching staff:**
Men: 48 fellows, 18 lecturers. *Women* 11 fellows, 13 lecturers.

College & admissions
Founded: 1263; women undergraduates first admitted in 1979. **Admission:** No undergraduates
admitted for archaeology and anthropology, earth sciences, geography, human sciences, theology,
biochemistry, classics and English, materials science, maths and statistics, philosophy and modern
languages, music, philosophy and theology.

Study opportunities
Library and information services: Library aims for at least basic coverage in all main subjects.
Separate college IT service. Ratio 1:20 workstations to students, access 24 hours/day. All student
rooms have data points (for access to library and internet). IT support from 2 full-time staff. **Study
abroad:** Formal exchange links in Lyon and Munich.

Living
Eating arrangements: Undergraduates not required to take meals in college; average undergraduate
spends approx £300 per term in hall. All meals in hall on cafeteria basis, JCR pantry for snacks and
breakfast. **Gate/guest hours:** Gate locked at midnight; all students have keys. 2 guest rooms. **Other
college facilities:** Nearby sports field and pavilion (with 2 squash courts). **Accommodation:** All
undergraduates offered rooms in college or annexes (usually bedsits) for at least 2 years and possibly
a 3rd. Average rent £1365 a term. Scarcely any first-degree students live at home.

Money
Scholarships: None at entrance. Awards made at end of 1st year. **Travel and project grants:** Grants
for academic purposes awarded annually on tutors' recommendations. **Term-time work:** College
allows term-time work (10% believed to work); limit of approx 6 hours pw. Some available in
college – library invigilation, computer officer. **Financial help:** Hardship fund available.

Student view

Good academically but with a relaxed attitude and a high level of student participation in
all sorts of college and university activities. JCR (Junior Common Room – the student body)

is central to college life, with a large common room, the Lindsay bar (student-run), a well-equipped gym, telephones, TV room, free tampons, condoms and rape alarms and taxi refunds for travel after dark. Heated political debates in JCR meetings that discuss a variety of college and wider issues. Extremely central location and beautiful surroundings. Good library facilities and 24-hour computer access. Great social events that are the envy of other colleges. Central sports facilities and a theatre to house the drama society. Active women's group as well as other societies including LGBT, ethnic minorities and overseas. College lawns open to all in the summer (with deckchairs!). Strong sense of community and diverse student body – many international students. Overall, a very active and forward-looking college with an emphasis on public service and a good balance between social and academic life.

Student footnotes

Housing: In college in first and final year; some live in rented accommodation for 1 year, others in Jowett Walk – self-catering accommodation owned by college. **Eats:** Some kitchens for self-catering. Relaxed dining hall (no formal hall) matches general atmosphere. Choice of JCR pantry, particularly renowned for great breakfasts and baked potatoes. **Drink:** Student-run bar, cheap with friendly atmosphere. **Nightlife:** Cheap summer ball, regular ents (bops, DJs, pantos). **Sports:** Largely a social activity but good football, rowing and cricket. **Financial help:** 20 Balliol bursaries annually to most deserving cases (£1k in 1st year, then £750 pa). Many other hardship funds such as maintenance grants, vacation residence, special projects and travel to the USA, Italy, Germany, etc. **Jobs:** Library invigilation and bar work during term. Long holidays to earn money. **Past students:** Ted Heath, Harold Macmillan (former prime ministers); Howard Marks (pro-cannabis campaigner); Graham Greene, Aldous Huxley (authors); Gerard Manley Hopkins (poet); Peter Snow (journalist); Adam Smith (father of modern economics); Chris Patten (last governor Hong Kong); Boris Johnson (London mayor); William Beveridge (economist and social reformer). **More info?** Contact JCR President at jcr.president@balliol.ox.ac.uk or check out the website (www.ballioljcr.org).

Oxford – Brasenose

Brasenose College, Oxford OX1 4AJ
☎ Tel 01865 277510
✉ Email admissions@bnc.ox.ac.uk
🖥 Website www.bnc.ox.ac.uk

Profile

Staff & students

Undergraduates: 196 men, 162 women. **Postgraduates:** 120 men, 82 women. **Teaching staff:** *Men:* 36 fellows, 14 lecturers. *Women:* 7 fellows, 17 lecturers.

College & admissions

Founded: 1509; women undergraduates first admitted in 1974. **Admission:** No undergraduates admitted to earth sciences; human sciences; metallurgy; modern history and English (joint school); oriental studies; theology; engineering, economics and management (EEM); material science, materials, economics and management (MEM); archaeology and anthropology, classics and oriental studies; philosophy and theology, computer science. **Largest fields of study:** PPE, law, modern history, economics and management (EandM).

Study opportunities

Library and information services: About 40,000 volumes on open shelves and a further collection of about 12,000 older books; 90 periodical subscriptions; separate modern history and law reading rooms. Separate college IT service: 250 computers with access to library and internet, open 24 hours/day (ratio 1:15 workstations to students).

Living

Eating arrangements: Breakfast, lunch and dinner in hall; tea available in New Buttery. **Gate/guest hours:** Unrestricted. **Other college facilities:** Bar, sports ground, pavilion, squash and tennis courts about 10 mins' walk from college; boathouse. **Accommodation:** College accommodation for most undergraduates who want it; rent approx £5248–£5511 pa. No first-degree students live at home.

Money

Scholarships: Awarded at the end of the 1st year. **Term-time work:** College does not allow term-time work. Work available in college only during summer conferences. **Financial help:** College discretionary fund for assistance in case of hardship.

Student view

Positioned along one side of Radcliffe Square, beside the towering dome of the Camera, BNC is ideally located. Very close to all main libraries (Bodleian, Radcliffe Camera and faculty libraries) as well as shops, pubs, cinemas and nightlife. Though not one of the most imposing or palatial Oxford colleges, the 16th-century Old Quad and adjoining (ironically named) miniature Deer Park are very picturesque. Small enough for a sense of community, large enough not to be claustrophobic. Almost all undergraduates housed – either on main college site or in the Frewin annexe in St Michael's Street. Some modern rooms, but mainly old 'character' rooms, which are steadily being renovated to a high standard (basins in all, ensuite for finalists). Normally solid academic performance (often in top 3 in Norrington table). Well known as the place for law and PPE (excellent tutors and library facilities). College library more comprehensive than it looks in most other subjects, and has extensive research stacks; lawyers have their own large specialist library. JCR is generally moderate although all political views are present. Incorporates students from a variety of backgrounds, schools and regions and is moving towards equal numbers of men and women; SCR very committed to widening intake. Friendly attitude throughout the college; everyone seems to find somewhere to fit in. Reputation as a strong rugby, rowing and hockey college and particularly strong in women's sports. Comprehensive facilities are close by, including 2 football pitches, rugby and hockey pitches, cricket field and nets, squash, tennis and netball courts, and excellent boathouse. Growing reputation for drama and music with a regular Summer Arts Festival, arts fund and a chapel choir of high standard. The college-run bar is excellent, widely known as one of the best, with popular bar staff; Gertie's, the college tea bar, serves hot and cold food and drinks just when you need it most. Purpose-built computer room for junior members houses modern computers. JCR has big-screen TV, DVD and video, a pool table and playstation, drinks machine, snacks and various constantly changing games machines. It runs societies as diverse as the Brasenose Players, Christian Union, women's group, Indolents (general sports club) and wine society.

Student footnotes

Housing: Accommodation guaranteed for Years 1, 3 and 4 (some 2nd years live out). **Eats:** 3 large meals in college a day, including good vegetarian options; 3-course meal in hall good value. Carfax chippy, Mehdi's Kebab Van. **Drink:** College bars (Grolsch, Carlsberg, Guinness), beer £1.80+ a pint. 4 central student pubs: Turf, King's Arms (always full), White Horse (very small), the Bear. **Nightlife:** Free college ents in bar, regular big-screen events. Usual smash-hit cinemas, plus the Phoenix (more arty). Lots of student drama. **Sports:** BNC sports facilities good and close to college. **Travel:** A few travel grants. Cheap bus to London and good national coach services. **Financial help:** Strictly means-tested. Have to be genuinely broke to get one. Vacation grants available. **Jobs:** Term-time work strongly discouraged by the college. Some college bar work available; always tight in town during term because of number of students. Lots more around during vacations. **Best features:** The bar. **And worst:** Closing time. **Informal name:** BNC (in writing); Nose (sporting supporters). **Past students:** Colin Cowdrey (cricketer), Michael Palin (comedian and TV personality), William Golding (author), Robert Runcie (former Archbishop of Canterbury), Sir Arthur Evans (archaeologist), John Buchan (writer), Lord Scarman (former appeal judge), Stephen Dorrell MP, William Webb-Ellis (inventor of rugby). **More info?** Contact JCR President (tel 01865 277830) or check out the website (www.jcr.bnc.ox.ac.uk).

Oxford – Christ Church

- Christ Church, Oxford OX1 1DP
- ☎ Tel 01865 276150
- ✉ Email admissions@chch.ox.ac.uk
- 🖥 Website www.chch.ox.ac.uk

Profile

Staff & students

Undergraduates: 232 men, 186 women. **Postgraduates:** 133 men, 100 women. **Teaching staff:** *Men:* 37 fellows, 10 research fellows, 28 lecturers. *Women:* 13 fellows, 8 research fellows, 13 lecturers.

College & admissions

Founded: 1546; women undergraduates first admitted in 1980. **Admission:** Undergraduates admitted to all subjects except the following as single Honours: computer science; earth sciences (geology); human sciences; physiological sciences; material sciences. Nor admitted to the joint schools of archaeology and anthropology; classics and English; history and economics; history and English; materials, economics and management; maths and computer science. **Largest fields of study:** PPE, history, law, English, modern languages, classics, geography, physics, mathematics, chemistry, engineering.

Study opportunities

Library and information services: Over 160,000 volumes; collections of early printed books and manuscripts; large law library with 24-hour access. Separate college IT service (ratio workstations to students 1:18): 20+ computers with access to library and internet; all student rooms have internet socket. IT facilities open 24 hours/day, support from full-time computing officer.

Living

Eating arrangements: All meals in hall. Breakfast approx £1.50, lunch and dinner approx £2.50–£2.70. **Gate/guest hours:** Undergraduates have own keys. Guests not admitted before 9am, and must have left by 2am. **Other college facilities:** Computer room, music room, art room, playing fields nearby, multigym, sports pavilion, squash courts, tennis courts, boathouse. Picture gallery (famous collection of Old Masters). As both a college and a cathedral, Christ Church has a strong musical tradition. **Accommodation:** All students in college accommodation, shared sets or bedsits (on-site rooms all with a fridge): rent £1064 a term (heat, light and laundry charges according to use).

Money

Scholarships: College entrance bursaries of up to £2k pa for students from low-income families. Also interest-free loans of up to £1k. Scholarships and other prizes awarded for meritorious work during residence. Book grants (£210) available for all undergraduates. **Travel grants:** Limited assistance provided to encourage travel by undergraduates, irrespective of subject of study. **Term-time work:** College does not allow term-time work. **Financial help:** Financial assistance fund available for those in unforeseen financial difficulty.

Student view — Alan Rimmer, JCR President (3rd year, Classics)

Living

What's it like as a place to live? Probably the grandest of Oxford's colleges, though not without its own warmth and strong community. **How's the student accommodation?** College accommodation provided throughout time here; quite a range of sizes and styles but generally excellent and competitive rates. **What's the student population like?** Christ Church retains a traditional stereotype but, although there is room for improvement, the facts show a balanced and diverse membership. **How do students and locals get on?** Town and gown has become more of an issue lately, but on the whole both sides keep themselves to themselves. More of a problem if you live out.

Studying

What's it like as a place to study? Facilities excellent across the board. Often too much to make the most out of. Traditional courses and intense terms. **What are the teaching staff like?** Probably the most eclectic bunch of tutors in the land, so hard to say what you'll find, other than some of the world's leading academics teaching on a one-to-one basis.

Socialising

What are student societies like? The traditional ones still dominate the social scene, but as wide a variety as you're likely to get anywhere. **What's a typical night out?** Pubs, club (maybe) . . . work. **And how much does it cost?** £20. **How can you get home safely?** Central Oxford is not without its dangers, but is fairly provincial. Colleges supply safety resources.

Money

Is it an expensive place to live? Not cheap, but short terms means costs are competitive. **Average price of a pint?** £2.50–£3. **And the price of a takeaway?** £4–£5. **What's the part-time work situation?** The university officially prohibits term-time work.

Summary

What's the best feature about the place? Unique in almost every way. **And the worst?** Work is pretty intense. **And to sum it all up?** Still probably the most intense and exciting student experience in the world.

Past students: William Gladstone, Sir Alec Douglas Home, Antony Eden, Sir Robert Peel (former Prime Ministers); Sir William Walton (composer); Sir Adrian Boult (conductor); Judge James Pickles; Peter Jay (economics editor); Mark Girouard (architectural historian); Lewis Carroll (author); Sir Leon Brittan (ex-European Commissioner); Nigel Lawson (former Chancellor of the Exchequer); W H Auden (poet); Auberon Waugh, Anthony Howard, David Dimbleby (journalists); Albert Einstein (relativity); John Locke (philosopher). **More info?** JCR President, c/o the college.

Oxford – Corpus Christi

Corpus Christi College, Oxford OX1 4JF
Tel 01865 276693
Email admissions.office@ccc.ox.ac.uk
Website www.ccc.ox.ac.uk

Profile

Staff & students
Undergraduates: 127 men, 110 women. **Postgraduates:** 74 men, 57 women. **Teaching staff:** *Men:* 28 fellows, 5 research fellows, 18 lecturers. *Women:* 5 fellows, 5 research fellow, 11 lecturers.

College & admissions
Founded: 1517; women undergraduates first admitted in 1979. **Admission:** Undergraduates not admitted to archaeology and anthropology, biological sciences, economics and management, engineering, geography, geology (earth sciences), human sciences, music (except for organ scholars), oriental studies, modern languages and related joint schools, theology. **Largest fields of study:** Classics, history and PPE.

Study opportunities
Library and information services: 80,000 volumes; 22 ethernet connections; 10 workstations open 24 hours/day with restricted borrowing hours. Separate college IT service: 20 computers with access to library catalogue and internet, own ethernet in student rooms (ratio 1:20 workstations to students). IT facilities open 24 hours/day; support from 1.5 full-time staff, 8 hours/weekdays.

Living
Eating arrangements: All meals available in college except for Saturday dinner and Sunday breakfast. **Gate/guest hours:** Keys available to all members. Some restrictions on frequency and duration of entertainment of guests in college. **Other college facilities:** Squash courts and playing fields; boathouse; music room. **Accommodation:** College accommodation available to all students; full-board approx £150 pw, term time only. No first-degree students live at home.

Money
Travel grants: Some available. **Term-time work:** College allows term-time work under certain restrictive conditions. **Financial help:** A maintenance support fund is available for any students who find themselves in unforeseen hardship.

465

Student view

Preeti Dhillon, JCR President (2nd year, History and Politics)

Living
What's it like as a place to live? It's a vibrant, safe and beautiful place to live. Steeped in history yet not stuck in the past, with all the modern high street shops and amenities. **How's the student accommodation?** Corpus provides accommodation for all 3 years which is incredible. It includes all utilities too. It is one of the cheapest in Oxford and is really well kept. **What's the student population like?** The population is about 50:50 state:independent school students. Same for the gender ratio. The students are mainly from the UK but there is a large international minority. Corpus is keen to increase the diversity of students. **How do students and locals get on?** There aren't any problems between students and locals, mainly because during term time the city is over-run with students, and locals go to clubs on different nights to the students.

Studying
What's it like as a place to study? Corpus has such a wonderful atmosphere for studying. The centuries-old library is well-stocked, open 24 hours and has wireless internet, as well as a number of computers. There are a number of courses not offered, as Corpus is small, such as geography and languages, but there is a wide enough range that there is a good mix of people and interests. Whilst Oxford is traditional and often conservative, Corpus has always been somewhat of a radical college and open to experimenting with new ways of teaching and learning. **What are the teaching staff like?** The teaching is world class. Most love teaching undergrads, though some will be more interested in their research and see undergrads as a nuisance, but this is the exception. The tutors are always accessible for those revision freak-outs and extra help that nearly everyone needs at some point. They make Corpus a place conducive to academic excellence.

Socialising
What are student societies like? Oxford knows how to do extra-curriculars. Corpus, though small, also has a good standing in clubs and societies with an especially strong drama group, the Owlets, and our own comedy collective and sports teams, from rowing to pool. There are also subject-specific societies, like Classics and Literary Society. They are a great way to socialise with people outside of your subject, and are open to all, and nearly everyone gets involved in something. Every year there is a sporting challenge against Corpus Cambridge, which is a highlight of the year. **What's a typical night out?** A typical night out starts out in the Beer Cellar (our student bar) before going onto a club (of which Oxford has a surprising amount). There are lots of pubs in Oxford, which are often frequented by those who don't like to club. Corpus has regular 'bops', which are so much fun as they are always themed so people get dressed up and dance the night away with the other Corpuscles. **And how much does it cost?** Depending on your tastes, £20–£30 probably. **How can you get home safely?** There are a number of initiatives in Oxford to ensure safety at night. The Nightbus is one of these; for just £1 it will get you home. There are a number of reliable and cheap taxi firms, but Corpus is so close to everything you can usually walk home. I've always felt safe in Oxford.

Money
Is it an expensive place to live? It's well known that Oxford is an expensive place to live. However, the student loan is usually enough to cover everything, and the college and

university both have fantastic provision for financial hardship. Corpus has really cheap food (about £2 a meal) so there's plenty of money for fun! I would say that, on average, a student spends £80–100 a week. **Average price of a pint?** £2 or so in the Beer Cellar (our student bar). **And the price of a takeaway?** £10. **What's the part-time work situation?** Part-time work is a no-no. You *can* theoretically work up to 6 hours pw but you have to get academic permission. The only people who work do so in the student bar or library. The terms are too short and the workload too intense to make it worth the extra stress of a job.

Summary

What's the best feature about the place? The community atmosphere. Corpus is small (about 200 undergrads) so it's full of friendly faces. **And the worst?** Paradoxically, the size of Corpus is also sometimes the worst feature as it can get claustrophobic, but this is easily cured with a few hours away from college. **And to sum it all up?** A challenging and fun atmosphere to spend some of the best years of your life in.

Past students: Erasmus; Sir Isaiah Berlin (philosopher and intellectual historian); Max Beloff (historian, first Principal of Buckingham University); J L Austin (philosopher); Sir Robert Ensor (historian and journalist); G W Most (classics); Vikram Seth (author); William Waldegrave, Brian Sedgemore, David and Ed Miliband (MPs). **More info?** Check out the JCR website (www.corpusjcr.org).

Oxford – Exeter

Exeter College, Oxford OX1 3DP
☎ Tel 01865 279648
🖷 Fax 01865 279630
✉ Email admissions@exeter.oxford.ac.uk
🖥 Website www.exeter.ox.ac.uk

Profile

Staff & students

Undergraduates: 219 men, 156 women. **Postgraduates:** 141 men, 90 women. **Teaching staff:** *Men:* 28 fellows 1 research fellows, 22 lecturers. *Women:* 11 fellows, 3 research fellow, 8 lecturers.

College & admissions

Founded: 1314; women undergraduates first admitted in 1979. First of ancient colleges to elect a woman as its Rector (Head) in 1993. **Admission:** Undergraduates admitted for all subjects apart from archaeology and anthropology, biological sciences, experimental psychology, geography, human sciences, metallurgy, oriental studies, PPP and theology.

Study opportunities

Library and information services: 40,000 books on open shelves; also similar number of antiquarian books and manuscripts. Library open 24 hours/day in term time. Separate IT service, access 24 hours/day. Ratio 1:17 workstations to students. 20 points with access to library and internet; various wireless internet points in college. IT support from up to 5 staff. All new students given introduction to IT facilities; regular surgery sessions by student computing assistants; IT skills courses run by university computing services. **Study abroad:** Language (and some law) students study abroad for a year.

Living

Eating arrangements: Self-service breakfast and lunch; served dinner available in early 17th-century hall daily throughout term; cost approx £10 per day (£1500 pa). Some self-catering facilities. **Gate/guest hours:** All members have late keys. No guests allowed between 2am and 8am unless they have been booked in overnight. **Other college facilities:** Bar, sports clubs, playing field, boathouse and multigym. College chapel choir (women and men), participation encouraged by generous choral scholarships. **Accommodation:** Nearly all undergraduates offered 3 or 4 years' residence in college-owned accommodation (usually all who do not want to live out). All 1st years, and some finalists, live on main college site; average rent £3150 pa. No first-degree students live at home.

Money

Scholarships: Scholarships and exhibitions awarded for meritorious work during undergraduate courses; organ and choral scholarships available. **Travel grants:** Generous provision from endowed funds for both academic and general travel. **Term-time work:** College only allows term-time employment in exceptional circumstances. **Hardship fund:** Well-endowed fund administered by the Rector and Tutors' Committee.

Student view
Edward Moores, JCR President (3rd year, MA Mathematics)

Living
What's it like as a place to live? Oxford is a fantastic place to live and study. The town is lively, well set out and packed on a weekend. The university is truly integrated with the town and, as the two live side by side, the atmosphere is a great one all year round. **How's the student accommodation?** The uni accommodation is good all round and not too expensive. The downside is that you have to move out at the end of each term. The private side is good as well, and all the students live in the same areas of town, making it a social and enjoyable place to live. **What's the student population like?** As diverse as can be! We get students from all over the country and the world, from all different backgrounds. Exeter College in particular is very welcoming and known for its friendly atmosphere. Many different groups of people come here, and you can't stereotype the students here. **How do students and locals get on?** Absolutely fine. A few issues now and again, but in general not a problem at all. Cowley especially has a great vibe to it.

Studying
What's it like as a place to study? Traditional courses, well taught, excellent facilities and world-class tutors – fantastic. **What are the teaching staff like?** A lot of them are top of the world in their fields, and thus it makes for an exciting learning environment. They take a keen interest in their students, and want to help us do well.

Socialising
What are student societies like? Hundreds of different societies that cater for all manner of interests and things that people may want to do here. World-famous Union where celebrities come and speak, and MPs from London frequently visit to put forward and defend their views on different motions. **What's a typical night out?** College Bar, then a club towards the west of town. **And how much does it cost?** £25. **How can you get home safely?** Well-lit streets with plenty of buses and a Union Safety bus available.

Money

Is it an expensive place to live? Student loan tends to go on accommodation, so you need an other source of income as well generally, but everyone gets by fairly easily. **Average price of a pint?** In college bars £1.80, in public bars £2.60. **And the price of a takeaway?** £3.50–£5. **What's the part-time work situation?** Lots of well-paid jobs around for holidays. Uni frowns upon work in term time, and nobody has time to work during term time anyway!

Summary

What's the best feature about the place? World-class teaching and tutorials, in a beautiful town with ancient buildings and a great atmosphere. A very highly rated degree at the end! **And the worst?** Lots of pressure to succeed and highly intense term times. **And to sum it all up?** A friendly and welcoming place, with so many opportunities to succeed, not only academically, but in any area of life that you would like to take part in.

Past students: Philip Pullman, Will Self, Martin Amis, J R R Tolkien (authors); Sir Roger Bannister (4-min mile); Tariq Ali (author, political campaigner); Richard Burton (actor); William Morris, Edward Burne-Jones (pre-Raphaelites); Sir Michael Levy, Robert Robinson (politicians); Alan Bennett (writer); Nevil Coghill (Chaucer expert); Ned Sherrin, Russell Harty (broadcasters); Sir Charles Lyall (orientalist); J A Froude (historian); Imogen Stubbs (actress); Reeta Chakrabarti (political correspondent).

More info? Contact JCR President on 01865 279614.

Oxford – Harris Manchester

⌨ Harris Manchester College, Oxford OX1 3TD
☎ Tel 01865 271006
✉ Email admissions@hmc.ox.ac.uk
💻 Website www.hmc.ox.ac.uk

Profile

Staff & students

Undergraduates: 49 men, 42 women. **Postgraduates:** 28 men, 27 women. **Teaching staff:** *Men:* 10 fellows, 5 lecturers. *Women:* 5 fellows, 12 lecturers.

College & admissions

Founded: 1786, in Manchester; moved to in Oxford 1889. Women undergraduates first admitted in 1907. Became part of the university in 1990 as college for mature students. Changed name in 1996 (from Manchester College). **Admission:** Mature students (21 and over) only. Undergraduates not admitted for most science courses. **Largest field of study:** Law; English; philosophy, politics and economics (PPE).

Study opportunities

Library and information services: 3 libraries: Tate (general); Carpenter (world religions); Old (books pre-1800); 40,000 volumes, 30 periodicals, 40 study places. Separate college IT service. Ratio 1:15 workstations to students. 2 computers with access to library, 6 to the internet. IT facilities open 24 hours/day; IT support from 1 full-time staff.

Living

Eating arrangements: Breakfast, lunch and dinner in college dining hall each weekday; breakfast/brunch at weekends. 17 meals a week included in college bills. **Other college facilities:** JCR bar. **Accommodation:** All 1st years who wish to live in college accommodation (90% of all students); no married accommodation available. 70 places available: full-board at £1433 per term (accommodation, heating and lighting, 17 meals a week). Students may live in privately owned accommodation.

Money

Term-time work: College allows term-time work, limit of 10 hours pw (10–15% believed to work). Some work available in college in kitchen, library, cleaning, occasional office work; night portering out of term time. **Financial help:** £7k own funds available.

Student view

One of Oxford's smallest undergraduate colleges with a distinguished history dating back to the Warrington academy of 1786. It has occupied its present buildings since 1893, with new 1980s accommodation added. It is Oxford's only college for mature students; students are from a wide range of educational, professional and national backgrounds. Very friendly but with a commitment to high academic standards and tutors who understand the special skills and needs of mature students. In the heart of the city, near the famed Bodleian Library and almost as famed King's Arms; close to many faculty libraries (essential) and to other colleges, concert halls and nightclubs. College accommodation is available for all first and final-year students, as well as most other undergraduates, in 16th-century houses or 2 neo-classical buildings. All rooms have phone and high-speed internet connection; all buildings have kitchens. Also a dedicated TV room with video/DVD player and JCR with free tea, coffee, newspapers and (more amazingly) a free pool table. By evening it becomes the friendliest and one of the cheapest JCR bars in Oxford. The historic chapel (windows by William Morris and Burne-Jones) remains Oxford's centre for Unitarian worship. Tate library is well-stocked (a good undergraduate library with a good study environment, including power and internet points for laptops); the Carpenter library is a distinguished archive. College has all the traditions of Oxford in a friendly and informal setting. The only requirements are the potential for high academic achievement and the energy for socialising as well. If you are over 21 and think you have what it takes to live and learn amongst the dreaming spires, then get in touch. It could change your life. For the better.

Student footnotes

Housing: Most undergraduates in college. **Eats:** College food excellent (and students living in are committed to a number of college meals). Hassan's mobile van in Broad Street cheap. **Drink:** Student-run JCR bar with extensions and competitive prices (Tetley's/Carlsberg); also cheap in Oxford Union bar. Close to King's Arms and Turf Tavern. **Nightlife:** JCR parties, BBQs, bands, discos, pubs, theatre and concert trips, frequent expeditions to nearby clubs. In college: choir, strong music tradition, wine society; also literary, law and history societies. **Locals:** Very friendly. **Sports:** Croquet lawn, pool table, gym, boat club. Men's and women's pool teams, college punt, croquet team. **Financial help:** University access funds. **Jobs:** JCR bar in term; cleaning, portering and waiting in holidays. **Best features:** Small, friendly, intimate and conveniently placed. **And worst:** Wet weather; JCR TV sometimes disappears. **Past students:** Joseph Priestley (discovered oxygen), John Dalton (chemist who split the atom), William Gaskell (playwright), James Martineau (philosopher), Josiah Wedgwood (of Wedgewood pottery), Sir Henry Tate (Tate and Lyle and Tate Gallery). **More info?** Contact JCR President (tel 01865 270999).

Oxford – Hertford

Hertford College, Oxford OX1 3BW
☎ Tel 01865 279400
✉ Email admissions@hertford.ox.ac.uk
💻 Website www.hertford.ox.ac.uk

Profile

Staff & students
Undergraduates: 165 men, 207 women. **Postgraduates:** 127 men, 93 women. **Teaching staff:** *Men:* 36 fellows, 6 research fellows, 23 lecturers. *Women:* 11 fellows, 13 lecturers.

College & admissions
Founded: 1284; women undergraduates first admitted in 1974. **Admission:** Places on the basis of exam and interview in December; entry highly competitive. **Academic features:** English, law, geography, engineering, Japanese and all mainstream subjects.

Study opportunities
Library and information services: Undergraduate and antiquarian libraries. College IT and library services converged. All student rooms have full internet connection. IT facilities open 24 hours/day; support from full-time IT officer and part-time student officers. **Study abroad:** Exchange programme for linguists.

Living
Eating arrangements: Swipe-card system, charged at end of term. **Other college facilities:** Chapel, JCR complex, lecture theatre, sports ground (for rugby, football, hockey, cricket), boathouse, punts, orchestra, choir, bar, rowing, squash and tennis courts, music practice room, multigym.
Accommodation: All undergraduates housed. 170 places in college, 297 in college houses. Standard rent £2391 pa (term time only), including bedding and heating. Fixed college facilities charge £252 for those living in college.

Money
Term-time work: College does not normally allow term-time work for undergraduates.

Student view

It's extremely central, in arguably the most beautiful area of Oxford. 3 interlinked quads, with architecture ranging from picturesque, ivy-clad sandstone to more modern buildings. 2 front quads are linked by the famous Bridge of Sighs – a definite tourist favourite! Directly opposite the Bodleian Library and within 10 mins' walk of most faculties, students enjoy a convenient lifestyle – made even more so by the fine dining hall on site. College offers accommodation to all students, for all years of their course. Rooms vary in size but all have ethernet access and internal phones. There are also 3 communal computer rooms and a well-stocked library (open 24 hours/day). College also has a gym, sports ground and pavilion with squash courts, boathouse, music rooms, common room with widescreen Sky

TV, coffee room and chill-out room. Most important is the fantastic student-run bar (with dangerously inexpensive cocktails), set in a sprawling complex of cellars. Hertford's students are an eclectic bunch, hailing from all over the UK and, indeed, the world. Known across the university as friendly and sociable, the atmosphere in college is one of relaxed study, with more than a smidgeon of play. Sports teams thrive, generally through mass participation rather than any great degree of skill. Music (accomplished chapel choir) and drama both prevalent, and students are involved in student journalism, charity work and many other university societies. Despite all this, recent academic records place it in the top 5 colleges – a testament to students' careful juggling of commitments and high quality of teaching in the tutorial-based system.

Student footnotes

Housing: All years guaranteed accommodation (all 1st years, most final years on site). **Eats:** Decent cheap food on site, twice weekly formal hall. Massive selection of pubs, cafés, restaurants around. **Drink:** Cheap, student-run college bar (beer £1.70 a pint); Turf Tavern, King's Arms 30 seconds away. **Nightlife:** Student nights in variety of clubs: Park End, the Bridge, Po Na Na and many others. Live comedy, music and theatre good. **Locals:** Variable but largely fine. **Sports:** College sports ground 1½ miles from college. Squash courts, grass tennis courts, gym (on site) and boathouse. **Travel:** Support for some course-compulsory travel. **Financial help:** University access funds. Keasbey and Alumni grants for Hertford students. **Jobs:** Work in the bar available (minimum wage); otherwise not allowed in term time (not really enough time). **Best features:** Diversity of people; friendly atmosphere. **Past students:** Evelyn Waugh, John Donne, Jonathan Swift, Gavin Maxwell (writers); Thomas Hobbes (philosopher); Natasha Kaplinsky (newsreader); Jaqui Smith (Home Secretary).

Oxford – Jesus

Jesus College, Oxford OX1 3DW
Tel 01865 279721
Email admissions.officer@jesus.ox.ac.uk
Website www.jesus.ox.ac.uk

Profile

Staff & students

Undergraduates: 187 men, 152 women. **Postgraduates:** 107 men, 72 women. **Teaching staff:** *Men:* 21 fellows, 17 research fellows, 16 lecturers. *Women:* 9 fellows, 5 research fellows, 7 lecturers.

College & admissions

Founded: 1571; women undergraduates first admitted in 1974. **Admission:** Undergraduates not admitted to the following subjects in Single or Joint Honours: ancient history, anthropology, archaeology, biochemistry, computer science, earth sciences, fine art, history of art, materials, oriental studies. No undergraduates admitted to Single Honours courses in physiological sciences or theology (though they may be studied in combination), or for Joint Honours physics and philosophy course.

Study opportunities

Library and information services: Modern lending and study library and well-equipped computer suite, both open 24 hours/day. Ethernet connection points in all student rooms. IT support from 3 full-time staff. **Study abroad:** Exchange links with Trier, Germany.

Living

Eating arrangements: Continental/cooked breakfast, cafeteria lunch and dinner, and set dinner in hall. Self-catering facilities in college-owned flats. **Gate/guest hours:** 8am to midnight; 24-hour key access for students. **Other college facilities:** Library, JCR, bar, music room, tennis courts, sports pitches, boathouse. **Accommodation:** All undergraduates guaranteed college accommodation for their whole course, on main college site or in college-owned flats at annex sites; all 1st-year rooms in college. Average charge: £3100 pa in college (term time only, including heat and light); £3400 pa in college-owned flats (40-week lease, utility bills not included).

Money

Term-time work: Students may work for a limited number of hours and with permission of tutor and senior tutor. **Scholarships:** Numerous scholarships, grants and bursaries. **Travel grants:** A number for travel to various parts of the world; Dodd Benefaction for vacation travel abroad.

Student view

It's great! It occupies one of the most convenient locations of all the Oxford colleges. Located on Turl Street, with the Bodleian Library, Radcliffe Camera, 2 cinemas, Cornmarket, High Street and the Oxford Union all within 2 mins' walk. Small geographical size hides a large community with a genuinely open atmosphere; academic successes matched by sporting prowess, major involvement in all things 'arty', and a full and lively social scene. If Jesubites are sometimes accused of being slightly insular, then that's because they are truly happy with their lot. College has top-class accommodation, offered to all years at affordable rent. Food is OK, very cheap, and works on a buffet system so you don't have to sign up for a load of meals at the start of each year. Resources for sporting, musical and artistic activities are also top-notch, and funds exist to help in all sorts of exciting (not only academic) pursuits. Spanking new JCR is the centre of social activity for undergraduates – with free pool table, wide-screen TV, DVD, satellite and video and an LCD projector with pull-down giant screen. Famous for its political apathy; JCR meetings are well attended and offer students the opportunity to have their say on the issues that affect them. College bar for socialising, drink at prices cheaper than most in town and JCR's weekly Friday night bops (and other JCR-organised events). Close-knit community makes socialising easy and fun! Everybody knows everyone so there is always a friend available to go out on the town or just stay in and watch a movie with. A college for anyone looking for a friendly, relaxed home where they can do well academically but have a life balanced by many other opportunities. Don't worry, not all students are Welsh! Open days are run several times a year and visits can often be arranged at other times.

Student footnotes

Housing: Excellent. All students offered accommodation for their entire course. **Eats:** OK, pretty cheap and no need to sign up in advance. **Drink:** College bar is fun and friendly. **Nightlife:** Lively, weekly, free college bops; frequent trips and social events. **Sports:** All free: table tennis, tennis, netball, basketball, hockey, cricket, rugby, football, pool, rounders, squash and rowing. Free gym. **Financial help:** Hardship funds available to all who need them. Academic scholarships offered. **Travel:** Everybody cycles. College also offers grants for students to travel overseas during vacations. **Jobs:** Work in college bar or during admissions period. **Best features:** Fun and friendly. Close-knit community. **And worst:** Considered insular by outsiders. **Past students:** Sian Lloyd, Magnus Magnusson (presenters); Ffion Hague (author); Harold Wilson (former Prime Minister); Lawrence of Arabia. **More info?** Visit http://jcr.jesus.ox.ac.uk.

Oxford – Keble

- Keble College, Oxford OX1 3PG
- ☎ Tel 01865 272727
- Fax 01865 272769
- ✉ Email admissions@keble.ox.ac.uk
- 💻 Website www.keble.ox.ac.uk

Profile

Staff & students
Undergraduates: 236 men, 177 women. **Postgraduates:** 143 men, 94 women. **Teaching staff:** *Men:* 40 fellows, 23 lecturers. *Women:* 12 fellows, 9 lecturers.

College & admissions
Founded: 1870; women undergraduates first admitted in 1979. **Admission:** Conditional offer or on basis of grades achieved plus interview. International and other alternative qualifications welcomed. Undergraduates not usually admitted for biochemistry; classics; earth sciences; EEM; European and Middle Eastern languages; experimental psychology; fine art; human sciences; MEM; metallurgy and science of materials; oriental studies; classics and oriental studies (joint); PPP; joint school of physics and philosophy.

Study opportunities
Library and information services: Over 45,000 books, 24-hour opening; some textbooks available on lease basis. College IT and library services largely converged. Ratio 1:20 workstations to students; approx 30 computers with access to library and internet. Most students have their own computers; ethernet points in all college rooms. Access to IT facilities 24 hours/day; IT support from 2 full-time staff. **Study abroad:** Exchange links arranged in some faculties.

Living
Eating arrangements: Keble hall (longest in Oxford) accommodates everyone in one sitting. Self-service breakfast, lunch and Sunday brunch; waitered service at dinner. Set lunch costs £1.89, dinner £3.77 for 3 courses. **Gate/guest hours:** Wicket gate keys available for all students. **Other college facilities:** JCR, bar, music room (grand piano and harpsichord), sports ground, boathouse, laundry, squash courts, gym, computer rooms. **Accommodation:** 80% of undergraduates in college accommodation (all 1st and 2nd years, most finalists) many rooms ensuite; average rent £1k per term (range £900–£1100 per term). Small proportion of students choose to live in privately owned accommodation. No first-degree students live at home.

Money
Scholarships: Awards given for meritorious work during undergraduate course. Organ and choral awards. **Travel grants:** A number of study and travel grants are provided by Keble Association. Academic prizes and competitive bursaries (£100–£1500) for worthwhile vacation projects involving travel. **Term-time work:** College does not allow term-time work. **Financial help:** Own funds available to help those hit by unexpected hardship.

Student view

It's the largest, most diverse and friendly college in the university. All 1st years get college accommodation, as do most other students who choose it. The rooms are excellent, most with ensuite facilities but few kitchens. Hall food is good; 3 meals a day are available, including substantial dinner. JCR has extensive facilities and organises regular and varied social events, from paintball to blind date. Keble has a strong sporting tradition but most clubs cater for all abilities. Superb college choir and drama flourishes (own theatre). The common theme for all Keble activities is enthusiasm. Whilst not the most political of colleges, it has a respected voice at university level (especially in journalism) and an active JCR committee. Most courses are offered, all world-class standard. If you work hard and play hard, then Keble is the right college for you.

Student footnotes

Housing: 2–3 years in college accommodation; college houses in 1 year. **Eats:** Food cheap in college: waiter-service dinner in hall for £3+. Locally, St Giles (greasy spoon), GandD's ice cream, Hussein's kebab van, Brown's (rich relations' treat). **Drink:** Large medium-priced, busy college bar, wide choice of beers. Parkend Club has cheap student nights. **Nightlife:** Cheap, cheesy, weekday Oxford student scene, different club each night. Developing alternative music scene, with new clubs opening for all tastes. London accessible by cheap bus (24 hours). University drama productions; excellent independent cinema. **Sports:** Loads at all standards; especially strong in rugby (male and female teams) and rowing. **Travel:** College and industrial travel scholarships. Good road and rail connections; close to London. **Hardship fund:** Generous university and college schemes for hard-up students. **Jobs:** Well-paid conference work; term-time jobs in library and bar. **Best features:** Friendly, large, challenging and diverse. **Past students:** Sir Peter Pears (singer), Rev. Chad Varah (founder of Samaritans), Michael Croft (National Youth Theatre), Imran Khan (cricketer and MP in Pakistan), Andreas Whittam Smith (founder of the *Independent*). **More info?** Enquiries to JCR President (tel 01865 272754) or visit the website (http://jcr.keble.ox.ac.uk).

Oxford – Lady Margaret Hall

- Lady Margaret Hall, Oxford OX2 6QA
- Tel 01865 274300
- Email admissions@lmh.ox.ac.uk
- Website www.lmh.ox.ac.uk

Profile

Staff & students

Undergraduates: 210 men, 208 women. **Postgraduates:** 80 men, 111 women. **Teaching staff:** *Men:* 17 fellows, 9 lecturers, 5 professors and supernumerary fellows. *Women:* 14 fellows, 3 lecturers.

College & admissions

Founded: 1878; men undergraduates first admitted in 1979. **Admission:** Interviews and written tests in some subjects (with a view to a conditional offer for pre-A-level candidates). Undergraduates not admitted for geography, geology, human sciences, material sciences or for oriental studies other than Hebrew.

Study opportunities

Library and information services: Open 24 hours; over 50,000 books on open shelves; specialist law library; science reading room. **IT facilities:** Internet connection in each student room, online access and PCs in the library, graduate computer room.

Living

Eating arrangements: Meals available in hall Sunday night to Friday night; cost £161 per term. JCR kitchen/pantries on all floors. **Gate/guest hours:** Gate closed at 7pm; all members of college issued with keys. Guest hours, 9am to midnight (2am at weekends). **Other college facilities:** Bar, several upright and 3 grand pianos, tennis courts, croquet lawn, boathouse, punthouse. Shared facilities for other sports. **Accommodation:** All 1st-year students able to live in college (85% of all undergraduates); single study bedrooms, many ensuite. Standard accommodation charge of £3411 pa (term time only).

Money

Scholarships: Awarded to undergraduates in residence on academic merit; organ and choral scholarships; various college prizes. Other grants in connection with academic work. **Travel grants:** Maude Royden exhibition for long-vacation travel. **Financial help:** College grants for unexpected hardship during course in addition to university bursaries.

Student view

Notably relaxed college with male/female ratio of 1:1. Beautiful, expansive gardens rolling down to the river where the college has its own punt house. Almost all students live in for 3 years; rooms are varied in shape and size but good basic standard with plenty of kitchens (legacy from its days as a women's college) and many ensuite rooms. Tolerant atmosphere with good state/private school balance, an anti-discrimination statute and amiable tutor-student relations. Its distance (10 mins' walk) from the town centre isn't a problem to socialising and working there; instead, LMH benefits from a strong college spirit, spacious feel and good on-site facilities. Its absence from the tourist trail in the summer is a virtue never to be underestimated.

Student footnotes

Housing: Very good, many rooms recently refurbished. **Drink:** Cheap (£1.70 a pint). **Eats:** Good college food, including vegetarian options; reasonably priced (meal from £2). Several popular cheap kebab vans in town; meal for £2–£3 in King's Arms. **Nightlife:** Frequent parties in college; many cheap JCR events in refurbished venue (JCR has own pa and drum kit). Always plethora of interesting student plays in Oxford, discounted student tickets. **Sports:** Good but relaxed. Rowing very strong in recent years. Squash and tennis courts and 5-a-side football pitch on site. Small fitness room with ergos and multigym on site (£10 pa); good facilities. **Travel:** Cheap travel by bike. Holiday fund (in memory of a former undergraduate) for students who have recently been unable to afford a good holiday. **Financial help:** Principal's fund and JCR living-out fund. All LMH students eligible for a limited loan (approx £150) from SCR. Good college system of advertising external hardship funds. **Jobs:** 7% work during term time; college jobs pool helps those who really need to. Most work in vacation; some work in college (helping with conferences and in library). **Best features:** Very, very friendly; own punts; loads of space; tolerant, sociable and academic atmosphere. **And worst:** Long walk home after nights out (particularly in winter). **Good news:** Punt refurbishments under way. **Past students:** Benazir Bhutto (former President of Pakistan), Lady Antonia Fraser (historian and author), Diana Quick (actress), Gertrude Bell (traveller and archaeologist), Dame Veronica Wedgwood (historian), Elizabeth Longford (historian and biographer), Eglantine Jebb (Save the Children), Baroness Warnock (philosopher), Matthew Taylor MP, Barbara Mills (first women direct of DPP), Caryl Churchill (playwright), Nigella Lawson (cookery writer), Ann Widdecombe MP, James Allen (presenter), Sam West (actor). **More info?** Enquiries to JCR President c/o the college.

Oxford – Lincoln

Lincoln College, Oxford OX1 3DR
☎ Tel 01865 279836
✉ Email admissions@lincoln.ox.ac.uk
🖥 Website www.linc.ox.ac.uk

Profile

Staff & students
Undergraduates: 146 men, 139 women. **Postgraduates:** 159 men, 131 women. **Teaching staff:** *Men:* 23 fellows, 8 research fellows, 1 praelectors, 15 lecturers. *Women:* 7 fellows, 2 research fellows, 1 praelector, 10 lecturers.

College & admissions
Founded: 1427. **Admission:** No undergraduates admitted for archaeology and anthropology, biology, classics, computer science, economics and management, EEM (engineering, economics and management), experimental psychology, fine art, geography, geology/earth sciences, history of art, human sciences, maths and computer science, materials science, oriental studies, PPP, theology.

Study opportunities
Library and information services: Aims to provide all essential texts for undergraduate disciplines and most texts for graduate taught courses. College IT and library services converged. Ratio 1:30 workstations to students. 16 computers with access to library and internet, open 24 hours/day; full-time computing officer plus student officers. Student rooms have ethernet access to university network and internet.

Living
Eating arrangements: Meals in hall; also snacks in bar, teas in JCR/MCR. **Gate/guest hours:** Gate closes 7–8pm during term, college members have 24-hour swipe card access. **Other college facilities:** Playing field; squash court; multigym; music practice rooms; bar; games room. Computer rooms open to all members. **Accommodation:** All undergraduates housed who require it; almost all students in college. Charges around £118 pw, term time only. No first-degree students live at home.

Money
Scholarships: College and Old Members' Trust awards for exceptional students. Book grants awarded annually, available to all students. Organ and choral scholarships. **Travel grants:** Up to £250 for undergraduates. **Financial help:** Grants and interest-free loans for students in financial difficulties.

Student view

Founded in 1427, its renowned medieval beauty is untarnished by grotty annexes arising from the dreams of 1960s planners. College is small and comfortable, with a cheeky stone imp as its mascot. Though quite traditional, it is also quite forward looking – high-speed internet access in every room, recently modernised kitchens (claiming to serve the best food in the university) and an excellent central location. Small, pretty college with a feeling of warmth and intimacy; relatively low number of undergraduates means everyone knows everyone. Students are a diverse bunch of individuals who participate in a multitude of activities on university, college and personal levels. Good informal support (especially older students keen to help younger counterparts), strengthened by an excellent welfare network. Healthy college sporting life; teams are enthusiastic and often successful. Students (both sexes) involved in a wide range, from the rugby, cricket, rowing, netball and football to trampolining, kayak polo and ultimate frisbee; emphasis on participation over ability. Comprehensive and well-maintained facilities: main fields a 10-min bike ride away; boat club, squash court and well-equipped multigym. Darts board, pool table and table football in college. Non-sporting clubs and societies range from incredibly successful choir to running children's holiday camps; and, of course, socialising remains a common priority. Lincoln is a strong community, perfectly suited to the trials and excitement of an Oxford degree. Not the largest or most famous college but is everything you could want – beautiful, central surroundings; a friendly, active JCR; and really good food!

Student footnotes

Housing: College accommodation for all; cheap for Oxford, with rooms from excellent (including self-catering houses) to fairly reasonable. **Eats:** College food excellent and popular; lunchtime snacks in college bar. Usual range of snack bars, fast-food in city centre; meal for £10-ish at Ask Tandoori Restaurant. **Drink:** College bar subsidised, well run with good selection; pint £1.80+. **Nightlife:** Lively for a small college: bops, videos, cabarets, boat parties, themed evenings, black tie meals, etc. Student clubs: Filth, the Bridge. **Locals:** Can be unfriendly, but only if provoked. **Sports:** Excellent multigym; good pavilion and playing fields. Increasingly successful sporting college, and it's all free, including boat club. **Travel:** Good – travel grants easily available for holidays of some intellectual value. **Financial help:** Excellent provision. Generous help given. **Jobs:** Some work (well paid) available in college in term time and vacation. **Best features:** Comfort; community. **And worst:** Claustrophobia. **Past students:** Sir Peter Parker (British Rail), John Le Carré (author), Edward Thomas (poet and essayist), John Wesley (founder of Methodists), Baron von Richthofen (the Red Baron), Dr Seuss (author). **More info?** Contact jcr.president@lincoln.ox.ac.uk.

Oxford – Magdalen

Magdalen College, Oxford OX1 4AU
Tel 01865 276063
Email admissions@magd.ox.ac.uk
Website www.magd.ox.ac.uk

Profile

Staff & students

Undergraduates: 232 men, 163 women. **Postgraduates:** 143 men, 99 women. **Teaching staff:** *Men:* 36 fellows, 4 research fellows, 23 lecturers, 10 professors. *Women:* 6 fellows, 5 research fellows, 12 lecturers.

College & admissions

Founded: 1458; women undergraduates first admitted in 1979. **Admission:** Entry by interview (pre- or post-A-level). Undergraduates not admitted to geography, geology or metallurgy, economics and management, earth sciences, history of art, history and economics, materials science, oriental studies or theology.

Study opportunities

Library and information services: Particularly strong in history, classics, PPE, law and sciences; Old Library with fine collection of Renaissance and 18th-century volumes. Separate college IT service: numerous computers accessible to library and internet (ethernet points in student accommodation). Ratio 1:30 workstations to students, 4 rooms with printers and scanners; many students bring their own computer. IT facilities open 24 hours/day; full-time computer officer.

Living

Eating arrangements: Community kitchens for self-catering or pay-as-you-dine in hall; cost of eating in college approx £7–£9 a day. **Gate/guest hours:** Gate keys issued to students. **Other college facilities:** JCR shop, wine cellar and bar; 11 tennis courts (8 grass, 3 hard), 3 squash courts, 17 college punts, sports ground in beautiful riverside setting, with probably best cricket square in Oxford. Free membership of JCR computing scheme. Choral foundation with very strong musical tradition. **Accommodation:** All undergraduates can be in college accommodation for duration of course (390 live in); rent approx £1065 per term, including heating, lighting, ethernet connection and cleaning (private accommodation more expensive).

Money

Scholarships: Scholarships and prizes awarded each year. Organ and choral awards. **Travel grants:** Funds for a number of purposes. **Term-time work:** Work outside college in term time not normally permitted. Holiday work available in bar, visitors' scheme and library; college helps find work with references and contacts. **Financial help:** Funds available according to need (all applicants' needs met recently).

Student view

Strikingly beautiful and architecturally coherent buildings – the Great Tower is one of Oxford's most famous landmarks. Extensive grounds (riverside walk, Deer Parks, Fellows' Garden) give a sense of space and calm rare in a comparatively congested city. Accommodation (mostly 'within walls') is some of Oxford's best but at average cost. All rooms have ethernet, phone connections, mini-fridges and washbasins; some are ensuite. 2 computer rooms offer printers, scanner, CD writer, etc. Sports facilities are outstanding – squash courts; gym; pitches for hockey, football, rugby, cricket with new changing and shower block, hard and grass tennis courts and very good rowing. Several performance venues for music and drama, including the new auditorium. College choir has an international reputation and sings daily for services in the beautiful on-site chapel. Students thrive in the atmosphere of freedom and independence – no image or routine is imposed and you can be who you want to be. Academically, it's quite hot but without huge pressure from tutors. Vast 24-hour-access library with up-to-date stock – new books are often bought immediately upon request – plus a special law library. The dons listen carefully to the student-run tutorial feedback system. Magdalen's bar is for all college members and helps to perpetuate the exceptional levels of integration between all parts of college – tutors, students and staff. JCR Committee is large, the most active in Oxford, and has taken the initiative in several student/tutor projects, including the new welfare-based personal tutor scheme. JCR funds used to improve facilities and services, which range from the bacon-dom of Sundays' JCR brunch to spanking new TVs and DVD players, from free pool table for the 2 common rooms to the JCR collection of art for hire. Societies in college range from film to discussion and debate to poetry. Drama and music have long-standing and impressive reputations.

Student footnotes

Housing: College accommodation guaranteed for all undergrads; quality ranges from palatial 18th-century sets (bedroom and sitting room) to the infamous concrete 1960s relic, the Waynflete. Rooms chosen by ballot, 3rd years have first pick. Some flats and houses, some married/family accommodation. **Eats:** Cheap in hall (approx £2.50+ for evening meal); good range, quality medium. Formal hall (sit down and be served) twice a week for the traditionalists. Bar serves potatoes, pasties, salads, soup, sandwiches, etc. Kitchen facilities vary from the supreme to the minimalist. JCR runs shops for basic provisions. **Drinks:** Bar not exceptionally cheap (£1.90 per pint lager, £1.70 spirits + mixer, £1.40 wine). JCR wineshop opens every term-time evening for students to buy booze on credit. **Nightlife:** JCR has its own ents equipment for fortnightly bops, plus several themed events per term. Oxford excellent for cinema, theatre, music, restaurants. Clubs cheesy rather than cool. **Sports:** Excellent facilities. Sport is for all levels: football excels, large boat club. **Travel:** Grants available for all undergrads, size depends on relevance to course, but requirements are fairly flexible. **Financial help:** Some college cash. No student should be unable to complete their course from lack of funds (some students entirely subsidised). Everyone qualifies for vac grants to help with cost of staying up in holidays to study. **Jobs:** Work available in college bar and JCR wineshop (other term-time work not really an option). Paid work (and free college accommodation) on offer in vacations. **Best features:** Friendly, very liberal atmosphere with space to develop. **And worst:** Surface impressions can be very misleading – the awe-inspiring surroundings should deter no one from applying. **Past students:** Oscar Wilde (author and playwright); C S Lewis (author); Sir John Betjeman (poet); A J P Taylor (historian); Lord Denning (Master of the Rolls); Kenneth Baker, John Redwood (politicians); Dudley Moore (comedian and actor); Charles Sherrington (physiologist); Andrew Lloyd Webber (composer); Erwin Schroedinger (physicist); William Hague MP. **More info?** Contact JCR President (tel 01865 276011, email president@magdjcr.co.uk) or check out the website (www.magdjcr.co.uk).

Oxford – Mansfield

- Mansfield College, Oxford OX1 3TF
- ☎ Tel 01865 270999
- Fax 01865 282910
- ✉ Email admissions@mansfield.ox.ac.uk
- Website www.mansfield.ox.ac.uk

Profile

Staff & students

Undergraduates: 143 men, 74 women. **Postgraduates:** 47 men, 36 women. **Teaching staff:** *Men:* 25 fellows, 8 lecturers. *Women:* 12 fellows, 5 lecturers.

College & admissions

Founded: 1886; undergraduates first admitted in 1955. **Admission:** Submitted work, written test where appropriate and interview (pre- or post-A-level candidates). Undergraduates are accepted for engineering science (including EEM), English, geography, history (including history and English, history and politics), human sciences, law (including law with law studies in Europe), materials science (including MEM), mathematics (including maths and statistics, maths and philosophy), oriental studies (Arabic, Hebrew and Jewish studies only), physics, PPE, theology (including philosophy and theology).

Study opportunities

Library and information services: 1st floor of main building is a study suite, with main, law and theology libraries and computer room; open to all students 24 hours/day. 14 Citrix Thin Clients (10 in computer room, 4 in library) plus printers, 30 ethernet points and wi-fi in libraries for student laptops; ethernet points in all student rooms on site and in annexe. 6 ethernet points plus wi-fi in JCR.

Living

Eating arrangements: All meals available in hall Monday–Saturday and evening meal on Sundays; cost from £12 per day. Cooking facilities in all college houses and on some staircases. **Gate/guest hours:** Unrestricted gate hours; some guest restrictions. **Other college facilities:** Shares Merton sports grounds and Hertford boathouse. Croquet, table tennis, bar. **Accommodation:** All 1st years and most finalists in college accommodation. 177 places available (61 ensuite), from £111.50 pw on site (+ bills), or £391.50 per month for 9-month tenancy off site (including utilities). All rooms self-catering, or meals in college hall. 2nd-year students live in privately owned accommodation for 1 year, approx £100 pw for self-catering.

Money

Scholarships: Scholarships and exhibitions awarded at any stage of an undergrad's course in recognition of high academic standards. Also a number of college prizes. **Travel grants:** 2 travel scholarships. **Financial help:** £3k own funds, average award £150. Limited number of maintenance awards for students with financial difficulties available.

Student view
James Naish, JCR President (3rd year, BA History)

Living
What's it like as a place to live? Mansfield prides itself on being one of the most open colleges in Oxford. This is reflected in the diverse student population and the large open quad that dominates the college. The atmosphere is welcoming and friendly and the food is amongst the best at the university. **How's the student accommodation?** Student accommodation at Mansfield is good value for money. The 60 rooms in E Block and the Garden Building have ensuite facilities but are smaller than the rooms in Blocks A, B, C and D, which were designed as double rooms but are occupied by only 1 person. All rooms have internet access, plenty of storage space and good views of the college. Current 2nd years are required to live off site but planning permission for a multi-million pound on-site development has been applied for. It is hoped that this will be developed within the next 3 years. **What's the student population like?** The student population at Mansfield is extremely diverse. Mansfield spearheads the FE Access Initiative and about 20% of its students come from overseas. Mansfield also has the highest state-sector entry of any college in the university. This makes for a unique student experience. Because Mansfield is one of the smallest colleges, there is a strong sense of community that establishes itself in a variety of academic and non-academic support groups – the 1887 Society attracts university-wide membership and is regularly spoken to by leading geographical scholars. **How do students and locals get on?** Town/gown conflicts are not what they used to be – in the early 13th century, a group of Oxford scholars left the town after a dispute with the locals and established Cambridge University. These

differences are long gone and students generally agree that the city is a relaxed place to study. Mansfield is located less than a 10-min walk from the High Street and enjoys a superb location, with the University Science Area less than 2 mins away.

Studying

What's it like as a place to study? Students at Oxford are taught using a tutorial system, which sees one-to-one or two-to-one teaching. This is excellent – students are able to discuss their essays with world-famous experts and exchange ideas with leading international scholars. The student:staff ratio is excellent and means that Oxford students have more course options than most. Study in the 2nd, 3rd and 4th years is extremely flexible. Mansfield students get excellent academic support – the 3 college libraries are well-stocked and the wooden-panelled Main Library is amongst one of the most attractive in the university. **What are the teaching staff like?** All Oxford colleges attract excellent scholars and Mansfield is no exception. The Reverend Dr John Muddiman is a leading New Testament scholar, and Professor Michael Freeden is the director of the Centre for Political Ideologies and founding editor of the *Journal of Political Ideologies*. Current Visiting Professor Jocelyn Bell Burnell is famous for first discovering radio pulsars, and Professor Ros Ballaster is a celebrated Jane Austen scholar. Honorary fellows of the college include the 39th president of the USA, Jimmy Carter.

Socialising

What are student societies like? Oxford has hundreds of student societies so there is something for everybody. At Mansfield there are a number of active academic societies including the 1887 Geography Society, the PPE Society and the Law Society. Non-academic-wise, rowing leads the way – the Mansfield Women's 1st VIII is a back-to-back blade-winning crew that hasn't been bumped for more than 2 years. The Mansfield/Merton Football Club is equally successful – in 2008 both the 1st XI and 2nd XI were promoted. Mansfield also has a combined rugby team with Merton. This team is forever improving and contains University Blues sportsmen. The Mansfield/Merton cricket team won the Premier Division title in 2007–08. The college is also home to Blues badminton players, a darts team, a pool team, Blues cyclists, a strong netball team, Blues triathletes . . . you name it, we have it. Mansfield is also home to an active film society and CU group. Mansfield students are also prominent in journalist circles where the 2 student papers – the *Oxford Student* and *Cherwell* – vie for top spot. One of the editors of the *Ox Stu* in Michaelmas Term 2008 was from Mansfield. **What's a typical night out?** The Mansfield Entz programme is amongst the best at the university. Each term there are 2 college 'bops' (themed fancy dress parties), 2 champagne and chocolate evenings, open mic and acoustic evenings, trips to Oxford Brookes' Pleasuredome and subsidised cinema/gig-going/sports-watching trips. Once a year, the JCR organises a club trip to London. Oxford is expensive but the JCR subsidises all its events so students don't have to pay a fortune. If a quiet trip to the pub is more your thing, Mansfield is excellently located for the Turf Tavern (Inspector Morse's local) and the King's Arms, which are both extremely popular with students.

Money

Is it an expensive place to live? Oxford can be an expensive place to live but that shouldn't put you off – the Oxford Opportunity Bursary and Mansfield College Hardship Funds ensure that all students get by without serious financial difficulties. Mansfield accommodation and food is reasonably priced and of good quality. **Average price of a pint?** £1.60 in the college bar. Between £2.50–£3.50 elsewhere. **And the price of a takeaway?** Varies greatly but can always be done for less than a £10. **What's the part-time work situation?** Mansfield students, and Oxford students generally, do not take jobs – we're only at university for 9 weeks at any one time and most of that time is devoted to study. It is generally accepted that part-time jobs should be taken during vacations.

Summary

What's the best feature about the place? Oxford – Its reputation, tutors, facilities, traditions, people. Mansfield combines beautiful neo-gothic architecture and an excellent position – aspects that make the older colleges so appealing – with an open-minded and progressive atmosphere that is free from many of the more bizarre anachronisms that you find elsewhere. Mansfield manages a good work/play balance. **And the worst?** Hours spent in the library rack up very quickly. If you don't enjoy independent study and a high-pressure environment, Oxford may not be for you. The strong sense of community found at Mansfield is a consequence of its small size. It is important that you get involved with university clubs – if you don't, you may find college life intolerably restrictive. **And to sum it all up?** Give Oxford and Mansfield a go – you won't regret it.

Past students: Rev Prof G B Caird (Dean Ireland's professor of the exegesis of holy scripture, Oxford University), Paul Crossley (pianist), C H Dodd (theologian, chairman of New English Bible translators), Michael White (music critic), Guy Hands (City of London), Chris Cragg (*Financial Times*), M von Trott (would-be assassin of Hitler), Donald McDonald (led the boat race mutiny). **More info?** Contact JCR President on 01865 270999.

Oxford – Merton

Merton College, Oxford OX1 4JD
Tel 01865 276310
Email admissions@admin.merton.ox.ac.uk
Website www.merton.ox.ac.uk

Profile

Staff & students

Undergraduates: 168 men, 134 women. **Postgraduates:** 180 men, 118 women. **Teaching staff:** *Men:* 19 fellows, 8 research fellows, 14 lecturers. *Women:* 8 fellows, 5 research fellows, 9 lecturers.

College & admissions

Founded: 1264; women undergraduates first admitted in 1980. **Admission:** By interview and conditional offer. **Largest fields of study:** Chemistry, literae humaniores, mathematics, history, physics, PPE and law.

Study opportunities

Library and information services: Over 80,000 volumes in lending library and fine Old Library (medieval manuscripts, chained early books). College library and IT services converged. 30 open-access PCs, including 4 with links to national and international library services (ratio workstations to students 1:20); 300+ points with access to internet. IT facilities open 24 hours/day; IT support from computer officer and 1–2 juniors.

Living

Eating arrangements: All meals available in hall using pre-paid meal swipe card: breakfast £1.50, lunch £2.50, dinner £3.50. **Gate/guest hours:** Gate closes by 11pm during term. Guests must leave college by 11pm. **Other college facilities:** Chapel, music room and organ; nearby playing fields, sports pavilion, boathouse. **Accommodation:** All undergraduates offered college accommodation, rent £2361–£2491 pa.

Money

Scholarships: Postmasterships and exhibitions awarded at end of 1st (and later) years for distinguished work. **Travel grants:** Various travel grants to 'subsidise well-thought-out plans for vacation travel'. **Term-time work:** No regulations governing part-time work but students expected to discuss it with tutor. Some vacation work in the library. **Financial help:** £20k own funds, average award £200. Special help: travel, book grants, hardship.

Student view — Alistair Haggerty, JCR President (2nd year, History)

Living

What's it like as a place to live? Beautiful historic buildings (including the oldest functioning library in Europe), very friendly staff, good facilities (well-stocked student bar, games room, gym), active and friendly undergraduate student body. **How's the student accommodation?** All accommodation is college-owned. Rents are very good value, among the cheapest of all the colleges. Rooms are almost always spacious and well maintained. All rooms are single; some have ensuite facilities. **What's the student population like?** Student population is relatively diverse. There is a growing international student community and students are drawn from a range of backgrounds. Almost 60% of students at Merton have come from state schools. The students are extremely friendly; everyone, almost without exception, gets on very well and there is a strong sense of community spirit. **How do students and locals get on?** Generally students seem to get on well with locals. The town vs gown tension is not particularly in evidence at Merton. Students are advised to walk in groups at night rather than alone, but this is more a precaution than a reaction to past problems.

Studying

What's it like as a place to study? Merton has a reputation for workaholics; however, whilst we do work hard, many students are heavily involved in college and university societies, and genuine workaholics are extremely rare. The culture at Merton encourages finding an effective balance between work and leisure. The courses are taught traditionally but are flexible in terms of the options you are able to choose. Facilities are excellent; there are 2 very well-stocked libraries, with helpful, knowledgeable library staff. **What are the teaching staff like?** Merton tutors are amongst the best in the university, with some amongst the most eminent in the world. Hence the college's consistently impressive academic results. They are also interested in the academic and social wellbeing of students. My experience of the tutors is that they are highly intelligent but also interesting people and good company.

Socialising

What are student societies like? University-wide societies are hugely diverse; ranging from conventional sports' teams to the Blackadder Appreciation Society'. Merton societies are less varied, but many students are involved with them. Particularly popular amongst Merton students are the music and drama societies. Many students are also involved in the college sports teams, which have experienced some notable successes in recent years (particularly in pool, darts, badminton and cricket). **What's a typical night out?** Start at the college bar and then proceed to a nightclub (Park End is a particular favourite of Mertonians). Alternatively there are some excellent pubs (particularly the Half Moon, which has some great live music). **And how much does it cost?** Including entrance and drinks, plus a kebab on the way home; around £15–£20. **How can you get home safely?** All entertainment venues are within walking distance, though there is also good taxi provision. The OUSU night bus can also be called to provide lifts to students for a very good price.

Money

Is it an expensive place to live? Oxford is an expensive city to live in. However, students are heavily subsidised by the college. With a bit of paid work over the summer you can make your student loan last the term. **Average price of a pint?** College bar = £1.80, Oxford City = £3. **And the price of a takeaway?** Kebab = £3.50, Indian = £6. **What's the part-time work situation?** All Oxford colleges disapprove of part-time work during term time.

Summary

What's the best feature about the place? The atmosphere. All students are extremely friendly, you can quickly become absorbed in interesting conversations and there are plenty of societies to get involved with. The student bar is a great centre for the social life of the college. We are also fortunate to be surrounded by some genuinely spectacular buildings. **And the worst?** It can be quiet, particularly around the exam periods. The college rules can also be on the draconian side at times, though the staff are generally very much on the side of the students. **And to sum it all up?** Merton is a warm, welcoming and inspiring college in one of Britain's finest universities. Whether you are after some great nights out, stimulating intellectual discussion or the opportunity to play sport (particularly pool) to a high standard, you will find it at Merton.

Past students: TS Eliot (poet); J R R Tolkein, Max Beerbohm (authors); Roger Bannister (4-min mile); Thomas Bodley (Bodleian Library), Crown Prince Naruhito of Japan. **More info?** Look at the website (www.mertonjcr.org).

Oxford – New College

New College, Oxford OX1 3BN
Tel 01865 279512
Email admissions@new.ox.ac.uk
Website www.new.ox.ac.uk

Profile

Staff & students

Undergraduates: 210 men, 200 women. **Postgraduates:** 125 men, 80 women. **Teaching staff:** *Men:* 30 fellows (+9 professors), 8 research fellows, 6 lecturers. *Women:* 10 fellows (+1 professor), 2 research fellows, 6 lecturers.

College & admissions

Founded: 1379; women students first admitted in 1979. **Admission:** Undergraduates admitted for all courses except classics and oriental studies, earth sciences, European and Middle Eastern languages, geography, history and English, materials science, theology, philosophy and theology.

Study opportunities

Library and information services: 100,000 volumes including substantial antiquarian collections. Separate college IT service; 6 points of access to library, 30 to internet (ratio 1:10 workstations to students); ethernet connections in all study bedrooms. IT facilities open 24 hours/day; 1 IT officer and assistant.

Living

Eating arrangements: All meals provided in hall (lunch £2.65). **Gate/guest hours:** Access by swipe card and library access system. **Other college facilities:** 8-acre sports ground 1km from college, squash courts, gym, college punts and boathouse. **Accommodation:** 95% undergraduates in college accommodation. £1050 per term for bed and dinner. Few students in privately owned accommodation, approx £85–£100 pw self-catering.

Money

Study grants: About 30 a year. **Financial help:** 30 students helped by government funds; £50k own funds, 100 helped. Other help by way of grants/loans and/or college jobs for those in financial difficulties.

Student view — Matthew Ranger, JCR President (2nd year, Law)

Living

What's it like as a place to live? The college is imperiously beautiful, the university is beautiful and the city is beautiful. You're engaging in a unique culture and living in one of the most impressive places in the country. **How's the student accommodation?** Brilliant. Most freshers get ensuite rooms at New College. If you want accommodation for the duration of your course, you'll probably be able to get it. Accommodation is more expensive pw than at other universities, but the terms at Oxford are so short that it pretty much evens out. **What's the student population like?** Far more friendly and diverse than the stereotypes let you believe. You'll meet people from across the country and across the world. Some of the diversity figures look rather gloomy, but current initiatives should allow them to improve. New College has a reputation for having some of the most sociable and friendly students (sounds horribly clichéd, but it is true). **How do students and locals get on?** The students and locals coexist perfectly, but you often feel that the university dominates the city, which helps to create the oft-talked about 'Oxford bubble' effect. College can be a bit insular, but the college environment allows for easy socialising.

Studying

What's it like as a place to study? Facilities are excellent. Most subjects are traditional, but you get a lot of flexibility with regard to what modules you study, especially in your last years. **What are the teaching staff like?** Amazing. They are the stars of the academic word. New College possesses many of Oxford's best tutors.

Socialising

What are student societies like? However obscure your interests are, you're probably going to find like-minded people and societies that cater for your quirks. College has great facilities for music and drama, and the New College Sports Ground is around the corner from college. **What's a typical night out?** Hang out in a friend's room, go to college bar, have a drink in a pub, go to a club. **And how much does it cost?** £20 for a heavy night. **How can you get home safely?** The SU runs a night-time Safety Bus, which will pick you up and take you home for £1. There are many decent cab companies. Usually, you will be out somewhere close to your accommodation (New College is centrally located), and central Oxford is fairly safe, so most people walk.

Money

Is it an expensive place to live? It's pretty expensive, and your bank balance will fall pretty quickly, but the terms are very short! **Average price of a pint?** £1.90 in college bar, £3 in pub. **And the price of a takeaway?** It depends. You usually go with the company that is offering the best deal, and deals don't usually last for a long time! Last year, Domino's offered a 50% off orders over £50 deal, which we used and abused.

What's the part-time work situation? The university doesn't really approve of jobs, and it's pretty unlikely that you'll have enough time to have one!

Summary

What's the best feature about the place? You're studying with and under some of the world's best minds in a beautiful city. **And the worst?** It can be pretty intense, and you occasionally just want to escape the 'Oxford bubble'. **And to sum it all up?** You'll cherish your memories of Oxford University, and New College is socially and academically one of the best colleges, so it's a privilege to study here.

Past students: Nigel Rees (broadcaster); Tony Benn (former Labour MP); Lord Longford (politician and social reformer); John Fowles (author); Hugh Gaitskell (former Labour leader); Naomi Woolf (social theorist); Kate Beckinsale, Hugh Grant (actors). **More info?** Enquires to JCR President (email president@jcr.new.ox.ac.uk) or check out the website (jcr.new.ox.ac.uk).

Oxford – Oriel

Oriel College, Oxford OX1 4EW
☎ Tel 01865 276555
✉ Email admissions@oriel.ox.ac.uk
🖥 Website www.oriel.ox.ac.uk

Profile

Staff & students

Undergraduates: 157 men, 143 women. **Postgraduates:** 119 men, 66 women. **Teaching staff:** *Men:* 26 fellows, 20 lecturers. *Women:* 11 fellows, 11 lecturers.

College & admissions

Founded: 1326; women undergraduates first admitted in 1985. **Admission:** Conditional or unconditional offers on the basis of UCAS form, written work/test and interview. All courses available except archaeology and anthropology; biological sciences; earth sciences; economics and management (EandM); engineering, economics and management (EEM); European and Middle Eastern languages; fine art; geography; history and English; history and politics; human sciences; history of art; law with law studies in Europe; materials science; materials, economics and management; mathematics and statistics; mathematics and philosophy; oriental studies; physiological sciences (except for medicine). **Largest fields of study:** PPE, history, law.

Study opportunities

Library and information services: Over 100,000 books; library open 24 hours, with wi-fi. **Study abroad:** Informal links with several European universities/colleges.

Living

Eating arrangements: All meals available in college at low cost (breakfast from £2, lunch £2.50, dinner £3.50). **Gate/guest hours:** Free access 24 hours/day for college members. Liberal guest rules. **Other college facilities:** Facilities for all major sports, gym, squash courts, common room, TV room, bar. **Accommodation:** All undergraduates can be accommodated in college for their entire course; charge £788–£1066 a term. No first-degree students live at home.

Money

Scholarships: University and college scholarships and exhibitions awarded for academic achievement. **Travel grants:** Small grants available. **Term-time work:** Some bar work and holiday work available in college. **Financial help:** College hardship funds, in addition to university bursaries.

Student view

Among the prettiest and oldest of colleges, right in the town centre and renowned for its friendly, intimate atmosphere (arguably the strongest college identity in Oxford). Accommodation for the whole course, with a choice of single or double rooms, flats for 3 or house for 4. Security is good. All meals in hall (choice of formal or informal dinner), reasonable standard and price; very good termly guest and annual subject dinners. Excellent library (open 24 hours), though the bar is more a focal point for student activity: not only the venue for several bops a term, but also has a pool table, dartboard and video games, quiz and pinball machines. JCR shop sells cheap snack food and drink, etc. TV room with Sky Digital (sports and movie channels). Good sporting reputation, especially for rowing (head of the river more than any other college in past 20 years); strong rugby, football, cricket, netball and lacrosse teams. Funding available from JCR for the many college societies for all interests, including philosophy, arts, literature, film. Drama society produces a play every summer in college's First Quad. Oriel provides an atmosphere where students can work and play, pursue their interests and generally enrich their lives. Student population is cosmopolitan and the atmosphere relaxed. Excellent support from fellow students and tutors, all of whom are always willing to listen and help with any problems. Easy to change course in the first term. Good prospects for career and graduate/research work.

Student footnotes

Housing: College accommodation for all years; reasonably priced. **Eats:** Provision for veggies in college (£2+ for lunch, £3 dinner). Great choice of places in town: Mehdi's kebab van (up to £3.50), Brothers, Chutney's Indian brasserie, Pizza Express, Chiang Mai Kitchen. **Drink:** College bar cheaper than pubs in town. **Nightlife:** Good college ents eg bops, summer ceilidhs, film screenings. Cinemas, plays, concerts and live bands in bars. Student clubs: Park End, Po Na Na's, Zodiac, Crunchies, Purple Turtle, Panic. **Locals:** No real problems; just need to be generally careful. **Sports:** College sports ground with squash and tennis courts; weights room in college; boathouse by river. **Travel:** College travel grants for academic purposes; student discount holidays and fares. **Financial help:** College takes this seriously. University funding and grants from college and college trusts for those in difficulty. **Jobs:** Bar shifts available; students employed out of term time by college, in library, helping with summer conferences, etc. and can stay in college cheaply. **Best features:** Friendly atmosphere. **Good news:** All college rooms have free and fast internet connection. **Past students:** Sir Walter Raleigh (Elizabethan courtier and explorer), Beau Brummel (Regency dandy), Cecil Rhodes (explorer), A J P Taylor (historian), Thomas More (Chancellor to Henry VIII), Norman Willis (actor), Matthew Arnold (poet), Sir Christopher Walford (ex Lord Mayor of London). **More info?** Contact JCR President on 01865 276587.

Oxford – Pembroke

Pembroke College, Oxford OX1 1DW
☎ Tel 01865 276412
✉ Email admissions@pmb.ox.ac.uk
💻 Website www.pmb.ox.ac.uk

Profile

Staff & students
Undergraduates: 190 men, 191 women. **Postgraduates:** 88 men, 50 women. **Teaching staff:** *Men:* 27 fellows, 7 research fellows, 35 lecturers. *Women:* 7 fellows, 5 research fellows, 12 lecturers.

College & admissions
Founded: 1624; women undergraduates first admitted in 1979. **Admission:** On basis of interview, school performance, reports and tests in certain subjects.

Study opportunities
Library and information services: Working collection of about 30,000 books covering all subjects taught. Separate college IT service. All bedrooms have access to internet. IT facilities open 24 hours/day; IT staff support 9.30am–5pm weekdays. **Study abroad:** A few formal exchange links.

Living
Eating arrangements: Breakfast and snacks from the pantry; lunch (including takeaway) available in hall; dinners charged at £672 pa. Kitchen closed on Saturday but arrangement to take meals in Christ Church. **Gate/guest hours:** No set hours. **Other college facilities:** Sports ground (1 mile from college), boathouse, bar, computer rooms. **Accommodation:** All 1st years in college accommodation and most finalists in the college annexe. 272 places available: rent depend on size of room, in range £2352–£4180 pa (term time only); or £2646–£4293 for 36 weeks. Self-catering facilities are available. No first-degree students live at home unless there are exceptional circumstances.

Money
Scholarships: Awarded at the end of the 1st year, based on performance in public examination. **Travel grants:** Limited funds available for small number of grants. **Term-time work:** College does not normally allow term-time work (2% believed to work). **Financial help:** Hardship grants offered to students in financial need.

Student view

Caroline Daly, JCR President (2nd year, Law with Legal Studies in Europe (with Spanish))

Living
What's it like as a place to live? It is an incredibly friendly environment. It feels like an oasis – in the very heart of Oxford yet somewhat hidden away. Its small physical size and lack of tourists means that the college has a strong sense of community. **How's the student accommodation?** All rooms are of a high standard. You can choose to pay more for a larger room or an ensuite. The most expensive rooms are absolutely stunning and there has been much renovation done in recent years. **What's the student population**

like? Pembroke has a reputation for being quite 'public school' but in my view, this is incorrect. The student population is diverse and all backgrounds are represented. Pembroke also benefits from an excellent Visiting Students Programme, where many Americans and a good few Europeans add to the diverse culture. **How do students and locals get on?** Pembroke is situated in the very heart of Oxford and as such, there are not many residential areas near by. Therefore, there aren't many locals around.

Studying

What's it like as a place to study? The courses are traditional with a very strong academic emphasis as one might expect from Oxford. There is a well-stocked library in Pembroke, which is open 24 hours/day during term. **What are the teaching staff like?** The teaching staff are excellent, many are renowned experts in their field yet all are genuinely interested in nurturing and teaching students.

Socialising

What are student societies like? Pembroke has a strong sporting tradition, with rowing being an obvious favourite. For the less sporty, there is an excellent choir along with many opportunities to take parts in musicals, concerts and drama. **What's a typical night out?** Pembroke is very sociable and regularly descends, en masse, to Oxford's many clubs. **And how much does it cost?** It really depends. Club entry is about £5. **How can you get home safely?** Most clubs are within walking distance from Pembroke (a couple are less than 200m away) therefore there is no need to take buses or taxis.

Money

Is it an expensive place to live? It can be an expensive city to live in but most people manage to keep a good control of their finances. **Average price of a pint?** £2.50. **And the price of a takeaway?** £3–£4. **What's the part-time work situation?** Students are discouraged from having jobs. It is almost impossible to hold down a job in the short and intense terms.

Summary

What's the best feature about the place? The JCR is the richest in Oxford, and students benefit from free pizza and drinks at all meetings as well as subsidised bops, trips and sport. Also, the open and friendly atmosphere. Pembroke retains the traditional charm of Oxford but manages to create a relaxed environment. **And the worst?** Rent can be high, but the rooms are of an excellent standard. **And to sum it all up?** Pembroke College provides the best of both worlds: a strong academic environment balanced by great opportunities to socialise and get involved in a wide range of activities.

Past students: Samuel Johnson (of dictionary fame), Michael Heseltine (former Conservative MP), John Snagge (BBC), Julian Critchley (journalist and former MP), Maria Eagle (Labour Minister). **More info?** Check out the website (www.pembrokejcr.co.uk).

Oxford – Queen's

The Queen's College, Oxford OX1 4AW
Tel 01865 279120
Email admissions@queens.ox.ac.uk
Website www.queens.ox.ac.uk

Profile

Staff & students
Undergraduates: 151 men, 199 women. **Postgraduates:** 89 men, 80 women. **Teaching staff:** *Men:* 28 fellows, 5 research fellows, 19 lecturers. *Women:* 4 fellows, 9 research fellows, 12 lecturers.

College & admissions
Founded: 1341; women undergraduates first admitted in 1979. **Admission:** Undergraduates not admitted for archaeology and anthropology, classical archaeology and ancient history, computer science, earth sciences, theology, modern history and English (but other joint schools involving English welcome).

Study opportunities
Library and information services: Over 140,000 volumes, including good coverage of all undergraduate subjects. College IT and library services converged. Ratio 1:20 workstations to students. 7 points with access to libraries, 30 to internet. IT facilities open 24 hours/day; 2 IT officers give support; weekly IT workshop.

Living
Eating arrangements: Breakfast available in hall, Florey Building and Iffley Road building; lunch and dinner in hall. Meals charged at cost, approx £6.50 a day. **Gate/guest hours:** Undergraduates can have their own keys. **Other college facilities:** Chapel with superb modern pipe organ and concert piano; convenient sports field; boathouse with several good eights; tennis courts; squash courts; beer cellar. **Accommodation:** All students in college accommodation. Rooms at approx £114.50 pw (term-time only), plus food at cost. No first-degree students live at home.

Money
Scholarships: Various scholarships and exhibitions offered to students on any course for distinguished work; college bursaries for excellence in non-academic activities (sports, etc); choral, organ or instrumental awards offered for distinguished performance (not restricted to students reading music). **Travel grants:** Some available. **Term-time work:** College does not allow term-time work.

Student view

Impressive Baroque buildings on the High Street – 'the grandest piece of classical architecture in Oxford' – and with the motto 'Queen's will provide'. Queen's does indeed provide students with the opportunity to combine an Oxford degree with as much sport, music, drama and socialising as they can. Unlike the impression given by its buildings, it is the friendliest and least-pretentious college of the lot. Originally the 'northern' college, it now attracts applicants from all over the country (and abroad). Not too large, so that students fit in quickly and get to know most other people. Accommodation provided for students for the full 3 years: off site for 1st and 2nd years; mixed-size rooms on the main college site in the final year. All rooms have ethernet links, some with internal phone lines. No self-catering facilities but college food (paid for on credit) is more than adequate for most, being cheap, available every day and often edible! Main college library is well stocked (and a specialist Egyptology library); its grandiose upper floor, with its ornate decoration, is definitely worth a visit. The most cherished undergraduate memories will involve the legendary beer cellar in some light or another (probably a hazy one). It may be smallish, and in a hole in the ground under Front Quad, but has a traditional pubby feel most nights. Darts is one of Queen's strongest sports and the popularity of the dartboards in the beer cellar will show you why. Numerous social events – don any random costume for fortnightly themed bops (original themes mean you will be able to link any costume into the theme); end-of-term events, sports victory celebrations and an unmissable triennial ball. The laid-back atmosphere means that in all aspects of life, the emphasis is on participation and enjoyment. Rugby, football, hockey and rowing teams all compete in the top divisions but there are also numerous successful 2nd and 3rd teams; inter-collegiate level sport is definitely favoured and successful at this level. Sports grounds and pavilion are on the banks of the Isis (not to be missed). Many well-reviewed Eglesfield Players performances (Eglesfield is college founder); Eglesfield Music Society holds weekly lunchtime recitals and the chapel choir (arguably the best mixed-voice ensemble) give regular public concerts in college chapel. The variety of their pursuits make Queen's students all very different individuals; the only characteristic they share is being genuinely nice, friendly people.

Student footnotes

Housing: All students can live in for the entirety of their course. Rents are reasonable. **Eats:** Good selection at a subsidised price (lunch £1.50–£3, 2-course dinner £3.14). Breakfast and lunch are self-service. **Drink:** Beer cellar has a wide variety at excellent prices (pint from £2+, spirits from £1.50+). Buttery also sells reasonably priced wine with dinner. Several good pubs close by. **Nightlife:** Excellent JCR-organised entertainments, fewer university-wide events. Range of clubs from small and expensive (Escape, the Bridge, Thirst) to large, cheap and cheesy (Park End, the Studio, OFS). Live acts at the Carling Academy on Cowley Road. **Locals:** Generally friendly as city is largely populated by academic types or visiting students. **Sports:** Excellent football, rugby and cricket pitches over the river from the College's shared boathouse. Tennis and squash courts. 10 mins' walk to university's main sports complex. Darts and ultimate frisbee also popular. **Travel:** Bus stops for local buses and park and ride as well as London services from outside main entrance. Train station 20-min walk. Bicycle popular method of commuting around town. **Financial help:** Jointly managed by JCR and college for those in severe financial difficulty. Further funds available from university. **Jobs:** Permission needed to work in term time but some offered in college administration. **Best features:** Friendly atmosphere, central location, 3–4 years accommodation. **And worst:** Huge variation in standard of student accommodation; can be slightly insular. **Past students:** Henry V, Rowan Atkinson (comedian), Leopold Stokowski (conductor), Brian Walden (TV presenter), Gerald Kaufman (politician), Edmund Halley (astronomer), Tim Berners Lee (inventor of World Wide Web). **More info?** Contact JCR President on 01865 279158.

Oxford – St Anne's

St Anne's College, Oxford OX2 6HS
☎ Tel 01865 274840
✉ Email enquiries@st-annes.ox.ac.uk
🖥 Website www.st-annes.ox.ac.uk

Profile

Staff & students

Undergraduates: 250 men, 202 women. **Postgraduates:** 145 men, 110 women. **Teaching staff:** *Men:* 39 fellows, 12 research fellows, 14 lecturers. *Women:* 13 fellows, 6 research fellows, 7 lecturers.

College & admissions

Founded: 1878; men undergraduates first admitted in 1979. **Admission:** College has tutorial fellows in all the main subjects. **Largest fields of study:** English, history, mathematics, medicine, modern languages, PPE.

Study opportunities

Library and information services: Large library; 110,000 books and many special collections. College IT service; points with access to internet and local libraries in all college rooms. Ratio 1:15 workstations to students, access 24 hours/day. Full-time computing officer.

Living

Eating arrangements: All meals available in hall but not compulsory. Self-catering facilities in college houses. **Gate/guest hours:** No gate hours. Guests may stay overnight if signed in. **Other college facilities:** Extensive computer systems; music practice rooms. Sports facilities shared with St John's; boathouse on river. **Accommodation:** Provided for almost all students throughout their course. Charges approx £3531 pa, including utilities and £375 towards meals.

Money

Scholarships: Scholarships and exhibitions awarded for good academic work and success in examinations. **Travel grants:** Generous funds available to undergraduates during their course. **Term-time work:** Discouraged but available in college in bar and library. **Financial help:** Funds available for individual cases of hardship.

Student view — Katie Mckinnon, JCR Secretary (2nd year, Medicine)

Living

What's it like as a place to live? It's a lovely part of Oxford, right next to the park. It's a little bit out from the centre of Oxford, but only a 10-min walk. **How's the student accommodation?** You can live in college for the duration of your course if you wish, although some choose to move into private accommodation nearby. It is reasonably priced and although some parts are worse than others, much of it is good. The canteen food is the best in Oxford colleges too. **What's the student population like?** Compared to many colleges, there is a good mix of people and backgrounds. There are many international students too. It is quite a large college, with good mixing between the years. **How do students and locals get on?** Most of Oxford is good in terms of mixing between locals and students, although there are some areas, particularly at the weekend, that some people prefer to avoid.

Studying

What's it like as a place to study? The courses are traditional, excellent in all subjects. The facilities are excellent, and many of the science and language facilities are very near to St Anne's. **What are the teaching staff like?** All of the staff are international researchers, but still find time to look after the students, in the tutorial system that is unique to Oxbridge. The workload is challenging, but means you learn a lot.

Socialising

What are student societies like? As well as the numerous university-wide societies, there are many St Anne's specific societies, including sports clubs like rowing, rugby, football, netball and all sorts. There are many other types too, such as a choir, orchestra, photography society, film society. **What's a typical night out?** There are club nights for every taste: the staple hits and cheese, as well as indie, electro, Italo disco, rockabilly,

493

anything. Right around the corner from St Anne's is an independent cinema and the famous Jericho Tavern gig venue, plus plenty of good restaurants. **And how much does it cost?** Most clubs have cheap entry (around £3–£4) and drinks deals, especially for students. **How can you get home safely?** St Anne's isn't far away from anything, but there are several taxi companies and a Safety Bus run by OUSU if you are desperate.

Money
Is it an expensive place to live? It isn't particularly cheap, and the student loan doesn't normally quite cover the term, but Oxford and St Anne's have good allowances for those in financial difficulties. **Average price of a pint?** In the college bar, a pint is £1.60. **And the price of a takeaway?** Not including the frequent student deals, almost anything is under £10 per person. **What's the part-time work situation?** Oxford and St Anne's don't really like part-time jobs, especially not over 10 hours pw – except for some in college, working in the bar or library. They prefer to help directly those people who are struggling financially.

Summary
What's the best feature about the place? St Anne's Library is one of the largest college libraries in Oxford, and anything it doesn't have, you can get them to order in. **And the worst?** We aren't exactly the prettiest of Oxford colleges. Some find the ramshackle mix of old and new endearing, though . . . Honest . . . **And to sum it all up?** St Anne's is definitely one of the friendliest, most welcoming colleges in Oxford, is busy but fun, and the college environment means that everything is on your doorstep.

Past students: Maria Aitken (actress); Frances Cairncross (economist); Baroness Young (Environment Agency); Iris Murdoch, Naomi Mitchison, Helen Fielding (authors); Libby Purves, Tina Brown (journalists); Joanna Richardson (actress); Dame Cicely Saunders (founder of hospice movement); Edwina Currie (former Conservative Minister); Sister Wendy (art historian); Elizabeth Jennings (poet); Martha Kearney (journalist).

Oxford – St Catherine's

St Catherine's College, Oxford OX1 3UJ
Tel 01865 271700
Email admissions@st-catherines.ox.ac.uk
Website www.stcatz.ox.ac.uk

Profile

Staff & students
Undergraduates: 262 men, 210 women. **Postgraduates:** 145 men, 101 women. **Teaching staff:** *Men:* 31 fellows, 10 research fellows, 29 lecturers. *Women:* 8 fellows, 3 research fellows, 17 lecturers.

College & admissions
Founded: 1962; women undergraduates first admitted in 1973. **Admission:** Undergraduates not admitted for classics, theology or ancient history, or archaeology and anthropology.

Study opportunities

Library and information services: 50,000 volumes. Overlapping college library and computing services. 33 workstations for students; all rooms have ethernet points (access to library and internet) for own PCs. Access to IT facilities 24 hours/day, IT staff support 8 hours/day.

Living

Eating arrangements: Hall, buttery; facilities on individual staircases. Students eat in hall on a pay-as-you-go basis, 3 meals for less than £8.50 a day. **Gate/guest hours:** Unrestricted. **Other college facilities:** JCR has debating pit, bar, buttery, TV room, theatre, and private dining room; Bernard Sunley Building with lecture and film theatre, outdoor and indoor theatres, music room (with harpsichord and grand piano), squash courts, several college punts, shared playing fields nearby. **Accommodation:** All 1st years in college; on-site accommodation for all 3rd years and vast majority of 2nd and 4th years. 453 self-catering single, 16 twin rooms in college at £106 pw; and 15 self-catering flats from £562 pm, rentable all year. Very few first-degree students live at home.

Money

Scholarships: Awarded for academic excellence at end of 1st year. **Travel grants:** Limited number for use in long vacation. **Term-time work:** College allows term-time work with tutor's permission; limit of 7½ hours pw. Some work available in college in bar, library, offices, security, dining hall. **Financial help:** Various funds and awards available.

Student view

Originally founded in the 19th century as a way of enabling bright students to study at Oxford, regardless of financial means. Catz is the youngest college (1962) and represents the best of 1960s architecture, with rows of long, low buildings making the most of the space and light. Although further from the city centre than many colleges, it is only a 10–15-min walk; anywhere in Oxford is easily accessible on a bike. It's one of the largest colleges, with a great diversity amongst its students – a high proportion of international and visiting students – and a great sense of community. New accommodation blocks allow almost all undergraduates to live in college for the entirety of their course. The social side of Catz is particularly impressive; it has a reputation as being one of the friendliest and liveliest of colleges. Large, well-equipped JCR bar complex, the centre of the social scene, is busy every night. Ents nights every other week and one major event each term (eg Catz Night, where the whole college lets its hair down). Catz is prominent in virtually every university society, from sport to drama, and there are many active college societies. College facilities include a music house (with Steinway grand), squash courts, free gym, sports fields, darkroom, punts, 3 computer rooms and a decent-sized theatre.

Student footnotes

Housing: Excellent rooms, especially brand new ensuite 2nd-year rooms; rent below university average. **Eats:** food generally good (not fancy but filling, wholesome and tasty). 3-course dinner a bargain at £2.90; other meals also good value; Scaff is informal alternative to dinner (always popular). **Drink:** Catz bar great place for chilled-out drink; £1.50 a pint of lager, spirits a bit more. Large range of alcoholic and non-alcoholic drinks. **Nightlife:** Good college ents: discos, bands, etc.; music, drama. College band, visiting bands in pubs, etc. Popular student clubs: Park End, the Bridge, Jongleurs, Filth. Oxford theatrical productions cheap and frequent. Numerous cinemas in town, mainstream to foreign/classic. **Locals:** Never see any. **Sports:** At least 1 Catz team in most sports (men's and women's), most competing at top level. College football, tennis and rugby teams consistently in top 3. College squash, tennis and netball courts, weights room, punts, shared boathouse, sports field (1 mile away). **Travel:** Generous travel awards (college and JCR). Coach to London runs regularly from town. **Financial help:** College founded to help poor students, so excellent in dealing with such matters. Financial help available to those in need. **Jobs:** In hall, bar and library during term. Longer-term jobs possible in vacation. **Best features:** Community spirit; very friendly and relaxed. **And worst:** Distance from centre. **Informal name:** Catz. **Past students:** Joseph Heller, Simon Winchester, Jeanette Winterson (authors); Sir Cameron Mackintosh (theatre producer); Peter Mandelson (politician); John Birt (former Director of BBC); Matthew Pinsent (rower).

Oxford – St Edmund Hall

St Edmund Hall, Oxford OX1 4AR
Tel 01865 279011
Email admissions@seh.ox.ac.uk
Website www.seh.ox.ac.uk

Profile

Staff & students

Undergraduates: 220 men, 171 women. **Postgraduates:** 91 men, 77 women. **Teaching staff:** *Men:* 28 fellows and senior teaching staff. *Women:* 12 fellows and senior teaching staff.

College & admissions

Founded: Before 1317; women undergraduates first admitted in 1979. **Admission:** Conditional or unconditional offers made via UCAS. Undergraduates not admitted for theology, classics, biology, human sciences, oriental studies, computer science. **Academic features:** All mainstream subjects plus Russian, Czech, fine art, earth sciences and materials science.

Study opportunities

Library and information services: Library in restored early English church: some 50,000 volumes, microfilm/fiche reader, workstations and laptop points available. Various computer rooms. All student rooms have ethernet connections. Access to IT facilities 24 hours/day; IT support from 2 staff members. **Study abroad:** Students on modern language and on law studies in Europe spend their 3rd year abroad.

Living

Eating arrangements: Cafeteria-style service, formal dinner every Sunday night; formal guest dinner 3 nights per term. Breakfast £1.70, lunch around £3, dinner £3.85. **Gate/guest hours:** No restrictions. **Other college facilities:** Computer rooms, music room, boathouse, all sports facilities, fitness gym, college bar. **Accommodation:** 75% of all undergraduates in college accommodation (all 1st, 3rd and 4th years; and most 2nd years who wish to). Room in college approx £3285 pa including heating; increases later in course, limited by indexation formula.

Money

Scholarships and bursaries: Awards after 1st year of study. Musical and other bursaries. Organ and choral scholarships. Support for academic projects. Small grants for travel and for developing language abroad. **Term-time work:** College does not allow term-time work. Some vacation work occasionally possible in college.

Student view

Teddy Hall, as it is affectionately known, is one of Oxford's friendliest colleges. There is a strong and loyal hall spirit, but this is not claustrophobic, and the small size of the college gives it an intimate and friendly atmosphere. Students are active both at college and university levels: teams excel in sports (especially women's teams) and there are also excellent music, drama and journalism traditions. JCR meetings very well-attended and remarkably free of party-political biases but with a strong reputation for student activism and radicalism. Teddy Hall ents are renowned and frequently draw students from other colleges. There is a growing LGB community. It's in the centre of Oxford, near shops, libraries and sports pitches. College is a blend of old and new: front quad is picturesque and medieval, and the library is in an 11th-century Norman church; more modern back quad is visually less impressive but better equipped (washing facilities, kitchens, etc.). Whatever your interests and beliefs, you are almost certain to find your niche here.

Student footnotes

Housing: College accommodation (in college and 2 annexes) for 3 years. Those living out look in JCR housing file, noticeboards. **Eats:** Food improving in college; always vegetarian option. Excellent guest nights (fierce competition for limited tickets). Loads of restaurants and curry houses in town, wide variety of prices (Friends, Chutney, Le Petit Blanc good). **Drink:** Lively and friendly college bar, with cheap drinks. Morrells is good brew. **Nightlife:** Wolfson Hall in college (largest student venue in Oxford), used to the full: discos, bops, LGB nights, blind date, charity events; videos in the JCR. Student clubs: Coven, Fifth Avenue, Zodiac. **Locals:** Friendly (though little contact). **Sports:** Good sport, especially athletics, rugby, football, netball and rowing. Boathouse. Other facilities have to be borrowed/rented; however, what it lacks in facilities it makes up for in team spirit. **Travel:** JCR refunds taxi fare after dark. Limited vacation travel grants available. **Financial help:** Some available (depends on individual circumstances). **Jobs:** Bar work in term time; work in holidays, eg porters or through agencies (lots about). **Best features:** Campaign activities; wide variety of interests; friendly. **And worst:** Small college; old-fashioned. **Informal name:** Teddy Hall. **Good news:** New international students' hardship fund. All bedrooms have internal phone and internet connections. **Past students:** Sir Robin Day (broadcaster), Terry Jones (Monty Python), General Sir Michael Rose (UN in Bosnia), Al Murray (comedian). **More info?** Enquiries to JCR President on 01865 279048.

Oxford – St Hilda's

St Hilda's College, Oxford OX4 1DY
☎ Tel 01865 276884
🖷 Fax 01865 276816
✉ Email college.office@st-hildas.ox.ac.uk
🖥 Website www.st-hildas.ox.ac.uk

Profile

Staff & students

Undergraduates: 57 men, 354 women. **Postgraduates:** 46 men, 100 women. **Teaching staff:** *Men:* 3 fellows and 25 lecturers. *Women:* 26 fellows, 11 research fellows, 21 lecturers.

College & admissions

Founded: 1893 as a women's college. Men first admitted in 2008. **Admission:** On the basis of academic results, interview and, in some subjects, submission of school written work. **Largest fields of study:** English, modern languages, PPE, law, history, mathematics, biological sciences.

Study opportunities

Library and information services: Good range of books for most Honours schools. Separate college IT and library services. Ratio 1:15 workstations to students, 30 points with access to library and internet. IT facilities open 24 hours/day; IT support from 2 staff members; courses on bibliographic databases.

Living

Eating arrangements: Maintenance fee includes swipe card for a certain number of meals in hall; additional credit can be bought as required. **Gate/guest hours:** During week, open to all 9am to 11pm and to accompanied visitors until 2am; overnight visitors must be signed in. **Other college facilities:** Music building, pianos and harpsichord, small chapel, tennis court, netball court, punts, computers and printers (with access to university computing facilities), JCR bar, buttery, washing machines and spin driers, cooking facilities. **Accommodation:** All 1st years in college accommodation (70% of all students). Rent £3150 pa (term time only), plus food. Students normally live in privately owned accommodation for 1 year. Virtually no first-degree students live at home.

Money

Travel grants: About £6k annually, including grants for undergraduates' travel abroad, for classics students and for historians' travel grants. **Term-time work:** College allows some paid term-time work, after consultation with tutors. Some work in college library; in JCR bar in holidays. **Financial help:** £25k own support funds (for undergraduates and graduates), average award £100–£200.

Student view
Katharine Tessell, JCR President (2nd year, Modern Languages)

Living

What's it like as a place to live? Friendly. Beautiful grounds, peaceful and well placed – close to town, bars, restaurants, etc. **How's the student accommodation?** Big rooms, some kitchen facilities. Many rooms recently refurbished and all are well furnished. **What's the student population like?** Very varied and friendly. High proportion of overseas students. Students from all backgrounds. **How do students and locals get on?** Pubs in Cowley a good mixture of Oxford, Brookes and locals. Generally friendly and get on well.

Studying

What's it like as a place to study? Focused on tutorial system. Traditional and intense. World-class facilities. Fantastic libraries. **What are the teaching staff like?** Excellent. Sometimes old-fashioned.

Socialising

What are student societies like? Loads of variety – sport, music, hobbies, politics. Often a very good way of making friends. **What's a typical night out?** Local pub then into town for a club. **And how much does it cost?** £20–£30 (if you drink lots!). **How can you get home safely?** Generally safe to walk, also Safety Bus and taxis.

Money

Is it an expensive place to live? About average for the south – not too expensive.

What's the part-time work situation? Uni strongly disapproves of part-time jobs but can work in college bar/buttery.

Summary

What's the best feature about the place? Beautiful setting and world-class teaching. **And to sum it all up?** A friendly, open and academically challenging place to live and study.

Past students: Marjory-Anne Bromhead (economist at World Bank), Nicola Le Fanu (composer), Kate Millett (feminist writer), Beryl Smalley (historian), A Bullard (vice-president, Amcon Corp, USA), Dame Helen Gardner (critic), Barbara Pym (novelist), Jacqueline Du Pré (cellist), Catherine Heath (writer), Hermione Lee (broadcaster), Gillian Shepherd MP, Baroness (Susan) Greenfield (science). **More info?** Enquiries to JCR President (tel 01865 276846, email jcr@st-hildas.ox.ac.uk).

Oxford – St Hugh's

St Hugh's College, Oxford OX2 6LE
Tel 01865 247900
Website www.st-hughs.ox.ac.uk

Profile

Staff & students

Undergraduates: 206 men, 199 women. **Postgraduates:** 135 men, 94 women. **Teaching staff:** *Men:* 62 fellows and lecturers. *Women:* 23 fellows and lecturers.

College & admissions

Founded: 1886; men undergraduates first admitted in 1987. **Admission:** College welcomes applications from all kinds of backgrounds. Undergraduates not admitted for classical archaeology and ancient history; geography; philosophy and theology.

Study opportunities

Library and information services: Large and well-stocked library plus law reading room. Computer rooms with 24-hour access; wi-fi available in library; all college study rooms have internet access (approx 500). IT support from full-time members of staff.

Living

Gate/guest hours: All undergraduates have keys. Overnight guests at weekend by arrangement. **Other college facilities:** Bar, tennis court, basketball court, croquet, large and pleasant garden, shared boathouse, squash courts and sports ground. **Accommodation:** All undergraduates offered study bedroom throughout their degree (40% of rooms ensuite, all with internet access); rent £3060 pa including maintenance charge.

Money

Scholarships: Scholarships and exhibitions (£200 and £3150, with some free vacation residence) for high performance in examinations; various essay prizes; organ scholarship. **Travel grants:** Limited amount of money available for students attending required courses. **Term-time work:** College does not allow term-time work. Some holiday work available in college.

Student view — **Barry Wright**, JCR President 2008 (3rd year, Mathematics)

Living

What's it like as a place to live? The college is a lovely place to live, with big lawns and gardens, as well as facilities like a gym and tennis courts on site. It's about a 15-min walk to the centre of town, and to faculty buildings. Since everyone lives on site, the atmosphere is very friendly and you always see people you know wandering around. **How's the student accommodation?** College accommodation is of a high standard, with rooms varying from the basic study bedroom up to bigger and more spacious ensuite rooms. Since where you live is decided by a ballot each year, you get the opportunity to live in different areas of the college as you progress, and live with all sorts of people. **What's the student population like?** The students here are from a vast array of different backgrounds, but all with one thing in common – they're all very friendly and helpful. There is a large international community, who mix well with home students, helped by the mixed nature of the accommodation. **How do students and locals get on?** Students mix reasonably well with locals, eg there isn't anywhere students should avoid going. But there is a bit of segregation as locals are not allowed into all the university buildings.

Studying

What's it like as a place to study? Hugh's is a great place to study, with top academics teaching, and some of the best teaching facilities in the world. There is a great library in college, as well as access to all the university's libraries, including the Bodleian, which has a copy of every book published in the UK. There are some quiet areas to get work done if you find your room too noisy, although most of college accommodation is fairly quiet. **What are the teaching staff like?** Being Oxford University, the teaching staff are almost all involved in research in their area(s) of expertise. Graduate students also take classes, going over work, but again they are some of the brightest people in the country. Despite their reputation, they are all approachable if you have questions or need help in any way.

Socialising

What are student societies like? There is a society for everything here – and if there isn't, you can create one! The university has a huge freshers' fair at the start of the year where all the societies gather and try to attract you to join! One major advantage of a collegiate university is that you can represent your college at various sports, without having to be a pro or train 7 days a week. Of course, if you want to do that, you can play for the university team, but this system means everyone has a chance to get involved. **What's a typical night out?** Students can do anything from going clubbing to attending magazine launch parties, or just have a quiet night in the college bar. Oxford also has an excellent range of public houses and restaurants. **And how much does it cost?** Club entry is fairly reasonable, although sometimes drinks can be a bit on the expensive side. However, there are lots of events throughout the year where this is not the case, and drinks are dirt cheap/free! **How can you get home safely?** The SU runs a safety bus scheme in case of emergencies, but there are lots of licensed taxis waiting outside all the major clubs and entertainment areas, so you can take one of those back to college. Others prefer to walk, which is also fairly safe if you stick to the main roads.

Money
Is it an expensive place to live? It is a fairly expensive place to live; Oxford is officially the 2nd most expensive place to live and study, after London. But the student loan and Oxford bursary system means that people generally have enough money to last the year, and if you run into problems, there are generous hardship funds to help you out. **Average price of a pint?** In the Hugh's bar, £1.50. In an average Oxford student bar, £1.80. In an Oxford pub, £2.90. **And the price of a takeaway?** We have a great kebab/burger van just down the road, where you can get a kebab for about £3 and a burger for £2 until 3 in the morning! **What's the part-time work situation?** Students are not encouraged to work. But if you really need to, you could get a job in the college bar, or one of the many local pubs who often look for part-time staff.

Summary
What's the best feature about the place? The close-knit community spirit of college, the amazing academics you work with, and just having a part of the 'Oxford Experience'. **And the worst?** The walk to town can feel a lot longer than the 10-15 mins if it's raining, and buses are not cheap! **And to sum it all up?** Work hard and play hard, but most of all it's a unique experience not to be missed!

Past students: Barbara Castle (former Labour Minister); Aung San Suu Kyi (Burma's pro-democracy activist); Jane Glover (conductor); Emily Davison (early suffragette); Peggy Ashcroft (actress); Mary Renault, Joanna Trollope (authors); Kate Adie (BBC reporter); Theresa May MP; Liz Forgan (journalist and broadcaster). **More info?** Contact JCR President on 01865 554195 or check out the website (www.hughsjcr.com).

Oxford – St John's

St John's College, Oxford OX1 3JP
Tel 01865 277300
Email admissions@sjc.ox.ac.uk
Website www.sjc.ox.ac.uk

Profile

Staff & students
Undergraduates: 212 men, 145 women. **Postgraduates:** 129 men, 86 women. **Teaching staff:** *Men:* 50 fellows, 15 research fellows, 13 lecturers, 1 lecteur. *Women:* 14 fellows, 13 research fellows, 13 lecturers, 1 lectorin.

College & admissions
Founded: 1555; women undergraduates first admitted in 1979. **Admissions:** Undergraduates admitted for all undergraduate degrees except earth sciences, materials science, and materials, economics and management (MEM).

Study opportunities
Library and information services: Over 75,000 books. 4 dedicated computer rooms, with Macs and PCs, open 24 hours/day. Almost all student rooms are networked. 2 full-time staff give IT support 8 hours/weekday. **Study abroad:** Formal exchange links in Munich, Geneva and Pisa – open to all students.

501

Living

Eating arrangements: Breakfast, lunch and early dinner self-service in hall (breakfast 85p–£2.20, lunch £2.20, dinner £2.80 approx); semi-formal dinner (£3.10 approx). Snacks available from college bar. **Gate/guest hours:** Late keys issued. **Other college facilities:** Sports ground (1 mile away) with rugby, soccer, hockey and cricket pitches, plus tennis courts. Boathouse in Christ Church Meadow. Squash court and gym in college. Music practice room and exhibition space for showing students' artwork. **Accommodation:** All undergraduates in college accommodation (some Jacobean, some Victorian, some modern), range £687–£819 per term. Specially adapted rooms for students with disabilities.

Money

Scholarships: Awards offered on examination results annually; organ and choral scholarships annually. Special funds for visually impaired undergraduates. **Special grants:** Book grants; music awards. **Financial help:** Some funding available for hardship grants and loans and for academic purposes.

Student view

The rumours are all true about the wealth of St John's and, as a student, the material advantages are obvious – accommodation for all undergraduates, cheap food in hall and facilities to rival any in Oxford (a well-stocked library, 3 excellent computer rooms, 2 squash courts and fitness room on site, a quad with wonderful theatre and so on). As one of the larger colleges, the sporting facilities are good – a sports ground only a mile away with rugby, football and hockey pitches, in addition to 6 tennis courts (hard and grass courts used by uni teams) and a boathouse. But what sets St John's apart from the rest of Oxford is not the legendary work ethic (which is shared by Univ and Merton and anyway comes from other students, rather than directly from tutors), but an apparently endless supply of ambition – many people become involved in extra-curricular activities, and it seems that the desire to achieve highly in finals is matched by endeavours beyond the library. Such dynamism leads to enthusiastic JCR debates and active drama, music and sports societies, as well as a really lively college social life. Students work hard but also take advantage of excellent extra-curricular facilities. The result is a vibrant and exciting place to earn a degree.

Student footnotes

Housing: College accommodation for all undergrads (excellent by national standards). Married flats 200m away. Fairly easy to get vacation residence for academic work, with some financial help. **Eats:** Cheap food in hall (3-course dinner £2.70), with veggie options; bar food. Takeaway pizza at Ask. **Drink:** Sub-pub prices in college bar; the Lamb and Flag next door. **Nightlife:** In college, great black-tie dinners, bops, karaoke, women's garden party, ball every 3–4 years. Out of college, lots: rock and jazz (OUJA) bands; Park End and Zodiac clubs, etc. **Sports:** Well-equipped gym in college, also croquet lawn and squash courts; sportsground 1 mile away; boat club. **Travel:** Special grants available. **Financial help:** Book grant for everyone; hardship fund for those in unexpected financial difficulties. Support funds for those from low-income families. **Jobs:** Work in term time forbidden (except for college or university); about 5% do (hard to fit in as workload heavy). About 75% find some sort of work in holidays, mostly at home rather than at Oxford. **Best features:** Sociable atmosphere. **Past students:** Philip Larkin (poet); Robert Graves, John Wain, Kingsley Amis (authors); Tony Blair (former Prime Minister). **More info?** Contact JCR President by leaving a message (tel 01865 277300, email jcr-president@sjc.ox.ac.uk).

Oxford – St Peter's

☑ St Peter's College, Oxford OX1 2DL
☎ Tel 01865 278900
✉ Email admissions@spc.ox.ac.uk
🖳 Website www.spc.ox.ac.uk

Profile

Staff & students
Undergraduates: 183 men, 174 women. **Postgraduates:** 60 men, 74 women. **Teaching staff:** *Men:* 27 tutorial fellows, 5 research fellows, 21 lecturers. *Women:* 3 tutorial fellows, 4 research fellows, 7 lecturers.

College & admissions
Founded: 1929; women undergraduates first admitted in 1979. **Admission:** Pre- and post-A-level candidates apply on the basis of A-level results (known or future), school record and interview. College welcomes applicants for joint schools; also applications from older candidates (especially in PPE). Undergraduates not accepted for PPP, experimental psychology, human sciences, computer science, engineering science, oriental studies, materials, classics, ancient history, fine art, Middle Eastern languages.

Study opportunities
Library and information services: Access 24 hours/day. Ample reading space, mainly undergraduate texts, with a few older and more specialist works; separate law and intellectual property law libraries. IT facilities – dedicated room, plus workstations in library, access 24 hours/day. 110 points with access to library and internet; all student rooms have ethernet connection; wireless access throughout main site. IT support from computer curator, IT officer and student support.

Living
Eating arrangements: Meals paid for using pre-pay swipe card. Informal dinner every night, formal dinner 3 times a week. **Gate/guest hours:** No restrictions except as to noise and good order. College locked at night but all students have keys. **Other college facilities:** Music room, chapel with organ and piano (used for worship, music, drama and other purposes), athletics and other sports facilities, JCR. **Accommodation:** All 1st years in college accommodation (nearly all undergraduates); no shared rooms or married accommodation. Rooms in college are £1k per term, plus food. Some 2nd years live in privately owned accommodation for 1 year: rent £85–£100 pw self-catering. First-degree students do not live at home.

Money
Scholarships: Academic scholarships and exhibitions awarded after 1st-year exams and thereafter on merit. Organ scholarship and 2 choral awards annually at entrance; instrumental awards for students in residence. **Travel grants:** Grants are made annually from various funds including Christian Deelman fund, a graduate travel fund and St Peter's Society. **Term-time work:** No college policy on term-time work (5% believed to work). Some vacation jobs in college in cleaning, secretarial, conference-hosting. **Financial help:** College and government sponsored funds, 20 students helped. Means-tested bursary scheme.

Student view

It's in the centre of Oxford – just off the major pedestrianised shopping area and at the heart of the city's many restaurants and coffee shops. The college is a small collection of buildings that includes the ancient New Inn Hall, St Peter's Chapel and a modern lodge in Linton House (complete with famed automatic doors). The friendly atmosphere ensures a busy social life to accompany the studious side of life. College library is open 24 hours; all rooms have free internet connections and much of the college is now wireless. A hectic social calendar is organised by the JCR, including fortnightly bops (discos) and annual arts festival. Newly refurbished bar, with heated patio, boasts cheap beer and termly theme nights. JCR has digital TV, video, DVD, pool and football tables, games and vending machines and newspapers (national and student) delivered daily. JCR also co-ordinates many college societies; many sports represented at all levels for men and women, including rowing, rugby, soccer, hockey, tennis, squash, badminton, athletics, netball, basketball, pool and darts. Drama and music are of an excellent standard with many performances throughout the year. Excellent college welfare system (regular hours and extensive peer support system). Good student representation on the college governing body ensures good relations with college authorities.

Student footnotes

Housing: 1st and 3rd year guaranteed live in; most live out in 2nd (but new builds mean practically everyone who wants to can live in). **Eats:** One small payment per term (currently £100), which can be spent on meals, then pay-as-you-go. Covers 3 meals a day during the week, 2 meals at weekends. Lots of places off site. **Drink:** £1.50 a pint in college bar. Cheap bar at union close by. **Nightlife:** Many JCR-organised events. Cinemas, theatres, nightclubs a stone's throw away. **Locals:** Most areas safe with indifferent locals; New Inn Hall Street is not well-lit and can be tricky late at night. **Travel:** College travel grants and scholarships. **Financial help:** University access fund; college hardship fund easily accessible. Academic and choral scholarships. **Jobs:** Term-time work discouraged but long vacations to allow for work. **Informal name:** SPC. **Best features:** Social atmosphere. **And worst:** Not as rich as some colleges. **Past students:** Sir Rex Hunt (former Governor of Faulkland Islands); Rev W Awdry (*Thomas the Tank Engine*); Sir Paul Reeves (Commonwealth Secretary-General); Ken Loach (film director); Sir Paul Condon (former Metropolitan Police Commissioner), Matt Frei (BBC journalist), Hugh Fearnley-Whittingstall (chef, River Cottage). **More info?** Enquiries to JCR President, contact details and more info on www.spcjcr.co.uk.

Oxford – Somerville

- Somerville College, Oxford OX2 6HD
- ☎ Tel 01865 270600
- ✉ Email admissions@some.ox.ac.uk
- 💻 Website www.some.ox.ac.uk

Profile

Staff & students

Undergraduates: 175 men, 195 women. **Postgraduates:** 35 men, 65 women. **Teaching staff:** *Men:* 20 fellows. *Women:* 20 fellows, 10 research fellows, 30 lecturers.

College & admissions

Founded: 1879; male undergraduates first admitted in 1994. **Admission:** Undergraduates not admitted for anthropology; geography; theology; earth sciences; economics and management; fine art; materials science; history and politics; engineering, economics and management, oriental studies.

Study opportunities

Library and information services: Over 120,000 volumes, with strong science, history, literature, languages and philosophy collections; computer terminals and microfilm/fiche reader. Separate college library and IT services. Ratio workstations to students 1:17, IT facilities open 24 hours/day. 110 points with access to library, all college rooms connected to the ethernet. 2 full-time IT support staff.

Living

Eating arrangements: Cafeteria system in hall, plus weekly formal hall (£7.50). Meals paid for on cash basis; 3 meals/day approx £12 per day. **Gate/guest hours:** Electronic access system. **Other college facilities:** Bar, gym, croquet, 2 boats, organ and several pianos. Small independent nursery for children of college members. **Accommodation:** Most students live in college accommodation (all 1st years and final years who choose it); average room rent approx £2808 pa (term time only). Some 9-month contracts, £4155 pa. Most 2nd-year students live in privately owned accommodation; average rent £85+ pw, plus bills.

Money

Scholarships: Various scholarships and exhibitions, both open and closed (usually £200 and £150 pa respectively), awarded at any time in an undergraduate's career for work of especial merit; also Bousfield Scholarships, for candidates from GDST schools. **Travel grants:** Various grants and awards. **Financial help:** Limited funds available for unexpected financial difficulties.

Student view

It became a mixed college in 1994, having been a women's college from 1879. It retains a pro-women environment, and has a friendly, relaxed and supportive atmosphere, with roughly equal numbers of males to females and a good state:independent school ratio. It's well-known for outward-looking social and political activism. Main quad is spacious, relaxed (one of the few in the university where students are allowed to walk on the grass) and much used in the summer. Buildings range from Victorian to the rather ugly 1960s (but if you live in them you don't have to look at them!). Library is one of the best and most beautiful in Oxford, and accessible 24 hours/day – vital in inevitable essay crises. Facilities include various TVs (including Sky and a big-screen TV in the bar), video and DVD player, photocopier, pool table, computer room (open 24 hours/day), music rooms, gym, darkroom and brand new college bar. Student support is strong, with welfare services provided by tutors and by student peer-support scheme; college provides financial hardship assistance and JCR travel grants. Accommodation is generally good, compulsory during your 1st year and guaranteed for your final year. Most students live out in their 2nd year, but the university, JCR and college provide some financial aid. Food is reasonable and cheap but cooking facilities also available; formal hall every week (a great chance to dress up and get drunk!). Academic pressure is generally high, depending on subject, but tutors and fellows usually supportive. It's a couple of mins' walk from the centre of Oxford, in a fashionable area boasting some of the city's best restaurants and bars. In-college entertainments are good (events popular with other colleges). Male undergraduates are beginning to make their mark in university sports, whilst the women's boat club is famous for dominating the river.

Student footnotes

Housing: College equalisation scheme helps students who have to live out; JCR helps in finding accommodation. **Eats:** College food generally ok – veggie and other choices; meal from £3. Sunday lunch at Radcliffe Arms for under a fiver. **Drink:** Cheap (beer from £1.50+ a pint) in newly refurbished bar. Lots of nearby pubs and bars. **Nightlife:** In-college entertainment very good; plenty of places nearby; nearly all clubs in walking distance. **Locals:** Very friendly, and avoids tourists. **Sports:** Newly refurbished gym. Members active in many university teams. **Travel:** Travel grants available. **Financial help:** College sympathetic. Hardship funds available, as well as vacation residence grants. **Jobs:** Officially not allowed during term time. Restaurant and bar work nearby. **Best features:** Friendly, unstuffy and supportive. **Past students:** Indira Gandhi (former Prime Minister of India); Iris Murdoch, Victoria Glendinning, Dorothy L Sayers (authors); Margaret Thatcher (former Prime Minister); Vera Brittain (writer and pacifist); Esther Rantzen (TV presenter); Ann Oakley (writer and sociologist); Kate Mortimer (economist); Dr Cicely Williams (paediatrician); Anne Scott James (journalist); Dame Kiri Te Kanawa (singer); Dorothy Hodgkin (chemist, protein crystallography); Shirley Williams (politician). **More info?** Email jcr.president@somerville.oxford.ac.uk.

Oxford – Trinity

Trinity College, Oxford OX1 3BH
☎ Tel 01865 279900
✉ Email admissions@trinity.ox.ac.uk
💻 Website www.trinity.ox.ac.uk

Profile

Staff & students

Undergraduates: 165 men, 143 women. **Postgraduates:** 86 men, 49 women. **Teaching staff:** *Men:* 24 fellows, 2 junior research fellows, 22 lecturers. *Women:* 1 fellow, 1 junior research fellow, 16 lecturers.

College & admissions

Founded: 1555; women undergraduates first admitted in 1979. **Admission:** Undergraduates not admitted for archaeology and anthropology, biological sciences, classical archaeology and ancient history, computer science, earth sciences, European and Middle Eastern languages, experimental psychology, fine art, geography, history and economics, history and English, history of art, human sciences, mathematics and computer science, music (except for the organ scholar), oriental studies (except with classics as main subject), physiological sciences (except for medicine), PPP.

Study opportunities

Library and information services: Combined arts, science and law library open 24 hours. Separate IT services. Every room has point with access to library resources and internet. IT support from computer manager in normal working hours plus JCR computer reps.

Living

Eating arrangements: All meals can be taken in hall. **Gate/guest hours:** Gate keys issued to college members. **Other college facilities:** Computer room, beer cellar, music society (organ, 2 pianos), squash court, gym, boathouse, playing fields and pavilion; spacious lawns and gardens. **Accommodation:** All 1st- and 2nd-year students accommodated if they wish (most undergraduates),

either in college or in student block about a mile away. Most charged £1076
per term.

Money

Scholarships: College exhibitions based on academic achievement after 1st year; scholarships awarded for final year. Designated college for the Jardine Scholarship (awarded by the Jardine Foundation to successful candidates from the Asia-Pacific area). **Travel grants:** Travelling bursaries, including one for a finalist (£1800); special fund for classical studies; college funds for academically approved projects. **Term-time work:** No outside employment permitted in term time; some in college (library, archives, gardens, kitchens). **Financial help:** Trinity bursaries, in addition to university support.

Student view — Richard Williams, JCR President (3rd year, Theology)

Living

What's it like as a place to live? We occupy a big site but in terms of numbers Trinity is small. This means you have a lot of personal space in the centre of a bustling city (and in pretty luxurious and beautiful surroundings at that). **How's the student accommodation?** College can provide accommodation for every year, which is usually more reasonably priced than the private market. Rooms vary in size and character, but are generally in very good condition and spacious. The most interesting rooms are 17th-century with a shared sitting room, and some are ensuite. **What's the student population like?** Students come from all over the country and around the world, from Manchester to Bermuda. The small student body allows for a close-knit, friendly community. **How do students and locals get on?** While there's a tradition of town vs gown, in reality there are few issues. During term time the centre of town is largely dominated by the student population, especially during the week.

Studying

What's it like as a place to study? The work is tough but engaging, providing a solid grounding in your subject before you go on to specialise in what really interests you, using internationally acclaimed resources and excellent guidance. **What are the teaching staff like?** They range from world-renowned academics to enthusiastic postgraduates. Depending on the subject, tutors are flexible as to the direction study will take.

Socialising

What are student societies like? The societies cater for just about any activity or interest, and there are always opportunities to start up something new, either in college or the wider university. Some, such as the Union Debating Society or the various college boat clubs, have a strong character and culture of their own. Student journalism, drama, sport, music and politics are especially strong. **What's a typical night out?** For a university better known for academic study than its thriving night life, Oxford has a surprisingly diverse range of club nights. From DandB to cheese, indie to dance, Oxford has something to suit a wide variety of tastes . . . whether you can get people to muster the enthusiasm to go out after a hard day's work is an entirely different matter. **And how much does it cost?** Every night a different club will put on a student night with drinks around £2, and free entry before a certain time. **How can you get home safely?** Most students live pretty centrally, close to clubs and well-populated areas, so getting home is fairly easy and safe. Otherwise colleges have funds to reimburse you for emergency taxis.

Money

Is it an expensive place to live? Trinity is generally among the more expensive colleges in Oxford, owing to our superior facilities – though there are also plenty of grants and scholarships available to help. **Average price of a pint?** £1.80 in the college bar. **And the price of a takeaway?** £5. **What's the part-time work situation?** Students are discouraged from finding part-time work, as our terms are only 8 weeks long, so the academic demands are intense. That said, you can earn a fair bit helping out in college behind the bar or working in the reception at the lodge.

Summary

What's the best feature about the place? The strong community feeling and pride in belonging to Trinity. **And the worst?** Everyone knows each other's business. Gossip abounds. **And to sum it all up?** A unique opportunity to combine the standard student experience with living in a palace, eating like a king and getting to know some incredible people.

Past students: Cardinal Newman; William Pitt the Elder; Sir Terence Rattigan (playwright); Lord Clark (Civilisation); Miles Kington (columnist); A V Dicey, W Anson (both great constitutional lawyers); R Hillary (author); Sir Hans Krebs (biochemist), R Porter (immunology), both Nobel Laureates; Sir Arthur Quiller-Couch (author); Ross and Norris McWhirter (Guinness Book of Records), Marmaduke Hussey (former Chairman of BBC); Robin Leigh-Pemberton (former Governor of the Bank of England). **More info?** Alternative prospectus available from the lodge, or contact the JCR President.

Oxford – University College

University College, Oxford OX1 4BH
☎ Tel 01865 276959
✉ Email admissions@univ.ox.ac.uk
🖥 Website www.univ.ox.ac.uk

Profile

Staff & students

Undergraduates: 222 men, 150 women. **Postgraduates:** 140 men, 69 women. **Teaching staff:** *Men:* 27 fellows, 6 research fellows, 10 lecturers. *Women:* 6 fellows, 5 research fellows, 4 lecturers.

College & admissions

Founded: 1249; women undergraduates first admitted in 1979. **Admission:** Undergraduates not admitted for archaeology and anthropology; biology; economics and management; geography; history and English; human sciences; philosophy and theology; theology; on some modern language courses, 1 language must be Russian.

Study opportunities

Library and information services: 2 libraries, 50,000 volumes, of which 35,000 on open shelves; 100 reader seats. 3 computer rooms (PCs, Macs, printers, scanner), open 24/7. Public access terminals (for email and internet) in graduate and undergraduate common rooms; all student rooms have telephone lines and internet points. IT drop-in clinics during term time.

Living

Eating arrangements: Charge of up to £9 a day for 3 meals in hall. **Other college facilities:** Music practice room. Squash court. Sports ground a mile from college (including hard and grass tennis courts). **Accommodation:** College accommodation available to undergraduates in first 3 years if wanted. 330 places available at rent of £113 pw, term time. Rent for room approx £2719 pa. No first-degree students live at home.

Money

Scholarships: Various scholarships and exhibitions, awarded after 1st year (except organ and choral scholarships, which are awarded upon entry). Book grants also available. **Travel grants:** A number awarded each year. **Term-time work:** College allows term-time work within college only (5–10% believed to work). **Financial help:** £80k own funds, 300 students helped; plus £5k other funds, awards £100–£150. Special help: own funds available for accommodation costs. Generous bursaries (up to £2k pa) for students from families with household income under £60k.

Student view

In the High Street, Univ is a very friendly and cosmopolitan college. Despite holding a consistently high position in Oxford's academic league table, it has a very vibrant social life. College bar is the central venue. College music society is ambitious and active (1 or 2 big productions each year). Sports teams successful – most people find themselves representing the college for some team – with high-profile men's and women's teams in rowing, football, hockey and rugby. JCR is apolitical and manages to avoid factiousness; committed to improving the living and working environment of the college. Univ prides itself on being tolerant in every respect, encouraging diversity and commitment. And then there's JCR tea each afternoon and legendary sweaty bops twice a term, followed up by free soup. There's even a karaoke machine. What more could you ask for?

Student footnotes

Housing: College accommodation for 2 years; on a par with other colleges. **Eats:** Cheap college food, including veggie option; main course from £1.50+. Loads of places in High Street (fairly expensive, except multitude of kebab vans including the famous Univ-based Ahmed's). **Drink:** College bar excellent; other college bars cheap. Popular pubs, eg Hobgoblin, Chequers, Wheatsheaf, the Turf, Far From the Madding Crowd. **Nightlife:** College ents cheap and frequent; Union Society club Purple Turtle a popular Univ haunt; lots of new bands playing Oxford; good cinemas. **Locals:** Generally friendly. **Sports:** Free facilities including sports ground and boathouse; squash court on site, and free use of state-of-the-art-gym just across the bridge at Magdalen College School. **Travel:** Various college travel grants, including several summer travel scholarships (£5k) and Keasbey Bursary fund for student travel. **Financial help:** Some £35k allocated by JCR each year; also several college funds and interest-free loans. **Jobs:** In dining hall (free food – excellent fringe benefit); plenty of jobs going about town, although it is requested by tutors that these are not sought. Most go home to work in vacations. **Informal name:** Univ. **Best features:** Inclusive community with friendly and diverse atmosphere. **Past students:** V S Naipaul, C S Lewis (authors); Percy Shelley, Andrew Motion (poets); Clement Attlee (former Prime Minister); Bill Clinton (former US President); Peter Snow (journalist); Bob Hawke (former Prime Minister, Australia); Stephen Hawking (Professor of Mathematics); Armando Ianucci (writer and performer); Prince Youssouppof (Rasputin's murderer), Michael York, Warren Mitchell (actors); Willie Rushton (comedian). **More info?** Contact JCR President (tel 01865 276606, email jcr.president@univ.ox.ac.uk) or get the alternative prospectus from the JCR Academic Affairs Officer at jcr.academic@univ.ox.ac.uk.

Oxford – Wadham

Wadham College, Oxford OX1 3PN
Tel 01865 277545
Email admissions@wadh.ox.ac.uk
Website www.wadham.ox.ac.uk/admissions

Profile

Staff & students

Undergraduates: 240 men, 235 women. **Postgraduates:** 105 men, 60 women. **Teaching staff:** *Men:* 29 fellows, 8 lecturers. *Women:* 12 fellows, 5 lecturers.

College & admissions

Founded: 1610; women undergraduates first admitted in 1974. **Admission:** Undergraduates not admitted for archaeology and anthropology; computer sciences; earth sciences; materials science; fine art; music; theology; geography; materials, economics and management (MEM); philosophy and theology; physiological sciences (except medicine).

Study opportunities

Library and information services: Large, modern library with space for 135 readers; computer room; both open 24 hours.

Living

Eating arrangements: Self-service breakfast, lunch and dinner in hall or student cafeteria. **Gate/guest hours:** No restrictions. **Other college facilities:** Large college theatre, computer room, common room and bar, laundrette, organ and grand piano, squash court, weight-training room; boathouse; sports ground 1¼ miles from college. **Accommodation:** 1st- and final-year students and some 2nd years offered college accommodation in single and shared sets and bedsitters; £984 per term covers rent, heat, light and dinner (breakfast and lunch extra). Plus 150 self-catering rooms in complex of shared flats 1¼ miles north of college, £361 per month including bills. No first-degree students live at home.

Money

Scholarships: Awarded for high performance in university examinations and excellent academic achievement. **Travel grants:** Various travel grants. **Term-time work:** College does not encourage students to take jobs in term time. **Financial help:** Loans or grants available in cases of hardship. Some grants/loans (eg living-out grant) available to all students.

Student view

A large and diverse student community. It has a fair admissions policy, fairly equal male: female ratio and shows no preference for state or private school applicants. Wadham claims to be 'an island of normality in a sea of intellectual and class snobbery'. Anachronistic JCR/MCR system abandoned in favour of unified SU, which is dynamic and politically active; a reputation for social and political consciousness, and environmental awareness. It has some of the best student ents in Oxford, offset by almost terminal laid-backness of some members. Sport teams vary from taking yourself very seriously to laughing a lot. Women's cricket extremely good laugh and Oxford's best, as is men's football; men's cricket, football and rugby 7s university champions. But the key thing about Wadham is that whoever you are, whatever you do, wherever you're from, you will be welcomed. SCR can be sympathetic and tutors generally likeable. College facilities are good: sports ground 15 mins away, library open 24 hours, theatre, squash and badminton courts, weights room. SU subsidised laundrette, TV, video, vending/games machines, photocopier, magazine, news sheet and own pa system; SU shop stocks everything (condoms, washing powder, stationery). Accommodation ranges from old, quaint and airy through to newer, goldfishbowl-like and warm, to brand new, disinfected and well-equipped (ie kitchens). All 1st years and finalists live in and many second and 4th years live in a new building by the sports ground; the rest of 2nd years live out. Relatively easy to change course in 1st term. Graduates go on to do everything, anything, and nothing. Wadhamites are extremely active in journalism, environmentalism, politics, arts, sports . . . they're everywhere, in every university society from tiddlywinks to the Green Party – and sometimes even in the library. The gardens are breathtaking; even the food is getting better.

Student footnotes

Housing: College accommodation, uniform costs (expensive); most students live out for 1 year (find it through noticeboards, estate agents). **Eats:** College lunch good value for pie/chips/beans (veg food better than meat); meals £2-ish. College dinners less impressive, £3; Surrounded by sandwich shops; St Giles Café (greasy, trucker atmosphere) a big favourite. Plenty of kebab/potato vans, burger bars, Indians, Chinese, pubs, cafés, restaurants, standard chains in town; meal from £5–£15. **Drink:** Wadham's bar looks like railway carriage but is friendly and cheap (pint from £2). College surrounded by pubs and other college bars. **Nightlife:** Excellent in college from bops to karaoke, live bands and some of Oxford's finest student DJs. Good cheap indie venues; plenty low-cost student drama in Wadham theatre; free, excellent SU discos. Excellent alternative cinemas and tons of ents in Oxford. All day summer music fest is a high point (Wadstock). **Locals:** Usually OK: a few dodgy areas (eg occasionally Cowley Road). **Sport:** Own sports ground; squash and badminton courts on site; most sports catered for; swimming pool 15 mins away. **Travel:** Travel grants available. Oxford on arterial routes to almost anywhere – by rail, coach, motorways. Car a nuisance (parking non-existent, fines exorbitant). **Financial help:** Good. College hardship funds for a few. Can also apply to university. Domestic bursar usually sympathetic to rent arrears problems. **Jobs:** University rules prohibit term-time work but a few have to. Most work in holidays (in college, Oxford or at home). **Best features:** Laid back and welcoming. **And worst:** The work. **Past students:** Christopher Wren (architect); Michael Foot (former Labour leader); Alan Coren (writer and humorist); Melvyn Bragg (author and broadcaster); Sue Brown (first woman to cox Blues boat); Lindsay Anderson (film and theatre director); Patrick Marber (playwright, actor); Rosamund Pike (Bond girl). **More info?** Wadham Alternative Prospectus from Education and Admissions Officer (email su.education@wadh.ox.ac.uk) or call SU President on 01865 277969.

Oxford – Worcester

Worcester College, Oxford OX1 2HB
Tel 01865 278300
Email admissions@worc.ox.ac.uk
Website www.worc.ox.ac.uk

Profile

Staff & students

Undergraduates: 223 men, 184 women. **Postgraduates:** 119 men, 79 women. **Teaching staff:** *Men:* 26 fellows, 19 research fellows, 24 lecturers, 7 professorial fellows. *Women:* 8 fellows, 12 research fellows, 15 lecturers, 2 professorial fellows.

College & admissions

Founded: 1714; women undergraduates first admitted in 1979. **Admission:** College welcomes both pre- and post-A-level candidates from all types of schools and colleges. Most offers AAA at A-level. Undergraduates not admitted for archaeology and anthropology; human sciences; materials science; materials, economics and management (MEM); oriental studies.

Study opportunities

Library and information services: Undergraduate library including individual reading cubicles; law library and a number of valuable antiquarian collections. Separate IT facilities, access 24 hours/day. Ratio 1:32 workstations to students. Internet connections in every student room. IT support from 4 full-time staff.

Living

Eating arrangements: Informal lunches available; choice of self-service or formal dinner; meals paid for as taken. **Gate/guest hours:** 24 hours/day. Undergraduates are issued with an access card. **Other college facilities:** Cellar bar, buttery, 26 acres of college grounds including mini-gym, 7 tennis courts, playing fields; boathouse. **Accommodation:** Undergraduates normally accommodated for the whole of their degree (in college grounds or within 300m); rent £750–£910 per term. No first-degree students live at home.

Money

Scholarships: Scholarships and exhibitions are awarded in the 2nd and subsequent years for excellence in academic work. 2 instrumental awards available annually to undergraduates in any subject. **Travel grants:** Available annually; also those undertaking fieldwork. **Term-time work:** Some term-time work sometimes available in college bar, hall, lodge and research work.

Student view

Imagine a place where verdant lawns and fragrant roses give way to a still and sparkling lake. Imagine a place where the sounds of a Sunday afternoon are that of leather on willow and the gurgle of another Pimms being poured. Imagine a place where you learn from your tutor as an equal, where your ideas are heeded and criticised. Imagine sitting down to a 3-course dinner in a historic hall, wearing academic gowns. Imagine living in noble, elegant buildings or in ancient, warm cottages. Imagine a vigorously fought karaoke competition taking place in the bar and the entire rugby team performing 'YMCA'. Worcester has all this and more; it is the secret garden of Oxford, with huge, rambling gardens, a lake and on-site playing fields. It upholds the old Oxford adage of 'work hard, play hard'. To the former, it has some of the greatest minds teaching challenging courses to a very high level and well-stocked, 24-hour libraries; to the latter, there is a great cellar bar under the cloisters, a buttery for sitting by a log fire sipping at coffees and chatting the days away, and a notoriously social student body ever itching to party. Whatever tickles your fancy, Worcester will be able to float your boat: great teams in all sports – rugby, rowing, soccer, hockey, cricket, lacrosse – drama society particularly active, and 2 chapel choirs are among the best in Oxford. With all this to offer, no wonder the average Worcester student was recently described as 'happy, well-adjusted, effortlessly brilliant, modest to the point of self effacement, Byronic in his wasted talents, a sparkling conversationalist and wit, and a respectable football player'.

Student footnotes

Housing: Most students in college accommodation (all 1st–3rd years); all students from 2009. **Eats:** Very cheap (£2 for 3-course dinner). Impressive formal halls every night except Saturdays. Lots of local restaurants and eateries. **Drink:** Very cheap college bar (£1.50 a pint). Oxford Union very close (cheap). Popular pubs: Radcliffe Arms, Turf Tavern, King's Arms. Popular bars: Thirst, Freuds, Duke of Cambridge. **Nightlife:** In-college parties, cocktail nights and discos. Filth, the Bridge and Park End provide cheesy nights out. Close to both arty and mainstream cinemas, and to the union for debates, speaker events and parties. **Music:** Classical concerts frequent and of very high quality. Pop, cult and student bands fairly easy to find, but no big stadium. Jazz very popular and prevalent. **Jobs:** College does not allow term-time jobs – there's too little time. **Hardship funds:** Available, as are generous book and travel grants. **Best features:** The fun, intelligent student body; the glorious grounds; the scrummy food; the dynamic and challenging courses. **And worst:** Degrees only last 3 years! **Past students:** Sir Alistair Burnet (journalist and broadcaster); Thomas de Quincey (author and essayist); Richard Lovelace (poet); Rupert Murdoch (media mogul); Donald Carr (cricketer); Richard Adams (author); Anna Markland (pianist); Lord Palumbo (property developer); the Sainsbury family. **More info?** Contact the JCR President (tel 01865 278380).

Peninsula Medical & Dental College

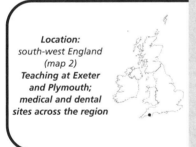

Location:
south-west England
(map 2)
*Teaching at Exeter
and Plymouth;
medical and dental
sites across the region*

Peninsula College of Medicine & Dentistry,
John Bull Building, Research Way,
Tamar Science Park, Plymouth PL6 8BU
☎ Tel 01752 437333
🖷 Fax 01752 517842
✉ Email pcmd-admissions@pcmd.ac.uk
🖥 Website www.pcmd.ac.uk

*Student enquiries: Undergraduate Admissions Office
Applications: UCAS*

In brief

Total Students: 20,170

 40% postgraduate
60% undergraduate

Undergraduates: 12,155

 98% full-time
16% mature on entry

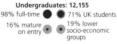 71% UK students
19% lower socio-economic groups

 52% female   48% male

- **Specialist medical and dental school**, partnership between Exeter and Plymouth universities and NHS in the south west.
- **Teaching staff:** 390 full-time and part-time.
- **Broad study areas:** Medicine, dentistry.

Freshers

- **Admissions information:** Typically offers for medicine are for 370–400 points from a maximum of 4 A/AS-levels, to include 320–340 from at least 3 GCE A-levels (minimum grade C in all subjects); at least 1 science subject A-level required (at grade A) and a non-science recommended. For dentistry, a relevant degree or GAMSAT.
- **First degree entrants:** 225 UK, full-time.

- **Points on entry:** 461 (average).
- **Accommodation:** All 1st years in university-approved accommodation.

Profile

Institution

Founded: 2002. **Structural features:** A partnership between universities of Exeter and Plymouth and the NHS in Devon and Cornwall. College is formed of a medical school, a new dental school and graduate school. **Site:** Exeter or Plymouth universities (Years 1–2); acute hospitals in Exeter, Plymouth and Truro; hospitals and dental education clinics across the region (Year 5). **Special features:** Research themes include diabetes, obesity and vascular risk; neuroscience and mental health; development and ageing; environment and human health; health services research; clinical education.

Courses

Academic features: Integration of academic and clinical aspects of course throughout. Years 1–2 delivered through small-group learning (SGL). Graduate-entry dentistry course. **Awarding body:** Joint award by University of Exeter and University of Plymouth. **Main undergraduate awards:** BDS, BM BS, BClinSci. **Length of courses:** 4 years (dentistry); 5 years (medicine).

Study opportunities & careers

Library and information services: Libraries and IT resources of both universities (see separate descriptions) and of the NHS. IT/multimedia a major tool in learning.

Student services & facilities

Student services, amenities and sporting facilities: See descriptions for *Exeter University* and *Plymouth University*. **Accommodation:** All 1st years are offered accommodation owned or approved by the universities; for details see *Exeter University* and *Plymouth University*. Years 2–5, either privately rented, university or hospital accommodation.

Money

Living expenses budget: Minimum budget of £5500 pa recommended (excluding tuition fees). **Financial help:** Bursaries of £1500 pa for UK students whose family income is up to £25k; tapered bursaries (£1k–£250 pa) for those whose family income is £25k–£45k. Additional help for students with a family income of up to £25k who attended a partner school/college or have specified local postcodes. **Tuition fees:** Home students pay £3225 pa for first degrees. International students pay £12,500 pa (pre-clinical), £20k (clinical).

Student view

It started in 2002, affiliated to universities of both Exeter and Plymouth. Students spend the first 2 years based in either Exeter or Plymouth (you are allocated before you arrive, though can swap if you prefer). In the 3rd year, students move either to the other main city or to Truro. There is a similar location swap in Year 4; and in Year 5 there are 2 further options of Torbay and Barnstaple. The rationale is to allow students to experience multiple teaching and clinical environments to reinforce their learning. Being a member of both universities has many advantages – eg twice the services, clubs, societies and socials. Medical students are integrated into the university where they are based, and have the same options as students on other courses. The nightlife is good in Plymouth and Exeter; Truro is quieter. Lots to be doing at all the sites when you aren't working, and pretty much all interests and pastimes are catered for. The south west has much to offer in terms of outdoor activities and is a beautiful area to work and study in. The lifestyle is laid back and friendly, and the school and clinical staff are enthusiastic and accommodating. In the clinical years, the ratio of students to clinicians is currently very low (around 2–3 to 1). Teaching is university-based in the first 2 years (problem-based learning, basic science teaching, lectures and placements in primary care). Last 3 years are in acute hospital trusts and primary care and involve a variety of clinical attachments. The course is new and constantly developing, though this shouldn't put you off applying. The advantages – good, new, accessible resources, modern course approach, welcoming staff and great setting – all add up to a great student experience. Where else can you go surfing in your lunch break?

Student footnotes
See *Exeter University* and *Plymouth University*.

Plymouth University

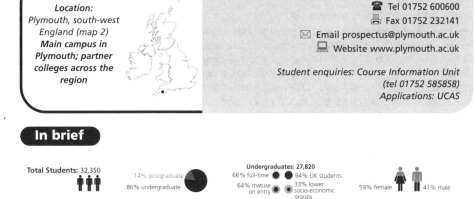

Location:
Plymouth, south-west England (map 2)
Main campus in Plymouth; partner colleges across the region

✉ University of Plymouth, Drake Circus, Plymouth PL4 8AA
☎ Tel 01752 600600
🖷 Fax 01752 232141
✉ Email prospectus@plymouth.ac.uk
💻 Website www.plymouth.ac.uk

Student enquiries: Course Information Unit (tel 01752 585858)
Applications: UCAS

In brief

Total Students: 32,350
14% postgraduate
86% undergraduate

Undergraduates: 27,820
66% full-time ● ● 94% UK students
64% mature ● ● 33% lower socio-economic groups on entry

59% female ● ● 41% male

- **A modern university.**
- **Teaching staff:** 1200 full-time and part-time.
- **Broad study areas:** Art and design, education, human sciences, science, technology, engineering, languages, health, computing, business, humanities, tourism, hospitality, medicine. You can look up the *Peninsula Medical & Dental College* separately.

Freshers
- **Admissions information:** Broad range of AS-levels welcomed, in combination with 2+ A-levels or equivalent; some courses have specific criteria. UCAS tariff used for many offers (Key Skills may count on some courses), others expressed in grades.
- **First degree entrants:** 3820 UK, full-time.
- **Points on entry:** 240–280 average.
- **Drop-out rate:** 8% in 1st year.
- **Accommodation:** Most 1st years housed.

Profile

Institution

Founded: 1970 as a polytechnic, later merging with colleges of education, art and agriculture; university status in 1992. **Structural features:** Peninsula Medical & Dental College, a joint enterprise with Exeter University. Involved in Combined Universities in Cornwall (CUC). Partner colleges in Devon, Cornwall and Somerset. **Site:** Main campus in Plymouth city centre; others in Taunton and Truro (nursing, midwifery). **How to get there:** Regular rail service from London Paddington, South Wales, Midlands and the north to Exeter and Plymouth; coach services from most major cities; by road via M5, and A38 from Exeter (3½ hours London to Plymouth); to Exeter and Plymouth airports from various cities in UK and beyond; ferry links from France and Spain to Plymouth.

Courses

Academic features: Modular degree scheme covering science, social science, arts and marine studies. 1st-year modules offered at partner colleges in Devon, Cornwall and Somerset, so students in south west can study nearer home. **Awarding body:** University of Plymouth. **Main undergraduate awards:** BA, BSc, BEd, BEng, BM BS, MEng, LLB, MMath, MChem, MGeol. **Length of courses:** 3 years; others 4 years (BEd, sandwich courses).

Study opportunities & careers

Library and information services: Specialist libraries on each site: total of 473,000 volumes, 2345 journal subscriptions (increasingly electronic), plus audio-visual materials. Information provision, £67 pa spent for each student (FTE). Network across all campuses and some student accommodation, including CD-ROM, national and international databases. General induction for new students on academic and information services. IT skills normally part of course programmes; short courses, workshops and seminars on computing. **Other learning resources:** Navigation simulator, computer-aided engineering facilities, diving school. Desk-top publishing, colour laser printer, binding and lettering equipment. **Study abroad:** Opportunities to study in Europe (through Socrates-Erasmus), North America or Australia. Students from any discipline can spend a term or a year at a partner institution and complete degree with no loss of time. Languages can be incorporated in most degree courses. **Careers:** Careers education programme; careers fair; information rooms and advice on each campus; computer-assisted guidance system.

Student services & facilities

Student advice and services: Counselling; disability assist service; chaplaincy; medical, legal and other welfare services on each campus. Nursery available. **Amenities:** SU building and offices; also shops, laundrettes, entertainments (visiting bands, DJs, etc.); sporting and non-sporting clubs and societies; Student community action volunteers group; student newspaper. **Sporting facilities:** All mainstream and a variety of other sports; university diving and sailing centre. Indoor recreation activities, eg aerobics, badminton, karate, yoga, fully equipped gym. **Accommodation:** Approx. half of 1st years in university halls. 2100 self-catering places available, £74–£80 pw, £94–£114 pw ensuite, some 40-week, some 52-week contracts. Most students live in privately owned accommodation for 2+ years (university has database of some 5000 rooms): average rent self-catering £55–£90 pw + bills, £80–£90 catered lodgings.

Money

Living expenses budget: Minimum budget of £6050–£6260 for academic year (excluding tuition fees) estimated by university. **Term-time work:** No limit to paid work imposed. Careers service runs earn-and-learn programme. Many jobs on campus. **Financial help:** Bursaries of £1045 pa for students whose family income is up to £25k, of £310 where it is £25k–£40k. Additional help eg for local students, those from designated schools or independent students needing to relocate. Some scholarships (of £350–£2k pa) for students on specified courses or eg achievement in marine sports. Also various funds from government and university; special help for childcare, travel and high course costs, students estranged from parents, serious on-going hardship. **Tuition fees:** Home students pay £3225 pa for first degrees. International students pay £8650 pa (classroom), £9150 (lab/studio).

Student view

Darren Jones, President and Chair of the Board of Trustees, University of Plymouth Students' Union (Graduate, BSc Human Bioscience)

Living
What's it like as a place to live? Plymouth is an amazing place to live; our central campus is within walking distance of the ever-expanding city centre, the famous Plymouth Barbican and the beautiful Hoe and coastlines. The city is also developing quickly with brand new buildings going up every year, including the most recent addition of the Drake Circus shopping centre. Plymouth is an exciting place to live and an amazing place to be a student. **How's the student accommodation?** Student accommodation is very good in Plymouth. 2 new on-campus accommodation blocks (halls) have now been built in addition to our other halls of residence just across the road from campus. The university also has an excellent accommodation service that accredits private accommodation throughout the city – accommodation that is comparably cheap with other city centre universities. **What's the student population like?** Plymouth has a very diverse student population spread out across the whole of the SW Peninsula. We also have the traditional academic community of undergraduates, postgraduates, mature and international students. Plymouth has always been a very friendly, laid-back place to be and a place that you will instantly make good friends in – perhaps for life! **How do students and locals get on?** There have been obvious issues with our expanding student community in the area but in comparison to other central universities we are pretty good. We are also doing much work to try and reduce any tensions that may exist.

Studying
What's it like as a place to study? We are coming to the end of an extensive building programme on campus, with brand new buildings being ready for student use. We also offer a wide range of degree programmes from the traditional science and arts degrees to the more quirky degrees such as surf science and technology. **What are the teaching staff like?** The teaching staff are lovely in Plymouth, with the spectrum of motivated and enthusiastic new academics to renowned academic stars; and the university is very proud of its ethos of staff–student relationships.

Socialising
What are the student societies like? We have around 100 different clubs and societies at UPSU, ranging from football, rugby and the yacht club, to fair trade, politics and Welsh societies! Our clubs and societies can form a central part of your non-academic life as a student at Plymouth; you may go to the Alps with our snow boarding and ski club (the 'Snowriders') or travel to Switzerland with our robotics society – anything is possible! All of our clubs and societies are very friendly and welcome beginners with an interest right through to pros! **What's a typical night out?** A typical night out UPSU style would be to start in the union for some of the cheapest drinks in the city (pint of Strongbow under £1.80!) and to meet with your friends before going to a sponsored club night and Cuba! and/or Ride before ending up (if you're really hardcore!) in Goodbodies for a 5/6am cooked breakfast. **How much does it cost?** Plymouth has some of the cheapest prices in the country and at the SU we offer some of the cheapest of the cheapest in the city! You can expect to have a full night out (from 9pm to 6am) for around £20. **How can you get home safely?** Plymouth has lots of taxis! UPSU works with Taxifast

who only ever charge a flat rate at any time, and because everything is so close together in Plymouth it always costs around £5, if not less!

Money

Is it an expensive place to live? Far from it – Plymouth is one of the cheapest places to be a student in the country, from accommodation costs to costs of living. **Average price of a pint?** In the SU the average price of a pint would be around £2 or less. **And the price of a takeaway?** Depending on what you want you can pay anything from a few pounds for a kebab/chips to around £10–£12 for pizza. **What's the part-time work situation?** There are part-time jobs available in the city with the main employers being the post office sorting office, telephone call centres the shopping centre, and of course the SU!

Summary

What's the best feature about the place? The location. **And the worst?** The location – believe it or not – as it can also be too far away from events in other places. **And to sum up it all up?** An excellent, friendly university with amazing people in a beautiful location that won't cost you the earth to study in.

More info? Enquiries to any UPSU executive member (tel 01752 663337) or from the website (www.upsu.com).

Portsmouth University

Location:
Portsmouth, south coast of England (map 2)
Single city-centre campus; partner colleges

University of Portsmouth, University House, Winston Churchill Avenue, Portsmouth PO1 2UP
☎ Tel 023 9284 8484
🖷 Fax 023 9284 3082
✉ Email admissions@port.ac.uk
🖥 Website www.port.ac.uk

Student enquiries: Assistant Registrar (Admissions)
Applications: UCAS

In brief

Total Students: 19,860

19% postgraduate
1% FE Students
80% undergraduate

Undergraduates: 15,940
86% full-time ● ● 93% UK students
18% mature ● ● 31% lower
on entry ● ● socio-economic
groups

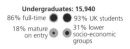

47% female  53% male

- **A modern university.**
- **Teaching staff:** 909 full-time and part-time.
- **Broad study areas:** Business, law, science, psychology, pharmacy, environmental studies, biological sciences, healthcare, engineering, computer science, creative technologies, architecture, art and design, film and media, journalism, humanities, languages, international studies, education.

Freshers

- **Admissions information:** AS-levels accepted in combination with 2+ A-levels or equivalent, depending on course. UCAS tariff used for all courses.

- **First degree entrants:** 3805 UK, full-time.
- **Points on entry:** 240 (average).
- **Drop-out rate:** 7% in 1st year.
- **Accommodation:** Most 1st years are housed.

Profile

Institution

Founded: 1869 as Portsmouth and Gosport School of Science and Art; became Portsmouth Polytechnic 1969; university status in 1992. **Site:** Single campus in city centre. **How to get there:** By train to Portsmouth and Southsea station; by coach to Portsmouth Harbour; by road via A3/M27 and onto M275.

Courses

Academic features: Many courses include foundation courses (in business, art, science, humanities and engineering). Final-year top-up degrees available in some areas. **Awarding body:** University of Portsmouth. **Main undergraduate awards:** FdA, FdSc, FdEng, BA, BSc, BEng, LLB, MEng, MPharm, MArch. **Length of courses:** 3–4 years (full-time).

Study opportunities & careers

Library and information services: Central library; total of 600,000 volumes, 19,500 periodicals, 1000 study places; short loan collection. Information provision, £102 pa spent for each student (FTE). New students given 1-hour introduction to library. Separate IT service with university-wide access to IT facilities, library and internet. **Study abroad:** 12% of students spend a period abroad. Formal exchange links with over 50 European universities and colleges, many open to non-language specialists. **Careers:** Information, advice and guidance service; recruitment service for work experience, volunteering, graduate jobs. Career management skills integrated into undergraduate degree programmes. Employability-based elective units (including learning through experience).

Student services & facilities

Student advice and services: Specialist support and advice on finance, housing, academic skills, careers and recruitment, information; disability advisers; health centre; international student advisers; counselling; chaplaincy; 38-place nursery. **Amenities:** Purpose-built SU with bars, coffee shop, café, nightclub, copyshop, bookshop, convenience store, jobshop and IT service centre.

Sporting facilities: Wide range over 3 sites (St. Paul's gymnasium, Nuffield Sports Centre and Langstone Campus sports grounds): indoor sports centre, state-of-the-art fitness studios and gymnasium, floodlit synthetic turf pitch, multi-use game area. Sports scholarships for elite athletes. **Accommodation:** Majority of 1st years offered a place in halls. 2940 study bedrooms, catered and self-catered, all with broadband, telephone and television service. Rent £75–£84 pw self-catering (£87–£102 ensuite), £89–£114 pw catered. Some rooms for students with disabilities. Average rent in local private accommodation £62–£65 pw plus bills for self-catering, lodgings £60–£70 pw, half board £70–£80 pw (usually including utilities).

Money

Living expenses budget: A minimum budget of £6k–£7k pa (excluding tuition fees) recommended by university. **Term-time work:** University allows part-time work in term time for full-time students (60% believed to work). SU Jobshop helps with term-time and vacation employment in local companies, retail outlets and university (eg SU bars, cloakroom, JobShop, customer service, administration, events, marketing, etc.). **Financial help:** Bursaries of £900 pa for UK students whose family income is up to £25k, of £600 pa for where family income is £25k–£32k. Additional bursaries for those from designated local colleges (£300 pa), for Foyer residents or those who have been in care (£1k pa), and for sports. Hardship fund of £500k (especially for students narrowly missing bursary entitlement). Also £515,833 government access to learning funds. Variety of other funds eg to help with accommodation, short-term loans (£16,258; 170 students helped), other funds and scholarships (£120,453; 197 students helped). **Tuition fees:** Home students pay £3225 pa for first degrees (reduced in placement year). International students pay £8350 pa (classroom), £9650 (lab/studio). Students may pay by instalment.

Student view) **Steve Topazio,** Education and Representation Officer (Graduate, Geography)

Living
What's it like as a place to live? Portsmouth is a vibrant and lively city with plenty to do. There is a nice mix of local residents, students and the Royal Navy, which provides a diverse community to live in. The nightlife is amazing, with a range of clubs and pubs offering great offers on food and drink. Gunwarf Quays is the main attraction in the city, with a bowling alley, cinema, restaurants and the world-famous Spinaker Tower, which offers fantastic views over the harbour and the Solent. **How's the student accommodation?** University accommodation ranges from basic to very plush. Depending on how much you want to spend, you can get a room with an ensuite, shared kitchen and living area, or if you opt for the cheaper option you can get your basic room with shared bathroom and kitchen. Private accommodation varies drastically, which is why it is always important to look around. The usual rent for private accommodation is £250 (per person per month, excluding bills) for a 3–4 bedroom house, although there are some houses for 5+. Most private rented accommodation is within 20–30 mins' walk of the university. **What's the student population like?** The student population is very friendly, with lots of interaction through the union in sports and societies. The population is also very diverse, with students from over 100 countries coming to the university. **How do students and locals get on?** Students, locals and the Navy tend to keep themselves to themselves, but through the work of the SU more community links are being made, which benefits everyone on the island.

Studying
What's it like as a place to study? Portsmouth is a fantastic place to study, the courses are very well taught and the resources available are second to none. A new library was opened in 2008 and a new teaching building in 2009. The Langstone campus offers many sports facilities and there is a university gym and 2 sports halls. **What are the teaching staff like?** As with most institutions, the teaching staff varies across the subjects. In the most part, academic staff are friendly and very well qualified and you even see the odd lecturer out in the union on a Wednesday night.

Socialising
What are student societies like? The SU offers over 100 sports clubs and societies catering for all interests. Visit www.upsu.net/au and www.upsu.net/societies to see a list of them all, but to give you a taste there are football, rugby, golf, sailing, hockey, boxing, juggling, go karting, rock, geography and fantasy role play! The union even offers volunteering opportunities and regularly raises money for its charities. **What's a typical night out?** Wednesday night is the best night out, starting with a few drinks in your local pub followed by a cheesy dressing-up theme at the SU, drinking the drink of Portsmouth – snakebite! **And how much does it cost?** On a Wednesday night you can expect to spend between £20 and £30 depending on your choice of drink. **How can you**

get home safely? The University Bus runs until midnight, but the quickest and cheapest way home is the local taxi firm; a typical journey home will cost you £4.

Money

Is it an expensive place to live? In most cases the student loan will pay for you to live a basic lifestyle at university. However most people work part time so they have a little bit of extra cash. The SU job shop advertises many local vacancies. Portsmouth is not an expensive place to live so long as you look around for the best deals! **Average price of a pint?** £1.80 in most pubs; some clubs offer special offers on certain nights. **And the price of a takeaway?** 9-inch pizza, garlic bread and can of coke for £7. **What's the part-time work situation?** The SU job shop helps students find part-time work; most jobs are above minimum wage. There are always jobs available, especially in the local call centre.

Summary

What's the best feature about the place? The seaside and beach, nothing better than having a BBQ by the beach after the summer exams. **And the worst?** Living near the sea – when winter comes you really know about it! **And to sum it all up?** The best city in the UK; it may be an island, but Portsmouth offers the best overall university experience. **More info?** Try visiting www.upsu.net.

Queen Margaret University

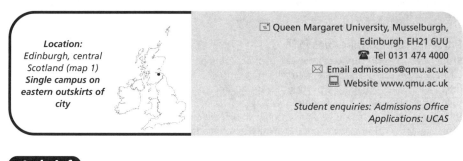

Location:
Edinburgh, central
Scotland (map 1)
Single campus on
eastern outskirts of
city

Queen Margaret University, Musselburgh,
Edinburgh EH21 6UU
Tel 0131 474 4000
Email admissions@qmu.ac.uk
Website www.qmu.ac.uk

Student enquiries: Admissions Office
Applications: UCAS

In brief

Total Students: 5655

22% postgraduate
78% undergraduate

Undergraduates: 4410
74% full-time
33% mature on entry
85% UK students
30% lower socio-economic groups

77% female
23% male

- **A modern university.**
- **Teaching staff:** 230 full-time.
- **Broad study areas:** Health sciences and health professional studies; social sciences; media and communication; drama and creative industries; business and enterprise.

Freshers

- **Admissions information:** UCAS tariff used in majority of courses; some offers expressed as grades.
- **First degree entrants:** 850 UK, full-time.
- **Points on entry:** 226 (average); range 180–336.
- **Drop-out rate:** 14% in 1st year.
- **Accommodation:** Majority of 1st years housed.

Profile

Institution

Founded: 1875; university status in 2007. **Site:** Single, purpose-built campus by Musselburgh, on south-east outskirts of Edinburgh. **How to get there:** Edinburgh easily accessible by train, coach from all over the UK, to Waverley railway station and central bus station (St Andrew's Square); airport 8 miles. Campus is next to Musselburgh railway station (6 mins from Waverley station); frequent bus service from city centre.

Courses

Awarding body: Queen Margaret University. **Main undergraduate awards:** BA, BSc. **Length of courses:** 3 years; 4 years (Hons).

Study opportunities & careers

Library and information services: Learning resources centre (LRC) with 120,000 books, 37,000 e-books, 700 journals, 16,500 e-journals; 1000 study places (some open 24/7). Books in heavy demand also held in reserve. Information provision, £109 pa spent for each student (FTE). LRC open 7 days/week all year, up to 12 hours/day in term time. IT service: 300 terminals, all with internet access, on wireless network. IT help desks in LRC. Induction on use of online catalogue and other services; e-resources workshops. **Study abroad:** European Erasmus links in many subjects (eg hospitality and tourism management, occupational therapy, drama). Also exchange opportunities in USA, Canada, Australia. **Careers:** Advice service; also Job Shop to help students get part-time and temporary work relevant to their degree.

Student services & facilities

Student advice and services: Counselling, disability support, advice on student funding, careers advice; mature student guidance; medical and healthcare service. **Amenities:** SU building, restaurants, cafés, shops, etc. **Sporting facilities:** Large sports hall, aerobics/dance studio, fitness suite, AstroTurf pitch. **Accommodation:** Majority of 1st-year students in university accommodation. 800 new self-catering rooms (all ensuite and with IT facilities); rent £91–£96 pw; 40 or 50-week contracts. Many students live in privately owned accommodation for 2 years: rent approx £300 per month for self-catering.

Money

Living expenses budget: Minimum budget of £5700–£6200 for academic year (excluding tuition fees) recommended by university; £8k for a full calendar year. **Term-time work:** Job Shop helps students find part-time and vacation work. **Financial help:** £255k discretionary and childcare funds, 265 students helped (awards range from £100–£2k). Special help: mature students; those with dependants, low income, disabilities or health problems; final-year students. Apply to student services office for help. **Tuition fees:** Scottish and EU students pay no fees during course; other UK students pay £1820 pa for first degrees (although tuition is free on some healthcare courses). International students pay £8800 (classroom), £9700 (lab/studio based).

Student view

Modern, attractive and rapidly expanding – in 2007 it gained full university status and moved to a brand new, purpose-built campus to the east of the city, by Musselburgh. Great facilities including a learning café; networked and wireless access for PCs and notebooks; TV, photographic and video-conferencing studios; and new sports facilities – to name but a few. On-site accommodation for some 800, mostly in flats for 4–5. Most live in private accommodation after 1st year; large numbers of students in Edinburgh, so accommodation in town is expensive and sometimes difficult to find. SU runs events most evenings such as karaoke, theme nights (Big Brother, Weakest Link, Who Wants to be a Millionaire, Pop Idol, etc.), quizzes, bingo, comedy nights, films, band nights and many more – the most popular student night being Wednesdays; SU making the most of the new venue at Musselburgh. Courses range from healthcare to business and many departments are known for their excellence (eg occupational therapy and physiotherapy); more arts and management courses being introduced. Most courses are modular; low drop-out rate. Most students are Scottish and under 22 but there is a growing contingent of mature and international students. High graduate employment rate in variety of fields; many courses also give a professional qualification.

Student footnotes

Housing: New self-catering halls. **Eats:** SU sells food and snacks at budget prices (£2+ for a meal). **Drink:** SU bar (£1.50 a pint); lively and friendly atmosphere. **Nightlife:** Union events most nights. Bands include tribute and student bands. **Locals:** Very friendly. **Sports:** New sports centre: large sports hall, aerobics/dance studio, state-of-the-art fitness suite, AstroTurf. **Travel:** Edinburgh offers many student concessions on trains and buses. **Financial help:** College loan system for students with good reasons. Access fund. **Jobs:** Some jobs on campus but most students find work in pubs, shops and restaurants in city centre. Vacancies advertised in jobshop. **Informal name:** QMU. **Best features:** Friendly, welcoming, fun, community spirit, you won't be a face in the crowd. **And worst:** Not in city centre. **More info?** Check out www.qmusu.org.uk.

Queen Mary

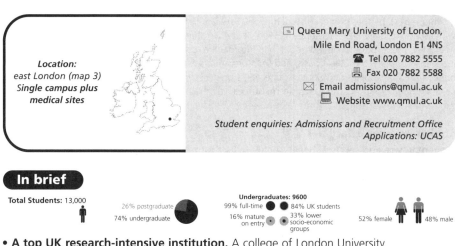

Location:
east London (map 3)
Single campus plus
medical sites

Queen Mary University of London,
Mile End Road, London E1 4NS
Tel 020 7882 5555
Fax 020 7882 5588
Email admissions@qmul.ac.uk
Website www.qmul.ac.uk

Student enquiries: Admissions and Recruitment Office
Applications: UCAS

In brief

Total Students: 13,000

26% postgraduate
74% undergraduate

Undergraduates: 9600
99% full-time
16% mature on entry
84% UK students
33% lower socio-economic groups

52% female   48% male

- **A top UK research-intensive institution.** A college of London University.
- **Teaching staff:** 1000 full-time.
- **Broad study areas:** Arts, engineering, informatics and mathematical sciences, medicine and dentistry, law, natural sciences, social sciences, management.

Freshers

- **Admissions information:** AS-levels accepted in combination with 2 (usually 3) A-levels or equivalent; Key Skills not considered. UCAS tariff used by most departments.
- **First degree entrants:** 2775 UK, full-time.
- **Points on entry:** 280 (average).
- **Drop-out rate:** 9% in 1st year.
- **Accommodation:** Almost all 1st years housed.

Profile

Institution

Founded: 1989, from merger of Westfield College (founded 1882) and Queen Mary College (1887); joined in 1995 by St Bartholomew's and the London Hospital medical colleges. **Structural features:** Part of London University. You can look up the medical and dental school (*Barts & The London*) separately. **Site:** Main campus on Mile End Road; clinical studies at Whitechapel, West Smithfield and Charterhouse Square sites. **How to get there:** 5 mins' walk from Stepney Green or Mile End underground stations, 10 mins from Bow Road station (Docklands Light Railway); No. 25 bus. **Special features:** Large number of visiting professors.

Courses

Academic features: Course-unit system allows students to make up tailor-made degree programme with guidance. **Awarding body:** University of London. **Main undergraduate awards:** BA, BEng, MEng, BSc, MSci, LLB, MBBS, BDS. **Length of courses:** 3 years; others 4 years; 5 years (medicine, dentistry).

Study opportunities & careers

Library and information services: 600,000 volumes, 2500 periodicals, 4000 e-journals. Information provision, £125 pa spent for each student (FTE). Separate IT facilities; approx 900 workstations, all with access to library and internet (ratio workstations to students 1:12). IT facilities open up to 14 hours/day; support from helpdesk, published information, computer services shop. New students have induction to library, on subject basis, and to information services, including basic PC skills and college network; IT skills courses on Windows, internet, system security, software (eg Excel, Quark XPress) and programs (eg Fortran). **Other learning resources:** Language laboratory. **Study abroad:** Formal exchange links with Europe and the USA. **Careers:** Information, advice and placement service.

Student services & facilities

Student advice and services: Health centre, welfare service, chaplains, counsellors, nursery, Nightline. **Amenities:** Shop, bookshop, travel centre and bank on site; SU building with nightclub, snackbar, bar. **Sporting facilities:** Multigym, gymnasium, squash courts on site; London University Union facilities (including swimming pool); sports ground in Essex (on tube line), hockey pitch in east London and boathouse in Chiswick. **Accommodation:** Offered to almost all single 1st-year students, priority to those who apply by 30 June and those who live furthest away. 2355 places available: self-catering places at £70–£98 (up to £114 pw ensuite; £63.50 if sharing), 38+ week contracts, Sept–June. Plus 220 intercollegiate places, £106 pw full-board (£91 sharing). Students live in privately owned accommodation for 1–2 years: self-catering rent £85–£100 pw plus bills, lodgings £85–£90. Ample private accommodation within a 3-mile radius.

Money

Living expenses budget: Minimum budget of £8k pa (excluding tuition fees) recommended.
Financial help: Bursaries of £1050 pa to UK students whose family income is up to £25k (a higher

rate of £4k pa for those with 3 A grades at A-level); £839 pa for tho
£34,600. Also £360k government funds, £25k own funds (awards rar.
£100–£3500); own funds for final-year students. Strictly limited help fo
exceptional financial hardship only. Some departmental scholarships avai.
awards office for help. **Tuition fees:** Home students pay £3225 pa for fir.
students pay £9k pa (classroom), £10,900 (lab/studio), £12,700–£14,600 (µ
£21,900–£23,350 (clinical).

Student view

It's a traditional university with a contemporary approach. It has been revamped to provide
modern, flexible courses that make graduates some of the most employable around. Mile
End site is hard to miss (impressive 1880s architecture) in London's vibrant East End, a mile
from the City and 5 mins from Canary Wharf. Unusually for London, it's a campus-based
college with halls (in newly opened student village) and most teaching on same site.
Medicine and dentistry is mostly at Whitechapel (Royal London Hospital) with another site
at Barts Hospital in West Smithfield (you can look up *Barts & The London* separately). Easy
access to centre of London and plenty of local culture. SU runs a number of bars, large
retail outlets and an academic advice service. Over 100 clubs and societies, from LGBT to
mountaineering – you're guaranteed to find something you like. Squash court, multigym
and sports hall on site (SU recently redeveloped its nightclub into a top London fitness
centre); extensive sports grounds at Chislehurst. Renowned for science, engineering,
languages, law, dentistry and medicine, but many top-quality smaller-scale arts and social
science departments. Large library with specialised study areas and extensive computer
facilities. Students from all backgrounds with large, well-integrated, international
community. Strong equal opportunities policy.

Student footnotes

Housing: Self-catering halls at Mile End overlooking Regent's Canal; and purpose-built student village
on site (2000 beds, café bar, shop, multigym and laundry, fitness centre). Plentiful local private
accommodation. **Eats:** Meal costs £3–£4 on campus; £4–£5 in local pubs. Excellent local Indian
cuisine; many cheap local restaurants; cheap bagels and curry in Brick Lane. **Drink:** SU bar has wide
range of drinks, regular promotions; pint from £1.80. Good East End pubs. London Pride is good local
brew. **Nightlife:** Regular weekly ents in top SU nightclub (club e1), including regular current chart
and pop nights; popular comedy and sports nights. London clubs, bars, pubs, theatres, cinemas all
accessible with lots of student discounts available. **Sports:** Sports hall, multigym and squash courts on
campus; excellent range of sports from men's rugby to women's football. **Travel:** STA branch on
campus. Good tube and bus links. Night buses from central London. **Financial help:** Some funds
available. **Jobs:** SU has a jobshop with lots of posts. Over 150 students work in SU. **Best features:**
Campus-based college, great location with lots of cultural diversity, friendliness of students and staff,
community atmosphere. **And worst:** Distance to sports grounds. **Informal name:** QMUL. **Past
students:** Peter Hain MP; Geoffrey Drain (author); Sir Roy Strong (art historian); Judge Alan Lipfriend;
Rhys Williams (rugby); Lady Falkender (secretary to Harold Wilson); Ruth Prawer Jhabvala, Malcolm
Bradbury, Andrea Newman (authors); Simon Gray (playwright); Patrick Moore (astronomer); Elizabeth
Andrews (former MP); Bruce Dickinson (of Iron Maiden). **More info?** Try www.qmsu.org.

Queen's University Belfast

Location:
Belfast, Northern Ireland (map 1)
Single site in centre of city plus medical site

Queen's University Belfast, University Road, Belfast BT7 1NN, Northern Ireland
☎ Tel 028 9097 2727
🖷 Fax 028 9097 2828
✉ Email admissions@qub.ac.uk
💻 Website www.qub.ac.uk

Student enquiries: Admissions Office
Applications: UCAS (but direct for nursing)

In brief

Total Students: 24,135

23% postgraduate
77% undergraduate

Undergraduates: 18,700
72% full-time — 95% UK students
19% mature on entry — 35% lower socio-economic groups

60% female — 40% male

- **A top UK research-intensive university.**
- **Teaching staff:** 831 full-time.
- **Broad study areas:** Applied social work; archaeology; business and management; Celtic studies; civil engineering; classics and ancient history; dentistry; economics; education; electrical and electronic engineering; English; history; law; maths, statistics and operational research; medicine; music; nursing; pharmacology and pharmacy; physics and astronomy; politics; psychology; theology and religious studies; town and country planning and landscape.

Freshers

- **Admissions information:** Offers in terms of grades rather than UCAS tariff points, usually based on 3 A-levels (with maybe an alternative offer based on 3 A-levels and an AS-level). Two AS-levels usually acceptable in lieu of a 3rd A-level, except for medicine and dentistry (who must have 3 A-levels plus an AS-level).
- **First degree entrants:** 3815 UK, full-time.
- **Points on entry:** 358 (average).
- **Drop-out rate:** 8% in 1st year.
- **Accommodation:** All 1st years who require it are housed; many live at home.

Profile

Institution

Founded: 1845 as Queen's College; university status in 1908. **Site:** Main site about 1 mile from city centre, undergoing major refurbishment; medical site about 1 mile from main site. **Special features:** International arts festival.

Courses

Awarding body: Queen's University Belfast. **Main undergraduate awards:** BA, BD, BDS, BEng, BMus, BSc, BTh, LLB, MB BCh, BAO, MEng, MPharm, MSci. **Length of courses:** 3 or 4 years; 5 years (BDS, MB BCh, BAO).

Study opportunities & careers

Library and information services: Main library (central site), and libraries for science, medicine, agriculture and food science; major new library in 2009. Total approx 2 million books plus extensive electronic resources. Information provision, £161 pa spent for each student (FTE). **Other learning resources:** NI technology centre, computer centres (open access), non-specialist language teaching as well as the Marine biology station, astronomical observatory, conservation laboratory, phytotron, palaeoecology centre, field centre, electron microscope unit, microprocessor laboratory. **Study abroad:** Range of courses include option to study at a partner university; European mobility programmes enable selected students to spend 3–9 months overseas. Some students may interrupt their course to work in Europe and USA. **Careers:** Information and advice service.

Student services & facilities

Student advice and services: One-stop student guidance centre has information on eg careers, accommodation, financial support. Health service, counselling service, student support officer. **Amenities:** Refurbished SU building with supermarket, secondhand bookshop, bars, discos, laundrette, bank, insurance company, travel agency, cinema on campus, bookshop, Officers' Training Corps. **Sporting facilities:** Playing fields and new sports facilities at physical education centre. **Accommodation:** All 1st years who require it are in university accommodation. 2100 self-catering places available (980 ensuite), most in purpose-built student village in walking distance of main campus; rent £72–£86 pw, including internet access; rooms in houses, without network, from £61 pw. Rents in privately owned accommodation, average £52 pw plus utilities (most within 2km). Up to 40% of first-degree students live at home.

Money

Living expenses budget: Minimum budget of £5500–£7k pa (excluding tuition fees) recommended by university. **Term-time work:** University allows full-time students to work in term time. Some work on campus in administration, SU, gardening, portering, catering, library and PE centre; vacancy list for work off campus and SU liaison with employers. **Financial help:** Bursaries of £1125 pa to UK students whose family income is up to £17,900; of £615 pa for those whose family income is £17,900–£22,900. Also £100 to all students with a family income of up to £32,900, for use at university bookshop or sports facilities. Special help: students in private accommodation with high rent, single parents, mature students with dependants and those with disabilities. Own funds usually for non-UK students suffering unforeseen hardship. Apply to SU student advice centre for help. **Tuition fees:** Home students pay £3225 pa for first degrees. International students pay £8970 pa (classroom), £10,990 (lab/studio), £12,150 (preclinical), £22,920 (clinical).

Student view

University area is one of the most beautiful in Belfast, bordering posh Malone Road. Facilities good: 2 diners, 2 bars and 2 large venues with licensed bars; also crèche facilities. Many students are local and live at home – often it's an extension of school and school friends. Academic standards high. Fair proportion of graduates go overseas for jobs; most remain at home. University undergoing major refurbishment. Accommodation, library, sports facilities all had a facelift. Public transport runs until 11pm; university area is centre of night life and SU is active. Major pop acts play in Belfast; regular discos and gigs in SU and town. Renaissance of pubs and eating places; also 4 major cinema complexes (including 1 10-screen cinema) showing national releases; Queen's Film Theatre has excellent alternative films. Annual festival, second only to Edinburgh in size and diversity. Main drug is alcohol. Police over-stretched but active in student area.

Student footnotes

Housing: Many live at home; others in halls for 1 year. Local housing through noticeboards, newspapers, SU welfare office and uni accommodation office (watch the small print: some seem more expensive but include utility bills so work out cheaper). **Eats:** Good variety in 2 restaurants in SU. Most local pubs do lunches and good food in bars (£4.50). **Drink:** Lots of good bars in university area. SU cheap, £2+ a pint, £2.50+ elsewhere. Speakeasy and Bunatee SU bars – specials all year round. Good brews are Harp, Smithwick's, Guinness. **Nightlife:** SU main venue for bands and discos. Shine (in SU) is a premier dance venue in Ireland. **Locals:** Very friendly; student area is pleasant. **Sports:** Excellent facilities on campus, including pool, gym, indoor football court; leisure centres, outdoor pitches. **Travel:** Cheap travel on railways. Hitching not practical. 15% off bus fare with Translink. **Financial help:** Bursar's loans and access funds. **Jobs:** Bar work, cloakrooms, bouncers, shop staff, library assistants – minimum wage; SU employs some 200 students. Most students do some kind of part-time work. 20% work locally in holidays; many find work at home. **Best features:** Large numbers of students but in close-knit community. **And worst:** Most students go home at weekends. **Past students:** Trevor Ringland, Nigel Carr, Philip Matthews (rugby players); Brian Mawhinney MP; Seamus Heaney (poet); Bernadette McAliskey (née Devlin, political activist); Kenneth Branagh (actor); Lord Tombs (former Chairman of Rolls-Royce); Brian Moore (writer); Paddy Kielty (TV presenter); Mary McAleese (President, Irish Republic). **More info?** Ring SU welfare officer or education office on 028 9097 3106, email su.president@qub.ac.uk or check out the website (www.qubsu.org).

RADA

Location:
central London
(map 3)
**Single site in
Bloomsbury**

Royal Academy of Dramatic Art,
62–64 Gower Street, London WC1E 6ED
☎ Tel 020 7636 7076
🖷 Fax 020 7323 3865
✉ Email enquiries@rada.ac.uk
💻 Website www.rada.org

*Student enquiries: Admissions
Applications: Direct*

In brief

Total Students: 230

15% postgraduate
85% undergraduate

Undergraduates: 200
100% full-time   85% UK students
10% mature
on entry

50% female   50% male

- **World-class specialist drama school.** Member of the Conservatoire for Dance & Drama.

- **Teaching staff:** 10 full-time, 35 part-time.

- **Broad study areas:** Acting, performance arts, theatre technical arts, theatre directing, theatre design, theatre costume, property making, stage electrics and lighting design, scenic art, scenic construction.

Freshers

- **Admissions information:** All eligible applicants are auditioned/interviewed.

- **First degree entrants:** 60 UK, full-time.

- **Drop-out rate:** Nil in 1st year.
- **Accommodation:** No RADA housing.

Profile

Institution
Founded: 1904, by Sir Herbert Beerbohm Tree; Royal Charter in 1920. **Site:** Gower Street (in heart of London University area); annexe in Chenies Street. **How to get there:** Close to many bus routes and several tube stations (Goodge Street, Tottenham Court Road, Euston, Warren St). **Structural features:** Founding member of Conservatoire for Dance & Drama.

Courses
Academic features: MA joint with King's College. Many short courses and summer schools. **Awarding body:** King's College London and University of London. **Main awards:** BA, graduate diploma, graduate certificate. **Length of courses:** 9 terms (BA acting); 6 terms (theatre technical arts, theatre design, theatre costume); 4 terms (specialist technical training); 3 terms (directing).

Study opportunities & careers
Library and information services: 25,000 volumes, 10 periodicals; video tape library. Specialist collections: G B Shaw collection. **Other learning resources:** 3 fully equipped theatres – Jerwood Vanbrugh (newly designed proscenium), the GBS and the John Gielgud Theatres. Broadcasting studio, scenery and property workshops, digital sound studio, design office and wardrobe. **Careers:** Information, advice and placement service.

Student services & facilities
Student advice and services: Access to all essential services. **Amenities:** Common rooms, refectory. **Accommodation:** No academy accommodation. Local rent approx £90–£120 pw.

Money
Living expenses budget: Minimum budget of £10,700 pa (excluding tuition fees) recommended by RADA. **Financial help:** Conservatoire bursaries of £1700 pa (£2100 in final year) for UK students whose family income is up to £25k; tapered down to £100 pa (£500 in final year) where family income is £39,300. **Tuition fees:** Home students pay £3225 pa for first degrees. International students pay £13,340 pa.

Student view

Acting, stage management and technical courses all very demanding and the hours are long. But then RADA training is possibly the best in the world. Because of this, very large numbers apply each year; selection is by audition or interview. Links to the profession are excellent – guest designers and directors work on all final-year productions. Agents and casting directors keep a watchful eye over final-year acting students, while second-year stage managers spend half a term on secondment, working with professionals. Life is not cheap.

Student footnotes
Housing: No London accommodation is cheap, and is not easy to find it nearby. RADA students have limited access to neighbouring student accommodation. **Eats:** Canteen on site, cheap subsidised food. Access to West End eateries. **Drink:** RADA Bar has special offers. Local actor and stage management bars. **Nightlife:** Public in-house shows are free to students, also some other

productions. Events in RADA Bar, eg karaoke, play reading, bands. Usual London nightlife. **Sports:** Local YMCA, etc.; ULU sports facilities nearby. **Financial help:** Excellent but limited (no student has ever been turned away because of lack of funds). **Good news:** Major refurbishment of Gower Street building; now houses one of the most advanced 200-seat theatres in Europe. **Past students:** Alan Bates, Sir John Gielgud, Dame Flora Robson, Susannah York, Lord Richard Attenborough, Glenda Jackson, Joan Collins, Ben Cross, Robert Lindsay, Lisa Eichhorn, Jonathan Pryce, Juliet Stevenson, Kenneth Branagh, Anton Lesser, John Hurt, Richard Briers, Albert Finney, Sir Anthony Hopkins, Sir Anthony Quayle, Ralph Fiennes, Mike Leigh, Jane Horrocks (actors).

Ravensbourne College of Design & Communication

Location:
south-east of London, within M25 (map 3)
Single site in Chislehurst, south-east London

Ravensbourne College of Design & Communication, Walden Road, Chislehurst, Kent BR7 5SN
☎ Tel 020 8289 4900
🖷 Fax 020 8325 8320
✉ Email info@rave.ac.uk
💻 Website www.ravensbourne.ac.uk

Student enquiries: Admissions Officer
Applications: UCAS (direct for foundation and postgraduate courses)

In brief

Total Students: 1500

2% postgraduate
17% FE Students
81% undergraduate

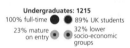
Undergraduates: 1215
100% full-time ● ● 89% UK students
23% mature ● ● 32% lower socio-economic groups
on entry

45% female 55% male

- **Specialist design and media college.**
- **Teaching staff:** 37 full-time, 180 sessional.
- **Broad study areas:** Design, broadcasting, film-making, fashion, graphic design, product design, architecture, animation, photography.

Freshers
- **Admissions information:** UCAS tariff used.
- **First degree entrants:** 205 UK, full-time.
- **Points on entry:** 210+ (average).
- **Drop-out rate:** 7% in 1st year.
- **Accommodation:** Some 1st years housed.

Profile

Institution
Founded: 1962, incorporating Bromley, Sidcup and Beckenham colleges of art. **Site:** 18-acre main site in Chislehurst. Moving in 2010 to new state-of-the-art campus in Greenwich. **How to get there:** Train from Charing Cross or London Bridge to Elmstead Woods; bus to college.

Courses

Academic features: English language support for international students. **Awarding body:** University of Sussex, City University. **Main undergraduate award:** BA. **Length of courses:** 2 or 3 years; 4 years (with Year 0).

Study opportunities & careers

Library and information services: 27,000 volumes in total, 170 journals, 3750 DVDs and videos, desktop publishing and computer image generation laboratories. Information provision, £60 pa spent for each student (FTE). 160 internet points; ratio of 1:3 workstations to students, access 12 hours/weekday. 15 full-time IT staff; 1-day induction for all new students plus top-up IT-skills training. **Other learning resources:** 2 broadcast studios equipped to industry standard with sound, video-editing and post-production equipment. Quantel and Discreet suite. Large-scale virtual reality set. 3-D printing and product prototyping workshop. Process and dye labs, printing rooms, etc. **Careers:** Information and advice service, work placements, industry days, student shows.

Student services & facilities

Amenities: SU bar; television studios/facilities. Regular events programme. **Sporting facilities:** Links with local sports centres and health clubs. **Accommodation:** Some 1st years in college accommodation. 100 self-catering places available (preference given to 1st years), rent approx £80 pw, term time only. Students live in privately owned accommodation for 2–3 years; rent typically £350 a month self-catering.

Money

Living expenses budget: A minimum of £5500 pa (excluding tuition fees) recommended by college. **Financial help:** Bursaries of £319 pa for UK students (on courses with £3225 fee), whose family income is up to £25k; of £500 pa for students from specified local schools or colleges. Further help eg for students from Ravensbourne foundation degree or diploma courses, talented students, those from specified schools and colleges, help with living, travel and work experience costs and £500 laptop voucher on selected courses. **Tuition fees:** Home students pay £3225 pa for first degrees. International students pay £9k pa (but early payment discount).

Student view

The town is quiet, with few local pubs, although there are some decent, friendly places to socialise. College has a good atmosphere. SU has grown a lot recently – regular union meetings enable every student's voice to be heard; it's ambitious and active politically as well as socially. SU bar was redesigned and built by students in the style of a cool London-style bar. It's packed every Thursday (event night) and hosts bands (indie to RandB, funk to jazz and house), all kinds of discos and fancy dress extravaganzas. Main attraction is the cheap beer, happy hours and a friendly atmosphere. There's also a film club and a monthly magazine, written and published by students. Easy access to London (only 15 mins by train). Bromley is close, with pubs (not too bad) and leisure centre (nice, not too expensive). College very relaxed until degree shows approach. Good reputation in industry. Because of small number of students, there's a lot of inter-departmental cooperation and everyone gets to know one another. It's an inspiring place to be because there's such a high concentration of creative people. Counselling tutor on hand 2 days a week. At Ravensbourne you get out what you put in!

Student footnotes

Housing: Not all 1st years in college housing but college has accommodation list; also look in *Bromley News Shopper* and estate agents. **Eats:** Good, cheap food in canteen, eg £3.50 for a filling hot lunch; vegetarians well catered for; occasional international themed food days. Chislehurst good for bars, cafes (excellent sandwich shop). **Drink:** £1.70+ a pint in SU bar. Lloyds in Bromley also good, as is Queen's Head (local, traditional). **Nightlife:** SU event nights, cheap entry (sometimes free). Also monthly external events where SU takes over local venue (eg Walkabout in Bromley) for disco, cheap eats and games. Film club. Only cinemas and pubs outside college – but central London close, with all big names. **Locals:** Fine. **Sports:** No on-site sports. Excellent Pavilion sports centre in Bromley (10 mins by bus). College rugby, football and basketball teams practise at various local venues; martial arts club. **Travel:** Good bus and trains – night buses from London. **Hardship fund:** Access fund available once a year – only given to those who really need it. **Jobs:** Local shops and bars; also Bromley and central London. **Best features:** Friendly atmosphere, great ethos. **And worst:** Lack of residential housing. **Informal name:** Rave. **Past students:** David Bowie (singer); Stella McCartney (fashion designer); Karen Franklin (*Clothes Show*); Maria Cornego (fashion designer).

Reading University

Location:
Berkshire, west of London (map 2)
Main campus
Reading, plus site 1 mile away

The University of Reading, Whiteknights, Reading RG6 6AH
☎ Tel 0118 987 5123
🖪 Fax 0118 931 4404
✉ Email student.recruitment@reading.ac.uk
💻 Website www.reading.ac.uk

Student enquiries: Sub-Dean of Faculty
Applications: UCAS

In brief

Total Students: 17,790

27% postgraduate
73% undergraduate

Undergraduates: 13,055

81% full-time — 91% UK students
13% mature on entry — 24% lower socio-economic groups

57% female — 43% male

- **A top UK research-intensive university.**
- **Teaching staff:** 1700 full-time and part-time.
- **Broad study areas:** Arts, humanities, social sciences, law, sciences (pure and applied), engineering, agriculture, food studies, surveying, education.

Freshers

- **Admissions information:** AS-levels accepted only in combination with 2+ A-levels or equivalent. UCAS tariff used to make offers on most courses, sometimes with specific grade and subject requirements (general studies and Key Skills usually excluded).
- **First degree entrants:** 2795 UK, full-time.
- **Points on entry:** 310+ (average).
- **Drop-out rate:** 5% in 1st year.
- **Accommodation:** All new students housed (guaranteed if apply by deadline).

Profile

Institution

Founded: 1892. **Site:** Whiteknights Campus, 320 acres, 1½ miles from centre of Reading; also buildings at Bulmershe Court, a mile away. **How to get there:** Close to M4 (junctions 10/11); frequent trains from London Paddington (22 mins) and Bristol; direct bus and train services from Heathrow and Gatwick airports. Frequent bus services from station and town (Nos 9, 20, 21).

Courses

Awarding body: University of Reading. **Main undergraduate awards:** BA, BSc, BEng, LLB, BA(Ed), MMath, MPhys, MChem, MEng. **Length of courses:** 3 years; 4 years (languages, art, food biosciences, typography, undergraduate Master's and sandwich courses).

Study opportunities & careers

Library and information services: Main library at Whiteknights plus Bulmershe library: total over 1.1 million volumes, 8000 online and 3500 print periodicals, multimedia material, archives, manuscripts. Special collections: Samuel Beckett Collection, Cole Library of Early Medicine, Overstone Library, Finzi poetry and music collections. Reading list material via short loan collections. Help desks, training sessions, etc. Information provision, £114 pa spent for each student (FTE). Separate IT service including university computer network, email and internet access; 600+ networked PCs and connections for laptops in library. IT help points, online guides, freshers' induction sessions, training sessions. **Other learning resources:** University museums (English rural life, Greek archaeology, and zoology), language laboratories (university-wide language programme), computer centre. **Study abroad:** 8% of students spend a period abroad. Formal exchange links with over 40 universities and colleges in Europe, most open to non-language specialists. **Careers:** Advisory service and resource centre.

Student services & facilities

Student advice and services: Counselling; study advisers; hardship and international student advisers; health centre (with doctors, dentists, psychiatrist); tutor system; mature student group; nightline; legal advice (through SU); chaplains. Playgroup, nursery. **Amenities:** Union building with bars, shops, travel and insurance services, etc; over 100 athletic and social clubs. Reading film theatre, bookshop, bank on campus. **Sporting facilities:** Sports hall, playing fields on campus; boathouses on Thames; sailing and canoeing on Thames and nearby gravel pits. **Accommodation:** Guaranteed for new students who apply by the deadline (25% of all students housed). 4500 halls places available, some ensuite: 2000+ full-board places £114–£153 pw, 30-week contracts; 2000+ self-catering £65–£104 pw ensuite, contracts 30, 37, or 50 weeks. Students live in privately owned accommodation for 1–2 years: rent £300–£450 pm for self-catering.

Money

Living expenses budget: Minimum budget of £5700 pa (excluding tuition fees) recommended by university for an academic year. **Term-time work:** University allows term-time work for full-time students, up to 16 hours pw Jobshop; part-time work available on and off campus. **Financial help:** Bursaries of £1350 pa for UK students whose family income is up to £25k; then bursaries tapering down to nil where family income is £60k. Other bursaries eg of up to £1k for students from specified Berkshire schools. Scholarships eg £2k in 1st year for high achievers; £800 pa for achievement in music. Also £350k government funds, 900 students helped; university funds as required (awards up to £3500). Special help: those with children (esp single parents), students with disabilities, mature students; university funds also for self-financing international students. Apply for help to student financial support office. **Tuition fees:** Home students pay £3225 pa for first degrees. International students pay £9630 pa (classroom) to £11,610 (science).

Student view
Rhiannon Horsley, RUSU President (Graduate, History)

Living
What's it like as a place to live? Lots going on, close to London, quite expensive.
How's the student accommodation? Lot of choice for halls, a range of options and prices. Quite a range for private accommodation; private accommodation ranges from about £260 pw to £320 pw, some nice, some not so; often get what you pay for. **What's the student population like?** Friendly; fairly middle class; large international student population makes it more diverse; a lot of people from Wales and the south. **How do students and locals get on?** Relationships with the local community are good and getting better; most local people realise that the university has a positive impact on Reading. Lots of students volunteering in the local community.

Studying
What's it like as a place to study? Good range, facilities vary, but lots of new buildings going up and refurbishment happening. Library is a bit shoddy, poor library opening hours. **What are the teaching staff like?** Depends, but on the whole quite student-focused and helpful.

Socialising
What are student societies like? Loads of societies – over 120 – which is a lot considering the size of uni. Most of the traditional ones like hockey, rugby, football, netball and more specialist ones, korfball, power kiting. Range of societies, from subject-based ones like history and chemistry to interest-based ones like debate, drama and even lock picking. Loads of students are involved; social centre of uni; focus placed on participation. Active campaigning groups including Amnesty and People and the Planet. Lots of volunteering groups, student media and 'raising and giving' society. **What's a typical night out?** Depends on who you are. Lots on, club nights, comedy night, etc. **And how much does it cost?** Depends how much you want to spend – a good time can be had for £15. **How can you get home safely?** Free night bus from the union, or a taxi.

Money
Is it an expensive place to live? Relatively expensive, especially compared to other places. **Average price of a pint?** £2 in the union, up to £3 in town. **And the price of a takeaway?** £6? Depends how much you eat!

Summary
What's the best feature about the place? Campus is vibrant and friendly. **And the worst?** Reading is expensive and the town lacks character. **And to sum it all up?** Great place to study: campus life is busy and vibrant with a great SU at the heart of Reading University.

Past students: Sir Richard Trehane (ex-Milk Marketing Board), Andy Mackay (Roxy Music), Steve Vines (journalist), Gillian Freeman (novelist and biographer), Susanne Charlton (BBC Weather), James Cracknell (Olympic rower), LTJ Bukem (DJ), Kenneth Branagh (actor). **More info?** Contact RUSU President (tel 0118 986 5133) or check out the (website www.rusu.co.uk).

Regent's Business School London

Location:
central London
(map 3)
**Single campus in
Regent's Park**

📄 Regent's Business School London,
Inner Circle, Regent's Park, London NW1 4NS
☎ Tel 020 7487 7505
🖷 Fax 020 7487 7425
✉ Email RBSL@regents.ac.uk
💻 Website www.RBSLondon.ac.uk

*Student enquiries: External Relations Department
Applications: UCAS or direct*

In brief

Total Students: 450

10% postgraduate
90% undergraduate

Undergraduates: 400
100% full-time ● ● 20% UK students
2% mature
on entry

40% female 60% male

- **Specialist business school.**
- **Teaching staff:** 25 full-time, 18 part-time.
- **Broad study areas:** Global business management, global marketing management, global financial management, global business and design management.

Freshers
- **Points on entry:** 160 (average).
- **Drop-out rate:** 1% in 1st year.
- **Accommodation:** Most 1st years housed.

Profile

Institution
Founded: 1996. **Site:** Single 26-acre campus in the heart of Regent's Park. **How to get there:** 5 mins' walk from Baker Street underground and buses.

Courses
Academic features: Small classes; international focus. In-company projects and multiple electives. January and September start dates. 1-year foundation year before degree course for those who need it. **Awarding body:** Open University. **Main undergraduate award:** BA. **Length of courses:** 3 years.

Study opportunities & careers
Library and information services: 38,000 volumes, 300 periodicals including daily newspapers from UK and overseas, 30 online catalogues with CD-ROM access, 300 academic videos and 120 study places. Specialist collection: Business and Institute of Linguists libraries. Information provision, £120 pa spent for each student (FTE). Separate IT services. 250 networked workstations with access to library and internet; open 24 hours/day with staffed helpdesk. 4–6 hour tuition for 1st-year students. **Other learning resources:** IBM and Apple computer laboratories. **Careers:** Information, advice and placement service.

Student services & facilities

Student advice and services: Personal tutors. **Amenities:** Music practice room, art gallery, sports bar, brasserie and bookstore. **Sporting facilities:** Tennis courts, weights room, multigym, dance studio, fitness classes. Students can also join ULU and use its sports facilities. **Accommodation:** 264 places in campus halls: full-board at £188 pw (shared room) to £270 pw, term time only. Many students in privately owned accommodation, rent for self-catering place in flatshare £90–£200 pw.

Money

Living expenses budget: Minimum budget of £8k pa (excluding tuition fees) recommended by the school. **Financial help:** Scholarships and bursaries available, worth up to 50% of fees. **Tuition fees:** £11,250 pa for home and international students (EU students receive some £1k pa towards their fees).

Robert Gordon University

Location:
Aberdeen, north of
Scotland (map 1)
2 sites in city

The Robert Gordon University,
Schoolhill, Aberdeen AB10 1FR
Tel 01224 262728
Fax 01224 263000
Email admissions@rgu.ac.uk
Website www.rgu.ac.uk

Student enquiries: Student Admissions
Applications: UCAS

In brief

Total Students: 12,985

32% postgraduate
68% undergraduate

Undergraduates: 8880
76% full-time
28% mature on entry
90% UK students
33% lower socio-economic groups

66% female 34% male

- **A modern university.**
- **Teaching staff:** 703 full-time.
- **Broad study areas:** Architecture, art and design, health and social care, nursing and midwifery, business and management, science and technology, information and media, engineering, law.

Freshers

- **Admissions information:** All qualifications considered.
- **First degree entrants:** 1525 UK, full-time.
- **Points on entry:** 200+ (average).
- **Drop-out rate:** 9% in 1st year.
- **Accommodation:** Majority of 1st years housed.

Profile

Institution

Founded: 1750, Robert Gordon Institute became a university in 1992. **Site:** 2 Aberdeen campuses – one in city centre and one in Garthdee. **How to get there:** Fast coach services from Edinburgh, Glasgow and all major cities to Aberdeen; rail services north and south; by road, A90 from south, A96 from north; flights from most major European cities to international airport on city outskirts. City centre campus a short walk from rail and coach stations; shuttle bus between sites.

Courses

Awarding body: Robert Gordon University. **Main undergraduate awards:** BA, BSc, BEng, MEng. **Length of courses:** 3 years (ordinary); 4 years (Hons); 5 years (sandwich Hons).

Study opportunities & careers

Library and information services: 250,000 volumes in total, 1600 periodicals, 1200 study places. Library and IT service converged. Ratio 1:7 workstations to students, 200 points with access to library, 700 points with access to internet, open 16 hours per day. Helpdesk support available. New students have library tour in first week plus compulsory IT course. Information provision, £95 pa spent for each student (FTE). **Study abroad:** 3% of students spend a period abroad. Number of formal EU exchange links (all open to non-specialists) and with Oregon State University and Illinois Institute of Technology. **Careers:** Information and advice service.

Student services & facilities

Student advice and services: Student finance and administration dept, accommodation office, student counsellors, careers officers, English language tutor, chaplaincy, medical advisory service, nursery, disabled student adviser, centre for student access. **Amenities:** SA with bars, games room, shop. **Sporting facilities:** New sports centre, with swimming pool, 2 gyms, climbing wall, bouldering room, 3 exercise studios and sports hall. **Accommodation:** 35% of 1st years in university accommodation (35% of 1st-year degree students live at home). 1250 self-catering places, some ensuite; rent £66–£86 pw, 35-week leases. Accommodation service gives help finding private accommodation; rent £55–£70 pw self-catering or BandB.

Money

Living expenses budget: Minimum budget of £5650–£8050 for the academic year (excluding tuition fees) recommended by university. **Term-time work:** University allows term-time work for full-time students (high percentage believed to work). Some work available on campus as janitors, porters, ground staff; university jobshop. **Financial help:** £398k government funds, 580 students helped (awards range from £100–£2k). Special help: Students with high accommodation costs, mature students with childcare costs, final year, self-financing, personal or medical costs, etc. Apply for help to student finance office. **Tuition fees:** Scottish and EU students pay no fees during course; other UK students pay £1820 pa for first degrees. International students pay £8750–£10,600 depending on course.

Student view

A modern university with excellent facilities, in a city with a lively social scene. Range of courses in 3 faculties (design and technology, health and social care and business) – all industry-focused and with the opportunity to gain professional work experience so not surprising that there is a good track record for graduate employment. Schoolhill Campus is in the city centre, close to shops, cafés and pubs. Newer Garthdee Campus, a short bus ride away, has modern glass buildings overlooking the River Dee and surrounded by lush parkland – a serene environment to study in. But student life is not all work and no play. RGU sports centre boasts a swimming pool, epic climbing wall, fitness gym and several areas for sports and fitness activities. For the more slothful, it also has a café bar where you can relax with friends. Aberdeen's nightlife is buzzing and, with such a large population of students, there's no shortage of clubs and pubs that cater for the student crowd and their modest budgets. Plenty of venues offering entertainment from live bands and guest DJs to themed nights and pub quizzes. With 2 bars, pool tables, a big screen TV and live entertainment 7 nights a week, RGU union is the perfect place to begin your night out.

Student footnotes

Housing: RGU accommodation on 6 sites around Aberdeen (priority to 1st years and international students). Unite and Armduir also provide student flats. For private accommodation, ask university, look in local paper or use one of many estate agents around city centre. **Eats:** Meals and snacks on campus (eg Costa Coffee, pasta bar). Restaurants and takeaways to suit all tastes, eg Chinese, Thai, Indian and Italian. Plenty of bars offer good-value pub grub. **Drink:** Union has scandalously cheap drinks: create your own cocktail at the Basement; Under the Hammer for a shared bottle of wine in an intimate atmosphere; for the adventurous, Siberia has flavoured vodkas from cola to curry! **Nightlife:** Venue for every musical taste as you would expect from a big city. Union puts on wide variety of ents, from rock nights to pub quizzes. **Locals:** Friendly; with so many students, it's easy to make friends. **Sports:** State-of-the-art sports facility (£10 million + recently spent on it): 25m swimming pool, 3 gyms, a climbing wall and a large sports hall; discounted student rates. Many sports clubs, eg football, rugby, badminton, snowsports, sailing, horse riding and rowing. Numerous sports facilities in Aberdeen, eg new Garthdee sports and alpine adventure park (short walk from Garthdee campus). **Travel:** University shuttle bus between campuses. Student travel agency on site. **Financial help:** Bursaries, grants and hardship loans available. **Jobs:** Variety of part-time and vacation jobs available; help from careers centre. **Informal name:** RGU. **Best feature:** Graduate employment rate. **More info?** Enquiries to SA (tel 01224 262292) or visit www.rguunion.co.uk.

Roehampton University

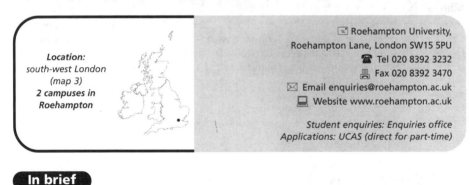

Location:
south-west London
(map 3)
2 campuses in
Roehampton

Roehampton University,
Roehampton Lane, London SW15 5PU
☎ Tel 020 8392 3232
🖨 Fax 020 8392 3470
✉ Email enquiries@roehampton.ac.uk
🖥 Website www.roehampton.ac.uk

Student enquiries: Enquiries office
Applications: UCAS (direct for part-time)

In brief

Total Students: 8535

21% postgraduate
79% undergraduate

Undergraduates: 6720
91% full-time
29% mature on entry

93% UK students
36% lower socio-economic groups

76% female   24% male

- **A modern university.**
- **Teaching staff:** 300 full-time and part-time.

- **Broad study areas:** Arts and humanities; education; social and life sciences.

Freshers

- **Admissions information:** AS-levels accepted in combination with 1 A-level or equivalent. UCAS tariff used.
- **First degree entrants:** 2215 UK, full-time.
- **Points on entry:** 210 (average).
- **Drop-out rate:** 13% in 1st year.
- **Accommodation** Majority of 1st years housed.

Profile

Institution

Founded: As Roehampton Institute in 1975, from the merger of 4 Victorian colleges: Digby Stuart, Froebel Institute, Southlands and Whitelands College; university status in 2004. **Site:** 2 sites: Roehampton Lane Campus (Digby Stuart, Froebel and Southlands); Whitelands Campus (10 mins' walk from main campus). **How to get there:** To Barnes station (15 mins' walk), Hammersmith or Putney Bridge tube stations; all connect by bus to campus.

Courses

Academic features: Most degrees are combinations of 2 subjects (over 500 possible combinations). **Awarding body:** Roehampton University. **Main undergraduate awards:** BA, BA(QTS), BSc, BMus. **Length of courses:** 3 years; 4 years (with study abroad or languages).

Study opportunities & careers

Library and information services: Library at each site; total of 506,660 volumes, 1500 periodicals, 840 study places. Specialist collections: early childhood, children's literature (including Bratton and Coleman collections), Froebel archive, Anne Hutchinson Guest Language of Dance. Information provision, £93 pa spent for each student (FTE). Library, IT and media facilities incorporated into learning resource centre. 500 workstations with access to library and internet, 130 available 24 hours/day (ratio 1:17 students). Helpdesks, technician support, talks, tours, induction packs and software training. **Study abroad:** 1% of students spend a period abroad. 60 European exchange links (many open to non-linguists) and others in USA and Australia. **Careers:** Counsellor on site.

Student services & facilities

Student advice and services: Welfare officers, doctor, medical centre, counsellors, chaplains, dyslexia support unit. **Amenities:** SU building on each campus; recreation officer. **Sporting facilities:** Facilities in and near colleges for wide variety of sports. **Accommodation:** 65% of 1st years in university accommodation (20+% of all students). 1370 places available, many ensuite and with internet connections: £88–£106 pw self-catering, £120 pw catered, contracts 37 weeks. Students live in privately owned accommodation for 2+ years, average £325–£370 pm (plus bills) for a flat share.

Money

Living expenses budget: Minimum budget of £7k pa (excluding tuition fees) recommended by university. **Term-time work:** University allows term-time work for full-time students. Some work available on campus in bars, catering, office, library, conferences, etc. (students employed wherever possible); also SU employment service helps find work off campus. **Financial help:** Bursaries of £500 pa for home students whose family income is up to £25k. Also scholarships of £1k pa for students with 320 points on entry. Also £300k government access to learning funds, including childcare and other grants and loans. **Tuition fees:** Home students pay £3225 pa for first degrees. International students pay £8875 pa.

Student view) **Gary Coates,** Students' Union President (Graduate, Drama, Theatre and Performance Studies, combined with Creative Writing)

Living

What's it like as a place to live? A fantastic community experience, with great access to all London amenities. **How's the student accommodation?** Ranging from brand new accommodation blocks, spacious and secure, all the way to 1940s old-style communal buildings. Ensuite and communal showers, data cabling in every campus room and bills are included. **What's the student population like?** A very strong sense of community, thanks to the collegiate system, varied ethnic and religious backgrounds as well as wide-spanning age range. A majority of students are from the south of England and London. The student population is 77% female. **How do students and locals get on?** The university has outlined increased activity with the wider community as one of it goals. To that end there are a number of events and activities whereby the gates of the university are flung open, including Brain Awareness Week, The Big Dance, Open Square Gardens and the recent Roehampton Festival.

Studying

What's it like as a place to study? Roehampton has a vast and varied range of courses, from anthropology to human rights to computing through to creative writing. Facilities include a purpose-built dance studio with sprung floor, surround sound and floor-to-ceilings mirrors; and state-of-the art biomechanics laboratories. **What are the teaching staff like?** Staff who are engaged in active research are also active members of the teaching staff, so that students benefit directly from their latest work. Published authors and leading researchers in their respective fields are among the university's teaching staff, who are engaging and genuinely interested in student development and learning. Dame Jacqueline Wilson (author of the very popular Tracey Beaker series), and Professor Allan Hobson (who discovered and defined rapid eye movements, and the Activation-Synthesis Hypothesis of dreaming providing a brain-based explanation of the nature of dreams) have both recently been appointed professorial fellows of the university.

Socialising

What are student societies like? The SU provides a wide range of societies, from the Deviant Society to the Japanese Culture Society. It's easy to establish a society as well – all you need are 5 guaranteed members and you can start your own! They aren't as socially renowned as our sports teams, but still highlight the diversity of our student body and how easy it is to liaise with other societies. **What's a typical night out?** Fez Club on a Wednesday, band nights, acoustic nights, the Clapham Grand and our very own cheese-fest, the Bop, every Friday with fancy-dress themes. Entry to most varies from free to a maximum of £5, with the exception of fresher's week events, the Christmas bash and summer ball. **How can you get home safely?** Free transport is provided to and from the external events; all others are within the campus grounds.

Money

Is it an expensive place to live? There are grants, bursaries, a range of scholarships and financial support available for students who need it. But being in London, prices are higher than other parts of the country. A large section of resident students have a part-time job to supplement their loan, which just about covers accommodation. **Average price of a pint?** On campus £1.70, off campus £2.90. **And the price of a takeaway?** Local pizza deals mean a large pizza can be bought for about £6, while most others will be between

£10 and £15. **What's the part-time work situation?** Jobs in the local area are available pretty much all the time; usually not much above the minimum wage, although lots of students work for casual catering companies, which sometimes pay more. There is also plenty of part-time work available on campus. The university has a jobs board for local companies to advertise for part-time positions, and an active careers service that aims to help students in the big bad world once they have graduated.

Summary
What's the best feature about the place? The layout. It's perfectly located outside the chaos of London city centre but easily accessible at the same time – only 20 mins from the heart of London. The campus is beautiful, with historic buildings, gardens and lakes that can be used for study or for leisure, all well maintained, and the colleges create 4 fantastic and diverse communities. **And the worst?** Cost of living. London is expensive and amenities such as the on-site book shop aren't the cheapest. **And to sum it all up?** A village community in the most exciting city in the world.

Past students: Ashley Ward (English athletics international); Toby Anstis, Alice Beers (presenters); Dan Kitson (comedian). **More info?** Contact SU on 020 8392 3221 or visit www.roehamptonstudent.com.

Rose Bruford College

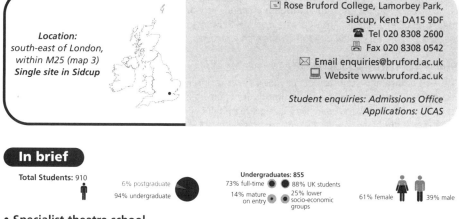

Location:
south-east of London,
within M25 (map 3)
Single site in Sidcup

Rose Bruford College, Lamorbey Park,
Sidcup, Kent DA15 9DF
☎ Tel 020 8308 2600
🖷 Fax 020 8308 0542
✉ Email enquiries@bruford.ac.uk
🖥 Website www.bruford.ac.uk

Student enquiries: Admissions Office
Applications: UCAS

In brief

Total Students: 910

6% postgraduate
94% undergraduate

Undergraduates: 855
73% full-time ● ● 88% UK students
14% mature ● ● 25% lower
on entry   socio-economic
              groups

61% female ● ● 39% male

- **Specialist theatre school.**
- **Teaching staff:** 21 full-time, large number of visiting tutors.
- **Broad study areas:** Acting, European and American theatre arts, music technology, theatre design, opera studies, scenic arts, digital arts, lighting design, costume production, stage management, actor musicianship, theatre studies, organising live arts.

Freshers
- **First degree entrants:** 205 UK, full-time.
- **Points on entry:** 230 (average).
- **Drop-out rate:** 8% in 1st year.
- **Accommodation:** Some 1st years housed.

541

Institution

Founded: By Rose Bruford in 1950. **Site:** Lamorbey Park in Sidcup, Kent (25 mins from London). **How to get there:** Easy access from M25, M20 and A2/M2. Good bus and train links (from Waterloo East, London Bridge).

Courses

Academic features: Full-time courses (accredited by the National Council for Drama Training) on all aspects of theatre – acting, actor musicianship, theatre design, stage management, lighting design, costume production, scenic arts, etc. Also distance learning courses in theatre studies and opera studies; summer school and international foundation course. New Master's and research degrees. **Awarding body:** University of Manchester. **Main undergraduate award:** BA. **Length of courses:** 3 years.

Study opportunities & careers

Library and information services: 40,000 books and audio recordings, 6,000 slides, 80 periodicals, 2000 videos, 100 reading places; audio-visual facilities. Converged library and IT services in learning resource centre; 1-hour induction session for all new students, with further information linked to projects throughout course. Ratio workstations to students 1:27 (open 10 hours/day), all with access to internet. Information provision, £28 pa spent for each student (FTE). **Other learning resources:** Barn Theatre, Rose Theatre (330-seat theatre in the round), recording studios, MIDI laboratory, lighting design studios, etc. **Study abroad:** Exchange programmes for European and American theatre arts degree programme. **Careers:** London showcase of students' work; professional placements; agents, casting directors and related employers invited to college productions.

Student services & facilities

Student advice and services: Student adviser on site; local doctors and dentists. **Amenities:** Extensive grounds; canteen; SU. **Accommodation:** Some places for 1st years in Greenwich University halls of residence, 20 mins' walk from college; rent £84–£104 pw (inclusive of the internet), 40-week contracts. Students in privately owned accommodation for 2+ years, rent £70–£90 pw self-catering. Very few students live at home.

Money

Living expenses budget: Minimum budget of £5500 pa recommended (excluding tuition fees). **Term-time work:** College has a flexible approach to term-time work. Occasional opportunities on campus. **Financial help:** Bursaries of £1k pa for UK students whose family income is up to approx £25k; of £300 pa for those whose family income is £25k–£35k; made automatically with student loan assessment, without further application. Also small bursaries from a number of trusts (eg Rose Bruford Memorial Trust, Edith Rudinger Gray Trust for opera studies); also college overseas bursary. **Tuition fees:** Home students pay £3225 pa for first degrees. International students pay £11,025 pa.

Student view

Based on 1 site in Sidcup, in Lamorbey Park, which is a peaceful, pretty backdrop to a hectic college life. It offers a range of degree courses covering all aspects of theatre practice, including both performance and production sides of theatre making. Classes take place in the studios, rehearsal rooms and workshops of the main campus, as well as the older Lamorbey House by the lake. 2 on-site theatres allow for an incredible number of productions per year, with involvement from all years and courses. Learning resources centre has IT facilities and the largest theatrical library aside from the British Library. Sidcup station is a 10-min walk from college with regular trains into London (20 mins) and local buses to various local shopping centres. Most students rent privately nearby, but there are some halls towards Eltham for 1st-year students. College tries to recreate the atmosphere of a full working theatre, so many hours are spent on practical work; academic aspects run alongside, so students leave with a thorough understanding of the industry. Courses can be very tiring but there is a good sense of unity and usually the buzz outweighs the stress. SU exists to help students through problems and to try and create a good social life for everyone: events include freshers' week, Christmas panto, ski trip, Christmas ball as well as a summer ball. College is small, so union reps are still taking their full-time courses as well as organising the union – but they manage! College clubs and societies include boys' and girls' football teams and a green society, and more introduced each year. Many student theatre companies put on productions on campus and in London, as well as further afield. Counsellor on site and a nurse visits weekly (offers advice and obligatory condoms). 3 years at Rosie B's are hectic but happy and the unsociable hours (particularly over production projects) prepare students fully for a career in the world of theatre.

Student footnotes

Housing: Few rooms in local university halls. Otherwise most students rent houses or lodge with local families; ask accommodation officer. **Eats:** Rose Café on campus. **Drink:** Metro Bar has large Bruford clientele; the Portrait (Sidcup). **Nightlife:** Nights out arranged to pubs/clubs; close to central London for all types of ents. College shows every term; student bands in college; SU event every other week. **Locals:** Friendly, if a bit posh. **Sports:** Good local facilities nearby. **Travel:** College refunds course travel expenses for productions. Get a young person's railcard. **Financial help:** Limited college trust funds and loans (access boards meet termly). **Annual living costs:** The minimum amount students say you need to live on each year (excluding tuition fees) is £6k pa. **Jobs:** Working during term time is difficult with the long hours, particularly in final year. Casual work, eg waiting, ushering, sometimes available. Holiday jobs essential. **Best features:** The atmosphere; mix of students. **Informal name:** Rosie B. **Past students:** Freddie Jones (*The Elephant Man*), Pam St Clement (*Eastenders*), Tom Baker (*Dr Who*), Nerys Hughes (*The Liver Birds*), Angharad Rees (*Poldark*), Barbara Kellerman (*The Sea Wolves*), Gary Oldman (the Harry Potter films), Barry Kilerby (*Mr Blobby*), Elaine Glover (*Footballers' Wives*), Diane Louise Jordan (presenter). **More info?** Contact SU 020 8308 2697.

Royal Academy Of Music

Location:
central London
(map 3)
Single site in Marylebone

Royal Academy of Music,
Marylebone Road, London NW1 5HT
☎ Tel 020 7873 7373
🖷 Fax 020 7873 7374
💻 Website www.ram.ac.uk

Student enquiries: Academic Registrar
Applications: Direct

In brief

Total Students: 800

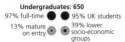

18% postgraduate
82% undergraduate

Undergraduates: 650
97% full-time
13% mature on entry
95% UK students
39% lower socio-economic groups

49% female   51% male

- **World-class music school.**
- **Teaching staff:** 20 full-time, 350 part-time.
- **Broad study area:** Music.

Freshers

- **Admissions information:** Students expected to hold A-levels or equivalent.
- **First degree entrants:** 40 UK, full-time.
- **Drop-out rate:** 1% in 1st year.
- **Accommodation:** Some 1st years housed.

Profile

Institution

Founded: 1822. **Site:** Central London. **How to get there:** Baker Street or Regent's Park underground stations; many buses. **Structural features:** Part of London University from 1999. Collaboration with King's College London on performance courses (undergrad and postgrad). **Special features:** Many distinguished visiting musicians, eg Sir Peter Maxwell Davies, Skampa Quartet, Vanbrugh Quartet. International composer festivals.

Courses

Awarding bodies: University of London; Royal Academy of Music. **Main awards:** BMus, MMus, MA. **Length of courses:** 4 years; 2 years (postgraduate).

Study opportunities & careers

Library and information services: Approx. 200,000 items in total, 40 periodicals and approx 10,000 books. Specialist collections: Sir Henry Wood, Sullivan Archive and Otto Klemperer collections of orchestral scores; Yehudi Menuhin archive. Separate IT service; 5 workstations with access to the library, 65 to the internet, open 16 hours/day (ratio of 1:11 workstations to students). 4 full-time, 2 part-time support staff; computer training, guidance and information given to all. **Other learning resources:** Concert hall, recital hall, living museum, opera theatre, 5 organs, electronic and recording studios. **Study abroad:** Member of Socrates, in which a permanent exchange programme operates between leading European conservatoires. Exchange links with conservatoires in Europe, USA and Australia. **Careers:** Information and advice.

Student services & facilities

Student advice and services: Student services; counsellor; disability adviser. **Amenities:** Music shop on site; RAM Magazine; canteen, licensed students' club; social facilities. **Accommodation:** Some students in London University or other halls of residence, rent approx £112–£180 pw for catered places (see university website, www.lon.ac.uk/accom). Most students live in privately owned accommodation for 2 years; rent £75–£100 pw.

Money

Living expenses budget: Minimum budget of £9500 for an academic year (excluding tuition fees) recommended by academy, £11,400 for a calendar year. **Term-time work:** College allows term-time work for students (30% believed to work). Term-time work in college bars, offices, library, security and fire stewarding; adverts for jobs elsewhere on noticeboards. **Financial help:** Bursaries of £615 pa for UK students whose family income is up to £17,900, of £410 pa where family income is £17,900–£28,100, and of £205 pa where it is £28,100–£38,300. Also some entrance scholarships, other awards and funds, particularly for postgraduate students. **Tuition fees:** Home students £3,225 pa for first degrees (other courses £8800–£14,850). International students pay £15,500 pa.

Student view

It's on the north side of Marylebone Road in the heart of London, housed in a compact campus; a classic sandstone and red brick Edwardian building at the front and extensions into the John Nash and Decimus Burton Victorian buildings of York Gate and York Terrace alongside. Facilities include 2 concert halls, a concert room, recital room, opera theatre, a museum housing a collection of fine instruments (including 13 Stradivariuses) and an annexe in the renovated York Gate building for practice, rehearsals and lectures. All students live out as there are no specific halls of residence, although the academy has numerous places within London University intercollegiate halls and international student house nearby. With several student flats and close proximity to Baker Street tube, accommodation is easily found; costs vary enormously, depending on location. All students enter the (very demanding) BMus performance course, which ensures an excellent degree. Highest standards of tuition from some of the finest members of the music profession. Practice and dedication is expected of students on a daily basis. Non-stop exciting programme of concerts, masterclasses and music series. There is no 'average' student except the one with a genuine love and energy for music. Many international and postgrad students. The RAM has an ever-developing social life in college. Students' union (RAMSU) has a policy of inclusivity across the student body in which over 50 nationalities are represented: freshers' week, jazz nights, bi-weekly parties, karaoke, cabaret, river parties, summer ball and barbecues. Absolutely the place to be if you want to become a performing musician.

Student footnotes

Housing: Accommodation office really helpful – plans for new hall of residence in pipeline. **Eats:** Excellent food at reasonable prices at RAM restaurant. Good snacks, etc. locally. **Drink:** RAM bar reasonably priced. 4 pubs within 400 yards. **Nightlife:** Bi-weekly parties, themed nights, termly balls. Automatic membership to ULU and its facilities. 20 mins' walk to West End; many excellent student offers on concerts, etc. throughout London. **Sports:** New yoga, Alexander Technique, Tai-Chi lessons; close to excellent ULU facilities. **Travel:** Socrates/Erasmus schemes and award system for summer schools. **Hardship fund:** Admin always willing to listen. Various forms of assistance. **Jobs:** Many gigs and teaching jobs (get yourself known!). Bar work and concert stewarding at RAM (concert work through RAM's own concert secretary). It's expensive to be a music student in London so many students need paid work. **Informal name:** RAM, The Academy. **More info?** Enquiries to RAMSU president (tel 020 7873 7337).

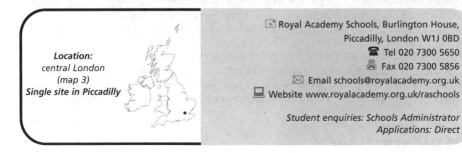

Royal Academy Schools

Location:
central London
(map 3)
Single site in Piccadilly

Royal Academy Schools, Burlington House,
Piccadilly, London W1J 0BD
☎ Tel 020 7300 5650
🖨 Fax 020 7300 5856
✉ Email schools@royalacademy.org.uk
💻 Website www.royalacademy.org.uk/raschools

Student enquiries: Schools Administrator
Applications: Direct

In brief

Total Students: 60

 100% postgraduate

100% full-time

50% female   50% male

- **A top postgraduate art school.**
- **Teaching staff:** 3 full-time, 3 part-time (The Keeper, Curator, Head of Fine Art, 3 year tutors) plus many visiting tutors.
- **Broad study areas:** Fine art – painting, sculpture, printmaking, video and installation.
- **Admissions information:** Application forms available late November; apply direct, fee £30.
- **Accommodation:** No school accommodation.

Profile

Institution
Founded: 1768. **Site:** In Burlington House, Piccadilly. **How to get there:** Green Park and Piccadilly underground stations; various buses.

Courses
Academic features: The course is postgraduate, with critiques, reviews, dissertations and annual exhibitions; most of the teaching done by visiting tutors. **Awarding body:** Royal Academy Schools. **Main award:** Postgraduate diploma. **Length of courses:** 3 years.

Study opportunities & careers
Library and information services: 15,000 volumes, various periodicals. Specialist collections: Old master drawings/prints.

Student services & facilities
Amenities: Shop, canteen, bar.

Money
Living expenses budget: Minimum budget of £8k pa (excluding tuition fees) recommended by schools. **Funding and fees:** All fees are currently covered by the Royal Academy. Maintenance grants and bursaries are available for students.

Student view

It's behind the Royal Academy gallery in the West End, which you reach via Burlington Gardens. An independent college (not part of the 'system'), running the only full-time 3-year postgraduate course in the country. The schools are focused on painting and sculpture (intake of approx 15 painters, 3–4 sculptors a year); printmaking a related study. Students encouraged to follow their own creativity. For 1st-year painters there is an introductory study period where the importance of drawing is emphasised. Each student has a personal working space and personal tutor; also a limited choice, on majority vote, to invite staff of their choosing (a wide variety of visiting artists and tutors). Being in central London, very good access to all the large galleries and many independent galleries, such as those in Cork Street a few moments away; possibilities for seeing all kinds of art work are vast. Free entrance to RA exhibitions including access to the main RA library and collections and opportunity to exhibit in main RA spaces. A small bar in the canteen and parties can be arranged. The RA schools are basically a set of studio spaces with regular tutoring, but being a small institution it does not operate in the same way that other colleges do. As a result, students are not hampered by the machinations of a larger college or university and there is more room for student influence in the running of the school.

Student footnotes

Eats: Canteen very cheap by London standards. Plenty of cheap alternatives in area. **Drink:** Subsidised college bar. **Nightlife:** Free admission to all RA exhibitions. **Financial help:** AHRB (Arts and Humanities Research Board) money and other charitable grants available for maintenance (RA covers the fees). **Travel:** Travel scholarships to selected students.

Royal Agricultural College

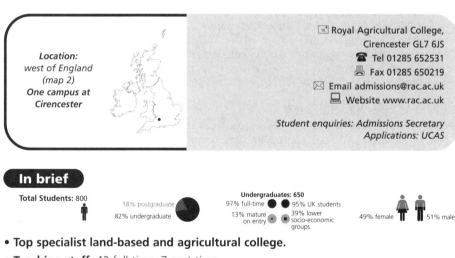

Location:
west of England
(map 2)
**One campus at
Cirencester**

Royal Agricultural College,
Cirencester GL7 6JS
☎ Tel 01285 652531
🖨 Fax 01285 650219
✉ Email admissions@rac.ac.uk
🖥 Website www.rac.ac.uk

*Student enquiries: Admissions Secretary
Applications: UCAS*

In brief

Total Students: 800

18% postgraduate
82% undergraduate

Undergraduates: 650
97% full-time   95% UK students
13% mature   39% lower
on entry   socio-economic
groups

49% female   51% male

- **Top specialist land-based and agricultural college.**
- **Teaching staff:** 42 full-time, 7 part-time.
- **Broad study areas:** Agriculture, business management, rural land and estate management, equine business, property management, international agribusiness management.

547

Freshers

- **Admissions information:** AS-levels accepted in combination with 2+ A-levels or equivalent.
- **First degree entrants:** 212 UK, full-time.
- **Points on entry:** 275 (average).
- **Drop-out rate:** 4% in 1st year.
- **Accommodation:** Most 1st years housed.

Profile

Institution

Founded: 1845. **Site:** 30-acre campus, 1 mile from Cirencester. **How to get there:** By road on A419 (from M4, Swindon or Gloucester) or A417 (from M5); train to Kemble via Swindon, 3 miles away; coach to Cirencester from London and Heathrow.

Courses

Academic features: Some courses lead to membership of Royal Institution of Chartered Surveyors (Rural Practice Division). **Awarding body:** Royal Agricultural College. **Main undergraduate awards:** BSc, FdSc. **Length of courses:** 3 years; 4 years (sandwich or with foundation year); 2 years (FdSc); 1 year (BSc top-up).

Study opportunities & careers

Library and information services: 40,000 volumes, 960 periodicals, reference works, statistical publications, 700 videos; 155 study places. Information provision, £190 pa spent for each student (FTE). Library and IT services partially converged; 70 workstations with access to library and internet (overall ratio 1:8 workstations to students). IT area open 24 hours/day, library 62 hours/week in term time. 2 IT support staff; training for new students in library and information services; lecture-based IT courses. **Other learning resources:** Own commercial farms, with different farming conditions (totalling 750 hectares); Rural Skills Centre. **Study abroad:** 10% of students spend a period in Europe. Formal exchange links with many universities in Europe, New Zealand and Canada. **Careers:** Careers adviser; information, advice and placement. Graduates are employed in farm, plantation, nursery and estate management; land agency; leisure management; conservation; rural investment and advisory services; food industry; retailing; marketing; journalism.

Student services & facilities

Student advice and services: Doctor, counselling service, dyslexia specialist, disability officer, student welfare officer, chaplain, personal tutors. **Amenities:** Common rooms with sofas and TV, SU bar, snack bar, SU shop. **Sporting facilities:** Sports pitches including floodlit all-weather hockey and tennis, facilities for squash, rowing, water sports and field sports, own gym, polo and clay pigeon shooting facilities nearby. Sports scholarships available. **Accommodation:** 90% of 1st years in college accommodation (40% of all students). 300 full-board places, £3450–£5490 pa (including 3 meals a day, utilities, daily cleaner), 30-week contracts. New self-catering places, 45-week contracts. Students live in privately owned accommodation for 2 years: 1-bedroom flats locally for £400–£600 a month (college helps find local accommodation). Very small numbers live at home.

Money

Living expenses budget: Minimum budget of £5500 pa recommended (excluding tuition fees). **Term-time work:** College allows term-time work for full-time students. Some work available on campus in bar, waiting at dinners and farm work (holidays only); some other holiday jobs displayed on noticeboards. **Financial help:** Bursaries of £1500 pa (which may be raised to £2k under certain conditions) for students whose family income is up to £25k; tapered bursaries (of £1500 to nil) for those whose family income is £25k–£60k. Also 32 college and industry-funded scholarships (up to £2k) awarded annually, including sports scholarships. **Tuition fees:** Home students pay £3225 pa for first degrees. International students pay £7300 pa.

Student view) **Stuart Homewood,** Student Union Chairman (2nd year, Agricultural Land Management)

Living
What's it like as a place to live? The RAC is a unique place to live. Set in the Gloucestershire countryside, it offers a fantastic environment for work and play. Must have the best views of any uni! **How's the student accommodation?** Accommodation at the college is warm and very comfortable. For 2nd and 3rd years there are lots of houses available in Cirencester, all lovely. **What's the student population like?** Rural, friendly. Great community spirit and largely English, international students from over 31 countries! **How do students and locals get on?** Very well on the whole.

Studying
What's it like as a place to study? Traditional buildings but very modern within them. At the forefront of agriculture and business. **What are the teaching staff like?** Very good, international, highly regarded in their fields.

Socialising
What are student societies like? The finest SU in the country! Balls second to none – people come from all over the country to attend them! **What's a typical night out?** Infamous college bar then town. **And how much does it cost?** Quite a lot (bar is good value though). **How can you get home safely?** On the buses provided (just for the college).

Money
Is it an expensive place to live? It is relatively expensive – but worth it. **Average price of a pint?** £1.80. **And the price of a takeaway?** £10–£15 (eat what you shoot!). **What's the part-time work situation?** Some jobs for college and local pubs – most students work in the holidays to pay for an enjoyable term ahead.

Summary
What's the best feature about the place? The people – and setting – cannot be matched. **And the worst?** Leaving. **And to sum it all up?** Oxbridge in the countryside – the finest socialising in the land.
More info? Enquiries to SU Chairman (tel 01285 889916).

Royal College of Art

Location:
central London
(map 3)
Main site in Kensington, sculpture in Battersea

Royal College of Art
Kensington Gore, London SW7 2EU
☎ Tel 020 7590 4444
🖨 Fax 020 7590 4500
✉ Email admissions@rca.ac.uk
🖥 Website www.rca.ac.uk

Student enquiries: Assistant Registrar
Applications: Direct

In brief

Total Students: 950

100% postgraduate

95% full-time

53% female   47% male

- **World-class postgraduate art college.**
- **Teaching staff:** 120 full-time and part-time.
- **Broad study areas:** Applied art; architecture and design; vehicle design; industrial design engineering; communications; fashion and textiles; fine art; conservation and curating.
- **Admissions information:** Applications by 19 January. Entry for Master's courses by competitive examination; usually about 410 places a year. Candidates normally aged over 21 with a first degree, send in portfolios of recent work.
- **Accommodation:** No college accommodation.

Profile

Institution

Founded: 1837; Royal Charter in 1967. **Site:** Opposite Hyde Park, beside the Albert Hall; Sculpture School in Howie Street, Battersea, just south of Battersea Bridge. **How to get there:** Underground (to Knightsbridge, South Kensington); buses for both sites. **Special features:** International reputation for work in areas from painting and sculpture to industrial design engineering, vehicle design and goldsmithing to communication art and design (illustration and graphics).

Courses

Academic features: Project or thesis work, following individual student proposals, forms an essential part of MPhil degree work. PhD work may be carried out in any discipline provided resources exist; minimum period of study is 2 full-time equivalent years. **Awarding body:** Royal College of Art. **Main awards:** MA, MPhil, PhD. **Length of courses:** 2+ years.

Study opportunities & careers

Library and information services: Integrated library, computing and audio-visual services. 72,000 books, 120 periodicals. Information provision, £84 pa spent for each student (FTE). Ratio workstations to students of 1:4 (access 13 hours/day); some 250 with access to library, 150 to internet. Central and course-based technicians give support; induction tour of library and information services for new students; range of IT courses, from introductory to advanced. **Other learning resources:** 4 major galleries, seminar rooms, 2 lecture theatres. **Study abroad:** College encourages student exchanges. **Accommodation:** No college accommodation. Student support office has a list; local rent approx £90–£110 pw to share a house, live with a family or a bedsit.

Money

Living expenses budget: Minimum budget of £12k pa (excluding tuition fees) recommended by college. **Term-time work:** College allows term-time work with permission of head of department. Some available in college: cloakroom and selling catalogues at degree shows; bar work; help with mailings, etc. **Financial help:** Application for state bursaries (not automatic) for English, Welsh and Northern Ireland candidates through RCA. Scottish candidates apply to the regional authority. Some RCA money also available. **Tuition fees:** Home students pay £4,780 pa, international students £22,850 pa.

Student view

Set in the heart of Kensington within walking distance of the museums (Victoria and Albert, Science and Natural History), its imposing 1960s architecture is a strong contrast to the surrounding Victorian splendour. The RCA, as it is informally called, is the world's only wholly postgraduate university institution of art and design and is the most concentrated community of young artists, designers and communicators to be found anywhere; a community focused on art in a design environment and design in an art environment. The college boasts an enviable list of graduates from David Hockney and Tracey Emin to James Dyson and Philip Treacy. The average age of students is 27, which adds to the maturity and vitality within the studios, alongside the vibrancy provided by the strong international mix of students. It is a rare experience and high standards are expected and achieved. Well-funded bursaries are available to eligible students though they will not fully cover the fees. The student support office is very helpful, offering friendly, constructive advice on housing and money issues. Students live in Battersea/Clapham, Shepherds Bush/Acton or East London. Bicycles are encouraged. The bar and RCAfé offer relaxation and a vast range of entertainment (debating and film societies, book club, chess, live bands, parties) whilst serving fair trade coffee, infusions or the cheapest drinks in West London. The SU area is the heart of the college where free speech reigns and student activity is abundant. Run by graduates with art at the top of their agenda.

Student footnotes

Housing: Accommodation and welfare office very helpful. No college accommodation; living in London is expensive. **Eats:** College canteen meals and snacks. RCAfé has great cappuccinos and sandwiches. **Drink:** Art Bar and RCAfé; both SU-run, prices very reasonable, pint of 1664 £2, Hoegaarden £2.50, Fosters £1.60. **Nightlife:** SU runs regular events, including DJ nights, karaoke, film evenings, amateur dramatics, discussion groups and big parties. **Sports:** Few college facilities but can use those at Imperial College. **Informal name:** RCA. **Past students:** David Hockney, Bridget Riley (painters); the Chapman Brothers, Henry Moore, Barbara Hepworth, Richard Wentworth (sculptors); Helen Chadwick (installation artist); James Dyson (inventor, vacuum cleaner pioneer); Julian McDonald, Ossie Clark (fashion designers); Philip Treacy (milliner); Ridley Scott (director); Tracey Emin (artist); David Connor (interior designer). **More info?** Ring SU on 020 7590 4211 or email su@rca.ac.uk.

Royal College of Music

Location:
central London
(map 3)
**Single site in
Kensington**

Royal College of Music, Prince Consort Road, South Kensington, London SW7 2BS
☎ Tel 020 7589 3643
🖷 Fax 020 7589 7740
✉ Email info@rcm.ac.uk
💻 Website www.rcm.ac.uk

*Student enquiries: Registry Services
Applications: CUKAS*

In brief

Total Students: 650

46% postgraduate

54% undergraduate

Undergraduates: 350

100% full-time ● ● 64% UK students

5% mature on entry ●

54% female 46% male

- **World-class music school.**
- **Teaching staff:** 200 full-time and part-time.
- **Broad study area:** Music.

Freshers

- **Admissions information:** Music A-level (grade C minimum) plus 1 other, or 2 AS-levels grade C. UCAS tariff not used.
- **First degree entrants:** 60 UK, full-time.
- **Points on entry:** 220 (average).
- **Drop-out rate:** 3% in 1st year.
- **Accommodation:** Most 1st years housed.

Profile

Institution

Founded: 1882, by Prince of Wales (later Edward VII). **Site:** South Kensington, close to the Albert Hall and Imperial College. **How to get there:** South Kensington and Gloucester Road underground stations; various buses. **Special features:** Regular performances, master classes and workshops with top international musicians, performance opportunities in London and across UK. Outreach and summer schools, working with local schoolchildren and teenagers.

Courses

Academic features: BMus with strong performance orientation. BSc physics with music, taught jointly with Imperial College. Range of postgraduate courses in performance and composition. Scholarships and prizes available. **Awarding body:** Royal College of Music. **Main awards:** BMus, PgDip, MMus, DMus. **Length of course:** 4 years; 1–2 years (postgraduate).

Study opportunities & careers

Library and information services: Reference and loan collections; 300,000 volumes, including rare early printed material and manuscripts. Information provision, £172 pa spent for each student (FTE). **Other learning resources:** Computing facilities and internet café, recording studios and research resources. Concert hall, recording studios and theatre on site. Specialist collections: portraits and performance history. Instrument museum. **Study abroad:** College has formal relationships with many musical organisations, including exchanges in Europe, North America and Australia. **Careers:** Information, advice and performance opportunities from communications department.

Student services & facilities

Student advice and services: Student services manager gives advice on finance and welfare; Alexander Technique training. Use of Imperial College counselling and health services and chaplaincy. **Amenities:** Britten Theatre, large concert hall and recital halls. Nearby music shop gives 10% discount to RCM students; facilities of Imperial College at special rates (including swimming pool and gym). **Accommodation:** 45% of students in college accommodation. 170 self-catering places in hall (with practising facilities), £106–£122 pw (£69 pw shared), 43-week contracts; some half-board accommodation for women available nearby. Other students live in privately owned accommodation, rent £80–£100 pw for self-catering. London rent are expensive; students need to ensure no objections to practising instruments. 5% of first-degree students live at home.

Money

Living expenses budget: Minimum budget of £6500–£10,500 pa (excluding tuition fees) recommended by college. **Term-time work:** College encourages professional work – considered an important part of professional development as performers (80% believed to work). Some work available on campus (stewarding, orchestral stage work, admin). Communications department helps find paid performing opportunities and teaching work. **Financial help:** Bursaries for UK/EU students whose family income is up to approx £25k (of £1k pa for UK students, £350 pa for EU students). All applicants are auditioned for a wide range of scholarships, many covering full fees. Some help also available for purchase of musical instruments. Hardship fund for those in demonstrable need. **Tuition fees:** Home students pay £3225 pa for first degrees. International students pay £15,280 pa.

Student view

RCM holds the key to an inspiring and stimulating student and professional life. Surrounded by the Imperial College, Royal College of Art, Albert Hall, numerous museums, as well as Hyde Park – an overwhelming sight every time you approach it. The professors are amongst some of the finest teaching today and the facilities are first-rate, especially the Britten Theatre. As well as a busy working life, there is an enthusiastic SA, which makes you feel welcome from day one and organises many social events throughout the year. Some of the highlights are freshers' week, rag week and the summer ball. It has a truly cosmopolitan atmosphere, with students on the standard 4-year course and some exchange students; many RCM students also take anything from 3 months to a year studying at a music college abroad. Students can get outside performance or teaching bookings through the college. RCM continues to provide the high standard of musical education it always has; you would be hard pushed to find a student who was not proud to be there.

Student footnotes

Housing: College hall in Shepherd's Bush is friendly, good value and easy to get to college. Lists of private accommodation from college. **Eats:** RCM canteen convenient (meal £3-ish) or Imperial College. Damario's Pizza Restaurant (£4+). **Drink:** SA bar (home from home) is place to relax and have fun (pint £1.80). **Nightlife:** Many local haunts for RCM students locally; West End just around the corner. **Sports:** Football team. Imperial College sports centre open to RCM students. **Financial help:** Scholarships available; hardship funds. Some interest-free loans to buy instruments from RCM Society. Welfare office gives advice. **Jobs:** External engagements and teaching. **Best features:** Good sense of community. **And worst:** Hectic; big working culture. **Past students:** Gustav Holst, Benjamin Britten, Michael Tippett, Ralph Vaughan Williams, Andrew Lloyd Webber, Oliver Knussen, Mark-Anthony Turnage (composers); Rick Wakeman, Colin Davis, Peter Pears, Janet Baker, Barry Douglas, Julian Bream, James Galway, Gwyneth Jones, Joan Sutherland, John Lill, Elizabeth Maconchy, Neville Marriner, Sarah Walker, David Willcocks (performers). **More info?** Contact SA on 020 7584 8195 or email sa.president@rcm.ac.uk.

Royal Holloway

Location:
Surrey, west of
London (map 3)
**Single campus near
Egham; partner
colleges**

⌨ Royal Holloway, University of London,
Egham, Surrey TW20 0EX
☎ Tel 01784 443979
🖨 Fax 01784 471381
✉ Email liaison-office@rhul.ac.uk
💻 Website www.rhul.ac.uk

*Student enquiries: Admissions and UK Recruitment
Applications: UCAS*

In brief

Total Students: 8335

28% postgraduate
72% undergraduate

Undergraduates: 5960
97% full-time ● ● 74% UK students
10% mature ● ● 24% lower
on entry   socio-economic
groups

58% female   42% male

- **A top UK research-intensive institution.** A college of University of London.
- **Teaching staff:** 450 full-time, 42 part-time.
- **Broad study areas:** Humanities, modern languages, social sciences, performing arts, sciences, management.

Freshers

- **Admissions information:** Each department has its own grade and subject requirements. AS-levels accepted in combination with 2+ A-levels or equivalent.
- **First degree entrants:** 1490 UK, full-time.
- **Points on entry:** 300 (average).
- **Drop-out rate:** 5% in 1st year.
- **Accommodation:** Almost all 1st years housed.

Profile

Institution

Founded: 1985 from merger of 2 19th-century London University colleges: Royal Holloway and Bedford College – both founded as women's colleges and first admitted men in the 1960s.
Structural features: A college of University of London. **Site:** 140-acre parkland campus, between village of Englefield Green and Egham town, 20 miles from central London; Founder's building, in style of Château of Chambord, and many new buildings. **How to get there:** Egham station (Waterloo–Reading line); buses. Close to Heathrow airport, M3, M4 and M25.

Courses

Awarding body: University of London. **Main undergraduate awards:** BA, BMus, BSc, MSci.
Length of courses: 3 years; 4 years (MSci or courses with languages).

Study opportunities & careers ⬢

Library and information services: 3 main libraries; several departmental collections; 500,000+ volumes in total, 1700 periodicals, 4000 electronic journals, 630 study places; restricted loan collections. Information provision, £116 pa spent for each student (FTE). Integrated library and computer service. 520+ computer workstations for student use in computer centre and academic departments. (Extra-curricular college certificates in computer applications or communication skills available by modular study.) **Study abroad:** 15% of students spend a period abroad. Formal exchange links with universities worldwide, many open to non-language specialists. **Careers:** Information, advice and placement.

Student services & facilities

Student advice and services: Dean of students, wardens, counsellor to students, doctors, FPA, psychiatrist, chaplains, inter-denominational chapel, SU welfare service. **Amenities:** Purpose-built SU building; cafés; theatres; orchestra and choirs. **Sporting facilities:** Wide variety of sports; playing fields, sports hall, gym, tennis and squash courts on site. **Accommodation:** 1st years usually housed if they accept a firm place and apply by the deadline (international students for their whole course). 3000 places available, some self-catering, some catered on a pay-as-you-go system: rent £81 (shared) to £120 (ensuite) pw, 30- or 38-week contracts; meals in catered halls cost additional £20–£25 a week. Students live in privately owned accommodation for 1–2 years: rent £65–£90 pw for house share, £60–£75 pw for lodgings. 5% of first-degree students live at home.

Money

Living expenses budget: Minimum budget of £7k+ pa (excluding tuition fees) recommended by college. **Term-time work:** College allows term-time work for full-time students, up to 16 hours pw (55% believed to work). Some work available on campus in bars, catering, portering, etc., particularly in SU; careers office has some info on (mainly holiday) work off campus. **Financial help:** Bursaries of £750 pa for students from England and Wales with a family income of up to £39,300; plus a further £500 pa if they have 320 points on entry (or equivalent) or if they enter with an Access certificate/diploma. Competitive entrance scholarships for those with 360 points on entry (of £3500 pa for those holding a bursary, of £1k pa for other UK or EU students, of £4k in 1st year for overseas students). Also awards for excellence in sport (golf, athletics), music (choral, organ and instrumental scholarships) and science (bioscience, earth science, computer science). Government funds, small general hardship fund plus a large number of college, departmental and faculty prizes. Apply to student financial adviser for help. **Tuition fees:** Home students pay £3225 pa for first degrees. International students pay £11,555 pa (classroom-based), £12,785 pa (lab/studio-based), £13,120 pa (management, economics).

Student view

It's based in Egham, Surrey, next to Windsor Great Park, yet only 40 mins from central London. The original building, Founder's Building, is stunning; the campus houses many departments and halls of residence in its 120 acres of parkland. Accommodation for all 1st years and some final years. SU is active socially and politically and provides almost 100 sports clubs and societies, eg LGB, James Bond appreciation, comedy, lacrosse. Sports teams have a strong record. It also provides a varied and enjoyable ents programme most days in the 1200-capacity venue.

Student footnotes

Housing: College accommodation good. Study bedrooms, some ensuite; some purpose-built for married students. Local area expensive (help from SU welfare, college accommodation office, local agents). **Eats:** SU coffee bar cheap, varied. Meal on campus £3+; cashless card system for buying food. Local places in Englefield Green, Windsor, Egham, Virginia Water: Don Beni's Pizzeria, Caffe Uno (3 course meals from £14+), several Chinese and Indian restaurants. **Drink:** SU operates 4 bars – good hours and good prices (Fosters £1.70+ a pint). Stumble Inn on campus (nice pub atmosphere, cheap prices); also Happy Man nearby. **Nightlife:** Very active SU ents, eg discos, comedy, chart bands. Musical theatre regulars at Edinburgh Fringe. **Locals:** Quite friendly (though some friction over parking). **Sports:** Playing field, fantastic sports hall and gym on campus. Egham sports centre good but costs; swimming in Staines. **Travel:** College bus service runs all day. At night, SU bus takes non-residential students home for small fee. Cheap deals through ski'n'snowboard club, European studies society. **Financial help:** Principal's Board and some access funds available. **Jobs:** Term-time work in SU bar, DJs, security, etc.; local pubs, office temping jobs; not much above minimum wage. College employment in holidays. **Best features:** Great atmosphere; very friendly. **And worst:** Hotbed of gossip. **Good news:** Improved computer facilities and new halls. **Past students:** George Eliot, Ivy Compton-Burnett (authors); Richmal Crompton (*Just William*); Felicity Lott (soprano); Janet Fookes (politician); David Bellamy (botanist); Kathleen Lonsdale (X-ray crystallographer); Jean Rook (journalist). **More info?** Enquiries to the SU President (tel 01784 486300) or visit www.surhul.co.uk.

Royal Northern College of Music

Location:
Manchester, north-west England
(map 2)
Single site in city centre

✉ Royal Northern College of Music, 124 Oxford Road, Manchester M13 9RD
☎ Tel 0161 907 5260
📠 Fax 0161 273 7611
💻 Website www.rncm.ac.uk

Student enquiries: Admissions Administrator
Applications: CUKAS

In brief

Total Students: 710

26% postgraduate
74% undergraduate

Undergraduates: 525

100% full-time ● ● 84% UK students
5% mature on entry ●

👩 👨
54% female   46% male

- **World-class music school.**
- **Teaching staff:** 35 full-time, 115 part-time.
- **Broad study areas:** Music, performing arts.

Freshers
- **Admissions information:** AS- and A-levels accepted, Key Skills viewed favourably. UCAS tariff not used.
- **First degree entrants:** 135 UK, full-time.
- **Drop-out rate:** 1% in 1st year.
- **Accommodation:** Majority of 1st years housed.

Profile

Institution
Founded: 1973 from Northern School of Music and Royal Manchester College of Music. **Site:** Modern buildings 1 mile south of city centre. **How to get there:** Manchester well connected by coach and rail (to Manchester Piccadilly and Victoria stations; 2 hours 40 mins from London), by road

(M6/M56, M61, M62, M67) and by air to Manchester International Airport (10 miles south of city centre). Many buses from city centre down Oxford Road.

Courses

Academic features: All undergraduate courses have 2 years broad musical education, 2 years specialisation. Joint courses run with University of Manchester and Manchester Metropolitan University. **Awarding body:** RNCM. Joint courses by University of Manchester and Manchester Metropolitan University. **Main awards:** BMus, GRNCM, PGDip, MMus, MPhil. **Length of courses:** 4 years for first-degree students.

Study opportunities & careers

Library and information services: Extensive reference and lending sections of books and performing material. Information provision, £88 pa spent for each student (FTE). Support from library and IT specialists; induction programme for all new students and IT courses. **Other learning resources:** Vast audio collection with playback facilities for records, tapes, CDs, videos and DVDs. Electronic studio keyboard laboratory, professionally staffed recording studio. Specialist collections: Collection of historic musical instruments, RNCM Archives. **Study abroad:** Exchanges in Europe through Erasmus scheme. **Careers:** Advisory service supporting professional studies element of degree programme.

Student services & facilities

Student advice and services: Chaplains, counsellors, welfare officer, medical referrals, instrument purchase and loan scheme. **Amenities:** Opera theatre, concert hall, recital room; junior common room; refectory with bar. Full programme of public events takes place throughout academic year. **Sporting facilities:** Arranged through SU and hall of residence. **Accommodation:** 80% of 1st years in college accommodation (30% of all students). 316 self-catering places in halls, rent £90.50 pw for 42-week contract. Most students live in privately owned accommodation for 2+ years: rent £60–£120 pw self-catering.

Money

Living expenses budget: Minimum budget of £6k pa (excluding tuition fees) recommended by college. **Term-time work:** College allows term-time work for full-time students (external concert engagements make significant contribution to professional development), 75% believed to work. Some work available on campus (bar, front of house) and help finding work in concerts/gigs for suitable students. **Financial help:** Bursaries of £1050 pa for UK/EU students from low-income families. Some support for students not eligible for bursaries. Also government funds and other funds used to alleviate student hardship, especially when students do not qualify for public support. Some entrance awards for students of outstanding promise. **Tuition fees:** Home students pay £3225 for first degrees. International students pay £13,150 pa (except vocal and conducting, which are £14,300 pa).

Student view

It's without doubt a world-class institution. Student life is one of focused musical study coupled with the fantastic cosmopolitan experience of living in Manchester. Facilities are good. 4 concert venues, 1 a designated opera theatre with its own workshop. Oxford Road Wing, recently opened, has large rehearsal spaces to complement the 5 existing spacious studios, as well as lots more state-of-the-art practice rooms (sound-proofed and air-conditioned). An equal mix of male and female students, and 2:1 ratio undergraduates to postgraduates. BMus course (a 4-year course) as well as a variety of postgraduate courses. SU provides welfare support and all sorts of social activities, including freshers' week – the best! There are 2 bars, 1 in the RNCMSU common room (JCR). Accommodation is relatively cheap. You can live in halls or rent a house. Halls can be a bit more but bills are included; rooms are ensuite and they are next to college so travel is quick and safe. You can get virtually anywhere in Manchester by bus; RNCM is on the busiest bus route in Europe so you will hardly ever have to wait for one.

Student footnotes

Housing: Find private accommodation through noticeboards (cheapest in Moss Side, Hulme, Whalley Range). **Eats:** Meal cheap in the SU; up to £8 at the Phoenix, Firkin, Babylon or in Rusholme (over 50 Indian restaurants, most cheap and very good – the famous Curry Mile!); good vegetarian; Chinatown in city centre. **Drink:** SU bar cheap, so are university SUs. **Nightlife:** Something for everybody in Manchester. Very vibrant gay village. Lots of student discounts at cinemas, theatres, shows, concerts at Manchester Evening News Arena plus many ents at SUs. **Locals:** Very friendly. Some dodgy areas to be avoided! **Sports:** Use of very good uni facilities. **Travel:** College fund for studying abroad. Numerous tours for ensembles. **Financial help:** Well-run hardship fund. **Jobs:** Loads of places to find work; Manchester and surrounding towns great for busking. **Best features:** Real sense of community. **And worst:** Fitting in everything you want to do! **Informal name:** RNCM. **Past students:** Peter Donohoe (pianist); Jane Eaglen, Amanda Roocroft (sopranos); Howard Jones (pop singer); Brodsky Quartet, Nossek Quartet, Nemo Brass. **More info?** Enquiries to SU President (tel 0161 907 5215).

Royal Scottish Academy of Music & Drama

Location:
Glasgow, central Scotland (map 1)
Single site in city centre

✒ Royal Scottish Academy of Music & Drama, 100 Renfrew Street, Glasgow G2 3DB
☎ Tel 0141 332 4101
✉ Email registry@rsamd.ac.uk
💻 Website www.rsamd.ac.uk

Student enquiries: Registry
Applications: CUKAS (music courses), UCAS (BEd music), direct (drama courses)

In brief

Total Students: 690

17% postgraduate
83% undergraduate

Undergraduates: 575

100% full-time ● ● 90% UK students
19% mature on entry ◉

57% female 43% male

- **Specialist music and drama school.**
- **Teaching staff:** 70 full-time, 600 part-time.
- **Broad study areas:** Music, drama, opera, film and television, technical and production arts, modern ballet.

Freshers

- **First degree entrants:** 175 UK, full-time.
- **Drop-out rate:** 7% in 1st year.
- **Accommodation:** All 1st years housed.

Profile

Institution

Founded: 1847. **Site:** Central Glasgow. **How to get there:** Glasgow well connected to all regions of the UK by train (4³/₄ hours from London to Glasgow Central, under an hour from Edinburgh), by coach (8¹/₂ hours from London to Buchanan bus station), by air (1 hour flight from London; Glasgow airport 7 miles from centre or Prestwick airport 22 miles) and by road (M8). Academy walking distance from Queen Street and Central stations and bus station. **Special features:** Many top professional concert artists and theatre directors in recitals, productions and masterclasses.

Courses

Academic features: Degrees in acting, technical and production arts, contemporary theatre practice, Scottish music, music performance (BMus), music education (BEd) and digital film and TV. **Awarding body:** RSAMD. **Main undergraduate awards:** BA, BEd, BMus. **Length of courses:** 3 or 4 years.

Study opportunities & careers

Library and information services: 80,000 music volumes, 13,800 books, 7600 sound recordings, 60 study places, 14 listening booths, computer lab. Converged library and IT services. Information provision, £64 pa spent for each student (FTE). Ratio workstations to students 1:23 (open 12 hours/day), 30 with access to library and internet. IT support staff; tours of library and IT services for new students. **Other learning resources:** Concert hall (360 seats), theatre (340 seats); TV studio; recital room; broadcasting studio; electro-acoustic recording studio. Opera school, including large performance space, rehearsal rooms and coaching rooms. **Study abroad:** Links and exchanges with colleges and conservatoires in Europe, Canada and the USA. **Careers:** Information and advice.

Student services & facilities

Student advice and services: Counsellor and welfare adviser. **Accommodation:** All 1st years housed; rent £101 pw, including bills and insurance; 44- or 50-week contracts. Advice and assistance in finding suitable privately owned accommodation; rent approx £70–£90 pw for self-catering.

Money

Living expenses budget: Minimum budget of £7k–£7500 pa (excluding tuition fees) recommended by Academy. **Financial help:** £22,700 government funds; £4k mature student bursary, 110 students helped. Entrance scholarships of £94k, 32 students helped. **Tuition fees:** Scottish and EU students pay no fees during course; other UK students pay £1820 pa for first degrees. International students pay £11,499 pa (£11,499–£13,824 MMus).

Student view

An orange brick building in the centre of Glasgow, full of modern facilities, surrounded by shops, pubs and eateries. Within a 10-min walk of 2 train stations, bus station and underground where transport is frequent; stay sensible and travel is safe. Parking is expensive but bike parking available. Good library has music scores, drama texts, books, CDs, videos and DVDs; CD and video/DVD players available to use. Library open 9am to 8pm (more limited Fridays–Sundays). Extensive IT suite with on-hand support. Healthy numbers of UK and international students covering a wide range of ages. Staff members are mostly approachable and the quality of teaching is high. Courses regularly reviewed, so stay relevant; workloads hard but realistic. Most students have jobs but it is hard to fit round long hours and course commitments. Glasgow is now one of Europe's most cosmopolitan cities offering excellent nightlife; full of students, so lively during week and at weekends. A substantial number of gay pubs and clubs. Lots of theatres, concert halls, cinemas and art museums. Always plenty going on in the arts; often cheap tickets for students. SU has sabbatical officer but no separate building or permanent bar as yet – catering staff provide subsidised bar for union events. A counsellor is available and SU also available to offer advice and help. There are footie tournaments, yoga and hill-walking, and students attend clubs and societies at neighbouring universities. Subjects well respected with good job prospects owing to academy's strong reputation. A few exchange places are available; apprenticeship schemes allocated by audition. A mix of coursework and examinations but much of assessment based on the practical. In the 1st year it's easy to change course and staff advise students individually according to needs.

Student footnotes

Housing: Plenty of safe housing. Many students live at home but 1st years in student flats in Liberty Living student village in Miller Street. Others rent flats through agencies; rent vary with location. **Eats:** Canteen and café bar open to students, staff or the public. **Drink:** Trader Joe's, Mollie Malone's, the Universal. **Nightlife:** Clubbing suits all tastes. Garage, Walkabout, Strathclyde Union, the Shack and Jumpin' Jacks are some favourites. **Sports:** Discounted access to nearby gyms. **Jobs:** Part-time, minimum wage work easy to find. Job centres nearby and opportunity for students to usher at shows/concerts in the college. Some students get professional work. **Hardship funds:** Hardship funds and loans are available and many students enter various competitions throughout the year. **Past students:** Billy Boyd, James McAvoy, Robert Carlyle, Tom Conti, Alan Cumming, John Hannah, Hannah Gordon, Daniella Nardini, Ian Richardson, Fulton Mackay, Phyllis Logan, Dawn Steele (actors); Ruby Wax (comedian); Lisa Milne (soprano), Angela Whelan (trumpeter), Sheena Easton, Bill McCue, Moira Anderson (singers).

Royal Veterinary College

Location:
central London
(map 3); Hertfordshire,
just north of M25
**Teaching split
between London and
Hertfordshire; partner
colleges**

Royal Veterinary College, University of London,
Royal College Street, London NW1 0TU
Tel 020 7468 5147/9/6
Fax 020 7468 5311
Email enquiries@rvc.ac.uk
Website www.rvc.ac.uk

*Student enquiries: Admissions
Applications: UCAS*

In brief

Total Students: 2050

26% postgraduate
74% undergraduate

Undergraduates: 1520
99% full-time ● ● 91% UK students
20% mature ● ● 30% lower
on entry socio-economic
groups

81% female   19% male

- **World-class research-intensive institution.** A specialist college of London University.
- **Teaching staff:** 161 full-time and part-time.
- **Broad study areas:** Veterinary medicine, bioveterinary science, veterinary pathology, veterinary nursing.

Freshers

- **Admissions information:** AS-levels are welcomed but all offers are based on 3 A-levels or equivalent. UCAS tariff not used.
- **First degree entrants:** 260 UK, full-time.
- **Points on entry:** 340+ (average).
- **Drop-out rate:** 3% in 1st year.
- **Accommodation:** Most 1st years housed.

Profile

Institution

Founded: 1791. **Structural features:** College of University of London. **Site:** Veterinary medicine and veterinary science at Camden Town (just north-east of Regent's Park); clinical studies and veterinary nursing on 230-hectare campus at Hawkshead (near Potters Bar, Hertfordshire). **How to get there:** Camden Town, buses and tubes (Camden Town, Mornington Crescent, Euston and King's Cross stations); Hawkshead, 20 mins by train from King's Cross to Brookmans Park or Potters Bar. **Special features:** 1-year preparatory year to widen participation (veterinary gateway programme).

Courses

Academic features: Integrated curriculum, including large proportion of directed learning and small group work; individual project in final year. 6-year degree programme combining veterinary medicine with BSc bioveterinary science. **Awarding body:** University of London. **Main undergraduate awards:** BVetMed, BSc, FdSc. **Length of courses:** 5 years (BVetMed, 6 with intercalated BSc); 3 years (BSc bioveterinary sciences, FdSc veterinary nursing), 4 years (BSc veterinary nursing); 3 years BSc; 2 years (FdSc).

Study opportunities & careers

Library and information services: Learning resources centres and computer suites at both sites; reference copies of standard texts. **Other learning resources:** Animal hospitals at both sites. Large animal clinical centre and small animal referral hospital at Hawkshead. **Study abroad:** BVetMed students may carry out components of extra-mural study overseas.

Student services & facilities

Student advice and services: Student support team including welfare and financial guidance officer and disability officer; physician and occupational health team visit both sites regularly. **Amenities:** ULU building in Malet Street, college refectory and SU rooms on both campuses. Playing fields and swimming pool at Hawkshead. **Accommodation:** Camden: 95% of 1st years live in self-catering accommodation provided either by the college (£115.50 pw, 48-week contract) or University of London intercollegiate accommodation (£130–£181 pw). Hawkshead: 1 hall for veterinary nursing students (£108 pw incl utility bills); 2 halls for clinical students (£124 pw incl breakfast and evening meal, plus lunch at weekends); £86 pw self-catering.

Money

Living expenses budget: Minimum budget of £800–£1k per month (excluding tuition fees) recommended by College. **Financial help:** Bursaries for UK students, dependent on family income and course: up to £1650 pa for veterinary medicine; up to £1750 pa for bioveterinary science; up to £2k for veterinary nursing; up to £5700 for students from gateway programme. Also merit scholarships. Government funds and limited college funds (awards range from £500–£3k; average £1k). Applications considered on individual merit. **Tuition fees:** Home students pay £3225 pa.

International students pay £8030 pa (science), £8300 (veterinary nursing), £18,400 pa (veterinary medicine).

Student view

It's split between 2 campuses: one in central London, Camden Town; the other, called Hawkshead, in rural Hertfordshire near Potters Bar. Life at the 2 campuses is very different. Camden is a relatively small site, where the first 2 years of veterinary science course and pre-clinical veterinary medicine are taught. Inside you will find a hive of activity with a warm, friendly atmosphere. When time allows, students relax in the common rooms or café; and there is a small branch of the student shop. On the other hand, Hawkshead is part of a large estate, the surrounding land run by the college farm. Remainder of veterinary medicine course and the veterinary nurses share this campus, plus some smaller courses (pathology, final year vet science and many of the postgrads). Small but active Students' Union Society (SUS) has a number of facilities at Hawkshead: common rooms, bar, sports fields, swimming pool. SUS is affiliated to the University of London Union (ULU) so all students can use its facilities, a short walk from the Camden campus. Although Hawkshead is in the countryside, access into London is very easy (regular trains to King's Cross); however, local travel is more difficult. Both sites have learning resources centres with 24-hour open-access PCs and state-of-the-art specialist libraries. For those wanting to study veterinary subjects who like the idea of a 'veterinary village', this is the place for you.

Student footnotes

Housing: College-owned shared flats at Camden for all 1st years and some 2nd years; catered and self-catered halls and shared houses at Hawkshead. Most students rent houses of their own. **Eats:** Refectory at both campuses, cheap and good. It is London so there is plenty of variety. **Drink:** ULU, and lots of bars and pubs in London. Buttery Bar at Hawkshead campus. **Nightlife:** It is the capital city! SUS organises a packed freshers' week and regular parties through the year. Social events with AVS (Association of Veterinary Students). **Sports:** Many clubs; if they aren't at RVC they will be at ULU! **Financial help:** Access fund and hardship funds, but the BVetMed is expensive, there's no way round it. **Travel:** Long holidays (where you are expected to do work experience on the BVetMed) and much opportunity to join projects based overseas. **Jobs:** Possible to find in London, if you have the time! **Best features:** Lots of like-minded, fun-loving people. **Worst features:** Too many like-minded people (but plenty of opportunities to meet students from other UL colleges). **Informal name:** RVC. **More info?** SUS General Manager (email sucommunications@rvc.ac.uk).

Royal Welsh College of Music & Drama

Location:
Cardiff, south-east Wales (map 1)
Single site in city centre

🖃 Royal Welsh College of Music & Drama, Castle Grounds, Cathays Park, Cardiff CF10 3ER
☎ Tel 029 2034 2854
🖷 Fax 029 2039 1301
✉ Email music.admissions@rwcmd.ac.uk or drama.admissions@rwcmd.ac.uk
🖥 Website www.rwcmd.ac.uk

Student enquiries: music 029 2039 1361; drama 029 2039 1327
Applications: CUKAS (music), UCAS (drama)

In brief

Total Students: 660

21% postgraduate
79% undergraduate

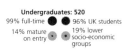
Undergraduates: 520
99% full-time ● ● 96% UK students
14% mature ● ● 19% lower
on entry socio-economic
groups

55% female 45% male

- **Specialist music and drama school.**
- **Teaching staff:** 30 full-time, 320 part-time.
- **Broad study areas:** Music; acting; theatre design; stage management; arts management; music therapy.

Freshers

- **Admissions information:** By interview or audition.
- **First degree entrants:** 145 UK, full-time.
- **Points on entry:** 200+ (average).
- **Drop-out rate:** 7% in 1st year.
- **Accommodation:** Most 1st years housed.

Profile

Institution

Founded: 1949, as Cardiff College of Music. Became Welsh College of Music & Drama in 1971 and Royal College in 2001. **Site:** Cardiff city centre, in grounds of Cardiff Castle. **How to get there:** Site close to main bus and railway stations. **Special features:** The national conservatoire of Wales. Visiting artists include Boris Berman, Jonathan Snowden, Margaret Price, Krzysztof Smietana, Donald Maxwell, Charles Rosen, Robert Tear, Julian Lloyd Webber, Gwyneth Jones. **Structural features:** Associated with University of Glamorgan.

Courses

Academic features: Emphasis on practical and performance-based training. Degrees in music, theatre design, stage management, technical theatre. **Awarding body:** University of Glamorgan. **Main undergraduate awards:** BMus, BA. **Length of courses:** 4 years (BMus), 3 years (BA).

Study opportunities & careers

Library and information services: Library with 50,000 items, including reference resources, scripts, scores, journals, CDs and DVDs; computer workstations provide word-processing, email and internet access. **Other learning resources:** 3 theatres on site; studios and workshops; 2 modern recital galleries, studio theatre, professional recording studio, courtyard performance space and 25 practice rooms in new Anthony Hopkins Centre. **Study abroad:** Some exchange opportunities. **Careers:** Information, advice and placement service.

Student services & facilities

Student advice and services: Student services, welfare team, counsellors, chaplaincy, police liaison. **Amenities:** Refectory, coffee shop, SU shop and bar. Concert and opera ticket concessions; strong practical association with BBC and WNO. **Accommodation:** 106 places in halls of residence (all ensuite, with telephone and data points); rent £80 pw, contracts 42 weeks. Privately owned accommodation locally: private halls, £70 pw + bills; shared houses at £210 pm self-catering + bills. SU holds lists of reputable landlords, housing agencies, etc.

Money

Living expenses budget: Minimum budget of £5k pa (excluding tuition fees) recommended by college. **Term-time work:** College allows part-time work. Some available in college – ushers, front of house, bars. **Financial help:** Some scholarships and bursaries. Access funds available. **Tuition fees:** Home students pay £3225 pa for first degrees (though Welsh residents may be eligible for annual fee grant). International students pay £11,045 pa.

Student view

It's in the picturesque surroundings of Cathays Park, just behind Cardiff Castle. Access is marvellous, only 10 mins' walk from the central bus station, railway station and city centre. College has new halls of residence at Cambrian Point, mostly for undergraduates (several postgrad places in flats at Severn Point); superb quality, city centre accommodation just 12 mins' walk from College, in a highly secure and comfortable environment. Individual music practice rooms on site and colour TV (with Sky digital package). If you don't fancy halls, it's easy to find houses in walking distance of college (in Cathays, Roath or Canton); a comprehensive SU housing list is part of student life pack sent to all new students. Variety of ages and nationalities at college, even though it is one of the smallest in the UK. Enthusiastic SU organises successful graduands' and freshers' balls. Freshers' week is packed full of entertainment; many other events throughout the year. Societies currently include LGBT, overseas society, girl's and boy's football, cricket, yoga, aerobics and Christian Union. College is friendly and intimate so you will soon discover fellow students with similar interests. As a capital, Cardiff has a plethora of pubs, clubs and takeaways to suit all tastes and, of course, cinemas and theatres. St David's Hall, the Cardiff International Arena, the Millennium Centre and the Millennium Stadium (spiritual home of Welsh rugby) are all in the heart of Cardiff, putting on a huge range of events. Relations between staff and students are good; much of the teaching is in small groups. The atmosphere for both music and drama students is less cut-throat than at some colleges, and the drop-out rate is low. Numerous concerts, annual full-scale opera and usually 6 drama department productions a term. Stage management pantomime is an annual must – mercilessly mocks everyone else in college! Whatever the course, the emphasis is always firmly on performance.

Student footnotes

Housing: Halls of residence; SU housing list for private housing. **Eats:** College canteen and coffee/sandwich bar (meal £3-ish). Outside college, abundance of good (and bad!) restaurants and takeaways from every corner of the world at varying prices. **Drink:** SU run college bar is cheap (£1.80 a pint). Plenty of local student pubs around to cater for Cardiff's large student population. Brains is local brewery. **Nightlife:** Regular SU events in college. Cardiff is full of things to do and plenty of busy, entertaining nightclubs. **Locals:** Very friendly; high student population in city. **Sports:** Union sports societies; access to Cardiff University sports centre; cheap student membership at the Welsh Institute of Sport. **Travel:** Main train and bus stations within walking distance. All student housing close to college. **Financial help:** Bursary funds and hardship funds. College staff helpful in giving advice. **Jobs:** Relatively easy to find part-time work in term time. College employs students as front of house staff as do local theatre and concert venues. **Informal name:** RWCMD or Royal Welsh Coll. **Best features:** Welcoming, friendly and very supportive college. **And worst:** Being small – everyone knows everyone else (good when you need a friend or good time but bad the morning after you've been a little naughty). **Past students:** Anthony Hopkins, Victor Spinetti, Simon Trinder (actors); Peter Gill (writer and director); Caryl Thomas (harpist); Iris Williams (singer); Anthony Stuart Lloyd (opera singer); Eve Myles (*Torchwood*). **More info?** Ring SU on 029 2037 2700.

St Andrews University

Location:
east coast of Scotland
(map 1)
2 sites, in and near St Andrews

University of St Andrews, College Gate,
St Andrews, Fife KY16 9AJ
☎ Tel 01334 476161
🖶 Fax 01334 463388
✉ E mail admissions@st-andrews.ac.uk
🖳 Website www.st-andrews.ac.uk

*Student enquiries: Admissions Application Centre
(tel 01334 462150)
Applications: UCAS*

In brief

Total Students: 8965

23% postgraduate
77% undergraduate

Undergraduates: 6940
85% full-time ● ● 65% UK students
5% mature ● ● 16% lower
on entry socio-economic
groups

56% female 44% male

- **A top UK research-intensive university.**
- **Teaching staff:** 350 full-time, 16 part-time.
- **Broad study areas:** Sciences (including biological, chemical, computational, physical, geographical, mathematical and medical), arts and social sciences (including modern languages, histories, film studies, philosophy, psychology, classics, anthropology, economics, English, Arabic and Middle East studies, management, geography, art history and international relations), divinity.

Freshers

- **Admissions information:** AS-levels accepted only in combination with A-levels. UCAS tariff not used. Entry requirements are relaxed for mature students.
- **First degree entrants:** 1225 UK, full-time.
- **Points on entry:** 340 (average).
- **Drop-out rate:** 2% in 1st year.
- **Accommodation:** All 1st years housed who want it.

Profile

Institution

Founded: 1413. **Site:** St Andrews town centre, plus North Haugh site 1/2 mile west of the centre. **How to get there:** Nearest station is Leuchars (5 miles away on main London–Aberdeen line), then bus; from Edinburgh, train takes 1+ hours, 2 hours by bus; good road links (M90 and A91).

Courses

Academic features: Admission to faculty rather than course so final choice of subject(s) can be delayed until end of 2nd year. Semester and modular system. **Awarding body:** St Andrews University. **Main undergraduate awards:** MA, BSc, MPhys, MChem, MSci, MTheol, MMath. **Length of courses:** 4 years (Hons); 3 years (general); direct 2nd year entry to some science Hons degrees.

Study opportunities & careers

Library and information services: 1 million volumes, 2750 periodicals, 1100 study areas. Information provision, £208 pa spent for each student (FTE). Separate IT services. Ratio workstations to students 1:5 (open 24 hours/day); some 800 workstations have library and internet access. Student IT advisory service (staffed by postgrads) and specialist support staff available; library introduction for all new students; free 6-hour IT skills training courses available (and more advanced courses if required). **Other learning resources:** Computing laboratory, Gatty marine laboratory, language centre. **Study abroad:** 10% of students spend a period abroad. Some 25 formal exchange programmes, many with multiple links, involving 9 other countries. **Careers:** Information, advice and placement service.

Student services & facilities

Student advice and services: Doctor, FPA, chaplain, student welfare service. Limited residential facilities for married and disabled students. **Amenities:** SA with coffee and snack bars, newspaper, arts and crafts area, shops, bars, etc. **Sporting facilities:** Modern physical education centre; 40 acres of playing field; 6 squash courts, all-weather athletics track, tennis courts, AstroTurf pitch, cricket bays. Many golf courses locally (including Old Course); local public leisure complex with indoor swimming pool. **Accommodation:** All 1st years who apply are in university accommodation (67% of all undergraduates). 2800 places available: 54% are full-board places, £4200–£5710 pa (£3785–£5145 pa shared), contracts term time or longer; 46% are self-catering places at £2k–£4410 pa (£3970 sharing). Students live in privately owned accommodation for 1+ years, rent from £330 pm plus bills self-catering. Under 5% of first-degree students live at home.

Money

Living expenses budget: Minimum budget of £12k pa recommended by university. **Term-time work:** University allows term-time work for full-time students. Limited work on campus as cleaners, etc. **Financial help:** Some financial needs-based scholarships. £247k government funds available, 600+ students helped; £25k own funds, 100 helped; plus £10k other funds. Special help for single parents, mature students and self-financing students. £50k used to provide short-term loans for 300 students. Apply to student support services for help (email sss@st.andrews.ac.uk); see website for further information. **Tuition fees:** Scottish and EU students pay no fees during course; other UK students pay £1820 pa for first degrees (£2895 for medicine). International students pay £11,350 pa, except pre-clinical students who pay £17,300.

Student view

Over 6000 students inhabit this historic town facing the North Sea, the 'home of golf' and the oldest university in Scotland (1410). Town is small, but lots of student facilities, with good mix of historic and new. University spread throughout old town; sciences mostly on 1960s campus-style North Haugh site. Very friendly, close-knit community of cosmopolitan students – about 20% international, 40% Scottish, 40% English. 1st years guaranteed a place in hall; most others live in university flats and private accommodation. SA is the hub of university life and is only club/venue in town. SA also provides welfare advice, live music, travel service, biggest charity campaign in Scotland (£30k raised last year), and oldest debating society in world. 100 societies, from serious (Amnesty International) to silly (Tunnock's Caramel Wafer Appreciation Society) to supportive (LGBT). Athletic union offers excellent facilities and wide range of sports for all abilities. Strong dramatic tradition; many theatre groups and musical societies. Leading independent student newspaper, the *Saint*. Balls for everything: halls, sports, societies. Traditions galore, red gowns, raisin weekend, pier walk, May morning dip in the North Sea. Modular course structure; entry by faculty, so requires no Honours specialisation before 3rd year. Small tutorial size and accessible tutors who are experts in their field. Many departments have excellent reputation including psychology, history (medieval, modern and Scottish), art history, computer science and physics, international relations and maths. Top graduate employment record. Strong alumni network across the world.

Student footnotes

Housing: All within walking distance, all very safe. **Eats:** Wide range. Meal on campus £2+. Indian, Chinese, Mexican, Littlejohns from £6 for main course. Many student deals. Coffee shops abundant. Tesco in centre of town. **Drink:** SA cheapest (£1.70+ a pint). Happy hour at most pubs. **Nightlife:** Pub oriented. Union for ents, bands, discos. Cinema, Byre Theatre, Crawford Arts Centre. Dundee and Edinburgh for occasional nights out, but most people stay around for the weekend parties. **Locals:** Reserved but friendly. **Sports:** 8 golf courses (cheap student passes). **Travel:** 5 miles to nearest train station, frequent buses to all main cities. **Financial help:** Through student support services. **Jobs:** Mostly in pubs, restaurants, shops. Occasional jobs with golf tournaments and tourist events. **Best features:** Biggest beach in Scotland, community spirit. **And worst:** Cold winter. **Past students:** John Knox (Scottish Reformation); Jean Paul Marat (philosopher); Sir Hugh Cortazzi (former British Ambassador to Japan); Fay Weldon, Zoe Fairbairns (authors); Hazel Irvine (presenter); Sara Douglas-Hamilton (wildlife presenter); John Suchet, Crispin Bonham-Carter (actors); Alastair Reid (poet); Eric Anderson (Provost of Eton); James Michener (author); Siobhan Redmond (actress); Michael Forsyth, Alex Salmond (politicians). **More info?** Enquiries to SA on 01334 462700 or visit www.yourunion.net.

St George's

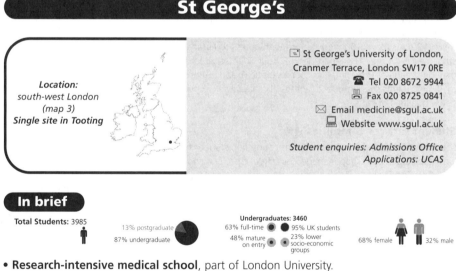

Location:
south-west London
(map 3)
Single site in Tooting

St George's University of London, Cranmer Terrace, London SW17 0RE
☎ Tel 020 8672 9944
🖷 Fax 020 8725 0841
✉ Email medicine@sgul.ac.uk
💻 Website www.sgul.ac.uk

Student enquiries: Admissions Office
Applications: UCAS

In brief

Total Students: 3985

13% postgraduate
87% undergraduate

Undergraduates: 3460
63% full-time
48% mature on entry
95% UK students
23% lower socio-economic groups

68% female   32% male

- **Research-intensive medical school**, part of London University.
- **Teaching staff:** 200 full-time, 310 part-time.
- **Broad study areas:** Medicine, radiography, physiotherapy, biomedical sciences, pharmacy, nursing, midwifery, social work, paramedic science.

Freshers

- **Admissions information:** AS-levels accepted in combination with 3 A-levels or equivalent. UCAS tariff not used; offers made in terms of grades.
- **First degree entrants:** 530 UK, full-time.

- **Points on entry:** 280 (average).
- **Drop-out rate:** 1% in 1st year.
- **Accommodation:** All 1st years housed who require it.

Profile

Institution

Founded: 1751. **Structural features:** Part of London University. Faculty of Health and Social Care Science in partnership with Kingston University. **Site:** Single site in Tooting, south-west London for medical studies and biomedical sciences. Nursing, midwifery, radiography and physiotherapy students study at both St George's and Kingston University (see separate profile). **How to get there:** Tooting Broadway underground station (Northern line); buses. **Special features:** Only free-standing medical school in the UK.

Courses

Academic features: Medical curriculum allows students to combine compulsory core with own choice of special study modules; much teaching in body-system modules, with emphasis on clinical relevance of basic sciences. All students on BSc and medical courses share common foundation programme. Graduate entry MBBS course. Modular health and social care science BSc. **Awarding body:** University of London. **Main undergraduate awards:** MB BS, BSc. **Length of courses:** 5 years (MB BS); 6 years (intercalated BSc); 4 years (graduate entry); 3 years (nursing, midwifery, radiography, physiotherapy, biomedical science).

Study opportunities & careers

Library and information services: 30,000 monographs, 90,000 journal volumes, 800 periodicals, 400 study places. Information provision, £234 pa spent for each student (FTE). Separate IT services (open 12 hours/day); 100 workstations with access to library, 140 to internet; ratio workstations to students 1:8. Staffed IT support desk; 2-hour orientation for new students on library catalogue, medical databases, internet, etc; courses on all IT applications offered. **Study abroad:** Most final year medical students spend up to 2 months abroad, largely outside Europe. **Careers:** Help available for newly qualified doctors.

Student services & facilities

Student advice and services: Student counsellor, student health service, chaplains. **Amenities:** Hospital chapel; bookshop managed by school club; bar, common rooms, prayer rooms, banks. **Sporting facilities:** Squash courts, aerobics training and weight-training rooms; large sports hall (badminton, volleyball, 5-a-side football, cricket nets); local Olympic-standard public swimming pool just off site; 10-acre sports ground at Cobham, rowing at Chiswick, sailing at Burnham-on-Crouch. **Accommodation:** 90% of 1st years in school accommodation (all those who require it). 332 self-catering places available at approx £99 pw, contracts term time only. Most students live in privately rented accommodation after 1st year, rent £75–£80 pw.

Money

Living expenses budget: Minimum budget of £9k for an academic year (excluding tuition fees) recommended by the school. **Term-time work:** No school policy on term-time work for full-time students. **Financial help:** Bursaries of £1260 pa for UK students whose family income is up to £25k, tapered down to £160 pa where family income is £50k. Also £1 million government funds, 120 students helped. Apply to Student Finance Support Officer for help. **Tuition fees:** Home students pay £3225 pa for first degrees, except NHS-funded courses and foundation programme to medicine (joint with Kingston University). International students pay £12,020 (BSc programmes), £15,200 pa (pre-clinical), £26,655 pa (clinical).

Student view

Large modern complex of buildings in Tooting, south-west London. All pre-clinical and approx half clinical teaching on site, with radiography and nursing split between both the main site and Kingston Uni. 1st years can apply for a place in self-catering mixed halls, 10 mins' walk from the medical school. Halls life is good (socially) and easy (financially and domestically). Tooting is good for eating and drinking; theatre, film and more require a short 5-min bus journey; central London is about 20 mins by tube. SU is apolitical, holding fortnightly discos in the newly refurbished SU bar, plus many other events (band nights, quiz nights, karaoke, formal balls every term) and specials (Christmas revue, rag week, freshers' fortnight). The bar is good value and rumoured to be the longest student bar in London; as well as the usual, it has guest beers, wines and malts on constant promotion. Hot and cold food now available at brand new SU café Eddie Wilson's. Most sports and leisure interests are catered for and new clubs constantly being formed. Sports ground is at Cobham (Surrey) but a sports hall on site has 3 squash courts, 3 multigyms and a weights room (membership only £20 pa). Successful clubs include hockey, football, netball, cricket, tennis, rugby and rowing. All clubs are remarkably active socially! School offers a range of subjects in health science, from 4- or 5-year medical courses, radiography, physiotherapy, pharmacy through to paramedic courses. Possible to intercalate a degree at the end of the 2nd year (or later). Student–staff relations are relaxed and friendly. Ideal if you want to become a capable and caring physician, and still enjoy every moment.

Student footnotes

Housing: Halls for all 1st years, local housing plentiful (find it through estate agents, ULU, word of mouth and on SU website). **Eats:** Curry! Tooting is curry centre of SW London. In med school, Eddie Wilsons offers good food at reasonable prices. **Drink:** Average pint £1.50+ in student bar. Pubs nearby include the Selkirk, the Trafalgar and Hoochie Mamas. **Nightlife:** SU events (well-equipped); comedy nights, quizzes, live bands. Plenty of local clubs; central London 20 mins away. **Locals:** Fine. **Sports:** Cheap, good on-site sports centre; cheap entry to local pool. **Travel:** School scholarships for electives. **Financial help:** Access funds; SGUL bursary for students on maintenance grant. Banks reasonable to healthcare professionals when it comes to overdrafts. **Jobs:** In student bar (up to £6.50/hour); nursing temp, medical secretary and lab work during holidays. **Best features:** Friendly atmosphere, expert training, curriculum, good clinical experience. **And worst:** 5 years can seem a long time! **Informal name:** George's. **Past students:** Henry Gray (Gray's *Anatomy*); Edward Jenner (smallpox vaccine); Thomas Young (physician and physicist); John Hunter (surgeon); Mike Stroud (physician and explorer); Harry Hill (comedian). **More info?** Contact SU President on 020 8725 2709, email stuuni@sgul.ac.uk or visit the SU website (www.students.sgul.ac.uk).

St Mary's University College

Location:
south-west London
(map 3)
Single site near Twickenham

✉ St Mary's University College, Waldegrave Road, Strawberry Hill, Twickenham TW1 4SX
☎ Tel 020 8240 2314
🖨 Fax 020 8240 2361
💻 Website www.smuc.ac.uk

*Student enquiries: Recruitment Office
Applications: UCAS*

In brief

Total Students: 4175

20% postgraduate
80% undergraduate

Undergraduates: 3325
83% full-time
16% mature on entry
93% UK students
33% lower socio-economic groups

66% female   34% male

- **University college, awarding its own degrees.**
- **Teaching staff:** 140 full-time.
- **Broad study areas:** Teaching, sport, health, humanities, media, arts.

Freshers

- **Admissions information:** At least 2 A-levels or equivalent required.
- **First degree entrants:** 845 UK, full-time.
- **Points on entry:** 160–200 (average).
- **Drop-out rate:** 8% in 1st year.
- **Accommodation:** Most 1st years housed.

Profile

Institution

Founded: 1850 as a Roman Catholic college for the education of teachers. **Site:** Single site including 18th-century Gothic house (built by Horace Walpole) just outside Twickenham town centre. **How to get there:** Bus and train (Strawberry Hill station).

Courses

Awarding body: St Mary's University College. **Main undergraduate awards:** BA, BSc, BA(ITT). **Length of courses:** 3 years; others 4 years.

Study opportunities & careers

Library and information services: 115,000 volumes, 3000 periodicals, 274 study places, reference copies of course books. Information provision, £56 pa spent for each student (FTE). Library and IT services converged. 160 workstations with access to library and internet, open 21 hours/day (ratio workstations to students of 1:15). IT support staff 8 hours/weekdays; induction tours for new students on library and information services and skills workshops; also specialist IT and computer driving licence workshops, i-learn café. **Other learning resources:** TV, drama studios, computer centre, theatre, radio suite, learning resources centre. **Study abroad:** Some students can exchange through Erasmus scheme. **Careers:** Information and advice on site through London University careers service.

Student services & facilities

Student advice and services: Medical centre, 2 nurses, visiting doctors; student services, counsellors, personal tutors, chaplains, wardens. **Amenities:** SU, campus bookshop, laundrette, café, refectory, sandwich shop open to resident and non-resident students. **Sporting facilities:** Gymnasium, dance studio, exercise physiology laboratory, sports hall, sport rehabilitation clinic, playing fields in Teddington. **Accommodation:** 75% of 1st years (and all international students) in college accommodation. 760+ places available: catered (includes 14 meals pw) rent £92–£130 pw, £77 pw shared; self-catering £89 pw; all for 38-week contracts. Students live in privately owned accommodation for 2 years, rent approx £85 pw self-catering.

Money

Living expenses budget: Minimum budget of £10k–£12k pa (excluding tuition fees) recommended by college. **Term-time work:** College allows term-time work for full-time students; much part-time work available locally, some on campus in bar, library and registry. **Financial help:** Bursaries of £500 pa for all UK students whose family income is up to £50k pa. Also sports scholarships of up to £1k. Access to learning fund to help priority groups. Apply to student finance adviser. **Tuition fees:** Home students pay £3225 pa for first degrees (£1255 for foundation degrees). International students pay £7200 pa.

Student view — Mark Woods, Student President (Sports Science)

Living

What's it like as a place to live? St Mary's is a great place to live as the campus provides a community atmosphere where there is always something going on to make everyone feel included. This personally meant for me that the transition from home life to university was as swift and easy as possible. The local area provides a wide range of activities available, especially with central London a 20-min train journey. **How's the student accommodation?** The student accommodation ranges in price to suit the individual student but all halls of residence provide sufficient facilities; the main differences in price due to ensuite facilities in the more expensive ones. **What's the student population like?** Since joining in 2005 I have felt part of the university both socially and academically. This is because of the family atmosphere St Mary's provides every year so everyone feels included, involved and welcome. St Mary's has a diverse student population with representatives from all over the globe. **How do students and locals get on?** There doesn't really seem to be much interaction; we both on the whole co-exist quite happily.

Studying

What's it like as a place to study? St Mary's is renowned for its teaching excellence within sport, drama and especially teaching, as well as providing high standards across all other subjects. Statistically St Mary's has the highest employment rate for those graduating with a teaching qualification. **What are the teaching staff like?** The teaching at the institution is of the highest standard, with all members of staff willing to assist as much as possible both during and outside lectures.

Socialising

What are student societies like? The SU has 31 clubs and societies providing for a wide range of interests – both at recreational level up to Olympic standard, with 13 representatives travelling to Beijing in 2008, whether it be sporting, such as football, rugby and netball, or other, such as drama, Christian Union or fire dancing. **What's a typical night out?** There is a wide variety of entertainment available to students, whether it be provided on campus or surrounding areas. With Central London a 20-min train journey away, the possibilities are endless, catering for everyone. **And how much does it cost?** Ultimately it depends where you go but there are loads of nightclubs that offer entrance and drink discounts to students. **How can you get home safely?** I'm sure it's the same everywhere else but the taxi drivers know where the most fares are going to be and so there are several points in town where there is normally a line of taxis – usually outside all of the nightclubs.

Money

Is it an expensive place to live? That's a hard one to answer really; it's different from student to student I guess. All depends on how much money they have, what bills are like, price of rent. As with everything there's a mix. **Average price of a pint?** On average £2. **And the price of a takeaway?** Depends on the takeaway, but most places have student discounts such as buy-one-get-one-free pizzas. **What's the part-time work situation?** The university has an excellent careers service able to assist in such matters. However, with various businesses in the local vicinity, as well as Twickenham stadium who pay £9 an hour on match days, part-time work is readily available.

Summary

What's the best feature about the place? Strong family atmosphere. **And the worst?** That you only spend 3 years here. **And to sum it all up?** St Mary's has provided me not only with excellent teaching facilities but has enabled me to grow as an individual.

Past students: Robert Ackerman (author); Patricia Mordecai (television director); Tom O'Connor (presenter); David Bedford (composer); John Callander (President of Commonwealth Institute); Pete Postlethwaite, Robert Beck (actors). **More info?** Enquiries to SU president on 020 8240 4315, email smucsu@smuc.ac.uk or check out the website at www.smsu.co.uk.

Salford University

Location:
Manchester, north-west England
(map 2)
Campus in Salford, west of Manchester

🖳 University of Salford, Salford, Greater Manchester M5 4WT
☎ Tel 0161 295 5000
🖷 Fax 0161 295 5999
✉ Email course-enquiries@salford.ac.uk
🖳 Website www.salford.ac.uk

Student enquiries: External Relations Office
Applications: UCAS

In brief

Total Students: 19,890

22% postgraduate
78% undergraduate

Undergraduates: 15,505
79% full-time ● ● 92% UK students
38% mature ● ● 41% lower
on entry socio-economic groups

56% female 🛉🛉 44% male

- **Research-intensive university.**
- **Teaching staff:** 2593 full-time and part-time.
- **Broad study areas:** Art and design technology; engineering; science; information technology; business; management; environment; healthcare and social work; media, music and performance; social sciences; languages and humanities.

Freshers

- **Admissions information:** AS-levels and Key Skills welcomed but in combination with A-levels or equivalent. UCAS tariff used to express entry requirements.
- **First degree entrants:** 3195 UK, full-time.
- **Points on entry:** 263 (average).
- **Drop-out rate:** 14% in 1st year.
- **Accommodation:** Guaranteed for all 1st years who apply by the deadline.

Profile

Institution 🛏

Founded: 1896 as the Royal Salford Technical Institute; university charter in 1967. **Site:** Campus 1½ miles from Manchester city centre. **How to get there:** Manchester easy to reach by road, rail, coach, air (Manchester airport in easy reach). For Salford, motorway links (M602), buses and trains from

Manchester; mainline railway station on campus. **Special features:** Integrated chairs where professors work part of their time in university and part in senior positions in their company, eg British Aerospace (aeronautical engineering), Unilever (applied chemistry), British Telecom (IT), Granada TV (media).

Courses

Academic features: Courses in wide range of subjects, eg aeronautical engineering, biomolecular science with cancer studies, computer and video games, complementary medicine, business and management, criminology, robotics and electronic systems engineering. Some 4-year degree programmes run jointly by university and local HE/FE colleges (students spend 2 years at each). 75% of students do some form of work placement as part of their degree; 'student capability schemes' improve skills in teamwork, verbal and written communication and presentation. **Awarding body:** University of Salford. **Main undergraduate awards:** BA, BSc, BEng, MEng, MChem, MPhys. **Length of courses:** 3 years; 4 years (eg for languages, undergraduate Master's, sandwich courses).

Study opportunities & careers

Library and information services: Combined library and computing service. 662,000 volumes; 2000 student study places in 3 main locations; access to large number of journals and e-books from networked PCs; recommended student texts; specialist music collections; archives for local canals and literary figures. Information provision, £122 pa spent for each student (FTE). 830 networked PCs, open access in core hours (some 24-hour); wireless internet access for laptops from many areas of campus; laptop loan scheme. Many services accessible from off campus. Extensive support for students through web pages, helpdesks, telephone helpline, email; rich ICT and information literacy skills training programme. **Study abroad:** Most students can take a language (eg physics with German or Spanish) and spend 6–12 months working or studying abroad. Exchange links with some 30 universities/colleges. **Careers:** Advice, guidance and information to support career choices. 90+% of graduates get a job or go onto further study within 6 months.

Student services & facilities

Student advice and services: Advice centre, health centre, psychotherapist, professional welfare officers, counsellors, international students' adviser, equal opportunities officer, chaplaincy; nursery (children 6 months–5 years). Some residential facilities for married and disabled students. **Amenities:** Restaurants, snackbars, bookshop, union shop and bank on campus; SU buildings with bars, insurance, hairdressers and travel bureau. Salford city art gallery on campus. **Sporting facilities:** Leisure centre with 4 squash courts, climbing wall, gyms, tennis courts, all-weather pitches, fitness room, floodlit AstroTurf (tennis and 5-a-side football); swimming pool, jacuzzi and sauna, 2 sports halls. Outdoor playing fields at student village, boathouse at Salford Quays. **Accommodation:** Guaranteed for 1st-year students applying before 1 September (all booking online). 3000+ single study bedrooms on 4 sites (all within a mile of university): self-catering £56–£75 pw, 40-week contracts. Rents include telephone line, internet access, personal possessions insurance. Also private halls at £84–£90 pw, 40- or 50-week contracts. Private rented accommodation £50–£65 pw.

Money

Living expenses budget: Minimum budget of £6600 for an academic year (excluding tuition fees) recommended by university, £8400 for a calendar year. **Financial help:** Bursaries of £310 pa for students whose family income is up to £25k; of £500 pa for those living within the Salford area; and of £1k pa for those with high entry points, studying abroad and for those studying designated courses (eg physics, modern languages), and others. Also £1.3 million government funds (access to learning) for UK students who may not traditionally have entered higher education (grants £100–£3500). Scholarships eg for women in engineering, accounting, environmental seience. Apply to student assistance office for help. **Tuition fees:** Home students pay £3225 pa for first degrees. International students pay £8400 pa (arts/humanities), £10,500 (science/engineering).

Student view

Main campus, Peel Park, 1½ miles from Manchester city centre, plus 2 others (Adelphi and Frederick Road). Strong links with industry (many courses allow for industrial sandwich years in UK or abroad) and good graduate employment record. Specialises in areas such as engineering, communications and healthcare, modern languages, technology, sociology and media (Adelphi media centre has links with Granada TV and university TV station, Channel M). Relatively easy to change course in first term. SU runs bars, nightclub, shops, swimming pool, gym, climbing wall, hairdresser, print shop and weekly SU publication, *Student Direct*. Student advice centre deals with range of problems and welfare issues – academic, international, finance, accommodation, legal and counselling. SU runs over 50 societies and sports clubs – an activity to suit every taste. Very active LGB group and Salford's very own student radio, Shock Radio. There is a volunteering unit where students get involved with community projects. Friendly atmosphere and a close knit community.

Student footnotes

Housing: University accommodation, 15 mins' walk from main campus, guaranteed for all 1st years; mixed housing; lively student village; some married quarters; ensuite and catered accommodation available. SU has list of private accommodation (can work out cheaper but involves the hassle of utility bills). **Eats:** Hot and cold snacks (eg paninis, pasties, burgers) all day in Lowry Bar. Meals in Pav Café 4–7 pm (plus all day for Sunday lunch). **Drink:** 2 main bars: the Pav and the Lowry. Drinks relatively cheap and always drink promotions. **Nightlife:** SU club nights (till 2am). On the doorstep of Manchester city centre, good variety of cinemas, restaurants, pubs, clubs, theatres, concerts, comedy clubs and loads of students. **Locals:** Pays to be vigilant, as with all big cities. **Sports:** Union runs very cheap leisure centre (including swimming pool, weights, sports hall, fitness centre, climbing wall, tennis/squash courts, 5-a-side football pitches, trampoline, etc.), automatic membership for gym/swim for those in uni accommodation. **Travel:** Union travel bureau on campus; cheap air, train and coach fares. **Financial help:** Access and hardship funds. Some interest-free loans from university. **Jobs:** Work in union bars, ents (technical and promotion), library and Manchester. Jobshop helps students find part-time or holiday work. Limited work in local industry. **Best features:** Leafy campus in heart of Manchester; friendly atmosphere. **And worst:** Too much rain. **Past students:** Peter Kay (comedian); Wes Butters (broadcaster); Emma Atkins, Sarah Lancashire, Nigel Pivaro (actors). **More info?** Enquiries to communications officer (tel 0161 736 7811, email communications-ussu@salford.ac.uk) or visit the SU website (www.salfordstudents.com).

School of Pharmacy

Location:
central London
(map 3)
**Single site in
Bloomsbury**

🖥 The School of Pharmacy, University of London,
29/39 Brunswick Square, London WC1N 1AX
☎ Tel 020 7753 5831
🖨 Fax 020 7753 5829
✉ Email registry@pharmacy.ac.uk
💻 Website www.pharmacy.ac.uk

Student enquiries: Assistant Registrar
Applications: UCAS

In brief

Total Students: 1385

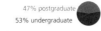

47% postgraduate
53% undergraduate

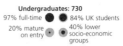

Undergraduates: 730
97% full-time ● ● 84% UK students
20% mature ● ● 40% lower
on entry socio-economic
groups

62% female ▮▮ 38% male

- **World-class specialist college of London University.**
- **Teaching staff:** 50 full-time.
- **Broad study areas:** Pharmacy.

Freshers
- **Admissions information:** Offers based on 3 A-levels or equivalent, not UCAS tariff.
- **First degree entrants:** 145 UK, full-time.
- **Points on entry:** 320 (average).
- **Drop-out rate:** 3% in 1st year.
- **Accommodation:** Most 1st years housed who are from outside London.

Profile

Institution
Founded: 1842, joined London University in 1925. **Structural features:** A school of London University. **Site:** Single site in London University area of Bloomsbury. **How to get there:** Russell Square underground station very close, easy walk to King's Cross, St Pancras, or Euston stations; many buses.

Courses
Awarding body: University of London. **Main undergraduate awards:** MPharm. **Length of courses:** 4 years.

Study opportunities & careers ⬢
Library and information services: 50,000 volumes, subscriptions to 200+ periodicals plus electronic access to 100s more, 75 study places; recommended books in reserve collection. Information provision, £223 pa spent for each student (FTE). Students also have borrowing rights at University College London. Separate IT service (open late using keycard system). Ratio workstations to students 1:9, access to the internet and library from 70 (plus students' own laptops) and access to wireless network. 4 IT support staff; 90-min induction to library and information services for all new students; weekly online searching seminars; other ad hoc IT courses. **Other learning resources:** Computer-assisted learning packages, English language and study skills. **Study abroad:** Undergraduates can study abroad (2nd semester of 3rd year) at partner university in the EU or USA. **Careers:** Information, advice and placement. Graduates employed as pharmacists in community (retail) practice, hospitals and industrial organisations.

Student services & facilities
Student advice and services: Health centre in Gower Street. **Amenities:** SU-run JCR. British Museum, ULU, etc. nearby. **Accommodation:** Most 1st years from outside London in university intercollegiate or private halls of residence; rent from £115 pw (£99 if sharing a room), 38-week contract. Most students live at home or in privately owned accommodation (£90–£120 pw for self-catering locally; down to £70 pw in Zones 2–3 involving 30+ mins travel). Help from London University housing service.

Money

Living expenses budget: Minimum budget of £800 per month (excluding tuition fees) recommended by school. **Term-time work:** Many students work part-time in local pharmacies (more than 10–12 hours pw not encouraged). **Financial help:** Bursaries of £500 pa for UK students whose family income is up to £25k (plus a supplementary bursary of £500 pa for those with high science entry qualifications); bursaries taper down to £100 pa (plus possible supplementary bursary of £100 pa) where family income is approx £35k. Also £47k government funds, 79 students helped. **Tuition fees:** Home students pay £3225 pa for first degrees. International students pay £12,300 pa.

Student view

It's next to Russell Square within 10 mins of Euston and King's Cross stations. A small independent college of London University, specialising in pharmacy. Has its own library and also access to UCL medical library. 2 computer rooms, both with email and internet access. Workload fairly easy-going if you keep on top of it; possible to include 3 months studying abroad. Many students come from the London area, though there is a large percentage of international students. Very few drop out and staff are approachable. Students from outside London are guaranteed 1 year in intercollegiate halls, 5 mins' walk; many students live at home (the cheapest option). SU runs a number of societies including Christian, Hindu, Islamic and Chinese. Few sports (mainly football) but students can join any of the dozens run by ULU. Union bar open every Friday, ULU every night. Many pubs and bars locally and Leicester Square (15 mins away) has many clubs. Odeon cinema at Tottenham Court Road is cheap; others at Piccadilly Circus. It's a very friendly college where virtually everyone knows everyone else by the end of 1st year.

Student footnotes

Housing: Intercollegiate halls guaranteed for 1 year (if from outside London). London not cheap. **Eats:** Good quality, cheap refectory in college, including some theme days. Many restaurants within 5 mins' walk (Chinese, Indian, Greek, Italian, hamburgers, etc.). **Drink:** Cheap student bar (cheap draft beer, quizzes, theme discos); ULU bar; numerous good pubs, eg Lord John Russell, the Rocket, O'Neill's. **Nightlife:** London has a lot of nightlife. Union bar and ULU bar. West End close. **Sports:** Some in college; ULU nearby has gym, pool, etc. and a multitude of societies and sports facilities. **Travel:** No travel scholarships. **Financial help:** Some. **Jobs:** Part-time jobs available, eg local chemists, in bars, etc. **Informal name:** SOP.

Scottish Agricultural College

Location:
Scotland (map 1)
Teaching centres in
Aberdeen, Ayr and
Edinburgh

Scottish Agricultural College,
Auchincruive Estate, Ayr, Scotland KA6 5HW
Tel freephone 0800 269453
Fax 01292 525349
Email recruitment@sac.ac.uk
Website www.sac.ac.uk/learning

Student enquiries: Admissions Office
Applications: UCAS

In brief

Total Students: 935

14% postgraduate
1% FE Students
85% undergraduate

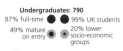
Undergraduates: 790
87% full-time ● ● 99% UK students
49% mature ● ● 20% lower
on entry socio-economic
groups

47% female 53% male

- **Specialist land-based and agricultural college.**
- **Teaching staff:** 100+ full-time and part-time.
- **Broad study areas:** Agriculture and agricultural science; applied animal, bioscience and food science; green technology; rural business management; countryside, rural resource management and conservation; environmental protection; sustainable environmental management and building design; horticulture; garden design and landscape management; activity, equine, food and nature tourism management; outdoor pursuits management; sports coaching and development; sport and recreation management.

Freshers

- **Admissions information:** Usual degree requirements, 3 Highers (at least grades BCC) or 2 Advanced Higher/A-level passes (grade C or above).
- **First degree entrants:** 145 UK, full-time.
- **Points on entry:** 200 (average).
- **Accommodation:** Many 1st years housed.

Profile

Institution

Founded: 1990, from amalgamation of North, West and East of Scotland agricultural colleges. **Site:** 3 sites: Aberdeen Campus (rural, 5 miles from city centre); Ayr Campus (from 2010, purpose-built campus, close to town centre); and Edinburgh Campus (urban, on Edinburgh University campus). **How to get there:** Ayr: new campus close to town centre, easy walking distance from rail and local bus services; coach service from Glasgow; regular rail service to Glasgow and Stranraer; by air, Prestwick Airport (5 miles), Glasgow (31 miles). Edinburgh: easily accessibly by road, rail (Waverley Station), coach and air; for campus, bus service from city centre or by road A701, A702, A7. Aberdeen: city location reached by rail (mainline), coach, air (airport 1¹/2 miles from campus); for campus, frequent bus service, 5 miles on A96 from city centre. **Special features:** Links with Glasgow, Robert Gordon (postgraduate) and Edinburgh universities. New Ayr Campus is joint venture with West of Scotland University.

Courses

Academic features: Strong project- and industry-based links, offering consultancy and veterinary services to the rural community with direct benefits to teaching and course content. Emphasis on communication, numeracy, business computing literacy and other transferable skills. **Awarding bodies:** Edinburgh and Glasgow universities. **Main undergraduate awards:** BSc, BA. **Length of courses:** 4 years (Hons); 3 years (ordinary).

Study opportunities & careers

Library and information services: 50,000 books, 300 journal titles, electronic journals and books. 200 study places. Converged IT and library services. Photocopying, colour printing and scanning facilities. Information provision, £200 pa spent for each student (FTE). 120 workstations with access to library and internet (12 hours/day); ratio workstations to students 1:5; IT helpdesk 8 hours/day. Library and information services induction session for all new students; 40-hour IT course for all. **Other learning resources:** Blackboard (web-based e-learning provision for all students, with email and internet access), laboratories, several farms including poultry farm, 2 countryside interpretation centres, food processing plant, glasshouse units, arboretum. **Study abroad:** Some students spend a period abroad. Many formal links with European universities/colleges. **Careers:** Library-based information and advice service.

Student services & facilities

Student advice and services: Student services on each site. **Amenities:** Range of clubs and societies at each centre; use of all university facilities at Edinburgh. **Sporting facilities:** Full range of sports facilities plus access to golf courses, water sports, hill-walking and climbing. **Accommodation:** 40% of 1st years in college accommodation (20% of all students). Own self-catering halls at Aberdeen and Ayr (rent in Ayr £60 pw, in Aberdeen £80 pw ensuite); use of Edinburgh University halls (£130–£180 pw full-board, £80–£100 pw self-catering, 30-week contracts). Privately owned accommodation varies from approx £55 pw in Ayr, £45–£95 pw in Edinburgh. 60% of first-degree students live at home.

Money

Living expenses budget: Minimum budget of £150 pw (excluding tuition fees) recommended by college. **Term-time work:** College allows term-time work for full-time students (50% of students have some part-time work). Some work available on campus. **Financial help:** Government funds plus college's own hardship funds (average award £300). Also some local trusts (usually with residential qualifications). **Tuition fees:** Scottish and EU students pay no fees during course; other UK students pay £1820 pa for first degrees. International students pay £7400 pa.

Student view
(Aberdeen)

The best of both worlds, city life and rural bliss – the campus is just 5 miles from the city centre, on the beautiful Craibstone Estate. Courses include agriculture, leisure with sport and recreation, countryside management, rural business management and sustainable environmental management. Also range of postgraduate courses (eg organic farming). Staff/student relations are good; class sizes reasonably small so lecturers know you by name. Students from all courses and years mix well and enjoy range of events organised by student representative council (eg fundraising, Torcher parade, ceilidhs, discos, games nights, etc.). Excellent library on campus and access to Aberdeen University library and sporting facilities. Exceptional computer facilities can be accessed 24 hours/day. 18-hole golf course, all-weather 5-a-side pitch, gym and sauna on campus. Aberdeen is the only SAC campus with a bar on site – very popular with students for starting the night off before heading into town. City has plenty of things to do: good shopping, ice-skating, 10-pin bowling, cinemas and swimming pools. Surrounding countryside is beautiful and great for hill-walking, climbing, winter sports, history tours, game and sea fishing.

Student footnotes

Housing: Self-catering halls, mostly for 1st years – bright, good-sized rooms, mainly ensuite. Internet/TV optional. Most then prefer to move on to privately owned accommodation (look in local paper, letting agents, noticeboards). **Eats:** Grab-and-go all day on campus, plus hot meal in evenings. Large selection of pubs, fast food and hotels near campus and in town. **Drink:** SAC Aberdeen bar, Aberdeen Uni SU, the Bobbin, Enigma, Hogshead, Slains Castle, Triple Kirks, etc. **Nightlife:** Agricultural Society (SAC and Aberdeen Uni students) organise ceilidhs, dances, annual ball, pub quizzes and crawls. In town, O'Neill's, Ministry, Priory, Espionage, Kef and Liquid. **Locals:** All very friendly; large student population. **Sports:** University facilities; city centre sports clubs. Football and newly formed rugby team. **Jobs:** Many students have part-time jobs, eg local shops, bars; some work for SAC staff on research; regular updates on noticeboards. **Past students:** Doddie Weir (Scotland rugby player). **More info?** Contact SU on 01224 711189.

Student view
(Ayr)

It's approximately 3 miles from the centre of Ayr, on the west coast of Scotland. Wide range of land-based courses – adventure tourism, countryside management, food technology, horticulture and agriculture – majority available from diploma to degree level. Environment is friendly and relaxed and enhanced by approachable staff and students. Study facilities more than adequate (computer labs, vast range of books in library). Accommodation all self-catering on campus, ranging from main halls of residence (Wilson Hall, with around 100 rooms) to self-catering cottages. Active SRC, based in the Cronin building, expresses views of students, arranges entertainments in campus bar and helps to keep student morale at all-time high. Also arranges all the sports and some of the societies, and always on hand to help with any queries or problems. Students can join the well-equipped gym in the Cronin building; Wednesday afternoons are free for sports and social activities. As members of BUCS, SUSF and NUS there is plenty to do.

Student footnotes

Housing: Cheap, cheerful and a good choice. **Eats:** Wide choice of college food and takeaways nearby. **Drink:** Student bar with regular events. **Nightlife:** Only 5-min journey to Ayr, range of pubs and clubs. Annual ball. **Travel:** Prestwick airport – 5 mins away by car, Troon Seacat terminal – 15 mins. Regular buses pass college entrance; Glasgow under an hour by train from Ayr. **Past students:** Sheila Swan (curling), Jim McColl (Beechgrove Garden). **More info?** Contact SRC President on 01292 525170.

Student view
(Edinburgh)

It's 4 miles south of the city centre, on the Edinburgh University science site (King's Building), and a great place to live and study. The city is steeped in history and culture; and there are some great pubs and clubs to complement student life (particularly Wednesday night, when the city is alive with students). The Agricultural Society is at the hub of SAC social life, with a full social calendar – stock judging nights, weekends in Dublin, a bad-taste night and annual black-tie ball. SAC students can join all Edinburgh Uni sports clubs; also has own sports teams (rugby, hockey, football), which train once/twice a week and compete in leagues. SAC has diversified from straight agriculture; courses now include rural resource management, environmental protection, horticulture with plantsmanship and garden design – all developed in consultation with industry. Friendships easily formed and support can be found in many forms, from fellow students and from academic and education staff.

Student footnotes

Housing: 1st years can be housed in Edinburgh Uni halls (Pollock Halls); private thereafter (look in The Scotsman or through agencies). **Eats:** Meals on campus reasonable; vending machines, shops and canteens on site. Lots of good, reasonable Indian restaurants locally. **Drink:** SU bar cheapest. Local places quite reasonable. **Nightlife:** Union organises various ents. Occasional local bands and student nights at local clubs. **Best features:** Social life – Wednesday night, without a doubt! **And worst:** Thursday mornings.

Sheffield Hallam University

Location:
Sheffield, north of England (map 2)
2 campuses in and close to city centre

✉ Sheffield Hallam University, City Campus, Howard Street, Sheffield S1 1WB
☎ Tel 0114 225 5555
🖷 Fax 0114 225 4449
✉ Email admissions@shu.ac.uk
💻 Website www.shu.ac.uk

Student enquiries: Admissions Office
Applications: UCAS

In brief

Total Students: 29,410

25% postgraduate
75% undergraduate

Undergraduates: 21,915
79% full-time
22% mature on entry
95% UK students
33% lower socio-economic groups

53% female   47% male

- **A modern university.**
- **Teaching staff:** 1563 full-time and part-time.
- **Broad study areas:** Applied science; architecture; art and design; business studies; computing; construction and property development; education; engineering; financial studies and law; humanities; leisure and food management; media; professions allied to medicine; psychology; sport; technology; tourism; urban studies.

Freshers

- **Admissions information:** UCAS tariff system used. Entry requirements specific to course.
- **First degree entrants:** 5445 UK, full-time.
- **Points on entry:** 270 (average).
- **Drop-out rate:** 8% in 1st year.
- **Accommodation:** All 1st-year students guaranteed accommodation

Profile

Institution

Founded: 1843 as Sheffield School of Design; merged in 1969 with college of technology to form Sheffield Polytechnic, and later with 2 teacher training colleges; university status in 1992. **Site:** 2 campuses: City Campus in city centre; Collegiate Campus in south-west of city. **How to get there:** Sheffield is well connected by rail (2½ hours from London, 1 hour from Manchester, Birmingham or Leeds) and road (M1 junction 33, then A630). City Campus is 2 mins from the train station and next to the main transport exchange (buses and supertram).

Courses 📖

Academic features: Emphasis on applied and vocational courses; high proportion of sandwich courses. Access and credit accumulation and transfer schemes in operation. **Awarding body:** Sheffield Hallam University. **Main undergraduate awards:** BA, BSc, BEng, MEng, LLB, FdEng, FdSc. **Length of courses:** 4 years (sandwich – standard for first degrees), 3 years (full-time), 2 years (FdEng/Sc).

Study opportunities & careers

Library and information services: Learning centre on both campuses, incorporating library, computing and multimedia: 532,000 volumes; extensive journal titles; reference collection of core texts; databases; internet resources; separate media collection; interactive media resource and computer games room. Information provision, £78 pa spent for each student (FTE). Learning centres open 24 hours in term time, 2000 study places (some group, some individual), 60% with PC, 10% with power for laptops. Support for information and IT queries available on and off campus during the week (in learning centres at weekends). Other facilities include free wi-fi access, laptop loan service, AV equipment loan service, colour and black and white printing, colour scanning, photocopying and video editing. Separate IT service provides an additional 750 IT-equipped study places across campuses, open 13+ hours per day, with access to 250+ industry-standard applications supporting all academic disciplines. **Study abroad:** Most language students spend a period abroad; option also open to sandwich students. Formal exchange links with a number of universities and colleges, including Hong Kong and Malaysia. **Careers:** Information, advice and guidance offered to all students and graduates of university.

Student services & facilities

Student advice and services: Medical centres (9 doctors, 6 nurses); multi-faith chaplaincy (17 advisers); law clinic (2 solicitors, a barrister); counselling service (13 counsellors); day nursery (74 places, age 6 months–5 years). **Amenities:** SU in city centre; catering outlets in all main buildings. University is in the heart of city, close to theatres, art galleries, museums, large retail outlets, pubs, clubs, places of worship, parks and open spaces. **Sporting facilities:** 2 fully-equipped fitness suites, 2 large sports halls, movement and dance studio, multi-use floodlit games area, soccer pitches, indoor cricket school, bowls hall, cricket squares. Professional coaches. Over 35 sports clubs. **Accommodation:** All 1st-year students offered accommodation (university-owned or managed, partnership or private-sector accommodation): self-catered rent £50–£120 pw, contracts 39–44 weeks; 413 catered places at £90 pw, contracts 39 weeks. Many 2nd- and 3rd-year students live in privately owned accommodation, average rent £50–£70 pw.

Money

Living expenses budget: Minimum budget of £700 a month (excluding tuition fees). **Term-time work:** University allows term-time work for full-time students; advisory limit of 15 hours pw. Student employment service helps find work on and off campus. **Financial help:** Bursaries of £700 pa for UK students whose family income is up to approx £25k; and of £300 pa for those from local partner schools or colleges. Care leavers guaranteed a bursary package of £1500 pa. Government access funds and emergency loans for short-term difficulties also available. **Tuition fees:** Home students pay £3225 per year for first degrees (except those funded by the Department of Health and for those on placement years). International students pay £8k–£10k pa.

Student view

Sheffield is far from what it once was: no longer just an industrial city but a place that is fast gaining a reputation as a trendy attractive city that has lots to offer – and one of the safest cities in the county. Courses are up-to-date and relevant, with excellent chances to gain practical knowledge and experience in industry. Students come from all over the world to benefit from the diverse experience of the university. Quality of teaching staff is a real draw, most being approachable and willing to help. Iconic SU building in the HUBS (Hallam Union Building for Students) – 'the best students' union I've ever seen' according to Kim Howells, then education minister. Hallam SU is very attractive; not only does it have great bars and a nightclub but an extensive range of student activities to get involved in and a fantastic advice centre. You can join a society, run a volunteering project or improve your course by becoming a student rep. If you are into sport, it is worth knowing that Hallam had 6 athletes competing for GB in last World University Games. With so much to do, there's something for everyone, no matter what your interests.

Student footnotes

Housing: Abundant, good quality and mainly affordable. All close to campuses. **Eats:** Tasty and cheap in the union Bar Phoenix. **Drink:** Union bar is cheap, lively and friendly; city is full of bars and coffee shops. **Nightlife:** Lots to do, whatever your tastes – big nightclubs, theatres, museums, bars, sporting events. **Locals:** Very welcoming to students. **Sports:** City has fantastic sporting facilities. **Travel:** University and union close to buses and train station (student discounts available). Taxis abundant. **Jobs:** Plenty of part-time jobs in city. University has good job-seeking service, Network. **Best features:** Atmosphere in Sheffield; really student-friendly city (recently called 'biggest village in Britain). **And worst:** The northern weather! **Past students:** Bruce Oldfield (fashion designer), David Mellor (cutlery designer), Nick Park (*Wallace and Gromit*), Howard Wilkinson (footballer), Richard Caborn (Sheffield MP). **More info?** Visit www.hallamunion.com.

Sheffield University

*Location:
Sheffield, north of
England (map 2)*
**Campus close to city
centre**

University of Sheffield, Western Bank, Sheffield S10 2TN
☎ Tel 0114 222 2000
🖨 Fax 0114 222 1234
✉ Email www.sheffield.ac.uk/asksheffield
🖥 Website www.sheffield.ac.uk

*Student enquiries: Student Recruitment, Admissions and
Marketing (tel 0114 222 1255)
Applications: UCAS*

In brief

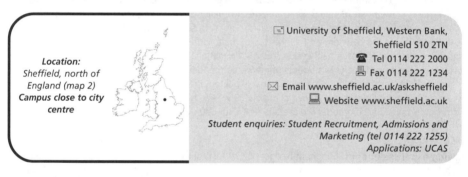

Total Students: 23,915
24% postgraduate
76% undergraduate

Undergraduates: 18,290
89% full-time 92% UK students
13% mature on entry 21% lower socio-economic groups

54% female 46% male

- **A top UK research-intensive university.**
- **Teaching staff:** 1288 full-time.
- **Broad study areas:** Arts, pure science, medicine (including dentistry, nursing, midwifery), law, engineering, social sciences, architecture.

Freshers

- **Admissions information:** AS-levels accepted in combination with 2+ A-levels or equivalent (at least 18 units); many courses have specific subject and grade requirements. Most offers expressed in terms of grades, small number use UCAS tariff.
- **First degree entrants:** 4785 UK, full-time.
- **Points on entry:** 310+ (average).
- **Drop-out rate:** 3% in 1st year.
- **Accommodation:** Almost all 1st years housed.

Profile

Institution

Founded: 1897, as University College from 3 existing colleges; university Charter in 1905. **Site:** Campus half a mile from city centre. **How to get there:** Sheffield well connected to other towns/cities by rail (eg 2$\frac{1}{2}$ hours to London, 1 hour to Manchester, 4 to Edinburgh) and road (close to M1, junctions 33/34). For university, use supertram and numerous buses.

Courses

Academic features: Courses in animal behaviour, biology with conservation and diversity, chemistry with enterprise management, motorsports engineering management, aerospace engineering with private pilot instruction. **Awarding body:** University of Sheffield. **Main undergraduate awards:** BA, BA (Law), BMus, BSc, MBiolSci, MChem, MComp, MMath, MPhys, MBChB, BDS, BMedSci, LLB, BEng, MEng. **Length of courses:** 3 or 4 years; 5 or 6 years (dentistry and medicine); 6 years (architecture).

Study opportunities & careers

Library and information services: 8 staffed sites (open 7 days/week in semester); over 1.4 million books and periodicals. Information centre (Information Commons) with 1300 study places, most in-demand books and periodicals, wireless access to university network. Information provision, £121 pa spent for each student (FTE). Library and IT service work together. 1780 student computers, in 35+ locations across campus, with access to library, university portal (Muse), academic software and the internet. IT facilities open 24 hours/day; IT support from staff, in person, by email or telephone helpdesk. Separate library and IT induction sessions for all new students; academic departments run IT skills courses tailored to their students. **Other learning resources:** Audio-visual and television centre, computing centre, drama studio, English language teaching centre, modern languages teaching centre, computer-aided design lab. **Study abroad:** Most students have opportunity to spend a period abroad (and counting towards their degree). Very active in Erasmus, with formal exchange links with over 180 European universities; 60+ links worldwide, eg in Australia, Canada, the USA, Mexico, Singapore and Hong Kong.

Student services & facilities

Student advice and services: Advice centre; counselling service (6 counsellors); disability and dyslexia support; health service (10 doctors); chaplaincy; nursery and holiday play schemes; nightline; student mentoring scheme. **Amenities:** Bars, food outlets, shops, travel agency, printing service, laundrette, banks, insurance office, jobshop, cinema, live music venue, nightclub. **Sporting facilities:** 150-station fitness centre with technogym, 1 large sports hall, 3 synthetic pitches, heated indoor swimming pool (with pool-side sauna and steam rooms), fitness/dance studio, 4 squash courts, indoor bouldering wall, 4 floodlit tennis courts; 45 acres of playing fields (5 miles away); rowing at Damflask reservoir (5 miles), sailing at Ogston reservoir (20 miles). **Accommodation:** 1st years guaranteed a place in university-owned or partnership accommodation. Approx. 5600 places available: self-catering at £70–£110 pw (up to £110 ensuite); catered places at £98–£122 pw (up to £122 pw ensuite) including meals for 31 weeks; all contracts 42 weeks. Most students live in privately owned accommodation for 2 years: £55–£70 pw for self-catering (+ bills). Approx. 9% of first-degree students live at home.

Money

Living expenses budget: Minimum budget of £6100 for academic year (excluding tuition fees) recommended by university, £7800 for 12 months. **Term-time work:** University allows term-time work for full-time students, to a limit of approx 15 hours pw. Some work available on campus in bars, offices, etc. Careers service jobshop run jointly with the union. **Financial help:** Bursaries of £680 pa for UK students whose family income is up to £16,800, of £420 pa where family income is £16,800–£34,600; further bursaries for students with 1 or more A-levels at grade A, those taking priority subjects and those involved in local university outreach schemes (maximum bursary of £3225 for students falling into each category). Also some departmental bursaries. Government funds and university's own schemes to help students in financial hardship. **Tuition fees:** Home students pay £3225 pa for first degrees. International students pay £9920–£11,510 pa (classroom-based), £13,050 (lab-based), £23,580 pa (clinical).

Student view

It's 10 mins' walk from Sheffield city centre – one of the UK's top cities, lively, growing and multicultural. But also only 10 mins' bus ride out to the Peak District. Low crime rate and Sheffielders are known as the friendliest people. Large student population is very diverse, including 3000+ international students from over 120 countries. SU is well-known nationally and active politically; runs 50+ sports clubs and 180 societies (all information available from *The Source* in the SU); also a nursery, a safety bus for female students, an LGB lounge, meeting area for mature students and Muslim prayer rooms. Its advice centre specialises in academic affairs, immigration, money and housing. SU is social hub with 3 night clubs, 2 bars, coffee shop and a large cinema theatre. There are up to 20 events/gigs week. Halls of residence are just 15 mins from the SU. Although SU is separate from the university and maintains its autonomy, they have good relationship.

Student footnotes

Housing: 6 good halls of residence; flats and university houses are high standard; some new accommodation. Private housing with approved landlords through uni accommodation service, SU noticeboard and private bureau. **Eats:** Meals good value on campus. Worldwide range of foods available. Some good veggie restaurants and cheap markets in Castle Square. **Drink:** Excellent SU bars with good prices, including interval café bar, well-known Bar One and Fox and Duck (Broomhill, a main student area). Fair trade and organic coffee at SU-run coffee shops (Coffee Revolution). **Nightlife:** SU gigs, weekly nightly include Late 1 on Monday, Tuesday club (drum and bass), Juice, Fuzz club (rock and indie), FROUK, Pop Tarts, Climax (LGB), Brighton Beach, Urban Gorilla, etc. Cinemas and SU film unit. Active SU theatre, many plays are shown at university's drama studio. Also Lyceum and Crucible. **Locals:** Fantastic. **Sports:** 50+ sports clubs. 5-star health and fitness facilities with an excellent swimming pool. **Travel:** Excellent travel shop; cheap tram, coach rail and flights. Very easy to travel around Sheffield. Well-connected rail network, regular buses to the Peaks. **Financial help:** University loans and grants and several other access funds. **Jobs:** Casual and part-time jobs in SU; jobshop in SU helps. 30% of students have term-time jobs, 60% in summer. Excellent volunteering opportunities in union. **Best features:** SU – widely regarded as one of the best. **And worst:** Hills. **Past students:** David Blunkett, Willy Hamilton (politicians); Amy Johnson (aviator); Eddie Izzard (comedian); Tony Miles, David Wetherall (footballers); Sir Peter Middleton (Barclays Bank); Jack Rosenthal (playwright); Carol Barnes (former TV newsreader); Helen Sharman (first Briton in space). **More info?** Ring SU president (tel 0114 222 8605) or visit www.shef.ac.uk/union.

SOAS

Location:
central London
(map 3)
Main site in
Bloomsbury; further
site King's Cross

🖥 School of Oriental & African Studies, University of London, Thornhaugh Street, Russell Square, London WC1H 0XG
☎ Tel 020 7898 4034
🖷 Fax 020 77898 4039
✉ Email study@soas.ac.uk
🖳 Website www.soas.ac.uk

Student enquiries: Student Recruitment Office
Applications: UCAS

Total Students: 4725

43% postgraduate
57% undergraduate

Undergraduates: 2675
98% full-time
27% mature on entry
63% UK students
20% lower socio-economic groups

58% female  42% male

- **A top UK research-intensive institution**, a specialist college of London University.
- **Teaching staff:** 200 full-time and part-time.
- **Broad study areas:** Languages, cultures and societies of Africa, Asia and the Near and Middle East – including law, economics, politics, history, linguistics, music, religions.

Freshers

- **Admissions information:** Average requirement is 280–360 points from 3 A-levels (excluding general studies) but many courses specify subjects and grades.
- **First degree entrants:** 525 UK, full-time.
- **Points on entry:** 315 (average).
- **Drop-out rate:** 8% in 1st year.
- **Accommodation:** Most 1st years housed by SOAS or London University.

Profile

Institution

Founded: 1916. **Structural features:** Part of London University. **Site:** Main site, Russell Square Campus (in London University area of Bloomsbury); Vernon Square Campus (at King's Cross, 20 mins' walk). **How to get there:** Main site close to Russell Square underground station, easy walking distance from several others; Vernon Square close to King's Cross, St Pancras and Angel underground stations; many buses to both sites.

Courses

Academic features: Unique range of African, Asian and Middle Eastern languages from Amharic to Vietnamese (all of which can be studied from scratch); full range of social science courses (including law, politics, economics and development studies) and humanities courses (anthropology to study of religions). Degree courses either single-subject or 2-subject. **Awarding body:** University of London. **Main undergraduate awards:** BA, BSc, LLB. **Length of courses:** 3 years; 4 years (for most languages).

Study opportunities & careers

Library and information services: 1.2 million volumes in 400+ languages (4000 items of music, poetry and plays; 50,000 photographs and slides), 4500 periodicals, 7000 electronic journals, 650 study places; reserve and short loan collections. Library is national library of the study of Asia and Africa. Information provision, £191 pa spent for each student (FTE). 200+ computers for student use, most with access to internet, some with non-roman print facilities; student residences online. IT helpdesk in working hours; new students offered training in standard applications. Specialist collections: regional libraries on Africa, Far East, South and South-East Asia, Near and Middle East; subject collections on law, geography, social sciences. Percival David Foundation of Chinese Art (1700 pieces of Chinese ceramics). **Other learning resources:** 5 language labs; many language tapes made in school's own recording studio; direct lines to BBC overseas services; satellite TV offering 30 channels. Close to Senate House Library, LSE library and British Library. **Study abroad:** Many language courses involve a period abroad. Extensive links with universities across Africa and Asia, some links in Europe and USA. **Careers:** Information and advice service; access to London University careers service.

Student services & facilities

Student advice and services: Welfare office; disability office; chaplains; access to doctors, dentists, FPA, psychiatrist, counsellor, optician, behavioural psychologist. **Amenities:** Refectory, snack bar and bar; also all facilities of ULU. **Sporting facilities:** All ULU facilities (including swimming pool). **Accommodation:** Most 1st years in SOAS or university accommodation. Approx. 760 ensuite self-catering rooms in school residence (with telephone and internet cabling): rent £120 pw, contracts 38–51 weeks/year. Also number of places in intercollegiate halls: £120–£145 pw (£96–£98 for shared room), including breakfast and evening meal and all weekend meals, 30-week leases. London University accommodation office helps with university and privately owned accommodation (based in ULU).

Money

Living expenses budget: Budget of up to £10k pa (excluding tuition fees) recommended by school. **Financial help:** Bursaries of £860 pa for UK students whose family income is up to £25k, of £420 pa where family income is £25k–£60k. **Tuition fees:** Home students pay £3225 pa for first degrees (£1570 in year abroad). International students pay £11,460 pa (£5730 for year abroad).

Student view

It's in Russell Square, not far from Holborn. London is an extremely bustling and energetic city; it's easily compared to a typical Moroccan street market and the variety and opportunities are amazing. Within a mile you will find something for every taste. In food terms, eg, you will find Asian, African, Italian, Arabic, Chinese and Japanese in small, cosy corner cafés and restaurants. It is not far from the British Museum, from shopping areas like Oxford Street and Tottenham Court Road, and from the underground world of goths and alternative music in Camden Town. Majority of students live in one of the many halls of residence nearby. 'Living' is perhaps the most educational part of getting a degree, particularly in London. You can live in an intercollegiate hall with people from all over London University (all rooms on corridors, and you eat dinner and breakfast communally); or in halls just for SOAS students (self-catering, all ensuite rooms and vibrant, intense places to live). Or you can rent private accommodation, which means you will have to deal with landlords and broken washing machines yourself; prices nearby are very competitive. Social life is extraordinary. SOAS bar is both a mis-education and an education – it is second to the library as a resource for information, political debate, colourful and passionate conversation. The effects may hold you back from lectures but the bar is indisputably the social centre of the galaxy; the heart of SOAS entertainments is open-mike night (full of spontaneity, vibrancy and surprise), ranging from music, dance and poetry to story-telling. Guest musicians come from obscure corners of the globe. The mixed-aged crowd is positively anti-ageist and enriching and hosts the best Arabic parties in London (featuring live acts from throughout the Middle East). Very active, very political SU: occupations, demonstrations and walk-outs against the war on Iraq. Several extremely active societies, eg Africa Society, Islamic Society, Palestine Society and the Climbing Society. Rubbish sports facilities.

Student footnotes

Housing: Most 1st years in intercollegiate or SOAS halls. **Eats:** SOAS food cheapish. **Drink:** SOAS bar cheap. **Nightlife:** SU events and all London awaits you. **Sports:** ULU pool, weights. Minuscule SOAS gym. **Financial help:** Some well-targeted funds. **Travel:** 10-min walk from halls. **Jobs:** Some work in SOAS bar and snack bar, or ULU (around the corner). **Best features:** It's a microcosm of the world!

And worst: It's a pretentious microcosm of the world! **Past students:** Paul Robeson (singer); Zeinab Badawi (presenter); David Lammy MP; Dom Joly (*Trigger Happy TV*). **More info?** Check out the SU website at www.soasunion.org.

Southampton Solent University

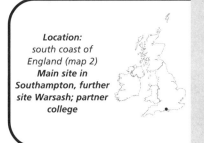

Location:
south coast of
England (map 2)
**Main site in
Southampton, further
site Warsash; partner
college**

✉ Southampton Solent University, East Park Terrace,
Southampton, Hampshire SO14 0YN
☎ Tel 023 8031 9000
🖷 Fax 023 8022 2259
✉ Email ask@solent.ac.uk
💻 Website www.solent.ac.uk

*Student enquiries: Registrar (prospectus from
marketing services)
Applications: UCAS*

In brief

Total Students: 17,455

 39% FE Students
4% postgraduate
57% undergraduate

Undergraduates: 9990
84% full-time   89% UK students
25% mature   36% lower
on entry   socio-economic
groups

 43% female   57% male

- **A modern university.**
- **Teaching staff:** 817 full-time and part-time.
- **Broad study areas:** Art and design, law, sport and tourism, maritime studies, media, psychology, business, computing and engineering, social sciences.

Freshers
- **Admissions information:** AS-levels accepted in combination with 1 (usually 2) A-levels or equivalent. UCAS tariff used.
- **First degree entrants:** 2500 UK, full-time.
- **Points on entry:** 220 (average).
- **Drop-out rate:** 13% in 1st year.
- **Accommodation:** Most 1st years housed.

Profile

Institution
Founded: 1984 as Southampton Institute; university status in 2005. **Site:** 2 sites: main campus in Southampton city centre; maritime academy at Warsash. **How to get there:** Southampton easily reached by rail (1¼ hours from London) or coach; by road via M3 or M27. Frequent buses within city. **Special features:** National champion yacht team.

Courses
Academic features: Courses in football studies, sports science, health and beauty, yacht and small craft design, media. **Awarding body:** Southampton Solent University. **Main undergraduate awards:** BA, BSc, BEng, LLB. **Length of courses:** 3 years; 4 years (sandwich courses, extended degrees).

Study opportunities & careers

Library and information services: 2 libraries; 237,000 books, 8560 periodicals, 762 study places. Information provision, £90 pa spent for each student (FTE). Separate IT service: 600 PCs and 140+ Macs with access to library and internet (ratio workstations to students 1:13). IT facilities accessible 12 hours/day, longer at peak exam and assignment times. **Other learning facilities:** Test tank, computer suite, 7 scale model ship, metrology lab, language labs, advanced manufacturing technology centre, digital media suites, digital television and editing centre. **Study abroad:** 3% of students spend a period abroad. **Careers:** Information, advice and placement service.

Student services & facilities

Student advice and services: Community services, including health centre; chaplain; SU welfare officer; student support network; assistive technology centre; jobshop. **Amenities:** SU with cashpoint, bookshop, bars, coffee lounge, games rooms. **Sporting facilities:** Sports hall, fitness suite, sports field (12 acres) 3 miles from campus; facilities for water sports on Solent (own jetty and facilities). **Accommodation:** 85% of 1st years in university accommodation. 2300 self-catering places in halls of residence, most for 1st years: £84.50 pw (£97 pw ensuite), for 40 weeks; some at £73.50 pw for 48 weeks. Privately owned accommodation costs £55–£65 pw for self-catering. 25% of students live at home.

Money

Living expenses budget: Minimum budget of £7k–£8k pa (excluding tuition fees) recommended by university. **Term-time work:** University allows term-time work for full-time students. Some available on campus through job pool (in faculty or services); off-campus jobs posted on noticeboards. **Financial help:** Bursaries of £1075 pa for UK students whose family income is up to £18,400; tapered down to £250 pa where family income is £39,300. Students in university halls receive £250 against accommodation costs. Also £567k government funds, plus opportunity bursaries; £4k own funds; 370 students helped. Special help for single parents, self-financing students, mature students; own funds used for those with cash-flow problems, late loan cheque, etc. Apply to student support office for help. **Tuition fees:** Home students pay £3225 pa on most first degree courses (£2050 pa for foundation degrees, £1795 on level zero). International students pay £8200 pa.

Student view) **Hayley Clarke,** Vice President of Communications, Magazine Editor and Head of Communications Committee (Graduate, BA Journalism)

Living

What's it like as a place to live? A busy, diverse city with a large student community – possessing 2 universities and several colleges. Southampton is dubbed the 'Green City' due to its many central parks and green spaces, which gives it a less hectic feel and is especially welcome in the summer when you can chill, or study, in the parks next to Solent campuses. **How's the student accommodation?** There are several different university-owned halls of residence, in all manner of shapes, sizes and noise levels! From the social hubs of Kimber and Lucia Foster, to the quieter digs, Hamwic and Chantry. They are based in 6 different locations, mostly for 1st-year students. 2nd and 3rd years can apply to live in Emily Davis halls, situated next to the train station and Asda. There are small, ensuite rooms available, or larger rooms for those willing to share a bathroom (it's not THAT bad!). Make sure you ask for a tour before you decide which one you'd like to live in. Private halls of residence owned by external company, UNITE, are also available and there is a large student community based in various inner city residential areas. Houses vary in price and standards – viewings are essential and our SU Advice Centre can help you with contracts, landlords and estate agents. **What's the student population like?** Solent's student community is very vibrant and diverse; from those who love art and media, to sporting, academic and business students. You'll meet all sorts of people on your courses, within your halls of residence and through clubs and societies – some of whom you may not normally have mixed with. Coming here is a real eye-opener that diminishes your average stereotypes. **How do students and locals get on?** Fairly well. There are many community links made through the university and SU with local residents, particularly within the highly student-populated areas. These include volunteering projects and community rubbish clear-ups. Beyond this, students tend to mingle amongst the locals at popular bars, clubs and shopping areas. Many have met great friends through part-time jobs or within specialist nightclubs (eg Lennon's = indie central).

Studying

What's it like as a place to study? Course amounts increase year on year. We have some niche courses from the likes of media and fashion styling, outdoor and water sports, to yacht and boat design. The music and media course facilities are brilliant and have recently been improved further. We also have brand new gym facilities for sports courses and media students have the enviable opportunity of being the only university to film at Glastonbury and Glade festivals every year! And if that wasn't enough, check out individual courses for trips abroad to India, France and the USA. **What are the teaching staff like?** There are plenty of specialist lecturers and staff, many of whom are willing to put on guest speaker sessions from industry professionals and devote extra time for tutorials, workshops and revision sessions.

Socialising

What are student societies like? The SU provides loads of sports clubs and societies for students to get involved in, as well as the chance to set up your own if it doesn't already exist! We currently have around 50 sports clubs and societies. Many sports teams compete in Varsity matches against neighbouring universities, such as Southampton University and Bournemouth University. Other popular sports include surfing, snowboarding, wakeboarding and martial arts . . . there's something for everyone. Our society of the year, twice in a row, is our student-run radio station, Sin Radio, which this year had close competition from the Afro-Caribbean society. A major attraction for many students coming here is the Southampton Stags American football team, which is a joint venture between Solent and Southampton universities. We also have a joint cheerleading club who support the games. **What's a typical night out?** Depending on your budget, many students either start drinking in their halls or the SU (eg Shots'n'Shares on a Friday night), then head on to our regular link-ups with local clubs, such as student-only venue, Kaos. **And how much does it cost?** On average £15–£20 . . . but it can easily be done on a tenner! **How can you get home safely?** Walk back with friends or housemates. All halls and most shared housing areas are within 10–15 mins away. There are also taxi services and late-night buses, which venture further out of the city. Within fresher's fortnight we put on the Big Night Out, where student guides (known as Angels) show our students the safest routes around the city, when visiting different bars and clubs.

Money

Is it an expensive place to live? No way; it's really cheap, especially for students. Various student discounts apply in shops, bars, clubs and restaurants when you show your university campus or NUS card. There are also many student-themed club nights and 2 student-only venues (Kaos and Jesters). **Average price of a pint?** Considering all the clubs and bars, £2.40 (£1.90 here at Solent SU). **And the price of a takeaway?** £3–£5, depending on what you want! There are LOADS of takeaway shops right next to the main student housing area. There's all sorts: pizza, Chinese, fish and chips, burgers and kebabs, etc. **What's the part-time work situation?** The SU provides students with jobs in the SU shop, café, bars and on reception, as well as jobs doing flyering and promotional work. The university has a great job shop and careers service, where you can either go straight to them or sign up for regular email notifications on internal and external vacancies. Popular student jobs include being a tour guide for students (through the university), working in our bars or becoming a freshers' Guardian Angel. There are also plenty of opportunities in the city centre, in various bars, clubs and shops, around 10 mins' walk from the university campus and accommodation.

Summary

What's the best feature about the place? Southampton is a busy city, without being too big and daunting. There are plenty of students here and endless amounts of entertainment. Solent is central to all of this and there is easy access to surrounding attractions, such as Bournemouth beaches, shopping or entertainment in Portsmouth and relaxing trips to the New Forest. **And the worst?** So many courses, sports clubs and societies to choose from and almost too many clubs nights to keep up with! You have to be motivated to get on with your studies, as there are plenty of fun distractions. **And to sum it all up?** An exciting place to be!

Past students: David Quayle (founder of BandQ), Mike Wedderburn (sports commentator). **More info?** Contact the SU president (tel 023 8038 6656, email supresident@solent.ac.uk) or visit the website (www.solentsu.co.uk).

Southampton University

Location:
south coast of
England (map 2)
Main campus, others
across city; art school
in Winchester

⌨ University of Southampton, Highfield,
Southampton SO17 1BJ
☎ Tel 023 8059 5000
📠 Fax 023 8059 3037
🖥 Website www.southampton.ac.uk

Student enquiries: Enquiries Office (tel 023 8059 5000)
Applications: UCAS (direct for part-time study)

In brief

Total Students: 24,735

31% postgraduate
69% undergraduate

Undergraduates: 17,120
84% full-time
19% mature on entry

92% UK students
20% lower socio-economic groups

60% female   40% male

- **World-class research-intensive university.**
- **Teaching staff:** 975 full-time, 160 part-time.
- **Broad study areas:** Law, arts and social sciences; engineering, science and mathematics; medicine, health and life sciences.

Freshers

- **Admissions information:** UCAS tariff used, with some course-specific requirements (subjects and grades).

- **First degree entrants:** 3540 UK, full-time.
- **Points on entry:** 345 (average).
- **Drop-out rate:** 4% in 1st year.
- **Accommodation:** All 1st years housed unless local.

Profile

Institution
Founded: 1862; received Royal Charter in 1952. **Structural features:** Includes Winchester School of Art (see separate profile). **Site:** Main campus plus 4 others, all 1/2–2 miles from city centre. **How to get there:** By road (M3 or M27); fast train from Waterloo (1 1/4 hours). Buses to university from city centre, station and airport.

Courses
Awarding body: University of Southampton. **Main undergraduate awards:** BA, BEng, BM, BMid, BN, BSc, LLB, MEng. **Length of courses:** 3 years; 4 years (languages, social work, MEng, double Honours, midwifery, nursing); 5 years (medicine).

Study opportunities & careers
Library and information services: Main library with 6 subsidiary specialist libraries; over 2.6 million books, journals and reports; 1900 study places; short loan collection, computerised catalogue on network; CD-ROMs and online information. Specialist collections: Agriculture to 1900, local history, parliamentary papers, history of relations between Jewish and non-Jewish peoples, Wellington papers, Mountbatten papers. Information provision, £139 pa spent for each student (FTE). Separate IT service (open 24 hours at some sites); 1700+ computers with access to library and internet (ratio workstations to students 1:17). Personal and telephone IT helpline during working day; joint library and information services programme for all new undergraduates. **Other learning resources:** Language centre. **Study abroad:** Many academic schools have exchange links with European institutions. **Careers:** Information, advice and placement service, and weekly newsletter. 75% of final-year students had career-related work experience.

Student services & facilities
Student advice and services: Student advice and health centres on campus; doctor, chaplain, counsellors, legal advice; adviser for students with disabilities (including assessment of needs), support for dyslexic students and those with mental health difficulties. Residential facilities for married and disabled students. 100-place nursery (must apply early). **Amenities:** SU shop, bookshop, travel agency, hairdresser, laundrette, banks, concert hall, theatre and art gallery. **Sporting facilities:** Playing fields set in 90 acres; 4 floodlit tennis courts; grass pitches for rugby, football, cricket, American football, lacrosse, etc. Sports centre with 8-badminton-court sports hall, 25m swimming pool, 140-station fitness suite, squash courts, dance studio, martial arts room. University boatyard with facilities for canoeing, kayaking, powerboating, sailing, windsurfing. Rifle range. Sports bursary scheme; talented athletes support scheme; community sports volunteering scheme. **Accommodation:** University accommodation guaranteed for all 1st years who apply by the deadline unless they live locally (25+% of all full-time students housed). 4000 self-catering places, £65.50–£109 pw, 39- or 51-week contracts; 1200 part-catered, £102–£146 pw, term time only. Students usually live in private rented accommodation for 1–2 years: £60–£65 pw (excluding bills) for self-catering house share.

Money
Living expenses budget: Minimum budget of £7200–£8800 for an academic year (excluding tuition fees) recommended by university. **Term-time work:** Student employment service helps

find local part-time and holiday work. Jobs advertised weekly. **Financial help:** Bursaries of £1k pa for UK students whose family income is up to £25k, of £500 pa where family income is £25k–£35k; also 150 competitive bursaries of £1k pa for specified students from Hampshire and the Isle of Wight; and 30 bursaries of £1k pa for students on 6-year medicine course. Many scholarships for academic excellence up to £2k pa; students may hold scholarship together with 1 or more bursaries. Also government funds and own fund. **Tuition fees:** Home students pay £3225 pa for first degrees (except those funded by the Department of Health and the foundation degree in health and social care). International students pay £9380 pa (classroom), £12k (lab/studio), £21,800 (clinical).

Student view

It's a quirky mix of campus and city university – a leafy haven just 3 miles from the main city centre. Grassy and attractive campus, home to a mixture of traditional red brick and modern buildings, including the refurbished 5-storey Hartley Library. Medical sciences and arts are each about 8 mins' walk from the main campus; oceanography and geology are based at a waterside campus in the city centre; also Winchester School of Art (15 miles away). Halls are all off campus, a short walk away (or bus trip on uni-link service). All 1st-year students with unconditional offers are offered a place in halls (self- or fully-catered); most are high quality, single study or ensuite bedrooms with shared cooking facilities. Students are represented on all faculty boards, SU committees and most university committees through union officers. Loads of bars and clubs in town, many with student nights. SU has weekly club night as well as bands and events. SU provides excellent range of services including a travel centre, shop, hairdresser, café and 4 bars; also home to the new uniplex cinema and 1600-capacity nightclub. SU advice and information centre provides representation and advice for all students on issues from housing or course-related problems to debt management.

Student footnotes

Housing: 1st years in halls; accommodation for disabled students; some married quarters. Private housing reasonable. **Eats:** Wide range of food at SUSU café (meal £2–£3), university piazza. Loads of takeaways near campus and halls; good food in pubs; plenty of good restaurants for when the parents visit. **Drink:** 4 SU bars; numerous hall bars, reasonably priced for the south (£1.70 Carling, £1.90 Caffreys). Also pubs in Portswood and Bevoir Valley (main student areas). **Nightlife:** SU has nightclub and excellent ents: discos, balls, comedy, films, quiz nights, karaoke and bands (small, local to large, well known, eg Razorlight). **Locals:** Good although students best avoid the Flowers Estate. **Sports:** Excellent sports facilities: new sports grounds, also 6 squash courts, sports hall, dance studio, sports complex with swimming pool, multigym. Loads of sports clubs. **Financial help:** SU/university hardship fund can give short-term loans. Also access fund for disabled, single parents, etc. **Jobs:** Some part-time work at SU; seasonal work, eg boat show in summer; bar and shop work always available. Jobshop and e-jobs service in careers advisory service. **Best features:** State-of-the-art facilities; cultural diversity. **And worst:** Student apathy. **Past students:** John Nettles (actor – *Bergerac*), Baroness Hooper (lawyer and conservative peer), Lord Tonypandy (former Speaker, House of Commons), Jenny Murray (Radio 4 presenter), Chris Packham (conservationist and author), Kathy Tayler (pentathlete), John Sopel (presenter), John Denham MP, Roger Black (athlete), John Inverdale (rugby), Stuart Maister (Broadview). **More info?** Enquiries to president (tel 023 8059 5217), or vice president comms (tel 023 8059 5226), email susu@soton.ac.uk or visit www.susu.org.

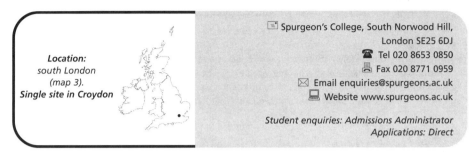

Spurgeon's College

Location:
south London
(map 3).
Single site in Croydon

Spurgeon's College, South Norwood Hill,
London SE25 6DJ
☎ Tel 020 8653 0850
🖨 Fax 020 8771 0959
✉ Email enquiries@spurgeons.ac.uk
💻 Website www.spurgeons.ac.uk

Student enquiries: Admissions Administrator
Applications: Direct

In brief

Total Students: 970

20% postgraduate
75% undergraduate

Undergraduates: 725
20% full-time
95% mature
on entry

80% UK students

25% female   75% male

- **Specialist theological college.**
- **Teaching staff:** 8 full-time, 18 part-time, 12 open-learning tutors.
- **Broad study area:** Theology.

Freshers
- **Admissions information:** Full-time applicants should apply by February.
- **First degree entrants:** 40 UK, full-time.
- **Accommodation:** Most 1st years housed.

Profile

Institution
Founded: 1856. **Structural features:** Private college, affiliated to Wales University. **Site:** 8-acre campus in South London. **How to get there:** By train to Norwood Junction or Crystal Palace; local buses. **Special features:** Theological college, training men and women for various forms of Christian service, especially as ordained Baptist ministers. Strong vocational bias. Ministerial applicants not normally accepted straight from school.

Courses
Academic features: Postgraduate research; taught Master's courses (including unique MTh in radical free church movements and conversion MA); part-time and open learning courses; diplomas and awards in counselling. **Awarding body:** University of Wales. **Main undergraduate awards:** BD, BTh. **Length of courses:** 1–3 years; 5–6 years (part-time).

Study opportunities & careers
Library and information services: 50,000 volumes, over 120 periodical series. Information provision, £200 pa spent for each student (FTE). IT facilities open 24 hours; 8 computers with access to library, mega-stream access to internet. **Other learning resources:** Audio-visual equipment.

Student services & facilities
Accommodation: 14 rooms in college at £2k pa; 16 self-catering flats/flatlets, including some for married students, £120–£500 per month, year-long contracts.

Money
Living expenses budget: Minimum budget of £7500 pa recommended (excluding tuition fees). **Term-time work:** College allows term-time work for full-time students, limit of 8 hours pw (20% believed to work). **Tuition fees:** Home and international students pay £5665–£6450 pa for first degrees (fees for loans for UK students; limited help for international students).

Student view

A theological college for training Baptist ministers and other Christian workers, as well as providing many part-time training and correspondence courses. Relatively easy to change between different training streams in first term (all share core units). It's in south London, close to all the facilities of central London. Crystal Palace National Sports Complex is 5 mins' away by car. Can accommodate some students in hall of residence (food and living expenses included in fees). Most students are mature on entry, some international. Social activities are organised for students and their spouses but majority are part-time so limited opportunities for socialising on a large scale. Full-time students are the hub of the community. There is a well-stocked computer-catalogued library and a bookshop on site. Sports facilities include tennis, snooker and table tennis. Occasional football matches against other colleges.

Student footnotes

Housing: College has some accommodation for married students and families off and on campus. Rooms on campus for single students. **Eats:** Available on site. The economically and gastronomically astute may be able to provide for themselves more cheaply. Akash Curry House in Croydon is cheap (take your own booze). **Drink:** No bar on campus. **Nightlife:** Nothing on campus. Student rates at Fairfield Halls and Warehouse Theatre in Croydon. **Locals:** Very friendly when approached. **Sports:** Weekly sports afternoon for those interested and able. Tennis court and croquet lawn on site. Crystal Palace sports stadium. **Travel:** Buy student railcard. **Financial help:** Students operate their own fund. College very flexible over fees and charges. **Jobs:** Some work available on campus outside term time, otherwise local shop work. **Best features:** Good community atmosphere and exceptionally helpful staff. **And worst:** Limited opportunities for socialising.

Staffordshire University

Location:
Staffordshire,
Midlands (map 2)
**Main campuses in
Stoke and Stafford;**
partner colleges

Staffordshire University, College Road,
Stoke-on-Trent ST4 2DE
☎ Tel 01782 294000
🖷 Fax 01782 292740
✉ Email admissions@staffs.ac.uk
🖥 Website www.staffs.ac.uk

Student enquiries: tel 01782 292746
Applications: UCAS

In brief

Total Students: 15,190

 22% postgraduate
78% undergraduate

Undergraduates: 11,795
 71% full-time   92% UK students
31% mature on entry   39% lower socio-economic groups

 51% female   49% male

- **A modern university.**
- **Teaching staff:** 613 full-time and part-time.
- **Broad study areas:** Arts, media and design; business; computing, engineering and technology; health; sciences; law.

Freshers

- **Admissions information:** UCAS tariff used on almost all courses. AS-levels and Key Skills (level 3) contribute to points but minimum of 2 A-levels or equivalent required.
- **First degree entrants:** 2545 UK, full-time.
- **Points on entry:** 240 (average).
- **Drop-out rate:** 11% in 1st year.
- **Accommodation:** Almost all 1st years housed who apply.

Profile

Institution

Founded: Roots in regional technical and art colleges, early 1900s; university established in 1992 from Staffordshire Polytechnic. **How to get there:** Stoke: easy access by road (M6 junctions 15/16 and A50) and rail (2 hours from London, 45 mins from Manchester). Stafford: short bus ride from town centre; well served by rail and road links (M6 junctions 13/14). Both campuses close to Birmingham, Manchester and East Midlands airports. University minibus between Stoke and Stafford (16 miles). **Structural features:** Strong links with local FE colleges through its Staffordshire University Regional Federation (SURF) network. **Special features:** 2 business villages and a creative village on campus. Major development of entertainment technology at Stafford campus.

Courses

Academic features: Pioneering fast-track 2-year degrees in certain subjects. Also bite-size courses and flexible distance learning options. Degrees in a broad range of subject areas including telecommunications, photography, journalism, sports law, motorsport technology, forensic science, music technology. New degree course in multiplayer online games design. **Awarding body:** Staffordshire University. **Main undergraduate awards:** BA, BSc, BEng, LLB, FdA, FdSc. **Length of courses:** 3 years (full-time); 2 years (fast-track degrees, FdA/Sc); 4 years (sandwich courses; extended degrees); 5 years (sandwich extended engineering degrees).

Study opportunities & careers

Library and information services: Libraries on Stoke and Stafford campuses: 300,000+ books, 2000 periodicals, networked CD-ROM workstations, 1330 study places. Separate IT service (open 12–14 hours/day); 2120+ computers (some on wireless network) with access to library and internet. IT support desks in all computer labs; new students have induction session; drop-in IT advice; IT skills courses in various subjects. **Other learning resources:** Science and engineering laboratories; design and fine art studios, forensic science crime scene house, purpose built law courts, television studio. **Study abroad:** Opportunities for study or work placement abroad. Links with universities across Europe, the USA and China in many subjects. **Careers:** Advice service. 90+% of students in employment or further study a year after graduation.

Student services & facilities

Student advice and services: Counsellors, health and chaplaincy service, support for disabled students, careers service. Nurseries at both main sites (0–5 years). **Amenities:** SU bars, snack bars, restaurants, bars, live music venues, shops, minibus service, banking facilities at Stoke and Stafford; film theatre at Stoke. Easy access to Peak District. **Sporting facilities:** Sports centres at Stoke and Stafford: fitness suite, dance/aerobics studio, sports hall (badminton, fencing, tennis); outdoor all-weather tennis courts, sports pitches for football and rugby. **Accommodation:** All 1st-year (and overseas) students who apply and meet the criteria are in university-managed accommodation. 1850 places available in halls, flats, shared houses or head tenancies; rent £52–£85 pw, 38-week contracts plus catering package for £27.50 pw (10 meals/week). Students live in privately owned accommodation for 2+ years, rent £35–£50 pw in Stoke, £48–£65 pw in Stafford plus bills.

Money

Living expenses budget: Minimum budget of £6k–£7k pa (excluding tuition fees) recommended by university. **Term-time work:** University supports term-time work for full-time students (35% believed to work). Some work available on campus in SU bar, library, etc. Workbank helps find jobs. **Financial help:** Bursaries of £1k for students whose family income is up to £20,800, of £850 where family income is £20,800–£25,500, and of £500 where it is £25,500–£30,800. Special help for those facing difficult circumstances (financial, social, illness, etc), particularly those who have already overcome difficulties to achieve educational success. **Tuition fees:** Home students pay £3225 pa for first degrees (but £2200 for foundation year/degree). International students pay £8850 pa.

Student view

It's in the Midlands and is a vibrant and creative place to be. 2 main campuses in Stoke (the larger of the 2, based in an industrial city, with terraced housing) and Stafford (a pleasant market town with more semi-detached housing). Cost of living at both is relatively low (cheaper in Stoke). For those that look, there is some excellent value accommodation available. University continues to gain a good reputation for innovation and progressive thinking. The SU also holds to these values and is continually developing strategies to provide the best possible experience for students. SU has 4 venues, 3 shops, a student advice service and much more. Diverse nightlife at union, which seeks to continually book quality acts to fill spacious venues. Centrally located in the UK, it is easily accessible and close to fields and the Peak District for time away from the city.

Student footnotes

Housing: Uni accommodation for 1 year, then student digs, which are easily found. Rents marginally lower in Stoke than Stafford. **Eats:** £2 for sandwiches on campus, £3 for meal. Plenty of takeaway options at good price. Locally, multiple balti houses, Italians, pubs. **Drink:** Union bar good value. Good, cheap bars and clubs in Stoke, fewer in Stafford (but it's only half an hour by car to Stoke). **Nightlife:** Good range of events in union. Local clubs including Liquid, Colleseum. **Sports:** University sports centre with AstroTurf pitches, gym, sports hall and a local swimming pool; comprehensive sports clubs. **Travel:** Good access. Stoke site right next to station. Easy to get to London; Manchester and Birmingham under 1 hour. Inter-site transport available. **Financial help:** Some access funds; few SU loans. **Jobs:** 10–15% of students work in pubs, cinemas, union during term time. Union job-board on main sites and university-run workbank. **Best features:** Location. **And worst:** The rainy weather! **More info?** Enquiries to SU president (tel 01782 294629 or via uni switchboard, tel 01782 294000), or visit www.staffsunion.com.

Stirling University

Location:
central Scotland
(map 1)
**Main Stirling campus,
plus 2 nursing sites**

The University of Stirling, Stirling FK9 4LA
☎ Tel 01786 473171
✉ Email recruitment@stir.ac.uk
💻 Website www.stir.ac.uk

*Student enquiries: Student Recruitment and
Admissions Service
(tel 01786 467046, fax 01786 466800)
Applications: UCAS*

In brief

Total Students: 10,510

27% postgraduate
73% undergraduate

Undergraduates: 7715
88% full-time ● ● 91% UK students
27% mature ◐ ◉ 32% lower
on entry socio-economic
groups

65% female 35% male

- **A top UK research-intensive university.**
- **Teaching staff:** 440 (140 research).
- **Broad study areas:** Natural sciences; management, finance and business law; education; arts; languages; social sciences, humanities.

Freshers

- **Admissions information:** AS-levels accepted in combination with 2+ A-levels or equivalent (highers and advanced highers for Scottish students). UCAS tariff not used; offers made on basis of specific grades.
- **First degree entrants:** 1350 UK, full-time.
- **Points on entry:** 250+ (average).
- **Drop-out rate:** 7% in 1st year.
- **Accommodation:** All 1st years housed who apply.

Profile

Institution

Founded: 1967. **Site:** 360-acre site 2 miles north-east of Stirling. Also campuses in Inverness and Stornoway (nursing and midwifery). **How to get there:** By air to Edinburgh or Glasgow airport; by rail (5½ hours from London, 45 mins from Edinburgh, 35 mins from Glasgow); by road (A9; M9, J11 to Bridge of Allan, through town and university on left). Regular buses direct to campus from Stirling city centre and station.

Courses

Academic features: Semester system; continuous assessment policy. Concurrent secondary education (teacher training) courses. **Awarding body:** University of Stirling. **Main undergraduate awards:** BA, BSc, BAcc, LLB. **Length of courses:** 4 years (Hons); 3 years (general).

Study opportunities & careers

Library and information services: 500,000 volumes, 2400 periodicals, 1000 study places; reference collection. Computerised catalogue and issue system. Specialist collections: Rare 19th-century books; government publications. Information provision, £115 pa spent for each student (FTE). Converged library and IT services. 400 computers with internet access (open 24 hours/day); ratio workstations to students 1:15. Staffed IT helpdesk for system and software problems; workshops for new students on eg Windows, email; credit-based IT skills courses for students of any discipline. **Study abroad:** Up to 10% of students spend a period abroad in their 3rd year. Formal exchange links with 50+ universities/colleges across Europe, Australia, the USA, Canada and Hong Kong. European-orientated course options. **Careers:** Information and advice. 4 careers advisers.

Student services & facilities

Student advice and services: Doctor, dentist, chaplains, counsellors and academic advisers on site; other services available locally. Limited residential facilities for married and disabled students. **Amenities:** Bookshop on campus; SA with shop and travel service; bank, supermarket, chemist; MacRobert Arts Centre (including cinema/theatre); radio station. Good facilities for disabled students (wheelchair routes, paraplegic toilets). **Sporting facilities:** Gannochy sports centre with wide range of indoor and outdoor sports; 50m swimming pool, golf course and indoor tennis centre all on campus. **Accommodation:** All 1st (and 4th) years who apply are guaranteed university accommodation (80% of 1st years; 60% of all students). 2440 self-catering places on campus at £60–£72 pw (up to £88 ensuite), 37-week contracts. More accommodation available off campus. Students typically live in privately owned accommodation for 1–2 years, average rent £180–£280 per month. 20% of first-degree students live at home.

Money

Living expenses budget: Minimum budget of £5k–£6k pa (excluding tuition fees) recommended by university. **Term-time work:** University allows term-time work. Some work available on campus in catering, bars, arts centre, SA bars. Careers service jobshop advertises outside part-time jobs; SA has jobsboard. **Financial help:** Some government funds for students domiciled in Scotland or EU (outside UK). Apply to student information and support service for help (tel 01786 467080). **Tuition fees:** Scottish and EU students pay no fees during course; other UK students pay £1820 pa for first degrees. International students pay £9100 pa (classroom), £11,200 (lab).

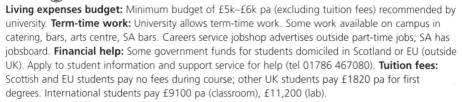

Student view

On the Airthrey Estate, it's backed by a massive hill, surrounded by woods and has a lake (sorry, loch) in the middle; easy to see why it's called one of Europe's most beautiful campuses. There are affiliated campuses in Inverness and Stornoway. Courses are very flexible and it's easy to change course in first term. It has an extremely active union with a wide variety of clubs and societies to cater for the 90 nationalities that form the university's population. Union also houses campus radio station, Radio Air 3, a TV station, Air TV, and its newspaper, *Brig*. Sports facilities excellent even before the opening of the Scottish National Tennis Centre, swimming pool and new fitness centre. Necessities can be bought on campus; most leave weekly shopping until they visit the town centre. Plenty of pubs and restaurants, and if you're bored with the town you can easily travel to Glasgow or Edinburgh for the day.

Student footnotes

Housing: Breezeblock halls/wooden chalets; moving towards market rent. Noticeboards and housing lists to help those living off campus; can be cheaper but usually whole-year contracts. **Eats:** Food, including veggie, in SA eateries excellent value; meal £2–£3.25 on campus. Westerton also good, from £5+. **Drink:** 4 bars, including a nightclub; good selection lagers and beers (from £1.90 a pint). **Nightlife:** Active ents scene (good enough to keep most students on campus); bands who have visited including Idlewild, Rachel Stevens and Wheatus. Glow is student club without club prices. **Locals:** Reasonably friendly. **Sports:** Excellent sports facilities on campus. Plenty of sports clubs. **Travel:** 3rd year exchange programme. Student travel shop. **Financial help:** Good. Access fund available to students (could be faster). **Jobs:** Union bars and kitchens; holiday work on campus/town (shops less so, unless you can guarantee long availability). **Best features:** Campus atmosphere. **Past students:** Tommy Sheridan (socialist politician); Dr John Reid MP; Jack McConnell MSP (First Minister); Iain Banks (author). **More info?** Contact SU President on 01786 467166, email susa-president@stir.ac.uk or visit the website (www.susaonline.org.uk).

Strathclyde University

Location:
Glasgow, central
Scotland (map 1)
2 campuses in city

University of Strathclyde,
Glasgow G1 1XQ
☎ Tel 0141 548 2814
✉ Email scls@strath.ac.uk
💻 Website www.strath.ac.uk

Student enquiries: Schools and Colleges Liaison
Service or see website
Applications: UCAS

In brief

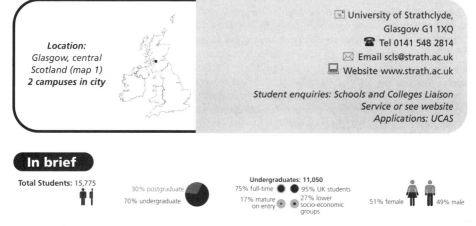

Total Students: 15,775

30% postgraduate
70% undergraduate

Undergraduates: 11,050
75% full-time
17% mature on entry
95% UK students
27% lower socio-economic groups

51% female   49% male

- **Research-intensive university.**
- **Teaching staff:** 860 full-time, 54 part-time.
- **Broad study areas:** Engineering; science; business; law, arts and social sciences.

Freshers
- **Admissions information:** AS-levels considered on individual basis. UCAS tariff not used.
- **First degree entrants:** 3140 UK, full-time.
- **Points on entry:** 360+ (average).
- **Drop-out rate:** 11% in 1st year.
- **Accommodation:** Most 1st-years housed who are not local.

Profile

Institution
Founded: 1796 as Anderson's Institution, then becoming Royal College of Science and Technology; gained Royal Charter as university in 1964, following merger with Scottish College of Commerce.

Site: John Anderson Campus, in city centre; education faculty currently at Jordanhill Campus (in West End) moves to main campus in 2011. **How to get there:** Glasgow well connected to all regions of the UK by train (4½ hours from London to Glasgow Central, 45 mins from Edinburgh), by coach (8 hours from London to Buchanan Bus Station), by air (1 hour flight from London; Glasgow Airport 7 miles from centre, Prestwick 22 miles) and by road (M8). University close to Queen Street and Glasgow Central stations and to bus station. **Special features:** School of social work joint with Glasgow University; centre of excellence in entrepreneurship education; large electrical and electronic engineering department.

Courses

Academic features: Flexible credit-based system for all courses. Assessment by coursework as well as final examination; practical training and experience are features of many degree courses. **Awarding body:** University of Strathclyde. **Main undergraduate awards:** BA, BEd, BEng, BSc, LLB, MEng, MSci, MPharm, MPhys, MChem. **Length of courses:** 4 years (Hons); 5 years (MEng); 3 years (Pass).

Study opportunities & careers

Library and information services: Andersonian Library has 1 million books, 7000+ periodicals (print and electronic); 2000+ reader places, 400 computer places and wi-fi zones for laptop use. Also open-access short loan collection, e-books, digitised exam papers and other learning materials. Major investment recently to, eg, digitise older texts, expand electronic resources and IT systems. Information provision, £140 pa spent for each student (FTE). Special collections: particularly strong in science, engineering, technology, language and literature, business studies and management; important collection of Government publications, documents published by international agencies, rare books and historical archives. Jordanhill library is major resource in education and teacher-training. **Study abroad:** 1+% of students spend a period abroad. Exchange links with universities and colleges in Canada, the USA, Australia, New Zealand, Japan and Singapore (100 pa students involved) and with 170+ universities/colleges across Europe, some open to non-language specialists; approx 150 pa students go to Europe on Socrates programmes. **Careers:** Extensive careers education programme, information and advice service (gives lifelong service to graduates); employers visits and vacancy bulletins.

Student services & facilities

Student advice and services: Health clinics on site; chaplaincy centres; disability service; counselling; financial advice service. Limited number of flats for married students. **Amenities:** Large SU with debates chamber, entertainment facilities including bars and nightclub, study and breakout space, welfare office, Sports Union. **Sporting facilities:** Sports centre with large twin-court games hall; gymnasium; weights room; cardiovascular room (70 exercise machines); 6 squash courts; swimming pool; 5 football, 2 rugby pitches, 1 all-weather hockey pitch. Range of exercise classes. Sports and golf bursaries. **Accommodation:** 40% of 1st years in university accommodation (20% of all students). 2000 places available (1400 for 1st years): most self-catering, rent £66–£88 pw for 37 weeks; some catered (at Jordanhill), £84 pw on 35-week contracts. Nearly 60% of students live at home.

Money

Living expenses budget: Minimum budget of £5500–£6600 recommended by university for academic year in university accommodation (excluding tuition fees). **Term-time work:** Majority of students work part-time and/or in holidays; careers service runs student employment service and lists hundreds of vacancies. Some work available on campus in SU, registries, accommodation. **Financial help:** £900k+ government funds (hardship and childcare funds), 1000 students helped; plus interest-free emergency loans. **Tuition fees:** Scottish and EU students pay no fees during course; other UK students pay £1820 pa for first degrees. International students pay between £8930 pa (classroom-based) and £11,465 pa (lab-based), £9960 pa (architecture).

Student view
Neil Campbell, Students' Association President (3rd year, Politics and Economics)

Living

What's it like as a place to live? Glasgow's an exciting city. **How's the student accommodation?** There is a good range of university halls, catering to different tastes and budgets, which is great for 1st year. There are also loads of private flats available in nearby areas and rent are fairly reasonable, especially as you move a little bit away from the city centre. **What's the student population like?** The uni has quite a mixture, from 1st years living at home to post-grads from all over the world. Glasgow has a massive student population, thanks to 3 unis and loads of colleges, so it's really diverse. **How do students and locals get on?** Most of Glasgow's pretty safe, certainly better than the reputation it seems to have! Strathclyde being in the centre means there aren't any local residents to get bothered by the noise.

Studying

What's it like as a place to study? Strathclyde is renowned for science, engineering and business and is not afraid of change and innovation. The library could be much better, but the new sports centre that is being build will be fantastic. **What are the teaching staff like?** Staff are helpful and friendly (usually), as well as being involved in cutting-edge research.

Socialising

What are student societies like? 44 sports teams, and as many if not more clubs and societies, catering to all tastes within the SU, which is a social hub for loads of students. It's really easy to get involved. **What's a typical night out?** There's no such thing in Glasgow! If you want it, you can find it. **And how much does it cost?** You can have a good night out for £20 easily, if you pick the right places. **How can you get home safely?** There're always loads of taxis, as well as night buses – particularly at weekends.

Money

Is it an expensive place to live? Glasgow is one of the cheapest places to live as a student in the UK. **Average price of a pint?** You can always find a deal somewhere, but £2.60 is probably average. **And the price of a takeaway?** You can get a good bit of stodge for £3. **What's the part-time work situation?** Lots of nearby shops and bars recruit students. The university has a good careers website with part-time vacancies for 15 hours pw or less. It's a fairly cheap city, so not much above national minimum wage.

Summary

What's the best feature about the place? The location. **And the worst?** The weather. **And to sum it all up?** A place of useful learning, right in the heart of Scotland's most exciting city. Great people, great times!

Past students: Craig Brown (ex-Scotland football manager), Dougie Donneley (BBC), Ed Byrne (comedian), Alex Kapranos (Franz Ferdinand), Tom Hunter (Entrepreneur), John Logie Baird (inventor of television), Sir Monty Finniston (Finniston report into British Engineering), Bobby McGregor (swimmer), David Livingstone (explorer), John Reith (Director General, BBC), Sir Adam Thompson (founder of British Caledonian); Malcolm Bruce, Douglas Henderson, Dick Douglas, Maria Fyfe, Clive Soley, Jim Murphy (politicians); James Kelman (writer). **More info?** Email vpocs@theunion.strath.ac.uk or visit www.strathstudents.com.

Sunderland University

Location:
north-east England
(map 2)
3 sites across
Sunderland town
centre; partner
colleges

University of Sunderland, Edinburgh Building, Chester Road, Sunderland SR1 3SD
☎ Tel 0191 515 3000
🖷 Fax 0191 515 3805
✉ Email student-helpline@sunderland.ac.uk
🖥 Website www.sunderland.ac.uk

Student enquiries: Student Recruitment Office, (tel 0191 515 3000, fax 0191 515 3805)
Applications: UCAS (GTTR for PGCE)

In brief

Total Students: 21,615

14% postgraduate
86% undergraduate

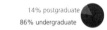

Undergraduates: 18,625
45% full-time 72% UK students
37% mature on entry 48% lower socio-economic groups

57% female 43% male

- **A modern university.**
- **Teaching staff:** 373 full-time, 58 part-time.
- **Broad study areas:** Creative and performing arts; business and management; computing; design; education; engineering; humanities; law; media; chemistry-based sciences; psychology; social sciences and caring professions; sports science and tourism.

Freshers

- **Admissions information:** All academic and vocational qualifications considered. UCAS tariff points system used.
- **First degree entrants:** 2285 UK, full-time.
- **Points on entry:** 180–300.
- **Drop-out rate:** 6% in 1st year.
- **Accommodation:** All 1st year students who want it are housed.

Profile

Institution

Founded: 1969 as Sunderland Poly, from colleges founded 1860 onwards; university status in 1992. **Site:** 2 city centre sites within 10-min walk. **How to get there:** Bus and coach services from Park Lane interchange, nearest airport Newcastle International, rail services from Sunderland station (or Durham/Newcastle nearby); by road, from A1M, take A690 then A19. Metro links 3 sites. **Special features:** Students from over 70 countries.

Courses

Academic features: Franchise scheme; modular credit scheme. **Awarding body:** University of Sunderland. **Main undergraduate awards:** BA, BSc, BEng, FdA, FdSc. **Length of courses:** 2 or 3 years (full-time); 4 years (sandwich); 3–5 years (part-time).

Study opportunities & careers

Library and information services: 3 libraries (2 open 24/7 in core teaching weeks): total of 4000+ books, 10,000 journals; many information resources available online. Library IT facilities include 300+ PCs, CD writers, scanners, networked printing facilities, wireless internet access (for use with own laptops). Information provision, £75 pa spent for each student (FTE). Separate IT service (access 24 hours/day); ratio workstations to students 1:6. Support from library staff and IT technicians throughout university; numerous induction sessions for new students on library and information services and IT skills; also subject workshops, surgeries, etc. **Other learning resources:** Art gallery; language centre; media resources unit; journalism suite; computer network with 24-hour access to mini-computers and main computer. **Study abroad:** Many students spend time abroad at partner universities in Europe, the USA, Canada, South America and Australia as part of their course. **Careers:** Information, advice and placement.

Student services & facilities

Student advice and services: Student services all in one-stop centre at City Campus: counselling service, financial adviser, professional welfare officer, solicitor through SU, chaplain, nursing sister on call for first aid, day nursery. **Amenities:** SU with 50 sporting and recreational societies (including ski club, all weather pitches), shop, bar and nightclub. Bookshop on site. **Sporting facilities:** New sports centre with fitness suite and sports hall; special access to Olympic swimming pool nearby. **Accommodation:** All 1st years and international students (and most continuing students) who want it are in university accommodation; 65% of all non-local students. 1500 self-catering places available, rent £52–£69.50 pw, 40-week contracts. Privately owned accommodation average rent £58 pw self-catering. 15% of first-degree students live at home.

Money

Living expenses budget: Minimum budget of £6k pa (excluding tuition fees) recommended by university. **Term-time work:** Some work available on campus in SU, library, student bars, clubs, societies, administration or as student ambassadors. Jobshop advertises on- and off-campus jobs. **Financial help:** Awards for all students who progress satisfactorily through their course (£965 over 3 years). Bursary of £525 pa for students whose family income is up to £39,300. Non-means-tested bursary of £525 pa for those on foundation degrees. Scholarships and support from sponsors and trusts on some courses. Further advice from student helpline. **Tuition fees:** Home students pay £3225 pa for first degrees (less in placement years). International students pay from £8150 pa (guaranteed scholarship of £1500).

Student view — Lara Clarke, President (Graduate, Performing Arts)

Living

What's it like as a place to live? It's an ace place to live. Everyone is friendly, it's easy to find your way around, it's not as big most other university towns. The nightlife is great too and if you fancy a drink, it's the cheapest place I know. **How's the student accommodation?** It's pretty much what you would expect from any university halls, but it's also warm and clean. As long as the people you are living with turn out to be ok . . . then you are sorted. Even if you end up with people from all over the country/world you will find something in common with all of them. The private landlords can be a bit tricky. The houses can be falling apart and have things wrong with them that you don't discover until you live there. The SU have a good house guide, however, so before anyone moves into a private house, make sure you come see us first . . . we don't bite . . . honest!! **What's the student population like?** We have a very diverse range of students, including many from all around the world. The majority of our students, however, are home students but don't let that put you off – I myself moved over from Ireland and I fitted in and found the best mates in the world straight away. **How do students and locals get on?** To be honest, there isn't really anywhere you are forbidden to go. Some pubs in town wouldn't be the most fun because that's were the older locals hang out, but if you go in you are more likely to get talking about Sunderland FC than any trouble. Weekend nights in town are very busy, though, and full of locals who may have had one too many to drink – so it's best to just go out on students' night on a Wednesday.

Studying

What's it like as a place to study? Depending on your course, the uni is expanding and the facilities are getting better one subject at a time. If you are a media student you are very lucky as we have one of the top media centres in the country, which houses its own radio and television studios. We have just had a new library built too, which is full of computers with high-speed internet which can only be used by our students. **What are the teaching staff like?** The staff are really quite good – of course I can only really speak for the tutors I had personally. I have been in meetings with deans of schools and principal lecturers who are constantly talking about trying to make the student experience better and, judging by the excitement and passion in those meetings, I think they are most definitely interested in what our students think.

Socialising

What are student societies like? Being part of a sports team I can honestly say it was the best decision I ever made at university. You meet so many people and go to so many fun events. Being part of a team helps build up loads of skills which look ace on your cv at the end of it all. Sunderland Uni has a great range of societies and teams as well, everything from the more traditional sports, like football and rugby, to the more out-there sports like American football, scuba diving and snowboarding. Then again, it's not all about sports; we have an amazing range of societies such as the Gaming Society, the Chinese Society, Ultimate Frisbee and Beer Pong! **What's a typical night out?** Well, all universities play sports on a Wednesday afternoon, competing in BUCS, which is a sports league for universities and colleges. After a day of playing, the best way to celebrate, or commiserate, is to meet up with all of the other teams and head out to the SU bar, then, after a small pub crawl, head to the SU venue. Don't get me wrong, though, it's not all about the drink; there are also great deals in other places. Student discount covers cinemas, bars, nightclubs, restaurants, the new Olympic-size swimming pool and many more places. **And how much does it cost?** Being a student before working for the SU, I know how hard it was to juggle money. So we try to get the places in town to offer us good deals at student-friendly places. On a student night, you would be hard pushed to pay more than £1.50 for a drink and entry is usually free or reduced upon presentation of your student card. Like I've said about other venues, they offer discounts (usually around 10%) when you pay with a student card. **How can you get home safely?** There are plenty of taxis all the time within the city centre, so it's never hard to get home. We also have a scheme with a local taxi firm that if it gets to the end of the night, you find that you have spent all of your money, you can still get a taxi as long as you give them your student card. The card then gets handed into the union and you can come in and collect it after you pay us the taxi fare.

Money

Is it an expensive place to live? Everyone tends to run out of money but I think this is just because, like myself, having a whole heap of money all at once burns a massive hole in your pocket. After your 1st year you get into the swing of things and there are loads of places to get a part-time job. In general though, it isn't a very expensive place to live. **Average price of a pint?** Never more than about £2 on a normal night, £1.50 on student nights. **And the price of a takeaway?** There is a pizza shop that does a 30-inch pizza, which is so so so huge, for £20 . . . and most of the takeaways have student offers too! **What's the part-time work situation?** The university say that, as long as you work less than 16 hours a week, it is ok to get a job. There are loads available as well, from bar jobs to call centres.

Summary

What's the best feature about the place? The amount of students. They are everywhere, it's brill. **And the worst?** Match days – all the streets are full of other people's cars. **And to sum it all up?** The best 4 years of my life.

Past students: Steve Cram (athlete). **More info?** Contact SU President on 0191 515 3584, email su.president@sunderland.ac.uk or visit the website (www.sunderlandsu.co.uk).

Surrey University

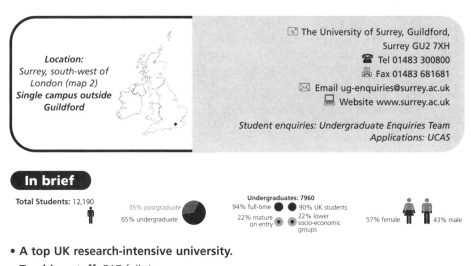

Location:
Surrey, south-west of London (map 2)
Single campus outside Guildford

The University of Surrey, Guildford, Surrey GU2 7XH
☎ Tel 01483 300800
🖷 Fax 01483 681681
✉ Email ug-enquiries@surrey.ac.uk
💻 Website www.surrey.ac.uk

Student enquiries: Undergraduate Enquiries Team
Applications: UCAS

In brief

Total Students: 12,190

35% postgraduate
65% undergraduate

Undergraduates: 7960
94% full-time
22% mature on entry
90% UK students
22% lower socio-economic groups

57% female   43% male

- **A top UK research-intensive university.**
- **Teaching staff:** 517 full-time.
- **Broad study areas:** Biomedical and molecular sciences; computing; dance; economics; electronic engineering; engineering; English literature; entrepreneurship; film studies; languages; law; management; midwifery; music and sound recording; nursing; physics; political, international and policy studies; psychology; social and media studies; tourism and hospitality.

Freshers

- **Admissions information:** 2 full A-levels or equivalent required, 3 specific subjects for some programmes. A range of other qualifications are accepted. Most offers grade-based; some based on UCAS tariff.
- **First degree entrants:** 2675 UK full-time.
- **Points on entry:** 353 (average).
- **Drop-out rate:** 7% in 1st year.
- **Accommodation:** All 1st years normally offered accommodation.

Profile

Institution

Founded: Royal Charter 1966, previously Battersea College of Technology. **Site:** Single campus, 1 mile outside Guildford. **How to get there:** Fast train from London Waterloo (40 mins) and south coast; close to A3. Campus 10 mins' walk from station, 15 mins' from Guildford town centre. **Special features:** Pioneered development of integrated professional training year (feature of most undergraduate degrees). Applications from mature students are welcomed. University also validates courses in a wide range of associated institutions.

Courses

Academic features: Some BSc/BEng incorporate foundation year for those without subject qualifications. **Awarding body:** University of Surrey. **Main undergraduate awards:** BA, BEng, BMus, BSc, MEng, MChem, MMath, MPhys. **Length of courses:** 3 years; 4 years (undergraduate Master's, courses with professional training or integrated foundation year); 4½ years (MEng); 5 years (professional training and foundation year).

Study opportunities & careers

Library and information services: 500,000+ volumes, 14,000 current periodicals (many electronically); 30,000 networked e-books and databases; 900 study places. Information provision, £176 pa spent for each student (FTE). Library and IT services converged; support and resources from SPLASH (Student Personal Learning and Study Hub). 450+ PCs, most available 24/7, with access to internet, university intranet, secure file space; free loan scheme for some specialist software. Online learning using interactive learning environment. Support for IT skills: paper and online information; IT training courses open to all; help from ITS helpdesk. **Study abroad:** 12% of students on professional training year spend it abroad. Approx. 85 Erasmus and 20 other international partnerships; some subject-specific, some university-wide. **Careers:** Information, advice and counselling.

Student services & facilities

Student advice and services: Counselling centre (8 staff); additional learning support (7 staff); student advice and information service (4 staff); multi-faith chaplaincy; health centre (6 nurses, 2 doctors) includes clinics on sexual health, contraception, asthma, smoking cessation, weight management, diabetes, travel. **Amenities:** SU has 5 bars, 3 restaurants, 1600-capacity nightclub. Licensed convenience store, bookshop, post office, laundrette, bank, restaurants on campus. **Accommodation:** All 1st years normally offered university accommodation (and most international and some final-year students). Self-catering places (44% ensuite), rent £57–£99 pw; contracts, term time or longer. Students live in privately owned accommodation for 1–2 years: rent £80–£85 pw for self-catering. 10% of first-degree students live at home.

Money

Living expenses budget: Minimum budget of £6300 pa (excluding tuition fees) recommended by university. **Term-time work:** University allows term-time work for full-time students (30% believed to work). Some work available on campus and in town centre. Careers service runs online jobshop. **Financial help:** Bursaries of £2050 pa for UK students whose family income is up to £10k, tapered (down to nil) where family income is £35k; bursary is doubled where a scholarship is also awarded. Scholarships of £1k pa available for students with high entry qualifications, some specifically for care-leavers or children of travellers, or on the basis of end-of-year assessments. Further scholarships available in specified subjects and for international students. £255,500 government access to learning funds; 80% who applied were helped (average award £907); limited own funds. Special help for hardship due either to exceptional and unexpected circumstances, or to additional costs incurred by non-traditional students. Apply to student advice and information service for help. **Tuition fees:** Home students pay £3225 pa for first degrees (except those funded by the NHS; £1285 for foundation years, £485 for professional training years). International students pay between £9k pa (arts) and £11,400 (science).

Student view

It has a medium-sized campus on the grassy Cathedral hillside, overlooking Guildford – 10 mins' walk to the railway (35 mins to London) and 15 mins to the bus station. Being on a hill it's not ideal for students with mobility problems. 1st years are in university accommodation, as are many final-year and all international students; which range from standard to very good (most rooms have a basin, some ensuite); kitchen shared between 4–14 and there are single- and mixed-gender floors. Good community spirit on campus and at the smaller residential site (3 miles from university with free bus service). Students living within a 3-mile radius are normally unable to have a car on campus. Laundrette, shop, bookshop, oriental food store, computer parts shop, post office and bank on campus, also a visiting fruit and veg market once a week. Large library (open until 1.30am), superbly-equipped sports hall and 24-hour-access PC labs. SU has excellent ents: discos every Wednesday, Friday and most Saturday nights, free films on Sunday nights. It produces award-winning media – *Barefacts* (weekly student newspaper) and GU2 (campus radio station). Social advice and support from university, also health centre with family planning advice and confidential counselling service; SU has dedicated education and welfare officers. Guildford is fairly expensive but the 3 nightclubs offer student discounts. Dozens of pubs, 2 theatres, a vast cinema complex, all coupled with the lovely Surrey countryside. Originally a technological university but now with thriving human sciences, performing arts, law and cultural departments. Courses are generally up to date, most modular, and most have a period in industry (some abroad) offering valuable experience. Workload varies from ok to hard, generally combining end-of-semester exams with assessed coursework. It is a culturally unique social centre – an easy place to make friends.

Student footnotes

Housing: University accommodation is affordable; few married/family flats. Off campus is a little more expensive; check out the accommodation office or take over friends' houses. **Eats:** Meal on campus £4–£5 (university or SU). In town, good choice (eg Pizza Express, Zizzi, etc.), range of prices. **Drink:** 5 union bars, complete range of drinking environments, wide range of beers and spirits (£1.80 a pint). Pubs more expensive. Good local brew – TEA from the Hogsback Brewery. **Nightlife:** Very good on site, with cabaret, bands (the Darkness, Shy FX, Mark Owen, Coolio, East 17, We are Scientists, the Jam, Pendulum), free lunchtime concerts, discos, balls and annual festivals. Theatres and Odeon cinema complex in town. **Locals:** Very friendly if you treat them well. No problem areas (Guildford's quite posh!) **Sports:** Good cheap facilities; friendly and competitive events. Floodlit AstroTurf pitch, superb indoor facilities, eg multi-purpose gym, climbing wall and a brand new multi-million pound sports centre in the planning. **Financial help:** University and government funds. **Jobs:** Lots on site (eg bars, catering outlets) and shop work and telephone sales in town at reasonable rates; employment agency on campus. **Best features:** Beautiful and culturally diverse campus. **And worst:** Expensive part of the country. **Past students**: David Varney (British Gas, etc.), Robert Earl (Planet Hollywood). **More info?** Enquiries to president SU on 01483 689227 or visit www.ussu.co.uk.

Sussex University

Location:
Brighton, south coast
of England (map 2)
**Single campus outside
city; associated
colleges**

⊞ University of Sussex, Falmer, Brighton,
Sussex BN1 9RH
☎ Tel 01273 678416
🖷 Fax 01273 678545
✉ Email ug.admissions@sussex.ac.uk
🖳 Website www.sussex.ac.uk

*Student enquiries: Undergraduate Admissions Office
Applications: UCAS*

In brief

Total Students: 12,445

25% postgraduate
75% undergraduate

Undergraduates: 9275
75% full-time ● ● 91% UK students
16% mature ● ● 22% lower
on entry socio-economic
groups

63% female 37% male

- **A top UK research-intensive university.**
- **Teaching staff:** 528 full-time and part-time.
- **Broad study areas:** Arts and humanities; biological sciences; chemical, physical and environmental sciences; computing and information technology; engineering; languages; mathematical and computing science; social sciences; medicine (you can look up the *Brighton & Sussex Medical School* separately).

Freshers

- **Admissions information:** AS-levels welcomed but in combination with 2+ A-levels or equivalent. Offers on basis of grades, not UCAS tariff.
- **First degree entrants:** 2075 UK, full-time.
- **Points on entry:** 290+ (average).
- **Drop-out rate:** 8% in 1st year.
- **Accommodation:** Guaranteed for all 1st years, who apply in time.

Profile

Institution

Founded: 1961. **Site:** Single campus, 4 miles from Brighton town centre. **How to get there:** To Brighton by road (M/A23 then A27), by coach or by rail (50 mins from Victoria, 30 mins from Gatwick airport). For university, frequent buses and trains from Brighton town centre to Falmer (station directly opposite campus, journey time 8 mins). Also ferries Dieppe–Newhaven, with direct train link to Falmer. **Structural features:** Medical school joint with Brighton University (*Brighton & Sussex Medical School*; you can look it up separately).

Courses

Academic features: Possible to combine some sciences with a language or American studies. **Awarding body:** University of Sussex. **Main undergraduate awards:** BA, BSc, BEng, LLB, MChem, MPhys, MEng, MMath, BM BS. **Length of courses:** 3 years; 4 years (courses with year abroad, undergraduate Master's) 5 years (BMBS).

Study opportunities & careers

Library and information services: 800,000+ volumes, 20,000 online and print journal subscriptions, 1000 study places, short loan collection, audio-visual section, CD-ROM databases. Special collections include Mass Observation (social history) and Virginia Woolf archives. Information provision, £177 pa spent for each student (FTE). Separate IT service. Ratio workstations to students 1:18; open 24 hours/day; all PCs have access to library and internet; adapted PCs for students with disabilities and special learning needs. IT support (email, telephone or in person), 8 hours/day; induction talks and information packs on library and information services for new students; courses in IT skills, computing and information handling. **Study abroad:** 15% of first-degree students spend a term/year abroad (possible with most subjects), normally 3rd year of 4-year course. Formal exchange links with universities in all EU and EFTA countries and many in North America. **Careers:** Information and advice (also for work out of term time).

Student services & facilities

Student advice and services: Health service, dentist, sick bay on campus, personal counselling and psychotherapy unit. Residential facilities for disabled students; crèche and nursery. **Amenities:** SU with concert hall, bar, club, restaurant, shops, campus student radio station and newspaper, banks, chemist, opticians, laundrette. **Sporting facilities:** 2 sports halls and fitness rooms; playing fields, tennis courts, etc. adjoining campus, sports injury clinic. **Accommodation:** University accommodation guaranteed for 1st years who apply by deadline. Around 3500 self-catering places available, including some family accommodation; rent £71–£97 pw (up to £110 pw ensuite); most 39-week contracts, some longer. Some students in university-managed accommodation beyond the 1st year (self-selecting groups); remainder live in privately owned accommodation: £85 pw + bills for self-catering. Over 15% of students live at home.

Money

Living expenses budget: Minimum budget of £7263 for the academic year (excluding tuition fees) recommended by university. **Term-time work:** University allows term-time work for full-time first-degree students (up to 70% believed to work); advisory limit of 15 hours pw. Some work available on campus in bar, catering, retail, admin, research, translation (but not in medical or academic records); also help in finding work off campus through well-established employment centre. **Financial help:** Bursaries of £1k pa for UK students whose family income is up to £25k. 200 scholarships (of £1k pa) awarded annually to students whose family income is up to £28k, who have no tradition of going to university; scholarships (usually £1k) for students with high entry qualifications on specified science courses; also sports bursaries. Students can qualify for more than 1 award. £483k government funds, 900 students helped; loans from vice-chancellor's fund for students experiencing short-term difficulties. **Tuition fees:** Home students pay £3225 pa for first degrees (except sandwich years and periods abroad). International students pay £9975 pa (classroom), £12,750 pa (lab/studio), £22,550 pa (medicine), which will increase by inflation each year; or students can opt for a higher fee, which is fixed for the duration of the course, of £10,500 pa (classroom), £13,270 pa (lab/studio) – not open to medical students.

Student view

Despite the fact that it was built in the early 1960s (along with many of Britain's greatest concrete monstrosities), it's actually one of the most beautiful campus universities in Britain. Set in the middle of the South Downs and just north of the lively seaside bohemia that is Brighton, the university as a whole takes its cue from the award-winning and challenging architecture of its campus. This is reflected in the open-minded, liberal and challenging attitude displayed in its teaching, particularly in the arts. Interdisciplinary studies feed this attitude, with 5 major schools offering courses rewarding in their variety. Science schools have an excellent reputation for attracting research grants, though their teaching is more formal and structured than in the arts. Large numbers of international and mature students, which gives it a rounded and diverse student population. The radical reputation of Sussex is deserved; best displayed in activities of the SU – an active campaigner on campus, local, regional, national and international issues (active in the fight for education accessible to all, now more involved in environmental campaigns). It also provides well-reputed advice services and runs a huge range of student activities catering for most interests. SU's cosmopolitan, anti-racist, anti-sexist and anti-homophobic attitudes reflect those of Sussex students and Brighton inhabitants. In fact, university's strongest point is Brighton: a student town with a lively social scene and a unique, laidback feeling. Loads of pubs and clubs to keep students busy and the beach is always a good place to sit and get away from it all when the studying becomes too much.

Student footnotes

Housing: Campus housing mainly single, self-catering; some double/family flats. In Brighton, high demand and high rent (and often poorly kept accommodation). **Drink:** Huge variety of bars in town; 6 bars on campus. **Eat:** Plenty of choice in all price ranges in town; campus has a good range of cafés, canteens and snack bars. **Nightlife:** Brighton has extremely active (but expensive) nightlife. On campus, regular club nights in the SU nightclub, live bands and films in bars, various cultural activities at the Gardner Arts Centre. **Sports:** Plenty of facilities; wide range of sports (competitive and non-competitive) for all levels of participation. **Travel:** Good public transport links (though trains and buses can be expensive). **Financial help:** Available via access funds, hardship loans and some funds from the academic schools; accessible with good advice from SU and faculties. **Jobs:** Excellent student employment office for jobs on and off campus. SU employs staff in bars and shops. Wages in Brighton are generally low; can be hard to find part-time or holiday work. **Best features:** Sussex is the sunniest campus in the UK. **Past students:** Thabo Mbeki (President, South Africa), Ian McEwan (author), Howard Brenton, Brian Behan (playwrights), Brendan Foster (athlete), Virginia Wade (tennis), Howard Barker (dramatist), Julia Somerville (presenter), Peter Jones (entrepreneur, *Dragon's Den*), Peter Hain MP, Simon Fanshawe (*That's Life*). **More info?** Visit www.ussu.info.

Swansea Met University

Location:
south-west Wales
(map 1)
3 sites across
Swansea

🖥 Swansea Metropolitan University,
Mount Pleasant, Swansea SA1 6ED
☎ Tel 01792 481000
🖨 Fax 01792 481085
✉ Email enquiry@smu.ac.uk
🖥 Website www.smu.ac.uk

Student enquiries: Registry
Applications: UCAS

In brief

Total Students: 5800

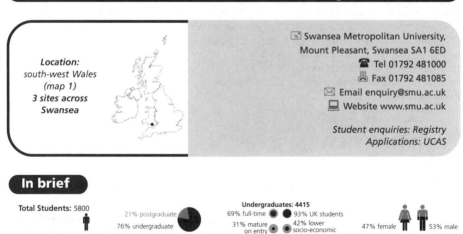

21% postgraduate
76% undergraduate

Undergraduates: 4415
69% full-time
31% mature on entry
93% UK students
42% lower socio-economic groups

47% female   53% male

- **A modern university**, a constituent member of Wales University.
- **Teaching staff:** 220 full-time, 86 part-time.
- **Broad study areas:** Art and design; accounting and finance; humanities; business and management; computing; education; automotive and motor sport engineering; built and natural environment; leisure and tourism; transport; digital media; theatre, film and TV studies.

Freshers

- **Admissions information:** AS-levels accepted in combination with 2+ A-levels or equivalent. UCAS tariff used.
- **First degree entrants:** 785 UK, full-time.
- **Points on entry:** 180 (average).
- **Drop-out rate:** 14% in 1st year.
- **Accommodation:** Many 1st years housed.

Profile

Institution

Founded: 1976 from colleges of art, technology and education. Swansea Institute from 1992; university status in 2008. **Structural features:** College of Wales University. **Site:** 3 main campuses: Mount Pleasant and Dynevor, both in town centre, and Townhill just outside; also Alexandra Road (architectural stained glass and music technology), close to Mount Pleasant. **How to get there:** Mainline rail from London Paddington (2 hours 50 mins) and frequent services from Cardiff, Bristol, Birmingham; close to M4; coach services to Quadrant Bus Station in Swansea, then buses 12/13 to Graiglwyd Square (for Townhill campus). Cardiff International airport 40 mins' drive; ferry services to Swansea from Cork.

Courses

Awarding body: University of Wales. **Main undergraduate awards:** BA, BSc, BEng. **Length of courses:** 3 years; 4 years (MEng, courses with year abroad).

Study opportunities & careers

Library and information services: 3 libraries (1 at each main campus); 130,000 volumes in total, 1300 periodicals, 660 study places. Library and information services converged. Information provision, £72 pa spent for each student (FTE). Technicians and computer unit provides IT support; new students have library tours, individual study sessions on eg internet; further IT skills courses to suit individual needs. **Other learning resources:** Visual aid centre, print room and resources centre. **Study abroad:** 5% of students spend a period abroad. Some European exchange links. **Careers:** Careers counsellors.

Student services & facilities

Student advice and services: Student financial adviser, counsellors, doctor, chaplains. **Amenities:** Student centre, SU bar, fitness centre. **Accommodation:** 50% of 1st years from outside the area in university accommodation. 565 self-catering places available (100+ ensuite), £56–£66 pw (£50 pw shared), 40-week contracts. Students live in privately owned accommodation for 1–4 years (plenty in the area): rent typically £45–£58 pw for self-catering (plus bills). 40% of first-degree students live at home.

Money

Living expenses budget: Minimum budget of £5k pa (excluding tuition fees) recommended by university. **Term-time work:** University allows term-time work for students; no work available on campus but an abundance of part-time jobs in surrounding area. **Financial help:** Bursaries of £305 pa for UK students from low-income families. Non-means-tested bursary of £500 pa for students who live 45+ miles from university. Financial contingency fund, 200+ students helped; plus emergency fund. Special help: single parents, or for mature, disabled, or self-financing students. Also bursaries and loans (can apply prior to starting course). Apply to student services for help. **Tuition fees:** Home students pay £3225 pa for first degrees (though Welsh residents may be eligible for annual fee grant). International students pay £6950 pa.

Student view) **Mimi Robinson,** Entertainments and Special Events Officer (2nd year, Graphic Design) and Harriet Brewster, Students' Union President

Living

What's it like as a place to live? Swansea is a great place to live, especially for the student population. The city centre has everything you need from shops to bars and restaurants, and the night life is fantastic with a vast range of clubs and pubs. Swansea is also very close to the Gower peninsula, with some lovely beaches, which makes it brilliant for summer activities and particularly surfing. **How's the student accommodation?** Student accommodation is provided in the form of halls of residence at 2 of Swansea Met's campuses – Townhill and Mount Pleasant. These all include kitchen and bathroom facilities and some rooms have ensuite showers. The rooms are a good size with storage and desk space provided. The best thing about them though is the view from the south-facing rooms; you can see the sea and the north coast of Devon on clear days. Living with groups of students is very helpful in the 1st year of university as you build friend groups and confidence along the way. If you do not live in halls, there are many houses around different areas of town that are for student use. These are advertised by the university to make sure the students leaving halls are going to safe, up-to-code houses for the following year. The quality of these houses is good, often having rooms for 4 or more people. Rent prices for both halls and housing are very reasonable and affordable. On average from £49 to £65 pw plus bills. **What's the student population like?** The student population at Swansea Metropolitan University is diverse and friendly. We have students from all walks of life, local, national and international students included, along with mature students and disabled students. It is not difficult to make friends here and as a result, all of our students study in a friendly, productive atmosphere. **How do students and locals get on?** Generally students keep themselves to themselves. In halls of residence, communication with the locals is less than it is in student housing. This is due to the fact that the student houses are in residential streets. Generally there is a good atmosphere between the 2 groups.

Studying

What's it like as a place to study? As one of the newest universities in the UK, Swansea Met is a brilliant place to study. The courses range from English to motorcycle engineering to fine art to music technology. There is something for everyone. The facilities across the campuses (we have 4) are top of the range. Dynevor Campus is our newest building and it houses the art and design departments. All the equipment and materials there are brand new, with plenty to go around. The Townhill, Mount Pleasant and Alexandra Road campuses are also excellent for equipment and resources catering for their specific subject specialities. **What are the teaching staff like?** The teaching staff at the university are all highly respected and are always interested in what the students are doing both in uni and in free time. The SU has an active involvement with the university, with course reps and union reps representing students at all levels from faculty up to governors. This maintains a positive relationship between students and staff, creating a far better atmosphere for students to study within.

Socialising

What are student societies like? The societies provided by the SU are very successful. There is a vast range of activities for our students to be involved in. These range from the traditional sports such as football and rugby to the dance society, climbing and mountaineering club and the surf club. Not all our clubs and societies are sport-based; we also have alternatives, such as the Enterprise Society and People and Planet. It is also made very easy for students to start up clubs that are not currently available. The sports teams, surf club and dance society are the most popular clubs with a big number of students joining up. **What's a typical night out?** A typical night out for our students begins in our student lounge, which is situated on Townhill Campus. When that closes, groups of students head into town, mainly to Wind Street where most of the nightlife in Swansea is situated. There are other venues that people drift to later in the night, such as the new Oceana and Sin City. A lot of the time you see groups of students in various costumes for fancy dress, be it for an organised event, someone's birthday or just a bit of fun; it's always fun. **And how much does it cost?** How much a night out costs depends on the student and the clubs they go to. Some places are more expensive than others. Usually you find students in town on a Wednesday, when most of the clubs hold their student nights. On a night like this you can spend as little as £10 – again, this depends on funds and the student in question. The good thing about Swansea is that you do not need to spend a lot of money to have a good night. **How can you get home safely?** The best way to get home safely after a night out is to get a taxi with a group of people all going in the same direction or to the same place. The SU provides information on making sure students use a licensed taxi service and has the numbers for these taxi companies. Walking back alone, as in any city, is not recommended in any case.

Money

Is it an expensive place to live? Swansea is not an expensive place to live in; rent prices are very low compared to the rest of the UK. Making your student loan last is up to your money management. **Average price of a pint?** Depending on where you go in Swansea, with such an array of bars and pubs, the cost of a pint is very variable, though starting at around £2.20. **What's the part-time work situation?** To assist with funding, a lot of students find part-time work in bars in the evenings and shops at weekends. Jobs are not everywhere; however, if you look it is most likely you will find them. And the university offers services to assist with job hunting, from checking CVs to having a list of jobs available in the area.

Summary

What's the best feature about the place? The location – very close to town, with views of the sea – but also the environment. With the Metropolitan being relatively small for a university, it gives students a greater choice of support and lecture time. From a degree prospective the courses are well thought out and are good value for money. From a social aspect it's not all just about the drinking; there is also a wide choice of beaches and a very good public transport system to go over to Cardiff or up in to the countryside. **And the worst?** The worst thing about Swansea could be the seaside climates: when it rains, it sometimes seems like it may never stop. But there are so many activities it can easily go unnoticed. **And to sum it all up?** I would sum up Swansea Metropolitan as being a community that cares for its students. There are no excuses for boredom as there are so many internal and external activities, though sometimes you have to look for them.

Past students: Mervyn Davies, Wayne Proctor, Andy Moore (Welsh rugby internationals); Glyn Garner (Bury FC). **More info?** Contact SU on 01792 298845 or visit www.metsu.org.

Swansea University

Location:
south-west Wales
(map 1)
*Single campus in
Swansea; partner
colleges*

University of Wales Swansea,
Singleton Park, Swansea SA2 8PP
☎ Tel 01792 295784
🖷 Fax 01792 295897
🖳 Website www.swansea.ac.uk

*Student enquiries: Schools and Colleges Liaison Office
Applications: UCAS*

In brief

Total Students: 15,525

18% postgraduate
9% FE Students
73% undergraduate

Undergraduates: 11,370
77% full-time ● ● 93% UK students
20% mature ● ● 29% lower
on entry ● socio-economic
groups

58% female   42% male

- **Traditional and research-intensive constituent member of Wales University.**
- **Teaching staff:** 1356 full-time and part-time.
- **Broad study areas:** Science, health and medicine, arts and social sciences, engineering, business, economics, law.

Freshers

- **Admissions information:** AS-levels accepted in combination with 2+ A-levels or equivalent (Welsh baccalaureate welcomed). UCAS tariff offers made for entry to most degree schemes.
- **First degree entrants:** 2760 UK, full-time.
- **Points on entry:** 316 (average).
- **Drop-out rate:** 7% in 1st year.
- **Accommodation:** Almost all 1st years housed.

Profile

Institution

Founded: 1920. **Structural features:** Part of Wales University. **Site:** Campus a mile west of city, on Swansea Bay near the Gower Peninsula. **How to get there:** Mainline rail from London Paddington (2 hours 50 mins), also frequent services from Cardiff, Bristol, Birmingham; close to M4; national coach services to Quadrant Bus Station. Cardiff International airport 40 mins' drive. Buses to campus from railway station, city centre and off-campus accommodation.

Courses 📖

Academic features: Many degrees modular. 4-year degrees in sciences and engineering with foundation year; also undergraduate Master's degrees. **Awarding body:** University of Wales. **Main undergraduate awards:** BA, BSc, BEng, BScEcon, LLB, MChem, MEng, MMath, MPhys. **Length of courses:** 3 years; 4 years (eg undergraduate Master's, courses with foundation year or period abroad).

Study opportunities & careers

Library and information services: 900,000+ volumes, 32,000 periodicals (including 24,700 electronic), 1300 study places (including 550 with PCs). Annual information provision spend, £176 per student (FTE). IT and library services converged, open 82 hours/week. 1850 PCs across university for student use with access to university wireless network. Induction sessions for all new students on library and information services; information skills courses (eg on the internet). **Other learning resources:** TV studio; portable digital recording units; digital photography and video conferencing; computer-assisted language labs. **Study abroad:** Many students (in most departments) can spend up to a year abroad in, eg, North America, Japan, Mexico, Australia or Europe. **Careers:** Information, advice and placement service; vacation employment, work experience.

Student services & facilities

Student advice and services: Integrated student services including student financial aid, international student advice, disability office and student counselling service. Also careers centre, health centre, dentist, chaplains, mosque, SU advice centre. Excellent facilities and support for disabled students (including adapted accommodation; assessment of needs service; dyslexia assessment and support; IT training; support for students with mental health problems; recording for the blind centre on campus). **Amenities:** SU building with shop, travel centre, laundrette, radio station, bar. CCTV unit; arts centre; gallery; theatre, cinema and Egypt Centre on campus. City has pubs/clubs, art galleries, theatres and wide range of restaurants/cafés. **Sporting facilities:** Main sports centre close by, with excellent facilities including national pool (50m and 25m pools), sports hall, climbing wall, fitness centre, 3 squash courts; outdoors, 6 tennis courts, rugby and soccer fields, 8-lane athletics track; indoor athletics training area and 2 artificial hockey pitches. Further 20 acres of sports fields 4 miles away. Range of activity programmes for all levels of ability. Sports scholarships available. Location ideal for water-based and other outdoor activities. **Accommodation:** 98% of 1st years normally in university accommodation. 3400 places available: self-catering £62–£67 pw (£83–£94 pw ensuite), 36- or 40-week contracts; part-catered places at £69–£85 pw + £24.50 weekly catering package, 36- or 40-week contracts. Small number of shared rooms at lower rates. Most students in privately owned accommodation after the 1st year: £55–£65 pw + bills (all self-catering).

Money

Living expenses budget: Minimum budget of £5500 for academic year (excluding tuition fees) recommended by university, £7060 for a calendar year. **Term-time work:** University supports term-time work for full-time students. Careers unit, Worklink, helps students find work on and off campus. **Financial help:** 90 bursaries (up to £3k) for top performers in selected subjects; some departmental bursaries (up to £2500). Also university scholarships (£1200–£3k pa); several sport scholarships each year (£1k pa). £565,150 government funds (awards £100–£3500), plus own funds of £23k for EU and overseas students. Special help eg for overseas students, non-traditional students, those with high travel costs, disability costs, final-year students and those with childcare costs. Apply to admissions office (scholarships) or student financial aid office. **Tuition fees:** Home students pay £3225 pa for first degrees (though Welsh residents may be eligible for annual fee grant). International students pay £8200–£11,900.

Student view
James Houston, President of Students' Union (Graduate, History)

Living
What's it like as a place to live? Changeable. It's hard to pin down but it's great! You can walk for 5 mins and be on a vast beach, or another 5 and you're in an incredible

hubbub with all the nightlife. But it does rain a lot! **How's the student accommodation?** Well it's certainly a mixture and it's not all great! But the best thing is there's loads of good stuff about, which means if you take the time to shop around you can get an amazing pad! **What's the student population like?** I'm biased maybe but I reckon they are some of the friendliest around. Being a campus uni, you always see someone you know and make friends every day. It's incredibly diverse but accepting at the same time. **How do students and locals get on?** During the week the locals are amazing and most residents and students get on. But we tend to keep away from town at the weekends as people come from far afield and it's safer and better for students to go to our own club nights.

Studying

What's it like as a place to study? Courses are great but contact time is totally changeable – which is great during heavy coursework periods but not so much at other times. But lecturers are readily available for one-to-one assistance. **What are the teaching staff like?** I can only speak for a few departments, but those that I have interacted with have been awesome. They're not always the top dogs in their fields, But they are the most passionate and supportive around!

Socialising

What are student societies like? Swansea is rammed with societies, many of which have flourished in the last few years. Our Afro-Caribbean and drama societies have put on amazing events whilst our radio guys have given the masses a BBC-like experience! **What's a typical night out?** One of the union bars and then either Oceana – dance/indie/RandB – or Sin City – rock/pop/indie. **And how much does it cost?** Cheap as chips – excellent student deals with the clubs, as we went into partnership. **How can you get home safely?** Dead easy with numerous taxis. Swansea isn't too big either so off-campus students can walk home extremely safely.

Money

Is it an expensive place to live? If you're reasonable it can go far but it does depend. Far too many events = £0.00! **Average price of a pint?** Our union £1.60. Town £2 (weekend £2.50). **And the price of a takeaway?** Very reasonable and Indian food is incredible and very competitive. **What's the part-time work situation?** Loads of jobs in the locality, particularly on the campus. The careers centre is great. You do have to get stuck in quick as the jobs go quickly.

Summary

What's the best feature about the place? The location! It's amazing how you can cross the road and be on one of the best beaches in the country. **And the worst?** The rain! It's seems to rain far too much but you do appreciate the sunshine more! **And to sum it all up?** Swansea is based in one of the best locations in the country, but its jewel is its students, who are the most welcoming, friendly people!

Past students: Donald Anderson MP; Gwynne Howell (opera singer); Mavis Nicholson, Alun Richards (authors); Ian Bone (founder of Class War); Nigel Evans MP; half of Manic Street Preachers; Paul Thorburn, Robert Howley (rugby players); Daniel Caines (athlete); Terry Matthews (billionaire); David Edwards (*Who Wants To Be A Millionaire* winner). **More info?** Contact union administrator on 01792 295466, email administrator@swansea-union.co.uk or visit the website (www.swansea-union.co.uk).

Teesside University

Location:
*north-east England
(map 2)*
**Single campus near
Middlesbrough town
centre; partner
colleges**

University of Teesside, Middlesbrough,
Tees Valley TS1 3BA
☎ Tel 01642 218121
🖷 Fax 01642 342067
✉ Email registry@tees.ac.uk
💻 Website www.tees.ac.uk

*Student enquiries: Admissions Officer, Academic Registry
Applications: UCAS*

In brief

Total Students: 22,660

2% FE Students
12% postgraduate
86% undergraduate

Undergraduates: 19,610
43% full-time ● ● 88% UK students
38% mature ● ● 48% lower
on entry ● ● socio-economic
groups

57% female   43% male

- **A modern university.**
- **Teaching staff:** 821 (including research staff).
- **Broad study areas:** Animation, games and visualisation; art and design, performing arts and music; business, accounting and marketing; computing; engineering; English and history; forensic science, criminology and law; health and social care; media and journalism; psychology; science, sustainability and the environment; social sciences; sport, exercise and leisure; web and multimedia.

Freshers

- **Admissions information:** AS-levels and Key Skills considered in addition to 2+ A-levels or equivalent. UCAS tariff used for offers where appropriate.
- **First degree entrants:** 2275 UK, full-time.
- **Points on entry:** 268 (average).
- **Drop-out rate:** 11% in 1st year.
- **Accommodation:** All 1st years guaranteed accommodation if Teesside is first (firm) choice.

Profile

Institution
Founded: 1969 as Teesside Polytechnic (from Constantine College founded in 1930); university status in 1992. **Site:** 1 main site near Middlesbrough town centre. **How to get there:** Bus and railway stations nearby; by road A19 and A66 (1 mile from Middlesbrough); Durham Tees Valley Airport.

Courses
Academic features: Many courses have links with industry, accreditation by professional bodies and work placements (UK and overseas). Strong record of graduate employment. **Awarding body:** University of Teesside. **Main undergraduate awards:** BA, BSc, BEng, LLB, FdA, FdEng, FdSc, FdSocSci, FdTech. **Length of courses:** 3 years; 4 years (sandwich); 2 years (Fd).

Study opportunities & careers

Library and information services: Learning resource centre (LRC): 384,223 books plus 17,266 journals (of which 15,466 electronic), 1300+ study places, video/DVD machines, wireless capability, etc. Access to online information off-campus. Annual information provision spend, £82 per student (FTE). 2090 computer workstations across the campus with internet access; ratio 1:7 workstations to students. LRC facilities open 96 hours/week in term time. Information skills training available for new students. **Other learning resources:** Projection-based auditoriums with virtual reality facilities; digital TV studio; purpose-built convergent newsroom; 30-room crime scene house, 10-vehicle examination laboratory, digital evidence laboratory, forensic laboratories; court room; health and social care laboratory space (dedicated areas that simulate, eg, intensive therapy, AandE units). **Study abroad:** Students can study abroad for up to 1 year in Europe or the USA, as integral part of some courses. **Careers:** Information, advice and guidance on careers, vacancies, jobs and further courses. Resources include magazines, DVDs, journals, and employer and occupational files.

Student services & facilities

Student advice and services: Advice on student health, finance, disabilities and international student matters; accommodation and counselling services, chaplains. Residential and other facilities for disabled students. 66-place nursery (enquire when applying). **Amenities:** Job centre, bookshop, media centre, TV and film archive, sport and recreation facilities. SU bar, café, club venue, shop, advice centre, clubs and societies. **Sporting facilities:** Sports centre includes 500-spectator sports hall, squash courts, sports and exercise labs, temperature-controlled environmental chamber, floodlit artificial pitch. Second centre with sports hall, gym, sauna. Also playing fields. **Accommodation:** All 1st years guaranteed accommodation if university is first choice – on campus or within easy walking distance. 1198 self-catering places in university-owned or managed halls, houses and flats. Rents in halls £63.50–£70 pw (£43 pw shared); 37-week contracts. Rents in managed housing scheme £37–£42 plus bills, 38-week contracts. Private accommodation locally approx £35–£50 pw.

Money

Living expenses budget: Minimum budget of £5k pa (excluding tuition fees) recommended by university. **Term-time work:** Job centre, run by SU, helps find part-time work. Term-time work available on campus in SU, library and information services, student services. **Financial help:** Bursaries of £1025 pa for UK students whose family income is up to £25k. 200 scholarships of £1k pa for academic attainment, 200 subject-based scholarships; bursaries of approx £1500 for international students paying their own fees. Also approx £700k access to learning funds, awards of £50–£3500. Special help for student parents, students with disabilities and mature students. Apply to student funding team for help. **Tuition fees:** Home students pay £3225 pa for first degrees. International students pay £8k pa (classroom), £8500 (lab-based) – fees are fixed for the whole course.

Student view — Mark Gillespie, Student Newspaper Editor (Graduate, Media Studies)

Living
What's it like as a place to live? Middlesbrough is a good place to live – close to town from campus and close to the nightlife. **How's the student accommodation?** Here the accommodation is reasonably good. **What's the student population like?** Friendly and diverse. **How do students and locals get on?** It could be much better but each leaves the other to their own devices.

Studying
What's it like as a place to study? A mix of traditional and non-traditional courses give a good variety of options. **What are the teaching staff like?** Interested in student matters.

Socialising

What are student societies like? A wide range of activities. Clubs and societies give our students every option to become involved. **What's a typical night out?** Union, bars, club, house party! **And how much does it cost?** £20–£25. **How can you get home safely?** Easily via taxi or walking home in a group.

Money

Is it an expensive place to live? All students are skint. **Average price of a pint?** £2, or £1.80 in the student bars. **And the price of a takeaway?** £3.50. **What's the part-time work situation?** The SU has a job centre to aid students who seek part-time work.

Summary

What's the best feature about the place? The university campus and union. **And the worst?** Beyond the train station – non-student land! **And to sum it all up?** M'boro is a great place for students, with a wide range of stuff to do plus a brilliant union; you're guaranteed have a good time here!

Past students: David Bowe MEP, Stephen Hughes MEP. **More info?** Visit the SU website (www.utsu.org.uk).

Thames Valley University

Location:
west of London, 3 sites (maps 2 and 3) **Sites in Brentford, Ealing, Reading and Slough; partner colleges**

Thames Valley University, St Mary's Road, Ealing, London W5 5RF
☎ Tel 0800 036 8888
✉ Email learning.advice@tvu.ac.uk
🖥 Website www.tvu.ac.uk

Student enquiries: Learning advice centres on each campus
Applications: UCAS

In brief

Total Students: 47,430

60% FE Students
4% postgraduate
36% undergraduate

Undergraduates: 17,200
52% full-time
62% mature on entry
85% UK students
40% lower socio-economic groups

65% female 35% male

- **A modern university.**
- **Teaching staff:** 340 full-time, 370 part-time.
- **Broad study areas:** Accounting, business and finance; art and design; computing and IT; construction and engineering; health, sports and exercise sciences; human and forensic sciences; law and criminology; media; music and performance; nursing and midwifery; psychology; tourism, hospitality and leisure.

Freshers

- **Admissions information:** AS-levels and Key Skills awards accepted in combination with 1+ A-level (GCE or VCE) or equivalent. UCAS tariff used.
- **First degree entrants:** 1630 UK, full-time.
- **Points on entry:** 165+ (average).

- **Drop-out rate:** 15% in 1st year.
- **Accommodation:** All 1st years housed if apply by deadline.

Profile

Institution

Founded: University status in 1992. West London Poly (1991), incorporating London College of Music, Ealing College, Queen Charlotte's College of Health Care Studies, Thames Valley College and (2004) Reading College and School of Arts and Design. **Site:** 4 sites: at Ealing and Brentford (both in west London), Slough (17 miles west from Ealing) and Reading (20 miles from Slough). **How to get there:** A4, M4 and A40; Slough and Reading sites close to bus and rail stations; Ealing and Brentford campuses near rail, tube and buses. Free mini-bus between sites.

Courses

Academic features: Modular scheme gives flexibility to all degree courses: specialist and major/minor subject combinations available. **Awarding body:** Thames Valley University. **Main undergraduate awards:** BA, BMus, BSc, LLB, FdA, FdSc. **Length of courses:** 3 years; 4 years (sandwich courses, year abroad); 2 years (FdA/Sc).

Study opportunities & careers

Library and information services: Learning resource centres at both sites: 270,000 volumes, 2000 periodical titles, 770 study places. Information provision, £46 pa spent for each student (FTE). Library and IT services converged. Total 550+ networked PCs with access to internet and CD-ROM network, open 24 hours/day. Ratio 1:14 workstations to students. IT support from dedicated staff members; 1/2 day induction to library and information services for new students; IT skills training online. **Study abroad:** Language and other students may spend a period abroad. Formal exchange links with 64 universities/colleges in western Europe. **Careers:** Information and advice service.

Student services & facilities

Student advice and services: Student services provides medical, counselling and welfare services. **Amenities:** Well-equipped SU. **Sporting facilities:** State-of-the-art fitness centre at Slough, small fitness suite at Ealing. **Accommodation:** All students housed if they apply by the deadline, in university halls or private accommodation. 810 ensuite places in halls at Brentford for 1st-year students, rent £113 pw (including bills and internet access), £159 pw for studio, contracts 44 or 52 weeks; 72 places at Reading, rent £89 pw (including bills and internet access), 40-week contracts. Accommodation service helps find local flats and lodgings 3–4 miles from campus, rent £70–£165 pw. Many students live locally.

Money

Living expenses budget: Minimum budget of £6930–£8k for academic year (£770 a month) recommended by university (excluding tuition fees); amount depends on campus. **Term-time work:** University allows term-time work for full-time students (limit of 15 hours pw). University employs students where possible (in and out of term), eg library, admin, design, telemarketing, etc.; university employment services helps find work locally. **Financial help:** Bursaries of £1030 pa for UK students whose family income is up to £25k; of £515 pa for students whose family income is £25k–£40k. Some scholarships for specific courses after the 1st year. Also £1.2 million government funds, 750 students helped (awards £100–£3500); priority groups include single parents, care leavers, disabled students and those experiencing exceptional financial hardship. £23k learner support (childcare), 27 students helped. Apply to student services for help (tel 020 8231 2573, email student.services@tvu.ac.uk). **Tuition fees:**

Home students pay £3225 pa for first degree courses. International students pay £7600 pa (classroom-based), £8900 pa (lab/studio-based).

Student view

Main campuses in Ealing (on the west side of London), Slough (17 miles to the west along the M4) and Reading (some 20 miles further west again); some teaching and new halls are at Brentford (close to Ealing). Ealing campus is 30 mins from Central London by tube (easy walking distance to Ealing Broadway and South Ealing stations). Slough campus is next to town centre, 2 mins' walk from the station. Good train and bus links and free inter-site minibus. Reading campus is a 5-min walk from the centre of town and a 10-min bus journey from the station. Friendly atmosphere, avoiding the impersonality of larger institutions. Wide range of extremely vocational courses, non-degree as well as degree. Lively, effective SU. Slough has an excellent gym. Ealing has a shop, cashpoints, games room, ents venue (Lawrence Hall) and bar; new atrium with shops and food court. All 3 campuses have an SU centre. SU runs wide range of social events and supports a number of clubs: standard sporting, cultural, social and political groups, ethnic groups (Afro-Caribbean, Asian, etc.). Also provides welfare and advice service to deal with problems (financial, legal, academic, etc.); confidential counselling service. New halls at Paragon development in Brentford; local rent high so many students commute from other parts of London. Good facilities for students with disabilities. Diverse range of students from many backgrounds. Student-driven university, innovative courses, sandwich years, opportunities to be involved with policy and decision-making processes. Free SU handbooks to all students and acclaimed SU mag – *The Valley* – produced termly, by and for students.

Student footnotes

Housing: Some halls now. Uni helps find local accommodation (publishes housing list); look on noticeboards on campuses and SUs; student-friendly estate agents. **Eats:** SU offers cheap range. Student discounts in some restaurants, eg Minsky's Diner (American-style in Ealing Broadway). Rose and Crown and Tandoori Villa good local places. **Drink:** Student bar cheaper than local pubs. Easy reach of trendy London clubs. **Nightlife:** Wide range of SU-based events – discos, live bands (including student bands from LCMM), bhangra, karaoke, club nights, jazz, theme nights, etc. SU and local club, Broadway Boulevard (weekly student night). Local cinemas and arts centre (Watermans); easy access to central London for theatre, clubs, films, etc. Close to Wembley and Twickenham. **Sports:** Student discounts at some centres, eg Gurnell swimming pool, Ealing squash courts, Brent Valley golf. **Hardship fund:** Access funds; financial advice team. **Jobs:** SU and university employ students (eg shops, bars). University job agency helps find work locally (part-time in term, full-time out of term). **Informal name:** TVU. **Best features:** Proximity to centre of London. **And worst:** Split site. **Past students:** Freddie Mercury (Queen frontman); Pete Townsend (the Who); John Bird (founder, *The Big Issue*); David Caddick (musical director, RSC); Martin Ellerby, Andrew Simpson (composers); Raphael Terroni (pianist); John Treleaven, Rosalind Sutherland (singers); Matt Tong (drummer, Bloc Party). **More info?** Ring SU on 020 8231 2726 or visit website (www.tvusu.co.uk).

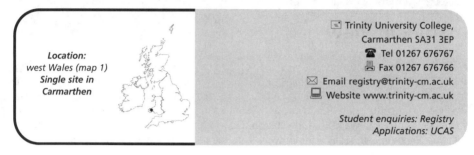

Trinity College Carmarthen

Location:
west Wales (map 1)
Single site in
Carmarthen

🖃 Trinity University College,
Carmarthen SA31 3EP
☎ Tel 01267 676767
🖷 Fax 01267 676766
✉ Email registry@trinity-cm.ac.uk
💻 Website www.trinity-cm.ac.uk

Student enquiries: Registry
Applications: UCAS

In brief

Total Students: 2390

12% postgraduate
88% undergraduate

Undergraduates: 2095
60% full-time | 89% UK students
27% mature on entry | 41% lower socio-economic groups

78% female | 22% male

- **College of higher education**, a constituent member of Wales University.
- **Teaching staff:** 86 full-time.
- **Broad study areas:** Creative arts and humanities; computing, business and IT; education and social inclusion; sport, health and outdoor education; teaching; theatre and performance; theology and religion; tourism.

Freshers

- **Admissions information:** AS-levels and Key Skills awards accepted in combination with 2+ A-levels or equivalent. UCAS tariff used.
- **First degree entrants:** 400 UK, full-time.
- **Points on entry:** 160+ (average).
- **Drop-out rate:** 11% in 1st year.
- **Accommodation:** All 1st years housed.

Profile

Institution

Founded: 1848, Church voluntary college; university college status in 2009. **Structural features:** Associate college of Wales University. **Site:** On outskirts of market town of Carmarthen, within easy reach of the Pembrokeshire and Brecon Beacons national parks. **How to get there:** Mainline rail and coach services from Swansea, Cardiff, Bristol, London. Close to M4 and A40. Ferries from Ireland to Fishguard, Pembroke and Swansea, airports at Swansea and Cardiff. **Special features:** Bilingual college. 35 US students in college and growing international community.

Courses 📖

Awarding body: University of Wales. **Main undergraduate awards:** BA(Ed), BA, BSc. **Length of courses:** 3 years.

Study opportunities & careers

Library and information services: Library with 116,000 volumes, 410 periodicals, 140 study places. Information provision, £69 pa spent for each student (FTE). Ratio of workstations to students 1:12 (IT facilities open 18 hours/day). All 350 computers have access to internet and library; wireless network. IT support staff 8 hours/weekday. Handbook and induction course to library and information services for new students; IT skills courses. **Other learning resources:** Modernised language and media labs; modern theatre; video conferencing facilities; screening room; broadcast suite. **Study abroad:** Opportunities to study in the USA, and in Europe funded by Erasmus. Formal exchange links with Eire, Italy, Netherlands, Austria, the USA and Spain. **Careers:** Guidance given.

Student services & facilities

Student advice and services: Counselling, study support, support with other specific needs. **Amenities:** Self-service restaurant, theatre, refurbished SU. **Sporting facilities:** Sports hall; indoor swimming pool; gyms; weights room; playing fields; multi-purpose floodlit all-weather playing surfaces; strong rugby tradition. **Accommodation:** Most 1st-year students in catered halls on campus, £90 pw (2 meals per day); self-catering college accommodation thereafter, £72 pw. Privately owned accommodation locally, £35–£50 pw.

Money

Living expenses budget: Minimum budget of £5k pa (excluding tuition fees) recommended by college. **Term-time work:** Work available in SU and conference centre. **Financial help:** Various bursaries eg for students from low-income families, those applying from FE colleges and those studying in Welsh. Also some subject scholarships of £600 pa, Also £81k financial contingency fund. **Tuition fees:** Home students pay £3225 pa for first degrees (though Welsh residents may be eligible for annual fee grant). International students pay £6500 pa.

Student view

A bilingual (English/Welsh) college in west Wales, set on the outskirts of the active, attractive market town of Carmarthen. It is surrounded by beautiful countryside, perfect for everything outdoors, with beaches, mountains, rivers and castles. Swansea, with its city life, is within range (about ½ hour). Founded for teacher training but now offers a wide range of courses, attracting students of all ages and backgrounds – from all parts of Britain, although there are also Irish, American, Canadian and European students. 3 halls of residence on campus offer both catered (good-quality food) and self-catering accommodation; cheap housing can also be found in town. A good place for sport with a strong rugby tradition, good facilities and some excellent teams. SU offers a wide range of active societies, excellent bar prices, regular discos, events and a good venue for touring bands. The college chapel holds daily voluntary religious services and there are very good welfare facilities. Being a small college, it is very friendly, a place where everyone knows everyone. To most, it soon becomes a home from home.

Student footnotes

Housing: Campus hostels generally good. Look on noticeboards, ask accommodation officer about private rentals. **Eats:** Good but pricey on campus (meal from £1.50). Takeaways, pub food, Indian, Chinese, etc. in town (£5–£15). **Drink:** £1.90 a pint in SU bar. Plenty of friendly pubs in town, often with specials nights (beer £1 a pint). **Nightlife:** SU has best ents at TTIC Bar and UNITY nightclub; regular discos, touring bands and DJs. Some 60 pubs and a cinema in town; limited clubs: Club Metro, Savannavis, Waterside. Can get SU transport to Swansea for nights out. **Locals:** Friendly.

Sports: Good sports facilities on campus, fitness centre, swimming pool, AstroTurf; sports fields a short distance away, good local leisure centre. **Travel:** Railway station and buses. **Financial help:** Money doctors, very popular access fund – best to apply early. **Jobs:** Some jobs on campus; plenty in town. Union jobshop and Go Wales. **Best features:** Very friendly; good social life. **And worst:** We all have to leave some day. **Past students:** Barry John, Carwyn James (Welsh international rugby players). **More info?** Contact SU on 01267 237794 or email supresident@trinity-cm.ac.uk.

Trinity College of Music

> Location:
> south-east London
> (map 3)
> Single site in
> Greenwich

🖂 Trinity College of Music, King Charles Court,
Old Royal Naval College, Greenwich, London SE10 9JF
☎ Tel 020 8305 4444
🖷 Fax 020 8305 9444
✉ Email admissions@tcm.ac.uk
💻 Website www.tcm.ac.uk

Student enquiries: Admissions Coordinator
(tel 020 8305 4402/5)
Applications: CUKAS

In brief

Total Students: 750

25% postgraduate
75% undergraduate

Undergraduates: 560
100% full-time ● ● 70% UK students
15% mature on entry ●

60% female | 40% male

- **Specialist music school.**
- **Teaching staff:** 18 full-time, 200 part-time.
- **Broad study areas:** Music performance and related subjects.

Freshers
- **First degree entrants:** 135 UK, full-time.
- **Drop-out rate:** 10% in 1st year.
- **Accommodation:** All 1st years housed.

Profile

Institution
Founded: 1872 (in Marylebone; moved to Greenwich, in 2001). **Structural features:** Merged with Laban in 2005 to form Trinity Laban – the UK's only conservatoire for music and dance. **Site:** Greenwich Old Royal Naval College. **How to get there:** DLR to Cutty Sark station; trains to Greenwich from London Bridge, Charing Cross and Waterloo East; by road via M25, A2, A20 and South Circular; by riverboat to Greenwich Pier; by air to London City Airport or Gatwick; on many bus routes.

Courses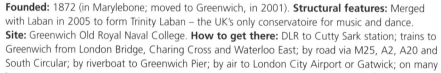
Academic features: Professional studies, musicianship, communication and teaching skills, contextual studies. BMus in Indian music; MMus in performance; specialist short courses. Trains musicians for a variety of careers in music. **Awarding bodies:** University of Westminster. **Main undergraduate awards:** BMus. **Length of courses:** 4 years; 1 year (PG/MMus).

Study opportunities & careers

Library and information services: 40,000 volumes, 60 periodicals, 50 study places. Specialist collections: CYM collection; Barbirolli collection of scores; Almeida collection of conducting scores; special instrument collection; Mander and Mitchenson theatre collection. Information provision, £47 pa spent for each student (FTE). Library and IT services converged. Ratio of workstations to students 1:10. Access to internet from 14 computers, library also online. IT facilities open 10+ hours/day, part-time consultant and library staff give IT support; handbook and induction programme to library and information services for new students; word and music-processing skills training within undergraduate courses. **Other learning resources:** Recording studio, video conferencing suite. **Careers:** Information, advice and placement.

Student services & facilities

Student advice and services: Doctor, psychiatrist, physiotherapist, welfare officer, international student affairs officer, Alexander Technique counsellor, career adviser. **Accommodation:** All 1st years housed in student village (15 mins' walk, joint with Greenwich University), rent from £99 pw, 40-week contract. Privately owned accommodation locally, rent £70–£95 pw for self-catering.

Money

Living expenses budget: Minimum budget of £7750–£10k pa (excluding tuition fees) recommended by College. **Term-time work:** College allows part-time work. Some work available in college, eg helping with auditions and examinations, library, setting up equipment. External engagements organised for chamber groups. **Financial help:** Bursaries of £1k pa for UK students whose family income is up to £25k, tapering down to £300 pa bursary where family income is £55k–£60k. Some scholarships (variable value). **Tuition fees:** Home students pay £3225 pa for first degrees. International students pay £12,950 pa.

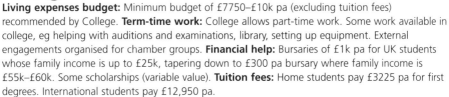

Student view

It's a small, friendly college with around 600 students studying all aspects of music, from jazz to church music, baroque to popular. A long history of musical education, having pioneered practical music exams from 1879, and introducing the first junior department to a conservatoire. Most students are British nationals but also a strong international contingent. Set in the Old Royal Naval College in Greenwich, a world heritage site and a fantastic venue in which to study. Brilliant new facilities, including over 80 practice rooms, keyboard lab, recording studio and a chill-out area in the basement. SU has always and continues to have a very good relationship with the staff and is proactive for its students, in a lively and social environment.

Student footnotes

Housing: New halls 5 mins' walk; others a bus ride away. Accommodation relatively cheap and easy to find in Greenwich area. **Eats:** College canteen, many inexpensive restaurants, pubs and cafés. **Drink:** Many pubs close by; many give student offers throughout the week. **Nightlife:** Regular SU parties in Greenwich and closer to town. **Sports:** Active SU arrangements for football, hockey, basketball, tennis and a local gym with student rates. **Travel:** Easy to travel into town via DLR, bus or train (10–20 mins). Excellent night bus services. **Financial help:** Good, with a supportive SU committee and warden. **Jobs:** Some part-time work in college, private teaching, gigs and bar work easy to find. **Best features:** Small, family-like atmosphere. **And worst:** Noise from film crews on location. **Informal name:** Trinity/TCM. **Past students:** Katrina Karneus (singer); Sir John Barbirolli,

Barry Wordsworth (conductors); Mike Dixon (*Pop Idol* coach); Sir John Taverner (composer); John Powell (film composer).

Trinity Laban

Location:
south-east London
2 affiliated colleges

▭ Trinity Laban, King Charles Court,
Old Royal Naval College, Greenwich, London SE10 9JF
☎ Tel 020 8305 4444
✉ Email info@trinitylaban.ac.uk
💻 Website www.trinitylaban.ac.uk

Student enquiries and application: to
constituent colleges

In brief

Total Students: 830

27% postgraduate
72% undergraduate

Undergraduates: 600
100% full-time ● ● 76% UK students
17% mature ● ● 15% lower
on entry ● ● socio-economic
groups

59% female 41% male

- **Specialist music and dance conservatoire**, incorporating Laban and Trinity College of Music.
- **Teaching staff:** 265 full-time and part-time.
- **Broad study areas:** Music performance and contemporary dance.

Freshers
- **First degree entrants:** 130 UK, full-time.
- **Drop-out rate:** 5% in 1st year.

Profile

Founded: 2005, from merger of Laban and Trinity College of Music. (You can look up both separately). **Special features:** The UK's only conservatoire for music and dance. Specialist education reflecting the increasingly collective world of artistic practice.

UCLan

Location:
north-west England
(map 2)
Main campus at
Preston; partner
colleges

▭ University of Central Lancashire,
Preston PR1 2HE
☎ Tel 01772 201201
📠 Fax 01772 892935
✉ Email cenquiries@uclan.ac.uk
💻 Website www.uclan.ac.uk

Student enquiries: Admissions Office
Applications: UCAS

In brief

Total Students: 29,845

15% postgraduate
85% undergraduate

Undergraduates: 25,415
61% full-time   95% UK students
33% mature   38% lower
on entry   socio-economic
groups

60% female   40% male

- **A modern university.**
- **Teaching staff:** 887 full-time, 224 part-time.
- **Broad study areas:** Business; cultural, legal and social studies; sciences; art, design and technology; health.

Freshers

- **Admissions information:** AS-levels accepted in combination with 2+ A-levels or equivalent.
- **First degree entrants:** 3845 UK, full-time.
- **Points on entry:** 200+ (average).
- **Drop-out rate:** 14% in 1st year.
- **Accommodation:** All 1st years guaranteed accommodation.

Profile

Institution

Founded: 1973 as Preston Poly; university status in 1992. **Site:** City centre campus in Preston. Also partner colleges and outdoor sports centre in North Wales. **How to get there:** National coach and rail services and close to M6. For university, 10-min walk from rail and bus stations; junction 31 from M6 south, junction 32 from north onto M55 then onto A6, then follow signs to university.

Courses

Academic features: Courses include fashion promotion, performing arts and journalism. Modular credit accumulation and transfer scheme throughout. **Awarding body:** University of Central Lancashire. **Main undergraduate awards:** BA, BSc, BEng. **Length of courses:** 3 years; 4 years (sandwich).

Study opportunities & careers

Library and information services: 7 libraries throughout Lancashire: 600,000 volumes, 3000 journals, 36,000 e-books, 26,000 e-journals; 1500 study places (group and individual); new learning zone; key resources collection, slide collection, audio-visual collection. Access all year round, 24/7 in term time; self-service issue and return. Also access to Lancashire county libraries. Specialist collections: Preston Incorporated Law Society Library; collection of illustrated books, local history and the Livesey and Wainwright collections. Information provision, £70 pa spent for each student (FTE). IT and library services converged. 520 PCs in library, with access to library resources and internet; 100 laptops for loan and use in library. Tours of the library, induction sessions, basic and advanced information literacy skills training, web- and paper-based support materials. Dedicated library and IT support, including roving helpers and help from support desk, or by telephone or email. **Study abroad:** Approx. 80 students pa spend a period abroad as part of course. Exchange programmes in the USA, China, Australia, Mexico and formal exchange links with 120+ European universities and colleges; opportunities for work placements overseas. **Careers:** Information officer; advice and placement service.

Student services & facilities

Student advice and services: Integrated student services including academic and careers advice, personal counselling, disability support, financial guidance. Health centre (including GPs, sports injuries, family planning). Multi-faith centre with representatives of most of major world faiths; Muslim prayer room. Pre-school centre for 70 children (6 months–5 years). **Amenities:** Arts centre, observatories, bookshop, SU with shops and bank, conference facilities, catering service. Shopping centres, cinemas and theatre in town. **Sporting facilities:** Sports centre with human performance laboratory, outdoor/indoor multi-sport complex (membership £80 pa). Preston Sports Arena, Lake District and Yorkshire Dales for outdoor pursuits. **Accommodation:** All 1st years guaranteed a place in university-owned or registered accommodation. 2000 self-catering places in flats for 1st-year students: £79 pw (up to £81 ensuite), all 42-week contracts Sept–June. Most students live in privately owned accommodation for 2+ years, ranging from places in large halls to shared houses, rent £50–£80 pw.

Money 🔮

Living expenses budget: Minimum budget of £6500 pa (excluding tuition fees) recommended by university. **Term-time work:** University allows term-time work for full-time first-degree students (30% believed to work); work available in library and SU. Campus Job Shop (The Bridge). **Financial help:** Bursaries of £310 pa for UK students on the full maintenance grant (ie family income of up to approx £25k). Also achievement grants for good performance; funding eg for work-related projects, overseas study trips; sport scholarships (£4k over the length of the course); and some music scholarships. Access to learning fund for home students with shortfall between income and expenditure or in unexpected hardship; priority groups include students with dependants, those with disabilities and final-year students. Loans for those in unexpected difficulties. Apply to Student Services for help. **Tuition fees:** Home students pay £3225 pa for first degrees. International students pay £8950 pa (classroom-based), £9450 (lab/studio-based).

Student view

It's a modern university with a 175-year heritage. It's large and one of the cheapest places to be a student. City Campus is about 5 mins' walk from Preston centre; newly built with fabulous facilities – a development mirrored in Preston, one of England's newest cities. University library open 24/7 in term-time, with loads of PCs, numerous study rooms and an internet café. Good transport in the area (though not needed often as most students live within 10 mins' walk). SU runs free, nightly safety buses from union (every 15 mins from 6pm to 2.30am); it also operates a scheme with a local taxi firm (so if you haven't any money, you can leave your NUS card with the driver and pay the union when you collect it). University student services and union's advice centre both give advice on managing your finances; hardship funds are available where necessary. Trendy courses include forensic science, games design, new music and media; or, for the adventurous, ecotourism and environmental management (field trips to Kenya) and motor sports (you can construct and race your own formula Ford vehicles); well-known for journalism, forensic science and fire safety engineering. Successful exchange programme (many students go to, eg, America, Australia, Europe) and many spend time in industry (on 4-year sandwich degrees). Assessment tends to be a mixture of course work and examinations; also presentations, producing exhibition work (especially on art and design courses) or laboratory logs. All courses modular, so usually straightforward to change course within a subject area. Students from all over the country, and many from partner institutions around the world; also lots of mature students – all catered for. University and the SU are working on improving the student experience and reducing drop-out rates (eg preparatory summer schools, student mentoring, structured induction programme, advice centre for new students). SU is the focal point for ents and services: it has a student bar (Source), a venue (53 Degrees), food outlets (Atrium), student shop (Essentials), advice centre, employment agency and 75+ sports clubs and societies. All tastes catered for, so whatever you're into, you can find it! Lots of good-quality housing, from traditional university-owned halls and cluster flats (some ensuite) to terraced houses shared with other students. Preston has a varied social scene, catering for everyone: bars and clubs, from alternative rock and thrash to trendy cocktail bars and cheesy student nights (usually student offers and friendly atmosphere); multi-screen cinemas, bowling and huge choice of restaurants. Also meetings of sports teams and societies and SU events such as the hugely popular Comedy Club (which attracts top acts).

Student footnotes

Housing: Housing relatively cheap and close to campus. **Eats:** SU has a full range of food offered in both Source bar and the Atrium. Nearby there are loads of takeaways and restaurants offering student deals. **Drink:** SU bars reasonable with a good selection of cheap bitter/lager. Loads of local friendly pubs with good student deals; major chains (eg Scream and O'Neill's). **Nightlife:** SU events excellent; loads of clubs offering music (alternative, cheese, clubby); also Guildhall, Charter Theatre, cinemas (8- and 10-screen). **Sports:** 70 different clubs and societies. Excellent university sports complex; Preston Sports Arena, 10 mins from campus, has everything. **Travel:** Mainline rail and bus routes. **Financial help:** SU Advice Centre. **Jobs:** SU jobshop (The Bridge) helps find work. Jobs plentiful. **Best features:** Friendly close-knit community; fact that you can roll out of bed 15 mins before your lecture and still not be late! **Worst features:** Notoriously wet Preston weather (but don't worry, there is plenty to do indoors). **Past students:** Joe Lydon (rugby league international). **More info?** Contact the President on 01772 894865 or check out the website (www.uclansu.co.uk).

UHI Millennium Institute

Location:
north of Scotland
(map 1)
Many teaching
centres across Scottish
Highlands and Islands

UHI Millennium Institute, Executive Office, Ness Walk, Inverness IV3 5SQ
☎ Tel 01463 279000
🖷 Fax 01463 279001
✉ Email info@uhi.ac.uk
💻 Website www.uhi.ac.uk

Student enquiries: Course information line (tel 0845 272 3600)
Applications: UCAS

In brief

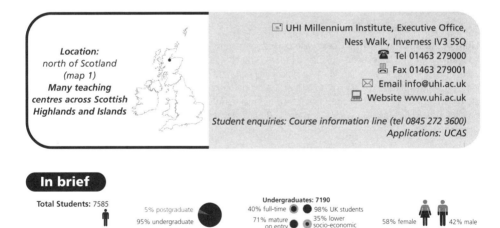

Total Students: 7585

5% postgraduate
95% undergraduate

Undergraduates: 7190
40% full-time ● ● 98% UK students
71% mature ● ● 35% lower
on entry socio-economic groups

58% female · 42% male

- **Modern, collegiate university**, the only higher education institution based in the highlands and islands of Scotland.
- **Teaching staff:** 485 full-time, 449 part-time.
- **Broad study areas:** Arts, culture and heritage, business and leisure, environment and natural systems sciences, health and social studies, information and engineering systems.

Freshers

- **Admissions information:** Standard entry requirements are 3 Highers or 2 A-levels, all at grade C, but prospective students without these are encouraged to apply.

- **First degree entrants:** 305 UK, full-time.
- **Drop-out rate:** 19% in 1st year.
- **Accommodation:** Some 1st-year students housed.

Profile

Institution

Founded: 2001. **Structural features:** 'Creating the University of the Highlands and Islands': 13 academic partner institutions and 1 research institution, plus many local learning centres (associated colleges, UHI learning centres) linked by UHI network throughout the Scottish highlands and islands. **Site:** Separate sites spread across the region. Learning centres in Arran, Bara, Bute, Harris, Islay, Lewis, Mull, Skye, Tiree, Orkney, Shetland, Uist and many mainland centres. Some sites in cities, some in small towns, some in villages. **Special features:** Aim is to reach high university standards but also to play a broader role in the educational, economic, social and cultural development of the region.

Courses

Academic features: Courses delivered at individual academic partner institutions and by distance learning, partly via UHI-linked materials, tutorials, video-conferencing and seminars. Not a virtual university but made up of real people in real buildings in real places. Teaching is in English (except Gaelic-related courses, which are taught in Gaelic). **Awarding body:** UHI Millennium Institute (some postgraduate degrees awarded by universities of Aberdeen and Strathclyde). **Main undergraduate awards:** BA, BSc, BEng. **Length of courses:** 3 years (ordinary degrees), 4 years (Hons).

Study opportunities

Library and information services: Each partner college offering taught courses has a library, computer suite with internet access, study rooms and video-conferencing facilities. Every student has access to email and internet facilities and technical help and support in all large colleges and local learning centres. Students can link to UHI academic partners from their local learning centre, with the aid of, eg, email contact with tutors, video-conferencing, internet access to library resources and online journals. Resources available at other UHI partners can be requested through the inter-site loan system.

Student services & facilities 👫

Student advice and services: Most partner colleges have a café/refreshments; several a student shop, recreation area/sports facilities, several have crèches. Most have student guidance and counselling and many have a careers office. **Students' Association:** UHISA aims to bring together people with common interests through the UHI information and ICT network but also runs face-to-face events, eg band competitions, tours and musical performances (see website at www.uhisa.org.uk). Also keen to promote sport within UHI through inter-site competitions, eg 5-a-side football championship; its athletics club competes in the Scottish university league. Diving, shinty, surfing, skiing and snowboarding clubs are planned. **Accommodation:** On-site halls of residence at 3 partner colleges. Others provide lists of local lodgings or private rented accommodation; some international students prefer to stay with host families.

Money 💰

Tuition fees: Scottish and EU students pay no fees during their course; other UK students pay £1820 pa for full-time first degrees. International students pay £6410 (arts), £7565 (science); fee is fixed for the duration of the course.

Ulster University

Location:
Northern Ireland
(map 1)
4 campuses across the province

🖳 University of Ulster, Cromore Road, Coleraine,
County Londonderry, Northern Ireland BT52 1SA
☎ Tel 028 7034 4141
✉ Email online@ulster.ac.uk
💻 Website www.ulster.ac.uk

Student enquiries: Registry Offices
Applications: UCAS (direct for part-time)

In brief

Total Students: 23,580

19% postgraduate
81% undergraduate

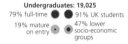
Undergraduates: 19,025
79% full-time ● ● 91% UK students
19% mature ● ● 47% lower
on entry socio-economic groups

59% female ● ● 41% male

- **Research-intensive university.**
- **Teaching staff:** 3400 full-time and part-time.
- **Broad study areas:** Art and design, business and management, computing and multimedia, engineering and built environment, informatics, life and health sciences, humanities, social sciences.

Freshers
- **Admissions information:** UCAS tariff used. Individual course requirements differ (see website).
- **First degree entrants:** 4755 UK, full-time.
- **Points on entry:** 291 (average).
- **Drop-out rate:** 15% in 1st year.
- **Accommodation:** Accommodation guaranteed for 1st years who apply by the deadline.

Profile

Institution
Founded: 1984, from merger of New University of Ulster and Ulster Polytechnic. **Site:** 4 campuses: Main campuses at Jordanstown (7 miles NE of Belfast) and Coleraine (on north coast, 50 miles north of Belfast). Also campuses in heart of Belfast and Magee in Londonderry. **How to get there:** All campuses have road and rail connections. Air and sea routes from mainland.

Courses
Academic features: New courses in architecture, marine science, criminology, marketing strategy and entrepreneurship, internet and communications engineering, property investment and development, leisure events and cultural management. **Awarding body:** University of Ulster. **Main undergraduate awards:** BA, BSc, BMus, BDes, BEng, MEng, LLB. **Length of courses:** 3 years; 4 years (eg sandwich; courses incl period abroad); 5 years (MEng).

Study opportunities & careers

Library and information services: Library on each site, main libraries at Coleraine and Jordanstown: 663,000 volumes, 3000 electronic books, 4600 periodicals, 1500 electronic journals. Information provision, £138 pa spent for each student (FTE). **Other learning resources:** Education technology unit; computer services; social skills training centre. **Study abroad:** Opportunities for study abroad and exchanges in universities/colleges in Europe (100+), the USA (140+), Hong Kong, Australia, Mexico and Canada, open to all students (knowledge of a language not required). Some dual awards available. **Careers:** Information, advice and guidance. Assistance with work experience and placements.

Student services & facilities

Student advice and services: Counsellors, psychologist, doctors, nurses, chaplains. Support for students with disabilities including adapted residences. Crèches (for under-5s) on all campuses. Joint universities deaf education centre (with Belfast University). **Amenities:** SU with extensive leisure facilities. **Sporting facilities:** Sports centres on Coleraine, Magee and Jordanstown sites with full facilities. **Accommodation:** 2300 campus places available (60% for 1st years): Coleraine, 400 places in on-campus halls, 405 off-campus, rent £60–£88 pw, £98 pw if sharing; Jordanstown, 700 on-campus, 170 off-campus, rent £47–£95 pw, £53 pw if sharing; Magee, 630 places, rent £51–£75 pw, £45 pw if sharing; many rooms ensuite and with telephone and internet connections. Students can apply for university-managed accommodation after the 1st year, or live in private sector; average rent £52 pw.

Money

Living expenses budget: Minimum budget of £5k for academic year (excluding tuition fees) recommended by university. **Living expenses budget:** Minimum budget of £125 pw (excluding tuition fees) recommended by university. **Financial help:** Bursaries of £1040 pa for students whose family income is up to £18,400, of £620 pa where it is £18,400–£21k, and of £310 where family income is £21k–£39,300. Scholarships for various subjects and for sports, of £250–£1500. Total available £190k government funds; £5500 endowment and other funds: special help for unanticipated need; crisis loans available, up to £50. **Tuition fees:** Home students pay £3225 pa for first degrees. International students pay £8540 pa.

Student view) Adrian Kelly, Site Vice-President, Coleraine

Living

What's it like as a place to live? Most students attending University of Ulster Coleraine tend to live in Portstewart after their 1st year. The halls are very responsible and provide great facilities for those students. Living in Portstewart is great also as there is a great community feeling in the student areas and the local community are very welcoming to the student population. **How's the student accommodation?** Uni accommodation is very nice and all amenities are available. It's also a great way of finding your feet before moving out of uni halls. Portstewart provides excellent standard of housing and is located close to the hub of student social life. It also has a great community feeling about the area. **What's the student population like?** The students come from a variety of locations and areas across the country and some internationals. Most students manage to hit the perfect balance between academic life and social life. Great community feeling amongst all students in the area. **How do students and locals get on?** Students generally live away from the main residential areas but, in general, students and the local population do get on very well. The SU sits on the local Portstewart Community Vision Group and liaises a lot with the locals and the local PSNI (police) officers.

Studying

What's it like as a place to study? It's a great place to study; the LRC (learning resource centre) is open to students 24/7 and staff are always very helpful. The facilities are great and readily available. Students generally have no problems in obtaining extensions on their work, providing there is a genuine reason. The relationship between students and staff is always relaxed also. **What are the teaching staff like?** Lecturers are always approachable and many are from either the UK or the Republic of Ireland. Some, in fact, used to study at the university themselves so can always relate to the students.

Socialising

What are student societies like? There are only a few nightclubs available in the area but this adds to the community feeling as most of the student population will always be in the same venue so people get to meet new individuals easier and quicker than in a big city. The SU hosts a disco every Monday night and also runs other forms of entertainment throughout the week. **What's a typical night out?** A typical night out would entail going round to a friend's house for a few drinks and meeting up with everyone else; music would always be on the go, with sometimes a DJ present. Students discuss the day's craic and the work load they have on, among other things. Then typically everybody heads to the Anchor or Kelly's around 11–11.30pm and enjoys their night. **And how much does it cost?** Generally costs as much as you want to spend. Typically £40 would cover taxis, admission and drinks easily. **How can you get home safely?** The local council runs a forum called Night Safe, where the area's licensees discuss issues including getting students home safe at night. Local taxis are always available and the local PSNI do regular patrols. With the community feeling amongst students, and the fact that our university is so small and most people know one another, everyone generally looks out for one another.

Money

Is it an expensive place to live? Generally it's not that expensive to live. However, with the price increase in oil and electricity, it is becoming harder for students to stretch their loans to cover each semester, so budgeting is essential. **Average price of a pint?** Union £2.30. Other areas £2.60. **And the price of a takeaway?** Not sure; depends what you're ordering. **What's the part-time work situation?** Jobs are hard to come by in the local area, as it is a small town that the students live in. Fortunately most students have weekend/part-time jobs back home at the weekends.

Summary

What's the best feature about the place? Its setting – students quite literally are only 5–10 mins from the beach. It's quieter than the cities, it's got plenty of green areas and has a nice feel about it. Any student who has come to this university will tell of its community feeling and relaxed atmosphere. **And the worst?** The building is quite old and dated-looking in places. **And to sum it all up?** Great feeling amongst students, who are close-knit and friendly; relaxed atmosphere to study in, with great lecturers who understand what you want from your degree.

Past students: Mark Robson (commentator), Kate Hoey MP, Brian Keenan (former hostage). **More info?** Ring SU President or Marketing Officer on 028 7032 4319, email president@ulst.ac.uk or visit the website (www.uusu.org).

University College Birmingham

Location:
Birmingham, West
Midlands (map 2)
Sites in city centre

University College Birmingham,
Summer Row, Birmingham B3 1JB
☎ Tel 0121 604 1000
✉ Email marketing@ucb.ac.uk
💻 Website www.ucb.ac.uk

Student enquiries: Marketing unit (tel 0121 693 5959)
Applications: UCAS (Admissions office for part-time
tel 0121 604 1040)

In brief

Total Students: 7135

45% FE Students
5% postgraduate
50% undergraduate

Undergraduates: 3480
74% full-time ● ● 68% UK students
31% mature ● ● 50% lower
on entry socio-economic
groups

70% female   30% male

- **Specialist college offering work-related courses.**
- **Teaching staff:** 197 full-time, 47 part-time
- **Broad study areas:** Business and marketing; childhood and education; hospitality, culinary arts food and retail management; recreation, sport and tourism; sports therapy and salon management; entertainment and events management.

Freshers

- **Admissions information:** Broad range of previous educational experience welcome.
- **First degree entrants:** 540 UK, full-time.
- **Points on entry:** 220 (average).
- **Drop-out rate:** 7% in 1st year.
- **Accommodation:** All 1st years housed who apply by deadline.

Profile

Institution

Founded: Late 19th century as a municipal technical school. **Structural features:** An accredited college of Birmingham University. **Site:** Heart of Birmingham's conference and hotel quarter, close to National Indoor Arena and Convention Centre. **How to get there:** By air, Birmingham International Airport (20 mins); by rail, Birmingham New Street station (few mins' walk); by road (M6/A38, M5/A46) into city centre. **Special features:** Specialist college offering full- and part-time HE and FE courses and work-related courses in food, tourism, hospitality, sports, marketing, salon management and early childhood studies. Many students progress from FE to HE.

Courses 📖

Academic features: Vocational course, industrial placements. Wide range of study possibilities through close relationship with Birmingham University and international tourism and hospitality industries. Broad range of previous educational experience welcome, including vocational qualifications; an effective route into higher education, particularly for mature students. **Awarding**

body: Birmingham University, University College Birmingham. **Main undergraduate awards:** FdA, FdSc, BA, BSc. **Length of courses:** 2 years (foundation), 3 years (Hons), 4 years (Hons with placement).

Study opportunities & careers

Library and information services: 72,000 books, 1000 journals, electronic database access from library or home. **Other learning resources:** Learning and skills development centre; spa health, beauty and fitness teaching centre; kitchens and restaurant facilities for teaching and use. **Careers:** Careers development centre and careers library.

Student services & facilities

Student advice and services: Counselling service, college nurse. **Amenities:** Guild of Students bar and 400 capacity venue. **Sporting facilities:** Own spa fitness club; sports hall at the Maltings Hall of Residence. **Accommodation:** All 1st years housed who apply by 31 August. 867 self-catering places in halls of residence, mainly for 1st years: rent £85 pw. Plentiful private accommodation locally, £60–£100 pw self-catering (plus bills). Help from Student Services Unit.

Money

Living expenses budget: Minimum budget of £6060 pa (excluding tuition fees) recommended by college. **Financial help:** College bursaries for full-time UK and EU full-time undergraduates: of £1050 pa for those whose family income is up to £25k; of £630 pa where it is £25k–£42,500; and £315 pa where it is £42,500–£60k. Bursary of £1575 pa for those on disabled students living allowance irrespective of family income. Limited number of scholarships. **Tuition fees:** Home students pay £3225 pa for first degrees (£1255 for Year 0). International students pay £7300 pa.

University College London

Location:
central London
(map 3)
Single site in
Bloomsbury

University College London,
Gower Street, London WC1E 6BT
☎ Tel 020 7679 2000
🖷 Fax 020 7679 7920
💻 Website www.ucl.ac.uk

Student enquiries: Study information centre
(tel 020 7679 3000, fax 020 7679 3001)
Applications: UCAS

In brief

Total Students: 20,170

40% postgraduate
60% undergraduate

Undergraduates: 12,155
98% full-time ● ● 71% UK students
16% mature ● ● 19% lower
on entry ● ● socio-economic
groups

52% female ⬤ ⬤ 48% male

- **World-class research-intensive institution**, a college of London University.
- **Teaching staff:** 4000+ full-time and part-time.
- **Broad study areas:** Mathematical and physical sciences, social and historical sciences, engineering sciences, life sciences, medicine, arts and humanities, built environment, law, Slavonic and Eastern European studies.

Freshers

- **Admissions information:** Minimum of 3 A-levels at grade B plus a pass in an additional AS-level, or equivalent international qualifications. UCAS tariff is not used.
- **First degree entrants:** 2480 UK, full-time.
- **Points on entry:** 440.
- **Drop-out rate:** 5% in 1st year.
- **Accommodation:** All 1st years housed (who apply by deadline).

Profile

Institution

Founded: 1826. **Structural features:** Founding college of London University. Absorbed a number of other London University institutions over the years (eg Institute of Archaeology, School of Slavonic and East European Studies, Institute of Child Health). **Site:** Heart of London University area in Bloomsbury. **How to get there:** Train (Euston station); underground (Warren Street, Euston Square, Goodge Street); many bus routes. **Special features:** Teaching on undergraduate degrees draws on innovative and cutting edge research at UCL and elsewhere. A global perspective encouraged in all programmes, to help students understand the global challenges we face and contribute towards their solutions. Work placement schemes and skills development actively supported.

Courses

Academic features: 3- or 4-year LLB course available. 4-year undergraduate Master's programmes in many branches of engineering, mathematical and physical sciences. Many degrees include the option of studying abroad for a year. **Awarding body:** University College London. **Main undergraduate awards:** BA, BEng, BSc, BSc(Econ), LLB, MBBS, MEng, MSci. **Length of courses:** 3 years; 4 years (undergraduate Master's, courses with year abroad); 5–6 years (medicine).

Study opportunities & careers

Library and information services: 2 main libraries and 14 specialist libraries – 2 million volumes, 12,000 periodicals, 2000 study places; special reference facilities for some course books; extensive specialist collections. Information provision, £259 pa spent for each student (FTE). Library and IT services converged. 1300 workstations (ratio 1:13 students), all with internet access; access to library from networked machines and 65 dedicated library machines; wireless network being rolled out throughout college. IT facilities in residences generally open 24 hours/day, otherwise 9–12 hours. Central helpdesk 8 hours/weekdays for personal, telephone and email enquiries plus departmental support; library tours and 30-min IT induction for new students; courses in IT training and use of electronic resources available. **Study abroad:** Formal exchange links with numerous European universities/colleges. **Careers:** Information, advice and placement service.

Student services & facilities

Student advice and services: Doctor, dentist, psychiatrist, solicitor, student counselling service. **Amenities:** Own theatre (Bloomsbury). **Sporting facilities:** Fitness centre; Somers Town sports centre; 90-acre athletic ground at Shenley. **Accommodation:** All single 1st years housed who apply by deadline. 4000 places in UCL and London University-managed residences. Halls £101–£145 pw; UCL self-catering houses £83–£145 pw; inter-collegiate halls £109–£157 pw; all 37-week contracts. Most students live out for part of their course; local rent approx £100–£110 pw for a room, £175 pw studio/flat.

Money

Living expenses budget: Minimum £220 pw (excluding tuition fees) recommended by UCL, so £8140 for academic year. **Term-time work:** UCL allows term-time work for full-time students provided it does not have an adverse effect on academic work. SU-run JobShop for student jobs in and out of university; careers service helps with holiday work. **Financial help:** Help for UK students with family income up to £50k pa: bursaries of £2700 pa for students whose family income is up to £11,600; of £2125 pa where it is £11,600–£13,700; of £1600 pa where it is £13,700–£15,800; tapered down to nil where family income is £50k. Bursaries approx doubled for students in 4th year of MSci and MEng. Scholarships for students prior to enrolling; various loans, bursaries, grants and scholarships for existing students (apply to entrance scholarships office, 020 7679 2005, or see www.ucl.ac.uk/scholarships). **Tuition fees:** Home students pay £3225 pa for first degrees. International students pay £11,810 pa (classroom), £15,460 (lab/studio), £23,060 (medical).

Student view
(Main campus)

The original University of London, in a gorgeous listed building in Bloomsbury, very central and a short walk from the West End. The union is the heart of student life, providing many social and developmental opportunities. Its pioneering clubs and societies centre is well-equipped and the base for some 150 groups (Afro-Caribbean to cycling and juggling, and even building a human-powered flight machine) and a variety of training workshops. UCL also owns the Bloomsbury Theatre, a successful fringe venue, which hosts many student productions including UCLU Opera, and drama, dance and film societies; students also have use of the Garage Workshop Theatre. Union runs an extensive sports ground at Shenley (94 acres); a sports centre in south Camden and the Bloomsbury fitness gym (good value for money) both close by. Many ents held in the 2 union club venues (Easy J's and Windeyer), including Happy Mondays, sports night, Wednesday comedy, and 3 fast-selling black-tie events each year. Within the 4 union sites there are 10 bars, 10 food outlets, 2 shops, a hairdresser and a print shop. Union also runs a fully staffed rights and advice centre for all problems from drugs to debt (in addition to the college's counselling service). Union runs WorkStation, which helps students find part-time jobs, either in college, the union or local community; a separate unit links students to voluntary work in the local community. There are numerous halls of residence, for most 1st- and many final-year students. Large proportion of students are from London and the home counties but college is proud of the number of its international students; over a third of students are postgraduate or part-time. UCL is a traditional college, consistently ranked in the top 5 nationally but, whilst work is demanding, many students find time to play hard too! With excellent prospects for graduates, it is a great university in 'the most exciting city in the world' – with the excitement right on the doorstep.

Student footnotes

Housing: Excellent halls near main campus; flats for couples; 2 bungalows for students with families. Private accommodation found through London University or UCL accommodation services, noticeboards or *Loot*. Many students live at home. **Eats:** 10 union food outlets dotted around, with plenty of variety and reasonably priced. UCL refectory a bit more expensive. Loads of restaurants in walking distance, many with student offers, eg Ravi Shanker, Archipelago. **Drink:** 10 UCL union bars on 3 sites with cheap prices. Pubs and bars locally quite expensive, especially in the West End. **Nightlife:** Ents on most nights at union: comedy, house nights, sports night, all free entry. Freshers' week events include Back2Skool, 2 Phat 4 Freshers and Freshers' Ball @ Koko. Usual London ents.

Locals: Pick and choose. Fairly safe area with common sense, eg don't travel alone late at night. **Sports:** State-of-the-art fitness centre on campus (discounted membership for students); Somers Town community sports centre; 2 sports grounds. **Travel:** Some departmental travel scholarships (always ask; they are kept very quiet). Most students travel on foot or by public transport (student discounts). **Financial help:** Access funds (mostly allocated in 1st term but some in 2nd). Union loans in extreme cases. Union produces money management guide. **Jobs:** WorkStation helps find temporary and part-time jobs. **Best features:** Location; quality of institution. **And worst:** Lack of union space. **Informal name:** UCL, UC, College. **Past students:** David Lodge (author); Jonathan Miller (theatre and opera director); Jonathan Dimbleby (broadcaster); David Gower (cricketer); Margaret Hodge MP; Fiona Armstrong (journalist); Dr Hilary Jones (TV-am); Coldplay; Derek Jarman (film-maker); Christopher Nolan (film director); Marie Stopes (birth control pioneer); Mahatma Gandhi (Indian independence movement); Ricky Gervais (comedian). **More info?** UCL union media and communications officer (tel 020 7679 7985, email mc.officer@ucl.ac.uk) or visit the website (www.uclunion.org).

Student view
(Slade Campus)

Small art school within a large university. It's in a beautiful setting in the main quadrangle of UCL. Undergraduate and graduate studios are arranged into painting, sculpture and fine art media. There are facilities for electronic media, sound, photography, print, film and video, bronze casting and general workshops. The history and theory of art area provides relevant and contemporary lectures. All the teaching staff are practising artists and tutor/student relationship is good. You are assigned a personal tutor who you see regularly but you can also arrange tutorials with both permanent and visiting tutors. Being within UCL means you have access to a good library and you can take subsidiary courses for a term within the BA degree, such as psychology or anatomy.

Student footnotes

Past students: Augustus John, Stanley Spencer, Gwen John, Derek Jarman, Mona Hatoum, Christopher le Brun, Rachel Whiteread, Douglas Gordon, Antony Gormley, Tomoko Takahashi (artists).

UWIC

Location:
Cardiff, south-east Wales (map 1)
4 sites across city; partner colleges

✉ University of Wales Institute Cardiff, Llandaff Campus, Western Avenue, Cardiff CF5 2SG
☎ Tel 029 2041 6044
🖷 Fax 029 2041 6286
✉ Email uwicinfo@uwic.ac.uk
🖥 Website www.uwic.ac.uk

Student enquiries: Recruitment and Admissions Unit
Applications: UCAS

In brief

Total Students: 10,910

29% postgraduate
1% FE Students
70% undergraduate

Undergraduates: 7605
88% full-time ● ● 91% UK students
47% mature ● ● 30% lower
on entry socio-economic
groups

55% female

45% male

- **A university college of the University of Wales.**
- **Teaching staff:** 552 full-time and part-time.
- **Broad study areas:** Architectural studies; art and design; biomedical science; business and management; dance; education and teacher training; food, nutrition and dietetics; health care and environmental health; hospitality, tourism and events; humanities; IT and computer studies; music production and technology; product design; psychology; social sciences; sport.

Freshers

- **Admissions information:** AS-levels accepted in combination with 2+ A-levels or equivalent. UCAS tariff used in addition to any course-specific requirements.
- **First degree entrants:** 2100 UK, full-time.
- **Points on entry:** 240 (average).
- **Drop-out rate:** 12% in 1st year.
- **Accommodation:** Almost all 1st years housed.

Profile

Institution

Founded: 1976 as South Glamorgan Institute from colleges of art, education, technology, food technology and commerce; became a college of the University of Wales in 1996, full member in 2003. **Structural features:** University College of the University of Wales. **Site:** 4 major sites in Cardiff (in easy travelling distance of each other and city centre): Colchester Avenue (business, hospitality), Cyncoed (education, sport), Howard Gardens (art and design) and Llandaff (art and design, health sciences and SU). **How to get there:** By rail to Cardiff Central (2 hours from London) or coach (central bus station next to train station); close to M4, 40 miles from M5 junction. Howard Gardens Campus close city centre train/bus stations; local bus services and UWIC's own bus service (UWIC Rider) connect all campuses and city centre.

Courses

Awarding body: University of Wales. **Main undergraduate awards:** BA, BSc. **Length of courses:** 3 years; others 4 years.

Study opportunities & careers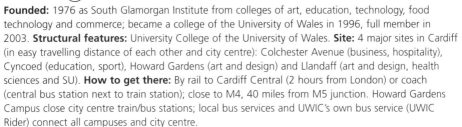

Library and information services: 4 libraries, total of 280,000 volumes, 1900 periodicals, plus audio-visual and electronic media; reference and short-term collections; 1000 study places. Special collections: Permanent collection of prints and books on the work of the designer Erté. Information provision, £77 pa spent for each student (FTE). Library and IT services converged. 1000 workstations with internet access, open 24 hours at Llandaff and Cyncoed. Staff support on all sites. **Study abroad:** Opportunities for students to spend time abroad. Formal exchange links with a number of EU universities/colleges, open to non-language students. **Careers:** Careers advisory service.

Student services & facilities

Student advice and services: Student services office, doctor, nurse, chaplain, counsellors, disability office, accommodation office and financial advisory service. **Sporting facilities:** Indoor sports centre; sports halls, national indoor athletics centre, Lawn Tennis Association complex, gymnasia, swimming pool, athletic track (international standard), indoor and outdoor tennis courts, rugby and football pitches; Wales Sports Centre for the Disabled; access to all sporting facilities of Cardiff University and to Welsh Institute of Sport. **Accommodation:** 90% of 1st years in UWIC accommodation or private halls. 1000 places available: self-catering £72.50, £78–£82 pw ensuite; catered £103.50–£106 pw; all on academic year (39-week) contracts. Accommodation service helps find private rented accommodation; local rent £50–£65 pw. 20% of first-degree students live at home.

Money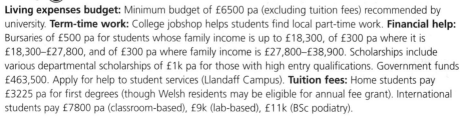

Living expenses budget: Minimum budget of £6500 pa (excluding tuition fees) recommended by university. **Term-time work:** College jobshop helps students find local part-time work. **Financial help:** Bursaries of £500 pa for students whose family income is up to £18,300, of £300 pa where it is £18,300–£27,800, and of £300 pa where family income is £27,800–£38,900. Scholarships include various departmental scholarships of £1k pa for those with high entry qualifications. Government funds £463,500. Apply for help to student services (Llandaff Campus). **Tuition fees:** Home students pay £3225 pa for first degrees (though Welsh residents may be eligible for annual fee grant). International students pay £7800 pa (classroom-based), £9k (lab-based), £11k (BSc podiatry).

Student view

It's based on 4 separate colleges, a young and vibrant institution with many excellent courses. UWIC Rider bus service runs through the city centre and connects all sites. Each site has its own character: Cyncoed is active, busy sports site; Colchester Avenue quieter and businesslike; Llandaff relaxed but hard working; Howard Gardens is creative but sometimes political. The university is currently undergoing major (£46 million) improvements over a 10-year period. 1st years in 2 halls of residence, in Cyncoed and Plas Gwyn (catered and self-catered available). Others in private, rented accommodation – plenty around if you look, many excellent. Students not only from Wales, but from all over the UK, Europe and elsewhere. You can change course quite easily in 1st term, usually within same subject area. Cardiff is a rapidly developing city, especially the Bay area; many tourist sites of historical, cultural and scientific interest. Plenty to do for any age or interest including the National Museum for Wales, the Castle, the Millennium Stadium, the Millennium Centre (grand arts centre with theatres for opera, dance, etc.), cinemas, theatres, clubs, pubs and range of shopping centres. Cardiff is well geared to its huge student population; good student deals, Excellent nightlife (ranked in top 5 UK nightlife hotspots) and new bars and clubs appear all the time; active gay scene. SU is developing rapidly; new SU building in 2009). It runs a coffee bar at Colchester Avenue and 2 popular bars (both named The Union) at Cyncoed and Llandaff, each with its own unique atmosphere; they are the safest and cheapest places to drink and entertainment usually free. SU Pulse Card (£10) gives discounts in SU outlets (shops, bars, etc.). SU Christmas ball is best-seller (students queue from 5am!); recent bands have included Big Brovaz, Kosheen, the Honeyz, Lisa Mafia. Good SU advice and representation at Llandaff and funds many successful sports clubs. Sporting facilities are excellent (2 specialist gyms, athletics track, swimming pool, AstroTurf, indoor tennis centre and National Indoor Athletics Centre NIAC) and plenty of sport to watch in the city (Cardiff Devils ice hockey, Cardiff FC and Cardiff Blues RFC, Glamorgan cricket, Network Q Rally of Great Britain).

Student footnotes

Housing: Most 1st years in halls. Plenty of good private accommodation around (noticeboards, word of mouth, UWIC housing list, information on SU website). **Eats:** Meal on campus approx £2.50+. JD Wetherspoons, Nando's, Old Orleans and Bar Ice all pretty good. **Drink:** Around £1.50 a pint (with Pulse Card). Most pubs have student nights. **Nightlife:** Excellent; student city: countless clubs, cinemas, etc. **Locals:** Usually great; some trouble areas, eg Bute Street, the docks, Ely. **Sports:** Plentiful on campus and in city. **Travel:** Locally good and cheap. Student discounts on trains and coaches; student bus service to all campuses and halls of residence. **Jobs:** Lots of part-time work, in city centre or in SU. Careers service runs jobshop. **Financial help:** Very popular service; SU will help and advise. **Best features:** The atmosphere. **Informal name:** UWIC. **Past students:** Gareth Edwards, John Bevan, John Inverdale, JJ Williams, Gareth Cooper, Tony Copsey (rugby players); Lynn 'the leap' Davies (Olympic athlete); Hugh Morris (MD, English Cricket); Mike Ruddock (rugby coach); Anne Diamond, Jill Dando (presenters); Michael Buerk (newsreader). **More info?** Contact SU on 029 20416190, email president@uwic.ac.uk or look on website (www.uwicsu.co.uk).

Wales University

Location:
Wales
9 teaching centres,
see accredited
institutions

University of Wales, University Registry,
King Edward VII Avenue, Cathays Park, Cardiff CF10 3NS
Tel 029 2037 6999
Email uniwales@wales.ac.uk
Web www.wales.ac.uk

Student enquiries: To each of the institutions listed below
(each has an individual profile in the book)
Applications: UCAS (see individual profiles)

In brief

Total Students: 103,500  20% postgraduate
5% FE Students
75% undergraduate

Undergraduates: 76,300
70% full-time ● ● 95% UK students

 59% female 41% male

- **Degree-awarding body for many university institutions in Wales.**
- **Teaching staff:** 4700 full-time and part-time.
- **Broad study areas:** Most of the main subject areas are taught at one or more of the accredited institutions. Medicine and dentistry are also offered at Cardiff University.

Profile

Institution

Founded: 1893, originally bringing together 3 existing colleges at Aberystwyth, Bangor and Cardiff.
Structural features: A federal university incorporating 9 institutions in Wales:

Aberystwyth University
Bangor University
Glyndŵr University
Lampeter (University of Wales, Lampeter)
Newport (University of Wales, Newport)
Swansea Met University
Swansea University
Trinity College Carmarthen
UWIC (University of Wales Institute, Cardiff)

Cardiff University, one of the original founding institutions, is an affiliated institution. Teaching, academic appointments and the selection of students are all the responsibility of the individual institutions. You can look up each of these institutions separately. **Length of courses:** 3 or 4 years; 4–6 years (medicine); 5 years (dentistry). **Tuition fees:** Each institution sets its own fees; see individual profiles.

Warwick University

Location:
West Midlands
(map 2)
Single campus near
Coventry

⌨ University of Warwick,
Coventry CV4 7AL
☎ Tel 024 7652 3648
✉ Email student.recruitment@warwick.ac.uk
💻 Website www.warwick.ac.uk

Student enquiries: Student Recruitment and Admissions
Applications: UCAS

In brief

Total Students: 30,320

33% postgraduate
67% undergraduate

Undergraduates: 20,375
52% full-time ● ● 84% UK students
11% mature ● ● 18% lower
on entry ● socio-economic
groups

56% female   44% male

- **World-class research-intensive university.**
- **Teaching staff:** 1770 full-time and part-time.
- **Broad study areas:** Arts, science, medicine, social studies.

Freshers
- **Admissions information:** Entry requirements usually include 3 A-levels plus a further AS-level. UCAS tariff not typically used.
- **First degree entrants:** 2565 UK, full-time.
- **Points on entry:** 340+ (average).
- **Drop-out rate:** 4% in 1st year.
- **Accommodation:** All 1st years housed who apply by given deadline.

Profile

Institution

Founded: 1965. **Site:** Single, landscaped campus, 2½ miles south-west of Coventry city centre. **How to get there:** To Coventry by rail (1¼ hours from London Euston, 11 mins from Birmingham International Airport), by coach (2½ hours from London) and by road (close to M1, M6, M40, M42). Frequent buses to campus from Coventry and Leamington Spa (both journeys 25 mins); students can get reduced bus pass. **Special features:** Many visiting professors. Arts and music centres; string quartet in residence. Successful science park; business school; close links with industry and local community.

Courses

Academic features: 4-year accelerated medical course (MBChB) for graduates. University provides adult and continuing education courses locally and validates an open access scheme; range of part-time degrees by day and/or evening study. **Awarding body:** University of Warwick. **Main undergraduate awards:** BA, BSc, LLB, BEng, MBChB, MChem, MEng, MMath, MMathStat, MPhys, MMORSE. **Length of courses:** 3 years; 4 years (including languages, undergraduate Master's).

Study opportunities & careers

Library and information services: 1 main library; total 1 million volumes, 11,000 periodicals (6000 electronic); 1980 study places; short-term loan period for books in heaviest demand. Specialist collections: modern records centre; BP archive centre. Information provision, £181 pa spent for each student (FTE). Separate IT service. Ratio workstations to students 1:9 plus further facilities in halls of residence; many students have own computers. 1000+ machines with access to library and internet. IT facilities open 24/7; comprehensive technical and advisory support. Induction courses on library and information services for all new students (reinforcing transition towards independent learning); IT skills courses and training suites. **Other learning resources:** Language centre, computing centre; new, integrated space (Learning Grid) for 300 students, in range of independent and group learning activities, open 24 hours/day all year. **Study abroad:** 5% of students spend a period abroad. Formal exchange links and Erasmus partnerships with 150+ universities in Europe and the Americas, many open to non-language specialists. **Careers:** Careers library, individual counselling, sponsorship officer, employers' recruitment visits.

Student services & facilities

Student advice and services: Doctors, psychiatrist, chaplains, law centre (in school of law), student counsellors and personal/residential tutor system. 47-place nursery. **Amenities:** Restaurants, new juice bar, fast food outlets, coffee bars and bars on campus. Modern SU building, student newspaper, travel and insurance offices; refectory; university arts centre (theatres, concert hall, music centre, cinema, art gallery, sculpture trail, bookshop); banks, hair salon, print shop, post office, Oxfam shop, large supermarket on campus. Close to Coventry (swimming pool, theatre, museums and galleries), Leamington, Warwick and Stratford (RSC). **Sporting facilities:** Extensive playing fields, sports pavilion, tennis courts, dri-play floodlit area, running track, trim track, 2 sports centres (25m pool, squash courts, well-equipped fitness room, gymnasia, aerobics studios, indoor climbing centre). **Accommodation:** All 1st years who apply in time are in university accommodation (50+% of all first-degree students). 5700 places in halls on campus, 1600 places off campus (almost all with internet access). Rents £70–£115 pw self-catering, 30- or 39-week contracts (some may be longer). Some final-year students return to campus (decided by ballot). Most 2nd and 3rd years live in self-catering places in university-managed properties (in Coventry, Kenilworth and Leamington Spa) or privately rented accommodation, rent typically £55+ pw plus bills.

Money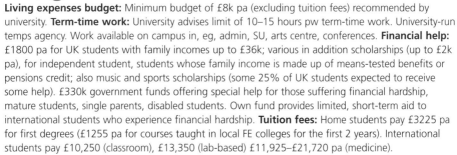

Living expenses budget: Minimum budget of £8k pa (excluding tuition fees) recommended by university. **Term-time work:** University advises limit of 10–15 hours pw term-time work. University-run temps agency. Work available on campus in, eg, admin, SU, arts centre, conferences. **Financial help:** £1800 pa for UK students with family incomes up to £36k; various in addition scholarships (up to £2k pa), for independent student, students whose family income is made up of means-tested benefits or pensions credit; also music and sports scholarships (some 25% of UK students expected to receive some help). £330k government funds offering special help for those suffering financial hardship, mature students, single parents, disabled students. Own fund provides limited, short-term aid to international students who experience financial hardship. **Tuition fees:** Home students pay £3225 pa for first degrees (£1255 pa for courses taught in local FE colleges for the first 2 years). International students pay £10,250 (classroom), £13,350 (lab-based) £11,925–£21,720 pa (medicine).

Student view

Mike Pidgeon, Communications Officer (Graduate, Engineering Business Management)

Living

What's it like as a place to live? Warwick campus was recently voted the best in the UK by the *Times Education Supplement*. Everything you need, from supermarkets to clubs, is, just around the corner. Nice, friendly chilled atmosphere where there's always something going on. **How's the student accommodation?** University-run accommodation on campus is nice but expensive. Some halls are better (and louder!) than others – Rootes has a reputation as being Party Central for freshers. Private accommodation in Leamington and Coventry varies massively, both in cost and quality – some are cheap as chips and amazing, whereas others cost a fortune and are complete dives. Make sure you check them out properly before you sign any contracts! **What's the student population like?** Warwick has an incredibly diverse student population, made up of people from over 120 different countries. Always interesting to make friends with people from far and wide. **How do students and locals get on?** Community relations are probably not the best in some areas of Leamington, but are getting much better – in part due to the work done in the community by Warwick Volunteers. Make sure you invite the locals to your house parties!

Studying

What's it like as a place to study? Courses are incredibly flexible – one of Warwick's main academic strengths. I changed mine a little all 3 years I was a student here! Courses are modern and highly regarded by employers. There's also a brand spanking new library, with lots of computers and uncomfortable fancy chairs, but there is still a slight lack of core textbooks, especially round exam time. **What are the teaching staff like?** Lecturers are almost always internationally regarded as experts in their field, carrying out top-notch research. Some are more interested in students than others, however – bit of a lottery as to who you get as your tutor!

Socialising

What are student societies like? Warwick SU has the highest number of societies of any SU in the UK – over 220. From socialism to string orchestra, break dancing to bridge, there is bound to be one that you like the look of. Add to this over 70 sports clubs run in partnership with the university. Clubs and socs are a major part of life for many people at Warwick. **What's a typical night out?** Warwick SU has been completely redeveloped this year to the tune of about £11 million – the new building open in time for Freshers '09, with pretty top-notch facilities. A typical night in the new union might be starting off for a few drinks in the terrace bar overlooking the main Piazza area, moving up to the union's pub for a pint or 2, then moving downstairs to the main venue for Top Banana – the longest-running student night in the country. **And how much does it cost?** Depends how much you drink! I can usually get by on about £15–£20, but then again I am a lightweight. **How can you get home safely?** Campus is well lit at night and regularly patrolled by the university's security department.

Money

Is it an expensive place to live? Much cheaper than most city unis. Accommodation costs in 1st year might be a struggle, but apart from that it's generally ok. **Average price of a pint?** Couple of quid. **And the price of a takeaway?** A fiver-ish. Depends what type of takeaway! **What's the part-time work situation?** There are plenty of part-time jobs in the union, doing things like bar work and stewarding. The uni also runs its own recruitment agency for students, definitely worth a look – some of the jobs they offer are pretty well paid.

644

Summary

What's the best feature about the place? Fantastic brand-new SU building. **And the worst?** Campus can become a bit of a bubble. **And to sum it all up?** Get involved in your union as much as possible – join clubs and societies, vote in elections and make the most of the new venue. Without the SU, Warwick would be a pretty dull place!

Past students: Sting (musician), Dave Nellist (Militant MP), David Davis MP, Lord Jeff Rooker, Stephen Pile (journalist), Simon Mayo (DJ), Timmy Mallett (TV personality), Estelle Morris (politician). **More info?** Contact SU President (02476 572784, email president@sunion.warwick.ac.uk) or visit the website (www.warwicksu.com).

West of Scotland University

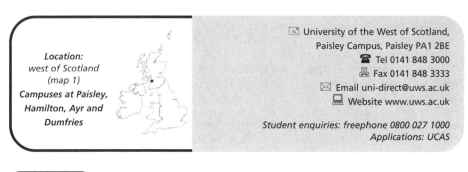

Location:
west of Scotland
(map 1)
Campuses at Paisley, Hamilton, Ayr and Dumfries

University of the West of Scotland, Paisley Campus, Paisley PA1 2BE
Tel 0141 848 3000
Fax 0141 848 3333
Email uni-direct@uws.ac.uk
Website www.uws.ac.uk

Student enquiries: freephone 0800 027 1000
Applications: UCAS

In brief

Total Students: 18,900

9% postgraduate
91% undergraduate

Undergraduates: 17,140
46% full-time
48% mature on entry
95% UK students
37% lower socio-economic groups

64% female   36% male

* **A modern university.**
* **Teaching staff:** 2000 full-time and part-time.
* **Broad study areas:** Business; education; engineering; science; social sciences; computing; design; sport; creative industries; languages, health, nursing and midwifery.

Freshers

* **Admissions information:** UCAS tariff not currently used.
* **First degree entrants:** 1730 UK, full-time.
* **Points on entry:** 170 (average).
* **Drop-out rate:** 17% in 1st year.
* **Accommodation:** Some 1st years housed.

Profile

Institution

Founded: 1897; university status (as Paisley University) in 1992. Merged with Bell College and changed to present name in 2007. **Site:** 4 campuses: Paisley Campus in Paisley town centre (business, computing, engineering, science, design, music, languages, health, nursing and midwifery, sport, social sciences); Ayr Campus, close to Ayr town centre on west coast (education, business, music, creative industries, health and nursing); Dumfries Campus near Dumfries town centre (business, health, nursing, computing and childhood studies); Hamilton Campus, south of Glasgow (business, computing, creative industries, engineering, science, design, health, nursing and midwifery, sport, social sciences). **How to get there:** M8 motorway, rail to Paisley (10 mins from Glasgow), close to Glasgow airport; A77 for Ayr; M74 for Dumfries; Hamilton is well-served with travel links and is centrally located; fast and frequent train service from Hamilton to Glasgow. **Special features:** Career-focused courses developed in partnership with business and industry; well-established links with FE colleges; thriving international student community. Scotland's biggest modern university and largest school of health, nursing and midwifery; £160 million projected investment programme planned.

Courses

Academic features: Practical courses developed with commerce and industry. Placement and work-based learning a feature of many programmes. **Awarding body:** University of the West of Scotland. **Main undergraduate awards:** BA, BAcc, BEd, BSc, BEng. **Length of courses:** 3–4 years (full-time); 4–5 years (sandwich); 4½ years (Hons engineering).

Study opportunities & careers

Library and information services: Over 220,000 volumes, 1200 periodicals, up to 1100 study places (100 at Ayr); short loan collection and electronically accessed material. Group reading rooms available. Library and resource centre at Paisley. Information provision, £89 pa spent for each student (FTE). Computing facilities and IT support. Library tours and email sessions for new students. **Study abroad:** Links with some 60 Erasmus partners across Europe. Opportunities for all students to study in the USA and Europe. **Careers:** Careers service across all 4 campuses.

Student services & facilities

Student advice and services: Personal tutor system; mentoring system for new students; finance and advice service; counselling; careers service; disability support; advice for international students; spiritual care team. Childcare available at Paisley and Hamilton. **Amenities:** SA with a variety of affiliated clubs and societies across all 4 campuses. **Sporting facilities:** Paisley: Robertson Trust sports centre on outskirts of town (sports hall, fitness suite, gymnasium, football, rugby and hockey pitches, jogging route and all-purpose training area). Hamilton: refurbished sports and leisure centre (multi-gym area, games hall and sauna). Dumfries: new sports facilities (games hall, gym and fitness studio). **Accommodation:** Preference given to 1st-year students from outside area. 235 self-catering places available at Paisley, 103 at Ayr, 156 at Hamilton; average rent £55–£63 pw, term time only. Privately owned accommodation £40–£60 pw for self-catering, £50–£70 BandB, £60–£90 for half-board. Many students live at home (common feature in west of Scotland).

Money

Living expenses budget: Minimum budget of £6500 pa recommended by the university (excluding tuition fees). **Term-time work:** 60% of full-time first-degree students believed to work. Some work available on campus, eg as guides for open days, enrolment, university reps, in SA, etc.; vacancies off campus advertised in careers service. **Tuition fees:** Scottish and EU students pay no fees during course; other UK students pay £1820 pa for first degrees. International students pay £7500 pa (classroom), £8300 (lab-based).

Student view   **David Devlin,** President (BA Psychology)

Living

What's it like as a place to live? The university has campuses around the former Strathclyde region of Scotland. The main campuses are in Ayr, Hamilton, Paisley and

Dumfries. The towns are lovely and the areas surrounding the university campuses are safe. However, as always, common sense is advisable. **How's the student accommodation?** The university's student accommodation is not the best; however, this is being reviewed at the moment and hopefully new residences will be in place by 2011. Private lets are generally ok, but the quality and price varies across our different campuses. **What's the student population like?** The student population is extremely friendly and extremely varied across our campuses. In the Hamilton campus you will experience more mature, Scottish students. In Paisley you will find possibly the most diverse set of students, ranging from mature students to school leavers and home students to international. Ayr has possibly one of the best student atmospheres across UWS. The smaller size of the campus means that you get to know everyone very quickly and have a laugh in the union building. **How do students and locals get on?** This varies from time to time and differs across the different campuses. In general there are few no-go areas; however, if that changes at any time, the SA will alert the students to this change.

Studying

What's it like as a place to study? The university is a great place to study. Investment has begun to make our teaching spaces the most advanced in Scotland. The Dumfries campus now has a new modern building and facilities and our Ayr campus is scheduled for redevelopment to begin shortly. Currently the Paisley and Hamilton teaching spaces are adequate and are also scheduled for redevelopment at some point after 2010. **What are the teaching staff like?** The lecturers are the best that anyone could ask for. You never need to be afraid to ask for help outside of class time.

Socialising

What are student societies like? UWS has a good number of sports clubs and societies. We are also looking for more to be set up. We have a fair number of people involved and the number increases all the time. **What's a typical night out?** A typical night out will involve going to the union for a drink then maybe on to a night club. However, in general our international population prefer to stay within the SU buildings. **And how much does it cost?** A good night out can be had for about £20–£30. **How can you get home safely?** The SA in Paisley offers a free bus service that returns students to the halls of residence. In Ayr and Hamilton the residences are on campus and are within walking distance from the union. If you travel outside of the unions, the best way to return home is by taxi. But remember, do not get into any unregistered taxis!

Money

Is it an expensive place to live? Not really. I would say that it's about average for everyone else in Scotland. **Average price of a pint?** £2.10 (but £1.80–£1.95 in the unions). **And the price of a takeaway?** £2–£3; however, some places are far more expensive than others. **What's the part-time work situation?** Jobs are readily available around the different areas of the university. Glasgow is close by to both the Hamilton and Paisley campuses and in the city it should be fairly easy to find a job. The pay for different jobs varies from minimum to extremely well-paid, depending on the company you work for. In general, call centres pay far more than other places and are more flexible for students. The university has just opened a Job Shop to help students find part-time work. They are very supportive of students who work part-time with their studies.

Summary

What's the best feature about the place? The people and the students. We are a very friendly bunch! **And the worst?** The weather. The west coast of Scotland is not famed for sunshine. **And to sum it all up?** The best modern university that Scotland has to offer (in my opinion).

Past students: Gavin Hastings (Scottish/British Lions rugby union international), Douglas Dryburgh (junior world curling champion), Craig Brown (Scottish national football coach), James Grady (footballer). **More info?** Contact the SA President (tel 0141 849 4161) for advice and SA Students' Handbook, or check out the website (www.sauws.org.uk).

Westminster University

Location:
Central and north-
west London
(map 3)
Main teaching
centres in West End
and Harrow

🖳 University of Westminster, 309 Regent Street, London W1B 2UW
☎ Tel 020 7911 5000
🖷 Fax 020 7911 5788
✉ Email admissions@wmin.ac.uk
💻 Website www.wmin.ac.uk

Student enquiries: Admissions Enquiries and
Student Finance Applications: UCAS

In brief

Total Students: 24,710

28% postgraduate
72% undergraduate

Undergraduates: 17,850
65% full-time ● ● 84% UK students
30% mature ● ● 44% lower
on entry socio-economic
groups

56% female 44% male

- **A modern university.**
- **Teaching staff:** 1200 full-time, 450 part-time.
- **Broad study areas:** Architecture and built environment; electronic systems and communications technologies; biosciences; business and management; law; media, arts and design; computer science; integrated health and complementary therapies; psychology and social sciences; languages, English and linguistics.

Freshers

- **Admissions information:** AS-levels accepted in combination with 2+ A-levels or equivalent. UCAS tariff used in addition to course-specific requirements.
- **First degree entrants:** 3670 UK, full-time.
- **Points on entry:** 216 (average).
- **Drop-out rate:** 13% in 1st year.
- **Accommodation:** Approx. 60% of 1st years housed who apply.

Profile

Institution

Founded: 1838, first as Royal Polytechnic Institution, then as Central London Polytechnic; university status in 1992. **Site:** 4 campuses: 3 in West End of London (between Oxford Street and Marylebone Road) and 1 in Harrow. **How to get there:** All West End sites within 20 mins' walk; all on major bus routes and tube lines. Harrow 25 mins by tube from central London.

Courses

Academic features: Degrees in complementary therapies; computer visualisation; mobile communication; commercial music; urban estate management; media studies; film, photographic and digital arts. **Awarding body:** University of Westminster. **Main undergraduate awards:** BA, BSc, BEng, LLB. **Length of courses:** 3 years; 4 years (language and sandwich courses).

Study opportunities & careers

Library and information services: 4 libraries: 437,000 volumes, 7100 periodicals, 1900 study places. Online catalogue system. Information provision, £97 pa spent for each student (FTE). Library and IT services converged. Access to library and internet from approx 5000 computers; ratio 1:5 workstations to students. IT facilities accessible 14 hours/day; staff support helpdesk 10 hours/weekday. New students have tours of library and lectures introducing information services; some schools offer IT skills training. **Study abroad:** Small number of students spends a period abroad. Some links with overseas universities/colleges. **Careers:** Careers centres in central London and Harrow.

Student services & facilities

Student advice and services: Visiting doctor, FPA, psychiatrist, international student adviser, student advisers and counsellors, chaplain, accommodation adviser; health and advice services in West End and at Harrow. 20-place nursery in central London, 16-place day-care facility at Harrow. **Amenities:** Refectory and/or bars at all sites. **Sporting facilities:** Athletics union with organised student clubs, fitness rooms (resistance and cardiovascular equipment); gymnasia; fitness and martial arts classes. Sports ground in Chiswick (various pitches, running track, tennis courts, boathouse, social rooms, bars). **Accommodation:** Approx. 60% of 1st years who apply are in halls; priority to students 25+ miles out of London. 1400 self-catering places, of which 620 at Harrow: rent £73–£153 pw; at Harrow, £102–£110 pw (£68 pw sharing); 38-week contracts, though some can be 50 weeks. Students live in privately owned accommodation for 2+ years: £80–£90 pw self-catering in Harrow, £125–£140 in central London.

Money

Living expenses budget: Minimum budget of £780 per month of study (excluding tuition fees) recommended by university, plus £400 start-up costs. **Term-time work:** Careers and student employment service advertises vacancies on www.wmin.ac.uk/careers. **Financial help:** Bursary of £319 for all UK students whose family income is up to £50k. Some scholarships, worth up to £4k pa, for highly qualified EU students, some restricted to those from partner colleges and schools. Also government funds, access to learning fund, grants and loans may be awarded to students facing unexpected financial hardship. **Tuition fees:** Home students pay £3225 pa for first degrees (but £1255 for foundation year; no fee for years abroad or on placement). International students pay £9830.

Student view

It has 4 campuses: 3 in the West End and the largest one at Harrow. Each contains several schools from bioscience to business and behavioural science to design and media. The vocational approach and outstanding careers service ensure that most graduates find decent jobs. London is expensive but part-time jobs are easy to come by (most students find one). 1st years from outside the capital get priority in halls; everyone else has to pick up a flat- or house-share. Harrow students live around the campus; West End students live as close as they can (often Kilburn or Brixton), though the rent are higher, of course. Very

649

diverse student body: a lot of part-time and mature students as well as a large number of international students. Changing course in first term is relatively easy and uncomplicated. All interests catered for in the various union societies and clubs. SU (UWSU) provides bars, shops and events; also campaigns, and support and representation, through the welfare and education department. Smoke media produces free fortnightly newspaper, *Smoke*, award-winning radio station and TV station (Smokescreen). High level of competitive sport through the athletic union – but also sport at all levels. Life in London can be hard but it can also be a lot of fun for not too much cash. Union's main objective is to ensure all students have a good time and there is someone there to pick them up if they fall down (even in the bar!).

Student footnotes

Housing: Halls for many 1st years and 3rd years. House/flat share around zone 2 (check out housing office, *Evening Standard*, *Loot* and agencies). **Eats:** Canteens open late on all campuses; hot meals cheap, snacks not. Off campus, huge variety in London, with hugely varying prices. **Drink:** Cheap union bars at Harrow and West End; other cheap places if you look. **Nightlife:** Nightclub at Harrow and spanking new state-of-the-art bar and club in Marylebone; regular entertainment and popular for student theme nights. **Locals:** Well, they are Londoners. But London is pretty safe. **Sports:** Sports halls and gyms at Harrow and Regent Street. Tennis, football, rugby, cricket, netball, boathouse, etc. at Chiswick. **Travel:** Coaches for sports and ents. Tube for day-to-day travel, or bike for the brave. **Financial help:** Some funds and a single process to get help. Valid cases given awards in month or two. **Jobs:** Comprehensive job lists from careers service; all advertised in union newspaper. **Best features:** Central London location and alternative quiet and calm of the Harrow campus (away from hustle and bustle). **And worst:** Expense of London life. **Past students:** Quentin Crisp (raconteur and humorist); Pamela Armstrong (actress); Fred and Judy Vermorel (authors); Peter Bruinvels MP; Alexander Fleming (discovered penicillin); Vic Reeves (comedian); Vivienne Westwood. Christopher Bailey (fashion designers). **More info?** Enquiries to SU President on 020 7915 5454 or visit the website (www.uwsu.com).

Wimbledon College of Art

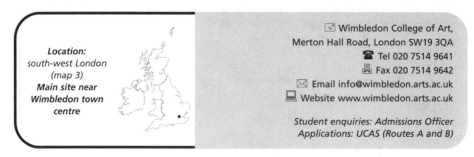

Location:
south-west London
(map 3)
**Main site near
Wimbledon town
centre**

🖃 Wimbledon College of Art,
Merton Hall Road, London SW19 3QA
☎ Tel 020 7514 9641
🖷 Fax 020 7514 9642
✉ Email info@wimbledon.arts.ac.uk
🖳 Website www.wimbledon.arts.ac.uk

*Student enquiries: Admissions Officer
Applications: UCAS (Routes A and B)*

In brief

Total Students: 1770

60% FE Students
5% postgraduate
35% undergraduate

Undergraduates: 640
90% full-time ● ● 85% UK students
30% mature ●
on entry ●

80% female ▮ ▮ 20% male

- **A top specialist art college**, part of Arts London.
- **Teaching staff:** 40 full-time, 50 part-time.

- **Broad study areas:** Fine art (painting, sculpture, print and digital media, time-based media, gallery studies), theatre design (set design for stage and screen, costume design and interpretation, technical arts and special effects, design for performance, lighting design and practice, multi-cultural theatre practice).

Freshers

- **Admissions information:** Students will normally have completed a foundation course; selection is by interview and portfolio.
- **First degree entrants:** 180 UK, full-time.
- **Drop-out rate:** 5% in 1st year.
- **Accommodation:** Some 1st years housed.

Profile

Institution

Founded: 1890. **Structural features:** Constituent college of Arts London (from 2006). **Site:** Main site and annexe in Wimbledon, south-west London. **How to get there:** Train (from Waterloo or King's Cross) or tube (District Line) to Wimbledon station; Northern Line to South Wimbledon; Tramlink to Dundonald Road; buses (Nos 163, 164, 152) to Nelson Hospital. **Special features:** Programme of visiting lectures by professional artists and designers. Artists and designers of international standing in residence for 7 weeks/term.

Courses

Academic features: Degrees in various aspects of fine art and theatre design; all include mandatory history of art and contextual studies. Most courses full-time, but also part-time fine art degree. Foundation degree in lighting design and practice. **Awarding body:** University of the Arts, London. **Main undergraduate awards:** BA, FdA. **Length of courses:** Most 3 years; 2 years (FdA); 6 years (part-time BA fine art).

Study opportunities & careers

Library and information services: 29,000 books, 100 periodicals, 50 study places. IT and library services converged. Ratio 1:30 workstations to students; 3 computers with access to library catalogue, 25 to internet. Purpose-built IT centre, access 10 hours/weekdays; 2 support staff. New students have induction to both library and IT centre; sessions on dissertation skills. Also access to facilities of the university's central Learning Zone. **Other learning facilities:** Slide collection, video tapes, CD-ROM databases. **Study abroad:** Erasmus exchange programmes with colleges in other European countries, opportunities for exchange in the USA and Australia. **Careers:** Departmental and specialist advice service.

Student services & facilities

Student advice and services: Easy access to university's central student services; see *Arts London*. College has its own trained counsellor, welfare officer, support for students with disabilities and for international students. **Amenities:** SU with common rooms, shop, canteen, etc.; workshop theatre. **Accommodation:** Some students in university's halls of residence, see *Arts London*. University accommodation service helps find privately rented accommodation (and extensive local network of private landlords and family stays), rent £75–£100 pw self-catering.

Money

Living expenses budget: Minimum budget of £6k–£10k pa (excluding tuition fees) recommended by College. **Term-time work:** College allows term-time work for full-time students (50+% believed to work). Some work available on campus. **Financial help:** See *Arts London*. **Tuition fees:** Home students pay £3225 pa (£1570 in placement year) for first degrees. International students pay £10,400 pa.

Student view

The 6th college to join Arts London, so has access to everything the university has to offer. Main building complex (on Merton Hall Road) and the Terry Bruen Building (Palmerston Road) are in quiet tree-lined residential areas, about 10 mins' walk from town centre. Wimbledon is well served by overground and underground stations, with quick access to central London, by Tramlink to Croydon (nearest stop Dundonald Road Station) and buses run frequently in the area. College is a friendly and vibrant environment in which to work. Good relations with helpful and committed staff. History of art and contextual studies (HACS) syllabus complements the studio practice well; workload is not overbearing. Good facilities; studios, film and video, bar and canteen in relatively new building. Learning resources centre has an IT centre with 30+ terminals with permanent internet access, colour print facilities and latest software. Canteen, open all day, serves snacks and full lunch menu (including salads at reasonable prices). Students from many backgrounds and countries; and opportunities for students to take part in the Erasmus scheme. SU is apolitical and its main activity is organising social functions in/out of college. It has many clubs and societies for whatever your interests, with access to any of the other university bars and facilities. College has a bar (with pool table and sound system), which is open in the evenings and used for parties and film club. New students tend to lodge locally, moving to shared accommodation once they've found their feet. College has its own small hostel for very few. Jobs are relatively plentiful in the area. Past students of the school have won Oscars, the Turner Prize and an Olivier Award.

Student footnotes

Housing: Ask housing officer. **Eats:** Canteen; vegetarian café; Greek, Italian, Chinese, Indian and McDonald's locally. **Drink:** SU bar, Leather Bottle and Prince of Wales. **Nightlife:** SU comedy nights, pool nights, film soc, and parties; theatre and cinema in Wimbledon; central London 10 mins. **Sports:** YMCA. **Jobs:** Restaurants and summer bar work in Wimbledon if you can get it. **Past students:** Louise Belson (freelance designer with RSC), Rolf Langenfass (designer, Vienna Opera), Iona McLeish (freelance designer, *Pal Joey*), James Acheson (costume designer), Raymond Briggs (author and illustrator).

Winchester School of Art

Location:
Hampshire, southern
England (map 2)
**Single site in
Winchester**

Winchester School of Art,
Park Avenue, Winchester SO23 8DL
☎ Tel 023 8059 6900
🖷 Fax 023 8059 6901
✉ Email askwsa@soton.ac.uk
🖥 Website www.wsa.soton.ac.uk

*Student enquiries: Marketing and Recruitment
(tel 023 8059 7005)
Applications: UCAS (Route A or B)*

In brief

Total Students: 1000 20% postgraduate
80% undergraduate

Undergraduates: 800  75% female   25% male

- **Specialist art college**, part of Southampton University.
- **Teaching staff:** 40 full-time and part-time.
- **Broad study areas:** Painting, printmaking, new media, sculpture, textile design and textile art, fashion, fashion marketing, graphic design, advertising design, photography, digital media.

Freshers

- **Admissions information:** Entry to BA studio programmes via A-levels or a foundation course (or advanced GNVQ or equivalent). Applications welcomed from mature and international candidates without standard UK qualifications.
- **First degree entrants:** 300 full-time.
- **Accommodation:** All 1st years housed unless they are local.

Profile

Institution

Founded: 1870; merged with Southampton University in 1996. **Structural features:** An academic school within Southampton University's faculty of law, arts and social sciences. **Site:** Winchester city centre. **How to get there:** M3; main London–Southampton railway (1 hour to London); 20 mins from south coast. **Special features:** 2-semester system. Teaching staff are practising painters, sculptors or designers. All students allocated their own studio space.

Courses

Awarding body: University of Southampton. **Main undergraduate award:** BA. **Length of courses:** 3 years.

Study opportunities & careers

Library and information services: 35,000 volumes, 120,000 slides, 7000 videos, 300 DVDs, 200 journal subscriptions, 100 study places; automated link with Hartley Library, Southampton University. Public-access computer workstations with latest graphics packages and wireless internet access. **Study abroad:** Opportunities to go on exchanges as part of course. Formal exchange links with universities and colleges across Europe. **Careers:** Information service by careers adviser and academic staff.

Student services & facilities

Student advice and services: Range of advice and support from Student Office, eg on careers, finance, and for international students, those with, eg, dyslexia. **Amenities:** SU, cafeteria, on-site art shop, own public gallery, art and design library. **Sporting facilities:** Recreation centre and park adjacent to college. **Accommodation:** All 1st years accommodated in student village: 378 self-catering study bedrooms (all ensuite and with wireless broadband) £82 pw, 40-week contract. Some rooms suitable for wheelchair users. Most students live in privately owned accommodation for 2 years; rent £60–£90 pw self-catering.

Money

Living expenses budget: Minimum budget of £7200–£8800 for an academic year (excluding tuition fees) recommended by university. **Term-time work:** School allows term-time work for full-time students. Some part-time jobs at school; many in local bars and shops. **Financial help:** Bursaries of £1k pa for UK students whose family income is up to £21,500, of £500 pa where family income is

£21,500–£30k; also competitive bursaries of £1k pa for specified students from Hampshire and the Isle of Wight. Also government funds and own fund. **Tuition fees:** Home students pay £3225 pa for first degrees. International students pay £9380 pa.

Student view · Alice Williams, President, WSA SU (Graduate, Painting)

Living

What's it like as a place to live? Small, friendly, sociable city. You can't walk 5 mins without bumping into a friend. **How's the student accommodation?** Art school – 1 hall, Erasmus Park, houses of 10, ensuite shower but share a kitchen. Private accommodation very good but quite expensive! **What's the student population like?** Friendly at the art school. Mostly students from the south, but growing international postgrad community. **How do students and locals get on?** Very integrated, students and city as one, everywhere accessible to everyone. An excellent community.

Studying

What's it like as a place to study? Has gone through a recent period of change but student numbers rocketing and league table positions rising. **What are the teaching staff like?** Some old guard left; they are excellent. A lot of new staff yet to make a mark.

Socialising

What are student societies like? No societies at Winchester School of Art, but access to hundreds at Southampton University. **What's a typical night out?** A meal in Ghandi's (Indian) followed by pubs and the Art School Union. **And how much does it cost?** Free entry mostly. Drink average price. **How can you get home safely?** Walking, cycling, taxi if you really need.

Money

Is it an expensive place to live? Quite expensive accommodation, but save on transport – can walk everywhere. **Average price of a pint?** At our union – £1.90! **And the price of a takeaway?** £5–£7. **What's the part-time work situation?** Bar and shop work. University approves of part-time jobs but does not actively help.

Summary

What's the best feature about the place? The art school community – friendly dynamic and creative. **And the worst?** Can be a bit insular and claustrophobic. **And to sum it all up?** If you are looking for London, go there; if you are ready to be inspired and make your own fun – come to Winchester.
More info? Contact SU president on 01962 840772 or check out the website (www.wsa.susu.org).

Winchester University

Location:
Hampshire, southern England (map 2)
Single site in Winchester, study centre in Basingstoke

🖃 The University of Winchester, Winchester, Hampshire SO22 4NR
☎ Tel 01962 841515
🖷 Fax 01962 842280
🖳 Website www.winchester.ac.uk

Student enquiries: Course Enquiries and Applications
Applications: UCAS

In brief

Total Students: 5300

20% postgraduate
80% undergraduate

Undergraduates: 4250
80% full-time
20% mature on entry
96% UK students
32% lower socio-economic groups

74% female   26% male

- **A modern university.**
- **Teaching staff:** 600 full-time and part-time.
- **Broad study areas:** Arts, performing arts, primary education, business, social sciences, humanities, health and social care.

Freshers

- **Admissions information:** A range of entry qualifications considered.
- **First degree entrants:** 1285 UK, full-time.
- **Points on entry:** 200+.
- **Drop-out rate:** 9% in 1st year.
- **Accommodation:** Almost all 1st year students housed if they apply by the deadline.

Profile

Institution

Founded: 1840 as a diocesan college for training teachers; university status in 2005. **Site:** Single site within walking distance of Winchester city centre overlooking the South Downs. **How to get there:** M3 from London or Southampton. Direct rail service from London Waterloo (one hour). 20 mins from south coast.

Courses

Awarding body: University of Winchester. **Main undergraduate awards:** BA, BSc, BA (QTS). **Length of courses:** 3 years; 3–4 years (primary education).

Study opportunities & careers

Library and information services: 250,000 books, DVDs, videos, sound recordings; 1000 journals; 450 study places (150 with networked PCs). Information provision, £103 pa spent for each student (FTE). 550 PC workstations across campus (in faculty buildings, library, IT centre) with wireless internet access; open 24 hours/day. Support from IT centre staff, surgery on appointment basis; IT training and helpdesk available to all students. **Other learning resources:** Audio, video and editing facilities and photographic equipment, theatre and arts centre, school resources centre. **Study abroad:** Exchange opportunities open to most first-degree students; linked with universities in the USA and Japan. **Careers:** Talks, information, advice and individual guidance from careers service.

Student services & facilities

Student advice and services: Nurse, welfare and disability advisers, international student adviser, counsellors, chaplain (university chapel), childcare provision, financial guidance, work experience and voluntary work opportunities, study skills co-ordination. **Amenities:** SU with bar, 1200-capacity venue, cinema and games room. Convenience store, bookshop, internet café, dining areas and laundry facilities on campus. **Sporting facilities:** Sports hall, human movement centre, netball, tennis, badminton, squash courts, dance studio, playing fields. City has Olympic-standard running track and athletic field, all-weather pitch close to campus. **Accommodation:** Campus accommodation likely for all 1st years who apply by the deadline, if the university is their firm choice; guaranteed if their home address is further than 25 miles (international students and those with medical requirements accommodated for their whole course). Self-catering £70–£82.50 pw (£90 pw ensuite), 40-week contract; catered places £107.50 pw, 31-week contracts.

Money 💰

Living expenses budget: Minimum budget of £7350 pa (excluding tuition fees) recommended by university. **Term-time work:.** Work is available locally and on campus (eg catering, accommodation office, estates, registry and SU), advertised by Jobshop. University has good relationships with local employers and volunteering charities. **Financial help:** Scholarships and bursaries: for all UK/EU students (of £375 over 3 years); for students with low family income (of £820 pa where family income is up to £25k, and of £410 where it is £25k–£39,300); for students from local partner colleges (up to total of £310 over 3 years); for those who have been in care (£2050 over 3 years); and for students with specified tariff points on eligible courses, eg archaeology (£4k over 3 years). For more information, visit Students and Money section of website. Enhanced funds to help unexpected hardship. Also government access to learning fund of £150k. **Tuition fees:** Home students pay £3225 pa for first degrees. International students pay £7740 pa.

Student view

It's attractively situated on a hillside, 10 mins' walk from Winchester city centre with picturesque views over fields. A combination of historic and modern buildings, the newest being 2 theatres (Stripe Theatre and Black-Box Theatre). Workload reasonable to heavy, with continuous assessment in most courses; not hard to change courses in the 1st year. Exchanges available with Canada, the USA, Europe and Japan. University accommodation for all 1st years (who apply in time) and some others. Social life centres around the new SU (especially for those based on campus), with nights ranging from cheese nights, live music, quizzes, promotions, stand-up comedy and much more. Wide range of pubs in Winchester, a good shopping centre and many hairdressers. Southampton (12 miles away) is 15 mins by train, London in an hour. Range of sports teams, compete locally and nationally. Regular student theatre productions and visiting companies. SU active socially and politically; provides welfare advice, social and sporting amenities, student newspaper, *Big Fish Little Pond* magazine and an annual handbook for freshers. Also respected LGB society and other minority societies. Nursery places available for limited number. Students come mainly from the Midlands and the south. It has a close-knit atmosphere, strong community spirit, safe environment and drop-out rate is fairly low.

Student footnotes

Housing: Around 1000 rooms (some ensuite), good standard; some catered on meal card system. Private accommodation accessible; prices similar to London. **Drink:** SU cheapest and largest venue; Guildhall Tavern and Greens very student-friendly. Pub prices average to high. **Nightlife:** Varied schedule, big event nights and 4 balls a year (freshers', graduation, Christmas, summer). Active events committee; SU performing arts company, abundant theatre groups. Good range of clubs and societies. **Sports:** Mostly free, can get discount at town leisure centre and pool. **Travel:** Regular bus service and many taxis, but everything is in walking distance. **Hardship fund:** Heavily in demand. Occasional short-term loans. **Jobs:** Usually plenty (pubs, shops, restaurants, light industrial, SU), reasonable rates. Large number get paid part-time work; 70% get work in holidays. **Informal name:** Winchester, Winch. **Buzzwords:** TP (teaching practice); BAPA (BA performing arts students); Bar End (sports ground). **Past students:** Martin Bashir (TV presenter), John McIntyre (BBC news reporter), Margaret Cox (Channel 4's *Time Team*). **More info?** Write to SU President, ring 01962 827418, email SU_President@winchester.ac.uk or check out the website (www.winchesterstudents.co.uk).

Wolverhampton University

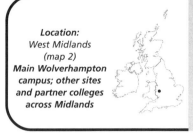

Location:
West Midlands
(map 2)
Main Wolverhampton campus; other sites and partner colleges across Midlands

✉ The University of Wolverhampton, Wulfruna Street, Wolverhampton WV1 1LY
☎ Tel 01902 322222
🖷 Fax 01902 322680
✉ Email admissions@wlv.ac.uk
💻 Website www.wlv.ac.uk

Student enquiries: Admissions Unit
Applications: UCAS

In brief

Total Students: 23,470

19% postgraduate
81% undergraduate

Undergraduates: 18,935
66% full-time ● ● 88% UK students
34% mature ● ● 52% lower
on entry socio-economic groups

59% female   41% male

- **A modern university.**
- **Teaching staff:** 713 full-time, 108 part-time.
- **Broad study areas:** Art and design, humanities, social sciences, engineering, business, languages, law, education, computing and IT, built environment, nursing and midwifery, applied sciences, health sciences, sport, performing arts and leisure.

Freshers

- **Admissions information:** AS-levels, Key Skills awards, etc. accepted in combination with 2+ A-levels or equivalent; BTEC and access learning also accepted.
- **First-degree entrants:** 3295 UK, full-time.
- **Points on entry:** 180 (average).
- **Drop-out rate:** 12% in 1st year.
- **Accommodation:** Most 1st years housed.

Profile

Institution

Founded: 1969 as Wolverhampton Poly; university status in 1992. **Site:** Main Wolverhampton site plus others in Compton Park, Telford and Walsall. Nursing courses in Burton, Walsall and Wolverhampton. **How to get there:** Accessible by train from most parts of the country; close to M5, M6, M54. Good local public transport (including train, tram and buses); free inter-site shuttle service.

Courses

Academic features: Students select from a wide choice of modular programmes; work placements encouraged. Strong emphasis on employment outcomes. **Awarding body:** University of Wolverhampton. **Main undergraduate awards:** BA, BEd, BSc, BEng, LLB, FdA, FdSc. **Length of courses:** 3 years; 4 years (including sandwich, year abroad); 2 years (FdA/Sc).

Study opportunities & careers

Library and information services: Learning centres on each site; 600,000 books, 6000 journals, 1831 study places. Specialist collections: Regional history of West Midlands, company and legal reports, European Documentation Centre. Information provisions, £133 pa spent for each student (FTE). Information skills training sessions. Separate IT services, open 8–24 hours/day (including support staff). 750 computers with access to library and internet. IT module available to all students. **Study abroad:** Formal exchange links with 100+ universities in Europe and 5 in the USA, open to students on most courses. **Careers:** Information and advice from careers and employment service.

Student services & facilities

Student advice and services: Advice and support includes personal counselling service, financial advisers, study skills advisers, multi-faith team, careers guidance and employment services, specialist support for disabled students and international students, education guidance (also advises applicants). Independent advice and support from SU. **Amenities:** Recreational and competitive sports, students' societies, social networking and volunteering opportunities provided by SU. **Sporting facilities:** Multi-floor sports hall, 2 squash courts and fitness suite at City campus; 12-court sports hall, fitness and conditioning suite, synthetic athletics track, synthetic floodlit pitch, grass pitches, tennis courts, swimming pool and dance studio at Walsall campus. **Accommodation:** 75% of 1st years in university accommodation. Over 2000 self-catering places in halls of residence on 4 campuses (1200 ensuite): rent £60–£90 pw, 37-week contracts. Most students live in privately owned accommodation for 2+ year, £40–£50 pw locally

Money

Living expenses budget: Minimum budget of £550 pm (excluding tuition fees) recommended by university. **Term-time work:** Some work available on campus in market research, clerical, library, catering, etc.; university jobshop helps students find work on and off campus. **Financial help:** Bursaries of £500 pa for UK students whose family income is £25k, of £300 pa where family income is £25k–£35k. Also up to £1k in 1st year for some students from West Midlands; some bursary and partial scholarships for international students. Extra help available from the access to learning fund. **Tuition fees:** Home students pay £3225 pa for first degrees (£1650 for foundation degrees). International students pay £8350 pa.

Student view

It has campuses in 3 different areas. The biggest (City Campus) and the smallest (Compton Campus) are a few miles apart in Wolverhampton; 2 others are in Walsall and Telford. Free buses go between the 3 sites and don't really take that long. Lots of development at all 3 sites: brand new teaching building at City, halls of residence at Walsall and SU at Telford – also a new innovative product development centre. As to studying, university has a really relaxed atmosphere. Libraries are big and spacious, with designated areas for quiet and group work. Many other learning areas, from Costa Coffee, to SU activities HUB, to the bar areas. SU is the heart of student life on all campuses. Not only does it have a bar, it offers advice on housing, finance, welfare, academic issues; training and development; extra-curricular activities such as societies and volunteering; social spaces and sports – and that's just the start. Freshers week is massive, with stalls for free stuff, live music and lots of fun for everyone. Always somewhere and something for everyone – well, nearly!

Student footnotes

Housing: Halls a must in 1st year (some rooms ensuite). Plenty of private housing (uni accommodation list). **Eats:** University food is tasty but pricey, in a really nice refectory. Good pub food, eg at the Tap and Spile in Wolves. **Drink:** Good union bar, fairly cheap; Banks, Whitbread, Scottish Courage, SandN. Loads of places in town to eat and drink. **Nightlife:** Places to go every night of the week. Good range of ents at the union. Some good nightclubs for when the union is quiet – try Heat in Walsall, Walkabout in Wolves. **Sports:** Loads in and out of the university; very active athletics union. **Jobs:** Plenty of work in bars and shops, reasonable pay. **Financial help:** Excellent welfare service both at uni and SU. **Best features:** Lively, friendly atmosphere. **Worst:** Split sites. **Informal name:** Wolves Uni. **More Info?** Visit the website (www.wolvesunion.org).

Worcester University

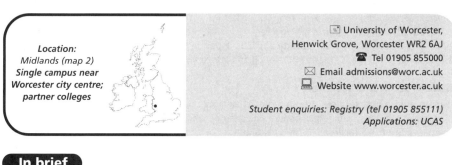

Location:
Midlands (map 2)
Single campus near Worcester city centre; partner colleges

University of Worcester,
Henwick Grove, Worcester WR2 6AJ
☎ Tel 01905 855000
✉ Email admissions@worc.ac.uk
💻 Website www.worcester.ac.uk

Student enquiries: Registry (tel 01905 855111)
Applications: UCAS

In brief

Total Students: 7750

21% postgraduate
79% undergraduate

Undergraduates: 6140

63% full-time ● ● 97% UK students
45% mature ● ● 39% lower
on entry socio-economic
groups

73% female 27% male

- **A modern university.**
- **Teaching staff:** 190 full-time, 90 part-time.
- **Broad study areas:** Education, horticulture, sciences, humanities, sociology and psychology, sport studies, nursing and midwifery.

Freshers

- **Admissions information:** UCAS tariff used; range of qualifications accepted including AS-levels, A-levels and Key Skills.
- **First degree entrants:** 1095 UK, full-time.
- **Points on entry:** 185+ (average).
- **Drop-out rate:** 10% in 1st year.
- **Accommodation:** Most 1st years housed who apply by the deadline.

Profile

Institution

Founded: 1946 as a teacher training college; university status in 2005. **Site:** Single campus, set in parkland 2 miles from Worcester city centre. **How to get there:** To Worcester by rail or road (close to M5). Bus service to university from city centre. **Special features:** Centres for early childhood, special needs and pollen research, county archaeological service. Welcomes mature students and international students.

Courses

Academic features: Foundation year for mature students without formal entry requirements. **Awarding body:** University of Worcester. **Main undergraduate awards:** BA, BSc. **Length of courses:** 3 years.

Study opportunities & careers

Library and information services: Over 130,000 volumes, 800+ periodicals, 3000 audio-visual items. 620+ study places, 100 access computers. Information provision, £57 pa spent for each student (FTE). Separate IT service. 350+ points with access to library and internet; ratio 1:30 workstations to students. IT facilities open 12 hours/weekdays, with helpdesk and other support. Induction sessions to library and information services for all new students; specialist advisers at other times. **Other learning resources:** Media services, dance and drama studios, computer centres, sports centre. Modular scheme advisers. **Study abroad:** Opportunity for students to spend a semester in the USA, Canada or Europe. **Careers:** Information and advice service.

Student services & facilities

Student advice and services: Health centre, chaplaincy, counselling, careers, students' advice centre in SU, advisory tutor system, equal opportunities centre, crèche. **Amenities:** SU bar, shops, newspaper. **Sporting facilities:** Playing fields, tennis courts, gymnasia, all-weather pitch, floodlit hard playing area on site; sports centre. **Accommodation:** 90% of 1st years in university accommodation (20% of all students). Places in halls and university-managed accommodation off-campus, £65–£95 pw self-catering, contracts 35 weeks or longer. Students live in private accommodation for 2+ years: £50–£60 pw self-catering or BandB. 10% of students live at home.

Money (£)

Living expenses budget: Minimum budget of £7250 pa (excluding tuition fees) recommended by university. **Term-time work:** University allows part-time work for students. Some work available on campus out of term time; for jobs off campus, jobs centre and ads. **Financial help:** Bursaries of £725 pa for UK students whose family income is up to £25k, of £625 pa where family income is £25k–£50K; £500 pa for all other UK/EU students. Limited number of scholarships (many of £1k) for academic achievement, support, eg, voluntary activities; also sports scholarships; international students' scholarships (up to £2k pa). Access fund available; also emergency and hardship loans. **Tuition fees:** Home students pay £3225 pa for first degrees. International students pay £8k pa.

Student view

Like the city of Worcester, it's not massive, yet the atmosphere is predominantly warm; not hard to feel a sense of belonging, especially around the approachable department staff and SU. Facilities on campus are reliable and functional. Socialite students can gravitate towards the bar (aptly named The Dive), which offers a range of entertainment and activities. Library offers a vast range of sources and facilities in a modern and pleasant environment. Very flexible modular scheme, where degree students create a personal timetable from a range of modules; also makes changing course in first term easy. Although campus can seem over-run with sports studies students; in fact students are on a diverse range of courses – archaeology to web development. Great commitment to overseas partners, so good opportunities to study alongside Europeans, Scandinavians and Americans both at home and abroad. City is only a short walk (even shorter bus ride) from the campus and satisfies all needs, with popular high street stores and independent outlets. Once bored with retail therapy, the local architecture, live music venues, theatre and county cricket ground are all within a small radius. Other Midland locations are within easy reach for the more intrepid nomads. All combines to offer more than simply an education.

Student footnotes

Housing: Good self-catered halls (6-bedroom flats, with living room and kitchen). Hall rent reasonable. Local private sector plentiful; university and SU hold housing lists; SU runs accommodation days. **Eats:** University refectory value for money; also SU snack area. **Drink:** SU bar cheap (loads of offers). **Nightlife:** SU cheap weekly ents programme, eg Lush, celeb DJs; final year and graduation balls; rag and freshers' weeks and lots of live music. **Locals:** Tolerant. Best to avoid Angel Place at night. **Sports:** Good facilities on and off campus. **Travel:** Train and bus services to Birmingham (1 hour). **Financial help:** Available for those with real problems; also loans and advice from university and SU. **Jobs:** Plenty locally, in and out of term time. **Best features:** Friendly campus and SU. **And worst:** Dead at weekends; road systems and parking are troublesome. **More info?** Ring SU President on 01905 740800 or visit the website (www.worcsu.com).

Writtle College

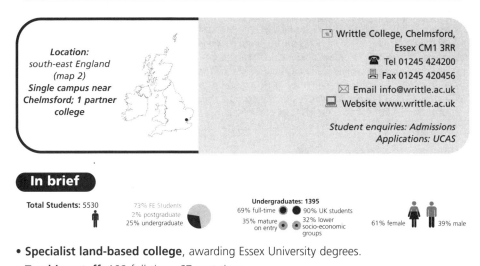

Location:
south-east England
(map 2)
Single campus near Chelmsford; 1 partner college

Writtle College, Chelmsford, Essex CM1 3RR
☎ Tel 01245 424200
🖷 Fax 01245 420456
✉ Email info@writtle.ac.uk
🖥 Website www.writtle.ac.uk

Student enquiries: Admissions
Applications: UCAS

In brief

Total Students: 5530

73% FE Students
2% postgraduate
25% undergraduate

Undergraduates: 1395
69% full-time ● ● 90% UK students
35% mature ● ● 32% lower
on entry ● socio-economic groups

61% female 39% male

- **Specialist land-based college**, awarding Essex University degrees.
- **Teaching staff:** 192 full-time, 67 part-time.
- **Broad study areas:** Animal science and management; equine studies and science; amenity horticulture and landscape management; interior and spatial design; agriculture; business management; commercial horticulture; floristry; sport; rural environment and conservation; garden design; sustainable food.

Freshers

- **Admissions information:** AS-levels and Key Skills accepted in combination with 2+ A-levels or equivalent such as BTEC National Diploma. UCAS tariff used.

- **First degree entrants:** 295 UK, full-time.
- **Points on entry:** 140 (average).
- **Drop-out rate:** 15% in 1st year.
- **Accommodation:** Majority of 1st years that apply are housed.

Profile

Institution
Founded: 1893. **Site:** Single campus on edge of Writtle village, 2 miles from Chelmsford. **How to get there:** Regular service from London to Chelmsford by rail (35 mins) and coach; just off A414, close to A12 and M11; Stansted airport half an hour drive. Regular bus service to college from Chelmsford.

Courses
Academic features: Modular courses; flexible learning methods. Optional industrial placement on all courses. **Awarding body:** University of Essex. **Main undergraduate awards:** BA, BSc, FdA, FdSc. **Length of courses:** 3 years (full-time); 2 years (FdA, FdSc).

Study opportunities & careers
Library and information services: 50,000 volumes, 500 periodicals, 100 study places. Separate IT services. Information provision, £41 pa spent for each student (FTE). Ratio of 1:6 workstations to students; 260 computers with access to library and internet. Access to IT facilities 14 hours/weekdays (9+ weekends); IT helpdesk 11 hours/weekday. 2-day induction to library and information services including tour; courses for all students on, eg, word-processing, spreadsheets. **Other learning resources:** 220-hectare estate including agricultural production units; fruit farm, commercial glass unit, equestrian centre, equine stud unit, small animal unit, amenity landscape centre, college shop, garden centre, computer-aided design centre, computer suites, science centre, interior design and floristry centre. **Study abroad:** 4% of students spend a period abroad. Formal exchange links with institutions in the EU, Canada, the USA, Australia, Nigeria, Nepal and Japan. **Careers:** Information, advice and placement service.

Student services & facilities 👫
Student advice and services: Counselling service, chaplains, learning support unit, careers centre, subsidised childcare nursery. **Amenities:** Recreation centre. Social centre with bar and disco. Adequate parking and motorbike storage space. **Sports:** Sports hall, squash, tennis, fitness centre, college playing fields. **Accommodation:** Majority of 1st years who apply housed in halls on campus. 400 places, contracts for full academic year; rent £3293 pa (shared) to £4107 pa (single ensuite), including meal allowance of approx 10 meals a week. Students live in privately owned accommodation for 2 years: £45–£70 pw self-catering. 40+% of first-degree students live at home.

Money 💰
Living expenses budget: Minimum budget of £4300 pa (excluding tuition fees) recommended by the college. **Term-time work:** College allows term-time work for full-time students (50% believed to work). Industrial Liaison Administrator helps find work off campus. **Financial help:** Bursaries based on a points system taking into account family income, strength of academic or vocational background and whether the student is taking a foundation degree; value up to £300 in Year 1, £400 in Year 2, £500 in Year 3. Also government and college access funds. **Tuition fees:** Home students pay £2835 pa for first degrees. International students pay £7500 pa.

Student view
Felicity Moy, Student Union (2nd year, FdSc Conservation and Environment)

Living
What's it like as a place to live? It has beautiful, lovely grounds, with beautiful views, situated in a country setting. **How's the student accommodation?** Accommodation is good, essential furniture is supplied and there are facilities for preparing light snacks and meals. **What's the student population like?** We have a diverse population of students from all over the world and all over the UK. **How do students and locals get on?** Students and locals get on fine and many students work in the local village shops and support local trade, which leads to good community spirit both on and off campus.

Studying
What's it like as a place to study? As a specialised college, we offer traditional and new land-based courses, with plenty of grounds to help with study. **What are the teaching staff like?** Most staff have an open-door policy and you can always contact a member of staff by email to discuss any concerns or queries.

Socialising
What are student societies like? As a small college, I think we offer a wide variety of clubs. There are plenty of sports to get involved in, with facilities on site and day/night/weekend trips away. **What's a typical night out?** The student bar on site is the place to be and offers both cheap soft drinks and alcoholic beverages. **How can you get home safely?** Because it's on campus, it is safe. If you go into town, it is advised to get a taxi to drop you back at the college. Chelmsford offers the same as most towns – pubs, clubs, etc. – and is situated very close to London and is on the Liverpool Street train line.

Money
Is it an expensive place to live? You have to budget but it is manageable and you can apply for help. **Average price of a pint?** £2. **And the price of a takeaway?** £5. **What's the part-time work situation?** Both jobs on and off site are available, some minimum wage but not all. Jobs are constantly advertised around campus.

Summary
What's the best feature about the place? The fact that we are a small campus, everyone knows everyone and looks out for each other. **And to sum it all up?** I fell in love with Writtle 3 years ago on an open day and still love it.
More info? Ring SU (tel 01245 422752) or look at www.writtlesu.com.

York St John University

Location:
York, north of England (map 2)
Single site near city centre

York St John University, Lord Mayor's Walk, York YO31 7EX
☎ Tel 01904 876598
Fax 01904 612512
✉ Email admissions@yorksj.ac.uk
Website www.yorksj.ac.uk

Student enquiries: Admissions Manager
Applications: UCAS

In brief

Total Students: 5555

 15% postgraduate
85% undergraduate

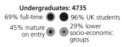
Undergraduates: 4735
69% full-time — 96% UK students
45% mature on entry — 29% lower socio-economic groups

 70% female — 30% male

- **A modern university.**
- **Teaching staff:** 206 full-time.
- **Broad study areas:** Education, humanities, occupational therapy, physiotherapy, performing arts, social sciences, business management, art and design, film and TV production.

Freshers

- **Admissions information:** AS-levels and Key Skills (level 3) accepted in combination with 2+ A-levels or equivalent. Also accept BTEC, Scottish Highers and Advanced Highers, Irish Leaving Certificate, Welsh Baccalaureate, International/European Baccalaureate Diploma, 14–19 Diploma. UCAS tariff used, along with course-specific requirements.
- **First degree entrants:** 1395 UK, full-time.
- **Points on entry:** 220 (average).
- **Drop-out rate:** 8% in 1st year.
- **Accommodation:** Majority of 1st years housed.

Profile

Institution

Founded: 1841 (as a diocesan teacher training college); university status in 2006. **Site:** Close to York city centre directly opposite York Minster and ancient city walls. **How to get there:** Good road and rail links: A1, M1, M62. **Special features:** Modular degrees on semester pattern.

Courses

Awarding body: York St John University. **Main undergraduate awards:** BA, BSc, BHSc. **Length of courses:** 3 years.

Study opportunities & careers

Library and information services: Learning centre with total of 187,000 volumes, access to 2000+ periodicals, course books for reference and loan; free inter-library loans. Group study facilities and quiet study areas. Converged IT and library services. Ratio 10:1 workstations to students; access 24 hours/day, support 12 hours/day. New students given bespoke overviews, user support documentation packs, introductory IT courses, various supportware. IT skills courses available. Information provision, £75 pa spent for each student (FTE). Specialist collections: 19th-century children's books. **Other learning resources:** Yorkshire film archive, learning resource area; Comenius centre (languages), religious education centre, performance and production spaces, music practice suites. **Study abroad:** 8% of students spend a period abroad. Formal exchange links with universities and colleges in Europe (17) and North America (8). **Careers:** Information, advice and guidance.

Student services & facilities

Student advice and services: Health centre, disability service, chaplaincy (chapel on campus), residency support team, student finance team, dyslexia and numeracy support unit, counselling, welfare service. **Amenities:** SU on site: bar, coffee bars, shops. **Sporting facilities:** Sports hall with climbing wall, basketball, netball, indoor football, cricket nets and volleyball, all-weather pitch, sports ground with football pitches. **Accommodation:** 95% of 1st years in university accommodation; rent £65–£73 pw self-catering (£77–£86 pw ensuite), 44–48-week contracts; £104 pw catered, 31-week contract. Most students in privately owned accommodation after 1st year, rent approx £62 pw self-catering.

Money 💰

Living expenses budget: Minimum budget of £5500 pa (excluding tuition fees) recommended by university. **Term-time work:** University allows term-time work for full-time students, to a suggested maximum of 16 hours pw. Some term-time work available on campus and summer work during clearing; university job bureau helps find work. **Financial help:** Bursaries of £1570 pa for UK students whose family's gross annual income is up to £18,300; of £1050 pa where it is £18,300–£20,900; and of £525 pa where gross family income is £20,900–£25k. Also £215,400 government funds, 123 students helped; £37k other funds, 12 students helped. **Tuition fees:** Home students pay £3225 pa for first degrees (£1255 for foundation degrees). International students pay £7800 pa.

Student view

Campus overlooks York city walls, with breathtaking views of the Minster and only mins away from the city centre. Recently gained university status and undergone some radical and exciting developments to improve the learning and teaching facilities. Student accommodation is all a short walk from campus. Extensive international exchange programme, so plenty of opportunities to study abroad during your degree. It's a small and vibrant university; great community and everyone can get involved at any level they choose – just socialising in the SU or becoming a student representative, either playing a sport or getting involved with union council or one of the societies. SU really is the epicentre of student life, providing a great venue to relax in as well as party! It has a varied START training programme, volunteering projects as well as 40+ sports and societies and loads of other opportunities to have the best possible student experience; also offers welfare and academic advice, so always someone to turn to if you have a problem. York is a warm, friendly, exciting and vibrant place to study!

Student footnotes

Housing: University halls for 1st years. Private housing advertised through university, SU, local agencies and newspapers. **Eats:** Meals in SU and elsewhere on campus (from £2.50). Everything at any price in York; many student discounts available. **Drink:** SU very friendly and cheap (£1.80 a pint). Yorkshire home of good beer, eg John Smiths. **Nightlife:** Theatre Royal, Art House Cinema, nightclubs Gallery and Toffs. **Locals:** Very friendly. **Sports:** Gym and AstroTurf plus other facilities. **Travel:** York mainline, 2–2½ hours to London, Edinburgh and Birmingham. **Financial help:** Access funds, limited childcare fund, Old John's opportunity fund – all easily accessible. **Jobs:** Work on campus outside term time, lots of local work in cafés, pubs, clubs, etc. **Best features:** Small, friendly, vibrant. **And worst:** Lecturers know everyone so you can't get away with not attending lectures! **Past students:** Geoff Cooke (rugby player). **More info?** Contact the SU on 01904 629 816 or visit the website (www.ysjsu.com).

York University

Location:
York, north of
England (map 2)
**Main campus close to
city; 1 site in centre**

The University of York, Heslington,
York YO10 5DD
☎ Tel 01904 430000
✉ Email admissions@york.ac.uk
🖥 Website www.york.ac.uk

*Student enquiries: Admissions and Schools Liaison
(tel 01904 433196, fax 01904 433538)
Applications: UCAS*

In brief

Total Students: 13,270

31% postgraduate
69% undergraduate

Undergraduates: 9105
85% full-time ● ● 90% UK students
11% mature ● ● 17% lower
on entry socio-economic
groups

58% female 42% male

- **A top UK research-intensive university.**
- **Teaching staff:** 11,090 full-time, 210 part-time.
- **Broad study areas:** Arts and humanities, social sciences, sciences and technology, medicine. (You can look up the **Hull York Medical School** separately.)

Freshers

- **Admissions information:** AS-levels accepted in combination with 2+ A-levels or equivalent. UCAS tariff not used.
- **First degree entrants:** 2030 UK, full-time.
- **Points on entry:** 413 (average).
- **Drop-out rate:** 4% in 1st year.
- **Accommodation:** All new, single 1st years offered accommodation.

Profile

Institution

Founded: 1963. **Site:** Main campus at Heslington – 200 acres of landscaped parkland about 1½ miles from city centre; campus largely traffic-free with cycle paths. Also medieval King's Manor in city centre (mainly archaeology). **How to get there:** By rail, London King's Cross 2 hours, Leeds 25 mins; bus to campus from central station (2 miles). By car, signposted off A64. **Structural features:** Hull York Medical School, joint with Hull University. **Special features:** Collegiate structure. York Students in Schools volunteering programme.

Courses

Academic features: Modular course structure. Extracurricular programmes include eg 14 languages (languages-for-all programme), York Award personal and professional skills training. IT courses for students without science or maths A-level. **Awarding body:** University of York. **Main undergraduate awards:** BA, BEng, BSc, MEng, MPhys, MMath, MChem. **Length of courses:** 3 years; 4 years (eg undergraduate Master's, sandwich courses); 5 years (medicine).

Study opportunities & careers

Library and information services: 4 libraries, 966,000 volumes, 8500 journal subscriptions (3500 print, 5000 electronic); 1007 reading places; multiple copies of course books; key text collection. Information provision, £197 pa spent for each student (FTE). Separate IT service: 1400 networked computers with access to library and internet. IT support from helpline and info email. Library session by subject for all new students; IT training available. **Other learning resources:** Language teaching centre. **Study abroad:** Some 85 students a year spend 3–12 months abroad (20 to the USA, rest to Europe). Formal exchange links with 75 universities and colleges overseas; range of subjects.

Student services & facilities

Student advice and services: Welfare team in each college. Student support office helps with eg managing money, welfare, etc.; student financial support unit; health centre; counselling service; on-site nursery (30 places); multi-faith chaplaincy; disability services; nightline service. **Amenities:** Wide range of catering outlets. 100+ student societies and sports clubs; student newspapers, TV and radio; concert programme; orchestras, music groups and choirs; art and drama studios; childcare facilities; cashpoints, supermarket, bookshop, travel centre, banks, post office, local store Some study bedrooms adapted for students with disabilities. **Sporting facilities:** 40 acres of playing fields on site; sports centre; 400-metre 7-lane athletics track; all-weather hockey pitch; 3 5-a-side football pitches; main sports hall; dance studio; boathouse on the River Ouse; gym. 2 swimming pools in city (2 miles away). **Accommodation:** All 1st years who want it, and are new to York, in university accommodation (40+% of all students, including all non-EU students). 3820 places (2500+ for 1st years), rent £82–£99 pw (college dining rooms, pay-as-you-eat system); most 38-week contracts (some 33- and 51-week lets). Most students live in privately owned accommodation for 1+ year: rent £60 pw self-catering + bills. Small number of first-degree students live at home.

Money

Living expenses budget: Minimum budget of between £7400–£9800 pa for an academic year recommended by university (excluding tuition fees). **Term-time work:** On campus agency, UniJobs, helps students find part-time work. **Financial help:** Bursaries of £1436 pa for students whose family income is up to £25k, of £718 pa where it is £25k–£35k, and of £360 pa where family income is £35–£40k. Scholarships eg for local students from low-income families, those studying maths, some nursing students. Government and university funds for students with unforeseen financial difficulties, administered by the Student Financial Support Unit. **Tuition fees:** Home students pay £3225 pa for first degrees. International students pay £9510 pa (classroom), £12,555 (lab/studio).

Student view

York is a beautiful place to study with quite a laid-back and easy atmosphere. Vast selection of pubs, both quaint and modern, combine with a growing number of coffee shops to create a very ambient and easy city in which to spend your university life. It's also very central, with good rail links to most major cities. Campus is based around a large artificial lake and consists of 8 colleges – each with a distinct identity and varying standards of accommodation and facilities. Most provide basic self-catering facilities but also have food outlets. Each college has a JCR committee responsible for the college's social, sports and welfare activities. This all makes it easy to integrate into college life. Most 2nd years find private accommodation quite cheaply. Good participation in SU, which offers a diverse range of events and services. RAG and student community action are extremely successful. Some 100 student societies with the country's oldest independent radio station, own TV station, political, religious, musical and subject-based societies and 2 (award-winning) student newspapers. Athletic union has around 50 clubs ranging from the traditional football, tennis and rugby to potholing, skateboarding and paintballing, which compete at college, regional and national levels. Highly rated for both academic standards and teaching; students expected to work hard. Modularisation has increased flexibility in many degree courses (you can often study modules outside your subject area). Departments vary in assessment methods: some are exam-based, others continually assessed. There are many opportunities to learn extra languages, computer skills, to study abroad or take a year in industry. The York Award scheme encourages students to take part in developing transferable skills and personal development. Nightlife in town is limited to 3 clubs; all do good student nights with a variety of music styles (although cheese reigns supreme). Campus offers more variety with a number of music-orientated societies and union events. Pubs in town provide better drinking than the campus. Sports facilities on campus are limited, though developing, and teams do well. Famous for intervarsity event with Lancaster – War of the Roses.

Student footnotes

Housing: Campus rooms all same price; some family flats in new complex. Uni and SU housing list for private accommodation. **Eats:** Campus food fairly cheap (£3 for a meal). Excellent food in some pubs; good selection of restaurants, varying prices. **Drink:** Cheap on campus. In town, pubs vary: reasonably priced, good traditional ales. **Nightlife:** On campus, good variety (small scale, as no large venue). In town, clubs from dance to plain cheese; lots of laughs but not for the serious clubber. Popular student-run cinema on campus; 1 popular, 1 arthouse in town. **Locals:** Friendly; no serious student/local hostility but some areas best avoided Fri/Sat nights. **Sports:** State-of-the-art AstroTurf pitch, mediocre sports centre. No swimming pool on campus but some close. **Travel:** Free SU minibus for local evening travel; reasonable rates from regular buses and taxis. **Financial help:** Union and university helpful. **Jobs:** Many students work in term time, good opportunities in pubs/clubs, shops, restaurants and SU (ents, doorstaff, driving); holiday work available on campus and in town. **Best features:** Ethos, which makes it relaxed, friendly, liberal and welcoming, encouraging diversity and providing opportunities. **Past students:** Tony Banks, Michael Brown and Harriet Harman (MPs), Harry Enfield and Victor Lewis-Smith (comedians), Moray Welsh (cellist), Paul Roberts (pianist), Genista McIntosh (National Theatre), Trevor Jones and Dominic Muldowney (composers), Tom Gutteridge and Sebastian Cody (TV producers), Greg Dyke (ex-director general, BBC), Christine Hamilton (media personality), Adam Hart-Davis (historian and presenter). **More info?** Get alternative prospectus; contact SU reception on 01904 433724 or visit the website (www.yusu.org).

SEARCH LISTS

Where your Subject is Taught

This search list shows you which universities teach your subject – as the whole or as the major part of a first degree course. (Beware – sometimes university prospectuses list these subjects differently, eg life sciences rather than biology.)

Accountancy

Aberdeen Uni • Abertay Dundee Uni • Aberystwyth Uni • Anglia Ruskin Uni • Aston Uni • Bangor Uni • Bath Uni • Bedfordshire Uni • Birkbeck • Birmingham City Uni • Birmingham Uni • Bolton Uni • Bournemouth Uni • Bradford Coll • Bradford Uni • Brighton Uni • Bristol Uni • Bristol UWE • Brunel Uni • Buckingham Uni • Bucks New Uni • Canterbury Christ Church Uni • Cardiff Uni • City Uni • Coventry Uni • Cumbria Uni • De Montfort Uni • Derby Uni • Dundee Uni • Durham Uni • East Anglia Uni • East London Uni • Edge Hill Uni • Edinburgh Uni • Essex Uni • Exeter Uni • Glamorgan Uni • Glasgow Caledonian Uni • Glasgow Uni • Gloucestershire Uni • Glyndŵr Uni • Greenwich Uni • Heriot-Watt Uni • Hertfordshire Uni • Huddersfield Uni • Hull Uni • Keele Uni • Kent • Kingston Uni • Lancaster Uni • Leeds Met Uni • Leeds Uni • Lincoln Uni • Liverpool Hope Uni • Liverpool John Moores Uni • Liverpool Uni • London Met Uni • London South Bank Uni • Loughborough Uni • LSE • Manchester Met Uni • Manchester Uni • Middlesex Uni • Napier Uni • Newcastle Uni • Newport • Northampton Uni • Northumbria Uni • Nottingham Trent Uni • Nottingham Uni • Oxford Brookes Uni • Plymouth Uni • Portsmouth Uni • Queen Mary • Queen's Uni Belfast • Reading Uni • Regent's Business Sch • Robert Gordon Uni • Royal Holloway • Salford Uni • Sheffield Hallam Uni • Sheffield Uni • Southampton Solent Uni • Southampton Uni • Staffordshire Uni • Stirling Uni • Strathclyde Uni • Surrey Uni • Swansea Met Uni • Swansea Uni • Teesside Uni • Thames Valley Uni • UCLan • Ulster Uni • UWIC • Warwick Uni • West of Scotland Uni • Westminster Uni • Winchester Uni • Wolverhampton Uni • York Uni • *See also:* Business studies

Acoustic engineering

Anglia Ruskin Uni • Birmingham City Uni • Cambridge Uni • Glyndŵr Uni • Huddersfield Uni • Salford Uni • Southampton Solent Uni • Southampton Uni • *See also:* Electrical engineering

Acoustics

See: Acoustic engineering; electronic engineering; music; physics; speech sciences

Acting

ALRA • Anglia Ruskin Uni • Bedfordshire Uni • Birmingham City Uni • Bristol Old Vic • Bucks New Uni • Central Saint Martins • Central Sch Speech/Drama • Chichester Uni • Cumbria Uni • Derby Uni • East London Uni • Essex Uni • Exeter Uni • Glyndŵr Uni • Guildhall Sch Music and Drama • Kingston Uni • Leeds Uni • London South Bank Uni • Manchester Met Uni • Middlesex Uni • Northampton Uni • Queen Margaret Uni • RADA • Rose Bruford Coll • Royal Scottish Academy Music/Drama • Royal Welsh Coll Music/Drama • Thames Valley Uni • Trinity Coll Carmarthen • UCLan • West of Scotland Uni • Wolverhampton Uni • York Uni • *See also:* Drama

Actuarial studies

City Uni • East Anglia Uni • Heriot-Watt Uni • Keele Uni • Kent • Kingston Uni • LSE • Manchester Uni • Queen's Uni Belfast • Southampton Uni • Swansea Uni • *See also:* Mathematics; social science; statistics

Administration

See: Business administration; estate management; housing administration; human resource management; public administration; social administration

Advertising

Bedfordshire Uni • Birmingham City Uni • Bournemouth Uni • Bradford Coll • Bucks New Uni • Canterbury Christ Church Uni • Central Saint Martins • Chester Uni • Coventry Uni • Creative Arts Uni • De Montfort Uni • Derby Uni • East London Uni • Edge Hill Uni • Falmouth Uni Coll • Glasgow Caledonian Uni • Gloucestershire Uni • Hertfordshire Uni • Huddersfield Uni • Lancaster Uni • Lincoln Uni • London Coll Communication • London Met Uni • Manchester Met Uni • Middlesex Uni • Newport • Northampton Uni • Robert Gordon Uni • Southampton Solent Uni • Sunderland Uni • Swansea Met Uni • Thames Valley Uni • Trinity Coll Carmarthen • UCLan • Ulster Uni • Winchester Sch Art • Worcester Uni • *See also:* Marketing

Advertising design

See: Graphic design

Aerodynamics

Brunel Uni • Cambridge Uni • Coventry Uni • Cranfield Uni (p/g only) • Hertfordshire Uni • Kingston Uni • Liverpool Uni • Nottingham Uni • Southampton Uni • Strathclyde Uni • Sussex Uni

Aeronautical engineering

Bath Uni • Brighton Uni • Bristol Uni • Bristol UWE • Brunel Uni • Cambridge Uni • City Uni • Coventry Uni • Cranfield Uni (p/g only) • Durham Uni • Farnborough Coll • Glamorgan Uni • Glasgow Uni • Glyndŵr Uni • Hertfordshire Uni • Imperial Coll • Kingston Uni • Leeds Uni • Liverpool Uni • Loughborough Uni • Manchester Uni • Nottingham Uni • Queen Mary • Queen's Uni Belfast • Salford Uni • Sheffield Uni • Southampton Uni • Staffordshire Uni • Strathclyde Uni • Surrey Uni • Sussex Uni • Swansea Uni • UHI Millennium Institute

Aesthetics

See: Art history; philosophy

African studies

Birmingham Uni • Coventry Uni • SOAS • *See also:* Archaeology; Asian studies; Middle Eastern studies

Afro-Asian studies

See: African studies; Asian studies

Agricultural botany

Aberdeen Uni • Glyndŵr Uni • Newcastle Uni • Nottingham Uni • Royal Agricultural Coll • *See also:* Agriculture; botany

Agricultural chemistry

See: Agriculture; chemistry

Agricultural economics

Aberdeen Uni • Aberystwyth Uni • Harper Adams Uni Coll • Queen's Uni Belfast • Reading Uni • Royal Agricultural Coll • Scottish Agricultural Coll • *See also:* Agriculture; economics

Agricultural engineering

Cranfield Uni (p/g only) • Harper Adams Uni Coll • Myerscough Coll • Royal Agricultural Coll

Agriculture

Aberdeen Uni • Aberystwyth Uni • Bangor Uni • Brighton Uni • Bristol UWE • Cranfield Uni (p/g only) • Cumbria Uni • Greenwich Uni • Harper Adams Uni Coll • Myerscough Coll • Newcastle Uni • Nottingham Trent Uni • Nottingham Uni • Queen's Uni Belfast • Reading Uni • Royal Agricultural Coll • Scottish Agricultural Coll • Wolverhampton Uni • Writtle Coll

Agronomy

See: Agriculture

Air transport engineering

City Uni • Cranfield Uni (p/g only) • Hertfordshire Uni • Imperial Coll • Kingston Uni • Loughborough Uni • UHI Millennium Institute

Aircraft engineering

See: Aeronautical engineering; air transport engineering

Akkadian

Cambridge Uni • SOAS • *See also:* Middle Eastern studies

American studies

Aberystwyth Uni • Birmingham Uni • Canterbury Christ Church Uni • Derby Uni • Dundee Uni • East Anglia Uni • Edinburgh Uni • Essex Uni • Hull Uni • Keele Uni • Kent • King's Coll London • Lancaster Uni • Leicester Uni • Lincoln Uni • Liverpool John Moores Uni • Liverpool Uni • London Met Uni • Manchester Met Uni • Manchester Uni • Northampton Uni • Northumbria Uni • Nottingham Uni • Portsmouth Uni • Sunderland Uni • Sussex Uni • Swansea Uni • UCLan • Ulster Uni • Warwick Uni • Winchester Uni • Wolverhampton Uni • Worcester Uni • York St John Uni

Amharic

See: Asian studies; oriental studies

Analogues

See: Computing; electrical engineering; electronic engineering

Analytical

See: individual subjects (eg chemistry)

Anatolia

See: Archaeology

Anatomy

Aberdeen Uni • Birmingham Uni • Bristol Uni • British Sch Osteopathy • Cambridge Uni • Cardiff Uni • Dundee Uni • Glasgow Uni • King's Coll London • Leeds Uni • Liverpool Uni • Manchester Uni • Newcastle Uni • Queen's Uni Belfast • Sheffield Uni • University Coll London *See also:* Medicine; human biology

Ancient history

Birmingham Uni • Bristol Uni • Cambridge Uni • Cardiff Uni • Durham Uni • Edinburgh Uni • Exeter Uni • King's Coll London • Lampeter Uni • Leeds Uni • Leicester Uni • Liverpool Uni • Manchester Uni • Newcastle Uni • Nottingham Uni • Oxford Uni • Queen's Uni Belfast • Reading Uni • Royal Holloway • St Andrews Uni • SOAS • Swansea Uni • University Coll London • Warwick Uni • Winchester Uni • *See also:* Classics; classical studies; history

Anglo-Saxon

Cambridge Uni

Animal science

Aberdeen Uni • Aberystwyth Uni • Anglia Ruskin Uni • Birmingham Uni • Brighton Uni • Bristol Uni • Bristol UWE • Cambridge Uni • Canterbury Christ Church Uni • Chester Uni • Cumbria Uni • East London Uni • Exeter Uni • Glasgow Uni • Gloucestershire Uni • Glyndŵr Uni • Greenwich Uni • Harper Adams Uni Coll • Imperial Coll • Leeds Uni • Lincoln Uni • Liverpool John Moores Uni • Manchester Met Uni • Myerscough Coll • Napier Uni • Newcastle Uni • Northampton Uni • Nottingham Trent Uni • Nottingham Uni • Plymouth Uni • Portsmouth Uni • Reading Uni • Royal Agricultural Coll • Royal Vet Coll • St Andrews Uni • Scottish Agricultural Coll • Sheffield Uni • Stirling Uni • Surrey Uni • Wolverhampton Uni • Worcester Uni • Writtle Coll

Animals

See: Agriculture; animal science; veterinary nursing/science; wildlife management; zoology

Animation

Abertay Dundee Uni • Anglia Ruskin Uni • Bedfordshire Uni • Birmingham City Uni • Bolton Uni • Bournemouth Uni • Bradford Uni • Bristol UWE • Bucks New Uni • Canterbury Christ Church Uni • Creative Arts Uni • Cumbria Uni • De Montfort Uni • Derby Uni • Dundee Uni • East London Uni • Edge Hill Uni • Edinburgh Coll Art • Falmouth Uni Coll • Glamorgan Uni • Gloucestershire Uni • Glyndŵr Uni • Greenwich Uni • Hertfordshire Uni • Kingston Uni • Lincoln Uni • London Coll Communication • London Met Uni • Manchester Met Uni • National Film Sch (p/g only) • Newport • Norwich Uni Coll Arts • Nottingham Trent Uni • Portsmouth Uni • Ravensbourne Coll • Robert Gordon Uni • Royal Coll Art (p/g only) • Southampton Solent Uni • Staffordshire Uni • Sunderland Uni • Swansea Met Uni • Teesside Uni • Thames Valley Uni • UCLan • Ulster Uni • West of Scotland Uni • Westminster Uni • Winchester Sch Art • Wolverhampton Uni • Worcester Uni • *See also:* Film studies

Anthropology

Aberdeen Uni • Birmingham Uni • Bristol Uni • Brunel Uni • Cambridge Uni • Durham Uni • East Anglia Uni • East London Uni • Edinburgh Uni • Glasgow Uni • Goldsmiths • Hull Uni • Kent

673

• Lampeter Uni • Lancaster Uni • Liverpool John Moores Uni • Liverpool Uni • London Met Uni • LSE • Manchester Uni • Newcastle Uni • Oxford Brookes Uni • Oxford Uni • Queen's Uni Belfast • Roehampton Uni • St Andrews Uni • SOAS • Southampton Uni • Sussex Uni • University Coll London • *See also:* Social anthropology

Applied

See: individual subjects (eg biology)

Aquaculture

Glasgow Uni • Salford Uni • Stirling Uni • Wolverhampton Uni

Arabic

Cambridge Uni • Durham Uni • Edinburgh Uni • Exeter Uni • Lampeter Uni • Leeds Uni • Manchester Uni • Oxford Uni • St Andrews Uni • Salford Uni • SOAS • Westminster Uni

Aramaic

See: Middle Eastern studies

Archaeology

Aberdeen Uni • Bangor Uni • Birkbeck • Birmingham Uni • Bournemouth Uni • Bradford Uni • Bristol Uni • Cambridge Uni • Cardiff Uni • Chester Uni • Durham Uni • East Anglia Uni • Edinburgh Uni • Exeter Uni • Glasgow Uni • Hull Uni • Kent • King's Coll London • Lampeter Uni • Leicester Uni • Liverpool Uni • Manchester Uni • Newcastle Uni • Nottingham Uni • Oxford Uni • Queen's Uni Belfast • Reading Uni • Sheffield Uni • Southampton Uni • Sussex Uni • UCLan • University Coll London • Warwick Uni • Winchester Uni • Worcester Uni • York Uni

Architectural design

Bedfordshire Uni • Bristol UWE • Central Saint Martins • Coventry Uni • Creative Arts Uni • Derby Uni • East London Uni • Edinburgh Uni • Glyndŵr Uni • Greenwich Uni • Huddersfield Uni • Kingston Uni • London Met Uni • Middlesex Uni • Napier Uni • Northumbria Uni • Nottingham Trent Uni • Nottingham Uni • Plymouth Uni • Portsmouth Uni • Ravensbourne Coll • Sheffield Hallam Uni • Sheffield Uni • Strathclyde Uni • UCLan • UWIC • Westminster Uni • Wolverhampton Uni • Writtle Coll

Architectural technology

Anglia Ruskin Uni • Birmingham City Uni • Bolton Uni • Brighton Uni • Bristol UWE • Coventry Uni • De Montfort Uni • Derby Uni • Glyndŵr Uni • Heriot-Watt Uni • Huddersfield Uni • Kingston Uni • Leeds Uni • Liverpool Uni • London South Bank Uni • Loughborough Uni • Napier Uni • Northampton Uni • Northumbria Uni • Nottingham Trent Uni • Plymouth Uni • Portsmouth Uni • Ravensbourne Coll • Robert Gordon Uni • Sheffield Hallam Uni • Southampton Solent Uni • Thames Valley Uni • UCLan • Ulster Uni • UWIC • Westminster Uni • Wolverhampton Uni

Architecture

Anglia Ruskin Uni • Architectural Association • Bath Uni • Birmingham City Uni • Brighton Uni • Bristol UWE • Cambridge Uni • Cardiff Uni • City Uni • Creative Arts Uni • De Montfort Uni • Derby Uni • Dundee Uni • East London Uni • Edinburgh Coll Art • Edinburgh Uni • Glasgow Sch Art • Glasgow Uni • Glyndŵr Uni • Greenwich Uni • Huddersfield Uni • Kent • Kingston Uni • Leeds Met

Uni • Lincoln Uni • Liverpool John Moores Uni • Liverpool Uni • London Met Uni • London South Bank Uni • Manchester Met Uni • Manchester Uni • Newcastle Uni • Nottingham Uni • Oxford Brookes Uni • Plymouth Uni • Portsmouth Uni • Queen's Uni Belfast • Ravensbourne Coll • Robert Gordon Uni • Royal Coll Art (p/g only) • Sheffield Hallam Uni • Sheffield Uni • Strathclyde Uni • UCLan • Ulster Uni • University Coll London • Westminster Uni • Wolverhampton Uni

Art

Abertay Dundee Uni • Aberystwyth Uni • Anglia Ruskin Uni • Bath Spa Uni • Bedfordshire Uni • Birmingham City Uni • Bolton Uni • Bradford Coll • Brighton Uni • Bristol UWE • Bucks New Uni • Camberwell Coll • Canterbury Christ Church Uni • Central Saint Martins • Chelsea Coll Art • Chester Uni • Chichester Uni • Colchester Inst • Coventry Uni • Creative Arts Uni • Cumbria Uni • Dartington • De Montfort Uni • Derby Uni • Dundee Uni • East London Uni • Edinburgh Coll Art • Falmouth Uni Coll • Glamorgan Uni • Glasgow Sch Art • Gloucestershire Uni • Glyndŵr Uni • Goldsmiths • Greenwich Uni • Hertfordshire Uni • Huddersfield Uni • Kent • Kingston Uni • Lancaster Uni • Leeds Met Uni • Leeds Uni • Lincoln Uni • Liverpool Hope Uni • Liverpool John Moores Uni • London Coll Communication • London Coll Fashion • London Met Uni • Loughborough Uni • Manchester Met Uni • Middlesex Uni • Newcastle Uni • Newport • Northampton Uni • Northumbria Uni • Norwich Uni Coll Arts • Nottingham Trent Uni • Oxford Brookes Uni • Oxford Uni • Plymouth Uni • Portsmouth Uni • Reading Uni • Robert Gordon Uni • Rose Bruford Coll • Royal Academy Sch p/g only • Royal Coll Art (p/g only) • Salford Uni • Sheffield Hallam Uni • Southampton Solent Uni • Southampton Uni • Staffordshire Uni • Sunderland Uni • Swansea Met Uni • Teesside Uni • Thames Valley Uni • Trinity Coll Carmarthen • UCLan • UHI Millennium Institute • Ulster Uni • University Coll London • UWIC • West of Scotland Uni • Westminster Uni • Wimbledon Coll Art • Winchester Sch Art • Wolverhampton Uni • Worcester Uni • York St John Uni • *See also:* Graphic design; photography; silversmithing; textiles; three-dimensional design

Art history

Aberdeen Uni • Aberystwyth Uni • Birkbeck • Birmingham City Uni • Birmingham Uni • Brighton Uni • Bristol Uni • Cambridge Uni • Central Saint Martins • Courtauld Inst • East Anglia Uni • East London Uni • Edinburgh Uni • Essex Uni • Falmouth Uni Coll • Glamorgan Uni • Glasgow Uni •Goldsmiths • Hull Uni • Kent • Kingston Uni • Lancaster Uni • Leeds Uni • Leicester Uni • Liverpool John Moores Uni • Manchester Met Uni • Manchester Uni • Middlesex Uni • Newcastle Uni • Newport • Northumbria Uni • Nottingham Uni • Open Uni • Oxford Brookes Uni • Oxford Uni • Plymouth Uni • Reading Uni • Roehampton Uni • St Andrews Uni • Sheffield Hallam Uni • SOAS • Southampton Uni • Sussex Uni • Swansea Met Uni • University Coll London • UWIC • Warwick Uni • Wimbledon Coll Art • Winchester Uni • York Uni

Art therapy

Derby Uni • *See also:* Art

Artificial intelligence

Aberdeen Uni • Aberystwyth Uni • Bedfordshire Uni • Birmingham Uni • Bradford Uni • City Uni • Cranfield Uni (p/g only) • De Montfort Uni • Durham Uni • East Anglia Uni • Edinburgh Uni • Essex Uni • Exeter Uni • Heriot-Watt Uni • Hertfordshire Uni • Huddersfield Uni • Imperial Coll • Leeds Met Uni • Leeds Uni • Liverpool Uni • Loughborough Uni • Manchester Met Uni • Manchester Uni • Newport • Nottingham Uni • Portsmouth Uni • Reading Uni • Robert Gordon Uni • Sheffield Uni • Southampton Uni • Sussex Uni • Ulster Uni • Westminster Uni

Arts management

Bristol Old Vic • Coventry Uni • Creative Arts Uni • Cumbria Uni • De Montfort Uni • Falmouth Uni Coll • Glasgow Uni • Glyndŵr Uni • Leeds Uni • London Coll Communication • London Met Uni

• London South Bank Uni • Middlesex Uni • Oxford Brookes Uni • Queen Margaret Uni • Rose Bruford Coll • Royal Coll Art (p/g only) • Royal Welsh Coll Music/Drama • Sheffield Hallam Uni • Ulster Uni • Winchester Uni

Asian studies

Birmingham Uni • Cambridge Uni • Edinburgh Uni • Leeds Uni • London Met Uni • Manchester Uni • Sheffield Uni • SOAS • UCLan • *See also:* Middle Eastern studies; South East Asian studies; oriental studies

Assyriology

See: Archaeology; Middle Eastern studies

Astronautics

See: Aerodynamics; space

Astronomy

Birmingham Uni • Cardiff Uni • Durham Uni • Edinburgh Uni • Glamorgan Uni • Glasgow Uni •Hertfordshire Uni • Kent • Kingston Uni • Leicester Uni • Liverpool John Moores Uni • Liverpool Uni • Nottingham Trent Uni • Nottingham Uni • Open Uni • Queen Mary • St Andrews Uni • Sheffield Uni • Southampton Uni • Sussex Uni • UCLan • University Coll London

Astrophysics

Aberystwyth Uni • Birmingham Uni • Bristol Uni • Cambridge Uni • Cardiff Uni • Durham Uni • Edinburgh Uni • Exeter Uni • Glasgow Uni • Hertfordshire Uni • Hull Uni • Keele Uni • Kent • King's Coll London • Lancaster Uni • Leeds Uni • Leicester Uni • Liverpool John Moores Uni • Liverpool Uni • Manchester Uni • Nottingham Trent Uni • Nottingham Uni • Queen Mary • Royal Holloway • St Andrews Uni • Sheffield Uni • Surrey Uni • Sussex Uni • UCLan • University Coll London • York Uni

Audio

Abertay Dundee Uni • Anglia Ruskin Uni • Birmingham City Uni • Bolton Uni • Brighton Uni • Bristol Old Vic • Bristol UWE • De Montfort Uni • Derby Uni • Essex Uni • Glasgow Caledonian Uni • Glyndŵr Uni • Huddersfield Uni • Lincoln Uni • London Met Uni • Ravensbourne Coll • Rose Bruford Coll • Salford Uni • Southampton Solent Uni • Surrey Uni • Thames Valley Uni • Westminster Uni

Audio-visual communication

See: Art; communication studies; electronic engineering

Audiology

Aston Uni • Bristol Uni • De Montfort Uni • Leeds Uni • Manchester Uni • Southampton Uni • Swansea Uni • University Coll London

Automotive engineering

Aston Uni • Bath Uni • Birmingham City Uni • Birmingham Uni • Bolton Uni • Bradford Uni • Brighton Uni • Brunel Uni • City Uni • Coventry Uni • Cranfield Uni (p/g only) • Derby Uni • Farnborough Coll • Glyndŵr Uni • Greenwich Uni • Harper Adams Uni Coll • Heriot-Watt Uni

• Hertfordshire Uni • Huddersfield Uni • Kingston Uni • Leeds Uni • Liverpool John Moores Uni • Loughborough Uni • Manchester Met Uni • Myerscough Coll • Newcastle Uni • Nottingham Uni • Oxford Brookes Uni • Sheffield Hallam Uni • Sheffield Uni • Staffordshire Uni • Strathclyde Uni • Sunderland Uni • Sussex Uni • Swansea Met Uni • Warwick Uni • Wolverhampton Uni

Avionics

Brunel Uni • City Uni • Coventry Uni • Cranfield Uni (p/g only) • Glasgow Uni • Glyndŵr Uni • Hertfordshire Uni • Leeds Uni • Liverpool Uni • Loughborough Uni • Manchester Uni • Queen Mary • Salford Uni • York Uni • *See also:* Aeronautical engineering

Bacteriology

Birmingham Uni • Edinburgh Uni • Imperial Coll • Newcastle Uni • Reading Uni

Banking

Anglia Ruskin Uni • Bangor Uni • Birmingham Uni • Bournemouth Uni • Buckingham Uni • Cardiff Uni • City Uni • Derby Uni • East London Uni • Glasgow Caledonian Uni • Leicester Uni • London Met Uni • Loughborough Uni • Middlesex Uni • Nottingham Trent Uni • Plymouth Uni • Portsmouth Uni • Reading Uni • Sheffield Hallam Uni • Stirling Uni • Ulster Uni • *See also:* Business studies; economics; finance; financial services

Behavioural science

Abertay Dundee Uni • Aberystwyth Uni • Anglia Ruskin Uni • Huddersfield Uni • Liverpool John Moores Uni • Portsmouth Uni • St Andrews Uni • Sheffield Uni • Surrey Uni • Westminster Uni • *See also:* Psychology; zoology

Bengali

Cambridge Uni • SOAS • *See also:* Asian studies; oriental studies

Berber

See: African studies

Biblical studies

Aberdeen Uni • Bangor Uni • Birmingham Uni • Cambridge Uni • Edinburgh Uni • Glasgow Uni • Gloucestershire Uni • Heythrop Coll • Lampeter Uni • London Sch Theology • Manchester Uni • Oak Hill Coll • St Andrews Uni • St Mary's Uni Coll • Sheffield Uni • Spurgeon's Coll • Trinity Coll Carmarthen • Winchester Uni • York St John Uni • *See also:* Religious studies; theology

Biochemical engineering

Aston Uni • Bath Uni • Birmingham Uni • Cambridge Uni • Cranfield Uni (p/g only) • Manchester Uni • Newcastle Uni • Sheffield Uni • Surrey Uni • Swansea Uni • University Coll London • *See also:* Biochemistry; biotechnology; chemical engineering

Biochemistry

Aberdeen Uni • Aberystwyth Uni • Anglia Ruskin Uni • Aston Uni • Bath Uni • Birkbeck • Birmingham Uni • Bradford Uni • Bristol Uni • Bristol UWE • Brunel Uni • Cambridge Uni • Cardiff Uni • Cranfield Uni (p/g only) • Derby Uni • Dundee Uni • Durham Uni • East Anglia Uni • East London Uni

• Edinburgh Uni • Essex Uni • Glasgow Caledonian Uni • Glasgow Uni • Greenwich Uni • Heriot-Watt Uni • Hertfordshire Uni • Huddersfield Uni • Imperial Coll • Keele Uni • Kent • King's Coll London • Kingston Uni • Lancaster Uni • Leeds Uni • Leicester Uni • Liverpool John Moores Uni • Liverpool Uni • London Met Uni • London South Bank Uni • Manchester Uni • Newcastle Uni • Northumbria Uni • Nottingham Trent Uni • Nottingham Uni • Open Uni • Oxford Uni • Portsmouth Uni • Queen Mary • Queen's Uni Belfast • Reading Uni • Royal Holloway • St Andrews Uni • Salford Uni • Sheffield Uni • Southampton Uni • Staffordshire Uni • Strathclyde Uni • Surrey Uni • Sussex Uni • Swansea Uni • UCLan • Ulster Uni • University Coll London • Warwick Uni • West of Scotland Uni • Westminster Uni • Wolverhampton Uni • York Uni

Biological chemistry

Aberdeen Uni • Aston Uni • Birkbeck • Bristol UWE • Derby Uni • Dundee Uni • East Anglia Uni • Edinburgh Uni • Exeter Uni • Glasgow Caledonian Uni • Greenwich Uni • Harper Adams Uni Coll • Heriot-Watt Uni • Hertfordshire Uni • Hull Uni • Kingston Uni • Leicester Uni • London Met Uni • Manchester Uni • Newcastle Uni • Nottingham Uni • Portsmouth Uni • Queen Mary • St Andrews Uni • Scottish Agricultural Coll • Sheffield Hallam Uni • Sheffield Uni • Southampton Uni • Surrey Uni • Sussex Uni • UCLan • Warwick Uni • West of Scotland Uni • *See also:* Biotechnology

Biology

Aberdeen Uni • Abertay Dundee Uni • Aberystwyth Uni • Anglia Ruskin Uni • Aston Uni • Bangor Uni • Bath Spa Uni • Bath Uni • Birkbeck • Birmingham Unil •Bolton Uni • Brighton Uni • Bristol Uni • Bristol UWE • Cambridge Uni • Canterbury Christ Church Uni • Cardiff Uni • Chester Uni • Coventry Uni • Cumbria Uni • Derby Uni • Dundee Uni • Durham Uni • East Anglia Uni • East London Uni • Edge Hill Uni • Edinburgh Uni • Essex Uni • Exeter Uni • Glamorgan Uni • Glasgow Caledonian Uni • Glasgow Uni • Gloucestershire Uni • Glyndŵr Uni • Greenwich Unil • Heriot-Watt Uni • Hertfordshire Uni • Huddersfield Uni • Hull Uni • Imperial Coll • Keele Uni • Kent • King's Coll London • Kingston Uni • Lancaster Uni • Leeds Met Uni • Leeds Uni • Leicester Uni • Liverpool John Moores Uni • Liverpool Uni • London Met Uni • London South Bank Uni • Manchester Met Uni • Manchester Uni • Middlesex Uni • Napier Uni • Newcastle Uni • Northampton Uni • Northumbria Uni • Nottingham Trent Uni • Nottingham Uni • Open Uni • Oxford Brookes Uni • Oxford Uni • Plymouth Uni • Portsmouth Uni • Queen Mary • Queen's Uni Belfast • Reading Uni • Roehampton Uni • Royal Holloway • St Andrews Uni • Salford Uni • Scottish Agricultural Coll • Sheffield Hallam Uni • Sheffield Uni • Southampton Uni • Staffordshire Uni • Stirling Uni • Strathclyde Uni • Sussex Uni • Swansea Uni • Teesside Uni • UCLan • Ulster Uni • University Coll London • Warwick Uni • West of Scotland Uni • Westminster Uni • Wolverhampton Uni • Worcester Uni • York Uni • *See also:* Botany; microbiology; zoology

Biomedical electronics

Birmingham Uni • Bournemouth Uni • Bradford Uni • City Uni • Liverpool Uni • Reading Uni • Strathclyde Uni • Ulster Uni

Biomedical science

Aberdeen Uni • Abertay Dundee Uni • Anglia Ruskin Uni • Aston Uni • Bangor Uni • Bedfordshire Uni • Birkbeck • Birmingham Uni • Bradford Uni • Brighton Uni • Bristol UWE • Brunel Uni • Cambridge Uni • Cardiff Uni • Chester Uni • Coventry Uni • Cranfield Uni (p/g only) • De Montfort Uni • Dundee Uni • Durham Uni • East Anglia Uni • East London Uni • Edinburgh Uni • Essex Uni • Exeter Uni • Glasgow Caledonian Uni • Glasgow Uni • Greenwich Uni • Harper Adams Uni Coll • Hertfordshire Uni • Hull Uni • Imperial Coll • Keele Uni • Kent • King's Coll London • Kingston Uni • Lancaster Uni • Leeds Met Uni • Leeds Uni • Leicester Uni • Lincoln Uni • Liverpool John Moores Uni • Liverpool Uni • London

Met Uni • London South Bank Uni • Manchester Met Uni • Manchester Uni • Middlesex Uni • Napier Uni • Newcastle Uni • Northumbria Uni • Nottingham Trent Uni • Nottingham Uni • Oxford Brookes Uni • Oxford Uni • Plymouth Uni • Portsmouth Uni • Queen Mary • Queen's Uni Belfast • Reading Uni • Robert Gordon Uni • Roehampton Uni • Royal Holloway • Royal Vet Coll • St George's • Sheffield Hallam Uni • Sheffield Uni • Southampton Uni • Staffordshire Uni • Strathclyde Uni • Sunderland Uni • Surrey Uni • Sussex Uni • Swansea Uni • UCLan • Ulster Uni • University Coll London • UWIC • Warwick Uni • West of Scotland Uni • Westminster Uni • Wolverhampton Uni

Biophysics

Aberdeen Uni • Birmingham Uni • Liverpool John Moores Uni • Nottingham Trent Uni • Portsmouth Uni • Strathclyde Uni

Biosocial science

See: Human sciences

Biotechnology

Aberdeen Uni • Abertay Dundee Uni • Aberystwyth Uni • Anglia Ruskin Uni • Aston Uni • Birmingham Uni • Bradford Uni • Bristol Uni • Bristol UWE • Cardiff Uni • Cranfield Uni (p/g only) • East London Uni • Edinburgh Uni • Glasgow Uni • Heriot-Watt Uni • Hertfordshire Uni • Hull Uni • Imperial Coll • Kent • Kingston Uni • Leeds Uni • Leicester Uni • Liverpool John Moores Uni • Liverpool Uni • Manchester Uni • Napier Uni • Newcastle Uni • Northumbria Uni • Nottingham Uni • Oxford Brookes Uni • Portsmouth Uni • Reading Uni • Royal Holloway • Scottish Agricultural Coll • Sheffield Uni • Strathclyde Uni • Surrey Uni • Sussex Uni • Swansea Uni • University Coll London • West of Scotland Uni • Westminster Uni • Wolverhampton Uni • *See also:* Biochemical engineering; biochemistry

Boat design

Coventry Uni • Newcastle Uni • Southampton Solent Uni • Southampton Uni • University Coll London

Botany

See: Plant science

Brewing

Brighton Uni • Heriot-Watt Uni • *See also:* Microbiology

Broadcasting

Bath Spa Uni • Bedfordshire Uni • Birmingham City Uni • Bournemouth Uni • Bradford Uni • Brighton Uni • Canterbury Christ Church Uni • Chester Uni • Coventry Uni • Creative Arts Uni • De Montfort Uni • Derby Uni • East London Uni • Falmouth Uni Coll • Farnborough Coll • Glamorgan Uni • Gloucestershire Uni • Glyndŵr Uni • Hertfordshire Uni • Huddersfield Uni • Kingston Uni • Leeds Uni • Liverpool John Moores Uni • London Coll Communication • London Coll Fashion • London Met Uni • National Film Sch (p/g only) • Nottingham Trent Uni • Portsmouth Uni • Ravensbourne Coll • Salford Uni • Southampton Solent Uni • Staffordshire Uni • Sunderland Uni • Teesside Uni • Thames Valley Uni • UCLan • UWIC • West of Scotland Uni • Westminster Uni • Winchester Uni • Wolverhampton Uni • *See also:* Communication studies; film studies; journalism; media studies

Building studies

Bedfordshire Uni • Bolton Uni • Brighton Uni • Bristol UWE • Brunel Uni • Coventry Uni • Derby Uni • Dundee Uni • Glamorgan Uni • Glasgow Caledonian Uni • Glyndŵr Uni • Greenwich Uni • Heriot-Watt Uni • Kingston Uni • Leeds Met Uni • Liverpool John Moores Uni • London South Bank Uni • Napier Uni • Newport • Northumbria Uni • Nottingham Trent Uni • Oxford Brookes Uni • Plymouth Uni • Portsmouth Uni • Reading Uni • Royal Agricultural Coll • Salford Uni • Sheffield Hallam Uni • Southampton Solent Uni • Swansea Met Uni • Thames Valley Uni • UCLan • Ulster Uni • University Coll London • UWIC • Westminster Uni • Wolverhampton Uni • *See also:* Architecture; building surveying; building technology; civil engineering

Building surveying

Aberdeen Uni • Anglia Ruskin Uni • Birmingham City Uni • Bolton Uni • Brighton Uni • Bristol UWE • Coventry Uni • East London Uni • Glamorgan Uni • Glasgow Caledonian Uni • Glyndŵr Uni • Greenwich Uni • Harper Adams Uni Coll • Heriot-Watt Uni • Kingston Uni •Leeds Met Uni • Liverpool John Moores Uni • London South Bank Uni • Loughborough Uni • Napier Uni • Newcastle Uni • Northumbria Uni • Nottingham Trent Uni • Plymouth Uni • Portsmouth Uni • Reading Uni • Robert Gordon Uni • Royal Agricultural Coll • Salford Uni • Sheffield Hallam Uni • UCLan • Ulster Uni • Westminster Uni • Wolverhampton Uni • *See also:* Quantity surveying

Building technology

Bedfordshire Uni • Birmingham Uni • Brighton Uni • Bristol UWE • Coventry Uni • Glamorgan Uni • Glasgow Caledonian Uni • Heriot-Watt Uni • Kingston Uni • Leeds Met Uni • Liverpool John Moores Uni • London South Bank Uni • Napier Uni • Nottingham Trent Uni • Portsmouth Uni • Reading Uni • Sheffield Hallam Uni • Strathclyde Uni • Ulster Uni

Bulgarian

University Coll London

Burmese studies

SOAS • *See also:* Asian studies; oriental studies

Business

See: Accountancy; business administration; business studies; economics; law; management

Business administration

Abertay Dundee Uni • Aberystwyth Uni • Anglia Ruskin Uni • Aston Uni • Bangor Uni • Bath Uni • Bedfordshire Uni • Birmingham Uni • Bournemouth Uni • Bradford Coll • Bradford Uni • Brighton Uni • Bristol UWE • Brunel Uni • Buckingham Uni • Bucks New Uni • Canterbury Christ Church Uni • Cardiff Uni • Chester Uni • City Uni • Coventry Uni • Cranfield Uni (p/g only) • Derby Uni • East London Uni • European Business Sch • Exeter Uni • Farnborough Coll • Glamorgan Uni • Glasgow Caledonian Uni • Gloucestershire Uni • Glyndŵr Uni • Greenwich Uni • Harper Adams Uni Coll • Heriot-Watt Uni • Hertfordshire Uni • Huddersfield Uni • Imperial Coll • Kent • Kingston Uni • Lancaster Uni • Leeds Met Uni • Leicester Uni • Liverpool John Moores Uni • London Business Sch (p/g only) • London Coll Fashion • London South Bank Uni • Loughborough Uni • Manchester Met Uni • Middlesex Uni • Napier Uni • Newport • Northampton Uni • Northumbria Uni • Nottingham Trent Uni • Oxford Brookes Uni • Plymouth Uni • Portsmouth Uni • Reading Uni • Regent's Business Sch • Royal Agricultural Coll • Salford Uni • Southampton Solent Uni • Stirling Uni • Strathclyde Uni • Swansea Met Uni • Swansea Uni • Teesside Uni • Thames Valley Uni • UCLan • UHI Millennium

Institute • Ulster Uni • University Coll Birmingham • UWIC • West of Scotland Uni • Westminster Uni • Winchester Uni • Wolverhampton Uni • Worcester Uni • Writtle Coll

Business economics

Aberdeen Uni • Aberystwyth Uni • Anglia Ruskin Uni • Aston Uni • Bangor Uni • Birmingham City Uni • Birmingham Uni • Bournemouth Uni • Bradford Uni • Brighton Uni • Bristol UWE • Brunel Uni • Buckingham Uni • Bucks New Uni • Cardiff Uni • Coventry Uni • Derby Uni • Dundee Uni • Durham Uni • East Anglia Uni • East London Uni • Edinburgh Uni • Essex Uni • European Business Sch • Exeter Uni • Glamorgan Uni • Glasgow Caledonian Uni • Glasgow Uni • Greenwich Uni • Heriot-Watt Uni • Hertfordshire Uni • Hull Uni • Imperial Coll • Keele Uni • Kent • Kingston Uni • Lancaster Uni • Leeds Met Uni • Leeds Uni • Leicester Uni • Liverpool Uni • London Met Uni • Loughborough Uni • LSE • Manchester Met Uni • Manchester Uni • Middlesex Uni • Napier Uni • Newcastle Uni • Newport • Northumbria Uni • Nottingham Trent Uni • Nottingham Uni • Oxford Brookes Uni • Plymouth Uni • Portsmouth Uni • Queen Mary • Queen's Uni Belfast • Reading Uni • Robert Gordon Uni • Royal Agricultural Coll • Salford Uni • Sheffield Hallam Uni • Southampton Uni • Staffordshire Uni • Stirling Uni • Surrey Uni • Sussex Uni • Swansea Met Uni • Swansea Uni • Teesside Uni • UCLan • UWIC • Warwick Uni • West of Scotland Uni • Westminster Uni • Winchester Uni • Wolverhampton Uni • Worcester Uni

Business studies

Aberdeen Uni • Abertay Dundee Uni • Aberystwyth Uni • Anglia Ruskin Uni • Aston Uni • Bangor Uni • Bath Spa Uni • Bedfordshire Uni • Birmingham City Uni • Birmingham Uni • Bolton Uni • Bournemouth Uni • Bradford Coll • Bradford Uni • Brighton Uni • Bristol UWE • Brunel Uni • Buckingham Uni • Bucks New Uni • Canterbury Christ Church Uni • Cardiff Uni • Chester Uni • Chichester Uni • Colchester Inst • Coventry Uni • Cranfield Uni (p/g only) • Cumbria Uni • De Montfort Uni • Derby Uni • Durham Uni • East Anglia Uni • East London Uni • Edge Hill Uni • Edinburgh Uni • Essex Uni • European Business Sch • Exeter Uni • Glamorgan Uni • Glasgow Caledonian Uni • Glasgow Uni • Gloucestershire Uni • Glyndŵr Uni • Greenwich Uni • Harper Adams Uni Coll • Heriot-Watt Uni • Hertfordshire Uni • Huddersfield Uni • Hull Uni • Imperial Coll • Kent • Kingston Uni.Lampeter Uni • Lancaster Uni • Leeds Met Uni • Leeds Trinity • Leeds Uni • Leicester Uni • Lincoln Uni • Liverpool Hope Uni • Liverpool John Moores Uni • Liverpool Uni • London Coll Fashion • London Met Uni • London South Bank Uni • Loughborough Uni • Manchester Met Uni • Manchester Uni • Middlesex Uni • Napier Uni • Newcastle Uni • Newport • Northampton Uni • Northumbria Uni • Nottingham Trent Uni • Nottingham Uni • Open Uni • Oxford Brookes Uni • Plymouth Uni • Portsmouth Uni • Queen Margaret Uni • Queen Mary • Regent's Business Sch • Robert Gordon Uni • Roehampton Uni • Royal Agricultural Coll • Salford Uni • Scottish Agricultural Coll • Sheffield Hallam Uni • Sheffield Uni • Southampton Solent Uni • Southampton Uni • Staffordshire Uni • Stirling Uni • Strathclyde Uni • Sunderland Uni • Surrey Uni • Sussex Uni • Swansea Met Uni • Swansea Uni • Teesside Uni • Thames Valley Uni • Trinity Coll Carmarthen • UCLan • Ulster Uni • University Coll Birmingham • UWIC • Warwick Uni • West of Scotland Uni • Westminster Uni • Winchester Uni • Wolverhampton Uni • Worcester Uni • Writtle Coll • York St John Uni

Byzantine studies

See: Classics; history

Canadian studies

See: American studies

Carbon dating

See: Archaeology

Caribbean studies

London Met Uni

Caring

See: Education; medicine; nursing; social administration; social work; youth and community work

Catalan

Aberdeen Uni • Birmingham Uni • Cambridge Uni • Kent • Lancaster Uni • Liverpool Uni • Sheffield Uni • Swansea Uni • *See also:* Spanish

Catering

Brighton Uni • Derby Uni • Glasgow Caledonian Uni • Gloucestershire Uni • Huddersfield Uni • Leeds Met Uni • Thames Valley Uni • Ulster Uni • University Coll Birmingham • UWIC • *See also:* Dietetics; hospitality management

Cell biology

Aberdeen Uni • Anglia Ruskin Uni • Aston Uni • Bath Uni • Birmingham Uni • Bradford Uni • Cambridge Uni • Coventry Uni • Dundee Uni • Durham Uni • East Anglia Uni • Edinburgh Uni • Essex Uni • Glasgow Caledonian Uni • Glasgow Uni • Heriot-Watt Uni • Huddersfield Uni • Hull Uni • Kent • Kingston Uni • Lancaster Uni • Leeds Uni • Leicester Uni • Manchester Met Uni • Manchester Uni • Newcastle Uni • Nottingham Trent Uni • Nottingham Uni • Oxford Brookes Uni • Portsmouth Uni • Reading Uni • Royal Holloway • St Andrews Uni • Sheffield Uni • Southampton Uni • Stirling Uni • Surrey Uni • Sussex Uni • Warwick Uni • Westminster Uni • Wolverhampton Uni • York Uni • *See also:* Microbiology

Cellular pathology

Bradford Uni • Bristol Uni • Glasgow Caledonian Uni • Reading Uni • St Andrews Uni • Sheffield Hallam Uni • Westminster Uni • *See also:* Pathology

Celtic studies

Aberdeen Uni • Aberystwyth Uni • Cambridge Uni • Edinburgh Uni • Exeter Uni • Glasgow Uni • Lampeter Uni • Liverpool Uni • Oxford Uni • Queen's Uni Belfast • Swansea Uni • Ulster Uni • *See also:* Irish studies; Scottish studies; Welsh studies

Central European studies

See: European studies

Ceramic science

See: Chemistry

Ceramics

Bath Spa Uni • Bedfordshire Uni • Birmingham City Uni • Bradford Coll • Brighton Uni • Bucks New Uni • Camberwell Coll • Central Saint Martins • Colchester Inst • Creative Arts Uni • Cumbria Uni • Falmouth Uni Coll • Glyndŵr Uni • Loughborough Uni • Robert Gordon Uni • Royal Coll Art (p/g only) • Sheffield Uni • Staffordshire Uni • Sunderland Uni • Swansea Met Uni • Thames Valley Uni

• Trinity Coll Carmarthen • UCLan • UWIC • Westminster Uni • Wolverhampton Uni • *See also:* Three-dimensional design

Chemical engineering

Aberdeen Uni • Aston Uni • Bath Uni • Birmingham Uni • Cambridge Uni • Edinburgh Uni • Heriot-Watt Uni • Imperial Coll • Leeds Uni • London South Bank Uni • Loughborough Uni • Manchester Uni • Newcastle Uni • Nottingham Uni • Oxford Uni • Queen's Uni Belfast • Sheffield Uni • Strathclyde Uni • Surrey Uni • Sussex Uni • Swansea Uni • Teesside Uni • University Coll London • West of Scotland Uni

Chemical physics

Bristol Uni • East Anglia Uni • Edinburgh Uni • Glasgow Uni • Liverpool Uni • Manchester Uni • Nottingham Uni • Sheffield Uni • Southampton Uni • Sussex Uni • University Coll London

Chemistry

Aberdeen Uni • Abertay Dundee Uni • Aston Uni • Bangor Uni • Bath Uni • Birkbeck • Birmingham Uni • Bradford Uni • Brighton Uni • Bristol Uni • Cambridge Uni • Cardiff Uni • Durham Uni • East Anglia Uni • Edinburgh Uni • Glamorgan Uni • Glasgow Uni • Glyndŵr Uni • Greenwich Uni • Heriot-Watt Uni • Huddersfield Uni • Hull Uni • Imperial Coll • Keele Uni • King's Coll London • Kingston Uni • Leeds Uni • Leicester Uni • Lincoln Uni • Liverpool John Moores Uni • Liverpool Uni • London Met Uni • Loughborough Uni • Manchester Met Uni • Manchester Uni • Newcastle Uni • Northumbria Uni • Nottingham Trent Uni • Nottingham Uni • Open Uni • Oxford Brookes Uni • Oxford Uni • Plymouth Uni • Queen Mary • Queen's Uni Belfast • Reading Uni • St Andrews Uni • Sheffield Hallam Uni • Sheffield Uni • Southampton Uni • Strathclyde Uni • Surrey Uni • Sussex Uni • Teesside Uni • UCLan • University Coll London • Warwick Uni • West of Scotland Uni • York Uni

Childhood studies

Aberystwyth Uni • Anglia Ruskin Uni • Bangor Uni • Bedfordshire Uni • Birmingham City Uni • Birmingham Uni • Bolton Uni • Bournemouth Uni • Bradford Coll • Bristol Uni • Bristol UWE • Canterbury Christ Church Uni • Chester Uni • Chichester Uni • Colchester Inst • Cumbria Uni • Derby Uni • East London Uni • Edge Hill Uni • Exeter Uni • Farnborough Coll • Gloucestershire Uni • Glyndŵr Uni • Greenwich Uni • Hertfordshire Uni • Hull Uni • Leeds Met Uni • Leeds Trinity • Leeds Uni • Lincoln Uni • Liverpool Hope Uni • Liverpool John Moores Uni • London Met Uni • Manchester Met Uni • Marjon • Middlesex Uni • Newport • Northampton Uni • Northumbria Uni • Nottingham Trent Uni • Open Uni • Oxford Brookes Uni • Plymouth Uni • Portsmouth Uni • Reading Uni • Roehampton Uni • Sheffield Hallam Uni • Strathclyde Uni • Sunderland Uni • Swansea Uni • Teesside Uni • Trinity Coll Carmarthen • UHI Millennium Institute • University Coll Birmingham • UWIC • Warwick Uni • West of Scotland Uni • Winchester Uni • Wolverhampton Uni • Worcester Uni

Chinese

Bristol UWE • Cambridge Uni • Edge Hill Uni • Edinburgh Uni • European Business Sch • Lampeter Uni • Leeds Uni • Liverpool John Moores Uni • Manchester Uni • Newcastle Uni • Nottingham Trent Uni • Nottingham Uni • Oxford Uni • Portsmouth Uni • Sheffield Uni • SOAS • UCLan • Westminster Uni • *See also:* Asian studies; oriental studies

Chiropody

See: Podiatry

Choreography

Bedfordshire Uni • Chichester Uni • Coventry Uni • Dartington • Derby Uni • Falmouth Uni Coll • Laban • London Contemp Dance Sch • Middlesex Uni • Northern Sch Cont Dance • Winchester Uni

Church history

Aberdeen Uni • Lampeter Uni • London Sch Theology • Oak Hill Coll • St Andrews Uni • Spurgeon's Coll • *See also:* Religious studies

Civil engineering

Aberdeen Uni • Abertay Dundee Uni • Anglia Ruskin Uni • Bath Uni • Birmingham Uni • Bolton Uni • Bradford Uni • Brighton Uni • Bristol Uni • Bristol UWE • Cambridge Uni • Cardiff Uni • City Uni • Coventry Uni • Cranfield Uni (p/g only) • Derby Uni • Dundee Uni • Durham Uni • East London Uni • Edinburgh Uni • Exeter Uni • Glamorgan Uni • Glasgow Caledonian Uni • Glasgow Uni • Greenwich Uni • Heriot-Watt Uni • Imperial Coll • Kingston Uni • Leeds Met Uni • Leeds Uni • Liverpool John Moores Uni • Liverpool Uni • London South Bank Uni • Loughborough Uni • Manchester Uni • Napier Uni • Newcastle Uni • Newport • Nottingham Trent Uni • Nottingham Uni • Oxford Uni • Plymouth Uni • Portsmouth Uni • Queen's Uni Belfast • Robert Gordon Uni • Salford Uni • Sheffield Uni • Southampton Uni • Strathclyde Uni • Surrey Uni • Swansea Met Uni • Swansea Uni • Teesside Uni • Ulster Uni • University Coll London • Warwick Uni • West of Scotland Uni • Wolverhampton Uni • *See also:* Engineering (general)

Classical studies

Aberdeen Uni • Birkbeck • Birmingham Uni • Bristol Uni • Durham Uni • Edinburgh Uni • Exeter Uni • Glasgow Uni • Kent • King's Coll London • Lampeter Uni • Leeds Uni • Liverpool Uni • Manchester Uni • Newcastle Uni • Nottingham Uni • Open Uni • Reading Uni • Roehampton Uni • Royal Holloway • St Andrews Uni • Swansea Uni • University Coll London • Warwick Uni • *See also:* Ancient history; classics

Classics

Birkbeck • Birmingham Uni • Bristol Uni • Cambridge Uni • Durham Uni • Edinburgh Uni • Exeter Uni • Glasgow Uni • Kent • King's Coll London • Lampeter Uni • Leeds Uni • Liverpool Uni • Manchester Uni • Newcastle Uni • Nottingham Uni • Oxford Uni • Reading Uni • Roehampton Uni • Royal Holloway • St Andrews Uni • Swansea Uni • University Coll London • Warwick Uni • *See also:* Classical studies; Greek; Latin

Climate

See: Geography; meteorology

Clothing

See: Fashion; textiles

Coastal engineering

See: Civil engineering

Cognitive science

Bradford Uni • Dundee Uni • Edinburgh Uni • Leeds Uni • Manchester Uni • Middlesex Uni • Royal Holloway • Sussex Uni • Westminster Uni • *See also:* Psychology

Commerce

Bedfordshire Uni • Birmingham Uni • Coventry Uni • European Business Sch • Glasgow Caledonian Uni • Huddersfield Uni • Liverpool Uni • Portsmouth Uni • Regent's Business Sch • West of Scotland Uni • See also: Business studies

Communication engineering

Anglia Ruskin Uni • Aston Uni • Bath Uni • Birmingham City Uni • Birmingham Uni • Bolton Uni • Bournemouth Uni • Bradford Uni • Bristol Uni • Brunel Uni • Cardiff Uni • City Uni • Dundee Uni • Durham Uni • East London Uni • Edinburgh Uni • Essex Uni • Farnborough Coll • Glamorgan Uni • Glasgow Caledonian Uni • Glyndŵr Uni • Greenwich Uni • Heriot-Watt Uni • Hertfordshire Uni • Huddersfield Uni • Hull Uni • Imperial Coll • Kent • Kingston Uni • Lancaster Uni • Leicester Uni • Liverpool John Moores Uni • Liverpool Uni • London Met Uni • Loughborough Uni • Manchester Uni • Napier Uni • Newcastle Uni • Newport • Northumbria Uni • Nottingham Uni • Plymouth Uni • Portsmouth Uni • Queen Mary • Ravensbourne Coll • Robert Gordon Uni • Sheffield Uni • Southampton Uni • Strathclyde Uni • Surrey Uni • Sussex Uni • Swansea Uni • Ulster Uni • University Coll London • West of Scotland Uni • Wolverhampton Uni • York Uni

Communication studies

Aberystwyth Uni • Anglia Ruskin Uni • Bangor Uni • Bedfordshire Uni • Birmingham Uni • Bournemouth Uni • Bradford Coll • Bradford Uni • Bristol UWE • Brunel Uni • Buckingham Uni • Canterbury Christ Church Uni • Cardiff Uni • Chester Uni • City Uni • Coventry Uni • Creative Arts Uni • East London Uni • Falmouth Uni Coll • Glamorgan Uni • Glasgow Caledonian Uni • Glyndŵr Uni • Goldsmiths • Huddersfield Uni • Kingston Uni • Lancaster Uni • Leeds Uni • Leicester Uni • Lincoln Uni • Liverpool John Moores Uni • Liverpool Uni • London Coll Communication • London Met Uni • Loughborough Uni • Manchester Met Uni • Middlesex Uni • Napier Uni • Newcastle Uni • Northumbria Uni • Nottingham Trent Uni • Nottingham Uni • Oxford Brookes Uni • Portsmouth Uni • Ravensbourne Coll • Robert Gordon Uni • Roehampton Uni • Sheffield Hallam Uni • Stirling Uni • Swansea Uni • UCLan • Ulster Uni • Westminster Uni • Wolverhampton Uni • York St John Uni • See also: Media studies

Community arts

Birmingham City Uni • Cumbria Uni • Dartington • East London Uni • Laban • Manchester Met Uni • Middlesex Uni • Royal Scottish Academy Music/Drama • Strathclyde Uni • Thames Valley Uni • West of Scotland Uni • Winchester Uni • York St John Uni

Community health

See: Health

Community studies

Bedfordshire Uni • Birkbeck • Birmingham Uni • Bolton Uni • Bradford Uni • Bristol UWE • Chichester Uni • Coventry Uni • De Montfort Uni • Derby Uni • Durham Uni • East London Uni • Glamorgan Uni • Glyndŵr Uni • Goldsmiths • Greenwich Uni • Huddersfield Uni • Liverpool John Moores Uni • London Met Uni • Manchester Uni • Marjon • Newport • Sunderland Uni • Sussex Uni • Trinity Coll Carmarthen • Ulster Uni • UWIC • Wolverhampton Uni • See also: Youth/community work

Community work

See: Youth and community work.

685

Comparative literature

Anglia Ruskin Uni • Bradford Uni • Buckingham Uni • East Anglia Uni • Essex Uni • Glasgow Uni • Goldsmiths • Kent • King's Coll London • Kingston Uni • Liverpool Uni • Manchester Uni • Surrey Uni • Warwick Uni

Complementary therapies

Anglia Ruskin Uni • Bedfordshire Uni • British Sch Osteopathy • Cumbria Uni • Derby Uni • East London Uni • Farnborough Coll • Glyndŵr Uni • Greenwich Uni • Lincoln Uni • London Coll Fashion • Middlesex Uni • Napier Uni • Salford Uni • Thames Valley Uni • UCLan • University Coll Birmingham • UWIC • Westminster Uni • Wolverhampton Uni • Worcester Uni

Computational mathematics

East Anglia Uni • Imperial Coll • Leicester Uni • London Met Uni • Manchester Uni • Nottingham Uni • Portsmouth Uni • Queen's Uni Belfast • Reading Uni • Sussex Uni • Swansea Uni

Computer engineering

Aberdeen Uni • Abertay Dundee Uni • Aberystwyth Uni • Anglia Ruskin Uni • Aston Uni • Bangor Uni • Bath Uni • Bedfordshire Uni • Birmingham Uni • Bolton Uni • Bournemouth Uni • Bradford Uni • Bristol Uni • Bristol UWE • Brunel Uni • Bucks New Uni • Cambridge Uni • Cardiff Uni • City Uni • Coventry Uni • Cranfield Uni (p/g only) • Derby Uni • Dundee Uni • Durham Uni • East Anglia Uni • East London Uni • Edinburgh Uni • Essex Uni • Exeter Uni • Glamorgan Uni • Glasgow Caledonian Uni • Gloucestershire Uni • Glyndŵr Uni • Greenwich Uni • Heriot-Watt Uni • Huddersfield Uni • Hull Uni • Imperial Coll • Kent • Lancaster Uni • Leicester Uni • Liverpool John Moores Uni • Liverpool Uni • London South Bank Uni • Loughborough Uni • Manchester Uni • Napier Uni • Newcastle Uni • Northampton Uni • Northumbria Uni • Nottingham Trent Uni • Oxford Brookes Uni • Plymouth Uni • Portsmouth Uni • Queen Mary • Reading Uni • Robert Gordon Uni • Sheffield Hallam Uni • Sheffield Uni • Southampton Uni • Strathclyde Uni • Sussex Uni • Swansea Met Uni • Swansea Uni • Teesside Uni • UCLan • Ulster Uni • Warwick Uni • West of Scotland Uni • Westminster Uni • Wolverhampton Uni • York Uni • *See also:* Computer technology

Computer science

Aberdeen Uni • Abertay Dundee Uni • Aberystwyth Uni • Anglia Ruskin Uni • Aston Uni • Bangor Uni • Bath Uni • Bedfordshire Uni • Birkbeck • Birmingham City Uni • Birmingham Uni • Bournemouth Uni • Bradford Uni • Brighton Uni • Bristol Uni • Bristol UWE • Brunel Uni • Buckingham Uni • Cambridge Uni • Cardiff Uni • Chester Uni • City Uni • Coventry Uni • Cranfield Uni (p/g only) • De Montfort Uni • Derby Uni • Dundee Uni • Durham Uni • East Anglia Uni • East London Uni • Edinburgh Uni • Essex Uni • Exeter Uni • Glamorgan Uni • Glasgow Caledonian Uni • Glasgow Uni • Gloucestershire Uni • Glyndŵr Uni • Goldsmiths • Greenwich Uni • Heriot-Watt Uni • Hertfordshire Uni • Hull Uni • Imperial Coll • Keele Uni • Kent • King's Coll London • Kingston Uni • Lancaster Uni • Leeds Uni • Leicester Uni • Liverpool John Moores Uni • Liverpool Uni • London Met Uni • Loughborough Uni • Manchester Met Uni • Manchester Uni • Middlesex Uni • Napier Uni • Newcastle Uni • Northampton Uni • Northumbria Uni • Nottingham Trent Uni • Nottingham Uni • Open Uni • Oxford Brookes Uni • Oxford Uni • Plymouth Uni • Portsmouth Uni • Queen Mary • Queen's Uni Belfast • Reading Uni • Robert Gordon Uni • Royal Holloway • St Andrews Uni • Salford Uni • Sheffield Hallam Uni • Sheffield Uni • Southampton Solent Uni • Southampton Uni • Staffordshire Uni • Stirling Uni • Strathclyde Uni • Sunderland Uni • Surrey Uni • Sussex Uni • Swansea Met Uni • Swansea Uni • Teesside Uni • Thames Valley Uni • Ulster Uni • University Coll London • Warwick Uni • West of Scotland Uni • Westminster Uni • Wolverhampton Uni • York Uni • *See also:* Computing

Computer technology

Aberdeen Uni • Abertay Dundee Uni • Aberystwyth Uni • Anglia Ruskin Uni • Aston Uni • Bath Uni • Bedfordshire Uni • Birmingham City Uni • Birmingham Uni • Bolton Uni • Bournemouth Uni • Bradford Uni • Bristol Uni • Bristol UWE • Brunel Uni • Bucks New Uni • City Uni • Coventry Uni • Cranfield Uni (p/g only) • De Montfort Uni • Derby Uni • East London Uni • Essex Uni • Farnborough Coll • Glamorgan Uni • Glasgow Caledonian Uni • Gloucestershire Uni • Glyndŵr Uni • Heriot-Watt Uni • Hertfordshire Uni • Huddersfield Uni • Hull Uni • Imperial Coll • Kingston Uni • Lancaster Uni • Lincoln Uni • Liverpool John Moores Uni • Liverpool Uni • London Met Uni • London South Bank Uni • Loughborough Uni • Manchester Uni • Middlesex Uni • Napier Uni • Newcastle Uni • Northampton Uni • Northumbria Uni • Nottingham Trent Uni • Nottingham Uni • Open Uni • Oxford Brookes Uni • Plymouth Uni • Portsmouth Uni • Reading Uni • Robert Gordon Uni • Sheffield Hallam Uni • Southampton Solent Uni • Southampton Uni • Sunderland Uni • Surrey Uni • Sussex Uni • Swansea Met Uni • Swansea Uni • Teesside Uni • Thames Valley Uni • UCLan • Warwick Uni • West of Scotland Uni • Westminster Uni • *See also:* Computer science

Computing

Aberdeen Uni • Abertay Dundee Uni • Aberystwyth Uni • Anglia Ruskin Uni • Aston Uni • Bangor Uni • Bath Uni • Bedfordshire Uni • Birkbeck • Birmingham City Uni • Birmingham Uni • Bolton Uni • Bournemouth Uni • Bradford Coll • Bradford Uni • Brighton Uni • Bristol UWE • Brunel Uni • Buckingham Uni • Bucks New Uni • Canterbury Christ Church Uni • Cardiff Uni • City Uni • Colchester Inst • Coventry Uni • Cumbria Uni • De Montfort Uni • Derby Uni • Dundee Uni • East Anglia Uni • East London Uni • Edge Hill Uni • Edinburgh Uni • Essex Uni • Exeter Uni • Farnborough Coll • Glamorgan Uni • Glasgow Caledonian Uni • Glasgow Uni • Gloucestershire Uni • Glyndŵr Uni • Goldsmiths • Greenwich Uni • Heriot-Watt Uni • Hertfordshire Uni • Huddersfield Uni • Hull Uni • Imperial Coll • Kent • Kingston Uni • Lancaster Uni • Leeds Met Uni • Leeds Uni • Leicester Uni • Lincoln Uni • Liverpool Hope Uni • Liverpool John Moores Uni • Liverpool Uni • London Met Uni • London South Bank Uni • Loughborough Uni • Manchester Met Uni • Manchester Uni • Middlesex Uni • Napier Uni • Newcastle Uni • Newport • Northampton Uni • Northumbria Uni • Nottingham Trent Uni • Nottingham Uni • Open Uni • Oxford Uni • Plymouth Uni • Portsmouth Uni • Queen Mary • Queen's Uni Belfast • Reading Uni • Robert Gordon Uni • Roehampton Uni • St Andrews Uni • Salford Uni • Sheffield Hallam Uni • Southampton Solent Uni • Southampton Uni • Staffordshire Uni • Stirling Uni • Strathclyde Uni • Sunderland Uni • Surrey Uni • Sussex Uni • Swansea Met Uni • Swansea Uni • Teesside Uni • Thames Valley Uni • Trinity Coll Carmarthen • UCLan • UHI Millennium Institute • Ulster Uni • University Coll London • UWIC • Warwick Uni • West of Scotland Uni • Westminster Uni • Wolverhampton Uni • Worcester Uni • *See also:* Computer science; information technology

Conflict

See: War studies

Conservation

Aberdeen Uni • Aberystwyth Uni • Anglia Ruskin Uni • Bangor Uni • Birkbeck • Bolton Uni • Bournemouth Uni • Brighton Uni • Bristol UWE • Camberwell Coll • Canterbury Christ Church Uni • Cardiff Uni • Central Saint Martins • Coventry Uni • Cumbria Uni • East Anglia Uni • East London Uni • Edinburgh Uni • Exeter Uni • Huddersfield Uni • Imperial Coll • Kent • Lancaster Uni • Leeds Uni • Lincoln Uni • Liverpool John Moores Uni • Manchester Met Uni • Myerscough Coll • Northampton Uni • Northumbria Uni • Nottingham Trent Uni • Oxford Brookes Uni • Plymouth Uni • Queen Mary • Reading Uni • Roehampton Uni • Royal Agricultural Coll • Royal Coll Art (p/g only) • Salford Uni • Scottish Agricultural Coll • Stirling Uni • Sussex Uni • Swansea Met Uni • Writtle Coll • York Uni • *See also:* Archaeology; biology; ecology; environmental studies

687

Construction

Anglia Ruskin Uni • Aston Uni • Bath Uni • Bedfordshire Uni • Birmingham City Uni • Bolton Uni • Bradford Coll • Brighton Uni • Bristol UWE • Colchester Inst • Coventry Uni • Derby Uni • Glamorgan Uni • Glasgow Caledonian Uni • Glyndŵr Uni • Greenwich Uni • Heriot-Watt Uni • Kingston Uni • Leeds Met Uni • Liverpool John Moores Uni • London South Bank Uni • Loughborough Uni • Napier Uni • Newport • Northampton Uni • Northumbria Uni • Nottingham Trent Uni • Oxford Brookes Uni • Portsmouth Uni • Reading Uni • Robert Gordon Uni • Royal Agricultural Coll • Salford Uni • Sheffield Hallam Uni • Southampton Solent Uni • Swansea Met Uni • Teesside Uni • Thames Valley Uni • UCLan • UHI Millennium Institute • Ulster Uni • University Coll London • West of Scotland Uni • Westminster Uni • Wolverhampton Uni • *See also:* Building studies

Consumer studies

Abertay Dundee Uni • Harper Adams Uni Coll • Kingston Uni • Liverpool John Moores Uni • London Met Uni • Manchester Met Uni • Queen Margaret Uni • Reading Uni • Teesside Uni • Ulster Uni • University Coll Birmingham

Contemporary decorative arts/crafts

Bradford Coll • Brighton Uni • Coventry Uni • Creative Arts Uni • Cumbria Uni • De Montfort Uni • Derby Uni • Glyndŵr Uni • Huddersfield Uni • Leeds Uni • Lincoln Uni • London Coll Communication • London Met Uni • Nottingham Trent Uni • Robert Gordon Uni • Teesside Uni • Ulster Uni

Control engineering

Aberdeen Uni • Anglia Ruskin Uni • Birmingham Uni • Brunel Uni • Cambridge Uni • Coventry Uni • Cranfield Uni (p/g only) • East London Uni • Huddersfield Uni • Hull Uni • Leicester Uni • Liverpool John Moores Uni • Loughborough Uni • Newcastle Uni • Newport • Reading Uni • Sheffield Uni • Strathclyde Uni • Sussex Uni • Teesside Uni

Corrosion

See: Materials science

Cosmetic technology

See: Chemistry

Costume design

Anglia Ruskin Uni • Bristol Old Vic • Creative Arts Uni • Cumbria Uni • Derby Uni • Edinburgh Coll Art • Glamorgan Uni • Huddersfield Uni • London Coll Fashion • Queen Margaret Uni • RADA • Rose Bruford Coll • Royal Scottish Academy Music/Drama • Wimbledon Coll Art • Worcester Uni • *See also:* Theatre design

Counselling

Abertay Dundee Uni • Anglia Ruskin Uni • Bolton Uni • Bradford Coll • Brighton Uni • Bristol Uni • Chester Uni • Chichester Uni • Colchester Inst • Cumbria Uni • Derby Uni • East London Uni • Glasgow Caledonian Uni • Greenwich Uni • Hertfordshire Uni • Huddersfield Uni • Hull Uni • Leeds Met Uni • London Sch Theology • Newport • Nottingham Uni • Roehampton Uni • Salford Uni • Sheffield Hallam Uni • Swansea Met Uni • Thames Valley Uni • UCLan • Ulster Uni • Wolverhampton Uni • York St John Uni

Country planning

See: Town and country planning

Countryside management

Aberdeen Uni • Aberystwyth Uni • Bournemouth Uni • Brighton Uni • Bristol UWE • Cumbria Uni • Derby Uni • Gloucestershire Uni • Harper Adams Uni Coll • Myerscough Coll • Newcastle Uni • Nottingham Trent Uni • Queen's Uni Belfast • Reading Uni • Royal Agricultural Coll • Scottish Agricultural Coll • Sheffield Hallam Uni • UHI Millennium Institute • Wolverhampton Uni • Writtle Coll • *See also:* Rural environment studies

Creative/performance writing

Aberystwyth Uni • Anglia Ruskin Uni • Bangor Uni • Bath Spa Uni • Bedfordshire Uni • Birkbeck • Birmingham City Uni • Birmingham Uni • Bolton Uni • Bournemouth Uni • Bradford Uni • Brunel Uni • Buckingham Uni • Bucks New Uni • Chester Uni • Chichester Uni • Cumbria Uni • Dartington • De Montfort Uni • Derby Uni • East Anglia Uni • East London Uni • Edge Hill Uni • Essex Uni • Falmouth Uni Coll • Glamorgan Uni • Gloucestershire Uni • Glyndŵr Uni • Greenwich Uni • Hertfordshire Uni • Huddersfield Uni • Hull Uni • Kent • Kingston Uni • Lampeter Uni • Lancaster Uni • London Coll Communication • London Met Uni • London South Bank Uni • Manchester Met Uni • Marjon • Middlesex Uni • National Film Sch (p/g only) • Newport • Northampton Uni • Northumbria Uni • Norwich Uni Coll Arts • Nottingham Trent Uni • Plymouth Uni • Portsmouth Uni • Queen Margaret Uni • Roehampton Uni • St Mary's Uni Coll • Salford Uni • Sheffield Hallam Uni • Southampton Solent Uni • Strathclyde Uni • Sunderland Uni • Sussex Uni • Teesside Uni • Thames Valley Uni • Trinity Coll Carmarthen • UCLan • UWIC • Warwick Uni • Winchester Uni • Wolverhampton Uni • Worcester Uni • York Uni

Criminal justice

Bangor Uni • Birmingham City Uni • Bradford Coll • Bradford Uni • Bucks New Uni • Cumbria Uni • De Montfort Uni • Derby Uni • East London Uni • Edge Hill Uni • Glamorgan Uni • Glyndŵr Uni • Greenwich Uni • Kingston Uni • Leeds Uni • Liverpool John Moores Uni • Middlesex Uni • Napier Uni • Newport • Northumbria Uni • Nottingham Trent Uni • Plymouth Uni • Portsmouth Uni • Sheffield Hallam Uni • Swansea Uni • UCLan • Ulster Uni • West of Scotland Uni • Westminster Uni • Wolverhampton Uni • *See also:* Law; criminology

Criminology

Abertay Dundee Uni • Aberystwyth Uni • Anglia Ruskin Uni • Bangor Uni • Bedfordshire Uni • Birmingham City Uni • Bolton Uni • Bradford Uni • Brighton Uni • Bristol UWE • Bucks New Uni • Canterbury Christ Church Uni • Cardiff Uni • Chester Uni • Coventry Uni • Cumbria Uni • De Montfort Uni • Derby Uni • Durham Uni • East London Uni • Edge Hill Uni • Essex Uni • Glamorgan Uni • Glasgow Caledonian Uni • Gloucestershire Uni • Greenwich Uni • Huddersfield Uni • Hull Uni • Keele Uni • Kent • Kingston Uni • Lancaster Uni • Leeds Met Uni • Leeds Uni • Leicester Uni • Lincoln Uni • Liverpool Hope Uni • Liverpool John Moores Uni • Liverpool Uni • London Met Uni • London South Bank Uni • Loughborough Uni • LSE • Manchester Met Uni • Manchester Uni • Middlesex Uni • Northampton Uni • Northumbria Uni • Nottingham Trent Uni • Open Uni • Plymouth Uni • Portsmouth Uni • Queen's Uni Belfast • Roehampton Uni • Salford Uni • Sheffield Hallam Uni • Sheffield Uni • Southampton Solent Uni • Southampton Uni • Staffordshire Uni • Stirling Uni • Sunderland Uni • Surrey Uni • Sussex Uni • Swansea Uni • Teesside Uni • Thames Valley Uni • UCLan • Ulster Uni • UWIC • Westminster Uni • Wolverhampton Uni

Croatian

See: Serbian/Croatian

Crop science/technology

Aberdeen Uni • Aberystwyth Uni • Bangor Uni • Cranfield Uni (p/g only) • Harper Adams Uni Coll • Newcastle Uni • Nottingham Uni • Reading Uni • Royal Agricultural Coll • Scottish Agricultural Coll • Southampton Uni • Wolverhampton Uni • Writtle Coll

Cultural studies

Aberdeen Uni • Abertay Dundee Uni • Anglia Ruskin Uni • Bath Spa Uni • Birmingham City Uni • Birmingham Uni • Brighton Uni • Bristol UWE • Bucks New Uni • Canterbury Christ Church Uni • Cardiff Uni • Derby Uni • Dundee Uni • East Anglia Uni • East London Uni • Falmouth Uni Coll • Glamorgan Uni • Glasgow Uni • Gloucestershire Uni • Goldsmiths • Hull Uni • Kent • King's Coll London • Kingston Uni • Lancaster Uni • Leeds Met Uni • Leeds Uni • Liverpool John Moores Uni • Liverpool Uni • London Coll Communication • London Coll Fashion • Manchester Met Uni • Manchester Uni • Middlesex Uni • Napier Uni • Newcastle Uni • Nottingham Trent Uni • Nottingham Uni • Oxford Brookes Uni • Queen Margaret Uni • Roehampton Uni • St Mary's Uni Coll • Salford Uni • Sheffield Hallam Uni • SOAS • Southampton Solent Uni • Sunderland Uni • Surrey Uni • Sussex Uni • UCLan • UHI Millennium Institute • Ulster Uni • UWIC • Warwick Uni • West of Scotland Uni • Westminster Uni • Wolverhampton Uni • Worcester Uni

Cuneiform studies

See: Middle Eastern studies

Curation

Central Saint Martins • Leeds Uni • London Coll Communication • London Coll Fashion • Wimbledon Coll Art

Cybernetics

Bradford Uni • Heriot-Watt Uni • Loughborough Uni • Reading Uni • Sussex Uni • *See also:* Computing; control engineering

Czech

Bristol Uni • Glasgow Uni • Oxford Uni • Sheffield Uni • University Coll London • Wolverhampton Uni

Dance

ALRA • Bath Spa Uni • Bedfordshire Uni • Brighton Uni • Canterbury Christ Church Uni • Chester Uni • Chichester Uni • Coventry Uni • Cumbria Uni • Dartington • De Montfort Uni • Derby Uni • East London Uni • Edge Hill Uni • Falmouth Uni Coll • Hull Uni • Kingston Uni • Laban • Leeds Uni • Lincoln Uni • Liverpool Hope Uni • Liverpool John Moores Uni • London Contemp Dance Sch • Manchester Met Uni • Middlesex Uni • Northampton Uni • Northern Sch Cont Dance • Northumbria Uni • Plymouth Uni • Roehampton Uni • Sunderland Uni • Surrey Uni • Teesside Uni • Thames Valley Uni • Ulster Uni • UWIC • Winchester Uni • Wolverhampton Uni • York St John Uni • *See also:* Drama; movement studies; performance arts

Danish

University Coll London • *See also:* Scandinavian studies

Data processing

Aberdeen Uni • Anglia Ruskin Uni • Bradford Uni • Cranfield Uni (p/g only) • Glasgow Caledonian Uni • Huddersfield Uni • Liverpool Uni • Staffordshire Uni • *See also:* Computing

Deaf studies

Bristol Uni • Middlesex Uni • Reading Uni • UCLan • Wolverhampton Uni

Decision theory

Manchester Uni • Strathclyde Uni • *See also:* Business studies; economics; politics

Demography

See: Geography; sociology; statistics

Dental technology

Birmingham Uni • De Montfort Uni • Manchester Met Uni • Portsmouth Uni • Queen Mary • UWIC

Dentistry

Aberdeen Uni • Barts & The London • Bedfordshire Uni • Birmingham Uni • Bristol Uni • Cardiff Uni • Dundee Uni • Exeter Uni • Glasgow Uni • Kent • King's Coll London • Leeds Uni • Liverpool Uni • Manchester Uni • Newcastle Uni • Peninsula Med and Dental Coll • Plymouth Uni • Queen Mary • Queen's Uni Belfast • Sheffield Uni • UCLan

Design

See: individual subjects (eg interior design; industrial design)

Development studies

Bath Uni • Birkbeck • Birmingham Uni • Bradford Uni • Chester Uni • Derby Uni • East Anglia Uni • East London Uni • Glamorgan Uni • King's Coll London • Leeds Met Uni • Leeds Uni • London Met Uni • LSE • Manchester Met Uni • Manchester Uni • Middlesex Uni • Open Uni • Portsmouth Uni • SOAS • Sussex Uni • Ulster Uni

Developmental biology

Aberdeen Uni • Edinburgh Uni • Glasgow Uni • Manchester Uni • Southampton Uni • University Coll London • *See also:* Biology

Deviance

See: Psychology; sociology; statistics

Dietetics

Chester Uni • Coventry Uni • Glasgow Caledonian Uni • Hertfordshire Uni • Huddersfield Uni • King's Coll London • Leeds Met Uni • London Met Uni • Nottingham Uni • Oxford Brookes Uni • Plymouth

Uni • Queen Margaret Uni • Robert Gordon Uni • Surrey Uni • Ulster Uni • UWIC • *See also:* Nutrition

Digital microelectronics

Anglia Ruskin Uni • Birmingham Uni • Bolton Uni • Bournemouth Uni • Bradford Uni • Dundee Uni • Heriot-Watt Uni • Hertfordshire Uni • Hull Uni • Imperial Coll • Kent • Kingston Uni • Liverpool John Moores Uni • Liverpool Uni • Sussex Uni • Westminster Uni • *See also:* Computing; electronic engineering; microelectronics

Directing

Bristol Old Vic • Central Saint Martins • Creative Arts Uni • Gloucestershire Uni • Middlesex Uni • National Film Sch (p/g only) • RADA • Ravensbourne Coll

Distilling

Heriot-Watt Uni

Divinity

See: Theology; religious studies

Drama

Aberystwyth Uni • ALRA • Anglia Ruskin Uni • Bath Spa Uni • Bedfordshire Uni • Birmingham City Uni • Birmingham Uni • Bolton Uni • Bristol Old Vic • Bristol Uni • Bristol UWE • Brunel Uni • Bucks New Uni • Central Saint Martins • Central Sch Speech/Drama • Chester Uni • Chichester Uni • Coventry Uni • Cumbria Uni • Dartington • De Montfort Uni • Derby Uni • East Anglia Uni • East London Uni • Edge Hill Uni • Essex Uni • Exeter Uni • Falmouth Uni Coll • Glamorgan Uni • Glasgow Uni • Glyndŵr Uni • Goldsmiths • Greenwich Uni • Guildhall Sch Music and Drama • Huddersfield Uni • Hull Uni • Kent • Kingston Uni • Lancaster Uni • Leeds Uni • Lincoln Uni • Liverpool Hope Uni • Liverpool John Moores Uni • London Met Uni • London South Bank Uni • Loughborough Uni • Manchester Met Uni • Manchester Uni • Marjon • Middlesex Uni • Northampton Uni • Northumbria Uni • Plymouth Uni • Portsmouth Uni • Queen Margaret Uni • Queen Mary • Queen's Uni Belfast • RADA • Reading Uni • Roehampton Uni • Rose Bruford Coll • Royal Holloway • Royal Scottish Academy Music/Drama • Royal Welsh Coll Music/Drama • St Mary's Uni Coll • Salford Uni • Sheffield Hallam Uni • Sheffield Uni • Staffordshire Uni • Sunderland Uni • Sussex Uni • Swansea Met Uni • Teesside Uni • Thames Valley Uni • Trinity Coll Carmarthen • UCLan • Ulster Uni • Warwick Uni • West of Scotland Uni • Winchester Uni • Wolverhampton Uni • Worcester Uni • York St John Uni • *See also:* Dance; performance arts

Drama therapy

Derby Uni

Drama training

Derby Uni • Glyndŵr Uni • Queen Margaret Uni • RADA

Dutch

Cambridge Uni • Nottingham Trent Uni • Nottingham Uni • Sheffield Uni • University Coll London

Earth sciences

Aberdeen Uni • Aberystwyth Uni • Anglia Ruskin Uni • Birkbeck • Birmingham Uni • Bournemouth Uni • Bradford Uni • Brighton Uni • Bristol Uni • Cambridge Uni • Cardiff Uni • Derby Uni • Durham Uni • East Anglia Uni • Edinburgh Uni • Exeter Uni • Glasgow Uni • Greenwich Uni • Hull Uni • Imperial Coll • Keele Uni • Kingston Uni • Lancaster Uni • Leeds Uni • Leicester Uni • Liverpool John Moores Uni • Liverpool Uni • Manchester Uni • Northampton Uni • Nottingham Uni • Open Uni • Oxford Uni • Plymouth Uni • Portsmouth Uni • St Andrews Uni • Scottish Agricultural Coll • Southampton Uni • Stirling Uni • Ulster Uni • University Coll London • West of Scotland Uni • Wolverhampton Uni • Worcester Uni • *See also:* Geology

East european studies

Birmingham Uni • Glasgow Uni • Manchester Uni • Nottingham Uni • University Coll London • *See also:* European studies

E-business

Aberdeen Uni • Anglia Ruskin Uni • Aston Uni • Bedfordshire Uni • Birmingham City Uni • Bolton Uni • Bradford Coll • Bradford Uni • Brunel Uni • Bucks New Uni • Chichester Uni • Coventry Uni • De Montfort Uni • Derby Uni • Dundee Uni • East London Uni • Exeter Uni • Glamorgan Uni • Glasgow Caledonian Uni • Gloucestershire Uni •Huddersfield Uni •Kingston Uni • Leeds Met Uni • Liverpool Hope Uni • Liverpool John Moores Uni • Liverpool Uni • London Met Uni • London South Bank Uni • Loughborough Uni • Napier Uni • Northampton Uni • Northumbria Uni • Nottingham Uni • Portsmouth Uni • Ravensbourne Coll • Robert Gordon Uni • Salford Uni • Southampton Solent Uni • Swansea Met Uni • Swansea Uni • Teesside Uni • UCLan • Ulster Uni • West of Scotland Uni • Westminster Uni • Winchester Uni

Ecology

Aberdeen Uni • Anglia Ruskin Uni • Bangor Uni • Bolton Uni • Bradford Uni • Brighton Uni • Cambridge Uni • Canterbury Christ Church Uni • Cardiff Uni • Coventry Uni • Cranfield Uni (p/g only) • Durham Uni • East Anglia Uni • Edinburgh Uni • Essex Uni • Exeter Uni • Hertfordshire Uni • Hull Uni • Imperial Coll • Lancaster Uni • Leeds Uni • Leicester Uni • Liverpool John Moores Uni • Liverpool Uni • Manchester Met Uni • Myerscough Coll • Newcastle Uni • Northampton Uni • Oxford Brookes Uni • Plymouth Uni • Portsmouth Uni • Queen Mary • Reading Uni • Royal Holloway • St Andrews Uni • Scottish Agricultural Coll • Sheffield Uni • Southampton Uni • Stirling Uni • Sussex Uni • University Coll London • Wolverhampton Uni • Worcester Uni • York Uni • *See also:* Biology; botany; zoology

Econometrics

Aberdeen Uni • Birmingham Uni • Bristol Uni • Brunel Uni • Essex Uni • Exeter Uni • Glasgow Caledonian Uni • Kent • Loughborough Uni • LSE • Nottingham Uni • Reading Uni • Sheffield Uni • Southampton Uni • Surrey Uni • Swansea Uni • York Uni • *See also:* Economics; mathematics

Economic history

Aberdeen Uni • Aberystwyth Uni • Anglia Ruskin Uni • Birmingham Uni • Cambridge Uni • Edinburgh Uni • Essex Uni • Exeter Uni • Glasgow Uni • Hull Uni • Liverpool Uni • LSE • Manchester Uni • Queen Mary • Royal Holloway • Stirling Uni • Strathclyde Uni • Sussex Uni • Swansea Uni • University Coll London • Warwick Uni • York Uni • *See also:* History

Economics

Aberdeen Uni • Abertay Dundee Uni • Aberystwyth Uni • Anglia Ruskin Uni • Aston Uni • Bangor Uni • Bath Uni • Bedfordshire Uni • Birkbeck • Birmingham City Uni • Birmingham Uni • Bradford Uni • Brighton Uni • Bristol Uni • Bristol UWE • Brunel Uni • Buckingham Uni • Cambridge Uni • Cardiff Uni • City Uni • Coventry Uni • De Montfort Uni • Dundee Uni • Durham Uni • East Anglia Uni • East London Uni • Edinburgh Uni • Essex Uni • European Business Sch • Exeter Uni • Glamorgan Uni • Glasgow Caledonian Uni • Glasgow Uni • Goldsmiths • Greenwich Uni • Heriot-Watt Uni • Hertfordshire Uni • Huddersfield Uni • Hull Uni • Keele Uni • Kent • Kingston Uni • Lancaster Uni • Leeds Met Uni • Leeds Uni • Leicester Uni • Liverpool John Moores Uni • Liverpool Uni • London Met Uni • Loughborough Uni •LSE • Manchester Met Uni • Manchester Uni • Middlesex Uni • Newcastle Uni • Newport • Northampton Uni • Northumbria Uni • Nottingham Trent Uni • Nottingham Uni • Open Uni • Oxford Brookes Uni • Oxford Uni • Plymouth Uni • Portsmouth Uni • Queen Mary • Queen's Uni Belfast • Reading Uni • Regent's Business Sch • Robert Gordon Uni • Royal Holloway • St Andrews Uni • Salford Uni • Sheffield Uni • SOAS • Southampton Uni • Staffordshire Uni • Stirling Uni • Strathclyde Uni • Surrey Uni • Sussex Uni • Swansea Uni • UCLan • Ulster Uni • University Coll London • UWIC • Warwick Uni • West of Scotland Uni • Westminster Uni • Wolverhampton Uni • York Uni

Education

Aberdeen Uni • Aberystwyth Uni • Anglia Ruskin Uni • Bangor Uni • Bath Spa Uni • Bath Uni • Bedfordshire Uni • Birmingham City Uni • Birmingham Uni • Bolton Uni • Bradford Coll • Brighton Uni • Bristol UWE • Brunel Uni • Buckingham Uni • Cambridge Uni • Canterbury Christ Church Uni • Cardiff Uni • Central Sch Speech/Drama • Chester Uni • Chichester Uni • Cumbria Uni • De Montfort Uni • Derby Uni • Dundee Uni • Durham Uni • East Anglia Uni • East London Uni • Edge Hill Uni • Edinburgh Uni • Exeter Uni • Farnborough Coll • Glamorgan Uni • Glasgow Uni • Gloucestershire Uni • Glyndŵr Uni • Goldsmiths • Greenwich Uni • Heriot-Watt Uni • Hertfordshire Uni • Huddersfield Uni • Hull Uni • Keele Uni • King's Coll London • Kingston Uni • Lancaster Uni • Leeds Met Uni • Leeds Trinity • Leeds Uni • Liverpool Hope Uni • Liverpool John Moores Uni • Liverpool Uni • London Met Uni • Loughborough Uni • Manchester Met Uni • Manchester Uni • Marjon • Middlesex Uni • Newport • Northampton Uni • Northumbria Uni • Nottingham Trent Uni • Open Uni • Oxford Brookes Uni • Plymouth Uni • Portsmouth Uni • Queen's Uni Belfast • Reading Uni • Roehampton Uni • St Mary's Uni Coll • Sheffield Hallam Uni • Southampton Uni • Stirling Uni • Strathclyde Uni • Sunderland Uni • Sussex Uni • Swansea Met Uni • Teesside Uni • Thames Valley Uni • Trinity Coll Carmarthen • UCLan • Ulster Uni • University Coll Birmingham • UWIC • Warwick Uni • West of Scotland Uni • Winchester Uni • Wolverhampton Uni • Worcester Uni • York St John Uni • York Uni • *See also:* Teacher training

Egyptology

Cambridge Uni • Liverpool Uni • Oxford Uni • Swansea Uni • University Coll London • *See also:* Archaeology; history; Middle Eastern studies

Electrical engineering

Aberdeen Uni • Anglia Ruskin Uni • Aston Uni • Bath Uni • Birmingham Uni • Bradford Coll • Bradford Uni • Brighton Uni • Bristol Uni • Bristol UWE • Brunel Uni • Cambridge Uni • Cardiff Uni • City Uni • Coventry Uni • Derby Uni • Dundee Uni • Durham Uni • East London Uni • Edinburgh Uni • Exeter Uni • Farnborough Coll • Glamorgan Uni • Glasgow Caledonian Uni • Glasgow Uni • Glyndŵr Uni • Greenwich Uni • Heriot-Watt Uni • Hertfordshire Uni • Huddersfield Uni • Imperial Coll • Leeds Uni • Leicester Uni • Liverpool John Moores Uni • Liverpool Uni • London Met Uni • London South Bank Uni • Loughborough Uni • Manchester Met Uni • Manchester Uni • Napier Uni • Newcastle Uni • Newport • Northumbria Uni • Nottingham Trent Uni • Nottingham Uni • Oxford Uni • Plymouth Uni • Portsmouth Uni • Queen Mary • Queen's Uni Belfast • Robert Gordon Uni • Salford Uni • Sheffield

Hallam Uni • Sheffield Uni • Southampton Uni • Staffordshire Uni • Strathclyde Uni • Sunderland Uni • Sussex Uni • Swansea Met Uni • Swansea Uni • Teesside Uni • UHI Millennium Institute • Ulster Uni • University Coll London • West of Scotland Uni • Wolverhampton Uni • *See also:* Electronic engineering; engineering (general)

Electromechanical engineering

Aston Uni • Bradford Uni • Farnborough Coll • Glasgow Caledonian Uni • Liverpool Uni • Loughborough Uni • Nottingham Uni • Robert Gordon Uni • Southampton Uni • Strathclyde Uni • Sussex Uni • Wolverhampton Uni • *See also:* Engineering (general)

Electronic engineering

Aberdeen Uni • Aston Uni • Bangor Uni • Bath Uni • Birmingham City Uni • Birmingham Uni • Bolton Uni • Bournemouth Uni • Bradford Coll • Bradford Uni • Brighton Uni • Bristol Uni • Bristol UWE • Brunel Uni • Cambridge Uni • Cardiff Uni • City Uni • Coventry Uni • De Montfort Uni • Derby Uni • Dundee Uni • Durham Uni • East London Uni • Edinburgh Uni • Essex Uni • Exeter Uni • Farnborough Coll • Glamorgan Uni • Glasgow Caledonian Uni • Glasgow Uni • Glyndŵr Uni • Greenwich Uni • Heriot-Watt Uni • Hertfordshire Uni • Huddersfield Uni • Hull Uni • Imperial Coll • Kent • King's Coll London • Lancaster Uni • Leeds Uni • Leicester Uni • Liverpool John Moores Uni • Liverpool Uni • London Met Uni • London South Bank Uni • Loughborough Uni • Manchester Met Uni • Manchester Uni • Napier Uni • Newcastle Uni • Newport • Northampton Uni • Northumbria Uni • Nottingham Trent Uni • Nottingham Uni • Plymouth Uni • Portsmouth Uni • Queen Mary • Queen's Uni Belfast • Ravensbourne Coll • Reading Uni • Robert Gordon Uni • St Andrews Uni • Salford Uni • Sheffield Hallam Uni • Sheffield Uni • Southampton Solent Uni • Southampton Uni • Staffordshire Uni • Strathclyde Uni • Sunderland Uni • Surrey Uni • Sussex Uni • Swansea Met Uni • Swansea Uni • Teesside Uni • UCLan • UHI Millennium Institute • Ulster Uni • University Coll London • Warwick Uni • West of Scotland Uni • Westminster Uni • Wolverhampton Uni • York Uni • *See also:* Electrical engineering; engineering (general)

Electronic mechanics

Bristol Uni • Coventry Uni • Glasgow Caledonian Uni • Glyndŵr Uni • Liverpool Uni • Newcastle Uni • Robert Gordon Uni • Strathclyde Uni • Sussex Uni • Swansea Met Uni • Wolverhampton Uni • *See also:* Electronic engineering

Electronics

Aberdeen Uni • Anglia Ruskin Uni • Aston Uni • Bangor Uni • Bath Uni • Birmingham City Uni • Birmingham Uni • Bolton Uni • Bournemouth Uni • Bradford Uni • Brighton Uni • Bristol UWE • Brunel Uni • Cardiff Uni • Coventry Uni • De Montfort Uni • Derby Uni • Dundee Uni • East London Uni • Edinburgh Uni • Essex Uni • Glamorgan Uni • Glasgow Caledonian Uni • Glasgow Uni • Glyndŵr Uni • Greenwich Uni • Heriot-Watt Uni • Hertfordshire Uni • Huddersfield Uni • Imperial Coll • Kent • Kingston Uni • Lancaster Uni • Leeds Uni • Leicester Uni • Liverpool John Moores Uni • Liverpool Uni • London Met Uni • Loughborough Uni • Manchester Uni • Napier Uni • Newcastle Uni • Northumbria Uni • Nottingham Trent Uni • Nottingham Uni • Plymouth Uni • Portsmouth Uni • Queen Mary • Robert Gordon Uni • Salford Uni • Sheffield Uni • Southampton Uni • Strathclyde Uni • Surrey Uni • Sussex Uni • Swansea Met Uni • Swansea Uni • Thames Valley Uni • UCLan • Ulster Uni • West of Scotland Uni • Westminster Uni • York Uni

Embroidery

Birmingham City Uni • Bradford Coll • Creative Arts Uni • Cumbria Uni • Edinburgh Coll Art • London Coll Fashion • Manchester Met Uni • Ulster Uni

Embryology

See: Developmental biology; medicine

Energy engineering

Cambridge Uni • City Uni • Cranfield Uni (p/g only) • De Montfort Uni • Edinburgh Uni • Exeter Uni • Glasgow Caledonian Uni • Glyndŵr Uni • Heriot-Watt Uni • Hertfordshire Uni • Lancaster Uni • Leeds Uni • Loughborough Uni • Napier Uni • Robert Gordon Uni • Scottish Agricultural Coll • Strathclyde Uni

Energy studies

Aberdeen Uni • Aston Uni • Cranfield Uni (p/g only) • De Montfort Uni • Dundee Uni • Exeter Uni • Glasgow Caledonian Uni • Heriot-Watt Uni • Leeds Uni • Scottish Agricultural Coll • Strathclyde Uni

Engineering (general)

Aberdeen Uni • Anglia Ruskin Uni • Aston Uni • Birmingham City Uni • Birmingham Uni • Bolton Uni • Bradford Coll • Bradford Uni • Brighton Uni • Bristol UWE • Brunel Uni • Cambridge Uni • Cardiff Uni • City Uni • Coventry Uni • Cranfield Uni (p/g only) • De Montfort Uni • Durham Uni • East London Uni • Exeter Uni • Glamorgan Uni • Glasgow Caledonian Uni • Glyndŵr Uni • Greenwich Uni • Harper Adams Uni Coll • Heriot-Watt Uni • Hertfordshire Uni • Huddersfield Uni • Hull Uni • Imperial Coll • King's Coll London • Kingston Uni • Lancaster Uni • Leicester Uni • Lincoln Uni • Liverpool John Moores Uni • Liverpool Uni • London South Bank Uni • Loughborough Uni • Manchester Uni • Napier Uni • Newport • Northampton Uni • Nottingham Trent Uni • Nottingham Uni • Open Uni • Oxford Uni • Plymouth Uni • Portsmouth Uni • Queen Mary • Robert Gordon Uni • Salford Uni • Sheffield Hallam Uni • Sheffield Uni • Southampton Solent Uni • Southampton Uni • Strathclyde Uni • Surrey Uni • Sussex Uni • Swansea Uni • Teesside Uni • Thames Valley Uni • UHI Millennium Institute • Ulster Uni • University Coll London • Warwick Uni • West of Scotland Uni • Westminster Uni • Wolverhampton Uni • *See also:* Electrical engineering; mechanical engineering

Engineering mathematics

Aberdeen Uni • Aston Uni • Birmingham Uni • Bristol Uni • Cranfield Uni (p/g only) • Exeter Uni • Hertfordshire Uni • Kingston Uni • Liverpool Uni • Loughborough Uni • Newcastle Uni • Nottingham Uni • Sussex Uni • *See also:* Mathematics.

English

Aberdeen Uni • Aberystwyth Uni • Anglia Ruskin Uni • Aston Uni • Bangor Uni • Bath Spa Uni • Bedfordshire Uni • Birkbeck • Birmingham City Uni • Birmingham Uni • Bolton Uni • Bradford Uni • Brighton Uni • Bristol Uni • Bristol UWE • Brunel Uni • Buckingham Uni • Cambridge Uni • Canterbury Christ Church Uni • Cardiff Uni • Chester Uni • Chichester Uni • Cumbria Uni • De Montfort Uni • Derby Uni • Dundee Uni • Durham Uni • East Anglia Uni • East London Uni • Edge Hill Uni • Edinburgh Uni • Essex Uni • Exeter Uni • Falmouth Uni Coll • Glamorgan Uni • Glasgow Uni • Gloucestershire Uni • Glyndŵr Uni • Goldsmiths • Greenwich Uni • Hertfordshire Uni • Huddersfield Uni • Hull Uni • Keele Uni • Kent • King's Coll London • Kingston Uni • Lampeter Uni • Lancaster Uni • Leeds Met Uni • Leeds Trinity • Leeds Uni • Leicester Uni • Lincoln Uni • Liverpool Hope Uni • Liverpool John Moores Uni • Liverpool Uni • London Met Uni • Loughborough Uni • Manchester Met Uni • Manchester Uni • Marjon • Middlesex Uni • Napier Uni • Newcastle Uni • Newport • Northampton Uni • Northumbria Uni • Nottingham Trent Uni • Nottingham Uni • Open Uni • Oxford Brookes Uni • Oxford Uni • Plymouth Uni • Portsmouth Uni • Queen Mary • Queen's Uni Belfast • Reading Uni • Roehampton Uni • Royal Holloway • St Andrews Uni • St Mary's Uni Coll

• Salford Uni • Sheffield Hallam Uni • Sheffield Uni • Southampton Uni • Staffordshire Uni • Stirling Uni • Strathclyde Uni • Sunderland Uni • Sussex Uni • Swansea Met Uni • Swansea Uni • Teesside Uni • Trinity Coll Carmarthen • UCLan • Ulster Uni • University Coll London • UWIC • Warwick Uni • Westminster Uni • Winchester Uni • Wolverhampton Uni • Worcester Uni • York St John Uni • York Uni

English as a foreign language

Anglia Ruskin Uni • Bedfordshire Uni • Bristol UWE • Buckingham Uni • Canterbury Christ Church Uni • Chichester Uni • Coventry Uni • Derby Uni • East London Uni • Essex Uni • Exeter Uni • Glamorgan Uni • Gloucestershire Uni • Heriot-Watt Uni • Hull Uni • Lampeter Uni • Lancaster Uni • Leeds Met Uni • Liverpool John Moores Uni • Manchester Met Uni • Manchester Uni • Middlesex Uni • Northampton Uni • Nottingham Trent Uni • Portsmouth Uni • Roehampton Uni • Salford Uni • Sheffield Hallam Uni • Southampton Solent Uni • Stirling Uni • Sunderland Uni • Sussex Uni • Swansea Uni • UCLan • West of Scotland Uni • Westminster Uni • Wolverhampton Uni

Entomology

See: Biology; zoology

Environmental archaeology

Bournemouth Uni • Bradford Uni • Edinburgh Uni • Lampeter Uni • Queen's Uni Belfast

Environmental biology

Aberdeen Uni • Aberystwyth Uni • Anglia Ruskin Uni • Bath Spa Uni • Birmingham Uni • Bolton Uni • Bristol UWE • Canterbury Christ Church Uni • Dundee Uni • Essex Uni • Exeter Uni • Glasgow Caledonian Uni • Glyndŵr Uni • Hull Uni • Imperial Coll • Kingston Uni • Lancaster Uni • Leeds Uni • Leicester Uni • Liverpool Uni • Manchester Uni • Napier Uni • Newcastle Uni • Northampton Uni • Nottingham Trent Uni • Nottingham Uni • Oxford Brookes Uni • Plymouth Uni • Portsmouth Uni • Queen Mary • Queen's Uni Belfast • Reading Uni • Royal Holloway • St Andrews Uni • Salford Uni • Scottish Agricultural Coll • Southampton Uni • Stirling Uni • Sussex Uni • Swansea Uni • University Coll London • West of Scotland Uni • *See also:* Biology; environmental science

Environmental chemistry

Aberdeen Uni • Anglia Ruskin Uni • Bangor Uni • Birmingham Uni • Bristol UWE • East Anglia Uni • Edinburgh Uni • Glasgow Uni • Lancaster Uni • Leeds Uni • Manchester Uni • Northumbria Uni • Nottingham Trent Uni • Nottingham Uni • Portsmouth Uni • Queen Mary • Reading Uni • Scottish Agricultural Coll • Sussex Uni • West of Scotland Uni • York Uni • *See also:* Chemistry; environmental science

Environmental engineering

Aberdeen Uni • Bath Uni • Birmingham Uni • Brighton Uni • Brunel Uni • Cambridge Uni • Cardiff Uni • Cranfield Uni (p/g only) • Edinburgh Uni • Exeter Uni • Glasgow Caledonian Uni • Glyndŵr Uni • Heriot-Watt Uni • Huddersfield Uni • Imperial Coll • Leeds Uni • Liverpool Uni • Loughborough Uni • Napier Uni • Northumbria Uni • Nottingham Trent Uni • Nottingham Uni • Portsmouth Uni • Queen's Uni Belfast • Robert Gordon Uni • Salford Uni • Sheffield Hallam Uni • Southampton Uni • Staffordshire Uni • Strathclyde Uni • Swansea Uni • UCLan • Ulster Uni • University Coll London • West of Scotland Uni

Environmental health

Bournemouth Uni • Bristol UWE • Cranfield Uni (p/g only) • Greenwich Uni • Leeds Met Uni • Manchester Met Uni • Middlesex Uni • Nottingham Trent Uni • Portsmouth Uni • Roehampton Uni • Salford Uni • Strathclyde Uni • Ulster Uni • UWIC • Wolverhampton Uni

Environmental management

Aberdeen Uni • Abertay Dundee Uni • Aberystwyth Uni • Anglia Ruskin Uni • Bangor Uni • Birkbeck • Birmingham Uni • Bournemouth Uni • Bradford Uni • Brighton Uni • Cardiff Uni • Cranfield Uni (p/g only) • Cumbria Uni • Exeter Uni • Glamorgan Uni • Glasgow Caledonian Uni • Gloucestershire Uni • Glyndŵr Uni • Greenwich Uni • Harper Adams Uni Coll • Hertfordshire Uni • Kingston Uni • Leeds Uni • Liverpool Hope Uni • Manchester Uni • Newcastle Uni • Northampton Uni • Oxford Brookes Uni • Queen's Uni Belfast • Royal Agricultural Coll • Salford Uni • Scottish Agricultural Coll • Southampton Solent Uni • Southampton Uni • Strathclyde Uni • Swansea Met Uni • UCLan • UHI Millennium Institute • UWIC • West of Scotland Uni • Wolverhampton Uni • Worcester Uni • Writtle Coll

Environmental science

Aberdeen Uni • Aberystwyth Uni • Anglia Ruskin Uni • Bangor Uni • Bath Spa Uni • Birkbeck • Birmingham Uni • Bournemouth Uni • Bradford Uni • Brighton Uni • Bristol UWE • Canterbury Christ Church Uni • Cardiff Uni • Cranfield Uni (p/g only) • Cumbria Uni • Dundee Uni • Durham Uni • East Anglia Uni • East London Uni • Edge Hill Uni • Edinburgh Uni • Essex Uni • Exeter Uni • Glasgow Caledonian Uni • Glasgow Uni • Gloucestershire Uni • Glyndŵr Uni • Greenwich Uni • Heriot-Watt Uni • Hertfordshire Uni • Huddersfield Uni • Hull Uni • Imperial Coll • Keele Uni • Kingston Uni • Lancaster Uni • Leeds Uni • Liverpool John Moores Uni • Manchester Met Uni • Manchester Uni • Middlesex Uni • Myerscough Coll • Newcastle Uni • Northampton Uni • Northumbria Uni • Nottingham Trent Uni • Nottingham Uni • Open Uni • Oxford Brookes Uni • Plymouth Uni • Portsmouth Uni • Queen Mary • Reading Uni • Roehampton Uni • Royal Holloway • St Andrews Uni • Salford Uni • Scottish Agricultural Coll • Sheffield Uni • Southampton Uni • Stirling Uni • Strathclyde Uni • Sussex Uni • Teesside Uni • UCLan • UHI Millennium Institute • Ulster Uni • UWIC • West of Scotland Uni • Wolverhampton Uni • Writtle Coll • York Uni

Environmental studies

Aberdeen Uni • Aberystwyth Uni • Anglia Ruskin Uni • Bangor Uni • Birkbeck • Birmingham Uni • Bolton Uni • Bournemouth Uni • Bradford Uni • Bristol UWE • Cardiff Uni • Coventry Uni • Cranfield Uni (p/g only) • Cumbria Uni • Edinburgh Coll Art • Edinburgh Uni • Exeter Uni • Glasgow Caledonian Uni • Gloucestershire Uni • Glyndŵr Uni • Hertfordshire Uni • Huddersfield Uni • Kent • King's Coll London • Kingston Uni • Leeds Uni • Leicester Uni • Liverpool John Moores Uni • Liverpool Uni • LSE • Manchester Met Uni • Manchester Uni • Middlesex Uni • Myerscough Coll • Newcastle Uni • Northumbria Uni • Nottingham Trent Uni • Nottingham Uni • Open Uni • Oxford Brookes Uni • Portsmouth Uni • Roehampton Uni • Royal Agricultural Coll • Royal Holloway • Salford Uni • Scottish Agricultural Coll • Sheffield Hallam Uni • Sheffield Uni • Southampton Solent Uni • Southampton Uni • Stirling Uni • Strathclyde Uni • Sussex Uni • Swansea Met Uni • UCLan • UHI Millennium Institute • Ulster Uni • University Coll London • UWIC • Wolverhampton Uni • Worcester Uni • Writtle Coll • York Uni • *See also:* Environmental archaeology; environmental science

Equine studies

Aberdeen Uni • Aberystwyth Uni • Brighton Uni • Bristol UWE • Bucks New Uni • Glyndŵr Uni • Greenwich Uni • Harper Adams Uni Coll • Lincoln Uni • Myerscough Coll • Northampton Uni • Nottingham Trent Uni • Oxford Brookes Uni • Plymouth Uni • Royal Agricultural Coll • Scottish Agricultural Coll • Wolverhampton Uni • Writtle Coll

Ergonomics

Loughborough Uni

E-Science

Hull Uni • Leicester Uni • Queen Mary

Estate management

Aberdeen Uni • Anglia Ruskin Uni • Bristol UWE • City Uni • Cumbria Uni • Glasgow Caledonian Uni • Glyndŵr Uni • Greenwich Uni • Harper Adams Uni Coll • Heriot-Watt Uni • Kingston Uni • Liverpool John Moores Uni • London South Bank Uni • Napier Uni • Northampton Uni • Northumbria Uni • Nottingham Trent Uni • Oxford Brookes Uni • Portsmouth Uni • Reading Uni • Royal Agricultural Coll • Sheffield Hallam Uni • Ulster Uni • West of Scotland Uni • Westminster Uni • Writtle Coll • *See also:* Urban estate management

Ethics

See: Philosophy; theology

EU studies

Aberdeen Uni • Aberystwyth Uni • East Anglia Uni • Edinburgh Uni • Essex Uni • Leeds Uni • London South Bank Uni • Newcastle Uni • Sussex Uni • University Coll London • *See also:* European studies

European business studies

Aberdeen Uni • Anglia Ruskin Uni • Aston Uni • Bath Uni • Birmingham Uni • Bournemouth Uni • Bradford Uni • Bristol UWE • Bucks New Uni • Canterbury Christ Church Uni • Cardiff Uni • City Uni • East London Uni • Edinburgh Uni • Essex Uni • European Business Sch • Greenwich Uni • Heriot-Watt Uni • Huddersfield Uni • Hull Uni • Kent • Kingston Uni • Lancaster Uni • Lincoln Uni • Liverpool John Moores Uni • Liverpool Uni • Loughborough Uni • Manchester Met Uni • Newcastle Uni • Northumbria Uni • Portsmouth Uni • Regent's Business Sch • Royal Agricultural Coll • Stirling Uni • Strathclyde Uni • Swansea Uni • Warwick Uni • Westminster Uni

European studies

Aberdeen Uni • Abertay Dundee Uni • Aberystwyth Uni • Anglia Ruskin Uni • Aston Uni • Bath Uni • Birmingham Uni • Bradford Uni • Bristol UWE • Cardiff Uni • Dundee Uni • East Anglia Uni • East London Uni • Edinburgh Uni • Essex Uni • Exeter Uni • Kent • King's Coll London • Kingston Uni • Lancaster Uni • Leeds Uni • Leicester Uni • Liverpool John Moores Uni • Liverpool Uni • London South Bank Uni • Loughborough Uni • Manchester Met Uni • Manchester Uni • Newcastle Uni • Northumbria Uni • Nottingham Trent Uni • Nottingham Uni • Open Uni • Portsmouth Uni • Queen Mary • Queen's Uni Belfast • Reading Uni • Royal Holloway • Salford Uni • Southampton Uni • Stirling Uni • Sussex Uni • Swansea Uni • Ulster Uni • University Coll London • West of Scotland Uni • Westminster Uni • Wolverhampton Uni • *See also:* Iberian studies; Scandinavian studies

Exhibition design

Huddersfield Uni • Lincoln Uni • London Coll Communication • Ravensbourne Coll • Royal Coll Art (p/g only) • Thames Valley Uni

Exploration

Cardiff Uni • University Coll London • *See also:* Mining; geology

Fashion

Bath Spa Uni • Bedfordshire Uni • Birmingham City Uni • Bolton Uni • Bournemouth Uni • Bradford Coll • Brighton Uni • Bristol UWE • Central Saint Martins • Colchester Inst • Coventry Uni • Creative Arts Uni • De Montfort Uni • Derby Uni • East London Uni • Edinburgh Coll Art • Falmouth Uni Coll • Glamorgan Uni • Glasgow Caledonian Uni • Glyndŵr Uni • Heriot-Watt Uni • Hertfordshire Uni • Huddersfield Uni • Kingston Uni • Leeds Met Uni • Leeds Uni • Lincoln Uni • Liverpool John Moores Uni • London Coll Fashion • London Met Uni • Manchester Met Uni • Manchester Uni • Middlesex Uni • Newport • Northampton Uni • Northumbria Uni • Nottingham Trent Uni • Portsmouth Uni • Ravensbourne Coll • Robert Gordon Uni • Royal Coll Art (p/g only) • Salford Uni • Sheffield Hallam Uni • Southampton Solent Uni • Southampton Uni • Sunderland Uni • Thames Valley Uni • UCLan • Ulster Uni • Westminster Uni • Winchester Sch Art • Wolverhampton Uni • *See also:* Textiles

Fermentation

See: Biochemistry; brewing; microbiology

Fertility

Southampton Uni

Film music

Bath Spa Uni • Bucks New Uni • Dartington • Glyndŵr Uni • Hertfordshire Uni • Leeds Coll Music • London Met Uni • National Film Sch (p/g only) • Southampton Uni • Thames Valley Uni • West of Scotland Uni • Worcester Uni

Film studies

Aberdeen Uni • Aberystwyth Uni • Anglia Ruskin Uni • Bangor Uni • Bath Spa Uni • Bedfordshire Uni • Birkbeck • Bolton Uni • Bournemouth Uni • Bradford Uni • Brighton Uni • Bristol UWE • Brunel Uni • Buckingham Uni • Bucks New Uni • Canterbury Christ Church Uni • Cardiff Uni • Central Saint Martins • Chester Uni • Creative Arts Uni • Cumbria Uni • De Montfort Uni • Derby Uni • Dundee Uni • East Anglia Uni • East London Uni • Edge Hill Uni • Edinburgh Coll Art • Essex Uni • Exeter Uni • Falmouth Uni Coll • Glamorgan Uni • Glasgow Uni • Gloucestershire Uni • Glyndŵr Uni • Goldsmiths • Greenwich Uni • Hertfordshire Uni • Hull Uni • Kent • King's Coll London • Kingston Uni • Lampeter Uni • Lancaster Uni • Leeds Met Uni • Leeds Trinity • Leeds Uni • Leicester Uni • Liverpool Hope Uni • Liverpool John Moores Uni • Liverpool Uni • London Coll Communication • London Coll Fashion • London Film Sch • London Met Uni • London South Bank Uni • Manchester Met Uni • Manchester Uni • Middlesex Uni • Napier Uni • National Film Sch (p/g only) • Newcastle Uni • Newport • Northampton Uni • Northumbria Uni • Nottingham Trent Uni • Nottingham Uni • Oxford Brookes Uni • Portsmouth Uni • Queen Margaret Uni • Queen Mary • Queen's Uni Belfast • Ravensbourne Coll • Reading Uni • Roehampton Uni • Royal Coll Art (p/g only) • Royal Holloway • Royal Scottish Academy Music/Drama • St Andrews Uni • St Mary's Uni Coll • Sheffield Hallam Uni • Southampton Solent Uni • Southampton Uni • Staffordshire Uni • Stirling Uni • Sunderland Uni • Surrey Uni • Sussex Uni • Swansea Met Uni • Swansea Uni • Thames Valley Uni • Trinity Coll Carmarthen • UCLan • Ulster Uni • Warwick Uni • West of Scotland Uni • Westminster Uni • Wimbledon Coll Art • Winchester Uni • Wolverhampton Uni • Worcester Uni • York St John Uni • *See also:* Media studies; video

Finance

Aberdeen Uni • Abertay Dundee Uni • Aberystwyth Uni • Aston Uni • Bangor Uni • Bath Uni • Bedfordshire Uni • Birkbeck • Birmingham City Uni • Birmingham Uni • Bournemouth Uni • Bradford Uni • Brighton Uni • Bristol Uni • Bristol UWE • Brunel Uni • Buckingham Uni • Bucks New Uni • Cardiff Uni • City Uni • Coventry Uni • Cranfield Uni (p/g only) • Cumbria Uni • De Montfort Uni • Derby Uni • Dundee Uni • Durham Uni • East Anglia Uni • East London Uni • Essex Uni • European Business Sch • Exeter Uni • Glamorgan Uni • Glasgow Caledonian Uni • Glasgow Uni • Glyndŵr Uni • Greenwich Uni • Heriot-Watt Uni • Hertfordshire Uni • Huddersfield Uni • Hull Uni • Imperial Coll • Keele Uni • Kent • Kingston Uni • Lancaster Uni • Leeds Met Uni • Leeds Uni • Leicester Uni • Lincoln Uni • Liverpool John Moores Uni • Liverpool Uni • London Business Sch (p/g only) • London Met Uni • London South Bank Uni • Loughborough Uni • LSE • Manchester Met Uni • Manchester Uni • Middlesex Uni • Newcastle Uni • Newport • Northampton Uni • Northumbria Uni • Nottingham Trent Uni • Nottingham Uni • Oxford Brookes Uni • Plymouth Uni • Portsmouth Uni • Queen Mary • Queen's Uni Belfast • Reading Uni • Regent's Business Sch • Robert Gordon Uni • Royal Agricultural Coll • St Andrews Uni • Salford Uni • Sheffield Hallam Uni • Sheffield Uni • Southampton Solent Uni • Southampton Uni • Staffordshire Uni • Stirling Uni • Strathclyde Uni • Sunderland Uni • Surrey Uni • Swansea Met Uni • Swansea Uni • Teesside Uni • Thames Valley Uni • UCLan • Ulster Uni • UWIC • Warwick Uni • West of Scotland Uni • Westminster Uni • Wolverhampton Uni • Worcester Uni • York St John Uni • York Uni • *See also:* Banking; financial services

Financial economics

Aberdeen Uni • Birkbeck • Birmingham Uni • Brighton Uni • Bristol UWE • Brunel Uni • City Uni • Coventry Uni • Dundee Uni • East Anglia Uni • Essex Uni • Exeter Uni • Kingston Uni • Leeds Uni • Leicester Uni • Liverpool Uni • London Met Uni • LSE • Manchester Met Uni • Newcastle Uni • Plymouth Uni • Reading Uni • Surrey Uni • Swansea Uni • UWIC • Winchester Uni

Financial services

Anglia Ruskin Uni • Bournemouth Uni • Bradford Coll • Buckingham Uni • Coventry Uni • Derby Uni • Glasgow Caledonian Uni • Greenwich Uni • Huddersfield Uni • London Met Uni • Manchester Met Uni • Napier Uni • Northumbria Uni • Nottingham Trent Uni • Reading Uni • Sheffield Hallam Uni • Southampton Solent Uni • Surrey Uni • UCLan • Ulster Uni • Westminster Uni • *See also:* Banking

Fine art

See: Art; painting; photography; printmaking; sculpture

Fine arts

See: Art history

Finnish studies

University Coll London • *See also:* Scandinavian studies

Fire safety engineering

Glasgow Caledonian Uni • Leeds Uni • Newport • UCLan • Ulster Uni

Fisheries management

See: Wildlife management

Fishery science

Aberdeen Uni • Stirling Uni

Food science

Aberdeen Uni • Abertay Dundee Uni • Bath Spa Uni • Bournemouth Uni • Brighton Uni • Chester Uni • Cranfield Uni (p/g only) • Glasgow Caledonian Uni • Harper Adams Uni Coll • Heriot-Watt Uni • Huddersfield Uni • Leeds Met Uni • Leeds Uni • Lincoln Uni • Liverpool John Moores Uni • London Met Uni • London South Bank Uni • Manchester Met Uni • Newcastle Uni • Northumbria Uni • Nottingham Trent Uni • Nottingham Uni • Oxford Brookes Uni • Queen's Uni Belfast • Reading Uni • Robert Gordon Uni • Royal Agricultural Coll • Scottish Agricultural Coll • Sheffield Hallam Uni •Strathclyde Uni • Surrey Uni • Teesside Uni • Thames Valley Uni • Ulster Uni • UWIC • Wolverhampton Uni • Worcester Uni • Writtle Coll • *See also:* Nutrition

Food technology

Aberdeen Uni • Abertay Dundee Uni • Chester Uni • Glamorgan Uni • Glasgow Caledonian Uni • Harper Adams Uni Coll • Heriot-Watt Uni • Huddersfield Uni • Leeds Uni • Lincoln Uni • London South Bank Uni • Reading Uni • Scottish Agricultural Coll • Sheffield Hallam Uni • Ulster Uni • UWIC

Footwear

Bolton Uni • De Montfort Uni • London Coll Fashion • Northampton Uni • *See also:* Textiles

Forensic science

Abertay Dundee Uni • Anglia Ruskin Uni • Bedfordshire Uni • Bournemouth Uni • Bradford Uni • Bristol UWE • Brunel Uni • Canterbury Christ Church Uni • Chester Uni • Coventry Uni • Cranfield Uni (p/g only) • Cumbria Uni • De Montfort Uni • Derby Uni • Dundee Uni • East Anglia Uni • East London Uni • Glamorgan Uni • Glasgow Caledonian Uni • Glasgow Uni • Glyndŵr Uni • Greenwich Uni • Heriot-Watt Uni • Huddersfield Uni • Hull Uni • Keele Uni • Kent • Kingston Uni • Leicester Uni • Lincoln Uni • Liverpool John Moores Uni • London Met Uni • London South Bank Uni • Manchester Met Uni • Manchester Uni • Newport • Northumbria Uni • Nottingham Trent Uni • Portsmouth Uni • Queen Mary • Robert Gordon Uni • Sheffield Hallam Uni • Staffordshire Uni • Strathclyde Uni • Sunderland Uni • Teesside Uni • Thames Valley Uni • UCLan • UWIC • West of Scotland Uni • Westminster Uni • Wolverhampton Uni • Worcester Uni

Forestry

Aberdeen Uni • Bangor Uni • Brighton Uni • Cumbria Uni • Edinburgh Uni • Myerscough Coll • Royal Agricultural Coll • UHI Millennium Institute • Wolverhampton Uni • Worcester Uni

French

Aberdeen Uni • Aberystwyth Uni • Aston Uni • Bangor Uni • Bath Uni • Birkbeck • Birmingham Uni • Bristol Uni • Bristol UWE • Buckingham Uni • Cambridge Uni • Canterbury Christ Church Uni • Cardiff Uni • Chester Uni • Coventry Uni • Durham Uni • East Anglia Uni • East London Uni • Edinburgh Uni • Essex Uni • European Business Sch • Exeter Uni • Glasgow Uni • Greenwich Uni • Heriot-Watt Uni • Hull Uni • Imperial Coll • Kent • King's Coll London • Kingston Uni • Lancaster Uni • Leeds Met Uni • Leeds Uni • Leicester Uni • Liverpool John Moores Uni • Liverpool Uni • London Met Uni • London Uni Inst Paris • Manchester Met Uni • Manchester Uni • Middlesex Uni • Newcastle Uni • Northampton Uni • Northumbria Uni • Nottingham Trent Uni • Nottingham Uni • Open Uni • Oxford Brookes Uni • Oxford Uni • Plymouth Uni • Portsmouth Uni • Queen Mary • Queen's Uni Belfast • Reading Uni • Roehampton Uni • Royal Holloway • St Andrews Uni • Salford Uni • Sheffield

Uni • SOAS • Southampton Uni • Stirling Uni • Strathclyde Uni • Sunderland Uni • Surrey Uni • Sussex Uni • Swansea Uni • UCLan • Ulster Uni • University Coll London • Warwick Uni • West of Scotland Uni • Westminster Uni • Wolverhampton Uni • York Uni

Freshwater biology

See: Marine biology

Fuel science

See: Chemistry; energy studies

Furniture design

Birmingham City Uni • Bucks New Uni • Creative Arts Uni • Cumbria Uni • De Montfort Uni • Edinburgh Coll Art • Kingston Uni • Leeds Met Uni • Lincoln Uni • London Met Uni • Loughborough Uni • Northumbria Uni • Nottingham Trent Uni • Plymouth Uni • Royal Coll Art (p/g only) • Sheffield Hallam Uni • Teesside Uni • UCLan • Ulster Uni • Wolverhampton Uni • York St John Uni

Furniture production

Bucks New Uni • Cumbria Uni • Edinburgh Coll Art • Lincoln Uni • London Met Uni

Garden design

Brighton Uni • Falmouth Uni Coll • Gloucestershire Uni • Glyndŵr Uni • Greenwich Uni • Leeds Met Uni • Myerscough Coll • Nottingham Trent Uni • Scottish Agricultural Coll • Wolverhampton Uni • Writtle Coll

Gender studies

East London Uni • Hull Uni • Leeds Uni • Queen's Uni Belfast • Sussex Uni • Swansea Uni • Warwick Uni • *See also:* Women's studies

Genetics

Aberdeen Uni • Aberystwyth Uni • Anglia Ruskin Uni • Birmingham Uni • Bristol UWE • Brunel Uni • Cambridge Uni • Cardiff Uni • Cranfield Uni (p/g only) • Dundee Uni • East Anglia Uni • Edinburgh Uni • Glasgow Uni • King's Coll London • Leeds Uni • Leicester Uni • Liverpool Uni • Manchester Uni • Newcastle Uni • Nottingham Uni • Portsmouth Uni • Queen Mary • Queen's Uni Belfast • Royal Holloway • Sheffield Uni • Southampton Uni • Sussex Uni • Swansea Uni • University Coll London • Warwick Uni • Westminster Uni • Wolverhampton Uni • York Uni • *See also:* Biology

Geochemistry

Glasgow Uni • Liverpool Uni • Manchester Uni • Portsmouth Uni • Reading Uni • *See also:* Geology; chemistry

Geography

Aberdeen Uni • Aberystwyth Uni • Bangor Uni • Bath Spa Uni • Birkbeck • Birmingham City Uni • Birmingham Uni • Bournemouth Uni • Bradford Uni • Brighton Uni • Bristol Uni • Bristol UWE • Brunel Uni • Cambridge Uni • Canterbury Christ Church Uni • Cardiff Uni • Chester Uni • Coventry Uni • Cumbria Uni • Derby Uni • Dundee Uni • Durham Uni • East Anglia Uni • Edge Hill Uni • Edinburgh Uni • Exeter Uni • Glamorgan Uni • Glasgow Caledonian Uni • Glasgow Uni • Gloucestershire Uni

• Greenwich Uni • Hertfordshire Uni • Huddersfield Uni • Hull Uni • Keele Uni • King's Coll London • Kingston Uni • Lancaster Uni • Leeds Met Uni • Leeds Uni • Leicester Uni • Liverpool Hope Uni • Liverpool John Moores Uni • Liverpool Uni • Loughborough Uni • LSE • Manchester Met Uni • Manchester Uni • Newcastle Uni • Northampton Uni • Northumbria Uni • Nottingham Trent Uni • Nottingham Uni • Open Uni • Oxford Brookes Uni • Oxford Uni • Plymouth Uni • Portsmouth Uni • Queen Mary • Queen's Uni Belfast • Reading Uni • Royal Holloway • St Andrews Uni • St Mary's Uni Coll • Salford Uni • Scottish Agricultural Coll • Sheffield Hallam Uni • Sheffield Uni • SOAS • Southampton Solent Uni • Southampton Uni • Staffordshire Uni • Stirling Uni • Strathclyde Uni • Sunderland Uni • Sussex Uni • Swansea Uni • UCLan • Ulster Uni • University Coll London • Westminster Uni • Wolverhampton Uni • Worcester Uni • York Uni

Geology

Aberdeen Uni • Birkbeck • Birmingham Uni • Brighton Uni • Bristol Uni • Cambridge Uni • Cardiff Uni • Derby Uni • Durham Uni • Edge Hill Uni • Edinburgh Uni • Exeter Uni • Glamorgan Uni • Imperial Coll • Keele Uni • Kingston Uni • Leeds Uni • Leicester Uni • Liverpool John Moores Uni • Liverpool Uni • Manchester Uni • Northampton Uni • Open Uni • Oxford Uni • Plymouth Uni • Portsmouth Uni • Royal Holloway • Southampton Uni • University Coll London • West of Scotland Uni

Geophysics

Aberdeen Uni • Birmingham Uni • Cambridge Uni • Durham Uni • East Anglia Uni • Edinburgh Uni • Imperial Coll • Lancaster Uni • Leeds Uni • Leicester Uni • Liverpool Uni • Southampton Uni • University Coll London • *See also:* Geology; physics

Geoscience

Aberdeen Uni • Aberystwyth Uni • Birmingham Uni • Bristol Uni • Cardiff Uni • Durham Uni • Edge Hill Uni • Glasgow Uni • Imperial Coll • Keele Uni • Leeds Uni • Leicester Uni • Liverpool Uni • Newcastle Uni • Plymouth Uni • Portsmouth Uni • Royal Holloway • St Andrews Uni

German

Aberdeen Uni • Aberystwyth Uni • Aston Uni • Bangor Uni • Bath Uni • Birkbeck • Birmingham Uni • Bristol Uni • Cambridge Uni • Cardiff Uni • Chester Uni • Coventry Uni • Durham Uni • Edinburgh Uni • Essex Uni • European Business Sch • Exeter Uni • Glasgow Uni • Greenwich Uni • Heriot-Watt Uni • Hull Uni • Imperial Coll • Kent • King's Coll London • Kingston Uni • Lancaster Uni • Leeds Met Uni • Leeds Uni • Leicester Uni • Liverpool Uni • Manchester Met Uni • Manchester Uni • Middlesex Uni • Newcastle Uni • Newport • Northampton Uni • Northumbria Uni • Nottingham Trent Uni • Nottingham Uni • Open Uni • Oxford Uni • Plymouth Uni • Portsmouth Uni • Queen Mary • Queen's Uni Belfast • Reading Uni • Royal Holloway • St Andrews Uni • Salford Uni • Sheffield Uni • Southampton Uni • Strathclyde Uni • Sunderland Uni • Surrey Uni • Sussex Uni • Swansea Uni • UCLan • Ulster Uni • University Coll London • Warwick Uni • West of Scotland Uni • Westminster Uni • Wolverhampton Uni • York Uni

Glass

Birmingham City Uni • Bucks New Uni • Creative Arts Uni • De Montfort Uni • Edinburgh Coll Art • Glyndŵr Uni • Robert Gordon Uni • Royal Coll Art (p/g only) • Sheffield Uni • Sunderland Uni • Swansea Met Uni • Wolverhampton Uni • *See also:* Three-dimensional design

Goldsmithing

See: Silversmithing

Government

See: Politics

Graphic design

Anglia Ruskin Uni • Bath Spa Uni • Bedfordshire Uni • Birmingham City Uni • Bolton Uni • Bradford Coll • Brighton Uni • Bristol UWE • Bucks New Uni • Camberwell Coll • Central Saint Martins • Chelsea Coll Art • Chester Uni • Colchester Inst • Coventry Uni • Creative Arts Uni • Cumbria Uni • De Montfort Uni • Derby Uni • Dundee Uni • East London Uni • Edinburgh Coll Art • Falmouth Uni Coll • Glamorgan Uni • Glasgow Caledonian Uni • Gloucestershire Uni • Glyndŵr Uni • Goldsmiths • Greenwich Uni • Hertfordshire Uni • Huddersfield Uni •Kingston Uni • Leeds Met Uni • Leeds Uni • Lincoln Uni • Liverpool John Moores Uni • London Coll Communication • London Met Uni • Loughborough Uni • Middlesex Uni • Napier Uni • Newport • Northampton Uni • Northumbria Uni • Norwich Uni Coll Arts • Nottingham Trent Uni • Plymouth Uni • Portsmouth Uni • Ravensbourne Coll • Reading Uni • Robert Gordon Uni • Royal Coll Art (p/g only) • Salford Uni • Sheffield Hallam Uni • Southampton Solent Uni • Southampton Uni • Staffordshire Uni • Sunderland Uni • Swansea Met Uni • Teesside Uni • Thames Valley Uni • UCLan • Ulster Uni • UWIC • Westminster Uni • Winchester Sch Art • Wolverhampton Uni • Worcester Uni

Greek (ancient/classical)

Birmingham Uni • Bristol Uni • Cambridge Uni • Durham Uni • Edinburgh Uni • Exeter Uni • Glasgow Uni •King's Coll London • Lampeter Uni • Leeds Uni • Liverpool Uni • Manchester Uni • Nottingham Uni • Oxford Uni • Reading Uni • Royal Holloway • St Andrews Uni • Swansea Uni • University Coll London • Warwick Uni • *See also:* Classical studies; classics

Greek (modern)

Cambridge Uni • Edinburgh Uni • Manchester Uni • Oxford Uni • SOAS

Gujarati

See: Asian studies

Harbours

See: Civil engineering

Hausa

SOAS • *See also:* African studies

Health

Aberdeen Uni • Abertay Dundee Uni • Anglia Ruskin Uni • Aston Uni • Bangor Uni • Bath Spa Uni • Bedfordshire Uni • Birmingham City Uni • Bolton Uni • Bournemouth Uni • Bradford Coll • Bradford Uni • Brighton Uni • Bristol UWE • Brunel Uni • Bucks New Uni • Canterbury Christ Church Uni • Chester Uni • Chichester Uni • City Uni • Colchester Inst • Cranfield Uni (p/g only) • Cumbria Uni • De Montfort Uni • Derby Uni • Durham Uni • East London Uni • Edge Hill Uni • Essex Uni • Farnborough Coll • Glamorgan Uni • Glasgow Caledonian Uni • Glasgow Uni • Gloucestershire Uni • Glyndŵr Uni • Greenwich Uni • Hertfordshire Uni • Huddersfield Uni • Hull Uni • Kent • King's Coll London • Kingston Uni • Leeds Met Uni • Leeds Trinity • Leeds Uni • Lincoln Uni • Liverpool Hope Uni • Liverpool John Moores Uni • Liverpool Uni • London Met Uni • Manchester Met Uni • Middlesex Uni • Napier Uni • Newport • Northampton Uni • Northumbria Uni • Nottingham Trent

Uni • Open Uni • Oxford Brookes Uni • Plymouth Uni • Portsmouth Uni • Queen Margaret Uni • Reading Uni • Robert Gordon Uni • Roehampton Uni • Royal Holloway • St Mary's Uni Coll • Salford Uni • Sheffield Hallam Uni • Southampton Uni • Staffordshire Uni • Strathclyde Uni • Swansea Met Uni • Swansea Uni • Teesside Uni • Thames Valley Uni • Trinity Coll Carmarthen • UCLan • UHI Millennium Institute • Ulster Uni • UWIC • West of Scotland Uni • Westminster Uni • Wolverhampton Uni • Worcester Uni • York St John Uni • York Uni

Hebrew

Aberdeen Uni • Cambridge Uni • Edinburgh Uni • Manchester Uni • Oak Hill Coll • Oxford Uni • St Andrews Uni • SOAS • University Coll London • *See also:* Middle Eastern studies; semitic languages

Hellenistic studies

See: Classics; Greek (ancient/classical)

Heritage studies

Bangor Uni • Birmingham Uni • Bournemouth Uni • Canterbury Christ Church Uni • Chichester Uni • Glamorgan Uni • Glyndŵr Uni • Huddersfield Uni • Manchester Uni • Newport • Nottingham Trent Uni • Scottish Agricultural Coll • Southampton Uni • UHI Millennium Institute • Worcester Uni

Highway/traffic

See: Civil engineering; town planning; transport studies

Hindi

SOAS • *See also:* Asian studies

Hindustani

See: Asian studies

Hispanic studies

Aberdeen Uni • Birkbeck • Birmingham Uni • Bristol Uni • Exeter Uni • Glasgow Uni • Hull Uni • Kent • King's Coll London • Leeds Uni • Liverpool Uni • Newcastle Uni • Nottingham Uni • Portsmouth Uni • Queen Mary • Royal Holloway • Sheffield Uni • Southampton Uni • Stirling Uni • Swansea Uni • University Coll London • *See also:* Iberian studies; Latin American studies; Portuguese; Spanish

History

Aberdeen Uni • Aberystwyth Uni • Anglia Ruskin Uni • Bangor Uni • Bath Spa Uni • Birkbeck • Birmingham Uni • Bolton Uni • Bradford Uni • Bristol Uni • Bristol UWE • Brunel Uni • Cambridge Uni • Canterbury Christ Church Uni • Cardiff Uni • Chester Uni • Chichester Uni • Coventry Uni • Cumbria Uni • De Montfort Uni • Derby Uni • Dundee Uni • Durham Uni • East Anglia Uni • East London Uni • Edge Hill Uni • Edinburgh Uni • Essex Uni • Exeter Uni • Glamorgan Uni • Glasgow Caledonian Uni • Glasgow Uni • Gloucestershire Uni • Glyndŵr Uni • Goldsmiths • Greenwich Uni • Hertfordshire Uni • Huddersfield Uni • Hull Uni • Keele Uni • Kent • King's Coll London • Kingston Uni • Lampeter Uni • Lancaster Uni • Leeds Met Uni • Leeds Trinity • Leeds Uni • Leicester Uni • Lincoln Uni • Liverpool Hope Uni • Liverpool John Moores Uni • Liverpool Uni • London Met Uni • Loughborough Uni • LSE • Manchester Met Uni • Manchester Uni • Newcastle Uni • Newport • Northampton Uni • Northumbria Uni • Nottingham Trent Uni • Nottingham Uni • Open Uni • Oxford Brookes Uni • Oxford Uni • Plymouth Uni • Portsmouth Uni • Queen Mary • Queen's Uni Belfast • Reading Uni • Roehampton Uni • Royal

Holloway • St Andrews Uni • St Mary's Uni Coll • Salford Uni • Sheffield Hallam Uni • Sheffield Uni • SOAS • Southampton Uni • Staffordshire Uni • Stirling Uni • Strathclyde Uni • Sunderland Uni • Sussex Uni • Swansea Uni • Teesside Uni • UCLan • UHI Millennium Institute • Ulster Uni • University Coll London • UWIC • Warwick Uni • Westminster Uni • Winchester Uni • Wolverhampton Uni • Worcester Uni • York St John Uni • York Uni • *See also:* Economic history; social history

History of art

See: Art history

History/philosophy of science

Aberdeen Uni • Birkbeck • Cambridge Uni • Cardiff Uni • Edinburgh Uni • Kent • Kingston Uni • Lancaster Uni • Leeds Uni • Newcastle Uni • Open Uni • St Andrews Uni • University Coll London

Horticulture

Brighton Uni • Bristol UWE • Glyndŵr Uni • Greenwich Uni • Myerscough Coll • Nottingham Trent Uni • Reading Uni • Scottish Agricultural Coll • Wolverhampton Uni • Worcester Uni • Writtle Coll

Hospitality management

Bedfordshire Uni • Bournemouth Uni • Brighton Uni • Bucks New Uni • Coventry Uni • Derby Uni • Glasgow Caledonian Uni • Gloucestershire Uni • Greenwich Uni • Huddersfield Uni • Leeds Met Uni • London Met Uni • London South Bank Uni • Manchester Met Uni • Middlesex Uni • Napier Uni • Northumbria Uni • Oxford Brookes Uni • Plymouth Uni • Portsmouth Uni • Queen Margaret Uni • Robert Gordon Uni • Salford Uni • Sheffield Hallam Uni • Strathclyde Uni • Surrey Uni • Thames Valley Uni • UCLan • Ulster Uni • University Coll Birmingham • UWIC • Wolverhampton Uni • *See also:* Catering

Housing management

Anglia Ruskin Uni • Birmingham City Uni • Bristol UWE • Glyndŵr Uni • Greenwich Uni • Heriot-Watt Uni • Leeds Met Uni • Liverpool John Moores Uni • London South Bank Uni • Middlesex Uni • Northumbria Uni • Salford Uni • Sheffield Hallam Uni • Stirling Uni • Ulster Uni • UWIC • Westminster Uni • *See also:* Urban estate management

Human biology

Aberdeen Uni • Aston Uni • Bedfordshire Uni • Birmingham Uni • Bradford Uni • Bristol UWE • Cambridge Uni • Chester Uni • Cranfield Uni (p/g only) • Durham Uni • East London Uni • Exeter Uni • Glamorgan Uni • Glasgow Caledonian Uni • Glasgow Uni • Heriot-Watt Uni • Hertfordshire Uni • Huddersfield Uni • Hull Uni • Keele Uni • King's Coll London • Kingston Uni • Leeds Met Uni • Leeds Uni • Liverpool Hope Uni • Liverpool Uni • London South Bank Uni • Loughborough Uni • Manchester Met Uni • Manchester Uni • Newcastle Uni • Northampton Uni • Northumbria Uni • Nottingham Uni • Oxford Brookes Uni • Plymouth Uni • Portsmouth Uni • Queen Margaret Uni • Robert Gordon Uni • Roehampton Uni • Salford Uni • Sussex Uni • Swansea Uni • Ulster Uni • Wolverhampton Uni • Worcester Uni • *See also:* Anatomy; physiology

Human communication

Bournemouth Uni • Bradford Uni • De Montfort Uni • Manchester Uni • Newcastle UniRobert Gordon Uni • Sheffield Uni • Ulster Uni • University Coll London • York St John Uni • *See also:* Communication studies; psychology

Human movement

See: Movement studies

Human resource management

Anglia Ruskin Uni • Aston Uni • Bath Uni • Bedfordshire Uni • Birmingham City Uni • Bolton Uni • Bournemouth Uni • Bradford Coll • Bradford Uni • Bristol UWE • Bucks New Uni • Canterbury Christ Church Uni • Cardiff Uni • Coventry Uni • Cranfield Uni (p/g only) • Cumbria Uni • De Montfort Uni • Derby Uni • East London Uni • Edge Hill Uni • Essex Uni • Glamorgan Uni • Gloucestershire Uni • Glyndŵr Uni • Greenwich Uni • Heriot-Watt Uni • Hertfordshire Uni • Huddersfield Uni • Hull Uni • Keele Uni • Kent • Kingston Uni • Lancaster Uni • Leeds Met Uni • Leeds Trinity • Leeds Uni • Lincoln Uni • Liverpool John Moores Uni • Liverpool Uni • London Met Uni • London South Bank Uni • LSE • Manchester Met Uni • Manchester Uni • Middlesex Uni • Napier Uni • Newport • Northampton Uni • Northumbria Uni • Nottingham Trent Uni • Oxford Brookes Uni • Plymouth Uni • Portsmouth Uni • Robert Gordon Uni • Roehampton Uni • Royal Agricultural Coll • Salford Uni • Southampton Solent Uni • Southampton Uni • Staffordshire Uni • Stirling Uni • Strathclyde Uni • Sunderland Uni • Swansea Met Uni • Thames Valley Uni • UCLan • Ulster Uni • UWIC • West of Scotland Uni • Westminster Uni • Winchester Uni • Wolverhampton Uni • Worcester Uni • York St John Uni

Human rights

Aberystwyth Uni • Bradford Uni • De Montfort Uni • East London Uni • Essex Uni • Kingston Uni • Leicester Uni • Roehampton Uni • SOAS • Staffordshire Uni • Sussex Uni • UCLan

Human sciences

Aberdeen Uni • Bolton Uni • Bradford Uni • Brunel Uni • Cranfield Uni (p/g only) • Durham Uni • Essex Uni • Hertfordshire Uni • Kingston Uni • Liverpool John Moores Uni • Loughborough Uni • Open Uni • Oxford Uni • Plymouth Uni • Queen Margaret Uni • Roehampton Uni • Sheffield Uni • Stirling Uni • Surrey Uni • Sussex Uni • Thames Valley Uni • University Coll London • Westminster Uni • *See also:* Biosocial science

Humanities

Aberdeen Uni • Anglia Ruskin Uni • Bath Spa Uni • Birkbeck • Birmingham Uni • Bolton Uni • Bradford Uni • Brighton Uni • Bristol UWE • Canterbury Christ Church Uni • Chichester Uni • De Montfort Uni • Derby Uni • Dundee Uni • East Anglia Uni • East London Uni • Essex Uni • Exeter Uni • Glamorgan Uni • Glasgow Uni • Gloucestershire Uni • Glyndŵr Uni • Goldsmiths • Greenwich Uni • Hertfordshire Uni • Huddersfield Uni • Hull Uni • King's Coll London • Kingston Uni • Lampeter Uni • Lancaster Uni • Leeds Met Uni • Leeds Trinity • Leicester Uni • Liverpool John Moores Uni • London Met Uni • Manchester Uni • Northumbria Uni • Nottingham Trent Uni • Nottingham Uni • Open Uni • Plymouth Uni • Portsmouth Uni • Reading Uni • St Andrews Uni • Salford Uni • Southampton Uni • Stirling Uni • Sussex Uni • Swansea Met Uni • Swansea Uni • Ulster Uni • UWIC • Westminster Uni • Wolverhampton Uni • Worcester Uni

Hungarian

University Coll London

Hydraulic engineering

See: Civil engineering

Iberian studies

Birmingham Uni • Bristol Uni • Swansea Uni • University Coll London • *See also:* Hispanic studies; Portuguese; Spanish

Icelandic

University Coll London • *See also:* Scandinavian studies

Illustration

Anglia Ruskin Uni • Bedfordshire Uni • Birmingham City Uni • Bolton Uni • Bradford Coll • Brighton Uni • Bristol UWE • Camberwell Coll • Central Saint Martins • Coventry Uni • Creative Arts Uni • Cumbria Uni • De Montfort Uni • Derby Uni • Dundee Uni • East London Uni • Edinburgh Coll Art • Falmouth Uni Coll • Glasgow Caledonian Uni • Gloucestershire Uni • Glyndŵr Uni • Hertfordshire Uni • Kingston Uni • Lincoln Uni • London Coll Communication • London Coll Fashion • London Met Uni • Loughborough Uni • Manchester Met Uni • Middlesex Uni • Northampton Uni • Norwich Uni Coll Arts • Nottingham Trent Uni • Plymouth Uni • Portsmouth Uni • Royal Coll Art (p/g only) • Southampton Solent Uni • Sunderland Uni • Swansea Met Uni • Teesside Uni • UCLan • Ulster Uni • UWIC • Westminster Uni • Winchester Sch Art • Wolverhampton Uni • Worcester Uni • *See also:* Graphic design

Immunology

Aberdeen Uni • Aston Uni • Bedfordshire Uni • Bristol Uni • Brunel Uni • East London Uni • Edinburgh Uni • Glasgow Caledonian Uni • Glasgow Uni • Leeds Uni • Leicester Uni • Napier Uni • Newcastle Uni • Strathclyde Uni • West of Scotland Uni • *See also:* Bacteriology; microbiology

Indian studies

See: Asian studies

Indonesian studies

SOAS

Industrial design

Anglia Ruskin Uni • Aston Uni • Birmingham City Uni • Bournemouth Uni • Bradford Uni • Bristol UWE • Brunel Uni • Coventry Uni • Cranfield Uni (p/g only) • Creative Arts Uni • De Montfort Uni • Hertfordshire Uni • Huddersfield Uni • London Coll Fashion • London South Bank Uni • Loughborough Uni • Middlesex Uni • Northumbria Uni • Nottingham Trent Uni • Ravensbourne Coll • Robert Gordon Uni • Royal Coll Art (p/g only) • Sheffield Hallam Uni • Swansea Met Uni • Teesside Uni • UCLan • Ulster Uni • UWIC • Westminster Uni • *See also:* Three-dimensional design

Industrial engineering

Aberdeen Uni • Bath Uni • Bradford Uni • Coventry Uni • Cranfield Uni (p/g only) • Exeter Uni • Huddersfield Uni • Manchester Met Uni • Nottingham Trent Uni • Royal Coll Art (p/g only) • UWIC

Industrial relations

Bath Uni • Kent • LSE • Stirling Uni • Wolverhampton Uni • *See also:* Business studies; economics; law; sociology

Industrial studies

Liverpool Uni

Informatics

Aberdeen Uni • Aston Uni • Bradford Uni • City Uni • Cranfield Uni (p/g only) • Dundee Uni • Edinburgh Uni • Glasgow Uni • Hertfordshire Uni • Kingston Uni • Lampeter Uni • Leeds Met Uni • Northumbria Uni • Nottingham Trent Uni • Portsmouth Uni • Ravensbourne Coll • Reading Uni • Salford Uni • Strathclyde Uni • Sussex Uni • Swansea Uni • Teesside Uni • Ulster Uni • Westminster Uni

Information design

See: Graphic design

Information science

Aberystwyth Uni • Bath Uni • Buckingham Uni • Coventry Uni • Cranfield Uni (p/g only) • Hertfordshire Uni • Hull Uni • Loughborough Uni • Manchester Uni • Northampton Uni • Portsmouth Uni • Robert Gordon Uni • Strathclyde Uni • Thames Valley Uni • University Coll London • West of Scotland Uni • Westminster Uni • Wolverhampton Uni

Information studies

Aberystwyth Uni • Birmingham City Uni • Bolton Uni • Coventry Uni • Glasgow Caledonian Uni • Leeds Met Uni • Liverpool John Moores Uni • Liverpool Uni • London South Bank Uni • Loughborough Uni • Manchester Met Uni • Northampton Uni • Northumbria Uni • Portsmouth Uni • Robert Gordon Uni • Salford Uni • Sheffield Uni • Sussex Uni • University Coll London • West of Scotland Uni • Westminster Uni • *See also:* Library studies

Information systems

Aberdeen Uni • Abertay Dundee Uni • Aberystwyth Uni • Anglia Ruskin Uni • Aston Uni • Bedfordshire UniBirkbeck • Birmingham City Uni • Bolton Uni • Bournemouth Uni • Bradford Uni • Brighton Uni • Brunel Uni • Buckingham Uni • Cardiff Uni • Chester Uni • City Uni • Cranfield Uni (p/g only) • Cumbria Uni • De Montfort Uni • East Anglia Uni • East London Uni • Glamorgan Uni • Glasgow Caledonian Uni • Gloucestershire Uni • Goldsmiths • Greenwich Uni • Hertfordshire Uni • Imperial Coll • Keele Uni • Kingston Uni • Leeds Met Uni • Liverpool John Moores Uni • Liverpool Uni • London Met Uni • London South Bank Uni • Manchester Met Uni • Manchester Uni • Napier Uni • Newcastle Uni • Northampton Uni • Nottingham Trent Uni • Oxford Brookes Uni • Portsmouth Uni • Reading Uni • Roehampton Uni • Royal Holloway • Salford Uni • Sheffield Hallam Uni • Staffordshire Uni • Stirling Uni • Strathclyde Uni • Surrey Uni • Sussex Uni • Swansea Met Uni • Swansea Uni • Teesside Uni • Thames Valley Uni • Trinity Coll Carmarthen • UWIC • West of Scotland Uni • Westminster Uni • Wolverhampton Uni

Information technology

Aberdeen Uni • Abertay Dundee Uni • Aberystwyth Uni • Anglia Ruskin Uni • Aston Uni • Bangor Uni • Bath Uni • Bedfordshire Uni • Birkbeck • Birmingham City Uni • Birmingham Uni • Bolton Uni • Bournemouth Uni • Bradford Coll • Bradford Uni • Brighton Uni • Bristol UWE • Brunel Uni • Bucks New Uni • Canterbury Christ Church Uni • Chester Uni • Chichester Uni • City Uni • Coventry Uni • Cranfield Uni (p/g only) • Cumbria Uni • De Montfort Uni • Derby Uni • East Anglia Uni • East London Uni • Edge Hill UniEdinburgh Uni • Essex Uni • European Business Sch • Exeter Uni • Farnborough Coll • Glamorgan Uni • Glasgow Caledonian Uni • Glasgow Uni • Gloucestershire Uni • Glyndŵr Uni • Goldsmiths • Greenwich Uni • Heriot-Watt Uni • Hertfordshire Uni • Huddersfield

Uni • Hull Uni • Keele Uni • Kent • Kingston Uni • Lampeter Uni • Lancaster Uni • Leeds Met Uni • Liverpool Hope Uni • Liverpool John Moores Uni • Liverpool Uni • London Met Uni • Loughborough Uni • Manchester Met Uni • Manchester Uni • Middlesex Uni • Napier Uni • Newcastle Uni • Newport • Northampton Uni • Northumbria Uni • Nottingham Trent Uni • Open Uni • Oxford Brookes Uni • Plymouth Uni • Portsmouth Uni • Queen Mary • Queen's Uni Belfast • Reading Uni • Robert Gordon Uni • Salford Uni • Sheffield Hallam Uni • Southampton Solent Uni • Southampton Uni • Staffordshire Uni • Strathclyde Uni • Sunderland Uni • Surrey Uni • Sussex Uni • Swansea Met Uni • Swansea Uni • Teesside Uni • Trinity Coll Carmarthen • UCLan • Ulster Uni • University Coll Birmingham • UWIC • Warwick Uni • West of Scotland Uni • Wolverhampton Uni • Worcester Uni • York St John Uni • York Uni

Instrumentation

Brunel Uni • Cranfield Uni (p/g only) • Liverpool Uni • Newport • Teesside Uni

Insurance

See: Actuarial studies; business studies; financial services

Interactive games production

Abertay Dundee Uni • Anglia Ruskin Uni • Bedfordshire Uni • Birmingham City Uni • Bolton Uni • Bournemouth Uni • Bradford Uni • Brighton Uni • Bristol UWE • Coventry Uni • Creative Arts Uni • Cumbria Uni • De Montfort Uni • Derby Uni • East London Uni • Glamorgan Uni • Glasgow Caledonian Uni • Gloucestershire Uni • Glyndŵr Uni • Greenwich Uni • Hertfordshire Uni • Hull Uni • Kingston Uni • Leeds Met Uni • Lincoln Uni • Liverpool Hope Uni • Liverpool John Moores Uni • London Coll Communication • London Met Uni • London South Bank Uni • Manchester Met Uni • Middlesex Uni • National Film Sch (p/g only) • Newcastle Uni • Newport • Portsmouth Uni • Queen's Uni Belfast • Ravensbourne Coll • Robert Gordon Uni • Salford Uni • Southampton Solent Uni • Staffordshire Uni • Sunderland Uni • Swansea Met Uni • Teesside Uni • Thames Valley Uni • UCLan • Ulster Uni • West of Scotland Uni • Westminster Uni • Winchester Uni • Wolverhampton Uni

Interactive multimedia

Anglia Ruskin Uni • Bath Spa Uni • Birmingham City Uni • Bolton Uni • Bournemouth Uni • Bradford Coll • Bradford Uni • Brighton Uni • Bucks New Uni • Coventry Uni • Creative Arts Uni • Cumbria Uni • De Montfort Uni • Derby Uni • Dundee Uni • Edge Hill Uni • Farnborough Coll • Glasgow Caledonian Uni • Gloucestershire Uni • Glyndŵr Uni • Greenwich Uni • Huddersfield Uni • Hull Uni • Leeds Met Uni • Lincoln Uni • Liverpool Hope Uni • Liverpool John Moores Uni • London Coll Communication • London Met Uni • Manchester Met Uni • Middlesex Uni • Newport • Northumbria Uni • Portsmouth Uni • Ravensbourne Coll • Robert Gordon Uni • Roehampton Uni • Rose Bruford Coll • Salford Uni • Sheffield Hallam Uni • Southampton Solent Uni • Staffordshire Uni • Sunderland Uni • Sussex Uni • Swansea Met Uni • Teesside Uni • UCLan • Ulster Uni • UWIC • West of Scotland Uni • Winchester Uni • Wolverhampton Uni • Worcester Uni • *See also:* Multimedia

Interior design

Anglia Ruskin Uni • Bedfordshire Uni • Birmingham City Uni • Bolton Uni • Bradford Coll • Brighton Uni • Bucks New Uni • Central Saint Martins • Chelsea Coll Art • Creative Arts Uni • De Montfort Uni • Dundee Uni • Edinburgh Coll Art • Falmouth Uni Coll • Glamorgan Uni • Glasgow Caledonian Uni • Glasgow Sch Art • Hertfordshire Uni • Huddersfield Uni • Kent • Kingston Uni • Leeds Met Uni • Lincoln Uni • Liverpool John Moores Uni • London Coll Communication • London Met Uni • Manchester Met Uni • Middlesex Uni • Napier Uni • Northumbria Uni • Nottingham Trent Uni • Plymouth Uni • Portsmouth Uni • Ravensbourne Coll • Robert Gordon Uni • Royal Coll Art (p/g only) • Salford Uni • Sheffield Hallam Uni • Southampton Solent Uni • Sunderland Uni • Swansea Met Uni • Teesside Uni • UCLan • Ulster Uni • UWIC • Westminster Uni • Wolverhampton Uni • Writtle Coll

International business

Aberdeen Uni • Abertay Dundee Uni • Anglia Ruskin Uni • Aston Uni • Bath Uni • Bedfordshire Uni • Birmingham City Uni • Birmingham Uni • Bournemouth Uni • Bradford Coll • Bradford Uni • Brighton Uni • Bristol UWE • Brunel Uni • Bucks New Uni • Canterbury Christ Church Uni • Cardiff Uni • Coventry Uni • De Montfort Uni • Derby Uni • Dundee Uni • East London Uni • Edge Hill Uni • Edinburgh Uni • European Business Sch • Glamorgan Uni • Glasgow Caledonian Uni • Glasgow Uni • Gloucestershire Uni • Greenwich Uni • Heriot-Watt Uni • Hertfordshire Uni • Huddersfield Uni • Hull Uni • Kingston Uni • Lancaster Uni • Leeds Met Uni • Lincoln Uni • Liverpool John Moores Uni • Liverpool Uni • London Business Sch (p/g only) • London Met Uni • London South Bank Uni • Loughborough Uni • Manchester Met Uni • Manchester Uni • Middlesex Uni • Northampton Uni • Northumbria Uni • Nottingham Trent Uni • Oxford Brookes Uni • Plymouth Uni • Portsmouth Uni • Reading Uni • Regent's Business Sch • Robert Gordon Uni • Roehampton Uni • Royal Agricultural Coll • Salford Uni • Sheffield Hallam Uni • Southampton Solent Uni • Staffordshire Uni • Stirling Uni • Strathclyde Uni • Surrey Uni • Swansea Uni • Teesside Uni • UCLan • Ulster Uni • UWIC • Warwick Uni • West of Scotland Uni • Westminster Uni • Wolverhampton Uni • *See also:* Business studies; European business studies

International development

Bath Uni • Bradford Uni • Chester Uni • De Montfort Uni • East Anglia Uni • East London Uni • Huddersfield Uni • Leeds Uni • Liverpool Uni • London Met Uni • LSE • Manchester Met Uni • Portsmouth Uni • Reading Uni • SOAS • Ulster Uni • Wolverhampton Uni • *See also:* Third World studies

International relations

Aberdeen Uni • Aberystwyth Uni • Aston Uni • Birkbeck • Birmingham Uni • Bournemouth Uni • Bradford Uni • Bristol UWE • Buckingham Uni • Cardiff Uni • Coventry Uni • De Montfort Uni • Derby Uni • Dundee Uni • Durham Uni • East Anglia Uni • Edinburgh Uni • Essex Uni • Exeter Uni • Hull Uni • Keele Uni • Kent • Kingston Uni • Lancaster Uni • Leeds Uni • Leicester Uni • Lincoln Uni • London Met Uni • Loughborough Uni • LSE • Manchester Met Uni • Middlesex Uni • Nottingham Trent Uni • Nottingham Uni • Open Uni • Oxford Brookes Uni • Plymouth Uni • Portsmouth Uni • Queen's Uni Belfast • Reading Uni • Royal Holloway • St Andrews Uni • Salford Uni • Sheffield Uni • SOAS • Southampton Uni • Sussex Uni • Swansea Uni • Warwick Uni • Westminster Uni • Winchester Uni • York Uni • *See also:* Politics; war studies

Internet technology

Aberdeen Uni • Abertay Dundee Uni • Aberystwyth Uni • Anglia Ruskin Uni • Aston Uni • Bangor Uni • Bedfordshire Uni • Birmingham City Uni • Bolton Uni • Bournemouth Uni • Bradford Uni • Brighton Uni • Bristol UWE • Brunel Uni • Bucks New Uni • Chester Uni • Coventry Uni • De Montfort Uni • Derby Uni • East Anglia Uni • East London Uni • Essex Uni • Exeter Uni • Farnborough Coll • Glamorgan Uni • Glasgow Caledonian Uni • Gloucestershire Uni • Glyndŵr Uni • Goldsmiths • Greenwich Uni • Heriot-Watt Uni • Hertfordshire Uni • Huddersfield Uni • Hull Uni • Kent • Kingston Uni • Leeds Met Uni • Leicester Uni • Lincoln Uni • Liverpool John Moores Uni • Liverpool Uni • London Met Uni • London South Bank Uni • Loughborough Uni • Manchester Met Uni • Middlesex Uni • Newport • Northampton Uni • Northumbria Uni • Nottingham Trent Uni • Open Uni • Plymouth Uni • Portsmouth Uni • Queen Mary • Ravensbourne Coll • Robert Gordon Uni • St Andrews Uni • Salford Uni • Sheffield Hallam Uni • Southampton Solent Uni • Sussex Uni • Swansea Met Uni • Swansea Uni • Teesside Uni • UCLan • UHI Millennium Institute • West of Scotland Uni • Westminster Uni • Wolverhampton Uni

Interpreting/translating

Aston Uni • East Anglia Uni • Heriot-Watt Uni • London Met Uni • Middlesex Uni • Roehampton Uni • Salford Uni • Sheffield Uni • Surrey Uni • Swansea Uni • Westminster Uni • Wolverhampton Uni

Investment

See: Business studies; finance; financial services

Iranian studies

See: Middle Eastern studies; Persian

Irish studies

Aberystwyth Uni • Liverpool Uni • St Mary's Uni Coll • Ulster Uni • *See also:* Celtic studies

Islamic studies

Birmingham Uni • Chester Uni • Exeter Uni • Lampeter Uni • Leeds Uni • Manchester Uni • St Andrews Uni • SOAS • UCLan • *See also:* Middle Eastern studies; religious studies

Italian

Aberdeen Uni • Bangor Uni • Bath Uni • Birmingham Uni • Bristol Uni • Cambridge Uni • Cardiff Uni • Durham Uni • East London Uni • Edinburgh Uni • Essex Uni • European Business Sch • Exeter Uni • Glasgow Uni • Greenwich Uni • Hull Uni • Kent • Lancaster Uni • Leeds Uni • Leicester Uni • Liverpool John Moores Uni • Liverpool Uni • Manchester Met Uni • Manchester Uni • Middlesex Uni • Nottingham Trent Uni • Oxford Uni • Plymouth Uni • Portsmouth Uni • Reading Uni • Royal Holloway • St Andrews Uni • Salford Uni • Sheffield Uni • Strathclyde Uni • Sussex Uni • Swansea Uni • University Coll London • Warwick Uni

Japanese

Birkbeck • Birmingham Uni • Cambridge Uni • Cardiff Uni • Edinburgh Uni • European Business Sch • Leeds Uni • Liverpool John Moores Uni • Manchester Met Uni • Manchester Uni • Newcastle Uni • Oxford Brookes Uni • Oxford Uni • Sheffield Uni • SOAS • UCLan • *See also:* Asian studies; oriental studies

Jazz

Birmingham City Uni • Birmingham Conservatoire • Hull Uni • Leeds Coll Music • Middlesex Uni • Thames Valley Uni • *See also:* Music

Jewellery

Birmingham City Uni • Bucks New Uni • Central Saint Martins • Creative Arts Uni • Cumbria Uni • De Montfort Uni • Dundee Uni • Edinburgh Coll Art • Glasgow Sch Art • Glyndŵr Uni • London Coll Fashion • London Met Uni • Loughborough Uni • Middlesex Uni • Robert Gordon Uni • Royal Coll Art (p/g only) • Sheffield Hallam Uni • Sunderland Uni • Ulster Uni • Wolverhampton Uni • *See also:* Silversmithing; three-dimensional design

Jewish studies

Manchester Uni • Oxford Uni • SOAS • University Coll London • *See also:* Hebrew

Journalism

Anglia Ruskin Uni • Bangor Uni • Bedfordshire Uni • Birkbeck • Birmingham City Uni • Bournemouth Uni • Brighton Uni • Bristol UWE • Buckingham Uni • Bucks New Uni • Canterbury Christ Church Uni • Cardiff Uni • Chester Uni • City Uni • Coventry Uni • Creative Arts Uni • Cumbria Uni • De Montfort Uni • Derby Uni • East London Uni • Edge Hill Uni • Falmouth Uni Coll • Glamorgan Uni • Glasgow Caledonian Uni • Gloucestershire Uni • Glyndŵr Uni • Greenwich Uni • Hertfordshire Uni • Huddersfield Uni • Kent • Kingston Uni • Leeds Met Uni • Leeds Trinity • Leeds Uni • Lincoln Uni •Liverpool John Moores Uni • London Coll Communication • London Coll Fashion • London Met Uni • Middlesex Uni • Napier Uni • Northampton Uni • Northumbria Uni • Nottingham Trent Uni • Portsmouth Uni • Queen Mary • Robert Gordon Uni • Roehampton Uni • Royal Holloway • Salford Uni • Sheffield Hallam Uni • Sheffield Uni • Southampton Solent Uni • Staffordshire Uni • Stirling Uni • Strathclyde Uni • Sunderland Uni • Teesside Uni • Thames Valley Uni • UCLan • Ulster Uni • West of Scotland Uni • Westminster Uni • Winchester Uni • Wolverhampton Uni • Worcester Uni • *See also:* Broadcasting; media studies

Jurisprudence

See: Law

Labour

See: Business studies; economics; industrial relations; law; politics; sociology

Land administration

See: Estate management

Land economy

Aberdeen Uni • Bournemouth Uni • Cambridge Uni • Queen's Uni Belfast • Reading Uni • Royal Agricultural Coll • Scottish Agricultural Coll • Sheffield Hallam Uni

Land surveying

See: Quantity surveying

Landscape architecture

Architectural Association • Birmingham City Uni • Bournemouth Uni • Edinburgh Coll Art • Falmouth Uni Coll • Gloucestershire Uni • Glyndŵr Uni • Greenwich Uni • Kingston Uni • Leeds Met Uni • Manchester Met Uni • Sheffield Uni

Landscape studies

Bangor Uni • Birmingham City Uni • Bournemouth Uni • Glyndŵr Uni • Greenwich Uni • Harper Adams Uni Coll • Kingston Uni • Myerscough Coll • Northampton Uni • Nottingham Trent Uni • Scottish Agricultural Coll • Sheffield Uni • Sussex Uni • Worcester Uni • Writtle Coll • *See also:* Architecture; horticulture

Languages

See: individual languages (eg French) or regional studies (eg African studies)

Laser

See: Physics

Latin

Aberdeen Uni • Bristol Uni • Cambridge Uni • Durham Uni • Edinburgh Uni • Exeter Uni • Glasgow Uni • King's Coll London • Lampeter Uni • Leeds Uni • Liverpool Uni • Manchester Uni • Nottingham Uni • Oxford Uni • Royal Holloway • St Andrews Uni • Swansea Uni • University Coll London • Warwick Uni • *See also:* Classics; classical studies

Latin American studies

Aberdeen Uni • Birkbeck • Bristol Uni • Edinburgh Uni • Essex Uni • King's Coll London • Leeds Uni • Liverpool Uni • London Met Uni • Middlesex Uni • Newcastle Uni • Nottingham Uni • Portsmouth Uni • Southampton Uni • Swansea Uni • University Coll London • Warwick Uni • *See also:* Hispanic studies; Portuguese; Spanish

Law

Aberdeen Uni • Abertay Dundee Uni • Aberystwyth Uni • Anglia Ruskin Uni • Aston Uni • Bangor Uni • Bedfordshire Uni • Birkbeck • Birmingham City Uni • Birmingham Uni • Bolton Uni • Bournemouth Uni • Bradford Coll • Bradford Uni • Brighton Uni • Bristol Uni • Bristol UWE • Brunel Uni • Buckingham Uni • Bucks New Uni • Cambridge Uni • Canterbury Christ Church Uni • Cardiff Uni • Chester Uni • City Uni • Coventry Uni • Cumbria Uni • De Montfort Uni • Derby Uni • Dundee Uni • Durham Uni • East Anglia Uni • East London Uni • Edge Hill Uni • Edinburgh Uni • Essex Uni • Exeter Uni • Glamorgan Uni • Glasgow Caledonian Uni • Glasgow Uni • Gloucestershire Uni • Glyndŵr Uni • Greenwich Uni • Hertfordshire Uni • Huddersfield Uni • Hull Uni • Keele Uni • Kent • King's Coll London • Kingston Uni • Lancaster Uni • Leeds Met Uni • Leeds Trinity • Leeds Uni • Leicester Uni • Lincoln Uni • Liverpool Hope Uni • Liverpool John Moores Uni • Liverpool Uni • London Met Uni • London South Bank Uni • LSE • Manchester Met Uni • Manchester Uni • Middlesex Uni • Napier Uni • Newcastle Uni • Newport • Northampton Uni • Northumbria Uni • Nottingham Trent Uni • Nottingham Uni • Open Uni • Oxford Brookes Uni • Oxford Uni • Plymouth Uni • Portsmouth Uni • Queen Mary • Queen's Uni Belfast • Reading Uni • Robert Gordon Uni • St Mary's Uni Coll • Salford Uni • Sheffield Hallam Uni • Sheffield Uni • SOAS • Southampton Solent Uni • Southampton Uni • Staffordshire Uni • Stirling Uni • Strathclyde Uni • Sunderland Uni • Surrey Uni • Sussex Uni • Swansea Uni • Teesside Uni • Thames Valley Uni • UCLan • Ulster Uni • University Coll London • Warwick Uni • West of Scotland Uni • Westminster Uni • Winchester Uni • Wolverhampton Uni • York Uni

Leather technology

London Coll Fashion • Northampton Uni

Leisure studies

Anglia Ruskin Uni • Bedfordshire Uni • Bolton Uni • Bournemouth Uni • Brighton Uni • Bristol UWE • Bucks New Uni • Canterbury Christ Church Uni • Coventry Uni • Cumbria Uni • Edge Hill Uni • Farnborough Coll • Glamorgan Uni • Glasgow Caledonian Uni • Glasgow Uni • Harper Adams Uni Coll • Huddersfield Uni • Hull Uni • Leeds Met Uni • Leeds Trinity • Liverpool Hope Uni • Liverpool John Moores Uni • Manchester Met Uni • Manchester Uni • Myerscough Coll • Napier Uni • Nottingham Trent Uni • Oxford Brookes Uni • Plymouth Uni • Portsmouth Uni • Salford Uni • Scottish Agricultural Coll • Sheffield Hallam Uni • Southampton Solent Uni • Sunderland Uni • Swansea Met Uni • Teesside Uni • UCLan • Ulster Uni • University Coll Birmingham • UWIC • West of Scotland Uni • Westminster Uni • Wolverhampton Uni • Writtle Coll • *See also:* Recreation studies; tourism

Levant

See: Archaeology

Library studies

Aberystwyth Uni • Liverpool John Moores Uni • Manchester Met Uni • Northumbria Uni • *See also:* Information studies

Life sciences

See: Biology

Linguistics

Aberdeen Uni • Aberystwyth Uni • Bangor Uni • Birkbeck • Brighton Uni • Bristol UWE • Cambridge Uni • East London Uni • Edinburgh Uni • Essex Uni • Glasgow Uni • Greenwich Uni • Hertfordshire Uni • Kent • King's Coll London • Kingston Uni • Lancaster Uni • Leeds Uni • Manchester Uni • Marjon • Newcastle Uni • Northumbria Uni • Nottingham Trent Uni • Nottingham Uni • Open Uni • Oxford Uni • Queen Mary • Queen's Uni Belfast • Reading Uni • Roehampton Uni • Salford Uni • Sheffield Hallam Uni • Sheffield Uni • SOAS • Southampton Uni • Sussex Uni • Swansea Uni • UCLan • Ulster Uni • University Coll London • Westminster Uni • Wolverhampton Uni • York St John Uni • York Uni • *See also:* individual languages (eg French)

Literature

See: individual languages (eg Chinese)

Logic

See: Mathematics; philosophy

Malay

See: South East Asian studies

Management

Aberdeen Uni • Abertay Dundee Uni • Aberystwyth Uni • Anglia Ruskin Uni • Aston Uni • Bangor Uni • Bath Uni • Bedfordshire Uni • Birkbeck • Birmingham City Uni • Birmingham Uni • Bolton Uni • Bournemouth Uni • Bradford Coll • Bradford Uni • Brighton Uni • Bristol Uni • Bristol UWE • Brunel Uni • Buckingham Uni • Bucks New Uni • Cambridge Uni • Cardiff Uni • Chester Uni • Chichester Uni • City Uni • Colchester Inst • Coventry Uni • Cranfield Uni (p/g only) • Cumbria Uni • De Montfort Uni • Derby Uni • East Anglia Uni • East London Uni • Edge Hill Uni • Edinburgh Uni • Essex Uni • European Business Sch • Exeter Uni • Farnborough Coll • Glamorgan Uni • Glasgow Caledonian Uni • Glasgow Uni • Gloucestershire Uni • Glyndŵr Uni • Greenwich Uni • Harper Adams Uni Coll • Heriot-Watt Uni • Hertfordshire Uni • Huddersfield Uni • Hull Uni • Imperial Coll • Keele Uni • Kent • King's Coll London • Kingston Uni • Lampeter Uni • Lancaster Uni • Leeds Met Uni • Leeds Trinity • Leeds Uni • Leicester Uni • Lincoln Uni • Liverpool John Moores Uni • Liverpool Uni • London Business Sch (p/g only) • London Coll Fashion • London Met Uni • London South Bank Uni • Loughborough Uni • LSE • Manchester Met Uni • Manchester Uni • Middlesex Uni • Napier Uni • Newcastle Uni • Newport • Northampton Uni • Northumbria Uni • Nottingham Trent Uni • Nottingham Uni • Open Uni • Oxford Brookes Uni • Oxford Uni • Plymouth Uni • Portsmouth Uni • Queen Margaret Uni • Queen Mary • Queen's Uni Belfast • Reading Uni • Regent's Business Sch • Robert Gordon Uni • Roehampton Uni • Royal Agricultural Coll • Royal Holloway • St Andrews Uni

• St Mary's Uni Coll • Salford Uni • Scottish Agricultural Coll • Sheffield Hallam Uni • Sheffield Uni • SOAS • Southampton Solent Uni • Southampton Uni • Staffordshire Uni • Stirling Uni • Strathclyde Uni • Surrey Uni • Sussex Uni • Swansea Met Uni • Swansea Uni • Teesside Uni • Trinity Coll Carmarthen • UCLan • UHI Millennium Institute • Ulster Uni • University Coll Birmingham • University Coll London • UWIC • Warwick Uni • West of Scotland Uni • Westminster Uni • Winchester Uni • Wolverhampton Uni • Worcester Uni • Writtle Coll • York St John Uni • York Uni • *See also:* Business studies; economics; estate management; European business studies; hospitality management; leisure studies; public administration; recreation studies

Manufacturing engineering

Aberdeen Uni • Anglia Ruskin Uni • Aston Uni • Bath Uni • Birmingham City Uni • Birmingham Uni • Bradford Uni • Brighton Uni • Bristol UWE • Cambridge Uni • Cardiff Uni • Coventry Uni • Cranfield Uni (p/g only) • Derby Uni • Durham Uni • East London Uni • Edinburgh Uni • Exeter Uni • Glamorgan Uni • Glasgow Caledonian Uni • Greenwich Uni • Heriot-Watt Uni • Huddersfield Uni • Hull Uni • Kingston Uni • Leeds Uni • Liverpool John Moores Uni • Liverpool Uni • Loughborough Uni • Napier Uni • Newcastle Uni • Newport • Northumbria Uni • Nottingham Trent Uni • Nottingham Uni • Open Uni • Plymouth Uni • Portsmouth Uni • Queen's Uni Belfast • Strathclyde Uni • Sussex Uni • Swansea Met Uni • Warwick Uni • West of Scotland Uni • *See also:* Production engineering

Marine architecture

Cranfield Uni (p/g only) • Newcastle Uni • Southampton Uni • University Coll London • *See also:* Naval architecture; naval engineering

Marine biology

Aberdeen Uni • Aberystwyth Uni • Anglia Ruskin Uni • Bangor Uni • Essex Uni • Glasgow Uni • Heriot-Watt Uni • Hull Uni • Kingston Uni • Liverpool Uni • Napier Uni • Newcastle Uni • Plymouth Uni • Portsmouth Uni • Queen Mary • Queen's Uni Belfast • St Andrews Uni • Southampton Uni • Stirling Uni • Swansea Uni • UHI Millennium Institute • Ulster Uni • *See also:* Maritime studies

Marine engineering

Cranfield Uni (p/g only) • Glasgow Uni • Greenwich Uni • Liverpool John Moores Uni • Newcastle Uni • Plymouth Uni • Portsmouth Uni • Southampton Solent Uni • Southampton Uni • Strathclyde Uni • University Coll London

Maritime studies

Greenwich Uni • Liverpool John Moores Uni • Plymouth Uni • Portsmouth Uni • Southampton Solent Uni • Southampton Uni

Marketing

Abertay Dundee Uni • Aberystwyth Uni • Anglia Ruskin Uni • Aston Uni • Bangor Uni • Bedfordshire Uni • Birmingham City Uni • Bolton Uni • Bournemouth Uni • Bradford Coll • Bradford Uni • Brighton Uni • Bristol UWE • Brunel Uni • Buckingham Uni • Bucks New Uni • Canterbury Christ Church Uni • Cardiff Uni • Chester Uni • Chichester Uni • Coventry Uni • Cranfield Uni (p/g only) • Creative Arts Uni • Cumbria Uni • De Montfort Uni • Derby Uni • Dundee Uni • East London Uni • Edge Hill Uni • European Business Sch • Exeter Uni • Glamorgan Uni • Glasgow Caledonian Uni • Gloucestershire Uni • Glyndŵr Uni • Greenwich Uni • Harper Adams Uni Coll • Heriot-Watt Uni • Hertfordshire Uni • Huddersfield Uni • Hull Uni • Keele Uni • Kent • Kingston Uni • Lancaster Uni • Leeds Met Uni • Leeds Trinity • Leeds Uni • Lincoln Uni • Liverpool Hope Uni • Liverpool John Moores Uni • Liverpool Uni

• London Coll Communication • London Coll Fashion • London Met Uni • London South Bank Uni • Loughborough Uni • Manchester Met Uni • Manchester Uni • Middlesex Uni • Napier Uni • Newcastle Uni • Newport • Northampton Uni • Northumbria Uni • Nottingham Trent Uni • Oxford Brookes Uni • Plymouth Uni • Portsmouth Uni • Queen Margaret Uni • Ravensbourne Coll • Regent's Business Sch • Robert Gordon Uni • Roehampton Uni • Royal Agricultural Coll • Royal Holloway • Salford Uni • Sheffield Hallam Uni • Southampton Solent Uni • Staffordshire Uni • Stirling Uni • Strathclyde Uni • Sunderland Uni • Swansea Met Uni • Swansea Uni • Teesside Uni • Thames Valley Uni • UCLan • Ulster Uni • University Coll Birmingham • UWIC • West of Scotland Uni • Westminster Uni • Winchester Uni • Wolverhampton Uni • Worcester Uni • Writtle Coll • York St John Uni • *See also:* Business studies

Materials science

Aberdeen Uni • Birmingham Uni • Cambridge Uni • Cranfield Uni (p/g only) • Imperial Coll • Leeds Uni • Liverpool Uni • Manchester Uni • Oxford Uni • Queen Mary • St Andrews Uni • Sheffield Hallam Uni • Sheffield Uni • Strathclyde Uni • Swansea Uni • *See also:* Chemistry; engineering; metallurgy

Materials technology

Aberdeen Uni • Birmingham Uni • Bradford Uni • Cranfield Uni (p/g only) • Exeter Uni • Imperial Coll • Leeds Uni • Liverpool Uni • Loughborough Uni • Northampton Uni • Plymouth Uni • Portsmouth Uni • Queen Mary • Sheffield Hallam Uni • Sheffield Uni • Strathclyde Uni • Swansea Uni

Mathematics

Aberdeen Uni • Aberystwyth Uni • Aston Uni • Bath Uni • Birkbeck • Birmingham Uni • Bolton Uni • Brighton Uni • Bristol Uni • Bristol UWE • Brunel Uni • Cambridge Uni • Cardiff Uni • Chester Uni • Chichester Uni • City Uni • Coventry Uni • Cumbria Uni • Derby Uni • Dundee Uni • Durham Uni • East Anglia Uni • Edinburgh Uni • Essex Uni • Exeter Uni • Glamorgan Uni • Glasgow Uni • Greenwich Uni • Heriot-Watt Uni • Hertfordshire Uni • Imperial Coll • Keele Uni • Kent • King's Coll London • Kingston Uni • Lancaster Uni • Leeds Uni • Leicester Uni • Liverpool John Moores Uni • Liverpool Uni • London Met Uni • Loughborough Uni • LSE • Manchester Met Uni • Manchester Uni • Newcastle Uni • Northampton Uni • Northumbria Uni • Nottingham Trent Uni • Nottingham Uni • Open Uni • Oxford Brookes Uni • Oxford Uni • Plymouth Uni • Portsmouth Uni • Queen Mary • Queen's Uni Belfast • Reading Uni • Royal Holloway • St Andrews Uni • Sheffield Hallam Uni • Sheffield Uni • Southampton Uni • Staffordshire Uni • Stirling Uni • Strathclyde Uni • Surrey Uni • Sussex Uni • Swansea Uni • UCLan • University Coll London • Warwick Uni • West of Scotland Uni • Wolverhampton Uni • York Uni

Mechanical engineering

Aberdeen Uni • Aston Uni • Bath Uni • Birmingham City Uni • Birmingham Uni • Bolton Uni • Bradford Uni • Brighton Uni • Bristol Uni • Bristol UWE • Brunel Uni • Cambridge Uni • Cardiff Uni • City Uni • Coventry Uni • Cranfield Uni (p/g only) • De Montfort Uni • Derby Uni • Dundee Uni • Durham Uni • Edinburgh Uni • Exeter Uni • Glamorgan Uni • Glasgow Caledonian Uni • Glasgow Uni • Glyndŵr Uni • Greenwich Uni • Heriot-Watt Uni • Hertfordshire Uni • Huddersfield Uni • Hull Uni • Imperial Coll • King's Coll London • Kingston Uni • Lancaster Uni • Leeds Uni • Leicester Uni • Liverpool John Moores Uni • Liverpool Uni • London South Bank Uni • Loughborough Uni • Manchester Met Uni • Manchester Uni • Napier Uni • Newcastle Uni • Newport • Northumbria Uni • Nottingham Trent Uni • Nottingham Uni • Oxford Brookes Uni • Oxford Uni • Plymouth Uni • Portsmouth Uni • Queen Mary • Queen's Uni Belfast • Robert Gordon Uni • Salford Uni • Sheffield Hallam Uni • Sheffield Uni • Southampton Solent Uni • Southampton Uni • Staffordshire Uni • Strathclyde Uni • Sunderland Uni • Surrey Uni • Sussex Uni • Swansea Met Uni • Swansea Uni • Teesside Uni • Thames Valley Uni • UHI Millennium Institute • Ulster Uni • University Coll London • Warwick Uni • West of Scotland Uni • Wolverhampton Uni • *See also:* Engineering (general)

Media and production

See: Broadcasting; film studies; graphic design; journalism; media studies; video

Media studies

Abertay Dundee Uni • Aberystwyth Uni • Anglia Ruskin Uni • Bangor Uni • Bath Spa Uni • Bedfordshire Uni • Birkbeck • Birmingham City Uni • Birmingham Uni • Bolton Uni • Bournemouth Uni • Bradford Uni • Brighton Uni • Bristol UWE • Brunel Uni • Buckingham Uni • Bucks New Uni • Canterbury Christ Church Uni • Cardiff Uni • Chester Uni • Chichester Uni • Colchester Inst • Coventry Uni • Creative Arts Uni • Cumbria Uni • De Montfort Uni • Derby Uni • East Anglia Uni • East London Uni • Edge Hill Uni • Falmouth Uni Coll • Farnborough Coll • Glamorgan Uni • Glasgow Caledonian Uni • Gloucestershire Uni • Glyndŵr Uni • Goldsmiths • Greenwich Uni • Hertfordshire Uni • Huddersfield Uni • Hull Uni • Keele Uni • Kingston Uni • Lampeter Uni • Lancaster Uni • Leeds Met Uni • Leeds Trinity • Leeds Uni • Lincoln Uni • Liverpool Hope Uni • Liverpool John Moores Uni • Liverpool Uni • London Coll Communication • London Coll Fashion • London Met Uni • London South Bank Uni • Loughborough Uni • Manchester Met Uni • Marjon • Middlesex Uni • Newcastle Uni • Newport • Northampton Uni • Northumbria Uni • Nottingham Trent Uni • Open Uni • Oxford Brookes Uni • Plymouth Uni • Portsmouth Uni • Queen Margaret Uni • Ravensbourne Coll • Robert Gordon Uni • Roehampton Uni • Royal Holloway • St Mary's Uni Coll • Salford Uni • Sheffield Hallam Uni • Southampton Solent Uni • Southampton Uni • Staffordshire Uni • Stirling Uni • Sunderland Uni • Surrey Uni • Sussex Uni • Swansea Met Uni • Swansea Uni • Teesside Uni • Thames Valley Uni • Trinity Coll Carmarthen • UCLan • UHI Millennium Institute • Ulster Uni • UWIC • West of Scotland Uni • Westminster Uni • Winchester Uni • Wolverhampton Uni • Worcester Uni • York St John Uni • *See also:* Broadcasting; communication studies; film studies

Media technology

Anglia Ruskin Uni • Aston Uni • Birmingham City Uni • Bolton Uni • Bournemouth Uni • Bradford Uni • Bristol Old Vic • Bristol UWE • Chester Uni • Chichester Uni • City Uni • Creative Arts Uni • Cumbria Uni • De Montfort Uni • Derby Uni • East Anglia Uni • Farnborough Coll • Glamorgan Uni • Glyndŵr Uni • Hertfordshire Uni • Huddersfield Uni • Hull Uni • Kingston Uni • Lampeter Uni • Lancaster Uni • Leeds Met Uni • Lincoln Uni • Liverpool Hope Uni • London Met Uni • London South Bank Uni • Manchester Met Uni • Oxford Brookes Uni • Portsmouth Uni • Ravensbourne Coll • Salford Uni • Sheffield Hallam Uni • Southampton Solent Uni • Staffordshire Uni • Surrey Uni • Sussex Uni • Swansea Met Uni • Teesside Uni • Thames Valley Uni • UCLan • West of Scotland Uni • Westminster Uni • Winchester Uni • York Uni

Medical engineering

Bath Uni • Birmingham Uni • Bradford Uni • Cardiff Uni • City Uni • Cranfield Uni (p/g only) • Hull Uni • Leeds Uni • Liverpool Uni • Queen Mary • Sheffield Uni • Surrey Uni • Swansea Uni

Medical imaging

Bradford Uni • Canterbury Christ Church Uni • Cumbria Uni • Derby Uni • Exeter Uni • Hertfordshire Uni • London South Bank Uni • Portsmouth Uni • Sheffield Hallam Uni • Ulster Uni • *See also:* Radiography

Medical laboratory science

Bedfordshire Uni • Birmingham Uni • Bradford Uni • East London Uni • Glamorgan Uni • Glasgow Caledonian Uni • Portsmouth Uni • Ulster Uni • UWIC

Medical microbiology

Aberdeen Uni • Anglia Ruskin Uni • Bradford Uni • Bristol Uni • Edinburgh Uni • Hertfordshire Uni • Leeds Uni • Newcastle Uni • Portsmouth Uni • Surrey Uni • *See also:* Microbiology

Medicinal chemistry

Aberdeen Uni • Anglia Ruskin Uni • Birmingham Uni • Bradford Uni • East Anglia Uni • Edinburgh Uni • Exeter Uni • Glasgow Uni • Huddersfield Uni • Hull Uni • Imperial Coll • Keele Uni • Kingston Uni • Leeds Uni • Leicester Uni • Liverpool John Moores Uni • Liverpool Uni • Loughborough Uni • Manchester Met Uni • Manchester Uni • Newcastle Uni • Nottingham Trent Uni • Nottingham Uni • Queen's Uni Belfast • Salford Uni • Sheffield Hallam Uni • Sheffield Uni • Southampton Uni • Strathclyde Uni • University Coll London • Warwick Uni • West of Scotland Uni • York Uni • *See also:* Chemistry; biomedical science; biochemistry

Medicinal physics

Birmingham Uni • Cardiff Uni • Exeter Uni • Hull Uni • Leeds Uni • Leicester Uni • University Coll London • West of Scotland Uni • *See also:* Physics

Medicine

Aberdeen Uni • Barts & The London • Birmingham Uni • Brighton and Sussex Med Sch • Brighton Uni • Bristol Uni • Cambridge Uni • Cardiff Uni • Dundee Uni • Durham Uni • East Anglia Uni • Edinburgh Uni • Exeter Uni • Glasgow Uni • Hull Uni • Hull York Med Sch • Imperial Coll • Keele Uni • King's Coll London • Lancaster Uni • Leeds Uni • Leicester Uni • Liverpool Uni • Manchester Uni • Newcastle Uni • Nottingham Uni • Oxford Uni • Peninsula Med and Dental Coll • Plymouth Uni • Queen Mary • Queen's Uni Belfast • St Andrews Uni • St George's • Sheffield Uni • Southampton Uni • Sussex Uni • Swansea Uni • University Coll London • York Uni

Medieval studies

Aberystwyth Uni • Birmingham Uni • Durham Uni • Edinburgh Uni • Glasgow Uni • Kent • Lampeter Uni • Lancaster Uni • Manchester Uni • Nottingham Uni • Queen Mary • St Andrews Uni • Swansea Uni • Winchester Uni • *See also:* History

Mediterranean studies

Birmingham Uni • *See also:* Archaeology

Mesopotamia

See: Archaeology

Metallurgy

Birmingham Uni • Bradford Coll • Cranfield Uni (p/g only) • Liverpool Uni • Sheffield Hallam Uni • Sheffield Uni • *See also:* Materials science

Metaphysics

See: Philosophy

Meteorology

East Anglia Uni • Edinburgh Uni • Leeds Uni • Reading Uni • *See also:* Geography

Microbiology

Aberdeen Uni • Aberystwyth Uni • Anglia Ruskin Uni • Birmingham Uni • Bradford Uni • Bristol Uni • Bristol UWE • Cambridge Uni • Cardiff Uni • Dundee Uni • East Anglia Uni • East London Uni • Edinburgh Uni • Glamorgan Uni • Glasgow Caledonian Uni • Glasgow Uni • Heriot-Watt Uni • Hertfordshire Uni • Huddersfield Uni • Imperial Coll • King's Coll London • Leeds Uni • Leicester Uni • Liverpool John Moores Uni • Liverpool Uni • London Met Uni • Manchester Met Uni • Manchester Uni • Napier Uni • Newcastle Uni • Northumbria Uni • Nottingham Trent Uni • Nottingham Uni • Portsmouth Uni • Queen Mary • Queen's Uni Belfast • Reading Uni • Scottish Agricultural Coll • Sheffield Uni • Staffordshire Uni • Strathclyde Uni • Surrey Uni • Sussex Uni • University Coll London • Warwick Uni • West of Scotland Uni • Westminster Uni • Wolverhampton Uni • *See also:* Bacteriology; biochemistry; biology; genetics; medical microbiology; virology

Microelectronics

Aberdeen Uni • Birmingham Uni • Bournemouth Uni • Bradford Uni • Brunel Uni • Dundee Uni • Edinburgh Uni • Heriot-Watt Uni • Hertfordshire Uni • Kingston Uni • Liverpool Uni • Robert Gordon Uni • St Andrews Uni • Salford Uni • Sheffield Uni • *See also:* Digital microelectronics; electronics; computer science

Middle Eastern studies

Birmingham Uni • Cambridge Uni • Edinburgh Uni • Exeter Uni • Leeds Uni • Manchester Uni • Oxford Uni • St Andrews Uni • Salford Uni • SOAS • *See also:* Asian studies

Midwifery

Anglia Ruskin Uni • Bangor Uni • Bedfordshire Uni • Birmingham City Uni • Bournemouth Uni • Bradford Uni • Brighton Uni • Bristol UWE • Canterbury Christ Church Uni • Cardiff Uni • Chester Uni • City Uni • Coventry Uni • Cumbria Uni • De Montfort Uni • Dundee Uni • East Anglia Uni • Edge Hill Uni • Glamorgan Uni • Glasgow Caledonian Uni • Greenwich Uni • Hertfordshire Uni • Huddersfield Uni • Hull Uni • Keele Uni • King's Coll London • Kingston Uni • Leeds Uni • Liverpool John Moores Uni • London South Bank Uni • Manchester Uni • Middlesex Uni • Napier Uni • Northampton Uni • Northumbria Uni • Nottingham Uni • Oxford Brookes Uni • Plymouth Uni • Portsmouth Uni • Queen's Uni Belfast • Robert Gordon Uni • St George's • Salford Uni • Sheffield Hallam Uni • Southampton Uni • Staffordshire Uni • Stirling Uni • Surrey Uni • Swansea Uni • Teesside Uni • Thames Valley Uni • UCLan • West of Scotland Uni • Wolverhampton Uni • Worcester Uni • York Uni

Mineral processing technology

Birmingham Uni • Exeter Uni • Leeds Uni • *See also:* Geology; mining

Mineralogy

See: Geology

Mining

Exeter Uni • Leeds Uni • *See also* Exploration; geology

Modern languages

See: individual languages (eg French) or regional studies (eg Scandinavian studies)

Molecular biology

Aberdeen Uni • Anglia Ruskin Uni • Aston Uni • Bangor Uni • Bath Uni • Birkbeck • Birmingham Uni • Bolton Uni • Bradford Uni • Bristol Uni • Bristol UWE • Cambridge Uni • Cardiff Uni • Cranfield Uni (p/g only) • Dundee Uni • Durham Uni • East Anglia Uni • Edinburgh Uni • Essex Uni • Exeter Uni • Glasgow Caledonian Uni • Glasgow Uni • Heriot-Watt Uni • Hertfordshire Uni • Huddersfield Uni • Hull Uni • Imperial Coll • King's Coll London • Kingston Uni • Leeds Uni • Leicester Uni • Liverpool John Moores Uni • Liverpool Uni • Manchester Met Uni • Manchester Uni • Newcastle Uni • Nottingham Trent Uni • Nottingham Uni • Open Uni • Oxford Brookes Uni • Portsmouth Uni • Queen Mary • Queen's Uni Belfast • Royal Holloway • St Andrews Uni • Scottish Agricultural Coll • Sheffield Hallam Uni • Sheffield Uni • Southampton Uni • Stirling Uni • Strathclyde Uni • Surrey Uni • Sussex Uni • UCLan • Ulster Uni • University Coll London • UWIC • Warwick Uni • Westminster Uni • Wolverhampton Uni • York Uni

Moral philosophy

See: Philosophy

Motor sport engineering

Birmingham City Uni • Bolton Uni • Bristol UWE • Brunel Uni • Bucks New Uni • City Uni • Coventry Uni • Cranfield Uni (p/g only) • Derby Uni • Farnborough Coll • Glyndŵr Uni • Hertfordshire Uni • Kingston Uni • Myerscough Coll • Northampton Uni • Oxford Brookes Uni • Sheffield Uni • Swansea Met Uni • UCLan • West of Scotland Uni

Movement studies

Bristol Old Vic • Central Sch Speech/Drama • Derby Uni • Laban • Northern Sch Cont Dance • St Mary's Uni Coll • Trinity Coll Carmarthen • *See also:* Dance; drama; physical education

Multimedia

Aberystwyth Uni • Anglia Ruskin Uni • Aston Uni • Bangor Uni • Bath Spa Uni • Birkbeck • Birmingham City Uni • Birmingham Uni • Bolton Uni • Bournemouth Uni • Bradford Coll • Bradford Uni • Brighton Uni • Bristol UWE • Brunel Uni • Buckingham Uni • Bucks New Uni • Chester Uni • Coventry Uni • Creative Arts Uni • Cumbria Uni • Dartington • De Montfort Uni • Derby Uni • East Anglia Uni • East London Uni • Edge Hill Uni • Falmouth Uni Coll • Farnborough Coll • Glamorgan Uni • Glasgow Caledonian Uni • Gloucestershire Uni • Glyndŵr Uni • Greenwich Uni • Heriot-Watt Uni • Hertfordshire Uni • Huddersfield Uni • Kent • Kingston Uni • Lancaster Uni • Leeds Met Uni • Leeds Uni • Lincoln Uni • Liverpool John Moores Uni • Liverpool Uni • London Coll Communication • London Met Uni • Loughborough Uni • Manchester Met Uni • Middlesex Uni • Napier Uni • Newport • Northumbria Uni • Norwich Uni Coll Arts • Nottingham Trent Uni • Oxford Brookes Uni • Plymouth Uni • Portsmouth Uni • Queen's Uni Belfast • Ravensbourne Coll • Robert Gordon Uni • Rose Bruford Coll • Salford Uni • Sheffield Hallam Uni • Southampton Solent Uni • Staffordshire Uni • Sunderland Uni • Sussex Uni • Swansea Met Uni • Swansea Uni • Teesside Uni • Thames Valley Uni • UCLan • Ulster Uni • UWIC • West of Scotland Uni • Westminster Uni • Winchester Uni • Wolverhampton Uni • Worcester Uni • *See also:* Interactive multimedia

Music

Aberdeen Uni • Anglia Ruskin Uni • Bangor Uni • Bath Spa Uni • Birmingham City Uni • Birmingham Conservatoire • Birmingham Uni • Brighton Uni • Bristol Uni • Brunel Uni • Bucks New Uni • Cambridge Uni • Canterbury Christ Church Uni • Cardiff Uni • Chichester Uni • City Uni • Colchester Inst • Coventry Uni • Dartington • Derby Uni • Durham Uni • East Anglia

Uni • Edinburgh Uni • Falmouth Uni Coll • Glasgow Uni • Goldsmiths • Guildhall Sch Music and Drama • Hertfordshire Uni • Huddersfield Uni • Hull Uni • Imperial Coll • Keele Uni • King's Coll London • Kingston Uni • Laban • Lancaster Uni • Leeds Coll Music • Leeds Uni • Liverpool Hope Uni • Liverpool John Moores Uni • Liverpool Uni • London Sch Theology • Manchester Met Uni • Manchester Uni • Middlesex Uni • Napier Uni • Newcastle Uni • Nottingham Uni • Open Uni • Oxford Brookes Uni • Oxford Uni • Plymouth Uni • Queen's Uni Belfast • Rose Bruford Coll • Royal Academy Music • Royal Coll Music • Royal Holloway • Royal Northern Coll Music • Royal Scottish Academy Music/Drama • Royal Welsh Coll Music/Drama • Salford Uni • Sheffield Uni • SOAS • Southampton Solent Uni • Southampton Uni • Staffordshire Uni • Strathclyde Uni • Sunderland Uni • Surrey Uni • Sussex Uni • Thames Valley Uni • Trinity Coll Music • UCLan • UHI Millennium Institute • Ulster Uni • UWIC • West of Scotland Uni • Westminster Uni • Wolverhampton Uni • York St John Uni • York Uni • *See also:* Film music; popular music

Music technology

Anglia Ruskin Uni • Bath Spa Uni • Bedfordshire Uni • Birmingham City Uni • Birmingham Conservatoire • Bolton Uni • Brighton Uni • Bristol Old Vic • Bristol UWE • Brunel Uni • Bucks New Uni • Canterbury Christ Church Uni • Chester Uni • Chichester Uni • City Uni • Coventry Uni • Dartington • De Montfort Uni • Derby Uni • Edge Hill Uni • Edinburgh Uni • Falmouth Uni Coll • Farnborough Coll • Glamorgan Uni • Glasgow Caledonian Uni • Glasgow Uni • Gloucestershire Uni • Glyndŵr Uni • Hertfordshire Uni •Huddersfield Uni • Hull Uni • Keele Uni • Kent • Kingston Uni • Lancaster Uni • Leeds Coll Music • Leeds Met Uni • Leeds Uni • London Met Uni • Manchester Met Uni • Oxford Brookes Uni • Portsmouth Uni • Queen's Uni Belfast • Ravensbourne Coll • Rose Bruford Coll • Royal Welsh Coll Music/Drama • Salford Uni • Southampton Solent Uni • Staffordshire Uni • Sunderland Uni • Surrey Uni • Sussex Uni • Swansea Met Uni • Teesside Uni • Thames Valley Uni • UCLan • Ulster Uni • UWIC • West of Scotland Uni • Wolverhampton Uni • Worcester Uni • York Uni

Music theatre

Bath Spa Uni • Bristol Old Vic • Bucks New Uni • Chichester Uni • Colchester Inst • Cumbria Uni • Edge Hill Uni • Gloucestershire Uni • Leeds Coll Music • Rose Bruford Coll • Thames Valley Uni • Trinity Coll Carmarthen • UCLan • *See also:* Music; drama; theatre studies

Music therapy

Derby Uni • Royal Welsh Coll Music/Drama • *See also:* Music

Mycology

See: Plant science

Mythology

See: Anthropology; classics; psychology

Nanoscale science/technology

Birmingham Uni • Cranfield Uni (p/g only) • Heriot-Watt Uni • Huddersfield Uni • Leeds Uni • Nottingham Uni • Queen Mary • Swansea Uni • Ulster Uni • University Coll London • York Uni

Nautical studies

See: Maritime studies

Naval architecture

Cranfield Uni (p/g only) • Glasgow Uni • Newcastle Uni • Southampton Solent Uni • Southampton Uni • Strathclyde Uni • University Coll London • *See also:* Marine architecture; naval engineering

Naval engineering

Glasgow Uni • Newcastle Uni • Portsmouth Uni • Southampton Uni • Strathclyde Uni • University Coll London • *See also:* Marine engineering

Near East studies

See: Middle Eastern studies; Asian studies

Neurobiology

See: Biology; physiology; psychology

Neuroscience

Aberdeen Uni • Birmingham Uni • Bristol Uni • Cambridge Uni • Cardiff Uni • Dundee Uni • Edinburgh Uni • Glasgow Uni • Keele Uni • King's Coll London • Leeds Uni • Leicester Uni • Liverpool Uni • Manchester Uni • Nottingham Trent Uni • Nottingham Uni • St Andrews Uni • Sheffield Uni • Southampton Uni • Surrey Uni • Sussex Uni • UCLan • University Coll London • Westminster Uni

New media publishing

Bournemouth Uni • Bradford Uni • Creative Arts Uni • Gloucestershire Uni • Huddersfield Uni • Leeds Uni • London Coll Communication • Norwich Uni Coll Arts • Oxford Brookes Uni • Ravensbourne Coll • Sheffield Hallam Uni • Teesside Uni • Winchester Uni • *See also:* Publishing

Norse

See: Anglo Saxon

Norwegian

University Coll London • *See also:* Scandinavian studies

Nursing

Abertay Dundee Uni • Anglia Ruskin Uni • Bangor Uni • Bedfordshire Uni • Birmingham City Uni • Birmingham Uni • Bournemouth Uni • Bradford Uni • Brighton Uni • Bristol UWE • Bucks New Uni • Canterbury Christ Church Uni • Cardiff Uni • Chester Uni • City Uni • Coventry Uni • Cumbria Uni • De Montfort Uni • Derby Uni • Dundee Uni • East Anglia Uni • Edge Hill Uni • Edinburgh Uni • Glamorgan Uni • Glasgow Caledonian Uni • Glasgow Uni • Glyndŵr Uni • Greenwich Uni • Hertfordshire Uni • Huddersfield Uni • Hull Uni • Keele Uni • King's Coll London • Kingston Uni • Leeds Met Uni • Leeds Uni • Lincoln Uni • Liverpool John Moores Uni • Liverpool Uni • London South Bank Uni • Manchester Met Uni • Manchester Uni • Middlesex Uni • Napier Uni • Northampton Uni • Northumbria Uni • Nottingham Uni • Open Uni • Oxford Brookes Uni • Plymouth Uni • Portsmouth Uni • Queen Margaret Uni • Queen's Uni Belfast • Reading Uni • Robert Gordon Uni • Royal Vet Coll • St George's • Salford Uni • Sheffield Hallam Uni • Southampton Uni • Staffordshire Uni • Stirling Uni • Surrey Uni • Swansea Uni • Teesside Uni • Thames Valley Uni • UCLan • Ulster Uni • West of Scotland Uni • Wolverhampton Uni • Worcester Uni • York Uni • *See also:* Midwifery

Nutrition

Aberdeen Uni • Abertay Dundee Uni • Bath Spa Uni • Bedfordshire Uni • Bournemouth Uni • Bradford Coll • Chester Uni • Coventry Uni • Glamorgan Uni • Glasgow Caledonian Uni • Glasgow Uni • Greenwich Uni • Huddersfield Uni • King's Coll London • Kingston Uni • Leeds Met Uni • Leeds Trinity • Leeds Uni • Lincoln Uni • Liverpool Hope Uni • Liverpool John Moores Uni • London Met Uni • London South Bank Uni • Manchester Met Uni • Middlesex Uni • Newcastle Uni • Northumbria Uni • Nottingham Trent Uni • Nottingham Uni • Oxford Brookes Uni • Plymouth Uni • Queen Margaret Uni • Queen's Uni Belfast • Reading Uni • Robert Gordon Uni • Roehampton Uni • St Mary's Uni Coll • Sheffield Hallam Uni • Surrey Uni • Teesside Uni • Thames Valley Uni • Trinity Coll Carmarthen • UCLan • Ulster Uni • UWIC • Westminster Uni • *See also:* Food science

Occupational psychology

See: Psychology

Occupational therapy

Bedfordshire Uni • Bournemouth Uni • Bradford Uni • Brighton Uni • Bristol UWE • Brunel Uni • Canterbury Christ Church Uni • Cardiff Uni • Colchester Inst • Coventry Uni • Cumbria Uni • Derby Uni • East Anglia Uni • East London Uni • Glasgow Caledonian Uni • Glyndŵr Uni • Huddersfield Uni • Leeds Met Uni • Liverpool Uni • London South Bank Uni • Northampton Uni • Northumbria Uni • Oxford Brookes Uni • Plymouth Uni • Queen Margaret Uni • Robert Gordon Uni • Salford Uni • Sheffield Hallam Uni • Southampton Uni • Teesside Uni • Ulster Uni • York St John Uni

Oceanography

Aberdeen Uni • Bangor Uni • East Anglia Uni • Liverpool Uni • Newcastle Uni • Plymouth Uni • Southampton Uni

Office organisation

Glasgow Caledonian Uni

Offshore engineering

Aberdeen Uni • Cranfield Uni (p/g only) • Heriot-Watt Uni • Liverpool John Moores Uni • Newcastle Uni • Robert Gordon Uni • Strathclyde Uni

Operational research

Aston Uni • Cardiff Uni • Coventry Uni • Exeter Uni • Heriot-Watt Uni • Lancaster Uni • Salford Uni • Sheffield Hallam Uni • Strathclyde Uni • Warwick Uni • West of Scotland Uni

Ophthalmic optics

Anglia Ruskin Uni • Aston Uni • Bradford Uni • City Uni • Glasgow Caledonian Uni • Liverpool Uni

Optometry

Anglia Ruskin Uni • Aston Uni • Bradford Uni • Cardiff Uni • City Uni • Glasgow Caledonian Uni • Manchester Uni • Ulster Uni

Organisational behaviour

Aston Uni • Bedfordshire Uni • Bradford Uni • Cranfield Uni (p/g only) • European Business Sch • Lancaster Uni • Sheffield Hallam Uni • Sussex Uni • UCLan

Organisational studies

Aston Uni • Cranfield Uni (p/g only) • Lancaster Uni • Manchester Uni • Sheffield Hallam Uni • Sussex Uni

Oriental languages

See: individual languages (eg Japanese)

Oriental medicine

East London Uni • Glyndŵr Uni • Middlesex Uni • Salford Uni

Oriental studies

Cambridge Uni • Lampeter Uni • Oxford Uni • SOAS • *See also:* Asian studies; South East Asian studies

Ornithology

See: Zoology

Orthoptics

Liverpool Uni • Sheffield Uni

Osteopathy

Anglia Ruskin Uni • Bedfordshire Uni • British Sch Osteopathy • Greenwich Uni • Leeds Met Uni • Middlesex Uni • Oxford Brookes Uni

Packaging technology

Creative Arts Uni • Glamorgan Uni • Sheffield Hallam Uni

Painting

Anglia Ruskin Uni • Bath Spa Uni • Bedfordshire Uni • Brighton Uni • Camberwell Coll • Canterbury Christ Church Uni • Central Saint Martins • Chelsea Coll Art • Coventry Uni • Creative Arts Uni • De Montfort Uni • Derby Uni • Dundee Uni • East London Uni • Edinburgh Coll Art • Falmouth Uni Coll • Glasgow Sch Art • Gloucestershire Uni • Glyndŵr Uni • Goldsmiths • Kingston Uni • Liverpool John Moores Uni • London Met Uni • Loughborough Uni • Manchester Met Uni • Middlesex Uni • Newcastle Uni • Norwich Uni Coll Arts • Robert Gordon Uni • Royal Academy Sch p/g only • Royal Coll Art (p/g only) • Sheffield Hallam Uni • Southampton Uni • Swansea Met Uni • University Coll London • UWIC • Wimbledon Coll Art • Winchester Sch Art

Palliative care

Bedfordshire Uni • Bristol UWE • Oxford Brookes Uni • Robert Gordon Uni • Sheffield Hallam Uni • Thames Valley Uni • Wolverhampton Uni

Parasitology

Aberdeen Uni • East London Uni • Glasgow Uni

Pathology

Aberdeen Uni • Bradford Uni • Bristol Uni • Cambridge Uni • Royal Vet Coll • St Andrews Uni

Peace studies

Bradford Uni • Coventry Uni • Lancaster Uni • Leeds Met Uni • London Met Uni • Queen's Uni Belfast • Reading Uni • Swansea Uni • York St John Uni • *See also:* War studies

Performance arts

Aberystwyth Uni • ALRA • Bangor Uni • Bath Spa Uni • Bedfordshire Uni • Birmingham Conservatoire • Birmingham Uni • Brighton Uni • Bristol Old Vic • Brunel Uni • Bucks New Uni • Canterbury Christ Church Uni • Central Sch Speech/Drama • Chester Uni • Chichester Uni • Colchester Inst • Coventry Uni • Cumbria Uni • Dartington • De Montfort Uni • Derby Uni • East Anglia Uni • East London Uni • Edge Hill Uni • Exeter Uni • Falmouth Uni Coll • Farnborough Coll • Gloucestershire Uni • Glyndŵr Uni • Goldsmiths • Hertfordshire Uni • Huddersfield Uni • Hull Uni • Kent • Kingston Uni • Laban • Lancaster Uni • Leeds Coll Music • Leeds Uni • Liverpool Hope Uni • Liverpool John Moores Uni • London Met Uni • Manchester Met Uni • Middlesex Uni • Newport • Northampton Uni • Northern Sch Cont Dance • Northumbria Uni • Nottingham Trent Uni • Plymouth Uni • Portsmouth Uni • Queen Margaret Uni • RADA • Roehampton Uni • Rose Bruford Coll • Royal Scottish Academy Music/Drama • St Mary's Uni Coll • Salford Uni • Sheffield Hallam Uni • Southampton Solent Uni • Staffordshire Uni • Sunderland Uni • Swansea Met Uni • Teesside Uni • Thames Valley Uni • Trinity Coll Carmarthen • Trinity Coll Music • UCLan • Ulster Uni • UWIC • Warwick Uni • West of Scotland Uni • Winchester Uni • Wolverhampton Uni • Worcester Uni • York St John Uni • York Uni • *See also:* Dance; drama

Persian

Cambridge Uni • Edinburgh Uni • Manchester Uni • Oxford Uni • SOAS • *See also:* Middle Eastern studies

Petroleum engineering

Aberdeen Uni • London South Bank Uni • Manchester Uni • Robert Gordon Uni • Strathclyde Uni • *See also:* Energy studies

Petrology

See: Geology

Pharmacology

Aberdeen Uni • Aston Uni • Bath Uni • Bedfordshire Uni • Birmingham Uni • Bradford Uni • Brighton Uni • Bristol Uni • Bristol UWE • Cambridge Uni • Cardiff Uni • Coventry Uni • Cranfield Uni (p/g only) • Dundee Uni • East London Uni • Edinburgh Uni • Glasgow Caledonian Uni • Glasgow Uni • Greenwich Uni • Hertfordshire Uni • Hull Uni • Imperial Coll • King's Coll London • Kingston Uni • Leeds Uni • Leicester Uni • Liverpool Uni • London Met Uni • Loughborough Uni • Manchester Met Uni • Manchester Uni • Newcastle Uni • Nottingham Trent Uni • Portsmouth Uni • St Andrews Uni • Sheffield Hallam Uni • Sheffield Uni • Southampton Uni • Strathclyde Uni • Sunderland Uni • Ulster Uni • University Coll London • West of Scotland Uni • Westminster Uni • Wolverhampton Uni • *See also:* Pharmacy

Pharmacy

Aston Uni • Bath Uni • Birkbeck • Bradford Uni • Brighton Uni • Cardiff Uni • Cranfield Uni (p/g only) • De Montfort Uni • East Anglia Uni • Greenwich Uni • Hertfordshire Uni • Huddersfield Uni • Keele Uni • Kent • King's Coll London • Kingston Uni • Leicester Uni • Liverpool John Moores Uni • Manchester Met Uni • Manchester Uni • Nottingham Uni • Portsmouth Uni • Queen's Uni Belfast • Reading Uni • Robert Gordon Uni • Sch Pharmacy • Strathclyde Uni • Sunderland Uni • UCLan • Ulster Uni • Wolverhampton Uni • *See also:* Pharmacology

Philosophy

Aberdeen Uni • Anglia Ruskin Uni • Bath Spa Uni • Birkbeck • Birmingham Uni • Bradford Uni • Bristol Uni • Bristol UWE • Cambridge Uni • Cardiff Uni • Dundee Uni • Durham Uni • East Anglia Uni • Edinburgh Uni • Essex Uni • Exeter Uni • Glamorgan Uni • Glasgow Uni • Gloucestershire Uni • Greenwich Uni • Hertfordshire Uni • Heythrop Coll • Hull Uni • Keele Uni • Kent • King's Coll London • Lampeter Uni • Lancaster Uni • Leeds Uni • Liverpool Hope Uni • Liverpool Uni • London Met Uni • LSE • Manchester Met Uni • Manchester Uni • Middlesex Uni • Newcastle Uni • Newport • Northampton Uni • Nottingham Trent Uni • Nottingham Uni • Open Uni • Oxford Brookes Uni • Oxford Uni • Queen's Uni Belfast • Reading Uni • Roehampton Uni • Royal Holloway • St Andrews Uni • St Mary's Uni Coll • Sheffield Uni • Southampton Uni • Staffordshire Uni • Stirling Uni • Sussex Uni • UCLan • University Coll London • Warwick Uni • Wolverhampton Uni • York Uni

Philosophy of science

See: History/philosophy of science

Phonetics

See: Linguistics

Photography

Anglia Ruskin Uni • Bath Spa Uni • Bedfordshire Uni • Birmingham City Uni • Bolton Uni • Bradford Coll • Brighton Uni • Bristol UWE • Camberwell Coll • Central Saint Martins • Chester Uni • Coventry Uni • Creative Arts Uni • Cumbria Uni • De Montfort Uni • Derby Uni • East London Uni • Edinburgh Coll Art • Falmouth Uni Coll • Farnborough Coll • Glasgow Sch Art • Gloucestershire Uni • Hertfordshire Uni • Kent • Kingston Uni • Leeds Met Uni • Leeds Uni • London Coll Communication • London Coll Fashion • London Met Uni • London South Bank Uni • Manchester Met Uni • Middlesex Uni • Napier Uni • Newport • Northampton Uni • Northumbria Uni • Norwich Uni Coll Arts • Nottingham Trent Uni • Plymouth Uni • Portsmouth Uni • Robert Gordon Uni • Roehampton Uni • Royal Coll Art (p/g only) • Royal Holloway • Sheffield Hallam Uni • Southampton Solent Uni • Staffordshire Uni • Sunderland Uni • Swansea Met Uni • Thames Valley Uni • UCLan • Ulster Uni • Westminster Uni • Winchester Sch Art • Wolverhampton Uni

Physical education

Bangor Uni • Bedfordshire Uni • Birmingham Uni • Bolton Uni • Brighton Uni • Brunel Uni • Canterbury Christ Church Uni • Chester Uni • Chichester Uni • Cumbria Uni • Derby Uni • East Anglia Uni • Edge Hill Uni • Edinburgh Uni • Gloucestershire Uni • Glyndŵr Uni • Greenwich Uni • Hertfordshire Uni • Hull Uni • Leeds Met Uni • Leeds Trinity • Leeds Uni • Liverpool John Moores Uni • Loughborough Uni • Marjon • Portsmouth Uni • Roehampton Uni • St Mary's Uni Coll • Sheffield Hallam Uni • Stirling Uni • Trinity Coll Carmarthen • Ulster Uni • UWIC • West of Scotland Uni • Wolverhampton Uni • Worcester Uni • York St John Uni • *See also:* Sports studies

Physical science

See: individual sciences (eg chemistry)

Physics

Aberdeen Uni • Aberystwyth Uni • Bath Uni • Birkbeck • Birmingham Uni • Bristol Uni • Cambridge Uni • Cardiff Uni • Dundee Uni • Durham Uni • Edinburgh Uni • Exeter Uni • Glasgow Caledonian Uni • Glasgow Uni • Heriot-Watt Uni • Hertfordshire Uni • Hull Uni • Imperial Coll • Keele Uni • Kent • King's Coll London • Lancaster Uni • Leeds Uni • Leicester Uni • Liverpool John Moores Uni • Liverpool Uni • Loughborough Uni • Manchester Uni • Newcastle Uni • Nottingham Trent Uni • Nottingham Uni • Open Uni • Oxford Uni • Queen Mary • Queen's Uni Belfast • Royal Holloway • St Andrews Uni • Salford Uni • Sheffield Uni • Southampton Uni • Strathclyde Uni • Surrey Uni • Sussex Uni • Swansea Uni • UCLan • University Coll London • Warwick Uni • West of Scotland Uni • York Uni

Physiology

Aberdeen Uni • Bedfordshire Uni • Birmingham Uni • Bristol Uni • Bristol UWE • British Sch Osteopathy • Cambridge Uni • Cardiff Uni • Dundee Uni • East London Uni • Edinburgh Uni • Glasgow Caledonian Uni • Glasgow Uni • Hertfordshire Uni • King's Coll London • Leeds Uni • Leicester Uni • Liverpool Uni • Loughborough Uni • Manchester Met Uni • Manchester Uni • Newcastle Uni • Nottingham Trent Uni • Oxford Uni • Portsmouth Uni • Queen's Uni Belfast • Reading Uni • Royal Holloway • St Andrews Uni • Sheffield Hallam Uni • Sheffield Uni • Southampton Uni • Strathclyde Uni • Sussex Uni • Swansea Uni • UCLan • University Coll London • Westminster Uni • Wolverhampton Uni

Physiotherapy

Bedfordshire Uni • Birmingham Uni • Bournemouth Uni • Bradford Uni • Brighton Uni • Bristol UWE • Brunel Uni • Cardiff Uni • Colchester Inst • Coventry Uni • Cumbria Uni • East Anglia Uni • East London Uni • Glasgow Caledonian Uni • Hertfordshire Uni • Huddersfield Uni • Keele Uni • King's Coll London • Kingston Uni • Leeds Met Uni • Leicester Uni • Liverpool Uni • Manchester Met Uni • Northumbria Uni • Nottingham Uni • Oxford Brookes Uni • Plymouth Uni • Queen Margaret Uni • Robert Gordon Uni • St George's • Salford Uni • Sheffield Hallam Uni • Southampton Uni • Teesside Uni • UCLan • Ulster Uni • York St John Uni

Planetary physics

See: Astrophysics

Plant science

Aberdeen Uni • Aberystwyth Uni • Birmingham Uni • Bristol Uni • Cambridge Uni • Cardiff Uni • Cranfield Uni (p/g only) • Durham Uni • East Anglia Uni • East London Uni • Edinburgh Uni • Glasgow Uni • Imperial Coll • Manchester Uni • Myerscough Coll • Newcastle Uni • Nottingham Trent Uni • Nottingham Uni • Oxford Uni • Reading Uni • St Andrews Uni • Scottish Agricultural Coll • Sheffield Uni • Southampton Uni • Stirling Uni • Wolverhampton Uni • Worcester Uni • Writtle Coll • *See also:* Agriculture; biology; horticulture

Plastics

See: Polymers

Podiatry

Aston Uni • Brighton Uni • East London Uni • Glasgow Caledonian Uni • Huddersfield Uni
• Northampton Uni • Plymouth Uni • Queen Margaret Uni • Salford Uni • Southampton Uni
• Sunderland Uni • Ulster Uni • UWIC

Policing

Birmingham City Uni • Bucks New Uni • Canterbury Christ Church Uni • Cumbria Uni • UCLan
• Wolverhampton Uni • *See also:* Criminology

Polish

Glasgow Uni • Oxford Uni • Sheffield Uni • University Coll London

Political economy

See: Economics

Politics

Aberdeen Uni • Aberystwyth Uni • Anglia Ruskin Uni • Aston Uni • Bath Uni • Birkbeck • Birmingham
City Uni • Birmingham Uni • Bradford Uni • Brighton Uni • Bristol Uni • Bristol UWE • Brunel Uni
• Buckingham Uni • Cambridge Uni • Canterbury Christ Church Uni • Cardiff Uni • City Uni • Coventry
Uni • Dundee Uni • Durham Uni • East Anglia Uni • East London Uni • Edinburgh Uni • Essex Uni
• Exeter Uni • Glamorgan Uni • Glasgow Caledonian Uni • Glasgow Uni • Goldsmiths • Greenwich
Uni • Huddersfield Uni • Hull Uni • Keele Uni • Kent • King's Coll London • Kingston Uni • Lancaster Uni
• Leeds Met Uni • Leeds Uni • Leicester Uni • Lincoln Uni • Liverpool Hope Uni • Liverpool John Moores
Uni • Liverpool Uni • London Met Uni • London South Bank Uni • Loughborough Uni • LSE • Manchester
Met Uni • Manchester Uni • Middlesex Uni • Newcastle Uni • Northampton Uni • Northumbria Uni
• Nottingham Trent Uni • Nottingham Uni • Open Uni • Oxford Brookes Uni • Oxford Uni • Plymouth Uni
• Portsmouth Uni • Queen Mary • Queen's Uni Belfast • Reading Uni • Robert Gordon Uni • Royal
Holloway • Salford Uni • Sheffield Hallam Uni • Sheffield Uni • SOAS • Southampton Uni • Stirling Uni
• Strathclyde Uni • Sunderland Uni • Surrey Uni • Sussex Uni • Swansea Uni • UCLan • Ulster Uni • UWIC
• Warwick Uni • West of Scotland Uni • Westminster Uni • Winchester Uni • Wolverhampton Uni
• Worcester Uni • York Uni

Pollution

Aberdeen Uni • Bradford Uni • Cranfield Uni (p/g only) • Lancaster Uni • Leeds Uni • Open Uni
• Scottish Agricultural Coll • Wolverhampton Uni • *See also:* Ecology; environmental science;
environmental studies

Polymers

Aberdeen Uni • Birmingham Uni • Cranfield Uni (p/g only) • Heriot-Watt Uni • Lancaster Uni • Leeds
Uni • London Met Uni • Loughborough Uni • Napier Uni • Queen Mary • Sheffield Uni • *See also:*
Chemistry; materials science

Popular music

Bath Spa Uni • Bucks New Uni • Canterbury Christ Church Uni • Chester Uni • Chichester Uni
• Colchester Inst • Dartington • Derby Uni • Glamorgan Uni • Gloucestershire Uni • Goldsmiths
• Hertfordshire Uni • Hull Uni • Lancaster Uni • Leeds Coll Music • Leeds Uni • Liverpool John Moores
Uni • Liverpool Uni • Manchester Met Uni • Napier Uni • Newcastle Uni • Northampton Uni • Salford

Uni • Southampton Solent Uni • Thames Valley Uni • UHI Millennium Institute • West of Scotland Uni • Westminster Uni • Wolverhampton Uni • *See also:* Film music; music

Population sciences

See: Geography; sociology; statistics

Portuguese

Birkbeck • Birmingham Uni • Bristol Uni • Cambridge Uni • Essex Uni • European Business Sch • Glasgow Uni • King's Coll London • Leeds Uni • Liverpool Uni • Manchester Uni • Newcastle Uni • Nottingham Uni • Oxford Uni • Queen Mary • Queen's Uni Belfast • Salford Uni • Southampton Uni • *See also:* Hispanic studies; Iberian studies; Latin American studies

Printing/typography

Anglia Ruskin Uni • Bradford Coll • Brighton Uni • Creative Arts Uni • Glyndŵr Uni • Leeds Met Uni • London Coll Communication • Plymouth Uni • Ravensbourne Coll • Reading Uni • Royal Coll Art (p/g only) • UWIC • Wimbledon Coll Art • Wolverhampton Uni

Printmaking

Anglia Ruskin Uni • Birmingham City Uni • Bradford Coll • Brighton Uni • Chelsea Coll Art • Creative Arts Uni • Derby Uni • Dundee Uni • East London Uni • Falmouth Uni Coll • Glasgow Sch Art • Glyndŵr Uni • Goldsmiths • Kingston Uni • London Coll Communication • London Met Uni • Loughborough Uni • Middlesex Uni • Newcastle Uni • Northampton Uni • Ravensbourne Coll • Reading Uni • Robert Gordon Uni • Royal Academy Sch p/g only • Royal Coll Art (p/g only) • Southampton Uni • Swansea Met Uni • Ulster Uni • UWIC • Wimbledon Coll Art • Winchester Sch Art

Probation

See: Social work

Product design

Abertay Dundee Uni • Anglia Ruskin Uni • Aston Uni • Bedfordshire Uni • Birmingham City Uni • Bolton Uni • Bournemouth Uni • Bradford Uni • Brighton Uni • Bristol UWE • Brunel Uni • Bucks New Uni • Camberwell Coll • Central Saint Martins • Coventry Uni • Creative Arts Uni • De Montfort Uni • Derby Uni • Dundee Uni • East London Uni • Edinburgh Coll Art • Falmouth Uni Coll • Glamorgan Uni • Glasgow Caledonian Uni • Glasgow Sch Art • Glasgow Uni • Goldsmiths • Greenwich Uni • Heriot-Watt Uni • Hertfordshire Uni • Huddersfield Uni • Hull Uni • Kingston Uni • Leeds Met Uni • Leeds Uni • Lincoln Uni • Liverpool John Moores Uni • Liverpool Uni • London Coll Communication • London Coll Fashion • London Met Uni • London South Bank Uni • Loughborough Uni • Manchester Met Uni • Middlesex Uni • Napier Uni • Northampton Uni • Northumbria Uni • Nottingham Trent Uni • Nottingham Uni • Plymouth Uni • Portsmouth Uni • Queen's Uni Belfast • Ravensbourne Coll • Robert Gordon Uni • Royal Coll Art (p/g only) • Salford Uni • Sheffield Hallam Uni • Southampton Solent Uni • Staffordshire Uni • Strathclyde Uni • Sussex Uni • Swansea Met Uni • Swansea Uni • Teesside Uni • UCLan • Ulster Uni • UWIC • West of Scotland Uni • Westminster Uni • Wolverhampton Uni • York St John Uni

Production engineering

Aston Uni • Bath Uni • Birmingham Uni • Bournemouth Uni • Bradford Uni • Bristol UWE • Cambridge Uni • Coventry Uni • Cranfield Uni (p/g only) • De Montfort Uni • Glamorgan

Uni • Glasgow Caledonian Uni • Greenwich Uni • Heriot-Watt Uni • Huddersfield Uni • Kingston Uni • Liverpool John Moores Uni • London South Bank Uni • Loughborough Uni • Newport • Portsmouth Uni • Robert Gordon Uni • Sheffield Hallam Uni • Staffordshire Uni • Strathclyde Uni • Swansea Uni • UCLan • West of Scotland Uni • Westminster Uni • Wolverhampton Uni

Professions allied to medicine

See: individual subjects (eg speech therapy)

Programming

See: Computing; computer science

Psychology

Aberdeen Uni • Abertay Dundee Uni • Aberystwyth Uni • Anglia Ruskin Uni • Aston Uni • Bangor Uni • Bath Spa Uni • Bath Uni • Bedfordshire Uni • Birkbeck • Birmingham City Uni • Birmingham Uni • Bolton Uni • Bournemouth Uni • Bradford Coll • Bradford Uni • Brighton Uni • Bristol Uni • Bristol UWE • Brunel Uni • Buckingham Uni • Bucks New Uni • Cambridge Uni • Canterbury Christ Church Uni • Cardiff Uni • Chester Uni • Chichester Uni • City Uni • Coventry Uni • Cranfield Uni (p/g only) • Cumbria Uni • De Montfort Uni • Derby Uni • Dundee Uni • Durham Uni • East Anglia Uni • East London Uni • Edge Hill Uni • Edinburgh Uni • Essex Uni • Exeter Uni • Glamorgan Uni • Glasgow Caledonian Uni • Glasgow Uni • Gloucestershire Uni • Glyndŵr Uni • Goldsmiths • Greenwich Uni • Heriot-Watt Uni • Hertfordshire Uni • Heythrop Coll • Huddersfield Uni • Hull Uni • Keele Uni • Kent • Kingston Uni • Lancaster Uni • Leeds Met Uni • Leeds Trinity • Leeds Uni • Leicester Uni • Lincoln Uni • Liverpool Hope Uni • Liverpool John Moores Uni • Liverpool Uni • London Met Uni • London South Bank Uni • Loughborough Uni • Manchester Met Uni • Manchester Uni • Middlesex Uni • Napier Uni • Newcastle Uni • Newport • Northampton Uni • Northumbria Uni • Nottingham Trent Uni • Nottingham Uni • Open Uni • Oxford Brookes Uni • Oxford Uni • Plymouth Uni • Portsmouth Uni • Queen Margaret Uni • Queen Mary • Queen's Uni Belfast • Reading Uni • Roehampton Uni • Royal Holloway • St Andrews Uni • St Mary's Uni Coll • Salford Uni • Sheffield Hallam Uni • Sheffield Uni • Southampton Solent Uni • Southampton Uni • Staffordshire Uni • Stirling Uni • Strathclyde Uni • Sunderland Uni • Surrey Uni • Sussex Uni • Swansea Met Uni • Swansea Uni • Teesside Uni • Thames Valley Uni • Trinity Coll Carmarthen • UCLan • UHI Millennium Institute • Ulster Uni • University Coll London • UWIC • Warwick Uni • West of Scotland Uni • Westminster Uni • Winchester Uni • Wolverhampton Uni • Worcester Uni • York St John Uni • York Uni

Public administration

Aston Uni • Birmingham Uni • Bradford Uni • De Montfort Uni • Kent • London Met Uni • London South Bank Uni • Manchester Met Uni • Northumbria Uni • Portsmouth Uni • Stirling Uni • Swansea Met Uni • Ulster Uni • West of Scotland Uni • Worcester Uni • *See also:* Social administration

Public health

Bradford Uni • Bristol UWE • De Montfort Uni • East London Uni • Greenwich Uni • Huddersfield Uni • Leeds Met Uni • Leeds Trinity • Liverpool John Moores Uni • London Met Uni • Manchester Met Uni • Oxford Brookes Uni • Sheffield Hallam Uni • Teesside Uni • Thames Valley Uni • UCLan • UWIC • Wolverhampton Uni • Worcester Uni • York St John Uni • *See also:* Environmental health

Public relations

Bedfordshire Uni • Birmingham City Uni • Bournemouth Uni • Bucks New Uni • Chester Uni • Derby Uni • Edge Hill Uni • Glasgow Caledonian Uni • Gloucestershire Uni • Greenwich Uni • Huddersfield Uni

• Leeds Met Uni • Leeds Trinity • Lincoln Uni • Liverpool John Moores Uni • London Coll Communication • London Coll Fashion • London Met Uni • Middlesex Uni • Northampton Uni • Queen Margaret Uni • Robert Gordon Uni • Sheffield Hallam Uni • Southampton Solent Uni • Sunderland Uni • Swansea Uni • Teesside Uni • Thames Valley Uni • UCLan • Ulster Uni • Westminster Uni • Wolverhampton Uni • Worcester Uni

Publishing

Bath Spa Uni • Creative Arts Uni • Gloucestershire Uni • London Coll Communication • Loughborough Uni • Middlesex Uni • Napier Uni • Norwich Uni Coll Arts • Oxford Brookes Uni • Ravensbourne Coll • Robert Gordon Uni

Quality control

See: Production engineering

Quantity surveying

Anglia Ruskin Uni • Birmingham City Uni • Bolton Uni • Bradford Coll • Bristol UWE • Glamorgan Uni • Glasgow Caledonian Uni • Glyndŵr Uni • Greenwich Uni • Heriot-Watt Uni • Kingston Uni • Leeds Met Uni • Liverpool John Moores Uni • London South Bank Uni • Loughborough Uni • Napier Uni • Northumbria Uni • Nottingham Trent Uni • Portsmouth Uni • Reading Uni • Robert Gordon Uni • Salford Uni • Sheffield Hallam Uni • Swansea Met Uni • UCLan • Ulster Uni • Westminster Uni • Wolverhampton Uni • *See also:* Surveying

Radar

See: Electronic engineering

Radio

See: Electronic engineering

Radio frequency engineering

Bradford Uni • Glyndŵr Uni • York Uni • *See also:* Electronic engineering

Radiography

Anglia Ruskin Uni • Bangor Uni • Birmingham City Uni • Bradford Uni • Bristol UWE • Canterbury Christ Church Uni • Cardiff Uni • City Uni • Cumbria Uni • Derby Uni • East London Uni • Exeter Uni • Glasgow Caledonian Uni • Hertfordshire Uni • Kingston Uni • Leeds Uni • Liverpool Uni • London South Bank Uni • Portsmouth Uni • Queen Margaret Uni • Robert Gordon Uni • St George's • Salford Uni • Sheffield Hallam Uni • Teesside Uni • Ulster Uni

Recreation studies

Aberdeen Uni • Aberystwyth Uni • Anglia Ruskin Uni • Bedfordshire Uni • Bolton Uni • Bournemouth Uni • Bucks New Uni • Cumbria Uni • Harper Adams Uni Coll • Leeds Met Uni • Liverpool Hope Uni • Myerscough Coll • Scottish Agricultural Coll • Sheffield Hallam Uni • Southampton Solent Uni • Swansea Met Uni • Ulster Uni • UWIC • West of Scotland Uni • *See also:* Leisure studies; sports studies; tourism

Religious studies

Aberdeen Uni • Bangor Uni • Bath Spa Uni • Birmingham Uni • Brighton Uni • Bristol Uni • Cambridge Uni • Canterbury Christ Church Uni • Cardiff Uni • Chester Uni • Chichester Uni • Cumbria Uni • Edinburgh Uni • Exeter Uni • Glasgow Uni • Gloucestershire Uni • Heythrop Coll • Hull Uni • Kent • King's Coll London • Lampeter Uni • Lancaster Uni • Leeds Trinity • Leeds Uni • Liverpool Hope Uni • London Sch Theology • Manchester Uni • Middlesex Uni • Newport • Nottingham Uni • Oak Hill Coll • Open Uni • Oxford Brookes Uni • Roehampton Uni • St Andrews Uni • St Mary's Uni Coll • SOAS • Spurgeon's Coll • Stirling Uni • Trinity Coll Carmarthen • UCLan • Winchester Uni • Wolverhampton Uni • York St John Uni • *See also:* Biblical studies; theology

Renaissance studies

See: History

Retail management

Bedfordshire Uni • Birmingham City Uni • Bournemouth Uni • Brighton Uni • Bucks New Uni • Canterbury Christ Church Uni • De Montfort Uni • Glasgow Caledonian Uni • Harper Adams Uni Coll • Huddersfield Uni • Leeds Met Uni • London Coll Communication • London Coll Fashion • London Met Uni • Loughborough Uni • Manchester Met Uni • Northampton Uni • Queen Margaret Uni • Robert Gordon Uni • Roehampton Uni • Southampton Solent Uni • Stirling Uni • Surrey Uni • Thames Valley Uni • UCLan • Ulster Uni • University Coll Birmingham • UWIC • Westminster Uni

Risk

See: Actuarial studies

Risk management

City Uni • Coventry Uni • Cranfield Uni (p/g only) • Glasgow Caledonian Uni • Lancaster Uni • Leicester Uni • Middlesex Uni • Portsmouth Uni • UWIC

Romanian

University Coll London

Rural environment studies

Aberdeen Uni • Aberystwyth Uni • Bangor Uni • Coventry Uni • Harper Adams Uni Coll • Newcastle Uni • Nottingham Trent Uni • Plymouth Uni • Reading Uni • Royal Agricultural Coll • Scottish Agricultural Coll • UHI Millennium Institute • Writtle Coll

Russian

Bath Uni • Birmingham Uni • Bristol Uni • Cambridge Uni • Durham Uni • Essex Uni • European Business Sch • Exeter Uni • Glasgow Uni • Heriot-Watt Uni • Leeds Uni • Manchester Uni • Nottingham Uni • Oxford Uni • Queen Mary • St Andrews Uni • Sheffield Uni • Surrey Uni • University Coll London • Westminster Uni • *See also:* Russian studies; Slavonic studies

Russian studies

Birmingham Uni • Bristol Uni • Durham Uni • Edinburgh Uni • Exeter Uni • Glasgow Uni • Leeds Uni • Manchester Uni • Nottingham Uni • St Andrews Uni • Sheffield Uni • Swansea Uni • University Coll London • Westminster Uni • *See also:* Russian; Slavonic studies

Safety

See: Environmental health

Sanskrit

Cambridge Uni • Edinburgh Uni • Oxford Uni • SOAS • *See also:* Middle Eastern studies

Scandinavian studies

University Coll London • *See also:* individual languages (eg Danish)

Scientific/technical graphics

Middlesex Uni • *See also:* Graphic design

Scottish studies

Aberdeen Uni • Dundee Uni • Edinburgh Uni • Glasgow Uni • St Andrews Uni • Stirling Uni • UHI Millennium Institute • *See also:* Celtic studies

Sculpture

Anglia Ruskin Uni • Bath Spa Uni • Brighton Uni • Camberwell Coll • Central Saint Martins • Chelsea Coll Art • Creative Arts Uni • De Montfort Uni • Dundee Uni • Edinburgh Coll Art • Falmouth Uni Coll • Glasgow Sch Art • Glyndŵr Uni • Kingston Uni • Leeds Uni • London Met Uni • Loughborough Uni • Newcastle Uni • Norwich Uni Coll Arts • Robert Gordon Uni • Royal Academy Sch p/g only • Royal Coll Art (p/g only) • Sheffield Hallam Uni • Southampton Uni • Sunderland Uni • University Coll London • Wimbledon Coll Art • Winchester Sch Art • Wolverhampton Uni

Seismology

See: Geology

Semiconductors

See: Electronic engineering

Semitic languages

Aberdeen Uni • Cambridge Uni • SOAS • *See also:* individual languages (eg Arabic)

Serbian/Croatian

Nottingham Uni • University Coll London • *See also:* Slavonic studies

Shipbuilding

See: Marine architecture; naval architecture

Silversmithing

Birmingham City Uni • Bucks New Uni • Camberwell Coll • Central Saint Martins • Creative Arts Uni • De Montfort Uni • Dundee Uni • Edinburgh Coll Art • Glasgow Sch Art • Glyndŵr Uni • London Met Uni • Loughborough Uni • Royal Coll Art (p/g only) • Sheffield Hallam Uni • Wolverhampton Uni • *See also:* Jewellery; three-dimensional design

Slavonic studies

Durham Uni • Glasgow Uni • Leeds Uni • Nottingham Uni • Sheffield Uni • University Coll London

Slovak

Oxford Uni • University Coll London

Social administration

Anglia Ruskin Uni • Bangor Uni • Bath Uni • Bradford Uni • Cardiff Uni • Hull Uni • Kent • LSE • Nottingham Trent Uni • Nottingham Uni • Robert Gordon Uni • Southampton Uni • Stirling Uni • UCLan • West of Scotland Uni • Westminster Uni

Social anthropology

Aberdeen Uni • Brunel Uni • Cambridge Uni • Durham Uni • East London Uni • Edinburgh Uni • Glasgow Uni • Goldsmiths • Hull Uni • Kent • Lampeter Uni • London Met Uni • LSE • Manchester Uni • Queen's Uni Belfast • Roehampton Uni • St Andrews Uni • SOAS • Southampton Uni • Sussex Uni • University Coll London • *See also:* Anthropology

Social biology

See: Biosocial science; human sciences

Social history

Aberdeen Uni • Aberystwyth Uni • Birmingham Uni • Brighton Uni • Bristol Uni • Edinburgh Uni • Essex Uni • Exeter Uni • Glasgow Uni • Hull Uni • Lancaster Uni • Leicester Uni • Liverpool Uni • LSE • Manchester Met Uni • Manchester Uni • Oxford Brookes Uni • St Andrews Uni • Strathclyde Uni • Sussex Uni • Swansea Uni • Teesside Uni • UCLan • UHI Millennium Institute • Warwick Uni • *See also:* Economic history; history

Social policy

Anglia Ruskin Uni • Bath Uni • Bedfordshire Uni • Birkbeck • Birmingham City Uni • Birmingham Uni • Bradford Uni • Brighton Uni • Bristol Uni • Bucks New Uni • Cardiff Uni • Coventry Uni • Durham Uni • East London Uni • Edge Hill Uni • Edinburgh Uni • Essex Uni • Glasgow Uni • Gloucestershire Uni • Glyndŵr Uni • Hull Uni • Kent • Leeds Uni • Lincoln Uni • Liverpool Uni • London Met Uni • London South Bank Uni • Loughborough Uni • LSE • Manchester Met Uni • Manchester Uni • Middlesex Uni • Newport • Nottingham Uni • Open Uni • Plymouth Uni • Portsmouth Uni • Queen's Uni Belfast • Reading Uni • Salford Uni • Sheffield Hallam Uni • Sheffield Uni • Southampton Uni • Stirling Uni • Sussex Uni • Swansea Uni • Trinity Coll Carmarthen • UCLan • Ulster Uni • Warwick Uni • West of Scotland Uni • Wolverhampton Uni • Worcester Uni • York Uni • *See also:* Social administration; social work

Social psychology

See: Psychology

Social science

Aberdeen Uni • Abertay Dundee Uni • Anglia Ruskin Uni • Bath Uni • Bedfordshire Uni • Birkbeck • Birmingham City Uni • Birmingham Uni • Bournemouth Uni • Bradford Uni • Brighton Uni • Bristol UWE • Cambridge Uni • Canterbury Christ Church Uni • Cardiff Uni • Chester Uni • City Uni

• Coventry Uni • Cumbria Uni • Durham Uni • East Anglia Uni • East London Uni • Edinburgh Uni • Essex Uni • Exeter Uni • Glamorgan Uni • Glasgow Caledonian Uni • Glasgow Uni • Gloucestershire Uni • Glyndŵr Uni • Goldsmiths • Hull Uni • Kent • King's Coll London • Kingston Uni • Lampeter Uni • Lancaster Uni • Leeds Met Uni • Leeds Uni • Leicester Uni • Lincoln Uni • Liverpool Hope Uni • Liverpool John Moores Uni • Liverpool Uni • London Met Uni • London South Bank Uni • Loughborough Uni • Manchester Uni • Middlesex Uni • Napier Uni • Newcastle Uni • Northumbria Uni • Nottingham Trent Uni • Nottingham Uni • Open Uni • Plymouth Uni • Portsmouth Uni • Queen Margaret Uni • Reading Uni • Robert Gordon Uni • Salford Uni • Sheffield Hallam Uni • Southampton Uni • Stirling Uni • Strathclyde Uni • Sunderland Uni • Sussex Uni • Swansea Uni • UHI Millennium Institute • Ulster Uni • West of Scotland Uni • Westminster Uni • Wolverhampton Uni • Worcester Uni • York Uni • *See also:* individual subjects (eg economics; politics; sociology)

Social statistics

See: Statistics; sociology

Social studies

Anglia Ruskin Uni • Aston Uni • Bangor Uni • Bedfordshire Uni • Birmingham City Uni • Birmingham Uni • Bradford Uni • Bristol Uni • Chester Uni • Chichester Uni • Coventry Uni • Durham Uni • East London Uni • Exeter Uni • Farnborough Coll • Glasgow Caledonian Uni • Gloucestershire Uni • Glyndŵr Uni • Lancaster Uni • Leeds Met Uni • Leicester Uni • Manchester Met Uni • Newcastle Uni • Northampton Uni • Nottingham Uni • Portsmouth Uni • Salford Uni • Sheffield Uni • Stirling Uni • Strathclyde Uni • Sunderland Uni • Sussex Uni • Trinity Coll Carmarthen • UCLan • UHI Millennium Institute • West of Scotland Uni • Winchester Uni • *See also:* Social science

Social work

Anglia Ruskin Uni • Bangor Uni • Bath Uni • Bedfordshire Uni • Birmingham City Uni • Birmingham Uni • Bournemouth Uni • Bradford Coll • Bradford Uni • Brighton Uni • Bristol UWE • Brunel Uni • Bucks New Uni • Canterbury Christ Church Uni • Chester Uni • Chichester Uni • Coventry Uni • Cumbria Uni • De Montfort Uni • Derby Uni • Dundee Uni • East Anglia Uni • East London Uni • Edge Hill Uni • Edinburgh Uni • Glamorgan Uni • Glasgow Caledonian Uni • Glasgow Uni • Gloucestershire Uni • Glyndŵr Uni • Goldsmiths • Greenwich Uni • Hertfordshire Uni • Huddersfield Uni • Hull Uni • Keele Uni • Kent • Kingston Uni • Lancaster Uni • Leeds Met Uni • Leeds Uni • Lincoln Uni • Liverpool Hope Uni • Liverpool John Moores Uni • London Met Uni • London South Bank Uni • Manchester Met Uni • Middlesex Uni • Newport • Northampton Uni • Northumbria Uni • Nottingham Trent Uni • Nottingham Uni • Open Uni • Oxford Brookes Uni • Plymouth Uni • Portsmouth Uni • Queen's Uni Belfast • Reading Uni • Robert Gordon Uni • Roehampton Uni • Royal Holloway • St George's • Salford Uni • Sheffield Hallam Uni • Sheffield Uni • Southampton Solent Uni • Southampton Uni • Staffordshire Uni • Stirling Uni • Strathclyde Uni • Sunderland Uni • Sussex Uni • Swansea Uni • Teesside Uni • Thames Valley Uni • UCLan • Ulster Uni • UWIC • West of Scotland Uni • Winchester Uni • Wolverhampton Uni • Worcester Uni • York Uni

Sociology

Aberdeen Uni • Abertay Dundee Uni • Anglia Ruskin Uni • Aston Uni • Bangor Uni • Bath Spa Uni • Bath Uni • Bedfordshire Uni • Birkbeck • Birmingham City Uni • Birmingham Uni • Bradford Uni • Bristol Uni • Bristol UWE • Brunel Uni • Bucks New Uni • Cambridge Uni • Canterbury Christ Church Uni • Cardiff Uni • Chester Uni • City Uni • Coventry Uni • Derby Uni • Durham Uni • East Anglia Uni • East London Uni • Edge Hill Uni • Edinburgh Uni • Essex Uni • Exeter Uni • Glamorgan Uni • Glasgow Caledonian Uni • Glasgow Uni • Gloucestershire Uni • Goldsmiths • Greenwich Uni • Huddersfield Uni • Hull Uni • Keele Uni • Kent • Kingston Uni • Lancaster Uni • Leeds Met Uni

• Leeds Uni • Leicester Uni • Liverpool John Moores Uni • Liverpool Uni • London Met Uni • London South Bank Uni • Loughborough Uni • LSE • Manchester Met Uni • Manchester Uni • Marjon • Middlesex Uni • Napier Uni • Newcastle Uni • Northampton Uni • Northumbria Uni • Nottingham Trent Uni • Nottingham Uni • Open Uni • Oxford Brookes Uni • Plymouth Uni • Portsmouth Uni • Queen Margaret Uni • Queen's Uni Belfast • Roehampton Uni • St Mary's Uni Coll • Salford Uni • Sheffield Hallam Uni • Sheffield Uni • Southampton Uni • Staffordshire Uni • Stirling Uni • Strathclyde Uni • Sunderland Uni • Surrey Uni • Sussex Uni • Swansea Met Uni • Teesside Uni • UCLan • Ulster Uni • UWIC • Warwick Uni • West of Scotland Uni • Westminster Uni • Wolverhampton Uni • Worcester Uni • York Uni

Software engineering

Aberdeen Uni • Abertay Dundee Uni • Aberystwyth Uni • Anglia Ruskin Uni • Bath Uni • Bedfordshire Uni • Birmingham City Uni • Birmingham Uni • Bolton Uni • Bournemouth Uni • Bradford Coll • Bradford Uni • Brighton Uni • Bristol UWE • Canterbury Christ Church Uni • City Uni • Coventry Uni • Cranfield Uni (p/g only) • De Montfort Uni • Derby Uni • Dundee Uni • Durham Uni • East Anglia Uni • East London Uni • Edge Hill Uni • Edinburgh Uni • Essex Uni • Exeter Uni • Farnborough Coll • Glamorgan Uni • Glasgow Caledonian Uni • Glasgow Uni • Greenwich Uni • Heriot-Watt Uni • Hertfordshire Uni • Huddersfield Uni • Hull Uni • Imperial Coll • Kingston Uni • Lancaster Uni • Leicester Uni • Liverpool Hope Uni • Liverpool John Moores Uni • Liverpool Uni • London Met Uni • Loughborough Uni • Manchester Met Uni • Manchester Uni • Napier Uni • Newcastle Uni • Northampton Uni • Northumbria Uni • Nottingham Trent Uni • Oxford Brookes Uni • Portsmouth Uni • Queen's Uni Belfast • Robert Gordon Uni • Salford Uni • Sheffield Hallam Uni • Sheffield Uni • Southampton Solent Uni • Southampton Uni • Staffordshire Uni • Stirling Uni • Strathclyde Uni • Sunderland Uni • Swansea Met Uni • Teesside Uni • UCLan • Ulster Uni • West of Scotland Uni • Westminster Uni • Wolverhampton Uni • York Uni • *See also:* Computing

Soil science

Aberdeen Uni • Aberystwyth Uni • Cranfield Uni (p/g only) • Nottingham Uni • Reading Uni • Royal Agricultural Coll • *See also:* Geology

Solid state electronics

See: Electronics

Solid state physics

See: Physics

South America

See: Latin American studies

South East Asian studies

Edinburgh Uni • Lampeter Uni • Leeds Uni • London Met Uni • Newcastle Uni • Sheffield Uni • SOAS • *See also:* Asian studies; oriental studies

Space

Aberystwyth Uni • Birmingham Uni • Brunel Uni • Cranfield Uni (p/g only) • Kent Kingston Uni • Lancaster Uni • Leicester Uni • Salford Uni • Southampton Uni • Surrey Uni • *See also:* Astronomy

Spanish

Aberdeen Uni • Aberystwyth Uni • Aston Uni • Bangor Uni • Bath Uni • Birkbeck • Birmingham Uni • Bristol Uni • Bristol UWE • Buckingham Uni • Cambridge Uni • Cardiff Uni • Chester Uni • Coventry Uni • Durham Uni • East Anglia Uni • East London Uni • Essex Uni • European Business Sch • Exeter Uni • Glasgow Uni • Greenwich Uni • Heriot-Watt Uni • Hull Uni • Imperial Coll • Kent • King's Coll London • Kingston Uni • Lancaster Uni • Leeds Met Uni • Leeds Uni • Leicester Uni • Lincoln Uni • Liverpool John Moores Uni • Liverpool Uni • Manchester Met Uni • Manchester Uni • Middlesex Uni • Newcastle Uni • Northumbria Uni • Nottingham Trent Uni • Nottingham Uni • Open Uni • Oxford Uni • Plymouth Uni • Portsmouth Uni • Queen Mary • Queen's Uni Belfast • Roehampton Uni • Royal Holloway • St Andrews Uni • Salford Uni • Sheffield Hallam Uni • Sheffield Uni • Southampton Uni • Stirling Uni • Strathclyde Uni • Sunderland Uni • Surrey Uni • Sussex Uni • Swansea Uni • UCLan • Ulster Uni • University Coll London • Warwick Uni • West of Scotland Uni • Westminster Uni • Wolverhampton Uni • York Uni • *See also:* Hispanic studies; Iberian studies; Latin American studies

Spanish studies

See: Hispanic studies; Iberian studies; Latin American studies; Spanish

Speech sciences

Central Sch Speech/Drama • East Anglia Uni • Leeds Met Uni • Manchester Met Uni • Reading Uni • Sheffield Uni • University Coll London

Speech therapy

Birmingham City Uni • City Uni • De Montfort Uni • East Anglia Uni • Leeds Met Uni • Manchester Met Uni • Manchester Uni • Marjon • Newcastle Uni • Queen Margaret Uni • Reading Uni • Strathclyde Uni • Ulster Uni • University Coll London • UWIC • *See also:* Speech sciences

Sports sciences

Aberdeen Uni • Aberystwyth Uni • Anglia Ruskin Uni • Bangor Uni • Bath Uni • Bedfordshire Uni • Birmingham Uni • Bolton Uni • Bournemouth Uni • Bradford Coll • Brighton Uni • Bristol UWE • Brunel Uni • Bucks New Uni • Canterbury Christ Church Uni • Chester Uni • Chichester Uni • Coventry Uni • Cumbria Uni • Derby Uni • Dundee Uni • Edge Hill Uni • Edinburgh Uni • Essex Uni • Exeter Uni • Glamorgan Uni • Glasgow Uni • Gloucestershire Uni • Glyndŵr Uni • Greenwich Uni • Heriot-Watt Uni • Hertfordshire Uni • Huddersfield Uni • Hull Uni • Kent • Kingston Uni • Leeds Met Uni • Leeds Trinity • Leeds Uni • Lincoln Uni • Liverpool John Moores Uni • London Met Uni • London South Bank Uni • Loughborough Uni • Manchester Met Uni • Marjon • Middlesex Uni • Myerscough Coll • Napier Uni • Northampton Uni • Northumbria Uni • Nottingham Trent Uni • Oxford Brookes Uni • Portsmouth Uni • Robert Gordon Uni • Roehampton Uni • St Mary's Uni Coll • Salford Unii • Scottish Agricultural Coll • Sheffield Hallam Uni • Southampton Solent Uni • Stirling Uni • Strathclyde Uni • Sunderland Uni • Swansea Uni • Teesside Uni • Thames Valley Uni • UCLan • Ulster Uni • University Coll Birmingham • UWIC • Westminster Uni • Winchester Uni • Wolverhampton Uni • Worcester Uni • York St John Uni

Sports studies

Aberdeen Uni • Abertay Dundee Uni • Aberystwyth Uni • Anglia Ruskin Uni • Bangor Uni • Bath Uni • Bedfordshire Uni • Birmingham Uni • Bolton Uni • Bournemouth Uni • Bradford Coll • Brighton Uni • Bucks New Uni • Canterbury Christ Church Uni • Chester Uni • Chichester Uni • Coventry Uni • Cumbria Uni • Derby Uni • Durham Uni • East Anglia Uni • East London Uni • Edge Hill Uni • Edinburgh Uni • Exeter Uni • Farnborough Coll • Glamorgan Uni • Glasgow Caledonian Uni

• Gloucestershire Uni • Glyndŵr Uni • Greenwich Uni • Heriot-Watt Uni • Hertfordshire Uni • Hull Uni • Kent • Kingston Uni • Leeds Met Uni • Leeds Uni • Lincoln Uni • Liverpool Hope Uni • Liverpool John Moores Uni • London Met Uni • Loughborough Uni • Manchester Met Uni • Marjon • Middlesex Uni • Myerscough Coll • Napier Uni • Newport • Northampton Uni • Northumbria Uni • Nottingham Trent Uni • Oxford Brookes Uni • Portsmouth Uni • Roehampton Uni • Royal Agricultural Coll • St Mary's Uni Coll • Salford Uni • Scottish Agricultural Coll • Sheffield Hallam Uni • Southampton Solent Uni • Southampton Uni • Staffordshire Uni • Stirling Uni • Strathclyde Uni • Sunderland Uni • Swansea Met Uni • Teesside Uni • Trinity Coll Carmarthen • UCLan • UHI Millennium Institute • Ulster Uni • University Coll Birmingham • UWIC • West of Scotland Uni • Westminster Uni • Winchester Uni • Wolverhampton Uni • Worcester Uni • Writtle Coll • York St John Uni • *See also:* Physical education

Stage management

ALRA • Bristol Old Vic • Central Sch Speech/Drama • Guildhall Sch Music and Drama • Kent • Middlesex Uni • RADA • Rose Bruford Coll • Royal Scottish Academy Music/Drama • Royal Welsh Coll Music/Drama • Swansea Met Uni • Winchester Uni

Statistics

Aberdeen Uni • Aberystwyth Uni • Anglia Ruskin Uni • Bath Uni • Birkbeck • Birmingham Uni • Brighton Uni • Bristol Uni • Bristol UWE • Brunel Uni • Cardiff Uni • City Uni • Coventry Uni • Derby Uni • East Anglia Uni • Edinburgh Uni • Essex Uni • Exeter Uni • Glamorgan Uni • Glasgow Caledonian Uni • Glasgow Uni • Greenwich Uni • Heriot-Watt Uni • Huddersfield Uni • Hull Uni • Imperial Coll • Kent • Kingston Uni • Lancaster Uni • Leeds Uni • Leicester Uni • Liverpool John Moores Uni • Liverpool Uni • London Met Uni • LSE • Middlesex Uni • Newcastle Uni • Northumbria Uni • Nottingham Trent Uni • Open Uni • Oxford Brookes Uni • Oxford Uni • Plymouth Uni • Portsmouth Uni • Queen Mary • Reading Uni • Royal Holloway • St Andrews Uni • Sheffield Hallam Uni • Sheffield Uni • Southampton Uni • Strathclyde Uni • Sussex Uni • Swansea Uni • University Coll London • Warwick Uni • West of Scotland Uni • Westminster Uni • Wolverhampton Uni • York Uni • *See also:* Mathematics

Strategic studies

See: War studies

Structural engineering

Aberdeen Uni • Bath Uni • Birmingham Uni • Bradford Uni • Cambridge Uni • Coventry Uni • Cranfield Uni (p/g only) • Edinburgh Uni • Glasgow Caledonian Uni • Heriot-Watt Uni • Imperial Coll • Leeds Uni • Liverpool Uni • Manchester Uni • Newcastle Uni • Nottingham Trent Uni • Plymouth Uni • Portsmouth Uni • Queen's Uni Belfast • Salford Uni • Sheffield Uni • Strathclyde Uni • University Coll London • West of Scotland Uni

Surf and beach management

Myerscough Coll • *See also:* Leisure studies; tourism

Surveying

Aberdeen Uni • Anglia Ruskin Uni • Birmingham City Uni • Bolton Uni • Brighton Uni • Bristol UWE • City Uni • Coventry Uni • East London Uni • Exeter Uni • Glamorgan Uni • Glasgow Caledonian Uni • Glyndŵr Uni • Greenwich Uni • Heriot-Watt Uni • Kingston Uni • Leeds Met Uni • Liverpool John Moores Uni • London South Bank Uni • Loughborough Uni • Napier Uni • Newcastle Uni

• Northumbria Uni • Nottingham Trent Uni • Plymouth Uni • Portsmouth Uni • Reading Uni • Robert Gordon Uni • Royal Agricultural Coll • Salford Uni • Sheffield Hallam Uni • UCLan • Ulster Uni • West of Scotland Uni • Westminster Uni • Wolverhampton Uni • *See also:* Quantity surveying

Sustainable development

Aberystwyth Uni • Anglia Ruskin Uni • Bangor Uni • Birmingham Uni • Creative Arts Uni • Falmouth Uni Coll • Glamorgan Uni • Greenwich Uni • Kingston Uni • Manchester Met Uni • St Andrews Uni • Scottish Agricultural Coll • Sheffield Hallam Uni • Teesside Uni • UCLan • UHI Millennium Institute • Winchester Uni • Wolverhampton Uni • Worcester Uni

Swahili

SOAS • *See also:* African studies

Swedish

University Coll London • *See also:* Scandinavian studies

Systems analysis

Aberdeen Uni • Abertay Dundee Uni • Anglia Ruskin Uni • Bournemouth Uni • Bristol UWE • Cardiff Uni • Cranfield Uni (p/g only) • Edge Hill Uni • Glasgow Caledonian Uni • Gloucestershire Uni • Kingston Uni • Leeds Met Uni • London Met Uni • Manchester Uni • Open Uni • Portsmouth Uni • Salford Uni • West of Scotland Uni • *See also:* Computer science; computing

Talmud

See: Jewish studies

Tamil

SOAS • *See also:* Asian studies; oriental studies

Teacher training

Aberdeen Uni • Anglia Ruskin Uni • Bangor Uni • Bath Spa Uni • Bedfordshire Uni • Birmingham City Uni • Birmingham Conservatoire • Bradford Coll • Brighton Uni • Bristol UWE • Brunel Uni • Canterbury Christ Church Uni • Central Sch Speech/Drama • Chester Uni • Chichester Uni • Cumbria Uni • Derby Uni • Dundee Uni • Durham Uni • East London Uni • Edge Hill Uni • Edinburgh Uni • Glasgow Uni • Gloucestershire Uni • Glyndŵr Uni • Goldsmiths • Greenwich Uni • Hertfordshire Uni • Huddersfield Uni • Hull Uni • Kingston Uni • Leeds Met Uni • Leeds Trinity • Liverpool Hope Uni • Liverpool John Moores Uni • London Met Uni • Manchester Met Uni • Marjon • Middlesex Uni • Newport • Northampton Uni • Northumbria Uni • Nottingham Trent Uni • Oxford Brookes Uni • Plymouth Uni • Portsmouth Uni • Reading Uni • Roehampton Uni • Royal Scottish Academy Music/Drama • St Mary's Uni Coll • Sheffield Hallam Uni • Stirling Uni • Strathclyde Uni • Sunderland Uni • Swansea Met Uni • Teesside Uni • Trinity Coll Carmarthen • Ulster Uni • UWIC • West of Scotland Uni • Winchester Uni • Wolverhampton Uni • Worcester Uni • York St John Uni • *See also:* Education

Teaching

See: Education; teacher training

Technical graphics

See: Scientific/technical graphics

Telecommunications engineering

Anglia Ruskin Uni • Aston Uni • Bath Uni • Bedfordshire Uni • Birmingham City Uni • Birmingham Uni • Bradford Uni • Coventry Uni • Essex Uni • Glasgow Caledonian Uni • Hertfordshire Uni • Hull Uni • King's Coll London • Lancaster Uni • London South Bank Uni • Loughborough Uni • Napier Uni • Newcastle Uni • Oxford Brookes Uni • Portsmouth Uni • Queen Mary • Sheffield Hallam Uni • Westminster Uni • Wolverhampton Uni

Television

See: Broadcasting; communication studies; film studies; media studies; TV studies

Textile technology

Bolton Uni • De Montfort Uni • Heriot-Watt Uni • Huddersfield Uni • London Met Uni • Manchester Met Uni • Manchester Uni

Textiles

Bath Spa Uni • Bedfordshire Uni • Birmingham City Uni • Bolton Uni • Bournemouth Uni • Bradford Coll • Brighton Uni • Bristol UWE • Bucks New Uni • Central Saint Martins • Chelsea Coll Art • Colchester Inst • Creative Arts Uni • De Montfort Uni • Derby Uni • Dundee Uni • East London Uni • Edinburgh Coll Art • Falmouth Uni Coll • Glasgow Sch Art • Glyndŵr Uni • Goldsmiths • Heriot-Watt Uni • Huddersfield Uni • Leeds Uni • Liverpool John Moores Uni • London Coll Fashion • London Met Uni • Loughborough Uni • Manchester Met Uni • Manchester Uni • Middlesex Uni • Northampton Uni • Norwich Uni Coll Arts • Nottingham Trent Uni • Plymouth Uni • Portsmouth Uni • Robert Gordon Uni • Royal Coll Art (p/g only) • Southampton Uni • Swansea Met Uni • Thames Valley Uni • UCLan • UHI Millennium Institute • Ulster Uni • UWIC • Winchester Sch Art • Wolverhampton Uni • York St John Uni

Thai studies

Leeds Uni • SOAS • *See also:* Oriental studies

Theatre design

Aberystwyth Uni • Birmingham City Uni • Bristol Old Vic • Camberwell Coll • Central Saint Martins • Central Sch Speech/Drama • Creative Arts Uni • Cumbria Uni • Edge Hill Uni • Glamorgan Uni • London Coll Fashion • Middlesex Uni • National Film Sch (p/g only) • Nottingham Trent Uni • RADA • Rose Bruford Coll • Royal Scottish Academy Music/Drama • Royal Welsh Coll Music/Drama • Trinity Coll Carmarthen • Wimbledon Coll Art

Theatre studies

Aberystwyth Uni • ALRA • Bangor Uni • Bath Spa Uni • Bedfordshire Uni • Birkbeck • Birmingham Uni • Bristol Old Vic • Bristol Uni • Bristol UWE • Central Sch Speech/Drama • Chester Uni • Colchester Inst • Coventry Uni • Dartington • De Montfort Uni • Derby Uni • East Anglia Uni • Essex Uni • Exeter Uni • Falmouth Uni Coll • Glamorgan Uni • Glasgow Uni • Glyndŵr Uni • Goldsmiths • Huddersfield Uni • Hull Uni • Kent • Lancaster Uni • Leeds Uni • Liverpool Hope Uni • London Met Uni • London South Bank Uni • Manchester Met Uni • Middlesex Uni • Plymouth Uni • Queen Margaret Uni • Reading Uni • Roehampton Uni • Rose Bruford Coll • Royal

Holloway • Royal Scottish Academy Music/Drama • St Mary's Uni Coll • Salford Uni • Staffordshire Uni • Surrey Uni • Sussex Uni • Swansea Met Uni • Thames Valley Uni • Trinity Coll Carmarthen • UCLan • Ulster Uni • Warwick Uni • Winchester Uni • Wolverhampton Uni • York St John Uni • York Uni • *See also:* Drama; acting

Theology

Aberdeen Uni • Bangor Uni • Birmingham Uni • Bristol Uni • Cambridge Uni • Canterbury Christ Church Uni • Cardiff Uni • Chester Uni • Chichester Uni • Cumbria Uni • Durham Uni • Edinburgh Uni • Exeter Uni • Glasgow Uni • Gloucestershire Uni • Heythrop Coll • Hull Uni • Kent • King's Coll London • Lampeter Uni • Leeds Trinity • Leeds Uni • Lincoln Uni • Liverpool Hope Uni • London Sch Theology • Manchester Uni • Nottingham Uni • Oak Hill Coll • Oxford Brookes Uni • Oxford Uni • Queen's Uni Belfast • Roehampton Uni • St Andrews Uni • St Mary's Uni Coll • Spurgeon's Coll • Trinity Coll Carmarthen • UHI Millennium Institute • Winchester Uni • York St John Uni • *See also:* Religious studies

Third World studies

Aberystwyth Uni • Bradford Uni • Derby Uni • East Anglia Uni • East London Uni • Middlesex Uni • Northampton Uni • Open Uni • SOAS • Sussex Uni • Westminster Uni

Three-dimensional design

Bath Spa Uni • Bedfordshire Uni • Birmingham City Uni • Bournemouth Uni • Brighton Uni • Bucks New Uni • Camberwell Coll • Central Saint Martins • Central Sch Speech/Drama • Chelsea Coll Art • Colchester Inst • Coventry Uni • Creative Arts Uni • De Montfort Uni • Derby Uni • Dundee Uni • Edinburgh Coll Art • Falmouth Uni Coll • Glasgow Sch Art • Goldsmiths • Greenwich Uni • Hertfordshire Uni • Huddersfield Uni • Kingston Uni • Leeds Met Uni • Liverpool Hope Uni • London Met Uni • Loughborough Uni • Manchester Met Uni • Northumbria Uni • Plymouth Uni • Portsmouth Uni • Ravensbourne Coll • Robert Gordon Uni • Royal Coll Art (p/g only) • Salford Uni • Sunderland Uni • Swansea Met Uni • Teesside Uni • Thames Valley Uni • UCLan • Wolverhampton Uni • York St John Uni

Topographical science

Glasgow Uni • Newcastle Uni • Swansea Uni

Tourism

Abertay Dundee Uni • Aberystwyth Uni • Anglia Ruskin Uni • Bath Spa Uni • Bedfordshire Uni • Bolton Uni • Bournemouth Uni • Bradford Coll • Brighton Uni • Bristol UWE • Bucks New Uni • Canterbury Christ Church Uni • Chester Uni • Chichester Uni • Coventry Uni • Cumbria Uni • Derby Uni • East London Uni • Exeter Uni • Glamorgan Uni • Glasgow Caledonian Uni • Gloucestershire Uni • Greenwich Uni • Harper Adams Uni Coll • Hertfordshire Uni • Huddersfield Uni • Hull Uni • Kent • Leeds Met Uni • Lincoln Uni • Liverpool Hope Uni • Liverpool John Moores Uni • London Coll Communication • London Met Uni • London South Bank Uni • Manchester Met Uni • Middlesex Uni • Napier Uni • Northampton Uni • Northumbria Uni • Oxford Brookes Uni • Plymouth Uni • Portsmouth Uni • Queen Margaret Uni • Robert Gordon Uni • St Mary's Uni Coll • Salford Uni • Scottish Agricultural Coll • Sheffield Hallam Uni • Southampton Solent Uni • Staffordshire Uni • Stirling Uni • Strathclyde Uni • Sunderland Uni • Surrey Uni • Swansea Met Uni • Teesside Uni • Thames Valley Uni • Trinity Coll Carmarthen • UCLan • UHI Millennium Institute • Ulster Uni • University Coll Birmingham • UWIC • West of Scotland Uni • Westminsterr Uni • Wolverhampton Uni • Writtle Coll • *See also:* Recreation studies

Town and country planning

Aberdeen Uni • Anglia Ruskin Uni • Birmingham City Uni • Bristol UWE • Cardiff Uni • Dundee Uni • Glasgow Caledonian Uni • Glyndŵr Uni • Greenwich Uni • Heriot-Watt Uni • Kingston Uni • Leeds Met Uni • Liverpool John Moores Uni • Liverpool Uni • London South Bank Uni • Manchester Uni • Newcastle Uni • Northumbria Uni • Nottingham Trent Uni • Oxford rrookes Uni • Portsmouth Uni • Queen's Uni Belfast • Reading Uni • Royal Agricultural Coll • Sheffield Hallam Uni • Sheffield Uni • University Coll London • Worcester Uni • *See also:* Environmental studies; urban studies

Toxicology

Aberdeen Uni • East London Uni • Hull Uni • Napier Uni • Plymouth Uni • UWIC

Traffic

See: Civil engineering; town and country planning; transport studies

Translation

See: Interpreting and translating

Transport studies

Aston Uni • Bedfordshire Uni • Birmingham Uni • Bolton Uni • Bristol UWE • Coventry Uni • Cranfield Uni (p/g only) • Cumbria Uni • Huddersfield Uni • Leeds Uni • Liverpool John Moores Uni • Loughborough Uni • Napier Uni • Salford Uni • Sheffield Hallam Uni • Swansea Met Uni • Teesside Uni • Ulster Uni • Wolverhampton Uni

Turkish

King's Coll London • Manchester Uni • Oxford Uni • SOAS • *See also:* Middle Eastern studies

TV studies

Aberystwyth Uni • ALRA • Bedfordshire Uni • Birmingham City Uni • Bournemouth Uni • Bradford Uni • Bristol Old Vic • Brunel Uni • Bucks New Uni • Canterbury Christ Church Uni • Chester Uni • Creative Arts Uni • Derby Uni • East Anglia Uni • Edge Hill Uni • Falmouth Uni Coll • Farnborough Coll • Glamorgan Uni • Glasgow Uni • Gloucestershire Uni • Hertfordshire Uni • Kingston Uni • Leeds Met Uni • Leeds Trinity • Leeds Uni • Lincoln Uni • Liverpool Hope Uni • Liverpool John Moores Uni • Manchester Met Uni • Manchester Uni • Middlesex Uni • National Film Sch (p/g only) • Northampton Uni • Nottingham Trent Uni • Nottingham Uni • Portsmouth Uni • Queen Margaret Uni • Reading Uni • Robert Gordon Uni • Roehampton Uni • Royal Scottish Academy Music/Drama • St Mary's Uni Coll • Salford Uni • Southampton Solent Uni • Staffordshire Uni • Sunderland Uni • Swansea Met Uni • Teesside Uni • Thames Valley Uni • UCLan • Warwick Uni • West of Scotland Uni • Westminster Uni • Wimbledon Coll Art • Wolverhampton Uni

Typography

See: Printing and typography

United States

See: American studies

Urban estate management

Aberdeen Uni • Bristol UWE • Glyndŵr Uni • Heriot-Watt Uni • Kingston Uni • Liverpool John Moores Uni • Northumbria Uni • Nottingham Trent Uni • Portsmouth Uni • Reading Uni • Westminster Uni

Urban studies

Aberdeen Uni • Birmingham Uni • Durham Uni • Edinburgh Coll Art • Glasgow Uni • Heriot-Watt Uni • Kent • Leeds Met Uni • Liverpool John Moores Uni • London South Bank Uni • Manchester Met Uni • Reading Uni • Salford Uni • Sheffield Hallam Uni • Sheffield Uni • Ulster Uni • University Coll London • Westminster Uni • *See also:* Environmental studies; town and country planning

Urdu

Cambridge Uni • SOAS • *See also:* Asian studies; oriental studies

Valuation

See: Estate management; quantity surveying; surveying

Veterinary nursing

Brighton Uni • Bristol Uni • Bristol UWE • Harper Adams Uni Coll • Middlesex Uni • Myerscough Coll • Napier Uni • Nottingham Trent Uni • Royal Vet Coll • UCLan

Veterinary science

Bristol Uni • Cambridge Uni • Edinburgh Uni • Glasgow Uni • Liverpool Uni • Nottingham Uni • Royal Vet Coll • Surrey Uni

Veterinary studies

Bristol UWE • Harper Adams Uni Coll • Myerscough Coll • Northampton Uni • Royal Vet Coll • Scottish Agricultural Coll

Video

ALRA • Bedfordshire Uni • Birmingham City Uni • Bolton Uni • Bradford Uni • Bristol Old Vic • Bucks New Uni • Creative Arts Uni • Dartington • De Montfort Uni • Derby Uni • Edinburgh Coll Art • Glasgow Caledonian Uni • Gloucestershire Uni • Hertfordshire Uni • Lincoln Uni • London Coll Communication • London Coll Fashion • London South Bank Uni • Manchester Met Uni • Middlesex Uni • National Film Sch (p/g only) • Newport • Portsmouth Uni • Queen Margaret Uni • Ravensbourne Coll • Robert Gordon Uni • Rose Bruford Coll • Royal Academy Sch p/g only • Royal Coll Art (p/g only) • Royal Scottish Academy Music/Drama • Salford Uni • Southampton Solent Uni • Sunderland Uni • Swansea Met Uni • Thames Valley Uni • West of Scotland Uni • Wimbledon Coll Art • Wolverhampton Uni • *See also:* Communication studies; film studies; media studies

Vietnamese studies

SOAS • *See also:* Asian studies

Viking studies

Nottingham Uni • University Coll London

Virology

Bristol Uni • Edinburgh Uni • Glasgow Uni • Leeds Uni • Warwick Uni

Virtual design

Bournemouth Uni • Bradford Uni • Coventry Uni • Creative Arts Uni • Dundee Uni • Glamorgan Uni • Goldsmiths • Hertfordshire Uni • Huddersfield Uni • Kingston Uni • Portsmouth Uni • Ravensbourne Coll • Regent's Business Sch • Salford Uni • Teesside Uni • Thames Valley Uni • UCLan • West of Scotland Uni • Wolverhampton Uni

Visual arts

Aberystwyth Uni • Anglia Ruskin Uni • Bath Spa Uni • Bedfordshire Uni • Birmingham City Uni • Bolton Uni • Bournemouth Uni • Bradford Coll • Brighton Uni • Bristol UWE • Bucks New Uni • Camberwell Coll • Canterbury Christ Church Uni • Central Saint Martins • Chelsea Coll Art • Chichester Uni • Coventry Uni • Creative Arts Uni • Cumbria Uni • Dartington • Derby Uni • East London Uni • Edinburgh Coll Art • Falmouth Uni Coll • Glamorgan Uni • Glasgow Sch Art • Glyndŵr Uni • Goldsmiths • Hertfordshire Uni • Huddersfield Uni • Hull Uni • Kent • Kingston Uni • Lancaster Uni • Leeds Uni • Leicester Uni • Liverpool John Moores Uni • London Coll Communication • London Coll Fashion • London Met Uni • Loughborough Uni • Manchester Met Uni • Manchester Uni • Middlesex Uni • National Film Sch (p/g only) • Northampton Uni • Northumbria Uni • Norwich Uni Coll Arts • Nottingham Trent Uni • Plymouth Uni • Ravensbourne Coll • Rose Bruford Coll • Royal Coll Art (p/g only) • Salford Uni • Sheffield Hallam Uni • Southampton Uni • Staffordshire Uni • Sunderland Uni • Teesside Uni • Thames Valley Uni • UCLan • Ulster Uni • UWIC • Westminster Uni • Winchester Sch Art • Wolverhampton Uni • Worcester Uni

Visual communications

See: Communication studies; graphic design

War studies

Aberystwyth Uni • Birmingham Uni • Bradford Uni • Hull Uni • Kent • King's Coll London • London Met Uni • Reading Uni • Swansea Uni • Wolverhampton Uni • *See also:* History; international relations; peace studies; politics

Waste studies

Bradford Uni • Cranfield Uni (p/g only) • Myerscough Coll • Northampton Uni • Scottish Agricultural Coll

Water resources

Bradford Uni • Cranfield Uni (p/g only) • Wolverhampton Uni

Watersports studies

See: Leisure studies; sports studies

Web development/design

Anglia Ruskin Uni • Bedfordshire Uni • Bolton Uni • Bradford Uni • Bristol UWE • Bucks New Uni • Canterbury Christ Church Uni • Creative Arts Uni • Cumbria Uni • De Montfort Uni • Derby Uni • East Anglia Uni • Edge Hill Uni • Gloucestershire Uni • Glyndŵr Uni • Hertfordshire Uni • Hull

Uni • Kent • Kingston Uni • Lincoln Uni • Liverpool Hope Uni • London Met Uni • Manchester Met Uni • Middlesex Uni • Northumbria Uni • Plymouth Uni • Portsmouth Uni • Queen's Uni Belfast • Roehampton Uni • Sheffield Hallam Uni • Southampton Solent Uni • Staffordshire Uni • Sunderland Uni • Sussex Uni • Swansea Met Uni • Teesside Uni • UCLan • Ulster Uni • West of Scotland Uni • Winchester Uni • Wolverhampton Uni • Worcester Uni

Welfare studies

See: Social administration; social work; youth and community work

Welsh language

Aberystwyth Uni • Bangor Uni • Cardiff Uni • Glamorgan Uni • Lampeter Uni • Swansea Uni

Welsh studies

Aberystwyth Uni • Bangor Uni • Cardiff Uni • Glamorgan Uni • Glyndŵr Uni • Lampeter Uni • UWIC • *See also:* Celtic studies

Wildlife management

Aberdeen Uni • Anglia Ruskin Uni • Bristol UWE • Coventry Uni • Cumbria Uni • East London Uni • Liverpool John Moores Uni • Manchester Met Uni • Nottingham Trent Uni • Plymouth Uni • Reading Uni • Royal Agricultural Coll • Salford Uni • Scottish Agricultural Coll • Writtle Coll

Wine studies

Brighton Uni • Coventry Uni

Women's studies

East London Uni • Edge Hill Uni • Lancaster Uni • Northumbria Uni • Queen's Uni Belfast • Westminster Uni • *See also:* Gender studies

Wood technology

Brighton Uni • Bucks New Uni

Yacht design

See: Boat design

Yacht/watersports studies

See: Leisure studies; sports studies

Youth and community work

Bedfordshire Uni • Bolton Uni • Bradford Coll • Bradford Uni • Brighton Uni • Brunel Uni • Canterbury Christ Church Uni • Chester Uni • Chichester Uni • Coventry Uni • Cumbria Uni • De Montfort Uni • Derby Uni • East London Uni • Edge Hill Uni • Exeter Uni • Gloucestershire Uni • Glyndŵr Uni • Goldsmiths • Greenwich Uni • Huddersfield Uni • Hull Uni • Lancaster Uni • Leeds Met Uni • Liverpool Hope Uni • Liverpool John Moores Uni • London Met Uni • Manchester Met Uni • Manchester Uni • Marjon • Middlesex Uni • Newport • Nottingham Trent Uni • Oak Hill Coll • Plymouth Uni • Portsmouth Uni • Sheffield Hallam Uni • Staffordshire Uni • Strathclyde Uni

• Sunderland Uni • Teesside Uni • Trinity Coll Carmarthen • UHI Millennium Institute • Ulster Uni • Winchester Uni • *See also:* Social work

Zoology

Aberdeen Uni • Aberystwyth Uni • Anglia Ruskin Uni • Bangor Uni • Birmingham Uni • Bristol Uni • Cambridge Uni • Cardiff Uni • Derby Uni • Dundee Uni • Durham Uni • Edinburgh Uni • Exeter Uni • Glamorgan Uni • Glasgow Uni • Hull Uni • Imperial Coll • Leeds Uni • Leicester Uni • Liverpool John Moores Uni • Liverpool Uni • Manchester Uni • Newcastle Uni • Nottingham Uni • Oxford Uni • Queen Mary • Queen's Uni Belfast • Reading Uni • Robert Gordon Uni • Roehampton Uni • Royal Holloway • St Andrews Uni • Salford Uni • Scottish Agricultural Coll • Sheffield Uni • Southampton Uni • Stirling Uni • Swansea Uni • University Coll London • West of Scotland Uni • *See also:* Animal science

Zulu

See: African studies

Professional Qualifications – Finding Out

If you are thinking of qualifying for a particular profession, you need to check out what's required direct with the professional body (or bodies). Most professions are graduate entry only – although a degree in itself is seldom sufficient qualification.

The websites and information packs of the professional bodies are usually excellent and tell you what is required, which degree courses they recognise, what you need to do to qualify and how long it takes. Contact details for each professional body are listed below.

Accountants, chartered

England and Wales: Marketing Manager, Student Recruitment and Promotion, The Institute of Chartered Accountants in England and Wales, Metropolitan House, 321 Avebury Boulevard, Central Milton Keynes MK9 2FZ; Tel 01908 248040; Email careers@icaew.com; Website www.icaew.co.uk. Publications: *ICAEW Guide to Training Vacancies* (online or hard copy on request).

Scotland: Marketing Administrator, Institute of Chartered Accountants of Scotland, CA House, 21 Haymarket Yards, Edinburgh EH12 5BH; Tel 0131 347 0161; Email caeducation@icas.org.uk; Website www.icas.org.uk. Publications: Free brochure.

Accountants, chartered certified

Careers Department, The Association of Chartered Certified Accountants, ACCA UK, 29 Lincoln's Inn Fields, London WC2A 3EE; Tel 020 7059 5000; Email students@accaglobal.com; Website www.accaglobal.com.

Accountants, public finance

Education and Training, Chartered Institute of Public Finance and Accountancy (CIPFA), 3 Robert Street, London WC2N 6RL; Tel 020 7543 5846; Email choices@cipfa.org; Website www.cipfa.org.uk.

Acoustics

Chief Executive, Institute of Acoustics, 77A St Peter's Street, St Albans, Hertfordshire AL1 3BN; Tel 01727 848195; Email ioa@ioa.org.uk; Website www.ioa.org.uk. Publications: *Acoustics Bulletin*; *Register of Members*; *Buyers' Guide*.

Actuaries

Careers Department, The Actuarial Profession, Napier House, 4 Worcester Street, Oxford OX1 2AW; Tel 01865 268228; Email careers@actuaries.org.uk; Website www.actuaries.org.uk. Publications: *List of Actuarial Employers*; *Beyond the Norm*.

Advocates (Scotland)

Intrants Programme Co-ordinator, Faculty of Advocates, Parliament House, Edinburgh EH1 1RF; Tel 0131 260 5795; Email scott.brownridge@advocates.org.uk; Website www.advocates.org.uk.

Air force

RAF; Tel 0845 605 5555; Website www.raf.mod.uk/careers.

Air pilots and air navigators

The Clerk, The Guild of Air Pilots and Air Navigators (GAPAN), Cobham House, 9 Warwick Court, Gray's Inn, London WC1R 5DJ; Tel 020 7404 4032; Email gapan@gapan.org; Website www.gapan.org. Publications: *So You Want to Be A Pilot?*

Architects

Careers Department, Royal Institute of British Architects (RIBA), 66 Portland Place, London W1B 1AD; Tel 020 7580 5533; Email info@inst.riba.org; Website www.architecture.com and www.careersinarchitecture.net.

Scotland: Membership Department, Royal Incorporation of Architects in Scotland (RIAS), 15 Rutland Square, Edinburgh EH1 2BE; Tel 0131 229 7545; Email info@rias.org.uk; Website www.rias.org.uk. Publications: *Chartered Architect.*

Army

Army Officer Entry; Tel 0845 7300 111; Website www.army.mod.uk.

Barristers (England and Wales)

Careers and Information, Bar Standards Board, 289 High Holborn, London WC1V 7HZ; Tel 020 7611 1444; Website www.barstandardsboard.org.uk.

Dentists

Education Department, British Dental Association, 64 Wimpole Street, London W1G 8YS; Tel 020 7563 4563; Email enquiries@bda.org; Website www.bda.org. Publications: *Careers in Dentistry.*

Dietitians

Education and Training Officer, The British Dietetic Association, 5th Floor, Charles House, 148/9 Great Charles Street, Queensway, Birmingham B3 3HT; Tel 0121 200 8080; Email info@bda.uk.com; Website www.bda.uk.com. Publications: *The Work of Registered Dietitians.*

Doctors

Education and Development Policy Officer, General Medical Council, St James Building, 79 Oxford Street, Manchester M1 6FQ; Tel 0845 357 3456; Email gmc@gmc-uk.org; Website www.gmc-uk.org. Publications: *Tomorrow's Doctors*; *The New Doctor.*

Engineers

Communications Manager, Engineering Council UK (ECUK), 246 High Holborn, London WC1V 7EX; Tel 020 3206 0500; Email info@engc.org.uk; Website www.engc.org.uk.

Healthcare profesionals

England: NHS Careers, PO Box 2311, Bristol BS2 2ZX; Tel 0845 60 60 655; Email advice@nhscareers.nhs.uk; Website www.nhscareers.nhs.uk and www.whatcanidowithmydegree.nhs.uk. Publications: Range of free literature covering most careers in the NHS.

Northern Ireland: School of Nursing and Midwifery, Medical Biology Centre, Queen's University, 97 Lisburn Road, Belfast BT9 7BL; Tel 028 9097 2233; Email nursing@qub.ac.uk; Website www.qub.ac.uk/nur.

Scotland: Careers Information Service, NHS Education for Scotland, 66 Rose Street, Edinburgh EH2 2NN; Tel 0131 220 8660; Email careers@nes.scot.nhs.uk; Website www.nes.scot.nhs.uk. Publications: Various careers leaflets.

Wales: Development and Education Officer, National Leadership and Innovation Agency for Healthcare (NLIAH), Innovation House, Bridgend Road, Llanharan, Wales CF72 9RP; Tel 01443 233 333; Email anne.duggan@nliah.wales.nhs.uk; Website www.wales.nhs.uk. Publications: *Your Guide to Careers in NHS Wales.*

Logistics and transport

Membership Services, The Chartered Institute of Logistics and Transport (UK), Logistics and Transport Centre, Earlstrees Court, Earlstrees Road, Corby, Northants NN17 4AX; Tel 01536 740104; Email enquiry@ciltuk.org.uk; Website www.ciltuk.org.uk. Publications: *Inside Careers Guide to Logistics and Transport Management.*

Management accountants

Student Services Centre, Chartered Institute of Management Accountants (CIMA), 26 Chapter Street, London SW1P 4NP; Tel 020 8849 2251; Email cima.contact@cimaglobal.com; Website www.cimaglobal.com. Publications: *Financial Management* magazine.

Mathematicians

Education Officer, The Institute of Mathematics and Its Applications, Catherine Richards House, 16 Nelson Street, Southend-on-Sea, Essex SS1 1EF; Tel 01702 354020; Email post@ima.org.uk; Website www.mathscareers.org.uk.

Merchant Navy

Careers Department, Merchant Navy Training Board, Carthusian Court, 12 Carthusian Street, London EC1M 6EZ; Tel 0800 085 0973; Email enquiry@mntb.org.uk; Website www.careersatsea.org.

Navy (Royal)

Royal Navy; Tel 0845 607 5555; Website www.royal-navy.mod.uk.

Occupational therapists

Education and Practice Department, College of Occupational Therapists, 106-114 Borough High Street, Southwark, London SE1 1LB; Tel 020 7357 6480; Email careers@cot.co.uk; Website www.cot.org.uk. Publications: *Occupational Therapy – Careers Handbook.*

Opticians

Registrar, General Optical Council, 41 Harley Street, London W1G 8DJ; Tel 020 7850 3898; Email goc@optical.org; Website www.optical.org. Publications: *A Career in Vision Care.*

Orthoptics

Careers Department, British and Irish Orthoptic Society, Tavistock House North, Tavistock Square, London WC1H 9HX; Tel 020 7387 7992; Email bios@orthoptics.org.uk; Website www.orthoptics.org.uk. Publications: *Parallel Vision* (monthly); *British and Irish Orthoptic Journal* (annual).

Pharmacists

Careers Department, Royal Pharmaceutical Society of Great Britain, 1 Lambeth High Street, London SE1 7JN; Tel 020 7572 2330; Email careers@rpsgb.org; Website www.rpsgb.org or www.pharmacycareers.org.uk. Publications: *Interested in Pharmacy?*

Physiotherapists

Learning and Development, The Chartered Society of Physiotherapy, 14 Bedford Row, London WC1R 4ED; Tel 020 7306 6666; Email enquiries@csp.org.uk; Website www.csp.org.uk. Publications: *Guide to Becoming a Chartered Physiotherapist*.

Podiatrists and chiropodists

Membership Team, The Society of Chiropodists and Podiatrists, 1 Fellmongers Path, Tower Bridge Road, London SE1 3LY; Tel 0845 450 3741/3722; Email enq@scpod.org; Website www.feetforlife.org. Publications: Podiatry Now (monthly); *British Journal of Podiatry* (quarterly).

Psychologists

Help Desk, The British Psychological Society (BPS), St Andrew's House, 48 Princess Road East, Leicester LE1 7DR; Tel 0116 254 9568; Email enquiry@bps.org.uk; Website www.bps.org.uk. Publications: *So You Want to be a Psychologist?*

Radiographers

Director of Professional Policy, The Society of Radiographers, 207 Providence Square, Mill Street, London SE1 2EW; Tel 020 7740 7200; Email info@sor.org; Website www.sor.org. Publications: *Radiography Education and Training Directory of Courses*.

Social workers

Information Services, General Social Care Council (GSCC), Goldings House, 2 Hay's Lane, London SE1 2HB; Tel 020 7397 5800; Email info@gscc.org.uk; Website www.gscc.org.uk.

Solicitors

England and Wales: Information Services, Solicitors Regulation Authority (SRA), Ipsley Court, Berrington Close, Redditch, Worcestershire B98 0TD; Tel 0870 606 2555; Email contactcentre@sra.org.uk; Website www.sra.org.uk. Publications: *Becoming a Solicitor*.

Scotland: Education and Training Department, The Law Society of Scotland, 26 Drumsheugh Gardens, Edinburgh EH3 7YR; Tel 0131 226 7411; Email legaleduc@lawscot.org.uk; Website www.lawscot.org.uk. Publications: *Becoming a Solicitor; Qualifying as a Solicitor, Pre-Diploma Training; Career Opportunities for LLB Graduates* (all available on the website or in hard copies on request).

Solicitors and barristers (Northern Ireland)

Careers Department, Council of Legal Education (Northern Ireland), Institute of Professional Legal Studies, 10 Lennoxvale, Belfast BT9 5BY; Tel 028 9097 5567; Email iplsenquiries@qub.ac.uk; Website www.qub.ac.uk/ipls.

Speech and language therapists

Information Department, Royal College of Speech and Language Therapists, 2 White Hart Yard, London SE1 1NX; Tel 020 7378 1200; Email postmaster@rcslt.org; Website www.rcslt.org. Publications: *A Career in Speech and Language Therapy*.

Surveyors

Careers Information, The Royal Institution of Chartered Surveyors (RICS), RICS Contact Centre, Surveyor Court, Westwood Way, Coventry CV4 8JE; Tel 0870 333 1600; Email contactrics@rics.org; Website www.rics.org.

Teachers

Careers Department, The Training and Development Agency for Schools (TDA), 151 Buckingham Palace Road, London SW1W 9SZ; Tel 0845 6000 991 (992 for Welsh speakers); Website www.tda.gov.uk.

Town planners

Careers and Membership Officer, Royal Town Planning Institute, 41 Botolph Lane, London EC3R 8DL; Tel 020 7929 9494; Email careers@rtpi.org.uk; Website www.rtpi.org.uk.

Toxicologists

Administrator, British Toxicology Society, PO Box 249, Macclesfield SK11 6FT; Tel 01625 267881; Email secretariat@thebts.org; Website www.thebts.org. Publications: *Careers in Toxicology*.

Translators and interpreters

Secretary, Institute of Translation and Interpreting, Fortuna House, South Fifth Street, Milton Keynes MK9 2EU; Tel 01908 325250; Email info@iti.org.uk; Website www.iti.org.uk. Publications: *ITI Bulletin* (bi-monthly).

Veterinary surgeons

Education Department, Royal College of Veterinary Surgeons, Belgravia House, 62–64 Horseferry Road, London SW1P 2AF; Tel 020 7222 2001; Email education@rcvs.org.uk; Website www.rcvs.org.uk. Publications: *Training to be a Veterinary Surgeon*.

LOOK AT THE PROSPECTUSES (WEBSITE OR PRINT).

Star Research-led Departments

The top departments, conducting internationally recognised research, are listed alphabetically by university (divided into *Super league* and *First division*) in the following subjects.

Accounting and finance
Agriculture, veterinary and food science
American and Anglophone area studies
Anthropology
Archaeology
Architecture and built environment
Art and design
Asian studies
Biological sciences
Business and management studies
Celtic studies
Chemical engineering
Chemistry
Civil engineering
Classics, ancient history, Byzantine and modern Greek studies
Communication, cultural and media studies
Computer science and informatics
Dentistry
Development studies
Drama, dance and performing arts
Earth systems and environmental sciences
Economics and econometrics
Education
Electrical and electronic engineering
Engineering general and mineral and mining engineering
English language and literature
European studies
French
Geography and environmental studies
German, Dutch and Scandinavian languages

Health – primary care, public health, etc.
History
History of art, architecture and design
Human biological and pre-clinical sciences
Iberian and Latin American languages
Italian
Law
Library and information management
Linguistics
Mathematics – pure
Mathematics – applied
Mechanical, aeronautical and manufacturing engineering
Medicine (clinical subjects)
Metallurgy and materials
Middle Eastern and African studies
Music
Nursing and midwifery
Pharmacy
Philosophy
Physics
Politics and international studies
Professions studies allied to medicine
Psychology
Russian, Slavonic and East European languages
Social work and social policy and administration
Sociology
Sport-related subjects
Statistics and operational research
Theology, divinity and religious studies
Town and country planning

Source: An analysis of the 2008 Research Assessment Exercise published by *Times Higher Education* (Issue No. 1876, December 2008).

Accounting and finance

First division: Bangor University, Bristol University, Essex University, Exeter University

Agriculture, veterinary and food science

First division: Aberdeen University, Aberystwyth University, Glasgow University, Leeds University, Nottingham University, Reading University, Royal Veterinary College Warwick University

American and Anglophone area studies

Super league: Sussex University

First division: Birmingham University, East Anglia University

Anthropology

Super league: Cambridge University, LSE, Roehampton University, SOAS

First division: Aberdeen University, Brunel University, Durham University, Edinburgh University, Goldsmiths, Kent, Manchester University, Oxford University, Queen's University Belfast, St Andrews University, Sussex University, University College London

Archaeology

Super league: Cambridge University, Durham University, Leicester University, Liverpool University, Oxford University, Reading University, Southampton University, University College London

First division: Birmingham University, Bradford University, Cardiff University, Exeter University, Lampeter University, Manchester University, Newcastle University, Nottingham University, Queen's University Belfast, Sheffield University, York University

Architecture and built environment

Super league: Bath University, Cambridge University, Edinburgh College of Art, Edinburgh University, Liverpool University, Loughborough University, Reading University, Salford University, Sheffield University, University College London

First division: Cardiff University, De Montfort University, Glasgow Caledonian University, Heriot-Watt University, Liverpool John Moores University, Newcastle University, Ulster University, Westminster University, Wolverhampton University

Art and design

Super league: Bournemouth University, Brighton University, Lancaster University, Loughborough University, Newcastle University, Open University, Oxford University, Reading University, Royal College of Art, University College London (incl Slade), Westminster University

First division: Arts London, Birmingham City University, Bristol UWE, Dundee University, Goldsmiths, Hertfordshire University, Leeds University, Newport, UWIC

Asian studies

First division: Oxford University, SOAS

Biological sciences

Super league: Bristol University, Dundee University, Manchester University, Oxford University, Royal Holloway, Sheffield University

First division: Aberdeen University, Bath University, Birkbeck, Cambridge University, Cardiff University, Durham University, East Anglia University, Edinburgh University, Exeter University, Glasgow University, Imperial College, King's College London, Leeds University, Newcastle University, St Andrews University, University College London, York University

Business and management studies

Super league: Bath University, Cambridge University, Cardiff University, Cranfield University, Imperial College, King's College London, Lancaster University, Leeds University, London Business School, LSE, Manchester University, Nottingham University, Oxford University, Strathclyde University, Warwick University

First division: Aston University, Birmingham University, Bradford University, City University, Durham University, Exeter University, Glasgow University, Kent, Leicester University, Loughborough University, Newcastle University, Queen Mary, Queen's University Belfast, Reading University, Royal Holloway, St Andrews University, Sheffield University, Southampton University, Surrey University

Celtic studies

Super league: Aberystwyth University, Cambridge University, Swansea University, Ulster University

First division: Bangor University, Cardiff University, Edinburgh University, Glasgow University

Chemical engineering

Super league: Birmingham University, Cambridge University, Imperial College, Manchester University, University College London

First division: Bath University, Newcastle University, Sheffield University

Chemistry

Super league: Bristol University, Cambridge University, Durham University, Edinburgh University, Imperial College, Leeds University, Liverpool University, Manchester University, Nottingham University, Oxford University, St Andrews University, Sheffield University, University College London, Warwick University, York University

First division: Bath University, Birmingham University, Cardiff University, East Anglia University, Glasgow University, Heriot-Watt University, Hull University, Southampton University, Strathclyde University, Sussex University

Civil engineering

Super league: Bristol University, Cardiff University, De Montfort University, Dundee University, Imperial College, Newcastle University, Nottingham University, Queen's University Belfast, Sheffield University, Southampton University, Swansea University

First division: Birmingham University, Bradford University, Heriot-Watt University, Leeds University, Loughborough University, University College London

Classics, ancient history, Byzantine and modern Greek studies

Super league: Cambridge University, Durham University, Exeter University, King's College London, Oxford University, University College London, Warwick University

First division: Birmingham University, Bristol University, Manchester University, Nottingham University, Reading University, St Andrews University

Communication, cultural and media studies

Super league: Cardiff University, East Anglia University, East London University, Goldsmiths, Leicester University, LSE, Nottingham Trent University, Royal Holloway, Sussex University, Ulster University, Westminster University

First division: Bedfordshire University, Bournemouth University, Bristol UWE, De Montfort University, Leeds Met University, Leeds University, Lincoln University, Oxford University, Salford University, Stirling University, Sunderland University

Computer science and informatics

Super league: Aberdeen University, Aberystwyth University, Bath University, Birmingham University, Bristol University, Cambridge University, Cardiff University, Durham University, Edinburgh University, Glasgow University, Imperial College, Lancaster University, Leeds University, Leicester University, Liverpool University, Manchester University, Newcastle University, Nottingham University, Open University, Oxford University, Plymouth University, Queen Mary, Royal Holloway, Southampton University, Sussex University, Swansea University, University College London, York University

First division: Bangor University, Birkbeck, Brighton University, City University, Dundee University, East Anglia University, Essex University, Exeter University, Goldsmiths, Heriot-Watt University, Hertfordshire University, Kent, King's College London, Lincoln University, Liverpool John Moores University, Loughborough University, Oxford Brookes University, Queen's University Belfast, St Andrews University, Sheffield University, Strathclyde University, Teesside University, Ulster University, Warwick University

Dentistry

Super league: King's College London, Manchester University, Queen Mary, Sheffield University

First division: Birmingham University, Bristol University, Cardiff University, Dundee University, Glasgow University, Leeds University, Newcastle University, Queen's University Belfast, University College London

Development studies

Super league: Manchester University, Oxford University

First division: East Anglia University

Drama, dance and performing arts

Super league: Bristol University, Exeter University, Glasgow University, Kent, King's College London, Leeds University, Manchester University, Queen Mary, Roehampton University, Royal Holloway, St Andrews University, Warwick University

First division: Aberystwyth University, Birmingham University, Central School of Speech and Drama, Dartington, De Montfort University, Goldsmiths, Hull University, Middlesex University, Queen's University Belfast, Reading University, Surrey University

Earth systems and environmental sciences

Super league: Birkbeck, Bristol University, Cambridge University, Cardiff University, Durham University, East Anglia University, Edinburgh University, Lancaster University, Leeds University, Liverpool University, Manchester University, Open University, Oxford University, Reading University, Royal Holloway, Southampton University, University College London

First division: Aberdeen University, Bangor University, Birmingham University, Glasgow University, Kent, Leicester University, Newcastle University, Plymouth University, Sheffield University, York University

Economics and econometrics

Super league: Aberdeen University, Birkbeck, Bristol University, Cambridge University, Edinburgh University, Essex University, Exeter University, Glasgow University, Kent, Leicester University, LSE, Manchester University, Nottingham University, Oxford University, Queen Mary, Royal Holloway, Sheffield University, Southampton University, Surrey University, University College London, Warwick University

First division: Birmingham University, Brunel University, City University, East Anglia University, St Andrews University, Stirling University, Sussex University, Swansea University, York University

Education

Super league: Cambridge University, King's College London, Oxford University

First division: Bristol University, Durham University, East Anglia University, Exeter University, Leeds University, Manchester Met University, Manchester University, Stirling University, Sussex University, Warwick University, York University

Electrical and electronic engineering

Super league: Bangor University, Glasgow University, Imperial College, Leeds University, Manchester University, Sheffield University, Southampton University, Surrey University, University College London

First division: Bath University, Birmingham University, Bristol University, Cardiff University, Essex University, Lancaster University, Liverpool John Moores University, Liverpool University, Loughborough University, Newcastle University, Nottingham University, Queen Mary, Queen's University Belfast, Strathclyde University, York University

Engineering general and mineral and mining engineering

Super league: Cambridge University, Heriot-Watt University, Imperial College, Leeds University, Manchester University, Nottingham University, Oxford University, Surrey University, Swansea University, Warwick University

First division: Aberdeen University, Bristol UWE, Brunel University, Durham University, Edinburgh University, Exeter University, Glamorgan University, Keele University, Lancaster University, Leicester University, Liverpool John Moores University, London South Bank University, Nottingham Trent University, Strathclyde University, Sussex University

English language and literature

Super league: Aberdeen University, Birkbeck, Birmingham University, Bristol University, Cambridge University, Cardiff University, De Montfort University, Durham University, East Anglia University, Edinburgh University, Exeter University, Glasgow University, Kent, King's College London, Leeds

University, Liverpool University, Manchester University, Newcastle University, Nottingham University, Oxford University, Queen Mary, Queen's University Belfast, Reading University, Royal Holloway, St Andrews University, Sheffield University, Southampton University, University College London, Warwick University, York University

First division: Anglia Ruskin University, Bangor University, Brunel University, Essex University, Goldsmiths, Hull University, Keele University, Lancaster University, Leicester University, Loughborough University, Nottingham Trent University, Open University, Stirling University, Strathclyde University, Sussex University, Swansea University

European studies

Super league: LSE

First division: Southampton University, Sussex University

French

Super league: King's College London, Oxford University, Warwick University

First division: Aberdeen University, Cambridge University, Durham University, Edinburgh University, Exeter University, Kent, Leeds University, Manchester University, Newcastle University, Nottingham University, Queen Mary, Reading University, St Andrews University, Sheffield University, University College London

Geography and environmental studies

Super league: Aberystwyth University, Bristol University, Cambridge University, Durham University, King's College London, Leeds University, LSE, Oxford University, Queen Mary, Royal Holloway, Sheffield University, University College London

First division: Aberdeen University, Birmingham University, Dundee University, Edinburgh University, Exeter University, Glasgow University, Hull University, Liverpool University, Loughborough University, Manchester University, Newcastle University, Nottingham University, Open University, Plymouth University, Queen's University Belfast, St Andrews University, Southampton University, Sussex University, Swansea University, Westminster University

German, Dutch and Scandinavian languages

First division: Birmingham University, Cambridge University, Durham University, Edinburgh University, Exeter University, King's College London, Leeds University, Manchester University, Newcastle University, Oxford University, Royal Holloway, St Andrews University, Swansea University, University College London

Health – primary care, public health, etc.

Super league: Aberdeen University, Bristol University, Cambridge University, Oxford University, Queen Mary, University College London

First division: Birmingham University, Cardiff University, Imperial College, King's College London, Leeds University, Manchester University

History

Super league: Aberdeen University, Birkbeck, Cambridge University, Essex University, Hertfordshire University, Imperial College, Kent, Liverpool University, LSE, Oxford Brookes University, Oxford University, Queen Mary, Sheffield University, SOAS, Southampton University, Sussex University, University College London, Warwick University

First division: Anglia Ruskin University, Birmingham University, Bristol University, Dundee University, Durham University, East Anglia University, Edinburgh University, Exeter University, Glamorgan University, Glasgow University, Hull University, Keele University, King's College London, Lancaster University, Leeds University, Leicester University, Manchester University, Nottingham University, Queen's University Belfast, Reading University, Royal Holloway, St Andrews University, Stirling University, Swansea University, Ulster University, Winchester University, York University

History of art, architecture and design

Super league: Birkbeck, Birmingham University, Courtauld Institute, East Anglia University, Essex University, Glasgow University, Manchester University, Nottingham University, Open University, St Andrews University, Sussex University, University College London, Warwick University, York University

First division: Aberdeen University, Bristol University, Cambridge University, Edinburgh University, Goldsmiths, Kingston University, Leeds University, Middlesex University, Oxford Brookes University, Plymouth University, Reading University, SOAS, Southampton University

Human biological and pre-clinical sciences

Super league: Manchester University, Oxford University, University College London

First division: Bristol University, King's College London, Liverpool University, Queen Mary, Sussex University

Iberian and Latin American languages

Super league: Cambridge University, King's College London, Manchester University, Nottingham University

First division: Birkbeck, Birmingham University, Durham University, Edinburgh University, Leeds University, Liverpool University, Newcastle University, Oxford University, Queen Mary, Queen's University Belfast, St Andrews University, Sheffield University

Italian

Super league: Cambridge University, Leeds University, Reading University, Warwick University

First division: Birmingham University, Bristol University, Manchester University, Oxford University, University College London

Law

Super league: Cambridge University, Cardiff University, Durham University, Kent, LSE, Nottingham University, Oxford University, Queen's University Belfast, University College London

First division: Birmingham University, Bristol University, Dundee University, Edinburgh University, Glasgow University, King's College London, Leeds University, Manchester University, Queen Mary, Reading University, Sheffield University, Southampton University, Strathclyde University, Sussex University, Ulster University

Library and information management

Super league: Sheffield University

First division: Brunel University, City University, Glasgow University, King's College London, Loughborough University, Napier University, Robert Gordon University, University College London, Wolverhampton University

Linguistics

Super league: Edinburgh University, Queen Mary, York University

First division: Essex University, Lancaster University, Manchester University, Sheffield University, UCLan, University College London, Wolverhampton University

Mathematics – pure

Super league: Aberdeen University, Bath University, Bristol University, Cambridge University, Edinburgh University, Heriot-Watt University, Imperial College, King's College London, Oxford University, Warwick University

First division: Birmingham University, Durham University, East Anglia University, Exeter University, Glasgow University, Leeds University, Leicester University, Loughborough University, Manchester University, Nottingham University, Queen Mary, Sheffield University, University College London, York University

Mathematics – applied

Super league: Bath University, Bristol University, Cambridge University, Durham University, Imperial College, Manchester University, Nottingham University, Oxford University, Portsmouth University, St Andrews University, Southampton University, Surrey University, Warwick University

First division: Brunel University, Edinburgh University, Exeter University, Glasgow University, Heriot-Watt University, Keele University, Kent, King's College London, Leeds University, Liverpool University, Loughborough University, Newcastle University, Queen Mary, Sheffield University, Strathclyde University, Sussex University, University College London, York University

Mechanical, aeronautical and manufacturing engineering

Super league: Birmingham University, Bristol University, Cardiff University, Greenwich University, Imperial College, Leeds University, Loughborough University, Nottingham University, Sheffield University

First division: Bath University, Brighton University, Brunel University, Cranfield University, Glasgow University, Liverpool University, Newcastle University, Queen's University Belfast, Southampton University, Strathclyde University, Swansea University, University College London

Medicine (clinical subjects)

Super league: Birmingham University, Cambridge University, Imperial College, King's College London, Manchester University, Newcastle University, Oxford University, Queen Mary, University College London

First division: Bristol University, Cardiff University, Glasgow University, Leeds University, Leicester University, Liverpool University, Sheffield University, Southampton University

Metallurgy and materials

Super league: Birmingham University, Cambridge University, Kent, Liverpool University, Manchester University, Oxford University, Sheffield University

First division: Imperial College, Queen Mary, Swansea University, Ulster University

Middle Eastern and African studies

Super league: Cambridge University, Edinburgh University, Oxford University

First division: Birmingham University, Durham University, Manchester University, SOAS

Music

Super league: Bangor University, Birmingham University, Bristol University, Cambridge University, City University, Glasgow University, Goldsmiths, Huddersfield University, Keele University, King's College London, Leeds University, Manchester University, Newcastle University, Nottingham University, Oxford University, Queen's University Belfast, Royal Academy of Music, Royal Holloway, Sheffield University, SOAS, Southampton University, Surrey University, Sussex University, York University

First division: Cardiff University, De Montfort University, Durham University, Edinburgh University, Liverpool University, Open University, Royal College of Music

Nursing and midwifery

Super league: Manchester University, Southampton University, Ulster University, York University

First division: City University, Hertfordshire University, Leeds University, Nottingham University, Stirling University

Pharmacy

Super league: Manchester University, Nottingham University, School of Pharmacy

First division: Bath University, Bradford University, Cardiff University, East Anglia University, King's College London, Queen's University Belfast, Strathclyde University

Philosophy

Super league: Birkbeck, Bristol University, Cambridge University, Edinburgh University, Essex University, King's College London, Leeds University, LSE, Middlesex University, Nottingham University, Oxford University, Reading University, St Andrews University, Sheffield University, Stirling University, University College London

First division: Bolton University, Dundee University, Durham University, Glasgow University, Manchester University, Queen's University Belfast, Sussex University, Warwick University, York University

Physics

Super league: Bath University, Cambridge University, Edinburgh University, Lancaster University, Nottingham University, St Andrews University

First division: Birmingham University, Bristol University, Durham University, Exeter University, Glasgow University, Heriot-Watt University, Hertfordshire University, Imperial College, King's College London, Leeds University, Leicester University, Liverpool University, Manchester University, Oxford University, Queen Mary, Queen's University Belfast, Royal Holloway, Sheffield University, Southampton University, Surrey University, Sussex University, Swansea University, University College London, Warwick University, York University

Politics and international studies

Super league: Aberystwyth University, Essex University, LSE, Oxford University, Sheffield University

First division: Cambridge University, Exeter University, Manchester University, Nottingham University, SOAS, Sussex University, University College London, Warwick University

Professions and studies allied to medicine

Super league: King's College London, Ulster University

First division: Aston University, Bristol UWE, Cardiff University, Glasgow Caledonian University, Glasgow University, Hull University, Lancaster University, Manchester University, Nottingham Trent University, Portsmouth University, Queen's University Belfast, Strathclyde University, Surrey University, Swansea University, University College London

Psychology

Super league: Birmingham University, Birkbeck, Cambridge University, Cardiff University, Glasgow University, Oxford University, Royal Holloway, St Andrews University, University College London, York University

First division: Bangor University, Bristol University, Durham University, Edinburgh University, Essex University, Exeter University, Goldsmiths, Leeds University, Nottingham University, Reading University, Sheffield University, Southampton University, Sussex University, Warwick University

Russian, Slavonic and East European languages

Super league: Manchester University, Oxford University, Sheffield University

First division: Bristol University, Cambridge University, Exeter University, Nottingham University, Queen Mary

Social work and social policy and administration

Super league: Bath University, City University, Edinburgh University, Kent, Leeds University, LSE, Oxford University, Sheffield University, Southampton University, University College London, York University

First division: Bedfordshire University, Birmingham University, Bradford University, Bristol University, Durham University, East Anglia University, Keele University, Lancaster University, London South Bank University, Manchester University, Nottingham Trent University, Nottingham University, Open University, Plymouth University, Reading University, Queen's University Belfast, Stirling University, Sussex University, Swansea University, Ulster University, Warwick University

Sociology

Super league: Essex University, Goldsmiths, Lancaster University, Manchester University, York University

First division: Aberdeen University, Cambridge University, Cardiff University, Edinburgh University, Exeter University, Newcastle University, Open University, Oxford University, Queen's University Belfast, Surrey University, Sussex University, Warwick University

Sport-related subjects

First division: Birmingham University, Bristol University, Liverpool John Moores University, Loughborough University

Statistics and operational research

Super league: Bristol University, Cambridge University, Imperial College, Kent, Leeds University, Nottingham University, Oxford University, Warwick University

First division: Bath University, Brunel University, Durham University, Glasgow University, Lancaster University, LSE, Manchester University, Newcastle University, Open University, St Andrews University, Sheffield University, Southampton University, University College London

Theology, divinity and religious studies

Super league: Aberdeen University, Cambridge University, Durham University, Manchester University, Oxford University, Sheffield University, University College London

First division: Birmingham University, Edinburgh University, King's College London, Lancaster University, Leeds University, Nottingham University, St Andrews University, SOAS

Town and country planning

Super league: Cambridge University, Cardiff University, Leeds University, Newcastle University, Sheffield University

First division: Aberdeen University, Glasgow University, Heriot-Watt University, Manchester University, Reading University, Sheffield Hallam University, University College London

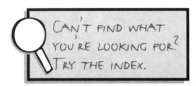

CAN'T FIND WHAT YOU'RE LOOKING FOR? TRY THE INDEX.

Six Categories of University

Universities are a pretty mixed bunch. Some have been around for 700 years; some colleges became universities last year. Some have 1500 students, some over 30,000 (London University has 43,000). Some are very concentrated, some federal. Each university has not only its own range of subjects, teaching and student mix, but also its own rationale and ethos.

You can check out descriptions of each university in the profiles, but here are six different categories of university, with a brief outline of their derivation.

Russell Group

This is a group of 20 research-intensive universities, so called because their first meeting was in Russell Square. They have very different origins, but teaching and learning are undertaken in a culture of research excellence. (For more information, visit www.russellgroup.ac.uk.)

Birmingham University	LSE
Bristol University	Manchester University
Cambridge University	Newcastle University
Cardiff University	Nottingham University
Edinburgh University	Oxford University
Glasgow University	Queen's University Belfast
Imperial College	Sheffield University
King's College London	Southampton University
Leeds University	University College London
Liverpool University	Warwick University.

Ancient universities

Some universities have been around for 400 years or more, so they have had plenty of time to establish world-class reputations. (In those days, universities were often closely connected to the Church.)

Aberdeen University	Glasgow University
Barts & The London	Oxford University
Cambridge University	St Andrews University
Edinburgh University	

Traditional research-led universities

Many of the country's top universities were established towards the end of the 19th century in cities around the country. They provided secular education and opened the doors to women, who had previously been excluded from university education. They include the federal universities of London and Wales. Others started life as university colleges of other universities (eg Newcastle University as a college of Durham University, Exeter University as a college of London University).

Birmingham University	Leicester University
Bristol University	Liverpool University
Courtauld Institute	London University (from merger of King's
Durham University	College and University College)
Exeter University	Manchester University
Hull University	Newcastle University
Leeds University	Nottingham University

Queen's University Belfast

Reading University

Sheffield University

Southampton University

Wales University (from merger of colleges at Aberystwyth, Bangor and Cardiff)

The 1960s universities

The 1960s saw a burgeoning of new universities, many now established as among the country's most successful research-led insitutions. Some are green-field campus universities and provided a very 'sixties' challenge to the established pattern.

East Anglia University

Essex University

Kent

Lancaster University

Sussex University

Stirling University

Warwick University

York University

Others – many of them technological universities – were established colleges (usually in cities) that were granted university status in the sixties.

Aston University

Bath University

Bradford University

Brunel University

City University

Cranfield University

Dundee University

Heriot-Watt University

Loughborough University

Salford University

Strathclyde University

Surrey University

1992 universities

Established polytechnics and colleges of HE were given university status in the 1990s. They are often called modern universities or new universities. Teaching rather than research is their primary concern (although some good research is done in many). They were originally set up to provide more vocational courses and, although some now have a broader range, their best courses still tend to be more practical and job-oriented (eg sports studies, retail management).

Abertay Dundee University

Anglia Ruskin University

Bedfordshire University

Birmingham City University

Bournemouth University

Brighton University

Bristol UWE

Coventry University

De Montfort University

Derby University

East London University

Glamorgan University

Glasgow Caledonian University

Greenwich University

Hertfordshire University

Huddersfield University

Kingston University

Leeds Met University

Lincoln University

Liverpool John Moores University

London Met University

London South Bank University

Manchester Met University

Middlesex University

Napier University

Northumbria University

Nottingham Trent University

Oxford Brookes University

Plymouth University

Portsmouth University

Robert Gordon University

Sheffield Hallam University

Staffordshire University

Sunderland University

Teesside University

Thames Valley University

UCLan

West of Scotland University

Westminster University

Wolverhampton University

Brand new universities

During the first years of the new millennium, several brand new universities were created –always from older institutions. Many started life as education colleges, but they also include the confederation of London art schools as the Arts University London (or Arts London, previously the London Institute). These brand new universities are often relatively small; and while they are all very new, they have many years of teaching experience.

Arts London
Bath Spa University
Bolton University
Bucks New University
Canterbury Christ Church University
Chester University
Chichester University
Creative Arts University
Cumbria University
Edge Hill University
Gloucestershire University

Glyndŵr University
Liverpool Hope University
Northampton University
Queen Margaret University
Roehampton University
Southampton Solent University
Swansea Met University
Winchester University
Worcester University
York St John University

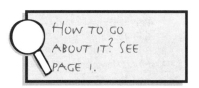

How to go about it? See page 1.

Drop-out Rates

This list shows you the rough proportion of full-time undergraduates who drop out by the end of their first year at each university.

To give you an idea of the UK picture, the average drop-out rate is 8.6% – ie nearly 1 in 10 students have left by the end of their first year, without transferring to another course. But the differences between universities are very great, ranging from under 1% to over 20%. Mature students are twice as likely to drop out than young entrants (over 15% compared to 7%) the explanation for some of the universities with high drop-out rates.

5% and under drop out in first year (excellent)

4	Arts London	4	Loughborough University
4	Aston University	5	LSE
3	Bath University	5	Manchester University
5	Birmingham University	4	Newcastle University
4	Bristol University	3	Nottingham University
5	Buckingham University	1	Oxford University
1	Cambridge University	0	RADA
5	Cardiff University	5	Reading University
3	Central School of Speech & Drama	1	Regent's Business School London
5	Chichester University	1	Royal Academy of Music
1	Colchester Institute	4	Royal Agricultural College
2	Courtauld Institute	3	Royal College of Music
3	Durham University	5	Royal Holloway
5	Edinburgh College of Art	1	Royal Northern College of Music
5	Edinburgh University	3	Royal Veterinary College
4	Exeter University	2	St Andrews University
2	Glasgow School of Art	1	St George's
2	Hull York Medical School	3	School of Pharmacy
3	Imperial College	3	Sheffield University
5	King's College London	4	Southampton University
5	Laban	5	Trinity Laban
5	Lancaster University	5	University College London
5	Leeds College of Music	4	Warwick University
5	Liverpool University	5	Wimbledon College of Art
0	London School of Theology	4	York University

6–10% drop out in first year (average and better)

10	Aberdeen University	10	Bucks New University
8	Abertay Dundee University	10	Canterbury Christ Church University
6	Aberystwyth University	8	Conservatoire for Dance & Drama
8	Bangor University	10	Creative Arts University
6	Bath Spa University	10	Cumbria University
7	Bournemouth University	10	De Montfort University
8	Brighton University	10	Dundee University
9	Bristol UWE	7	East Anglia University
9	Brunel University	8	Essex University

10	European Business School London	8	Plymouth University
8	Falmouth University College	7	Portsmouth University
10	Farnborough College	9	Queen Mary
7	Glasgow University	8	Queen's University Belfast
7	Gloucestershire University	7	Ravensbourne College of Design & Communication
9	Goldsmiths		
7	Greenwich University	9	Robert Gordon University
9	Harper Adams University College	8	Rose Bruford College
9	Heriot-Watt University	7	Royal Scottish Academy of Music & Drama (RSAMD)
9	Hertfordshire University		
10	Huddersfield University	7	Royal Welsh College of Music & Drama
6	Hull University		
9	Keele University	8	St Mary's University College
7	Kent	8	Sheffield Hallam University
9	Kingston University	8	SOAS
9	Lampeter University	7	Stirling University
9	Leeds Met University	6	Sunderland University
6	Leeds University	7	Surrey University
6	Leicester University	8	Sussex University
7	Lincoln University	7	Swansea University
10	Marjon	10	Trinity College of Music
9	Northumbria University	7	University College Birmingham
6	Norwich University College of the Arts	9	Winchester University
7	Nottingham Trent University	10	Worcester University
9	Oxford Brookes University	8	York St John University

11–15% drop out in first year (higher than average)

12	Anglia Ruskin University	12	Newport
13	Bedfordshire University	12	Northampton University
12	Birmingham City University	12	Northern School of Contemporary Dance
11	Bradford University	14	Queen Margaret University
11	Chester University	13	Roehampton University
11	City University	14	Salford University
11	Coventry University	13	Southampton Solent University
14	Derby University	11	Staffordshire University
13	East London University	11	Strathclyde University
13	Edge Hill University	14	Swansea Met University
13	Glasgow Caledonian University	11	Teesside University
13	Heythrop College	15	Thames Valley University
11	Leeds Trinity	11	Trinity College Carmarthen
12	Liverpool Hope University	14	UCLan
11	Liverpool John Moores University	15	Ulster University
14	London Met University	12	UWIC
13	London South Bank University	13	Westminster University
11	Manchester Met University	12	Wolverhampton University
13	Middlesex University	15	Writtle College

16% and more drop out in first year (high drop out)

22 Bolton University	18 Napier University
18 Glamorgan University	19 UHI Millennium Institute
16 Glyndŵr University	17 West of Scotland University

WHERE IS IT?
SEE MAPS,
PAGES 86–89.

Glossary and Addresses

Glossary

A1 – AS-level (alternative term).

A2 – second half of an A-level.

Access courses – prepare students without the standard entry qualifications (particularly mature students) for a degree course.

AEA – Advanced Extension Award.

AH level – Advanced Higher levels, Scottish qualification taken in school; recognised by universities towards satisfying their entrance requirements.

A-level – Advanced level, qualification taken in school and widely recognised by universities towards satisfying their entrance requirements.

AP(E)L – Assessment of Prior (Experiential) Learning.

AS-level – Advanced Subsidiary level, qualification taken in school and widely recognised by universities towards satisfying their entrance requirements.

Assembly Learning Grant – a non-returnable grant made to students resident in Wales from low-income families.

Bachelor's degree – most first degrees lead to a bachelor's degree. Depending on the course, once you have graduated, you can put designated initials after your name – most usually BA (Bachelor of Arts) or BSc (Bachelor of Science) but also, eg, BEd (Bachelor of Education), BN (Bachelor of Nursing) or LLB (Bachelor of Laws).

BFI – British Film Institute.

British Council – offers information and advice for international students studying in the UK. It also now runs the Erasmus scheme in the UK (which provides UK students with EU financial support for study elsewhere in the EU).

BUCS – British Universities and Colleges Sports Association.

Bursaries – non-returnable money available from universities for students, usually from low-income families or from other vulnerable groups. Government bursaries are also available to, eg, students on health courses (NHS bursaries); student grants are called bursaries in Scotland.

Career Development Loan – CDLs are offered by a partnership of the Learning and Skills Council and some high street banks to cover vocational education or training for up to two years.

CATCH – application system for pre-registration nursing and midwifery courses in Scotland.

Clearing – UCAS system for applicants to apply for places in August–September.

Conditional offer – a course offer that requires achievement in outstanding exams.

CUKAS (Conservatoires UK Admissions Service) – the national application system for practice-based music courses at some seven conservatoires.

DCSF – Department for Children, Schools and Families.

Degrees – first degree courses last three or four years full-time and usually lead to a bachelor's degree (though there are exceptions, eg in Scotland and some undergraduate Master's courses).

Higher degrees, including most Master's degrees, PhD, etc. usually require a first degree as a prerequisite.

Department for Employment & Learning (Northern Ireland) – government department responsible for education in Northern Ireland.

DipHE – a higher education qualification awarded after two years full-time study at a university, and should give credit to the first two years of an Honours degree.

Diplomas – new qualification for 14–19 year olds, being introduced in England.

DIUS – Department for Innovation, Universities & Skills.

DSA – Disabled Student Allowance, paid to UK students with various disabilities and assessed alongside their other grants and loans.

ECDL – European Computer Driving Licence.

ELB – Education and Library Board; local board in Northern Ireland to which students can apply for student support.

EU – European Union.

Extra – UCAS system to allow those without a place to apply for courses between January and summer Clearing.

FdA and FdSc – foundation degrees (arts and sciences).

FE – further education.

Fee Grant – a grant for students resident in Wales, who are also studying in Wales, to cover part of their tuition fees.

Firm offer – Term for the offer that an applicant has accepted as a first choice.

First degrees – what it says on the tin: the first degrees open to you when you leave school and enter higher education. Courses normally last three or four years full-time and usually lead to a bachelor's degree (though there are many exceptions).

Foundation degree – a higher education qualification, awarded after two years full-time study at a university or college; courses are designed in conjunction with employers to meet skills shortages. The FD should give credit to the first two years of an Honours degree, although you may need to take an extra term or summer school.

FT – full-time (of students and staff).

FTE – full-time equivalent (eg FTE student).

Further Education – FE covers courses leading to qualifications also offered by schools, together with vocational qualifications. However, the distinction between FE and HE (higher education) is muddied because some universities and HE colleges offer FE courses, and some FE colleges offer all or part of degree courses.

GCSE – General Certificate of Secondary Education, usually taken at school at age 16. Grade C in English and maths GCSE (or equivalent) are required for many first degree courses.

GNVQ – General National Vocational Qualifications.

HE – higher education.

HEFCE (Higher Education Funding Council in England) – the government funding body for universities in England. There are parallel bodies in Scotland (SHEFC) and Wales (HEFCW).

Higher degrees – include most Master's degrees, PhD, etc.; you usually need a first degree in order to undertake a higher degree.

Higher education – refers to the education undertaken by students aged 18+, which is designed to build on qualifications largely taken at school. HE courses lead to a degree (or HND, FDA, DipHE, etc.) and are offered by all universities and colleges of higher education; confusingly, some HE courses are also offered, in whole or in part, by some FE colleges..

Highers – Scottish qualification taken in school; recognised by universities towards satisfying their entrance requirements.

HNC/D – Higher National Certificate/Diploma.

Home students – students ordinarily resident in the UK or EU for the purposes of assessing which tuition fee they pay. Home students pay a fee decided by the university, up to a limit decided by the government; most will be entitled to a student loan to cover the tuition fee.

Honours degree – first degrees that are classified into four classes of Honours (firsts, upper and lower seconds, third-class Honours).

IB – International Baccalaureate.

ICT – information and communications technology.

IGCSEs – International General Certificate of Secondary Education taken primarily by 14–16 year-olds.

Independent student – UK governments assess loans and grants for independent students without reference to their parents' income. Independent students are aged 25 or over, are married or have supported themselves for at least three years, or have no living parents.

Insurance offer – the offer an applicant has accepted as a second choice through UCAS.

International Baccalaureate – qualification taken in most international schools and at an increasing number of schools in the UK, recognised by universities as satisfying their entrance requirements.

International students – students from outside the EU. They pay tuition fees that reflect the full cost of providing the tuition and they are not usually entitled to any financial assistance from the UK government.

ISIC – International Student Identity Card, which allows students to get discounts across the world.

IT – information technology.

ITT – Initial Teacher Training.

JCR – Junior Common Room, the undergraduate student community (and its common room); mostly used at colleges of the universities of Oxford and Cambridge.

LEA – Local Education Authority.

LGBS – Lesbian, Gay, Bisexual Society.

LLB – Bachelor of Laws.

Maintenance grant – a non-returnable grant made to students from low-income families resident in England and Northern Ireland (similar grants in Wales are called Assembly Learning Grants; in Scotland, SAAS Bursaries).

Master's degrees – are usually higher degrees, taught or research based. However, some first degrees lead to Master's (many courses at Scottish universities; and throughout the UK some extended undergraduate science courses leading to, eg, MEng). On successful completion of a Master's degree, you can put designated initials after your name, eg MA (Master of Arts), MBA (Master of Business Administration) or MEng (Master of Engineering).

MB BS (or MB BCh) – Bachelor of Medicine and Surgery.

MCR – Middle Common Room, the graduate student community (and its common room); mostly used at colleges of the universities of Oxford and Cambridge.

National Council for Drama Training (NCDT) – an accreditation organisation for drama courses.

NUS (National Union of Students) – a confederation of students' organisations in universities throughout the UK.

OFFA – Office of Fair Access.

Office of the Independent Adjudicator for Higher Education (OIA) – provides an independent system of complaint against universities in England and Wales.

PAMs – professions allied to medicine.

PPE – Oxford University's course, and test for entrants to, politics, philosophy and economics.

Pre-U – a post-16 qualification (developed by Cambridge University International Examinations), which prepares students for university studies.

PT – part-time (of students or staff).

QAA (Quality Assurance Agency for Higher Education) – ensures that universities across the UK maintain standards in higher education qualifications

QTS – Qualified Teacher Status.

Research quality – research assessment exercises are undertaken every few years for all universities and colleges at the same time. Quality and quantity of research varies widely between universities and between departments. Some universities are research-led, others are not. (See the star research departments in different subjects on pages 754–64 and the top research-intensive universities on page 12.) The most recent Research Assessment Exercise was published in December 2008.

SA – Students' Association (sometimes used as an alternative to Students' Union).

SAAS – Student Awards Agency for Scotland.

SAAS bursary – non-returnable grants made to students resident in Scotland from low-income families; YSB for those studying in Scotland, SOSB for those studying outside Scotland.

Scholarships – non-returnable money, traditionally awarded by universities to students of talent; often now bursaries by another name.

School – a term used by many universities to mean something like a department or faculty (confusing if you are still at school).

SCR – Senior Common Room; the community of teaching staff and fellows (and its common room).

Skill (National Bureau for Students with Disabilities) – a national organisation providing information and support for students with disabilities; it has national HQs in England, Scotland, Wales and Northern Ireland.

SLC – Student Loans Company.

Socrates – EU education action programme with various programmes within it, eg Erasmus and Lingua. All UK universities have some involvement in the student mobility programme and all subjects are covered. To spend time in the EU on one of these programmes, your institution must be a participant; and if your course is approved, you may get help with the extra costs involved.

SOSB (Students Outside Scotland Bursary) – a non-returnable grant made to students from low-income families who are resident in Scotland but studying outside Scotland.

SRC – Students' Representative Council (sometimes used as an alternative to Students' Union).

Student Awards Agency for Scotland (SAAS) – administers loans and grants to students resident in Scotland.

Student loan – two separate government-funded loans for home students: one to cover tuition fees (paid direct to the university); one for maintenance. Student loans are repaid once you are earning.

Student Loans Company (SLC) – administers government-funded student loans and grants across the UK.

SU – Students' Union, the local students' representative organisation in a university or college. The SU will provide, eg, representation on university committees, welfare and entertainment services.

Teaching quality – the quality of higher education teaching is assessed as part of a rolling programme, subject by subject. The published results evaluate the quality of the learning experience in the overall teaching of that subject, and there are hundreds of subject reports on individual universities and colleges. Some of them were written long ago, so things will probably have changed a good deal; others are much more recent. Reports are available on the QAA website.

Training Development Agency for Schools (TDA) – the national agency for information on teaching and the training of teachers.

Tuition fees – the fees students are charged by universities to cover their tuition. Home students usually pay up to a maximum dictated by the government. International students pay the full cost of providing the tuition.

UCAS – the UK application system for most first degree courses.

UK Council for International Student Affairs (UKCISA) – provides an advisory service for international students.

ULU – University of London Union.

Unconditional offer – an offer of a place to an applicant which requires no further examination passes.

Undergraduate – usually refers to a student on a first degree course; some universities use the term to describe all students who are not graduates (including those on non-degree courses).

Young Students' Bursary (YSB) – is a non-returnable grant made to students from low-income families who are resident in Scotland and also studying in Scotland.

Addresses

British Council, 10 Spring Gardens, London SW1A 2BN; Tel 020 7930 8466; all enquiries to British Council Information Centre: Tel 0161 957 7755; Email general.education.enquiries@britishcouncil.org; Website www.britishcouncil.org.

Conference of Drama Schools (CDS Ltd), The Executive Secretary, PO Box 34252, London NW5 1XJ; Tel 020 7692 0032; Email info@cds.drama.ac.uk; Website www.drama.ac.uk. For copies of the CDS Guide (from French's Theatre Bookshop): Tel 020 7255 4300; Email theatre@samuelfrench-london.co.uk.

CUKAS (The Conservatoires UK Admissions Service), administered by UCAS, Rosehill, New Barn Lane, Cheltenham, Gloucestershire GL52 3LZ. Contact direct to CUKAS helpline: 0871 418 0470; Website www.cukas.ac.uk.

Department for Children, Schools and Families (DCSF), Sanctuary Buildings, Great Smith Street, Westminster, London SW1P 3BT; Tel 020 7925 5000; Email info@dcsf.gsi.gov.uk; Website www.dcsf.gov.uk. Public enquiries: Tel 0870 000 2288.

Department for Employment and Learning (Northern Ireland), Student Support Branch, Room 407, Adelaide House, Adelaide Street, Belfast BT2 8FD; Tel 028 9025 7715; Email studentsupport@delni.gov.uk; Website www.studentfinanceni.co.uk.

Department for Innovation, Universities and Skills (DIUS), Castle View House, East Lane, Runcorn, WA7 2GJ. For all general enquiries: Tel 020 7215 5555; Email info@dius.gsi.gov.uk; Website www.dius.gov.uk.

Educational Grants Advisory Service (EGAS), c/o Family Welfare Association, 501–505 Kingsland Road, London E8 4AU; Helpline: 020 7254 6251; Email fwa.headoffice@fwa.org; Website www.egas-online.org.

Erasmus (based at British Council Wales), British Council, 28 Park Place, Cardiff, CF10 3QE; Tel 029 2039 7405; Email erasmus@britishcouncil.org; Website www.britishcouncil.org/erasmus.

EU Customer Service Team, Tel 0141 243 3570; Email EU-Team@SLC.co.uk; Website www.studentfinancedirect.co.uk.

GTTR (Graduate Teacher Training Registry), Rosehill, New Barn Lane, Cheltenham, Gloucestershire GL52 3LZ; Tel 0871 4680 469; Email enquiries@gttr.ac.uk; Website www.gttr.ac.uk.

HEFCE (Higher Education Funding Council in England), Northavon House, Coldharbour Lane, Bristol BS16 1QD; Tel 0117 931 7438; Fax 0117 931 7203; Email hefce@hefce.ac.uk; Website www.hefce.ac.uk.

ISIC. For ISIC card applications: Tel 0870 1627 546, Post: ISIC Mail Order (ISIC Applications, 5th Floor, St George's House, 56 Peter Street, Manchester M2 3NQ) NUS Helpline: 0870 841 3224; Email isic@nussl.co.uk; price £7 (£7.50 by mail order); Website www.isiccard.com.

National Council for Drama Training (NCDT), Tel 020 7407 3686; Email info@ncdt.co.uk; Website www.ncdt.co.uk.

NHS bursaries and grants, *England:* NHS Student Grants Unit, Hesketh House, 200–220 Broadway, Fleetwood, Lancashire FY7 8SS. Helpline: 0845 358 6655; Email enquiries@nhspa.gov.uk; Website www.nhsstudentgrants.co.uk.

Northern Ireland: Contact your local Education and Library Board.

Scotland: Student Awards Agency for Scotland (SAAS); see below.

Wales: NHS Wales Student Awards Unit, 2nd Floor, Golate House, 101 St Mary Street, Cardiff CF10 1DX; Tel 029 2050 2355.

NUS (National Union of Students) NUS HQ, 2nd Floor, Centro 3, 19 Mandela Street, London NW1 0DU; Tel 0871 221 8221; Email nusuk@nus.org.uk; Website www.nusonline.co.uk.

Office of the Independent Adjudicator for Higher Education (OIA), 5th Floor, Thames Tower, Station Road, Reading RG1 1LX; Enquiries Team: Tel 0118 959 9813; Email enquiries@oiahe.org.uk; Website www.oiahe.org.uk.

One Parent Families, 255 Kentish Town Road, London NW5 2LX; Helpline: 0800 018 5026; Email info@oneparentfamilies.org.uk; Website www.oneparentfamilies.org.uk.

Open & Distance Learning Quality Council (ODL QC), 16 Park Crescent, London W1B 1AH; Tel 020 7612 7090; Email info@odlqc.org.uk; Website www.odlqc.org.uk.

QAA (Quality Assurance Agency for Higher Education), Head Office, Southgate House, Southgate Street, Gloucester GL1 1UB; Tel 01452 55700; Email comms@qaa.ac.uk; Website www.qaa.ac.uk.

Skill (National Bureau for Students with Disabilities), *England:* Head Office, Unit 3, Floor 3, Radisson Court, 219 Long Lane, London SE1 4PR; Tel 020 7450 0620; Helpline: 0800 328 5050; Email skill@skill.org.uk; Website www.skill.org.uk.

Northern Ireland: Unit 2, Jennymount Court, North Derby Street, Belfast BT15 3HN; Tel 028 9028 7000; Email adminfo@skillni.org.uk; Website www.skillni.org.uk.

Scotland: Norton Park, 57 Albion Road, Edinburgh EH7 5QY; Tel 0131 475 2348; Email admin@skillscotland.org.uk; Website www.skill.org.uk/scotland.

Wales: The Executive Centre, Temple Court, Cathedral Road, Cardiff CF11 9HA; Tel 029 2078 6506; Email rachel@skillwales.org.uk; Website www.skill.org.uk/wales.

STA Travel, Customer Relations Manager, 6 Wrights Lane, London W8 6TA; National call centre: 0871 2300 040.

Student Awards Agency for Scotland (SAAS), Gyleview House, 3 Redheughs Rigg, Edinburgh EH12 9HH; Tel 0845 111 1711; Email qeu@scotland.gsi.gov.uk; Website www.saas.gov.uk.

Student Loans Company (SLC), 100 Bothwell Street, Glasgow G2 7JD. Tel (general enquiries) 0845 026 2019. For specific enquiries on your loan arrangements, see the SLC website (www.slc.co.uk).

Student Support England, Tel 0845 602 0583; Website www.studentfinanceengland.co.uk.

Student Support NI Website www.studentfinanceni.co.uk

Student Support Wales Website www.studentfinancewales.co.uk

Training and Development Agency for Schools (TDA), 151 Buckingham Palace Road, London SW1W 9SZ (but moving to Manchester by end 2010); Tel 020 7023 8000; Website www.tda.gov.uk. Teaching information line: 0845 6000 991 (992 for Welsh speakers).

UCAS (Universities and Colleges Admissions Service), Rosehill, New Barn Lane, Cheltenham, Gloucestershire GL52 3LZ; Tel 01242 222 444; Help and advice for applicants from Customer Service Unit: Tel 0871 468 0 468; Email enquiries@ucas.ac.uk; Website www.ucas.com. (UCAS Card enquiries: Tel 0871 468 0471).

UKCISA (UK Council for International Student Affairs), 9–17 St Albans Place, London N1 0NX. General (not student) enquiries: Tel 020 7288 4330; student advice line: Tel 020 7107 9922; Website www.ukcisa.org.uk.

UK Visas, UK Border Agency, Visa Service Directorate, King Charles Street, London SW1A 2AH; Tel 0845 010 5555; Email direct from website; Website www.ukvisas.gov.uk.

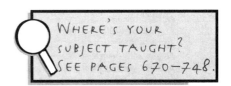

WHERE'S YOUR SUBJECT TAUGHT? SEE PAGES 670–748.

INDEX